CLARENDON STUDIES IN THE HISTORY OF ART

General Editor: Dennis Farr

MURAL PAINTING IN BRITAIN 1840–1940

Image and Meaning

CLARE A. P. WILLSDON

OXFORD
UNIVERSITY PRESS

OXFORD
UNIVERSITY PRESS

Great Clarendon Street, Oxford OX2 6DP
Oxford University Press is a department of the University of Oxford.
It furthers the University's objective of excellence in research, scholarship,
and education by publishing worldwide in

Oxford New York

Athens Auckland Bangkok Bogotá Buenos Aires
Cape Town Chennai Dar es Salaam Delhi Florence Hong Kong Istanbul
Karachi Kolkata Kuala Lumpur Madrid Melbourne Mexico City Mumbai
Nairobi Paris São Paulo Shanghai Singapore Taipei Tokyo Toronto Warsaw

and associated companies in Berlin Ibadan

Oxford is a registered trade mark of Oxford University Press
in the UK and certain other countries

Published in the United States
by Oxford University Press Inc., New York

First published 2000

British Library Cataloguing in Publication Data
Data available

Library of Congress Cataloging in Publication Data
Data applied for

ISBN 0–19–817515–9

1 3 5 7 9 10 8 6 4 2

Typeset Kolam Information Services Pvt Ltd, Pondicherry, India
Printed in Great Britain
on acid-free paper by
Butler & Tanner Ltd. Frome, Somerset

For my parents
Dr John A. Willsdon, and Dorothy I. Willsdon

ACKNOWLEDGMENTS

The origins of this book lie in my delight when undertaking research as an undergraduate at Cambridge on the Scottish painter John Duncan, at the wealth of subtle and intriguing relationships of image and meaning to be found in nineteenth- and twentieth-century murals. It quickly became clear during further research, for a Ph.D. at Cambridge on aspects of mural painting in London from 1890 to 1930, that there was no standard work or national survey extending from Prince Albert's bold revival of fresco at Westminster in the 1840s to the changes of style and taste which accompanied the Second World War. The present book is the outcome. For nurturing and encouraging the seeds from which it has grown, I am deeply grateful to Dr John Gage, who supervised my doctoral thesis, Professor G. D. S. Henderson, Dr Paul Joannides, and Duncan Robinson, Director of the Fitzwilliam Museum (University of Cambridge); as well as to Professor Martin Kemp (University of Oxford) and Professor Joseph Mordaunt Crooke (University of London). In turn, I owe a special debt of gratitude to Dr Dennis Farr, CBE, General Editor of the Clarendon Studies in the History of Art, who encouraged me to write this book, and gave invaluable guidance in my exploration of the vast and little-charted realm of art history, with disconcertingly indistinct borders, which formed its subject. I would also like to thank both Dr Farr and Anne Ashby, my editor at OUP, for keeping faith with my project even when the recurrent volumes of material coming to light from my fieldwork made it clear that the published outcome would be longer than originally envisaged.

The extensive fieldwork in Britain and abroad on which the book is based has been greatly assisted by generous support from the British Academy, the Carnegie Trust for the Universities of Scotland, and the Faculty of Arts of the University of Glasgow. Study Leave awarded by the University of Glasgow has likewise been invaluable. The preparation of the book was much enriched by the opportunity to examine at first hand a wealth of fascinating murals in a number of European countries in the course of a project funded by the Leverhulme Trust to investigate Continental systems for research and documentation of murals.

Many of the photographs in this book are published for the first time, and I am indebted to the British Academy, Marc Fitch Fund, and Scouloudi Foundation of the Institute for Historical Research, London for their support, as well as to the University of Glasgow Publication Fund for contributing to the cost of colour illustrations. I would also like to express my appreciation for the funding for illustration in colour of murals in their care which has been generously given by the Worshipful Companies of Skinners and Drapers, and Lloyd's Register of Shipping, London.

Amongst the many other scholars who have encouraged and assisted me in the research for this book, special thanks are due to Dr Ann Saunders, Dr John Bold, and Geoffrey Stell. I am particularly grateful for the insights into nineteenth- and twentieth-century Continental mural painting and art which I have gained from stimulating discussions with Jan T. Ahlstrand (Lund), Professor Frank Büttner (Munich), Hofrat Dr Werner Kitlitschka and Professor Walter Krause (Vienna), Dr Judith Ogonovszky-Steffens (Brussels), and Professor Richard Thomson, and

character of mural painting as an art with something to say; a medium inextricably bound to the circumstances, beliefs, and aspirations of its times, but which, for its makers and viewers alike, could simultaneously carry evocative, psychological power. The completion of a mural might be marked by public ceremonial in the form of an unveiling reported by the press, whilst, following the First World War, a mural memorial could act as a potent focus for community remembrance or personal catharsis. In dealing with such art, it is not sufficient to apply abstract theory, or plot stylistic changes, and I would ask readers to forgive my impertinence as I venture into other disciplines in search of illumination, and to bear with the width of historical and contextual material which, in consequence, I bring into play. By offering both an account and an interpretation of murals in Britain from 1840 to 1940, however, I hope that this book will provide a rewarding reference source for as wide a range of readers as possible, from art and architectural historians and those directly concerned with conservation and preservation, and those who cherish their local murals, to all who have an interest in a deeper understanding of Britain's past and her relationships with Continental history and traditions.

Of necessity, I have had to be selective in the range of examples discussed, but the reader will find a supplementary list of murals in locations across Britain in the appendices, along with a guide to mural techniques. It should be noted that the inclusion of a building in the book does not imply that visitors may gain access to it, or that murals in it are still extant. I would be rewarded if, as a result of this book, readers are prompted themselves to explore the riches of Britain's mural tradition, and to send me information on any futher murals which fall within the broad period of 1800 to the present day.

misadventure or intent, they are likewise generally too large in scale, or specific in symbolism, to attract a ready purchaser, and may not even be recognizable as former murals. Lord Leighton and Sir Stanley Spencer, for example, were both much interested in mural art and painted murals but it is their portable, exhibitable easel works for which they have conventionally been best remembered. In bringing to light work by a wealth of frequently accomplished, but since forgotten artists, as well as presenting murals by luminaries such as Leighton, Watts, Brangwyn, and Bakst, it is hoped that this book will not only extend our knowledge of art in Britain, but also lead to a rounder, more nuanced picture of its character and Continental connections.

In an age when art history has tended to give primacy to so-called avant-garde trends, the frequent role of murals as vehicles for the preservation or maintenance of beliefs and ideals has also contributed to their neglect. The seemingly conservative representational and narrative idiom of many nineteenth- and twentieth-century murals has, for example, all too frequently been dismissed as somehow irrelevant or undeserving of attention, so that its inner—and sometimes surprisingly radical—meanings have remained undetected. Both in trying to reconstruct the character of lost works, and in dealing with extant murals, I have turned to hitherto unpublished period sources and archives to search out not only basic data on artists, subjects, and dates, but also vital clues to the meanings which murals would have held for their artists, patrons, and viewers. In so doing, I have tried to remain alert to the nature of such written sources as themselves a witness, like the murals to which they relate, to particular times and places. By correlating the mural images with period texts, it has in turn become apparent that the very character of mural painting, as an art of ideas intended normally to form a permanent presence in a particular setting, demands imaginative sensitivity to the vision of future time which was cherished by its makers and users. Now living, at the start of the new millennium, in the future to which they looked, it is, of course, appropriate to seek to identify and evaluate a British mural tradition. This book is itself, however, in turn intended to be a first stage in a long-term project to record and document Britain's mural heritage from 1800 to the present day. As such, it is hoped that it will find its place alongside the systematic steps now being taken in other European countries to establish records of their nineteenth- and twentieth-century murals, and that it will be seen as a legitimate sequel to the extensive research undertaken in recent years on medieval murals in Britain, as well as to projects such as the *Corpus der mittelälterlichen Wandmalerei* in Austria, its German partner on Baroque murals, and the 1986 exhibition at the Petit Palais in Paris of decoration for the city's *mairies.*

The book also contributes to a richer appreciation of the role of visual imagery and symbolism in general as formative factors within the evolution of social, cultural, and political ideals of the nineteenth and twentieth centuries. In the course of its preparation, I have had the good fortune to be able to discuss some of the murals included in it with the artists who actually painted them, or their immediate descendants. As a centenarian, the late Robertson Weir, for example, described to me his mural training under Maurice Greiffenhagen in Glasgow, in the very School of Art by Charles Rennie Mackintosh, which, but a few years previously, he had actually seen in process of erection. So too, the late James Byam Shaw told me of modelling as a child for one of the historical figures in the mural at Westminster by his father, John Byam Shaw—and thereby literally enacting the past within the present, for portrayal in a work of art intended to endure for posterity in the seat of national government. My appreciation of such encounters properly belongs to the Acknowledgements section in this book, but they have been a vivid reminder of the essential

PREFACE

This book is believed to be the first nationwide study of mural painting from 1840 to 1940 published in any western country. It is based on some twenty years of research not only throughout Britain, but also in Continental centres whose murals influenced British artists or formed part of a shared European tradition. Whilst it draws upon work by over four hundred and fifty muralists and explores the contributions both of well- and now lesser-known names, it constitutes more than a simple catalogue or chronology. Mural painting, whether in prehistoric caves, Italian Renaissance churches, or 'New Deal' American post-offices and schools, has traditionally fulfilled diverse and powerful symbolic purposes—ritual, religious, social, political, psychological, commemorative, or commercial, to name but a few. In attempting a first *compte rendu* of this art-form in Britain from the accession of Queen Victoria in 1837 to the watershed in styles, attitudes, and patronage marked by the Second World War, I have therefore sought to situate the examples discussed within a larger historical and cultural framework. Social trends, changing conceptions of national identity, attempts to project private, public, or corporate *personae*, and the 'invention of tradition' in the face of technological advance or political change, as well, of course, as developments in easel art, architecture, and monumental sculpture, for example, are considered as integral facets of this framework.

In its day, mural painting of the nineteenth and early twentieth centuries was seen by its exponents as a pinnacle of artistic achievement, sealing reputations, setting standards for wider emulation, and sometimes promising social status. In the case of certain artists, such as Sir Frank Brangwyn, it could also involve a subtle and multi-layered embodiment of private ideals within public art. A mural might quietly be imbued by its painter with unexpected and even subversive implications, which thereby gained gravitas from association with 'High Art'. For its patrons, however, in an era when first photography and later film, radio, and television were still to come of age, mural painting played a wide diversity of sometimes very different roles. In attempting to understand the complex of creative tensions which could be sparked by the varied and at times conflicting purposes of artist and patron, I have tried to reconstruct some of the distinctive beliefs and states of mind from which the works arose, or were intended to be viewed—whether in considering the great State murals on the walls of Parliament or the Foreign Office, or examples of the many hundreds of local mural schemes which were carried out in civic and village halls, schools, churches, theatres, shops, private houses, and business premises. An important aim, given its virtual neglect in British art history and heritage, has been to demonstrate that mural painting is an integral and richly complex element in the history both of British and European art, as well as one which served both public and private purposes.

An inherently vulnerable art-form, murals have all too often been destroyed, defaced, or discarded in course of architectural renovation, or as a result of changes in ownership and taste. At the same time, by their physical nature, they inevitably stand outwith the commercial circuits of exhibition and auction which keep easel works in the public eye. If detached from the wall by

Belinda Thomson (Edinburgh). I likewise wish to thank Peter Cormack, John Christian, Alan Crawford, and Stephen Wildman for information and suggestions which aided my exploration of late nineteenth-century and Arts and Crafts Movement murals.

At every stage in preparing this book, I have met with extraordinary generosity, enthusiasm and freely offered help on the part of countless other individuals, families, and organizations. Doors of every kind have been literally unlocked, from the portals of power of State and civic buildings to the time-worn gateways of historic schools and churches, flamboyant theatre foyers, and venerable entrances to companies and clubs. I have been allowed to photograph the walls of private homes, pore over dusty records, and trace the contours of tantalizing bumps on emulsioned surfaces for clues to treasures no longer visible. My quest for the essential details of locations, titles, painters, and patrons has been patiently met by many hundreds of respondents in church offices, local authorities, business and industry, livery companies, specialist archives, and regional and National galleries, who have grappled with my questionnaires and enquiries, shared specialist knowledge, or pointed me in the direction of unsuspected sources of information. If my persistence has tested their patience, I apologize; their contributions have richly enhanced this study, and I am profoundly grateful to them. To name everyone who has assisted my research for this book would require space far beyond that available here, but I hope that those not mentioned will none the less consider themselves included in my thanks.

I owe a particular debt of gratitude to a number of muralists, including the late Robert Baker, the late Edward Payne, and the late Robertson Weir, as well as to relatives of muralists or mural patrons, including Rodney Brangwyn, Elizabeth Bulkeley, the late Sir John Stuart Knill, Bt., Christine M. Martin, T. J. Fenton, Noel Florence, Marina Rainey, the late James Byam Shaw, CBE, Christina Byam Shaw, Rosalind Thomas, Josephina de Vasconcellos, and Una Douglas Wallace, who provided unique insights into the lives and work of their forbears and in some cases were also able to show me collections of paintings or writings by them.

Of the numerous curators, archivists, and private individuals who brought murals, documents, and information to my attention, or otherwise assisted my quest for original material, I would like to record special appreciation of the help given by Gordon Anderson; Lady de Bellaigue, Royal Archives; Dimitris G. Dondos, Bridgewater House; Malcolm Hay and Phyllis Rogers, Palace of Westminster; Sidney Hutchison, CVO, Royal Academy of Arts; C. H. James, British School at Rome; and Anne Sutton and Ursula Carlyle, Mercers' Company. I would also like to thank Myles Glover, former Clerk of the Worshipful Company of Skinners, for his warm encouragement of my study of the company's Brangwyn murals and related archives; and Robert J. and N. Naismith and Dr Michael Shea, CVO and Mona Shea, who have so generously allowed me to view works and scrutinize their walls at Ramsay Garden in Edinburgh.

For their particular help in giving information about or access to murals, sketches, archives, or other source material, I am grateful to David Beevers, Preston Manor and Rottingdean Grange, Brighton; Dr G. Brandwood; George Breeze, Cheltenham Art Gallery and Museums; Dr Chris Brookes, Exeter University; Janice Carpenter and Ann Compton, University of Liverpool Art Collections; John Champness, Lancashire County Council; Revd John O. Drackley, Derby; John Evans, Gillingham; Rachel Fear, Royal West of England Academy; Alan Griffiths, Diocesan Liturgy Commission, University of Southampton; William Hardie, Glasgow; Margaret Hartley, Bradford Art Galleries and Museums; Guy Holborn, Lincoln's Inn Library; Rodney Hubbock, Winchester Diocesan Advisory Committee; Dr John Jones, Dean and Archivist, Balliol College, Oxford;

Richard Jefferies, Watts Gallery; Rt. Hon. Lord Joicey; John M. Keyworth, Bank of England; Dr C. Kightly, Lincoln Diocesan Tourism Consultancy; Elspeth King, Smith Art Gallery and Museum, Stirling; Alistair Laing, National Trust (England); George Learmonth, Birmingham Museums and Art Gallery; Christopher Lloyd, LVO, Surveyor of the Queen's Pictures; Joseph McBrinn; D. J. J. McEwen, Headmaster of St Edmund's College, Ware; Dominic Marechal, Koninklijke Musea voor Schone Kunsten van België; Sir Oliver Millar, GCVO, former Director of the Royal Collection and Surveyor of the Queen's Pictures; Edward Morris and Joseph Sharples, Walker Art Gallery, Liverpool; R. G. Penman, Malvern College, Worcs; Dr John Physick, CBE; Dr C. C. G. Rawll, All Saints' church, Margaret Street, London; Alan Rome, Cathedral Architect to the Deans and Chapters of Bristol, Salisbury and Wells, and Mary Rome; Revd Peter Smith, Berwick church, Polegate; K. S. Sales, Woodgreen, Hants; Susan Stanway, Roedean School; Sir Hugh Stucley Bt.; Julian Treuherz, Manchester City Art Galleries; Philip Vainker, Royal Pavilion Art Gallery and Museum, Brighton; John Vaughan, Victorian Society Liverpool; Meta Viles, former Assistant Librarian, Royal Scottish Academy; Peter and Janet Webster, Cardiff; Dr Andrew White, Lancaster City Council; Matthew Williams, Cardiff Castle; Vicky Tuck (Principal) and staff, Cheltenham Ladies' College; and the staffs of the Corporation of London Record Office; House of Lords Record Office; Library and Archives, King's College, and Newnham College, Cambridge; University of Liverpool Archives; Lanark Division of Strathclyde Department of Education; and Tate Gallery Archive. I am also most grateful for assistance with information about Continental murals given by staff at the Institut Royal du Patrimoine Artistique, and Service des Monuments et Sites in Brussels; the Inventaire Générale, Service d'Edifices Civiles et Culturelles, and Service des Monuments Historiques, Paris; the Landesamt für Denkmalpflege, Bayerische Verwaltung für staatlichen Schlösser, Gärten und Seen, and Neue Pinakothek, Munich; the Nationalmuseum, Stockholm, the Skissernas Museum, Lund; and the Skitsesamling, Køge.

Thanks are also due to Peyton Skipwith and Andrew Mackintosh Patrick of the Fine Art Society, for allowing me to consult material in their archives; and to Margaret Ballardie, the late Anna Hulbert, and Pauline Plummer, as well as R. L. Snowden of the Stenhouse Conservation Centre, Edinburgh, for alerting me to murals they had conserved. The assistance of the Ancient Monuments Society, Council for the Care of Churches, *Country Life*, Historic Houses Association, National Association of Decorative and Fine Arts Societies, National Trust, Victorian Society, *Scots Magazine*, and Society for the Protection of Ancient Buildings is likewise gratefully acknowledged. I would like to record especial appreciation of the contribution made by staff at English Heritage and Historic Scotland (National Monuments Record) and by the Photographic Unit of the University of Glasgow, in helping with illustrations for the book.

Quotations from and references to material in the Royal Archives, Windsor are by the gracious permission of Her Majesty Queen Elizabeth II. Quotations from the Castle Howard Archives are by kind permission of the Hon. Simon Howard, and those from archives relating to the murals at Chelsea Town Hall and the Chelsea Pageant are courtesy of The Royal Borough of Kensington and Chelsea Libraries and Arts Services, which has also permitted the reproduction of Plates XXIV, 103, and 104. Material from the Roberson Archive at the Hamilton Kerr Institute, University of Cambridge is quoted by permission of the Syndics of the Fitzwilliam Museum to whom rights in this publication are assigned. Plates V–VIII, 1, 14, 33–6, and 38–40 are reproduced by courtesy of the Mercers' Company and the Joint Grand Gresham Committee, and I am grateful to the Mercers' Company for permission to quote from material in its archives. Quotations in Chapter 11 from

Minutes and MS material relating to the decoration of the Tate Gallery Restaurant are from the Tate Gallery Records, and by kind permission of the Tate Gallery Archive, which has also kindly allowed reproduction of the photograph in Plate 221.

Plates II–IV, XIV–XV, XVIII, 12, 18–25, 27–9, 48–50, 53, 66–71, and 222–3 are reproduced by kind permission of the Palace of Westminster. Plate XXIX is reproduced with kind permission of the Special Trustees of Guy's Hospital and Plate 168 by kind permission of Southend Museums Service. Plate 102 is reproduced with the kind permission of the Trustees of the National Museums and Galleries of Northern Ireland. Plate 201 is reproduced by courtesy of the Corporation of London; Plate 180 by courtesy of the Freer Gallery of Art, Smithsonian Institution, Washington, DC (accession 04.61); Plate 214 by courtesy of the Estate of John Roberts; and Plate 100 by courtesy of Felix Rosenstiel's Widow & Son Ltd, London on behalf of the Estate of Sir John Lavery. Plate 202 a, b, c is copied from photographs by Bedford Lemere & Co, London, courtesy of the National Gallery of Canada.

The following individuals and organizations have also given kind permission for quotation of written material and/or illustration of artwork, or have allowed me to take photographs of work in their possession (where permission relates in part or in whole to illustrations, the relevant plate numbers are noted in brackets):

Aberdeen City Council (212); the Alice Trustees (195); the Vicar and PCC, All Saints' church, Margaret St, London (XXVI); Gordon Anderson (Belleroche Diaries; 76); the Athenaeum, Liverpool (XLI, 217); the Trustees of Balcombe Victory Hall (109–10); Balliol College, Oxford (XXXV); the Governor and Company of the Bank of England (203–6); Bayerische Staatsgemäldesammlungen, Munich (5–6); Bayerische Verwaltung der staatlichen Schlösser, Gärten und Seen, Munich (16); Berwick Church, Sussex (138–9); Birmingham City Archives (Hardman collection); Birmingham Museums and Art Gallery (XXXIV, 99, 183); Birmingham School of Art Archives, University of Central England (99); British Architectural Library, RIBA, London (207); the Bodleian Library, University of Oxford (G.A.fol.B24) (170–1); the Estate of Mary Adshead (196); Bristol Museums and Art Gallery (105–7); Bridgewater House, London (XXXVI); Brighton, Hove and Sussex Sixth Form College (XXXIII, 165); the British School at Rome; Rodney Brangwyn (X, XI–XIII, XIX–XX, XL, 8, 13, 41–7, 61, 72–85, 87, 135, 200, 202 a, b, c); Stad Brugge Stedelijke Musea (87); Burgtheater, Vienna (51); Cardiff County Council (Cardiff Castle—XXXVII, 179; Sports and Leisure Department—XXXVIII); the Cheltenham Ladies' College (158); Christ Church, Cheltenham (XXVIII), Christ's Hospital, Horsham (135); the City Art Centre, Edinburgh (154); Annabel Cole (160, 193–4); Combe Bank School (182); Conseil d'Etat, Paris (52); Corporation of London Records Office; Anthony Crane (XXXII, 182–3); the Crown Estate (XXXIX, 177, 188); Lucy Dynevor (MSS by Sir William Rothenstein); the Master and Wardens of the Worshipful Company of Drapers (IX); Ecole nationale supérieure des Beaux-Arts, Paris (144); the Elmley Foundation and the Madresfield Estate (133–4); Essex County Council (113–14); the Faringdon Collection Trust (184); Ferens Art Gallery: Hull City Museums and Art Galleries (75); Noel Florence (104); the Foreign and Commonwealth Office, London (XVI, 54 a, b–59); the Hon. Mrs Crispin Gascoigne (Harcourt Papers); Glasgow City Council (100–1); the Librarian, Department of Special Collections, University of Glasgow (XIX, XX, 185); Guardian Royal Exchange (30); Charlotte and Stephen Halliday (XLI, 197, 217, 221); Harris Museum and Art Gallery, Preston (159); Hunterian Art Gallery, University of Glasgow (211—Mackintosh Collection; 213); Kent Archives Service (Combe Bank Archive); Holy Trinity church, Kilmarnock (126); the Imperial War Museum, London (War Artists' Archive;

XVII, 62–5); the High Commission of India, London (88–9); King's College, University of Cambridge (192–3); Kirklees Metropolitan Council (169); Kunsthistorisches Museum, Vienna (224); Leeds Museums and Galleries (City Art Gallery) (XL, 111–12); the Treasurer and Masters of the Bench of Lincoln's Inn (142); Liverpool City Council (XXIII, 108); the University of Liverpool (178, 196); Lloyd's Register of Shipping (XLII, 200); London Metropolitan Archives; the Clerk of the Records, House of Lords (Cameron Papers; R. J. B. Walker's *Catalogue*); Lord Lytton (109–10); the Estate of Charles Mahoney (167); Mairie de Paris (2, 37, 91); Local Studies Unit, Manchester Central Library (City Council Archives); Manchester City Art Galleries (I, 15, 93–7); Marconi Marine (VSEL) Ltd (219); Middlesex Hospital, London (164 a, b); Morley College, London (166); William Morris Gallery, London (13); R. J. Naismith (186); the John Nash Estate (111); National Gallery of Scotland (XLIV); the Trustees of the National Library of Scotland (Nora Geddes's *Reminiscences*); National Maritime Museum, London (218); National Museums and Galleries of Wales (73–4); the National Trust (Buscot Park: 184; Plas Newydd: 9, 10, 198–9; Sandham Memorial Chapel: 136–7; Waddesdon Manor: 195; Wallington Hall: 173–4); the New Forest Parish Councils of Emery Down, Minstead and Lyndhurst (119); Newnham College, Cambridge; Österreichische Galerie Belvedere Wien (11); the Librarian of the Oxford Union Society (140–1); Petit Palais, Musée des Beaux-Arts de la Ville de Paris (31); Musée de Picardie, Amiens (60); Laurence Pollinger Limited and the Estate of Lord Neville Lytton (109–10); the Prendergast School (167); Marina Rainey (XVI, XXXIX, 54 a, b–59, 188); Republik Österreich/Parlamentsdirektion (3); Rochdale Metropolitan Borough Council (XXII, 92); Rochdale Local Studies Library; Royal Academy of Arts, London (7, 78–80, 84–5, 150); Royal West of England Academy (XXXII); St Edmund's College, Ware (146); St James the Less church, Vauxhall (118); St James the Less Episcopal church, Edinburgh (129 a, b); St John the Baptist church, Brighton (123); St Jude's church, Hampstead (132); Provost of St Mary's Cathedral, Edinburgh (128); St Mary's church, Clapham (116); St Michael and All Angels church, Garton-on-the-Wolds (125); St Ninian's Episcopal church, Pollokshaws, Glasgow (130); St Peter's Roman Catholic Cathedral, Lancaster (127); Scottish National Portrait Gallery, Edinburgh (XXXI, 156); Dr Michael Shea, CVO and Mona Shea (XXX, 152–3); the Worshipful Company of Skinners (X–XIII, 41–7); the South African High Commission, London (XXI, 90); the Estate of Joseph Southall (XXXIV); Stadtarchiv Düsseldorf (32); Strathclyde University Archives (Sir Patrick Geddes papers); the Studio Trust (77, 187); Tate Gallery, London (XLIII, 215–16); Rosalind Thomas and Woodgreen Village Hall Management Committee (XXV, 115, 225); Vauxhall St Peter's Heritage Centre (124); V&A Archive; the Board of Trustees of the Victoria and Albert Museum (61, 117–18, 121, 147–9); Wakefield Metropolitan District Council (98); Una Douglas Wallace (212); the Watts Gallery Archives, Compton (143); the Whitworth Art Gallery, The University of Manchester (189–90); Wigmore Hall, London (210); Stephen Wildman.

The following plates are © 1961 Estate of Vanessa Bell, courtesy Henrietta Garnett (138, 193–4); © 1978 Estate of Duncan Grant, courtesy Henrietta Garnett (139, 161, 192–4); © Estate of Mrs G. A. Wyndham Lewis. By Permission (15, 163, 191); © Mayor Gallery, London (220).

Whilst every effort has been made to trace owners of copyright, the author and publisher regret that in some cases this has not been successful. I would welcome any information which would enable full acknowledgement to be given in any future edition of the book.

My greatest debt of thanks is due to my parents, to whom this book is dedicated. Their perceptive observations and challenging insights have enriched my searches and interpretations, whilst their understanding, patience, and unwavering support have enabled me to bring the book to its present conclusion and look beyond it to the horizons of mural research.

CONTENTS

COLOUR PLATES

BLACK AND WHITE PLATES

PHOTOGRAPHIC CREDITS

ABBREVIATIONS AND NOTE ON USE OF APPENDICES B–E

ABBREVIATIONS

BD	Diaries of Count William de Belleroche (collection of Gordon Anderson)
BEA	Bank of England Archive/Museum, London
BSRA	Archives of the British School at Rome, London
CFA	Commissioners on the Fine Arts, Palace of Westminster, London (1841–1863)
CHA	Castle Howard Archives
CLRO	Corporation of London Records Office
CP	Command Paper, published by HMSO, London
Cam.P.	Sir D. Y. Cameron Papers, Historical Collections: House of Commons Library, MS No. 106, in the custody of the House of Lords Record Office, Palace of Westminster
GCM	Gresham Committee Minutes, Mercers' Company Archives, London
HA	Harcourt Archive, Bodleian Library, Oxford (MS Dep. 457)
HA(B)	Hardman Archive, Birmingham City Archives
HLRO	House of Lords Record Office, Palace of Westminster
IWM	Imperial War Museum, London, War Artists Archive
LMA	London Metropolitan Archives
MCA	Mercers' Company Archives, London
MTA	Manchester Town Hall Archives, Local Studies Unit, Manchester Central Library
Min.SCFA	Minutes of Evidence taken before the Select Committee on the Fine Arts (1841, published in Parliamentary Papers, Palace of Westminster)
NLS	National Library of Scotland, Edinburgh
PP	Parliamentary Paper(s)
PRO	Public Record Office, London
p.w.u.	present whereabouts unknown
RA	Royal Academy of Arts, London
RA(F)	Roberson Archive, Fitzwilliam Museum, Cambridge
RA(W)	Royal Archives, Windsor Castle
Rep.SCFA	Report from the Select Committee on Fine Arts (1841, published in Parliamentary Papers, Palace of Westminster)
SCA	Archives of the Worshipful Company of Skinners, London
RIBA	Royal Institute of British Architects, London

SCHLO	Select Committee on the House of Lords Offices (1925–30 re decoration in Royal Gallery, House of Lords, Palace of Westminster)
SCPW	Select Committee on the Palace of Westminster (1906–7)
SUA	Sir Patrick Geddes Archive, Strathclyde University Archives, Glasgow
TGA	Tate Gallery Archive, London

APPENDICES

Appendices B–E contain selected supplementary examples (not necessarily extant) of mural painting and relate each to a specific chapter (see 'Contents'). Within these chapters, reference to an item in the related appendix is indicated by a number.

1

An *Art extraordinaire*

On 15 March 1895, a 'special van' sent by Roberson's, the artists' suppliers and colourmen, drew up at the Royal Academy of Arts in London. According to the company's archives, nine of their employees set to work 'fitting into large case 17ft × 13ft' a 'Picture by Sir Fred. Leighton PRA', which they loaded onto the van and took across London to the Royal Exchange, next to the Bank of England and the Mansion House in the City.[1] Their labours ran into overtime. A few weeks earlier, on 28 February, eight of Roberson's men had already expended considerable energy in removing from their stretchers both Leighton's painting and another of the same proportions by his fellow Academician Robert W. Macbeth, and in 'putting one on [a] cylinder and restraining the other'. By 10 May, however, gathering once more at the Royal Exchange, the workmen were ready to start 'unpacking from case and fitting to wall and fixing . . . the picture by Sir Frederic Leighton Bart, PRA', taking care to make 'special arrangement for its safety and security'. With a certain note of pride in a difficult job well done, Roberson's Personal Account Book records that 'this picture required extremely careful handling', and by 27 May the triumphant stage had been reached of 'making two Large Curtains in dark green Serge for opening ceremony fitted with cords rings etc'.[2] The first mural had been installed in the series of thirty which was carried out for the Exchange between 1895 and 1927 by prominent artists of the day. Gratifying success had been achieved with a modern French version of the technique for securing murals to the wall called *marouflage* (see Appendix A), which was being pioneered in Britain at the Exchange (Leighton having carried out his painting on canvas in his own studio). Now the Lord Mayor of London agreed to officiate at a formal unveiling ceremony when the green serge curtains were drawn aside, revealing Leighton's mural to a gathering of the great and the good of the City. Entitled *Ancient Commerce* (Plate 1), it portrayed a scene of Phoenician traders bartering with early Britons on the shore of Cornwall, and it offered, appropriately for its location, a reminder of Britain's historic tradition of trade, as well as a suitably 'authentic' effect: Leighton had painted the cloud-swept sky from studies made on the Cornish coast. R. W. Macbeth's mural, showing Queen Victoria opening the new Exchange in 1844 after its predecessor's destruction by fire, was unveiled shortly afterwards.

If Roberson's dry business archives come to life with unwonted immediacy in recording these first contributions to the mural scheme at the building known by the late nineteenth century as 'the heart of Empire', it is hardly surprising. Native mural painting in Britain did not have an

[1] Roberson's Personal Account Book (1895), HKI 313–1993, p. 93, RA(F). [2] Ibid.

unbroken, firmly established tradition like its counterpart in France, Germany, or Austria. Although accomplished work, in both churches and private houses, had been completed in medieval and Renaissance Britain, the Reformation had severely curtailed religious patronage and secular commissions had increasingly fallen to Continental artists.[3] James Barry had painted an ambitious and original scheme of symbolic decoration at the Society of Arts in the 1770s and 1780s and in 1811 William Blake had dreamt of painting walls with 'figures one hundred feet in height',[4] inventing his own characteristically bizarre fresco medium for the purpose, but another thirty years elapsed before any substantial and coordinated effort to re-establish a native 'school' of mural painting. This was the decoration of the new Palace of Westminster, begun in the early 1840s. Fired alike by the interest in medieval wall-painting which accompanied the Gothic Revival in architecture, and the enthusiasm of Prince Albert and of artists such as William Dyce and Sir Charles Eastlake for the recent revival of early Italian fresco technique by the German Nazarene artists in Rome and Munich, the British turned to mural painting with vigour and *élan*, but more in a spirit of experiment than of habit. By the 1890s, however, when the Royal Exchange murals were begun, paintings could be found on the walls of the Paris Hôtel de Ville (Plate 2) as well as nearly every Parisian Mairie (district town hall) and their German counterparts, and also in the Parliament buildings, law-courts, universities, schools, and even hospitals and railway stations of countless Continental towns and cities (Plate 3). In France, Delacroix and Ingres had painted ceilings in the Louvre, whilst Puvis de Chavannes, Besnard, and the Nabis were carrying forward their beacon in decorations for the Sorbonne, the Panthéon (Plate 4), or private houses; in Austria, the hand of Klimt was sought for commissions in the great public buildings of Vienna; whilst in Germany the work of the Nazarenes for King Ludwig I (Plates 5, 6) had been followed by that of the Düsseldorf and Munich 'Schools', and mural painting was a central preoccupation of Symbolists such as von Stuck. For the British, despite the work at Westminster, this form of art was still something of a novelty. French workmen had to be called over to demonstrate the *marouflage* method at the Exchange; this in itself was an attempt to overcome the technical problems which painting directly onto the wall had thrown up in the Westminster decoration and in a number of other British schemes from the 1850s to the 1880s. Whereas the fictional French painter Claude Lantier in Emile Zola's 1886 novel *L'Oeuvre* could dream of making his name, almost as a matter of course, through the opportunity

> to have miles upon miles of walls to cover, to decorate the railway stations, the markets, the municipal offices, everything that will be built . . . Only strong heads and muscles will be wanted, for there will be no lack of subjects . . . The whole of modern life! Frescoes as high as the Panthéon! A series of canvases big enough to burst the Louvre![5]

British artists and patrons were developing this form of art largely by trial and error—a situation which continued into the twentieth century.

The results naturally revealed elements of inspiration from Continental examples, but they also showed—as in Leighton's use at the Exchange of a painting medium (spirit fresco) recently

[3] See E. Croft-Murray, *Decorative Painting in England* (1965–70); of the native work undertaken, the most significant includes James Thornhill's at Greenwich Hospital (1708–12) and St Paul's Cathedral (1719–21); William Hogarth's at St Bartholomew's Hospital (1735–6) and, along with work by Joseph Highmore, at the Foundling Hospital (1746–7); and James Barry's *Progress of Civilisation* murals at the Royal Society of Arts (1777–*c.*1784).

[4] Quoted in M. Butlin, *William Blake* (Tate Gallery, London, 1978), p. 104.

[5] E. Zola, *His Masterpiece*, trans. E. A. Vizetelly (Gloucester, 1986), pp. 36–7.

invented in Britain—a concern to shape a distinctive 'native' art form. Though Lantier envisaged murals of 'modern life', the British often preferred other forms of iconography. Very 'contemporary' events and attitudes were nevertheless expressed frequently by means of historical or literary subjects in the murals they produced. The century from 1840 saw a significant number of British artists of stature turning their hand to mural painting: not only Dyce and Leighton but also G. F. Watts, Daniel Maclise (Plate 7) and Ford Madox Brown, to the Newlyn painters, Percy Wyndham Lewis, Duncan Grant, Sir Stanley and Gilbert Spencer, and Sir Frank Brangwyn (Plate 8). Their work represents a distinctive—and at its best, very original and remarkable—contribution to the national heritage. This book is intended to offer a first survey and critical discussion of what they achieved; a body of art which can fairly be termed the 'British mural revival'.

The work considered in the following chapters was felt in its time to be a kind of *art extraordinaire*, making painters into heroes, viewers into visionaries, and buildings into architecture. Mural painting lent authority, imbued respect, revealed religion, and fostered faith. Thoughts, dreams, and ideals might be given vivid presence in hall or home alike, and artistic genius unleashed. Present could be joined with future, time with place, and man with fellow man. In public buildings, churches, or schools, murals might offer a focus for ritual and remembrance, or provide propaganda and instruction. The turn-of-the-century polymath and patron Sir Patrick Geddes went to see the easel pictures on show at the Manchester International Exhibition in 1887 and, evidently finding the murals by Madox Brown then under way at the city's Town Hall to be far more exciting, demanded:

> Instead of this endless labour on little panels, scattered hither and thither to flap idly upon rich men's walls, grant any of these painters one continued task for his fellow citizens, old or young—make him work for hall or school, for street or square, and see the result; see how the dormant thoughts will flash into activity and the languid nerves be strung.[6]

When, in turn, some twenty-five years later, Geddes was able to promote a pioneering exhibition in London of mural cartoons, samples of fresco, and murals due for installation in various buildings, one of the exhibition's reviewers simply stated that 'The whole question of wall painting . . . is bound up with and forms part of the march of the nation.'[7]

Murals, however, were not just for civic show and cathedral walls, or the great State buildings such as the Palace of Westminster and the Foreign Office, which were decorated in the course of the century from 1840. In private houses, they could invite reverie and retreat; in theatres and on board ship, entertainment and 'escape'. Walter Crane, one of the artists who, despite his Ruskinian belief that 'all really great works of art are public works,'[8] carried out the majority of his mural schemes for private patrons, wrote that 'The mural painter is not only a painter, but a poet, historian, dramatist, philosopher.'[9]

Mural painting was an art with things to say. Painting onto the wall direct, with a medium such as the fresco adopted at the Palace of Westminster on the Nazarene model in the 1840s, gave physical unity to an image and its location, and might invoke powerful symbolism and ritual meaning. At the same time, the kind of iconic, even 'psychological' power of wall-painting

[6] P. Geddes, *Every Man His Own Art Critic* (Manchester and London, 1887), p. 27.

[7] Anon: 'Exhibition of Mural Decoration at Crosby Hall', *Builder*, 102 (14 June 1912), p. 690.

[8] W. Crane, *The Bases of Design* (1902), p. 16.

[9] W. Crane, 'Of Decorative Painting and Design' in *Arts and Crafts Essays*, ed. W. Morris (1893), p. 45.

identified by John Duncan, one of the artists who painted murals for Geddes—'something eternal everlasting to which may bow their heads generation after generation, to which will pray one human family, another . . . another'[10]—could, of course, be sought through any method intended to create a lasting picture in a particular place. As Ruskin himself argued in 1859, with questionable logic but undoubted conviction, 'All the greatest art which the world has produced is . . . fitted for a place, and subordinated to a purpose . . . Portable art—independent of all place,—is for the most part ignoble art.'[11]

Just as the numerous advocates of this *art extraordinaire*—from Prince Albert to Ruskin in the nineteenth century and Roger Fry to Bishop Bell of Chichester in the twentieth—were never satisfied with the amount of patronage available, so mural decoration was an art form which took painting to its limits and extremes. 'England's Michelangelo',[12] as G. F. Watts was dubbed, is believed to have attempted in 1852 to portray not merely the Creation of man painted by his Renaissance role model, but *The Progress of the Cosmos*—and on the walls of Euston Station, with the startling implication that the steam of Watts's engine was born from primal ether. Jakob Götzenberger represented 'infinity' in Bridgewater House a few years later, and in the 1870s, Walter Crane painted what he called 'life' as seen 'through Time's glass' at Combe Bank, near Sevenoaks, to complement the meetings of Charles Darwin, T. H. Huxley, and the Royal Society. To succeed in mural painting betokened virility—B. R. Haydon committed suicide when rejected for a commission at the Palace of Westminster—and its very practice demanded radical measures. Daniel Maclise, faced in 1857 with two 13.72m wall-spaces to decorate in the Royal Gallery at Westminster, had first to procure from Roberson's an astonishing '10 Frames cov'd with sized paper and clamped together to form Cartoon'[13] on which to plot each of his mural designs, and then had to be persuaded by Prince Albert and a visit to observe mural methods in use in Berlin that the technical problems he foresaw were actually surmountable. In the 1890s, canvas large and strong enough to fill the 5.18m high spaces around the ambulatory of the Royal Exchange had to be imported from the Low Countries, and several of the artists commissioned—Stanhope Forbes, Henrietta Rae, Ernest Normand, and W. L. Wyllie—had to install pit and pulley arrangements in their studios to cope with painting their panels. In the event it was over thirty years before the Exchange decoration was complete. In the early 1930s the Bank of England had to foot the bill (£1,000) for fitting out a former chapel for a trial 'installation' of the murals for its newly remodelled building so as to ensure the harmony of ensemble sought by its artists and architect. Around 1937 Rex Whistler made an elaborate sketch of the 'labyrinth of scaffolding, ladders etc' (Plate 9) he expected to require for his murals at Plas Newydd, Anglesey, though a photograph of him at work on them (Plate 10) suggests that simpler devices sufficed in the event.

Hubert Wellington, Principal of the Edinburgh College of Art in the 1930s, called mural painting 'a very special branch of the art of painting . . . [which can] be likened to Grand Opera'.[14] If for Crane the muralist was a 'poet, historian, dramatist, philosopher', it is not surprising that the 'grand opera' involved not only priest, politician, and diplomat, but also tragic hero. Nineteenth-century Ecclesiologists like Beresford-Hope wanted church walls to manifest the spiritual; town councillors demanded strategic celebrations of civic pride, but Sigismund Goetze

[10] J. Duncan, MS Notebook (1917–20), p. 46, Acc. 6686(iii), NLS.

[11] J. Ruskin, *The Two Paths* (1859), quoted in *Papers of the Society of Mural Decorators*, ed. M. Sargant-Florence (1936), pp. 115–16.

[12] See W. Blunt, *England's Michelangelo* (1975).

[13] Roberson's Personal Account Book (12 Oct. 1857), HKI 245–1993, p. 30, RA(F).

[14] H. Wellington, reported in 'Mural Painting unveiled in Heriott-Watt College', *Scotsman* (16 Dec. 1939).

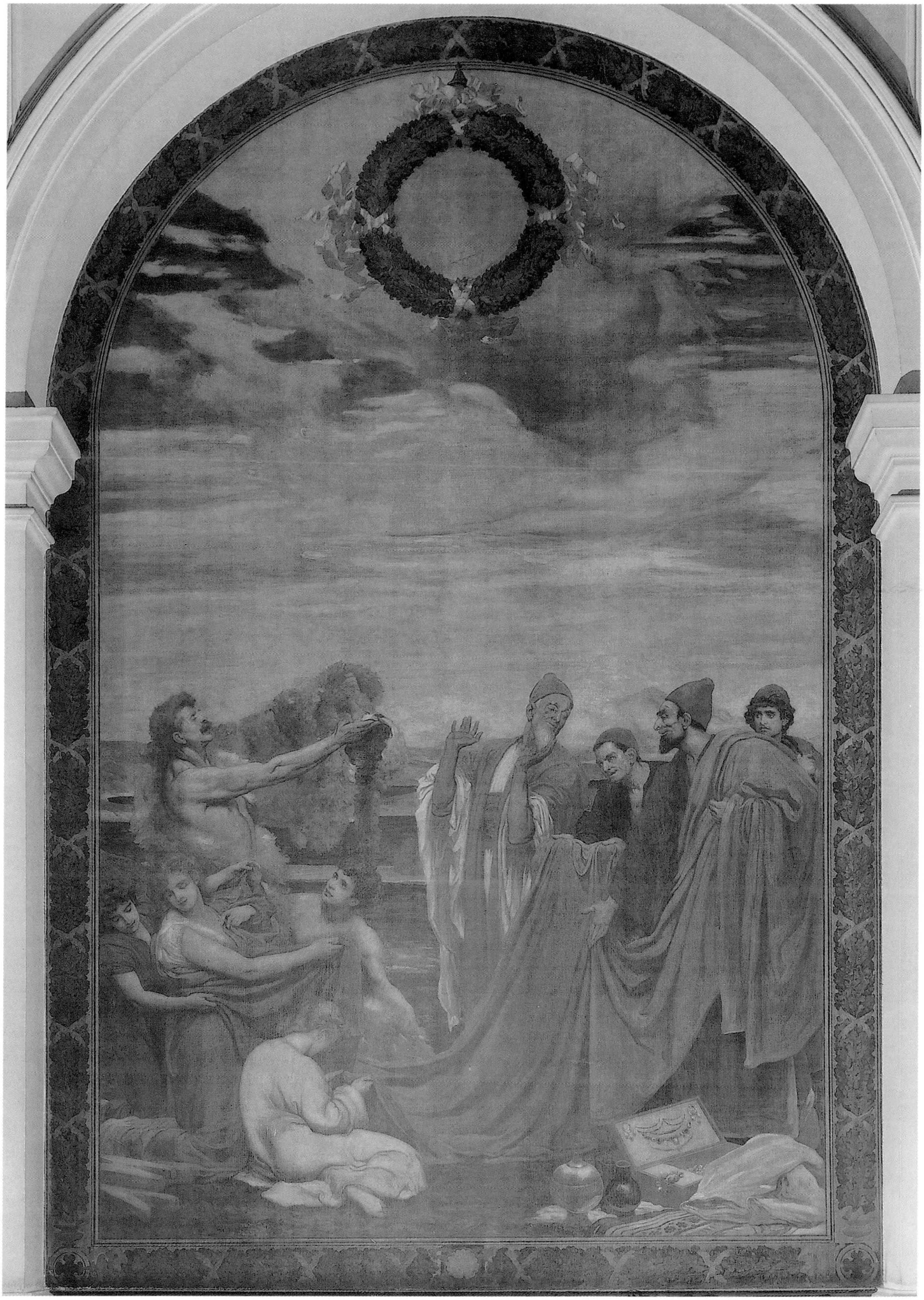

1. Frederic, Lord Leighton, *Phoenicians trading with the Early Britons on the Coast of Cornwall (Ancient Commerce)*, Royal Exchange, London. Presented by Frederic, Lord Leighton, 1895

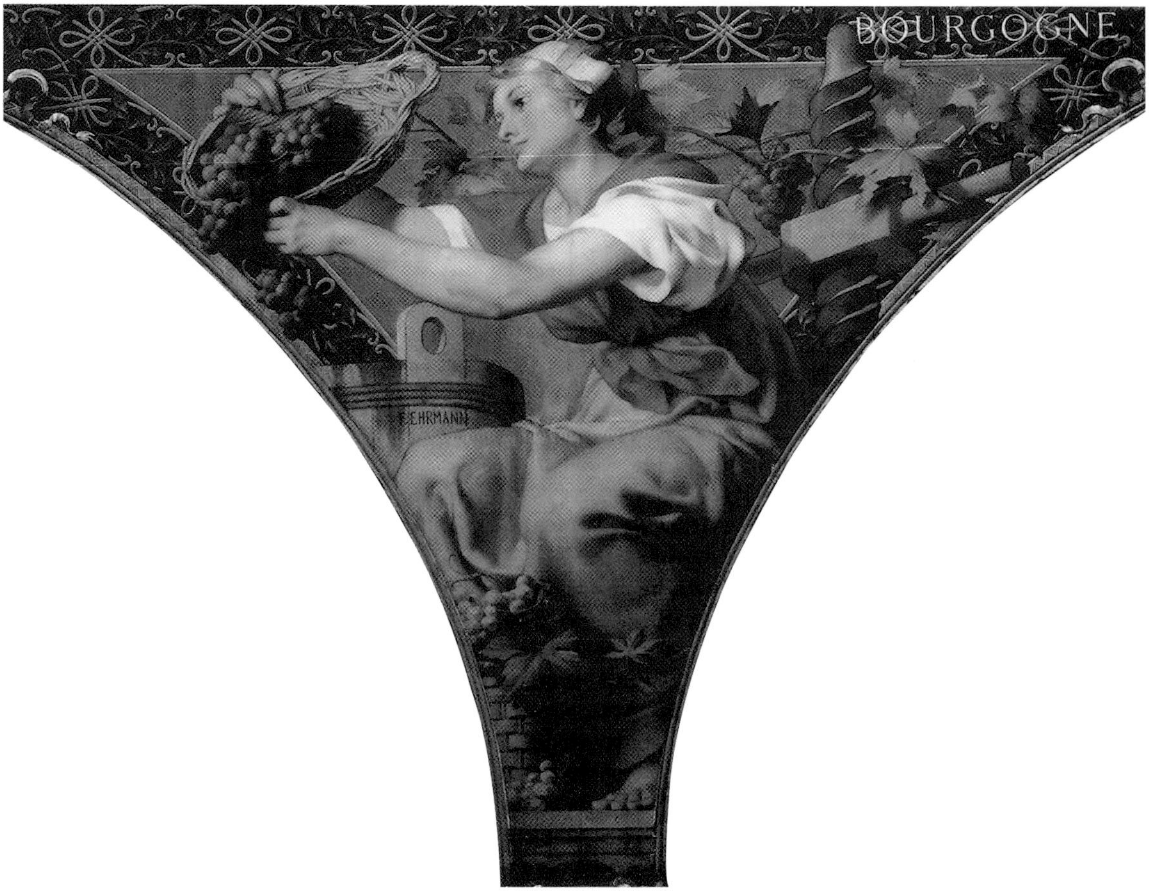

2. François-Emile Ehrmann, *Bourgogne*, Salle des Fêtes, Hôtel de Ville, Paris, 1891

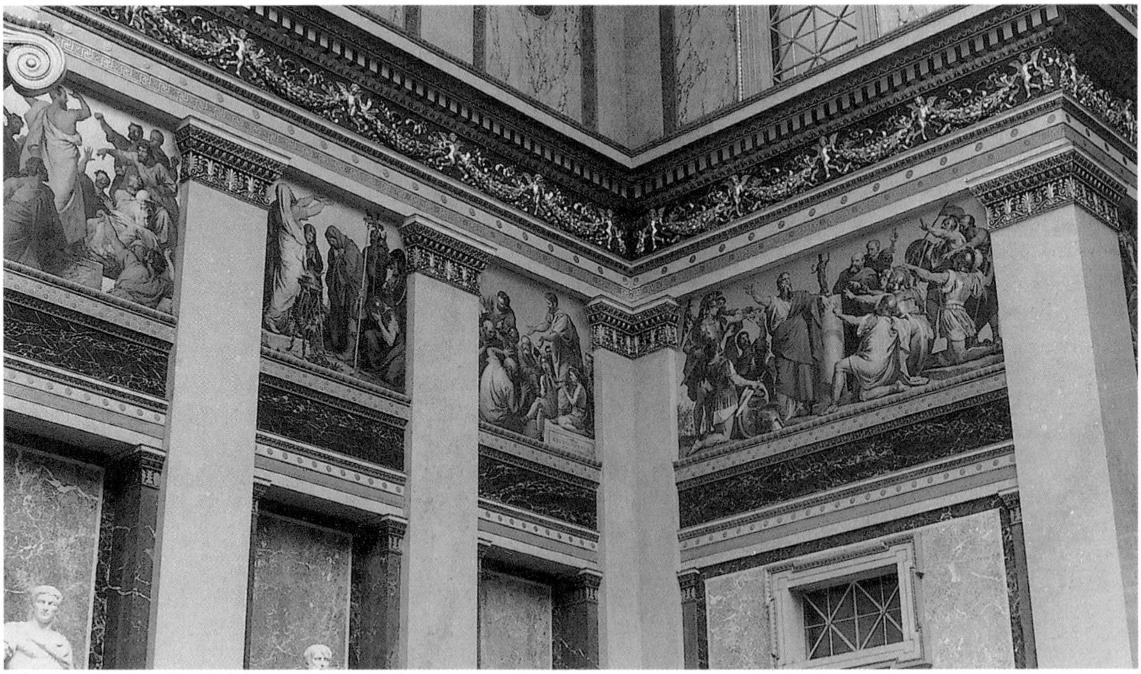

3. August Eisenmenger, *Demosthenes speaking to the People; Caius Graccus on the Speaker's Tribune; Decimus dedicating himself to death; Solon allowing the Athenians to swear by the laws*, session chamber of the House of Representatives, former Reichsrat (now Bundesversammlung), Parlament, Vienna, 1886

in his commission at the Foreign Office, and Brangwyn in the Royal Gallery at Westminster both faced outright rejection of a completed mural scheme, as a result of changed political contexts in the 1920s and 1930s. So too in 1935 Duncan Grant's and Stanley Spencer's mural work for the liner *Queen Mary* met with adamant refusal from the Cunard director Sir Percy Bates. Goetze negotiated a compromise and changed his iconography; Brangwyn lost his battle to the 'English officials',[15] and the forces of Bloomsbury rallied to the defence of Grant, prompting a debate about larger principles of artistic freedom. Spencer simply pulled out of his commission and retreated to a private 'Church House', a kind of mural project without an actual building.[16] Such diversity of plot and cast demands an equal range from the historian of nineteenth and early twentieth-century murals, who by turns must reach into literature, politics, music, philosophy, or science in quest of understanding, and who must be prepared to place murals in the history not just of the so-called 'march of the nation', but also of wider historical, historiographical, cultural, technological, or social factors.

Perhaps because of its character as an art often 'larger than life' in scope as well as scale, mural painting in Britain from 1840 to the Second World War has been gingerly treated (if at all) by modern art historians. Even at a European level, it was possible as recently as 1980 for the historian of nineteenth-century German fresco, Magdalena Droste, to write of murals as 'a form of painting, which since the beginning of the [twentieth] century have, setting aside a few exceptions, been aesthetically taboo'.[17] Bridging painting and architecture, murals have tended not to be seen as part of the history of either; they cannot generally be exhibited unless through sketches or reproductions; and they may be difficult of access and even harder to photograph. They fall ready victims to changes of taste or the reconstruction or demolition of buildings, or they may be removed and reconstituted as independent pictures. Art created for a particular place, with a concomitant function and meaning shaped by patron, painter, and purpose, has, in Britain in particular, rested uneasily with the legacy of Clive Bell's belief that 'The representative element in a work of art may or may not be harmful. Always it is irrelevant.'[18] Although William Morris, William Burges, the Aesthetic Movement, and 'British Impressionism', like nineteenth-century sculpture and architecture, have found appreciation in the wake of John Betjeman's crusade for Victorian art and architecture, there has hitherto been no catalogue or listing, let alone a developmental survey, of British decorative painting of the period, and only sporadic discussion in articles or within the context of monographs on individual artists or histories of art movements of certain, not necessarily representative, examples. C. E. Keyser's rudimentary *List of Buildings in Great Britain and Ireland having Mural and other Painted Decorations* of 1883 has astonishingly remained the main reference.[19] Extensive research has been carried out into medieval British murals,[20] but 'avant-garde' or abstract styles and 'Modernism' have been the dominant subject of

[15] BD (undated).

[16] See R. Carline et al. *Stanley Spencer RA* (1980), pp. 29–30 and 122; a sketch by Spencer for a possible setting for the scheme is in the Tate Gallery (see F. MacCarthy, *Stanley Spencer*, 1997).

[17] 'Eine Malerei . . . die seit Beginn dieses Jahrhunderts, von wenigen Ausnahmen abgesehen, ästhetisches Tabu ist', M. Droste, *Das Fresko als Idee* (1980), p. 11 (author's translation).

[18] Clive Bell, *Art* (1914), p. 20, quoted in *British Art*, ed. S. Compton (1987), p. 15.

[19] See C. F. Keyser, *Buildings in Great Britain having . . . Painted Decoration* (1883); his book was described as 'authoritative' even as recently as 1993 (see P. Burman in *Thomas Gambier Parry*, ed. D. Farr (1993), p. 24).

[20] This includes the work of the Conservation of Wall-Painting Department at the Courtauld Institute, University of London; Prof. E. W. Tristram of the RCA gave major impetus to medieval wall-painting conservation and studies from the 1920s to the 1950s, and his copies of such decoration, which first reached public attention through the 'British Primitives' exhibition at Burlington House in 1923, followed those of J. T. Smith earlier (see Smith, *Antiquities of Westminster*, 1807) and in this sense form part of the wider history of mural painting at the period.

studies of twentieth-century British painting.[21] It has apparently seemed easier to dismiss, rather than seeking to reconcile with the 'Modernist' canon, an art-form which was often conservative in style by virtue of its very nature as an attempt to embody in lasting form a patron's particular purposes—even though these might involve radical 'content'.

In the last fifteen years or so on the Continent, in contrast, belief that 'A global and objective view of the painting of a nation or a period cannot be gained without taking account of its great decorative paintings'[22] has led to such exhibitions as *Le Triomphe des Mairies*, with its exhaustive documentation of nineteenth-century murals in Paris town halls and the Hôtel de Ville,[23] as well as surveys of individual mural artists like the 1997 *Eduard von Engerth* exhibition in Vienna.[24] It likewise underpins such books as Werner Kitlitschka's *Malerei der Wiener Ringstrasse*. Since the work by Droste, Vaughan, Büttner, and others, German mural art from the Nazarenes onwards has become a recognized field of study. Elsewhere on the Continent, nineteenth- and early twentieth-century historical and Symbolist murals in Belgian civic buildings, and Risorgimento murals in Italy have been the subject of doctoral theses.[25] Meanwhile, in Austria, Klimt's Beethoven frieze (Plate 11) has been rescued from ignominious decay and installed as the *pièce de résistance* of the regilded Secession Building in Vienna for which it was originally created, and Sweden and Denmark have museums for twentieth-century mural sketches and designs.[26]

The metaphorical tide, however, is beginning to turn. As early as 1973, using period sources, John Physick's pioneering *Marble Halls* catalogue 'rediscovered' the decorative schemes of a number of important lost Victorian buildings. More recently, in 1985, Richard Cork's *Art Beyond the Gallery in Early Twentieth Century England* opened new horizons in the field of 'Modernist' or avant-garde British art by bringing to attention some of its murals and architectural sculpture. Helen Smith has catalogued numerous domestic decorative schemes in England of the period 1850–1890; German research has been undertaken on selected British murals of the 1920s and 1930s, and Julie Codell has recently argued the case for recognition of Madox Brown's murals at Manchester Town Hall as a significant element in his *oeuvre* which contributed to wider nineteenth-century debates on the nature of history.[27] My own research on London mural

[21] See, for example, the emphasis in *British Art*, ed. Compton and C. Harrison, *English Art and Modernism* (1994).

[22] 'On ne peut avoir une vision globale et objective de la peinture d'un pays ou d'une époque sans aborder l'art des grand décorations', T. Burollet, *Symboles et Réalités* (1984), p. 50 (author's translation).

[23] Burollet et al., *Le Triomphe des Mairies* (1987); J. Foucart's *Les Peintures de l'Opéra de Paris de Baudry à Chagall* (Paris, 1980) was an important early step in the revival of interest in French 19th/20th century mural painting.

[24] *Eduard von Engerth* (Historisches Museum der Stadt Wien, 1997).

[25] M. Droste, *Das Fresko* (1980), W. Vaughan, *German Romantic Painting* (1980), F. Büttner, *Peter Cornelius*, 1 (1980) and 2 (1999); for German murals, see also E. Trier and W. Weyres, *Kunst des 19. Jahrhunderts im Rheinland*, vol. 3, *Malerei* (Düsseldorf, 1979); R. Andrée et al. (eds), *Die Düsseldorfer Malerschule* (exh. cat., Kunstmuseum, Düsseldorf 1979); H. T. Wappenschmidt, *Ausstattung des deutschen Rathaussaales* (1981); Burollet, *Symboles et Réalités* (1984) and B. Rommé (ed.), *Moritz von Schwind—Fresken und Wandbilder* (exh. cat. Staatliche Kunsthalle Karlsruhe, 1996); H. Börsch-Supan's *Die Deutsche Malerei* (1988) collates the German murals 1800–70 given in key published sources. For Belgian murals, see J. Ogonovszky-Steffens, 'La Peinture monumentale d'histoire dans les édifices civils en Belgique (1842–1923). Naissance, histoire, caractéristiques' (Ph.D. thesis, Brussels, 1994), 'Regards sur la peinture monumentale d'histoire en Belgique au XIXè siècle', in *Charles Degroux et le Réalisme en Belgique*, ed. J. Dewilde and J-M. Duvosquel (exh. cat., Stedelijk Museum, Ypres, 1995), pp. 63–70, 'Un Idéal de Mur', in M. Draguet et al., *Splendeurs de l'Idéal. Rops, Knopff, Delville et leur Temps* (exh. cat., Musée de l'Art Wallon de la Ville de Liège, 1997), pp. 179–97; and for Italian murals, see S. von Falkenhausen, *Italienische Monumentalmalerei im Risorgimento, 1830–1890: Strategien nationaler Bildersprache* (Ph.D. thesis, Tübingen, 1991, published Berlin, 1993). For French public murals, see also P. Vaisse, 'Le Troisième République et les peintres: recherches sur les rapports des pouvoirs publics et de la peinture en France de 1870 à 1914' (Ph.D. thesis, Paris IV, 1980).

[26] For the Beethoven frieze, see Willsdon, 'Gustav Klimt's Beethoven Frieze', in *Art History*, 19 (1996), pp. 44–73. Mural sketches are collected by the Skissernas Museum, Lund, Sweden, and the Skitsesamling, Køge, Denmark.

[27] H. Smith, *Decorative Painting* (1984); mural painting of the Arts and Crafts Movement in Birmingham has been explored in A. Crawford (ed.), *By Hammer and Hand* (1984) and there is a short chapter on English mural painting 1900–35 in J. Christian (ed.), *The Last Romantics* (1989). For the German research, see M. Braesel, *Die*

schemes has borne fruit in the *Survey of London* volume on County Hall (1991) and Ann Saunders's London Topographical Society monograph on the Royal Exchange (1997), for example, where painted and sculptural decoration is embraced as integral to the buildings' histories; as the present book went to press, chapters were published by T. Barringer on Leighton's murals at the Victoria and Albert Museum within the context of a reappraisal of his *oeuvre*, and C. Poulson on Dyce's Royal Robing Room murals at Westminster in relation to nineteenth-century Arthurian iconography.[28] Comprehensive conservation of the murals at the Palace of Westminster is under way, with radical results.[29] The time is ripe to attempt a history and reappraisal of the wider spectrum of nineteenth- and early twentieth-century mural painting in Britain.

Some of the neglect of the British counterpart to the Continental murals discussed by Burollet, Kitlitschka, and others undoubtedly stems from its distinctive character as an art of 'reinvention', with associated problems of interpretation. The 1840s offer a natural *point de départ* for this book because they saw the setting up of a Commons Select Committee to consider 'the Promotion of the FINE ARTS of this Country in connexion [*sic*] with the Rebuilding of the Houses of Parliament',[30] followed by a Royal Fine Arts Commission to put this idea into practice, and thereby re-establish a native 'school' of mural painting. Meanwhile, the Roman Catholic Emancipation Act of 1829 and the rise of the Anglo-Catholic Oxford Movement opened the way for a reintroduction of decoration in churches.

J. T. Smith's *Antiquities of Westminster*, published in 1807, had provided a vivid reminder, through its illustrations of the thirteenth- and fourteenth-century wall-paintings in the original Palace of Westminster (Plate 12), of Britain's vigorous pre-Reformation decorative tradition; with the rebuilding of the Houses of Parliament following the 1834 fire, completed in 1852, an opportunity was presented to renew this. Coinciding as it did with 'the commencement of a new reign'[31] such a development of native talent might, it was hoped, also match—and perhaps even outdo—the decorative tradition of the Nazarenes in modern Germany, and it could also be seen as a response to such recent French schemes as the huge patriotic paintings in the Galerie des Batailles at Versailles and the murals of Delacroix and Ingres.[32] The launch of mural painting at Westminster in this sense forms the flowering of the pride in national identity which had sprung from the wars against Napoleon at the start of the century, and Wellington's and Nelson's victories were indeed the subject of Maclise's enormous murals there.

Following first the Municipal Corporations Act of 1835, and in 1888 the formation of County Councils,[33] the new citadels of local government, the town and county halls, sought in turn to emulate the example of the Houses of Parliament by commissioning murals to embody their values and principles. A multitude of other kinds of building—from theatres to restaurants, schools, museums, and, from around 1900, the new commercial premises which accompanied the

Englische Wandmalerei der 1920er und 1930er Jahre (Ph.D. thesis, Kiel, published Frankfurt and New York, 1996). For Manchester Town Hall, see J. Codell, 'Ford Madox Brown, Carlyle, Macaulay, Bakhtin', in *Art History*, 21 (1998), pp. 324–66.

[28] See Willsdon, *Aspects of Mural Painting in London* (1988), H. Hobhouse (ed.), *County Hall* (1991), and A. Saunders (ed.), *The Royal Exchange* (1997); T. Barringer, 'Leighton in Albertopolis' (1999); and C. Poulson, 'The Queen's Robing Room Frescos' (1999).

[29] See M. A. C. Hay in *Apollo*, 135 (1992), pp. 301–11.

[30] Rep. SCFA, PP VI (18 June 1841), p. iii.

[31] E. Edwards, *The Administrative Economy of the Fine Arts in England* (London, 1840), p. 189.

[32] For these schemes, see L. Rosenthal, *Du Romantisme au Réalisme* (Paris, 1914), pp. 299–341; M. Chaudonneret, 'Historicism and Heritage in the Louvre: From the Musée Charles X to the Galerie d'Apollon', *Art History*, 14 (1991), pp. 488–520; F. Haskell, *History and its Images: Art and the Interpretation of the Past* (New Haven and London, 1993), pp. 281–2; and Willsdon in Macmillan's *Grove Dictionary of Art* (s. v. 'Mural', 1996).

[33] See C. Cunningham, *Victorian and Edwardian Town Halls* (1981), pp. 8ff. for the history of municipal democracy.

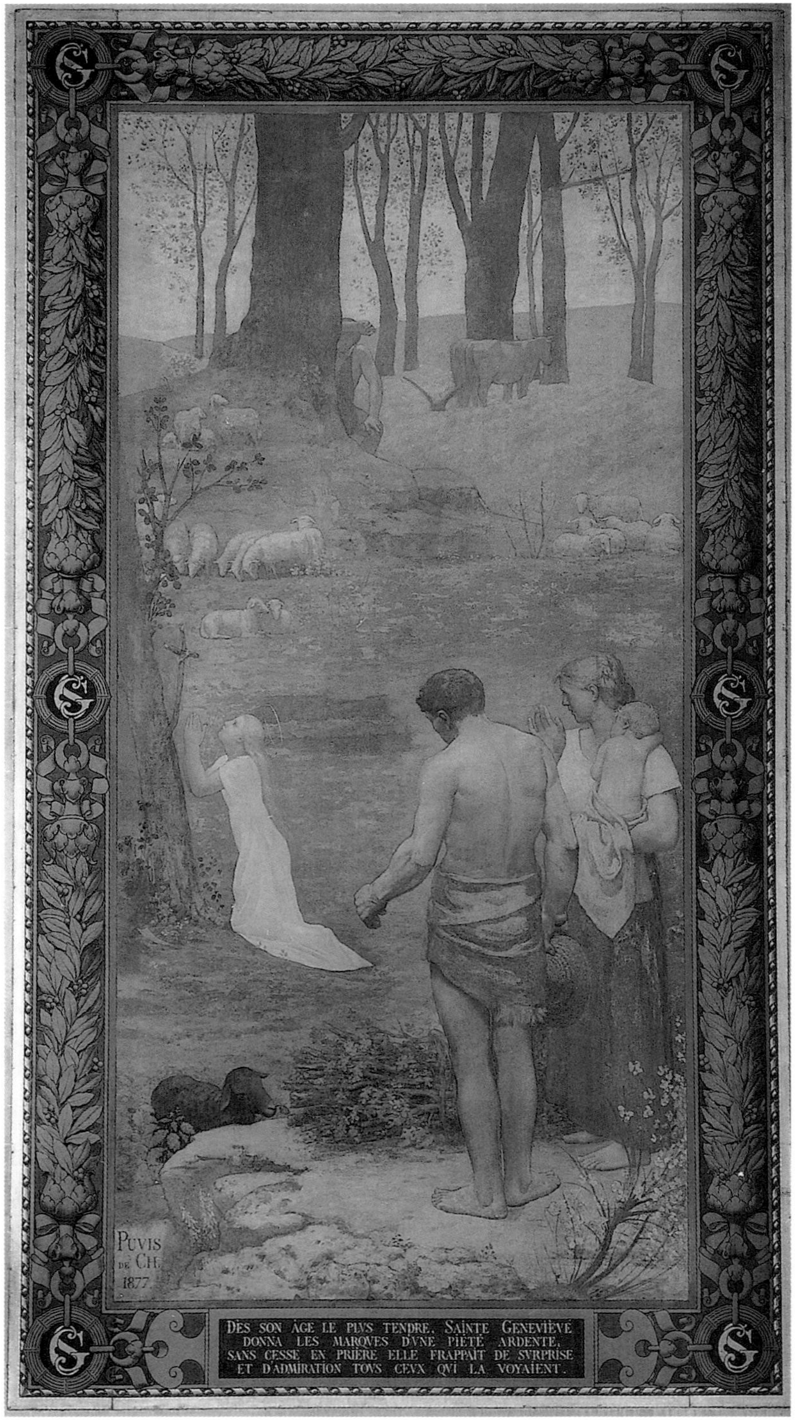
PUVIS DE CH. 1877
DÈS SON ÂGE LE PLUS TENDRE, SAINTE GENEVIÈVE
DONNA LES MARQUES D'UNE PIÉTÉ ARDENTE,
SANS CESSE EN PRIÈRE ELLE FRAPPAIT DE SURPRISE
ET D'ADMIRATION TOUS CEUX QUI LA VOYAIENT.

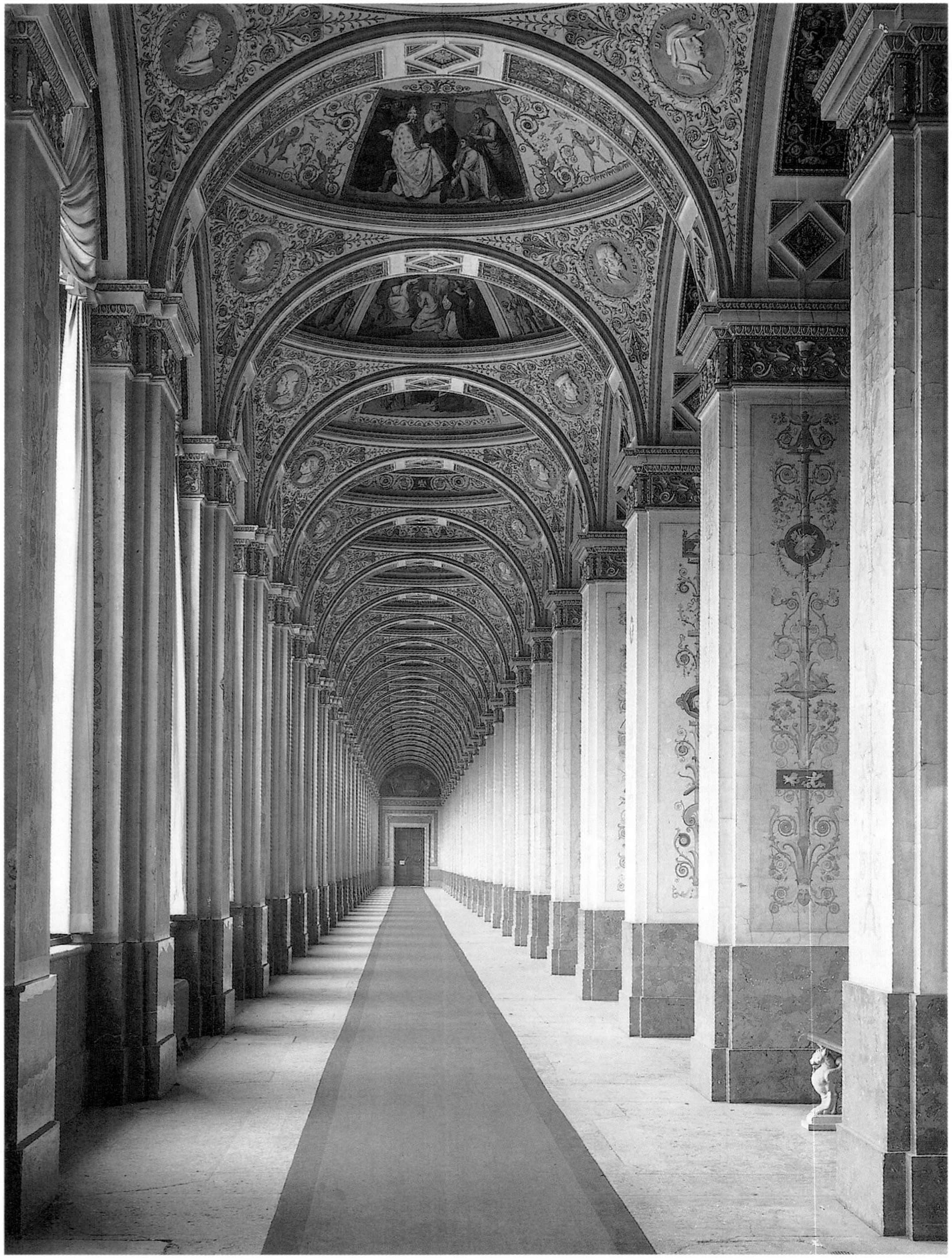

4 (*above, left*). Pierre Puvis de Chavannes, *Childhood of Ste. Geneviève*, Panthéon, Paris, 1877

5 (*above, right*). View westwards of the decoration illustrating the history of art designed by Peter Cornelius, 1827–*c.*1838, and executed by his pupils in the *Loggiengang*, Alte Pinakothek, Munich, *c.*1830s (destroyed)

6 (*right*). *Rubens,* detail from ceiling decoration illustrating the history of art, designed by Peter Cornelius, *c.*1837, and executed by his pupils in the 14th Loggia, Alte Pinakothek, Munich, 1838–40 (destroyed)

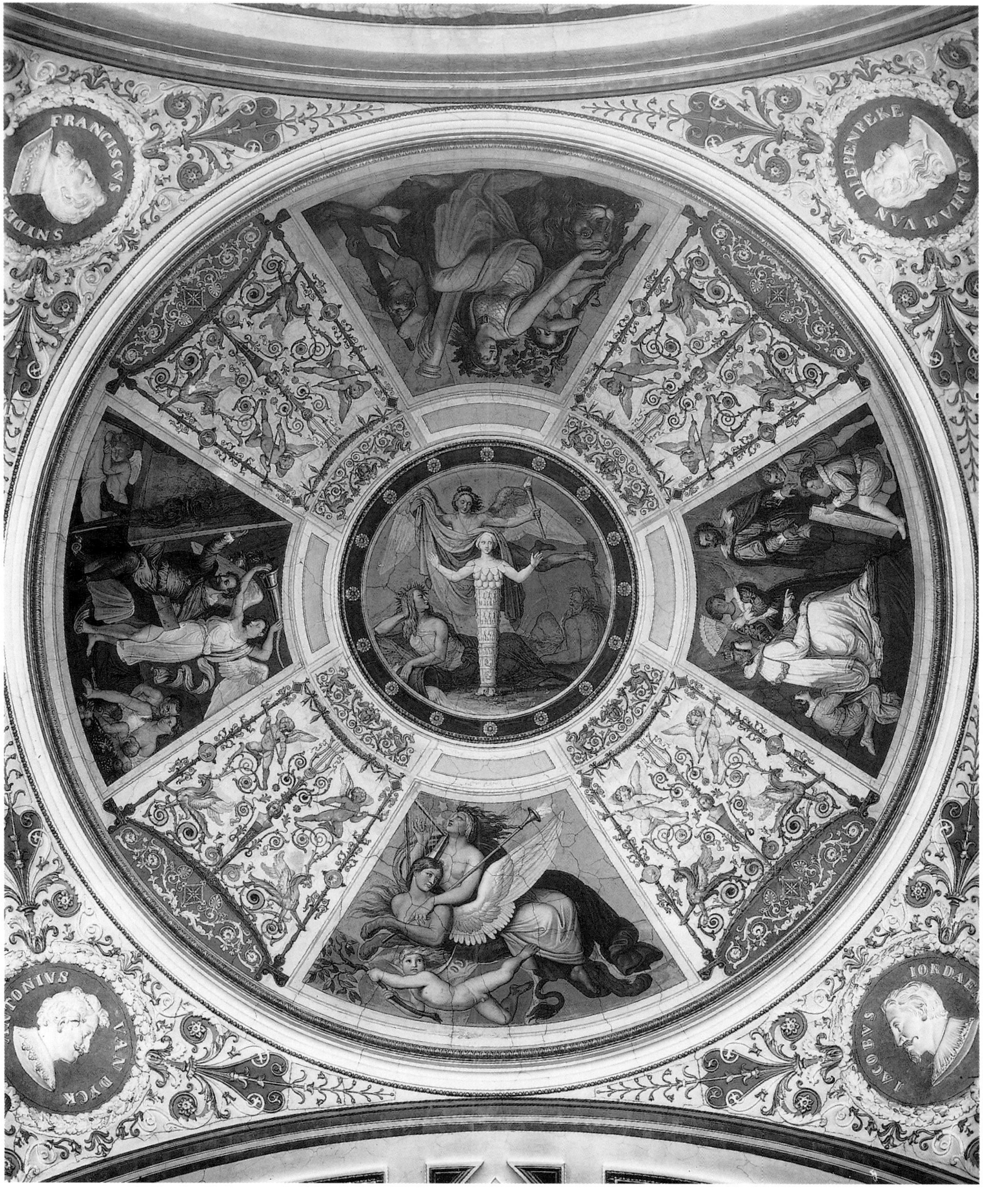

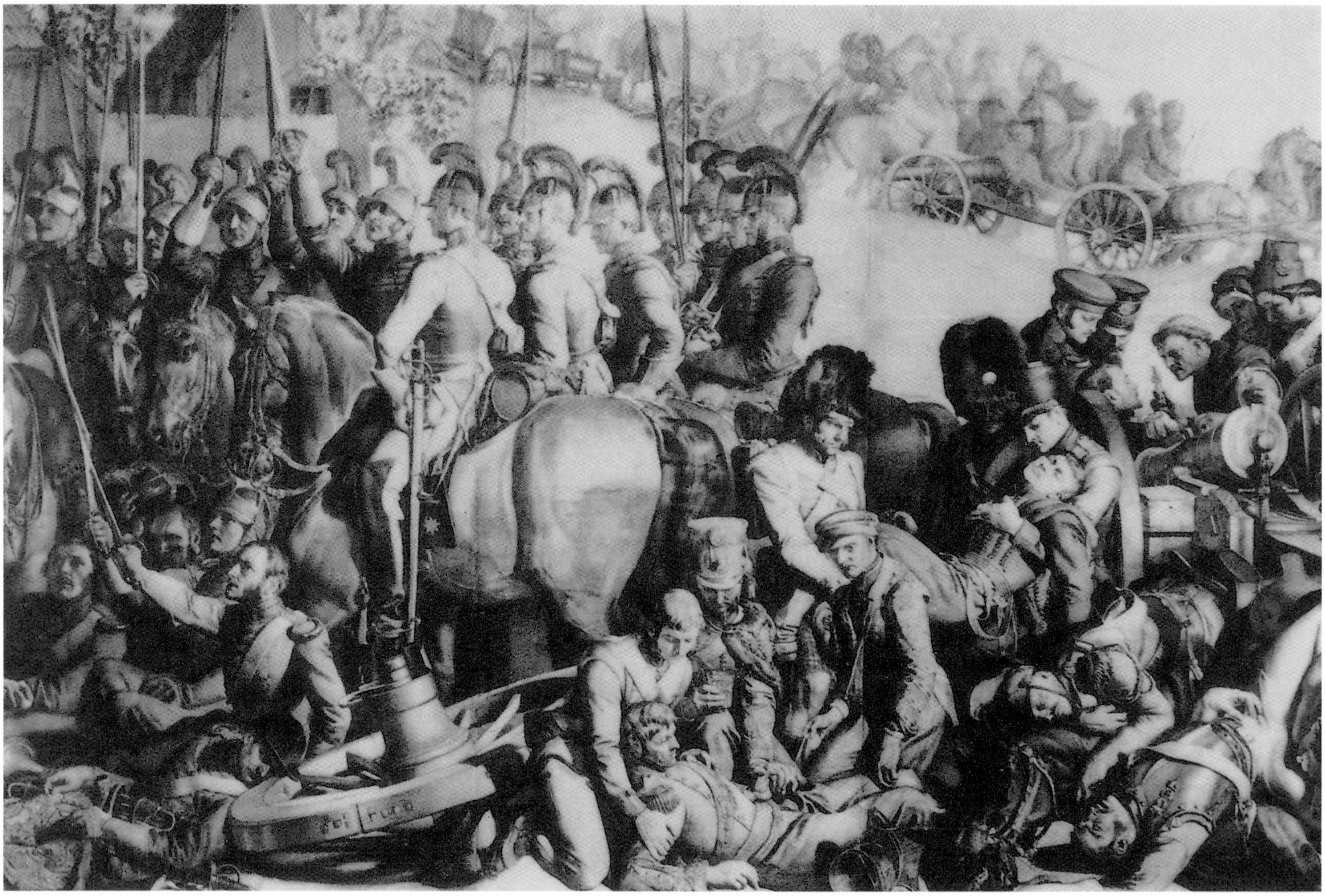

7. Daniel Maclise, detail from cartoon for *The Meeting of Wellington and Blücher after Waterloo*, Royal Gallery, Palace of Westminster, London, *c.*1859–62. London, Royal Academy of Arts

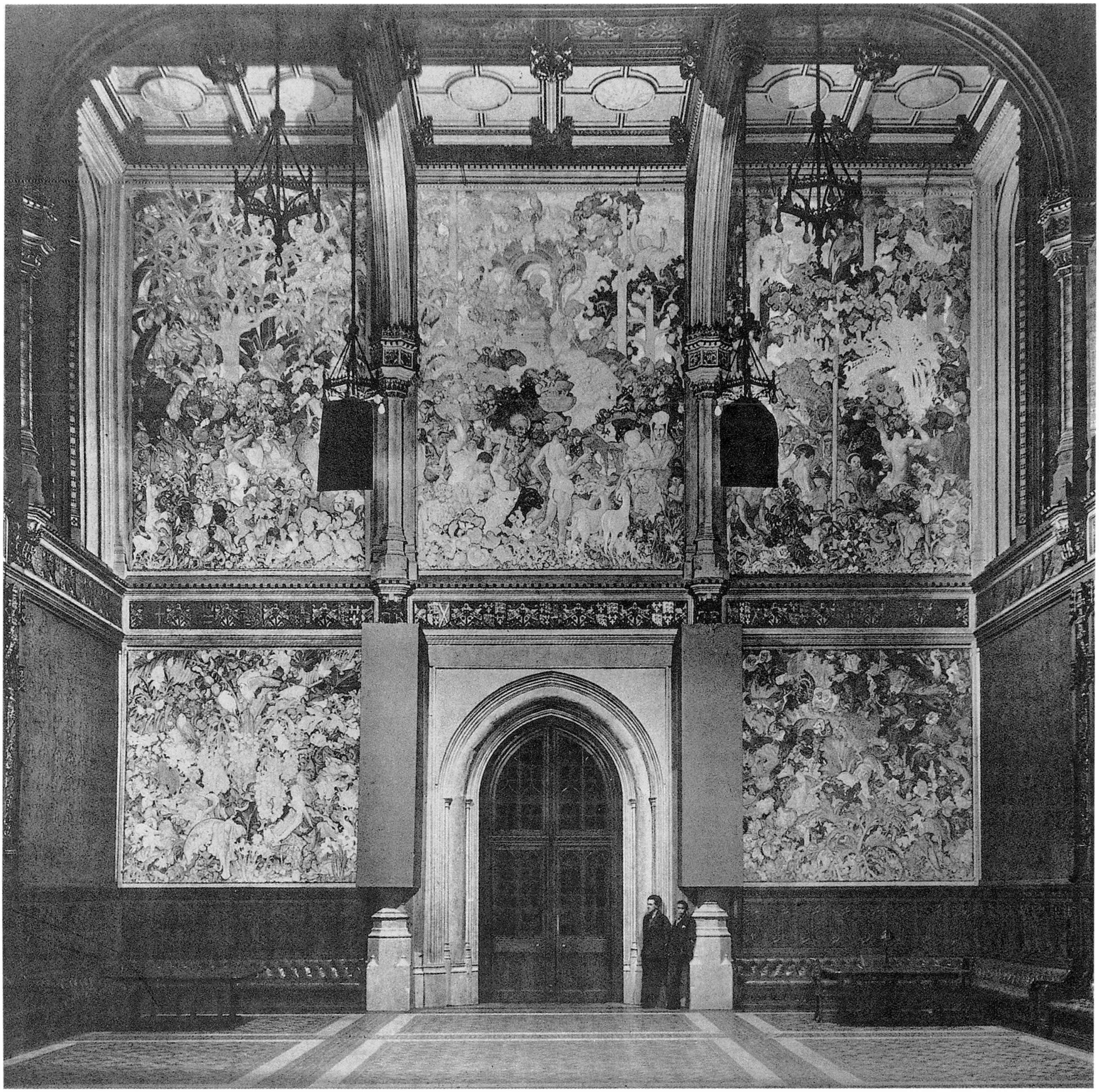

8. Photograph of end wall in the Royal Gallery, Palace of Westminster, London, with five of Sir Frank Brangwyn's *British Empire* panels temporarily placed *in situ*, 1930

expansion of Britain as an imperial power—also turned to mural painting to create mood and ambience or to express status, aspiration, or ideals. Where in previous centuries patronage had centred in State, ecclesiastical, and private hands, there was now a vast expansion of its type and scope, involving complex patterns of appropriation and assimilation as 'new' kinds of patron sought to project their identity by association not just with past architectural styles, but also with their forms of decoration. Lacking an established decorative tradition as found on the Continent, these patrons took note of what they saw on foreign walls, when, for example, as city councillors they visited the Paris Hôtel de Ville for one of the numerous reciprocal civic receptions of the late nineteenth century, or when, as in Manchester and Glasgow, civic deputations were sent expressly to report on Continental mural schemes; indeed, Geddes reported on the new Paris decorations at the 1889 Edinburgh Art Congress. Artists themselves often trained in Paris, Düsseldorf, or Antwerp and saw foreign work at first hand in the great international exhibitions in Paris or Vienna, or at the Paris Salon, where murals were exhibited before installation. Prior to his murals at Westminster, E. A. Armitage had actually helped with Paul Delaroche's mural at the Ecole des Beaux-Arts in Paris. Later in the century, Charles Rennie Mackintosh's connections with the Vienna Secession and Brangwyn's Belgian upbringing and début as a muralist on the walls of Samuel Bing's Maison de l'Art Nouveau in Paris (Plate 13) are reminders of the close artistic relationships with the Continent which underpinned the development of mural painting in Britain.

Back at home, however, without the established commission and payment procedures which were often standard in Continental countries, British patrons naturally 'invented' their own. The system of donation of murals adopted at the Royal Exchange and in the twentieth-century Palace of Westminster schemes can be seen as essentially a derivative of the existing practice of subscription for statuary, and, at the Exchange, it was perhaps also a reflection of philanthropic traditions in the City of London.[34] In 1869 the Society of Arts recorded as the biggest of all the French government's heads of expenditure for the following year the staggering sum of £26,000 for the decoration of buildings[35]—a figure which reflected the much more centralized, as well as more firmly established, tradition of patronage in France. In Britain at this period, in contrast, a wary eye was being kept on the cost of the new decorations at the South Kensington Museum by the Board of Trade, from whose pocket they were funded; its most extravagant fees were £3,000 each for Leighton's two large lunettes for the South Court. So too, whilst State, government, or city were the principal patrons of much contemporary Continental mural painting, and operated tightly organized procedures of competition and selection by committee which kept a close rein on the choice of styles and iconography, the sheer variety of types of mural patronage in Britain, and their nature as new 'inventions', often made for idiosyncratic procedures and outcomes as well as some brilliant achievements. It is perhaps hardly surprising that even as late as the 1930s Brangwyn's ill-fated murals for Westminster were the result of a hybrid arrangement whereby Lord Iveagh as a private individual had 'donated' what was effectively a State War Memorial. When the Royal Fine Art Commission was called in after Iveagh's premature death to sort things

[34] The Wellington Memorial (1844) and George Peabody (1869) statues outside the Exchange had been funded by subscription; philanthropy in the City was, of course, illustrated in the example of Sir Thomas Gresham himself, whose foundations included the Royal Exchange (1566) (see Saunders, *The Royal Exchange*, pp. 18–19).

[35] 'Fine Arts', *Journal of the Society of Arts*, 17 (23 July 1869), p. 707; in 1864, the *Journal* (9 Dec.; 13, p. 109) noted that 'a sum equal to £11,584' had been spent on mural painting in the church of St Augustin in Paris alone.

out, its chairman, Lord Crawford and Balcarres bemoaned 'the muddle of the House of Lords affair, what with one committee and another, and the Lord Great Chamberlain bedevilling the whole business . . . a source of lamentable confusions'.[36]

Whilst freedom from 'bureaucracy' might be expected to enable an artist to come up with splendid results—as Brangwyn's murals could perhaps have been had he been allowed to install them—the lack of a consistent patronage system in Britain, combined with the absence of both a continuous 'history' of mural painting and the kind of established tradition of systematic training in mural art found in France and Germany,[37] often led to more variable artistic quality than on the Continent. There was a vast amount of work by commercial companies in Britain, especially in churches, which is of only modest merit, whilst artists previously experienced only in easel painting found themselves, like Maclise, having to invent new strategies to cope with walls. These had varying degrees of success, but they raise the issue of possible implications for the artists' easel works, and of the nature and status of large-scale 'decorative' easel paintings like Leighton's *Daphnephoria*, created in 1874–6 for Lythe Hill, the Surrey home of his fellow artist Stewart Hodgeson.[38] The latter type of work became popular in Aesthetic circles. Walter Crane's comment that 'The term Decorative Painting implies the existence of painting which is not decorative; a strange state of things for an art which primarily and pre-eminently appeals to the eye'[39] of course parallels the debate in France at the *fin de siècle* about the definition of 'decorative painting'.[40]

The recognition of mural painting as a distinctive art form received new impetus in 1881 through Leighton's introduction of a prize for mural decoration at the Royal Academy, which provided a British version of the Prix de Rome, and in 1911 the British School at Rome was established, with special emphasis on decorative painting and the study of Renaissance murals in Italy. Growing out of the use of students as 'executive' muralists in the decoration of the South Kensington Museum in the 1860s and 1870s, decorative painting had meanwhile been accorded its own 'school' at the Royal College of Art in 1901 and was also introduced to the curricula at the Slade School and certain art schools outside London. Those trained to be mural painters were in the event often sadly thwarted by what Wyndham Lewis called the 'cyclopean dividing wall in time' of the First World War.[41] It is an irony that by the early 1930s when such training was bearing fruit in schemes like Gilbert Spencer's for Balliol College, Oxford, and Alan Sorrell's for Southend Public Library (both by former students respectively of the Slade and the British School at Rome) the requirement at the Royal College of Art for all Drawing and Painting students to study mural painting had just been dropped.[42] In contrast to other European and a number of Commonwealth countries, Britain meanwhile ended up, as a result of both the abandonment of a Ministry of Information project of 1919 and the Brangwyn Royal Gallery fiasco, with no national First World War Memorial.

In dealing with such a multi-faceted art-form, involving as it does an often complex interaction between patron, painter, and viewer, and their wider social, political, and historical contexts, as

[36] Letter from Lord Crawford and Balcarres to Lord Peel (20 June 1928), Work 11/279, PRO.

[37] e.g. at the Ecole des Beaux-Arts in Paris, the Akademie in Düsseldorf, and the Akademie der bildenden Künste and the Kunstgewerbeschule in Vienna. This training often consisted of 'master painters' employing students to work on decorative schemes as assistants.

[38] Now in the Lady Lever Art Gallery, Port Sunlight.

[39] Quoted in J. M. Brydon et al., 'Decorative Painting', in *Transactions of the RIBA*, 7 (1891), p. 277.

[40] See R. Thomson, *Monet to Matisse* (1994), pp. 131ff.

[41] W. Lewis, 'The Writer and the Absolute' in W. Michel and C. J. Fox (eds), *Wyndham Lewis on Art* (1969), p. 13.

[42] See *Prospectus* of the Royal College of Art, 1927–8.

well as widely variable artistic quality, traditional art-historical methodologies of stylistic analysis own or study of techniques and sources are, on their own, not much help. Many manuals and textbooks discussing historical methods of mural painting were published both in tandem with and following the revival of mural painting at Westminster,[43] and technical aspects have correspondingly tended to dominate the limited amount of modern interest in nineteenth- and early twentieth-century British mural painting,[44] but these are only part of the story. In the interests of a more integrated and rounded approach, technique is discussed in this book only in so far as it has a bearing on the larger significance or character of a mural: the 'psychological', political, or social implications of the subjects chosen for the walls of a particular building may in many cases be more revealing of meaning and purpose than the materials or even the style with which they were painted. Whilst *in situ* media such as true fresco, encaustic, or substitutes including waterglass were frequent in the period 1840–60, and were welcomed by Prince Albert for enabling a broadness of style he felt desirable in 'High Art' intended to communicate great thoughts, these largely gave way by the later nineteenth century (as on the Continent, and despite Leighton's attempts to popularize 'spirit fresco') to oil or other media on canvas fixed to the wall; this can be taken as the method employed in the work discussed unless otherwise stated. Where technique becomes significant, in fact, is most often in relation to philosophies of the 'integration' of murals with their setting, or with an architectural style, as in the case of what has been called 'fresco as an idea' in nineteenth-century German mural painting.[45] The German tradition of symbolism derived from the physical unity of iconography and its location was particularly influential in Britain through Prince Albert's promotion of fresco, and 'art-architecture' in turn became a rallying cry of Burges and the Gothic Revivalists. In the twentieth century, in the wake of T. G. Jackson's *Architecture a Profession or an Art?* of 1892, ideals of interrelationship between decoration and architecture were transferred to the context of 'Edwardian Baroque' in buildings such as the Old Bailey. Even in the 1930s these ideals remained vigorous, not only in the decoration of the Bank of England, but also on board ships and in the theoretical association of fresco technique with 'Modernist' architecture.

In considering decorative art in Britain during the period from 1840 to 1940, whether murals, sculpture, or indeed, other art-forms with a particular symbolic role, concepts 'borrowed' from other disciplines, such as the 'invention of tradition' discussed by the historians Cannadine and Hobsbawm,[46] may indeed offer a more helpful aid to interpretation than conventional art-historical methodologies, such as attribution and the tracing of influences and stylistic chronologies, and may in turn illuminate an artist's choice of idiom. Aesthetic canons of judgement, though necessary, are not sufficient. The realistic murals illustrating historical episodes, such as

[43] e.g. E. Latilla, *Treatise on Fresco* (1842); M. P. Merrifield, *Treatise on Painting* (1844) and *The Art of Fresco Painting* (1846); T. Goodwin, *The Art of Mural Decoration* (1866); C. J. Herringham, *The Art of Cennino Cennini* (1899); Hamilton Jackson (1904); Vallance (1908); Ward (1913). Peter Cornelius's fresco technique was detailed in Appendix 3 of the *First Report* of the CFA at Westminister (22 April 1842), PP XXV, and Sir Charles Eastlake described this and other techniques to the CFA, e.g. Appendix 14 to its *Third Report* (1844), PP XXXI. Exhaustive accounts of new techniques were systematically published in the *Journal of the Society of Arts* through the second half of the 19th century. Impetus was given to technical studies by the RA's professorship of Chemistry ('the only one of its kind in Europe'); its incumbent from 1879 to 1911, A. H. Church, conducted a Parliamentary Enquiry into the condition of the Westminster frescoes from 1895 to 1906 and advised on the preservation of numerous other mural schemes, as well as investigating Roman and other early techniques (see obituaries of Church in *Transactions of the Chemical Society*, 109 (1916).

[44] e.g. Farr (ed.), *Joseph Southall* and *Thomas Gambier Parry*; Crawford (ed.), *By Hammer and Hand*; and Hay, Vaughan and Powers in *Apollo* (1992); as well as to some extent Smith, *Decorative Painting* and Christian (ed.), *The Last Romantics*.

[45] Droste, *Das Fresko*, p. 11 (see n. 17).

[46] E. Hobsbawm and T. Ranger (eds) *The Invention of Tradition* (1983).

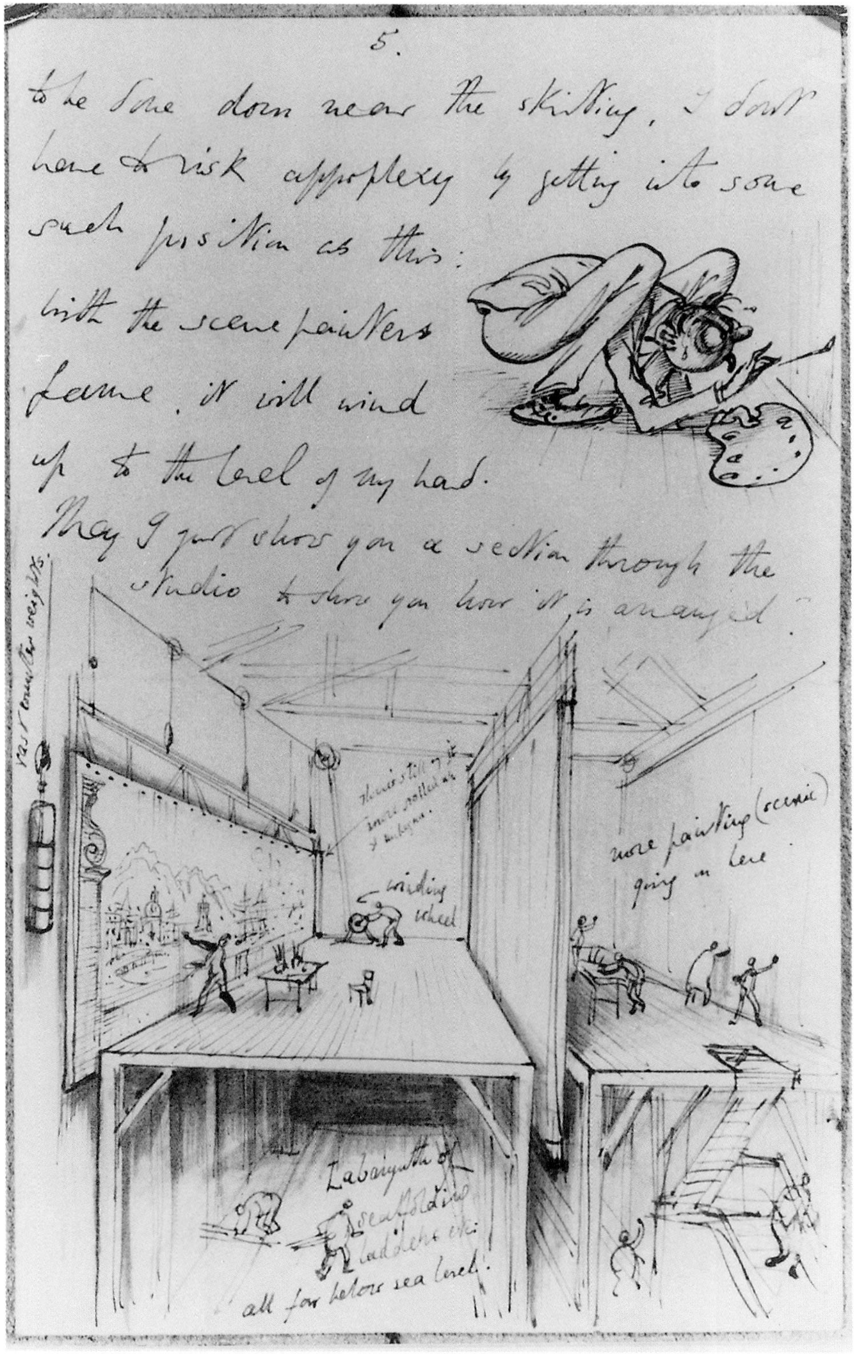

9. Rex Whistler, sketches of self-portrait and proposed working method for his murals at Plas Newydd, Anglesey, 1937

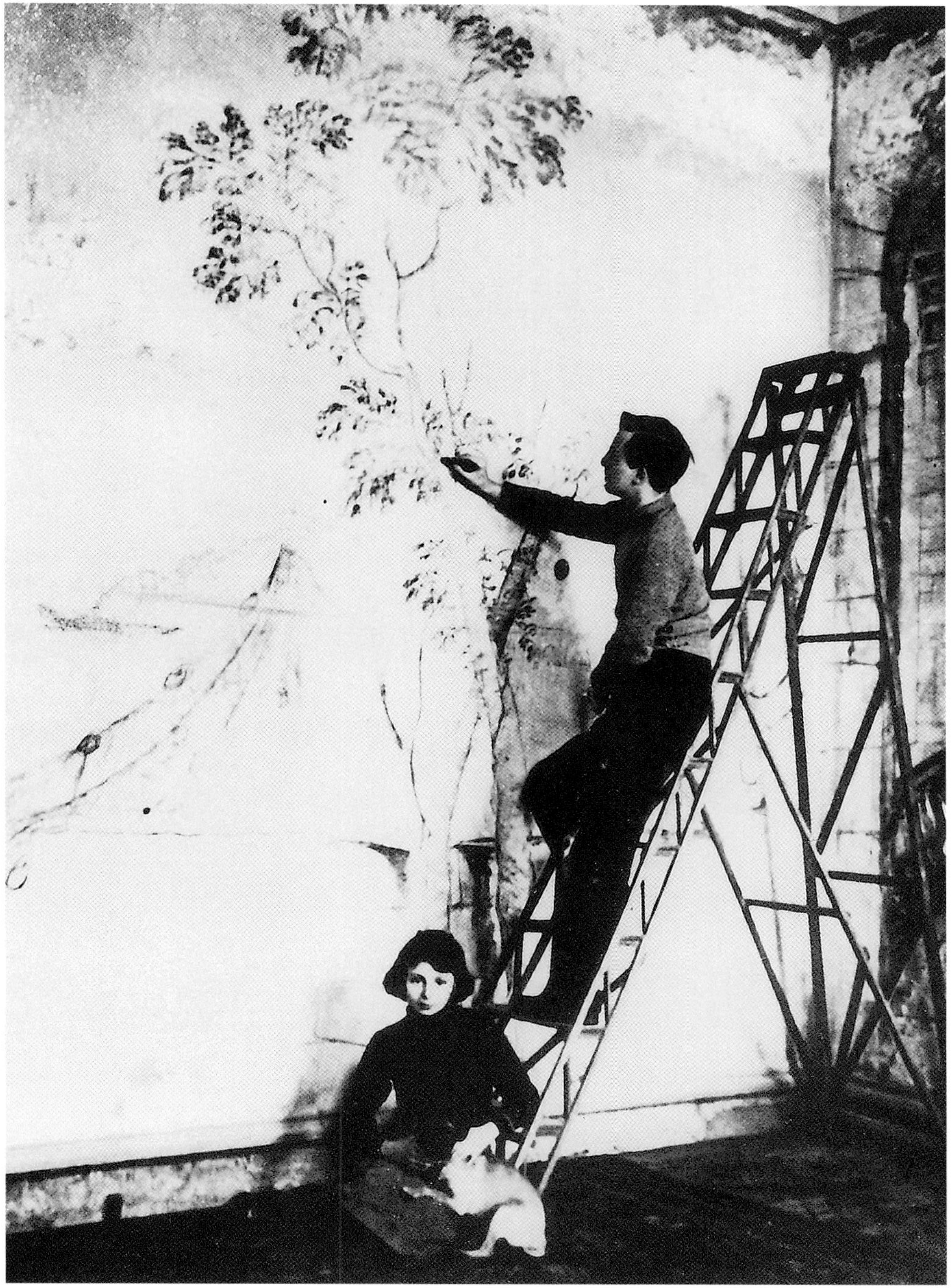

10. Photograph of Rex Whistler working on his murals at Plas Newydd, Anglesey, late 1930s

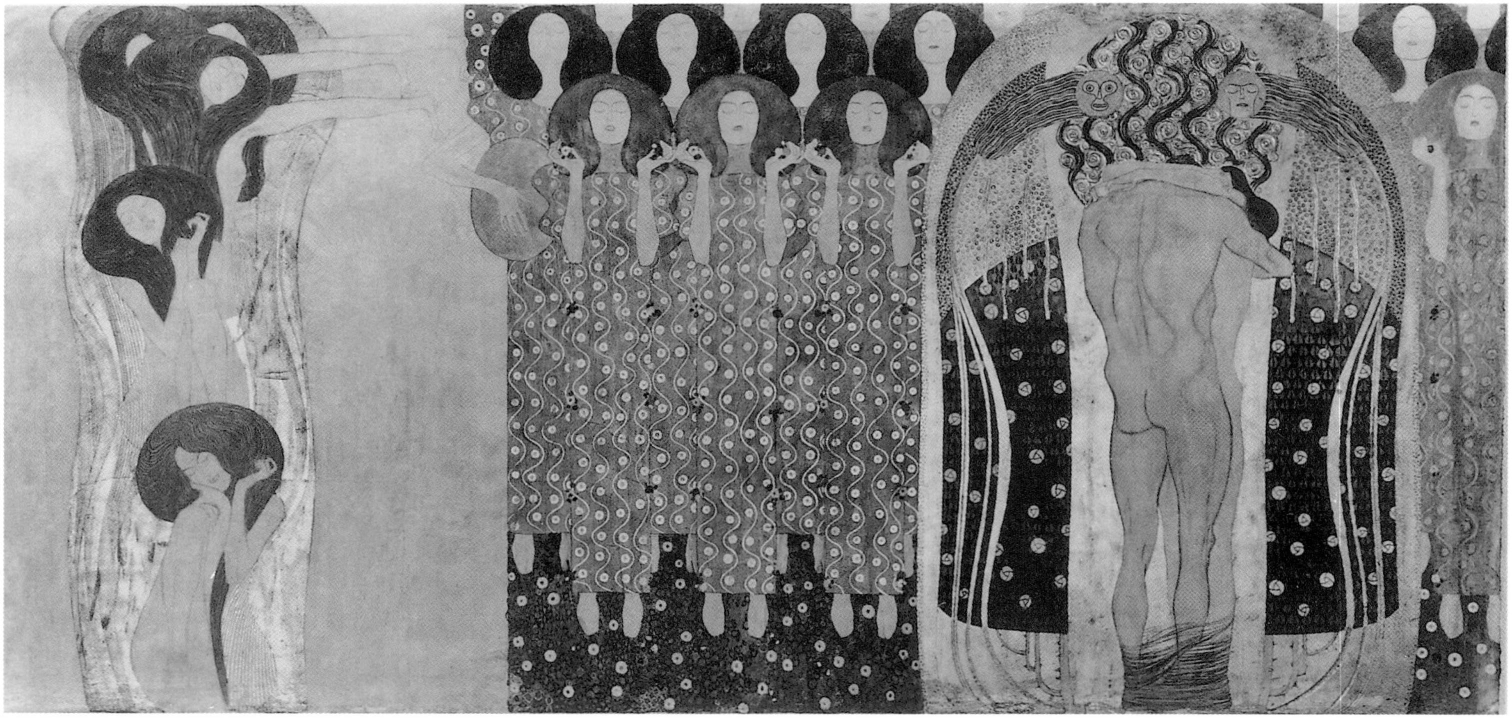

11. Gustav Klimt, *The Arts, Choir of Paradise Angels*, and *This Kiss to the Whole World*, final section of *Beethoven* Frieze for XIVth Vienna Secession Exhibition, 1902. Vienna, Österreichische Galerie

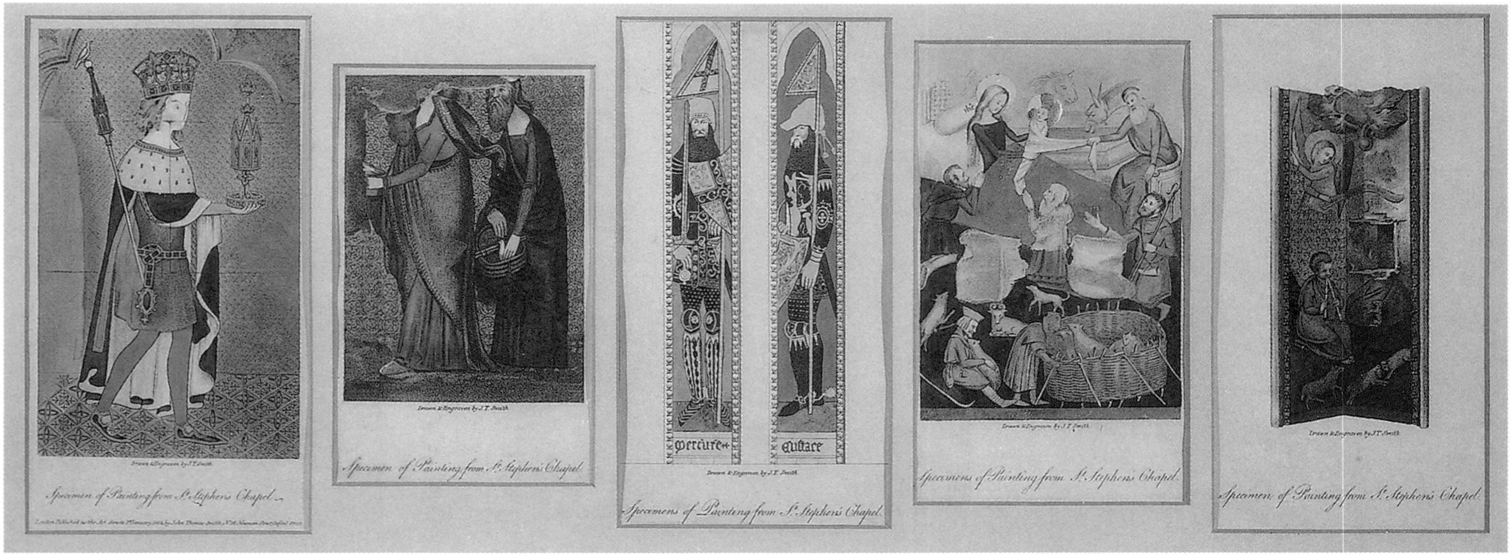

12. J. T. Smith, *Specimens of Painting from St. Stephen's Chapel*, colour line engravings published in 1804 and used as illustrations in *The Antiquities of Westminster* (1807). London, Palace of Westminster

Ford Madox Brown's, painted in the 1870s and 1880s in Manchester's new Town Hall (Plate I), or the ambitious scheme at the Royal Exchange (Plate 14) find their place within the revival of civic ritual and historical pageants which swept through Europe in the nineteenth century.[47] Like such 'invention of tradition', manifest also in the trade guild processions which marked the opening of Waterhouse's new Town Hall, Brown's effort to bring the past to life upon the walls spoke of its continuum with present-day Manchester, conferring legitimacy on the role of the city's new tribunes of the people in the post-Reform Act era, much as did the building's Gothic Revival architecture. Similarly, the panels at Westminster in 1906 by artists whom Hermann Muthesius called the 'Neupräraffaeliten' ('the Neo-Pre-Raphaelites')[48] can be recognized as integral with the new Liberal Government's national programme of reform. The murals at the Royal Exchange, in contrast, looked back to the past to preserve ancient privileges in the teeth of political change. If such interpretations seem to marginalize the painter as a mere propagandist, a pawn in the hands of the patron, then we have to remember that the very regard in which mural painting was held by many artists themselves in the nineteenth and early twentieth centuries was itself born of the same ploy, not merely learning from but actually identifying with the past, and thereby giving an almost 'psychological' twist to the justification of the new by clothing it with costumes borrowed from the 'great masters' of past art. Watts tried to reinvent the mural painting of Michelangelo, Raphael, and Titian, and Morris the medieval guilds, just as, in a way not essentially dissimilar, policemen dressed in suits of armour from the Tower of London watched over a banquet attended by Queen Victoria at the Guildhall in 1852, making history into 'actuality'.[49] The psychological force for the Victorians of such 'acting' is nowadays, in the age of television and computer images, perhaps difficult to recapture, and indeed demands recognition of a 'history of ways of seeing' as much as of murals.

The pronounced and long-lasting preference in Britain for historical iconography in mural painting (even in private houses), in which past events or legends were imbued with modern significance, contrasts markedly with the enthusiasm in French and German decoration from the 1870s onwards not only for the 'modern life' subjects envisaged by Claude Lantier but also their use as 'allégorie réelle'.[50] Nor is there any real British counterpart to the symbolic, 'universal' personifications of Marianne which were a stock-in-trade of French town-hall decoration, for example. The numerous murals in Britain, like those at the Royal Exchange, which represent history in life-like form undoubtedly find close parallels in the work of the German 'Düsseldorf School' muralists, or of Belgians such as Albert and Juliaan De Vriendt, but at the same time their keen sense of continuity between past and present coheres specifically with developments in the writing of history by W. Stubbs, J. R. Green, and, in the twentieth century, G. M. Trevelyan. In turn it helped shape perceptions of the past: the Royal Exchange murals were reproduced as textbook illustrations even as late as the 1950s.[51] This 'past–present' phenomenon in mural painting is, of course, closely related to beliefs that Britain's modern Empire found its origins in Tudor and

[47] See D. Cannadine, 'The Transformation of Civic Ritual', *Past and Present*, no. 94 (1982), pp. 107–30, and W. Hartmann, *Der historische Festzug seine Entstehung und Entwicklung im 19. und 20. Jahrhundert* (Munich, 1976).

[48] H. Muthesius, 'Kunst und Leben in England', *Zeitschrift für bildende Kunst*, NF 13 (1902), p. 66.

[49] See 'Seven Centuries of the Lord Mayoralty', Supplement to the *London Argus* (8 Nov. 1900), p. 11.

[50] e.g. H. Gervex and E. Blanchon portrayed contemporary scenes including a modern abattoir at the Mairie of the XIX Arrondissement (1879). For 'allégorie réelle' (the 'représentation du vécu' to present an ideal or a concept), see Burollet, *Le Triomphe des Mairies*, p. 38.

[51] e.g. in Cassell's *Stream of Time* (1952); in 1953 a British Transport film-strip on Cornwall included Leighton's *Ancient Commerce* Exchange mural (see MCA).

Stuart times,[52] as well as in aspects of eighteenth-century history. As a kind of 'suspension of disbelief', the visualization of history in murals is also a first cousin of theatre, and several mural artists were also stage and costume designers for plays and pageants. When placed in the larger context of mural painting in Britain since 1840, the so-called 'avant-garde' decorative art of Wyndham Lewis (Plate 15) and the Omega artists in the early twentieth century thus defines itself as much in terms of revolt against such subjective identification with the past as in relation to the modern Continental easel painting put on show by Roger Fry in his Post-Impressionist exhibitions, or the 'exotic' performances of the Ballets Russes. At the same time, its attempt to integrate art and architecture can be recognized as a direct heir of Ruskin's ideal of 'combination',[53] the Gothic Revivalism of Westminster and of Manchester's Town Hall, and the ideas of the Arts and Crafts Movement: Fry had learnt decorative painting from C. R. Ashbee. 'The New Art History' has made much in recent years of the sociologist Bourdieu's 'field of cultural production', but what he has called 'understanding works of art as a *manifestation* of the field as a whole'[54] has to be a basic starting-point in dealing with the century of murals from 1840.

It would be misleading to suggest that murals in Britain through the century from 1840 were mainly a kind of large-scale history painting, though they do indicate that historical subjects were popular in British art for much longer than has been suggested by Sir Roy Strong in considering easel painting.[55] Literary themes, including the 'patriotic' *Morte d'Arthur* legend as interpreted by Malory and Tennyson, were a mainstay in mural art, and 'escapism', 'retreat', and related purposes often underpinned such choices in leisure and private buildings. The ideal of integration found some of its most fascinating and psychologically complex means of expression in schemes which drew upon the Germanic tradition of the *Gesamtkunstwerk* and sought to bring together literature, painting, and music, or created synaesthetic effects. This phenomenon—which of course is essentially cognate with the sense of fluidity between past and present in painting history—is evident in Prince Albert's private commissions and was reborn in a variety of schemes of the late nineteenth and early twentieth centuries which constitute a distinctive form of British Symbolism, such as John Duncan's work at Pitreavie Castle, Gerald Moira's in the Wigmore Hall, or Sigismund Goetze's at Grove House. Whilst the theories of the Gothic Revivalists and their adaptation by the Arts and Crafts Movement have been extensively discussed by architectural and design historians, the evidence of mural painting in Britain suggests that Continental examples, including the work of the Nabis and French Symbolists and the ideas of Nietzsche, were often as important in the evolution of the concept of the 'integrated interior'.

If the logic of integration, like the role of the patron, seems to diminish the artistic autonomy of the painter of mural art, and perhaps therefore to account in part for the continued neglect of mural painting in the so-called 'Post-modernist' age with its gods of freedom and plurality, the 'constraints' of working for a place and a patron were felt by Sir William Rothenstein to be actually beneficial. Having painted a mural in the scheme undertaken at the Palace of Westminster in 1924–7, he argued: 'we had not only the subject given to us, but a certain perspective, a certain size of figure; so far from being a handicap, something definitely imposed is an immense

52 See, for example, the writings of the historians J. A. Froude and M. Creighton in the late 19th/early 20th centuries; their ideas were popularized in e.g. C. R. L. Fletcher and R. Kipling, *A School History of England* (Oxford, 1911).

53 See Chapter 9 ('Mind and Body'), n. 5.

54 P. Bourdieu, *The Field of Cultural Production* (Cambridge 1993), p. 37; for an example of the application of this theory, see A. Lewis, 'On Not Explaining Late Degas' (review article), *Art History*, 20 (June 1997), pp. 319, 323.

55 R. Strong, *And When Did You Last See Your Father* (London, 1978), pp. 44, 72.

advantage.'[56] As will be seen, the iconographical limitations imposed on Brangwyn at the Royal Gallery in the House of Lords at the same period were arguably the very spur to his novel and imaginative interpretation of his commission, yet, as with other mural schemes, tastes and attitudes changed in the time that it took to complete a project on such a scale. On this occasion, as with Goetze's Foreign Office work, the murals became 'obsolete' during the very course of their production because of concurrent changes in social and political philosophies. Subconscious recognition of this dilemma perhaps accounts for the value placed on the preparatory cartoons for the 1840s decoration at Westminster through their public exhibition; a phenomenon which accords with what has been identified in nineteenth-century Austria and Germany as *Kartonkunst*[57] and which was, of course, reborn in Geddes's 1912 exhibition.

In this story of survival and revival, 1940 offers a natural terminus, not only on account of the Second World War, but also as the close of the decade which saw Brangwyn's Royal Gallery scheme—painted for the very hall where Maclise had celebrated Britain's perceived supremacy in Europe in the previous century—mark the end of mural painting at Westminster. When Edward Croft-Murray tackled mural painting in Britain in his *catalogues raisonnés* of 1962 and 1970, however, he stopped at 1837, taking the view that the decoration at the Palace of Westminster launched in 1841 was an end and not a beginning.[58] T. S. R. Boase's landmark article of 1954 on the nineteenth-century work at Westminster has remained the most substantial discussion of it for more than forty years, even though it is now recognized as a document of its time.[59] The nineteenth-century mural 'revival' at Westminster has in effect been treated as a poor relation in British art history; a kind of misguided footnote both to a glorious medieval and Renaissance legacy of British wall-painting, and to the splendours of Rubens's Banqueting Hall ceiling in Whitehall or of Thornhill and foreigners like Verrio and Zucchi in the eighteenth century. The attempt to reinvigorate Prince Albert's earlier effort to promote a British 'school' of monumental art in 1906 at Westminster has also been all but overlooked other than in relation to the architectural history of the Houses of Parliament,[60] even though its artists were drawn from one of the two strands in modern British art which Muthesius had identified in 1902 as representing its most promising trend, namely 'decorative tendencies'.[61] The other strand was the work of Sir Frank Brangwyn, who, although he was the principal British professional muralist of his day, has subsequently been remembered mainly for his graphic art and easel paintings, and for his furnishings and applied art,[62] or else sometimes dismissed as offering 'no sense of any serious intellectual involvement'[63] as a painter.

In attempting to offer a first anatomy of mural painting from 1840 to 1940, I have deliberately given close attention to the evolution of the great State schemes at the Palace of Westminster which spanned the century, since they were consciously intended to provide a lead in the revival of British mural painting. A chapter is likewise devoted to State patronage at the Foreign and Commonwealth Office and to the ambitious schemes at the Royal Exchange and by Brangwyn

[56] W. Rothenstein, 'The Decoration of Buildings', *Journal of the RIBA*, 38 (1931), p. 203.

[57] This is discussed in W. Kitlitschka, *Die Kartons für die Bildausstattung des Wiener Opernhauses* (exh. cat., Albertina, Vienna, 1973), pp. 7–8.

[58] Croft-Murray, *Decorative Painting*, vol. 2, p. 77.

[59] See M. Bond, *Works of Art in the House of Lords*, pp. 14–15.

[60] Some of the murals are discussed in Bond, *Works of Art*; see also Boase in M. H. Port (ed.), *The Houses of Parliament* (1976).

[61] See Chapter 11 ('Work and Play'), n. 76.

[62] e.g. in J. Freeman, *The Art of Frank Brangwyn* (exh. cat., Brighton, 1980). A reappraisal of Brangwyn's *oeuvre* is given in Macmillan's *Dictionary of Art* (Willsdon, s.v. 'Brangwyn', 1996), pp. 672–3.

[63] A. Causey, 'An Artist Hidden by his Reputation', *Illustrated London News* (22 April 1967), p. 26.

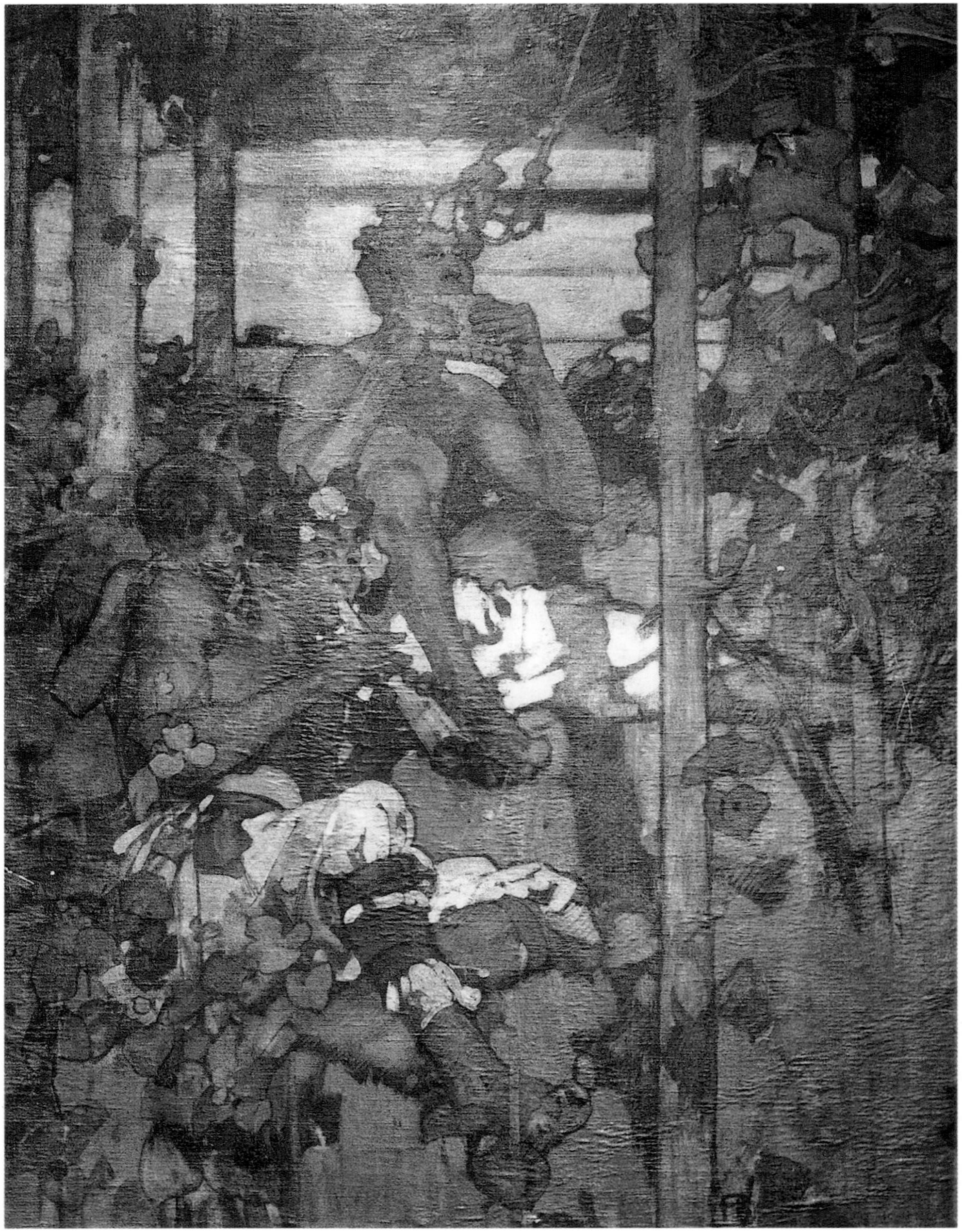

13. Sir Frank Brangwyn, *Music*, detached panel from Siegfried Bing's Maison de l'Art Nouveau, 22 rue de Provence, Paris, *c*.1895. (Cut down from original size as shown in the *Studio*, 12, 1897, 14). London, William Morris Gallery

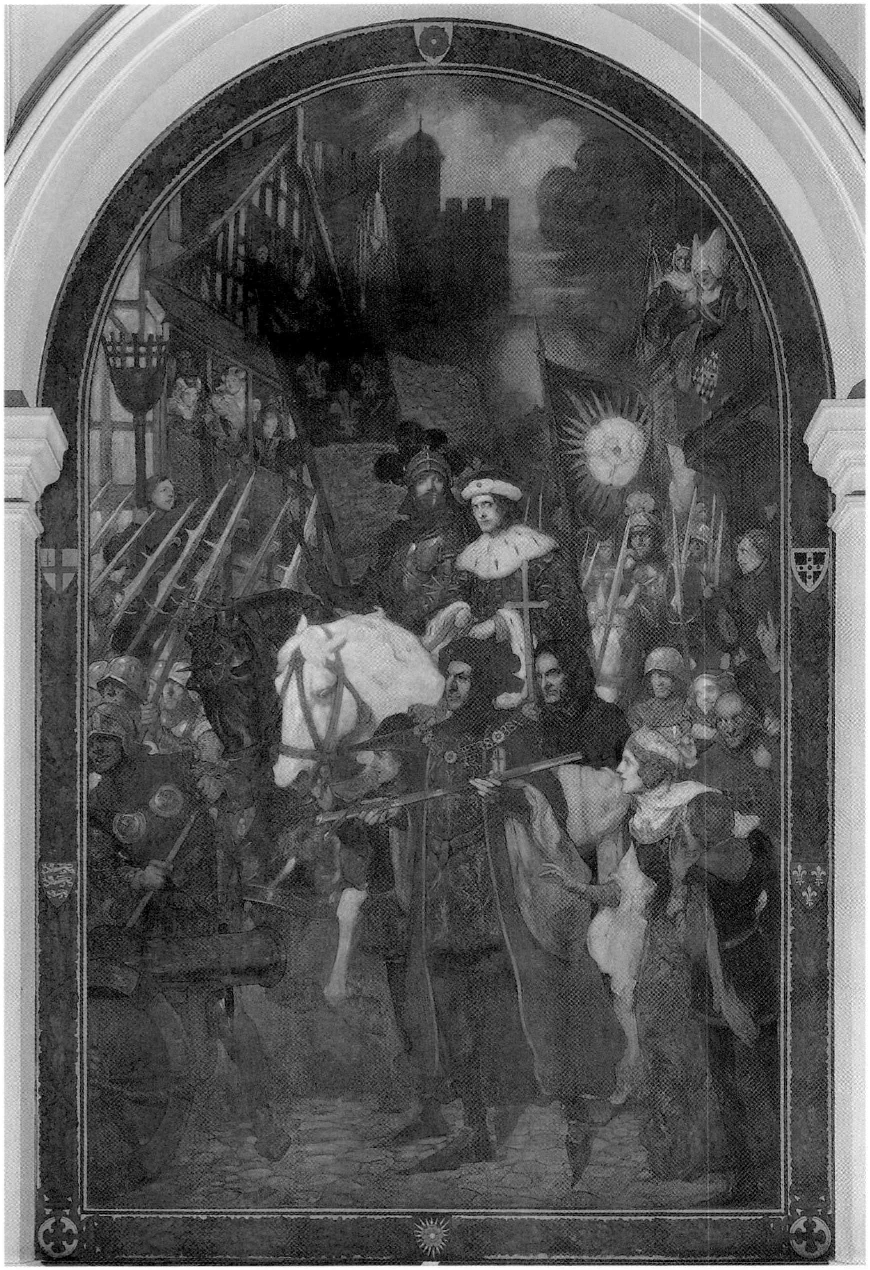

14. John H. Amschewitz, *Henry VI Battle of Barnet, 1471. The Trained Bands marching to the support of Edward IV*, Royal Exchange, London. Presented in memory of Ellis Abraham Franklin by his sons, 1911

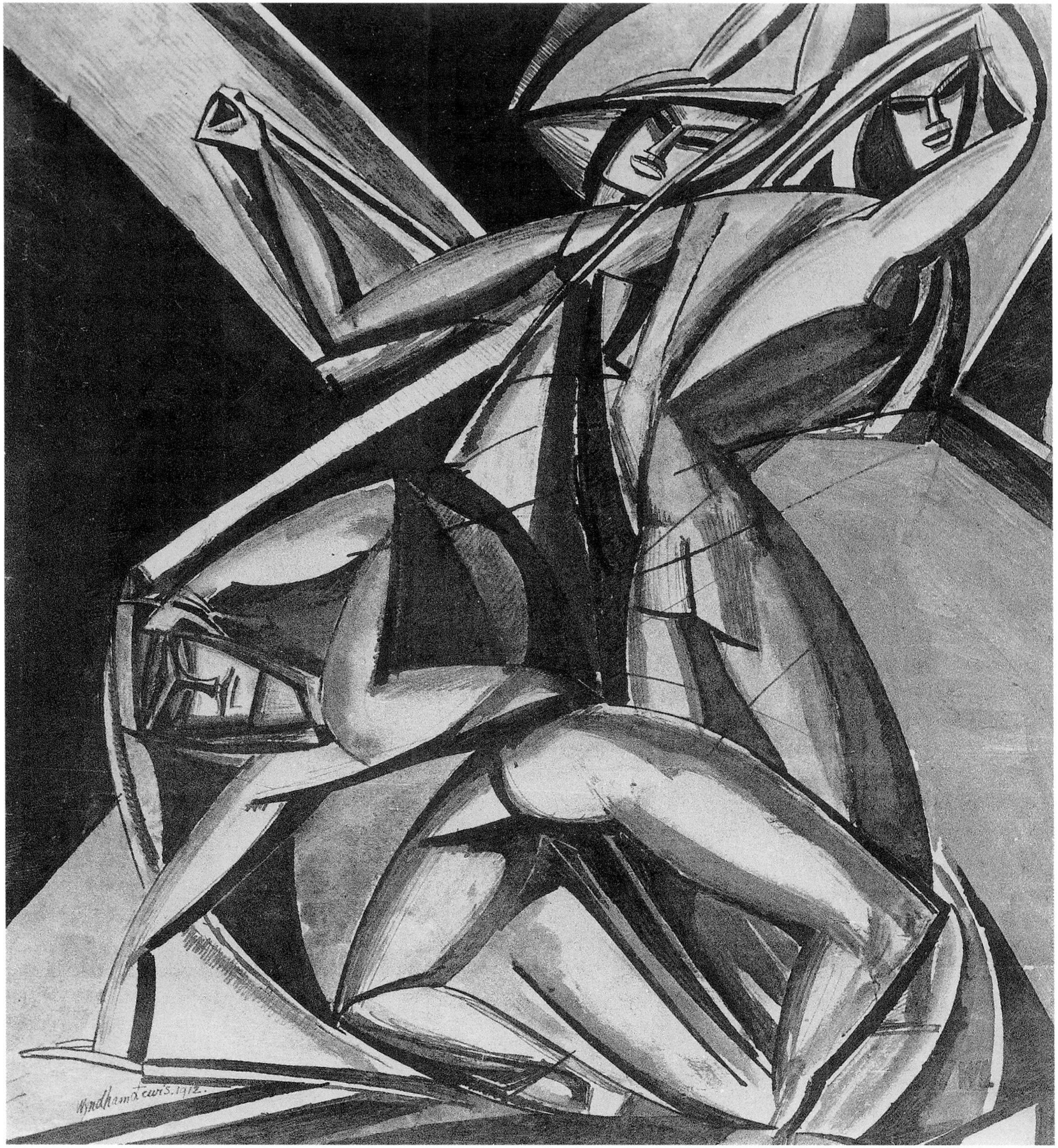

15. Percy Wyndham Lewis, *The Dancers* (study for *Kermesse?*), 1912. Ink and watercolour. Manchester, City Art Galleries

at Skinners' Hall, which stand out as influential landmarks in the period. By looking at all these schemes from a wider contextual standpoint, the reasons why Crane regarded the mural artist as a 'poet, historian, dramatist, philosopher' become abundantly clear. Dyce, Charles West Cope, Maclise, John Byam Shaw, Henry A. Payne, Edwin Abbey, Frank Salisbury, Colin Gill, and Sir George Clausen at Westminster and Leighton, Stanhope Forbes, Ernest Crofts, and a number of other artists at the Exchange stand out as painters of insight and imagination, whilst Brangwyn in particular emerges, in his mural art, as someone who, far being from a lightweight 'decorator', was instead an original, deeply thoughtful, inventive and accomplished painter.

Alluding to the difficulties with technique experienced by Maclise and his colleagues at Westminster, one of Brangwyn's most ardent contemporary supporters, Frank Rutter, came to the conclusion that the Lords had 'ignobly rejected as a free gift Frank Brangwyn's golden casket of crushed jewels, the *British Empire Panels*, the crowning master-work of the man who has been honoured in all countries but his own as the world's greatest decorative painter' because 'the British Houses of Parliament never have been decorated and never want to be decorated.'[64]

Almost as a corollary to the prevailing view of murals as the grandest form of painting, imposing the greatest artistic demands, a curious defeatism—even an inferiority complex—seems simultaneously to have dogged the practice and theory of decorative painting in nineteenth- and early twentieth-century Britain. It upsets the neatness of a linear reading of developments from 1840 to 1940; it undoubtedly contributed to the neglect of the field by subsequent art historians; and it underlines the need for subtle, imaginative, and wide-ranging tools of analysis in seeking to identify and disentangle the multifarious threads of British mural art. For, even in 1863, as Ruskin was attempting before his time to persuade the Royal Academy to teach mural painting, 'possibly [as] the principal branch'[65] of its curriculum, a Select Committee was conducting a gloomy post-mortem on the disintegration and decay of the murals at Westminster, and a halt was called to further decoration there. As one of the Westminster artists, John Callcott Horsley, later wrote, 'none of us knew that fresco painting required not only fresh plaster on which to work, but fresh air to preserve the work when done . . . The Thames was the main sewer of vast London and . . . was charged with foul and most destructive gases . . . [whilst] coal gas was pouring forth its destructive powers night and day.'[66] His colleague Cope lamented, 'how much of life has been wasted, as it were, writing in the sand. Time's effacing fingers began to obliterate at one end, while we were painfully working at the other.'[67]

The sense of failure in the wake of the Westminster 'experiment' provoked a giddy roller-coaster of fresh 'revivals' and further 'regrets', one sometimes simultaneous with the other. Already before his work on the mural for the Royal Exchange, Leighton was promoting his adoption both at Lyndhurst Church in 1864 and at the South Kensington Museum in the 1870s of Gambier Parry's new 'spirit fresco' (see Appendix A), as the pioneering of a genre: 'mural painting of a high class is an object for which I am ready to make personal sacrifices.'[68] Madox Brown's spirit fresco murals at Manchester Town Hall were also hailed as a 'first', whilst in the 1890s the same role was claimed at the Royal Exchange, a token of 'a bright future for . . . historic art'.[69] The latter scheme was a key

[64] F. Rutter, *Art in my Time* (London, 1933), p. 206.

[65] J. Ruskin, Evidence to the Royal Academy Commission (8 June 1863) §23, in *Complete Works*, ed. E. T. Cook and A. Wedderburn (London, 1903–12), vol. 14, p. 482.

[66] Quoted in Bond, *Works of Art*, p. 34.

[67] Ibid.

[68] See Chapter 9 ('Mind and Body'), n. 56.

[69] Unattributed newspaper cutting, *c.*1892, in MCA.

stimulus to the second 'revival' of mural painting at Westminster in 1906. Yet in 1913 the culture of 'regret' was again in evidence, when the decorative artist and Arts and Crafts theorist Robert Anning Bell wrote of the history of decorative painting in Britain as 'the most lamentable'.[70] In the 1920s Sir William Rothenstein, Director of the Royal College of Art, Henry Tonks of the Slade School, and Charles Aitken, Director of the Tate Gallery, also endeavoured, in varying degrees of common purpose with the British School at Rome, to 'revive' what was felt to be a 'lost' art of mural painting, as Fra Newbery had already at Glasgow School of Art at the turn of the century. Sir Henry Newbolt, writing on the completion of the 1924–7 scheme of murals in St Stephen's Hall in the Palace of Westminster (the first major commission to artists from the British School at Rome), believed that 'a new age has unexpectedly and almost unconsciously produced a new flowering of decorative art in this country.'[71] The official British assessment of national achievement at the 1925 Decorative Arts Exhibition in Paris, however, was almost a rerun of Anning Bell's pre-war comments.[72] Sir John Rothenstein's retrospective exhibition of 'Mural Painting in Britain since 1918', held at the Tate Gallery in 1939, was conceived as a plea for the encouragement of mural decoration,[73] with the implication that its exhibits were but a beginning. It is perhaps not surprising that this culture of self-deprecation was perpetuated, if subconsciously, in the emphasis on architecture rather than its decoration in Sir Nikolaus Pevsner's *Buildings of England*, and that, even as its first volumes were being prepared, the catalogue for an Arts Council exhibition in 1951 of work by the 'Society of Mural Decorators' proclaimed that 'The decorative treatment of walls and other large surfaces is virtually a lost art in this country.'[74]

Faced with this flux and reflux in the perception of mural painting in Britain through the century from 1840 and even beyond, it seemed desirable in writing this book to look for underlying constants by arranging the discussion of individual mural schemes according to the principal types of patronage or building—State; educational and welfare; private; church; business and leisure, and so on. If this risks a sequence of individual, though complementary, 'histories' rather than a single evolutionary sweep, it is hoped that it might better do justice to the subtleties of interrelationships between artist, patron, and function, and avoid positing a simplistic pattern of 'linear' development at the expense of interpretative depth. Such an arrangement, of course, inevitably creates artificial boundaries, as in the case of the decoration of the South Kensington Museum, which was funded by Parliament but is dealt with in the context of 'Mind and Body' rather than State commissions because of its role as an 'educational' building. Significant cross-connections of this kind are identified at the start of the relevant chapters. Likewise, the arrangement of murals by functional type, rather than within a single integrated chronology, means that the 'story' of the particular contribution to the evolution of mural painting of individual enthusiasts such as Sir Patrick Geddes, or of teachers such as Henry Tonks, and artists like Leighton and Brangwyn, is inevitably spread across a number of chapters ('Mind and Body' as well as 'Private Houses' for Geddes, for example). I have nevertheless felt this

[70] R. Anning Bell, 'Mural Decoration', in *Ghent Catalogue* (1913), p. xxxiv. This was translated into French for the catalogue of the Decorative Arts Exhibition in Paris in 1914.

[71] H. Newbolt, *The Building of Britain* (n.d.), p. 2.

[72] G. Sheringham, 'Mural Decoration' in *Report . . .* (1925): e.g. 'the art is on the point of expiring for lack of understanding' (p. 52).

[73] 'Introduction', J. Rothenstein, *Mural Painting* (1939); a substantial review by Percy Horton of the 1939 Tate exhibition was published in the *Studio*, 118 (July, 1939), pp. 2–9.

[74] P. James, preface to H. Feibusch, *Society of Mural Painters First Exhibition* (1951); cf. Pevsner's comment on the 19th and 20th centuries in *The Buildings of England: London*, vol. 1 (Harmondsworth, 1957): 'Painting developed away from fresco and wall-painting, and nearly all that mattered was expressed in terms of the easel picture' (p. 106).

to be a sacrifice worth making in order to allow something of the range of trends in what might be called the 'philosophy' of mural painting in Britain to become apparent through analysis of the different generic forms and their various manifestations. Although, for reasons of space, the geographical range of the book is confined to present-day Britain (i.e. murals in Southern Ireland are not covered, apart from occasional comparative references[75]), and murals by British-based artists working abroad, such as those by Sargent for Boston Public Library, are excluded, the contributions of foreigners working in Britain are discussed as an integral part of its mural history. Murals now lost and known only from period sources are likewise considered, and in order to provide as wide a range of representative material as possible, certain chapters are accompanied by appendices containing selected supplementary examples. Again for reasons of space, decoration consisting purely of patterns or heraldry or, as in some churches, primarily of inscribed texts, has been omitted unless in some way significant within a larger pictorial or abstract scheme. Mural painting in Britain since 1800 deserves to come of age in art history, and I hope very much that this book will be a first step in its recognition, providing a platform for its informed preservation as a rich and integral part of the national heritage.

[75] For Southern Irish murals, see P. McEvansoneya, 'History, Politics and Decorative Painting: James Ward's Murals in Dublin City Hall', *Irish Arts Review*, 15 (1999), pp. 142–7; this in any case notes that 'decorative mural paintings of any type in Ireland post 1820 are rare' (p. 142).

2

Royalty and Reform: State Patronage at the Palace of Westminster, 1841–1864

SUBJECTS AND SYMBOLISM

In 1843 the history painter Benjamin Robert Haydon recorded in his journal a chance encounter with one of his former pupils, Sir Charles Lock Eastlake:

> 'Do you remember,' said he, 'coming with me into Westminster Hall, and drawing a gigantic limb on the wall with the end of the umbrella, saying, "This is the place for art"?' I did not. He said I actually did so, thirty years ago; and he remembered my jumping up to reach high.[1]

The occasion of this exchange was the first exhibition of cartoons for murals for the new Palace of Westminster, and Haydon went on to reflect 'Now here we were, master and pupil, marching about, and the first act of this great drama just beginning.'[2]

The drama had had a lengthy prologue, as Haydon indicates, and it was to have many more acts before its final curtain in 1933. Haydon's umbrella demonstration, reminiscent of Blake's desire to paint 'figures . . . one hundred feet in height'[3] was part of a tide of Romantic idealism which flowed from the experiments with sequences of large history or literary paintings made at the end of the eighteenth century by Boydell, Fuseli, and Robert Bowyer. There had been a project in 1809 at the British Institution for Government prizes for painting, but it came to naught, 'the country being at that time still engaged in a tedious and expensive war'.[4] When a Select Committee was appointed in 1841 by the new Tory Prime Minister, Sir Robert Peel (with himself as one of its members) to look into 'the Promotion of the FINE ARTS of this Country, in connexion [*sic*] with the Rebuilding of the Houses of Parliament',[5] the outcome was to prove an even more dramatic confrontation between Romantic dreams and *Realpolitik*. Haydon, bitterly disappointed by his failure to secure any prizes in the series of competitions to find suitable painters for murals at Westminster, committed suicide; the whole enterprise launched by the 1841 Committee was the first State support for the arts in Britain since Charles I's subsidy of the Royal Tapestry factory at Mortlake and George III's foundation of the Royal Academy of Arts in 1768, and it very quickly became inextricably bound up with matters of government.

[1] B. R. Haydon, *Diary* (1 June 1843), ed. W. B. Pope (1963), vol. 5, p. 280.
[2] Ibid.
[3] See Ch. 1, n. 4.
[4] W. B. Sarsfield Taylor, *Painting in Oil and Fresco* (1839), p. 363.
[5] Rep. SCFA (18 June 1841), PP VI, p. iii.

The Royal Fine Arts Commission, appointed on the recommendation of the 1841 Select Committee to determine artists and subjects, was chaired by Prince Albert and had Haydon's pupil Eastlake as its Secretary; the luminaries among its membership included men who had already served on the Select Committee, such as Peel himself and the Members of Parliament, Sir Robert Inglis and Thomas Wyse; other politicians including Peel's Whig opposite, Lord John Russell, and Lord Francis Egerton of Bridgewater House, along with the poet Samuel Rogers and the historian Henry Hallam. Avowedly chosen so that 'party distinctions' were 'excluded',[6] it was ultimately dependent on Parliament's vote of £4,000 per annum 'for the purpose of promoting and encouraging the Fine Arts in the United Kingdom'[7] with 'direct reference to the moral wants of our nation'.[8] There is a very real sense in which the Commission's promotion of murals and sculpture in the Palace of Westminster (the architects, Sir Charles Barry and A. W. N. Pugin, were confined, to their chagrin, to the non-figurative ornament and stained glass) became an attempt to answer a question first put before Queen Victoria's accession by the man who was to be commemorated in the largest murals of all, the Duke of Wellington: 'How is the king's government to be carried on in a reformed Parliament?'[9] Regarded by Victoria as '*Britain's* pride, her glory, her hero, the greatest man she ever had produced',[10] Wellington had preserved Britain's monarchy and liberties by his victories over Napoleon, but new kinds of freedom were now being coveted by Victoria's subjects as the Chartists marched on London in the 1840s, seeking universal manhood suffrage and constitutional reforms.

Whilst the 1832 Reform Act had opened Westminster to a new generation of radical Members of Parliament, and dealt a death blow to the Hanoverian tradition of direct political intervention by the monarchy, the building itself nevertheless remained a royal palace, as Eastlake pointed out to the Commission:

> The edifice now in progress at Westminster, is strictly and officially called 'Her Majesty's Palace at Westminster, in which Her Parliament is wont to assemble'. It is, therefore, a Royal Palace permanently devoted to the purposes of Government and Legislation; and the circumstance of the Parliament, or Lords and Commons, meeting within its precincts, represents the combination of those elements of power with those of the Throne, which is characteristic of the English Constitution.[11]

When he married Queen Victoria, Prince Albert had been advised by his German tutor, Baron Stockmar, 'Be you . . . the Constitutional genius of the Queen,'[12] and he made strenuous efforts to restore the sensitive balance of power between sovereign and Parliament after the notorious Bedchamber affair, which led Thackeray to call the Queen 'a machine worked by ministers . . . which has no right for the sake of her little partialities to stop the march of parties in England'.[13] At the same time, however, Albert was so warm an admirer of Peel that the Queen called the latter his

[6] Letter from Prince Albert to Sir Robert Peel (13 Oct. 1844), RA(W), F29/4.

[7] *Report to the Queen's Most Excellent Majesty* of the CFA (22 April 1842), PP XXV, p. 5. (This was the first report of the CFA).

[8] *The General Object of the Commission . . .*, Appendix 2, ibid., p. 10.

[9] Quoted in 'Sir Robert Peel', *Encyclopaedia Britannica*, 11th ed. (New York, 1911), vol. 21, p. 42.

[10] Quoted in R. Mullen and J. Munson, *Victoria Portrait of a Queen* (London, 1987), p. 60. This was despite Victoria's initial vitriolic attack in 1840 against Wellington when he opposed a Bill to give Albert precedence after the Queen in Parliament or as she determined; see R. Rhodes James, *Albert, Prince Consort* (London, 1983), pp. 89–90.

[11] C. L. Eastlake, *Observations on the principles which may regulate the selection of subjects for Painting in the Palace of Westminster . . .*, Appendix 12, *Third Report* of the CFA (1844), PP XXXI, p. 35.

[12] Letter from Baron Stockmar to Prince Albert (18 May 1841), quoted in Rhodes James, *Albert*, p. 121.

[13] Quoted in Mullen and Munson, *Victoria*, p. 33.

'second father'[14] and herself was won over to become a dedicated supporter of Peel's 1841–6 ministry. By 1846, Albert was so enthusiastic about Peel that he made a public appearance in the House of Commons in support of the Premier's fatal speech for Free Trade, a move widely interpreted as partisan and one he never repeated, but it was entirely consistent with his deeply felt belief that a sovereign had 'an immense responsibility upon his shoulders with regard to his Government and the duty to watch and *control* it'.[15]

Against this backdrop was born the scheme for the decoration of the Palace of Westminster; Peel's remark to the House of Commons a few days prior to his Free Trade speech that 'It is no easy task to insure [*sic*] the harmonious and united action of Monarchy, Aristocracy, and a reformed House of Commons'[16] might indeed stand as the epitaph for the travails of the Royal Fine Arts Commission. Although Eastlake, Hallam, Lord Mahon, and a number of its other members had vital parts to play in the elaborate process of consultation and enquiry to determine the most suitable methods, subjects, and styles for the new murals, the stamp of Prince Albert, working in close cooperation with Peel until the latter's death in 1850, is felt at every turn. Lord Granville's comment to Queen Victoria shortly before the Commission was dissolved in 1863 after the Prince's death is highly revealing: Albert had 'decided all the historical questions and the manner in which every portion of the Palace of Westminster was to be decorated'.[17]

If Albert made no further appearances on the political stage after his Commons venture of 1846, then the history of the Westminster murals suggests that Lady Eastlake was correct to speak of Albert's chairmanship of the Commission as only a '*supposed* neutral ground in public matters on which a royal individual . . . could safely tread'[18] (my italics). There is evidence to show that the mural project became in fact an alternative means for Albert to affirm the role of the monarchy in the British Constitution which he prized so highly.

Not only for Victoria and Albert but also for the politicians, however, it was the very sharing of power between monarch and Parliament in Britain which seemed to offer the most potent safeguard against the tremors of revolution on the Continent which were to erupt in France in 1848; the British Constitution was in turn a model to which the Continent aspired.[19] The eventual decision by the Royal Fine Arts Commission to use significant episodes in the constitutional history of the nation as the major theme for the murals can be seen as a direct reflection of the sentiment already voiced by one of its members, the historian Hallam:

> Climates more propitious may impart more largely the enjoyments of existence; but in no other region have the benefits that political institutions can confer been diffused over so extended a population; nor have any people so reconciled the discordant elements of wealth, order, and liberty.[20]

Although Haydon claimed to have attempted from 1812 onwards to persuade 'all the Ministries in succession, down to Sir Robert Peel'[21] of the desirability of mural painting in the House of Lords, it was perhaps only in the 1840s that the political moment was ripe for the logic behind Barry and Pugin's Gothic building style to be carried to its ultimate conclusion through the addition of

[14] Ibid., p. 49.

[15] Prince Albert, quoted in Rhodes James, *Albert*, p. 171.

[16] Peel, speaking in the House of Commons (19 Jan. 1846), quoted in Rhodes James, *Albert*, p. 162.

[17] Letter from Lord Granville to Queen Victoria (17 Nov. 1862), RA(W) F31/98.

[18] Lady Eastlake, obituary of Prince Albert in *Quarterly Review*, 111 (1862), quoted in T. S. R. Boase, 'The Decoration of the New Palace of Westminster', *Journal of the Warburg and Courtauld Institutes*, 17 (1954), p. 324.

[19] See Rhodes James, *Albert*, pp. 184ff.

[20] H. Hallam, *View of the State of Europe during the Middle Ages*, 2nd ed. (London, 1878), p. 269, quoted in R. Strong, *And When Did You Last See Your Father* (1978), p. 143.

[21] B. R. Haydon, journal entry (19 Sept. 1843), in T. Taylor (ed.), *Life* (1853), vol 3, p. 238.

mural decoration. Gothic had been selected as a 'national' architectural style: the wall-painting, sculpture, and stained glass used as a matter of course by the medieval builders[22] were likewise adopted now as symbolic rather than merely stylistic features. In the context of changing relations between monarch and Parliament, occasioned by the Reform Act, and of Britain's vision of herself as 'guardian of peace in Europe' because of her Constitution, consideration of the choice of subjects for the new murals and how to ensure their permanence became the two burning issues in the Commission's extensive process of enquiry and deliberation. Whilst State sponsorship of mural painting by the personal action of the monarch, as in Bavaria, or of the Emperor, as in France, was a matter of course on the Continent, and above all, in the hands of the Nazarenes in Prince Albert's native Germany, had become a very real instrument for shaping national identity[23] (Plate 16), Britain had no such continuous tradition and was effectively having to invent one from scratch. If Prince Albert ultimately failed to carry the Commission in his belief that German artists should be employed—Eastlake, for one, threatened to resign his secretaryship at the prospect—then he secured the next best alternative of the Germanophile and German-trained artists Dyce and Maclise for the principal decorations, whilst the choice of iconography and the sequence of its execution both reveal subtleties of monarchical emphasis which can be attributed to his hand. Since less than half of the total of over 130 murals planned was ever carried out, and of this only 39 were by 'fine' artists (as opposed to students required to copy existing paintings) the history of the project is primarily one of theories and ideals. What was produced cannot be fully understood without first considering the motives and the dreams of the Royal Fine Arts Commission; these in turn were to be of immense influence on the subsequent history of mural painting in Britain, even though the actual works which resulted from them at Westminster were relatively few in number.

THE SUBJECTS

The Select Committee of 1841 and the early meetings of the Royal Fine Arts Commission were almost exclusively concerned to establish the best means of founding a British 'school' of 'high art' through the Westminster decoration and it was only gradually that their ideals came to a focus, first with the competition for large-scale cartoons in 1842 and then by 1844 with attempts to find specific subjects for the winning and selected artists to paint on the walls of the Palace itself.

Sir Charles Barry recommended to the Commission in 1843 that the murals should have 'reference to events in the history of the country'[24] and Eastlake as Secretary made the broad recommendation that 'The purpose of the building must regulate the selection of subjects,'[25] but the cartoon competition of 1842 merely stipulated that 'Each artist is at liberty to select his subject from British History, or from the works of Spenser, Shakespeare or Milton.'[26] The artists already

[22] See M. Bond (ed.), *Works of Art in the House of Lords* (1980), pp. 11ff. for a brief summary of this earlier decoration; copies of the medieval wall paintings in the original Palace of Westminster had been published in J. T. Smith, *Antiquities of Westminster* (1807).

[23] See K. Andrews, *The Nazarenes* (1964), pp. 55ff.; W. Vaughan, *German Romanticism and British Art* (1979); and F. Büttner, *Peter Cornelius*, vol. 1 (1980) and 2 (1999), and 'The Official Art of Romanticism as a Synthesis of the Arts', pp. 307ff. in K. Hartley (ed.), *The Romantic Spirit in German Art* (1994).

[24] Sir Charles Barry, *New Houses of Parliament. Architect's Report as to Internal Decorations* . . . Appendix 1, *Second Report* of the CFA (1843), PP XXIX, p. 7.

[25] C. L. Eastlake, *Styles and Methods of Painting suited to Decoration of Public Buildings*, Appendix 6, ibid., p. 61.

[26] *Notice respecting a Competition in Cartoons*, Appendix 1 to *First Report* of the CFA (22 April 1842), PP XXV, p. 7. The cartoons entered for the competition were exhibited in summer 1843 in Westminster Hall.

had marked preferences. The highest prizes (of £300 each) were awarded for E. A. Armitage's *Caesar's first Invasion of Britain* (Plate 17), G. F. Watts's *Caractacus led in Triumph through the Streets of Rome*, and C. W. Cope's *The First Trial by Jury*, whilst the overwhelming bias of the historical entries was pre-Norman and of the literary ones Milton.[27] Sir Martin Archer Shee, President of the Royal Academy, had already told the 1841 Select Committee that the selection of mural subjects should be arrived at 'in conjunction' with the artists so that each might 'consider if the subject were suited to the powers of his art'[28] and in 1844 even a historian like Henry Hallam could see 'that, in the selection and management of subjects, a painter will prefer, wherever the choice is truly free, those which give most scope for the beauties of his art . . . the human form to a considerable degree uncovered . . . [in] action . . . [showing] energy or . . . grace . . . female beauty . . . repose of massy and broad draperies . . . for want of which we soon turn from many representations of modern events.'[29] Hallam advised that 'for the most part of our history, as might be supposed, does not afford any plentiful harvest of what is so essential in historic painting' and he therefore proposed that subjects should not 'be confined to our own British history'.[30]

This provoked a strenuous defence of the suitability of British and colonial historical subjects from the historian and antiquarian Lord Mahon, in the form of a letter to Peel: 'I would no more consent to admit foreign scenes to decorate a British House of Parliament, than I would an alien to sit among its members.'[31] Mahon was not actually a member of the Commission, but Peel must have found his approach more congenial than that of Hallam, since the latter was a Whig. Mahon was appointed an additional Commissioner, along with Macaulay, in 1845, becoming chairman of a small committee charged by Prince Albert (who was also one of its members) with selecting subjects. His own recommendations were clearly aimed at Albert: a battery of English subjects 'in which Royal blood bears some part' and involving queens in particular as well as 'the first Council of Queen Victoria'.[32]

That Albert conceived of the Westminster decoration as an opportunity to present a direct commentary on the nature of the British Constitution and the special role he saw for the present-day monarch within both it and modern Europe is revealed by a draft memorandum, annotated by Peel, which he produced for the Commission around 1844. Arguing that 'The most difficult subject, perhaps, which this Commission has to consider and report upon to the Queen is the selection of proper subjects for paintings which are to adorn the walls of the chief halls in the new Palace,' he proposed that the murals 'should . . . record the chief events of British history, that they should characterise the peculiar parts of the Edifice, where they are put up, & that they should furnish the artist with the means of exhibiting his skill in the *highest* branch of the Art.'[33]

He went on, however, to recommend his own suggestion that the Guard Chamber and Robing Room should have 'poetical' or 'allegorical' subjects and the Royal Gallery an ambitious scheme representing 'the great achievements of this country the direction of which has been the proudest part of the Royal Prerogative'. These last would feature 'an allegorical representation of Peace and

[27] See the discussion of the entries and prize works in Boase, 'Decoration' (1954), pp. 325ff.

[28] Sir Martin Archer Shee in Min. SCFA (25 May 1841), PP VI, § 273 and § 271.

[29] H. Hallam, *Observations on the Principles which may regulate the selection of subjects for painting in the Palace of Westminster*, Appendix 8, *Third Report* of the CFA (3 May 1844), PP XXXI, p. 22.

[30] Ibid.

[31] Lord Mahon, *Letter on the same subject*, Appendix 10, *Third Report* of the CFA (3 May 1844), PP XXXI, p. 28.

[32] Ibid., p. 27.

[33] Prince Albert, *Memorandum* to Peel (*c*.1844), RA(W), F30/32.

16. Julius Schnorr von Carolsfeld, *Siegfried and Kriemhild*, Saal der Helden, Nibelungensäle, Residenz, Munich, *c.*1832. Fresco

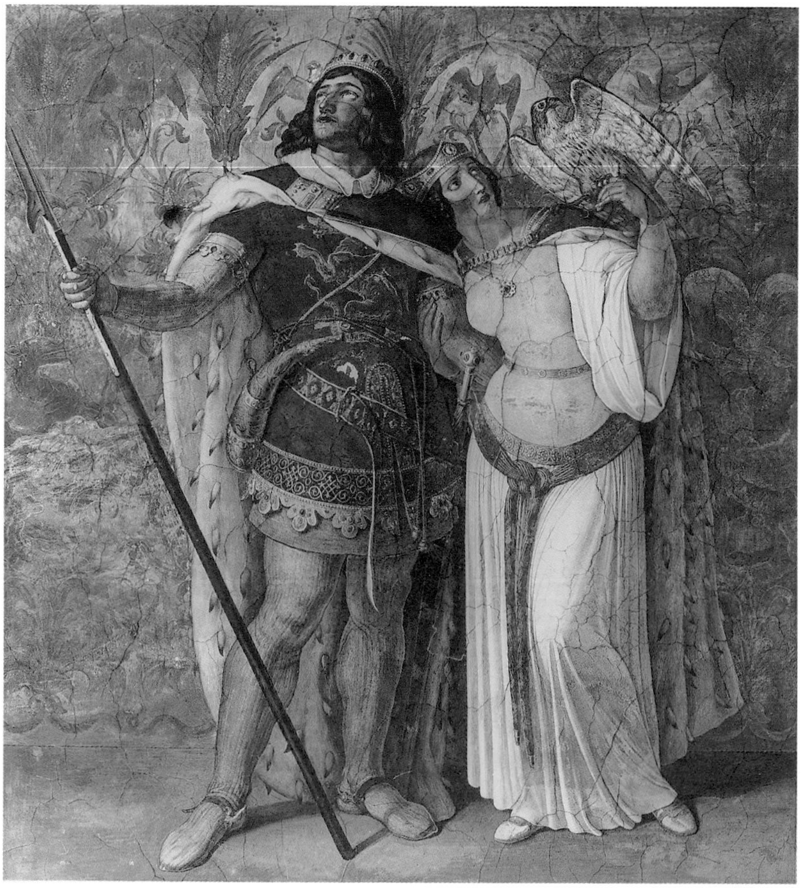

17. Edward A. Armitage, *Caesar's first Invasion of Britain*, engraving of drawing from prize cartoon for the 1842 Palace of Westminster cartoon competition, exhibited in 1843 at Westminster Hall. From J. J. and W. Linnell, *The Prize Cartoons* (London, 1844)

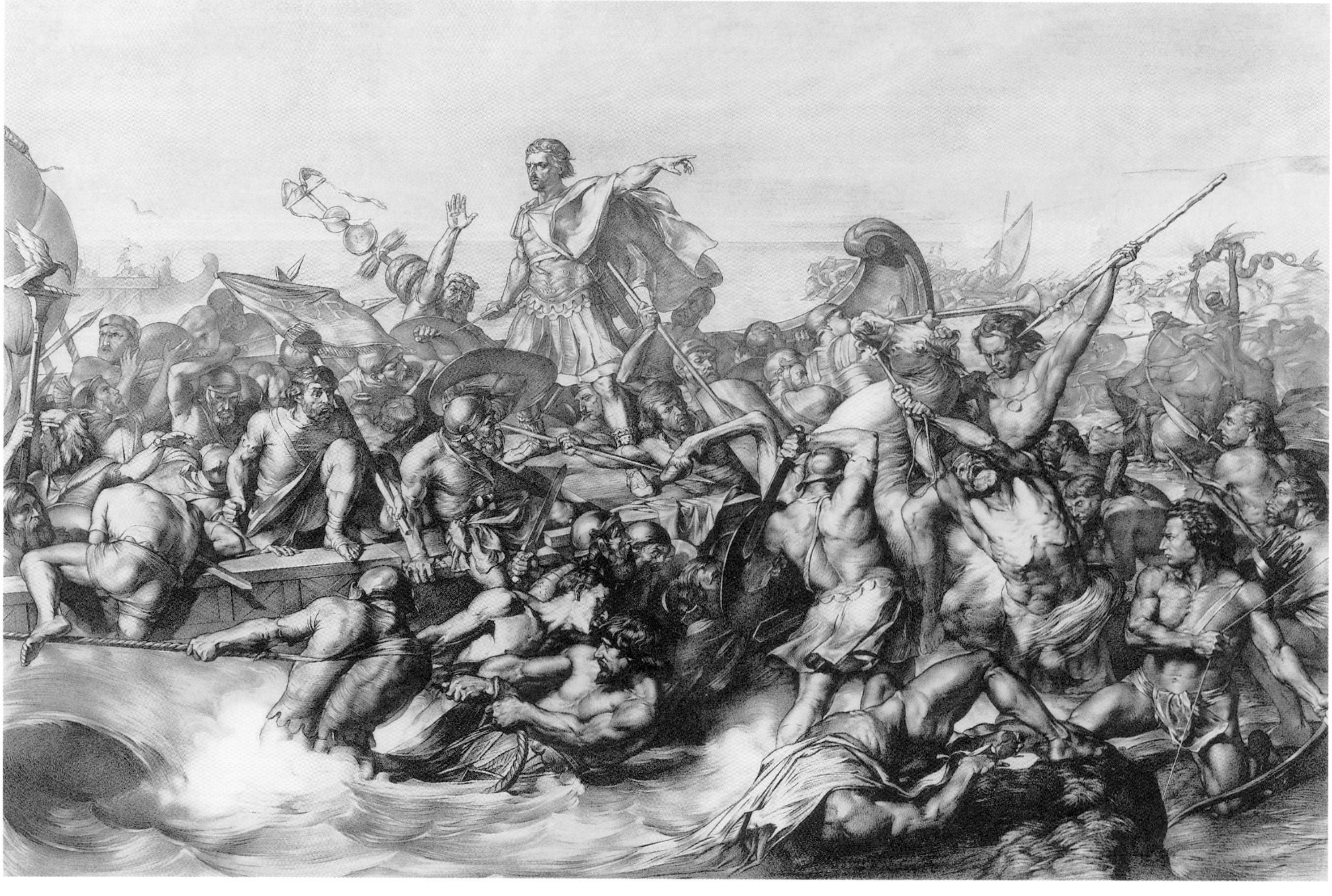

War', the battles of Trafalgar and Waterloo, 'which terminated at sea and on land the great struggle of the nations of Europe and established that Peace which the world has enjoyed ever since,' and a sequence of further historical episodes to flank 'Queen Victoria surrounded by the sovereigns of Europe who came to prove to her their respect for her person and their readiness to cooperate with her in the maintenance of universal peace'.

In St Stephen's Hall, 'the site of the old H. of C. [*sic*]', would be illustrated 'the particular epochs of the History of the Constitution' starting with 'Alfred giving laws' and concluding with 'The Passing of the Reform Bill'.[34]

Meanwhile, the Commission had decided to launch the murals in the Chamber of the House of Lords and had selected themes of *Justice*, *Religion*, and *Chivalry*. It reported in August 1846 that Dyce had completed the first fresco, of *The Baptism of King Ethelbert* (Plate 18). With this flagship subject, which drew attention to the spiritual authority of the monarch, *in situ* in the central panel of the room, the rest of its panels (each 5 × 2.86m in size) were started. Calamity, however, had struck. Peel had been defeated in the Commons in July 1846, just the month before the Commission's report and on the occasion of Albert's controversial appearance in Parliament. With a Whig government now in power, for which Victoria and Albert had no sympathy, it is most revealing that the 1846 Report went on to argue 'that it would not be expedient, with reference to the claims which may hereafter be urged for the commemoration of great events, to complete the series of paintings on the walls of the . . . Palace at the present period'.[35] An undertaking was nevertheless made to select subjects for the whole Palace and, when these were presented with the 1847 Report, it was clear that the Whig interpretation of history had gained the upper hand.

The subjects of Peace and War envisaged in 1844 by Albert for the Royal Gallery were transferred to the entry to St Stephen's Hall, where the old House of Commons had sat: Parliamentary ideals had triumphed over the 'Royal Prerogative' he had wished to commemorate. Although his Waterloo and Trafalgar subjects had been preserved, they were now present as part of a series illustrating 'the military history and glory of the Country',[36] rather than as adjuncts to an apotheosis of Queen Victoria. Albert's ideas for St Stephen's Hall were likewise modified to exclude his modern subjects, and his monarchical emphasis ('Alfred giving Laws') was replaced with illustrations of how the common people and barons had founded the Constitution.[37] Macaulay's and Hallam's typically Whig emphasis on the Parliamentary battles with the Stuarts as the origins of the modern Constitution was chosen for the Peers' and Commons North Corridors; poetry was to be illustrated in the Upper Waiting Hall, and plenty of historical women were in evidence throughout. Colonial subjects were in the Central Corridor and Painted Chamber; 'Scripture subjects' to demonstrate 'the idea of Justice on Earth, and its development in Law and Judgement'[38] were to fill the Peers' Robing Room; twenty-eight Tudor portraits were selected for the Royal Antechamber. The Queen's Robing Room was to be ornamented with subjects from the legend of King Arthur, and the artists' preferences for early subject-matter were met by the exclusion of any episodes later than the Glorious Revolution. Although the prevailing emphasis of the mural scheme as a whole was thus far less emphatically royalist than Albert's earlier proposals, the royal dimension had by no means been lost. It is significant that apart

[34] Ibid.

[35] *Sixth Report* of the CFA (4 Aug. 1846), PP XXIV, p. 8.

[36] *Report of the Committee appointed to select Subjects in Painting and Sculpture, with a View to the Future Decoration of the Palace of Westminster*, Appendix 1, *Seventh Report* of the CFA (1847), PP XXXIII, p. 13.

[37] Ibid., pp. 9–10.

[38] Ibid., p. 11.

from 'experimental' decoration on poetry themes in the Upper Waiting Hall, the Queen's Robing Room with its Arthurian subjects was the next location to be painted. Dyce was selected and began designing in 1848.

Meanwhile, the Lords' Chamber was being completed. Maclise told a friend that the upper part of his fresco of *The Spirit of Chivalry* (Plate 19) was 'to be a type of the House of Lords . . . as the principal figure is meant to be typical of the Queen herself'.[39] Symbolically based on a Renaissance Madonna, she bears a laurel crown and is paid homage by representatives of State, Church, and army, and the arts and sciences. A partner mural of chivalry in history by Cope reinforces the royal emphasis by illustrating *Edward III conferring the Order of the Garter on the Black Prince* (Plate 20)—an episode whose authenticity was vigorously defended by Albert and Peel despite a challenge from the historian Sir Harris Nicholas.[40] It had direct relevance to Prince Albert himself, since his 'acceptance' into the British Royal Family had been marked by conferral of the Order of the Garter, but it can also be seen to relate to his vision of the British monarchy as the guardian of European peace and the cardinal instrument of the modern Parliamentary Constitution. Just as the victories over Napoleon of Wellington and Nelson had, as Albert put it, 'established that Peace which the world has enjoyed ever since', so the Order of the Garter had been given, according to Peel (quoting from Nicholas himself) after the 'glories of the Campaign in France'.[41] The Black Prince was regarded as one of the fathers of the modern Constitution because he had supported the 'Good Parliament',[42] and two clerical figures at the right of Cope's original sketch for the mural were indeed noted by the press as 'not very bad likenesses of Sir Robert Inglis and Sir Robert Peel'.[43] Inglis was 'a strong Tory' Member of Parliament.[44]

The ideas involved in both Maclise's and Cope's *Chivalry* murals were to find symbolic echoes not only in the two vast murals to be undertaken by Maclise from 1857 in the Royal Gallery—the *Death of Nelson* and the *Meeting of Wellington and Blücher at Waterloo*—but also in the more extensive treatment of chivalric ideals as embodied in the *Morte d'Arthur* by Malory, which were painted by Dyce in the Royal Robing Room from 1851 to 1864. It is easy to see why the Black Prince subject was of such importance to Albert and Peel: Edward III's Garter Order had been a part of his creation, in the wake of his French triumphs, of a Round Table of knights modelled on Arthur's. The other murals in the House of Lords Chamber can similarly be identified as focal emblems in the context of fears for national security amid the Continental uprisings, and the sense on the part of Peel and Albert alike that Britain's strongest defence was her mode of government through parliamentary and monarchical cooperation. Dyce's *Baptism of King Ethelbert*, for example, the first mural completed, and the historical partner to J. C. Horsley's allegorical *Spirit of Religion*, illustrates the Anglo-Saxons who, in addition to having Germanic origins like Albert himself and many of Queen Victoria's ancestors, were widely seen as having laid the foundations of Britain's modern democracy and political institutions.[45] Prince Albert had made this association clear in his proposal for a sequence of Constitutional subjects for St Stephen's Hall, which began with 'Alfred Giving Laws' and concluded with 'The Passing of the Reform Bill'. Although Albert's scheme was eventually revised, G. F. Watts's *Alfred inciting the Saxons to prevent the*

[39] Quoted in Ormond, *Daniel Maclise* (1972), p. 85.

[40] See letters from C. Cope (30 Sept. 1844), RA(W) F29/64, and Peel (8 Oct. 1844), RA(W) F29/66 to Eastlake, who left the matter to Prince Albert to resolve.

[41] Letter from Peel to Eastlake (8 Oct. 1844).

[42] Cf. 'Edward IV', *Encyclopaedia Britannica*, 11th ed. (1911), vol. 8, p. 995: 'the death of the Black Prince robbed the Commons of their strongest support.'

[43] *Literary Gazette* (5 July 1845), p. 443, quoted in R. J. B. Walker, *Catalogue* (1959–77), vol. 3, p. 31.

[44] Boase, 'Decoration' (1954), p. 321.

[45] See Strong, *And When Did You Last See Your Father?*, pp. 116ff.

Landing of the Danes, along with another Anglo-Saxon subject by F. R. Pickersgill, *The Burial of Harold*, was awarded a premium in the competition held in 1847 for paintings in oil for the Palace; now it hangs in Committee Room 10. Watts's own account of his subject emphasized its 'religious and patriotic feeling'[46] in the same way that *Ethelbert* in the House of Lords Chamber represents the spiritual foundation of the Constitutional ideals held dear by Victoria, Albert, and Peel. Indeed, although the sequence of Westminster competitions held from 1842 was devised essentially to test artistic merit and the Commissioners were augmented to increase their range of expertise,[47] the award of premiums suggests that iconography as much as style was at stake. Two of the 1847 premiums (where the judges included Peel) were for Anglo-Saxon subjects, and a third for a subject, *The Battle of Meamee*, strongly reminiscent of Albert's proposal that a mural of 'the submission of the Indian Rebel chiefs'[48] might flank the one he wished to have of Queen Victoria and the European nations in the Royal Gallery.

This emphasis on iconography is clearly instanced by the final pair of murals in the Lords' Chamber, *The Spirit of Justice* by Maclise (Plate 21) and *Prince Henry acknowledging the Authority of Chief Justice Gascoigne* by Cope (Plate 22). Whilst Cope's picture commemorated a lawyer who had refused to sentence prisoners at the behest of the King, thereby upholding the principle that judges are subject to the authority of Parliament and not the monarch, Cope's conception of the theme was apparently shaped by Albert, who provided Eastlake with a sketch which the latter described to Cope; Cope then produced his own for Eastlake's approval.[49] The mural tellingly gives prominence not to Gascoigne but to Henry, as a principled monarch who selflessly concedes the justice of Gascoigne's stance. Maclise, meanwhile, made what would have been understood as a pointed reference to Albert's concern at what he had called 'the blackest stain on civilised Europe',[50] the slave trade, by including a negro slave as one of the beneficiaries of his symbolic figure of *Justice*. Albert had pressed Peel's Foreign Secretary, Lord Aberdeen, to act on the slavery issue some years earlier, and he was also urging intervention from the Anglican Church; the judges who sit beneath *Justice* in his picture are ecclesiastical as well as lay.

The extent to which Albert exercised a controlling hand over the work in the Chamber can be gauged by the fact that when *Mr Punch* of the famous magazine joined in the fresco revival at Westminster in 1847 by starting a mural himself, the caption read: 'Prince Albert can hardly be persuaded to quit my *atelier*...'[51] His influence was also important in the other mural work of the 1840s, in the Royal Robing Room and the Upper Waiting Hall,[52] whilst even the Macaulay-Hallam style subjects in the Peers' and Commons' Corridors, which were 'intended to do justice to the heroic virtues displayed on both sides',[53] stood for that very reason in evident contrast to the militant hero-worship of Cromwell by the Radicals and Chartists, which was still felt in the mural iconography at Rochdale Town Hall in the early 1870s;[54] they were, of course, drawn up under the

46 G. F. Watts, quoted, ibid., p. 115.

47 Criticism was made of the lack of artistic representation on the Commission (see Boase, 'Decoration' (1954), p. 334); Viscount Mahon, the Tory historian who was later the prime mover behind the National Portrait Gallery, and T. B. Macaulay, the Whig historian, were appointed to the CFA in 1844.

48 Prince Albert, Draft Memorandam to Peel (see n. 33).

49 See Walker, *Catalogue*, vol. 3, p. 34.

50 Prince Albert's first public speech (June 1840), to the Society for the Extinction of the Slave Traffic and the Civilization of Africa, quoted in Rhodes James, *Albert*, p. 109.

51 'Punch's own Picture', illustrated in M. Bond (ed.), *Works of Art*, p. 31; the subject of his picture, aptly enough, is *Prince Henry*, for which Albert had provided a sketch.

52 See, for example, Eastlake's comment to Prince Albert (13 Dec. 1853, RA(W) F31/13) that 'Mr. Dyce has expressed his readiness to make the alterations suggested by Your Royal Highness in his last executed fresco in the Queen's Robing Room.'

53 *Seventh Report* of the CFA (op. cit.), p. 10.

54 See Chapter 7. The sizes of the murals are: *Hospitality*—3.42 × 6.64m; *Courtesy* and *Generosity*—3.42 × 1.78m each; *Mercy*—3.42 × 3.11m; *Religion*—3.42 × 4.43m.

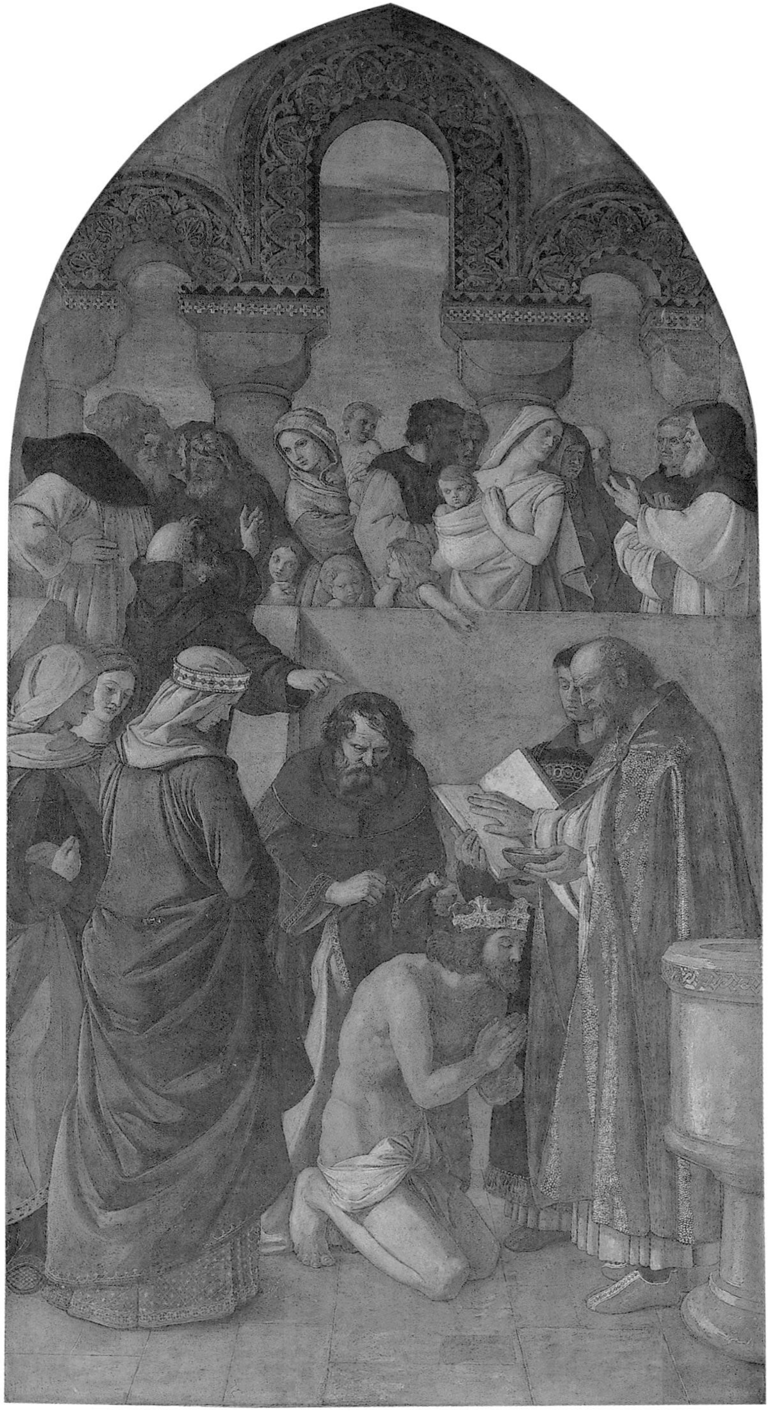

18. William Dyce, *The Baptism of King Ethelbert*, 1846, House of Lords Chamber, Palace of Westminster, London

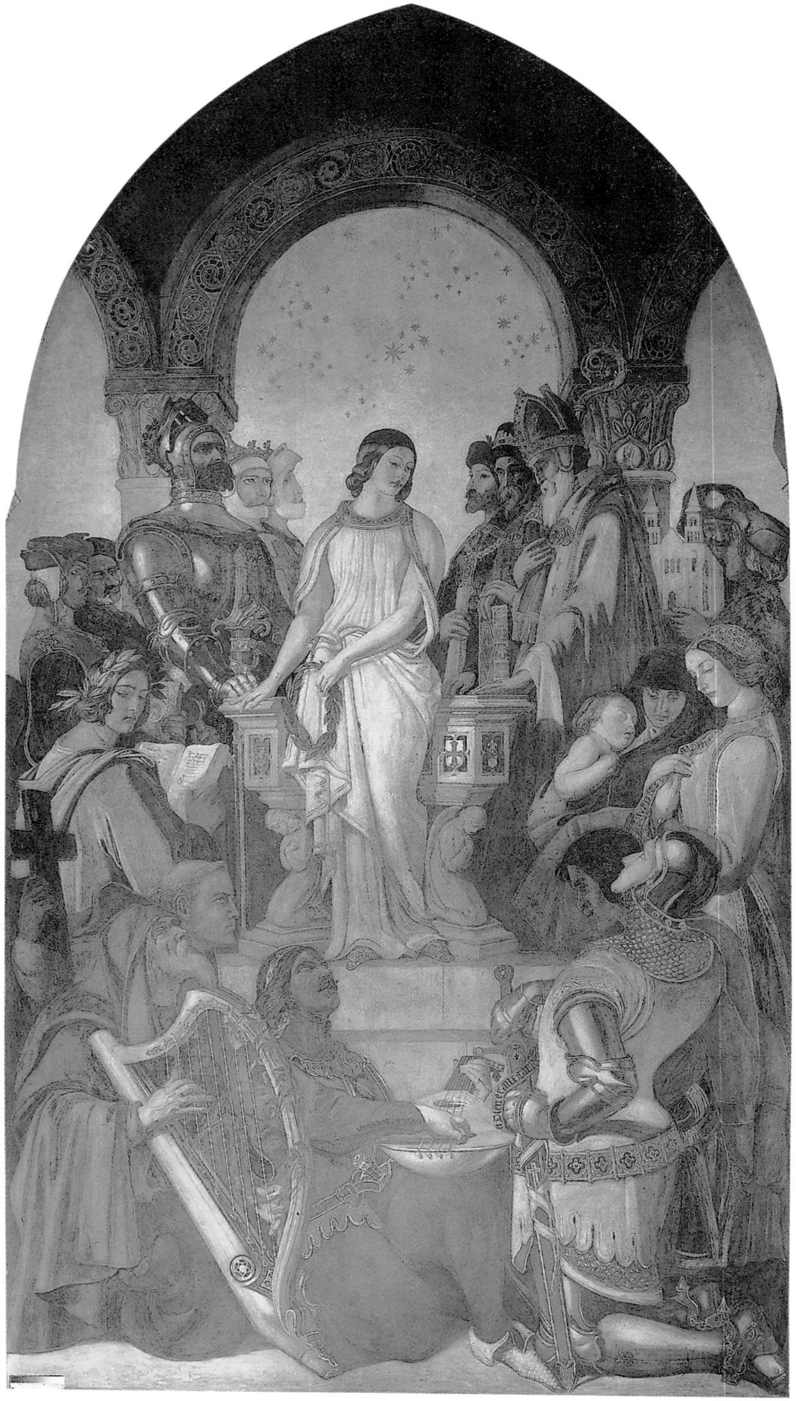

19. Daniel Maclise, *The Spirit of Chivalry*, 1847, House of Lords Chamber, Palace of Westminster, London

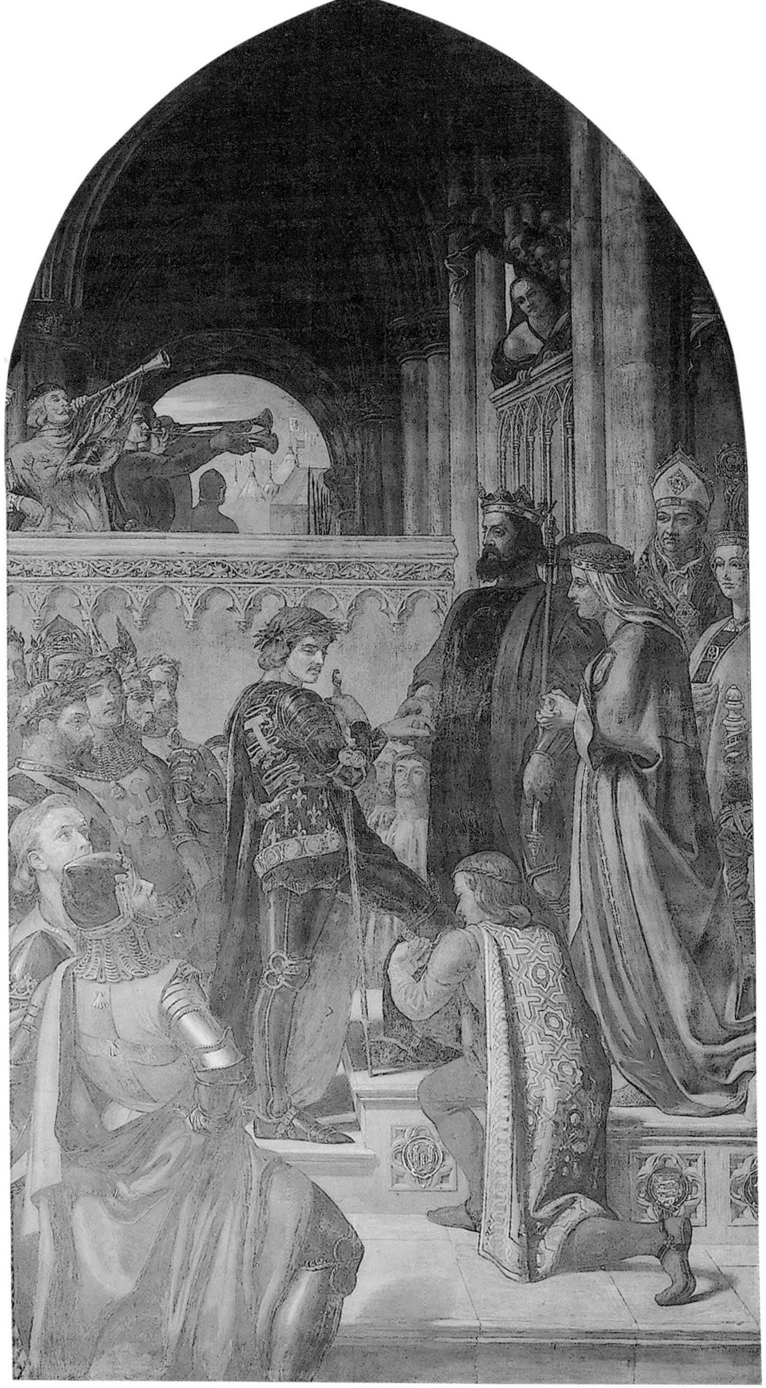

20. Charles West Cope, *Edward III conferring the Order of the Garter on the Black Prince*, 1848, House of Lords Chamber, Palace of Westminster, London

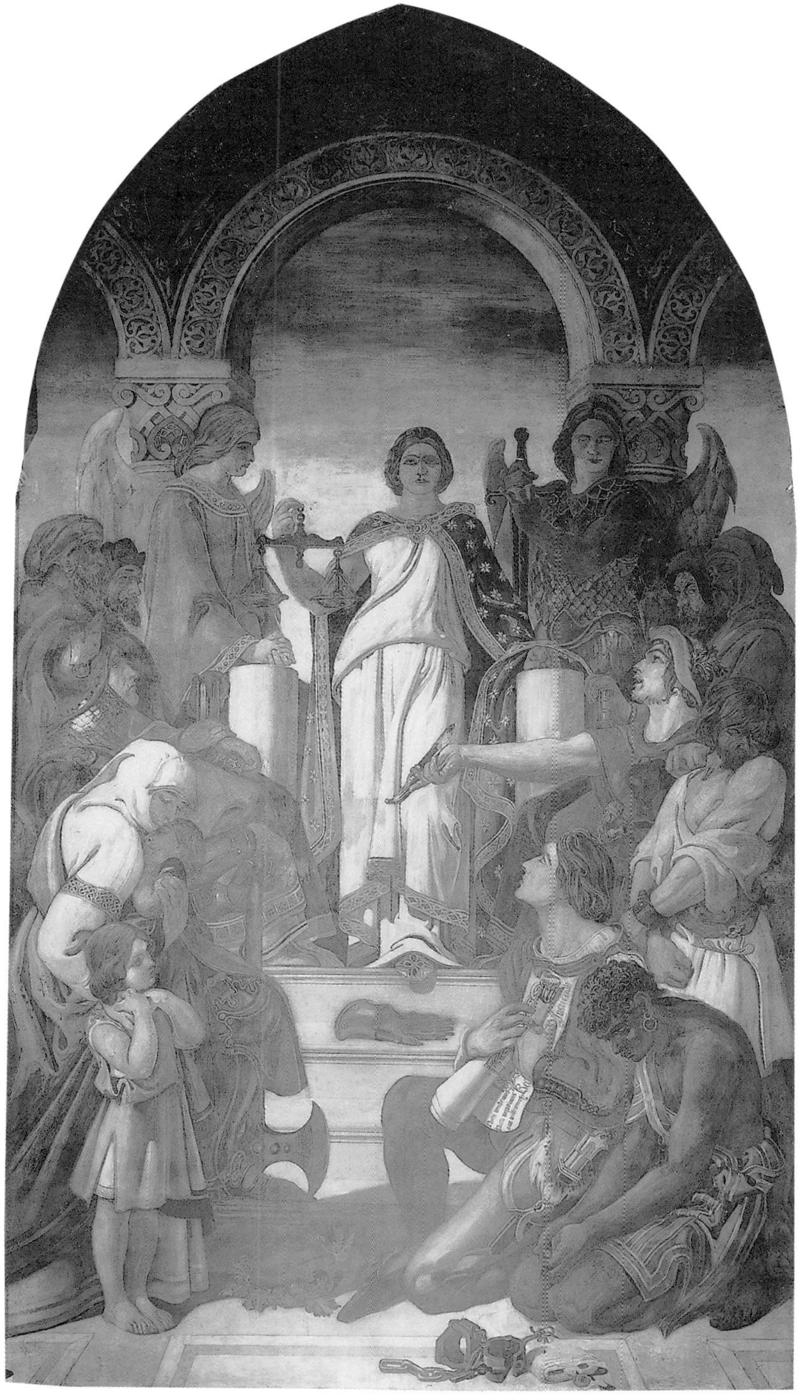

21. Daniel Maclise, *The Spirit of Justice*, 1849, House of Lords Chamber, Palace of Westminster, London

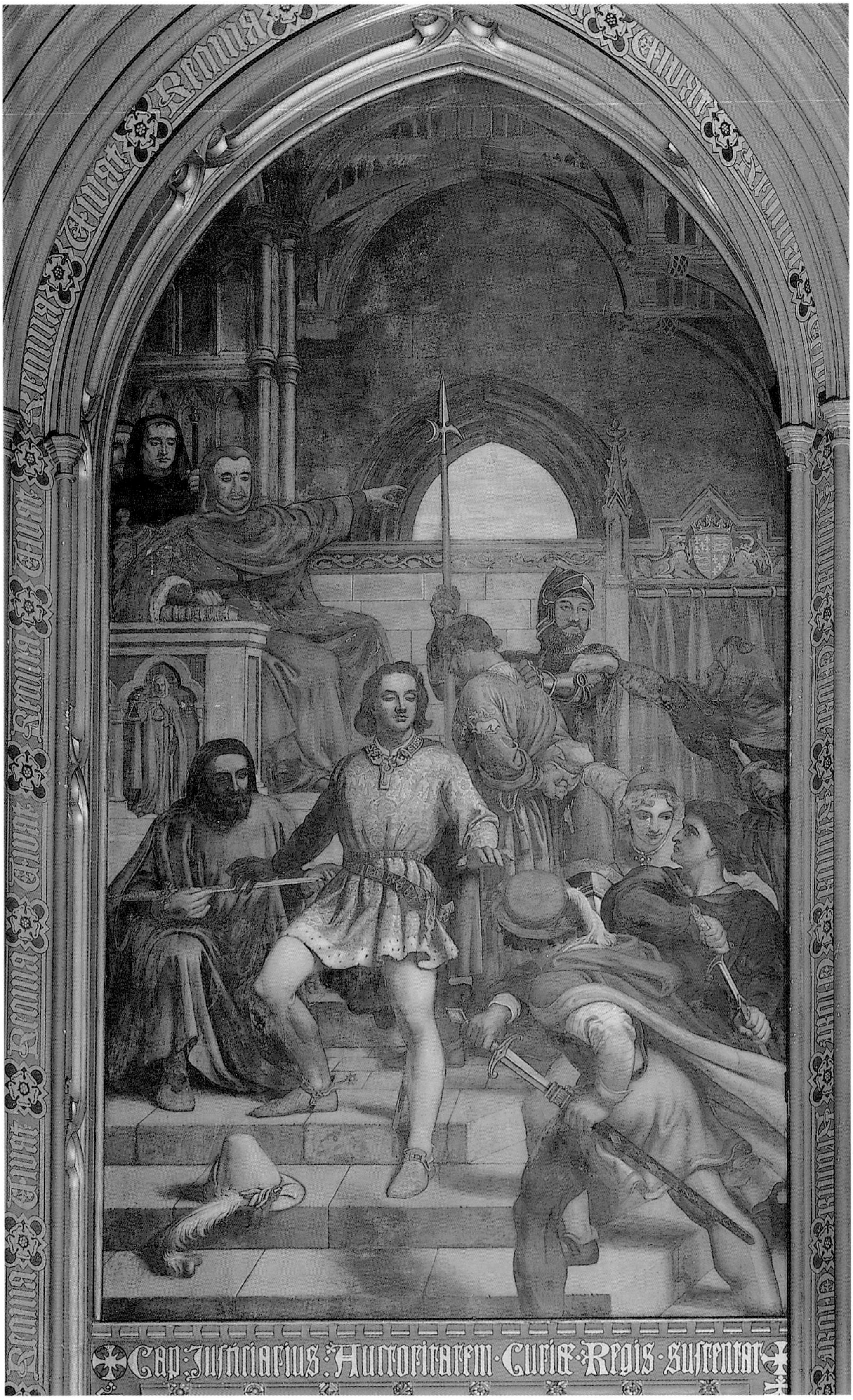

22. Charles West Cope, *Prince Henry acknowledging the Authority of Chief Justice Gascoigne*, 1849, House of Lords Chamber, Palace of Westminster, London

impending shadow of the Chartist revolt of 1848. Though Peel had lost the Premiership in 1846, his influence still seems to have been powerful in the Royal Commission.

Such political overtones within the Royal Rooms of the Palace celebrate its nineteenth-century function and stand in marked contrast to the commemoration of cultural history—Greek and German literature and art—which was featured in the decoration of King Ludwig I of Bavaria's recent Palace and State buildings in Munich, the most immediate prototype for the Westminster project (Plates 5, 6). Yet even in the Royal Robing Room, where themes from early national legend (Malory's *Morte d'Arthur*), again carried out in fresco, suggest direct imitation of Ludwig's use of the *Nibelungenlied* in his Königsbau (Palace)[55] (Plate 16), there is a distinctively topical reference, for this room is where the monarch sets out on his or her route at the State Opening of Parliament.

The Arthurian subjects entrusted to Dyce were selected to illustrate the larger moral principles of *Hospitality* (Plate II), *Courtesy*, *Mercy*, *Generosity*, and *Religion* (Plate 23). In answer to a letter from Dyce enquiring whether to take a 'historical' or 'allegorical' view of the *Morte d'Arthur*,[56] Prince Albert was adamant that his murals should show 'particularly . . . those scenes which exemplify the moral qualities venerated in Chivalry, with the Round Table attended by Arthur and his knights forming the centrepiece of the room'.[57]

He thus made explicit the interrelationship of the Robing Room with the Lords' Chamber, where *Chivalry* (Plate 19) is illustrated, and where the Queen would preside over the whole of the Lords and Commons from her throne during the State Opening ceremony itself. If Albert's dream of placing a mural of the Queen presiding over not just Parliament, but indeed the Empire and the European nations, in the Royal Gallery was never achieved, there was certainly an inner symbolism to the Round Table themes in the Robing Room which was not lost on Dyce, who explained that he had followed Malory's text, where 'Merlin . . . interprets the Round Table to signify the World.'[58]

Given the kind of allusion to be found in the Chamber murals, it seems likely that some kind of similar association was also intended between the episodes selected by Dyce in consultation with the Prince, and Victoria and Albert's own lives. *The Admission of Sir Tristram to the Fellowship of the Round Table (Hospitality)* (Plate II) for example, suggests the same kind of 'admission ritual' as *Edward III conferring the Order of the Garter on the Black Prince* (Plate 20) in the Chamber and would have suggested not only the Prince's own entry into the British Royal Family, but also—in the light of Dyce's explanation of the 'Round Table' as the world—his aspirations to deeper involvement in affairs of State and foreign policy.[59] In the 1840s when the murals were started, Victoria was additionally much concerned that 'something must be done at once to place the Prince's position on a constitutionally recognised footing, and to give him a title adequate to that position.'[60] The mural of *Courtesy*, on the other hand, suggests a more personal commemoration of Victoria and Albert's own romance: Sir Tristram meeting Yseult, 'learned her to harp and she began to have great fantasy unto him'.[61]

[55] Cf. also Prince Albert's reference in an undated letter to Peel (RA(W) F29/1; early 1841?) to showing him 'a very fine Edition' of the *Nibelungenlied* 'which has lately appeared', illustrated by the Düsseldorf artists Bendemann and Hübner.

[56] Letter from Dyce to Eastlake (20 July 1848), RA(W) F30/61.

[57] Letter from Prince Albert to Eastlake (21 July 1848), National Art Library, Victoria and Albert Museum, London, Pressmark: 86. GG. 18 (33).

[58] Letter from Dyce to Eastlake (20 July 1848) (see n. 56).

[59] See, for example, Albert's support for Peel's Free Trade principles in 1846 and his own 'firm grip on foreign affairs' from the late 1840s (Rhodes James, *Albert*, p. 170).

[60] Queen Victoria, writing to Peel in 1845, quoted, ibid., p. 154.

[61] Malory, *Morte d'Arthur*, quoted in Bond, *Works of Art*, p. 46.

Dyce appears to have been responsible for proposing the device of illustrating the Arthurian legend in terms of 'personifications of certain moral Qualities',[62] a clear reflection of the familiarity with Nazarene mural painting that had recommended him to Albert for the Westminster commissions. In the Royal Gallery, however, a more literal, narrative approach was required for the eighteen historical episodes eventually determined by the Commissioners as its decorative scheme in place of Albert's more symbolic proposal with the nations paying homage to Queen Victoria. Although Albert's preferred artist, Maclise, had requested that he be employed in the Royal Gallery 'as containing subjects, on the whole, more interesting to me',[63] the history of his commission shows that Albert took pains to ensure that Maclise never lost sight of his original inner meaning for the Royal Gallery.

Maclise, significantly, was commissioned (in 1857) to begin with *The Meeting of Wellington and Blücher after Waterloo* (Plate 24) and *The Death of Nelson* (Plate 25, Plate III), the two largest murals, with titles which had originally been part of Prince Albert's proposals, as illustrations of British victories which had 'established that Peace which the world has enjoyed ever since'. Already in the 1850s, Albert had noted 'Is the sovereign not the natural guardian of the honour of his country, is he not *necessarily* a politician . . . ?'[64] By 1857 Britain had experienced the Crimean War and was facing troubles in India, as well as what Albert perceived to be a very real threat to European peace in the person of the new French Emperor. Both he and Victoria were convinced that, as Victoria put it, 'The position of the Queen's army is a pitiable one'[65] and argued vigorously with the Foreign Secretary for it to be strengthened. The Royal Gallery decoration can be seen as a deliberate attempt to assert Britain's historic military and naval dominance over the French within this context: a plea, in fact, from the Monarch to Parliament. It is perhaps not without significance that Maclise's commission for *The Meeting of Wellington and Blücher* coincided almost exactly with the completion, amidst a climate of strengthening Prussian might, of a mural by Adolphe Menzel of the self-same subject, though in a very different style, for the Crown Prince's palace in Berlin (1858, now in the Neue Pinakothek, Munich).

Maclise's cartoon for *Wellington* (Plate 7), exhibited to the enormous approbation of his fellow artists in 1859,[66] bore eloquent testimony to his delight in meticulously accurate historical detail, from his portraits of Russian generals, based on originals supplied by the Berlin connoisseur Dr Waagen, to the uniforms of Wellington and Blücher, 'copied from coats, caps and arms actually worn in the field on the day of the battle'.[67] When he tried to execute this detail *in situ*, however, he ran into serious difficulties and resigned his commission after less than a month. The incident highlights the extent to which subject-matter had become inextricably interwoven with style and technique in the thinking behind the whole Westminster scheme, and the significance for Albert of what he called 'the style of fresco'[68] which had been selected.

Maclise found that fresco made the kind of detail he desired impossible. The method of painting onto wet plaster involved joining one day's labour to that of the previous day, small portion by small portion; furthermore, what he called 'my poor earthy lime-burnt tinges' were competing

[62] Letter from Dyce to Eastlake (20 July 1848) (see n. 56).

[63] Maclise, quoted in Boase, 'Decoration' (1954), p. 348.

[64] Quoted in Rhodes James, *Albert*, p. 218.

[65] Comment from the period of the Indian Mutiny, quoted, ibid., p. 260.

[66] Forty-three artists presented Maclise with a gold porte-crayon 'not so much as a token of our esteem and admiration as of the honest pride which, as artists and fellow-countrymen, we feel in the success of the cartoon you have lately executed' (quoted in Boase, 'Decoration' (1954), p. 348). (The size of the actual murals is 3.69 × 11.93m each.)

[67] W. J. O'Driscoll *Memoir of Maclise* (1871), p. 138, quoted in Ormond, *Maclise*, p. 109.

[68] Letter from Albert to Eastlake (10 Aug. 1859), RA(W) F31/58.

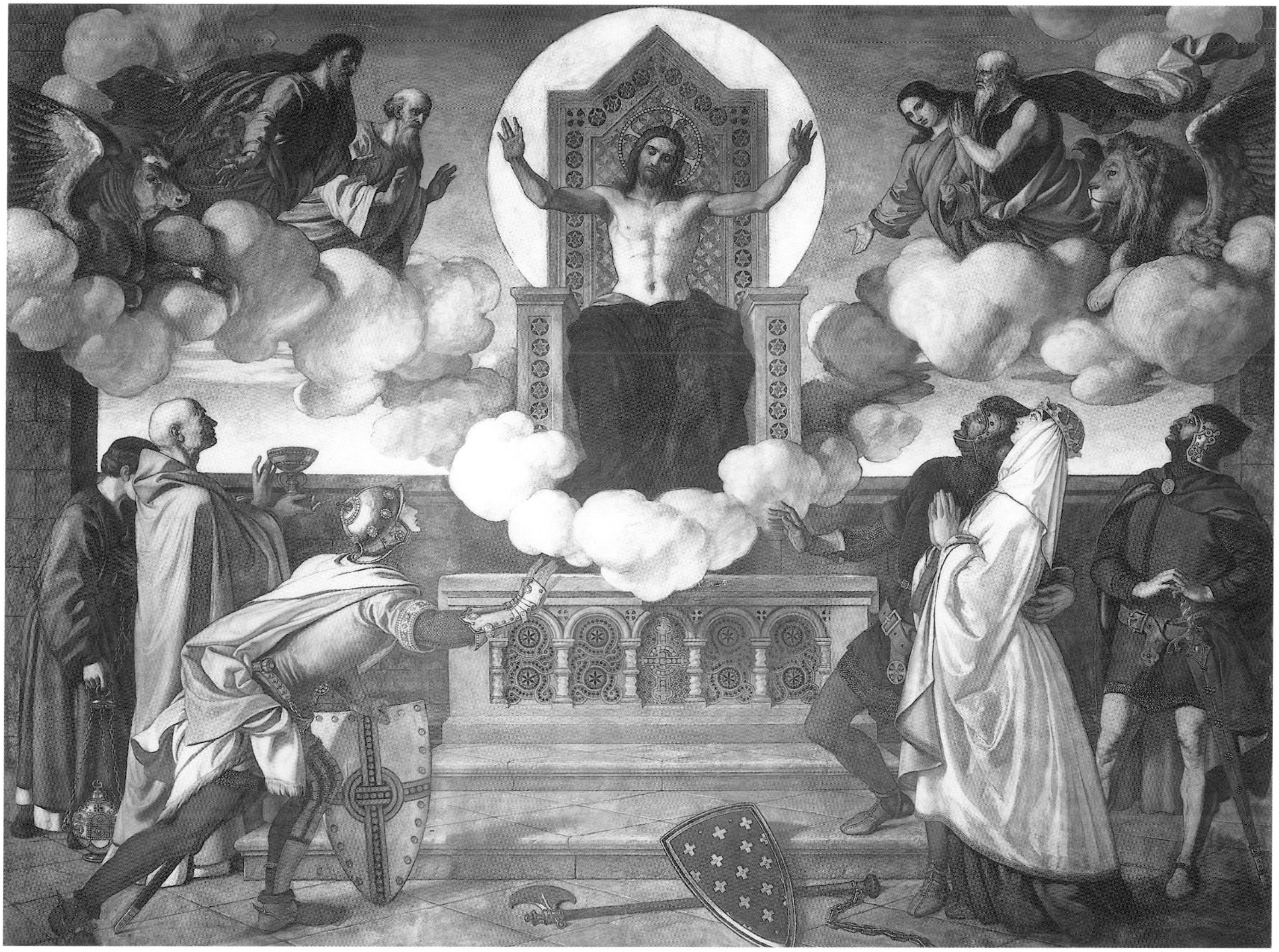

23. William Dyce, *Religion. The Vision of Sir Galahad and his Company*, Royal Robing Room, Palace of Westminster, London, 1851

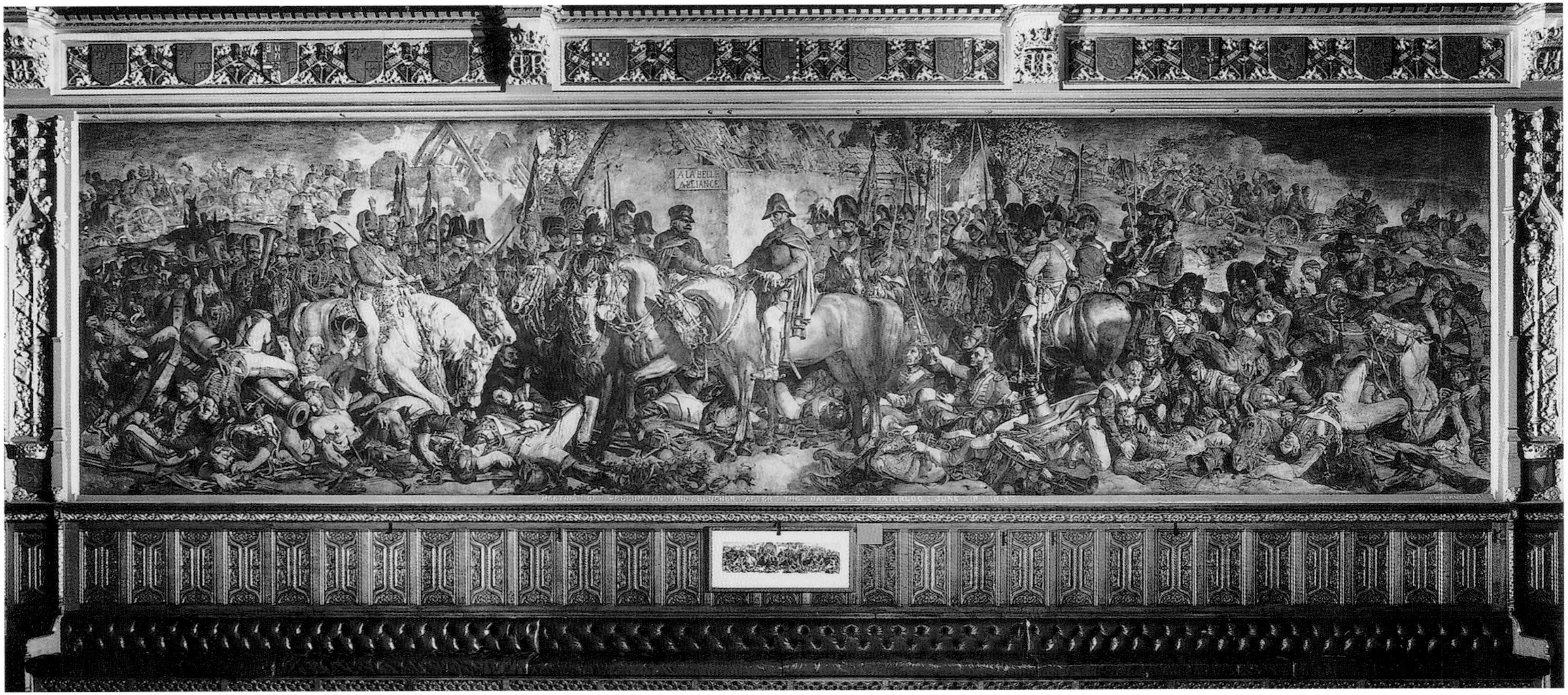

24. Daniel Maclise, *The Meeting of Wellington and Blücher after Waterloo*, Royal Gallery, Palace of Westminster, London, *c.*1859–62

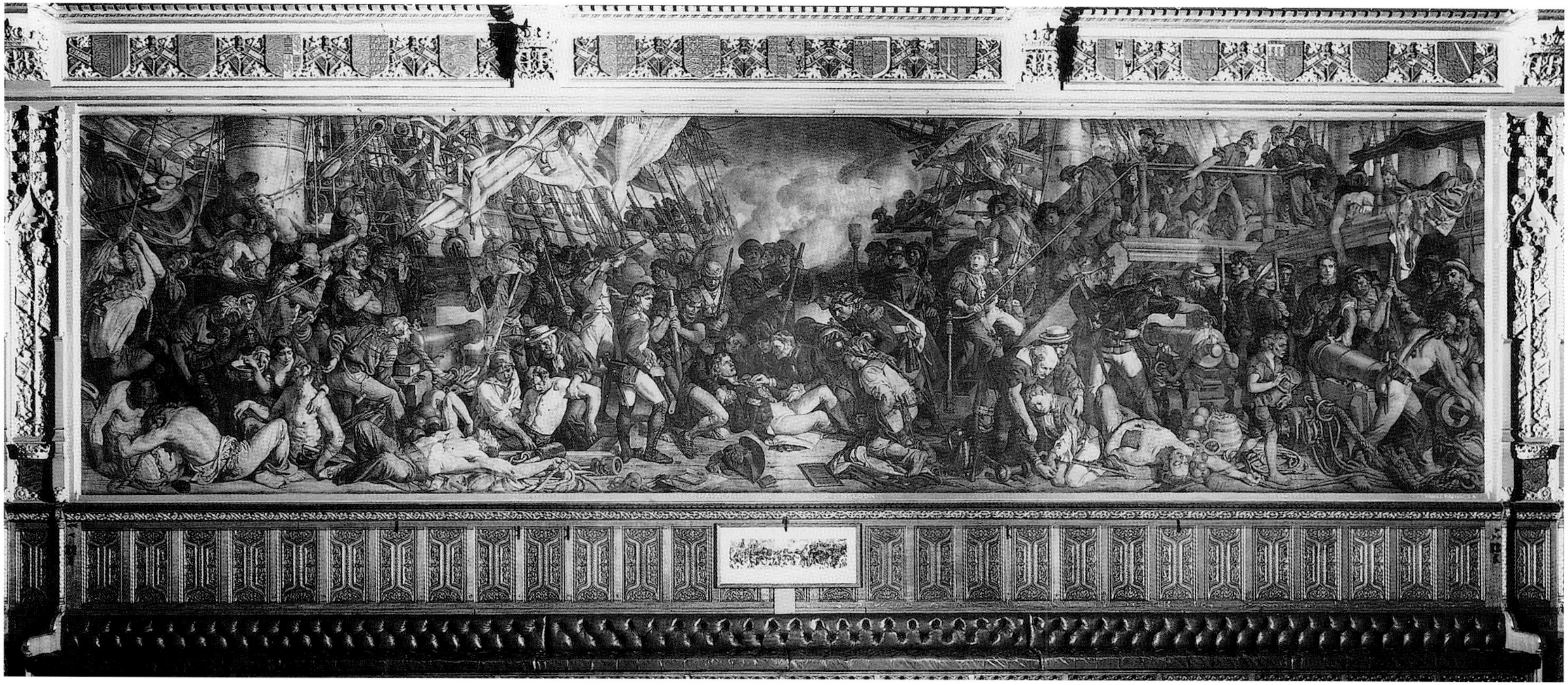

25. Daniel Maclise, *The Death of Nelson*, Royal Gallery, Palace of Westminster, London, 1863–5

with 'the heraldic devices . . . in gules, and gold, and azure . . . emblazoned in form and colour over the forty-six feet of compartment . . . in their dazzling passage'[69] because of the sun shining on the walls through the stained glass of the Gallery. Albert, however, having seen his royalist Peace of Nations allegory for the end wall disallowed, was clearly most reluctant that any overemphasis on detail should threaten to obscure the murals' larger significance. He wrote to Eastlake that

> The spot which is to be decorated by painting, absolutely requires *monumental treatment*, and feeling this, the Comm*rs* selected the style of fresco . . . All organic substances, like oil and wood, ought to be eliminated as perishable, from a monumental work . . . If Mr. Maclise feels disgusted at the dry and rigid materials for his production and longs for oil, it is because he feels pain in the struggle to have to cast away the peculiar means of producing effects in finishing of minute details, in which he knows he excels. But a grand historical work requires the sacrifice of these details, and fresco is a protection to Mr. Maclise against himself, and secures his rising by this work to a height, as an Artist, which he cannot himself comprehend as yet.[70]

'The fresco style' was, in effect, a deeply symbolic vehicle, the means to secure the 'large and simple forms' and 'very direct action' which its great German practitioner Peter Cornelius had told one of the members of the Commission, Thomas Wyse, were necessary for the appreciation of art 'by the lower classes of the community'.[71] Just as the Tractarians and Ecclesiologists were looking to the Nazarene fresco revival for clarity of pictorial statement in churches,[72] so at Westminster it was the didactic and moral purpose motivating the Royal Fine Arts Commission under Albert's chairmanship that turned the medium into the message.

Maclise, however, remained insistent that he could not work in fresco, even when Albert agreed to remove the stained glass and himself designed a system of reflectors to diffuse the light. Eventually, Prince Albert sent him to Berlin to learn the new technique of water-glass being employed there; Maclise talked to one of its chief exponents, Wilhelm Kaulbach, and studied its use also in Munich and Dresden. It was a process of watercolour painting fixed to the wall with liquid silica, and it maintained the matt surface admired in fresco (see Appendix A).[73] After some traumas, Maclise was converted and the technique was also adopted by other Westminster artists. In order to understand the role played by 'the style of fresco' in the attempts to create a national tradition of 'High Art' at Westminster, the nature of the murals carried out in both fresco and water-glass, and its significance within Albert and the Commission's iconographical programme, we now need to look more fully at the train of events which led up to Maclise's crisis.

'THE STYLE OF FRESCO'

The sheer bravado of embarking on a mural project of unprecedented scale in Britain, and in a medium whose British practitioners (so the Select Committee of 1841 had been told) numbered precisely three,[74] sounds exactly the sort of Peelite enterprise which was scorned by Disraeli as

69 Maclise, quoted in Bond, *Works of Art*, p. 61.

70 Letter from Albert to Eastlake (10 Aug. 1859) (see n. 68).

71 Evidence of Thomas Wyse, quoted in Rep. SCFA (18 June 1841), PP VI, p. vii.

72 See Chapter 8.

73 See Prince Albert's diagram and explanation of this scheme in his letter to Eastlake (10 Aug. 1859) (see n. 68). For a discussion of the historical evolution and technical characteristics of water-glass, see J. Pursche, 'Betrachtung zur Malerei mit Alkalisilikaten' (1998).

74 Evidence from Dyce, Min SCFA (28 May 1841), PP VI, § 393–4.

'Ring[ing] the changes on great measures and great experiments'.[75] It can be seen, however, as a very conscious attempt on the part of Peel, Albert, and the Commission to demonstrate that Britain could equal, if not surpass, modern Continental achievement in 'High Art'. Just as Britain's Constitution earned her respect throughout Europe, so too might her art: what more natural than to celebrate one by means of the other?

The Select Committee of 1841 was the direct outcome of the Select Committee on Arts and Manufactures of 1835, which had had its attention drawn by witness after witness to the way in which the arts on the Continent were supported by the government and hence were far more advanced than in Britain. One of the most forthright speakers was Gustav Waagen, who loaned Maclise the original portraits for use in *Wellington and Blücher*. He advised government-supported art studios as at the 'school of Düsseldorf', public exhibitions to extend a knowledge of art among the people, state purchase of works of art, and 'the employment of artists in public buildings', lack of which was 'the principal reason why England is so deficient in historical works of painting'.[76] He suggested that the new Houses of Parliament might be used for the purpose and that fresco would be a suitable form of decoration. The Committee's Report resulted in the establishment of the Government Schools of Design in 1837, but also recommended government patronage of fresco painting. Following a request by the President of the Board of Trade, Henry Labouchere, for government money to support experiments in fresco, the 1841 Select Committee was created, with Labouchere and also William Ewart, who had chaired the 1835 Committee, amongst its members.

Just as the German Gewerbeschule were recommended by the artist William Dyce to the Council of the new School of Design when it sent him to report on Continental practice, so it was the German tradition of mural painting in fresco, instigated by the Nazarenes, which the Committee on the Fine Arts decided was the best model for the decoration of Parliament. Likewise, the immensely popular cartoon exhibition of 1843, attended by some half a million people, and its successors for trial pieces of fresco and for oil painting, were a reflection of Waagen's recommendations, although it is likely that the 1809 British Institution plan for State prizes for artists was also a direct inspiration.

Evidence from the Member of Parliament Thomas Wyse on the beneficial effects of King Ludwig of Bavaria's patronage of mural painting in Munich—'I have seen the peasants of the mountains of the Tyrol holding up their children, and explaining to them the scenes of the Bavarian history almost every Sunday'[77]—and advice which Wyse had received direct from Cornelius, Director of the Munich Academy where Ludwig's artists were trained, and himself responsible for some of the most important Bavarian State murals[78] (Plates 5, 6) were given prominence in the 1841 Committee's report. Eastlake likewise delivered a 'Paper on Fresco Painting' to the Committee, in which he drew attention to the way in which 'The efforts to create a new style of art, in Germany . . . were intimately connected with the struggle for political independence,' arguing that 'If . . . we are to look to the Germans, the first quality which invites our attention is their patriotism.'[79]

[75] Words given to the 'gentleman in Downing Street' (Peel) by Disraeli in *Sybil* (1845) to poke fun at Peel's approach to government (Book VI, ch. 1, p. 348 of the edition by S. M. Smith, Oxford, 1991).

[76] G. Waagen, *Minutes of Evidence to the Select Committee on Arts and Manufactures* (1835), PP V, pp. 8–9.

[77] T. Wyse in Min. SCFA (11 June 1841), PP VI, p. 65.

[78] Cornelius's chief work in Munich was the series of Greek mythology frescoes in the Glyptothek; see A. Jameson, *Visits and Sketches* (1834), pp. 216ff.; and Büttner, *Cornelius*, vol. 1 (1980).

[79] C. L. Eastlake, *Paper on Fresco Painting*, Appendix to Min. SCFA (1841), PP VI, pp. 74–5.

It is hardly surprising that Peel recommended Eastlake to Albert as the Secretary of the Royal Commission on the Fine Arts which was born of the Committee, whilst not only Wyse, but also George Vivian, a connoisseur who had studied monumental art in Munich, Henry Bellenden Ker, a warm admirer of the Nazarene Julius Schnorr von Carolsfeld (Plate 16), and Sir Benjamin Hawes, who had commissioned 'a ceiling or two'[80] himself from Cornelius, were appointed as members. Also placed on the Commission was Lord Shrewsbury, who as a Roman Catholic like Wyse shared the Ecclesiologists' sympathy with the Nazarenes' Neo-Catholic ideal of 'purifying' Germany through the qualities of simplicity and directness associated with fresco, and who had himself commissioned Nazarene decoration for his new church at Cheadle.[81]

Admiration for the Germans' expression of 'national ardour'[82] through fresco painting, and its consequent effects in elevating morality and improving standards of design in the nation at large, became recurrent keynotes of the Commission's Reports and advice to the Queen. They consulted Schnorr, and in 1841, when Cornelius was visiting London, he was persuaded to provide the Commission with an extensive report on fresco technique for the guidance of the Westminster artists, even though he was actually nursing hopes that some of his students in Munich might be chosen instead. As early as 1814 in Germany he had voiced his 'innermost conviction' that 'the reintroduction of fresco painting as it was in Italy during the time of the great Giotto up to the time of the divine Raphael' was

> the infallible remedy to give German art the basis for its direction to a new age, worthy of the spirit of the nation . . . Instead of merely wanting to unite incompatible external properties in the manner of empty eclecticism, it centres as a focal point all the life rays radiating from God in a blazing fire that benevolently lights and warms the world. From a spiritual and physical viewpoint, these works belong actually to that spot on the earth where they were created; they are in most beautiful unison with God, nature, time, and surrounding life.[83]

Fresco (see Appendix A), in which the pigment is applied onto the wet plaster of the wall and as it dries becomes physically bonded to it by carbonation, thus united the very ideals which were at the heart of the scheme for decoration at Westminster: expression of national sentiment, its intimate relationship with moral and spiritual authority, and the opportunity it offered for the dissemination of these ideals through the establishment of a national 'school' of British art and design. Albert's and Peel's celebration through the mural iconography of Britain's identity and international authority as embodied in her Constitution was thus directly matched by the medium which literally fused it with the walls—themselves in the 'national' Gothic style—of her government.

Meanwhile, the very constitution of the Royal Fine Arts Commission itself was a subtle coalition of those who, like Peel, Wyse, Hawes, and Albert himself, must have seen German-style art, if not German artists, as the natural extension of their Free Trade sympathies, as well as the means to improve British art achievement, and those who had Ecclesiological leanings to the Nazarene ideal. The elision of sacred and secular in Maclise's Madonna-like *Chivalry* (Plate 19), as in his *Pietà*-type composition for *Nelson* (Plate III) and in Dyce's presentation of Arthurian legend (Plate 23, Plate II), was thus in a sense prefigured by the make-up of the Commission itself, but it was a notable feature of Ludwig's mural projects and was clearly taken up at Westminster as an

[80] B. Hawes, Min. SCFA (1841), PP VI, p. 752.
[81] See Chapter 8.
[82] C. L. Eastlake, *Paper on Fresco Painting*, p. 74.
[83] P. von Cornelius, letter to Joseph Goerres (3 Nov. 1814), in E. G. Holt, *From the Classicists to the Impressionists* (1966), pp. 99–100.

obvious device with which to endow monarch and Parliament alike with moral power. Albert in particular would have been intimately familiar with the murals by Cornelius and his pupils in the Aula of Bonn University, where he had been educated; they offer a direct prototype for Dyce's compositional dependence in the Royal Robing Room on the Vatican Stanze by Cornelius's 'divine Raphael'.

There was also no shortage of interest on the part of the British art press in German art, with a plethora of descriptions of the Munich Glyptothek and Residenz murals, technical treatises on fresco, and travelogues on the German monuments emerging in the wake of the decision to decorate at Westminster.[84] Any entrant to the Westminster competitions should not have been lacking in inspiration. The 1842 competition remit was for 'precision of drawing . . . and a style of composition less dependent on chiaro-scuro than on effective arrangement';[85] the murals of Cornelius in Munich, and of Schnorr von Carolsfeld, and especially Friedrich Overbeck, were clearly in the Commissioners' minds.[86] German tendencies were not, however, notably evident in either the cartoons submitted or the premiums awarded. Armitage's *Caesar's first Invasion of Britain* (Plate 17) which gained one of the three £300 premiums, used a figure arrangement reminiscent of Géricault's *Raft of the Medusa*, with its apex format and dramatic silhouetting of Caesar against the sky, and its effect stemmed largely from chiaroscural rather than linear qualities.[87] Armitage had trained under Paul Delaroche and was eventually requested to submit a further cartoon with certification that it had been wholly completed in England, after rumours that Delaroche had helped him. Some of the few obviously Germanic (in terms of linear) compositions were not recognized at all, such as H. J. Townsend's *Fight for the Beacon*, with its stiffly frozen column of flailing figures against the open sky, and the work of the Bell Scott brothers who had studied in Germany. J. Z. Bell, one of the few British practitioners of fresco and Director of the new Manchester School of Design, was one of the better-known artists, but his *Cardinal Bourchier Urging the Dowager Queen of Edward IV to give up the Duke of Gloucester* was felt to show 'meanness of character and expression' by the press.[88] W. E. Frost (*Una and the Satyrs*) and H. C. Selous (*Boadicea haranguing the Iceni*) (Plate 26) were typical of the group of entrants who weakly attempted to imitate Rubens and Etty with histrionic conglomerations of naked flesh.[89] It seems that only in the subsequent competitions and invitations to artists did Germanism come to the fore. The trend can once again be attributed to Albert's intervention.

The artist who was eventually given the major work in the first phase of Westminster decoration was William Dyce, who had not entered the cartoon competition of 1842, but was invited to submit a design after it. Dyce's appointment was Albert's personal action; if Albert had been forced to abandon his wish for German artists at Westminster, then he clearly attempted to ensure

[84] e.g. W. Bell Scott, *British, French and German Painting* (1841) and J. G. Crace, 'The Decorations of Munich' (1851); see also Chapter 1, n. 44, and the account of British appreciation of German art in Vaughan, *German Romanticism*. A. Jameson, *Visits*, had already published detailed accounts of modern German murals including those at Munich.

[85] C. L. Eastlake, *Notice Respecting a Competition in Cartoons*, Appendix 1, *First Report* of CFA (1842), p. 8.

[86] Jameson, for example, had spoken of the popular British perception of the Germans' 'formal, hard, and elaborate execution' (*Visits*, 1834, p. 137) and Dyce had told the SCFA (Min. SCFA, 28 May 1841, §427) that German frescoes were 'hard and crude in style'; conversely, Cornelius, according to Prince Albert (*Memorandum* to Peel, *c.*1841, RA(W) F29/7), criticized British artists for 'dazzling the eye by richness of colouring' and 'pleasing the senses by a voluptuousness of forms'.

[87] Illustrated in Boase, 'Decoration' (1954), pl. 46; see also F. K. Hunt, *The Book of Art* (1846) and J. J. and W. Linnell, *The Prize Cartoons* (1844) for illustrations of Westminster cartoons, of which only a few appear to have survived, e.g. Watts's and Cope's in the Victoria and Albert Museum, London.

[88] *Athenaeum* (1843), p. 652, quoted in Boase, 'Decoration' (1954), p. 329, who also illustrates Townsend's and Bell's cartoons (pls. 46 and 47).

[89] Frost's work is illustrated in ibid., pl. 47.

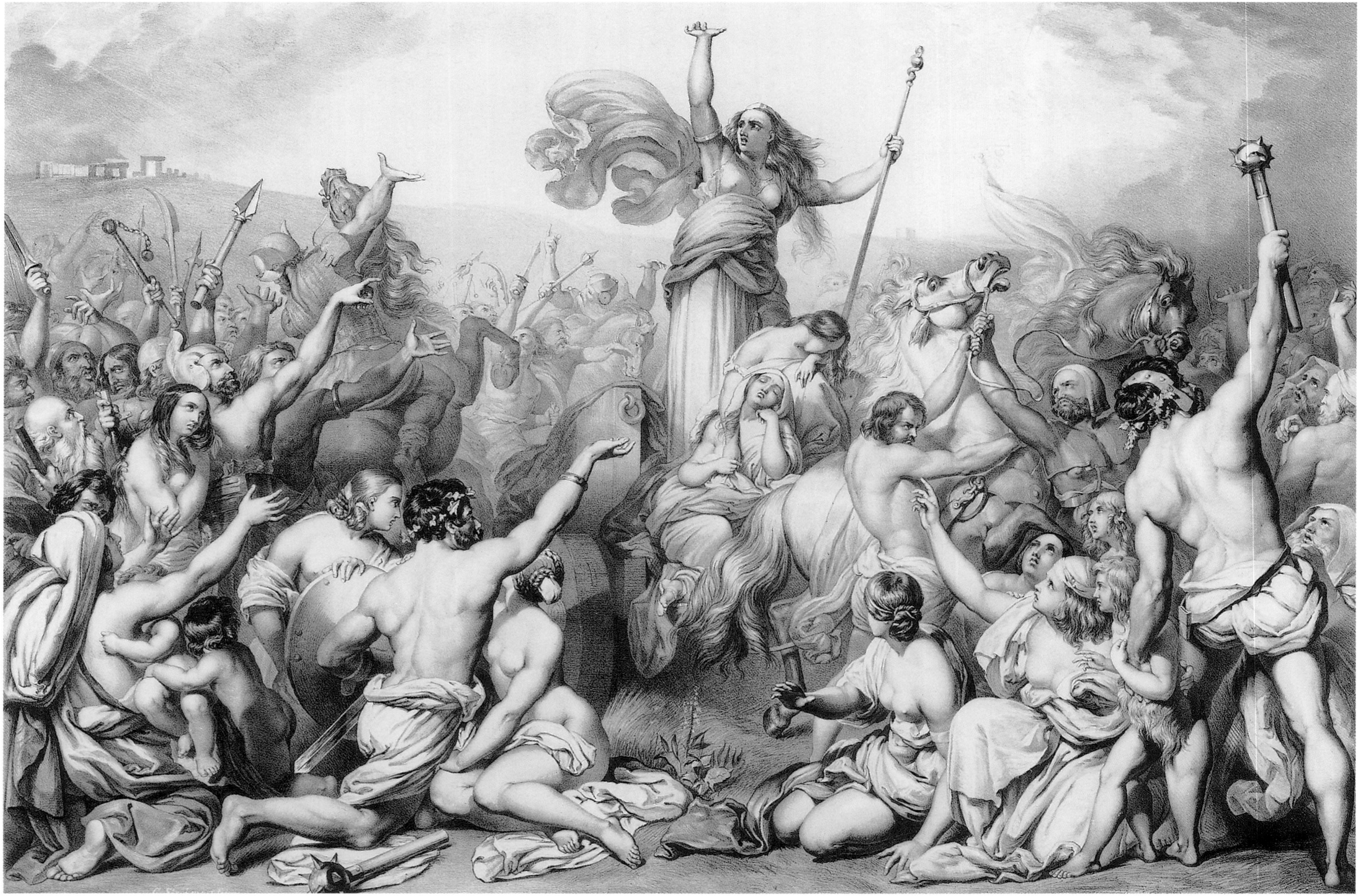

26. H. C. Selous, *Boadicea haranguing the Iceni*, engraved line drawing of entry for 1842 Palace of Westminster cartoon competition. From J. J. and W. Linnell, *The Prize Cartoons* (London, 1844)

that the very nearest alternative was adopted. Dyce had been in close association with the Nazarenes at the start of his career in Rome, was familiar with German practices through his Council of Design visit abroad, and had particularly admired Schnorr's *Nibelungenlied* frescoes (Plate 16) then in progress for the Munich Residenz. He had been one of the strongest supporters of fresco when questioned by the Select Committee; Cornelius had reputedly asked Albert 'What need have you of Cornelius to come over and paint your walls when you have got Mr. Dyce?'[90]

The reality was that the 1842 competition had been a splendid way of making money for the Commission (entry to the exhibition cost a shilling for the first fortnight before it was thrown open to free viewing, and the proceeds allowed the award of ten extra £100 prizes), but a failure in the matter of finding suitable artists. Sir Martin Archer Shee had already advised the 1841 Select Committee that 'artists of reputation'[91] would not be willing to enter a competition, and the majority of the 1843 entries were from young and lesser-known painters. Dyce himself had pronounced that 'competition is very inapplicable in painting' since even though an artist's sketch might be 'successful . . . it does not follow that his picture will be of equal merit.'[92] When further competitions were held, in 1845 and (for oil paintings) in 1847, there was impatience amongst the artists. Not only Dyce, but also Cope (who *had* won a £300 premium in 1843, albeit for a more Raphaelesque than Nazarene composition), Horsley, Richard Redgrave, and William Cave Thomas had been directly invited to submit cartoons for the Lords' Chamber after the 1842–3 competition. However, no decision on whether they would actually be employed was made until 1846, after the subject-matter had been selected for the Lords' Chamber and Dyce's *Ethelbert* (Plate 18), with its strong royal symbolism, had been completed there. The latter was designated a model to guide the other artists in 'the size of their principal figures, their style of colouring, and the degree of completeness in the execution of their works'.[93] Whatever Dyce did not actually paint himself was thus to be as Dyce-like—and therefore Germanic—as possible. The decorative commissions which had meanwhile been given in 1845 for the Upper Waiting Hall (poetry subjects) went to Cope (who had gone to study with Hess in Munich), Cave Thomas (who had studied with Cornelius), Horsley (a close friend of the Berlin artists Hensel and Magnus), J. R. Herbert, J. Severn (who had been a close associate of the Nazarenes in Rome), and Tenniel (who went to Munich); in the event Thomas declined and Armitage and Watts contributed. In 1848 the Queen's Robing Room (Plate 23, Plate II) was entrusted to Dyce in its entirety. Supported by Albert, Peel had been instrumental in ensuring that Barry's architectural design afforded full ceremonial opportunity for the Queen—'such an arrangement of the Royal Robing Room as shall enable the sovereign to pass through the Victoria [i.e. Royal] Gallery direct to the House of Lords in State'[94]—when she opened Parliament. The choice of Albert's favourite painter can be seen as a directly symbolic means to affirm this vision in the years after 1846 when Peel had lost the premiership. The 'fresco style' had become all but synonymous with Albert and Peel's vision of the role of the monarchy in modern government; a means to perpetuate it after the 'iconographical' crisis of 1846, which had caused such radical Whig revisions of Albert's subject proposals.

In this context, it is hardly surprising that Maclise's revolt against fresco in the Royal Gallery provoked such consternation on the part of Albert, nor that Albert took personal steps to ensure British competence in the technique before the Westminster work was begun. Despite his original

90 Quoted in Bond, *Works of Art*, p. 30.
91 Shee, Evidence, Min. SCFA (25 May 1841), § 209.
92 Dyce, Evidence, Min SCFA (28 May 1841), § 482.
93 *Fifth Report* of CFA (1846), PP XXIV, p. 287.
94 Quoted in Bond, *Works of Art*, p. 44.

airy prediction to Peel that fresco would be easy for the British—'the English will be vastly superior to any other nations, as they have shown themselves in all technical arts. Colours and mechanical improvements will be brought here to greater perfection than they exist in Germany, judging of the superiority of all existing painting materials over those of the Continent'[95]—the Prince was closely involved in arrangements for numerous technical reports[96] and he organized a series of opportunities for fresco practice. Dyce was given work at Osborne House, and with Eastlake, Maclise, William Etty, Sir Edwin Landseer, Thomas Uwins, Clarkson Stanfield, and the miniaturist Sir William Ross in a garden pavilion at Buckingham Palace.[97] Even when the Westminster decoration started, Eastlake referred to the Upper Waiting Hall (Plate 27), where several of the Buckingham Palace artists were again employed, as 'a place of trial with a view to test their abilities'.[98]

Whilst in Munich in 1845, Cope 'had a long conversation on the subject of frescoes with Professor Hess', whom he had 'found at work in the Basilica of St. Boniface—the best modern frescoes I have yet seen'.[99] These were part of Ludwig's mural schemes; one of the few, in fact, where the German artists were working within medieval-style architecture as at Westminster, and therefore of particular interest to the British.

If Albert's enthusiasm for fresco as a 'royal' medium reflected an attempt to shape British State mural patronage in the mould of the essentially private patronage of the Bavarian princes with which he had grown up, there is an ominous footnote to Cope's reminiscence. Hess impressed on him that 'much depends upon the wall being in the proper state.'[100] When the frescoes at Westminster began to disintegrate before the artists' very eyes as they worked upon them in the later 1850s, awkward questions began to be heard in Parliament about the scope of the Royal Fine Arts Commission's powers.[101]

THE FRUITS OF THEIR LABOURS

Haydon had dismissed all but Ford Madox Brown's unsuccessful entry for the cartoon competition as unworthy of execution, whilst Ruskin had been equally damning of the project in discussion with Joseph Severn:

95 *Memorandum* from Prince Albert to Peel (*c.*1841), RA(W) F29/7.

96 Cf. the account of fresco technique in the *Statements of Director Cornelius* . . . Appendix 3 to *First Report* of the CFA (1842), pp. 18ff.; C. L. Eastlake's letter to Prince Albert (15 Aug. 1842) informing him that 'Mr [C. H.] Wilson the agent employed to travel on the Continent to collect information relating to the objects of the Commission is arrived in London' and Wilson's *Report*, Appendix 3, *Second Report* of CFA (1843), PP XXIX, p. 16; C. L. Eastlake, *Styles and Methods of Painting suited to Decoration of Public Buildings*, Appendix 6, *Second Report* of CFA (1843), PP XXIX and *Methods of Painting adapted to Mural Decoration*, Appendix 14, *Third Report* of the CFA (1844), PP XXXI; *Observations on Fresco-Painting, by Mr. Dyce* (31 Aug. 1846), Appendix 4, *Sixth Report* of CFA (1846), PP XXIV, p. 11; *Stereochrome Painting* . . . (summary of a lecture at the Royal Institution by its Vice-President and Secretary, Revd J. Barlow), Appendix 3, *Tenth Report* of CFA (1854), PP XIX; *Report by Daniel Maclise, Esq., RA, on the 'Waterglass' or 'stereochrome' method of painting*, Appendix 3, *Twelfth Report* of CFA (1861), etc., J. N. Fuchs, 'Manufacture, Properties and Application of Waterglass, including a Process of Stereochromatic Painting', *Journal* of the Society of Arts (17 June 1859 et seq.), pp. 521ff., was 'translated by desire and communicated by HRH the Prince Consort, President of the Society of Arts'. Letters to Sir Charles and Lady Eastlake from Continental artists, including Schnorr von Carolsfeld, on mural techniques are in the National Art Library, Victoria and Albert Museum, London, Pressmark: 86. M. 3–4.

97 See Chapter 10.

98 Letter from Eastlake to Prince Albert (28 July 1851), RA(W) F31/1. The size of each fresco in the Upper Waiting Hall is approximately 2.47 × 1.22 m.

99 C. H. Cope, *Reminiscences* (1891), pp. 152–3.

100 Ibid., p. 153.

101 Cf. the complaint by 'Mr. Coningham' in an extract (late 1850s/early 1860s) apparently from *Hansard*, RA(W), F31/63 'that the Commission of Fine Arts was at the bottom of all this jobbing in the fine arts. The Commission had done no good, and the sooner it was abolished the better'; see also n. 126 below.

With your hopes for the elevation of English art by means of fresco I cannot sympathise. I have not the remotest hope of anything of the kind . . . It is not the material nor the space that gives us thoughts, passions or powers. I see on our Academy walls nothing but what is ignoble in small pictures, and would be disgusting in large ones.[102]

By 1858, the *Quarterly Review* was of the opinion that the majority of the Westminster murals revealed 'little else than coarse unfinished daubing, hasty, inaccurate drawing and academical "tours de force" scarcely superior to what may be seen on the papered walls of a French café' and were 'vulgar in taste, poor in invention, commonplace in treatment, and have no relation whatever to the architectural features of the place: they exhibit, in short, an utter ignorance of the object of mural painting.'[103] Its diagnosis of what had gone wrong—the employment of 'painters who had already been formed in a school opposed in all its views and tendencies to fresco, and had neither the requisite acquaintance with, nor feeling for, this branch of their art' and their 'want of a due appreciation and knowledge of the true aim of painting when combined with architecture'[104]—was an uncomfortable echo of Eastlake's own observations to the Select Committee of 1841 that 'the peculiar merits of the English school are of a nature which are perhaps the least fit to be displayed in fresco . . . the department of the art which is least attainable in fresco is *chiaroscuro*, particularly in masses.'[105]

As the 1842 competition had shown, the English were 'colourists' where the Germans were 'linear'; for this very reason, Eastlake had hoped the British might develop their own distinctive style by referring directly to the great Italian examples which had inspired the Germans and where his own true sympathies lay. Prince Albert, on the other hand, whilst giving a notable lead in the purchase by the British of early Italian works of art,[106] had firmly held up German models as the paradigm for the Westminster artists to follow. Although Dyce's Arthurian murals in the Royal Robing Room (Plate 23, Plate II), so reminiscent of Ludwig's *Nibelungenlied* subjects, show the distinctive archaisms of Overbeck in their stiff figure postures and have a typical German tripartite symmetry, their overall compositional basis is derived from Raphael's Vatican Stanze. There is also much more realism and chiaroscural emphasis in, for example, his Evangelists floating on volumetric clouds above the knights of the Holy Grail in *Religion* (Plate 23) than in the work of Cornelius. His most Germanic composition, *The Departure of the Knights of the Round Table on the Quest for the Holy Grail* (National Gallery of Scotland), which borrows its rearing horseman and close-knit medieval crowd directly from Schnorr's painting *The Battle of Lipadusa*, was never used, and he seems to have isolated and modified the horseman motif from it to form an entirely original, 'close-up' scene for *Generosity*, which is very different in its cropped composition from the balanced geometry of the German designs, although it still retains a typically Germanic shallowness of foreground. The baptism motif and onlookers in Dyce's *Ethelbert* (Plate 18), meanwhile, in the Lords' Chamber, reveal a debt to Masaccio's Brancacci chapel frescoes and Pintorricchio respectively.[107] Dyce himself had considerable misgivings about the Germans' colouristic skills[108] and must have been pleased when Eastlake described his work as

[102] Letter from J. Ruskin to J. Severn (21 Sept. 1845) in *Works*, ed. Cook and Wedderburn (1903–12), vol. 4, p. 394.

[103] Anon., 'Fresco Painting', *Quarterly Review*, 104 (1858), pp. 320–1.

[104] Ibid., p. 320.

[105] Eastlake, Evidence, Min. SCFA (4 June 1841), PP VI, § 577.

[106] See J. Steegman, *Victorian Taste* (1970), p. 61.

[107] Dyce had gone to Italy at the Commissioners' request on being selected to paint *Ethelbert*, where he studied these and other works; see his *Observations on Fresco Painting* (n. 96 above).

[108] See n. 86 above.

'superior . . . in colouring' to murals he had 'lately inspected . . . at Berlin, Dresden and elsewhere'.[109] However, Eastlake also admitted to Prince Albert that despite this quality, Dyce 'does not, under the present circumstances, compete with the Germans in magnitude of design or multitude of figures—nor in the grasp of thought which such comprehensive themes suggest, and in which the German artists show their great invention'.[110]

Amongst the most intractable difficulties encountered by the artists were in fact the 'circumstances' of their work, even though these had already been criticized by Cornelius in his 1842 advice to the Royal Commission: 'The available spaces for painting in Gothic buildings are . . . unfavourable; the pointed arch, sometimes introduced superficially on walls, and the acute forms produced by the simplest groinings in the ceilings are . . . difficult to fill satisfactorily.'[111]

The vertical, pointed-arched panels in the Chamber led to crowding of the figural incident in Horsley's *Spirit of Religion* in particular, and it was perhaps only Maclise of the artists involved who found a satisfactory solution by framing his compositions, *The Spirit of Chivalry* (Plate 19) and *The Spirit of Justice* (Plate 21), with a round arch beneath the actual pointed one of their architectural surround, and by arranging his figures in rising tiers which culminate in a dais. The MP Sir George Bowyer indeed argued in the House of Commons that the subjects of the Lords' Chamber had been rendered 'perfectly unintelligible'; Dyce's *Baptism of King Ethelbert* (Plate 18) showed the king 'to all appearance . . . prepared for a whipping rather than a baptism. The King could not have stripped for the purpose of immersion, for the font was also shown in the picture, and was so small he could no more get into it than into a tea cup.'[112]

In confronting the reality of 'the greatest Italian masters never having been called upon to paint in a Gothic building', even Eastlake found himself involved in chronological gymnastics to justify his advocacy of Raphael, speaking of how 'The Tudor style of Gothic . . . is coeval with the highest development of art in Italy.'[113] Sir Charles Barry's Gothic design had, in fact, been deliberately chosen in preference to Tudor style, and in the event he too, despite having designed the Palace 'so that they [the Lords] would be in a mess if painting was not introduced'[114] came to the conclusion that the most suitable part for decoration was actually the bit he had not designed, the Old Westminster Hall.[115] Richard Redgrave, who had been one of the six artists commissioned after the competition to provide cartoons, sketches, and samples of fresco for the House of Lords Chamber, but whose work was ultimately rejected, was perhaps not surprisingly among the sternest critics of the artists' conditions there:

> The situations selected for them by the Commissioners were quite unsuited to the proper display of high art in any medium. The three paintings opposite the throne are so deeply recessed that they are seen as in a dark hole, and with the three opposite to them, have to contend against a side light, admitted on their level, and through richly stained glass; and they also suffer from the great absence of repose, arising from the extensive employment of colour-gilding throughout the forms in the general decoration of the chamber. Tapestry would have been a far more suitable decoration.[116]

[109] Letter from Eastlake to Prince Albert (15 Oct. 1852), RA(W) F31/5.
[110] Ibid.
[111] *Statements of Director Cornelius* (n. 96), p. 20.
[112] Sir George Bowyer, reported in extract (*c*.1860/61), apparently from *Hansard*, RA(W) F31/93.
[113] Eastlake, *Styles and Methods of Painting suited to Decoration of Public Buildings*, p. 65.
[114] Sir Charles Barry, quoted by B. R. Haydon (10 July 1841) in Taylor, *Life*, vol. 3, p. 169.
[115] Barry, Evidence, Min. SCFA (18 May 1841), PP VI, § 74.
[116] S. and R. Redgrave, *British Painters*, (1947), p. 464.

These were virtually the same problems as Maclise was to complain about in the Royal Gallery, and the artists in general were not hesitant to voice their dissatisfaction over a range of issues. When Cope's and Horsley's original designs for the Lords' Chamber were rejected, they wrote jointly to Eastlake to complain that

> no reason . . . being given for such apparent dissatisfaction, we are unable to effect those alterations, which we might either be desirous of making ourselves, or at the insistence of His Royal Highness and the Commission. We may here be allowed to say that one great cause of the want of uniformity in the designs, has arisen from the system sanctioned by the Commission, namely the encouragement of individual competition, even among the commissioned artists.[117]

Although Eastlake at the outset had advised that 'the artists should be left as unfettered as possible'[118] with regard to subject choice, he had also recognized an imperative for 'one directing head',[119] a principle urged by Cornelius, Haydon, and numerous writers in the press. If 'the fresco style' was the Commissioners' answer to this and the means whereby they hoped to found a British school of High art, then, as the Lords' Chamber reveals, British response to the German model was more idiosyncratic than consistent. A number of the artists employed at Westminster certainly had connections with the government's new German-style School of Design, and some of its students, directed by Richard Burchett were indeed chosen by Barry to provide the one section of mural painting for which he was responsible, the Tudor portraits in the Prince's Chamber. These were roundly criticized in Parliament for being 'copies' of period originals, but to modern eyes their figured gold backgrounds ensure a highly successful harmony with their architectural setting. Without an established source of decorative artists, however, such as the Munich Academy under Cornelius in Germany, or the Ecole des Beaux-Arts whose prizewinners secured State commissions in France, it was perhaps inevitable that the most successful schemes at Westminster are otherwise those where only one artist was employed, such as Maclise's Royal Gallery (even though it was never finished) and the Peers' and Commons North corridors by Cope (Plate IV) and Edward Matthew Ward (Plate 28) respectively. Dyce's Royal Robing Room was perhaps executed over too long a period to be entirely harmonious, and the more naturalistic, strongly recessional effect in his *Hospitality* (Plate II) sits uneasily with the shallow stage format of his earlier scenes (Plate 23). It is as though he had abandoned his belief that fresco painting was essentially decorative rather than illusionary. The Upper Waiting Hall with its eight panels of poetry by Watts, Armitage, Cope, Horsley, Herbert, and Tenniel is essentially a 'patchwork'[120] such as the Select Committee had been concerned should be avoided. Tenniel's *Saint Cecilia* there is one of the unhappiest examples of the mawkishness which the twin ideals of 'female beauty' and Raphael could produce. Watts's *The Red Cross Knight* (St George and the Dragon) from Spenser's *The Faerie Queene* (Plate 27) is less arresting than his oil of *Alfred inciting the Danes*, which was rewarded in the competition for easel paintings for Westminster, but still has a comparably monumental emphasis on a central figure group. Cope's *Death of Lara* (Byron) introduces an atmospheric landscape in which the dying figure is an intriguing echo of Holman Hunt's recent *Rienzi*. Herbert's scene from *King Lear* is, in contrast, a return to the Nazarene-style, round-arched architectural

[117] Letter from Cope and Horsley to Eastlake (25 July 1845), RA(W) F30/16.

[118] Eastlake, Evidence, Min. SCFA (4 June 1841), PP VI, § 661.

[119] Ibid., § 584.

[120] Question from Col. Rawdon of the SCFA, to Shee, Min. SCFA (25 May 1841), PP VI, § 292.

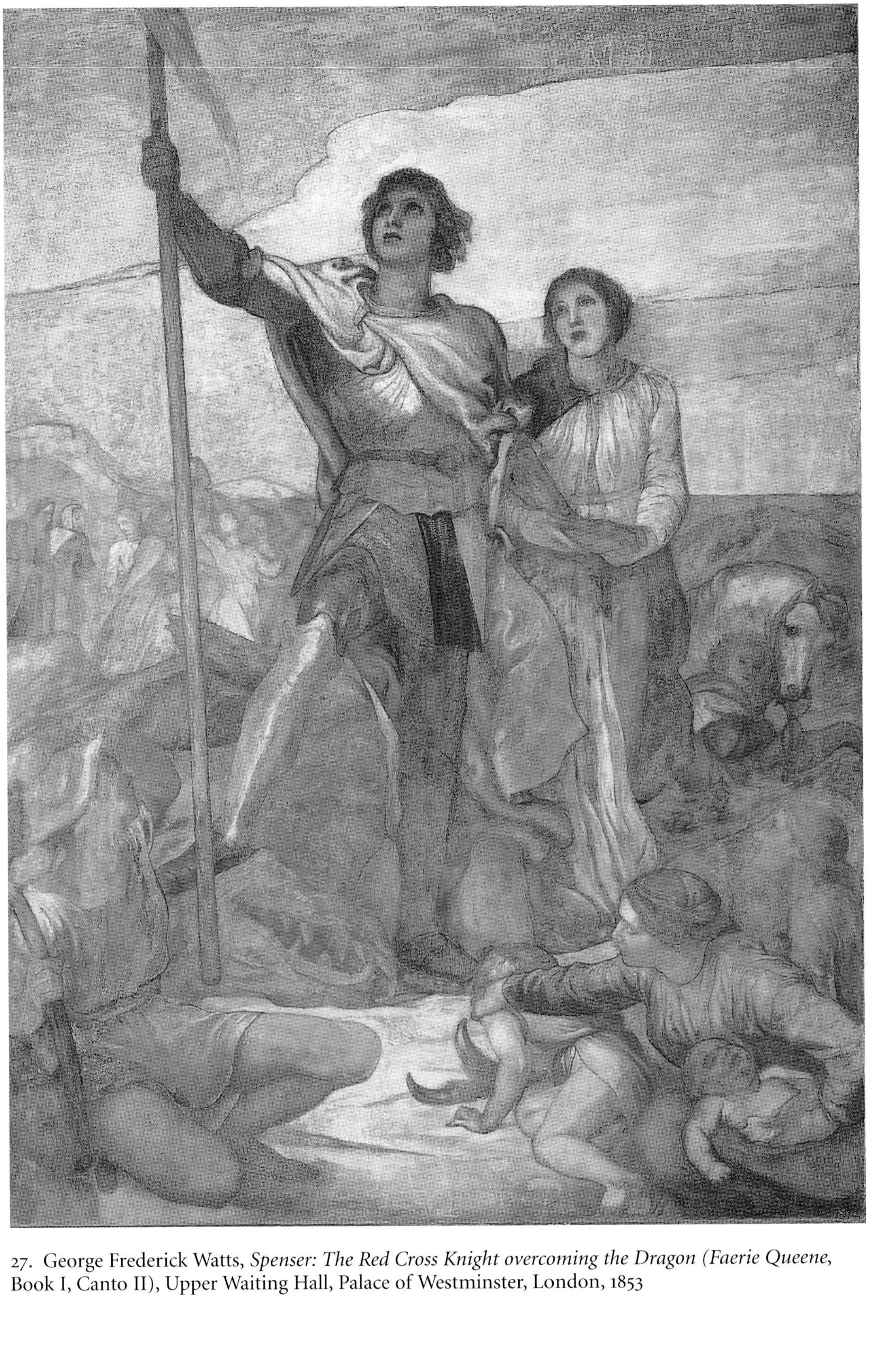

27. George Frederick Watts, *Spenser: The Red Cross Knight overcoming the Dragon (Faerie Queene,* Book I, Canto II), Upper Waiting Hall, Palace of Westminster, London, 1853

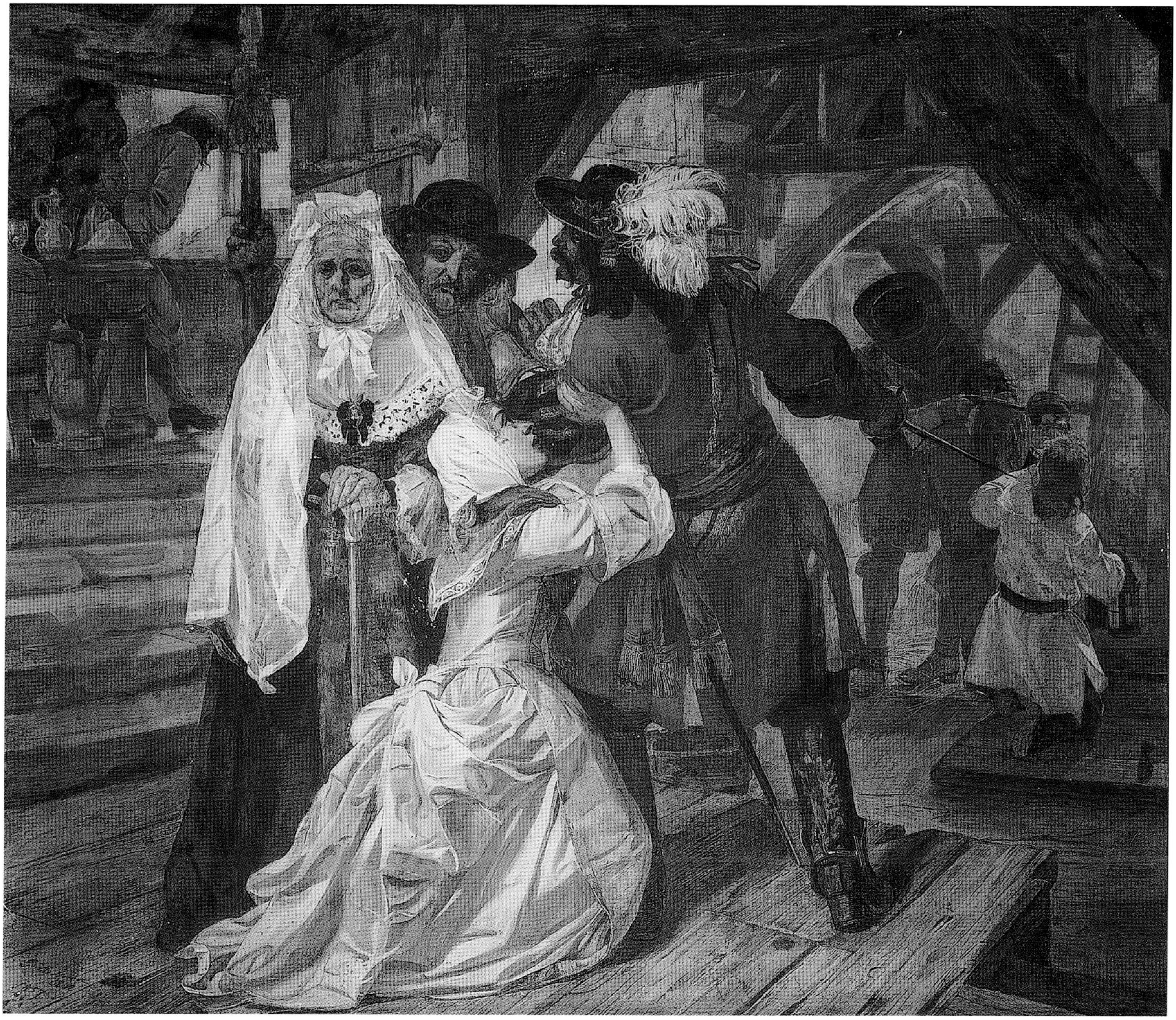

28. Edward Matthew Ward, *Alice Lisle concealing the Fugitives after the Battle of Sedgemoor*, Commons' Corridor, Palace of Westminster, London, 1857

interior which characterizes Dyce's Robing Room work and Maclise's in the Lords' Chamber; Armitage's *Father Thames* is a rather solid echo of the classical 'Parnassus' hemicycle he had assisted his French teacher Paul Delaroche in painting at the Ecole des Beaux-Arts in Paris, a work which had been glowingly described to the Select Committee by a number of its witnesses. The scheme as a whole reveals tensions between Germanic and French trends, whereas Maclise's Royal Gallery work succeeds in its skilful synthesis.

The conception of the Royal Gallery recalls the recent Pavillon du Roi of Louis Philippe at Versailles with its *grandes batailles*, and Maclise's *Death of Nelson* (Plate 25) and *Wellington and Blücher* (Plate 24, Plate III), untrammelled by Gothic arch settings, also exploit to the full the panoramic shallow foregrounds filled with human incident and religious overtone to be found in Gros's Napoleonic battle pictures. These features are subtly combined, however, with a range of highly realistic detail more reminiscent of Moritz von Retsch, Alfred Rethel, and even Kaulbach. The geometry of ship's rigging and masts, guns, and gangway punctuates the rolling smoke of the Battle of Trafalgar in *The Death of Nelson*, vividly justifying Eastlake's arguments to the Commission in 1844 that 'to insist . . . that a work of art should be absolutely faithful to the description from which it is taken . . . might sometimes be fatal to its success',[121] since Nelson did not in fact die above deck as shown. The red jackets of the soldiers create vibrant notes in the turmoil; injured and dying are comforted in the foreground whilst the hero himself, Christ-like, is the centre of a secular *Pietà*. Maclise's care in seeking authenticity was none the less noted by contemporaries. T. J. Gullick recorded that 'to paint Nelson's coat Mr. Maclise was allowed to borrow the actual relic from Greenwich Hospital, with its bloodstains, and those embroidered orders, the wearing which perhaps cost him his life'; and that in *Wellington*, 'nothing is represented . . . that has not a foundation in fact. Nothing has been painted without authority, from the forage cap worn by Blücher on the occasion, to the regulation button of every regiment, and even the stitches in the bridle and headgear of the horses. The War Office has, we understand, given the painter every assistance,—in some instances having whole uniforms made.'[122]

The detail, however, is subordinate to the larger dramatic and decorative effect. Although Albert had hoped that the water-glass technique eventually adopted by Maclise would enable him to preserve the 'large and simple forms'[123] identified by Cornelius as the vital characteristics of fresco, it is arguable that in work of such large dimensions as the Royal Gallery panels, it was Maclise's very delight in anecdotal interest that saved him from the vacuity of some of the frescoes in the Lords' Chamber and Upper Waiting Hall. Water-glass did not have to be carried out in mosaic-like sections like fresco, but allowed a 'total' approach to the picture surface which Maclise relished and which was far closer to conventional oil painting.

The sense of the mural as a whole and its harmonious integration with the architectural setting and with its neighbours were, nevertheless, achieved with a considerable degree of success by E. M. Ward (Plate 28) in his Stuart scenes in the Commons' (North) Corridor, which were begun in fresco, although water-glass was adopted for the last two. They are much smaller then either Maclise's or the Lords' Chamber murals and combine the domestic genre of Delaroche's history style—loving details of costumes and interiors—with a more architectonic sense than Cope's

[121] C. L. Eastlake, *Observations on the Principles . . . considered with reference to the nature and various styles of the Formative Arts*, Appendix 12, *Third Report* of the CFA (see n. 96), p. 32.

[122] T. J. Gullick, *National Pictures in Westminster* (1865), pp. 34, 32.

[123] Cornelius, quoted by Wyse in Evidence, Min. SCFA (11 June 1841), (see n. 74), § 861.

parallel commission for the Stuart scenes in the Peers' Corridor. Both Cope's (Plate IV) and Ward's corridor work, undertaken during the late 1850s and 1860s after the iconographical significance of 'the style of fresco' had begun to wane, mark a distinctive return to the more atmospheric reconstruction of history, derived from Delaroche, with which the British artists had perhaps always been happiest. It also has an affinity with the contemporary Flemish and Belgian historical realism which was to inspire Ford Madox Brown at Manchester Town Hall later in the century. If German parallels are to be found, they are more with the new Düsseldorf style of historical realism than with the original more stylized approach of Cornelius, though the work was still carried out in fresco. This new realism reaches its climax with the highly accomplished, well-composed, and somewhat Pre-Raphaelite style of J. R. Herbert's *Moses* and *Daniel* (Plate 29) murals in the 'Moses Room', now painted in oil on canvas, and of very large dimensions.[124]

Even in the 1840s and early 1850s in the Lords' Chamber and Royal Robing Room, however, there had been traces of something more full-blooded. Dyce's personification of *Mercy* and Maclise's *The Spirit of Chivalry* (Plate 19) are both reminiscent of *The Queen of Beauty*, who participated in the Eglinton Tournament immediately preceding the Westminster murals,[125] and Victoria and Albert's elaborate *bals costumés* likewise offer direct prototypes for the realistic representation of historic costumes in the murals. The use of the past to refer to the present, which is apparent from Albert's own comments about the mural subjects, was thus clearly projected just as the Eglinton and ball guests had identified with historical characters by wearing their costumes.

One of the artists' recurrent concerns was money. Cope succeeded in increasing his remuneration for the Peers' Corridor from £450 to £700 per panel; with such changes to the Commissioners' estimates, the Treasury began to ask questions. By 1861 Albert was writing to Lord Palmerston to point out that the Commissioners' 'position is not that of a Government Department, nor of trustees of a public institution, asking for expenditure for their speciality, but of a body appointed by the Crown, on an understanding with Parliament.'[126]

To the end it was royal control which he struggled to maintain in the face of what Parliament was increasingly convinced was public money 'grossly and wantonly wasted',[127] although he won a stay of execution in 1861 for the Commission by arguing that if 'the Encouragement of the Fine Arts is either no longer an object to Parliament, or we possess no longer the public confidence' it should be dissolved.[128] A few months later he was dead: his place was at first taken nominally by the Queen, but by 1864 the Commission had been wound up, its ambitious programme for the complete decoration of the Palace cut short, and ongoing commissions to Maclise and others terminated. Maclise struggled on until his *Death of Nelson* was finished in 1865; Herbert's free-hanging pictures of Moses and Daniel subjects were not ultimately completed by the artist until around 1880.

[124] Ward's Commons' North Corridor murals are each 2.07 × 2.38 m; Cope's Peers' Corridor murals are each 2.20 × 2.86m. Herbert's *Moses* is 3.20 × 6.43m and his *Daniel* 3.20 × 7.32m. For Madox Brown's Manchester Town Hall scheme, see Chapter 7.

[125] Cf. J. Bouvier's lithograph of *Lady Elizabeth Seymour as the Queen of Beauty* at the Tournament (National Portrait Gallery, London), illustrated in S. Stevenson and H. Bennett, *Van Dyck in Check Trousers* (Scottish National Portrait Gallery and National Museum of Antiquities of Scotland, Edinburgh, 1978), pl. 113.

[126] Letter from Prince Albert to Lord Palmerston (19 Feb. 1861), RA(W), F31/73.

[127] B. Osborne (MP), (5 July 1861/1862 [?] in an unidentified extract, apparently from *Hansard*, RA(W) F31/93), criticizing expenditure since 1846 of '60,000L' on the Westminster decoration. He also quoted the Chancellor of the Exchequer's view that 'the ornamentation of the Houses of Parliament had been in many instances enormously and ludicrously overdone.'

[128] Letter from Prince Albert to Palmerston (19 Feb. 1861) (see n. 126).

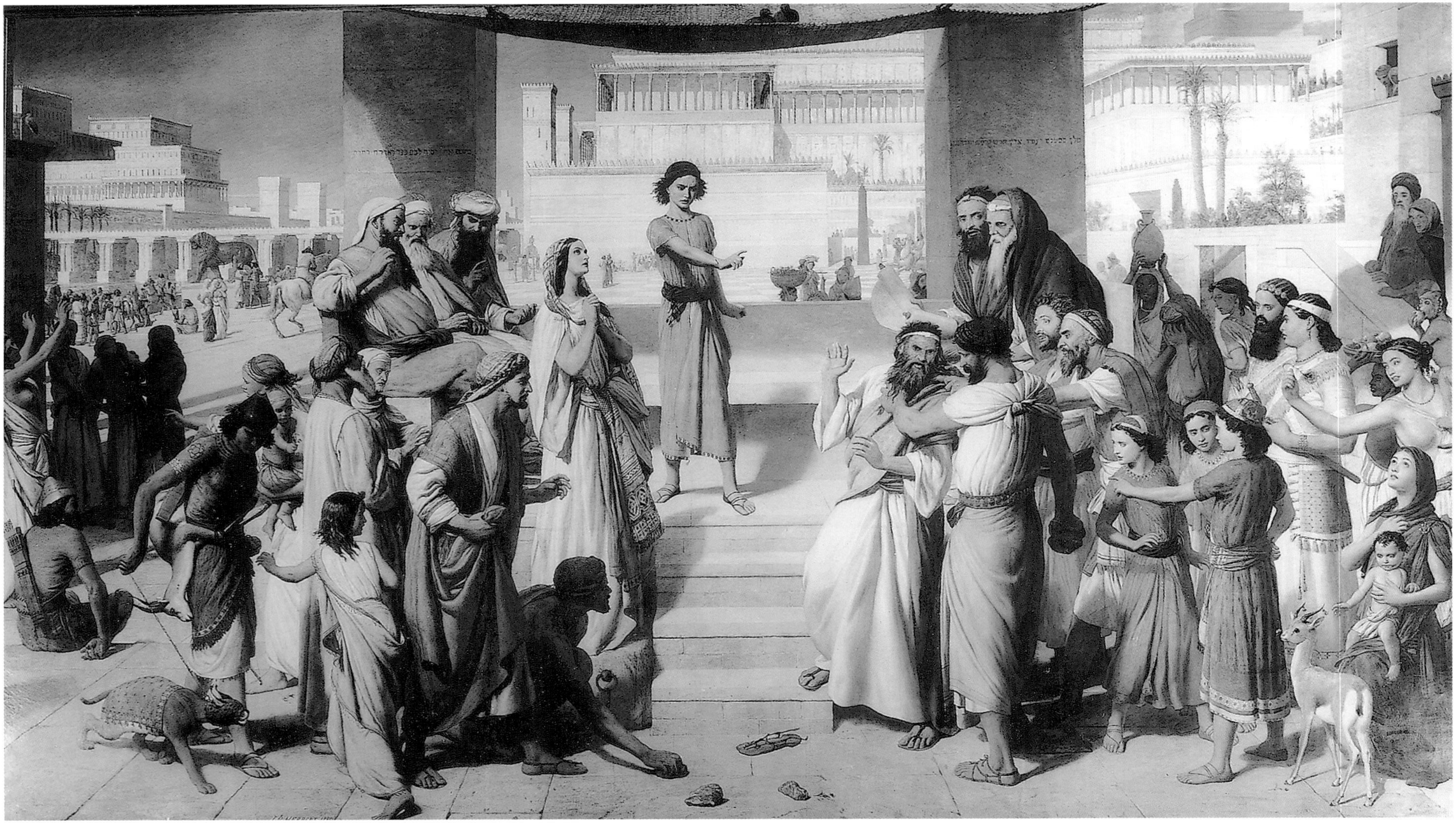

29. John Rogers Herbert, *The Judgement of Daniel*, Moses Room, Palace of Westminster, 1868–80

The most generally cited reason for the demise of the Westminster scheme, apart from the Prince's own death, was 'the style of fresco' itself. Whilst in the 1840s and especially before the 'crisis' of 1846, the Commission had been preoccupied with fresco, by 1854 it was seeking reports on alternative media, such as stereochrome or water-glass,[129] and with Maclise's resignation of his Royal Gallery commission in 1859, water-glass was formally adopted as the medium for subsequent work. Meanwhile, worrying reports appeared in the *Journal* of the Society of Arts, of which Albert was Patron, on the problems which Cornelius himself had experienced in Germany as a result of errors in the preparation of the mortar.[130] Barry had advised that three or four years should be allowed to elapse before the plaster would be sufficiently dry for successful fresco work at Westminster, and by the 1850s, even though panels of slate affording an airspace in front of the walls were adopted in the Upper Waiting Hall, the murals were, in the words of the Redgraves:

> hardly completed when decay seized them; the colours underwent destructive changes, flesh tints became painfully livid, greens disappeared, blues and browns changed places—a general mildew seized the whole. The ground itself was soon destroyed, it blistered, became loose and disintegrated, and these eight works are now beyond the reach of criticism.[131]

Whilst Maclise converted manfully, with Cope and Ward in his wake, to water-glass, and Landseer completed as an easel painting his never-to-be-installed *Monarch of the Glen* (John Dewar and Sons Ltd) originally intended as an oil decoration for the Lords' Tearoom,[132] the post-mortem began. Speakers at the Society of Arts tried to salvage the reputation of fresco, but had to concede its incompatibility with the London smoke, despite earlier promises of the efficacy of bread pellets as a cleaner.[133] In 1862 a Committee was formed to investigate the decay. True fresco was discredited and theories on its failure abounded. For the rest of their lives, Cope and Horsley retouched devotedly both their own and other artists' work; Dyce himself restored his *Ethelbert* in 1862. Cope sadly noted in recollection, 'how much of life has been wasted in, as it were, writing on the sand.'[134] Even Maclise's water-glass began to fade before his eyes, like his strength itself. He died in 1870, six years after Dyce.

Yet it is arguable whether the fresco fiasco was the ultimate reason for the cessation of painting at Westminster. With both Peel and Albert gone, the ideological momentum had gone as well; Mahon had soldiered on to the final report of the Royal Fine Arts Commission, but its only other signatories were Albert and—a telling sign of the times—a radical MP. The European context was dramatically different from that of 1841 or even the 1850s: Britain enjoyed an *entente cordiale* with

[129] See n. 96 above.

[130] Fuchs, 'Manufacture' (24 June 1859: see n. 96), p. 538.

[131] Redgrave, *British Painters*, p. 465.

[132] Landseer was asked to paint three murals of scenes of the hunt for this location, but the House of Commons, frustrated by what it saw as the CFA's incompetence, had refused to sanction the intended fee of £1,500 (see Redgrave, *British Painters*, p. 465 and R. Ormond, *Sir Edwin Landseer* (London, 1981), p. 174); see also Chapter 10, n. 23 below.

[133] e.g. the paper 'On Fresco Painting as a suitable Mode of Mural Decoration' read by J. Beavington Atkinson (10 Feb. 1864) to the Society, and the correspondence arising (both in *Journal* of the Society of Arts, 12 (12 Feb. 1864), pp. 194ff.).

[134] Cope, *Reminiscences*, p. 257. A 'Committee of Artists employed in the Decoration of Westminster Palace', helped by the chemist F. Wright, was set up in 1871 to investigate the decay in all the murals (*Report*, 1872), and although Cope retouched his murals in 1874–5/1880, by 1888 all the frescoes except Cope's *Judge Gascoigne* were in extremely poor condition (Walker, *Catalogue*, see n. 43); a factor which clearly influenced the choice of mosaic in the late 19th century for the panels of saints in the Central Lobby. Prof. A. H. Church restored many of the murals in 1894–5, when all the Poets' Hall (Upper Waiting Hall) works except Tenniel's *Dryden* had to be covered with paper because their condition was so bad. Some further cleaning was undertaken in 1937 and 1951; and comprehensive conservation was begun in the 1980s (when the 'Poets' Hall' work was rehabilitated; see Hay in *Apollo*, 135 (1992)).

France and had demonstrated her leadership in design technology to the rest of the world in the International Exhibitions of 1851 and 1862. Easel painting rather than mural art had caught the public attention through the Manchester Art Treasures Exhibition of 1857. The elaborate commentary on Constitutional history which had been so important an aspect of the murals in the 1840s was archaic and irrelevant for a Parliament now reformed beyond what Wellington could ever have dreamt. Meanwhile, although fresco had been abandoned, there were new developments promising far greater flexibility of execution and style in mural painting. Spirit fresco had been invented and successfully demonstrated by Gambier Parry, one of the members of the 1862 committee on decay, whilst the Germans themselves, with the French and Belgians, were widely using the traditional method of *marouflaged* oil already used in Britain by Rubens for his famous Whitehall Banqueting House ceiling. When the decoration of Westminster was revived in the early twentieth century after Queen Victoria's death, it was in this method, and with an entirely revised iconographical programme and mode of patronage.

The Westminster project had, however, thrown up almost all the issues which were to dog the British in their revival of mural painting from the mid-nineteenth century onwards: durable technique; the best mode of artist selection and patronage; the relationship of murals to architecture; development of an appropriate style for the patron's purposes by artists accustomed to easel painting; presentation of narrative and symbol; and how to 'paint for posterity' whilst retaining relevance to the moment. It is doubtful if, with the exception of Maclise's work, a truly successful result had been obtained; Dyce's interest waned, whilst Cope's and Ward's Corridor murals are capable and competent, but are not nearly as innovative as the contemporary easel paintings of the Pre-Raphaelites. Perhaps the artists were somewhat inhibited by the shadow of the Royal Fine Arts Commission; and yet without the often sensitive encouragement and remarkable stimulus of Prince Albert, Haydon might have continued to plead for monumental art in vain for another twenty years. A start had been made, and when State mural painting resumed in the twentieth century, many important lessons had been learned. Where the 1840s mural scheme at Westminster had been envisioned by Prince Albert as a form of propaganda for his ideal of a greater political role for the monarchy, however, the murals begun there in 1906 were to be a manifesto for a very different kind of Constitution, in which power would lie with 'the people', and in which the very character and composition of the House of Lords, that crucial locus of so much of the earlier decoration, would themselves be transformed.

Meanwhile, the use of murals to present a message came to the fore in a building which had been constructed only a few years after the new Palace of Westminster, and where initial plans for decoration were indeed influenced by the work at Westminster. This was the Royal Exchange in the City of London. Popularly known by the late nineteenth century as 'the heart of Empire', the Exchange did not, however, receive pictorial—as opposed to pattern or heraldic—decoration, until 1892, when an extensive and innovative scheme was begun there, which in turn inspired murals in the halls of the Drapers' and Skinners' livery companies in the City. The character of these schemes as an arguably yet more ambitious form of 'propaganda' than Prince Albert's only partially successful project (though now, of course, in the context of London, rather than national government), and of the Skinners' work as the first important mural scheme in Britain by Sir Frank Brangwyn (whose abortive Royal Gallery murals for Westminster marked the conclusion of State patronage in 1933), forms an essential bridge between the nineteenth-century work at

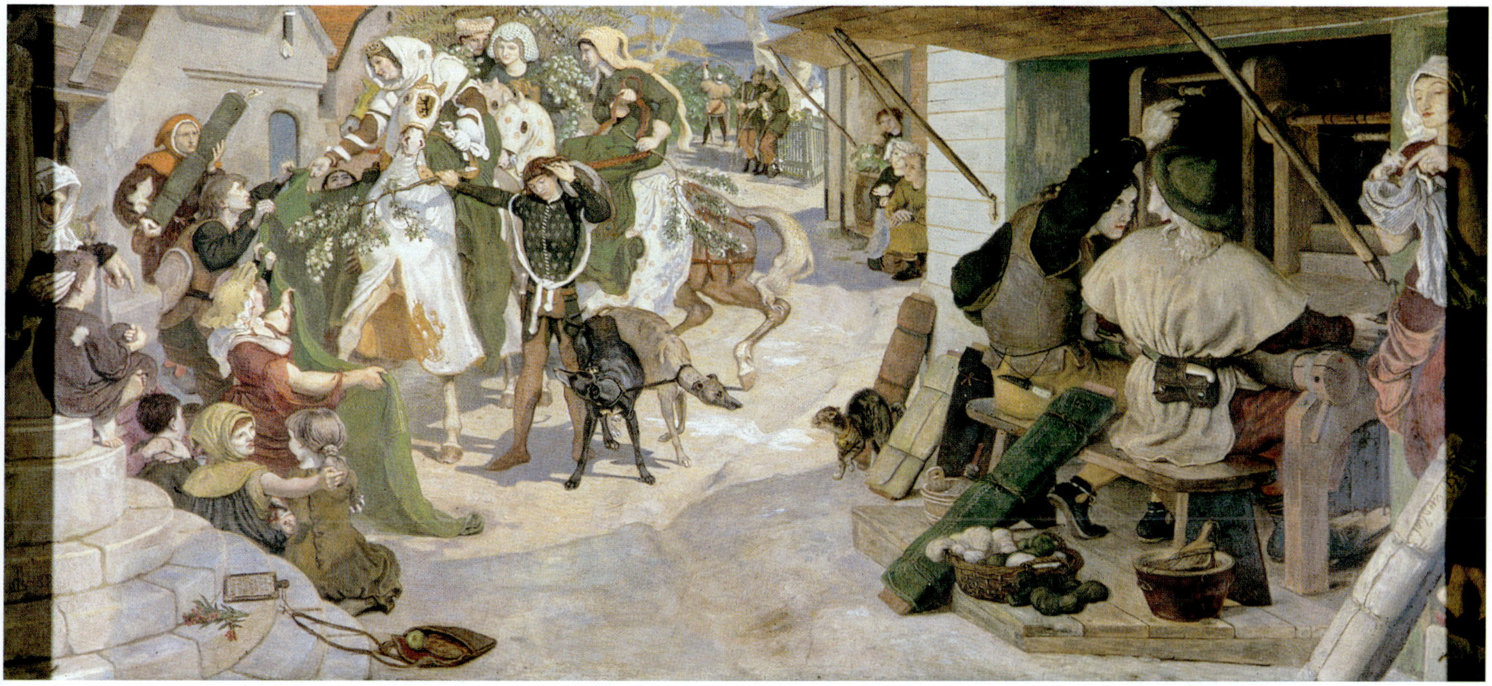

I. Ford Madox Brown, *The Establishment of Flemish Weavers in Manchester AD 1363*, Manchester Town Hall, 1881–2

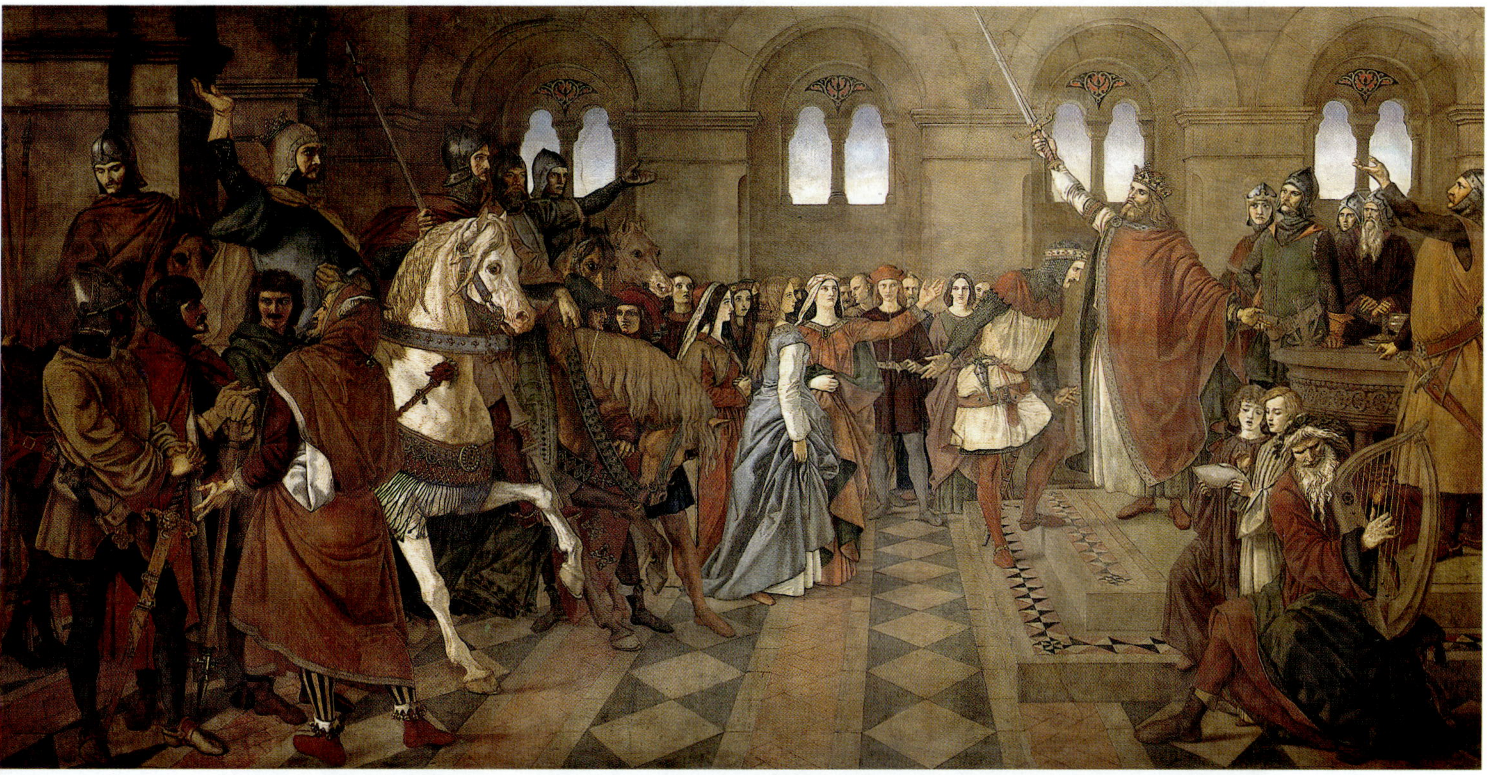

II. William Dyce, completed by Charles West Cope after Dyce's death, *Hospitality. The Admission of Sir Tristram to the Fellowship of the Round Table*, Royal Robing Room, Palace of Westminster, London, 1864–6

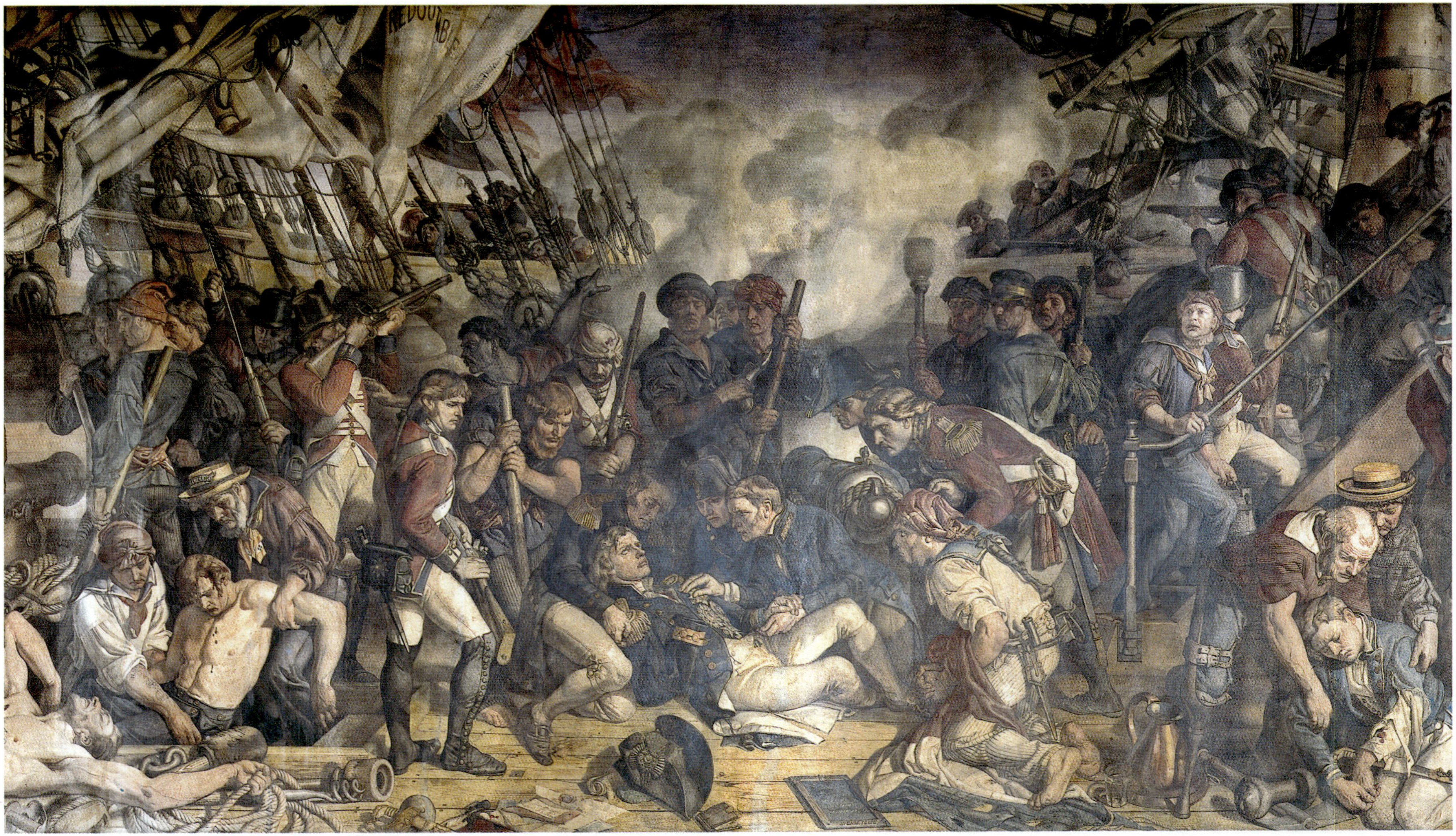

III. Daniel Maclise, detail from *The Death of Nelson*, Royal Gallery, Palace of Westminster, London, 1863–5

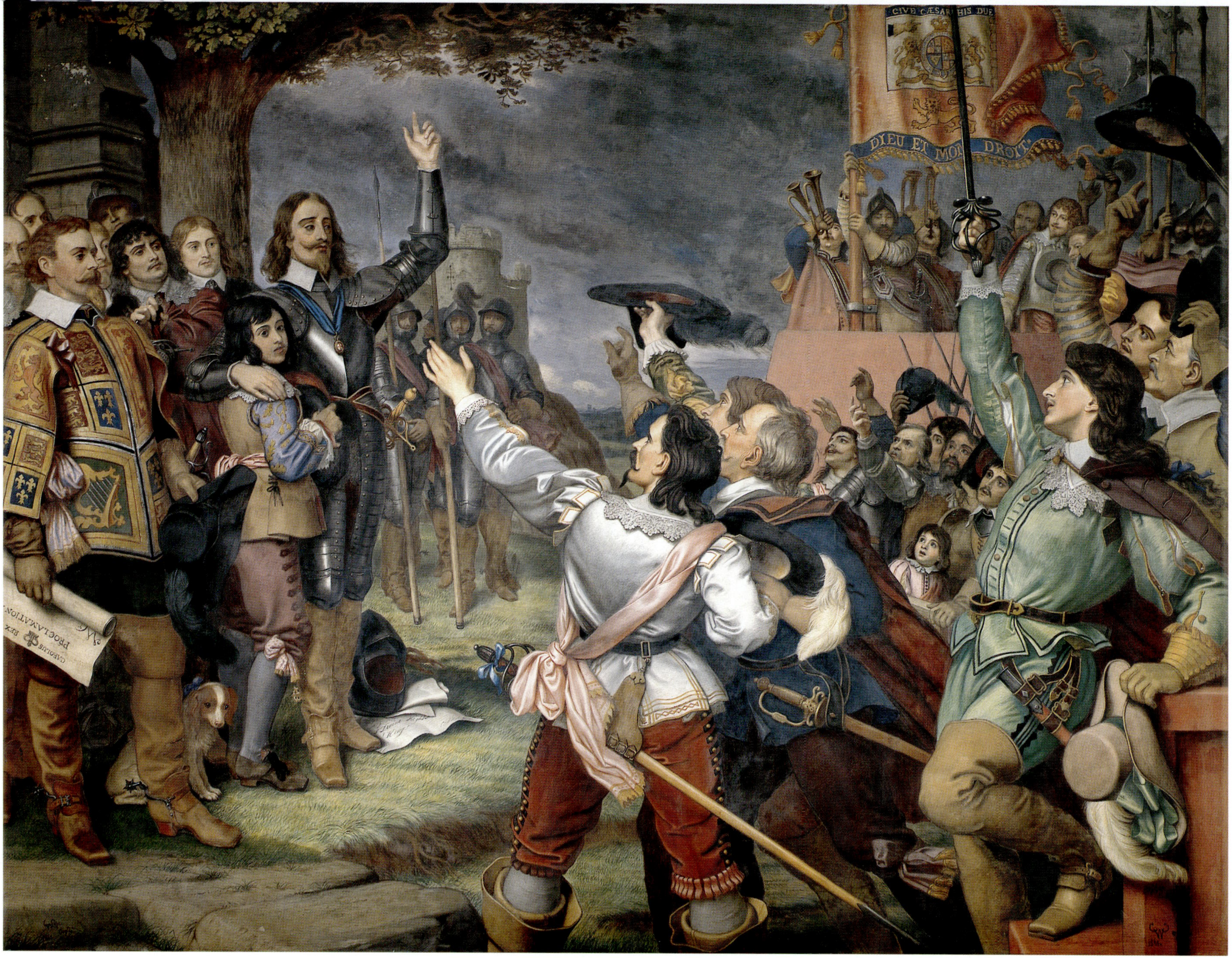

IV. Charles West Cope, *King Charles I raising his Standard at Nottingham, 1642*, Peers' Corridor, Palace of Westminster, London, 1861

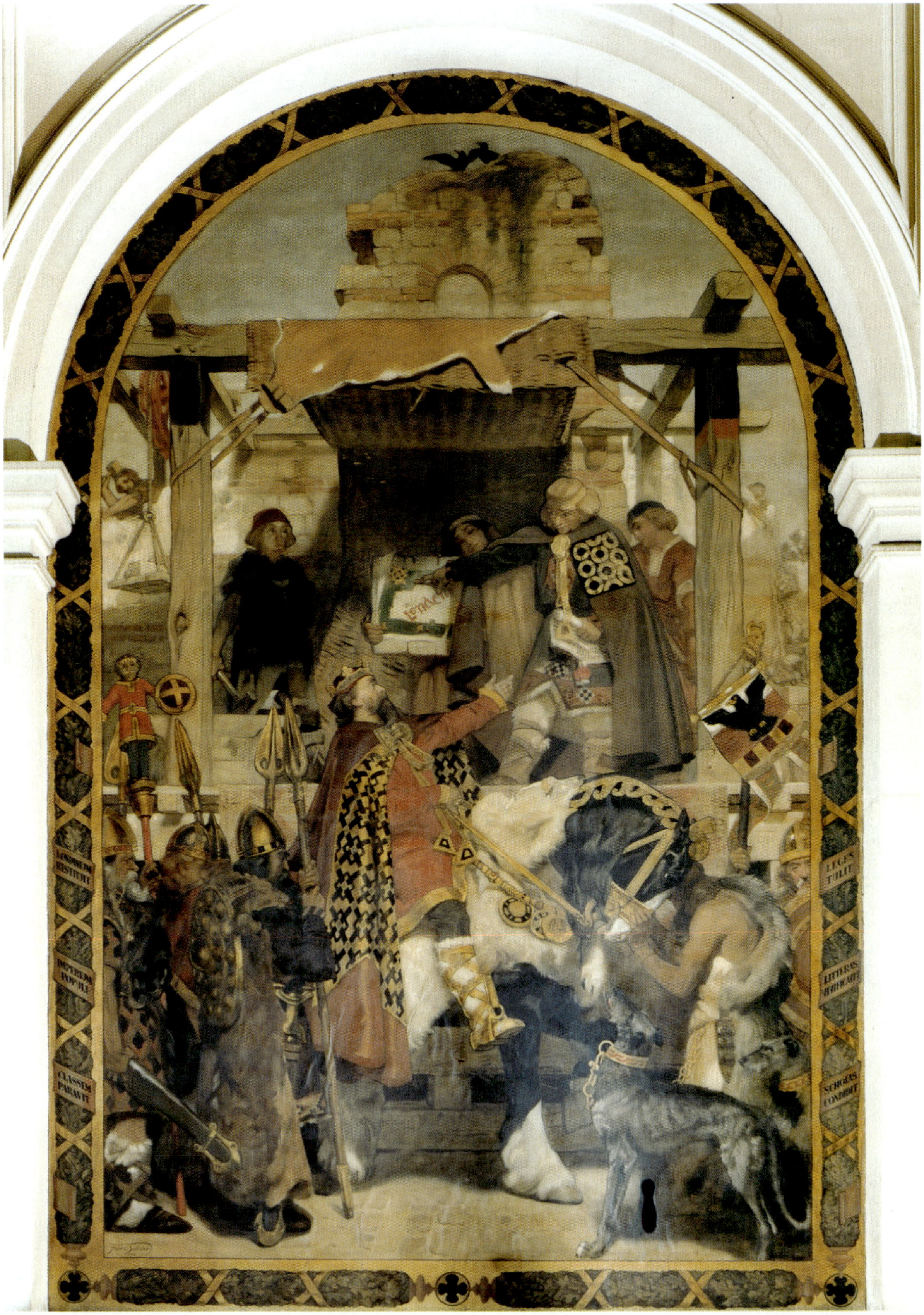

V. Frank O. Salisbury, *Alfred the Great repairing theWalls of the City of London*, Royal Exchange, London. Presented by Sir Charles Wakefield (afterwards Viscount Wakefield), 1912

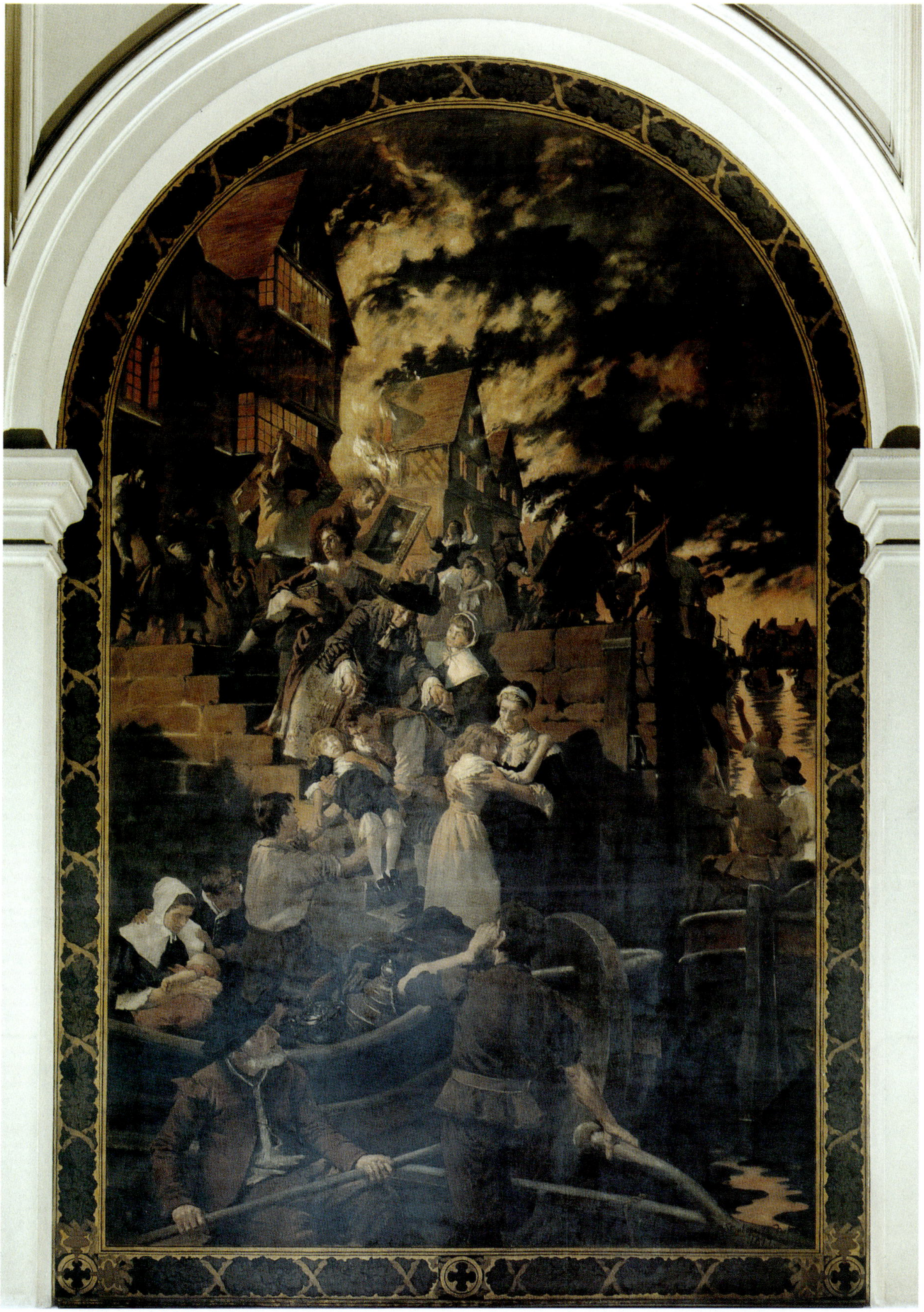

VI. Stanhope A. Forbes, *The Great Fire of London, 1666*, Royal Exchange, London. Presented by the Sun Fire Office, 1899

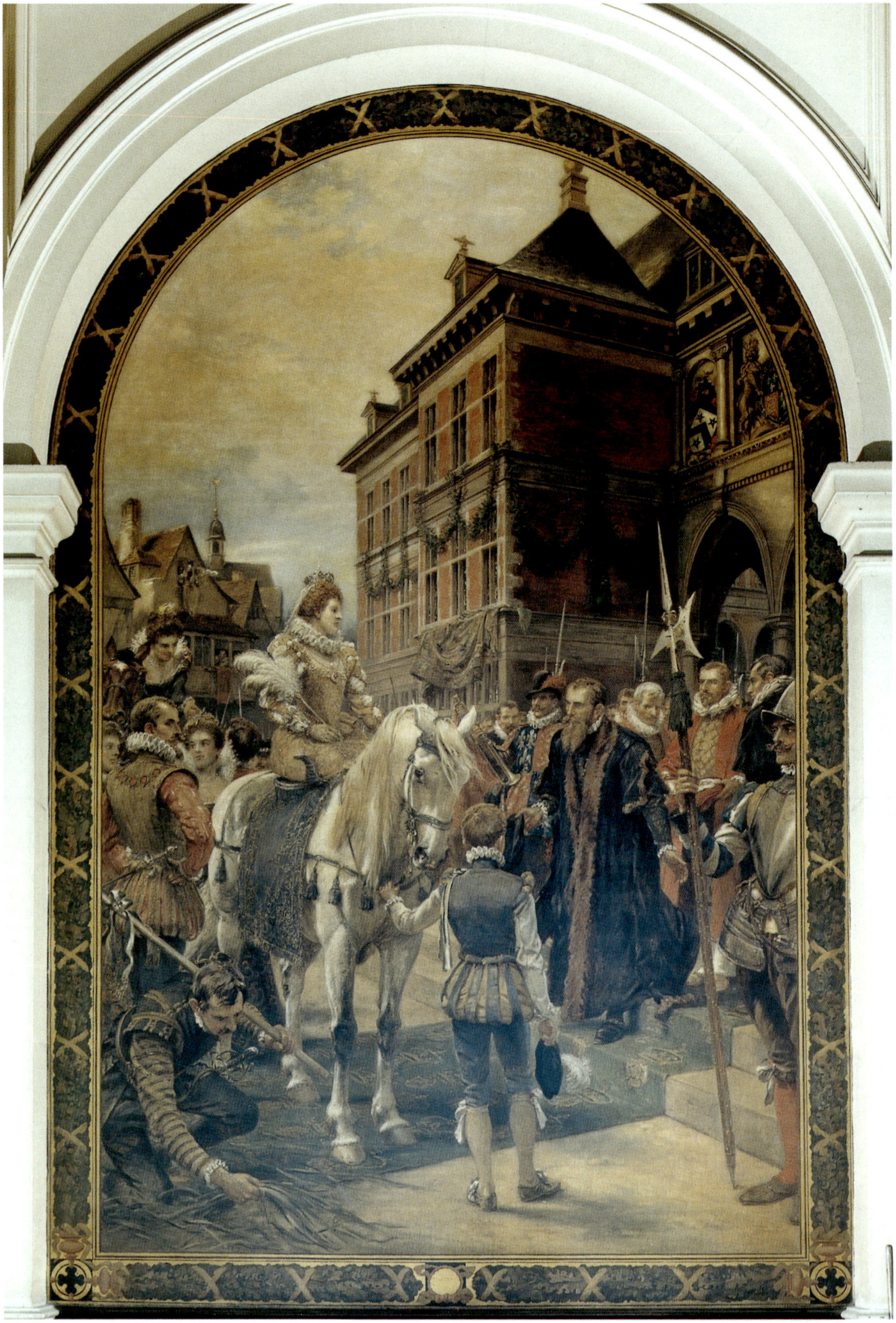

VII. Ernest Crofts, *The Opening of the first Royal Exchange by Queen Elizabeth, 23 January 1570–71*, Royal Exchange, London. Presented by the Mercers' Company, 1899

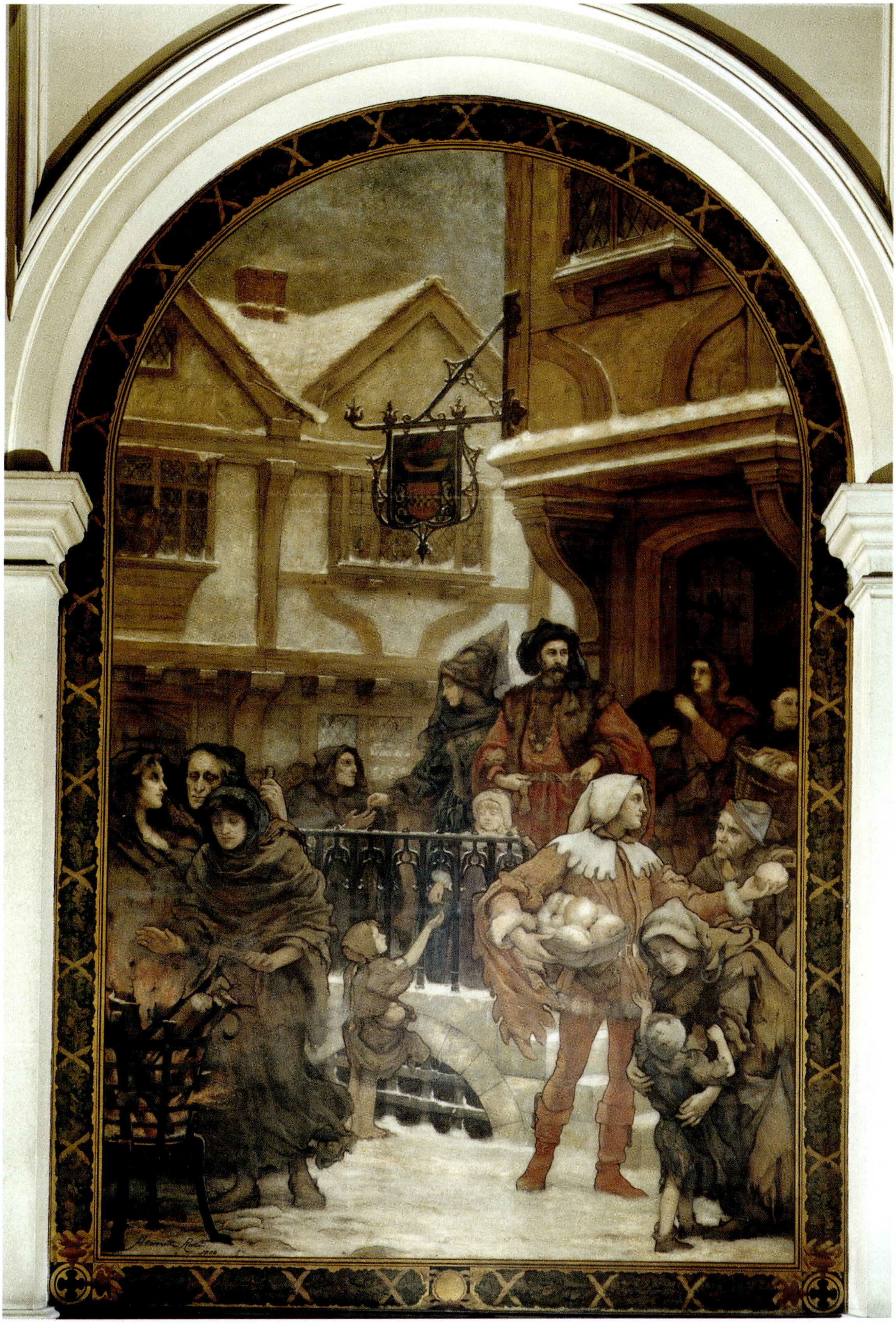

VIII. Henrietta Rae, *Sir Richard Whittington dispensing his Charities*, Royal Exchange, London. Presented by Sir Abe Bailey, KCMG, 1900

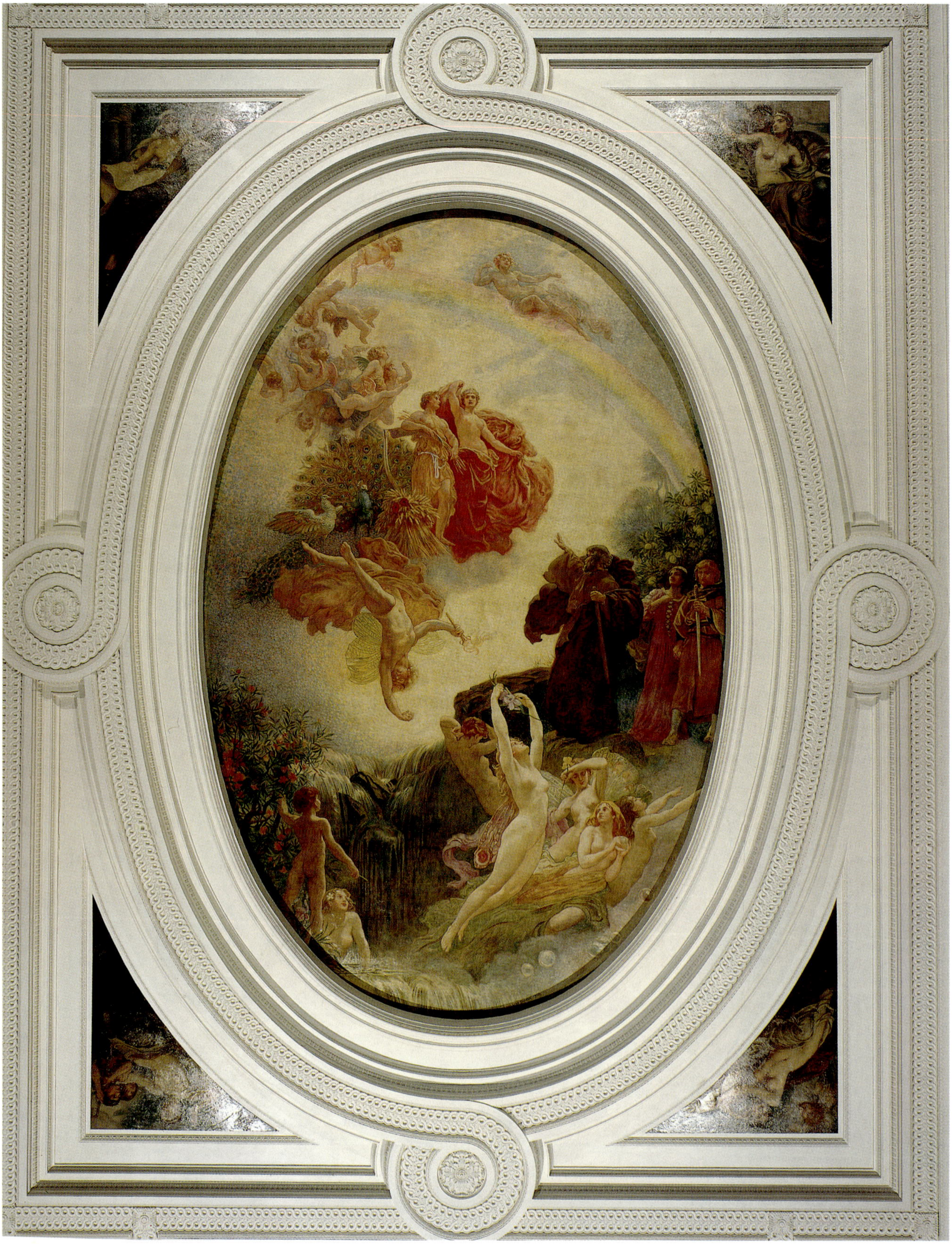

IX. Herbert J. Draper, *The Tempest* (Shakespeare)(Prospero summoning the deities), ceiling painting, Banqueting Hall, Drapers' Hall, London, 1901

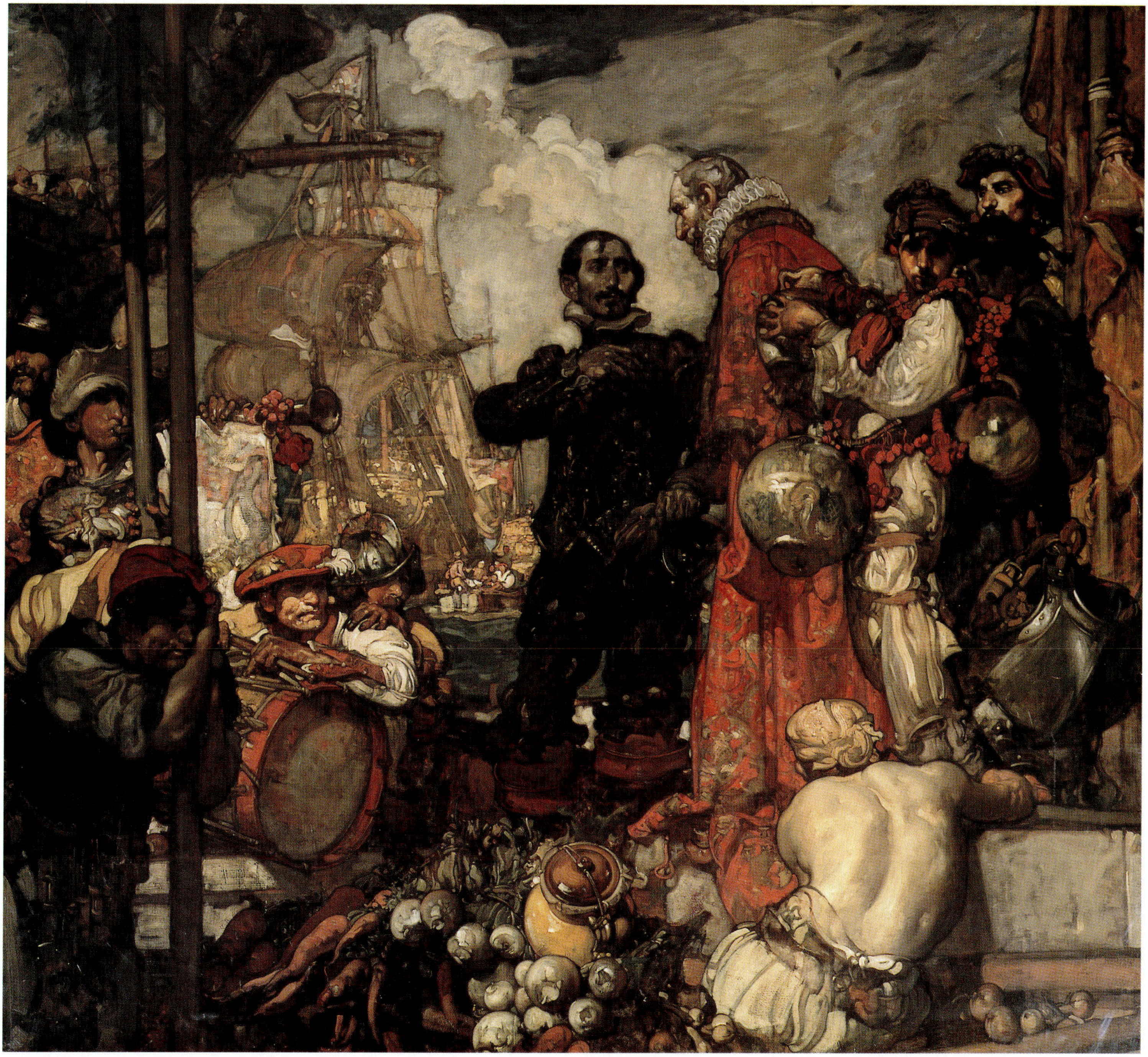

X. Sir Frank Brangwyn, *The Departure of Sir James Lancaster for the East Indies, AD 1594*, Banqueting Hall, Skinners' Hall, London, 1904

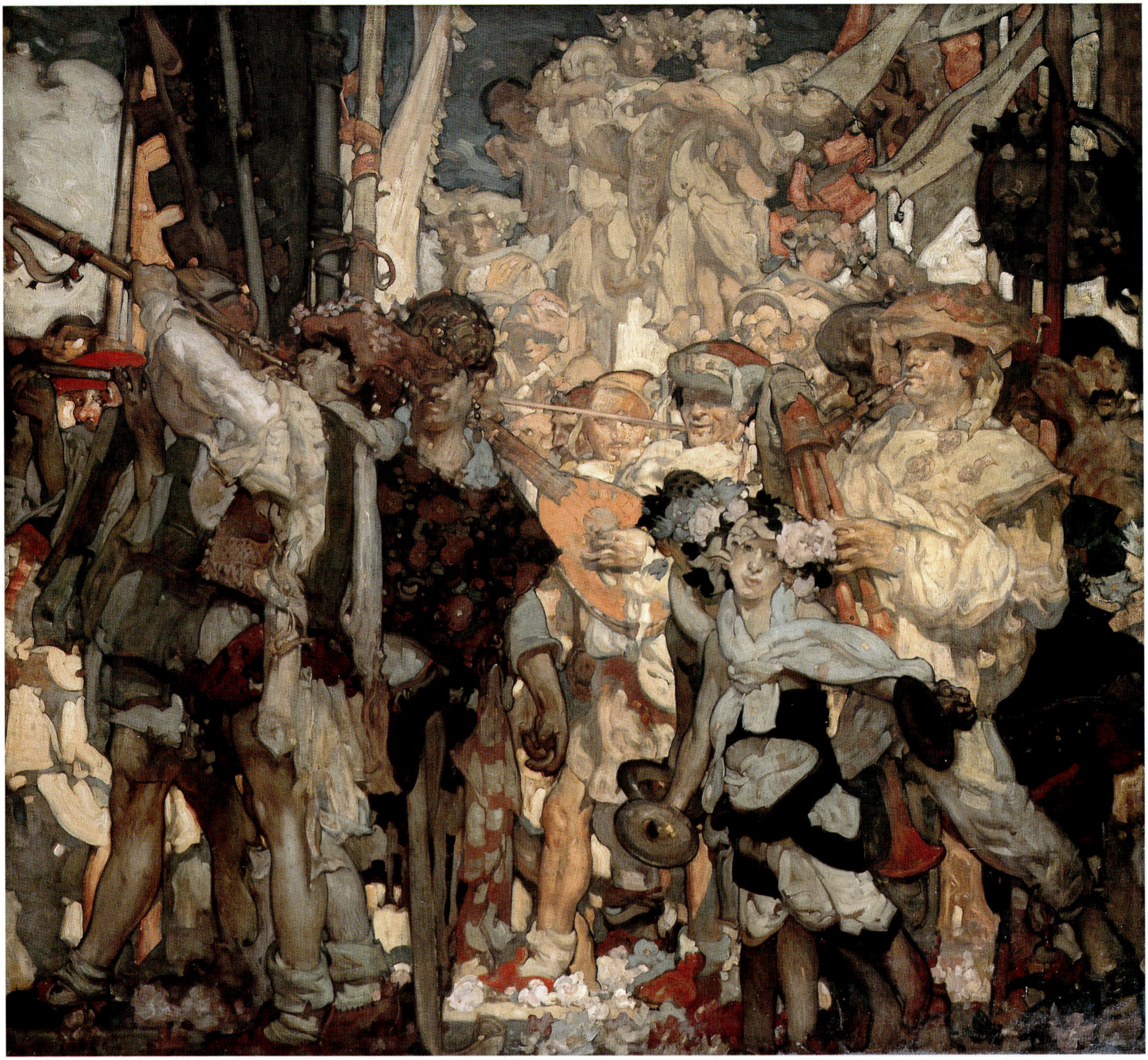

XI. Sir Frank Brangwyn, *A City Pageant on Lord Mayor's Day in Olden Times*, Banqueting Hall, Skinners' Hall, London, 1902–9

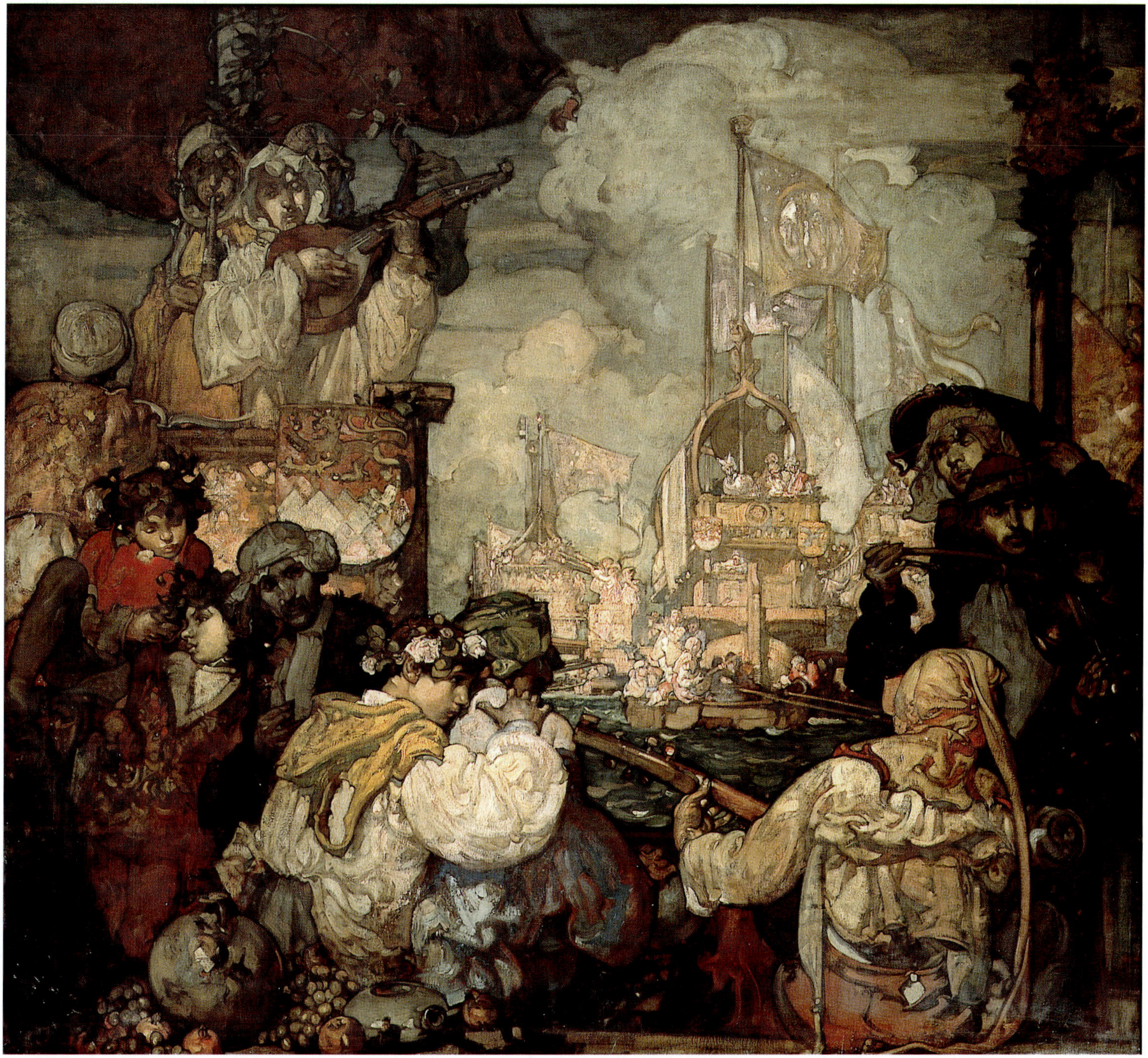

XII. Sir Frank Brangwyn, *A River Procession of the City's and Companies' Barges to Westminster AD 1453*, Banqueting Hall, Skinners' Hall, London, 1902–9

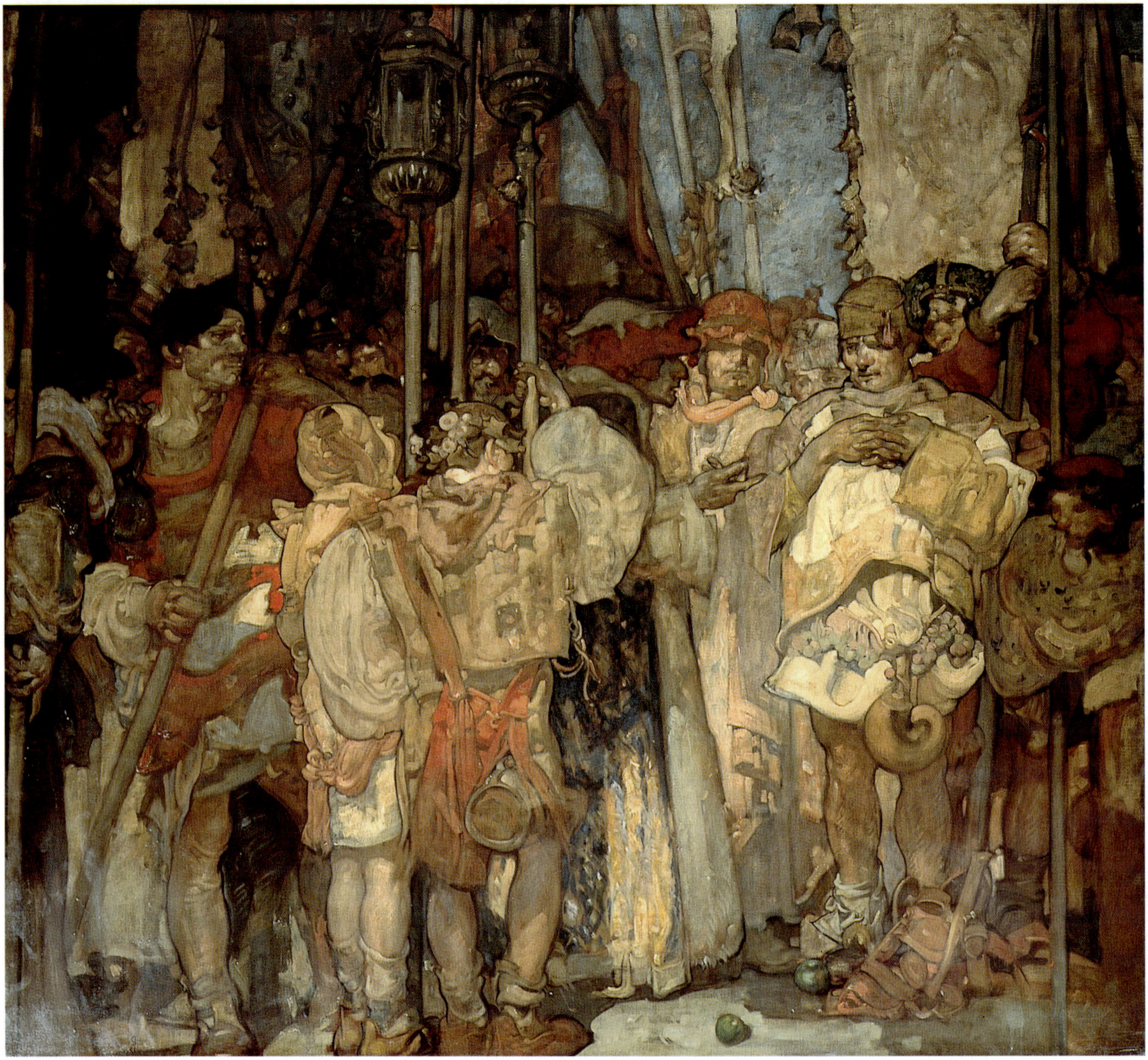

XIII. Sir Frank Brangwyn, *An Incident in the Strife between Skinners and Merchant Taylors, AD 1483*, Banqueting Hall, Skinners' Hall, London, 1902–9

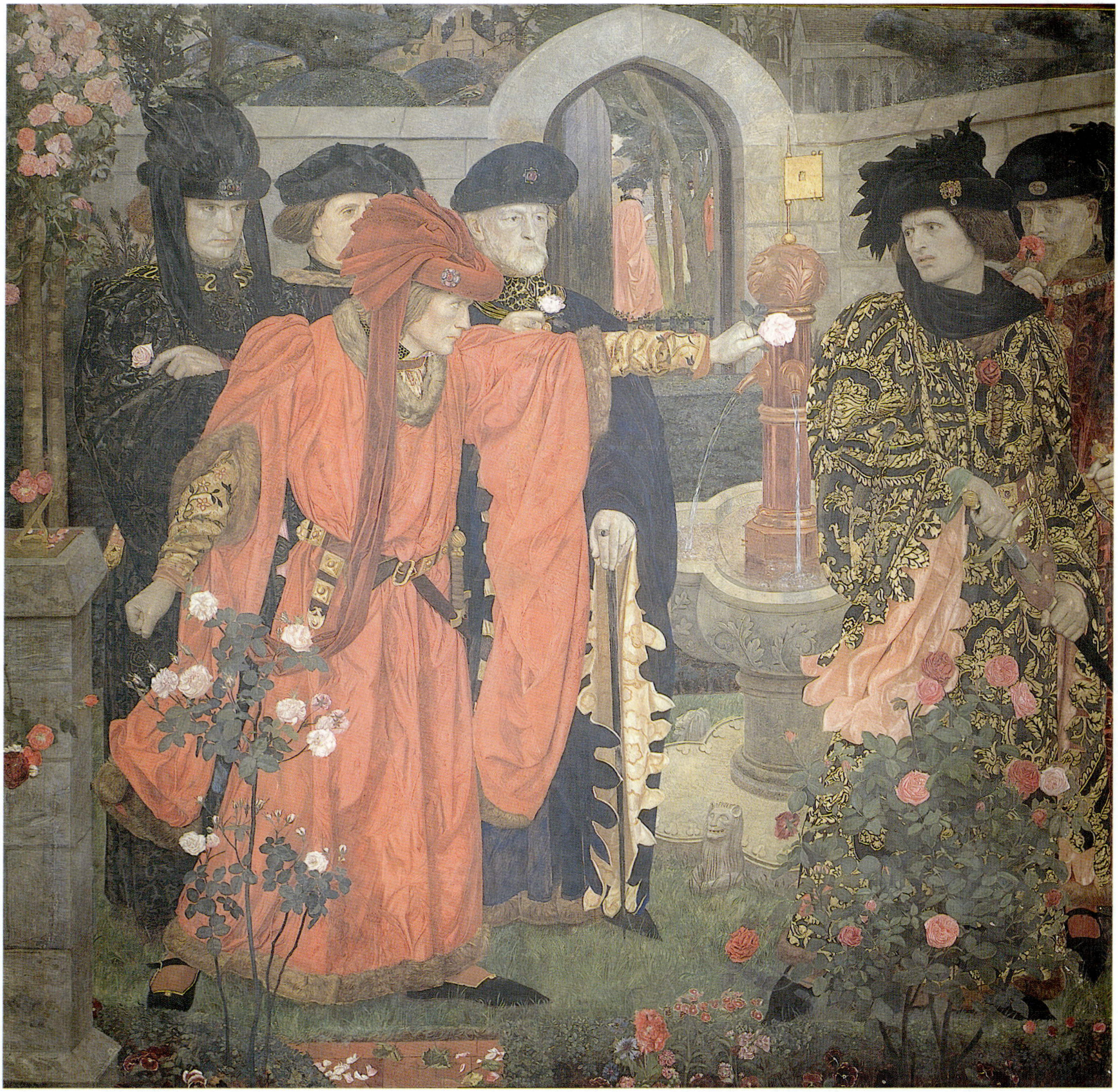

XIV. Henry A. Payne, *Plucking the Red and White Roses in the Old Temple Gardens*, East Corridor, Palace of Westminster, London, 1908–10. Presented by Lord Beauchamp

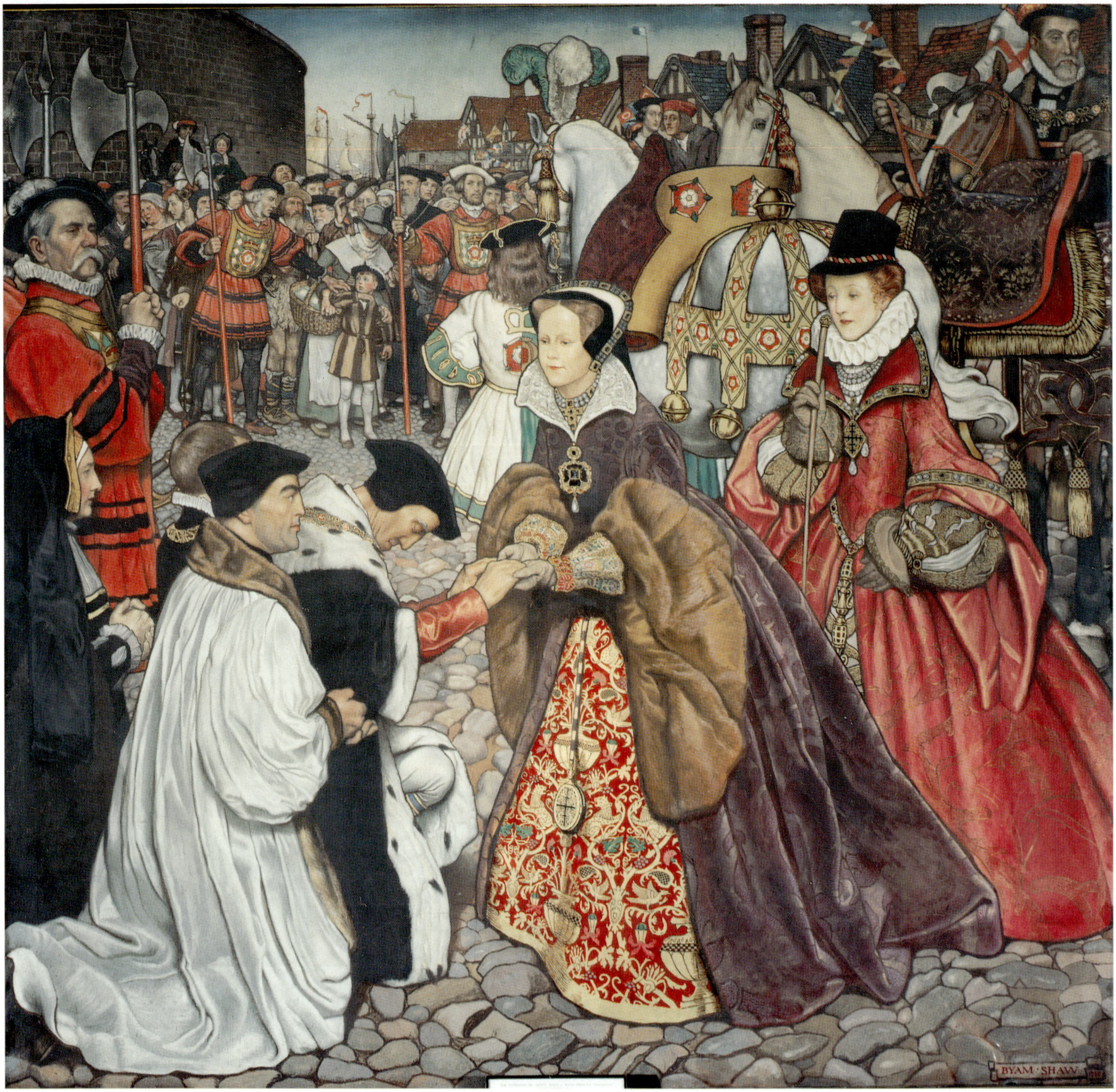

XV. John Byam Shaw, *The Entry of Queen Mary I with Princess Elizabeth into London 1553*, East Corridor, Palace of Westminster, London, 1908–10. Presented by Lord Airedale

XVI (*facing, above*). Sigismund Goetze, *Britannia Pacificatrix*, 1912–20, Ambassadors' Staircase, Foreign and Commonwealth Office, London. (Photograph taken prior to installation)

XVII (*facing, below*). Sir Stanley Spencer, *Travoys arriving with the Wounded at a Dressing Station at Smol, Macedonia, 1916*, for 'Hall of Remembrance', 1918–19. London, Imperial War Museum

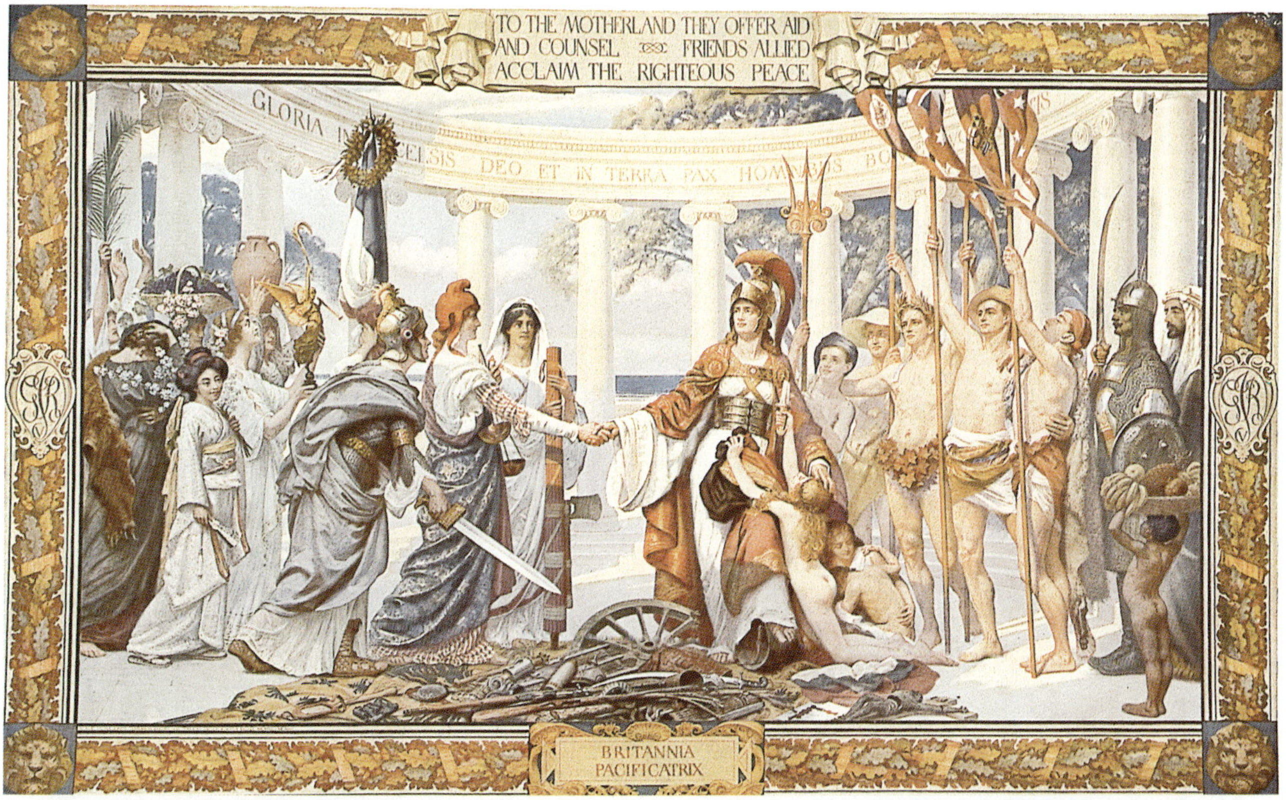
TO THE MOTHERLAND THEY OFFER AID
AND COUNSEL FRIENDS ALLIED
ACCLAIM THE RIGHTEOUS PEACE
BRITANNIA
PACIFICATRIX

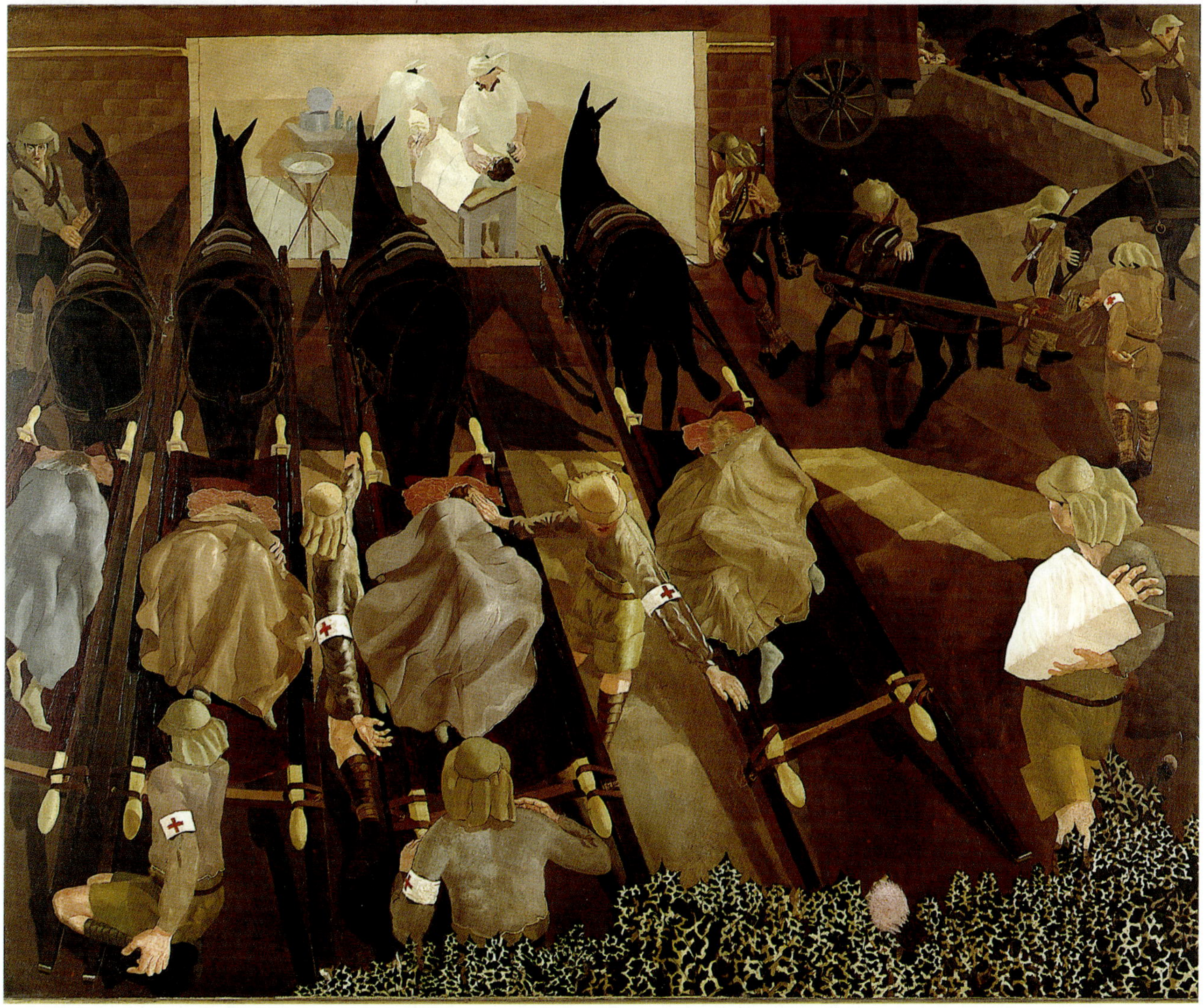

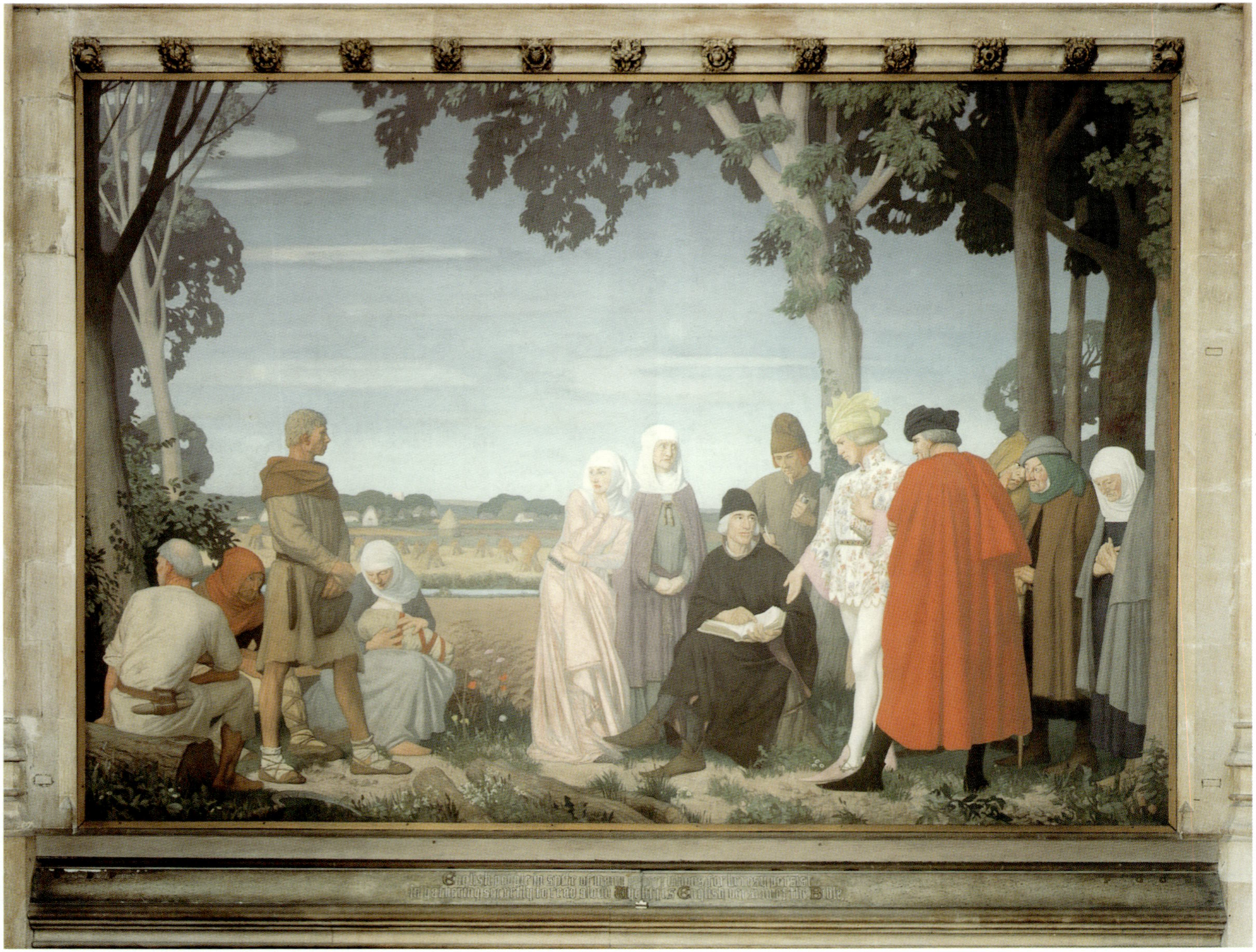

XVIII. Sir George Clausen, *The English People, in spite of prosecutions for heresy, persist in gathering secretly to read aloud Wycliffe's English Bible*, St Stephen's Hall, Palace of Westminster, London, 1925–7. Presented by the Duke of Portland

Westminster and the second 'revival' of State mural painting from 1906. It is therefore helpful to consider the work at the Royal Exchange and the livery companies, the subject of the next chapter, before this further phase of State patronage, not least because of the role played by the Exchange scheme as a 'showcase' for 'spirit fresco', and, above all, *marouflage*—which did much to restore British confidence in mural painting after the problems experienced at Westminster in the earlier nineteenth century.

3

Pageantry and Propaganda: Murals in the Royal Exchange and London Livery Company Halls

In 1891 the *City Press* gave its readers a hefty pat on the back: 'The born Londoner is a quicker-brained man than the average Englishman, more fluent of words, easier to teach, more helpful, and decidedly more enterprising. He has higher decision, energy and pluck than the usual Englishman.'[1] The very next year saw a vivid demonstration of such 'enterprise', 'decision', and 'energy' when a scheme was announced for the installation of twenty-four murals, each approximately 5.23 m high by 3.40 m wide, in the panels around the ambulatory of the Royal Exchange. As befitted the historic centre of commerce, founded by Sir Thomas Gresham in 1566 and controlled jointly by the City and Gresham's own livery company (the Mercers'), prominent City business and livery companies were each invited to donate one of the new murals. A press report noted that 'if, as it deserves to be, the undertaking is at once recognised as a precedent, a precept, and as an example, a bright future may, without being over sanguine, be predicted for the professors of historic art in this country' and proposed that

> the City Companies should come forward and demand the assistance of our historical painters for the embellishment of their halls and of the court rooms . . . [which] in their architectural proportions are sumptuous, but which . . . are almost devoid of decoration . . . were the immense area of wall space available . . . adorned by panels filled with historical subjects, the barrenness and the monotony would give way to symmetry of form and richness of colour . . . Public taste would surely be improved.[2]

Although the decoration of the Royal Exchange, with subjects taken principally from City of London history, was only to be completed in 1924, with six smaller portrait panels being added by 1927, and its example was in the event rather less extensively emulated than this journalist envisioned, it did prompt two of the most accomplished of any mural schemes in the century from 1840, those at the Drapers' and Skinners' Halls. With the Exchange work, these form the immediate context not only for the resumption of mural decoration at Westminister in 1906, but also for the quickening throughout Britain in the early twentieth century of patronage for mural painting in town and city halls and commercial companies, as well as in other London institutions

[1] 'London and the Londoners', unattributed cutting from the *City Press* (5 Aug. 1891), PB129–1993, RA(F).

[2] Loose untitled newspaper cutting in MCA, apparently from 1892.

like the Old Bailey, which will be explored in later chapters. Whilst the Exchange, Drapers', and Skinners' decoration provides a direct and intriguing link between the use of history painting for contemporary political allusion at Westminster in the 1840s to the 1860s and the interrelationship of art and politics in a number of the town hall schemes, its history is, none the less, inextricably entwined with that of the Londoners celebrated in the *City Press*, and it originates in a unique conjunction of changes in London's government with developments in patronage and influences from Continental mural painting.

Of the various livery company schemes, Brangwyn's work for the Skinners stands out as the most significant. Whereas at the Exchange the perceived urgency of the message underpinning the choice of iconography and artists led to a certain disregard of the overall aesthetic effect of the ensemble, Brangwyn's scheme, painted of course by a single artist rather than a group, and following in direct sequel to his mural at the Exchange, represents a triumph of decorative and symbolic unity in which the very differences in objective between patron and artist were in fact a creative spur. The interrelationship of 'message' with 'medium' in this scheme is one of remarkable sublety and power, and the success of the Skinners' murals established Brangwyn's British reputation. During the later 1900s he received further commissions from commercial companies, such as Lloyd's Register of Shipping, as well as overseas commissions,[3] whilst the personal philosophy of life and art expressed in his work at Skinners' Hall already contains in embryo that of his later Royal Gallery scheme.

THE MURALS AT THE ROYAL EXCHANGE

When the third and present Royal Exchange was constructed between 1842 and 1849, B. R. Haydon had advised its architect, Sir William Tite, that 'a series of beautiful fresco illustrations of our rise, from the earliest to the latest period of commercial greatness' should be painted around the central courtyard along with 'chiaroscuro portraits of the greatest men who have contributed to that rise'.[4] The Gresham Committee (representing the City and Mercers as responsible for the building) felt his price of £3,580 to be too high. Instead, apparently on the advice of Prince Albert, the Munich artist Frederick Sang was employed to provide heraldic work on the ceiling and walls, in the wax-based medium of encaustic (Plate 30) (see Appendix A), which Tite recommended as 'lately introduced into Germany and . . . [in the] Church of the Madeline [*sic*] and other buildings at Paris'.[5] Like the Madeleine, his building was in the form of a classical temple, and he told the Gresham Committee that 'in the Roman baths in Rome though exposed to dampness and every vicissitude of the weather for 1800 or 2000 years the paintings in Wax . . . still preserve their freshness and vividness of colour.'[6] Even though historical subjects as at Westminster were beyond the budget, he clearly hoped to outdo Parliament when it came to technique. In due course in 1860 Prince Albert 'proceeded to a very minute inspection of the

[3] For Lloyd's Register, see Chapter 11; Brangwyn's foreign commissions included decoration at Cuyahoga County Court House, Cleveland, Ohio (1912–14), the Panama Pacific International Exhibition, San Francisco (1914), and the Missouri State Capitol (1915).

[4] Letter from Haydon to Tite (11 July 1844) in T. Taylor (ed.), *Life*, vol. 3 (1926), p. 258.

[5] Report from Tite to 'the Sub-Committee appointed to consider the subject of additional Sculptural Decorations at the New Royal Exchange', GCM (26 April 1844). For Sang's decoration, see the *Illustrated London News* (9 Nov. 1844).

[6] Tite, 'Report'.

decorations the general appearance of which and of the harmony of colouring [he] . . . expressed himself very much pleased'.[7] But by the late nineteenth century, despite several renewals by Sang, the decoration was in a sad state of repair. The Exchange's central courtyard was open to the air and, probably in part for this reason, decoration in the earlier buildings had consisted of statues, which represented Gresham himself and the monarchs. In 1883–4, however, the courtyard was roofed over and in 1890 Crace's company (which had painted ornamental motifs in the Mercers' and Fishmongers' Halls) felt able to recommend 'a good oil painting' in place of encaustic and also 'a scheme of pictorial illustration in the large wall panels'.[8] The Gresham Committee now turned to Lord Leighton for advice, clearly seeking something of greater artistic stature than a trade decorator could offer. Although the Committee initially proposed the employment of Royal Academy students, Leighton persuaded it that 'well-known artists of proven ability'[9] should be commissioned. It was at this point that Haydon's proposal seems to have been revived, but in terms of 'scenes . . . illustrating English history or the history of the City of London',[10] rather than purely 'commercial' subjects. A working committee was appointed, including Leighton, Poynter, and P. H. Calderon as representatives of the Royal Academy, and also the Master of the Mercers' Company, Deputy Joseph Snowden, and the Lord Mayor, who was Chairman of the Gresham Committee. By 1892 they were ready to choose subjects. This, however, was the year when Sir Stuart Knill became Lord Mayor and therefore the leading figure in the working committee. A few years previously, when he was an alderman, he had donated a mural scheme of allegorical personifications for the Guildhall, which amounted to propaganda for the cause of the City Corporation in the context of a perceived threat from the new London County Council (LCC).[11] For, in 1884, a Royal Commission on the livery companies had found them corrupt and denounced them as failing in their historic function as protectors and benefactors of trades and providers of charity and welfare; in 1889, just as the Corporation of London celebrated the seven-hundredth anniversary of the foundation of the City's mayoralty, the London County Council had in consequence come into being on a tide of demand for municipal reform. Its election manifestos presented an ambitious programme of municipalization in a multitude of areas traditionally controlled by the companies, the Corporation, and private enterprise—from dockyards, poor relief, and building to education.

Knill's hand, in turn, can be recognized behind the distinctive emphasis on the traditions and historic rights of the City of London, and its livery companies and ancient businesses, which now emerged in the subjects chosen for the Exchange decoration in 1892, and which indeed underpinned the very method of donation by these same companies and businesses which was adopted to fund the scheme. The continuity of past and present implied by the two subjects which were the first to be completed and unveiled, in 1895—the panel donated and painted by Leighton himself showing *Ancient Commerce* (Plate 1) and the one donated by Deputy Snowden and painted by Robert W. Macbeth, showing the opening of the third Royal Exchange by Queen Victoria in 1844—was, in subsequent murals, demonstrated directly in relation to the City's very system of government. For each of the next group of panels was unveiled in conjunction with the annual Lord Mayor's procession and the hand-over of office from one mayor to the next. Just as in the

7 GCM (3 March 1860).

8 'Report from Mr. J. D. Crace' in GCM (20 June 1890), p. 328.

9 Letter from Leighton to Gresham Committee (13 July 1892) in MCA, and GCM (1 July 1892), pp. 26–9.

10 See letter from Eaton (Secretary of the RA), to J. Watney of the Mercers' Company (18 June 1890), pp. 28–9, GCM.

11 See Chapter 7.

Guildhall scheme, a firm message of revolt was being expressed against the LCC and its aspirations for greater power.

In the 1890s the Lord Mayor's procession had only recently been reinvented so as to regain something of its splendour in earlier centuries, when it had been a river-based pageant.[12] Whereas Knill's Guildhall programme of allegorical personification and anti-LCC slogans had been carried out by a commercial company (Hardman's), something much more vivid was now afoot at the Exchange; an art, indeed, which might match the very spectacle of the mayoral procession, when the people of modern London, some dressed in the costumes of their forebears and others, by the 1890s even riding new-fangled motorcars,[13] acted out their history in welcoming their new leader. In the context of the threat to the City and companies, it becomes possible to understand why a 'fine art' tradition, with its legacy of association with the patronage of great art by the merchant princes of the Renaissance, was now being preferred to the patterns or emblematic motifs of the 'trade' decorators like Hardman's or Crace's. Leighton, of course, had told his students at the Royal Academy in 1883 that 'art has an organic connection with the temper of the times,'[14] and had already called in his first address as President of the Royal Academy for the artist to have 'in modern society a lawful place, a meaning, a justification'[15] as in Renaissance Italy. His artistic credo thus meshed seamlessly with the purposes of Knill and the Gresham Committee, just as City councillors and mayors would by the 1890s have become fully familiar, through many reciprocal civic functions in late nineteenth-century Europe, with the recent schemes of decoration by prominent artists in Continental 'civic palaces' like the Hôtel de Ville in Paris.[16] Whereas at the Hôtel de Ville concern to reflect 'the true and real picture of political, economic and social life of the present people of Paris, in the surroundings where they live and have their being'[17] had led to the inclusion of a number of contemporary scenes (Plate 31), and modern iconography was standard in many of the Paris Mairies,[18] at the Exchange it was almost exclusively the past which was made vividly 'present' through the murals. The decoration of the building would thus have driven home to the modern merchants of London the continuing relevance of the *historic* rights and powers of the City and its institutions, just as the choice of spirit fresco, already 'proven' by Leighton in murals at Lyndhurst Parish Church and the South Kensington Museum, and by Madox Brown at Manchester Town Hall[19] (Plate I), and felt to be a 'durable' medium which would ensure the lasting presence of the decoration, was made in preference to the 'oil' recommended by Crace's company. The painting of the murals as if they were easel works on canvas in the studio, with *marouflage* being employed to fix them to the Exchange walls, marked an important break with the procedure in these earlier schemes (somewhat ominously, the motto of the Parisian firm of Binant from which advice on *marouflage* was

[12] The procession had originally been water-based. It saw a new lease of life around 1889 in conjunction with the 700th anniversary of the mayoralty. See R. Withington, *English Pageantry: A Historical Outline*, vol. 2 (New York, 1963).

[13] See 'Lord Mayor's Day Closing Ceremonies of the Civic Year', unattributed press cutting of *c.*1890s, PB116–1993 in RA(F).

[14] Leighton, RA Address of 1885 in *Addresses delivered to the Students of the Royal Academy by the Late Lord Leighton* (London, 1897), p. 99.

[15] Leighton, RA Address of 1879 in ibid., p. 9.

[16] These visits were regularly recorded in the Minutes of Common Council and the LCC Reports in the late 19th and early 20th centuries. The Lord Mayor visited the 1889 Paris International Exhibition, for example, and in 1891 the German Emperor Wilhelm II was present at a reception at the Guildhall.

[17] T. Burollet, *Le Triomphe des Mairies* (1987), p. 68 (author's trans.). Lhermitte's *Les Halles* (Pl. 31), no less than 4.75 × 6.90 m. in size, must have given a particularly dramatic sense of modern city life 'invading' the very building. It was detached from the Hôtel de Ville walls early this century.

[18] Ibid., p. 34; examples include the murals by H. Gervex and E.-H. Blanchon of 1879 in the Mairie of the XIXth *arrondissement*, illustrating local industry (including work in an abattoir) and civic duties such as registration of a birth.

[19] For Lyndhurst Church, see Chapter 8; for the South Kensington Museum, see Chapter 9; for Manchester Town Hall, see Chapter 7.

obtained was *Nil desperandum.*[20]

In their distinctive London context, the Exchange murals were thus a means to make overtly permanent the passing (but of course highly symbolic) show of the newly revived mayoral procession; several of their artists, such as Seymour Lucas, Frank Salisbury, and Edwin A. Abbey were also designers for historical pageants and the 'realistic' Shakespearean theatre productions of Sir Henry Irving or Sir Herbert Beerbohm Tree. Whilst there were, despite the increasing emphasis on modern iconography in Parisian murals, plenty of Continental examples of 'realistic' re-creation of history in such work as Jean-Paul Laurens's in the Panthéon or that of the Düsseldorf school[21] (Plate 32), as well as a long-standing tradition in Germany of a typological relationship between past and present,[22] the Exchange murals can be seen as sharing in the 'invention of tradition' identified by Cannadine and others in the renewal from the late nineteenth century of ancient civic ceremonials such as the Oyster Feast in Colchester.[23] Through the Exchange project, civic ritual was being translated into what, for the Corporation and the Mercers, was effectively a 'new' medium—pictorial decoration. This process, calling into play all the famed 'enterprise' and 'energy' of the Londoner, explains much of the character of the Exchange scheme as an experiment, involving mistakes as well as triumphs, but it also underlines the need to evaluate it within its wider historical, social, and political context, rather than merely from an aesthetic angle or as some kind of dusty history painting of no significance because apparently remote from avant-garde trends in art. If we are more familiar with 'propaganda art' in the context of post-Revolutionary Russia, early twentieth-century Mexico, or 'New Deal' North America,[24] the Exchange scheme shows that murals were already fulfilling a related function in the 1890s and 1900s in Britain.

In the context of the 'struggle for London' of the 1890s, the distinctive political colour of the reciprocal relationship between past and present in the Exchange decoration is clearly revealed by a speech made in 1897 by Sir George Faudel-Phillips, the outgoing Lord Mayor, when he unveiled the mural by Solomon J. Solomon showing *Charles I demanding the Five Members at the Guildhall* (Plate 33). Commenting that 'London required such large-hearted and enthusiastic citizens' as its donor, the City MP and financier Sir Samuel Montagu, he went on to observe, 'in point of fact, as London was being extended until it had attained the dimensions of a large and populous county . . . it was becoming not only the greatest, but one of the most beautiful cities in the world.'[25] This was an ironic allusion to the new county of London and the audience shouted 'Hear, Hear!' Montagu's mural shows King Charles's arrival at the Guildhall in 1642 in quest of the 'Five Members' he had tried to arrest at Westminster, who had taken shelter in the City. This incident was traditionally believed to mark the origin of the right of City MPs, like Montagu

[20] See *1895 Toile Binant Marouflage Extrait de l'Annuaire du Bâtiment (Sageret). Année Courante*... PB77–1993, RA(F).

[21] e.g. Peter Janssen's murals of local and city history at the University of Marburg (1893), intended to arouse patriotism through 'grosse starklebige Vergangenheit' ('the past as great and large as life', period description quoted in D. Bieber, *Peter Janssen als Historienmaler. Zur Düsseldorfer Malerei des späten 19. Jahrhunderts*, vol. 1 (Bonn, 1979), p. 374); cf. also E. Bendemann's murals (for both artists see Trier and Weyres, and R. Andrée et al. cited in Chapter I, n. 25). Janssen visited Britain in 1887 and exhibited in London and Paris as well as Germany.

[22] e.g. the murals by A. Rethel (a friend of Leighton) of the life of Charlemagne, painted at Aachen Town Hall in the 1840s and intended to symbolize the '"Jammer" der Gegenwart' ('"misery" of the present', Trier and Weyres, *Kunst des 19. Jahrhunderts* p. 174).

[23] See E. Hobsbawm and T. Ranger (eds), *The Invention of Tradition* (1983) and D. Cannadine, 'Civic Ritual' (1982).

[24] For the Russian work, see I. Golomstock, *Totalitarian Art* (London, 1990); for Mexican and New Deal murals, see M. Park and G. E. Markowitz, *Democractic Vistas: Post-Offices and Public Art in the New Deal* (Philadelphia, New York, and London 1984); essays by J. Quirarte and E. Cockcroft in *The Latin American Spirit: Art and Artists in the United States, 1920–1970* (Bronx Museum of the Arts, exh. cat., New York, 1988); and D. Rochfort, *Mexican Muralists: Orozco, Rivera, Siqueiros* (London, 1993).

[25] 'Lord Mayor's Day Closing Ceremonies...' (see n. 13).

himself or the incoming Lord Mayor in 1897, Alderman Davies, to sit on the Treasury Bench on the first day of Parliament, but it had also precipitated an earlier constitutional struggle in the City, when the allegiance of its Trained Bands was transferred from a Royalist Mayor to Parliament itself.[26] As if to underline this package of symbolism, *King John sealing the Magna Carta* (Plate 34), painted by Ernest Normand, was unveiled in 1900 directly opposite *Charles I*, and again in conjunction with the Lord Mayor's inauguration. Not only did Magna Carta contain a clause protecting the privileges of London's citizens, but, as was pointed out in the press at the time of the 1900 Lord Mayor's procession when the panel was unveiled, King John had been responsible for conferring on the City Corporation the right to elect its mayor.[27] Both *Charles I* and *Magna Carta* would thus have directed attention to the historic origins and power of the City of London Corporation and the role of the City not merely in local but also national government, performing a quasi-ritual function as a focus of ceremony on the occasion when the continuity and resilience of the Corporation in modern London were asserted through the installation of the new Lord Mayor. In *Charles I*, the Mayor (shown in his full robes of office and accompanied by his mace-bearer and other civic dignitaries) is indeed placed alongside Charles, almost as an equal, as he welcomes him at the Guildhall entrance. It is significant, however, that despite the allusion to City MPs' privileges in its subject, this mural presents a sympathetic portrait of the king, framing him protectively within the arc shape of one of the wheels of his State coach behind, and emphasizing the harmony of City and Crown by mirroring this shape in turn in the curves of the Mayor's chain of office, his bow of obeisance, and his doffed, feathered cap. Similarly, Charles stands strategically at the centre of the City coat of arms which ornaments the red carpet of honour. Cromwell, of course, his arch enemy, had been adopted by Lord Rosebery, leader of the LCC, as the figurehead of its Liberal and Progressive politics, and the Gresham/RA Committee had not surprisingly rejected a proposal in 1896 of a mural of Cromwell for the Exchange.[28]

Although, in keeping with the earlier tradition of statues of monarchs in the building and its 'Royal' appellation, kings or queens feature prominently in many of its other murals, the mayoralty and the Corporation are always, tellingly, well to the fore or more so. Albert Chevallier Tayler's *Sir Henry Picard, Master of the Vintners' Company, entertaining the Kings of England, Scotland, Denmark and Cyprus* (1903) shows a medieval feast given by a mayor to the monarchs;[29] at her recent Jubilee celebrations in the City, Queen Victoria in turn had entertained four kings. The Mayor, standing in the centre foreground with his City sceptre prominently displayed, intercedes on behalf of Richard III in Sigismund Goetze's *The Crown offered to Richard III at Baynard's Castle* (given by Carl Meyer, a central figure in the campaign to erect a Shakespeare Memorial Theatre). E. A. Abbey's mural of *Reconciliation of the Skinners' and Merchant Taylors' Companies* (Plate 35), presented jointly by the two companies in 1904, shows Lord Mayor Billesden resplendent in his robes of state upon a scarlet dais in the Guildhall as if a king himself, his chain of office and City sceptre gleaming, as he settles the companies' dispute over precedence in civic processions in 1484. It is perhaps a comment on

[26] See C. Russell, *The Fall of the British Monarchies 1637–1642* (Oxford, 1991), p. 431.

[27] 'Seven Centuries of the Lord Mayoralty', *Supplement to the London Argus* (9 Nov. 1900), p. 4.

[28] GCM (15 May 1896); the offer was made by H. Hadwyn, to be funded by public subscription.

[29] The feast was given by Picard (Mayor in 1357) for Edward III and the foreign monarchs; see John Stow's *Annales of England*, quoted in an extract from A. Crawford, *A History of the Vintners' Company* (London, 1977) kindly supplied to the author by the Vintners' Company.

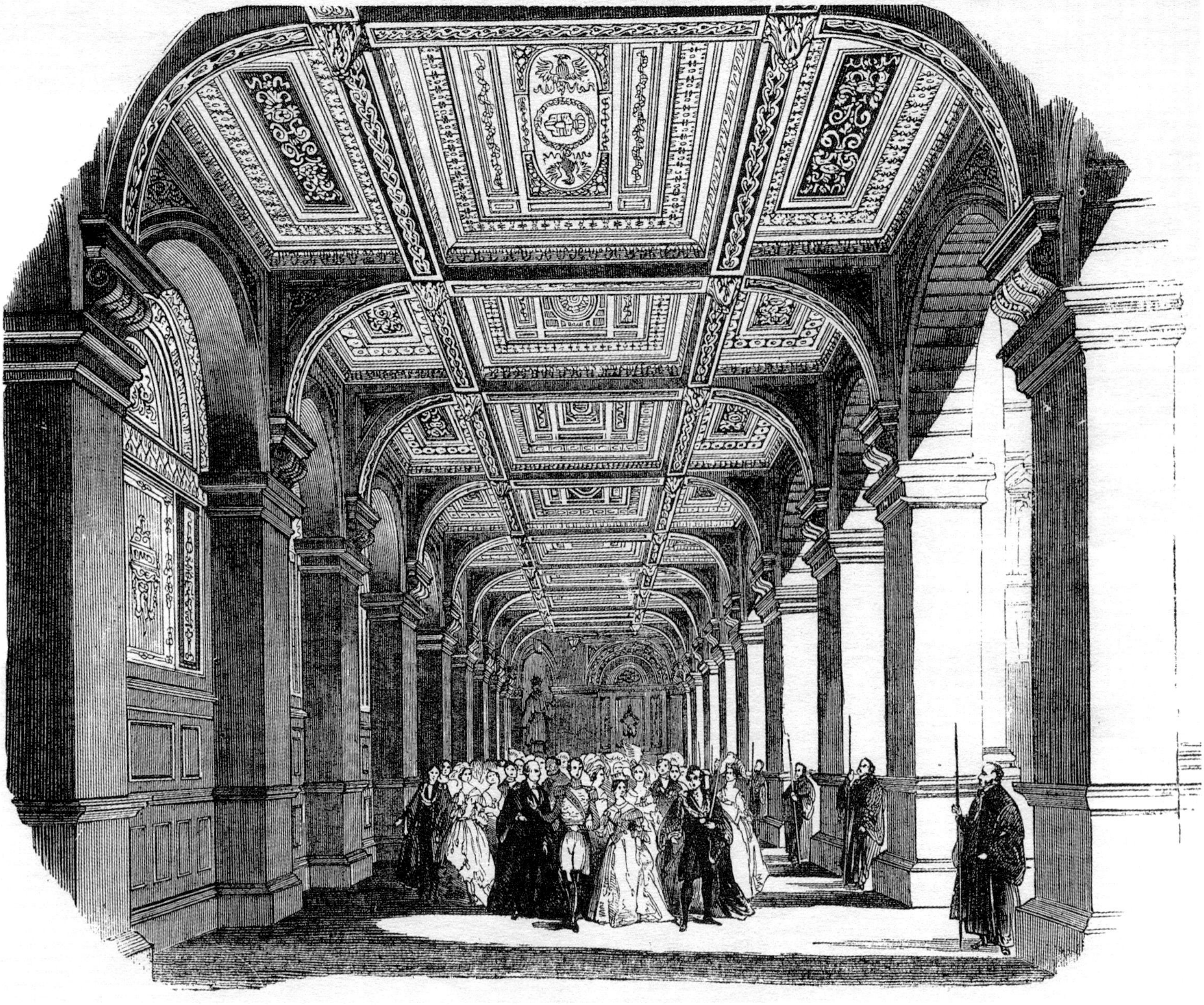

30. Unknown artist, *The Procession in the North Ambulatory*, engraving in the *Illustrated London News*, 2 November 1844 (the opening of the third Royal Exchange by Queen Victoria; Frederick Sang's encaustic decorations visible on the walls and ceiling). Guardian Royal Exchange collection

31 (*facing, above*). Léon Lhermitte, *Les Halles*, 1895, formerly Hôtel de Ville, Paris. Paris, Petit Palais, Musée des Beaux-Arts de la Ville de Paris

32 (*facing, below*). Friedrich Klein-Chevallier, *Jan Wellem inspects his Chief Builder Matheus Alberti's Designs for a Palace in the New Part of the City of 1708*, 1894–6, formerly Rathaussaal, Düsseldorf (destroyed). Period photograph, Düsseldorf, Stadtarchiv

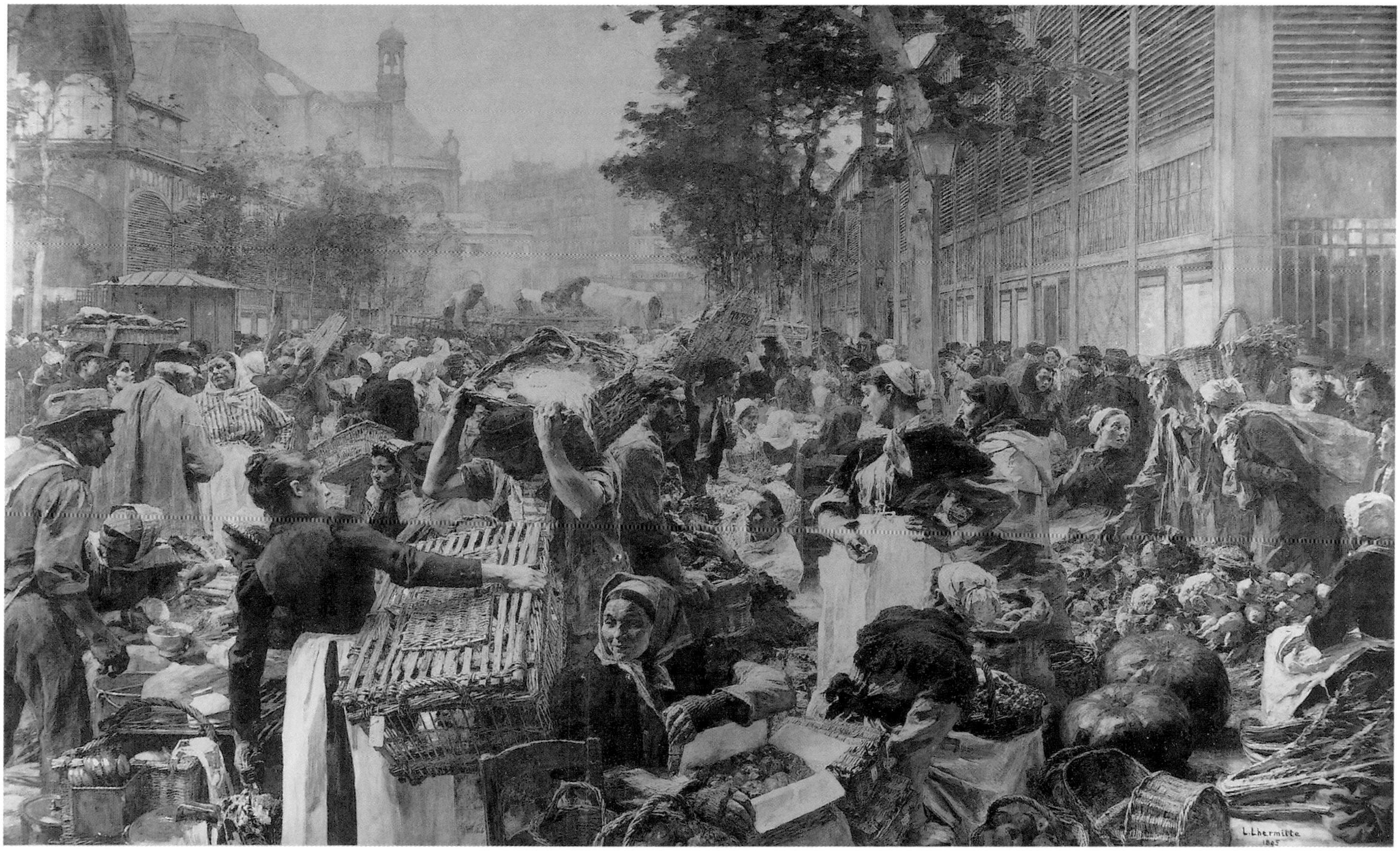
L.Lhermitte

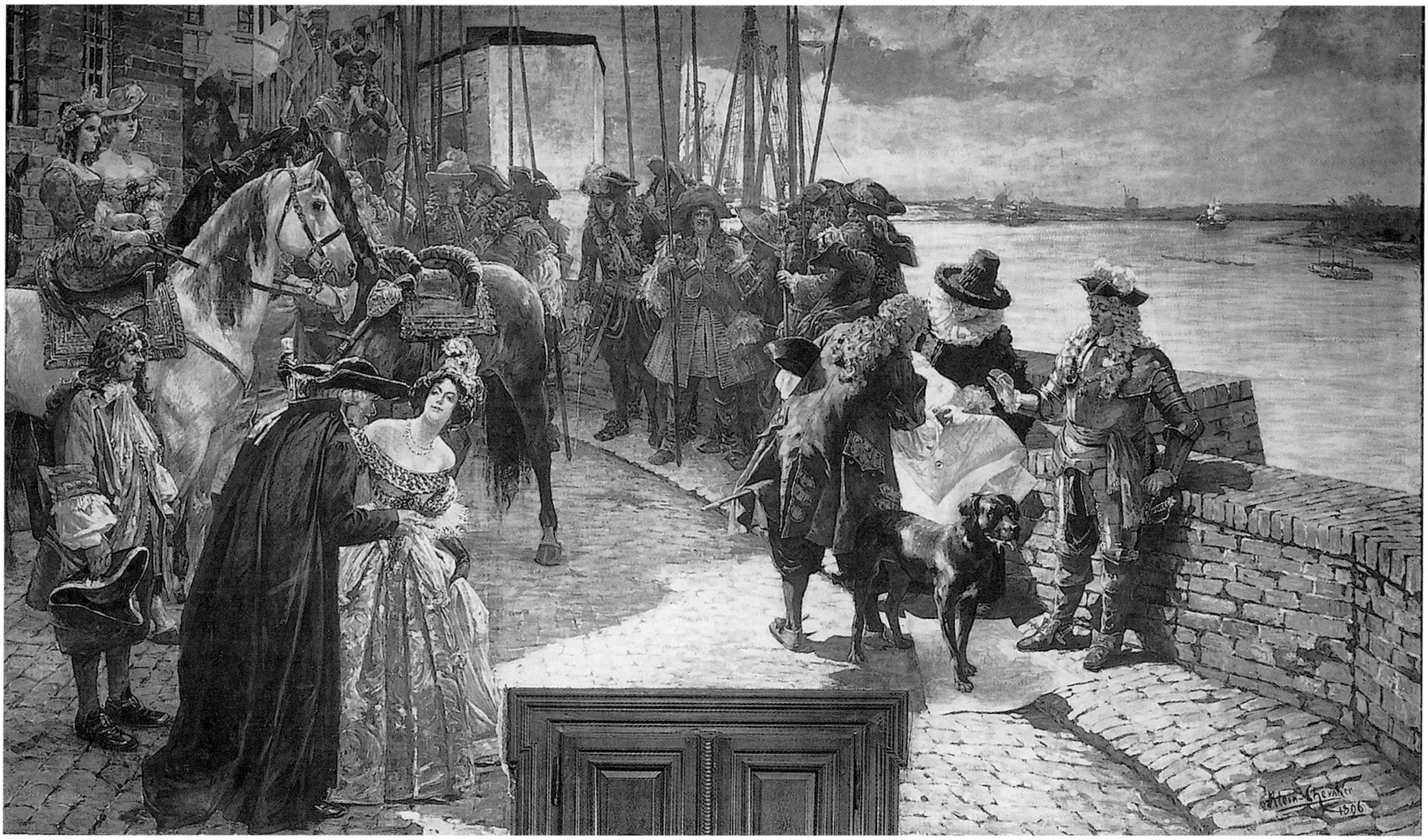

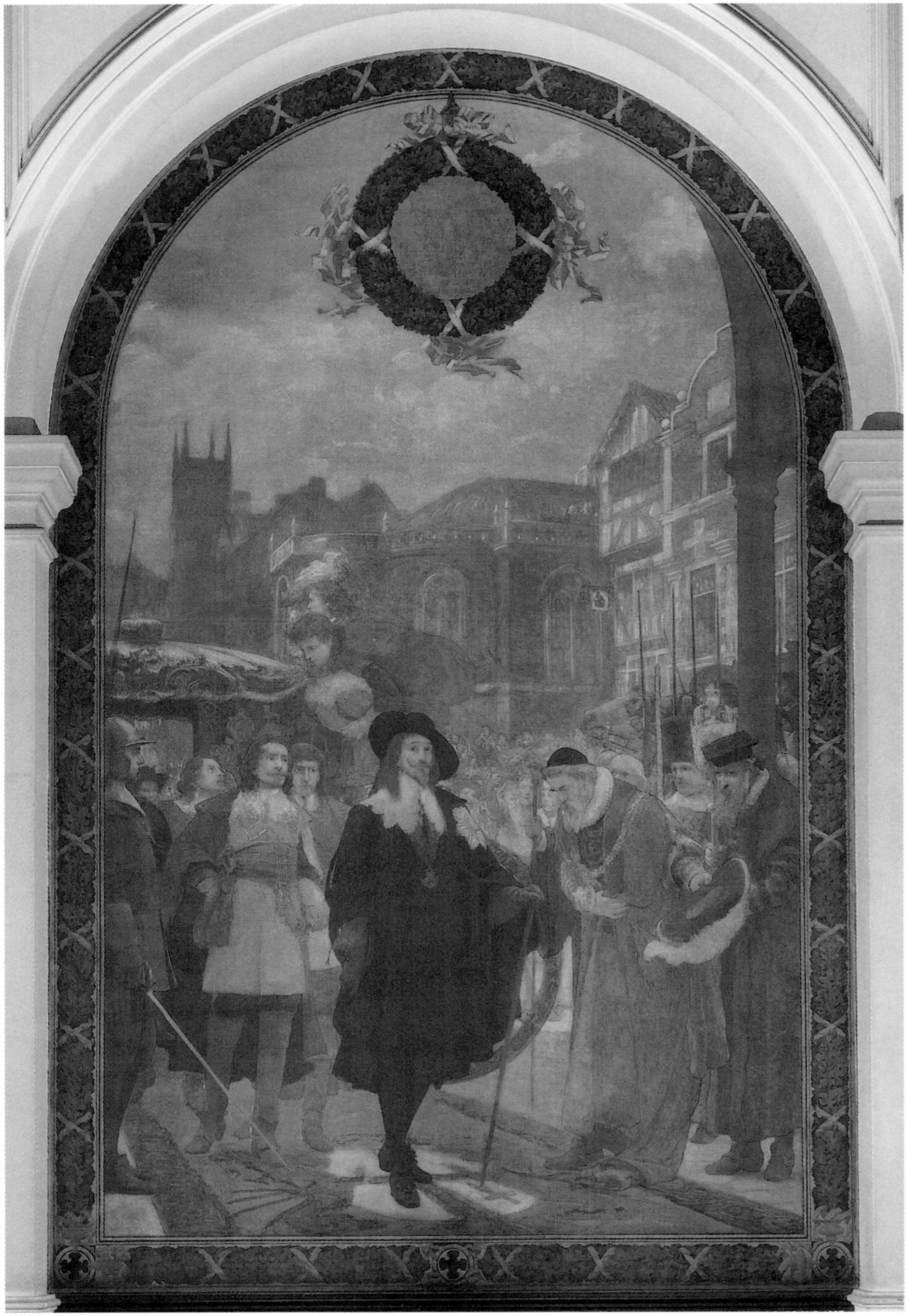

33. Solomon J. Solomon, *Charles I demanding the Five Members at the Guildhall, 1641–2*, Royal Exchange, London. Presented by Sir Samuel Montagu, Bart., MP, 1897

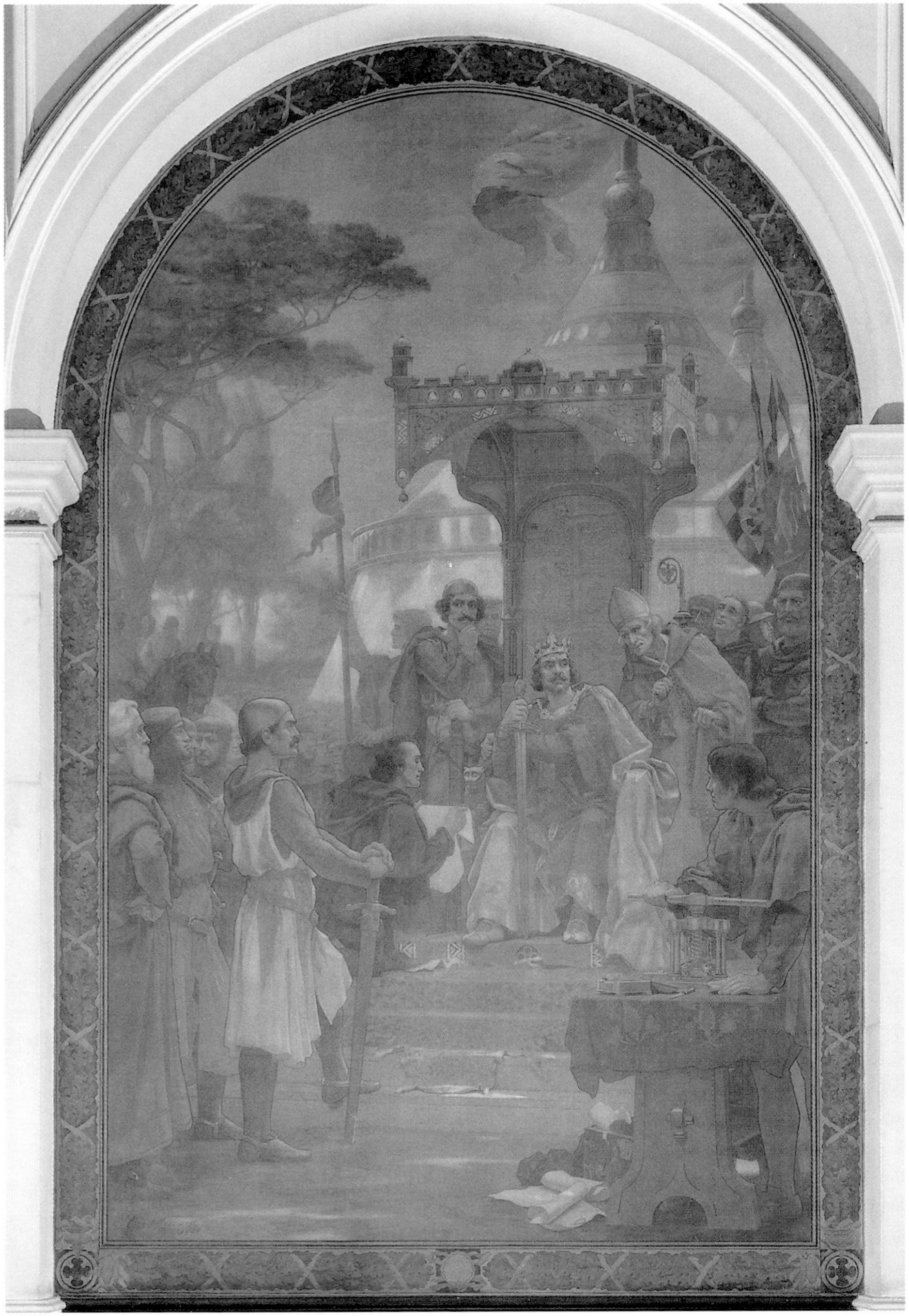

34. Ernest Normand, *King John sealing Magna Carta*, Royal Exchange, London. Presented by John Paddon, 1900

the effectiveness of the City's propaganda at the Exchange that the LCC should apparently have chosen to fight back in 1899, the year after the unveiling of Goetze's mural, by means of Walter Crane's *Masque of Beauty*, whose Demon Bumblebeadalus mocked the Corporation's regalia:

> And what if a tub-thumping socialist boggles
> At your mace and your furs and your goggles?[30]

A speech of the period by Sir Stuart Knill, who chaired the Gresham/RA Committee when it drew up the mural programme, argued for the livery companies' contemporary relevance by reference to their past achievements in the very areas of welfare, trade, and construction which the LCC was threatening to municipalize, and it offers further clues to the significance of the Exchange decoration, as it cites subjects illustrated in the murals. Seymour Lucas's *William the Conqueror granting a Charter to the Citizens of London* (Plate 36), for example, shows the incident which Knill identified as being when the Conqueror addressed the Portreeve or Chief Magistrate as 'the official to whom secular authority was given'.[31] As the panel donated by the Corporation itself in 1898, its iconography would thus have drawn attention to the Portreeve's historic responsibility for City government; the Gresham Committee in fact insisted that Lucas should amend his design so 'that the Bishop standing in front of the Portreeve should be placed at the back of him so as to make his figure more important'.[32] Even in the final composition, however, this Bishop is still suitably prominent: he was Bishop William of London, reputed as having obtained from William the Conqueror 'great liberties for the City of London'.[33] Again, Knill's speech explained that 'It is in Alfred's time that we first hear of a municipal government . . . King Alfred, rebuilding London after its fourth destruction by fire, placed it in the keeping of Alderman Othelred [*sic*], and a frith gild or peace gild was established.'[34] The architect portrayed in Frank Salisbury's mural of *Alfred the Great repairing the Walls of the City of London* (Plate V) holds up his commission from Ethelred as he listens to Alfred's instructions; the donor of the mural was Alderman Wakefield, later Lord Mayor and Viscount. Although this mural was not completed until 1912, it can be read as bearing witness to the ongoing concern about increase in the LCC's powers which also underscores Brangwyn's work at Skinners' Hall in the 1900s. Salisbury's composition, with its taut geometric scaffolding framing Alfred on his black stallion like some Roman Imperator, and its touches of gilding and notes of bold red, green, and black, presents a highly decorative, almost heraldic effect, whilst the Latin inscriptions around its border ('He rebuilt London,' 'He established the sovereignty of the people,' etc.) confirm Alfred's implied line of inheritance from Roman London. The Corporation had proudly compared its achievements in building and in housing provision with those of ancient Rome,[35] and Salisbury not only copied his shields from Anglo-Saxon manuscripts but also based his London Wall on surviving fragments of the original. His imagery in fact points to the mural's role as part of a larger group of 'building and construction' subjects in the

[30] *Beauty's Awakening A Masque of Winter and Spring*, 'presented by members of the Art Workers' Guild' in June 1899 at the Guildhall (quotation from text as printed in the *Studio*, Special Number (1899), p. 28).

[31] S. Knill, *A Pot-Pourri of London Antiquities* (London, 1890).

[32] GCM (5 Feb. 1897).

[33] J. Carpenter, *Liber Albus*, quoted in C. Welch, *Illustrated Account of the Royal Exchange and the Pictures Within* (London, 1913), p. 68.

[34] Knill, *Pot-Pourri*.

[35] Anon., *Fifty Years' Progress in the City*, in the *Remembrancer's Lord Mayor's Day Book* (1887), p. 9, CLRO.

scheme, which would have had potent significance in the context of the LCC's campaign for housing for the poor and an integrated renewal and building plan for the City.[36]

Since Alfred rebuilt London after its destruction by fire, Salisbury's panel provides a symbolic counterpart to Stanhope Forbes's scenes, more atmospheric in style, of *The Great Fire of London 1666* (presented by the Sun Fire Office, and unveiled in 1899) (Plate VI), and *The Destruction of the Second Royal Exchange in 1838* (presented by Royal Exchange Assurance in 1920). Other building or rebuilding subjects include *William II building the Tower of London*, by Charles Goldsborough Anderson, and of course, *The Opening of the first Royal Exchange by Queen Elizabeth*, by Ernest Crofts (Plate VII). Such thematic correspondences between the panels turn the scheme into less of a chronological than a cyclic account of history, vividly projecting the identities between past and present which were its *raison d'être* and also laying a direct foundation for the symbolic parallelism between Tudor and modern Britain to be developed in 1906 at Westminster by the very party whose members included Lord Rosebery and other supporters of the LCC! As Igor Golomstock has proposed in considering the 'realist' vision of history in the very different political culture of 'totalitarian art', apparently opposite ideologies may often adopt common strategies or styles to express their ideals.[37] In interpreting the significance of the murals at the Exchange, whether individually or as an ensemble, we need to be sensitive to their larger symbolic and even sociological function as an 'iconic' art form, focusing the ideals and aspirations of those Londoners of whom the *City Press* wrote so proudly in 1891. Yet, at the same time, the very potency of this art lay precisely in its 'realist' idiom, which, by inviting viewers to recognize themselves in the citizens of London past, made actual the continuum of history so central to the Corporation's and the companies' bid for survival. Even Salisbury's more overtly decorative approach involves historical accuracy, whilst despite their emphasis on monarchs and mayors, the murals also repeatedly give prominence to the ordinary people of bygone times. This can be compared with Continental examples like Francis Tattegrain's history murals at the Hôtel de Ville (Plate 37) or Jean-Paul Laurens's *Death of Sainte Geneviève* at the Panthéon in Paris, and work by German muralists of the late nineteenth century, but it also reflects the vision of British history as shaped less by kings, battles, and politicians than by the people and their traditions, customs, and the palimpsest of building which was to be found in the writings of W. Stubbs, E. A. Freeman, and J. R. Green.[38]

Sir Richard Whittington dispensing his Charities (Plate VIII), for example, the mural by Henrietta Rae, wife of Ernest Normand who painted *Magna Carta* the same year (1900), was presented by the financier Sir Abe Bailey and celebrates the Mercers' traditional role in welfare provision—so savagely criticized in the Livery Companies' Commission Report—in that Lord Mayor Whittington was one of their most illustrious members (as well as a City MP). It gives primary attention, however, to the common folk of London who benefit from Whittington's welfare, reinventing in secular form the kind of imagery associated with a religious subject such as *Christ Preaching to the Sick*[39] to suggest to the modern viewer Freeman's conviction that 'it is something to know

[36] See H. M. Hyndman, *A Commune for London* (London, 1887) and 'Questions to Candidates', *Star* (6 Dec. 1888); housing was a particular election issue in 1892, when the Exchange iconography was determined.

[37] Golomstock, *Totalitarian Art*, p. vii.

[38] See for example, Freeman's *History of the Norman Conquests of England* (Oxford, 1867–79); Green's *History of the English People* (London, 1877–80), and Stubbs's *The Constitutional History of England in its Origin and Development* (Oxford, 1866); in contrast to Macaulay's view of history as a roll-call of heroes, these writers believed in what Freeman called 'the unity of history' (quoted by J. W. Burrow, *A Liberal Descent: Victorian Historians and the English Past* (Cambridge, 1981), p. 222).

[39] e.g. in Rembrandt's prints of this subject.

ourselves of the blood and speech of the actors of that day and its morrow.'[40] Two poor young women warm themselves in the left foreground at a brazier in the snow-covered street outside Whittington's house, whilst a mother at the right stoops to lift her toddler son so that he can reach the loaves being distributed by one of Whittington's servants; the easily legible style makes the mural a close counterpart to Peter Janssen's quest 'for compelling realism' in his similarly paternalistic Düsseldorf mural *Die Burgherrin verteilt Brot* at Schloss Burg an der Wupper (1899).[41] The donor's wife was the model for Whittington's in the mural.

Goldsborough Anderson's *William II building the Tower of London* and Stanhope Forbes's *The Opening of the First Royal Exchange* likewise make a powerful appeal to the ordinary people of London whose allegiance, of course, was vital to the continued existence of the Corporation and livery companies. The Anderson mural was presented in 1911 by an individual Mercer, William Wallis Aston, and the Forbes in 1899 by the Mercers as a company. Both pictures thus speak of the historic role of the Mercers, joint controllers of the Exchange, in shaping London's physical identity and commercial prosperity, but they also assert the modern relevance of the company through the immediacy of their style and compositions. True to his training in Düsseldorf, Crofts (Plate VII) represented Sir Thomas Gresham with a life-like vigour (taking his portrait from one attributed to Holbein)[42] which brings him into the very presence of the viewer in a manner far removed from the quasi-religious veneration invited by the individual statues in niches in the earlier Exchange buildings. The 'icon' is brought to life: dressed in his Mercers' robes, Gresham descends the steps of his fine new Bourse to greet his monarch and her retinue as if an equal, whilst the angled viewpoint allows the composition to encroach by implication into the very space occupied by the viewer. The servant in the immediate left foreground is indeed partly cut off by the frame of the mural as if to suggest that the reeds he strews are falling in the path of the modern merchants who would have passed the mural on their business in the Exchange in the 1890s. An even more dramatic elision of past and present and of painted and actual worlds is achieved in Forbes's *Great Fire* (Plate VI), which explicitly proposes the centrality of art as the very agent of historical continuity, and in turn explores the psychological mechanism of this power. This panel was presented by the Sun Fire Office and unveiled in 1899. Lurid flames (painted from direct observation of the forge at Newlyn) billow across the night sky, turning the river peach and copper as children and possessions are hurried by the frightened citizens into waiting boats. Prominent amongst the salvaged items is a portrait—the likeness of an ancestor which is so valued that life must be risked to preserve it. The human rescue chain, meanwhile, which suggests another appropriation of a religious image, this time the spiralling, vertical column of figures in Tintoretto's *Presentation of the Virgin* (Santa Maria dell'Orto, Venice), descends with dynamic urgency to the viewer's very feet. By implication we are made to stand in one of the rescue boats cut off by the lower edge of the picture. Passed down the chain, the portrait thus follows in direct succession to the sleeping children of a new generation, symbolically encapsulating the link not only with the past but also with the future into which the viewer is drawn. The portrait is at once both an illusion—the likeness of a person—and an emblem, representing continuity and endurance.

[40] Freeman, *History*, quoted in Burrow, *A Liberal Descent*, p. 108.

[41] The phrase is I. Markowitz's ('packende Realistik') quoted in Trier and Weyres, *Kunst des 19. Jahrhunderts*, p. 185. Janssen's mural was part of a scheme for a 'national monument of the Grand Duchy of Berg'.

[42] See A. Saunders (ed.), *The Royal Exchange* (1997), pl. 1; the portrait is now attributed to William Key.

Forbes's panel is one of the most imaginative and successful responses to the purposes of the Gresham Committee, introducing a more universal element into their politics, and perhaps again inviting association with antiquity since Pliny described how concern to safeguard a portrait housed at Rhodes led King Demetrius to refrain from conquering the city by fire.[43] The illustration in the mural of the river in turn points to the prominence given in the Exchange iconography to imagery of the Thames, shipping, and as a complementary motif, the sea—just as Goldsborough Anderson's *William II* likewise deals not only with building (the construction of the Tower of London) but also with water transport and trade. In this panel, the stone for the Tower is brought by boat along the Thames and the common labourers in the foreground at the water's edge are of course the ancestors of the dockworkers in Brangwyn's *Modern Commerce* (Plate 38), the only contemporary subject in the 1892 programme. Anderson's composition, despite its more literal style, suggests a conscious symbolic mirroring of Brangwyn's panel, which had been completed a few years earlier in 1906, whilst the figure of William II on horseback behind takes up the motif of Salisbury's *Alfred* of 1911, acting as a pivot between the 'shipping' and 'building' themes. Other river or sea subjects include E. A. Cox's *Philip the Good presenting the Charter to the Merchant Adventurers* (1916), a reminder of the Tudor navigators whose enterprise was felt to have laid the foundations of the modern British Empire. Again, however, there was also a modern political element within the theme. Municipalization of the Port of London was a key aim of the LCC; the Progressive Sidney Webb's claim that 'The bulk of the shipping trade of the Capital of the Empire lies at the mercy of an unregulated crowd of private wharfingers and the boards of directors of four giant dock companies'[44] would have struck particularly near the bone for the donor of Brangwyn's panel, Sir Thomas Lane Devitt, a prominent Skinner and President of the Shipping Federation, as well as for Sir Frederick Green, its chairman and the donor of Cox's panel; both men were also directors of shipping companies. The dockers in *Modern Commerce* (one a reverse image of the man shouldering a packing crate in Léon Lhermitte's recent Hôtel de Ville mural of *Les Halles* (Plate 31)) are, like those later to be illustrated in Brangwyn's Lloyd's Register of Shipping scheme for Devitt,[45] the very men whose labour the LCC wished to control itself.

Despite the correspondences of iconography and motifs between panels, and the prevailing allegiance to the 'realistic' re-creation of past events, the overriding *visual* effect at the Exchange quickly became one of disunity. Although Leighton had laid down requirements for a common horizon line and colour scheme, these lapsed fairly soon after his death in 1896, just as oil also gradually replaced spirit fresco; nevertheless *marouflage* continued as the installation technique. Despite the appointment of Sir Lawrence Alma-Tadema as an artistic adviser in Leighton's place, in practice little further attempt seems to have been made to match the tightly knit thematic programme of the murals with a correspondingly integrated artistic effect, though the Gresham Committee's amendment to Lucas's sketch suggests that a watchful eye was kept on matters of iconography. The continuing practice of artists painting the murals in their studios rather than *in situ* militated against overall harmony, whilst the system of patronage whereby, subject to the approval of the Gresham Committee, a donor was able to choose his artist, provided only loose control over style beyond a general preference for Royal Academicians and an increasingly

[43] See Pliny, *Natural History*, Book XXXV, ch. 36, trans. J. Bostock and H. T. Riley (vol. 6, London, 1857), p. 266; I am grateful to staff at the University of Edinburgh Department of Fine Art for bringing this to my attention.

[44] S. Webb, *The London Programme* (London, 1891), p. 65.

[45] See Chapter 11.

conservative tendency (a proposal for a mural by Eric Kennington was turned down in the later 1900s).[46] The protracted progress of the scheme was in any case hardly conductive to unity. Subjects selected from Knill's list were painted as donors came forward. Although Leighton's panel (Plate 1) has a naturalistic seascape setting (the clouds were observed in Cornwall to ensure an authentic effect in its incident of *Phoenicians trading with the Early Britons on the Coast of Cornwall*), and Lucas's *William the Conqueror* (Plate 36) is effectively a window in the wall, placing the figures in a shadowy Norman interior, the contrastingly decorative effect of Salisbury's *Alfred* forms part of a small sub-group of murals in which the kind of 'Neo-Pre-Raphaelite' mural style adopted shortly afterwards in the East Corridor at Westminster can be seen in embryo.[47] Yet even this grouping does not appear to reflect any particular thematic or iconographical factor.

The primacy for the Gresham Committee of subject and symbolism is clear from their resistance around 1917 to proposals to modify the programme devised in 1892 so as to incorporate the contemporary themes proposed by various donors as a means of reflecting the significance of the First World War.[48] By this time, however, the original propaganda motive *vis-à-vis* the LCC was far less pressing, and in effect a new and chillingly topical form of 'art with a message' was introduced through the replacement of *Scene of a Folk-Mote in St. Paul's Churchyard* (i.e. a people's assembly or council), a subject planned back in 1892, with *Their Majesties King George V and Queen Mary visiting the Battle Districts in France, 1917* (Plate 39). Whilst the *Folk-Mote*, had it been painted earlier, would have made a powerfully symbolic counterpart in the Corporation versus LCC debate to *Magna Carta* (Plate 34) and *Charles I demanding the Five Members* (Plate 33), the replacement subject was clearly intended to encourage morale in a nation bowed by the tragic news from the Front. Here now was not just an icon for the City, but also for the nation: the mural was exhibited in various other British cities before installation at the Exchange in the presence of representatives of the Services. It was presented by Sir William Dunn, Lord Mayor, and its artist, Salisbury, recalled subsequently how Dunn swept aside his fears that the Gresham Committee would reject a modern subject: 'The Lord Mayor said "Nonsense! I will not have a word of objection. I am chairman ex-officio and I have a subject of worldwide interest and national importance, and furthermore, here is a letter from the king promising all the help necessary to the painter." '[49] If Salisbury still hankered after a historical subject which would permit the kind of decorative effects of his *Alfred*, he found himself designated a colonel, given a car 'without speed limit', and instructions to follow the King and Queen through France on their 1917 visit. Despite the more naturalistic, 'documentary' style of the resultant painting as compared with *Alfred*, it none the less continues the adaptation of religious imagery common in many of the earlier murals, with the King, standing on high ground, holding field-glasses and talking to Field-Marshall Sir Douglas Haig, elevated above the viewer in the upper section of the mural as if a khaki-clad saint, whilst a scene of Queen Mary visiting a military hospital is placed in a separate lower section, like a predella panel.

[46] Information kindly supplied to the author by Guardian Royal Exchange Assurance; see also GCM (28 Nov. 1919, 16 Jan. 1920, and 28 May 1920) and letter to the Mercers' Company from Royal Exchange Assurance (11 July 1919), MCA. Kennington was proposed by the Royal Exchange Assurance Company, an aspiring donor, for *The Peace Thanksgiving*, a subject ultimately painted by Salisbury for Sir Horace Marshall. The Company instead presented Stanhope Forbes's *The Destruction of the Second Royal Exchange in 1838* (1920).

[47] See Chapter 4.

[48] e.g. an offer from the Australian Government in 1912 of a mural illustrating the opening of its Parliament was turned down by the Gresham Committee after John Horseley Palmer, a leading Mercer and the donor of *The Foundation of St. Paul's School, 1509* objected to 'the insertion of a picture . . . of a modern subject, in no way directly connected with the City', which would be 'both incongruous and inartistic' (GCM, 12 Jan. 1912, p. 367).

[49] F. O. Salisbury, *Sarum Chase* (1953), p. 38.

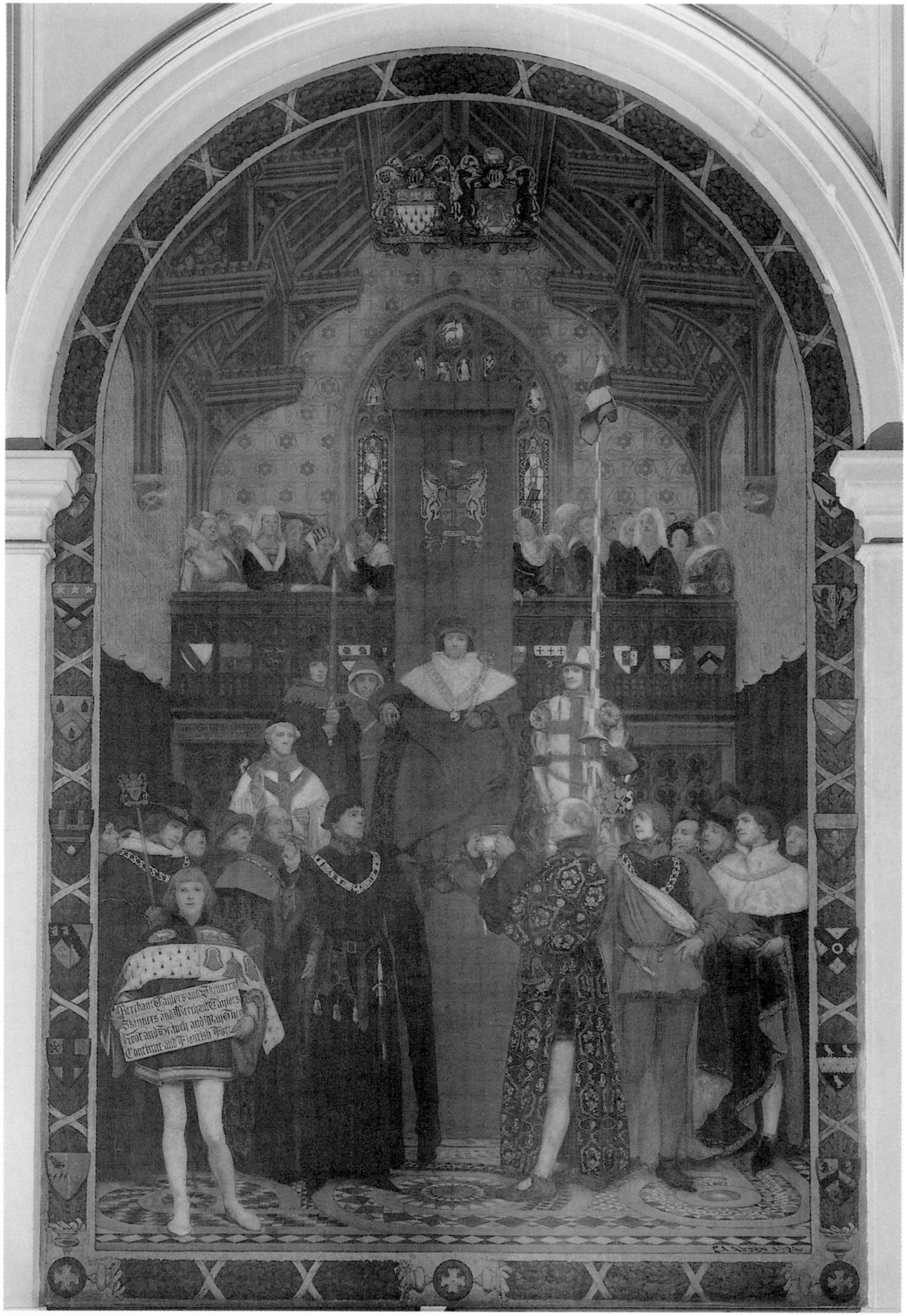

35. Edwin A. Abbey, *Reconciliation of the Skinners' and Merchant Taylors' Companies by Lord Mayor Billesden, 1484*. Royal Exchange, London. Presented by the two companies, 1904

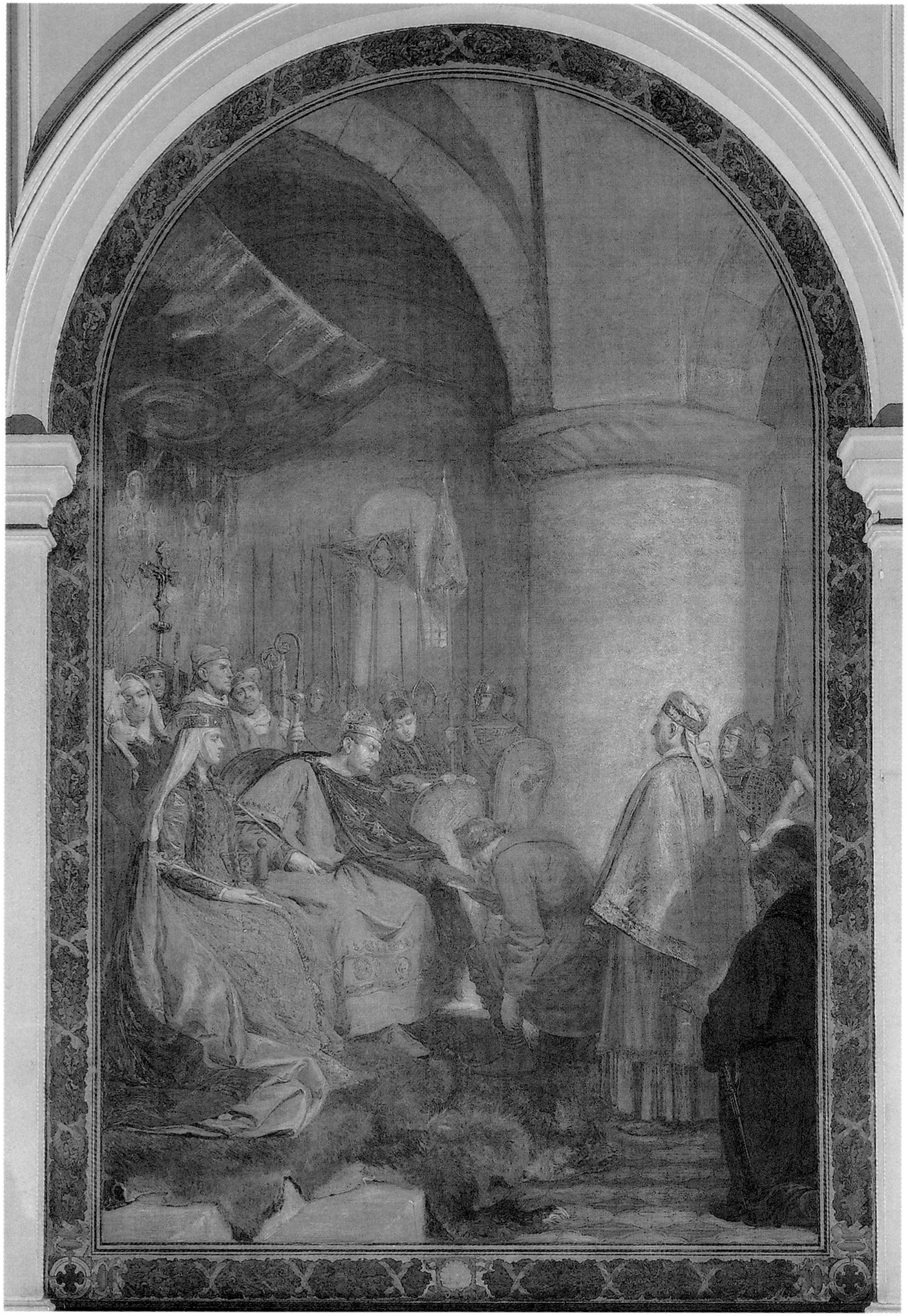

36. J. Seymour Lucas, *William the Conqueror granting a Charter to the Citizens of London*, Royal Exchange, London. Presented by the Corporation of London, 1898

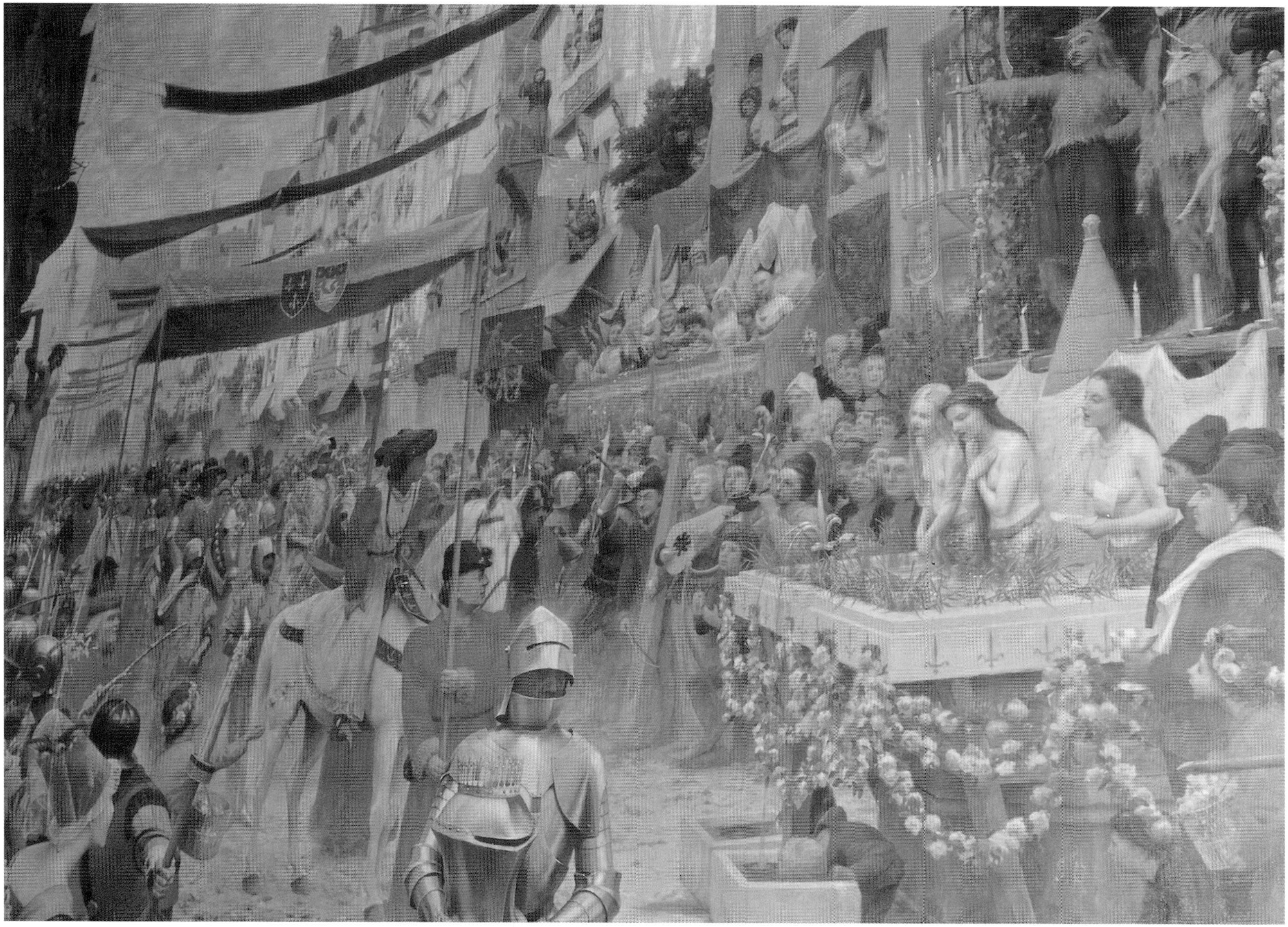

37. F. Tattegrain, detail of *Entry of Louis XI into Paris*, Salon de Passage, Hôtel de Ville, Paris, 1891

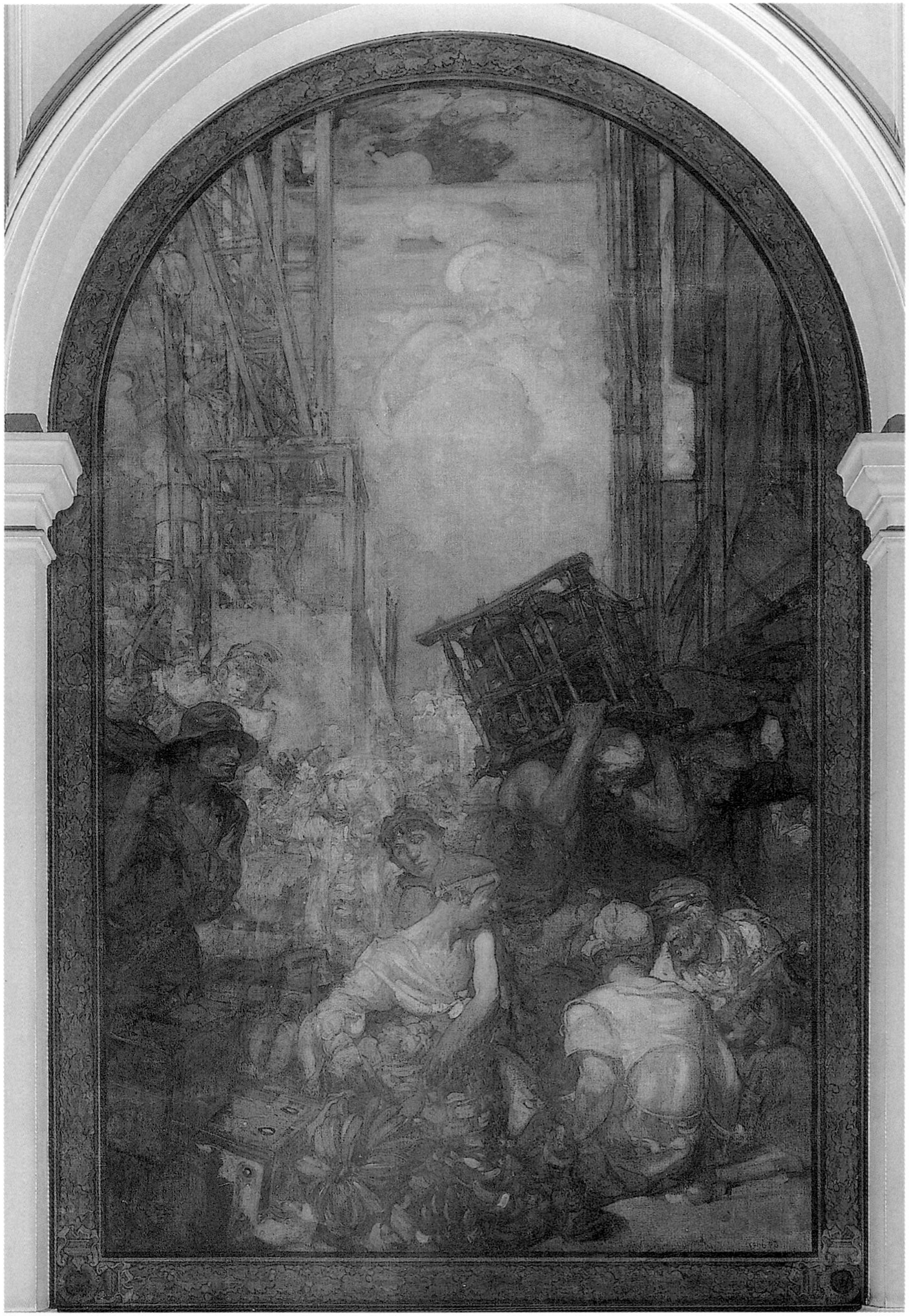

38. Sir Frank Brangwyn, *Modern Commerce*, Royal Exchange, London. Presented by Sir Thomas Lane Devitt, Skinner, 1906

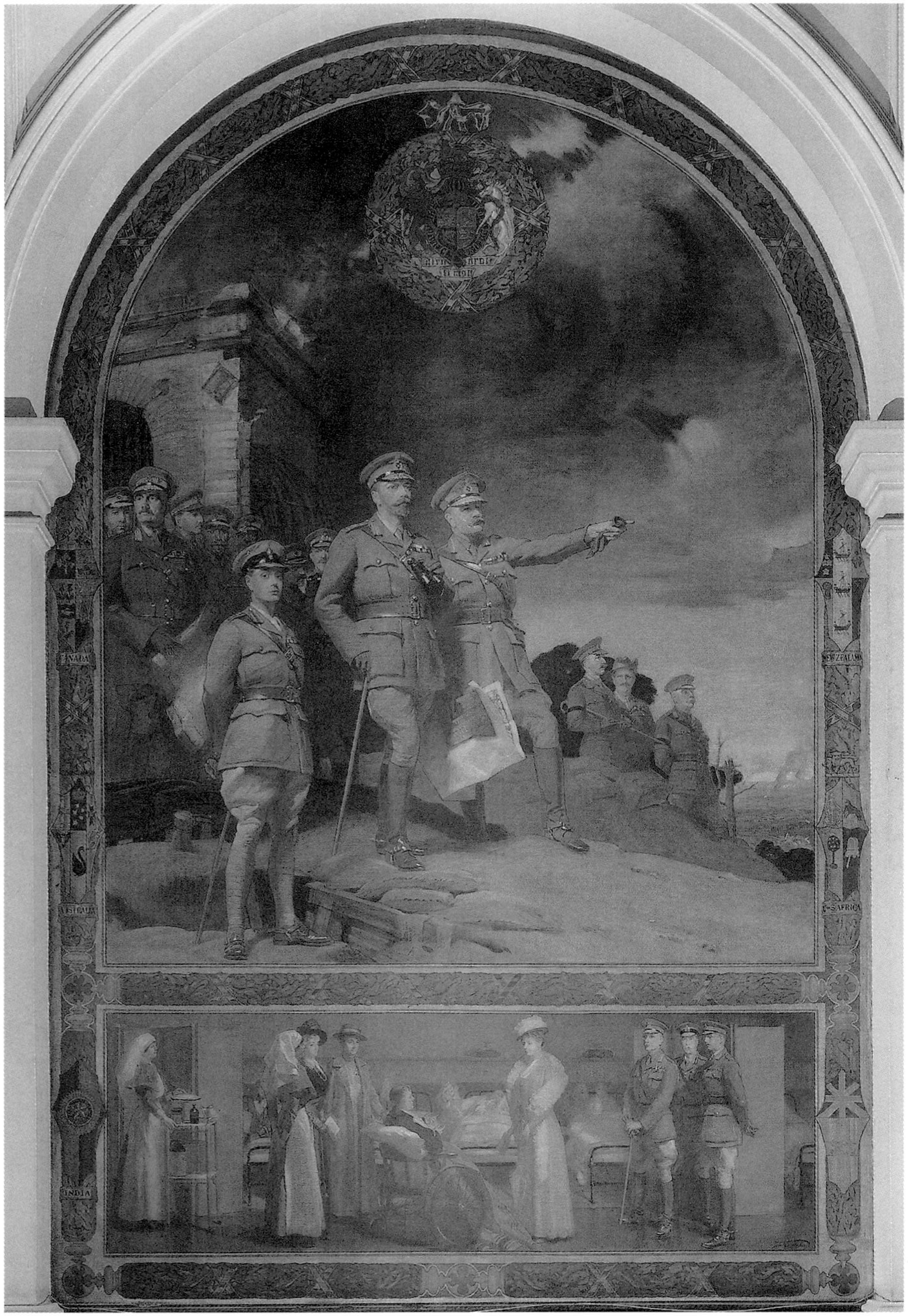

39. Frank O. Salisbury, *Their Majesties King George V and Queen Mary visiting the Battle Districts in France, 1917*, Royal Exchange, London. Presented by Sir William H. Dunn, Bart., Lord Mayor, 1917

The original Exchange programme was further modified after the war to include several memorials. Salisbury painted the *National Peace Thanksgiving on the Steps of St. Paul's Cathedral, 6 July 1919*, again portraying the King and Queen, now with the Archbishop of Canterbury and the Bishop of London. This was presented by Sir Horace Marshall, Lord Mayor at the declaration of peace, and unveiled in 1919 by the Duke of York, the future King George VI. Salisbury's earlier 'heraldic' flair is now a shadow of its former self, present only in the banners and ecclesiastical robes; portraiture has replaced propaganda. The idiom is similar to his *Burial of the Unknown Warrior* panel for St Stephen's Hall at this period, but the earlier ritualistic aspect of the mural scheme as a focus for group ceremonial had of course been reinvented, for in place of mayoral pageantry, the unveiling of the War Memorial panels now provided an occasion for a communal commemoration and remembrance. William L. Wyllie's *Blocking of Zeebrugge Waterway, St. George's Day, 23 April 1918*, presented by the Eagle, Star and British Dominions Company Ltd, was unveiled in 1920, for example, in the presence of survivors of the event, including Lieutenant W. B. Leake, whose guidance in a humble motor-launch of British sailors to safety from enemy fire it portrays. The painting was prepared from detailed sketches of what Wyllie, himself a seaman, called 'everything that had to do with the occasion' as well as from eye-witness accounts.[50] With its dramatic nocturnal effects inspired by Wyllie's artistic hero Turner, and the suggestive cross-shape etched by the motor-launch's mast on the sky illuminated by battle-fire, emotive content still dominates, continuing the tradition of Forbes's *Great Fire*. Likewise, the tribute in the War Memorial panels to the common soldier—and in Lucy Kemp-Welch's *Women's Work in the Great War* (Plate 40), to his female counterpart—is a natural sequel to the emphasis on ordinary people in the earlier murals. Welch's panel, donated by the Empress Club, whose members had been active in the Emergency Voluntary Aid Committee, was the last of the pictorial murals and was unveiled in 1924 by Princess Mary, who expressed pleasure at 'so interesting & striking a picture—& one [which] ... will become a very historical addition to those already in the building'.[51] With its backdrop of an azure sunlit sea for women dressed in khaki who demonstrate a variety of contributions to the war effort (land-working, book-keeping, industrial work with a machine tool, etc.), the mural, like Wyllie's, of course complements the sea and river theme of the 1892 programme. Wyllie's *Zeebrugge* might indeed be read as a conscious sequel to the tribute to British naval supremacy contained in A. C. Gow's *Nelson Leaving Portsmouth, 18 May 1803 to join HMS Victory*, presented by the Corporation of Lloyd's on the centenary of the event and one of the few subjects showing an incident outside London (though none the less carrying London associations).[52] Interpreted from a wider, thematic standpoint rather than a purely stylistic one, and in terms of its significance as 'ritual', 'invented tradition', and 'propaganda', the Exchange scheme in fact reveals a remarkable degree of integration, despite its long period of execution and the changes introduced to its programe after 1917. The smaller portrait panels of prominent businessmen from the City's past, commissioned during the 1920s to complete it, were mostly copied from period paintings.[53]

[50] M. L. Wyllie, *We Were One: A Life of W. L. Wyllie* (London, 1935), p. 228.

[51] Letter from Princess Mary's Lady in Waiting to Colonel Watney of the Mercers' Company (30 April 1924) in Royal Exchange Box 3.6, MCA.

[52] Nelson was given the Honorary Freedom of the City of London and a sword from the Court of Common Council (presumably that shown in the mural); see Welch, *The Royal Exchange*, pp. 91–2.

[53] See Willsdon in Saunders (ed.), *The Royal Exchange*, pp. 332–3 and Royal Exchange Box 4.1 in MCA; the panels include copies by E. B. Patry of Sir Thomas Lawrence's portrait of *Sir Francis Baring* at Stratton and Zoffany's of *Sir Richard Glyn* at Bridewell Royal Hospital.

In the 1900s, however, with the Exchange's great mural experiment still under way, and at a period when the ideal of unity between art and architecture was being keenly advocated by Sir William Richmond and the Art Workers' Guild, amongst others,[54] it was the variety of styles under one roof in the building which provoked comment and criticism. This variety, of course, was itself a symptom—if not a conscious symbol—of the very principles of free enterprise and independence for which the Corporation and companies stood, in contrast to the centralizing and regulatory aspirations of the LCC. E. A. Abbey, who with Salisbury had contributed to the Neo-Pre-Raphaelite subgroup of Exchange murals, spoke frankly of 'the hideous result [which] . . . the court of the Royal Exchange presents—which is a standing example of how *not* to do it,'[55] when employed to supervise the resumption of mural painting at Westminster in 1906.[56] If the care taken by the new Liberal regime (which supported the LCC) to ensure coordination in the scheme might seem to suggest a political as well as an aesthetic motive, livery companies themselves had in fact already shown concern to improve upon the effect at the Exchange when murals were commissioned from one artist, rather than a group, in the 1900s at Drapers' and Skinners' Halls. At the latter, 'harmony' indeed became a deeply symbolic vehicle for the Skinners' distinctive purposes.

LIVERY COMPANY MURALS

Drapers' Hall

Although J. G. Crace's decorating company had carried out some modest designs in the Drapers' Court Dining Room, and the French painter Félix Joseph Barrias had illustrated the Legend of the Golden Fleece on its ceiling in 1868, the new 'fine art' at the Exchange must have been the immediate spur to the Drapers' Company's decision in 1901 to commission decoration from Herbert J. Draper (whose name was coincidental) for the large oval (Plate IX) and smaller supplementary panels on the ceiling of its Great Hall. Barrias, who contributed to the mural work at Charles Garnier's Paris Opéra,[57] had also painted a decoration as part of the scheme by Crace for the Mercers' Hall in the 1880s,[58] but Draper was firmly part of the new 'British school' of muralists being fostered by Leighton. Having studied in Paris and Rome, he had won Leighton's RA Prize for the Decoration of a Portion of a Public Building, and Poynter—one of the members of the Exchange's Gresham Committee—much admired his completed Drapers' Hall work. Whilst the scheme can be seen as part of the effort by the London livery companies to demonstrate their authority in the context of the changes in London government, it is less overtly propagandist than the Royal Exchange work. Draper was allowed to select his own theme, and finding that there was no subject from the company's history 'that lent itself to allegorical treatment, or to the light and fanciful arrangement that a ceiling painting demands',[59] he submitted two possible designs. One, 'a symbolical treatment of the reign of Queen Victoria', would have continued the royal and

[54] See Chapter 11.

[55] Letter from Abbey to Lord Carlisle (17 July 1908), CHA, J22/84

[56] See Chapter 4.

[57] See J. Foucart, *Les Peintures de l'Opéra de Paris de Baudry à Chagall* (Paris, 1980).

[58] Information kindly supplied by the Mercers' Company; see J. Imray, *The Mercers' Hall* (London, 1991) for Crace's scheme.

[59] Quoted in M. A. Greenwood, *Pictures and other Works of Art and Interest at Drapers' Hall* (1930); MS text kindly made available by the Worshipful Company of Drapers.

commemorative emphasis of the Exchange decoration, but the Drapers preferred his other design, 'the symbolical pageant from Shakespeare's *Tempest* when Prospero summons various deities symbolising the four elements . . . by the commanding power of intellect, compelling the forces of nature'.[60] The Drapers were, of course, traditionally providers of education, supporting a number of schools; in 1901 they would have been watching anxiously the LCC's designs on the control of education in London, which bore fruit in Arthur Balfour's 1902 Education Act and 1903 Education (London) Act. Their commission forms a counterpart to the Shakespearean murals completed in 1901 at Howell's School for Girls, a Drapers' Company institution in Cardiff.[61] The theme of 'intellect' was, indeed, underlined in the company's Hall by the addition of personifications of *Science, History, Literature*, and *Ethics*, which were completed by Draper in 1910 in the spandrels.[62] The sum of £2,000 which Draper was paid for his *Tempest* subject, and the £3,000 he received for the two supplementary rectangular panels on the ceiling of *Dawn* and *Evening* from *A Midsummer Night's Dream*, reflect the importance of the scheme for the company, which was clearly concerned to secure high-quality work.

If Draper's classically inspired nudes and figures in flowing drapery reveal a debt to Leighton, the subtle, high-keyed colour effects in his panels suggest inspiration from the pointillist mural painting recently developed in Paris by Henri Martin at the Hôtel de Ville, as well as the shimmering light in work by Albert Besnard, such as his recent ceiling panel at Samuel Bing's Maison de l'Art Nouveau shop in Paris, and decoration for the Sorbonne.[63] The central figures of Draper's main oval panel, shown *di sotto in su* as in a Baroque illusionist ceiling painting, take shape against a backdrop of tiny colour-points which coalesce in the eye of the spectator down below to give the effect of luminous sky; reflected light gives warmth to the nude skin. A rainbow appropriately frames one end of the composition. Style as much as subject creates the 'light and fanciful arrangement' felt by Draper to be necessary for a ceiling painting. Whilst the strategic placement of *Dawn* above the Master's chair perhaps suggests the Drapers' pride in their contribution to the origins of London's historic government—a number of historians, for example, regarded the livery companies as 'the source of muncipality'[64]—the decorative scheme also finds kinship with Continental Symbolism's interest in dream experience. The pointillist colour lends an almost hallucinatory quality, much as a psychological dimension of the *Midsummer Night's Dream* story can be sensed in the Klimt-Matsch partnership's murals in the Empress Elizabeth's Villa Hermes near Vienna.[65] Draper's decorations, painted in the studio and presumably installed by *marouflage*, were warmly acclaimed by the press.[66] Where the artistic quality of the Exchange scheme is somewhat variable—hardly a surprising outcome given the unfamiliarity of mural painting for most of its artists—Draper's work shows a high degree of competence and forms a most successful complement to the classical-style interior at Drapers' Hall, looking towards the more complex symbolic pointillism created a few years later by Sigismund Goetze at Grove House.[67]

[60] Ibid.

[61] See Appendix C, no. 14.

[62] According to Draper, this iconography was suggested by Guy Dawber (Greenwood, see n. 59).

[63] Besnard's 1896 Sorbonne mural (*Life Is Born from Death*) is discussed and illustrated in D. Silverman, *Art Nouveau* (1989), pp. 226–7.

[64] See G. Unwin, *The Guilds of London* (London, 1906), p. xxxviii, who quotes Brentano and Hazlitt.

[65] See W. Kitlitschka, *Die Malerei der Wiener Ringstrasse* (1981), pp. 168–70.

[66] See Anon, 'Mr. Herbert Draper's Painted Ceiling for the Livery Hall of the Drapers' Company', *Studio*, 29, No. 123 (15 June 1903), pp. 33–41.

[67] See Chapter 10.

Skinners' Hall

In the 1890s, Leighton had refused a proposal that Brangwyn should contribute to the Exchange scheme, on the grounds that he was too inexperienced.[68] Although Brangwyn had won his spurs in mural painting as the artist of no less prominent a commission than the frieze of Oriental *Potters* around the exterior of Bing's Maison de l'Art Nouveau, as well as its interior panels of *Music* (Plate 13) and *Dancing*, and was highly acclaimed on the Continent as an easel painter, he was relatively unknown in Britain. His selection by the Skinner, Sir Thomas Lane Devitt, as the artist of his Exchange panel was approved by the Gresham Committee in 1900—after Leighton's death—and was in a sense a leap of faith. When the Skinners' Company, even before the completion of this panel, asked Brangwyn in 1902 on Devitt's recommendation[69] to provide decoration for the newly renovated seventeenth-century Banqueting Hall in their headquarters at 8 Dowgate Hill, this was his first major British commission, and one of its murals, *The Departure of Sir James Lancaster for the East Indies* (Plate X) secured his election as an Associate of the Royal Academy in 1904. In 1912, following his work for the Skinners, he was asked to provide a large-scale painting for Carpenters' Hall, and (again on Devitt's recommendation) to decorate Lloyd's Register of Shipping's new Dining Room,[70] and he wrote to the Clerk of the Skinners' Company: 'I shall never forget the obligation I am under to the Skinners' Company for having given me an opportunity that has seldom if ever fallen to the lot of a British artist in this country.'[71]

Brangwyn's Skinners' Hall scheme can be set in the same context of livery company anxiety at the growth of LCC power as the Exchange and Drapers' decoration, and it enabled him to work for an institution whose origins lay in the kind of medieval guild of craftsmen which had inspired his early mentors, A. H. Mackmurdo and William Morris,[72] and with which he was familiar from his own upbringing in Bruges with its many ancient guilds. It was originally intended that he should provide mural paintings to complement gesso relief panels recently completed by Robert Anning Bell on the themes of *Industry, Education, Hospitality, Charity, Commerce*, and *Science*, which reflect the various areas of the company's traditional involvement in trade, welfare, and instruction (like the Drapers, the Skinners owned schools). Where Bell, a leading member of the Art Workers' Guild, had produced classical-style personifications in the tradition of Walter Crane, Devitt was keen that Brangwyn should paint contemporary subjects. If he had in mind something like *Modern Commerce* at the Exchange, his fellow Skinners were, however, less enthusiastic at the prospect of what would surely have amounted, in the hands of an artist as steeped in the traditions of Flemish Baroque genre and modern French 'realism' as was Brangwyn, to very overt comment indeed on the condition of London. Instead, the tried and tested formula of history painting, as in all but Brangwyn's own panel at the Exchange, was chosen, and a series of titles relating to the company was drawn up after much deliberation. An early watercolour sketch illustrating the effect of possible designs when set in the warm, brown, wood-panelled room with its carved Baroque

[68] Brangwyn wrote independently to Leighton requesting the opportunity to paint a Royal Exchange mural, but was turned down as not being an 'artist of proven ability' (GCM 8 June 1894).

[69] The Skinners accepted Devitt's recommendation on the advice of C. H. Holme, editor of the *Studio*, and the artist Alfred East (see Devitt's letter of 15 Nov. 1902 to Draper, Clerk of the Skinners' Company, enclosing their recommendations, in SCA).

[70] See Chapter 11.

[71] Letter from Brangwyn to the Clerk of the Skinners' Company (28 April 1912), SCA.

[72] Brangwyn spent his early years in Bruges where his father was an ecclesiastical designer and architect, and after the family moved to London in 1875, was guided informally by Harold Rathbone and A. H. Mackmurdo, and employed as a copyist in Morris's workshop in Oxford Street from *c.*1882 to 1884 and occasionally subsequently.

flower swags (Plate 41) shows that, lacking previous experience of history painting, Brangwyn too looked directly to the Exchange for inspiration.[73] The figures examining some kind of draped material on a seashore in this sketch, for example, suggest the topic of *British Merchants Bartering for Skins with (say) Russian Traders* which Brangwyn, clearly looking to Leighton's *Ancient Commerce* at the Exchange, had included in his own list of suggested subjects.[74] This design can be recognized as the first step towards what in the eventual scheme became *Pelts and Furs at the City Mart* (Plate 42), a subject which the Skinners presumably preferred as combining a reference to their history (the mural shows Walbrook, an early site of skin-trading where Skinners' Hall was later built),[75] with an Exchange-style allusion to the topical issue of markets in London. The LCC had recently taken control of these from the City. The mural would thus have been as much protest as propaganda. A vertical panel, it portrays Skinners in their distinctive red livery gowns purchasing skins in the background, whilst their 'primitive' forebears, sprawled at rest in the immediate foreground, eat green apples with the knives of their trade. Instead of occupying the central position on one of the long walls of the hall, as had Brangwyn's 'Russian skin trade' subject in his watercolour sketch, the mural was installed to form the initial subject in the sequence of ten from the Skinners' history which run around the side walls of the Banqueting Hall. A symbolic subject of *Harmony* (Plate 43) was installed above the gallery to link these historical episodes, and in the early 1930s Brangwyn added two corner panels of *Education* and *Charity* (Plate 44) (showing modern-day figures) as replacements for Bell's reliefs. It had quickly become apparent that Brangwyn's robust and vigorous style was out of keeping with Bell's work, which had therefore been moved.[76]

Brangwyn's preparatory sketches indicate that as early as 1900 he was experimenting with one of the Banqueting Hall subjects, *The Founding of Tonbridge School*[77] (Plate 45). Since this illustrates the theme of education present in Bell's reliefs, it is possible that even before his formal commission, Brangwyn had thus been approached by the Skinners with a view to the introduction of greater immediacy in their decorative scheme. Although they discarded Devitt's proposal for contemporary themes, the description of the murals published by W. H. Draper, Clerk of the Company, on their completion in 1909, certainly makes it clear that the scheme was intended to extend the same kind of invitation to the viewer to recognize kinship with the people of the past as occurred in the Exchange: 'The Skinners who entertained General Monk in 1660 and King William in 1689 were, as regards the trade of the Skinners the same, no more or less, as the Skinners who in 1794 honoured Admiral Lord Howe, or in 1895 Speaker Peel, or in 1909 Lord Rosebery.'[78]

Although pressure was put on Brangwyn to complete the scheme as soon as possible following his formal commission in 1902, in the event it was not ready until 1909. This may explain the Skinners' willingness now to honour Rosebery, whose name, as we have seen at the Exchange, had been closely associated with the LCC; of greater significance in Draper's description, however, is its 'cyclic' interpretation of history, which indeed is literally exemplified in Brangwyn's portrayal of himself as the 'primitive' Skinner eating an apple in the foreground of *Pelts and Furs* and in

73 The sketch is owned by the Skinners' Company.

74 List of 'Mr. Brangwyn's suggested subjects' (10 July 1902), SCA.

75 See W. H. Draper, *Historical Paintings of the Skinners* (1909), Introduction.

76 From the SCA, it appears that Bell was originally asked in *c.* 1902 to provide six gesso panels for the south end of the hall, but his commission was halted in 1904. Brangwyn offered in April 1912 to replace free of charge the panels Bell had completed. These are approximately 2.89 × 1.52 m in size; the main horizontal panels in Brangwyn's 1902 scheme are each approximately 2.89 × 3.20 m, and the vertical panels in it are each approximately 2.89 × 1.60 m. *Harmony* is approximately 1.52 × 3.96 m.

77 Sketch by Brangwyn in Dundee Art Gallery, no. 4/65/117.

78 Draper, *Paintings*, Introduction.

40. Lucy Kemp-Welch, *Women's Work in the Great War, 1914–1918*, Royal Exchange, London. Presented by C.Williamson Milne on behalf of the Empress Club, 1922

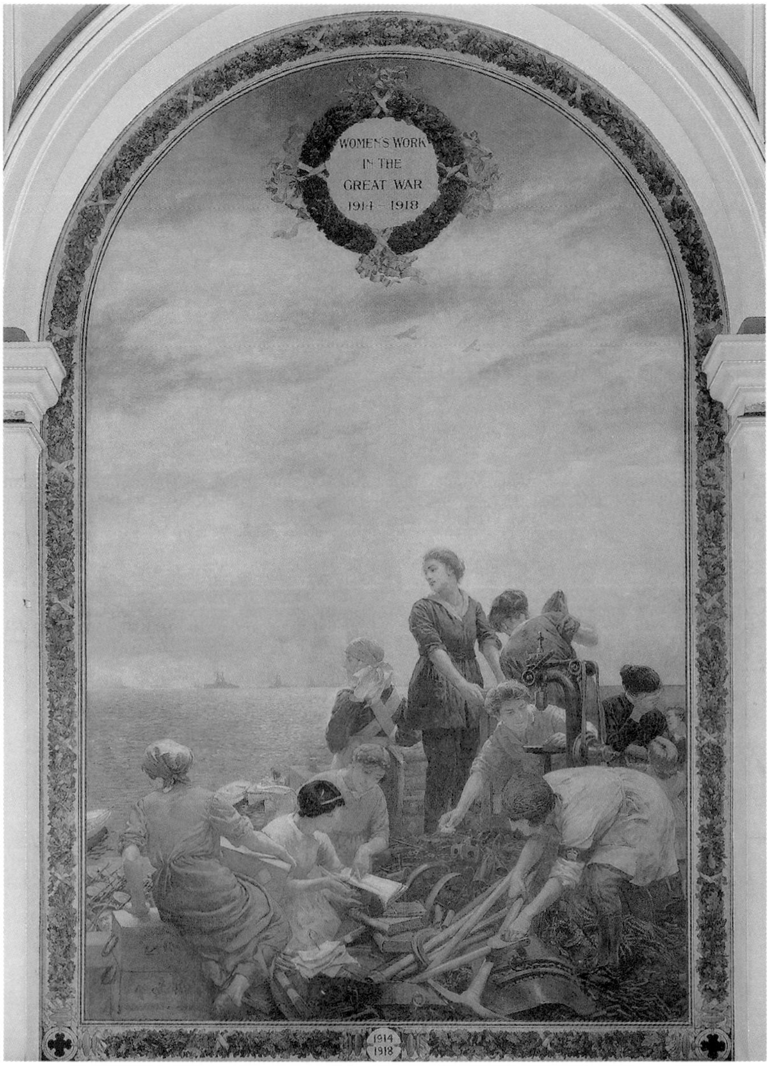

41. Sir Frank Brangwyn, detail from watercolour sketch indicating proposed scheme of murals for Skinners' Hall, London, *c.*1902. London, Worshipful Company of Skinners

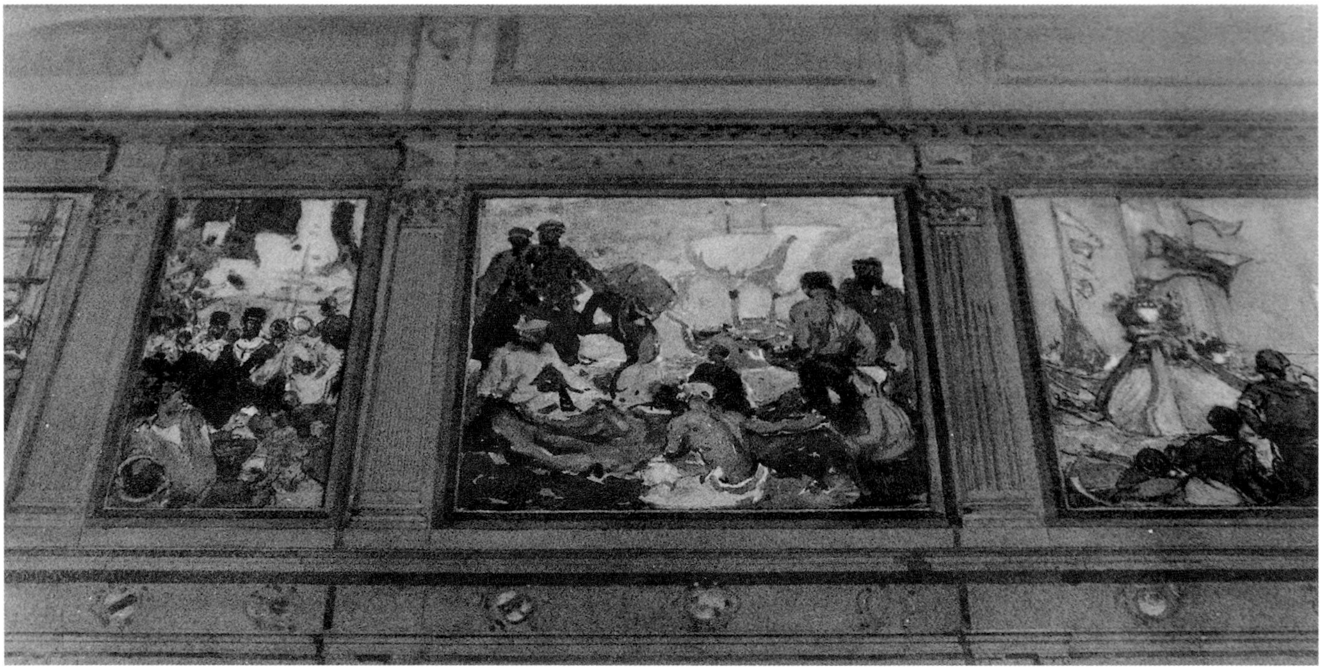

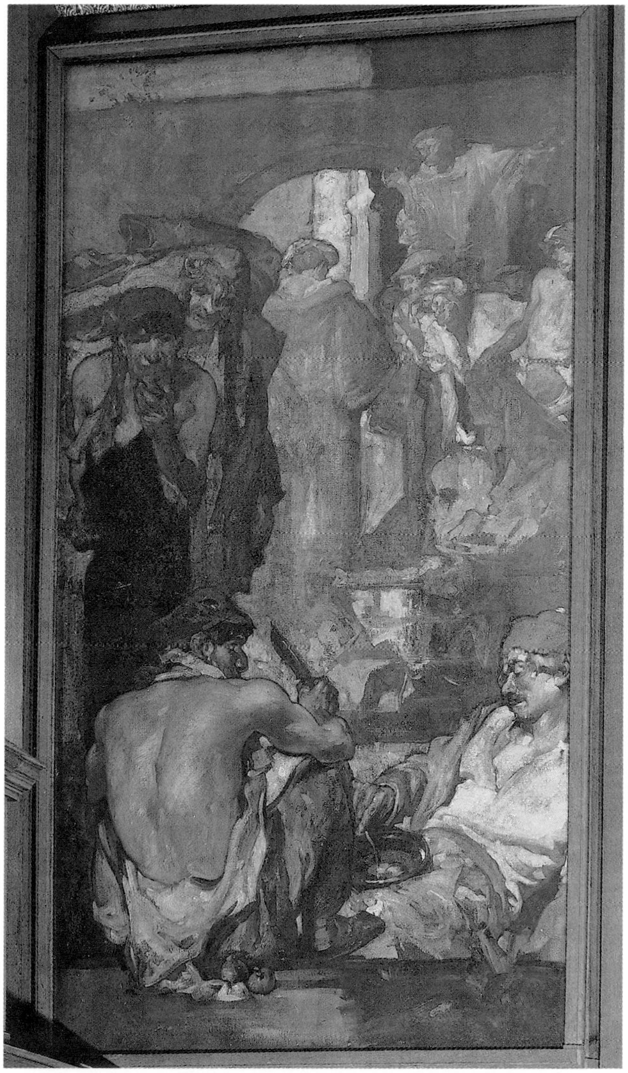

42. Sir Frank Brangwyn, *The Guild of Corpus Christi surveying Pelts and Furs at the City Mart in the Days before the Granting of their Charter*, Banqueting Hall, Skinners' Hall, London, 1902–9

43. Sir Frank Brangwyn, *Harmony*, Banqueting Hall, Skinners' Hall, London, 1909

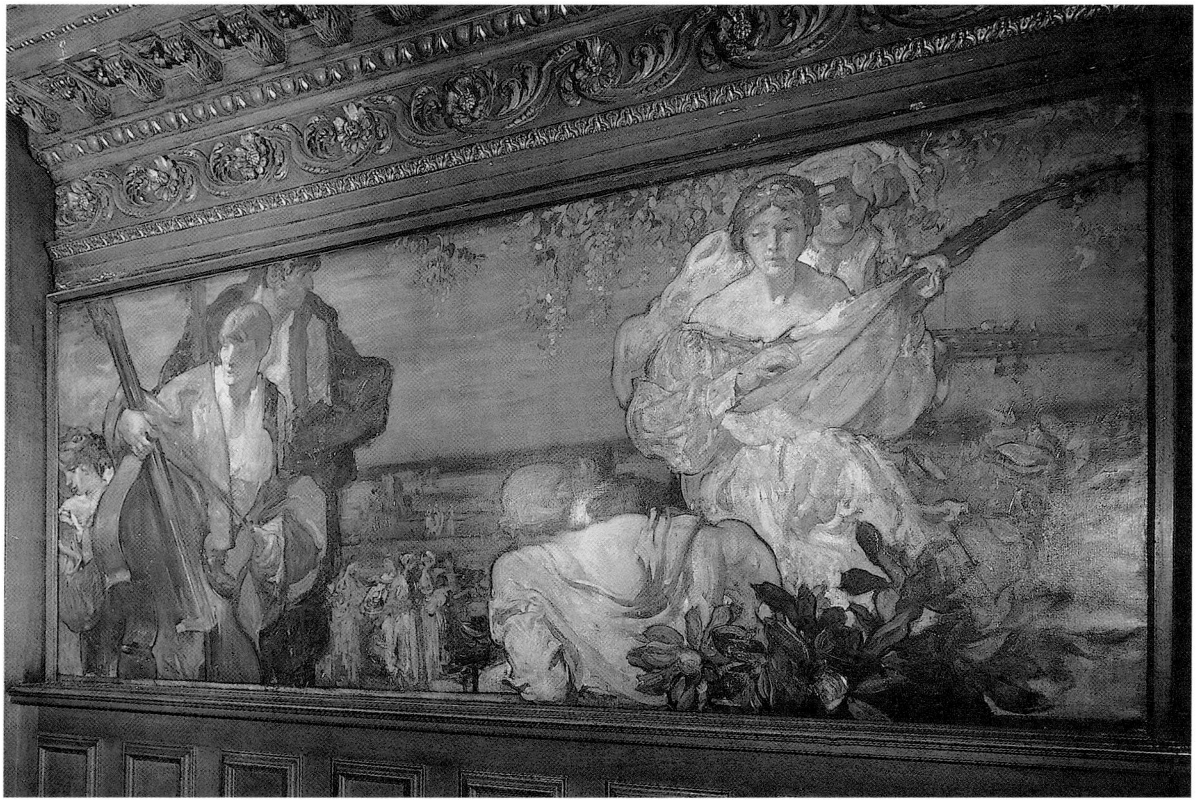

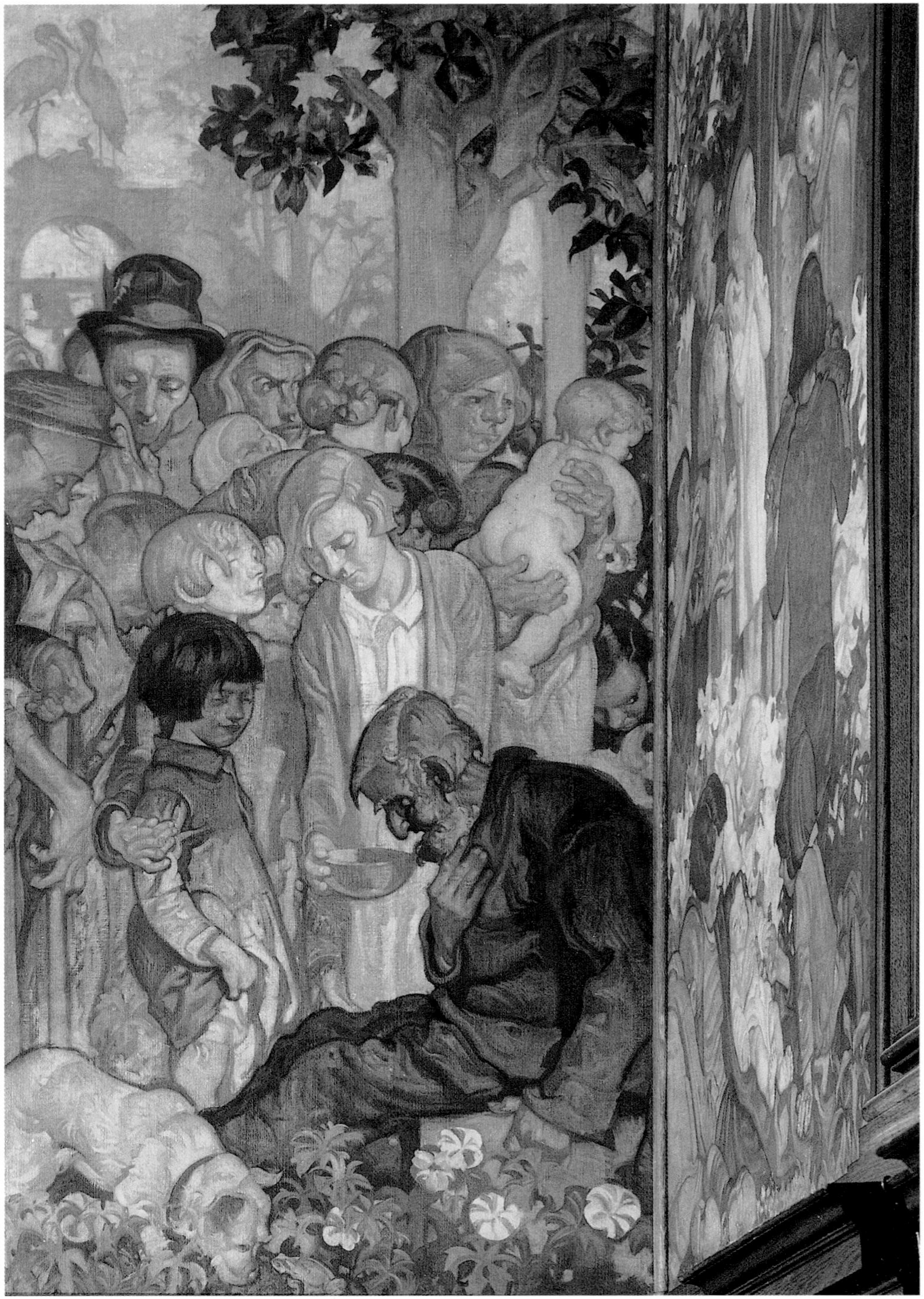

44. Sir Frank Brangwyn, *Charity*, Banqueting Hall, Skinners' Hall, London, 1937

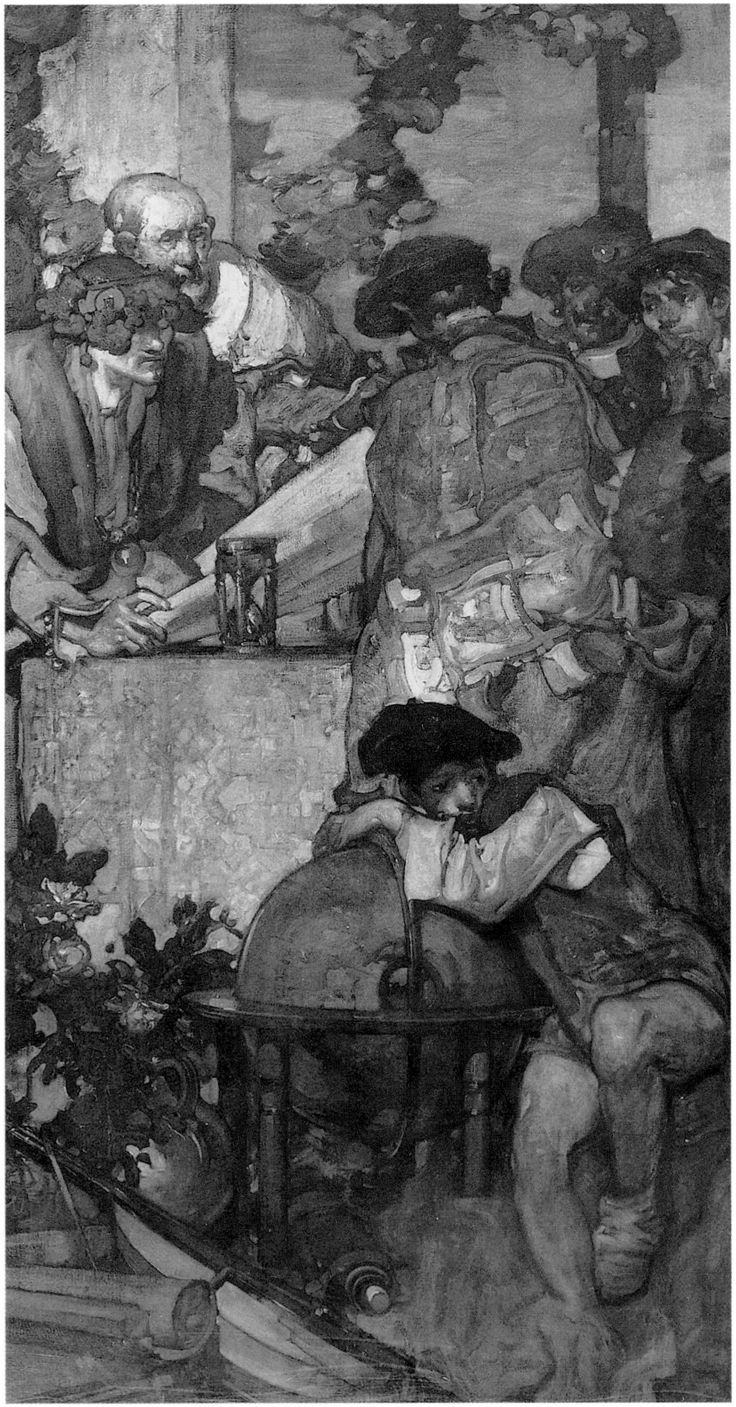

45. Sir Frank Brangwyn, *The Founding of Tonbridge School by Sir Andrew Judd, AD 1553*, Banqueting Hall, Skinners' Hall, London, 1902–9

a further apparent self-portrait in early versions of *River Procession*.[79] He provided scenes of modern London dock life as head- and tailpieces for Draper's booklet. Where artistic disunity was felt to dog the work at the Exchange, despite its close-knit iconographical programme, in Brangwyn's hands at Skinners' Hall the far more tightly coordinated, richly imaginative synthesis of style and subject which took shape in itself projects history's 'cycle'. The scheme shows that Brangwyn's art cannot be dismissed as mere 'wallpaper',[80] and that his own much-quoted self-description as a 'decorator', 'born with a gift for filling up spaces', who took as the highest compliment the comment that his work 'looked like a Persian carpet',[81] should not be taken at face value; rather, it needs to be placed in conjunction with his belief, as expressed late in life, that 'Art should have meaning or message, and, be accessible to all—and, should be such, as to waken the feelings of the fellowship of man.'[82] The decorative unity of his interpretation of the Skinners' subjects symbolizes not only the Skinners' concern with the continuation of their historic traditions and rights within modern London, and their motto *In Christo Fratres*, but also a personal belief in universal brotherhood, later to reach its most ambitious expression in Brangwyn's 'British Empire' panels for the House of Lords (1924–33). Whilst his self-portrait as one of the rough, half-naked men with knives in the foreground of *Pelts and Furs* demonstrates a sympathy with the common man which is evident in the foregrounding of the ordinary citizens of London in the other murals too, this is more than mere reflection of Brangwyn's outrage that 'History never records the poor',[83] or the emulation of a device favoured by Belgian muralists such as Henri Leys, Egide Guffens, and Jan Swerts,[84] and of course used in the Royal Exchange. It can be recognized as presenting the ultimate logic of Brangwyn's ideal of fellowship, for it implies that the common people who work with their hands are artists too. This philosophy emerged simultaneously in Brangwyn's Venice Biennale exhibition decorations,[85] and whilst it reveals the influence of William Morris, it also corresponds with the strongly social emphasis of the Arts and Crafts Movement in Brangwyn's native Belgium. The unity of his scheme provides a British counterpart, for example, to the creation of an 'artistic microcosm' as a 'model of harmony for the social macrocosm' by Brangwyn's Belgian friend and fellow contributor to Bing's Maison de l'Art Nouveau, Henri Van de Velde.[86] In a sense, Brangwyn's colouristic, exuberant art at Skinners' Hall, with its generous baskets of fruit or flagons of wine bringing the art of Jordaens to mind, and its reinterpretation of Mantegna's *Triumphs of Caesar* (Hampton Court Palace, London) in the composition of *City Pageant* (Plate XI) is far closer to the sensual, even hedonistic association of art and life in *fin-de-siècle* Belgium, in which 'carnivals, masks and Corpus Christi processions were part of the lived experience of social radicals preaching

[79] A sketch in the Guildhall Art Gallery, London for *River Procession* and Brangwyn's design for this mural in his Skinners' Company watercolour (see n. 73 above) both include a small figure waving from high on a mast who compares closely with Brangwyn's own posture in *Self-Portrait with the Miners* (1907, Glynn Vivian Art Gallery, Swansea). The elongated body and hunched shoulders of the self-portrait Skinner eating an apple in *Pelts and Furs* are reminiscent of postures often represented by G. Klimt and G. Minne (e.g. the *Standing Youth* bronze of 1898 by the latter, which, with work by Klimt, Brangwyn gave to the William Morris Gallery, Walthamstow).

[80] D. Sutton, 'The Art of Frank Brangwyn', *Country Life*, 112, no. 2910 (24 Oct. 1952), p. 1282.

[81] Quoted in BD (13 Aug. 1952).

[82] Undated remark, ibid.

[83] Undated remark, ibid.

[84] Cf. the foregrounding of servant figures in Leys's *Feestmaal van het St. Lucasgilde*, Koninklijk Museum voor schone Kunsten, Antwerp; Brangwyn's servants also recall prototypes in Rubens's *Feast of Herod* (National Galleries of Scotland, Edinburgh) and Tintoretto's *Marriage at Cana* (Santa Maria della Salute, Venice).

[85] See Chapter 11.

[86] Silverman, *Art Nouveau*, p. 272; for Brangwyn's Belgian contemporaries and Bing, see also M. Eidelberg and S. Henrion-Giele, 'Horta and Bing: An Unwritten Episode of L'Art Nouveau', *Burlington Magazine*, 119 (Nov. 1977) and G. Weisberg, 'Bing and Brangwyn', *Jaarboek*, Brugge (1987), pp. 277–86.

Morris's gospel'[87] than to the stricter medievalism of Morris himself. *City Pageant in Olden Times* is in fact an illustration of a Corpus Christi Day procession.

The arrangement of the murals in the Skinners' Banqueting Hall itself draws attention to a number of wider recurrent themes which underpin the historical programme and thus give it symbolic unity. Subjects are paired typologically, again as at the Exchange, with the 'primitive feast' in *Pelts and Furs*, for example, hanging opposite the 'modern' banquet given in 1689 by Lord Mayor Pilkington (a Skinner) to welcome William and Mary to the Company's new Hall on the Walbrook site (Plate 46), but in turn also implying continuity with the modern function of the Hall as the venue for banquets. It was under William and Mary that the City's and the companies' traditional rights, lost under Cromwell, were restored, and the subject thus forms an appropriately symbolic finale to the scheme. Similarly, *A River Procession of the Cities and Companies' Barges to Westminster AD 1483* (Plate XII) stands opposite the river incident which marked the Skinners' contribution not merely to London history, but to the origins of Empire, *The Departure of Sir James Lancaster for the East Indies, 1594*. Such correspondences are made visible by the flowing, curvilinear dynamic of the scheme, which guides the eye from one mural to the next via the undulating banners of *City Pageant in Olden Times* or repeated, generous shapes such as the globe upon which the schoolboy leans in *The Founding of Tonbridge School by Sir Andrew Judd*, or the flagons carried by servants in *Lancaster* and *Pilkington's Banquet*. Although Brangwyn experimented with a composition for *Pilkington's Banquet* very similar to Leys's *Feestmal van het St. Lucasgilde*,[88] he gradually modified this to resemble more closely Tintoretto's *Marriage at Cana*, with a high table set beneath arches in the background, which now allowed the foreground to be filled with these rounded, unifying motifs—not only flagons, but also a pumpkin and other fruit. Similarly, the relegation of Pilkington and his royal guests to the background in this ultimate composition, as tiny figures at the high table, so that the servants bearing these provisions occupy the foreground, is echoed in Brangwyn's abandonment of an early idea, apparently for another Skinners' mural, in which figures pay obeisance to a 'king' on a dais.[89]

The figures in close-up in the foreground of the murals—from the apple-eaters with their knives in *Pelts and Furs* to the Skinners bearing parchment rolls, and the page-boys in *Edward III granting the Charter on 1st March 1327*, or the servants in *Pilkington's Banquet*, in fact become members of a greater procession through time which spills beyond the confines of *River Procession* or *City Pageant* to make of the ensemble a seamless whole, embracing the viewer by implication in its march. Even before the viewer is aware of the detail of the historical incidents, their visual rhythm, punctuated with the vibrant orange of carrots on the quay in *Lancaster*, the pinks and crimsons in the pageant costumes, or the finery of those receiving General Monk, and the glowing red of the Skinners' robes worn by Lancaster and by his forebears in *Pelts and Furs*, projects the Skinners' message—and in turn, also Brangwyn's—of human fellowship. Whilst this suggests affinities with Van de Velde's theory of 'psychophysical'[90] and kinaesthetic line, as evident in the fluid, intercommunicating spaces of his Bloemenwerf house,[91] or even with the Nietzschean

[87] Silverman, *Art Nouveau*, p. 173.

[88] See n. 84.

[89] Thumbnail sketch in sketchbook 808 48A, RA. This book also contains other rough sketches which may be identified as related to Skinners' Hall murals since the sketches do not necessarily show either the entire mural or their exact designs; e.g. that labelled 'The Astrologue Mr. Taylor' (the source for Sir Andrew Judd in *Tonbridge School*) and that of 'Neptune and his sea . . . [illegible]' (cf. the pageant topics in the Skinners' 'Subjects suggested for the Decoration of Skinners' Hall' (5 May 1902), SCA). See Willsdon, *Aspects of Mural Painting* (1988), ch. III for identification of other Skinners' Hall sketches.

[90] Silverman, *Art Nouveau*, p. 368.

[91] Ibid., p. 272.

philosophy of 'eternal recurrence' espoused by the Vienna Secession, of which Brangwyn was a corresponding member, the colouristic *richesse* and repetition of motifs perhaps have most in common with the Baroque tradition of emblematic art Brangwyn so admired in the work of Rubens and the Flemish seventeenth-century masters. As such, of course, these traits are naturally suited to the Baroque architecture of the Hall.

At a further level of significance, Brangwyn's repeated images do indeed operate as emblems or visual leitmotifs. Fruit, flowers, and musical instruments all present the themes of restoration, munificence, royalty, and mayoralty which, with those of the sea and shipping (reflecting Devitt's background) underpin the historical episodes. These themes echo aspects of the Exchange programme, but now, through Brangwyn's imagery, they are given a much tighter focus, reflecting the ideals of the Skinners' Company at one level, and at another, more subtle one, Brangwyn's own evolving philosophy of life. The theme of shared plenty and munificence, for example, can be followed from the green apples eaten by the early Skinners at Walbrook in *Pelts and Furs*, through those discarded half-eaten on the ground in the disruptive *Strife between Skinners and Merchant Taylors, 1483* (Plate XIII) to the golden, ripened apples at the magnificent banquet laid on for William and Mary, who 'restored' the companies' rights. The emblematic apples not only point to munificence in the sense of the Skinners' traditional charitable and beneficent role, but also adumbrate Brangwyn's celebration of man's shared enjoyment of the fruits of the earth in his British Empire panels for Westminster.

Although originally the Skinners considered a Tudor emphasis in their subjects, their ultimate choice gave greater prominence to medieval and Restoration episodes. Several of the subjects, such as the banquet for William and Mary, emphasize moments in the company's history when links with the monarchy and the government of the City were fostered. *Edward III granting the Charter 1327* partners *The Reception of General Monk at Skinners' Hall 1660* opposite, which marks the occasion when news was brought of the Restoration of the monarchy; whilst *Strife between Skinners and Merchant Taylors* illustrates the struggle between the two companies for precedence in the City's processions, which was resolved by the mayor. The Skinners' munificence, whether represented by the symbolic apples of Pilkington's Banquet, the 'Symbols of plenty'[92] carried on the Corpus Christi Festival car by boys in *City Pageant in Olden Times*, or the provision of education in *The Founding of Tonbridge School, 1553*, is perhaps the most insistent theme of all, and relates very closely to those of restoration, mayoralty, and river and shipping activity. In suggesting this relationship, floral and musical imagery plays a central role.

Musicians garlanded with flowers feature in both *A River Procession of the City's and Companies' Barges to Westminster AD 1453* and *City Pageant*. Like *The Reception of General Monk at Skinners' Hall, 1660* and *Pilkington's Banquet*, both these subjects continue the theme already prominent at the Exchange of the expression of the Corporation's and the companies' identity through traditional ceremonial. At Skinners' Hall, this probably received additional impetus from the recent accession of Edward VII, who, keen to revive the royal pageantry which had been neglected during Queen Victoria's widowhood, progressed through the City at his Coronation in 1902, when the Skinners decorated the exterior of their Hall. Despite its title, *River Procession* in fact appears to portray another royal progress—that down the river in 1662 of the new Queen Catherine of Braganza. Whilst this would not have been inappropriate to the Skinners' monarchist

[92] Draper, *Paintings*, p. 42.

sympathies (Brangwyn was asked, after all, to remove two armed Roundheads from his initial design for *General Monk*, thus playing down the Cromwellian association also avoided at the Exchange), Brangwyn was, of course, a Roman Catholic, and his preference for the subject perhaps reflects this. He had already included 'Queen Henrietta's Procession to Hampton Court' in his own early list of proposed subjects for the murals, echoing that of 'Queen Henrietta brought to London in the Royal Barge AD 1625' in the Skinners' own first plans. Although the Skinners eventually selected the 1453 'City and Companies' water procession topic, it is the 'antique-shap'd open Vessell, cover'd with a State or Canopy of Cloth of Gold, made in the forme of a Cupola, supported with high Corinthian pillars, Wreath'd with flowers' in which John Evelyn saw Catherine of Braganza in 1662, as well as the 'various inventions, musiq, and peales of ordinance' which accompanied her on the Thames, that are actually illustrated in Brangwyn's *River Procession*. This is confirmed by Draper's 1909 booklet, which associates Evelyn's account with the mural.[93]

Draper diplomatically suggests, however, that the painting is evocative, rather than strictly illustrative, of the 1453 procession which Brangwyn had been supposed to portray—'Mr. Brangwyn's panel takes us back . . . even past the "triumph" which Evelyn saw'[94]—but the musicians wearing floral garlands round their heads who, clearly in response to Evelyn's description, Brangwyn introduced in the immediate foreground of *River Procession*, operate as a subtle pointer to the larger symbolism of the scheme as a whole. A traditional element of the Skinners' historic ceremonial costume was a flower-garlanded 'crown'. This is worn by the Skinners in *City Pageant in Olden Times*, and it is what identifies this mural as an illustration of the annual Corpus Christi festival. It was on this occasion that the Masters and Wardens of the Company were elected in the 'ceremony of the cocks and caps'[95]—and when, therefore, the continuity of the company and its involvement in munificent provision, education, and welfare were vouchsafed. The 'cocks' are special drinking cups, and the 'caps' were a form of headgear around which flowers are thought to have been wound. Brangwyn also illustrates the flower-garlanded crown or 'cap' however, in other murals, in contexts when it would not normally have been worn, for example, in *The Founding of Tonbridge School*. The flower garlands worn by the musicians in *River Procession* are essentially a more generalized version of this crown, and they are also worn by the servants lifting the flagons and fruit in *Pilkington's Banquet*—those other emblems of munificence—as well as by the musicians in *City Pageant*. Here, a clue to the symbolic association in the murals of flowers, music, and munificence is offered by Draper's phrase 'Symbols of plenty', which refers to the musicians' instruments—bagpipes, cymbals, trumpet, and also lute. Just as the floral crown or garland is a leitmotif linking the different eras of the Skinners' history, so too is the lute, whose rounded shape complements the motifs of fruit and flagons. It is played in the barge at the left of *River Procession*, whilst it is also shown prominently in *Tonbridge School* as one of the gifts which, through the Skinners' charity, place 'the whole world'[96] at the feet of the boy

[93] Brangwyn's 'Henrietta' subject is in the list of 'Mr. Brangwyn's suggested subjects' (see n. 74 above); for the Skinners' 'Henrietta' proposal, see 'Subjects suggested for the decoration of the Skinners' Hall' (5 May 1902), SCA. For Evelyn's description, see *The Diary of John Evelyn*, ed. E. S. de Beer (Oxford, 1955), p. 333 (23 Aug. 1662). Brangwyn did in fact illustrate the Skinners' subject of *River Procession of the City's and Company's Barges 1453* in a small oil which is very similar to one of the murals in Brangwyn's preliminary watercolour scheme (see n. 73 above) and was presented to the Guildhall Art Gallery, London in 1908 (no. 861, catalogued as *The Lord Mayor's Show in Olden Days)*.

[94] Draper, *Paintings*, p. 25.

[95] See description of *City Pageant* in an anonymous booklet (*c.* 1909) in SCA about the Skinners' Hall murals 'by Frank Brangwyn'. It is not clear whether this attribution refers to text or paintings.

[96] Description of *Tonbridge School*, ibid.

receiving education, who cradles a globe.[97] Music is the central subject of *Harmony*, the one overtly allegorical mural in the scheme and the panel which, in its position above the gallery, forms the pivot of the typological arrangement of the historical scenes. Here, the female lutenist at the right and the men playing double basses at the left—suggesting harmonious union between the sexes—provide music for dancers seen within a fertile open landscape behind, with flowering wisteria now hanging above the musicians' heads, and a fruiting fig tree occupying the right-hand foreground. Though Brangwyn originally experimented with an alternative allegorical subject for this position, called *The Fruits of Industry*,[98] his eventual theme thus brings together the very motifs—musical instruments, flowers, and fruits—which recur throughout the scheme and interlink the various phases of the Skinners' history. Although Brangwyn's original *Fruits of Industry* design would have provided a climax to the apple sequence in the murals (it included a figure bearing a basket of fruit), his eventual *Harmony* design thus allowed a more comprehensive synthesis. Its fruit, flower, and musical leitmotifs focus the themes of restoration, munificence, and plenty but they also point to the wider one of brotherhood implicit in Brangwyn's foregrounding of the common man or woman, who, often partly cut off by the mural frame, seems even to encroach upon the viewer's space.

Brangwyn's 'organic' imagery of fruit and flowers can, of course, be compared with the dominance of nature as a general source of inspiration in Art Nouveau, but its association at Skinners' Hall with a cyclic view of past and present suggests that Brangwyn drew in particular on Siegfried Bing's 'understanding of historical time as governed by the eternal and essential forces of nature'.[99] Bing acted as an artistic adviser to the 'liberal' French government during the 1890s, when Brangwyn was decorating his Maison de l'Art Nouveau. Bing's vision of the artistic regeneration of modern France as an organic process, in which a new style would germinate, flower, and scatter its seed, and of nature as a power to 'eliminate social differences'[100] again suggest that the imagery Brangwyn devised for Skinners' Hall sought to move beyond the politics of the struggle for London to a more universalist ideal of community life, which, ironically, was in fact perhaps closer to the 'Socialism' of the hated LCC than to the conservatism of the City and the livery companies. Yet by 1915, when plans for the decoration of County Hall were being developed, a proposal from Brangwyn was turned down;[101] likewise, he was passed over by the new Liberal government at Westminster.[102] His name had become closely identified with the private and conservative interests of the City; his art, perhaps, was somehow too emotively compelling for a State and nation where the use of mural art as a form of propaganda was still far less familiar than on the Continent. It was still abroad, indeed, in the requests for the loan of his Skinners' panels, for example, from the organizers of the International Exhibitions in Dresden, Venice, and Paris of 1911, 1913, and 1914 respectively, that he continued to find much appreciation, whilst it was in America that he received his principal commissions from 1912 to 1915. Though the Skinners, not surprisingly in view of the London symbolism of their scheme, refused to lend their panels, they

[97] Another 'round' shape, the globe is a traditional emblem of omnipotence (cf. the sculpture of God the Father by Artus Quellin II in Bruges Cathedral, which Brangwyn would have known in childhood).

[98] P.w.u.; reproduced in H. Furst, *The Decorative Art of Frank Brangwyn* (1924) facing p. 1.

[99] Silverman, *Art Nouveau*, p. 185.

[100] Ibid.

[101] See Chapter 7.

[102] This was despite (or, given the desire at Westminster in the 20th century to 'improve' upon the effect at the Royal Exchange, perhaps because of) the information given to the Select Committee on the Palace of Westminster (7 Dec. 1906, § 983) by Sir John Watney, Clerk to the Gresham Committee, that his Committee had approved Devitt's choice of Brangwyn for his Exchange panel because 'We know all about Mr. Brangwin [*sic*]. He is an exceedingly good decorative artist.'

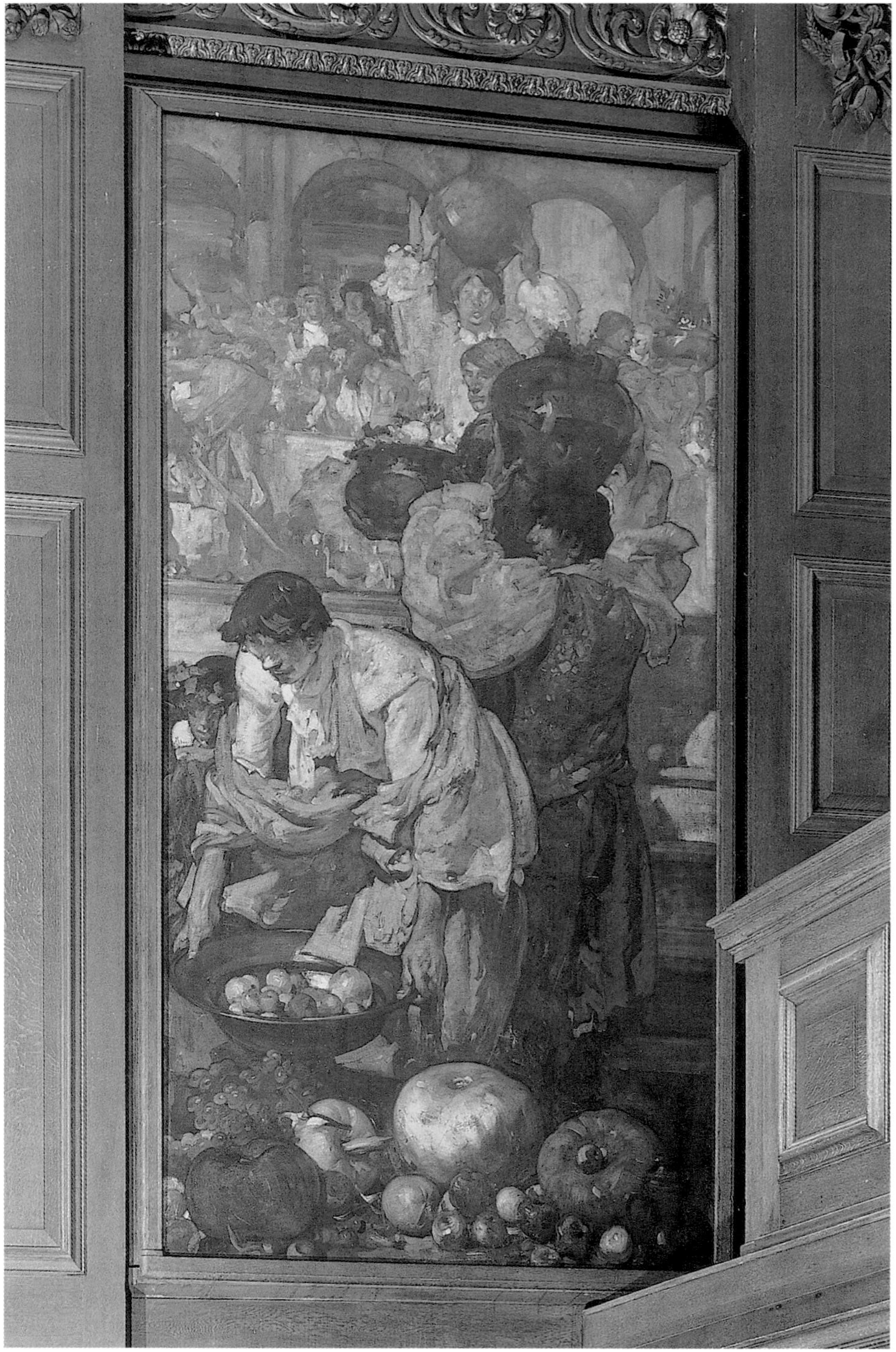

46. Sir Frank Brangwyn, *Lord Mayor Pilkington entertaining King William III and Queen Mary*, Banqueting Hall, Skinners' Hall, London, 1902–9

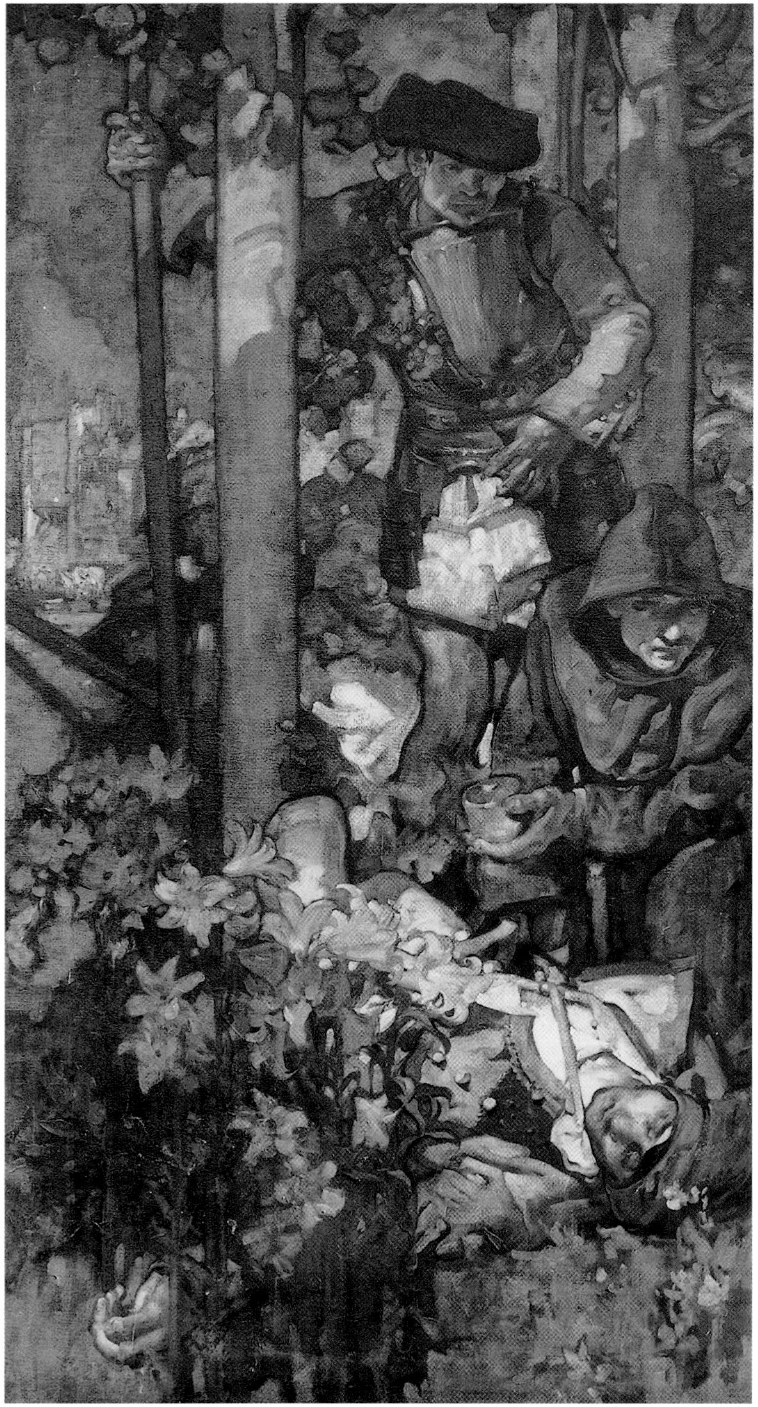

47. Sir Frank Brangwyn, *An Incident in the Defence of London Bridge by Sir Andrew Judd, AD 1554*, Banqueting Hall, Skinners' Hall, London, 1902–9

welcomed visitors to the murals. Amongst those at the unveiling ceremony was Brangwyn's friend, Sir Henry Newbolt, who in the 1920s was to advise on the St Stephen's Hall murals at Westminster, with their closely coordinated quest for stylistic harmony, but now in the very different idiom of the British School at Rome.

In 1929 it was in turn Colin Gill, one of the contributors to the St Stephen's Hall scheme, whom the Fishmongers' Company chose to decorate their newly remodelled Hall.[103] Although his four grisaille lunettes showing sea and river nymphs as part of H. S. Goodhart-Rendell's classical remodelling of the Hall were still essentially a continuation of the 'invention of tradition' seen in the earlier Royal Exchange and livery company schemes, their 'neoclassicism' now spoke of order and stability in times of growing economic depression. In a sense, the contemporary working clothes and almost Hogarthian sense of observed life in the *Education* and *Charity* (Plate 44) panels (the first showing an apprentice in a carpenter's shop and the second children caring for an old man) with which Brangwyn completed his Skinners' scheme a few years after, were more directly related to the reality of the age, but, of course, they still presented a world of manual rather than machine labour. The old man in *Charity* is the latter-day recipient of the succour given by man to his fellow man already portrayed in *An Incident in the Defence of London Bridge by Sir Andrew Judd, AD 1553* (Plate 47) in the earlier portion of the scheme, where a dying insurgent is cared for by his enemy, and where the origin of a similar episode in Brangwyn's first scheme for his later British Empire murals for Westminster can be identified.[104] The Skinners' Hall work had, in fact, enabled Brangwyn to develop a repertoire of symbolic motifs which not only project his personal ideals within the scheme itself, but also reverberate through his subsequent *oeuvre*. The pageant car and procession in *City Pageant*, for example, is the original model of the howdah motif later used in Brangwyn's decorations for the 1924 Wembley exhibition, and in his Westminster murals; the overtones of plenty and beneficence present in the servants bearing provisions in *Pilkington's Banquet* are carried forward into the religious context of Brangwyn's *Last Supper* stained-glass panel for Lord Iveagh at Dublin Cathedral in 1931–6, and are likewise reinterpreted in the native figures bearing the fruits of Empire in the panels Iveagh donated to the House of Lords. If the Royal Exchange and livery companies' patronage of mural painting in the late nineteenth and early twentieth centuries represents a landmark in the involvement of the fine as opposed to the trade artist in decoration in Britain, and in turn took the use of art for propaganda into a new phase of political urgency whose direct sequel lies in the revival of mural painting at Westminster from 1906, the contribution of Brangwyn is a distinctive and original achievement which asserted the identity of the individual artist as much as that of his patrons. Though Wyndham Lewis was to *Blast* Brangwyn in 1914, it was a sense of the artist's autonomy which, as we shall see in the context of private house and 'leisure' decoration (Chapters 10 and 11), underpinned the mural painting which he and other members of the so-called avant garde developed in the twentieth century. At Skinners Hall, however, the purposes of artist and patron reached a point of harmonious symbiosis which, by its very nature, was but rarely achieved, and which stands out in the history of mural painting from 1840 to 1940 as one of its great moments.

[103] See C. Barham, 'The City Halls of London Fishmongers' Hall', *Country Life* (19 Jan. 1929), pp. 82–90.

[104] See Chapter 6; the motif and composition of the *Defence of London Bridge* mural were perhaps derived from W. Shakespeare Burton's *Wounded Cavalier* (*c.* 1856; Guildhall Art Gallery, London).

4

Pictures and Politics: State Patronage at the Palace of Westminster, 1906–1913

East Corridor and First Scheme for St Stephen's Hall

If the nineteenth-century murals at Westminster were essentially the fruits of a German mode of patronage, in which royal initiative was the motive force, by 1906 very different exemplars and attitudes lay behind the establishment of a Select Committee 'to enquire and report with respect to the unfinished condition of the rooms of the Palace of Westminster appropriate to the Service of this House'.[1] For one, it was to report to the House of Commons; for another, it took a distinctive position, now that Queen Victoria was dead, of strict, albeit respectful independence from royal involvement:

> [It was] at first intended that Earl Stanhope should fill the post which the Prince's death had vacated, but it was found that such a course would be repugnant to the feelings of Her Late Majesty, who not unnaturally shrank from seeing another occupy the place which Her Illustrious Consort had so long and so successfully filled.[2]

Instead of operating under the direction of a member or representative of the Royal Family, the artists who were chosen to revive decoration at Westminster were instead made answerable to the First Commissioner of Works, Lewis Harcourt, MP, with Lord Carlisle, the amateur artist and patron of Morris and Burne-Jones, as his nominal artistic adviser. This was because the landslide Liberal government, which came to power in 1906, just before the Select Committee produced its report the following year, had seized eagerly on its proposals that decoration at Westminster be restarted in the East Corridor as one of the most frequented parts of the building, 'through which many menbers of the public pass in daytime, when Parliament is sitting, on their way to the Committee Rooms upstairs'.[3] Where Prince Albert had concentrated on the House of Lords and the 'royal' parts of the Palace, the focus in the early twentieth century was very firmly to be on the parts most tangibly associated with the 'voice of the people' in the government of their country, and since the East Corridor was part of the House of Commons, any matters to do with its fabric were technically the responsibility of the First Commissioner of Works.

[1] Motion of Lord Stanmore to the House of Lords (19 July 1906).

[2] Draft Report of the SCPW (1907), CHA, J22/84.

[3] Anon. booklet, *The Decoration of the Houses of Parliament* (1910), p. 8.

Harcourt's responsibilities were indeed considerable in respect of the new mural project. When the Select Committee published its report in 1907, after almost two years of intensive questioning of a range of witnesses, from the President of the Royal Academy, Sir Edward Poynter, to John Singer Sargent, W. R. Lethaby, William Holman Hunt, and Edwin Abbey, he had written to its chairman, Lord Stanmore, to disagree strongly 'with the idea of my having a Council of Advice. My experience is that Advisory Committees seldom do anything and that what they do is almost invariably a compromise and certainly wrong,'[4] and in the event it was decided that he should be the virtual director of the mural scheme. If Albert's had been the controlling voice in the 1840s, then it was thus still one man who held effective power in the 1900s, but a man, as we shall see, with very different purposes. Harcourt announced:

> I have the authority of the Cabinet to accept with much gratitude the offer of private donors of pictures for all or any of the vacant wall spaces in the Small Corridor leading from the Central Lobby of the Houses of Parliament [i.e. the East Corridor] and I am authorised to settle the proper subjects for these pictures in consultation with the donors and any others whose advice I may wish to take . . . It was also agreed that the donors should select their own artists subject of course to my approval on behalf of the Government.[5]

This model was clearly no longer to be the kind of direct State intervention in the arts so eagerly called for by Haydon and his Romantic contemporaries at the start of the nineteenth century, and attempted through the controversial vote of money by Parliament in the 1840s and 1850s for what was effectively Albert's project, but instead the type of private support for mural painting pioneered by the donor system at the Royal Exchange in the previous decade. Much interest had been taken in this by the members of the 1906–7 Select Committee, and although it had recommended that the £4,000 allocated annually by the Commons to Albert's Royal Commission should be continued, Harcourt, acting on behalf of the Prime Minister, Sir Henry Campbell Bannerman, now quietly dropped this system and pursued the Committee's alternative recommendation that 'every effort should be made to encourage the defrayal of works from private sources.'[6]

Harcourt had been responsible for introducing in 1906 the Plural Voting Bill, which aimed to undermine the Conservative majority in the House of Lords. This had the result during the period 1906–10, when the murals were being painted, of Campbell Bannerman and his successor, H. H. Asquith, creating a large number of new Liberal peers, whose influence, it was hoped, would facilitate acceptance in the House of Lords of the battery of new radical legislation which the Liberal government wished to institute. One of the main objectives of the new Liberal government was in fact the reform of the Tory-dominated Lords, and particularly its power of veto, which of course threatened Liberal bills. There is evidence to suggest that Harcourt was most anxious to obtain uniformity of style in the new murals—something widely felt to be lacking at the Royal Exchange—and in turn to use both this and their iconography for political purposes. He told Lord Carlisle, himself a Liberal sympathizer, 'I have personally written to three of our Liberal Peers whom I may be able to persuade to become donors,'[7] and his tongue-in-cheek complaint in 1910 about the inefficiency of the hereditary system clearly reveals his political outlook: 'When the House of Lords is properly abolished and we are no longer bothered by Belted Earls, these things

4 Letter from Harcourt to Stanmore (23 July 1907), HA.
5 Letter from Harcourt to Carlisle (21 May 1908), HA.
6 *Report* of the SCPW, *House of Lords Journal* (10 July 1907).
7 Letter from Harcourt to Carlisle (19 June 1908), CHA, J22/84.

will be properly managed under the direction of your unrepentant friend, Loulou'[8] (this was his pet name).

Although ostensibly paid for by private rather than State finance, the East Corridor murals (Plates XIV, XV, 48–50) were thus as political in character as those promoted by Prince Albert had been Peelite and royal. Of the donors, Lord Stanmore was the only Conservative, but his inclusion was only natural, given his enthusiasm for the revival of the Westminster decoration and his leadership of the original Select Committee; the others were Carlisle himself; and Lords Airedale, President of the National Liberal Foundation; Wandsworth, President of the London and Home Counties Radical Union; Winterstoke, one of the 'new' peers; and Beauchamp, a dedicated convert to Liberalism who later became Leader in the Lords and First Commissioner of Works, with responsibility for the mural scheme launched in succession to the East Corridor, in St Stephen's Hall.

A comment by Lord Carlisle to Harcourt that in offering his panel, 'the choice of the painter and of the subject would be subject to your approval,'[9] reinforces the evidence that despite an earlier admission on the part of Harcourt of artistic ignorance,[10] it was he who ultimately determined not only the iconographical, but also the artistic character of the murals. In practice, therefore, just as competitions had been held in the nineteenth century, but Albert's choice of Dyce had held ultimate sway, so now in 1907–8, when the quest for artists began, it was a highly individual decision which was made. This was despite the fact that thirteen out of the sixteen artist and architect witnesses to the 1906 Select Committee had preferred the Continental norm of selection by competition—an intriguing *volte-face* of artistic attitude, when compared with the feeling *against* competition voiced by artist witnesses to the 1842 Committee, and one which was probably influenced by new awareness of the highly developed systems of competition in the German and French town halls by the turn of the century.

Harcourt does not seem to have sought out artists with particular political sympathies. Rather, he took steps to promote what might, within the limited terms of officially acceptable figurative art in Britain at the time, be termed a 'radical' school to match the 'reformist' purposes of his own party:

> In order that some common decision may be come to as to the scale, colour and medium and in order that the general treatment shall be harmonious and avoid the divergence of style which appears in the Royal Exchange, Mr. Abbey has kindly consented to advise me and assist the artists in arriving at a general scheme.[11]

Edwin Abbey, who was Visitor at the Royal Academy of Arts, was a close friend of Lord Carlisle, and had been commissioned in 1901 to paint the Coronation of King Edward VII, a task in which two RA pupils, Frank Cadogan Cowper and Ernest Board, had helped him. With Frank Salisbury, Denis Eden, Henry Payne, and John Byam Shaw, these young artists formed a distinctive group in early twentieth-century British art which Abbey himself labelled 'Primitif'[12] and which was dubbed 'Neo-Pre-Raphaelite' by the German critic Hermann Muthesius. The germ of this grouping had first emerged in mural work through Abbey's and Salisbury's contributions to the Royal

[8] Letter from Harcourt to Carlisle (14 July 1910), CHA, J22/84.

[9] Letter from Carlisle to Harcourt (17 May 1908), CHA, J22/84.

[10] Harcourt in *Minutes of Evidence taken before the SCPW* (19 March 1907), § 1203 and 1204 (published in *Proceedings of the Lords Present, and Minutes of the Proceedings at Each Sitting*, Palace of Westminster, London, 1906–7).

[11] Letter from Harcourt to Solomon (24 July 1908), HA.

[12] Letter from Abbey to Carlisle (17 July 1908), CHA, J22/84.

Exchange (Plate 35; Plate V). Together with Brangwyn and Gerald Moira, Muthesius saw the 'Neo-Pre-Raphaelites', who were struggling to break free of Royal Academy traditions, as the most promising hope for a revival of decorative art in Britain.[13] Normally using the more reliable marouflaged oil on canvas in place of Albert's fresco, their style had close affinities with the 'Birmingham School' of decorative art led by Joseph Southall, and Henry Payne had in fact already contributed to the Liberal-backed Birmingham Town Hall mural scheme,[14] as well as carrying out the decoration of the private chapel at Madresfield Court in Worcestershire of Lord Beauchamp, his donor at Westminster.[15] Apart from Abbey and Salisbury, he was the only one of the group to have had any prior mural experience, and Abbey, not surprisingly, soon complained that his artists were 'difficult cattle to drive in a team'.[16] He imposed common adherence to a red, gold, and black colour-scheme and stipulated that 'the foreground men must be 5ft.6in. high—and the horizon line 4 ft. from the ground line—and the V.P. in the centre . . . and local colour shapes rather than light and shade shapes'[17]—an evident attempt to enforce the kind of ground rules which had initially ensured harmony at the Royal Exchange, but which had been so dramatically broken there. In the East Corridor remarkable homogeneity was in fact achieved, with Eden's quasi-heraldic *John Cabot and his Sons receive the Charter from Henry VII to sail in Search of New Lands 1496* (Plate 48) being the only departure from the more realistically envisaged historical approach of the other murals. Even this panel, however, preserves the high tonality, realism of portraiture, and shallow picture space which characterize the other pictures, and Abbey seems to have imposed a number of compositional alterations on the artists' original sketches to ensure visual balance in the figural gestures of the murals either side of *Cabot*, which is thereby cleverly framed at the centre of one of the corridor walls.

It is questionable, in fact, whether the artists ever fully appreciated the political purposes of their patrons. Payne wrote somewhat plaintively to Lord Carlisle after he had completed his mural (Plate XIV) 'Could you tell me what was really meant by the title of the "Origin of Parties"?'[18] In order to see more clearly why the 'Neo-Pre-Raphaelite' style should have appealed so strongly to Harcourt and his donors, we need to consider the significance of the subjects which were finally selected for the artists to illustrate, after much deliberation on the part of Harcourt and his advisers.

In questioning the witnesses to the Select Committee in 1906–7, Stanmore won approval for his suggestion that 'if we had pictures of Queen Elizabeth and costumes of her age, it would form an interesting history, would it not'[19] because it was felt to offer greater visual appeal than modern alternatives such as 'jubilees and coronations'. Seymour Lucas, one of the several Royal Exchange artists to be questioned, felt these were undesirable because 'we have our newspapers nowadays which will give us all that information.'[20] The result of the Committee's enquiries, however, was a recommendation that the iconography already laid down in Prince Albert's scheme should be adopted, even though Stanmore privately expressed a preference for 'more modern subjects', perhaps indicating a sympathy with what turned out to be Harcourt's purposes. Albert's Commission had envisaged for the East Corridor a programme of six paired subjects, in three of which

[13] See H. Muthesius, 'Kunst and Leben in England', *Zeitschrift für bildende Kunst*, 13 (1902), especially p. 69.
[14] See Chapter 7.
[15] See Chapter 8.
[16] Letter from Abbey to Carlisle (10 Oct. 1910), CHA, J22/84.
[17] Letter from Abbey to Carlisle (10 Nov. 1908), CHA, J22/84. Each mural is 2.06 × 2.11m in size, and is painted on canvas on wood.
[18] Letter from Payne to Carlisle (27 Oct. 1910), CHA, J22/84.
[19] Stanmore in *Minutes of Evidence* (see n. 10), (3 Dec. 1906) § 484.
[20] Seymour Lucas in ibid. (3 Dec. 1906), § 485.

48. Denis W. Eden, *John Cabot and his Sons receive the Charter from Henry VII to sail in Search of New Lands 1496*, East Corridor, Palace of Westminster, London, 1908–10. Presented by Lord Winterstoke

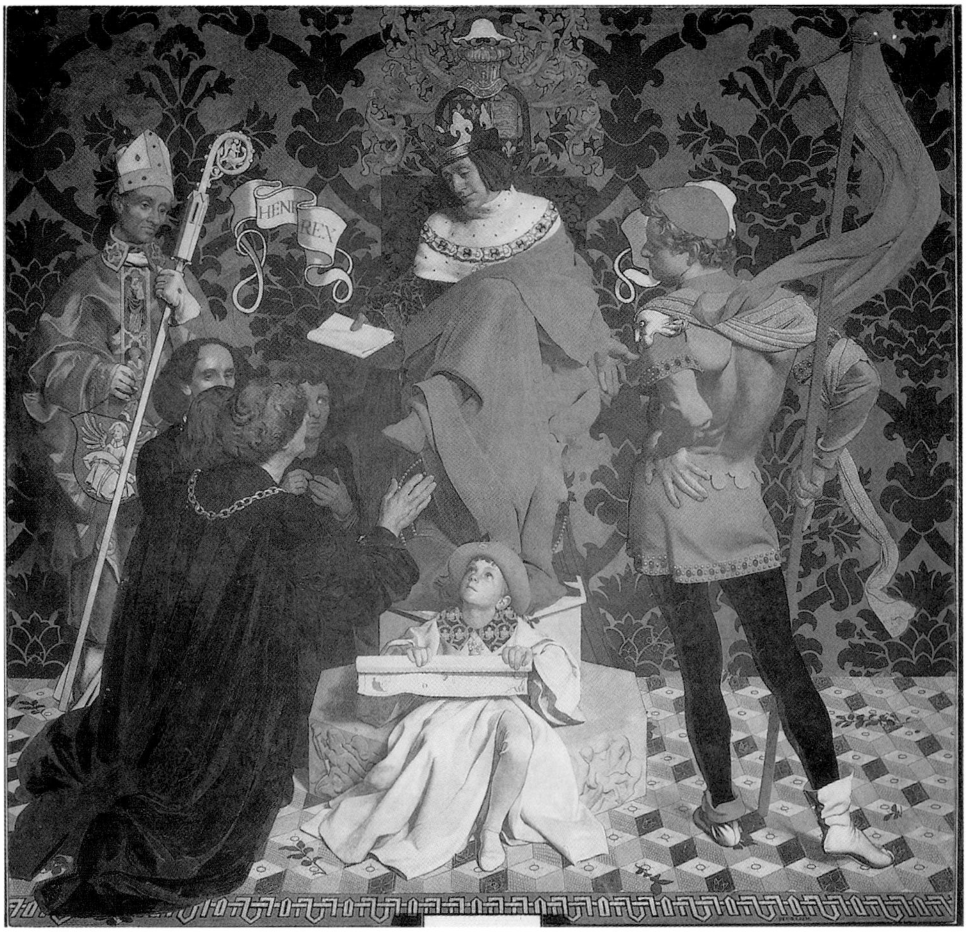

49. Frank Cadogan Cowper, *Erasmus and Thomas More visit the Children of Henry VII at Greenwich 1499*, East Corridor, Palace of Westminster, London, 1908–10. Presented by Lord Carlisle

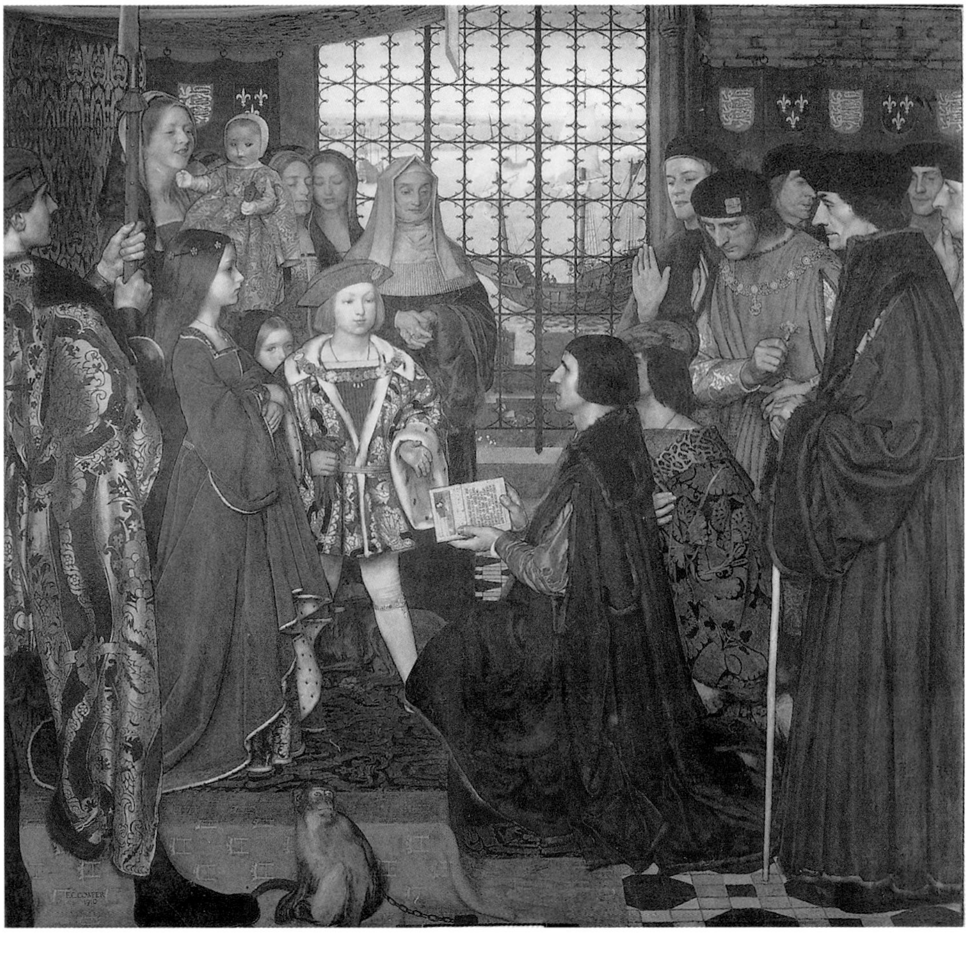

'Britain appears sunk in ignorance, heathen superstition and slavery; in the other three, she appears instructing the savage, abolishing barbarous rites, and liberating the slave,'[21] but Carlisle and Harcourt came to the conclusion that historical subjects 'of a somewhat similar character'[22] to those already in the other corridors leading off the Central Lobby would be desirable, and Tudor themes were selected as the natural complement to Cope's and Ward's Stuart panels in these (Plate IV; Plate 28). This choice fulfilled Carlisle's ideal that the murals should combine 'the picturesque with some important historical or social movement',[23] but it overlooked the fact that there was already extensive Tudor illustration in both Burchett's portrait murals and the bronze bas reliefs of sixteenth-century subjects carried out by William Theed in the Prince's Chamber of the House of Lords in the 1850s, and more subtle reasons can be found for the titles eventually determined.

If Carlisle was principally motivated by his taste for Morris and Burne-Jones, whose creation at Kelmscott of a 'heaven on earth, an old Elizabethan house'[24] was a retreat from modern society, Harcourt turned to a range of advisers whose Tudor subject proposals supplied extremely precise modern references. Prime amongst these were Lord Morley, one of Asquith's new peers and responsible for reading the Bill which stated that, if necessary, King George V would create new peers to restrict the Conservative domination of the House of Lords; and the budding young historian, George Macaulay Trevelyan.

A Liberal sympathizer, Trevelyan was the great-nephew of the Whig historian Thomas Babington Macaulay, who had been on Albert's Royal Fine Arts Commission, but whose voice had been somewhat overruled by its pro-monarchical elements. Through Trevelyan's suggestions for the East Corridor and their application by Harcourt, a new direction was given to Macaulay's conception of history as an attempt to understand the past for the sake of the present.[25] His approach harmonized perfectly with the choice of the East Corridor for the revival of decoration because it was the part of Westminster most frequented by the public. Later to write the *English Social History* (eventually the *Illustrated English Social History*), with its aim of evoking in vivid terms the everyday life and character of the past, Trevelyan was already pleading for an appreciation of the educational value of history and a return to the narrative and literary styles of Scott, Macaulay, and Carlyle, who could make history 'come alive' for the common man. Reacting to the 'scientific' view of history as calculable cause and effect,[26] he argued that to convey the significance of past events to modern man, the historian must write 'living, many-coloured and romantic' history.[27]

The episodes selected by Harcourt for the East Corridor were based on accounts by historians whom Trevelyan regarded as 'literary'—the late nineteenth-century writers J. A. Froude and Mandell Creighton, and the incumbent of the new chair of constitutional history at University College London, and Liberal sympathizer, A. F. Pollard—and also on episodes in Shakespeare's *Henry VII* and *Henry VIII*. They narrate the story of the Reformation, which Creighton felt was the period when

> for the first time did they [the English] fully appreciate the benefits of their geographical position, and set to work to make the most of them. Commerce, industry, seamanship, adventure, all assumed those

[21] *Seventh Report* of the CFA (1847), PP XXXIII, p. 11.

[22] Letter from Carlisle to Harcourt (17 May 1908), CHA, J22/84.

[23] Letter from Carlisle to Harcourt (20 June 1908 (?)), HA.

[24] Letter from W. Morris to C. J. Faulkner (17 May 1871), quoted in *The Letters of William Morris to his Family and Friends*, ed. P. Henderson (London, 1950), p. 41.

[25] See 'Introduction' to Macaulay's *History of England*, ed. H. Trevor-Roper (Harmondsworth, 1967).

[26] J. R. Seeley was one of those seeking to develop a more 'scientific' approach to the interpretation of the past.

[27] G. M. Trevelyan, *Clio a Muse and other Essays Literary and Pedestrian* (London, 1913), p. 39.

forms with which we have ever since been familiar. The modern Englishman came into definite existence.[28]

With Henry VIII as its figurehead (in the murals he symbolically occupies the central place of the sequence) the Reformation period was felt by Froude to have shaped national identity, above all through its break with Rome. He was one of the first to reappraise Henry VIII, seen by Dickens as 'a spot of blood and grease': 'what manner of man Henry was, and what the statesman and churchmen were who stood by him and assisted him in reshaping the English constitution, becomes a practical question of our own time.'[29] It was precisely the 'reshaping of the English constitution' which the Liberals so keenly sought in 1906–10.

A descriptive booklet by Sir Martin Conway, the art critic, which was published in conjunction with the unveiling of the murals in 1910, and various papers filed with the official records of the commission, reveal the significance of the murals in this context. *Plucking the Red and White Roses* (Plate XIV), for example, the first mural (by Henry Payne) was an illustration of Shakespeare, but also the event which ushered in the Tudor dynasty, 'the old nobility of England [having] exterminated themselves and exhausted the country, which was once more glad to be under the rule of a strong monarch'.[30] Hence its subtitle, which puzzled Payne, 'The Origin of Parties', for the Wars of the Roses had led to the emergence of 'modern' political structures, and just as Henry VI had been a 'strong monarch', so it was to George V that the Liberals looked when he agreed in 1910 to create a hundred new non-hereditary peers, if necessary, to secure the reform of the Lords' powers.

Denis Eden's *John Cabot and his Sons receive the Charter from Henry VII to sail in Search of New Lands 1496* celebrates Reformation seapower, which Froude felt underpinned the modern British Empire; it was donated by Lord Winterstoke, who not only had a personal link with Cabot in that both were Bristolians, but was also, with Harcourt, a key advocate of the Liberal policy of Free Trade. Harcourt himself was additionally urging the strengthening of Britain's naval defence power at the period of the murals[31] and was responsible for introducing Winterstoke's mural when Carlisle felt that an offer by Lord Swaythling of *The Commons Petitioning Queen Elizabeth to Marry* by Solomon J. Solomon would not harmonize in style with the other planned murals. The latter was eventually placed over the stair at the end of the East Corridor, discreetly separated from the main sequence. Its style is not in fact dissimilar to the other murals (Solomon was selected by Swaythling because he 'did a panel for me at the Royal Exchange which was very satisfactory',[32] but the subject was, of course, one where the Commons did not achieve success, and it is possible also that its Jewish donor and artist were not felt to be compatible with the predominant correspondence between Tudor religious and modern political 'reformation' in the mural symbolism. *Cabot* was moreover a particularly topical subject in 1907 since Newfoundland, which he discovered, was given Dominion status at the Imperial Conference of that year; Sir Martin Conway described it as 'the first stone . . . of our Colonial Empire'.[33] Eden was directed to base his picture on the account of the episode by H. F. Wilson, Joseph Chamberlain's private

[28] M. Creighton, *The English National Character*, Romanes Lecture, Sheldonian Theatre, Oxford (17 June 1896).

[29] J. A. Froude, *The Divorce of Catherine of Aragon The Story as told by the Imperial Ambassadors resident at the Court of Henry VIII.* Supplementary volume to the *History of England* (London, 1891), p. 3.

[30] Typed description of the episode filed with letter from Payne to Carlisle (27 Oct. 1910), CHA, J22/84.

[31] e.g. in Harcourt's speech to the constituents in Rossendale Division at Crawshawbooth, as reported in *The Times* (3 Oct. 1908): 'We depended for the defence of our country and our homes on the command of the sea.'

[32] Letter from Swaythling to Harcourt (2 July 1908), HA.

[33] W. M. Conway, *The Historical Paintings in the Houses of Parliament* (1911), p. 11.

secretary in the Colonial Office, and the mural was clearly intended to suggest the Liberals' role in creating the modern Empire.

The third panel illustrates Froude's belief that the origin of modern England could best be seen 'through the eyes of Erasmus'.[34] Painted by Frank Cadogan Cowper and donated by Lord Carlisle himself, it is *Erasmus and Thomas More visit the Children of Henry VII at Greenwich* (Plate 49). Its place within the larger evolution of the Reformation is graphically conveyed in the way the nine-year-old prince receiving Erasmus is echoed with the effect of a zoom lens in the next panel of Henry VIII's break with Rome, where Henry is juxtaposed with the kneeling Catherine of Aragon (Plate 50); further evidence, no doubt, of Abbey's coordinating hand. The mural's subtitle of *The New Learning* points specifically to the Liberals' concern with universal education, regardless of religious persuasion. This was focused in the 1906 Education Bill, whose rejection by the Lords had been the principal incentive for the move to reform the Lords.

The central Henry VIII subject by Salisbury (Plate 50), which follows, shows the trial of Queen Catherine which initiated 'the breach with Rome'; Conway's booklet argues 'this breach was not religious but purely political.'[35] The distinctive association between Liberalism and Nonconformity is continued in Ernest Board's *Latimer Preaching at Paul's Cross*, whilst the final panel, *Mary Tudor entering London* (Plate XV), by John Byam Shaw, illustrates an incident of religious toleration. Concern with laws on marriage and divorce led to a Royal Commission in 1909, which cited Henry's divorce as the earliest legislation in Britain. Lord Stanmore, who gave the panel and chose its title, was portrayed by Salisbury as the bishop to the right of Wolsey, thus making a very direct allusion to the Froudian view of Henry as 'assisted' by the 'statesmen and churchmen . . . who stood by him' in his reform of the English constitution. The Latimer subject meanwhile draws attention to current Liberal concerns both with education and with helping the poor by means of Free Trade price reductions: Latimer's subject was the 'break-down of any system of poor relief' and a situation where 'education was sadly hampered.'[36]

With such clear allusions to contemporary politics, it is hardly surprising that Harcourt imposed strict secrecy on the murals' progress until their unveiling:

> What I realise and which the artists do not is that if any of these sketches are shown there will be a demand from M.Ps. that designs for all the frescoes shall be exhibited in the tearoom of the House of Commons before the work is completed or accepted. If this happens all the Philistines and others would descend upon my devoted head with the probable result that I should be forbidden to accept or erect any of the frescoes which have been so generously offered through me to the Houses of Parliament.[37]

His approach, however, so different from the deliberate cultivation of a 'democratic' image by the Royal Fine Arts Commission through its vast public exhibitions of mural sketches in the 1840s, perhaps backfired. Harcourt was much disappointed when the murals were still incomplete at Christmas 1909, probably because of the impending General Election of January 1910. When they were unveiled later in 1910, their symbolism seems to have gone largely unremarked by the critics, with the exception of the single suggestive headline in the *Illustrated London News* of 'Coals of

[34] J. A. Froude, *Life and Letters of Erasmus*, Lectures delivered at Oxford 1893–4 (London, 1894), p. 431.

[35] Conway, *Historical Paintings*, p. 13.

[36] Ibid., p. 5.

[37] Letter from Harcourt to Stanmore (23 March 1909), HA.

Fire! Gifts from Lords to the Commons',[38] which did not attempt to discover detailed significance in the actual subjects.

The fact was that the British were still largely unaccustomed to propagandist purposes in mural art. The Royal Exchange, Skinners' Hall, and several of the town halls, such as Manchester, Rochdale, and to some extent Birmingham, had experimented with the use of history for 'modern' goals, but none of these schemes had involved such close control over the endeavours of its artists as appears to have happened in the East Corridor. The symbolism in the earliest murals at Westminster in the 1840s and 1850s was perhaps only partly successful: Prince Albert's choice of subjects had been diluted by the Commission and his symbolic conception sabotaged by a technical fiasco. In many ways what was being attempted in 1906–10 in the East Corridor finds its closest counterpart in the use of historical episodes for specific contemporary references by many of the post-unification German town halls, or in the illustration at the Berlin Reichstag in the 1900s of the Battle of Sedan, where the French flag was explicitly portrayed being dragged through the mud, so provoking apoplexy in Franco-German diplomatic circles. The employment at Westminster in 1906–10 of the 'Abbey School' also finds parallels in the deliberate revival in Germany and Austria at the same period of the style of the 'Dürerzeit' for nationalistic, if not party political purposes, by such as the Hagenbund and the Klimt-Matsch decorative partnership. A parallel symbolic revival of fifteenth- and sixteenth-century styles also took place in *fin-de-siècle* Belgium. Salisbury, for example, had made a special study of the 'Cologne Primitives'. The frozen, angular postures of his Queen Catherine and Henry VIII, and especially Catherine's stiffly convulsed fingers, with which he experimented in sketches to achieve the right degree of expression,[39] are derived from artists such as Rogier van der Weyden or Memling, whose work he saw in Frankfurt when visiting his brother who lived there. Although his motif of a kneeling figure before a seated church leader was adapted from Tiepolo[40] and Cadogan Cowper quotes from Raphael's *Miracle of the Mass at Bolsena* (Vatican, Rome)[41] in his figure of Sir Thomas More, the principal inspiration for the murals is the art of Holbein, Dürer, and work of the early German, Flemish, and Tudor periods, which Lord Carlisle, who collected such art himself, encouraged the East Corridor team to study in the London exhibitions of 1906–7.[42] A reference scrapbook assembled by Payne includes reproductions of Dürer and other German woodcuts whose idiom finds an echo in the flattened picture space of *Plucking the Red and White Roses*, whilst Byam Shaw decorated his studio walls with reproductions including Holbein's *Duchess of Milan* (National Gallery, London) and Van Eyck's drawing of St Barbara (Koninklij Museum voor Schone Kunsten, Antwerp). Such enthusiasms, of course, reflect an awakening appreciation of the decorative qualities of Holbein's *Ambassadors*, acquired by the National Gallery in 1901, as well as W. R. Lethaby's advocacy, as a reaction against the High Victorian obsession with the classical, of Holbein and Van Eyck as new sources for the modern artist.[43] As a 'progressive' choice by a

[38] 'Coals of Fire! Gifts from Lords to the Commons', *Illustrated London News* (5 Nov. 1910); the date of this article (Guy Fawkes Night) would of course have added a further critical innuendo.

[39] These sketches were amongst a file of preparatory work by Salisbury for his East Corridor mural which was sold at Christie's, London (25 Sept. 1985).

[40] Cf. Tiepolo's *Marriage of Barbarossa* fresco in the Kaisersaal at the Residenz, Würzburg, which was copied by Salisbury in one of the Christie's sketches.

[41] Cowper had visited Italy in 1903.

[42] See letter from Cowper to Carlisle (29 April 1909), CHA, J22/84, thanking him for an invitation to the *Early English Portraiture* exhibition at the Burlington Fine Arts Club; other relevant exhibitions which the East Corridor artists could have seen in London include those of *Early Flemish Art* (Guildhall) and *Early German Art* (Prince's Gallery) (both 1906).

[43] See W. R. Lethaby, *The Study and Practice of Artistic Crafts*, Address delivered to the students of the Birmingham Municipal School of Art (15 Feb. 1901) (London and Birmingham, 1901), p. 11.

type of patron who, by definition, is unlikely to espouse the extreme avant-garde, the commissioning of the 'Abbey School' by Harcourt may be compared with the deliberate employment of the innovatory Secessionists in Austria in 1900–4 by the Culture Minister, Dr Koerber, as a symbol of his government's modernization policies.

The style of the East Corridor murals is in fact a complex amalgam of the 'decorative and ornamental' admired by Lethaby in early German art with both highly realistic and psychologically suggestive elements. The artists wanted 'that little corridor to look like a richly gilded and painted and mediaeval casket or shrine, of which the historical wall paintings were intended to be part of the decoration,'[44] and Muthesius had identified the goals of the 'Abbey School' as 'primarily of a decorative nature . . . in the matter of colour they strive for a rich, dense carpet effect,'[45] but it was perhaps their ability to lend the aura of actuality to the past which appealed most to their patrons, seeking to embody Trevelyan's 'living, many coloured and romantic history'. Making the past appear credible was in the essence of Harcourt's purpose, very much as it had also been for the patrons at the Royal Exchange, despite their different politics. If the modern citizen of Britain passing through the East Corridor could recognize himself in the scenes of Reformation history, their message would be clear, and Harcourt forbade the embellishment of the corridor envisaged by the artists, who were clearly aiming at the kind of *Gesamtkunstwerk* achieved by Payne at Madresfield Chapel. An excess of decoration might well have distracted from the symbolic message, and Abbey's scrupulousness in historical authenticity—he drew in his own art on a vast reference collection of 'tapestries . . . arms and armour, etc . . . chests of drawers full of superbly designed materials—velvets, brocades and silks of various periods and special manufacture'[46]—must have been a major reason why he was asked to coordinate the artists.

The artists, however, were also exploring realms beyond the literal re-creation of history, just as they yearned for a more strongly decorative impact, and the results can be regarded as some of the most successful mural painting of the entire 1840–1940 period in Britain. Salisbury, Board, and Byam Shaw all based key historical figures in their murals on authentic period portraits,[47] whilst Payne set his Tudors and Lancastrians in the real garden, filled with identifiable old English flowers and plants, of his own house at Amberley in Gloucestershire. The sharply characterized crowd of ordinary people, modelled on his friends and family, in Shaw's *Entry of Mary*, and the re-creation of the half-timbered city setting are also comparable with the realistic historicism of Continental murals such as Ernst Klimt's *Hans Wurst at the Jahrmarkt* in the Vienna Burgtheater (Plate 51) and Tattegrain's *Entry of Louis XI into Paris* in the Hôtel de Ville in Paris (Plate 37). The figural postures, for example, are often symbolic rather than merely 'Tudric' in the manner of the popular Elizabethan pageants and Liberty designs of the period.

The starkly outstretched arm of the Duke of York at the left of Payne's *Plucking the Red and White Roses* and the tiny distant figures seen through the garden gateway, derive from the semi-decorative panel of *Beauty receiving the White Rose from her Father* (1898–9, Birmingham Art

[44] Cowper, quoted in E. V. Lucas, *Edwin Austin Abbey, Royal Academician: A Record of his Life and Work* (London, 1921), pp. 461–2.

[45] '[Die Ziele dieser Schule sind] in allererster Linie . . . dekorativer Art . . . In der Farbe wird eine reiche satte Teppichwirkung angestrebt', Muthesius, 'Kunst und Leben' (1902), p. 66.

[46] M. H. Spielmann, 'Edwin Austin Abbey RA', *Magazine of Art* (1899), p. 196.

[47] e.g. Wolsey in Salisbury's mural is based on the portrait in Christ Church, Oxford (a photograph of this was amongst Christie's preparatory material (see n. 39 above)) and his Queen Catherine derives from other Christie's sketches which Salisbury made of Holbein's miniature of her in the Horace Walpole Collection at the British Museum; Board's Edward VI is based on Scrotes's profile portrait in the National Gallery, and Byam Shaw's of Elizabeth I on the portrait of her as a young queen in the Royal Collection (artist unknown).

Gallery) by Payne's mentor Southall, but they introduce a new, strongly dramatic sense. This drama is also very evident in the curious spatial estrangement of the protagonists in Board's *Latimer* mural, where Latimer is relegated to the extreme left, and his portrait source in a picture by Guillim Scrotes manipulated to a sharp profile, so as to counterpoise the figure of Edward at the right. Such 'theatrical' gestures perhaps reflect familiarity with the typically dramatic arrangements of Jean-Paul Laurens's historical panels in the Paris Hôtel de Ville.[48] There was, however, a very tangible theatrical element in Salisbury's mural, for it followed Sir Henry Irving's Lyceum Theatre production of Shakespeare's *Henry VIII* in placing the Cardinals at the centre back and Henry at the left, rather than the arrangement already in use in a painting of *The Trial of Queen Catherine* by Abbey himself, which had more literally illustrated the account of the episode given in both Shakespeare and Cavendish's *Life of Wolsey*.[49] Not only Salisbury and Abbey but also Byam Shaw were involved in designs for Shakespeare's plays and historical pageants; several of these pageants were mounted by the Liberals.[50]

Three of the East Corridor murals illustrated Shakespearean subjects, and the scheme can be seen as contributing on the one hand to a quest on the part of the Liberals for a national cultural identity (in 1908 they also strongly supported Harley Granville Barker's plans for a National Theatre, for example)[51] and on the other to the development of distinctive new trends in theatrical production in the early twentieth century. For just as Trevelyan aimed to write 'living history', so Irving conceived of the theatre as something with psychological force, 'a living power, to be used for good, or possibly for evil, an educational medium of no mean order';[52] and Sir Herbert Beerbohm Tree wrote of the 'mission of the modern theatre to give the public representations of history which shall at once be an education and a delight'.[53] Salisbury's original conception of Henry as standing rather than seated during Catherine's supplication was a deliberate departure from the historical sources for greater emotive effect: 'I felt that this [the seated posture] was wrong, as after careful study of Henry's character I had decided that this was the crisis of his life, and he, in spite of his sovereignty, would have been standing.'[54] It was subsequently adopted, at his suggestion, in Beerbohm Tree's 1910 production of *Henry VIII*. In this, Salisbury underlines the new symbolic emphasis of William Poel's Elizabethan Stage Society, and of his friend Edward Gordon Craig, whose journal the *Mask* had published in 1909 an article by A. Hevesi which proposed very different principles for Shakespearean production from Irving's and Tree's 'pageantry of realism': 'poetic suggestions shall be supported on a modern stage by painted scenic suggestion. Not an illusion of reality . . . but a harmonisation of his melodies of speech in form and colour.'[55] The highly controlled gorgeousness of the red, gold, and black colour scheme which unites the East Corridor work, Eden's 'heraldic' contribution, and Salisbury's own increasingly

[48] Laurens himself had participated in the 1908 Franco-British Exhibition in London, and had been one of the selection jury at the Paris 1900 exhibition, where work by Abbey and Cowper had been shown.

[49] G. Cavendish's *Life of Wolsey* (1641) had been edited by F. S. Ellis in 1893 for William Morris's Kelmscott Press. Salisbury also painted the Cardinal's robe from Irving's in the Lyceum *Henry VIII* (first staged in 1892), which was loaned to him by Edith Craig.

[50] Following his East Corridor mural, Byam Shaw, along with his pupil, Eleanor Fortesque Brickdale, and Seymour Lucas, advised on costume for the *Pageant of London* in the 1911 *Festival of Empire*, whose vice-presidents included Harcourt, Asquith, and other members of the Liberal government.

[51] See Anon., 'Towards a National Theatre' in the Liberal journal, the *Nation* (18 Jan. 1908).

[52] Quoted in L. Irving, *Henry Irving the Actor and his World* (London, 1951), p. 679.

[53] H. Tree, *An Apology and a Footnote* in *Henry VIII and his Court* (London, 1910), p. 104.

[54] F. O. Salisbury, *Sarum Chase* (1953), p. 22.

[55] A. Hevesi, 'Shakespeare as a Scenographer', *Mask* (1909–10), p. 8. It was after seeing him as Tree's Henry VIII that the pioneer of symbolic staging in Germany, Max Reinhardt, invited to Berlin one of Tree's actors, Bourchier, to provide an example for his own actors.

economical approach to mural painting, which left behind the elaborate historical detail of his East Corridor panel for a more emblematic presentation, as at Chelsea and Liverpool Town Halls, can be seen as a reflection of this. Of the British muralists of the early twentieth century, however, it was perhaps to be Brangwyn above all who developed the art of 'suggestion' and 'melodies in form and colour' to its full potential. Abbey had hoped the East Corridor would be a first step in a 'revival of interest in mural painting in England',[56] a familiar echo of the aspiration of Prince Albert's Royal Fine Arts Commission. His death in 1911, along with the interruption caused by the First World War in the development of the new British School at Rome, which he founded with Rothenstein as a means to encourage a British school of mural art, meant that there was no real sequel to the 'East Corridor style'. Work by Board and Salisbury in its idiom at Bristol and Chelsea remained an isolated echo; by the 1920s when artists from the British School at Rome were employed in St Stephen's Hall at Westminster, very different goals were in sight.

When the East Corridor work was unveiled in 1910, it was already Brangwyn whom the Liberal journal, the *Athenaeum*, considered would have been a more appropriate choice for it.[57] Although he was not to gain a commission at the Palace of Westminster until the ill-fated project for War Memorial murals in the Royal Gallery in 1924, pressure was now mounting in other quarters too for the kind of modern iconography which had become the norm in many French public mural schemes, and in which Brangwyn excelled, as had been demonstrated by his recent Royal Exchange (Plate 38), Venice Biennale, and Lloyd's Register of Shipping panels of industrial labour.[58] Roger Fry, although not a supporter of Brangwyn, also drew attention to the contemporary life subjects of William Rothenstein in autumn 1910, just after the East Corridor unveiling, in the Liberal weekly, the *Nation*,[59] and both Fry himself at the Borough Polytechnic in 1911 and Rothenstein through his involvement at County Hall began to demonstrate opportunities for contemporary iconography in mural art.[60] Meanwhile in Germany, at the Berlin Reichstag (Parliament) building, historical and modern events had been juxtaposed in the murals completed in 1909, whilst the compromise programme of part symbolic, part historical material eventually determined for the final phase of the Neue Hofburg decoration in Vienna was loudly denounced by *Ver Sacrum*[61] as being retrograde and conservative.

Had Harcourt been allowed by circumstances to complete the scheme of decoration he envisaged for Westminster, British State mural painting might have become part of this trend to contemporaneity in the same way as the schemes of modern trade and labour by Henri Martin in the French Upper Chamber, begun in 1913 and completed in 1926 (Plate 52). In 1909, as the East Corridor was being completed, he sought titles for a series of 'historico-political' panels for St Stephen's Hall,[62] which would have contained contemporary incidents and also left space for future generations to fill. Although not actually part of the House of Commons, the decoration of St Stephen's Hall was nevertheless placed under Harcourt's supervision by the Prime Minister and the Lord Great Chamberlain,[63] and both his choice of subjects and his selection of Abbey as once

[56] Quoted in Lucas, *E. A. Abbey*, p. 462.

[57] Anon., 'Mr. Brangwyn's Paintings and Etchings', *Athenaeum*, no. 4334 (19 Nov. 1910), p. 633.

[58] For Brangwyn's Royal Exchange panel, see Ch. 3; for his Venice Biennale and Lloyd's Register of Shipping work, see Ch. 11.

[59] R. Fry, 'The Art of Mr. William Rothenstein', *Nation* (11 June 1910), p. 382.

[60] For the Polytechnic, see Ch. 9; for County Hall, see Ch. 7.

[61] See A. Lhotsky, 'Die Baugeschichte der Museen und der neuen Burg', *Festschrift des kunsthistorischen Museums zur Feier des fünfzigjahrigen Bestandes*, Part 1 (Vienna, 1941), pp. 153 ff.; already in 1898 *Ver Sacrum* had protested at historical subjects for the Maria-Theresien-Saal (Jahrgang I, vol. 4, p. 21).

[62] Letter from Harcourt to 'Prime Minister' (24 June 1909), HA.

[63] Letter from Harcourt to Lord Cholmondely (24 June 1909), HA.

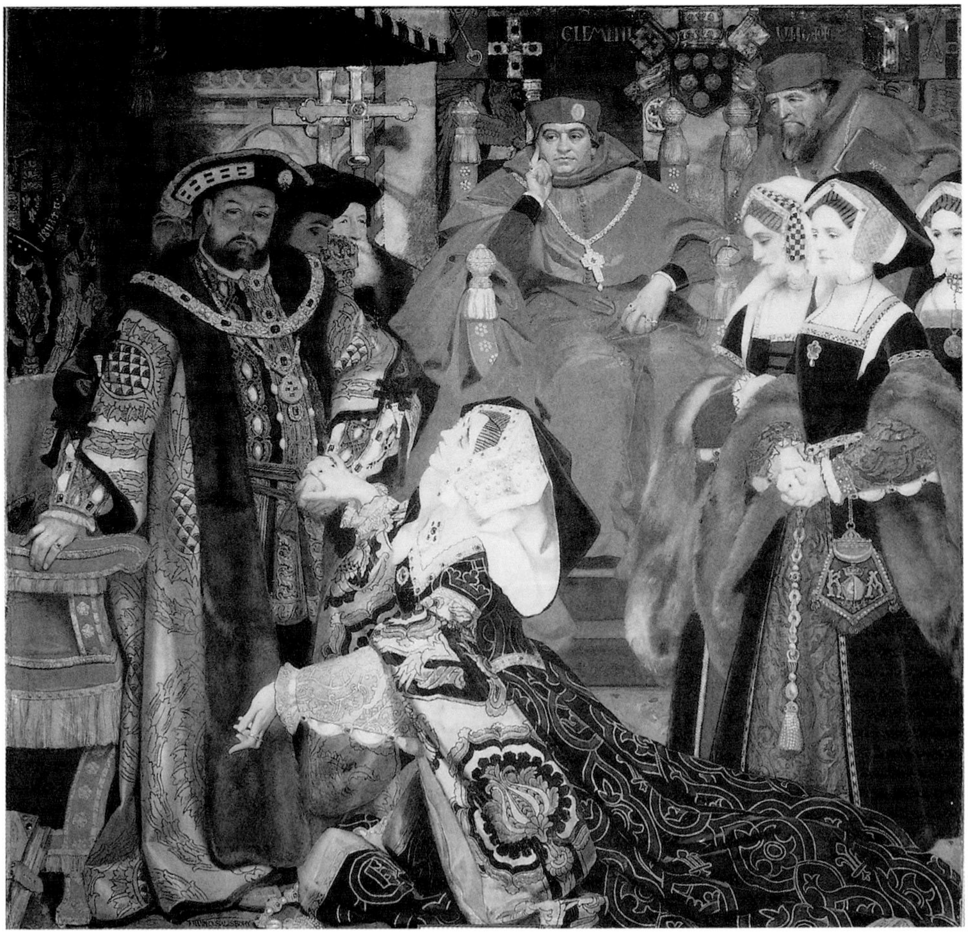

50. Frank O. Salisbury, *Henry VIII and Catherine of Aragon before the Papal Legates at Blackfriars 1529*, East Corridor, Palace of Westminster, London, 1908–10. Presented by Lord Stanmore

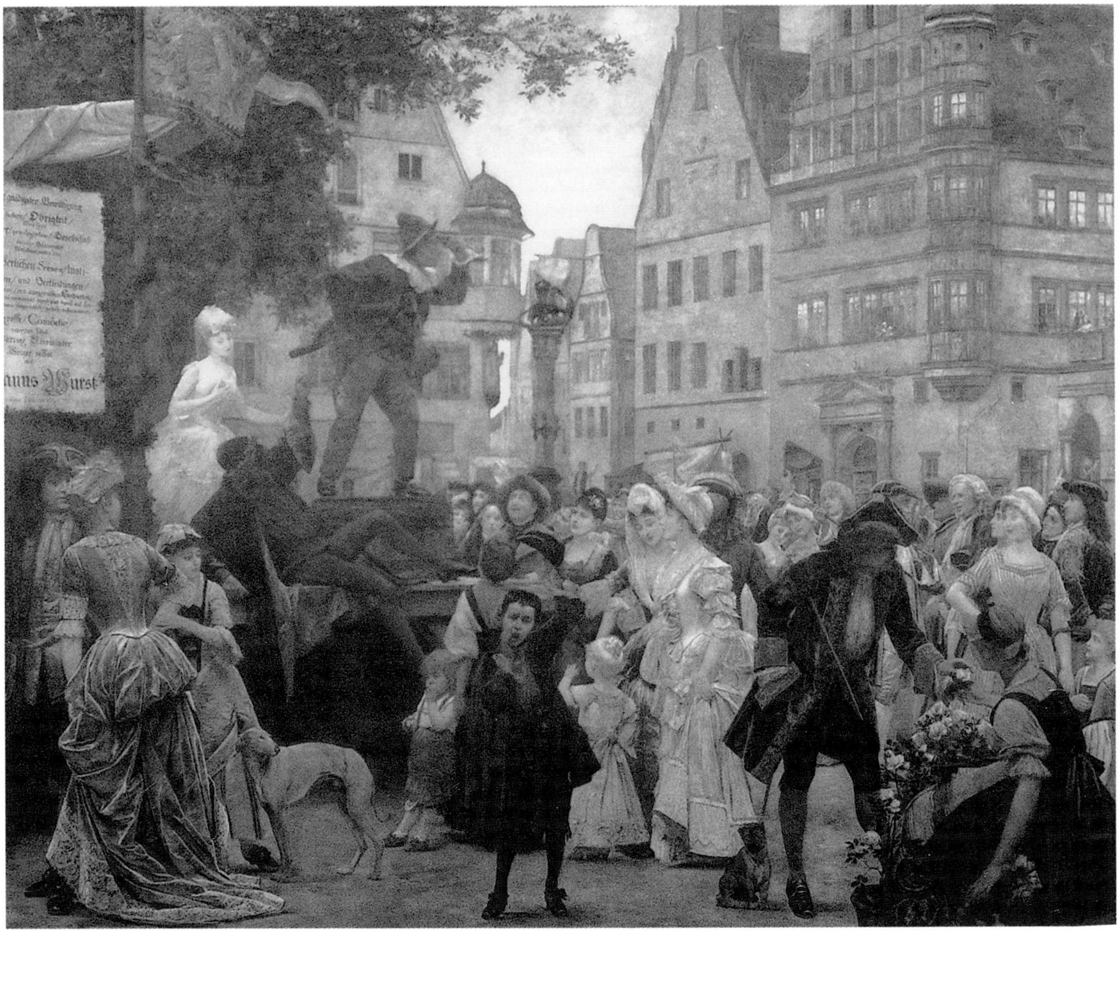

51. Ernst Klimt, *Hans Wurst at the Jahrmarkt*, ceiling decoration, Burgtheater, Vienna, 1886–8

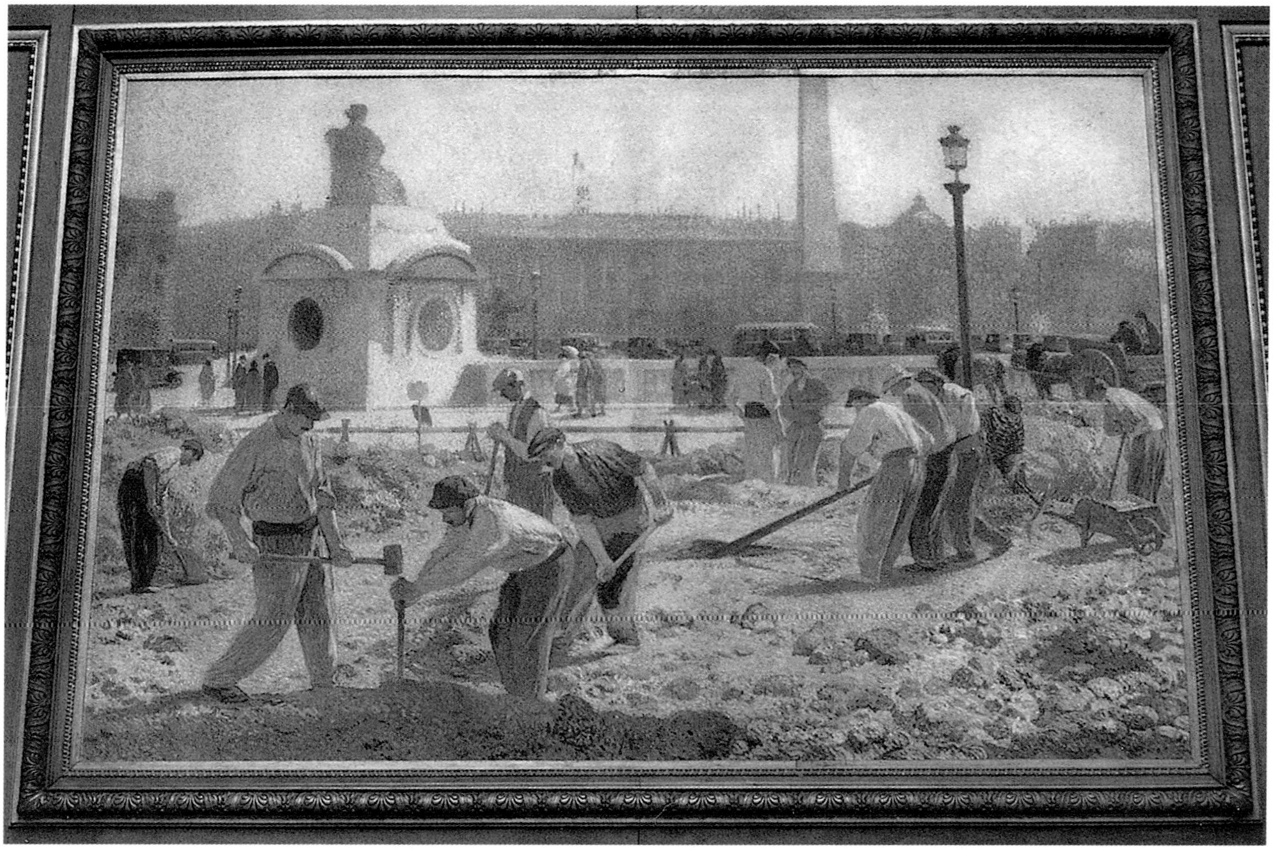

52. Henri Martin, *Industrial Labour* (roadmenders in the Place de la Concorde, Paris), panel from scheme illustrating *Working France presents itself to the Conseil d'Etat*, Salle d' Assemblée Générale du Conseil d'Etat, Palais Royal, Paris, 1926

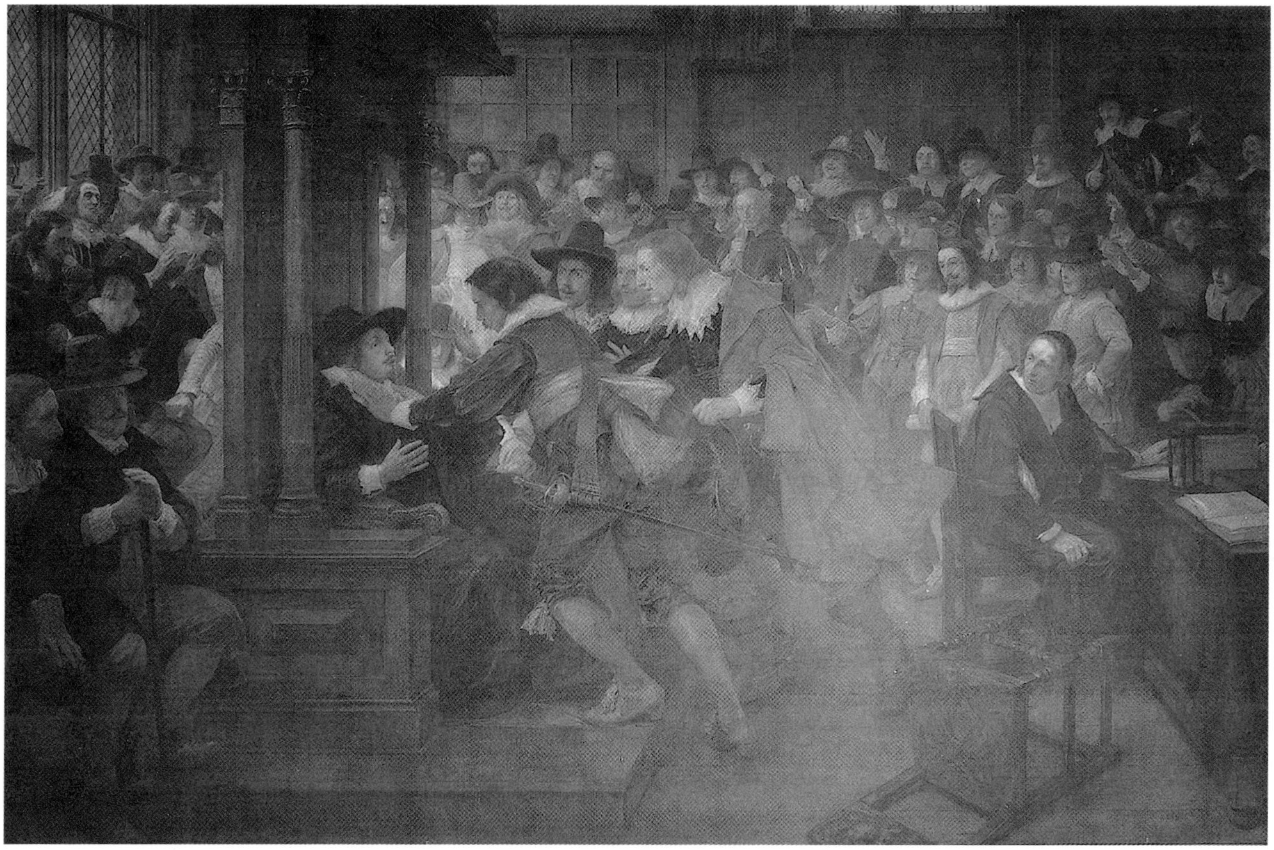

53. Andrew Carrick Gow, *The House of Commons, 2 March 1628–9*, formerly St Stephen's Hall (now in Committee Room 14), Palace of Westminster, London, 1912

again the coordinating artist promised an even more radical outcome than in the East Corridor. Lord Carlisle complained that the committee Harcourt enlisted to assist him to choose titles for the eight panels (Prince Albert's were abandoned) was 'purely literary . . . the literary gents will not understand that pictures are different from tracts';[64] he consented to join it, but its real voice lay with members and advisers like Trevelyan, Morley, H. A. L. Fisher, Minister of Education, and the party propagandist Augustine Birrell. Their eventual themes were 'The growth of privileges at Parliament from the Middle Ages to Modern Times'[65] and the final episode was to be *King George V Opening his First Parliament in 1911*—the business of which was the Parliament Bill to curtail the powers of the Lords, as a step towards their abolition. Other titles included such symbolic portents of reform as 'Passage of last bill in the House of Lords, 1832'; the scheme would have been a very literal invasion of the House of Lords by the Commons who wished to abolish it.

At Abbey's death, artistic direction was passed to a Royal Academy Committee, and the Academy donated a panel to launch the scheme, of *The House of Commons, 2 March 1628–9 (Holles and Valentine holding the Speaker in the Chair)* (Plate 53), a theme against which the constitutional historian Anson had noted 'may forecast the events of the twentieth century'.[66] By A. C. Gow, the panel marked a break with the tightly symbolic use of artistic style which had characterized the East Corridor, for Gow was a far more traditional Royal Academician and history painter than the 'Primitives' Abbey had favoured; Abbey, Carlisle, and Harcourt had expressly excluded him from participation in the East Corridor work.[67] By concentrating on the advice of 'the literary gents' and failing to find a suitable replacement for Abbey, Harcourt had unwittingly lost the very means to present his message which had proved so successful in the East Corridor. Gow's picture is well composed, but with none of the decorative and psychological drama which captures the attention in the East Corridor. Like Seymour Lucas's *The Flight of the Five Members*, the only other panel completed before the outbreak of war, it belongs to the kind of anecdotal history painting first developed by Ward and Cope at Westminster in the 1850s, and consolidated by many of the Royal Exchange panels. The East Corridor murals were chosen to represent Great Britain at the Ghent International Exhibition of 1913, but a distinctive character for State mural painting was not to re-emerge until the St Stephen's Hall decoration was begun again in 1924, with different titles and new artists. Meanwhile, however, the issue of political and propagandist purposes versus artistic professionalism in the State's patronage of mural art was to come to a head through the decoration of the Foreign Office, and the abortive project after the First World War for a national 'Hall of Remembrance'. These were schemes that in turn brought to light the very problems which were eventually to seal the fate of British State mural painting with the collapse of Brangwyn's Royal Gallery commission in 1933. In their different ways, the murals at the Foreign Office, the Hall of Remembrance, St Stephen's Hall, and the Royal Gallery were now all profoundly influenced by the context or aftermath of the war.

[64] Letter from Carlisle to Harcourt (25 June 1909), HA.

[65] Letter from Harcourt to Carlisle (undated), CHA, J22/84.

[66] Letter from Anson to Harcourt (4 Nov. 1909), HA.

[67] Lord Winterstoke had wished Gow to paint his mural for the East Corridor but was persuaded by Abbey, Carlisle, and Harcourt to accept Eden instead. Gow had contributed to the Royal Exchange scheme.

5

War and Peace: State Mural Schemes, 1912–1927

SIGISMUND GOETZE'S MURALS FOR THE GREAT (AMBASSADORS') STAIRCASE AT THE FOREIGN OFFICE, LONDON (1912–27)

Although murals were apparently envisaged by Sir George Gilbert Scott in his initial Gothic design of 1857 for the Foreign Office, when the building was eventually completed, in classical idiom, the decoration was entrusted to Clayton and Bell's company and for the most part consisted of pattern motifs and such effects as the stencilled 'powdering of stars'[1] in the Foreign Secretary's Room. Only the dome above the Ambassadors' Staircase appears to have received more pictorial treatment, boasting personifications of the various countries of the world and, in the spandrels, of the 'four quarters of the globe', by 1868.[2] Scott, however, had written of the desirability of murals of 'Scripture history, the progress of science', and famous poets' work in non-ecclesiastical buildings in the Gothic style[3]—just such a building as his Foreign Office would have been had his first design been accepted—and a more ambitious figurative mural scheme than Clayton and Bell's can thus be regarded as one of the victims of the architectural 'Battle of the Styles' which in the later nineteenth century had ousted the association of the Gothic with national identity, epitomized by Westminster, in favour of Italian Renaissance-inspired classicism.

At some point in the later nineteenth century, five seventeenth-century Brussels tapestries, probably those formerly in the old Foreign Office in Downing Street, seem to have been installed, but by 1905 these had been transferred to the British Embassy in Paris. In 1912 the Archbishop of Canterbury, Randall Davidson, was moved at the Royal Academy banquet to deplore the way the British were 'content to see the walls of a fine public office covered with nothing better than maps and almanacs with an occasional photogravure' and to muse on 'what Home Secretaries we might evolve, what Chancellors of the Exchequer, what Budgets, might be ours if the surroundings were quite other' than 'drab . . . walls'.[4] He drew attention in contrast to the way that Princes of Renaissance Italy

[1] H. Smith, *Decorative Painting* (1984), p. 84 (see photographs in National Monuments Record).

[2] Anon., 'The Grand Staircase at the New Foreign Office', *Illustrated London News*, 53 (1868), p. 99 (see illustration on pp. 100–1).

[3] Smith, *Decorative Painting*, p. 43, summarizing George Gilbert Scott, *Remarks on Secular and Domestic Architecture* (1857).

[4] Report of Davidson's speech in the *Spectator* (11 May 1912).

were in touch with great ideals, great aspirations . . . surrounded by beautiful things at the time when they had their ordinary work to do, and if the Committee was dull or the Chairman stupid, and the drudgery was wearisome, they had by a mere glance at the walls an opportunity of getting new thoughts, aspirations and of transmuting the prose into poetry.[5]

His words inspired Sigismund Goetze, artist of one of the Royal Exchange panels and a regular exhibitor at the Royal Academy, the Paris Salon, and the Société des Artistes Français, to 'place his services at the disposal of the Government to paint a panel or completely decorate a room in one of the great public buildings'.[6] The Government seems to have seized the offer eagerly; Goetze was prepared to donate the murals, and someone from the Office of Works was 'instructed . . . to take him round various Public Buildings in order to see what struck his fancy'.[7] He selected the walls at the top of the Ambassadors' staircase in the Foreign Office, and Lord Beauchamp, who had by now replaced Harcourt as First Commissioner of Works, but who had been a donor and a strong supporter of the Westminster East Corridor work, approved the artist's 'ideas for a suitable decorative scheme'[8] in 1913 and requested him to prepare colour sketches, which were exhibited for six weeks at the Foreign Office in May 1914 in a lit scale model[9] (Plates 54a and b). A commission was given to Goetze as a result of these by the Prime Minister and Sir Edward Grey, Secretary of State for the Foreign Office. They appointed a 'small committee', however, 'to consider all matters of detail in connection with the panels so as to ensure that the subjects represented were not likely to clash in any way with diplomatic amenities';[10] this consisted of two Foreign Office officials and Sir Lionel Earle as the representative for the First Commissioner of Works.

The Foreign Office Ambassadors' staircase was, after all, a particularly prominent location. The subjects which Goetze displayed in his 1914 model can in fact be recognized as having a very precise diplomatic purpose in the context of the outbreak of war that year, and for that very reason were to become out of date, and indeed a liability in Foreign Office eyes once the war was over. Meanwhile, as Goetze records, 'owing to the War, the Foreign Office required every wall space available'[11] and installation of the murals, which Goetze carried out in spirit fresco on canvas in his studio for *marouflage* afterwards in the manner of the early Royal Exchange work, was deferred. By 1919, when the question of installation arose again, Grey had been succeeded by Lord Curzon and Sir Lionel Earle by Sir Alfred Mond.

Goetze's scheme consists of five large panels (so large, indeed, that special canvas had to be imported from Belgium) illustrating personifications of Britannia. *Britannia Sponsa* ('The Seafarers') (Plate 55) in which 'successive waves of overseas tribes land to obtain possession of Britannia'[12] provides a symbolic partner at one end of the stair gallery to *Britannia Colonorum Mater* (Plate 56) at the other, in which the mature Britannia sends her sons overseas to gain new territory, whilst *Britannia Bellatrix* (Plate 57) and *Britannia Nutrix* (Plate 58) illustrate the Britons being instructed in the arts of war and peace respectively, and flank *Britannia Pacificatrix* (Plate XVI)—Britannia the peacemaker—on the long wall. Three smaller overdoor panels illustrate *Silence*, *Strength* (Plate 59), and *Dulce et decorum est pro patria mori* by means of further

[5] Report of Davidson's speech in the *Morning Post* (6 May 1912).

[6] Sir Alfred Mond, *Mural Decoration of the Foreign and Commonwealth Office*, Memorandum (13 Feb. 1920), Cab 24/98 630, CP 630, File No. 3/D/8, PRO, p. 104.

[7] Ibid.

[8] S. Goetze, *Mural Decorations at the Foreign Office* (n.d., *c.*1921), p. 1.

[9] This model is now held in the Empire and Commonwealth Museum, Bristol.

[10] Mond, *Mural Decoration*, p. 105.

[11] Goetze, *Mural Decorations*, p. 2.

[12] Ibid., p. 3.

personifications. The 'classical' idiom follows in sequel to the decoration Goetze had recently completed in his own home, Grove House, in Regent's Park, London.[13]

In 1912–14, when Goetze received and started his commission, Sir Edward Grey was facing the mounting international crisis which would culminate in the First World War. His only hope lay in maintaining a balance of power in which a Triple Alliance of Britain, France, and Russia could match German threats and preserve British control of central and eastern Asian territory felt to be vital to the survival of the British Empire.[14] British forces were seriously 'unprepared' and if Britain was to preserve its 1904 Entente with France, it needed at least to offer a clear appearance of military and naval strength.[15] The murals would have provided an obvious propaganda opportunity in such a diplomatically strategic position as the staircase used by the representatives of visiting foreign governments. The French in particular were accustomed to conduct their political affairs in buildings decorated with murals, such as the Palais Bourbon in Paris, where Delacroix's *Orpheus teaching the Greeks the Arts of Peace* and *Attila and the Huns trampling Italy and the Arts* offer close precedents for Goetze's iconography. The most immediate source for Goetze's scheme, however, is that by Puvis de Chavannes at the Musée de Picardie in Amiens (1861–5 and 1880–2), a mural sequence already drawn to the attention of the 1906 Select Committee on the decoration of the Palace of Westminster by Lord Beauchamp, and one which Goetze saw on a tour of France and Germany he undertook in 1913 to study work relevant to his Foreign office commission. Both individual motifs in the Foreign Office murals, like Britannia nursing a child in the 'Arts of Peace', and the general image of bride/mother/nation personified relate directly to Puvis's murals, which include *Ave Picardia Nutrix* (Plate 60) as well as *La Guerre.* Such correspondences would have been a direct appeal to French sensibilities in particular in 1912–14, whilst Goetze's luminous, almost Post-Impressionist handling of coloured shadows on naked, classically posed flesh is entirely in harmony with early twentieth-century French 'official' art styles like Besnard's or Béraud's. The clearest message of all, however, would have been from Goetze's brooding, muscular warrior of primitive times representing *Strength* (Plate 59), who is dressed in animal skins and literally towers above the heads of visitors walking along the stair gallery beneath; and from the youth of Britain hoisting sail and launching a primitive boat from the shore in *Britannia Colonorum Mater* (Plate 56). With the Britons learning the 'Arts of War', this last offered a tangible celebration of the naval supremacy which Grey was convinced must be maintained in order to preserve the Entente Cordiale and of the willingness to mount a defence which it was believed would keep the crucial balance of power. Grey, furthermore, had a strong personal commitment both to thorough military training and to the skills of negotiation implied by the *Britannia Pacificatrix* (Plate XVI) theme.

Goetze recorded that by the time war broke out, he had 'the first' murals ready for installation,[16] and Mond referred to two being ready at that stage.[17] These would presumably have been *Britannia Sponsa* (Plate 55) and *Britannia Nutrix* (Plate 58). With their themes of the possession of Britain by overseas tribes in the earliest days of her history, and of Britain's cultivation of the

[13] *Britannia Sponsa* is approximately 8.45 × 4.64 m; *Britannia Colonorum Mater* is approximately 6.93 × 4.64 m; *Britannia Bellatrix* is approximately 5.18 × 4.64 m; *Britannia Nutrix* is approximately 5.18 × 4.64 m and *Britannia Pacificatrix* is approximately 7.46 × 4.64 m. For Grove House, see Chapter 10.

[14] See K. Wilson, 'British Power in the European Balance 1906–14', in D. Dilks (ed.), *Retreat from Power. Studies in Britain's Foreign Policy of the Twentieth Century*, vol. 1 1906–1939 (London, 1981), pp. 40–1.

[15] Sir H. Wilson, quoted ibid., p. 27.

[16] Goetze, *Mural Decorations*, p. 4.

[17] Mond, *Mural Decoration* p. 105.

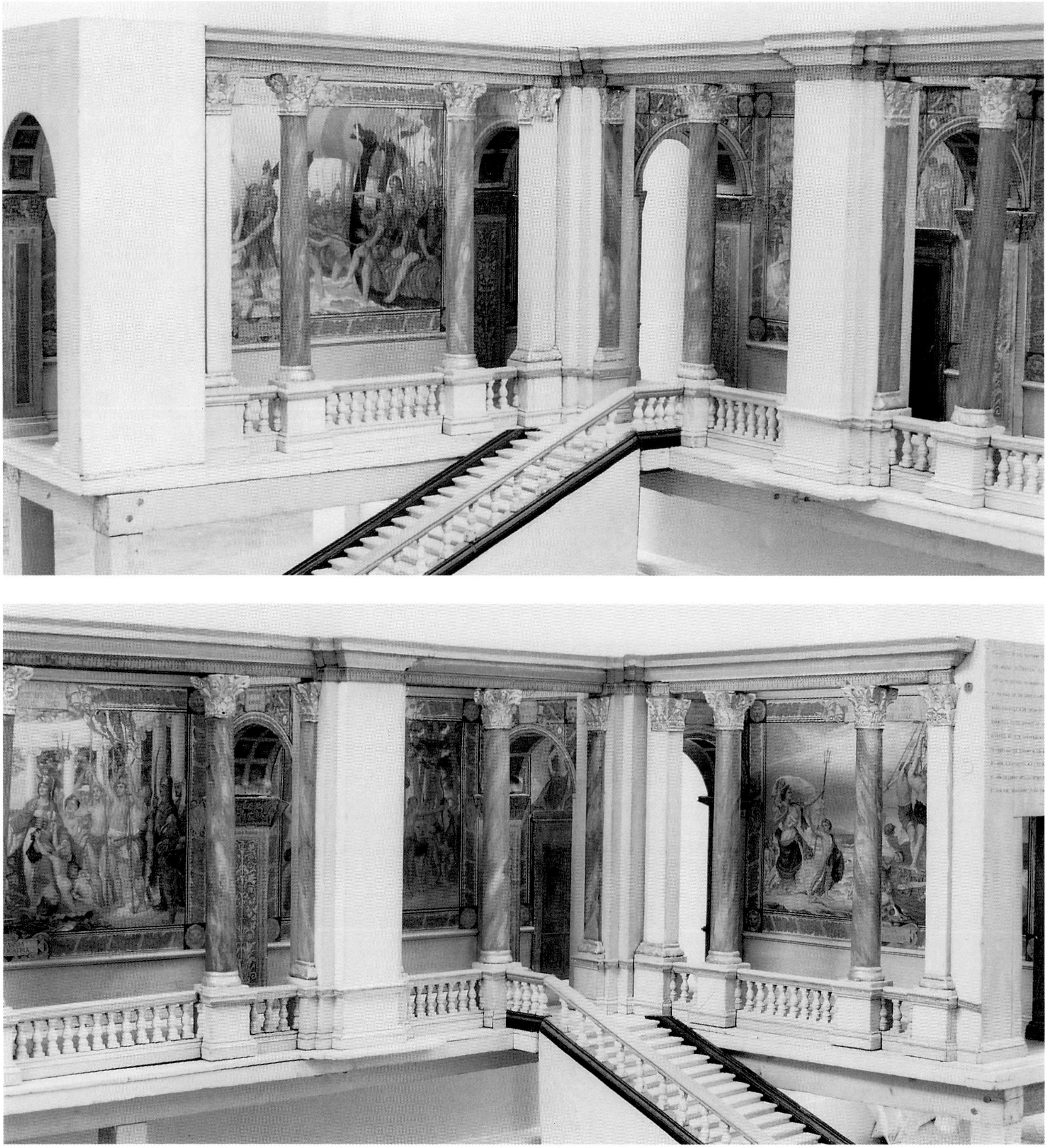

54. (a) and (b). Sigismund Goetze, scale model of the Ambassadors' Staircase, Foreign Office, London, containing sketches of his murals there; begun 1914, and including the revised version of 1919–21 of *Britannia Pacificatrix* (b). Bristol, Empire and Commonwealth Museum

55 (*facing, above*). Sigismund Goetze, *Britannia Sponsa*, 1912–20, Ambassadors' Staircase, Foreign and Commonwealth Office, London. (Photograph taken prior to installation and squared up in pencil, possibly by Goetze)

56 (*facing, below*). Sigismund Goetze, *Britannia Colonorum Mater*, 1912–20, Ambassadors' Staircase, Foreign and Commonwealth Office, London. (Photograph taken prior to installation.)

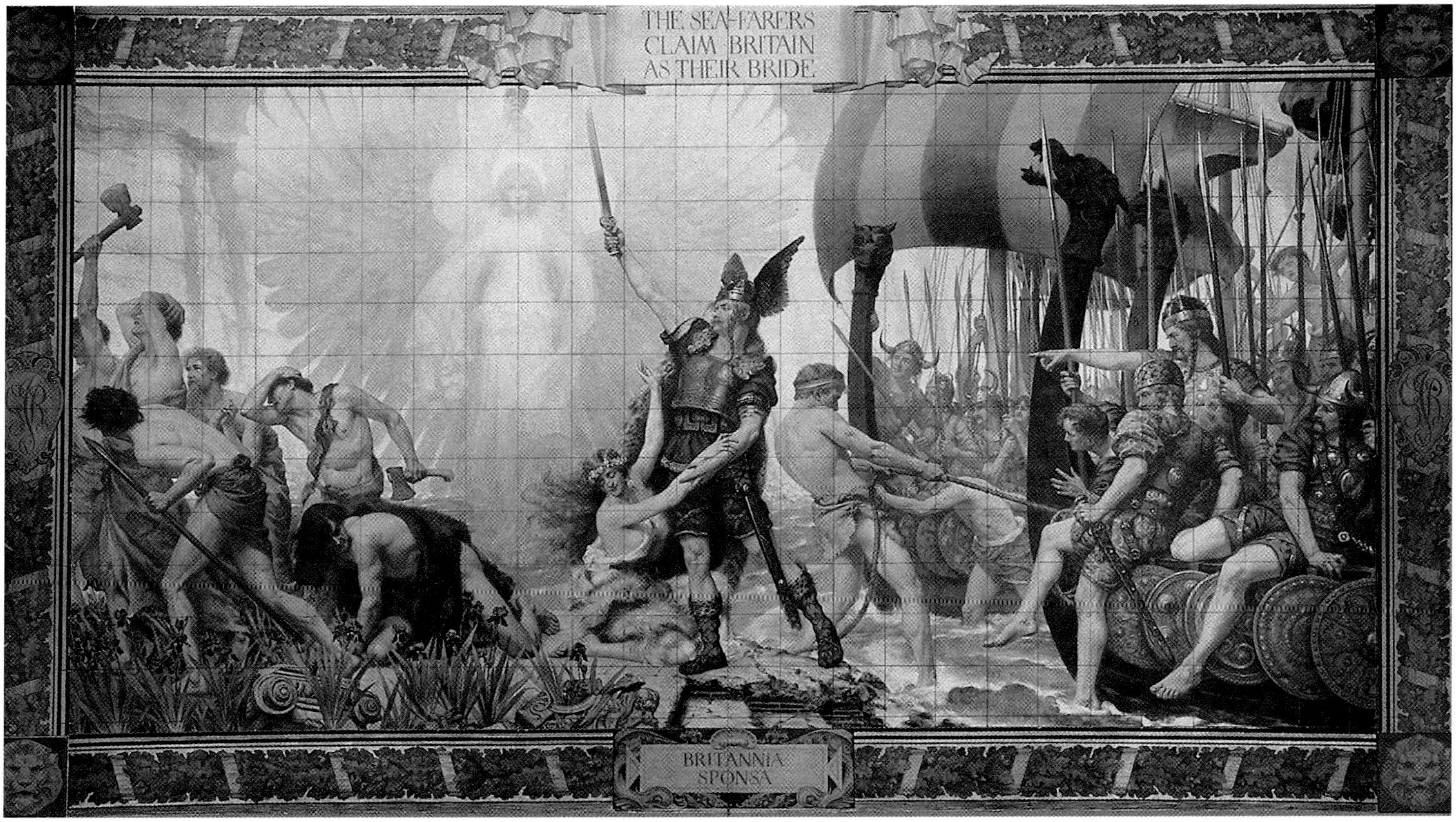
THE SEA-FARERS
CLAIM BRITAIN
AS THEIR BRIDE
BRITANNIA
SPONSA

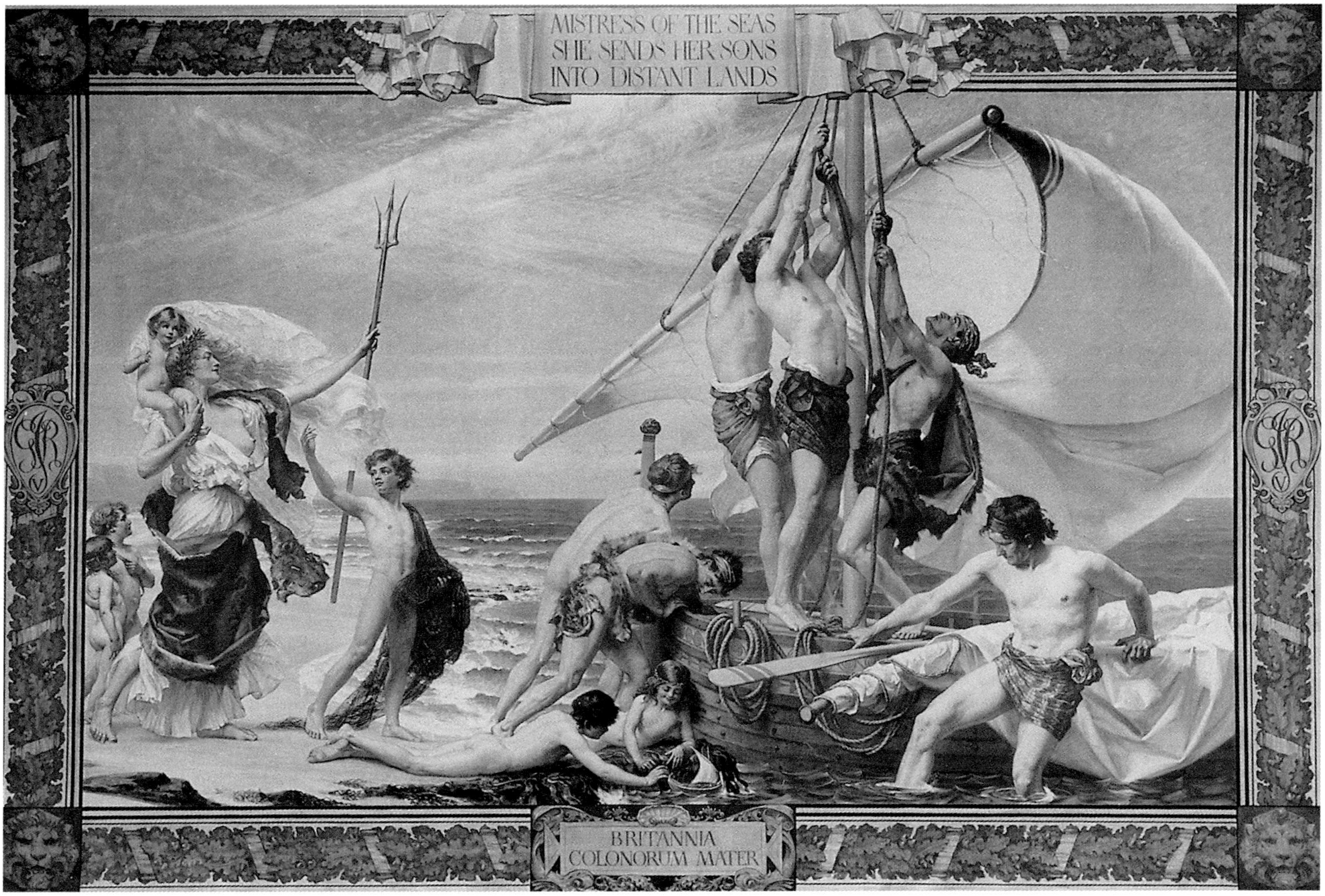
MISTRESS OF THE SEAS
SHE SENDS HER SONS
INTO DISTANT LANDS
BRITANNIA
COLONORUM MATER

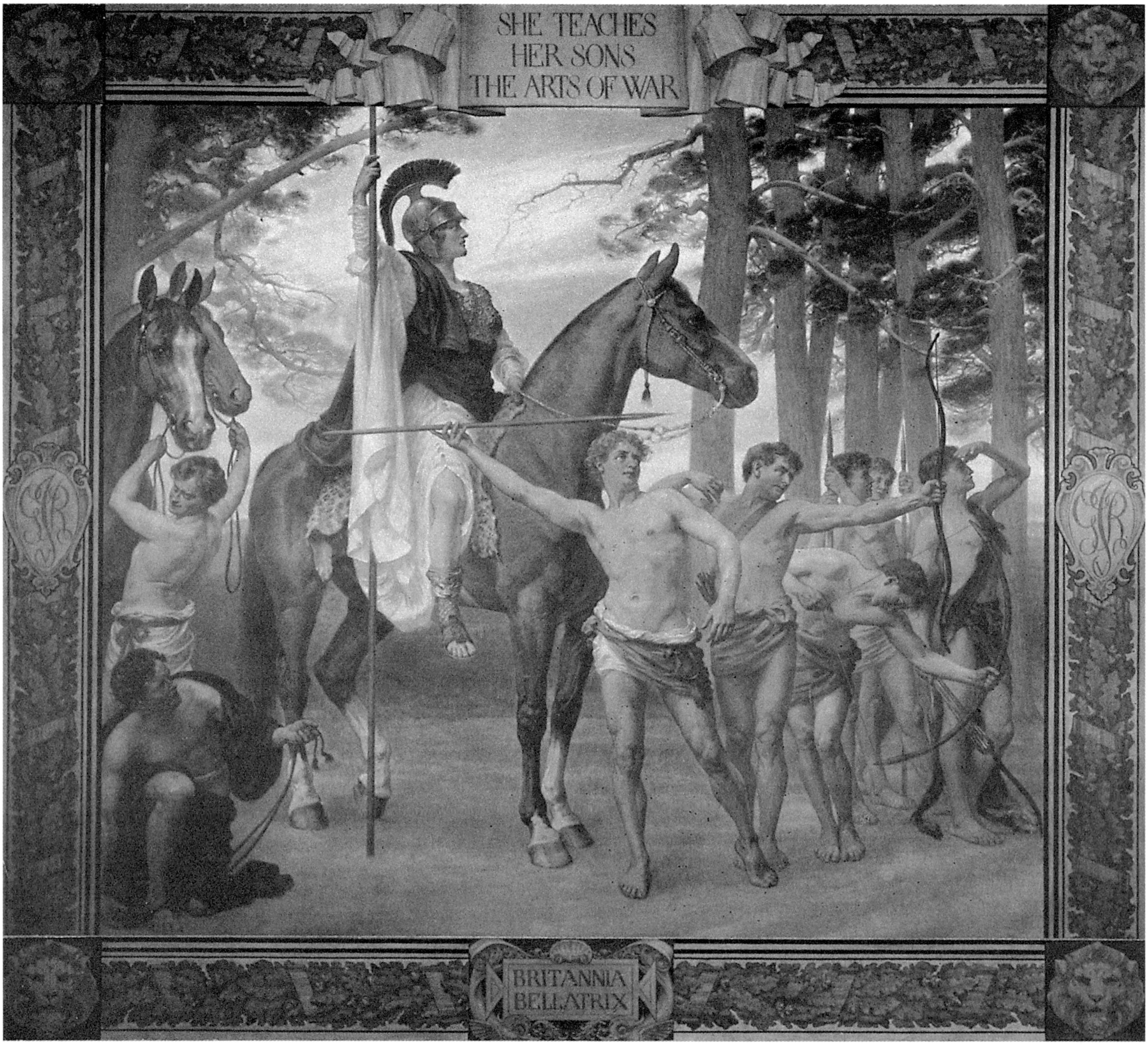

57. Sigismund Goetze, *Britannia Bellatrix*, 1912–20, Ambassadors' Staircase, Foreign and Commonwealth Office, London. (Photograph taken prior to installation.)

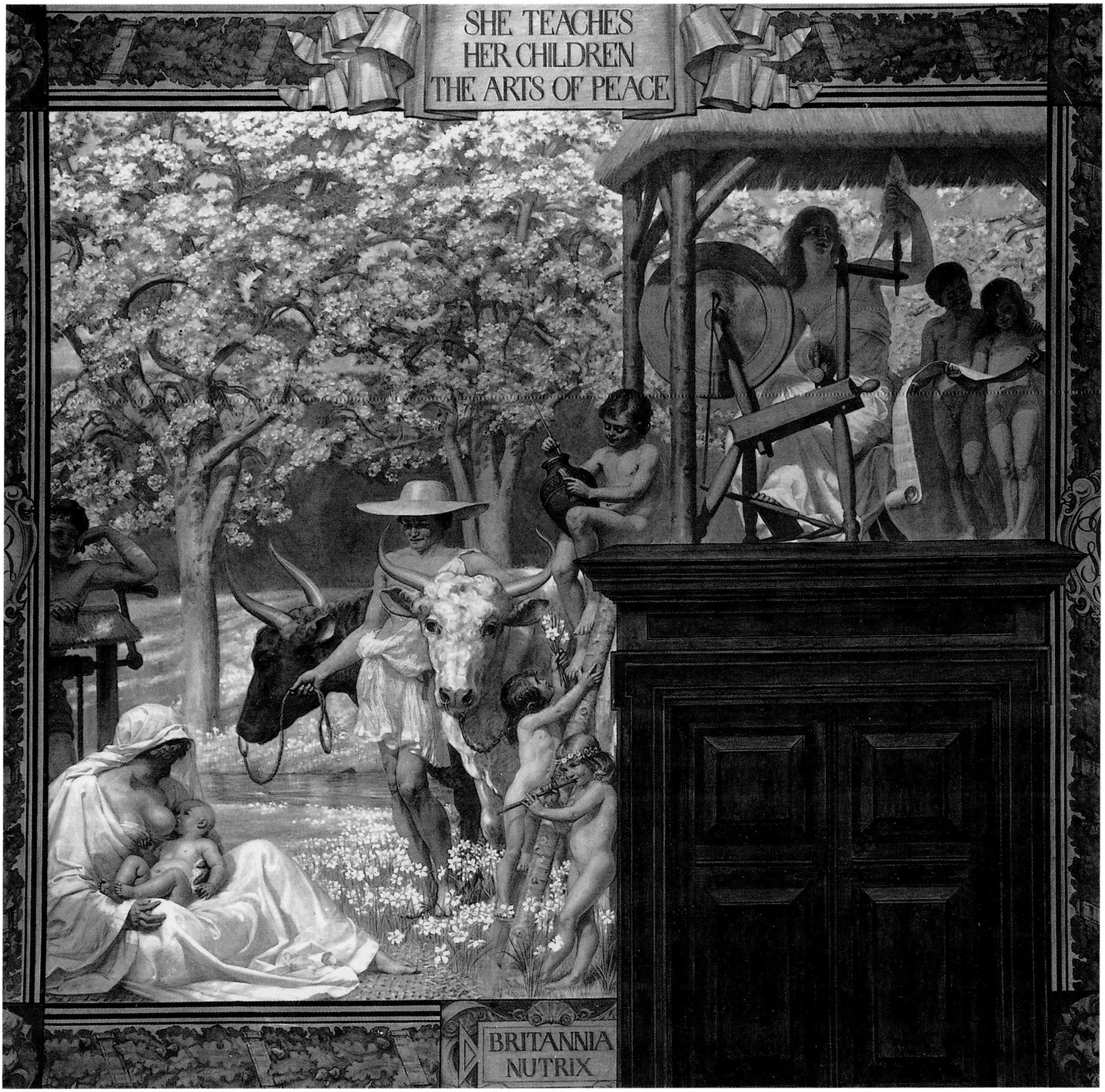

58. Sigismund Goetze, *Britannia Nutrix*, 1912–20, Ambassadors' Staircase, Foreign and Commonwealth Office, London. (Photograph taken prior to installation, with mock door.)

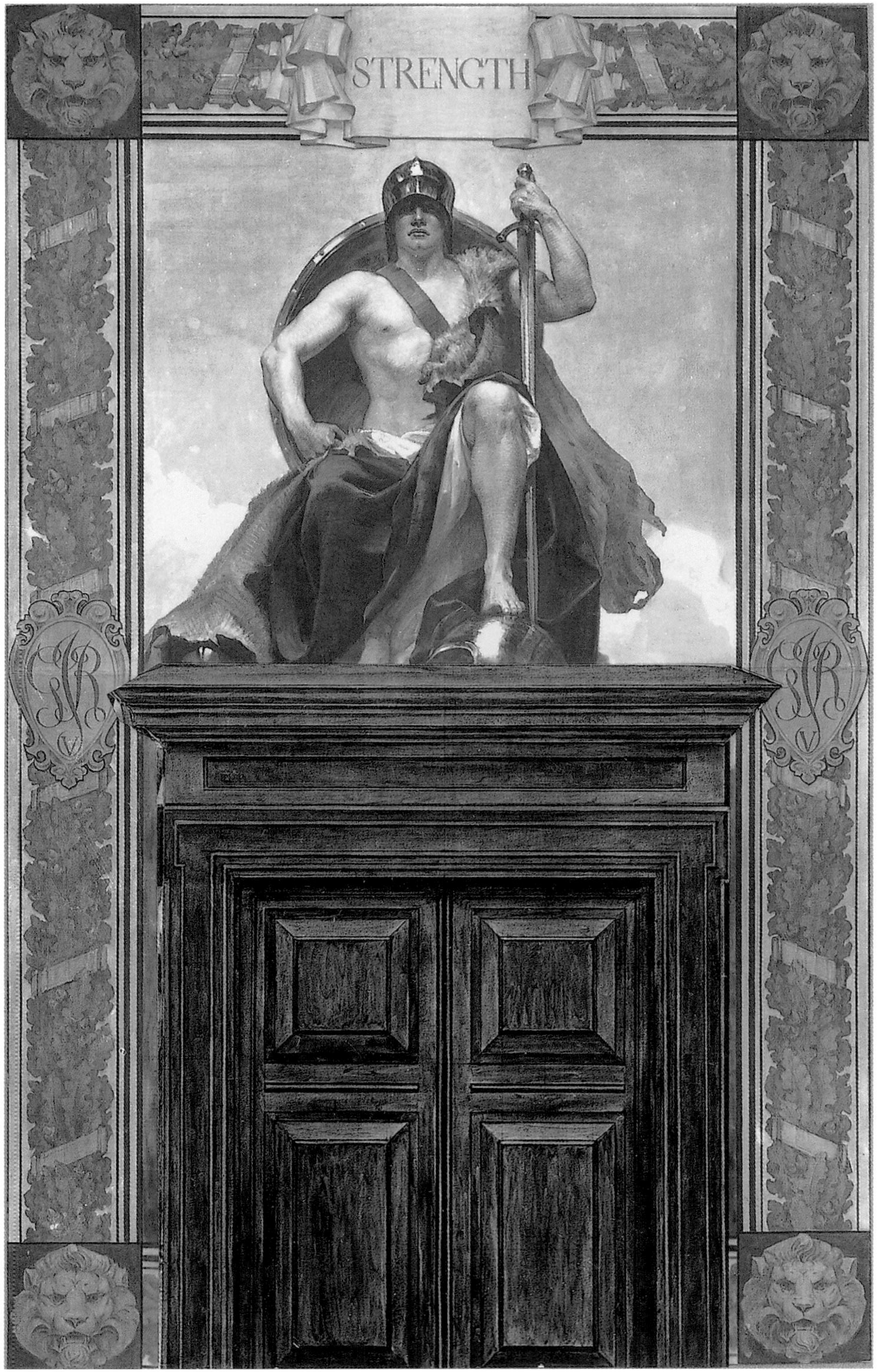

59. Sigismund Goetze, *Strength*, 1919–20, Ambassadors' Staircase, Foreign and Commonwealth Office, London. (Photograph taken prior to installation, with mock door superimposed on the print, presumably by Goetze.)

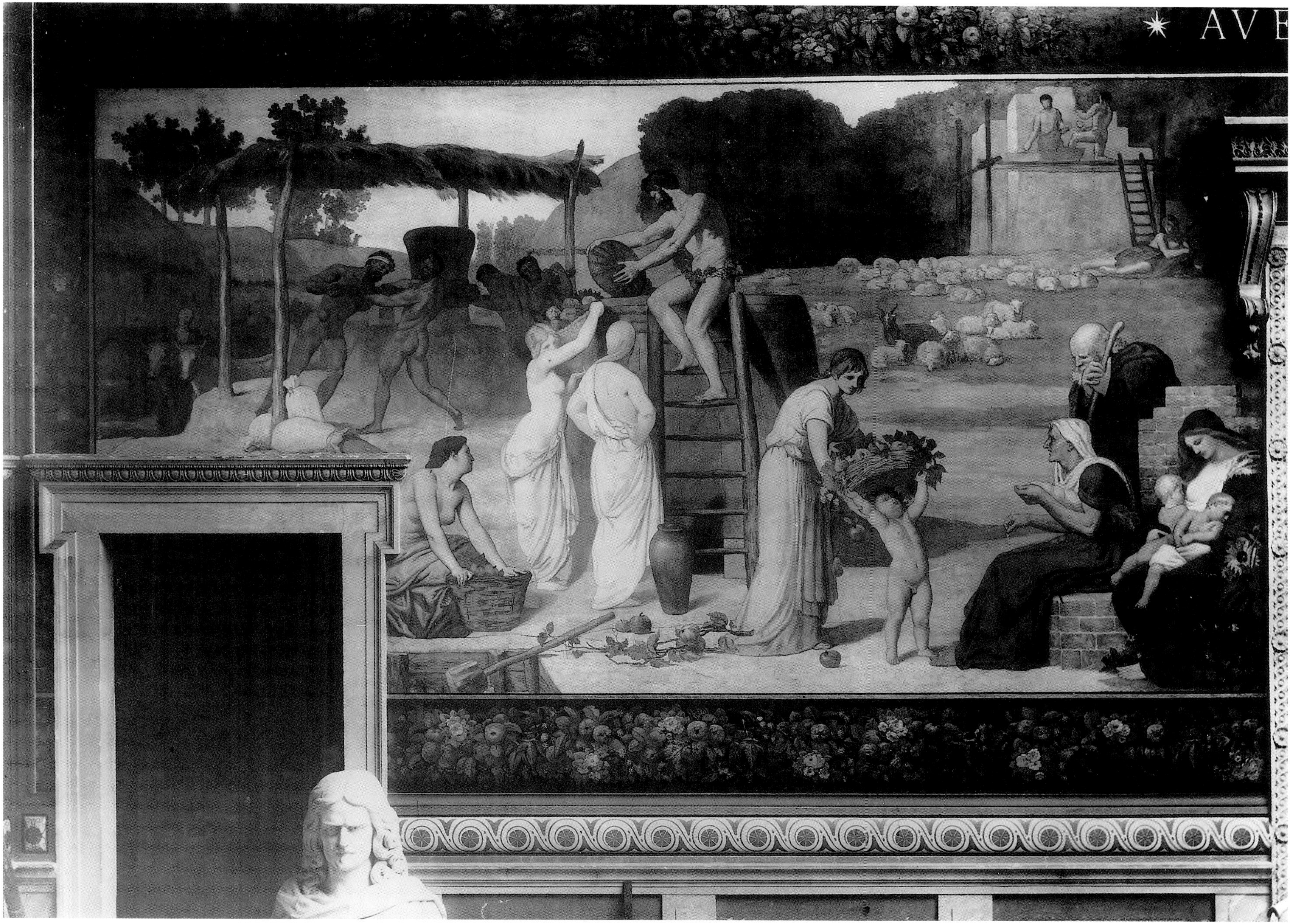

60. Pierre Puvis de Chavannes (1824–98), *Ave Picardia Nutrix* (right portion), 1865, Amiens, Musée de Picardie

arts of peace, it is hardly surprising that Goetze was not allowed to install these. Had his scheme been further advanced, its larger message would have vividly projected Grey's 'balance of power' politics; as it was, it neither matched these in its incomplete state in 1914 nor, when completed in 1919, did it match the new post-war ideals of Curzon and his colleagues. Its apparent glorification of aggression was no longer relevant, but then neither was its conception of diplomacy. Goetze had originally envisaged an illustration of 'the grasping of the "hands across the sea" of the two great English-speaking races, Great Britain and the USA'[18] for his central *Britannia Pacificatrix* panel (Plate XVI), but when this was overtaken by the negotiations for the League of Nations, he seems to have amended, or been asked to amend, his plans. His new design must have been but salt in a wound for Curzon, for prominently accompanying the chief protagonists of Britannia and a personification of the United States, draped in the Stars and Stripes, is a personification of France who points to the 'Scrap of Paper',[19] the Treaty of Sèvres, in the negotiation of which Curzon was deeply involved during 1920–1 when the fate of Goetze's murals was being decided. Men and women representing the other signatory countries stand on either side of Britannia, against a backdrop of the sea viewed through a colonnade inscribed 'Gloria in excelcis Deo et in terra pax . . . '; and one of these is 'Prince Feisal'.[20] By 1920, however, the Prince had declared sovereignty and thereby sabotaged Britain's attempts to make an amicable settlement with France on the matter of its territory in Syria. The Treaty of Sèvres, in turn, fast became a failure for Curzon because it led to a separate peace agreement between France and the Greek and Turkish nationalists, in which Britain was not involved, and consequently to the downfall of Lloyd George's government in 1922. On the eve of these events, Geotze's prominent positioning of France as the virtual centrepiece at the top of the Ambassadors' staircase, 'with her Tricolour garlanded with laurels' and pointing 'to the debris of Despotism and Militarism which she has been fighting to destroy',[21] was singularly unfortunate. Curzon, however, rejected the panels 'On artistic grounds';[22] a curious judgement, given his close supervision of Thornycroft's sculptural memorial to him as Viceroy of India, in which the approach is comparable to Goetze's;[23] and his taste in his own house at Kedleston,[24] but one which can be clearly explained by the political context. With their high, light tonality and classical overtones, Goetze's murals are, in fact, an ideal counterpart to the light marble and Portland stone of the Foreign Office interior, and his figure groupings are cleverly placed to be clearly legible within the columnar framework of the stair gallery.[25] Given the great size of the murals, significant motifs are carefully included for symbolic effect at eye level—broken arms and war debris at the feet of *Britannia Pacificatrix*, for example, or the cameo of children (could these be those of Goetze's relation by marriage, Sir Alfred Mond?) playing with a toy boat in *Britannia Colonorum Mater*.

Hoping to gain support for his judgement, Curzon proposed that advice be sought from a Committee composed of the Directors of the National and Tate Galleries and of the Victoria and

[18] Goetze, *Mural Decorations*, p. 6.

[19] Ibid., p. 7.

[20] Ibid., p. 8.

[21] Ibid., p. 7.

[22] Mond, *Mural Decoration*, p. 106.

[23] Cf. the memorial's combination of 'the ethnic with the ideal and narration with symbol' (S. Beattie, *The New Sculpture*, New Haven and London, 1983, p. 320).

[24] Only a few years later, Curzon was to commission a sculpture war memorial for his private chapel at Kedleston whose idealized style is a close equivalent to Goetze's in painting.

[25] Goetze explained that he had 'had throughout in mind the effect of his composition as seen between the great marble columns, the architectural lines of which, instead of interfering with the grouping of the figures, are used to assist in emphasising the main features of the designs' (Goetze, *Mural Decorations*, p. 7).

Albert Museum, and a 'Royal Academy Painter nominated by the President of the Royal Academy'.[26] Goetze protested that 'not one of the first three gentlemen proposed has ever written a line upon or evinced an interest in the art of mural decoration'[27] and his side was taken by Mond, who reasoned with Curzon that 'If it is open to any other Minister, who is merely a temporary occupant of a Government Building to veto decisions previously arrived at, I do not see how any artist of merit could be expected to undertake Government work.'[28] The longer the arguments continued, the more out of date the iconography became. Goetze's *Britannia Colonorum Mater* represents the British colonies as subordinates—literally children of the mother nation—yet by 1919 they were demanding and receiving an increased measure of independence in recognition of their role in Britain's victory in the war. Perhaps acting on instructions following the Japanese insistence on a racial equality clause in the League of Nations, Goetze gave prominence in *Britannia Pacificatrix* to a kimono-clad figure with blossom, as well as to the African, Asian, and American signatories; yet such harmony sits uneasily with his glorification in the other murals of Britain as a conqueror, ruler, and settler of other nations.

Perhaps there were other reasons too for Curzon's attitude to the murals. The new contemporaneity of the Official War Artists such as Muirhead Bone, Rothenstein, Nevinson, and Orpen, who worked *in situ* on the battlefields, stood in stark contrast to Goetze's idealized conceptions of British military and naval strength. And yet both Goetze's allegorical approach and the highly selective and often strongly stylized renderings of war by the War Artists[29] in fact form but two sides of one coin. Although the artists were asked to produce 'a record of the facts',[30] they were also required to adapt this to portray certain themes; and just as the War Artists' work was subjected to the scrutiny of the censor, so Goetze's murals had been subject to the authority of the Lord Great Chamberlain, who had commissioned them in conjunction with the First Commissioner of Works. The Lord Chamberlain was responsible for theatrical and film censorship and, given his prohibitions against not merely 'realistic horrors of warfare' (perhaps in part why allegory had been chosen in the first place for the Foreign Office), but also 'references to controversial politics',[31] it is likely that Curzon and the Cabinet feared some irregularity in Goetze's work. The play *Versailles*, for example, on the subject of the League of Nations, was censored in 1919; clearly, the State would likewise have been unprepared to countenance the kind of uncompromising treatment of war to be presented only a few years later by Neville Lytton at Balcombe Victory Hall,[32] though this was a local rather than a national project. In turn, the frank representation of the nightmare of war which emerged in the 'Hall of Remembrance', begun in 1918 by the Ministry of Information, never reached display as a permanent mural scheme.

Goetze's murals thus stood at a crossroads in the evolution of State patronage of art. They reflected the Government's continuing experiment with what Lord Carlisle had called 'pictures as

[26] Mond, *Mural Decoration*, p. 106.

[27] Ibid.

[28] Sir Alfred Mond, *Mural Decoration at the Foreign Office*, Memorandum (6 May 1920), Cab. 24/105, CP 1221, File No. 3/D/8, PRO, p. 193.

[29] See S. Malvern, 'War as it is: the Art of Muirhead Bone, C.R.W. Nevinson and Paul Nash 1916–17', *Art History*, 9, no. 4 (Dec. 1986), pp. 487–575, for a discussion of this aspect of the War Artists' work.

[30] Quoted in the 'Introduction' to *First World War Artists* (exhibition at Kelvingrove Museum and Art Gallery, Glasgow, Jan. 1987); source not specified.

[31] Rules 18 and 15 of the British Board of Film Censors, quoted in N. Pronay and D. W. Spring (eds), *Propaganda, Politics and Film 1918–1945* (London, 1982), p. 103.

[32] See Chapter 7.

tracts' in the interrupted St Stephen's Hall scheme at Westminster, and yet they can also be seen as a conscious attempt to secure work with a distinctive 'art motive',[33] the principle which purportedly drove the Ministry of Information's efforts to create a memorial of the war through its 'Hall of Remembrance', and the criterion by which Lord Curzon sought to reject Goetze's work in 1920–1. Conversely, Goetze's murals were, by the date of their completion, entirely out of step with the new 'documentary' aim of creating a 'Pictorial Record'[34] of war which guided the Imperial War Museum when (chaired, in fact, by Mond) it took over in 1919 the Ministry of Information's responsibilities for collecting war art, and, in the process, shelved the Ministry's 'Hall of Remembrance'. Curzon and the Cabinet suggested alternative locations for Goetze's scheme, such as town halls; Goetze, supported by Mond, clung to Beauchamp's original commission. Curzon gave ground on condition that the murals be hung on stretchers like easel paintings; Goetze insisted on *marouflage*, seeking the very permanence of union with the wall which in the nineteenth century had made fresco the *sine qua non* at Westminster. Sir Charles Holmes, Director of the National Gallery, eventually succeeded in having the murals temporarily installed for inspection; after 'opinions favourable to the pictures had been expressed by leading British, French and Belgian artists',[35] they were finally accepted and permanently fixed in 1921.

It has been suggested that Curzon was hostile to Goetze's work because he believed the artist to be German, and in 1921, immediately after the murals were accepted by the Cabinet, *Plain English* certainly published an article on 'Our Foreign Frescoes' which both condemned Goetze's murals as the work of 'a foreign Jew' and critized the involvement of Mond (who was of German-Jewish descent).[36] Goetze, who was not a Jew and whose ancestors had come to Britain from central Europe over a century before, brought a successful action against *Plain English.* (In any case on his 1913 visit to study Continental murals, he had found those in Germany 'mainly . . . of a character to be sternly avoided', and had described Kaulbach's 'colossal' murals at the Neues Museum in Berlin as a 'blatant absurdity'.)[37] The rapidly changing nature of propaganda, diplomatic relations, and also styles in art both during and after the war suggests, in fact, that Curzon was perhaps prepared by 1921 to tolerate the murals because they were now unlikely to do much harm. Whilst in 1914 Grey's and Beauchamp's enthusiasm for the decoration of the Foreign Office can be placed in the context of its radical opening up to the public through the establishment of its News Department and Press Bureau, by 1919 its propaganda machine had grown vastly sophisticated. Allegorical murals with Latin titles could hardly compare either with the panoply of verbal, eye-witness, and photographic information on Britain's foreign policies being issued to the press, or with the use of art for propaganda through the Official War Artists scheme.

Goetze's style and iconography, rooted in a classical idiom reaching back through Leighton and French academic tradition to High Renaissance painting, were also out of touch, not just with Vorticism and the avant-garde, or the Official War Artists' records of the Front, but with the directness and accessibility of the art of Sickert and the Camden Town Group as well. Likewise, his

[33] M. and S. Harries, *The War Artists* (1983), p. 149.

[34] Ibid. Interestingly, Goetze did model the figure of Australia in *Britannia Pacificatrix* on Bert Hill, the Australian soldier who had returned with the body of Goetze's nephew Francis Mond, killed on the Front (information kindly supplied by Marina Rainey); see also C. Dakers, 'Sigismund Goetze', *Decorative Arts Society Journal*, no. 21 (1997), p. 61 for the identity of other models for this mural.

[35] *Extract Draft Conclusions of Cabinet* 88(21) (22 Oct. 1921), FO 366/795, PRO.

[36] See Dakers, 'Sigismund Goetze' (1997), p. 62.

[37] Quoted in ibid., p. 55.

heroic half-nude *Strength* (Plate 59) stood a world apart from Brangwyn's ordinary soldiers fighting hand-to-hand in his brutally frank *Put Strength in the Final Blow* war poster (Plate 61). None the less, the ideal, perfect figures through which Goetze's anachronistic message was conveyed must have seemed at the least naïve, at worst an affront, to a nation preoccupied with remembering the dead, caring for the maimed, and rehabilitating—where possible—the traumatized. By 1921 they would have been equally at odds with the vision not of one superior, but of many cooperating peoples, building a 'world fit for heroes' through a united League of Nations. Goetze was a victim of changing political circumstances. What future could there be, in this situation, for British State mural painting? Was it destined to echo the compromise of Vienna's Neue Hofburg decoration, an uneasy combination of realistic and historical material? The conflicting answers offered by the subsequent British 'State' mural schemes—the 'Hall of Remembrance', St Stephen's Hall, and the Royal Gallery in the Palace of Westminster—show clearly that Goetze's Foreign Office paintings stand at a turning-point, if not a crisis, in the history of mural art in Britain.

Was Goetze's work itself an unresolved compromise? It has many happy echoes of his subtle and sensitive nude painting in murals on the theme of Ovid's *Metamorphoses* in his own home, Grove House; his pianist wife Constance was the model both there and for several of the Foreign Office figures, just as the irises in the foreground of *Britannia Sponsa* had already appeared in *Aesacus et Hesperiae* at Grove House (they were probably painted from specimens in Goetze's own splendid garden there). Yet the *Pacificatrix* panel at the Foreign Office lacks the telling contemporaneity of some of Goetze's allegorical easel paintings[38] and it is hard not to conclude that the conflicting pressures exerted by his patrons at the start and close of his commission effectively repressed a more personal vision. Compared with Brangwyn at Skinners' Hall, or later at the Royal Gallery in Westminster, he did not, perhaps, ultimately possess the inclination or imaginative flexibility to synthesize his own and his patrons' ideas in an innovative manner which could lead forward the 'British School of Mural Painting' so eagerly anticipated by the Palace of Westminster 1906 Select Committee, the Archbishop of Canterbury, and British artists themselves. Perhaps this is why his Grove House work, done for his own private satisfaction, has more spontaneity and originality.

The very concept of art as propaganda was in any case undergoing radical change by 1919. With the Armistice, the *raison d'être* of the Ministry of Information was of course removed, but its abortive 'Hall of Remembrance' project, begun in 1918 under the initiative of the British War Memorials Committee set up by Lord Beaverbrook when he became Minister of Information, had, in fact, already effectively moved beyond propaganda. Even though it never took shape as a mural scheme, this project is of interest not just for its individual paintings, but also for the insight it offers into the near-rejection of Goetze's work and the thinking behind the decoration from 1924 of St Stephen's Hall at the Palace of Westminster. It also throws light on the history of Brangwyn's abortive war memorial scheme for the Royal Gallery at Westminster, likewise begun in 1924, which will be considered in the next chapter.

[38] e.g. *Despised and Rejected of Men* (see reproduction in Witt Library, London), in which the naked, crucified Christ was placed amidst a crowd of fashionably dressed early twentieth-century citizens in the manner of J. Béraud's *Mary Magdalene in the House of the Pharisee* (1891, Walker Collection, Paris).

THE HALL OF REMEMBRANCE

The Hall of Remembrance was intended as a British counterpart to the 'vast series of decorative paintings on a heroic scale',[39] eventually housed in the Manitoba State Legislative Building, which had been launched as a Canadian National War Memorial by Lord Beaverbrook. Muirhead Bone, one of the principal art advisers to the British War Memorials Committee, saw the objective of the Hall as the communication of 'dreams' and 'feelings' that, 'expressed by our artists in terms of beauty', might 'speak to succeeding generations in a voice which never grows unintelligible or stale . . . the power of Art . . . is as clear and telling as the "moral voice within us".'[40] Beaverbrook's committee none the less still clearly saw the scheme, at least at the outset, as a vehicle for more specifically political ideals. Just as Goetze's Foreign Office work was reorientated after the war to convey the ideology of League of Nations politics, so the 'super-pictures' on the scale of Uccello's *Rout of San Romano* paintings, which were envisaged as the centrepiece of the Hall, were supposed to illustrate the concerted work of the Allies in the conduct of the war, and included 'The War Council' (to be painted by Sir William Orpen).[41] So too, whilst several of the artists listed by the committee as suitable potential contributors, such as Augustus John, had already been involved in the Canadian scheme, many can be recognized as exponents of the audacious approaches to 'reality' which during the hostilities had ensured that the art produced by the Ministry of Information's Official War Artists was consistent with the censor's strictures on 'realistic' representations of the trauma of war. As C. E. Montague, one of the Ministry's first propaganda writers, who acted as the censor of war correspondents' despatches, had commented: 'we are all in a league to hide . . . some extreme, mysterious horror which is . . . war "as it is" . . . which, if leaked out, would make the world lay down its arms on the spot.'[42] Although, in striking contrast to Goetze's allegorical iconography, it was planned that the 'super-pictures' of Allied cooperation should be complemented with 'a comprehensive survey of the general subjects of life in England during the War', including such documentary subjects as 'Navy and Mercantile Marine', and even 'Clerical and other work by women', the artists proposed thus included Charles Rennie Mackintosh ('outré designer and architect [who] would set out a room or exhibition in a striking and original manner that might be useful'); Stanley Spencer ('Painter of figure pictures imbued with imaginative qualities of remarkable order Pictures by him have been purchased by Contemporary Art Society for the Nation'); Mark Gertler (whose name was entered beside the theme of 'The Tube on a Raid Night'); and Wyndham Lewis, the Vorticist advocate of Futurism's cult of violence and war—as well as, interestingly, Brangwyn.[43]

In the event, the choice of artists was remarkably catholic, but Mackintosh, Gertler, and Brangwyn, as well as other names, were discarded, and the plans developed into something reminiscent of the kind of closely integrated 'Hall of Heroes' War Memorial which had been

[39] *The Canadian War Memorial Fund Its History and Objectives*, pamphlet in file 460 a/10, IWM.

[40] Harries, *The War Artists*, p. 94.

[41] The 'super-pictures' description is in a letter from R. Ross, the 'connoisseur and gallery-owner' (Harries, *War Artists*, p. 31) to the British War Memorials Committee (8 April 1918), IWM, in ibid. (Ross acted as adviser to the Committee); for Orpen's involvement, see *Minutes* of British War Memorials Executive Committee (27 March 1918), IWM, in ibid.

[42] Montague, 1917 Preface to the last five issues of the *Western Front* volume of illustrations by the Official War Artists, quoted in Malvern, 'War as it is' (1986), p. 495.

[43] Proposed subjects are from *Minutes* of British War Memorials Executive Committee (20 (?) March 1918), IWM; comments on potential artists are in *Memorandum of Proceedings of Preliminary Meeting of Imperial Permanent Memorials Committee* (6 March 1918), IWM.

installed in 1916 by the Arts and Crafts Exhibition Society at its Royal Academy Exhibition.[44] Bone recommended that the Hall of Remembrance be located within a garden on Richmond Hill as 'a kind of Pavilion' with music playing in one of its galleries and an oratory containing decoration on the theme of ' "the coming Brotherhood of Man", for which we all pray',[45] as its climax. Such a *Gesamtkunstwerk* scheme would, of course, have projected aptly the political harmony represented by Allied cooperation, and D. Y. Cameron's suggestion of pairing the subjects of the large murals and adopting a common horizon line was welcomed by the Committee. Cameron himself painted *The Battlefield of Ypres*—a bleak yet strangely tranquil panorama of the empty Western Front, which he significantly explained as 'not a portrait of any one spot—photographers can do that'[46]—and he worked closely with his partner artist, Charles Sims, to ensure coordination between their pictures. The power of the scheme, however, had it ever been realized as a mural ensemble, would arguably have resulted from the intensity of lived experience and personal vision present in certain *individual* pictures and transcending both theory and agenda (whether political or Arts and Crafts). As Orpen commented to the Secretary of the British War Memorials Committee when Sargent's *Gassed*[47] (Plate 62), the intended centrepiece of the Hall, was voted 'Picture of the Year' at the Royal Academy in 1919, 'don't tell an artist what to do . . . instead of "America and France" you have *Gassed* by J.S.S. . . . So much for ordering artists about.'[48] Sargent's harrowing procession of blinded soldiers, stumbling and lurching through the sickly pink finality of an evening on the Western Front in the 'awfully long strip of a picture'[49] he was required to fill, spoke not of the particularity of strategic alliance, but instead of the numbing futility of war as such, and of the universality of the human condition. Stanley Spencer's *Travoys arriving with the Wounded at a Dressing Station at Smol, Macedonia, September 1916* (Plate XVII), with its visionary flood of blinding light emanating from a field operating theatre seen beyond a fan-like formation of waiting stretchers drawn by mules, was likewise an act of personal catharsis, and a deeply felt affirmation of spiritual 'redemption' after the 'scene of horror' on the Eastern Front in Macedonia, where he had served in the RAMC.[50] Tonks's 'Uccello' painting, *An Advanced Dressing-Station in France, 1918*, with its more diffuse composition of wounded soldiers, stretcher cases, and orderlies against a backdrop of smoking burnt-out ruins, seems melodramatic by contrast.

Highly individual contributions were also provided by Paul Nash in his *Menin Road* (Plate 63), a battlefield vista all but devoid of human content, whose sombre morass of brown and purple mud punctuated with stagnant puddles, debris of war, and devastated trees is yet momentarily lit by eerie shafts of yellow sunlight (tokens of possible renewal?); and by Henry Lamb in *Irish Troops in the Judean Hills surprised by a Turkish Bombardment* (Plate 64). Lamb's painting has something of Spencer's crystalline intensity, but suggests a frightening hallucination rather than the healing vision offered by Spencer's *Travoys*. Its aerial viewpoint and sharp-edged, jagged smoke clouds

[44] See Chapter 11 and D. Farr et al. *Joseph Southall* (1980).

[45] Bone to IWM Art Sub-Committee (29 Jan. 1919), quoted in Harries, *War Artists*, p. 94. Ross had already suggested that 'a special wing at the Tate Gallery' might be used to house the paintings (*Minutes* of British War Memorials Executive Committee, 21 March 1918, IWM), and recommended a wood-panelled setting as in the 'famous Scuola or Guild rooms of Venice, decorated by Carpaccio, Tintoretto and Tiepolo' (letter of 8 April 1918, IWM). On Bone's advice, the architect Charles Holden was then asked to prepare designs for a purpose-built pavilion.

[46] Quoted in Harries, *War Artists*, p. 102.

[47] All the paintings intended as murals for the Hall of Remembrance were painted in 1918–19 and are now in the Imperial War Museum, London.

[48] Letter from Orpen to A. Yockney (18 April 1919), Orpen File, IWM, quoted in R. Cork, *A Bitter Truth* (1994), p. 222.

[49] Letter from Sargent to Yockney (14 Oct. 1918), IWM, quoted in ibid., p. 220. The painting is 1.28 m high by 6.10 m wide.

[50] Quoted in Harries, *War Artists*, p. 111.

engulfing helpless, mannequin-like soldiers capture the psychological moment of panic reaction to enemy fire, but offer no hint of resolution, as in Nash's and Spencer's paintings. In turn, in Wyndham Lewis's *A Battery Shelled* (Plate 65), the very process of artistic response to the experience of war is placed under scrutiny, in a multi-layered, deeply disturbing composition which plays out Lewis's recognition of the untenability of his earlier sympathy with Futurism's glorification of violence and battle. Just as the personification and allegory of Goetze or of the majority of the RA Hall of Heroes murals were now felt inappropriate, so the mechanistic, geometric human forms characteristic of Lewis's Vorticist phase are set in his painting like alien robots amidst a plain of churned mud rendered as an angular pattern of metallic green strewn with the machinery of war, whilst at the left foreground, significantly turning his back on the scene, is a figure identified as Lewis himself. He is accompanied by Edward Wadsworth and a man who can be taken as another former Vorticist, and all three are portrayed as (relatively) life-like, flesh and blood beings. As survivors of the war, this trio and its 'alter ego' bring to mind, as Cork has pointed out, Freud's proposal that 'our own death is indeed, unimaginable, and whenever we make the attempt to imagine it we can perceive that we really survive as spectators.'[51] The image clearly illustrates Lewis's description of the war as 'a sleep, deep and animal, in which I was visited by images of an order very new to me. Upon waking I found an altered world: and I had changed too, very much. The geometrics which had interested me so exclusively before, I now felt were bleak and empty. They wanted filling.'[52]

Compared with such a philosophical response to war, the fussy patterning of dark against light in William Roberts's *A Shell Dump, France* seems contrived and superficial, just as C. R. W. Nevinson's *The Harvest of Battle*, which likewise returned to a more naturalistic idiom, lacks the monumentality of Sargent's *Gassed*. Put together as a decorative ensemble, the paintings produced for the Hall of Remembrance would undoubtedly have failed; it is questionable whether the requirement for first-hand experience of war, built upon the achievements of the Official War Artists project, from which the scheme evolved, could so soon after the event have been matched to the discipline of painting for a particular building and location. Whereas in France a national war memorial was being created by an artist who had neither been involved in combat nor present at the Front, Claude Monet, on a theme which sought not to illustrate the war but rather to offer a vision of regeneration, the *Nymphéas* (Orangerie, Paris), in the Hall of Remembrance the chosen iconography was perhaps still too recent and emotively charged for successful translation into an art-form intended to speak for time immemorial. Augustus John, indeed, found it impossible to make any response to his commission.

The decision to abandon the Hall of Remembrance as a mural scheme in 1919 when it came under the purview of the Imperial War Museum, and the substitution of 'record' for 'art motive' in the collection policy of the Museum, were perhaps a tacit recognition of this dilemma. When the State turned to murals again at St Stephen's Hall in the Palace of Westminster in 1924, not only was war explictly avoided as a theme, but the progressive strain of art espoused by the Official War Artists and in the Hall of Remembrance was replaced with the more predictable and conservative style of the British School at Rome, which can be recognized as once again directly related to political objectives. The choice of this style can, none the less, be seen as a direct sequel both to the ideal of coordination attempted by Cameron at the Hall of Remembrance (Cameron, a member of

[51] Quoted in Cork, *A Bitter Truth*, p. 226. [52] Quoted in ibid.

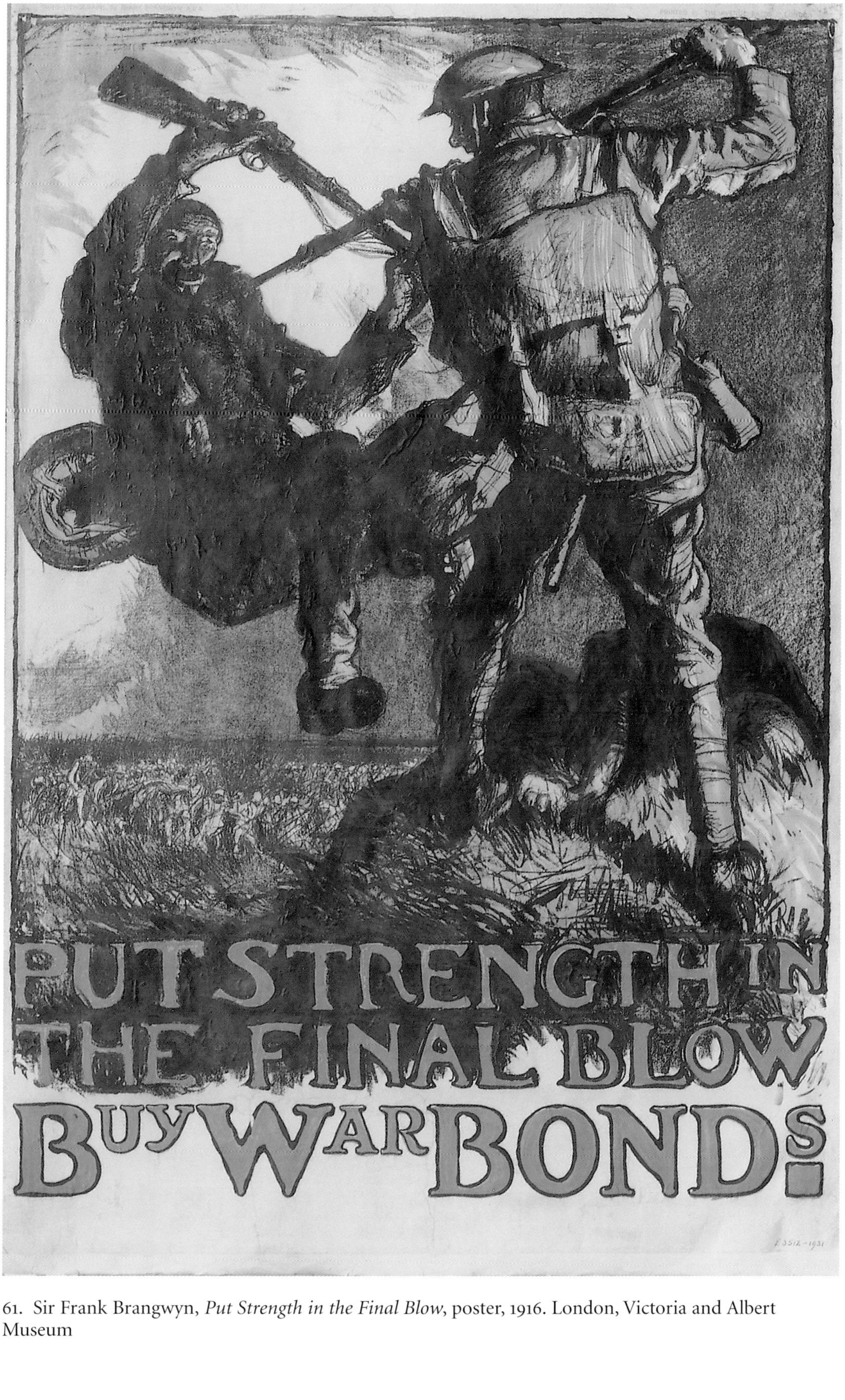

61. Sir Frank Brangwyn, *Put Strength in the Final Blow*, poster, 1916. London, Victoria and Albert Museum

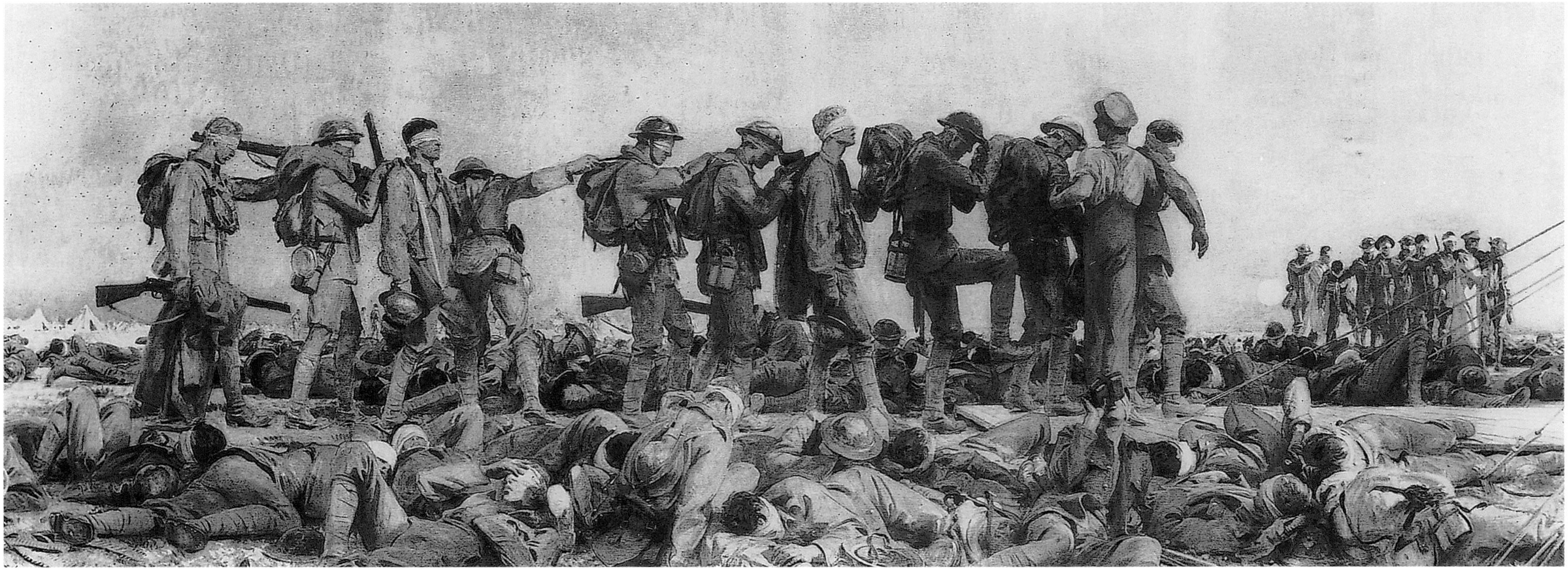

62. John Singer Sargent, *Gassed*, signed 'Aug. 1918', for 'Hall of Remembrance', 1918–19. London, Imperial War Museum

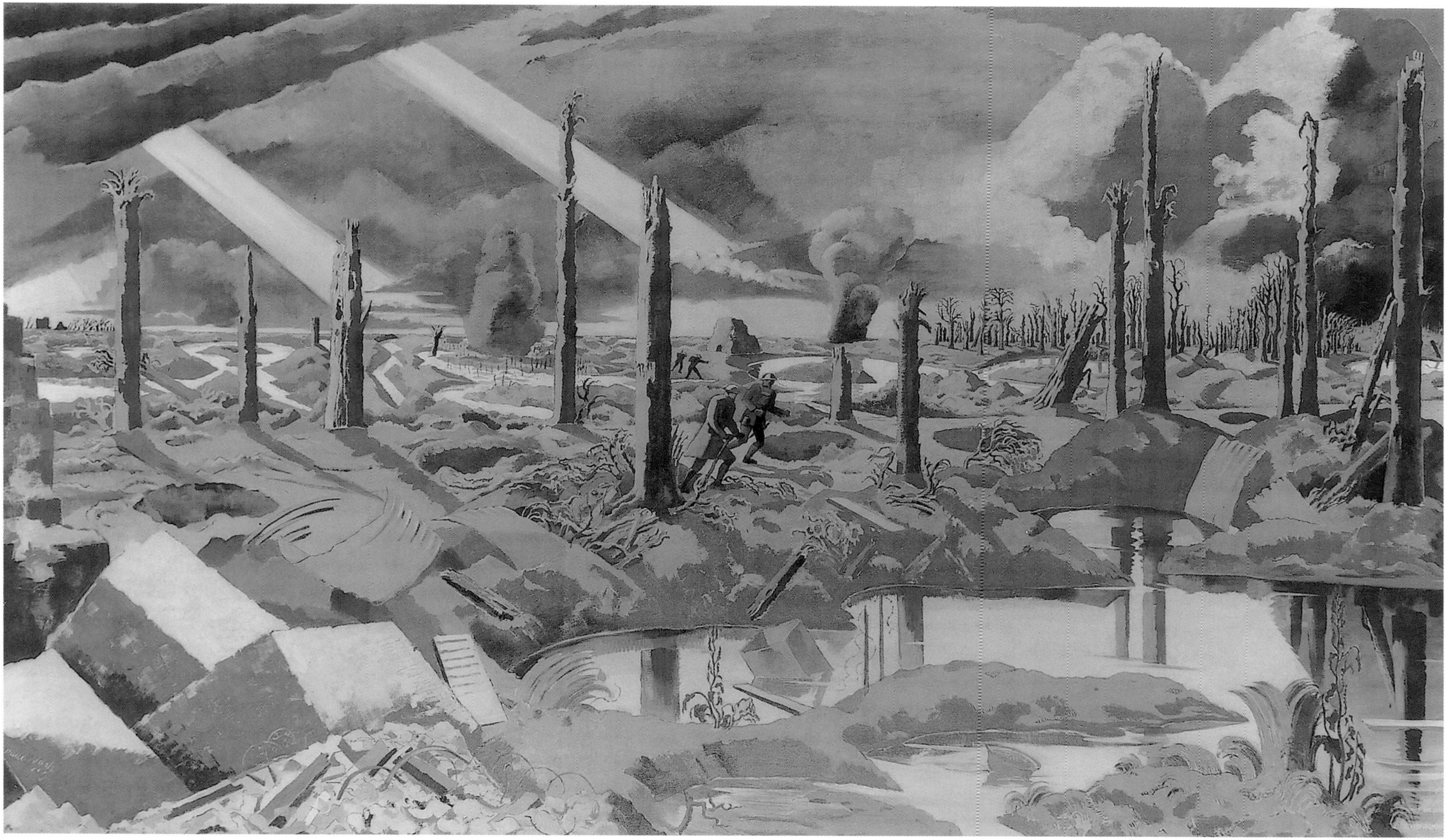

63. Paul Nash, *The Menin Road*, for 'Hall of Remembrance', 1918–19. London, Imperial War Museum

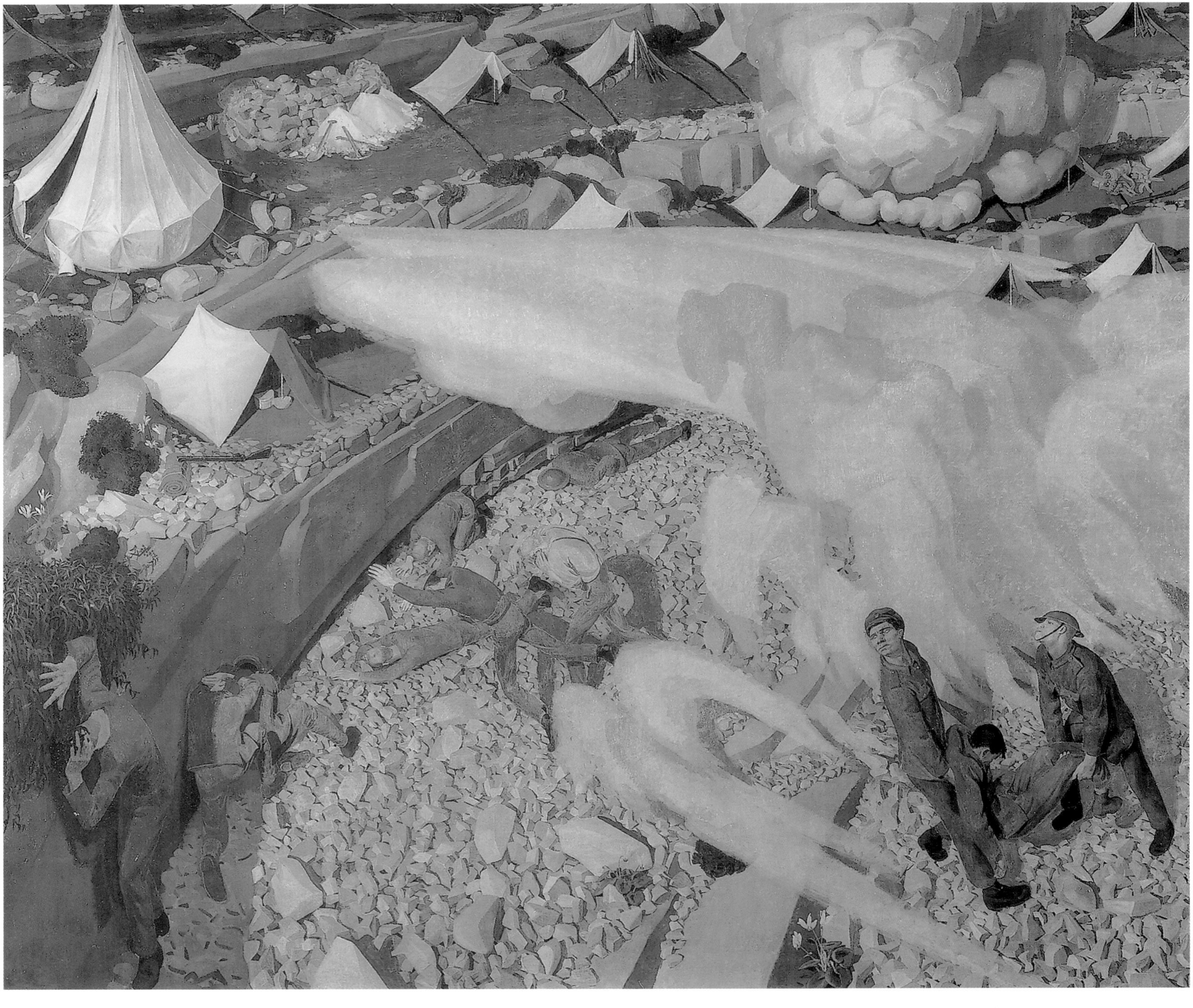

64. Henry Lamb, *Irish Troops in the Judean Hills surprised by a Turkish Bombardment*, for 'Hall of Remembrance', 1918–19. London, Imperial War Museum

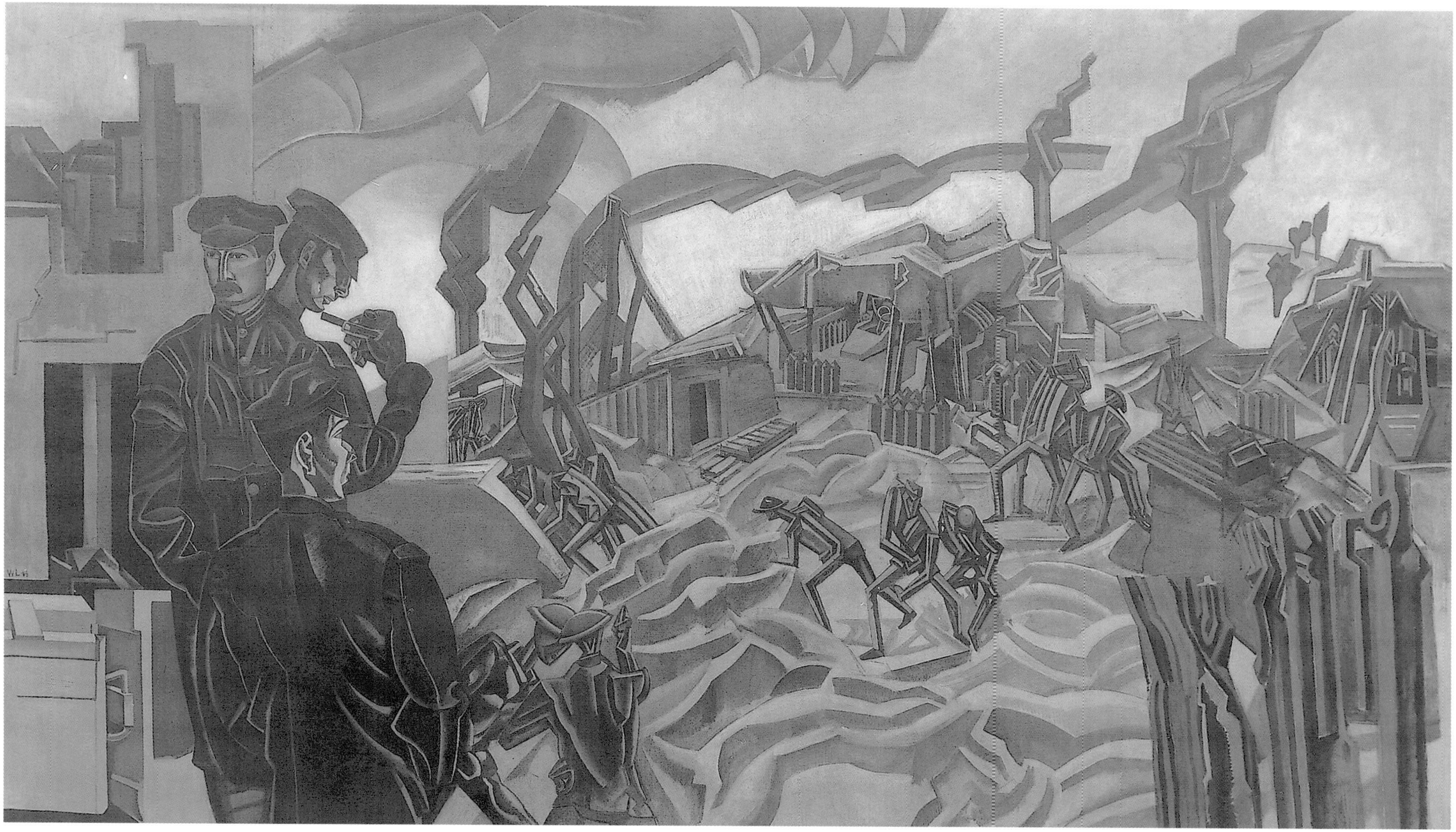

65. Percy Wyndham Lewis, *A Battery Shelled*, for 'Hall of Remembrance', 1918–19. London, Imperial War Museum

the School's Faculty of Painting, became artistic supervisor at St Stephen's Hall) and to the reference to early Italian art (Uccello's *Rout of San Romano* in the Uffizi, Florence).

ST STEPHEN'S HALL, PALACE OF WESTMINSTER (1924–1927)

The tensions between an individual artist's concern to express a personal vision and the State's ideals as patron which had become manifest in the Foreign Office commission to Sigismund Goetze resurfaced even more acutely in the murals carried out in the 1920s for St Stephen's Hall. Far from diminishing, the influence of the censor was by then still more powerful, whether in film, literature, or in mural painting; the medium *par excellence*, perhaps, in which, on account of its permanence, the censor's *bête noire* of a 'theme repeated over and over again'[53] could arguably be most dangerous. By 1935, shortly after the Lords' rejection of Brangwyn's Royal Gallery panels, which were begun simultaneously with the decoration of St Stephen's Hall, a situation had been reached where 'no controversy' was regarded as in practice equivalent to 'No reality'.[54] Whereas the East Corridor murals at Westminster in 1906–10 could escape the Lord Great Chamberlain's strictures in his function as censor against 'references to controversial politics'[55] through historical parallelism which involved a high degree of realism, and the memorial motive at the Hall of Remembrance had seen a short-lived, though still relative, openness to representation of 'the horrors of war', by the 1920s and 1930s the increased sophistication and strictness of the censorship machinery had excluded such devices.[56] The iconography and style of Goetze's Foreign Office murals; the semi-symbolic or carefully selective lithographs of contemporary war (often using avant-garde styles) by the Official War Artists; the abandonment of the Hall of Remembrance scheme; the work at St Stephen's Hall, and finally Brangwyn's Royal Gallery murals, can be regarded as reflecting successive stages in the evolution of this situation, and also as revealing an enduring view on the part of the British government of mural painting as a form of message, or even a 'tract'.

At St Stephen's Hall, the censor's prohibition of the portrayal of contemporary politicians was probably a material factor in the decision in 1924 to remove a panel showing *The Burial of the Unknown Warrior*[57] (Plate 66) which had been completed in 1918 by Frank Salisbury as a contemporary contribution to Harcourt's and Beauchamp's unfinished scheme. With the two panels by Gow (Plate 53) and Seymour Lucas which had been installed in 1912 and 1915 respectively,[58] it was relegated, after much public outcry, to a Committee Room, and an entirely new series of historical subjects was commissioned, whose parameters trod a delicate line between 'no realism' on one hand and, on the other, an overt appeal to the common man—whose support was now critical in the immediate wake of the extension of the franchise to all men and women over the age of 30. The Speaker of the House of Commons, W. H. Whitley, who was placed in control of the scheme, on behalf of the Lord Great Chamberlain, along with the First Commisssioner of

[53] Quoted from the *British Board of Film Censors Annual Report* (1935) in Pronay and Spring (eds), *Propaganda, Politics and Film*, p. 113.

[54] Ibid., p. 111.

[55] Ibid., p. 105.

[56] Ibid., p. 107.

[57] See HLRO, undated MS by W. H. Whitley; cf. also the note in Minute Sheet (19 Dec. 1924), Work 11/264, PRO, recording the Office of Works' dissatisfaction with Salisbury's painting and the Speaker's having 'ambitious ideas by which the whole of those panels in St. Stephen's Hall might be treated by some artist as a comprehensive whole'.

[58] See Chapter 4. Salisbury's painting (like Gow's and Lucas's) is on canvas; it is 2.67 × 4.11 m in size.

Works and the chairman of a newly formed Royal Fine Art Commission, intended the eight new panels to 'tell a story to . . . the ordinary citizen and to the schoolchildren who visit the home of their Parliament'.[59]

Although he noted that 'The ideas and memories which will present themselves may be employed in two ways: by symbolic or by direct representation,' it was the 'direct' method on which he insisted[60] for such a public and significant part of Westminster as St Stephen's Hall, described by the poet and naval historian Sir Henry Newbolt as 'the exact spot where many of the great struggles of our Parliamentary history took place: where words were spoken and decisions taken which have ever since affected the course of our national life'.[61]

Whitley was later to become Chairman of the BBC and a prime mover in the inauguration of the Empire Broadcasting Service in 1933; he acted in association with Newbolt in determining the St Stephen's Hall scheme, as he was later to do at the BBC, and although Newbolt sought the advice of the historians G. M. Trevelyan, A. F. Pollard, and C. H. Firth, it was Whitley who took the decisions.[62] The St Stephen's Hall murals (Plates 67–71; Plate XVIII) can be seen as a first experiment in the use of mural painting as part of the British Government's growing commitment to popular education and, in particular, to the dissemination of ideals of Empire. Their theme was 'The Building of Britain'; their individual subjects, from British history up to the Act of Union of 1707, were intended as a means to make the viewer aware of his place in a continuing chain of history and as 'not merely literal illustrations to a prosaic narrative' but topics which would 'go beyond fact to symbolise the inner meaning of certain events—to awake us to the greatness and wonder of our growth as a nation, our evolution from a group of tribal states to a worldwide Commonwealth'.[63] Their educative purpose, as material for photographic reproduction as well as viewing *in situ*, was made plain by Whitley at the Royal Academy Banquet of 1929, after they were completed:

> The real recompense [to the artists] would come when those pictures were, as he hoped they soon would be, on the walls of every school in the Empire, telling the story of the Building of Britain . . . What a difference it would make if in all our great towns there were buildings, municipal, university, commercial, each containing a series of paintings to tell the story of local and national endeavour . . . [to] carry a message through to future generations.[64]

It was not, however, the Royal Academy to which Whitley had turned for the artists to realize this vision, but the British School at Rome, which had been established by Abbey before the war as effectively a break-away institution intended to return painting and sculpture to the monumental purposes they had served during the Italian Renaissance, and to give British artists the kind of training structure, involving study in Italy, which was available to the French through their Academy in Rome. Like D. Y. (later Sir David) Cameron, who was selected to coordinate the new St Stephen's scheme, the majority of its artists were either tutors at the school (William

[59] Notes by Whitley on the significance of the St Stephen's Hall panels, Work 11/197 (PRO file in HLRO).

[60] Ibid.

[61] H. Newbolt, *The Building of Britain* (*c.* 1927), p. 1.

[62] e.g. see letter about choice of mural titles from Lord Crawford and Balcarres (Chairman of the Royal Fine Art Commission) to Sir D. Y. Cameron (coordinator of the St Stephen's Hall scheme) (25 June 1925), Cam. P.: 'and a good deal depends on what the Speaker thinks and if he feels sympathetic.'

[63] Newbolt, *Building of Britain*, p. 4. The murals, again painted on canvas, are each 3.05 × 4.42 m in size.

[64] Report of Whitley's speech in *The Times* (6 May 1929). When the murals were completed, Whitley indeed persuaded the Fine Arts Publishing Company, Bell's, and a number of other publishers to issue reproductions of them as posters for schools and history text-book illustrations, much as had already occurred with the Royal Exchange murals from 1913 (see Chapter 3 n. 51 and Willsdon in A. Saunders (ed.), *The Royal Exchange* (1997), n. 75).

Rothenstein), or recently qualified scholars (e.g. A. K. Lawrence and Colin Gill). Although a number of the artists such as George Clausen were also members or visitors at the Royal Academy, their primary sympathies lay with the new Rome School; the panel of King John signing Magna Carta (Plate 67) allotted to the Secretary of the Royal Academy, Charles Sims (who had contributed to the Hall of Remembrance) proved the most controversial on account of its more realistic and dramatic approach.

Realism, in other words, was to be tempered and approached through the eyes of Piero della Francesca, Lorenzetti (whose *Allegories of Good Government* in the Palazzo Pubblico in Siena provided a direct source of inspiration for motifs in Clausen's pastoral subject of *The English People gathering to read Wycliffe's Bible*) (Plate XVIII), and the early Italian Renaissance artists, which were upheld as the key exemplars at the British School at Rome, just as the historical episodes were to conclude well before modern times. This approach can be seen as a recognition that abstract classical personifications, as at the Foreign Office, could no longer speak to the voter in the street and the Commonwealth school-child, whose attention Whitley hoped to capture 'directly'. As one of 'Mr. Punch's correspondents at the Front' pointed out after 1919:

> Dawn to me will no longer be personified as a rosy-fingered damsel or a lovely swift footed deity, but as a sturdy little man in khaki, crimson-eared with cold, heralded and escorted by frozen wafts of outer air, bearing in one knobbly fist a pair of boots, and in the other a tin mug of black and smoking tea.[65]

Equally inaccessible, however, were the Vorticist experiments of some of the Official War Artists; as *Punch* also recorded, speaking as a mother:

> 'They give me a dreadful feeling. I can't bear to look at them. Is it really like that at the front?'
> The Warrior (who has seen terrible things in battle): 'Thank heaven, no, mother.'[66]

The style of the British School at Rome and the range of subjects at St Stephen's Hall were an obvious compromise between the censor's constraints and the kind of direct confrontation with reality being adopted despite him at the same period, not only at Balcombe Victory Hall by Neville Lytton, but also in the historically accurate pageant costumes and displays of the 1924 Wembley Empire Exhibition. Whilst the appeal of the murals was to be 'direct, so that he who runs may read',[67] Whitley was at the same time clearly resistant to the kind of art which had been praised only a few months before the first plans were laid for the St Stephen's Hall murals by none other than the then Prime Minister, Ramsay MacDonald: pictures representing 'the fundamental eternal verities and the struggles of humanity, not in the persons of dead people, but in the persons of his own generation'.[68] These were the pictures of Frank Brangwyn, whose largest public exhibition to date at Queen's Gate had just become the first art exhibition in Britain ever to have been opened by a Prime Minister. Censorship seems not to have been a deterrent for MacDonald to the portrayal of the real and the modern; he had already 'lent a ready ear' to proposals from one of their most devoted advocates, William Rothenstein, that artists be allowed to decorate 'the waiting rooms of hospitals, canteens, employment bureaux, village halls'.[69] Although MacDonald referred to the

[65] Quoted in C. Groves, *Mr. Punch's History of the Great War* (London, 1920), p. 208.

[66] Caption to a cartoon by Frank Reynolds showing a 'mother' and 'soldier' at an exhibition of 'War Pictures' in the style of Nevinson and Lewis (presumably the RA 1919 exhibition of paintings for the new Imperial War Museum), reproduced in ibid., p. 240.

[67] Whitley, *Second Draft* of *Suggested Terms of Reference for a Scheme for Decorating the 8 Panels in St. Stephen's Hall, with Pictures, for consideration on Wednesday, April 1st, 5.30*, Cam.P.

[68] Quoted in R. Brangwyn, *Brangwyn* (1978), p. 226.

[69] Entry in notebook of Sir William Rothenstein, TGA 7911.10.1.

'difficulty of carrying out a plan of the kind'[70] (perhaps an allusion to the censor's control), he had been the moving spirit behind the mounting of the Wembley Exhibition, and its illusionistic displays had no doubt passed the censor because, unlike permanent mural paintings, it was a temporary event. He had, however, lost office before the completion of preparations for the Wembley Exhibition. When it opened, it was with Neoclassical architecture for its government buildings and publicity lettering based on Trajan's column; a symbolic packaging which marked the new Conservative Government's identification of the British Empire with that of Ancient Rome, and one that contrasted visibly with Labour's attempts to propagate an alternative image of 'federal union for the British Commonwealth'.[71]

The essential message of modern security as guaranteed by continuity through the ages, which is implicit in this Roman symbolism, provides the immediate context for the iconography and style of *The Building of Britain* at St Stephen's Hall. Decorations in the Wembley pavilions, such as the classical personification of Empire on the glass roof of the British Government building[72] and the mural for its basilica of *The Altruists* by the Rome Scholar A. K. Lawrence, a modern nude subject, but inspired by Piero della Francesca, had in fact turned the exhibition into a curious hybrid of a Conservative overlay on Labour ideas. At St Stephen's Hall, however, this Conservative imagery came into full operation. It provides the backdrop to the rejection of Brangwyn's murals commissioned by Lord Iveagh for the Royal Gallery, as well as to the Office of Works' insistence that Epstein replace his planned contemporary portrait for the Hudson Memorial in Hyde Park with something more 'symbolic', which resulted in his *Rima*, based on the Ludovisi throne relief and unveiled by the new Prime Minister, Stanley Baldwin, in 1925. It explains A. K. Lawrence's outburst at being required to paint at St Stephen's Hall *Queen Elizabeth commissioning Sir Walter Releigh* when he would have preferred 'a great war fantasy' with its 'chief subject'

> a stricken infantryman, mortally wounded, being attended to by a R.A.M.C. doctor and man . . . I should introduce the figure of a young peasant woman offering aid . . . incidents also to suggest the uncomplaining suffering borne not only by stricken men, but by the nervous and apprehensive men . . . the whole to be composed into a design which shall *not* be an incomprehensible allegory but as clear an expression as possible of the magnificent *dignity* of our people in enduring the catastrophe of war.[73]

His vision suggests he had seen Lord Lytton at work in Balcombe, but Clausen too, who had the coordinator Cameron's highest regard amongst the artists, attempted to persuade his patrons that

> the question 'what is it all about?' should be so obvious that no-one should ever ask it . . . I fear the result at St. Stephen's will be much the same as at the Royal Exchange—disconnected episodes, conveying no general impression. This I think is the case with the series at Westminster done by the 'Abbey pupils'. . . there is no unity in the series as a whole . . . What is in my mind, in quite a crude way— . . . is a series of panels representing, say, Religion, Kingship, Law, Military power, naval power, Industry, Agriculture, the education of youth, colonising, etc.[74]

Lord Devonport likewise, who had offered to donate the first panel, was reported in a letter from Newbolt to Cameron marked 'Private—Poison—Safety First!' as having voiced his objections to the historical subjects of the murals 'on the grounds that they were 1) all unknown to the public

[70] Ibid.

[71] D. Lavin, 'History, Morals and the Politics of Empire: Lionel Curtis and the Round Table' in J. Bossy and P. Jupp (eds), *Essays Presented to Michael Roberts* (Belfast, 1976), pp. 119–29.

[72] Described in *The Times* (23 April 1924), p. xviii.

[73] Letter from Lawrence to Cameron (4 Aug. 1925), Cam.P.

[74] Letter from Clausen to Cameron (22 June 1925), Cam.P.

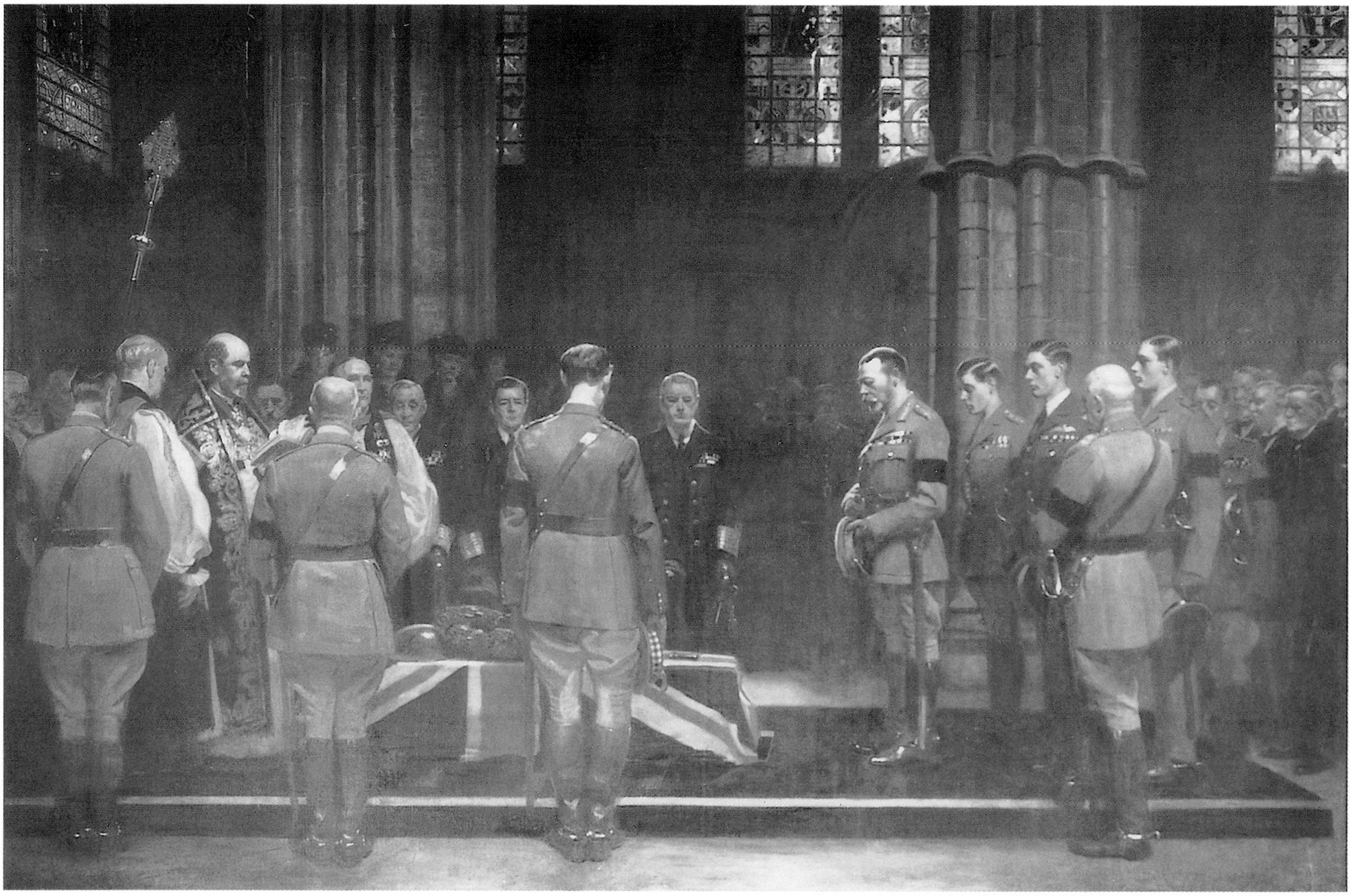

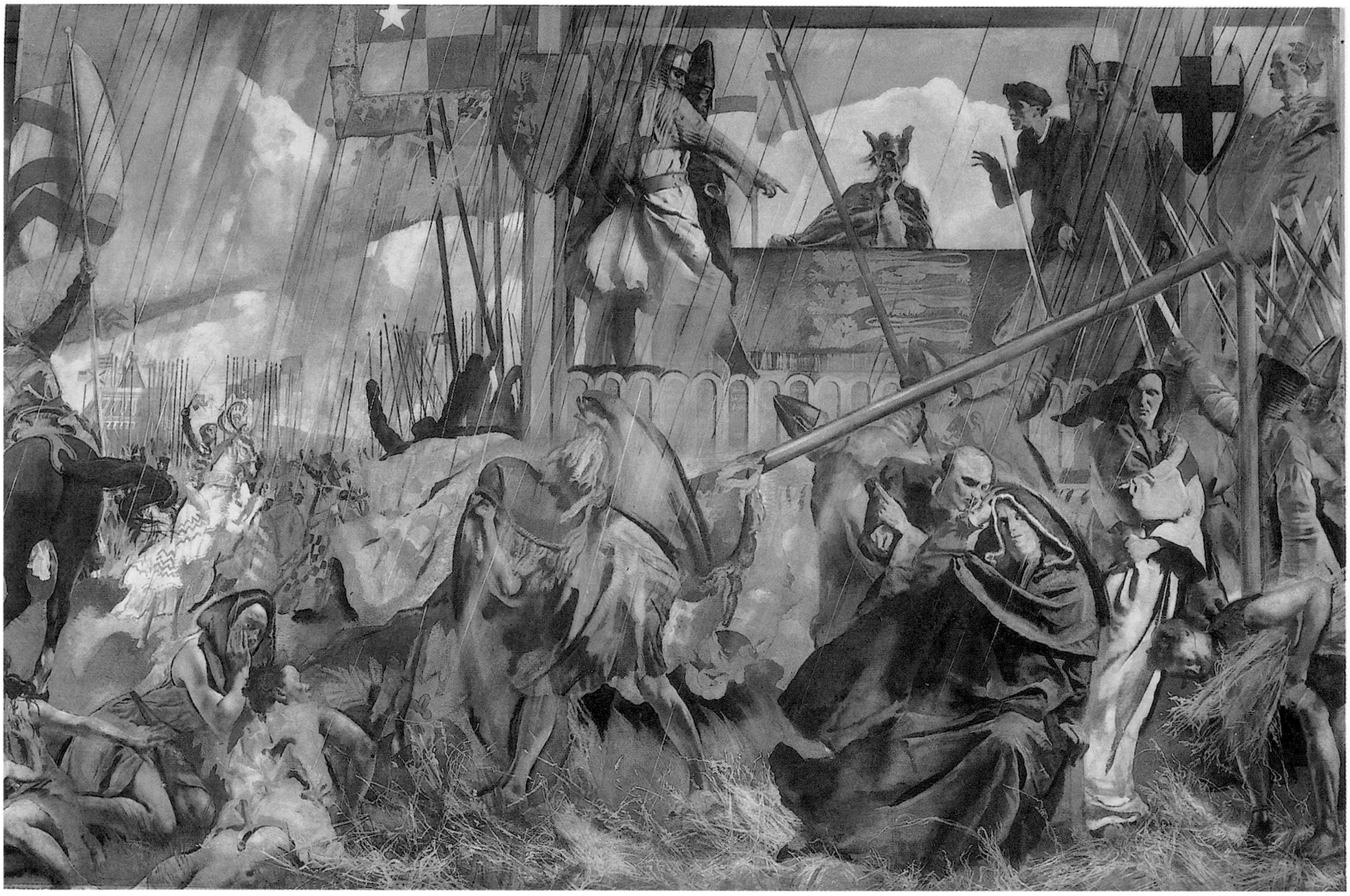

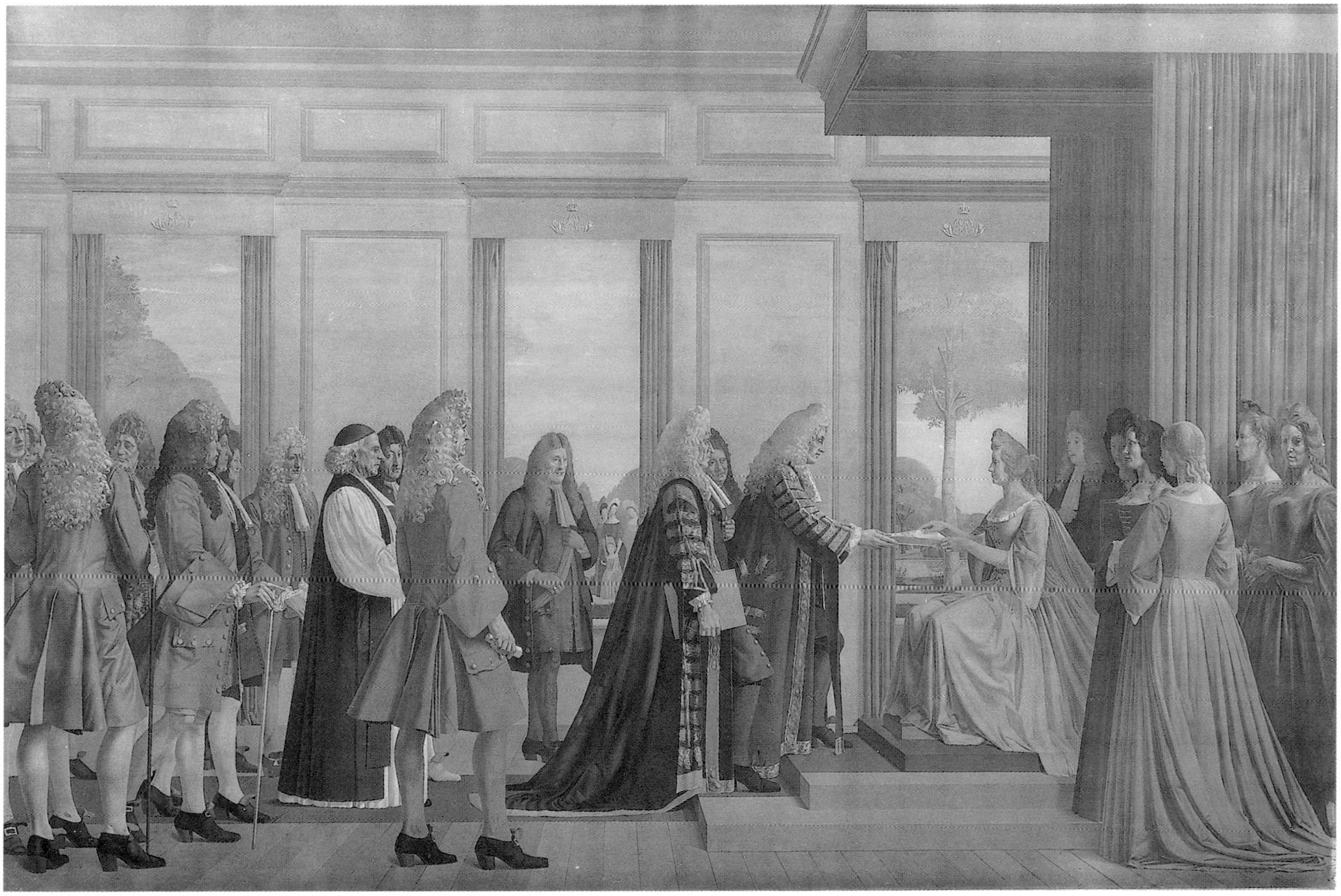

68. Sir (Walter) Thomas Monnington, *The English and Scottish Commissioners present to Queen Anne at St. James's Palace the articles of agreement for the Parliamentary union of the two countries, 1707*, St Stephen's Hall, Palace of Westminster, London, 1925–7. Presented by the Viscount Younger of Leckie

66 (*facing, above*). Frank O. Salisbury, *The Burial of the Unknown Warrior, 1920*, formerly St Stephen's Hall, Palace of Westminster, London, 1920–1

67 (*facing, below*). Charles Sims, *King John, confronted by his Barons assembled in force at Runneymede, gives unwilling consent to Magna Carta, the foundation of justice and individual freedom in England, 1215*, St Stephen's Hall, Palace of Westminster, London, 1925–7. Presented by the Viscount Burnham

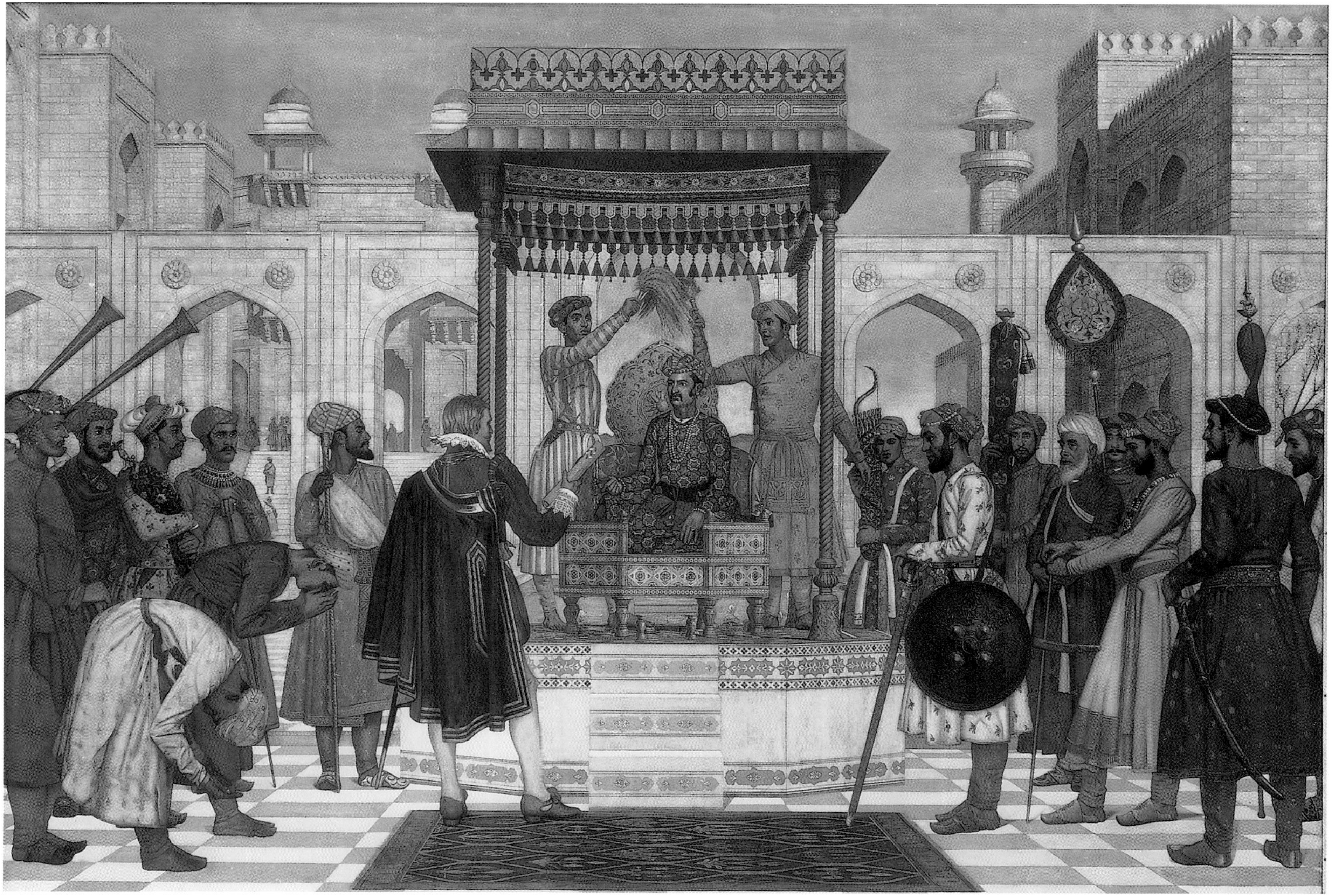

69. Sir William Rothenstein, *Sir Thomas Roe, envoy from King James the first of England to the Moghul Emperor, succeeds by his mingled courtesy and firmness at the Court of Ajmir in laying the foundation of British influence in India, 1614*, St Stephen's Hall, Palace of Westminster, London, 1925–7. Presented by the Duke of Bedford

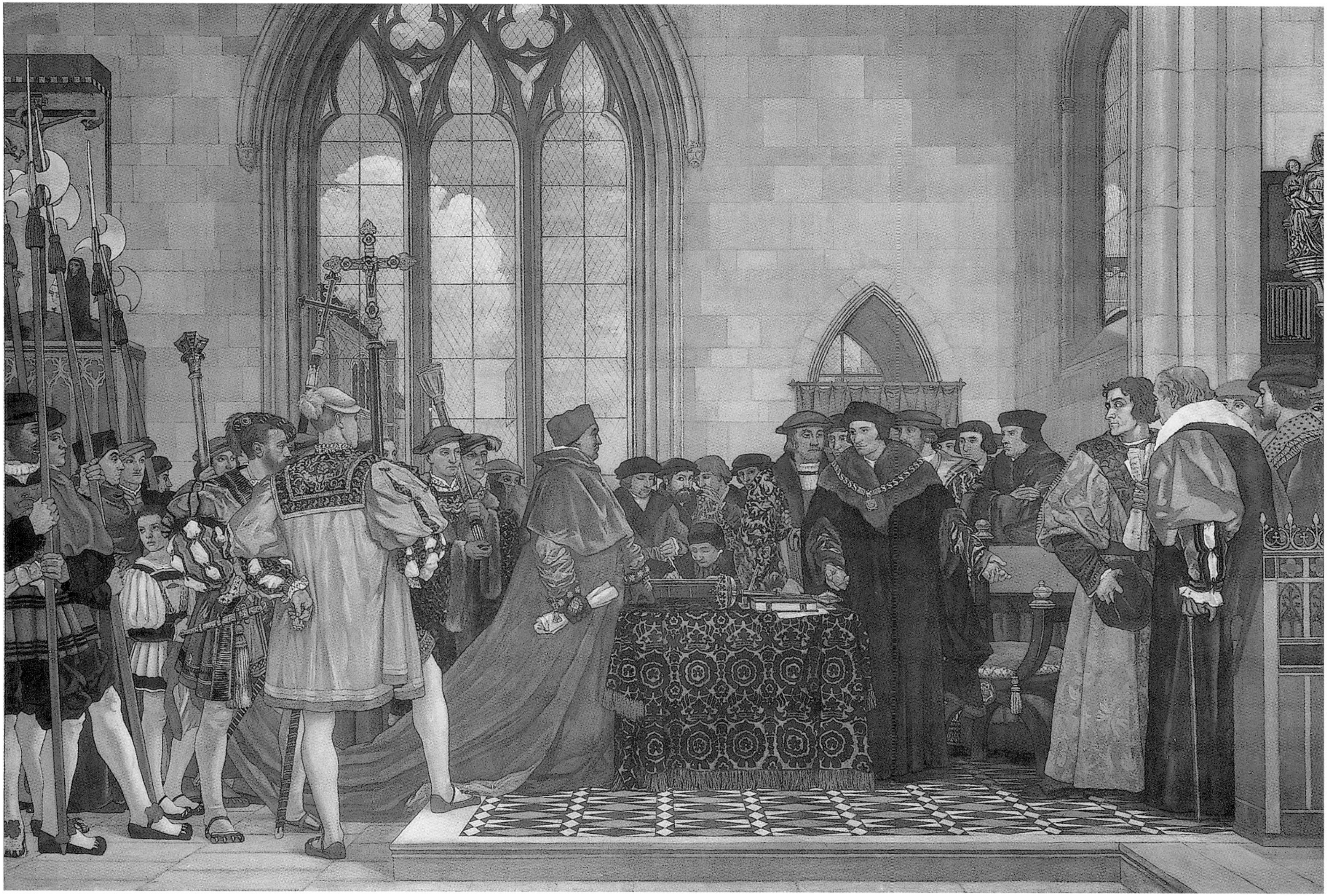

70. Vivian Forbes, *Sir Thomas More, as Speaker of the House of Commons, in spite of Cardinal Wolsey's imperious demands, refuses to grant King Henry VIII a subsidy without due debate by the House, 1523*, St Stephen's Hall, Palace of Westminster, London, 1925–7. Presented by the Viscount Fitzalan

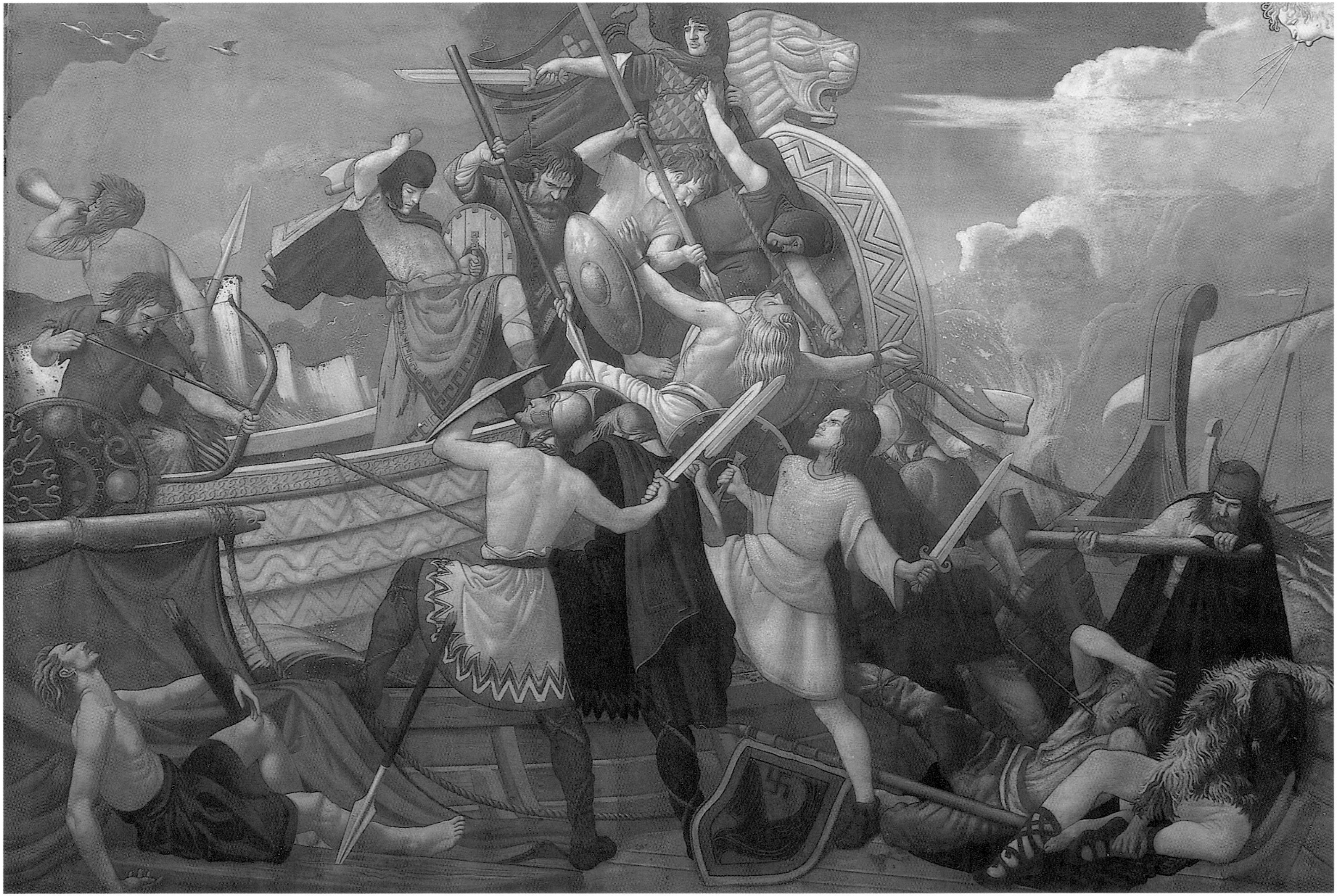

71. Colin Gill, *King Alfred's Longships, newly built for the defence of the realm, attack vessels of the Danish invaders storm-beaten in Swanage Bay, 877*, St Stephen's Hall, Palace of Westminster, London, 1925–7. Presented by the Duke of Devonshire

2) all old and hackneyed'.[75] Newbolt thought Devonport instead wanted 'scenes from 1689 down to the present day, with the Food Supply in Wartime as one of the "General Subjects"'.[76] As Newbolt stated, however, 'war is to be kept out of it as far as possible':[77] the approach was not just the consequence of censorship restrictions, but in a more positive sense, a direct continuation of the use for political purposes of State mural painting which had been evident from the 1840s schemes onwards. All the subjects chosen in fact illustrate aspects of Baldwin's goal of 'peace in our time' and his vision of the values of conciliation, consensus, and pastoral idealism in the maintenance of Imperial stability. These ideals were also Trevelyan's; he now saw history as 'ordered progress', having moved after the war to a more right-wing position.[78] Although the artists wished to choose their own historical themes, and in the case of Clausen and Lawrence, to develop larger symbolic statements, Whitley, working through Cameron, appears to have kept close contact, not only over the allocation of subjects but also the detail of designs; Newbolt wrote an explanatory booklet to convey the ideals behind the scheme. This booklet was itself a tacit admission that, as Clausen and Devonport had predicted, the significance of the particular subjects chosen could not be conveyed simply by visual means alone.

Newbolt's explanation shows clearly how the British School at Rome style of Neoclassicism was intended to project Baldwin's ideology. The final panel, for example, was originally allocated to Orpen, who had been one of the artists chosen to contribute to the Hall of Remembrance; but eventually it was transferred to W. T. Monnington, presumably because his style was felt to be more rigorously 'classical' and because Orpen had raised controversy with his bitter view of the Armistice in *To the Unknown British Soldier in France* (1922, altered subsequently, IWM).[79] Monnington's panel of *The English and Scottish Commissioners present to Queen Anne at St. James's Palace the articles of agreement for the Parliamentary union of the two countries* (Plate 68) typifies the conciliation and consensus undercurrent to the scheme; Newbolt described its subject as an act 'to hold the Empire together' and explained

> Mr Monnington has brought back . . . the stateliness of the Augustan age. There is a classical serenity in the lines of the Mall, seen through the Palace window; in the graceful figures of the Queen and her ladies, and no less in the bearing of the Commissioners in their superhuman costume.[80]

The later eighteenth and nineteenth centuries were seen as characterized above all by wars;[81] this conclusion to the mural sequence instead emphasizes harmony, and Monnington's restrained colour scheme of delicate greys, blacks, and browns offset by isolated notes of scarlet and blue in certain costumes only, and by the calm, Piero della Francesca sky which closes off the extremely shallow pictorial space, aptly complements the static geometry described by Newbolt. It is an intriguing prelude to Monnington's eventual move to abstract mural design, based on

[75] Letter from Newbolt to Cameron (25 July 1925), Cam.P.

[76] Ibid.

[77] Letter from Newbolt to Cameron (16 May 1925), Cam.P.

[78] See 'G. M. Trevelyan: the Uses of Social History' in A. Briggs, *The Collected Essays of Asa Briggs: Images, Problems, Standpoints, Forecasts*, vol. 2 (Brighton, 1985), pp. 240–2. Trevelyan was in close friendship and ideological sympathy with Baldwin and Newbolt quotes from his writings in his pamphlet about the murals; the East Corridor murals and those in St Stephen's Hall can be regarded as integral with Trevelyan's evolving re-evaluation of the nature of history, which culminated in his *English Social History* (1942). The emphasis on the pre-19th-century era at St Stephen's Hall also correlates closely with that in Trevelyan's *History of England* (1926).

[79] See Harries, *War Artists*, pp. 147–9.

[80] Newbolt, *Building of Britain*, p. 22.

[81] Ibid., p. 3. The Cambridge *History of the British Empire* (J. H. Rose, A. P. Newton and E. A. Benians, 1929) described the 18th century as 'first and foremost a century of great wars' (p. 8) and *The Act of Union* was the only 18th-century episode in the scheme, which Whitley had originally planned should tell 'the story of the building of the British Commonwealth' and not merely Britain (MS by Whitley in HLRO).

mathematical calculation, at Bristol Council House in the 1950s, but it also synthesizes the predominant colours and the sense of ordered composition in the preceding murals. (Sims's stormy *King John gives unwilling consent to Magna Carta* (Plate 67) is the most animated panel and its critical reception was perhaps unfair since he had been instructed to include a storm as a symbolic means to emphasize the larger cosmic significance of the event as 'the foundation of justice and individual freedom in England'.)[82]

Given the respect in which he was held, it is not surprising that Clausen was chosen to paint the mural which perhaps focuses some of the most central tenets of Baldwin's and Trevelyan's philosophies. The characters gathered to hear the reading of Wycliffe's English Bible (Plate XVIII) represent various ages, classes, and occupations, from 'the ploughman, perhaps named Piers . . . with his wife and baby' to the 'boyish squire . . . and others of more rustic breed', and are thus a model society in microcosm; they meet in 'a landscape then as now ideally English, with its quiet ploughlands undulating between shady trees and grey church tower'.[83] Trevelyan's and Baldwin's affection for rural values and a belief in their power within the fabric of history is underscored by the highly controlled colour harmonies of gentle pinks, blues, and touches of vibrant red in the costumes, with clear echoes of the Italian 'primitive' styles which not only the British School at Rome, but also writers including Roger Fry, were bringing to the forefront of critical appreciation in the early twentieth century.[84] It is an intriguing paradox that, far from reflecting the respect for 'abstract' form which led Fry to his appreciation of Piero della Francesca and others, the use of such sources by the St Stephen's Hall artists was thus in the service of a very specific political ideal.

Some aspects of the iconography rest inevitably on verbal explanation, for example, William Rothenstein's portrayal of Sir Thomas Roe, King James I's envoy to the Moghul Emperor 'laying the foundation of British influence in India . . . by his mingled courtesy and firmness at the Court of Ajmir'[85] (Plate 69). The information that Roe was an MP and 'a City man by birth—a grandson . . . of the Lord Mayor of London . . . and of Sir Thomas Gresham'[86]—combines with the visual attention given to the ordinary citizens of London opening their gates to the barons and joining with them to exact John's signature of Magna Carta, to acknowledge the new popular participation in Britain's government and to appeal to the man in the street. On a more general level, however, the careful attention to compositional order and relationships both within and between individual panels can be seen as the visual counterpart to the conciliation and consensus ideals embodied in Roe's diplomacy. The description by Newbolt of the Act of Union portrayed by Monnington as 'an act to hold the Empire together' is subtly reinforced by the visual dialogue between its tall classical windows framing blue sky and the pointed Indian arches, which open onto a similar sky behind the tightly choreographed ensemble of figures in Rothenstein's *Roe*, which he painted after extensive study of Indian miniature paintings. *Sir Thomas More, as Speaker of the House of Commons . . . refuses to grant King Henry VIII a subsidy without due debate by the House*, by Vivian Forbes (Plate 70), likewise includes a tall Gothic window framing blue sky with white clouds as part of its backdrop, and perhaps comes as close as any of the murals to parallelism with

[82] Ibid., p. 9.

[83] Ibid., pp. 12, 11.

[84] Cf. Fry's 1917 exhibition of *Copies* at the Omega Workshops, in which the work of Piero della Francesca was represented.

[85] The full title of the mural is *Sir Thomas Roe, Envoy from King James the First of England to the Moghul Emperor, succeeds by his mingled courtesy and firmness at the Court of Ajmir in laying the foundation of British Influence in India.*

[86] Newbolt, *Building of Britain*, p. 19.

modern times. As the 'people's representative', who speaks for both 'the Commons of England' and 'the burgesses and Knights of the Shire',[87] More is not only the heir to the efforts of the Magna Carta Londoners and barons, but surely also a type for Whitley himself, the Speaker of the House of Commons in the early twentieth century. Once again, however, any such correspondence is carefully subordinated in Newbolt's text to the larger principle of 'the ancient liberty of the House [of Commons]'[88] which More's action defends.

This evident avoidance of any contemporary allusion, such as might evoke the kind of censorship received at the period by Miss Smith Dampier's play, *The Queen's Minister*, which involved recent politicians in its *dramatis personae*,[89] perhaps produced a somewhat sterile result and failed to evoke the best from the various artists. Clausen, as we have seen, wanted an even more symbolic emphasis on essentially abstract themes of 'Religion, Kingship, Law . . . ', an approach which reflected his French Symbolist affinities, whereas Lawrence preferred an expression of the epic through overtly modern topics. The avoidance of war subjects resulted in a choice of iconography in which Newbolt could argue that, for example, *King Alfred's Longships newly built for the defence of the realm, attack vessels of the Danish invaders storm-beaten in Swanage Bay, 877* (Plate 71) was an illustration less of battle than of the preservation of British liberties and hence of the foundation of the British Empire, because the incident resulted in the creation of the British navy,[90] but such subtlety of verbal argument inevitably threatened to make the scheme again one of 'tracts' rather than 'pictures'. In the circumstances, the choice of Colin Gill for *King Alfred* was one of the happiest of the project, for his flattened, somewhat decorative forms and quasi-emblematic treatment of the theme (the storm is signified not by naturalistic effects as in Sims's *Magna Carta*, but by a puffing zephyr's face at the top right) lifted it nearer to the symbolic plane intended by Whitley. Other murals show a less successful attempt to balance realistic and symbolic approaches, Lawrence's, for example (*Queen Elizabeth commissions Raleigh . . .*), tending to the kind of exaggerated, stage-décor type of conception which also seduced Frank Salisbury in his Liverpool Town Hall murals of the period.[91] Glyn Philpot, so confidently experimental in private mural commissions,[92] responded to Newbolt's interpretation of Richard I's Crusades as a defence of 'the wisdom of peaceful age, the happiness of peaceful youth'[93] with sensitively painted clergy and choirboys at the left of his mural, but tried to evoke Richard's transformation of militarism 'into something poetical and devoted'[94] with over-dramatized, self-conscious postures for the king and his soldiers at the right.

When the murals were unveiled in 1927, Herbert Furst, the great Brangwyn advocate, found they showed no 'living, so to speak . . . concrete relation to life . . . all the subjects seemed remote and hardly in contact with the present at any point.'[95] In the House of Commons, the question was asked as to whether the artists had known of the miners' strike, which was taking place as they painted their panels.[96] For a public which in the late 1920s was demanding modern reality and war-subject films,[97] Whitley's 'direct' appeal was still too rarefied. When, a few years later, Colin

[87] Ibid., pp. 3, 16.
[88] Ibid., p. 3.
[89] See D. Knowles, *The Censor, the Drama and the Film* (London, 1934), pp. 122–3.
[90] Newbolt, *Building of Britain*, pp. 5–6.
[91] See Chapter 7.
[92] See Chapter 10.
[93] Newbolt, *Building of Britain*, p. 8.
[94] Ibid.
[95] H. Furst, 'The Building of Britain', *Apollo* (Sept. 1927), p. 114.
[96] Question from Mr. Lawson to Captain Hacking, *Parliamentary Debates* (17 Dec. 1925).
[97] See J. M. MacKenzie, *Propaganda and Empire* (Manchester, 1984), pp. 90–1.

Gill was chosen along with several of the other St Stephen's Hall artists to carry out murals in the Bank of England, these were significantly of modern-day events in the life of the Bank.[98]

Meanwhile, what Ramsay MacDonald, the Labour Premier, had appreciated as Brangwyn's ability to present 'the fundamental and eternal verities and struggles of humanity, not in the persons of dead people, but in the persons of his own generation'[99] was still to prove unacceptable for a State building. Whereas the idiom of the British School at Rome threw an effective distance, even in modern subjects at the Bank of England, between the viewer and the subject, Brangwyn's contemporaneity was of a different order. If already during the war, the uncompromising directness of his posters like *Put Strength in the Final Blow* (Plate 61), in which a Tommy throttles a Hun, had meant he was never employed as an Official War Artist or even for the Hall of Remembrance, then his selection by Lord Iveagh to paint the War Memorial he wished to present to the Royal Gallery of the House of Lords was to prove, in the unfolding political context of the 1920s and early 1930s, a red rag to a bull.

98 See Chapter 11.

99 R. Brangwyn, *Brangwyn*, p. 226.

6

Celebrating the Empire, 1924–1938

Despite the emphasis on 'peace in our time' in the St Stephen's Hall scheme begun in 1924, public pressure for a tangible State acknowledgement of the part played by ordinary men and women in the achievement of the peace was so strong that the Speaker of the House of Commons, W. T. Whitley, had to give assurances to the Lord Great Chamberlain that Frank Salisbury's immensely popular *Burial of the Unknown Warrior* (Plate 66) would still be accessible for public viewing after its removal to make way for the new St Stephen's murals. Following the abandonment of the Hall of Remembrance and the absorption of its paintings into the Imperial War Museum's collections under the more restricted heading of 'record of war', in 1924 there was still no State War Memorial in the British seat of government, such as Beaverbrook's Canadian War Memorial scheme, for example, had achieved in Manitoba. It was effectively left to a private individual, Lord Iveagh, to propose a memorial for Westminster, when in 1925 he offered to donate mural decorations for its Royal Gallery. Here, Daniel Maclise's sequence of huge battle paintings, begun under Prince Albert's Royal Fine Arts Commission in the 1850s, had been abandoned with only two panels complete (Plates 24, 25; Plate III). Iveagh's gift was intended to complement a sculptural memorial in the Gallery, also paid for through the private donations of peers, and made by John Tweed. Though it thus had its origins in the motive of a memorial, the history of the resultant mural scheme, which ultimately illustrated the peoples, fauna, and natural products of the nations of the British Empire, is intimately bound up with that of evolving attitudes towards the emergent 'Commonwealth' of nations in the 1920s and early 1930s, and it provides a direct prelude to the celebration of national identity within this new context by native artists at a number of the High Commission offices created in London in the 1930s. At the same time, the Royal Gallery scheme brought to a climactic head both the troubled relationship of art, politics, and propaganda, which had played such a dominant role in the development of State patronage in Britain since 1840, and the issue of the censor's influence which had been recurring since Goetze's work at the Foreign Office. In terms of Brangwyn's personal development as a muralist, it represents the logical culmination of features first adumbrated in his work at Skinners' Hall (Plates 42–7; Plates X–XIII).

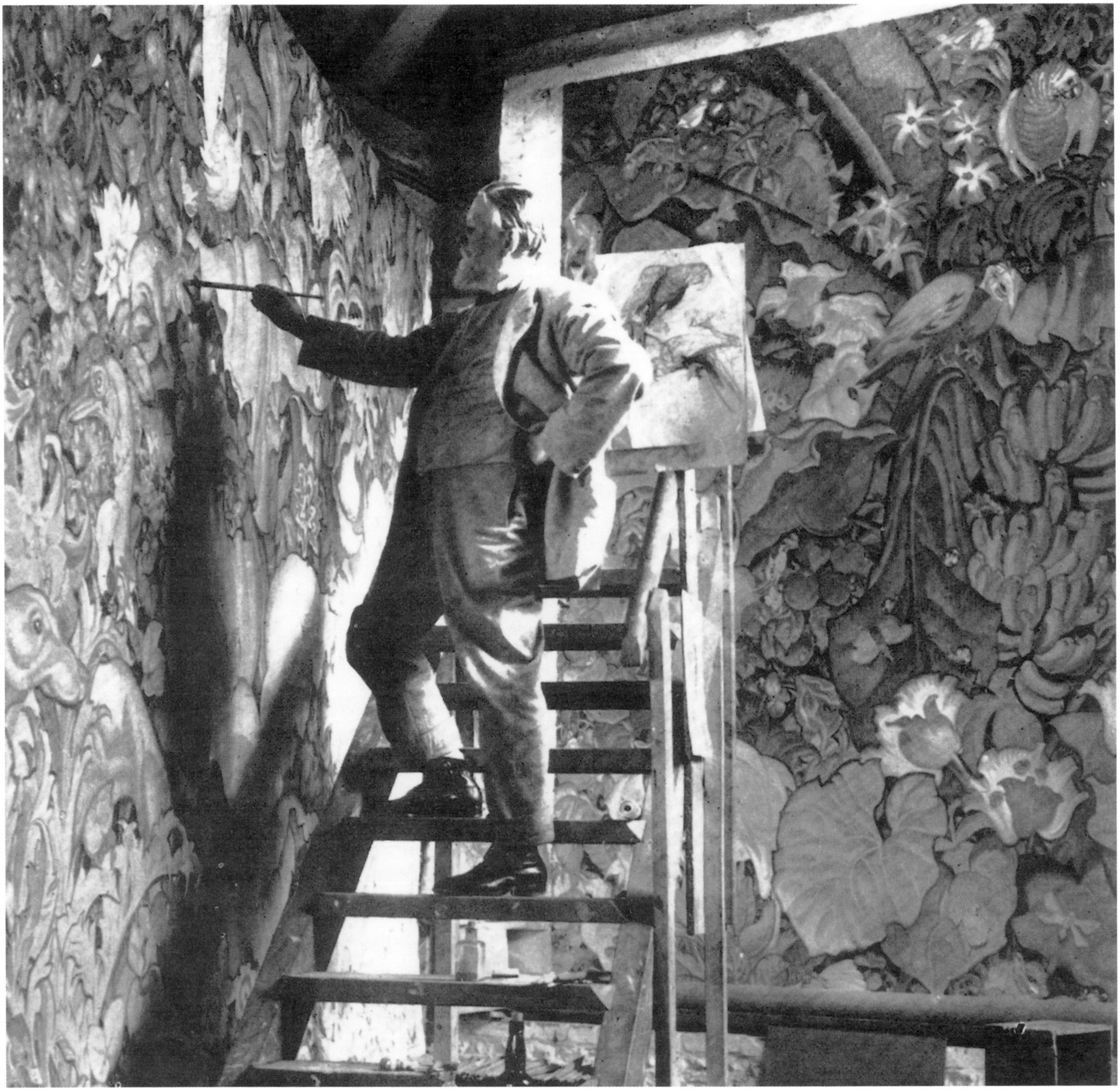

72. Sir Frank Brangwyn working on his *British Empire* murals for the Royal Gallery, House of Lords, in his studio at Ditchling, early 1930s

BRANGWYN'S 'BRITISH EMPIRE' MURALS FOR THE ROYAL GALLERY OF THE HOUSE OF LORDS, 1924–1933

Lord Iveagh selected Brangwyn as the artist of his War Memorial gift. Brangwyn had contributed to the Canadian War Memorial and, in fact, he had been consulted by the 1906 Select Committee on the decoration of the Palace of Westminster scheme. At that stage, however, he had been too busy with other commissions, notably Skinners' Hall, to contemplate a response, despite the suggestion in 1910 by the art critic of the *Athenaeum* that his style 'would probably fit aptly enough with a Gothic setting' like Westminster.[1] After the war, even though his name was dropped without explanation from the initial list of artists for the Hall of Remembrance, a number of American voices also urged that he would be a suitable choice as the artist of a British National War Memorial.[2] His pageant designs for the 1924 Wembley Exhibition and the opening of his Queen's Gate one-man show by the Labour Premier, Ramsay MacDonald, in the same year, would have associated his vividly immediate style, however, with a very different political outlook from that which, after the Conservative victory of 1924, underpinned Whitley's scheme at St Stephen's Hall.

Although Iveagh's offer was accepted by the Select Committee on the House of Lords Offices, which had administrative responsibility for alterations to the fabric of the Palace of Westminster, it is thus perhaps not surprising that the scheme encountered opposition from an early stage from the Royal Fine Art Commission, which advised the Government on art matters; even after undergoing various revisions of iconography, in 1930 it was ultimately to prove unacceptable to the House of Lords when it was nearing completion. Changes on the political scene, Lord Iveagh's death in 1927, and the influence of the Lord Great Chamberlain as censor all contributed to make Brangwyn's style and subjects, and even the original motive of a War Memorial, seriously out of step with the climate of 1930, thereby bringing the revival of mural painting in the Houses of Parliament, which had been launched by the East Corridor work of 1908–10, to a conclusion. The nature of Iveagh's agreement with Brangwyn was essentially that of a private patron and Brangwyn was tenaciously resistant to attempts by the Royal Fine Art Commission to gain access to his work, which was done in his studio in oil, tempera, and a mixture of the two, for future installation in the House of Lords. By 1928 Lord Crawford and Balcarres, Chairman of the Commission, was lamenting his lack of authority in this situation, taking a remarkably rosy view of the Foreign Office scheme, which had so nearly been rejected, and showing frustration that there had merely been 'a simple agreement'[3] between the artist and Lord Iveagh:

> the model which should have been followed was the procedure adopted when the Foreign Office rooms were redecorated, or else that of St. Stephen's Hall. In each case the work proceeded along ordered lines of sequence and caution with excellent results; whereas the muddle of the House of Lords affair, what with one committee and another, and the Lord Great Chamberlain bedevilling the whole business, has been a source of lamentable confusions.[4]

[1] *Athenaeum*, no. 4334 (19 Nov. 1910), p. 633.

[2] e.g. A. Defries, 'Frank Brangwyn RA: A Master Craftsman', *American Magazine of Art*, 15, no. 2 (Nov. 1924), p. 566.

[3] Letter from C. H. Bland (Secretary of the Trustees of Lord Iveagh's Estate) to Lord Peel (11 May 1928), Work 11/279, PRO.

[4] Letter from Lord Crawford and Balcarres to Peel (20 June 1928), ibid.

Unlike France, Germany, and Austria (or even Canada and the United States, where Brangwyn had undertaken government commissions), Britain still had no established State patronage procedures, and the St Stephen's Hall arrangements had been essentially ad hoc. The Royal Gallery scheme throws into relief the matter of how far an artist's personal vision of his commission and that of his patrons, who in this case had specific political as well as artistic purposes, can ever be reconciled, but it is also arguable that it was the very constraints that were imposed on Brangwyn in terms of subject choice that actually stimulated him to create one of his most fascinating and symbolic mural schemes. Far from being 'lots of bananas etc',[5] as Lord Crawford called it when it was rejected by the Lords, Brangwyn's scheme can actually be seen to carry a very individual and powerful message in its 'British Empire' programme, which has consistently been overlooked in the years since its creation, when abstract and non-figurative trends have often been preferred by historians of British art. Although his Royal Gallery panels were eventually bought by Swansea City Council (Brangwyn was Anglo-Welsh) for its new Guildhall against stiff competition from American and Commonwealth bidders, and installed there in 1933, Brangwyn was bitter at their rejection from Westminster. Impatient with the intervention of the Royal Fine Art Commission and perhaps overlooking the inevitable political implications of decorating the principal assembly hall of the British State, where international convocations as well as national events like the State Opening of Parliament took place, he felt his commission had been treated 'as if it took place in the time of Henry VIII'.[6] He regarded his murals as

> my 'opus importato'. . . I've put all my life's study into this work *and this does represent F. B.* All my sketches, easel pictures and studio knock-ups would be all right if they were shown with these panels . . . They would all lead up to the House of Lords decorations—people would understand them better.[7] (Plate 72)

The Royal Gallery murals in fact relate closely to aspects of Brangwyn's earlier work, whilst their evolution involved a process of refinement of ideas about the brotherhood of man and his relationship with the natural world which have their origins in his formative experiences as an assistant to William Morris and muralist for Samuel Bing. Whilst the Lords and the Royal Fine Art Commission gave their reasons for the rejection of the murals as stylistic disharmony with their intended setting—'their insistent motives ill accord with the Waterloo Chamber . . . large paintings of tropical flora and fauna flanking the War Memorial and the historic cartoons would appear inappropriate'[8]—there are political factors which suggest that Brangwyn's theme of the plenitude of the British Empire was actually what was unacceptable. As in the case of the earlier State mural schemes in the East Corridor and St Stephen's Hall at Westminster, and the Foreign Office, what was sought by the patrons was primarily a form of propaganda for particular ideals.

Brangwyn's original brief for the murals appears to have laid down 'that the scheme of decoration was to harmonise with the scheme of the war memorial'[9] and his first designs were for typical scenes from the recent war which would have complemented both Tweed's allegorical sculpture and Maclise's two existing 'documentary' murals of the Battle of Waterloo and the *Death of Nelson.* A variety of sketches for subjects of *The Call to Arms and the Departure for the Front* (intended as a large panel for the north wall), *The Trench, The Clearing Station, The Signing of the Armistice, A*

[5] Quoted in BD (21 July 1948).
[6] Ibid. (undated).
[7] Ibid. (15 Mar. 1944).
[8] *Fourth Report* of the SCHLO, CP HL84 (1929–30).
[9] *Third Report* of the SCHLO (9 July 1925).

Heavy Gun in Action (Plate 73), and *A Tank in Action* (Plate 74) were prepared and the last two were actually completed for installation.[10] It is likely that Brangwyn was drawing on his experience of painting similar war subjects for the Canadian War Memorial, and he would also have been aware of the Hall of Remembrance iconography (Plates 62–5; Plate XVII) and the war scenes being completed at Balcombe Village Hall by Neville, Lord Lytton.[11] Brangwyn lived nearby at Ditchling.

A Tank has an oblique viewpoint and tightly organized geometry of design, with the huge machine rearing as a backdrop to tumbling cohorts of soldiers who are part silhouetted, part sharply detailed by the eerie flashes of gunfire; it is perhaps as near as Brangwyn ever came to the jagged forms of Roberts and Wyndham Lewis. *A Gun* is composed around a typically Brangwyn-esque mass of curling, voluminous smoke, punctuated by the lean and broken trunks of bare trees, amidst which the muscular, bare-backed gunners strain to load the barrel of their instrument of death; the motif translates into a context of war the celebration of manual effort and rhythmic figural movement to be found in so many of Brangwyn's earlier murals, like those for the Venice Biennale of 1906 and for Lloyd's Register of Shipping in London of 1912.[12] Prominent in the foreground is the motif of man's succour to his brother man—now undertaken by medical personnel and steel-helmeted Tommies—which had first appeared at Skinners' Hall in the mural of *The Defence of London Bridge* (Plate 47), as well as in the Biblical scenes Brangwyn painted at Christ's Hospital, Horsham[13] and in many of his other decorations and illustrations. The colours are subtle, nuanced shades of evening pinks and purples; a few fragile flowers bravely survive beside the exaggeratedly cumbersome boots of the anxious soldiers. The powerful realism, which even verges on the grotesque, and the dramatic incidents, as well as the echo of a *Pietà* in the foreground episode of *A Gun*, take clear account of the style and content of the Maclise paintings alongside which Brangwyn's work was to stand, whilst continuing the highly personal awareness of war as both the arbiter between life and death and the agent in attaining Brangwyn's ideal of the brotherhood of man, which had been so much a feature of his Winnipeg Memorial, *Soldiers at War* lithographs for the Canadian War Record Office, and Belgian Relief Fund poster commissions.

Even though *A Tank* and *A Gun* had been substantially completed, a decision was taken at the end of 1925 to replace war subjects with what Brangwyn described as 'what had been saved for the Empire as a result of the War'.[14] The change of plan has traditionally been attributed to Brangwyn, but its circumstances do not appear to be clearly documented and it is surely revealing that it followed directly on the resolution of the House of Lords Select Committee on the War Memorial for the Royal Gallery to 'nominate four Lords to act for the House in relation with those responsible for the decoration': these were the Lord Chancellor, the Lord Chairman, the Lord Great Chamberlain, and the First Commissioner of Works.[15] The First Commissioner was, of course, also one of those responsible for supervising the St Stephen's Hall murals, where a deliberate decision had been taken that 'war should be kept out of it as far as possible,' whilst the Lord Great Chamberlain, as official censor, could clearly not allow 'realistic horrors of warfare', nor ignore the current trends in film censorship where 'no controversy' was increasingly

[10] Panels now in the National Museum of Wales, Cardiff.
[11] See Chapter 7.
[12] See Chapter 11.
[13] See Chapter 8.
[14] Work 11/279, PRO.
[15] Resolution of the House of Lords Select Committee on the War Memorial (9 July 1925).

equivalent to 'no reality'.[16] Brangwyn apparently wrote 'a strong letter' in 1925 to the Lord Great Chamberlain, protesting that Lord Iveagh had stipulated that there was to be 'no interference with the artist while he was working':[17] this suggests that some attempt had been made to see his work in progress. The king certainly seems to have been unaware as late as November 1925 of any dissatisfaction with the chosen war iconography since he 'asked Lord Iveagh at Elveden how the work was progressing'.[18]

Whether the decision to abandon the war themes was Brangwyn's or the censor's, it was in fact to result in an arguably far richer and more subtle expression of the significance and implications of war on Brangwyn's part than his first designs, where dependence on the Official War Artists is still to be felt in, for example, *A Tank's* centrifugal, two-dimensional composition which recalls William Roberts's *First German Gas Attack at Ypres* (1918, National Gallery of Canada) for the Canadian War Memorial. Sketches for *The Trench* (Plates 75, 76) likewise include a frieze of men on a high horizon carrying a stretcher as in Sargent's *Gassed* (Plate 62) and also in Lytton's Balcombe murals. Brangwyn seems at first to have experimented with a scheme of purely heraldic decoration, perhaps suggested to him by the new Committee of Lords since it recalls Sir Charles Barry's original idea that the Royal Gallery might be decorated with 'a gorgeous enrichment of matter more allied to the College of Arms than of Arts'.[19] Then he explored the juxtaposition of the less violent of his war scenes—a subject suggesting the *Departure for the Front* at a dockside—with panels in the lower registers of the walls illustrating the different races, countries, products, flora, and fauna of the British Empire[20] (Plate 77). Finally he concentrated on the Empire material alone, creating figurative subjects for six 6.09 by 3.96 m vertical panels which were presumably intended for the upper sections of the end walls of the Royal Gallery (Plate 8), and predominantly floral and animal compositions for ten 3.65 m square lower panels, four of which may have been meant to flank the Maclise pictures. A further small square panel was produced, apparently in error. The panels are in oil and/or tempera.

The First World War was an experience which had clearly touched Brangwyn on a profound emotional level, as a symbolic private sketch in a notebook of a skull labelled 'F. B. 1918' reveals.[21] His personal sorrow at the state of Belgium, his native country, is apparent from his Relief Fund posters and *Mater Dolorosa Belgica* painting of 1915.[22] Already in sketchbooks dating from the period of the war, however, a sense emerges from his drawings of how reconciliation and renewal could be born of combat and destruction. In this can be discovered the seeds of the eventual iconography of the Royal Gallery work, showing why it was that Brangwyn believed his preparatory material would 'lead up' to his panels, and that it should be shown with them to enable people to 'understand them better'. Whereas Lytton's presentation of the aftermath of war at Balcombe Village Hall remains profoundly pessimistic, featuring the maimed amidst the grieving in the witnesses to reconstruction, and concentrating almost exclusively on experiences of the war itself, the fraught gestation process of the Royal Gallery work and the apparent pressure on Brangwyn to avoid a direct representation of battle brought about a remarkable pictorial catharsis for his initial anger at the carnage in which the final panels of the Royal Gallery represent the ultimate logical stage.

[16] N. Pronay and D. W. Spring: *Propaganda, Politics and Film, 1918–1945* (London, 1982), p. 111.

[17] *Note on the Position of the Scheme for the Royal Gallery*, Work 11/279 2028/3 Part I, PRO.

[18] R. Brangwyn, *Brangwyn* (1978), p. 237.

[19] Quoted in ibid., p. 233.

[20] Design held by Glynn Vivian Art Gallery, Swansea.

[21] Sketchbook 815/84, RA.

[22] *Mater Dolorosa Belgica* is in the William Morris Gallery, Walthamstow.

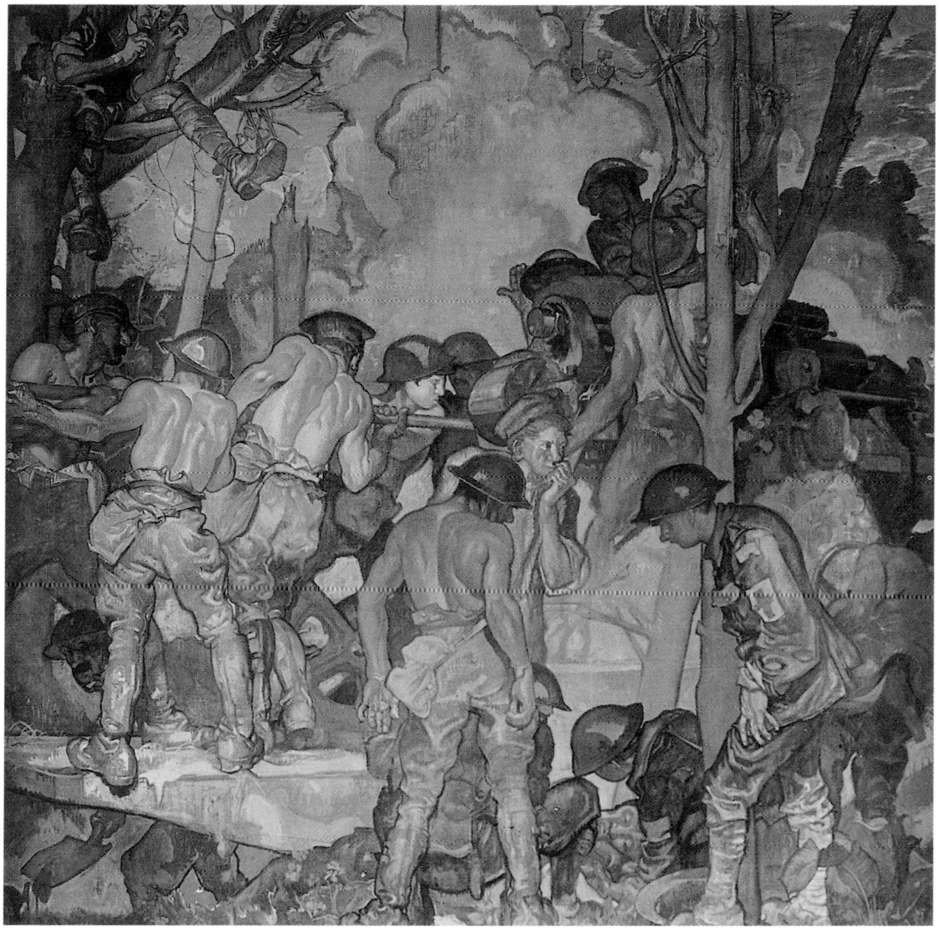

73. Sir Frank Brangwyn, *A Heavy Gun in Action*, discarded panel for Royal Gallery, Palace of Westminster, begun *c.*1924 and completed in 1927. Cardiff, National Museum of Wales

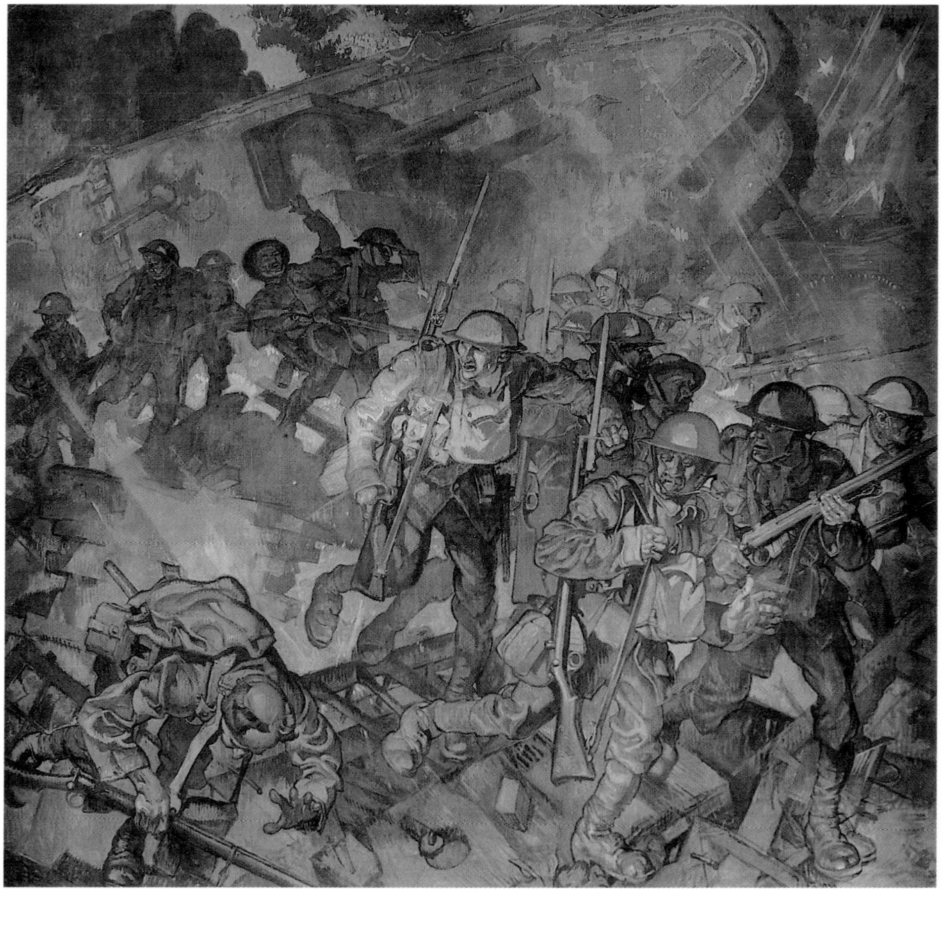

74. Sir Frank Brangwyn, *A Tank in Action*, discarded panel for Royal Gallery, Palace of Westminster, begun *c.*1924 and completed in 1929. Cardiff, National Museum of Wales

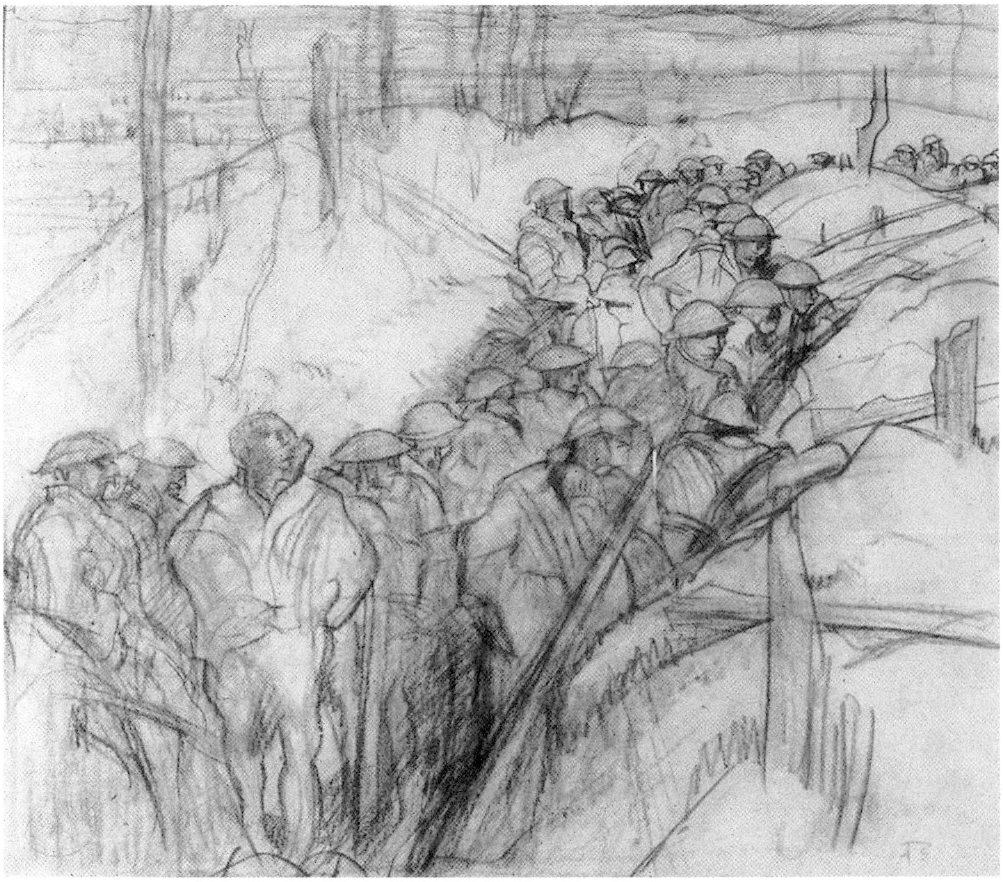

75. Sir Frank Brangwyn, *Soldiers in a Trench*, study for first scheme for Royal Gallery, House of Lords, *c.*1924. Hull, Ferens Art Gallery

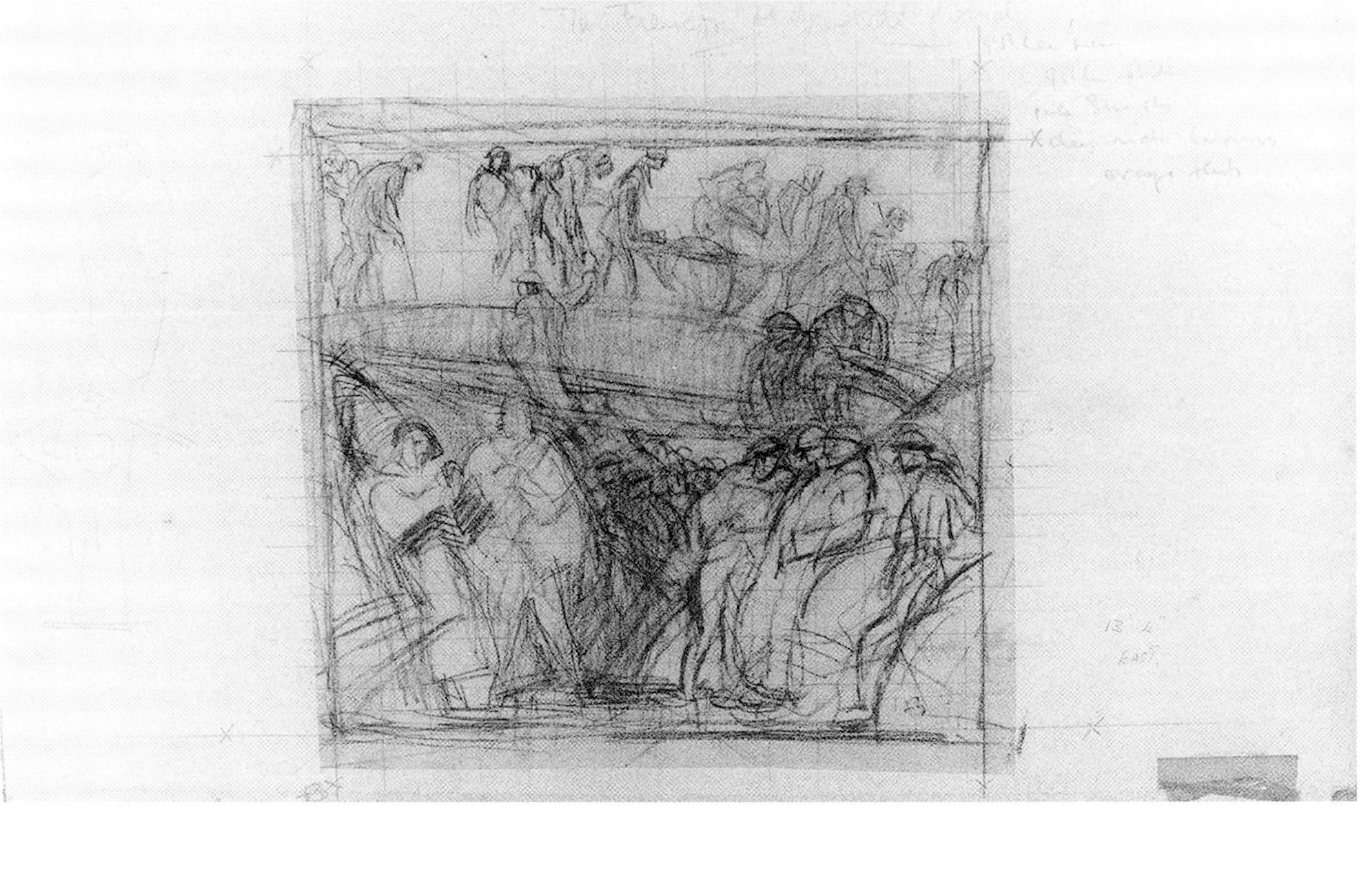

76. Sir Frank Brangwyn, sketch for *The Trench* for first scheme for Royal Gallery, House of Lords, *c.*1924. Collection Gordon Anderson

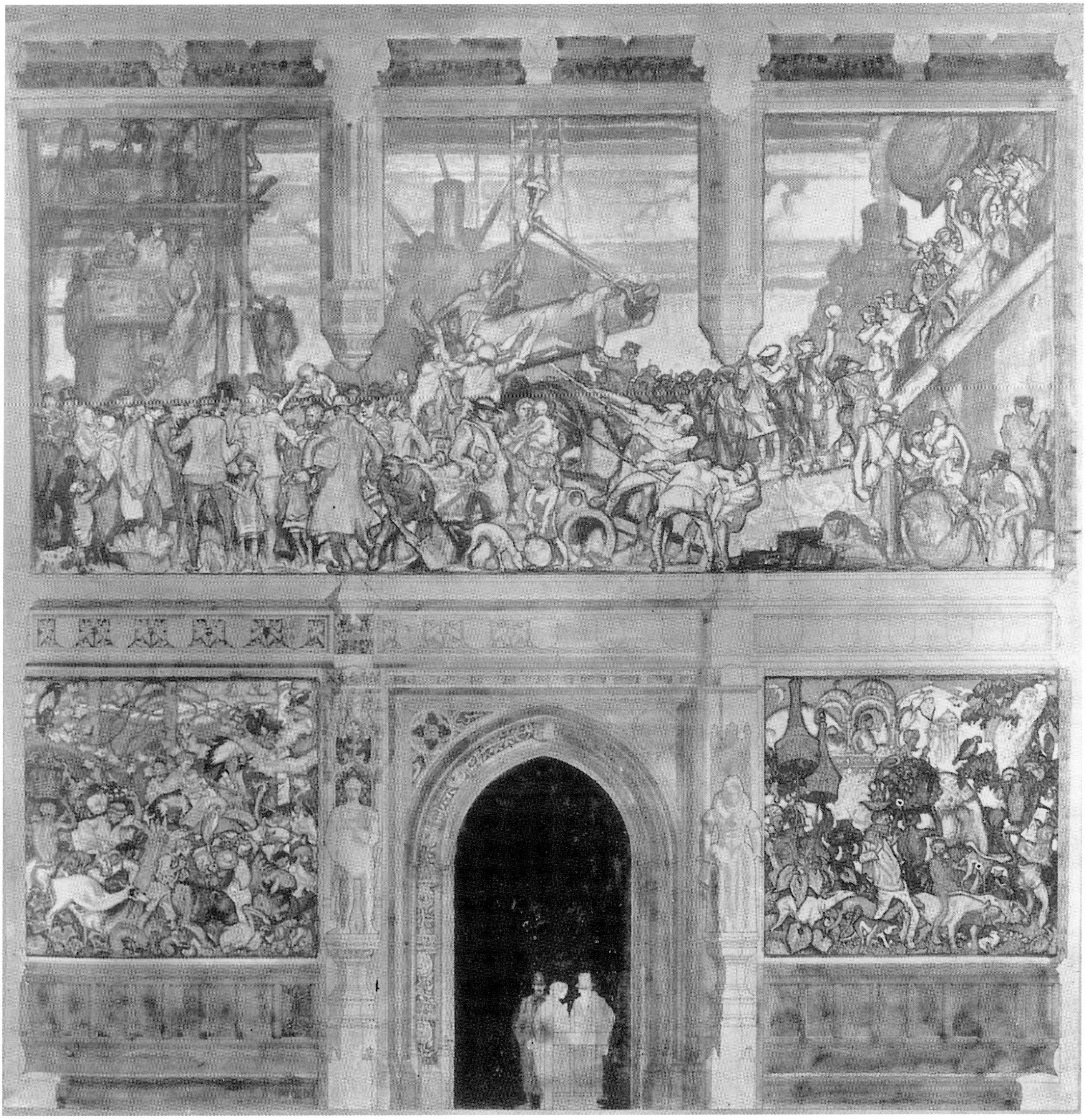

77. Sir Frank Brangwyn, design for one of the end walls of the Royal Gallery, Palace of Westminster, London, showing murals of war and peace *in situ*, *c.*1924–5 (photograph *c.*1931)

A group of thumbnail sketches made soon after the outbreak of the war illustrates field-workers scything not corn but skulls; others portray scenes of barricades and battlefields under the general caption 'The glories of war?'[23] One of the most bitter (Plate 78) juxtaposes wounded soldiers tending each other—the theme of succour which Brangwyn had so often illustrated in earlier work—with a distant ploughing scene. A pathetic personal note is added by a portrait of the artist's beloved dog apparently lying dead. Later pages illustrate 'gas masked stretcher men' which closely prefigure those in two charcoal and chalk designs for *The Trench*. Alongside 'Poland snow-plain' we find three haystacks in the fog, entitled 'The Mists of Autumn arise around the fruits that ripen FB'; other sketches show an outdoor Mass in a snowfield and 'The Last Mass' in a newly ploughed field, and are set beside a trench scene (Plate 79). However sombre, an implied association is being built up between the events of war and the seasonal cycle of man's tilling of the land. By 1917, however, Brangwyn's private sketches[24] show not only 'plowing' but also 'sowing' and include the germ of the embarkation scene (Plate 80) to be developed, probably by reference also to his 1915–16 poster *The Last Boat out of Antwerp*, in the 'transitional' designs for the Royal Gallery, where war scenes are combined with views of an Empire wheat harvest and an Indian howdah procession (Plate 77).

Between the period of the thumbnail wartime sketches and the first war programme for the Royal Gallery, Brangwyn had carried out not only the Canadian War Memorial commission, but also one for Stations of the Cross as a War Memorial for Arras Cathedral. Both took up the Christian symbolism of his *Mater Dolorosa Belgica*, the Canadian mural in fact illustrating soldiers beside a wayside cross. The final Empire scene he developed for the Royal Gallery transmutes this traditional Christian iconography into a more personal synthesis of images for man's salvation, regeneration, and fellowship with his brother man. Just as Stanley Spencer was re-presenting the Christian Resurrection iconography through a Cookham scenario in his Burghclere chapel murals at the same period,[25] so Brangwyn can be seen as also reinterpreting conventional religious imagery to create his own statement of the Christian theme of renewal. Despite their vastly differing styles, both artists offer a positive view forward in the wake of the war, which contrasts forcibly with the disillusionment of Lytton and so many of the intelligentsia of 1920s Britain, which is encapsulated in Robert Graves's *Goodbye to All That* (1929).

The fruits of Empire imagery of the final House of Lords designs (Plates 81–3; Plates XIX–XX) thus grows out of earlier, war motifs in Brangwyn's sketches and studies. The recurrent theme of the peoples of the Empire harvesting and sharing as brothers the plenty of their nations, which underpins the entire scheme of murals as finally conceived, may seem far removed from the ugliness of war, but when the sketches and final panels are placed in juxtaposition, their individual motifs reveal a transmutation of Brangwyn's earlier war iconography, showing his deeper message of reconstruction out of ruin. A preliminary study for *The Trench*[26] (Plate 75) is both a development of the pocket war-time pencil sketch labelled *Last Mass* (Plate 79) and a sensitive pictorial study of something Brangwyn said he had 'been personally moved by', 'The light of sunset on blue snow'.[27] It clearly relates to further explorations by Brangwyn of the conventional association of winter with death and devastation in a war-time sketch headed 'Winter . . . Snow on Hills' which shows a man on a ladder, propped against a bare tree and looking out towards snowy

[23] Sketchbook 799/8H, RA.
[24] e.g. Sketchbook 774/8H, RA (*c.*1915).
[25] See Chapter 8.
[26] 49 × 42.6 cm, ink, red and black chalk on paper.
[27] Undated comment in BD.

hills, vainly trying to pluck fruit (Plate 84). In one of the final House of Lords panels (Plate XX), we see the symbolic transformation of this: a man climbing a ladder to lay bricks for a new bridge whilst figures beneath him carry baskets of harvested fruit; in another of the panels, children reach up to pluck fruit from richly leaved trees against a background of verdant hillsides dotted with houses.

A comparable transformation occurs in respect of the couple labelled 'Peace Nov. 1918' and shown arm in arm, silhouetted in meditation against an empty plain and sun-flooded sky, at the start of one of Brangwyn's war-time sketchbooks (Plate 85). The man holds a gun or perhaps a sword, the woman a baby; the motif implies the survival and revival of fellowship beyond conflict and it is extended and enlarged, becoming linked to the fruit-picking or harvesting motif in the Empire panels. In these, couples bearing fruit and produce, some man and wife, others Red Indians, or even a child riding an animal, are used as a recurrent unifying motif. They are the sequel to similarly paired couples of figures symbolizing harmony or renewal in Brangwyn's pre-war murals at Skinners' Hall (Plates 42–3; 45–7; Plates X–XIII) whilst they also bring to mind Millet's use of the couple as an emblem of harmony.[28] Brangwyn greatly admired Millet. He may well also have been aware from his period of work in Paris during the 1890s of the recent Panthéon murals by Ferdinand Humbert (Plate 86), which made symbolic associations between the seasons and human experience. Both 'blue snow', as a setting for a warrior bidding farewell to his wife, and a family picking fruit from a ladder feature in Humbert's murals. Their arrangement in contrasting pairs (*Liberty/Patriotism* is represented by the farewell, for example, and partners *Prosperity/Family* where the fruit-picking occurs) also suggests a prototype for Brangwyn's 'transitional' scheme for the House of Lords, in which war and Empire harvest scenes were paired (Plate 77).

Brangwyn's compositions in his final panels, with their high horizons and successive, densely filled zones of human and animal activity, accumulating one above the other in almost mosaic-like profusion, are essentially different from either the recessional 'views' of Humbert or the spare, stage-set scenarios of the St Stephen's Hall murals (Plates 67–71; Plate XVIII). They offer a direct development of Brangwyn's high horizons in his Skinners' Hall work, whilst creating an effect of richly worked, all-over surface design reminiscent of the designs of Brangwyn's early mentor, William Morris. Fronds and branches of foliage, flowering trees, and the baskets overflowing with fruit carried by the various natives can too easily be interpreted as a purely decorative extravaganza; an interwoven tapestry of subtly harmonized warm reds, ochres, and oranges marked by cool blue shadows and glimpses of distant purple mountains. What has so often been dismissed as 'wallpaper'—and what Lord Crawford and Balcarres called 'lots of bananas etc'—is in fact Brangwyn's very message. The interrelatedness of the designs and their profusion of detail would have complemented splendidly the Gothic ornament of the Royal Gallery and the Pre-Raphaelitism of Maclise, but it is also the embodiment of Brangwyn's vision of man's brotherhood, not only with his fellow man, but also with the animal and vegetable kingdoms. The Indian dancer emerging from screens of tropical foliage in one of the smaller panels for example, is a tangible emblem of the same vision of regeneration as inspires the howdah procession attended by natives with fruit and flowers, and monkeys and apes (Plate XIX). The dancer, an emblem of art, literally 'grows' pictorially from the tropical plants surrounding her; their fruits in turn are

[28] e.g. Millet's *Going to Work*, Glasgow Museum and Art Gallery, Kelvingrove.

harvested in honour of the prince or king aboard the howdah, who is clearly evolved from Brangwyn's earlier pageant of plenty at Skinners' Hall (Plate XI) and *Rajah's Birthday* oil painting (1908, Leeds City Art Gallery), as well as his Wembley pageant designs of 1924. Whereas in Brangwyn's 'transitional' design (Plate 77) the howdah procession members bearing fruits are overtly juxtaposed with the soldiers carrying guns and caps, who board ship for war in the panel above, in the final designs there is a more subtle symbolism.

Originally, it appears that Brangwyn envisaged each of his panels as representing groups of specific Colonies or Dominions. Preliminary cartoons[29] (Plate 87) are labelled with names of countries, and the Lord Great Chamberlain referred in a letter of 1928 to 'the Empire of the East and the Empire of the West' as being illustrated by the large panels 'whilst the lower panels were to represent the different Dominions'.[30] An annotation on one of the colour cartoons (Glynn Vivian Art Gallery, Swansea), however, shows how Brangwyn gradually moved away from this literal, geographical description to a more universal meaning. This is written on the carpet borne by a figure who repeats one of the dockyard workers Brangwyn had earlier portrayed in his Lloyd's Register of Shipping murals: 'Man in his pursuit of . . . [illegible, but apparently either 'wealth' or 'war'] has put heavy burdens on his fellow.' In celebrating 'what had been saved for Empire as a result of war', Brangwyn clearly remained keenly aware of the suffering it had entailed and which he had initially illustrated in his war scenes—or if the word is 'wealth', of the inequalities which still existed even afterwards in peacetime. Whilst first sketches and cartoons for the murals[31] include motifs illustrating British control over and assistance to her Empire—such as the ship under construction and railway viaduct with a 'city' whose apparent foundation date of '1740' is inscribed alongside—the actual murals either dispense with these motifs or subordinate them. The reference to the foundation of a city by settlers, which recalls the imagery of Brangwyn's Canadian Grand Trunk Railway Office mural in London[32] is omitted and the ship under construction is replaced by a coloured boy bearing a large basket of bananas (Plate XX). Red Indians are meanwhile introduced to accompany surveyors and woodcutters who appear in the background of another panel. As executed, Brangwyn's scheme projects the implication which lies behind the carpet-bearer annotation—that the British Empire should be acknowledged as an independent fellowship of all races rather than an unequal partnership in which Britain exploited dependent countries. In this sense, the howdah bearing a native king or prince (Plate XIX) becomes an emblem of a wider sympathy with colonial identity in the murals, born of Brangwyn's ideal of the universal fellowship of mankind, which can only have contributed to the murals' negative reception in 1930 by the Lords.

For by that date, pressure from the colonies and dominions for independence from Britain was mounting rapidly. It was not without reason that the final mural in the 'Building of Britain' sequence in St Stephen's Hall had been dedicated to 'an act designed to hold the Empire together'; its commemoration of the union of England and Scotland, like the illustration in the same scheme of Sir Thomas Roe's negotiations with the Indian Moghul, was an emblem of the unity of Empire and reflected Britain's growing anxieties in the 1920s at the Empire states' demands for independence by way of recognition of their contribution to Britain's victory in the war. Whereas the 1924

[29] Examples are held by the Glynn Vivian Art Gallery, Swansea, the Victoria and Albert Museum, London, and the Stedelijke Musea, Bruges; that in Plate 29 is 1.56 × 3.44 m.

[30] Letter from the Lord Great Chamberlain to Sir Lionel Earle (29 Mar. 1928), Work 11/279 2028 Part I, PRO.

[31] Glynn Vivian Art Gallery, Swansea.

[32] See Chapter 11.

Wembley British Empire exhibition had celebrated the peace and prosperity regained, the Imperial Conference of 1926 had begun to show cracks in the edifice of Empire, and by April 1930, when the decisive debate in the House of Lords on the fate of Brangwyn's murals took place following their temporary installation, concern was at its height. Another Imperial Conference was to be held in the Royal Gallery itself in October 1930, and this in fact led to the Statute of Westminster. In these circumstances it is not surprising that both Lord Lee of Fareham and Lord Crawford and Balcarres, Chairman of the Royal Fine Art Commission, stressed the urgency of a decision on Brangwyn's murals and opposed an amendment by the new Lord Iveagh that the matter be referred back to the House of Lords Offices Committee for a later decision. Furthermore, with the coming to office of MacDonald's second Labour Cabinet in 1929, Lord Sankey had become Lord Chancellor, one of the sub-committee of four with responsibility for overseeing Brangwyn's work. Whilst MacDonald himself might have been expected to be sympathetic to Brangwyn, having praised his work so warmly in 1924, the fate of the murals was in the hands of the Lords, and Sankey was profoundly opposed to the independence movement. Motifs such as the native boy sipping from a cup (Plate 82), originally drawn by Brangwyn as simply a seated figure not engaged in eating or drinking, but subsequently modified to illustrate the same idea of rightful enjoyment of plenty which he had earlier illustrated in the drinkers of his *Pelts and Furs*, or the negress bearing fruit upon her head (Plate 81) or in her arms, who appears in several of the panels and who sat for Brangwyn in his studio at Ditchling, would only have added fuel to the Lords' debate.

In addition to the perceived threat of colonial independence, there was by 1930 considerable opposition in the Lords to what was known as the 'Empire Free Trade' faction within their ranks, represented by Lords Beaverbrook and Rothermere. This was felt to threaten British imports into the dominions—a highly important market in the context of the deepening slump in British trade at that time.[33] Whereas in 1924, when the British Empire Exhibition took place, politicians had been keen to promote the purchase in Britain of Empire goods, in 1930 the position was reversed. The last thing the British Government wanted to be reminded of was 'the Empire, in all its majesty and multitudinous resource'.[34]

What the Royal Fine Art Commission described as 'the insistent motives' of Brangwyn's murals would have carried far too uncomfortable an implication; the very exuberance of his compositions—'brilliant in colouring, fertile in invention and full of fancy in their luxuriant variety and treatment'[35] as the Commission put it—was out of step not so much with the Royal Gallery as with political purpose, and a literal invasion of the plenty of the Commonwealth's raw products into the very room where the forthcoming independence conferences were to be held. Moreover, Brangwyn's replacement of British settlement imagery with native characters enjoying their countries' resources was also inappropriate in the context of recent legislation, such as the 1927 'Harvester Scheme' to encourage the British unemployed to emigrate to Canada, the 1929 Colonial Development Act, and the schemes for British colonization in Australia proposed by George Lansbury, who as First Commissioner of Works was now one of the supervisors of Brangwyn's work. Although the Lords were apparently following the Royal Fine Art Commission's advice that

[33] See C. L. Mowatt, *Britain between the Wars* (London, 1955), p. 367.

[34] Brangwyn's description of his theme, given after the change of programme in 1925, and quoted in R. Brangwyn, *Brangwyn*, p. 238.

[35] *Fourth Report* of the SCHLO, CP HL84 (1929–30).

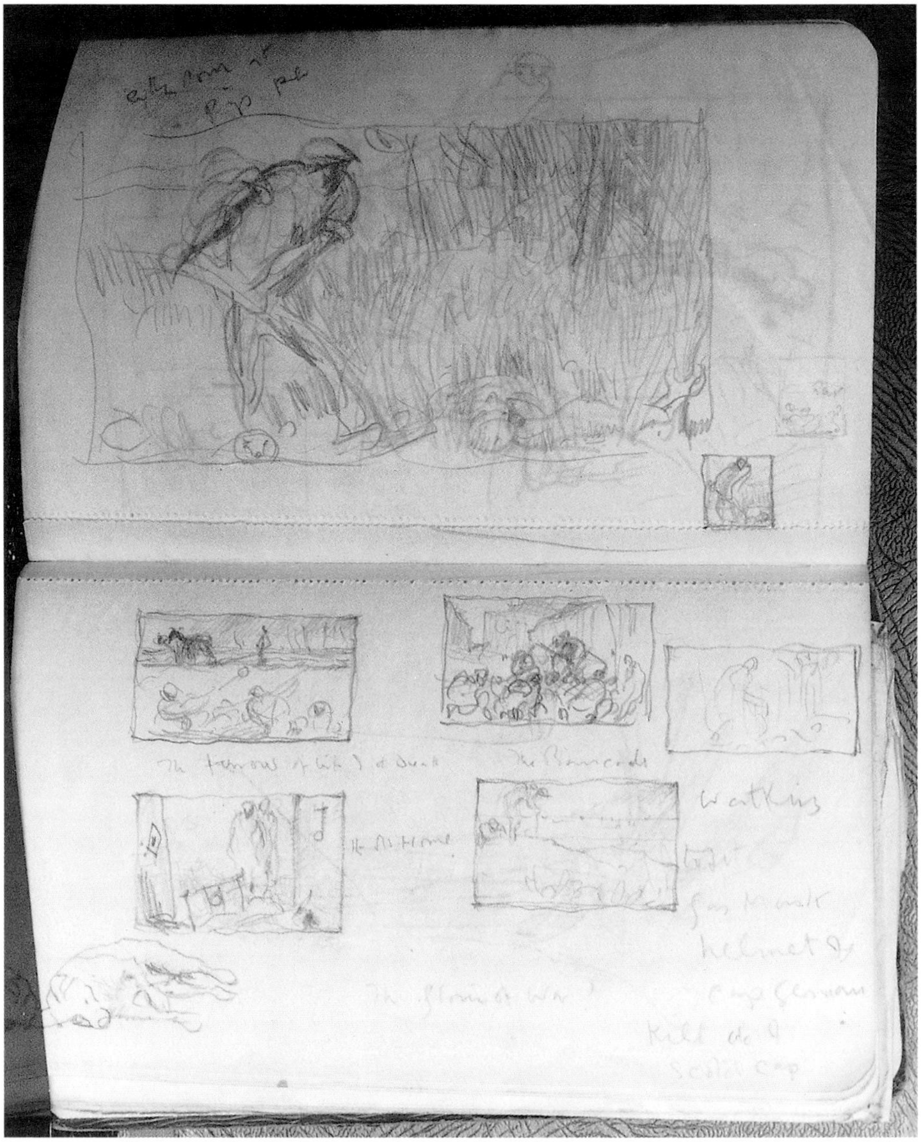
Watkins

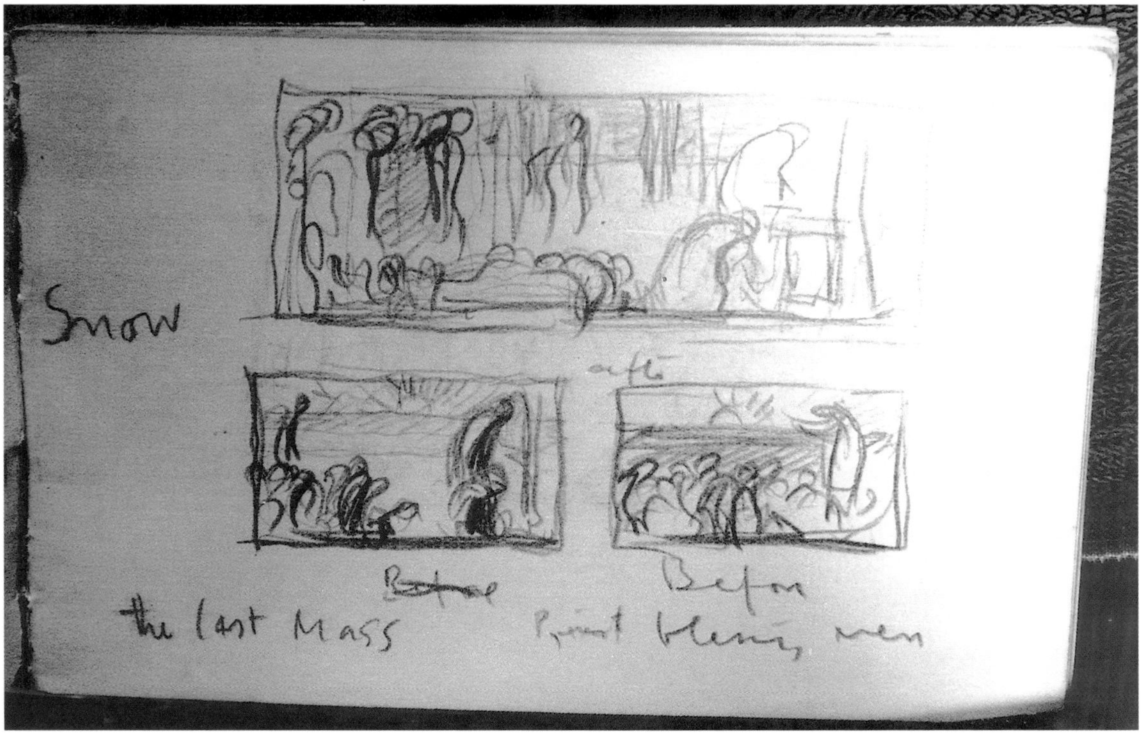
Snow
Befor
the last Mass

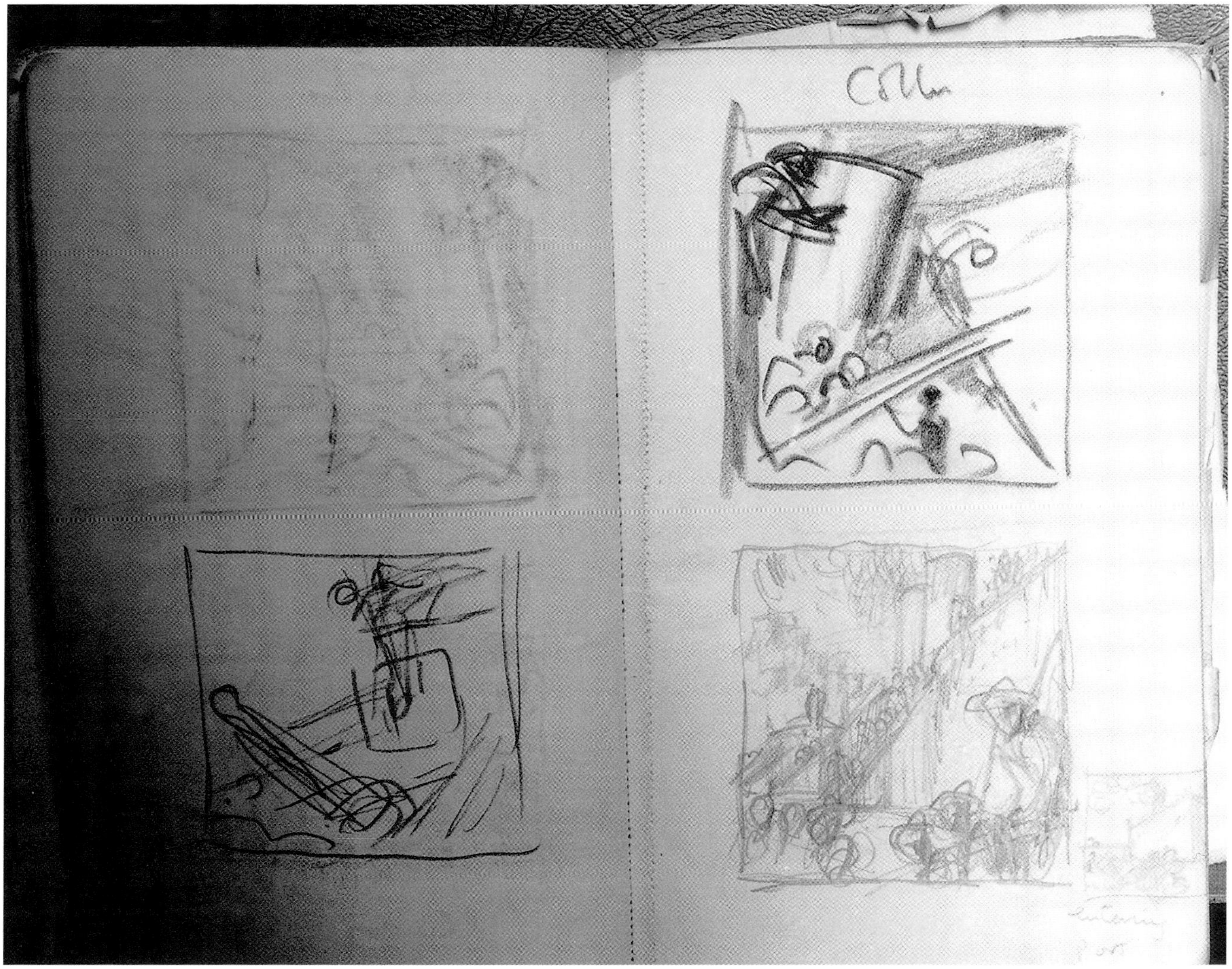

80. Sir Frank Brangwyn, 'entering port', 1917. Pencil. Sketchbook 773/8H, Royal Academy of Arts, London

78 (*facing, above*). Sir Frank Brangwyn, man ploughing in a field with a dead body (upper page); and war scenes (lower page, inscribed by Brangwyn 'The Glories of War?', with the artist's dog apparently lying dead). *c.*1914–18. Pencil. Sketchbook 799/8H, Royal Academy of Arts, London

79 (*facing, below*). Sir Frank Brangwyn, 'Snow' and 'the last Mass', *c.*1915. Pencil. Sketchbook 774/8H, Royal Academy of Arts, London

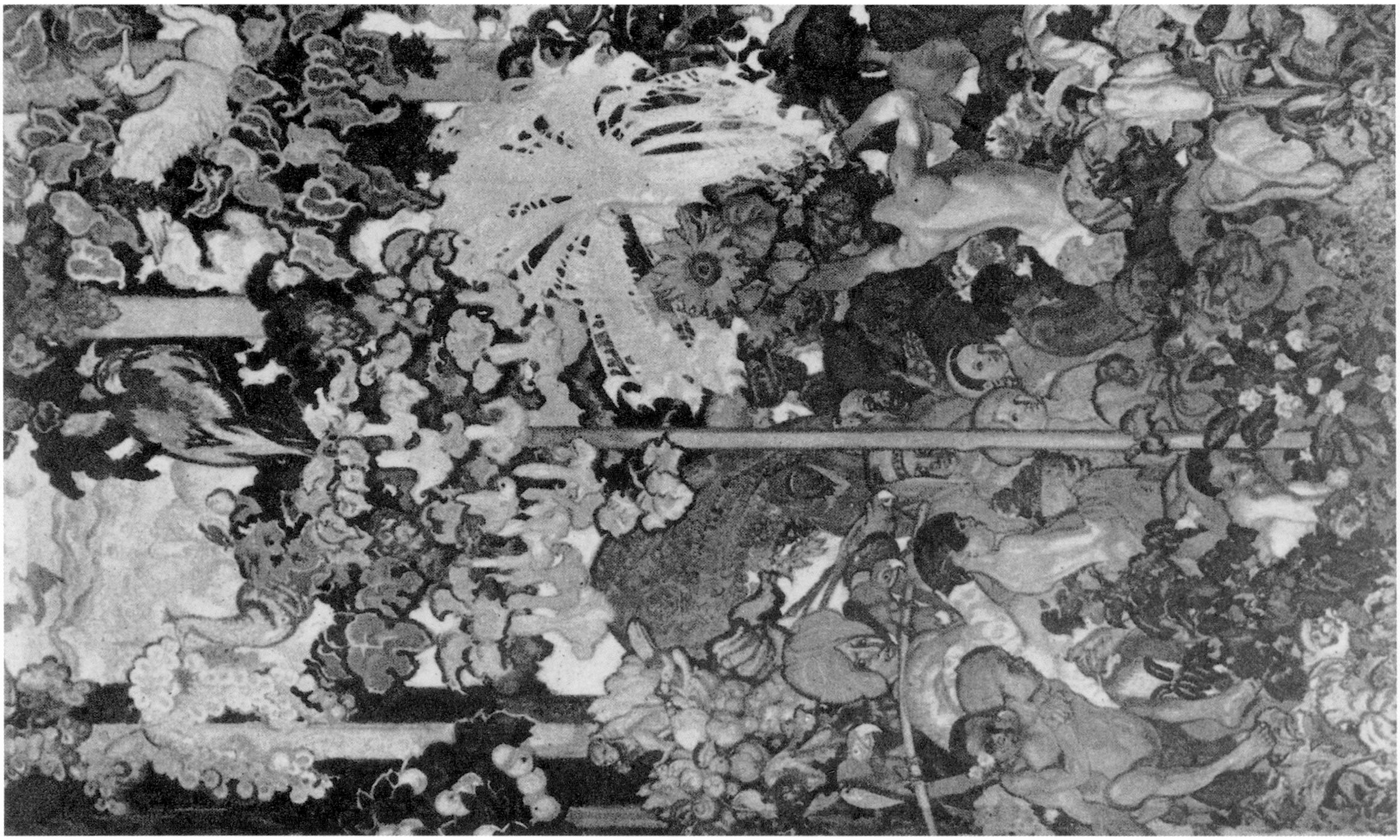

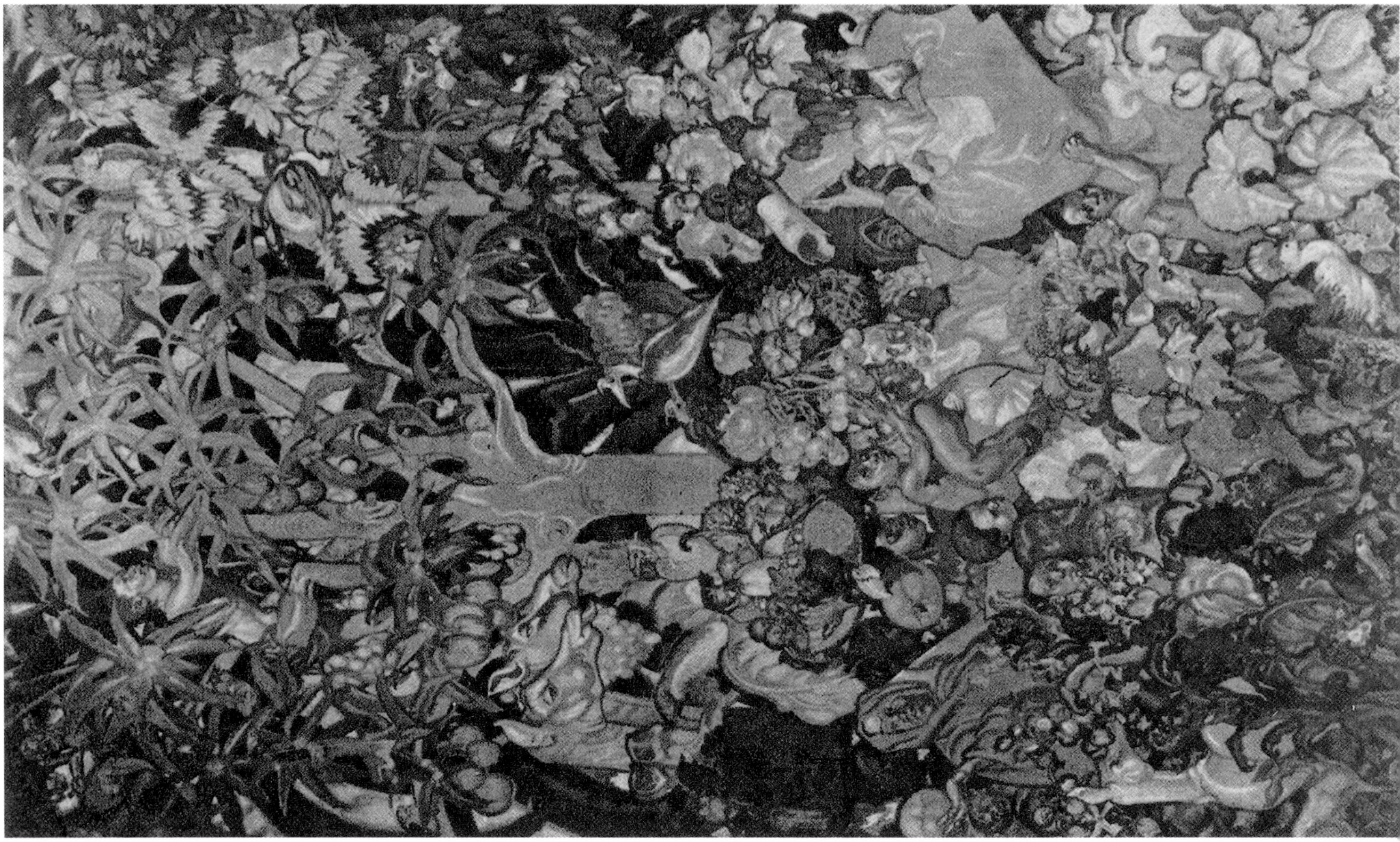

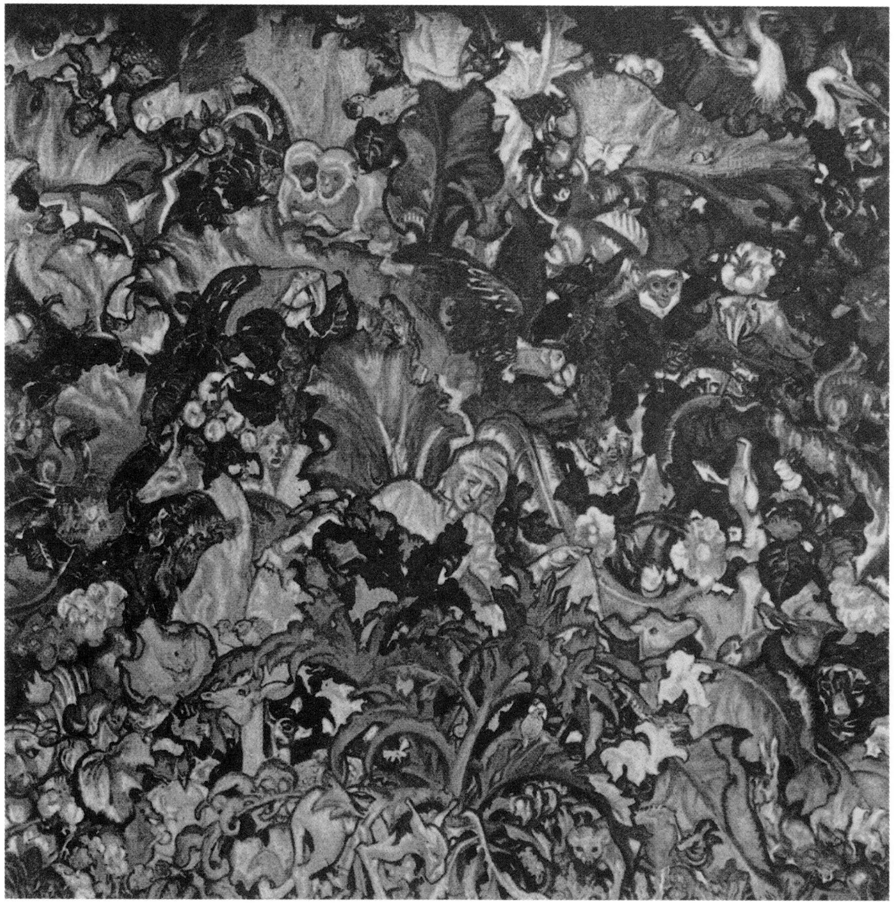

83. Sir Frank Brangwyn, *British Empire* mural for east or west wall, Royal Gallery, Palace of Westminster, London, 1924–33, now in Guildhall, Swansea (photograph *c.*1930)

81 (*above, left*). Sir Frank Brangwyn, *British Empire* mural, for left panel, upper north wall, Royal Gallery, Palace of Westminster, London, 1924–33, now in Guildhall, Swansea (photograph *c.*1930)

82 (*above, right*). Sir Frank Brangwyn, *British Empire* mural, for right panel, upper north wall, Royal Gallery, Palace of Westminster, London, 1924–33, now in Guildhall, Swansea (photograph *c.*1930)

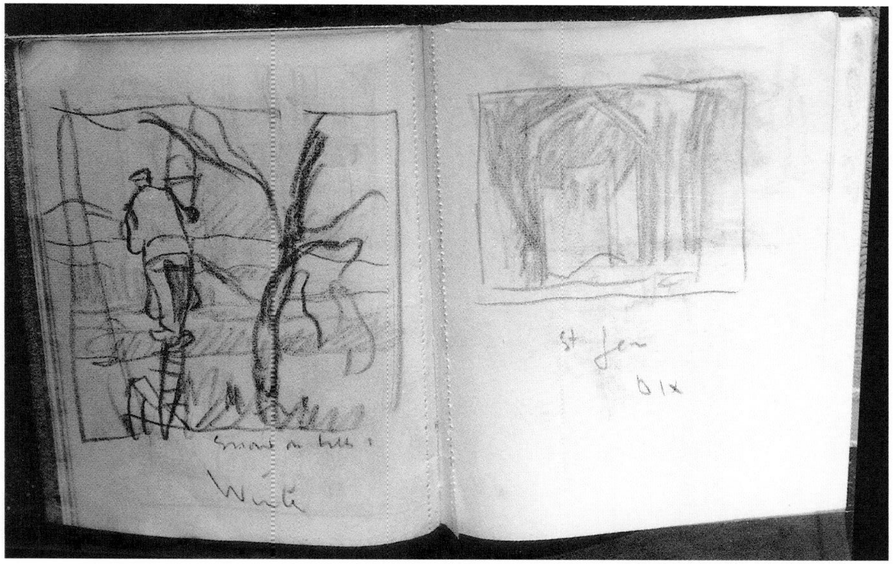

84. Sir Frank Brangwyn, 'Winter', *c.*1918. Pencil. Sketchbook 815/84, Royal Academy of Arts, London

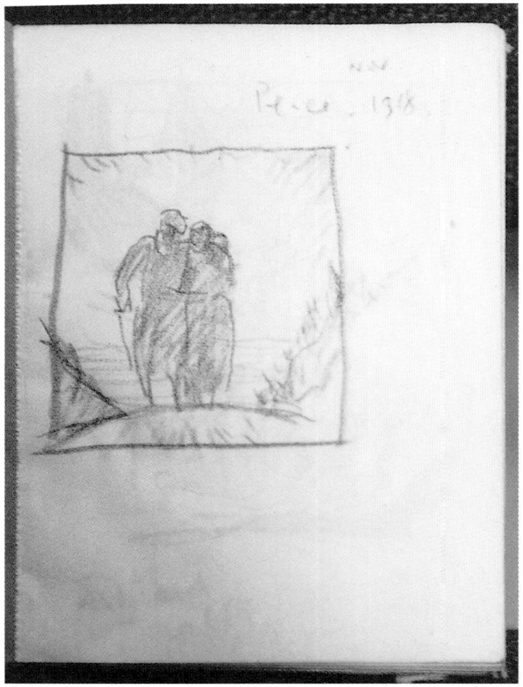

85. Sir Frank Brangwyn, 'Peace Nov. 1918', 1918. Pencil. Sketchbook 815/84, Royal Academy of Arts, London

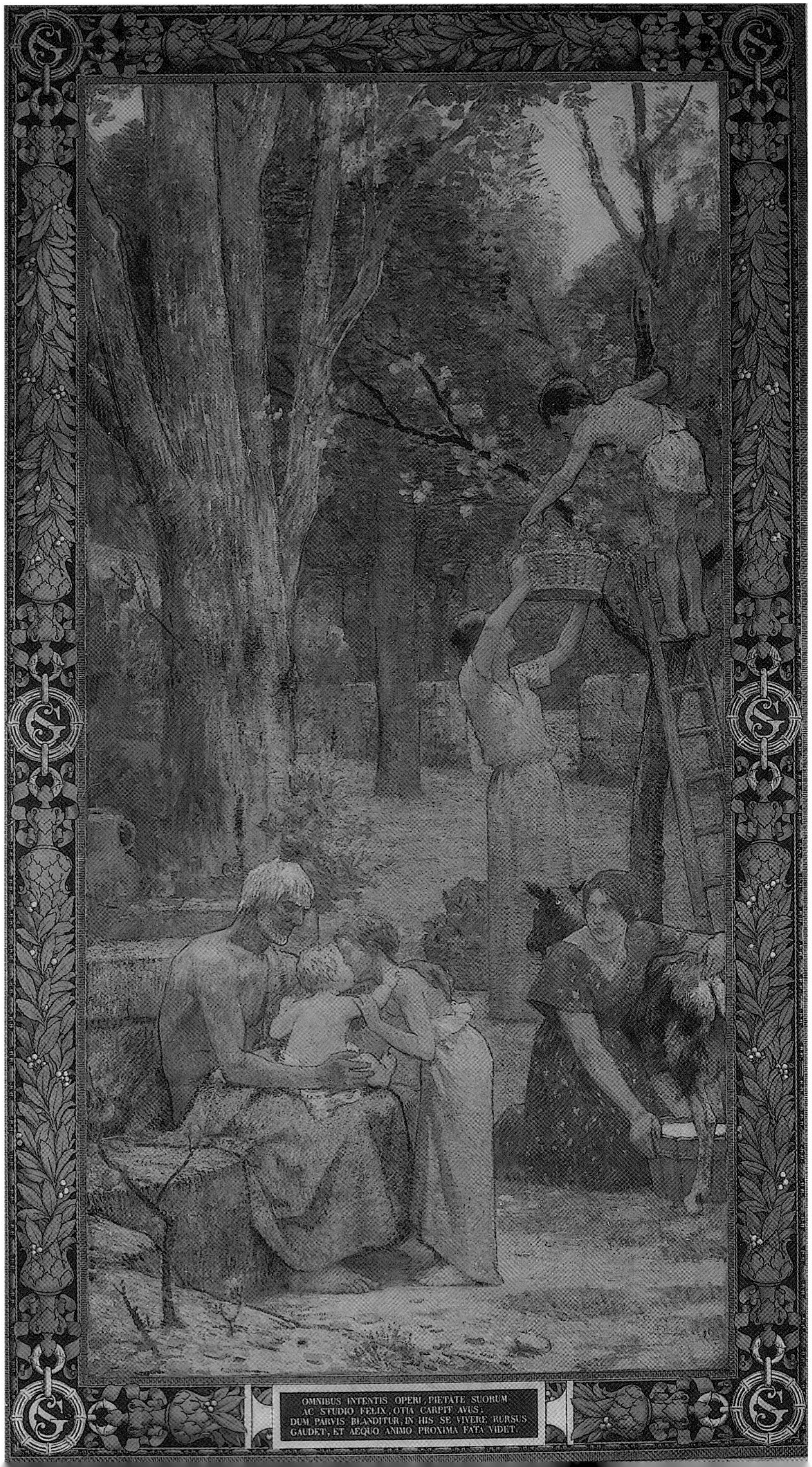

86. Ferdinand Humbert, *Prospérité/Famille*, 1898–1900, Panthéon, Paris

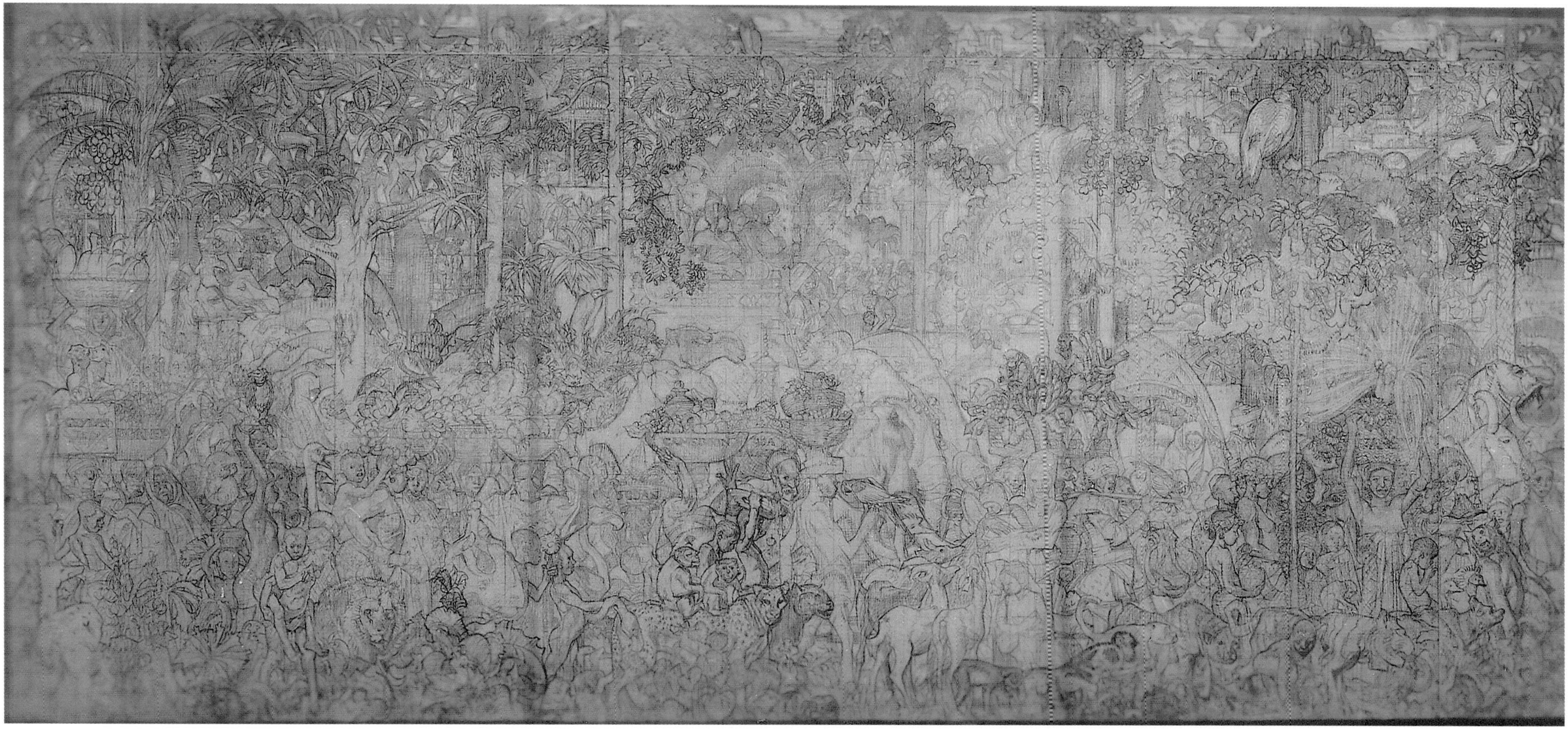

87. Sir Frank Brangwyn, cartoon for *British Empire* murals for upper north wall, Royal Gallery, Palace of Westminster, London, *c.*1924–33. Bruges, Stedelijke Musea

'Mr Brangwyn's paintings will not harmonise with their surroundings . . . the large paintings of tropical flora and fauna flanking the War Memorial [i.e. Tweed's sculpture] and the historic cartoons [i.e. Maclise's murals] would appear inappropriate'[36] in their rejection of the panels, these factors suggest deeper political motives. This reading of the situation is supported by contributions to the Lords' debate of 1930 on the murals. Lord Newton, for example, proposed that the murals 'might . . . be appropriate in what I believe is the Daíl Éirann, or they might go abroad and be considered appropriate for the palace that I understand the League of Nations is now constructing at Geneva'. Ireland was pressing its claims to independence, whilst the League of Nations had become virtually synonymous with the colonial and dominion independence movement. It is significant that after the rejection of the panels, it was the *Daily Mail*, owned by the Empire Free Trader Lord Rothermere, which orchestrated their acceptance by Swansea City Council, after a showing at the Ideal Home Exhibition of 1933.

The fate of Brangwyn's Royal Gallery work throws into focus the continuing conception of mural art as propaganda, which had characterized British State patronage even from Prince Albert's first schemes for the decoration of Westminster in the 1840s. Just as Albert had wanted to make the Royal Gallery a vehicle for his vision of the power of the monarchy in the government of Britain, and indeed, Empire too, so the Lords in 1930 were essentially looking at the message behind the appearance of Brangwyn's scheme. Paradoxically, however, there were simultaneous signs that new alternative forms of propaganda were being preferred, and even that propaganda should be disguised and 'indirect'. By 1933, Viscount Lee of Fareham was highlighting, in a talk to the Royal Empire Society, the way in which the 'indirect, persuasive, instructional value' of films could enable the 'projection of England to the four corners of the earth'.[37] Films sent to the Commonwealth took the place after 1933 of the Empire Marketing Board; at the same time, the Speaker of the House of Commons, J. H. Whitley, who had initiated the St Stephen's Hall murals, was launching the Empire Broadcasting Service as 'This new link with the Homeland'.[38] Both films and radio were part of the changed situation of the 1930s. Brangwyn's abandonment of war themes had been appropriate in 1925, in the context of Baldwin's vision of 'peace in our time', but by 1930, Mussolini was already announcing that 'right unaccompanied by might is an empty word.'[39] Far from promoting pacifism, the censors were now actually agin it;[40] rearmament was starting; and Britain was actively seeking colonial support for her defence. Political events had moved too fast for Brangwyn to keep pace, exactly as had occurred in respect of Goetze's Foreign Office scheme. After they had rejected Brangwyn's work, the Lords resolved that no further money should be made available for the decoration of the Royal Gallery, and British State mural patronage was effectively terminated. The decision can be seen as part of the wider concern amongst Conservatives—who were then in a majority in the Lords—at any situation where the government might be felt to be controlling propaganda. As the historian J. M. Lee has noted, 'In an era when Hitler's Germany was beginning to develop an international reputation for government-controlled propaganda services, the prospect of a British propaganda organisation . . . was not very welcome.'[41]

[36] Ibid.

[37] Talk given on 20 March 1933.

[38] J. H. Whitley, 'Empire Broadcasting and the New Service', *United Empire*, 24 (1933).

[39] Quoted in Mowatt, *Britain between the Wars*, p. 373.

[40] See J. M. MacKenzie, *Propaganda and Empire* (Manchester, 1984), p. 79.

[41] J. M. Lee, 'The Dissolution of the Empire Marketing Board, 1933, Reflections on a Diary', *Journal of Imperial and Commonwealth Studies*, no. 1 (Oct. 1972), p. 52.

At the same time, however, it is only too evident that in ostensibly relying on the advice of the Royal Fine Art Commission in respect of Brangwyn's murals, the Lords were looking to a body whose membership had clear sympathies with the Neoclassicism of the British School at Rome, exemplified in the St Stephen's Hall scheme. The association of this style with Conservative ideals, which had been latent in the classical packaging of the Wembley Exhibition, had been confirmed by the election of Whitley in 1929 to the Executive Committee of the British School at Rome; Viscount Lee of Fareham, another of the Royal Fine Art Commission members, was moreover, one of the major collectors of early Italian art in Britain (his pictures later formed a nucleus of the Courtauld Collection). It is hardly surprising that the Commission was unsympathetic to Brangwyn's work, with its strong inspiration from Baroque and Renaissance Flemish sources, and its robust realism, which had won Ramsay MacDonald's appreciation in 1924. Brangwyn's close-up motifs of flowers and animals, even though tinged with something of the Art Deco idiom that would emerge fully blown in his Rockefeller Center murals in 1930–4 in New York, would have been only too reminiscent of the images in John Grierson's 1920s films for the now disbanded Empire Marketing Board. In rejecting his murals the Lords were, paradoxically, perhaps in fact acknowledging the very power of their visual and symbolic impact.

If the flower-garlanded elephants bearing the triumphant howdah procession through an Empire Eden in Brangwyn's central panel for the north wall of the Royal Gallery seem the polar opposite of Max Ernst's Surrealist *Celebes* of 1921 (Tate Gallery, London)—a metallic, nightmare beast inspired by the form of a Sudanese corn-bin but standing in a barren, war-torn landscape—there are aspects of the 'British Empire' panels which none the less suggest that the 'insistence' of their imagery was actually a reflection of unresolved anxieties and tensions on the part of Brangwyn. His treatment of these themes would have seemed unpalatable in the context of early 1930s politics, but the murals also have a strangely impersonal, even detached, quality. The vigour which made his work at Skinners' Hall seem so spontaneous and alive is now slightly forced, even artificial; the incessant rhythmic forms suggest a world too tightly structured to be truly free, and nature's spaces, here crowded with abundance, verge almost on the obsessive and claustrophobic. No longer presenting particular identities, as in the preliminary cartoons with their annotations and labels, the teeming figures, beasts, and plants evoke a paradise which, though in a very different way, is almost as surreal as the hell-scape of *Celebes.* Embedded in this riot of nature, the children and adults sometimes seem subordinate to the convulsions of plant forms.

Seeking, like Ernst, to purge the horrors of war—perhaps even to resolve a 'crisis of faith' after the aggression of works such as his *Put Strength in the Final Blow* war poster (Plate 61)—it is as though Brangwyn was as yet unable, or unwilling, paradoxically, to empathize fully with 'what had been saved'. Like Monet in his *Grandes Décorations* for the Orangerie in Paris, he looked to nature's cycle to heal the wounds of war. Yet, after his various false starts, and working in fiercely guarded self-isolation, this seems to have resulted in a conservative return to the 'safety' of familiar models—the Flemish tapestries and William Morris designs which had been amongst his earliest experiences of art—rather than a truly innovative response. As his sketches and studies reveal, Brangwyn was engaged in an anguished catharsis, seeking renewal of his earlier faith in man's eternal brotherhood. Freed from the horrors of portraying the Western Front by the shift to scenes of peace, his eventual iconography depended entirely for its message on a symbolic counterpoint with Maclise's adjacent 'Waterloo' murals. Once separated from these its 'land of plenty' may seem almost escapist. Whether by choice or *diktat*, the imagery of human suffering and Christian compassion which, but a few years earlier, had drawn forth the near Expressionist intensity of Brangwyn's *Stations of the Cross* designs for Arras Cathedral (Stedelijke Musea, Bruges), has been all but excised from the murals themselves. The snatches of comment which Brangwyn inscribed beside certain figures in his preliminary cartoons reveal his humanitarian instincts, yet somehow these have failed to materialize in the iconography and manner of the completed works. The result is arguably a 'glorious failure': splendid images of fruitfulness and brilliant light, but not reaching the deeper spiritual truths or human emotions which at Arras, or at Skinners' Hall, as well as in other schemes such as that at Christ's Hospital, Horsham (to be discussed in Chapter 8) arose out of a direct confrontation with the darker sides of life, or even death itself, rather than their inference through contrast with another artist's work.

MURALS AT INDIA HOUSE (1929–1932) AND SOUTH AFRICA HOUSE (1933–1938)

If Brangwyn's Royal Gallery work marked an end to mural patronage by the British Government, the power of mural painting to project identity was taken up by the Empire and Commonwealth nations themselves through the decorations at India House and South Africa House, both recently built by Sir Herbert Baker, in which native artists were employed. Where Frank Salisbury had contributed prominently to the pre-war decoration of Baker's and Lutyens's government buildings in Delhi, the work of Indian painters at India House (Plates 88–9) can be seen as an assertion of identity in the wake of the Statute of Westminster, and in the very period immediately preceding the Government of India Act of 1935, which envisaged a measure of federal self-government for the different Indian provinces. Likewise, the predominance of South African painters in the distribution of commissions at South Africa House, and the balance there between subjects from the country's Dutch and British history, speaks of the principles of native 'Fusion' politics during the 1930s and of Jan Smuts's guiding vision of self-government based on 'Anglo-Afrikaner reconciliation'.[42] The South Africa House scheme (Plate 90; Plate XXI) was proudly illustrated in an article in the *Studio* in 1934 by its High Commissioner, C. T. te Water, as a showcase for 'the interaction of the two dominant white races of South Africa, of the "European" culture of the one upon the "African" culture of the other'[43] in the creation of 'a white race to be counted . . . as indigenous to Africa as are the black races which surround it',[44] and it can be seen as part of a larger cultural affirmation of this ideal through the establishment of a South African National Gallery and a National Academy of Arts in Cape Town in 1932. The founder members of the Academy included one of the South Africa House painters, J. Pierneef, who also carried out murals in Johannesburg Railway Station in the 1930s.[45]

The murals at India House, painted in tempera, fell heir of course, to the long and distinguished tradition of Indian mural painting, which had also aroused the interest of the Society of

[42] N. Mansergh, *The Commonwealth Experience* (London, 1969), p. 377.

[43] C. T. te Water, 'The Cultural Heritage of South Africa', *Studio*, 108 (1934), p. 170.

[44] Ibid., p. 164.

[45] Illustrated in ibid., pp. 174–5.

Mural Decorators and Painters in Tempera, and their iconography is exclusively from Indian legend, history, and custom. As such it won the approval of Rabindranath Tagore.[46] Where Rothenstein at St Stephen's Hall had illustrated the coming of a British emissary to the Moghul Court felt to have laid foundations for British rule in India, one of the four great incidents from Indian history in the continous frieze around the Central Dome at India House (by R. Ukil, S. Choudhury, D. K. Barma, and L. M. Sen) illustrates the meeting of Alexander the Great with the captive Indian King Porus (Plate 88). This was the occasion when the latter's 'chivalrous bearing so pleased Alexander that he returned his Kingdom to him';[47] a suggestive theme in the context of India's independence aspirations in the 1920s and 1930s. At the same time, however, the Indian artists selected (following a competition held by the Government in India, acting through a committee chaired by the Chief Commissioner of Delhi, Sir John P. Thomson)[48] were, on Baker's advice, dispatched for training under Sir William Rothenstein at the Royal College of Art, and thereafter to Italy to study Renaissance paintings at first hand; a similar but more limited scheme was also introduced for the South Africa House artists.[49] If this suggests that the Imperial hand remained uppermost, to the extent that Indian or South African tradition was re manufactured as a product in the style of the British School at Rome, it is important to remember that Rothenstein had a strong sympathy with Indian culture and was a friend of Tagore. Where he himself reflected something of the style of Persian manuscripts in his cleanly silhouetted figures in *Sir Thomas Roe* at St Stephen's Hall, the distinctive outlined forms, costumes of bright lemon yellow, tangerine, blue, and viridian, and the stylized foliage and flat perspective of the India House paintings make only small concessions to Western art, although the Central Dome frieze has a gilded backdrop like an early Italian panel painting. Traditional Indian pattern motifs border the roundels in the pendentives beneath, which illustrate the Indian stages of life from *Jamma* (Birth) to *Nirvana* and employ symbolic colour progressions in which the red of the unborn spirit develops, for example, into the orange of childhood's 'carefree existence'.[50] In the pendentives of the Entrance Hall, R. Ukil's and S. Choudhury's eight female personifications of the Indian seasons, including exotic native flowers, have an almost Art Nouveau ebullience which reminds the viewer that such Western artists as Mucha, Bakst, and Bossanyi were themselves already indebted to Indian and Oriental sources. Scenes from Indian musical and religious traditions by Choudhury, Ukil, and Sen decorate a number of other rooms in the building.

The message of an at least equal, rather than a subordinate relationship of Indian to British culture is perhaps most clearly evident in the nature of the murals as a realization of Baker's 'British School at Rome' tenet of reciprocal harmony between art, craft, and architecture; a tenet which was to reach its most ambitious statement at the Bank of England a few years later.[51] Yet even this was perhaps a relative matter: for all its 'Indian' sculptural and design ingredients,[52] India House remains a resolutely neoclassical structure, as tangible a monument to British Imperialism as Baker's earlier but similar Secretariat and Parliament House buildings in New Delhi itself. An analogous effect occurs in his massive South Africa House in Trafalgar Square. Here, three mural paintings carried out in 1933 by the British painter J. H. Amschewitz illustrate

[46] Information from S. Mukherji, *Murals in India House High Commission of India, London*, pamphlet kindly supplied by India House.

[47] Ibid., p. 4.

[48] Ibid., p. 1.

[49] See H. Baker, *Architecture and Personalities* (1944), p. 134.

[50] Ibid., p. 3.

[51] See Chapter 11.

[52] e.g. the inlaid floor of the Entrance Hall illustrating the symbols of the different Indian provinces, and the use of Indian wood and carving styles throughout the building.

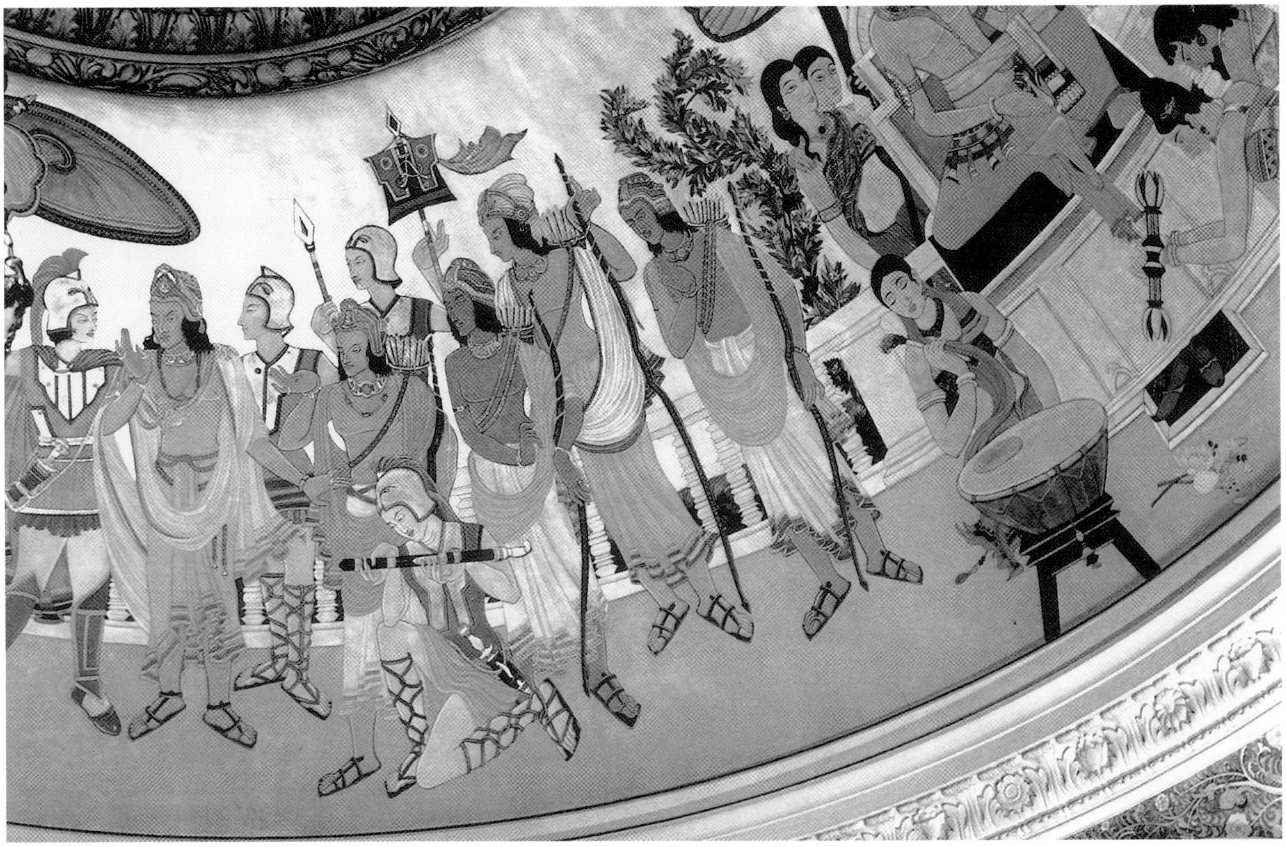

88. R. Ukil, S. Choudhury, D. K. Barma, and L. M. Sen, *The Meeting of Alexander the Great and King Porus*, detail from Central Dome, India House, London, 1929–32

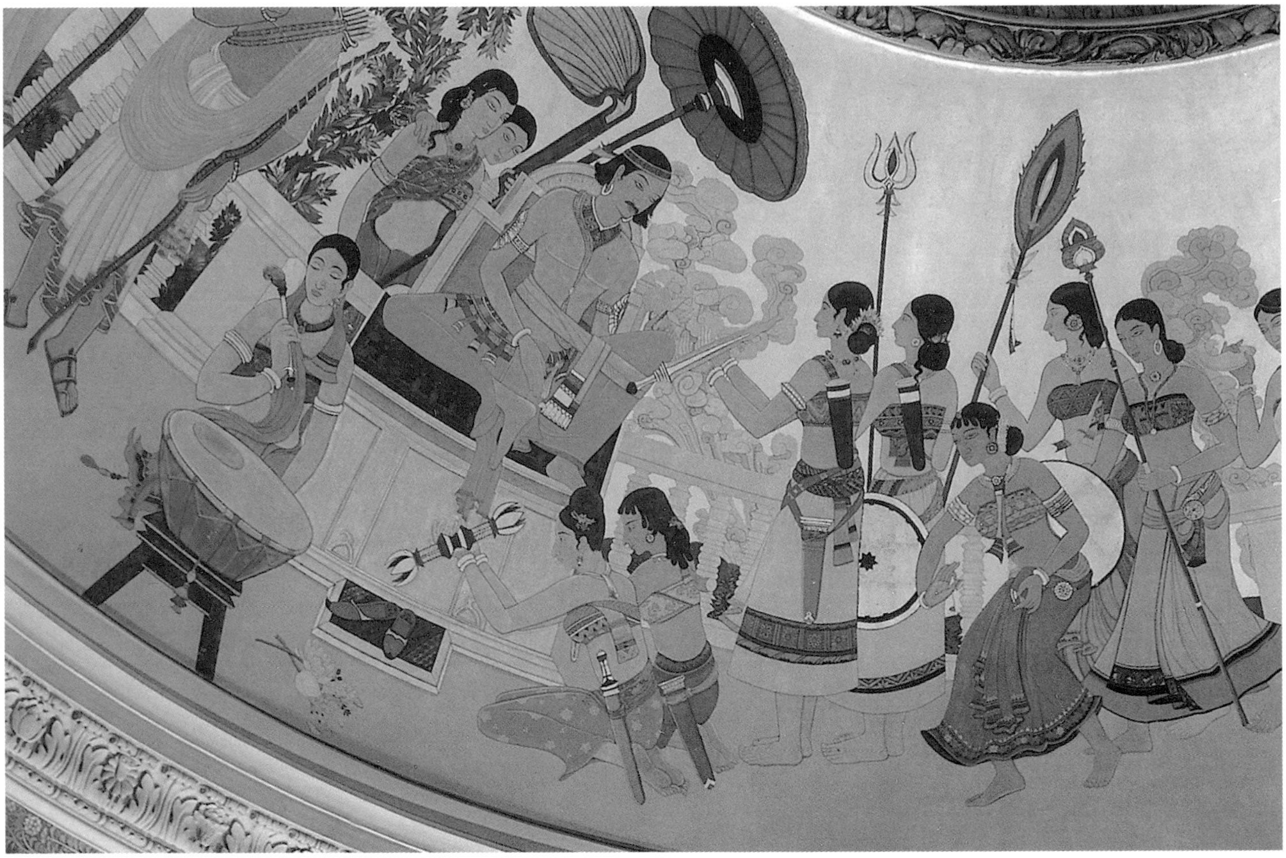

89. R. Ukil, S. Choudhury, D. K. Barma, and L. M. Sen, detail from Central Dome, India House, London, 1929–32

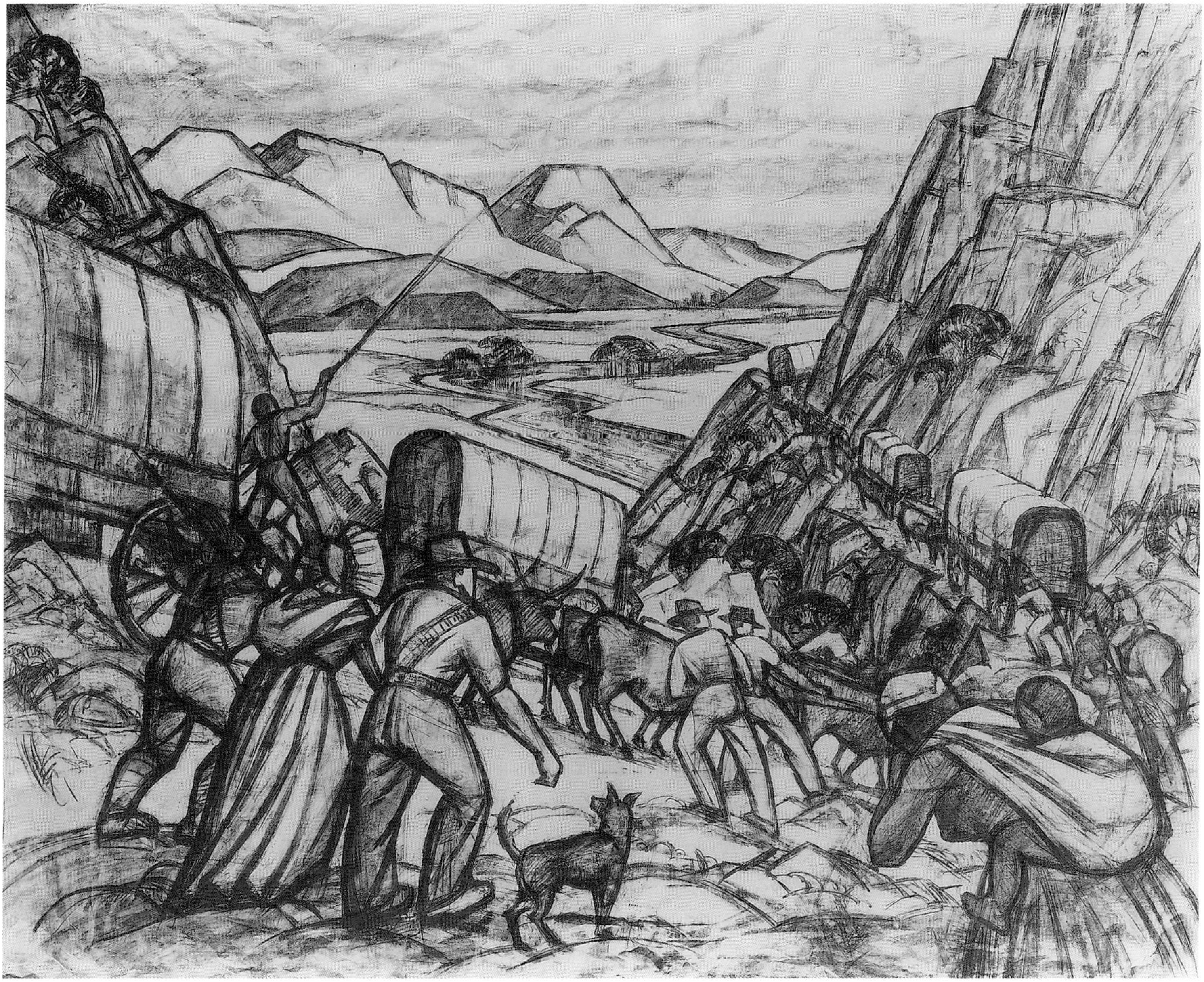

90. Jan Juta, sketch for *The Great Trek*, South Africa House, London, *c.*1933–4

the discovery of South Africa by Prince Henry the Navigator, Bartholemew Dias, and Vasco da Gama (Plate XXI) respectively; those by the South African Jan Juta show Dutch settlement and the Voortrekkers, whilst landscape panels in a modified Post-Impressionist style by another South African, R. Gwelo Goodman, illustrate the Dutch pastoral tradition of the Cape Town region and are accompanied by murals of characteristic local flora and fauna. J. Pierneef's murals show the Transvaal. Amschewitz's billowing cloudscapes, a muscular sailor in the foreground suggesting respect for the contribution of the common man to history, and vibrant orange and turquoise harmonies reveal a strong—perhaps too literal—influence from Brangwyn and develop trends evident in his Liverpool Town Hall murals.[53] The murals by Juta showing the building of the castle at Cape Town, Jan Riebeeck's landing, and *The Great Trek* (Plate 90), however, are closer to the British School at Rome style of Colin Gill, mixed in *The Great Trek's* static bulky figures and exaggerated mountain perspective with something perhaps of Diego Rivera's Mexican mural idiom. Pierneef's contributions include a boldly geometric rendering of one of the goldmines near Johannesburg: the gold standard had, of course, been abandoned by Britain in 1931, opening the way to a predominantly economic, rather than political, foundation for the Commonwealth.[54] Again, a desire to loosen Imperial ties thus seems implicit. A series of panels showing 'the traditional Zulu way of life' (including a 'Feast of the Fruits') was added in 1938. Unlike Brangwyn's British Empire panels, however, it is not a vision of 'universal brotherhood' which these evoke, but rather a sense of a separate, even an alien tradition, for they were intended as decoration for a self-contained 'Mural Room' devised by Baker. Painted by the South African artists, Eleanor Esmonde White and Leroux-Smith Leroux, their earth colours and style derived from Bantu art (though in a tempera medium) essentially offer a picturesque, anthropological, contribution to the decorative programme rather than any reflection of the rising political claims to black representation which would dominate post Second World War South African affairs.

It is easy to read such murals solely from an early twenty-first century perspective, as no more, despite their 'native' accents, than ineluctable Imperialism. Set in the context of the 1930s, and of the rejection of Brangwyn's British Empire panels at Westminster, however, their message can be seen as a more subtle contribution to a changing balance of power within the Commonwealth. In several cases, notably at India House, this was expressed in work of undoubtable artistic merit.

[53] Amschewitz's *Prince Henry*... and *Portuguese Navigators* flank the entrance to the Ambassador's Room; Juta's murals decorate one of the principal corridors and the Exhibition Room, Gwelo Goodman's the Anteroom, and Pierneef's another corridor and the balcony area.

[54] See M. Kitchen, *The British Empire and Commonwealth: A Short History* (Basingstoke and London, 1996), p. 78.

7

Patron and Icon at the Town Hall

When mural painting was revived at Westminster, one of the keenest hopes was that State patronage 'would incite the municipal bodies in the provinces and other corporate bodies to apply the arts also to the decoration of their town halls and other public buildings'.[1]

As early as 1842, Sir Charles Eastlake, Secretary of the Royal Fine Arts Commission at Westminster, spelt out the crucial association between medium and message which was to become the *Leitmotiv* of mural patronage at town, county, and village halls over the succeeding hundred years:

> the places in which it is possible and desirable to employ the higher branches of art will be the national and municipal buildings; all localities in a word, where painting can be displayed to the public in its highest and most didactic form.[2]

Ruskin simply put it that 'There should not be a single ornament put upon great civic buildings, without some intellectual intention.'[3]

In considering the development of civic mural patronage, stylistic and aesthetic factors have to be seen in their historical and political context, just as the architecture itself of a town or village hall is related to the aspirations and ideals of those who commissioned it. The emphasis on the integration of art and architecture, which gathered momentum throughout the period from Ruskin's Gothic Revival to the Arts and Crafts Movement and the Edwardian Baroque, combines with a very specific attempt to make murals a vehicle of propaganda, pride, or public principle. Whilst the Westminster mural experiment was driven by a larger aim to establish a national school of decorative painting, civic murals perhaps inevitably became, despite Eastlake's hopes, the expression of more local purposes, and need to be seen as part of the 'civic ritual'[4] evident at the Royal Exchange. Like architectural sculpture, but also like the nineteenth-century revival of ceremonials such as the Lord Mayor's Procession in London or the Oyster Feast in Colchester,[5] they formed the backdrop to an increasingly elaborate stage set, where mayors and councillors sought to make visible their new role as 'tribunes of the people' in an age of radical political, social, and technological change. In 1867 the editor of *The Economist*, Walter Bagehot, foretold that 'the more democratic we get, the more we shall get to like state and show,'[6] and by 1882, the

[1] Question from Ewart to Dyce, Min. SCFA (28 May 1841), PP VI, §494.

[2] C. L. Eastlake, *General View of the Object of the Commission*, Appendix, *First Report* of the CFA (London, 1842), PP XXV, p. 13.

[3] *The Seven Lamps of Architecture* (1849), quoted in J. H. G. Archer (ed.), *Art and Architecture in Victorian Manchester* (1985), p. 162.

[4] D. Cannadine, 'Civic Ritual', *Past and Present*, no. 94 (1982).

[5] Ibid..

[6] Quoted in E. Hobsbawm and T. Ranger (eds), *The Invention of Tradition* (1983), p. 122.

Birmingham councillor J. T. Bunce was advising in his book *Municipal Boroughs and Urban Districts*, that 'The work of the town . . . should be done with such stateliness of manner as to dignify the corporate life.'[7]

Bunce was responsible for devising the iconography of the Arts and Crafts-influenced murals which were painted in the 1890s for Birmingham Town Hall; for patrons with such aims it was natural that spirit fresco, perceived as offering a modern substitute for the 'true fresco' of the great murals of the Italian Renaissance, should become one of the answers to the technical problems which tended to dampen enthusiasm for mural patronage in the years immediately following the Westminster mural revival. By the end of the nineteenth century, both spirit fresco and the use of oil on canvas attached to the wall had become standard practice, following Madox Brown's successful work at Manchester Town Hall between 1879 and 1893 (Plate I) which included some spirit fresco, and Leighton's adoption of spirit fresco combined with *marouflage* at the Royal Exchange (Plate 1). Such technical developments led to the paradoxical situation in which the example of the town halls, along with that of the Exchange, acted as a significant spur to the resumption of mural painting at Westminster from 1906.

In what was thus often a subtle and complex process of interaction between civic patron, architect, and decorators, the mural painter could play a highly important role, as was graphically explained by J. M. Brydon, the architect of Chelsea Town Hall, to the Royal Institute of British Architects in 1891:

> The soul of the Vestryman is stirred within him, the voice of the Common Councillor is heard in the land; and the architect, as he steers between the Scylla of stencils and the Charybdis of distemper, longs for the assistance of the trusty painter pilot, whose brush helps him to bring the *Argosy* into the sure haven of Art.[8]

One of the features of town hall mural painting is the rise of the 'fine' artist in place of the decorating company like Heaton, Butler, and Bayne, who provided the majority of the mural decoration at Rochdale Town Hall in the 1860s, but ceded the principal mural of the scheme to the Pre-Raphaelite-inspired artist Henry Holiday. Again, Madox Brown's work at Manchester was a leading example in this respect. The change reflects the growing interest in the iconographical potential of mural painting within 'civic ritual' (as compared with the frequently non-figurative painted decoration or stencil work of the companies), as much as the influence of foreign example, Lord Leighton's promotion of mural painting as a 'fine' art, and the Arts and Crafts Movement's emphasis on art in relation to architecture.

Foreign example and British response

In the absence of a successful national mural school or style after the Westminster fresco débâcle, German, Belgian, and French murals were the natural model for schemes such as Manchester (where Waterhouse, the architect, attempted to employ Belgian muralists, but was forced to abandon his plans by affronted local artists) or Glasgow, where the new Municipal Chambers were styled on their completion in 1888 'our new Hôtel de Ville',[9] and a deputation was sent to the Continent to gather inspiration from murals in France and Italy. Alfred Rethel's historical mural

[7] Quoted in Cannadine, 'Civic Ritual' (1982), p. 119.

[8] J. McKean Brydon in Brydon et al., 'Decorative Painting', (1891), p. 279.

[9] P. Geddes, 'On National and Municipal Encouragement of Art upon the Continent' (printed paper in SUA, given to the Edinburgh Art Congress, 1889), p. 8.

cycle for Aachen Town Hall (1847–52) aroused much interest in Britain and by the late nineteenth century there were frequent reciprocal visits between British and foreign councillors. New French work like the immensely ambitious Hôtel de Ville scheme (Plates 2, 91) was not only seen at the Salon, prior to its installation, by many British artists who were training in Paris, but was also extensively reported in the British art and architectural press. The progress of the murals in the new Paris Mairies, or *arrondissement* municipal halls, and of the German town halls created in the wake of unification (Plate 32), as well as of twentieth-century projects such as Stockholm Town Hall, was likewise well documented.[10] However, although the German Rathäuser introduced contemporary iconography as early as the 1870s[11] and the French Mairies from 1879,[12] historical imagery persisted in the overwhelming majority of the British schemes, even into the 1920s and 1930s, and can be seen as a reflection of the 'invention of tradition' in association with 'civic ritual', which, in essence, still motivated the nostalgic rural life iconography of the twentieth-century Village Hall scheme at Woodgreen in Hampshire. Wishing to authenticate their status and powers, the new or enlarged city and county councils sought credibility by reference to past customs or events, so that historical subjects frequently paralleled contemporary civic achievements or aspirations. This takes up one of the features of Rethel's Aachen scheme and contrasts with the overt illustrations of, for example, municipal providence in Henri Gervex and Emile Blanchon's contemporary life scenes at the nineteenth *arrondissement* Mairie. So too, whilst Rochdale's *Observer* likened its newly decorated, £155,000 Town Hall to the House of Lords in 1871, its iconography was, in fact, a direct appeal for the reform of central government, and so makes a striking contrast with so many of the post-1870 German town hall schemes. Dependent to a significant degree on state support, these were often a glorification of the new unified national identity rather than an expression of local or radical politics. In this respect the emphasis on specifically local iconography in other British schemes, from Manchester and Birmingham to Bristol, Nottingham, Glasgow, or Edinburgh, also contrasts with the omnipresent national Marianne emblem which adorned the French provincial town halls.

From Ruskin to Rothenstein: the theoretical context

Ruskin's concern for 'intellectual intention' in the decoration of civic buildings was born of his belief in the Gothic as the one style of architecture in which painting, sculpture, and carving might interact in the presentation of a moral message, and it was natural that the new patrons at the town halls should from the start look to the Gothic to express their quest for historical self-justification. Whilst Barry and Pugin had established the association between the Gothic style and national identity at the Palace of Westminster in the 1840s, however, Ruskin's was a more integrative conception. For the architects who followed his lead, and who were to be chosen to design the majority of the new town halls created after the Municipal Corporations Act of 1835—Godwin, Sir

[10] See W. Vaughan, *German Romanticism* (1979) for British interest in Aachen and other German schemes; the leading articles in the *Builder* on 'The Modern Hôtel de Ville, Paris' (20 April 1889), p. 290 and 'Decorations of the Paris Mairies' (18 Nov. 1899), pp. 455–7; and the 'Letter from Paris' column in the *Builder* during the 1890s, e.g. 1 Mar. 1890, 1 Aug. 1891, 14 Nov. 1891 (reports on the Hôtel de Ville decoration); Hôtel de Ville murals exhibited before installation were discussed in 'French Art of the Year' in the *Builder* (21 May 1892), p. 395. Geddes (*Encouragement of Art*, p. 9) drew attention to the work of the 'Verschönerungsvereine' (embellishment societies) in German cities. The decoration of Stockholm City Hall was reported in the *Studio* (90, 1925, p. 205).

[11] See H. T. Wappenschmidt, *Studien zur Ausstattung des deutschen Rathaussaales* (1981).

[12] See T. Burollet et al., *Le Triomphe des Mairies* (1986).

George Gilbert Scott, Street, and Waterhouse, for example—the materials of a building were no longer subordinate, as for Pugin, to its design. Instead, the materials as manifest in the decoration and furnishing of a building were the very substance of its form, and carried its meaning. Art was no longer added, but integral.

Street was an assessor for the Manchester Town Hall competition, won by Waterhouse, whilst Waterhouse sat in judgement over a remarkably high proportion of town hall competitions from the late 1850s onwards. Waterhouse's dedication to the absolute necessity of mural painting in his interior at Manchester led him to mastermind its planning without any fee, and Manchester became the one municipal mural scheme which was incessantly cited by artists and architects alike well into the twentieth-century in support of further patronage.[13] Meanwhile, there were other significant Gothic revival schemes like those at Rochdale (by Scott's pupil W. H. Crossland), and at Bradford. Much of the 'Art as Unity' philosophy of the Arts and Crafts Exhibition Society and the Art Workers' Guild in the later nineteenth century has its origins in the Ruskinian Gothic, and the Guild's Master in the 1880s, Walter Crane, emerges as an important figurehead whose Socialist sympathies led to his support for the reform of London government in the 1890s. His 1899 Guildhall Masque, *Beauty's Awakening*, offered a witty parody of what were felt to be the tired formulae of Hardman's armorial and emblematic decoration in the Guildhall; it showed personifications of Ruskin's *Seven Lamps of Architecture* being awakened from sleep so that London might once again 'be the leader of cities in the symbolising of her greatness by the Beauty of her Outward Show'.[14] His actors included Henry Holiday, who had painted the chief mural at Rochdale Town Hall, and their satire on 'civic ritual'[15] was not only a riposte to the Royal Exchange's 'mural propaganda', but also a challenge to municipal patrons to accept their new conception of mural painting as something 'universal'. It was a medium, according to Crane, which should speak 'a succinct language' of 'pictorial emblem, symbol or allegory'.[16] Symbolic personifications, in contrast to the more descriptive or narrative depiction of historical episodes used by the earlier town halls, became a typical feature of a number of turn-of-the-century schemes like that at Wakefield County Hall. The symbolic murals installed as late as 1911–14 in Chelsea Town Hall are essentially the outcome of the Art Workers' Guild principles held by its architect J. M. Brydon, just as the building itself reflects the new eclecticism in architecture which now embraced the Classical and Baroque, also under the 'Art as Unity' banner. Crane, and the example of Manchester, in turn directly inspired Sir William Rothenstein's pleas for civic mural patronage in the post-1918 period, which bore fruit in the London County Hall and Leeds Town Hall projects, and most significantly in the village hall decoration movement of the 1930s. Rothenstein, however, was as much inspired by the French decorative tradition, and it would be misleading to overemphasize the role of the Ruskin and Crane legacy.

Important impetus for civic patronage of 'fine' artists came from Lord Leighton's instigation of a 'prize for the decoration of a portion of a public building' at the Royal Academy in 1881, in emulation of the French art training system; and from the example of the Royal Exchange,[17] which encouraged patrons who, as at Bristol Old Council House or Liverpool Town Hall, decided to

[13] See, for example, W. Rothenstein, *A Plea for a Wider Use of Artist-Craftmen* (1916).

[14] '"Beauty's Awakening A Masque of Winter and Spring", Presented by Members of the Art Workers' Guild', *Studio* (Special Number, 1899), p. 4.

[15] Ibid., p. 28; see Chapter 3.

[16] Quoted in G. Smith and S. Hyde, *Walter Crane* (1989), p. 14.

[17] See Chapter 3.

insert murals into an existing building. Leighton also kept alive the strong tradition of historical iconography, which was further revitalized by the emphasis at Westminster from 1906 and the post-war work of the British School at Rome. Artists from the latter were responsible for one of the last major municipal mural schemes, that at Essex County Hall in the 1930s.

By 1925 at the Paris Decorative Arts Exhibition, the Report of the Department of Overseas Trade had concluded that new techniques and the economic climate would henceforth ensure that 'very few Town Halls will be dignified by twenty-foot panels of William the Conqueror landing at Hastings or William of Orange landing at Brixham,'[18] yet even beyond the 1940s, a historical scheme was carried out by James Duff at Dundee, and another in 1961–4 at Newport Civic Centre by Hans Feibusch. It was perhaps only with the 1951 Festival of Britain and its emphasis on celebration of a post-war technological age that a new mood began to develop in civic mural painting, in which work such as Monnington's abstract ceiling decorations at Bristol Council House, inspired by aerodynamic engineering, began to replace the entrenched preference for historical iconography. There is a sense in which civic, county, and village hall mural schemes need to be seen as essentially conservative in character, their very meaning inextricably associated with their purpose as decoration for buildings which have been called 'secular shrine[s] to civic antiquity',[19] yet this by no means prevented the production of work which in several instances was of very high quality and originality.

PRINCIPAL SCHEMES: 1871–1914

Although a large number of new town halls were built from the 1850s in the wake of the 1835 Municipal Corporations Act, it was not until 1888 that county councils were established and 1899 that the London Government Act was passed, which subdivided the capital into twenty-eight metropolitan boroughs.[20] The lead in the building and decoration of new town halls thus came from the provinces, and the first civic mural schemes are to be found in the radical north of England. Rochdale's centrepiece was an eleven metre long mural in its Great Hall of *The Signing of the Magna Carta*, completed by Henry Holiday in 1871 (Plate XXII). The Rochdale Town Hall, built by W. H. Crossland, is one of the most complete expressions of Ruskinian Gothic, and its stained glass, sculpture, tiling, carving, and murals create a medieval-style integrated ensemble which at the same time carries a rich tapestry of allusion to the origins of Rochdale's modern economy (cotton manufacture) and its status as one of the most prominent centres of the drive for electoral reform. The Anti-Corn Law Leaguer and Reformer, John Bright, laid the foundation stone in 1866, whilst his colleague Richard Cobden was Rochdale's Member of Parliament from 1859. The 'art-architecture' of Rochdale Town Hall thus juxtaposes painted panels in the former council chamber, illustrative of the history of cotton manufacture from Egyptian times to the modern flannel loom (Plate 92), with statuary of Cobden and Bright on the main stairway, and stained glass whose foreign and British civic escutcheons celebrate the virtues of Free Trade.

[18] G. Sheringham, 'Mural Decoration' in *Reports . . .* (1925), p. 53.

[19] Cannadine, 'Civic Ritual' (1982), p. 118.

[20] See C. Cunningham, *Victorian and Edwardian Town Halls* (1981), pp. 8 ff. for the development of municipal legislation in the 19th century.

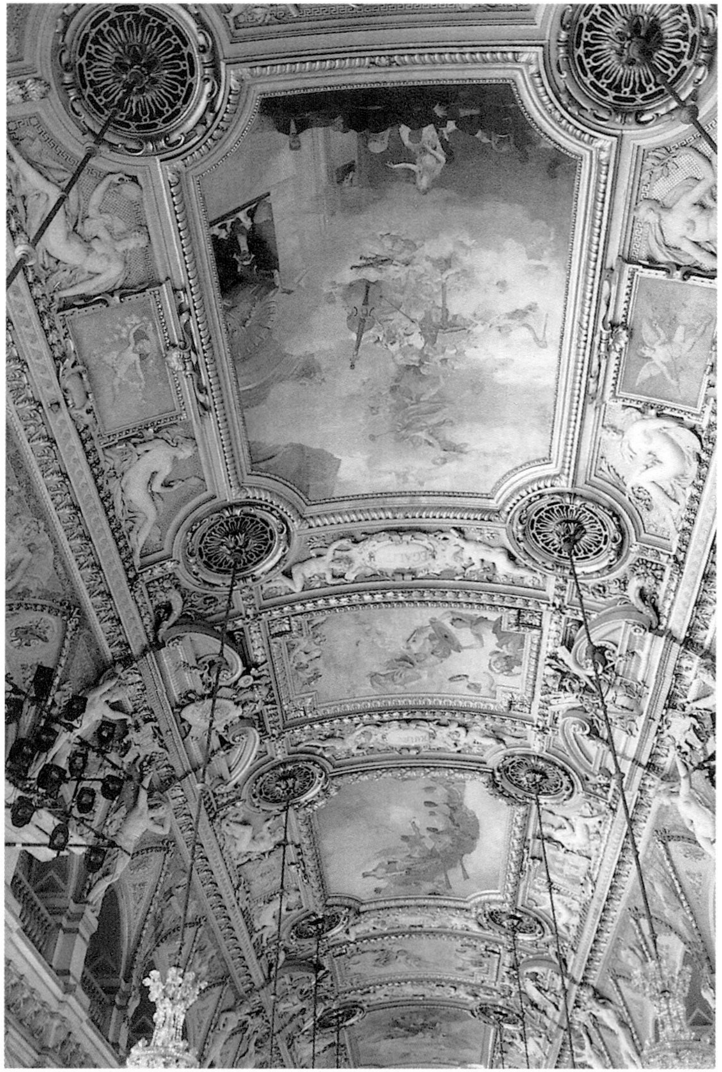

91. Henri Gervex, *Music*; Gabriel Ferrier, *Perfume*; Benjamin Constant, *The City of Paris welcoming the World to its Festivities*; Gabriel Ferrier, *Flowers*; Aimé Morot, *Dance through the Ages*, ceiling of Salle des Fêtes, Hôtel de Ville, Paris, 1889–90

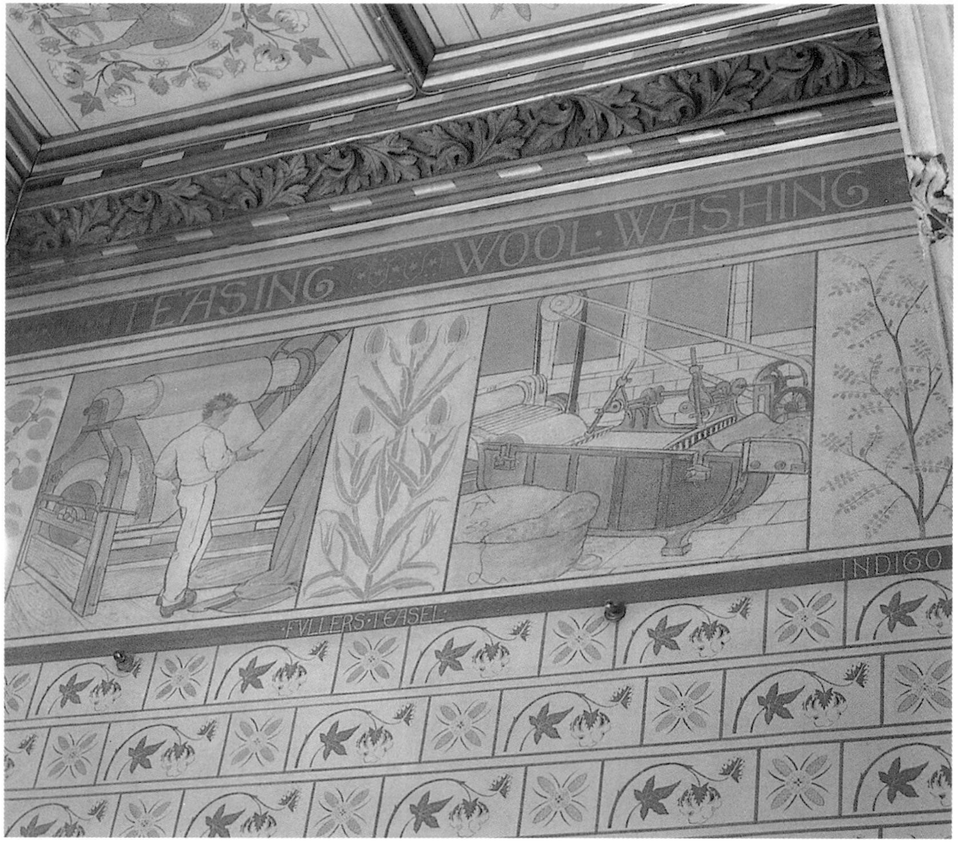

92. 'Mr Allen' (of Heaton, Butler and Bayne), illustrations of the history of weaving and spinning, in the former Council Chamber (now the Reception Room) of Rochdale Town Hall, *c.*1871

Distinctive amongst northern towns for its unusually high level of popular participation in local government,[21] Rochdale found a focus for its aspirations for similar representation at Westminster in the design of its Great Hall. Not only does its hammerbeam roof derive from that of Westminster, but its juxtaposition of Holiday's mural of the Magna Carta with a procession of the British monarchs in the stained glass refers specifically to Reform, and it is significant that a 'fine' artist was selected for the all-important Magna Carta subject. Holiday had designed stained glass for Heaton, Butler, and Bayne, but had won his reputation as a decorative painter in the Pre-Raphaelite style in commissions for William Burges's private houses. Elsewhere, the decorating company of Heaton, Butler, and Bayne provided the Council Room cotton murals and the twenty-seven panels of Rochdale trades in the vestibule to the mayor's suite, itself a treasure-house of further mural painting illustrating Night and Day with song-birds mocking a sleeping owl, and a liberal profusion of butterflies, stars, and flowers. Best and Lea, a local firm, did the 'game, wild ducks, pheasants and objects of the chase'[22] on the walls of the Refreshment Room.

Although *The Signing of the Magna Carta* had been included in the original plans for the mural subjects at Westminster, since it symbolized the origins of the modern parliamentary system, it is revealing that in the event, only a series of metal statues of 'Barons .... who cooperated in obtaining Magna Carta'[23] was installed, for Cartwright, Cobbett, and other Radicals had appropriated the theme, along with the Bill of Rights and Oliver Cromwell, as an emblem of the Chartists' goal of 'universal manhood suffrage'. After the Chartists' 'Monster National Petition' of 1848, it is not surprising that Magna Carta was effectively played down as a Westminster subject but given the grandest treatment at Rochdale, where it is flanked by Oliver Cromwell, who was tellingly included as one of the monarchs in the stained glass. It is possible that Holiday's *Magna Carta* was a specific memorial to one of the leading Chartists, the Rochdale councillor and alderman Thomas Livsey, who drew no fewer than 40,000 mourners to his funeral in 1864, and was described by Cobden as 'a self sacrificing friend and *protector*'[24] of working men—by implication a modern Cromwell.

Whereas the Select Committee at Westminster had planned to give equal representation of the noble and royal aides in *Magna Carta*, Holiday's mural allows the barons, those spiritual ancestors of the modern Members of Parliament for whom householders had just won the right to vote in 1867, to dominate the scene. Arranged in a frieze, they move from left to right to confront King John, and so guide the eye across to the window at the right showing Oliver Cromwell. The dais where they bring John to sign the charter corresponds with the real dais at the opposite end of the hall, linking the modern councillors of Rochdale with the barons who represented John's people. Although in a Gothic Revival hall, Holiday's figures have a statuesque monumentality which graphically reflects his intriguing comment that 'my life has been a continued protest against mediaevalism,'[25] as well as his 1867 visit to Italy and Pompeii. They are at the same time, however, robustly naturalistic and wear costumes researched from period tomb effigies, vividly bringing

[21] See J. Garrard, *Leadership and Power in Victorian Industrial Towns 1830–80* (Manchester, 1983), pp. 108–9 ff.

[22] Anon., *Rochdale Town Hall*, p. 13 (typescript, 1920, in Archive Dept., Rochdale Local Studies Library).

[23] *Account of the Amount of all Commissions for Works of Art to various Artists for the Decoration of the New Palace of Westminster* . . . (*Return* to the House of Commons, 13 Aug. 1853), p. 6.

[24] Quoted in Garrard, *Leadership and Power* p. 128.

[25] H. Holiday, *Reminiscences* (1914), p. 164, quoted in P. Cormack, *Henry Holiday* (1989), p. 1.

home the mural's message of past into present, much as the stained glass in the Magistrate's Court showing another Chartist hero, John Hampden, offered a literal illustration of Macaulay's description of Freedom, which 'o'er Hampden's life its beams of glory pour'd'.[26] Present in the stained glass, Hampden would have 'illuminated' the processes of truth. Holiday, later to become a Socialist, indeed modelled the barons in his mural himself, dressing for reference photographs in a specially made suit of chain mail, and so causing consternation in his five-and-a-half-year-old daughter, who thought he was off to war! The concern with realism is continued in the outline stencils of Heaton, Butler, and Bayne, and Best and Lea, who reputedly referred to Patent Office records to ensure accurate illustration of the various kinds of cotton machinery (Plate 92). William Burges's influence can perhaps also be felt in their naturalistic reinterpretations of mediaeval heraldic motifs.

Although Rochdale was a splendid fanfare to herald the start of municipal mural patronage, there were only partial and sometimes disappointing echoes in the other Gothic Revival town halls of the later nineteenth century. Daniel Maclise, however, painted two historical murals at Halifax, which like Rochdale was clearly seeking to align itself with Westminster where he had been an artist, whilst Holiday was again employed at Bradford, perhaps in recognition of his political sympathies. His work here (now lost) seems to have been more modest. The Town Hall at Preston, built by Sir George Gilbert Scott, no longer survives, but apparently had extensive decoration in the Ruskinian tradition, which included a painted allegory on the stairway of *Manufacture and Commerce*, symbolically placed above portraits of great men of past and present, who included the Free Trader, Corn Law Reformer, and Prime Minister, Sir Robert Peel, who had been commemorated in stained glass at Rochdale. The hall had a further thirty-six portraits showing Chaucer, Raphael, Dr Johnson, and Sir Humphry Davy, amongst other representatives of the arts, sciences, and politics. At Bolton, however, painted figures with trumpets were considered a disaster and quickly eradicated; elsewhere, there were a number of non-figurative schemes like that of 1874 at Winchester County Hall by Hardman's company (now lost) where the Tree of Jesse format for the names of the knights of the shire, like that by Holiday for the Magna Carta barons' names at Rochdale, must have been an intriguing appropriation of religious imagery to promote veneration of a civic patron's identity and lineage. Even Manchester remained more project than reality since only Madox Brown's twelve panels of local history in the Great Hall (Plate I; Plates 93–7) came to fruition out of a Rochdale-style plan for extensive integration of art and architecture.

Non-figurative mural painting was again provided here by Heaton, Butler, and Bayne, and Best and Lea, but the architect Alfred Waterhouse, acting out of 'a conviction which I so strongly feel that the building furnishes a great opportunity for pictorial embellishment of the highest order',[27] had more ambitious plans for five rooms of murals illustrating history, legend, 'manners and customs', and 'arts and science'.[28] Having failed to persuade Stacy Marks, who had done murals for him at Eaton Hall, to accept a commission, he secured the services of the local artists E. J. Gregory,

[26] Quoted in P. Karsten, *Patriot Heroes in England and America: Political Symbolism and Changing Values over Three Centuries* (Madison, Wis., 1978), p. 117.

[27] Report from Waterhouse to the Chairman of the New Town Hall Sub-Committee (1 Aug. 1877), M79/35, MTA. Waterhouse had provided space for murals in the principal courtroom of his Assize Courts in Manchester (1859) but this was not in the event painted.

[28] Letter from Councillor Joseph Thompson to the Chairman of the New Town Hall Sub-Committee (8 Oct. 1878), M79/10, MTA. These subject 'heads' appear to have been suggested by Thompson.

J. D. Watson, and Frederic J. Shields, and also of Ford Madox Brown. Meanwhile, he seems to have become impressed by what was being achieved in Continental mural schemes, visiting Belgium with a Council deputation and reporting in June 1876 that

the two living artists whose work appears to me to accord best with Gothic architecture are Mons. Guffins and Mons. Swertz [*sic*] . . . Those who have recently seen the council chamber of the Town Hall at Courtrai will remember the excellent work of these artists there, realising one's ideal of what mural painting should be. The medium employed is waterglass, believed to be indestructible, the same as that adopted by Herbert in his picture of 'Moses', in the library of the House of Lords.

I had an interview with Mons Guffins at Brussels, Mons Swertz being at the time engaged in his office of Director of the Institute of Fine Arts at Prague. Mons Guffins entered very warmly into the idea of executing some work for the Manchester Town Hall, which had been brought under his notice by Mr. Beresford Hope; and in a letter I have since received from him, I learn that his charge would be about the same as that asked by the English artists who have been consulted in the matter.[29]

Egide Guffens and Jan Swerts had in fact already carried out mural work in Britain in the chapel of Ince Blundell Hall in Liverpool; Beresford-Hope was the influential editor of the *Ecclesiologist*, who had long been promoting the merits of Nazarene-inspired mural painting in church architecture of the Gothic Revival.[30] The Manchester Academy and artistic fraternity, however, was thrown into consternation. Shields protested personally to Alderman Heywood:

By inviting or receiving foreign painters, you taunt English artists with incapacity whilst you rob us of a rare opportunity of disproving your doubts or objections. Have English painters failed when tried? Witness the noble works of Barry in the Society of Arts, at London . . . witness the Houses of Parliament . . . my one object is if possible to dissuade your Committee . . . and to entreat them that this first opportunity for the decoration of a great civic building in England may be given to English painters whose hearts and art are in sympathy with their brethren.[31]

From Waterhouse's remark to Councillor Joseph Thompson, 'The more I talk to the painters, the more confused I become. Those were palmy days when . . . we had only to get the money and then set Guffens and Swerts to work!'[32] his enthusiasm for Belgian artists seems to have been shared by the town council. When the commission for the decoration of the Great Hall with twelve historical panels was eventually given to Shields and Brown 'conjointly',[33] it appears that Waterhouse still contrived to involve Guffens in making an initial selection of subjects for the murals from a scheme of some 250 which had been drawn up by Councillor Thompson, before placing this 'Belgian' selection before Brown and Shields. The iconography conflated ideas for the other rooms in the building, as well as the Hall itself, to weave themes of science, industry,

[29] Report from Waterhouse to the New Town Hall Sub-Committee (21 June 1876), M79/35, MTA. F. Shields recorded that members of the committee had also visited Austria to examine the work of potential mural artists (letter 10 Oct. 1876 in E. Mills, *The Life and Letters of Frederic Shields* (1912), p. 199). Although they would have been too early to see the historical murals painted during the 1880s by Ludwig Mayer in the Vienna Rathaus, they presumably studied the realistic evocations of scenes from opera painted during the 1860s at the Vienna Opera House by Moritz von Schwind.

[30] See Chapter 8. For Guffens and Swerts, see J. Ogonovzsky-Steffens, 'Egide Guffens', in *Nouvelle Biographie Nationale*, vol. 4 (Brussels, 1997), pp. 206–8.

[31] Letter from Shields to Heywood (11 Oct. 1876), M9/75/2/2, MTA.

[32] Letter from Waterhouse to Thompson (15 Dec. 1876), quoted in J. H. G. Archer (ed.), *Art and Architecture in Victorian Manchester*, p. 170.

[33] Letter from Waterhouse to Brown (12 June 1877), M9/175/2/2, MTA. The fee agreed was £50 per square yard, with the cost of materials being met by the Corporation.

education, and Christianity into what Brown called 'the most comprehensive epitome of the rise and progress of Manchester that can be compressed into 12 pictures'.[34]

Having modelled his Town Hall on a Flemish medieval cloth hall, it was natural that Waterhouse should have preferred Guffens and Swerts. In finally opting for Madox Brown, who had to submit each design for Waterhouse's approval, and who in the event took over the whole commission when Shields dropped out, he was actually choosing the nearest alternative. Brown had trained under the great Flemish muralist, Gustav Wappers, and he and Shields announced themselves willing to travel to Antwerp to learn water-glass technique from the son of Baron Leys, who had recently completed the murals in Antwerp Town Hall.[35] Waterhouse was not surprisingly concerned about durability, since frescoes by Agostino Mario Aglio had dismally perished in Manchester's earlier nineteenth-century Town Hall. The Manchester councillors' sympathy for Belgian artists can be readily explained by their Free Trade ideals, which were already emblematized by Heaton, Butler, and Bayne's 'heraldic bearings of the various cities and countries connected with Manchester in trade' in the Great Hall, and by its statues of Gladstone and Charles Pelham Villiers, the Member of Parliament and Free Trader. Foreign artists' work in the Great Hall would have dedicated the Town Hall even more literally to the cause of Free Trade than was even Manchester's Free Trade Hall itself, where murals had been provided in the 1850s by students of the very Manchester Academy which had protested against Guffens and Swerts. Waterhouse's personal vision of 'art-architecture' thus dovetailed exactly with the political ideals of his patrons. The almost Baroque exuberance of design which characterizes many of Brown's murals, and is so different from the easel work of his Pre-Raphaelite phase, prompts the question of whether he may even have been instructed to emulate the modern Belgian school of historical painting in which Rubens's influence was still strong.

Free Trade is clearly behind the subject of *The Establishment of Flemish Weavers in Manchester AD 1363* (Plate I) which echoes in its theme, dynamic composition, and the prominence of the common man, the mural of *Edward III of England and the Antwerp Merchants*, recently completed by Swerts in the Antwerp Exchange, whilst *The Trial of Wyclif* (Plate 94) is a Reformation subject in which Brown's interpretation suggests that an allusion to Manchester's nineteenth-century reformers such as Bright was intended. Liberalism (which held power in Manchester) was, of course, traditionally associated with Nonconformism, and Thompson, who devised the subjects, was a leading Congregationalist who had had a chapel built by Waterhouse. Brown noted in his description of the mural that 'recent researches in Germany show that many of the Latin texts published by John Huss a century later were in reality composed by Wyclif.'[36] His *Wyclif* composition offers an intriguing glimpse back, but through Belgian spectacles, to the *Hussite Sermon* by the Düsseldorf painter K. F. Lessing. A flagship of the Düsseldorf tradition, also used by Rethel at Aachen, in which history was made to symbolize modern national and social ideals or events, Lessing's picture was severely hieratic in its Nazarene-type figure arrangement. Whilst Brown echoed its general format, he tellingly skewed the composition and introduced foreshortening and a high viewpoint, as if in response to Wappers's criticism of the German Düsseldorf school as lifeless.

[34] Letter from Brown to Waterhouse (15 June 1877), M9/175/2/2, MTA.

[35] Ibid.

[36] *Mural Paintings in the Large Hall Town Hall Manchester* (Manchester City Council booklet, 1969, containing Brown's descriptions of his murals), p. 9.

It is perhaps surprising, given the Reform overtones of *Wyclif*, that the Town Hall Committee refused to accept Brown's and Shields's wish to paint an illustration of the 'Peterloo meeting' as the final mural in the sequence, but the councillors' preference for the German and Belgian method of alluding to the present via the past can be taken as a reflection of the strength of their concern to justify their power through association with tradition. The parallelism between past and present, which is clear throughout their range of subjects, was aptly conveyed by Brown's 'Pre-Raphaelite' realism, which led him to study every detail for his murals in the open sunlight. Over the fifteen years necessarily spent on this painstaking approach, his style became increasingly variable, and the murals painted before around 1883 are markedly superior to the later ones.

The Opening of the Bridgewater Canal (Plate 95), which echoes the close-up of a boat interior used in 1852–5 by Brown in his *Last of England* (Birmingham Museum and Art Gallery), but places it within a horizontal composition full of steep foreshortening, shows a strong sensitivity to the demands of the mural as architectural ornament in its almost heraldic counterpoint of black, white, and red barges and soldiers' uniforms. At the same time, viewed as a contribution to the type of history painting promoted at Westminster, whose heroes or heroines are clearly identifiable within centralized or hierarchical compositions, this mural seems flawed; its caricatural, over-sized babies in the boat suggest an incongruous throwback to Brown's early idol Hogarth, and there are similar infelicities of scale in the mural of *Chetham's Life's Dream*, which commemorates the famous Manchester school. Seen, however, as an assertion of the role of art itself in the ongoing manufacture of Manchester history, as a pictorial narrative which privileges the commonplace, and even the bathetic as a guarantor of history's veracity, Brown's murals can be recognized, as Codell has argued, as deliberately 'anti-heroic', offering an alternative historiography which corresponds with Manchester's belief in its Town Hall as an emblem 'of the labour and responsibilities of the community . . . appealing to men of every rank and station each in his way to unite in helping forward the common interest of all'.[37] Brown's presentation of the seeming randomness of history and the denseness of its overlay—in which, for example, the moment of scientific revelation marked by *Crabtree watching the Transit of Venus* (Plate 96) conjoins with the banality of his wife's activity of knitting—corresponds with the delight in history as a construct of humdrum details to be found in the writings of Carlyle and Macaulay, whom Brown greatly admired.[38] *Crabtree* (one of two scientific subjects) is, nevertheless, most rigorously composed, and is one of the most successful murals in the scheme in terms of its relationship with the architectural setting. Situated at the far end of the hall, its beam of sunlight focused on the astronomer's instruments creates a strong directional thrust which balances the horizontal of the adjacent dais in the hall. Filled with loving detail of the scientist's paraphernalia, it also maintains the momentum of allusion to Manchester's economics with its background bales of woven cloth and Mrs Crabtree's knitting. These motifs guide the eye backwards to *Flemish Weavers* (Plate I) and forwards to *John Kay Inventor of the Flying Shuttle*, just as Brown alerts the viewer to many other thematic cross-references in the descriptive text which he devised to accompany the murals. As in other early murals (1879–84), like *The Baptism of Edwin*, *The Expulsion of the Danes from Manchester* (Plate 93), and *The Proclamation regarding Weights and Measures* (Plate 97), the

[37] *Manchester Guardian*, 13 September 1877, quoted in J. Codell, 'Ford Madox Brown', *Art History*, 21 (1998), pp. 356–7, who also points out a number of 'parodic' or ironic uses by Brown of figure postures in earlier 19th-century history paintings such as Maclise's *Meeting of Wellington and Blücher* and G. F. Watts's *Alfred inciting the English to resist the Danes* (both Palace of Westminster).

[38] See Codell, 'Ford Madox Brown', pp. 338 ff.

composition of *Crabtree* uses a shallow foreground 'stage' backed by a wall with a window or opening. This device is remarkably close to several of Guffens's designs for the Hotel van Schilde in Antwerp of 1889, (Koninklij Museum voor schone Kunsten, Antwerp), suggesting the possibility that Guffens saw or knew Brown's work as a result of his contact with Waterhouse. Brown's easel work was certainly known by Belgium's avant-garde Les Vingt.

Despite the original plan to use water-glass, Brown employed the new spirit fresco, though on a dry ground, for all but the last four murals which were done in his studio in oil, then marouflaged, due to his ill health. When Sir Coutts Lindsay, Director of the Grosvenor Gallery, proposed in 1880 that a further scheme be painted at Manchester he advocated marouflaged oil, but this probably conflicted with Waterhouse's principles of execution *in situ* and was rejected. Since Brown was paid only a little over £3,300 for his entire scheme, Lindsay's estimate of £9,000 was probably also unattractive, even though he promised 'an example of decorative art hitherto unknown in this country', to be painted by G. F. Watts, W. B. Richmond, A. Legros, and Burne-Jones, and 'illustrating the four great poets of England—Shakespeare, Milton, Spenser and Chaucer'. Another scheme involving Royal Academy artists (W. F. Yeames, P. H. Calderon, and W. B. Richmond) and Walter Crane, and reminiscent of the one he had just started at the Royal Exchange, was suggested by Lord Leighton when Waterhouse approached him in 1895. Despite Waterhouse's appeal to municipal sensibility, however, with the proposal that the subjects include 'what I suppose to be the greatest work of the Corporation—the Thirlmere Water Supply',[39] no further commissions were given.

Manchester thus remained an incomplete torso, but it had created an immense amount of interest amongst artists, architects, and patrons alike, and in the 'anti-heroic', explicitly localized emphasis of Madox Brown's imagery, it had introduced a new form of civic, as opposed to Westminster-inspired historical mural painting. In the civic mural schemes of the turn of the century, however, French influences and the new theories of Crane and the Arts and Crafts Movement tended to replace the sense of rivalry with Westminster and reference to German and Belgian examples which was evident at Rochdale and Manchester. Gibson and Russell's Art Nouveau cum Jacobean County Hall at Wakefield, for example, reflects Crane's overtly symbolic emphasis, with its landscape frieze representing the 'field' of the town's name in Committee Room B and its extensive sequence of personifications of *Peace, Plenty* (Plate 98), *Art*, and *Science* by Charles Grange Lowther. These have affinities with the kind of work found in a number of the Paris Mairies and mark a departure from the more politicized iconography of the earlier schemes; they portray the ideals after which the modern county strove and are appropriately placed on the upper level of the stairway beside the council offices, showing enlightenment and progress after the Viking ship illustrative of the Dark Ages which decorates its lower level. *Justice* and *Peace* (a winged female sheltering a wren symbolic of weakness, and leaning on an olive tree with a rose grafted onto it beside broken swords) likewise provide a suggestive progression from the Wars of the Roses frieze by H. C. Fehr in an adjacent anteroom. The variety of medium (Fehr used

39 For Lindsay's comment, see *Report on the Decoration of the Town Hall of Manchester by Sir Coutts Lindsay to the Committee on Decoration* (12 May 1880), M79/13, MTA; Waterhouse's proposal is in a letter to the Lord Mayor of Manchester (16 Jan. 1895), M79/15, MTA. Given the Decoration Committee's earlier visit to Austria, was Waterhouse aware of the plans drawn up in 1880 at Vienna Town Hall by its architect Friedrich von Schmidt for illustration on its walls of the City of Vienna's 'three great works of peace-time', which included the creation of the water-supply and the regulation of the Danube (see W. Kitlitschka, *Die Malerei der Wiener Ringstrasse* (1981), p. 41)?

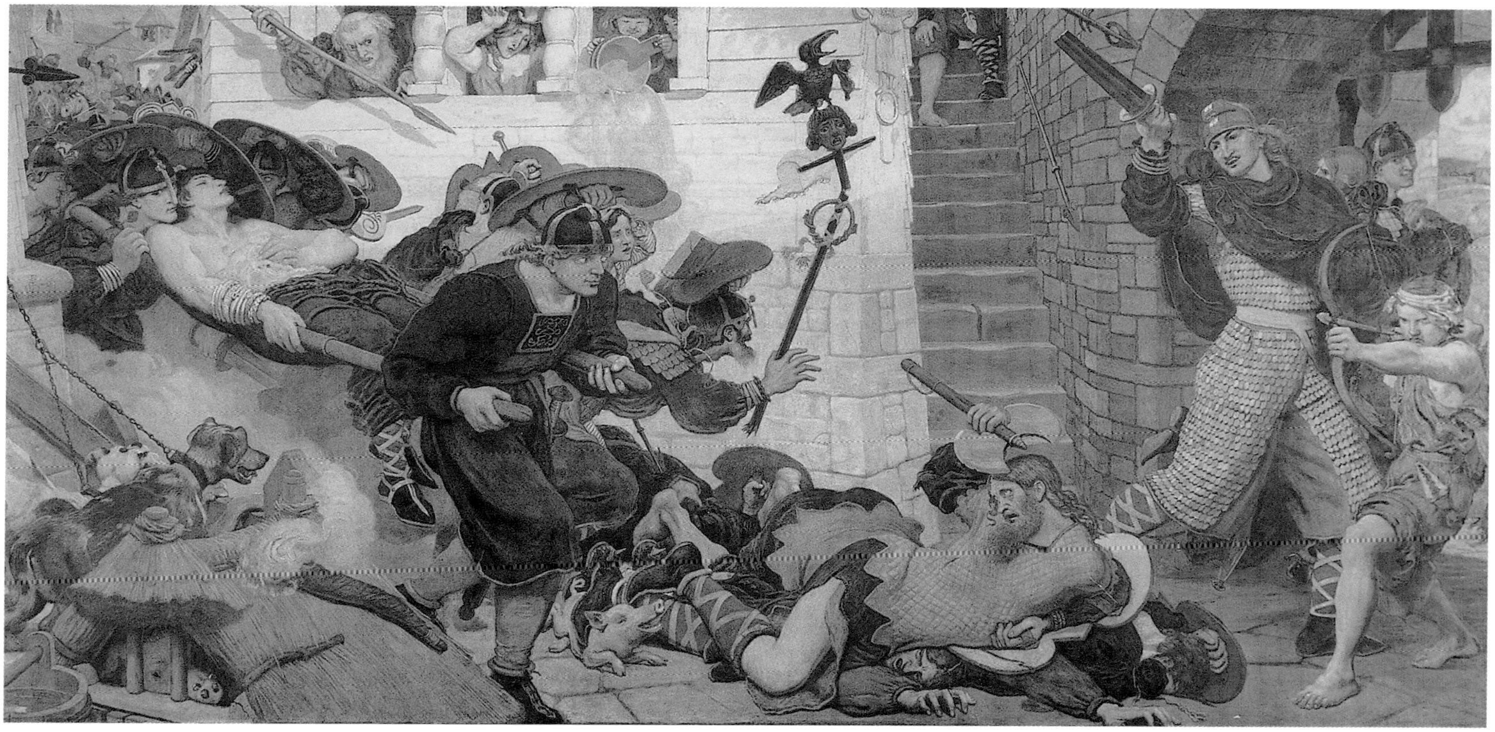

93. Ford Madox Brown, *The Expulsion of the Danes from Manchester*, Manchester Town Hall, 1880–1

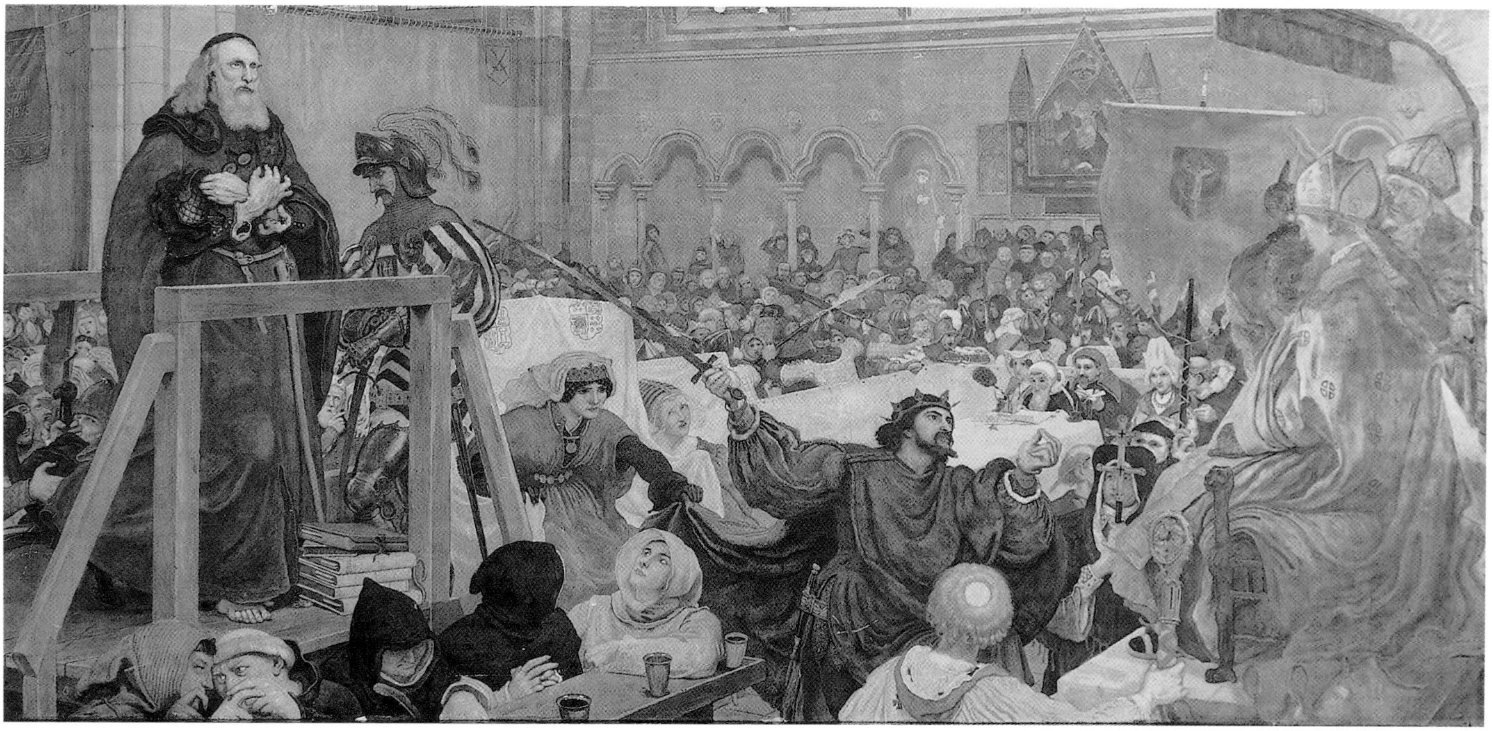

94. Ford Madox Brown, *The Trial of Wyclif*, Manchester Town Hall, 1885–6

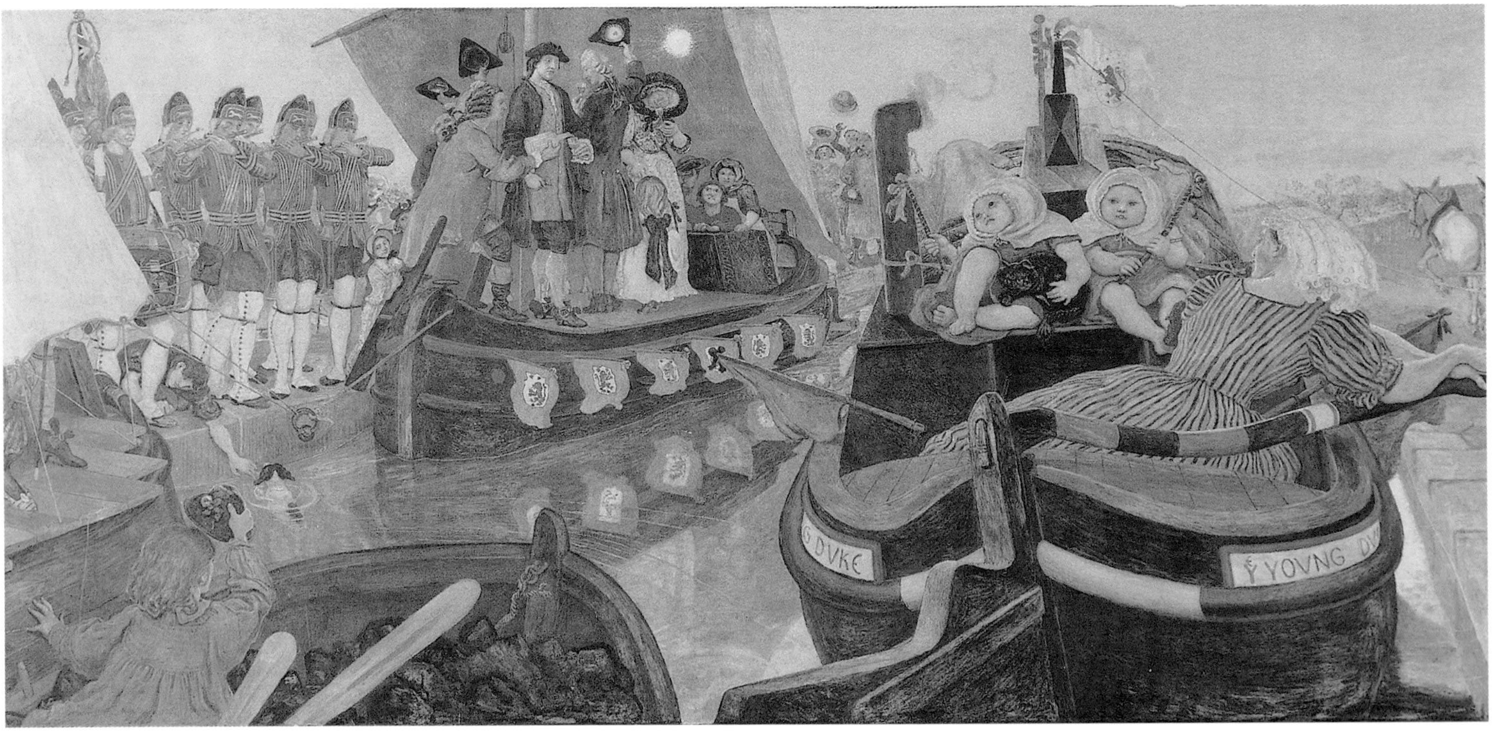

95. Ford Madox Brown, *The Opening of the Bridgewater Canal AD 1761*, Manchester Town Hall, 1890–2

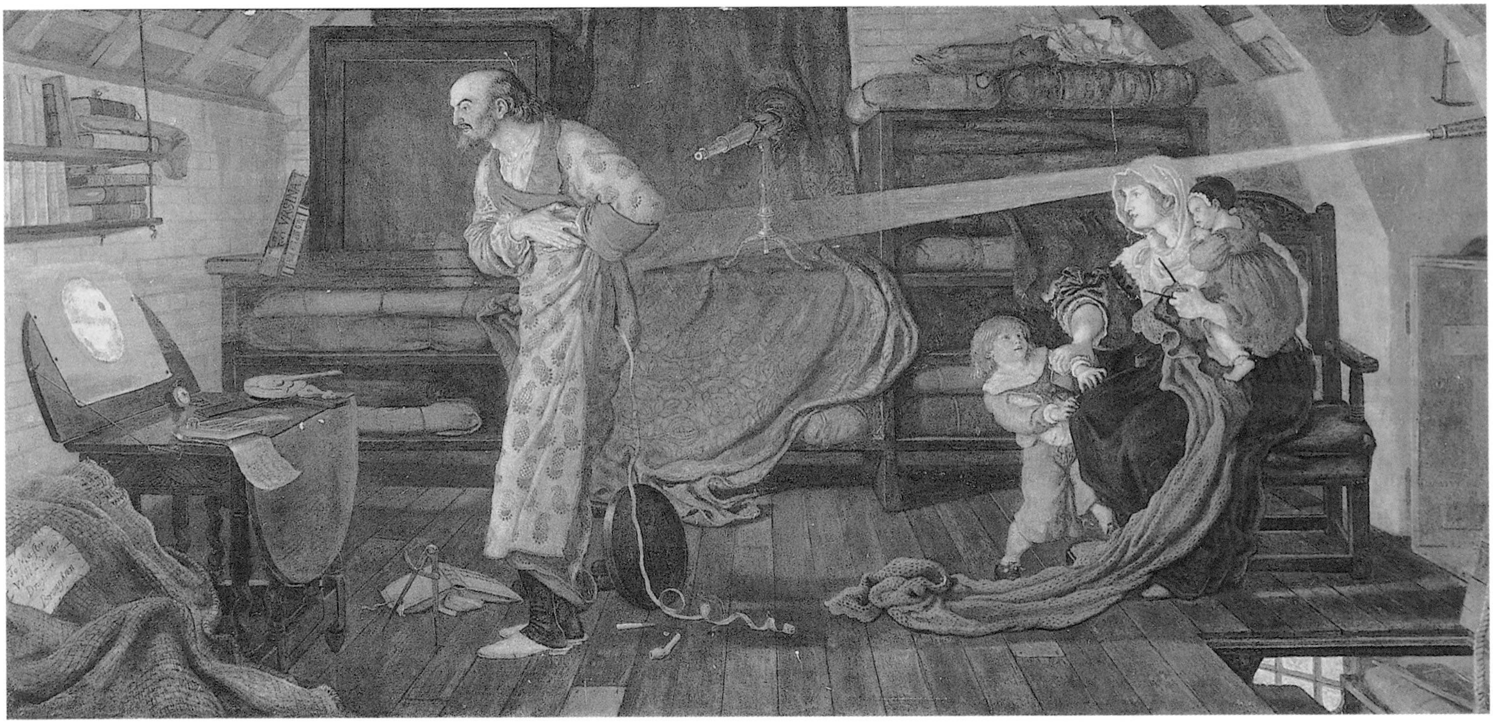

96. Ford Madox Brown, *Crabtree watching the Transit of Venus AD 1639*, Manchester Town Hall, 1881–3

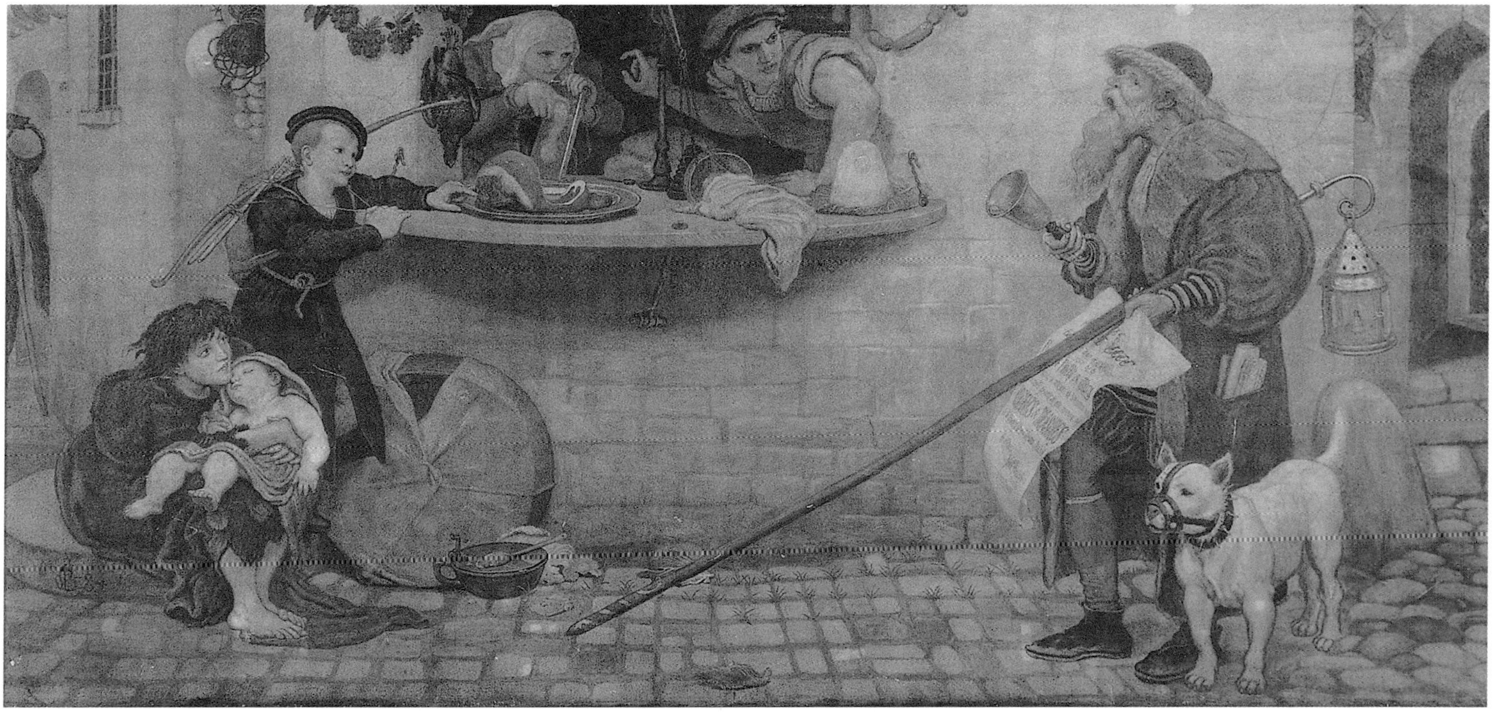

97. Ford Madox Brown, *The Proclamation regarding Weights and Measures AD 1556*, Manchester Town Hall, 1881–4

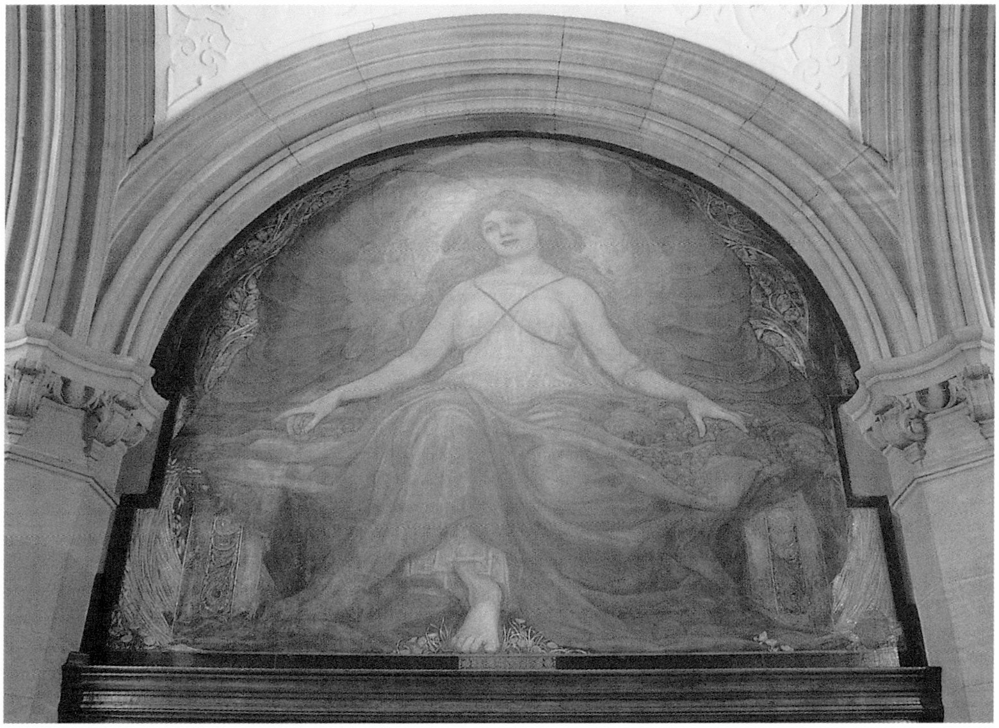

98. Charles Grange Lowther, *Plenty*, Wakefield County Hall, 1902

coloured plaster bas relief) and the symbolic placement of the iconography within the building is very much in harmony with the 'Art as Unity' ideals of Crane and the Arts and Crafts architects, and the 'fine' as opposed to 'trade' artist is now clearly to the fore. Madox Brown himself had given strong impetus to these developments with his contribution to Morris's *Arts and Crafts Essays*[40] and his essay 'On Mural Painting' in the second catalogue of the new Arts and Crafts Exhibition Society (1889), whilst both his and Crane's views on the didactic character of mural painting found natural favour with civic patrons. Yet at Lancaster Council Chamber in *c.*1887, E. L. Eaton of the local decorating firm of Eaton and Bulfield was responsible for a highly accomplished scheme of twelve small-scale civic history panels: as Lethaby pointed out in a letter to the Arts Workers' Guild, the battle against the 'trade' decorator was not yet won:

> The drifting apart of Architecture, Painting and Sculpture is shown on the one hand in the trade decoration of our buildings, and on the other in the subject painting and portrait sculpture of our galleries. But any real art-revival can only be on the lines of Unity of all the aesthetic arts.[41]

It was in London that this battle was to be most keenly fought at the *fin de siècle.* The provinces, meanwhile, saw the triumph of Arts and Crafts ideology at Birmingham Town Hall, where students of the Municipal School of Art painted ten panels (now lost) (Plate 99) of history and allegory for the 'Liberal elite' of Joseph Chamberlain's city.[42] In Glasgow, four Francophile 'Glasgow Boys' provided atmospheric scenes from the city's past, including Sir John Lavery's innovative modern life subject of *Shipbuilding on the River Clyde* (Plates 100, 101). The Birmingham scheme was directed by E. R. Taylor, a disciple of Walter Crane, and a number of its panels were exhibited at the Arts and Crafts Exhibition Society; they included *Song*, the first mural work by H. A. Payne, who later contributed to the 'Neo-Pre-Raphaelite' murals in Westminster's East Corridor. The Glasgow scheme was, in part, prompted by complaints from the social reformer and leader of the Celtic Renaissance, Sir Patrick Geddes, that William Young's new Venetian Renaissance-style City Chambers were 'magnificently decorated . . . yet obviously only in the lower planes of art . . . well wrought mahogany . . . but no mural paintings'.[43]

A deputation of civic officials sent to inspect new murals at the Sorbonne, the Panthéon, and the Hôtel de Ville in Paris, and those by Puvis de Chavannes at Amiens, gave an ecstatic report (1894) and the resultant commission at Glasgow was followed by William Hole's historical murals in Edinburgh City Chambers (1904–9). Both schemes involve an intriguing blend of the local with the national, Glasgow complementing Alexander Roche, George Henry, E. A. Walton, and Lavery's large city history panels with William Findlay's personifications of the Scottish rivers whose conception as 'floating' women clearly recalls Puvis. Lavery's *Modern Shipbuilding* (1901, Plate 100), with its bold composition of intersecting diagonals and horizontals, punctuated by red boat funnels and labourers with ropes and machinery, corresponds more closely than any other British civic mural at this date to the modern life iconography to be seen in the Paris Mairies and is one of the most effective demonstrations of the merits of commissioning murals from 'fine' rather

[40] For Fehr's technique, see 'Studio Talk', the *Studio*, 13 (1898), pp. 46–7; Brown wrote 'Of Decorative Painting and Design' in W. Morris (ed.), *Arts and Crafts Essays* (1893), pp. 39 ff.

[41] Undated letter quoted in H. J. L. J. Massé, *The Art Workers' Guild* (1935), p. 8.

[42] See A. Crawford (ed.), *By Hammer and Hand* (1984), pp. 63–5 and 'The Wall Paintings by Art Students in the Town Hall, Birmingham', *Studio*, 1 (1893), pp. 237–40. Three sketches by C. M. Gere for his *Escape of Priestley* mural are held by the University of Central England (Plate 99 is in pencil on card, size 6.4 × 15.2 cm).

[43] Geddes, *Encouragement of Art*, p. 8.

than 'trade' artists, which were being so strongly urged. Lavery was even allowed to choose a contemporary rather than a historical subject.

In London, in contrast, there was a much more conservative approach at the Guildhall, which for Walter Crane and the Art Workers' Guild must have brought the issue of 'fine' versus 'trade' to a head. What the *Building News* called 'undoubtedly the most glorious municipal chamber in the kingdom',[44] built by Horace Jones in 1884, had been ornamented with 'artistic frescoes representing the various trades and crafts of the . . . Livery Companies'[45] along with coats of arms, signs of the zodiac, and flowers and fruits of the months in a scheme (no longer extant) which sounds typical of the kind of 'trade' decoration used twenty years before in Rochdale's secondary rooms. In 1890 the further scheme (also now lost) which Alderman Sir Stuart Knill donated for the lobby of the chamber, featured St George and the Dragon, and was painted by the Birmingham firm of Hardman's, to which he was related. Both schemes gave pertinent reminder of the livery and City companies' historic rights and privileges in the face of the threat to City government which was being posed by the 1888 Local Government Act's creation of the London County Council, and by complaints like Sidney Webb's and the LCC Progressives' that the City was 'a sort of obsolete appendix at the centre' of the metropolis.[46]

Knill was exceedingly anxious to hasten the completion of his murals. Roger Watts, manager of Hardman's, wrote in August 1891 to the firm's principal artist, Joseph Pippet: 'We have been doing "Yeoman's work" fighting the Alderman for you! He wants to know *why on earth* you are not back three weeks ago!—and which train you are coming by!! We are keeping his hair cool.'[47] The reason becomes clear in subsequent letters where Watts tells Pippet: '[Knill] has a very glum countenance about it—and says we shall destroy his chances of being Lord Mayor if we play him false etc. and a lot more!!!!! He is so [?] incensed because we unfortunately did not do the city arms . . . *first*';[48] and 'he wants the *End Wall* (city arms) to be the next one tackled—and we shall all sleep easier in our beds when it is once more started!'[49]

In advance of the report of a Royal Commission which in 1893 was to recommend that the City be subsumed in a London administration, the urgency of the 'End Wall' iconography was all too clear: its City arms were surrounded by 'those of the twelve Livery Companies, bound together by branches of a rose tree', with the motto 'Now join your arms and with your arms your hearts, that no dissention [*sic*] hinder government.'[50] This was the culminating emblem which gave City versus LCC significance to the fight of St George and the dragon portrayed on the north wall. St George's victory 'protects the City, whose friends the Citizens with their Mayor, are anxiously awaiting the result of the combat'.[51] There is perhaps no more vivid example of the use of mural painting to create a 'civic shrine to municipal antiquity', and Knill, who had already commissioned decoration from Hardman's at Southwark Cathedral, was indeed criticized by some at the Guildhall for seeming 'to turn it into a chapel'.[52] The murals were apparently done

[44] *Building News* (2 Sept. 1892), p. 312. Though the Council Chamber was new, the 17th-century Alderman's Courtroom was preserved and retained its allegorical decoration (1727) by James Thornhill, symbolizing the City of London.

[45] J. J. Baddeley, *A Guide to the Guildhall of the City of London* (London, 1898), p. 82.

[46] A. C. Gardiner (a Liberal journalist), quoted in A. Briggs, *Victorian Cities* (London, 1963), p. 345.

[47] Letter from Watts to Pippet (5 Aug. 1891), p. 358, Decoration Day Book 1892–Jan. 1920, No. 65, HA(B).

[48] Ibid., letter from Watts to Pippet (10 Aug. 1891), p. 383.

[49] Ibid., letter from Watts to Pippet (9 Sept. 1891).

[50] 'The Decoration of the Outer Lobby of the Council Chamber', *Report of the City Lands Committee* No. 29 (16 June 1892), CLRO. The scheme must have been a development of the tree motif used by Hardman's at Winchester (for which see period photograph, ref. 65M89/Z250, in Hampshire Record Office).

[51] 'The Decoration of the Outer Lobby' (see n. 50).

[52] Letter from Watts to Pippet (10 Aug. 1891), (see n. 48).

'in the style of the Guildhall about 1400' with the 'rich, handsome mediaeval effect and a cream background like vellum'.[53]

Although this kind of imitative revivalism was directly satirized in the targeting of 'civic apathy, corruption, incompetence, bribery etc'[54] through parody of the iconography of the Guildhall murals in the Art Workers' Guild masque *Beauty's Awakening*,[55] Crane and his companions were unable to obtain 'the direct representation of art on the London County Council'.[56] If they hoped to appeal to the Progressive majority in the new LCC, it was ironically not until after a shift in the council to Conservatism that the building of the new County Hall from 1916 gave an opportunity for mural decoration, and even this was in the event abortive. The LCC did, however, commission murals in its schools during the 1900s, whose artists were, as at County Hall, pupils at the art colleges under its jurisdiction.[57] If the battle for the experienced fine artist was not entirely won—offers from Sir Frank Brangwyn and Charles Shannon to provide the decoration for County Hall were turned down—then there was no victory for trade decoration either. After the turn of the century civic mural painting was almost invariably the province of artists who had first established their reputation in easel painting, until the introduction of training in 'decorative painting' in the Royal College of Art and a number of other institutions, along with the rise of the British School at Rome, bore fruit in commissions of the later 1920s and the 1930s.

The situation had its disadvantages as well as merits. Like Ford Madox Brown at Manchester, easel artists who undertook mural commissions had to experiment for solutions, with varying degrees of success. Unlike Brown, however, they were at least generally able to work in their familiar medium of oil, since the method of *marouflage* had become a standard practice in Britain as it had long been on the Continent. This was perhaps as important a reason as any for the decline in patronage of the trade decorators, whose technical expertise with *in situ* decoration, as exemplified at the Guildhall, was no longer required to ensure a durable result. Meanwhile, there was a further development of the coloured plaster bas-relief technique used at Wakefield in the history scenes at Colchester Town Hall, a building of 1899 by the Art Workers' Guild member, John Belcher. These show that even the aesthetic idealism of the Arts and Crafts fraternity could be as intimately related to the civic patron's iconic purposes as were Hardman's designs at the Guildhall, for the bas reliefs, like the neo-Baroque 'palace' which houses them, were exactly contemporary with Colchester's revival of ancient civic ritual in the form of its Oyster Feast and so form part of a larger nexus of historical self-justification on the part of the council. Despite William Morris's frustration at finding himself 'ministering to the swinish luxury of the rich',[58] there is a very real sense in which the integrative ideals evolved out of Gothic Revivalism by the Arts and Crafts artists, and further developed by the Edwardian Baroque or 'Free Style' architects, provided the natural answer to civic patrons' concern to demonstrate visibly both their status and their commercial and industrial wealth. Crane's appeal in 1897 for civic patronage as at Manchester—'if every municipality would do likewise, we should soon have an English

[53] Hardman's 'Proposed Design for decorating the outer vestibule. Guildhall' (9 Sept. 1890) approved by City Lands Committee (29 Sept. 1890), CLRO.

[54] Massé, *The Art Workers' Guild*, p. 54.

[55] e.g. St George's battle with the dragon at the Guildhall was parodied by Truehearte's with the dragon Aschemon in the Masque.

[56] Massé, *The Art Workers' Guild*, p. 49.

[57] These commissions arose out of the 1912 exhibition of mural designs at Crosby Hall; see Chapter 9.

[58] W. R. Lethaby, *Philip Webb and his Works* (Oxford, 1935), p. 94, quoted in N. Pevsner, *Pioneers of Modern Design* (Harmondsworth, 1975), p. 24.

School of mural painting'[59] in fact met with a fair degree of response, but in a range of styles and subjects he could never have envisaged.

Liverpool Town Hall in 1901 commissioned spandrels of modern industrial labour from Charles Furse (Plate XXIII) who had studied at the Royal Academy. Close in style to French work such as André Rixens's realistic personification of *Fire* as a brawny blacksmith at the Paris Hôtel de Ville, these were partly funded by public subscription in the manner of sculptural monuments or the Royal Exchange murals, and they develop the contemporary iconography introduced by Lavery at Glasgow. Four lunettes of historical industry and King John's Charter to the city were, in fact, added to the entrance hall by one of the Royal Exchange artists, J. H. Amschewitz, in 1909. Trained at the Royal Academy too, his transformation of the symbolic tendencies of Crane with a decorative colourism and muscular figure style learnt from Brangwyn offered, like Furse's work, a convincing answer to the Francophile critic D. S. MacColl's attack of 1899 on Pre-Raphaelite influence in decorative painting:

> how is a school to express the triumphs of force, of labour, of man's energy that was born and bred to express only moody love sickness? It is this paradox that has always made the carrying of art to the people by William Morris and Mr. Crane a piece of high comedy. They propose to decorate the world, and the art they have in their hands is stolen from a woman's bower . . . For big public art ampler and more vital roots of design are necessary than those struck by the decorators of the Arts and Crafts.[60]

One of the most ambitious of the Beaux-Arts Baroque schemes was painted in 1906 by a cousin of Sir Coutts Lindsay, Robert Ponsonby Staples, for Belfast City Hall. This consisted of two large triptychs illustrating *Shipbuilding in Belfast* (Plate 102) and *Linen-Making in Belfast*, but these striking contemporary subjects, which would have developed the iconography of Lavery's Glasgow City Chambers panel, were never in the event installed.[61] Plans for murals to be painted by Clausen at Lanchester and Rickards's Neo-Baroque Cardiff City Hall sadly came to naught, but murals were installed in existing buildings at Chelsea and Bristol which clearly demonstrate the developing role of the easel painter as mural decorator, and can also be seen as a specific reaction to the revival of mural decoration at Westminster from 1906.

Although Chelsea's architect, J. M. Brydon, had spoken eloquently to the Royal Institute of British Architects in 1891, along with his fellow Art Workers' Guild member W. B. Richmond, on the need for murals to be a part of architecture, it was not until 1911 that Chelsea Borough Council and the Chelsea Arts Club jointly launched a scheme for nine murals, as a result of a proposal from the local Member of Parliament, E. J. Horniman (of the eponymous Museum in London) to Lord Carlisle, First Commissioner of Works at Westminster. The four murals ultimately carried out (Plate XXIV; Plates 103–4) were donations, in the manner of the 1906 Westminster work, from prominent Chelsea individuals including Earl Cadogan, Horniman, and Mayor Christopher Head. John Singer Sargent, who had contributed to the Boston Public Library murals in the United States, was consulted and, along with his fellow Chelsea Arts Club member P. W. Steer, and E. A. Rickards who had built Cardiff Town Hall, judged a competition to select the artists. These

[59] W. Crane, *Art and Life and the Building and Decoration of Cities* (1897), quoted in Crawford, *By Hammer and Hand*, p. 62.

[60] Article by D. S. MacColl in the *Saturday Review* (21 Oct. 1899) in D. S. MacColl Papers, Special Collections, Glasgow University Library.

[61] Staples worked in consultation with the architect A. Brumwell Thomas; see J. McBrinn, 'Belfast's Other Murals', *Causeway* (1997), pp. 40–1. A mural by J. Luke was installed in 1951. In 1902–3, J. W. Carey had painted thirteen historical murals in the Ulster Hall, newly acquired by Belfast Corporation, which show maritime, commercial, and industrial life in Belfast, mainly since 1760 (ibid., p. 39).

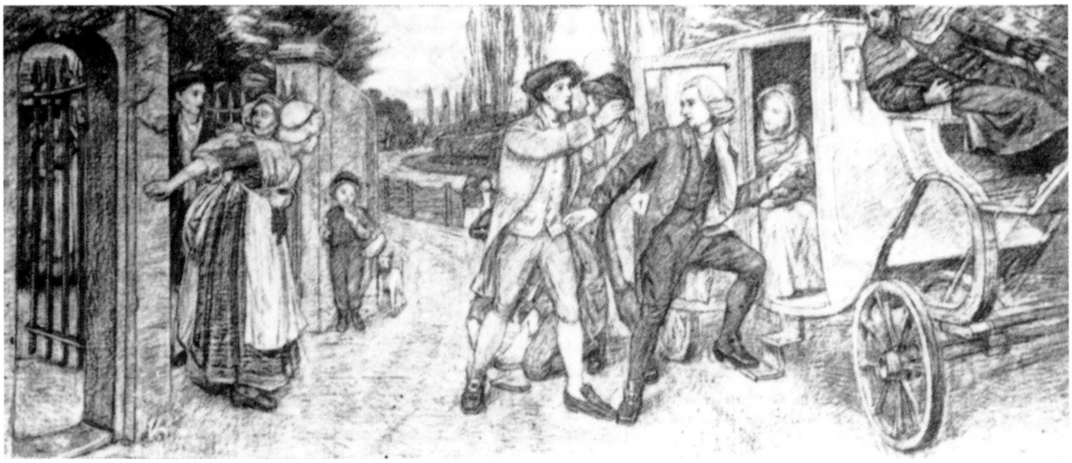

99. Charles March Gere, study for *The Escape of Priestley*, mural formerly in Birmingham Town Hall, early 1890s

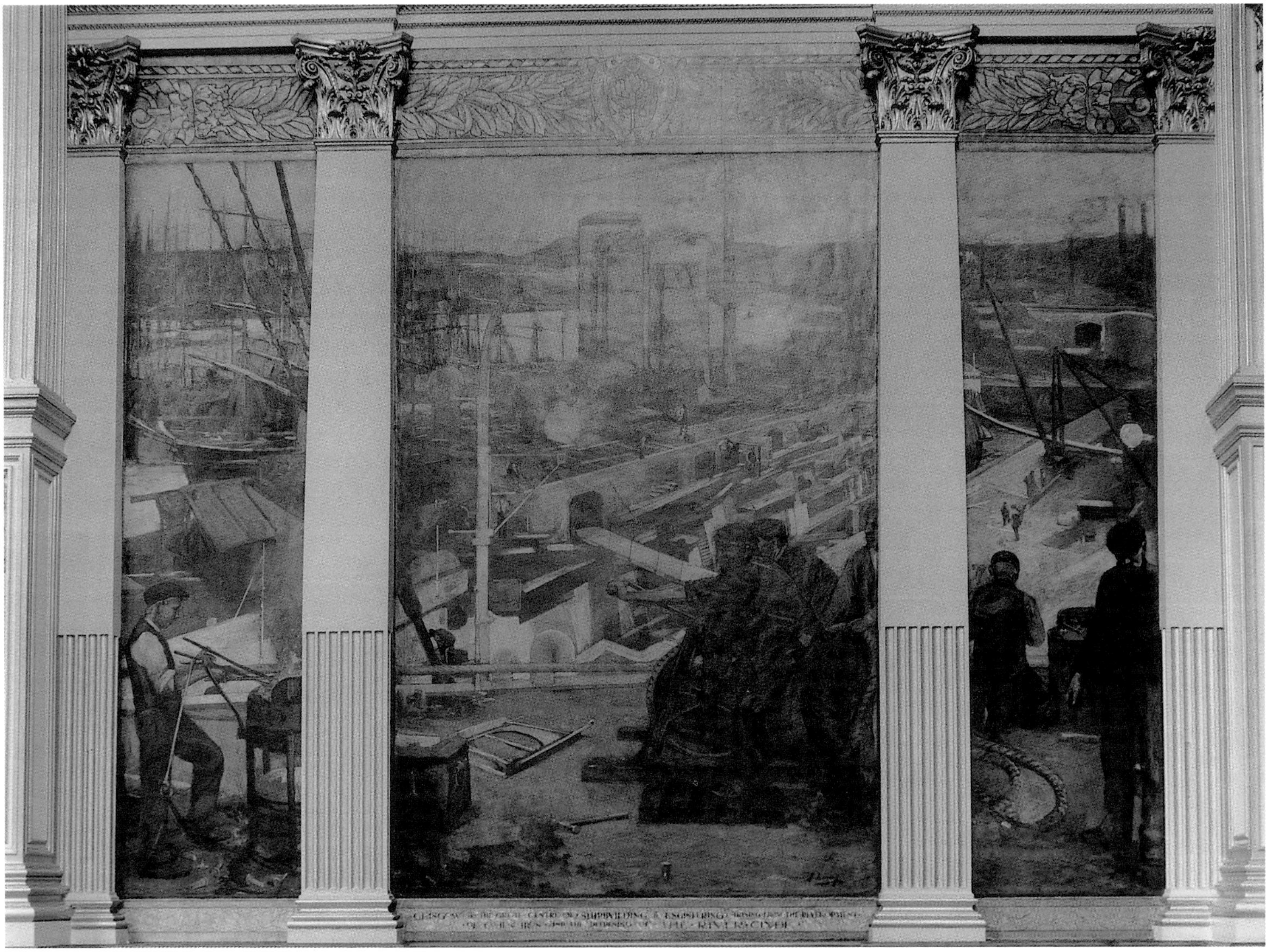

100. Sir John Lavery, *Modern Shipbuilding on the Clyde*, Banqueting Hall, Glasgow City Chambers, 1901

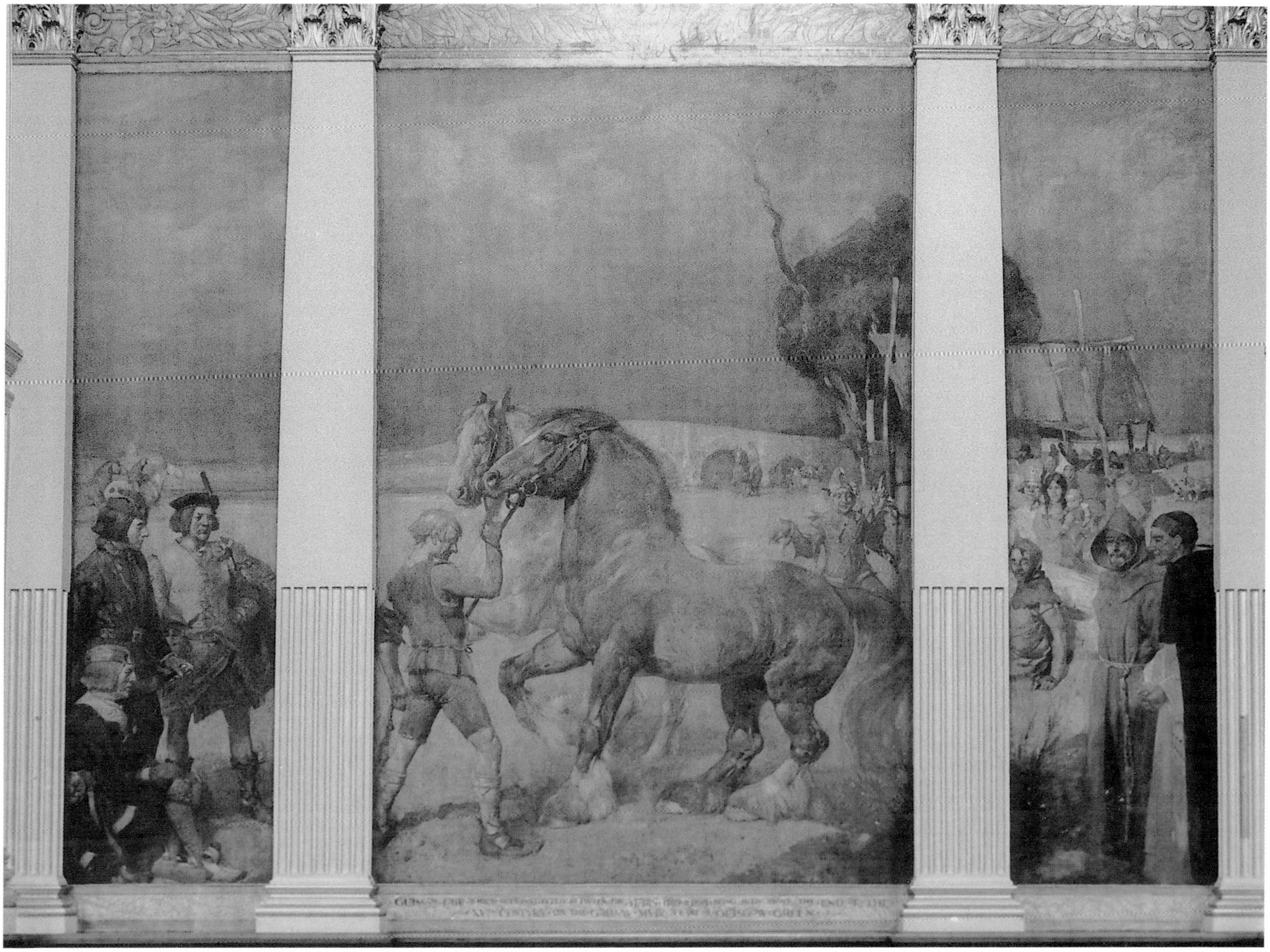

101. Edward A. Walton, *Glasgow Fair in Olden Times*, Banqueting Hall, Glasgow City Chambers, *c.*1900

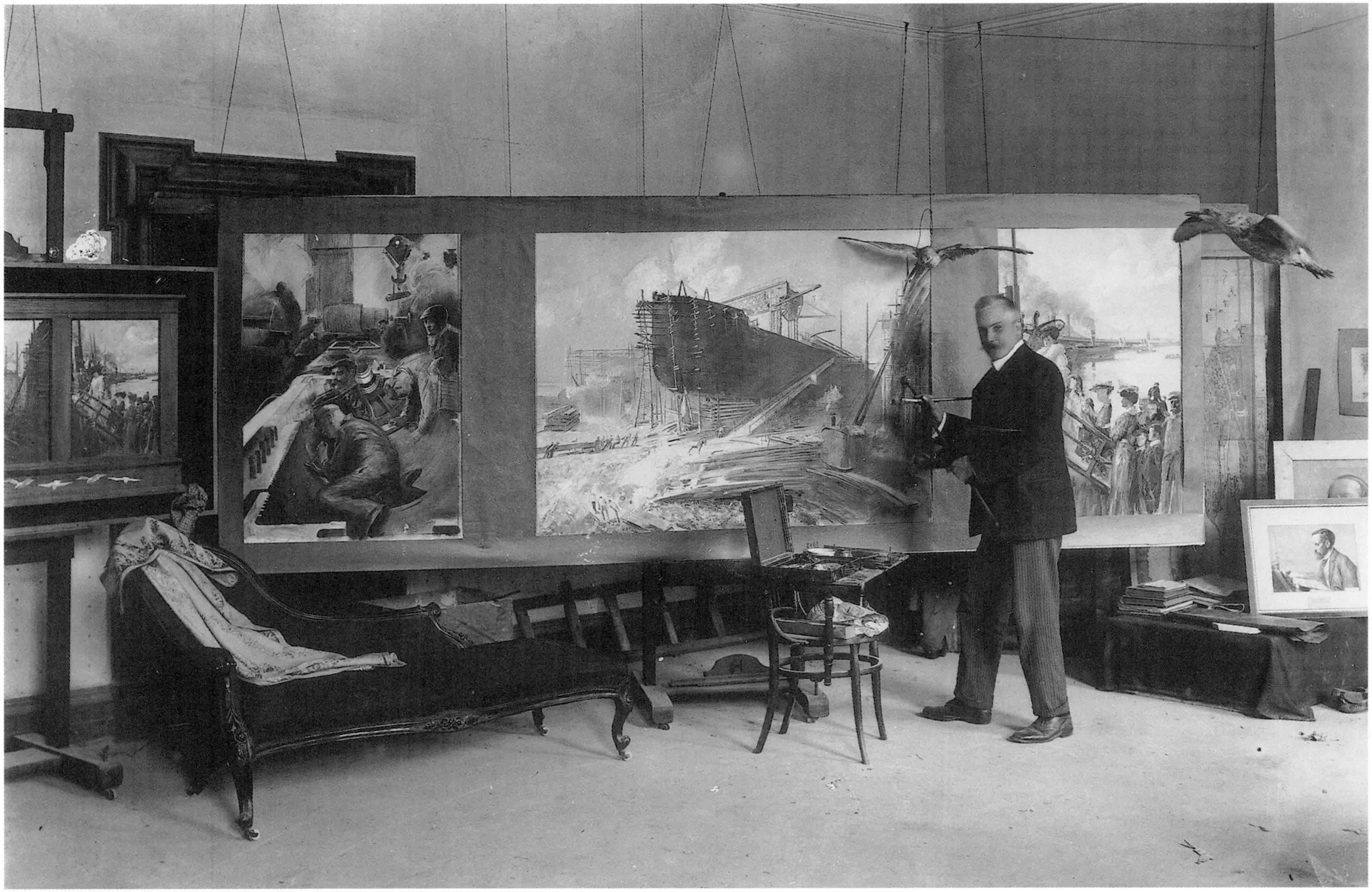

102. Period photograph of Robert Ponsonby Staples painting *Shipbuilding in Belfast*, for Belfast City Hall (not installed), 1906

were Frank O. Salisbury, who had just completed a mural at Westminster, Charles Sims, who was to contribute to the St Stephen's Hall murals there, and the local artists George R. Woolway and Mary Sargant-Florence, a leading light in the new Society of Mural Decorators and Painters in Tempera, who was prevailed upon to work in tempera on canvas marouflaged to the wall.[62] Their subjects of *Art* (Plate XXIV) *History, Literature* (Plate 103), and *Politics, Religion and Science* (Plate 104) have some similarities, especially those by Salisbury and Sims, with the Holbein-and Pre-Raphaelite-inspired 'Neo-Primitive' style of the Westminster East Corridor, but they are more overtly symbolic, presenting female personifications of their themes surrounded by representative personalities from various historical periods. Salisbury's *Art* (Plate XXIV) for example, sits like some Northern Renaissance Madonna on a gilded ornamental throne with pillars derived from those by Holbein in Chelsea Parish Church, whilst Holbein, Wren, Turner, Rossetti, Whistler, Charles Keene, Cecil Lawson, Maclise, Holman Hunt, Lawes-Wittewronge, and E. A. Abbey occupy the centre left foreground and a page cum cherub clasps a placard with the artists' names at the right. The rationale for this somewhat bizarre ensemble lies in its associations with Chelsea, with Abbey and Maclise presumably included because of their work at Westminster. The panels are successfully interrelated by the common compositional device of a balcony overlooking the Thames, or in Salisbury's work, a 'stage' from which the dome of St Paul's can just be glimpsed on the distant horizon. This, with the illustration of costumed characters from the past, suggests that the murals were perhaps intended as a pictorial commemoration of the *Midsummer Masque of Chelsea's History* which had been performed beside the river in the Old Ranelagh Gardens at the Royal Hospital as part of the 1908 Chelsea Pageant. Cadogan, Horniman, and Sargent had all been prime movers in this event, as had the founder of the Elizabethan Stage Society, William Poel.

Poel's more evocative than literal theatrical style of 'melodies of speech in form and colour'[63] can perhaps be seen as the motive for the more symbolic approach to history in the Chelsea murals, with their juxtaposition of characters from all ages and of the real and the allegorical, and their recurrent colour schemes of reds, golds, pinks, and blues. They thus mark a distinctive departure from the Rochdale, Manchester, and also Westminster East Corridor tradition of illustration of specific historical incidents, and look towards the more purely symbolic iconography to be developed by Salisbury in his Liverpool Town Hall murals of 1923.

The Chelsea pageant of 1908 had been firmly didactic, designed to create 'living history' in the belief that this was 'the basis of all education . . . the appeal to the eye is the most instant and impressive of all appeals.'[64] Whilst the murals can be seen as sharing the celebration of Chelsea's contribution to the British Empire and nation, and of the role in this of her writers, artists, scientists, and thinkers, they also, as might be expected from their relationship with the Westminster East Corridor scheme, embody a rather more specific contemporary political significance. Even as the Pankhursts were chaining themselves to the railings at Westminster for the vote, the Chelsea muralists were subtly giving prominence to women. Elizabeth I is at the centre of Sims's *History*, with Nell Gwynne and Henry VIII's wives at either side, whilst Elizabeth Fry and the eighteenth-century author and religious writer Mary Astell are given pride of place in *Politics,*

[62] See N. Heaton, 'Encaustic treatment of tempera painting in Chelsea Town Hall, 1914' (1924) in J. Batten (ed.), *Papers of the Society of Mural Decorators*, vol. 2 (1925), p. 74. The other panels appear to be in marouflaged oil.

[63] A. Hevesi, 'Shakespeare as a Scenographer', *Mask* (1909–10), p. 8.

[64] *Chelsea Historical Pageant Old Ranelagh Gardens Royal Hospital* (25 June–30 July 1908) (Souvenir volume in Chelsea Public Library), p. 7.

Religion and Science (Plate 104) by Mary Sargant-Florence—who was herself a suffragette. Salisbury's artists pay their homage to female beauty, and the very principle of the female muse who appears in each panel emblematizes the suffragette vision of women as active contributors to the achievements of the nation. Sargant-Florence rendered her muse as an angel with the distinctive right-angled wings[65] used by the suffragettes as an emblem. Lady Carlisle, whose husband had helped to launch the scheme, was an active supporter of votes for women; Sims was to be chosen in 1923 to paint a picture for the House of Commons of the introduction of Lady Astor, the first woman MP, to Parliament.

This apparent hidden agenda perhaps explains some of the controversy which surrounded the installation of the murals—one councillor complained the hall was being turned into 'an exhibition of criminals'[66]—but the inclusion of Oscar Wilde in *Literature* (Plate 103) seems to have been the most contentious issue. Although the new British School at Rome's 1913 decorative painting competition, won by Colin Gill, was for a mural of *Music* to complete the Chelsea scheme, the intervention of the war was probably why this was never realized. Chelsea, however, became, like Manchester, a flagship for the campaign for civic patronage of art. Sir Claude Phillips, Director of the National Gallery, called its decoration

> a matter which concerns not only the borough itself, but, quite as definitely, if more remotely, the whole of London, nay, the whole of the United Kingdom. The decoration of *mairies* and municipal halls generally with paintings of the monumental order has long been the rule in France, but has never yet been deemed a necessity in England . . . The art that is destined to adorn the secular temples and palaces of the people may, nay, must, be not only decorative, satisfying to the eye, but didactic—expressive of great moments in the psychological life of a nation, of great syntheses, of great symbolisms.[67]

If the four murals of 1912–14 in the Machynlleth Council House in Wales by Murray Urquhart, illustrating the life of Owain Glyndwr, show that Phillips's ideal of mural painting on walls far beyond London was already on the way to fulfilment,[68] the schemes at Bristol and Liverpool were perhaps the most immediate sequel to his plea. Like the choice at Machynlleth of Urquhart, a Scottish painter trained in London and Paris, the work at both Bristol and Liverpool confirms the role of the 'fine' artist which was given impetus by Chelsea's competition and by Phillips's plea for more than mere 'decoration'. The nine Bristol panels (Plates 105–7), apparently begun just before the First World War, were for the most part carried out by members of the Bristol Savages Sketching Club, and as independent easel-type oil paintings which were exhibited at Bristol Art Gallery in 1923 prior to their installation in the Old Council House. Their historical subjects relate directly, as Phillips demanded, to the city's involvement not only in the development of local trade and shipping, but also in the history of the royal family and in national politics, from support for Cromwell (*Mistress Dorothy Hazard and the Women of Bristol defending the Frome Gate, 1643* (Plate 105)) to the *Chairing of Edmund Burke*. Liverpool's Memorial Hall of 1923 was entirely

[65] Cf. S. Pankhurst's angels in her decorations for the WSPU Exhibition at the Prince's Skating Rink, 1909, illustrated in L. Tickner, *The Spectacle of Women: Imagery of the Suffrage Campaign 1907–14* (London, 1987), pl. 13.

[66] 'A Chelsea Portrait Debate on Objections to a Town Hall Panel', anon. unidentified newspaper article in 'F. J. Welch's Scrapbook' of period cuttings, etc., Chelsea Public Library. A motion that the panel be moved was passed at the Council meeting of 13 May 1914, but letters from the Chelsea Arts Club, E. J. Horniman, and others appear to have won a stay of execution and, with the intervention of the war, the plan seems to have been dropped (see Chelsea Borough Council Minutes May 1914–May 1915).

[67] C. Phillips, 'Decoration of Chelsea Town Hall', *Daily Telegraph* (15 Dec. 1912).

[68] For Urquhart's Machynlleth scheme, see P. Lord, *Imaging the Nation* (1999), p. 12.

symbolic, but both it and Bristol can be seen, like Chelsea, as direct responses to the Westminster East Corridor. Lord Winterstoke, who had been a donor at Westminster, launched the Bristol work before the war, and it included a mural by his Westminster artist, Ernest Board (Plate 107), as well as one by F. G. Swaish. Both were pupils of the East Corridor's supervising painter, E. A. Abbey. The Liverpool panels were by Frank Salisbury, who had contributed at both Westminster and Chelsea as well as at the Royal Exchange.

In some ways, Bristol perhaps represents a bid to outdo the earlier schemes, for it combines both of the styles identified by Hermann Muthesius as holding the greatest promise for the future of British decorative art[69]—not only the East Corridor 'Neo-Pre-Raphaelite' idiom, but also the more Baroque- and Continental-influenced art of Brangwyn and Gerald Moira, Professor of Decorative Painting at the Royal College of Art. These two artists had already shared in the decoration of the prestigious Lloyd's Register of Shipping in London (see Chapter 11), and at Bristol now joined the 'Neo-Pre-Raphaelites' E. Board and F. G. Swaish. Other panels, like J. Hassall's *The State Entry of Queen Elizabeth into Bristol*, show compositional and thematic similarities to the Royal Exchange work.

Although the panels were executed over a period of some seven years or so, the 'disunity' so much criticized in the Royal Exchange decoration was largely avoided by what appears to have been a careful selection process (each artist produced trial sketches which in some cases, such as Board's, were significantly modified to emphasize history or spectacle) and by the use of recurrent motifs, like Bristol Cathedral and the keep of Bristol Castle. The latter, for example, is decoratively flattened by means of a subtle colour scheme of delicate pink, cream, pale green, and blue, and juxtaposed with sailing-ships in Swaish's mural of its construction in 1125. It thereby prefigures the heraldic use of the Castle as part of the city insignia on the sail of the ship in the Neptune pageant watched by the King in Board's *King Edward IV being entertained by William Canynge at his House in Redcliffe Street 1461* (Plate 107).

Whilst Moira's luminously sun-lit *Mistress Dorothy Hazard* (Plate 105) is perhaps another example of a suffragette allusion, since the artist was a member of the Art Workers' Guild and closely associated with its suffrage sympathizers Crane and Holiday, it is probably Brangwyn's panel which carries the most personal symbolism, echoing the kind of self-identification with the common man which had emerged in his recent Skinners' Hall historical work. His *Chairing of Edmund Burke* is clearly relevant in its iconography to the political activities of Lord Winterstoke, but also shows Brangwyn's personal sympathy with the seething mass of the citizenry who doff their hats to Burke as he is chaired aloft before the mighty structure of the cathedral, flanked by fluttering pennants in the sky of rolling clouds. Waving from aloft on a high pole is a tiny supporter who occurs in two Skinners' Hall preparatory sketches and who, from his use in the 1907 *Self Portrait with Miners* (Glynn Vivian Art Gallery, Swansea), seems to have stood for the artist himself. The mural thus reflects, like the work at Skinners' Hall, Brangwyn's regret that 'History never records the poor or obscure or their vices. It is for those in high places that this privilege is held,'[70] and the common citizens, rather than Burke, have prominence in the design. Such role-reversal, also used in the Guffens and Swerts murals which influenced Madox Brown at Manchester, is again a reminder of Brangwyn's Belgian background.

[69] See Chapter 4.

[70] Undated remark in BD; Brangwyn's two Skinners' Hall sketches are in his sketchbooks in the RA.

The Bristol scheme is one of the most successful of the twentieth-century civic commissions, without the derivative mannerism of Mary Sargant-Florence's work at Chelsea or the somewhat over-theatrical conception of Salisbury's Liverpool War Memorial. It is unfortunate that Brangwyn was never given the opportunity to carry out an entire civic scheme as he was in the United States, at Cuyahoga County Court House in 1912, where his 17.5 × 1.9 m *King John Signing the Magna Carta* was a vivid demonstration of his power to invest even such a conventional historical theme with a new expressive symbolism such as Sir Claude Phillips had envisioned for 'the secular temples and palaces of the people'. Sketches by Brangwyn for civic history subjects for Hull Town Hall, like his proposals for London County Hall, were never carried out, apparently because of the war.

The impact of the First World War, and subsequent developments

When Salisbury came to carry out his Liverpool panels, whose themes of *Infancy*, *Duty's Call*, *Sacrifice*, *Renown*, *Immortality*, and *Remembrance* were inspired by a poem an unknown mourner sent him on the death of her son in the war, the transformation of his original 'Neo-Pre-Raphaelite' style, begun in his Royal Exchange, St Stephen's Hall, and Chelsea Town Hall murals, was completed. A design he had produced for the *History* subject eventually painted by Sims at Chelsea seems to have been the starting-point for the Michelangelo Sybil-inspired female personifications who dominate each of his panels, and the inscription placed around *Renown* (Plate 108)—'Brute Force cannot prevail against the ideals of justice and freedom'—was a subtitle he had given as early as 1911 to a picture of knights in shining armour on white horses and about to be crowned with laurel wreaths by a heavenly host, called *Eternal Victory* (sold at Christie's, London, 25 September 1985). He had dedicated it to the Allied Nations: in a similar spirit, *Triumph* at Liverpool surmounts a smaller panel illustrating the arms of Great Britain's allies in the war. It is as though, in the face of the appalling carnage of the 77,500 citizens of Liverpool whom he had been commissioned to commemorate, he attempted to retreat to the dream world of Romantic chivalry with which he had started his career in easel pictures like *The Passing of Queen Eleanor* (1908, St Albans Abbey). Yet he could not regain the taut, psychologically dramatic compositions of his East Corridor work at Westminster (Plate 50) and *Alfred* at the Exchange (Plate V). His Liverpool figures are blandly simplified and static; conventional symbols which also entirely lack the decorative vigour of his crisply detailed lunettes of 1919 at the Victoria Memorial at Calcutta. Where he is most successful is in the small group of secondary panels realistically illustrating scenes of wartime effort, such as *Undaunted* with its pair of sailors hauling in a taut rope, their naked arms and torsos straining in rhythmic counterpoint to the rigging and nets and in parallel to the horizon. The scene is bathed in a natural sunshine which is absent from the main allegorical panels and plays over the glass weights on the fishing nets to make an inspired echo of the symbolic orbs held by *Renown* and *Triumph*.

How to acknowledge the trauma of war and yet transcend it, preserving Phillips's pre-war vision of 'great syntheses . . . great symbolism' in a way that might speak as a living, but also lasting statement of a city's commemorative impulse; this was the issue with which mural painters now grappled. In the early 1920s, when the controversial realism of the Royal Artillery Memorial sculpture in Hyde Park aroused heated debate, and the apparent nihilism of an abortive scheme at Leeds Town Hall of local industrialized landscapes met with disfavour, death was perhaps still too near for the actuality of either war or the post-war environment to be visually acceptable in public art. Whereas the war poetry of Rupert Brooke and Wilfred Owen speaks to the mind's eye and in private, mural painting in a town or village hall directly engages the physical eye, and in a very public way. As a formal, ritual focus for a community's grief and commemoration, it was perhaps not surprising that the inherently stylized character of sculptural or architectural monuments such as village crosses or cenotaphs, or else stained glass, was generally preferred to mural painting, even though mural painting was included in the recommendations of the Royal Academy's War Memorial Advisory Committee.[71] With the abandonment by the Imperial War Museum of the Hall of Remembrance project, the Liverpool scheme and one at Balcombe Victory Hall in Sussex, completed in 1924 by Neville, Lord Lytton[72] (Plates 109–10), were the only civic or village mural memorials of note.

Just as the system of extensive public subscription from a wide variety of local institutions and individuals perhaps made the Liverpool murals a memorial as much through the *act* of their installation as through their style and iconography, so at Balcombe the scheme seems more a personal quest for catharsis on the part of Lytton than a true image for a community. A survivor from the Front, where he had been coordinating Editor of the Official War Correspondents, Lytton had contributed before the war to the Arts and Crafts Exhibition Society. At Balcombe, no longer restricted by the censorship imposed on the Official War Artists,[73] his murals echo much of the harsh literalism of his sketches of life in the trenches, published in 1921.[74] They also reveal, however, an ambivalence in their imagery which speaks poignantly of the shell-shocked survivor seeking desperately to reconcile censored and actual war experiences in a world which was supposed to be 'brave' and 'new', yet whose past seemed more attractive. This world is symbolized by the Tudoresque cottage architecture of the village hall itself, built by Lady Denman as a contribution to the renewal of the local community, many of whose members had fallen with Lytton's own Sussex Regiment, and whose surviving relatives were, of course, the users of the Victory Hall. The building's domestic style naturally invited an intimate, personal relationship with such people, rather than the ceremonial associated with the grandeur of Liverpool Town Hall, and this, of course, would have made the immediacy of Lytton's imagery the more emotive. Both Lord Denman and Lytton's brother, the second Earl of Lytton, had been members of the Select Committee responsible for the revival of mural painting at Westminster in 1906, and Lytton's iconography is an interesting echo of his father's radical proposals there for modern-life iconography. It also echoes, however, the theme of the fragility of life and the suffering in death of the poetry of Lytton's father-in-law, Wilfrid Scawen Blunt.

The scheme contrasts illustrations of *Dolor* and *Spes* in the form of war scenes, and those of its aftermath: peace is too positive a word for *Spes*, for the fluid processional composition of figures moving around the hall dado creates ambiguity as to where and when war ends, and these scenes are still heavily tinged with the presence of suffering. *Dolor* presents an almost cinematic sequence of 'stills' of a soldier's sequence of actions in marching forward to confront and throttle an

[71] See 'Studio Talk', *Studio*, 76, no. 314 (May 1919), pp. 138–41, and Anon., 'Suggestions for the Treatment of War Memorials', *Journal of the RIBA*, 3rd ser., 25 (April 1918), pp. 143–4 and 'The Royal Academy and War Memorials' (July 1918), pp. 208–9.

[72] Stanley Spencer was invited in 1919 by Muirhead Bone to undertake a war memorial for the Village Hall at Steep, but despite producing a study which adumbrates ideas later developed in his Burghclere Chapel scheme, this project came to nothing (see R. Carline et al., *Stanley Spencer* (1980), p. 97 and cat. no. 64).

[73] See Chapter 5.

[74] N. S. Lytton, *The Press and the General Staff* (London, 1921).

opponent (Plate 110), followed by his despairing gesture towards the enemies he had maimed or killed, where his open hands suggest an Owen-like sense of the futility of the combat. After this, *Spes* with its mourning women, widow, child in black, and legless survivor has a bitter note. Nearby, Lady Denman and her builders start reconstruction, whilst Lytton and his future wife play a flute and a guitar (Plate 109), perhaps in allusion to the painter's friendship with Arnold Dolmetsch, who lived near Balcombe and was seeking to preserve early English musical traditions. Watching the group is an Australian doctor, who likewise looks towards the local Chanctonbury Ring in the misty distance as if musing on the even earlier origins of Balcombe's community; a nearby dancing girl seems to perform 'to the music of time' since she echoes in reverse the pose of Venus in Botticelli's *Primavera* (Uffizi, Florence). Was Lytton aware of Walter Pater's interpretation of this figure as 'the goddess of pleasure' who yet always had 'some shadow of death in the grey flesh'?[75]

Whilst Lytton's soldier in hand-to-hand combat is strongly reminiscent of Brangwyn's controversial *Put Strength in the Final Blow* poster of 1916 for the Belgian Relief Fund (Plate 61), and his stretcher-bearers of those in Sargent's *Gassed* (Plate 62), his figures lack their dynamism and vision. Repetitive in gesture and scale, their khaki clothes blend with the swirling smoke to create an overall bleached pallor which is accentuated by Lytton's use of true fresco; the figures, indeed, are too widely spaced and evenly lit for the scenes to be fully realistic, and yet they are too literal to be completely symbolic. It is perhaps no coincidence that only a matter of months after the murals had been unveiled, Brangwyn, who lived at nearby Ditchling, abandoned his plans for battle scenes at the Front in his Royal Gallery War Memorial at Westminster for a celebration of the Empire's plenitude and brotherhood—'what had been saved from the War'.[76]

A similarly positive outlook on the commemoration of the fallen had, interestingly, already been planted in the civic sphere by an artist who was in many respects diametrically opposed in both outlook and style to Brangwyn, yet who shared with him a common upbringing in the ideology of William Morris and the Arts and Crafts Movement, and a common admiration for French decorative painting. This was William Rothenstein (later Sir William), who had become highly influential as a theorist and teacher through his position as Principal of the Royal College of Art from 1920. Already in 1916, whilst the war was still in progress, Rothenstein had published a *Plea for a Wider Use of Artists and Craftsmen* in which he argued the need for civic patronage of artists as a means to reshape and renew a shattered world, in part through memorials expressive of 'something of this heightened sense of the beauty of familiar things . . . the changing life of the farm, the immemorial habits of men turning their hands to all the needs of the soil and of the seasons'[77] and above all in town halls. These he envisaged as

> the symbolic centre of the life and creative industry of the whole neighbourhood; each succeeding year should add something to its completeness. The fabric of these buildings is, in most cases dignified and impressive, but within, its walls are cold and empty . . . we look in vain for any visible sign in the objects of use and ornament which we see about us of a living local culture and imagination.[78]

He concluded his plea with a recollection of Manchester Town Hall's murals, and the request:

[75] W. Pater, *The Renaissance* (London, 1870), quoted in E. H. Gombrich, *Symbolic Images* (Oxford, 1978), p. 204 n. 23.

[76] See Chapter 6.

[77] W. Rothenstein, *A Plea for the Wider Use of Artist-Craftsmen* (1916), pp. 16–20.

[78] Ibid., pp. 18–19.

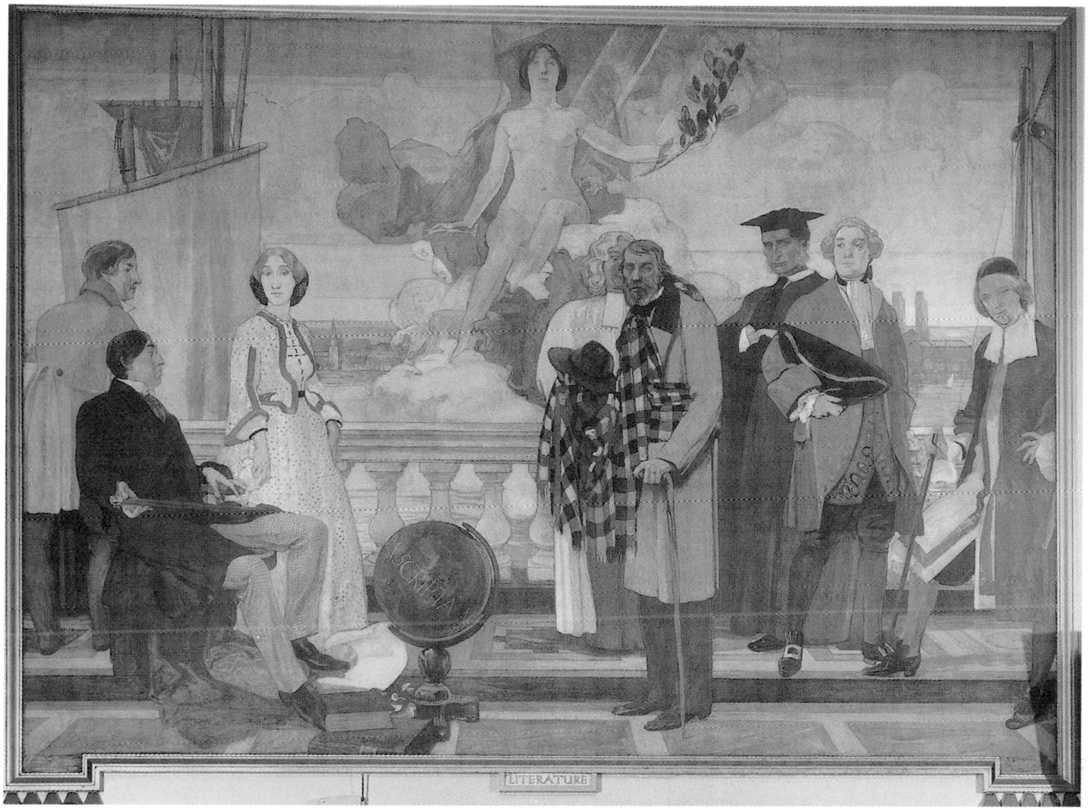

103. George R. Woolway, *Literature*, Chelsea Town Hall, *c.*1911–13

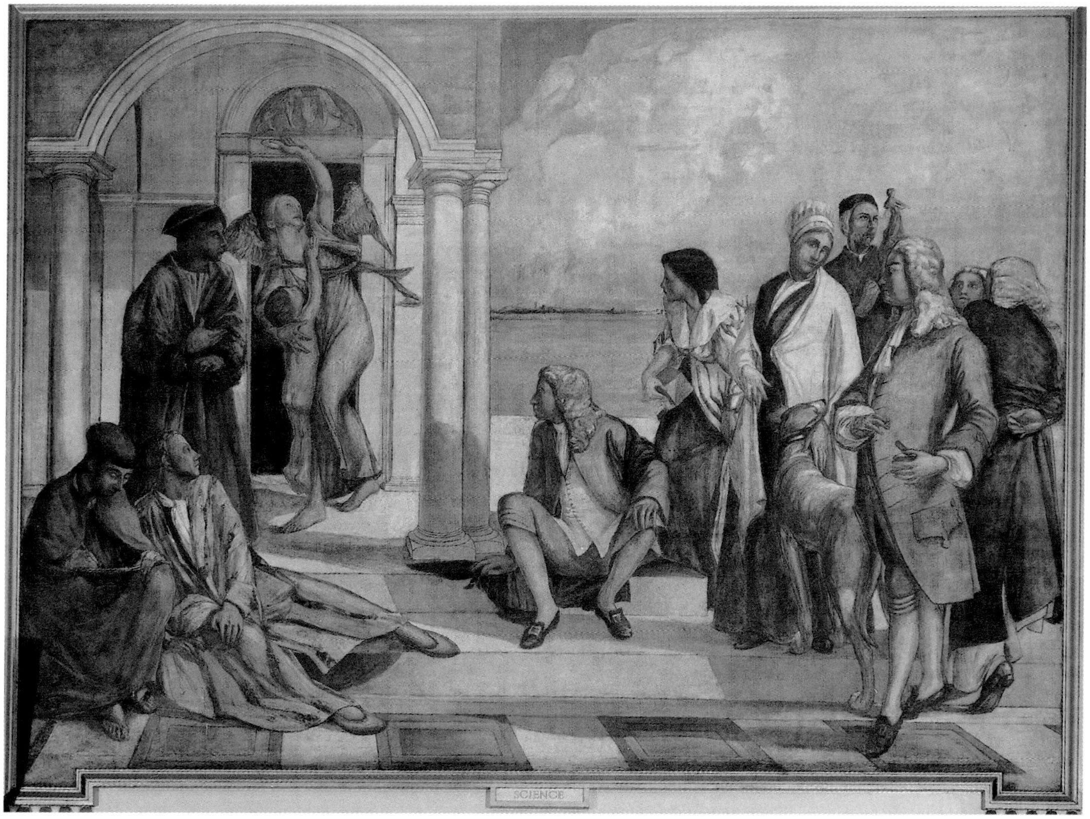

104. Mary Sargant-Florence, *Politics, Religion and Science*, Chelsea Town Hall, *c.*1911–13

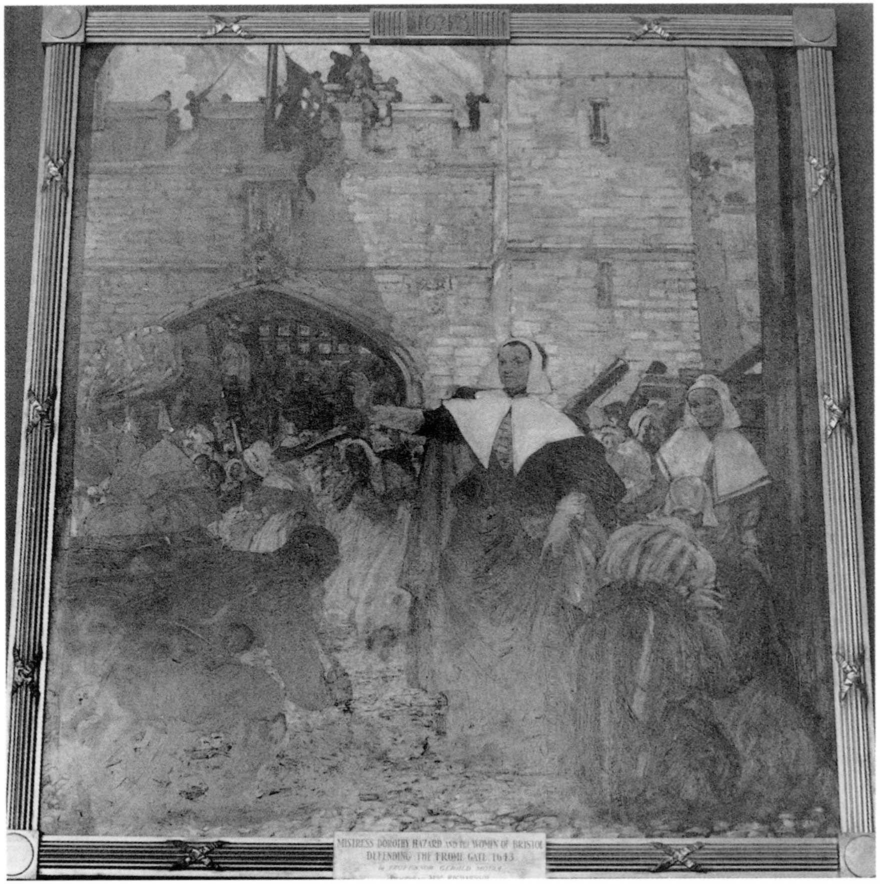

105. Gerald Moira, *Mistress Dorothy Hazard and the Women of Bristol defending Frome Gate 1643*, Bristol Old Council House, *c.*1914–23

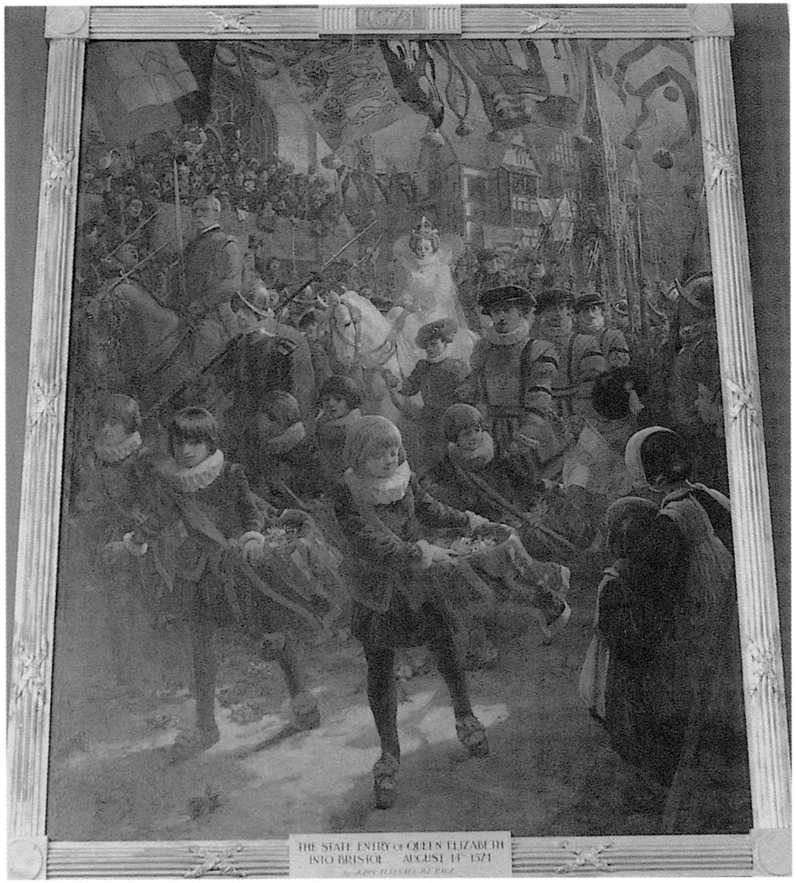

106. John Hassall, *The State Entry of Queen Elizabeth into Bristol, August 14th., 1574*, Bristol Old Council House, *c.*1914–23

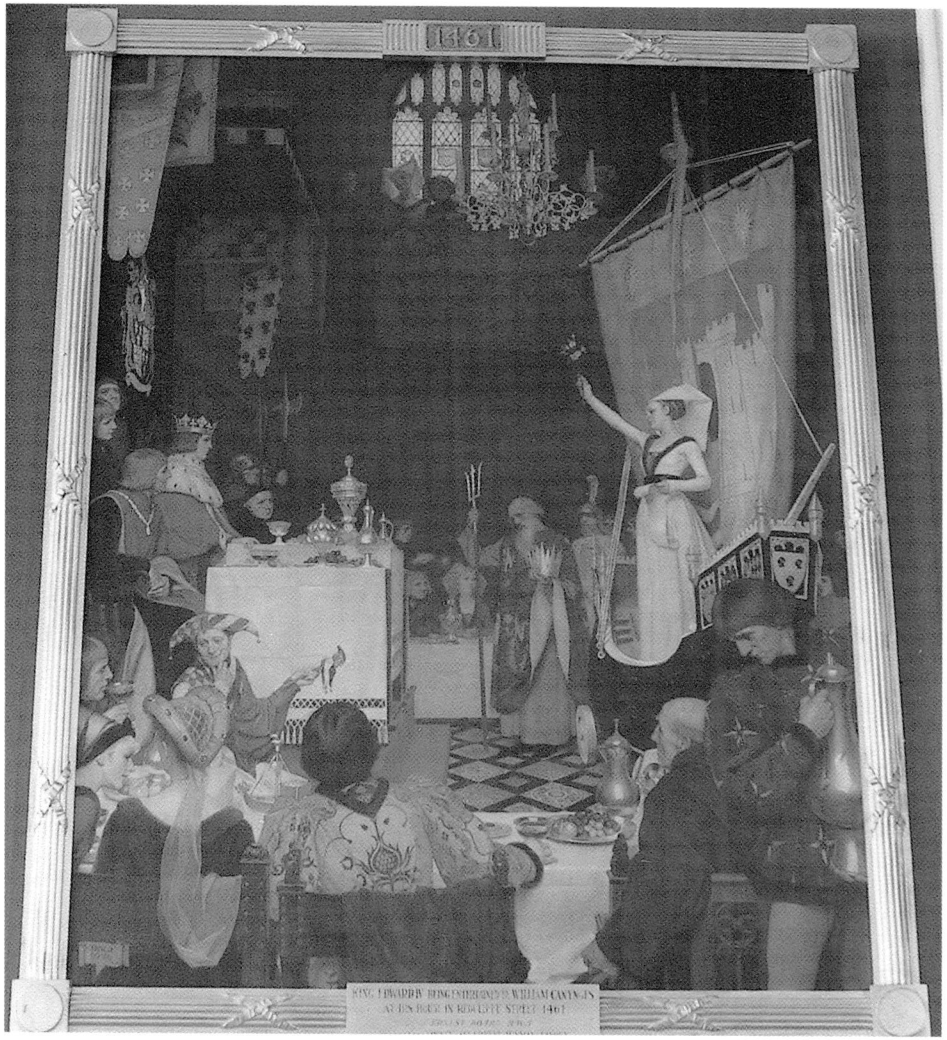

107. Ernest Board, *King Edward IV being entertained by William Canynge at his House in Redcliffe Street 1461*, Bristol Old Council House, *c.*1914–23

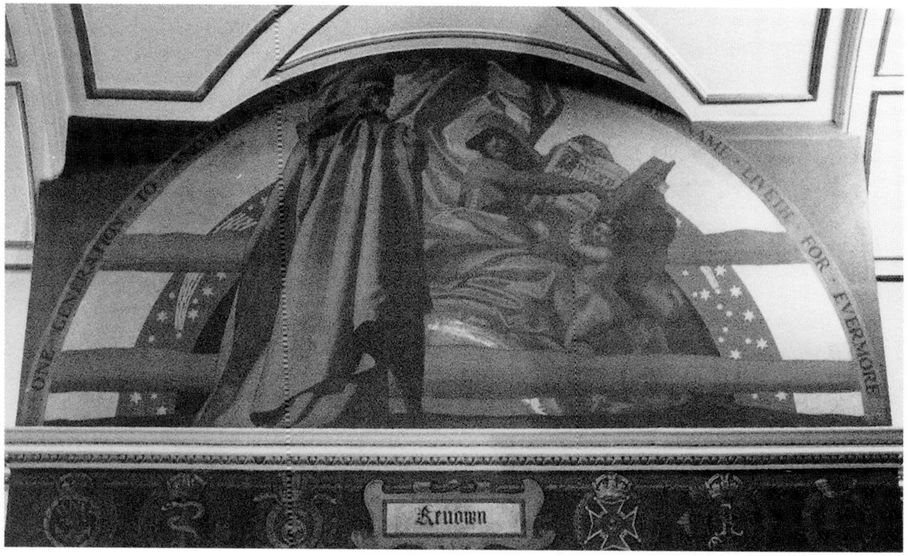

108. Frank O. Salisbury, *Renown*, from First World War Memorial in the crypt, Liverpool Town Hall, *c.*1919

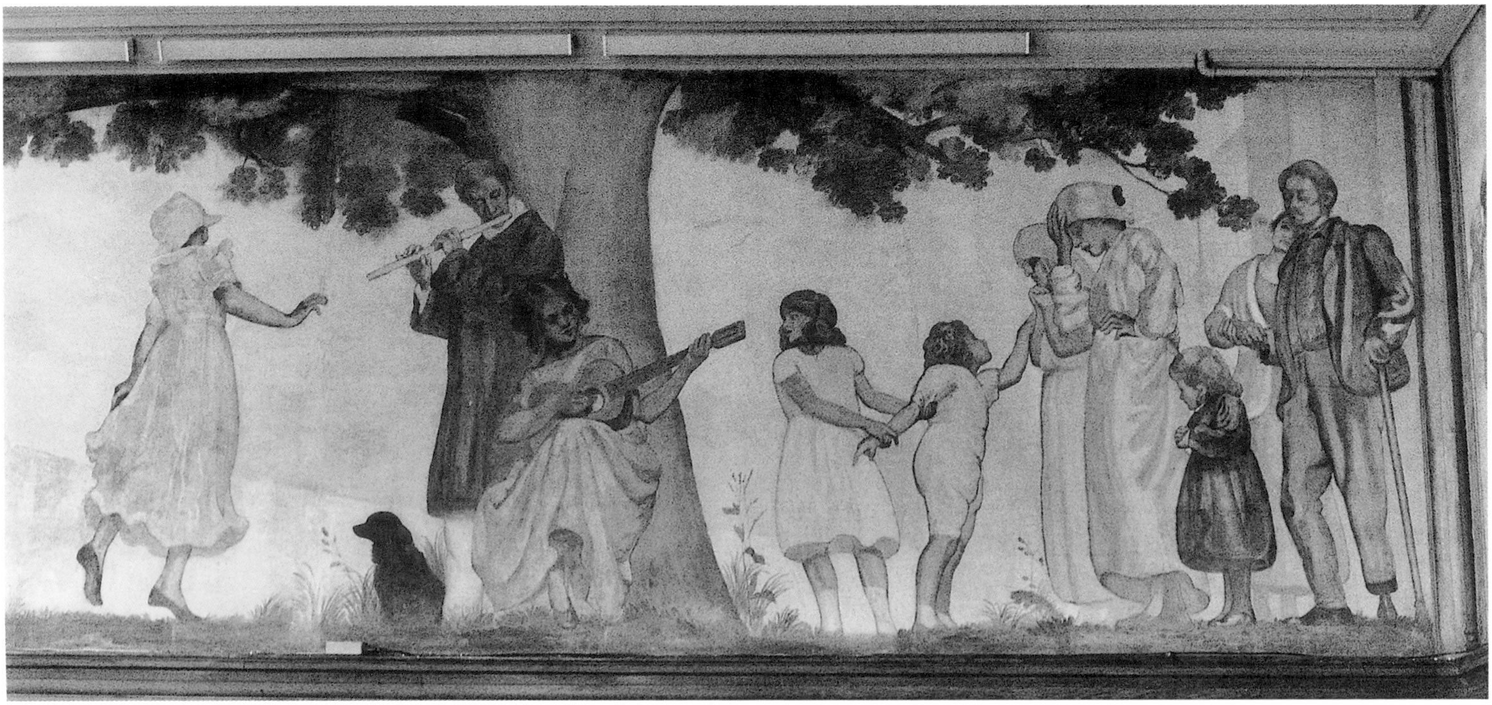

109. Neville, Lord Lytton, detail showing a dancing girl, the artist playing a flute, and his future wife playing the guitar, with war survivors, from *Spes* section of the First World War Memorial, Victory Hall, Balcombe, Sussex, completed 1924

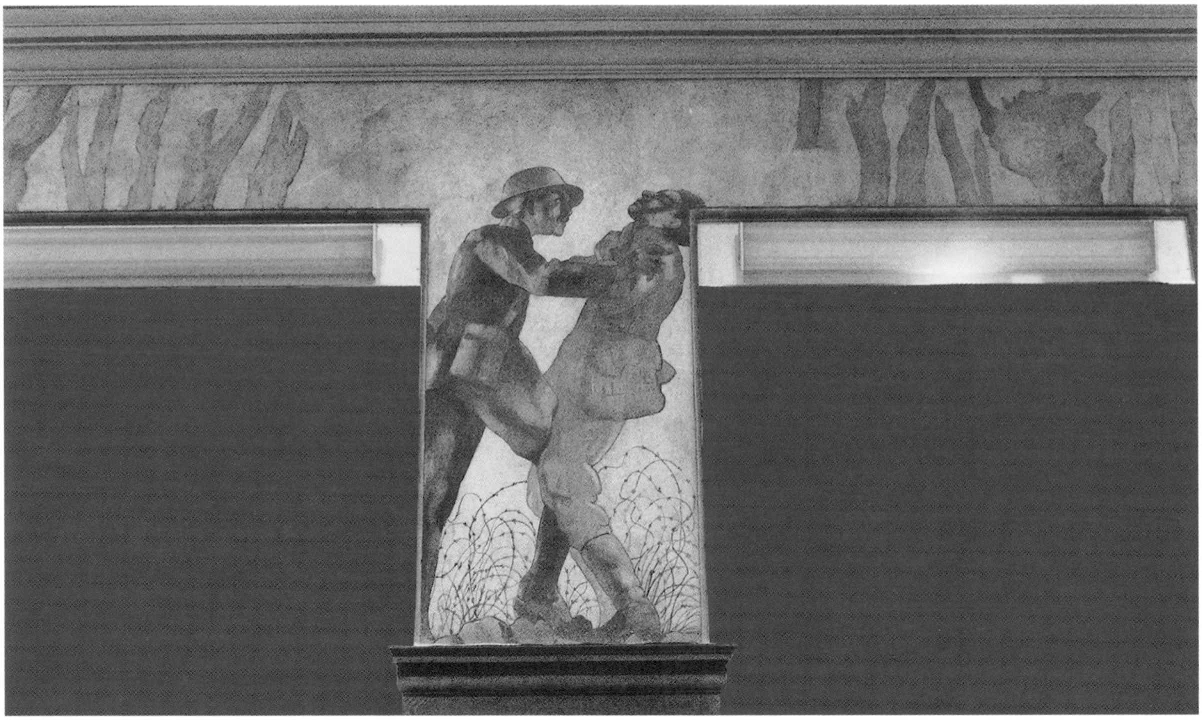

110. Neville, Lord Lytton, detail showing soldiers in hand-to-hand combat, from *Dolor* section of the First World War Memorial, Victory Hall, Balcombe, Sussex, completed 1924

Let some of our young artists be given similar tasks in other towns; let them illustrate the growth of the special industries associated with them, the local scenes among which they have arisen, ceremonies and events connected with local history, processional portrait groups of distinguished citizens, past and present—and why not also scenes recording honourable local service in the war?[79]

It is possible that Rothenstein's ideas had first begun to take shape when he sat on the committee of the *Exhibition of Designs for Mural Painting and for the Decoration of Schools and Other Buildings* held at Crosby Hall in Chelsea in 1912.[80] Also on the committee had been the Art Workers' Guild members Crane, Moira (who worked at Bristol), Lytton, and Halsey Ricardo, as well as the Mayor of Chelsea, the Chelsea judge Sargent, and the Chelsea artist Mary Sargant-Florence; Michael Sadler (Vice-Chancellor of Leeds University); Henry Tonks, and W. E. Riley (the LCC architect). Sir Patrick Geddes, the advocate of murals at Glasgow City Chambers and the influential patron of murals at University Hall in Edinburgh, was a prime mover of this exhibition.[81] One of its direct outcomes was the involvement of the LCC with art, for which Crane had first made a plea in his Guildhall masque. It put murals in a group of its primary schools, whilst the year after the Crosby Hall exhibition, Halsey Ricardo put the case for the employment of student artists in the mural decoration of the new London County Hall, then being built. This proposal also reflected the advocacy of 'participation by students in real work on public buildings and elsewhere'[82] by means of municipal patronage, in a far-reaching Parliamentary Report of 1911 on the Royal College of Art, to which Ricardo had contributed. After the war it was Rothenstein, along with Henry Tonks of the Slade, and other directors of the London art schools, who was also instrumental in the creation of eight lunettes for the corridors on the principal floor of County Hall by their students on the theme of *Life in the London Parks controlled by the London County Council.* This iconography directly echoed not only the late nineteenth-century Mairie illustrations of Paris parks, but more recently, the Borough Polytechnic murals of 1911–12 by Fry, Grant, and Etchells,[83] and the subject of civic amenities which was being illustrated in the early 1920s at Stockholm City Hall with such frescoes as Prins Eugen's *The City by the Water*, a view of one of Stockholm's parks.[84] Tonks was critical of Stockholm City Hall as architecture, and it is conceivable that he for one hoped to outdo its decoration; Rothenstein was clearly putting into practice both his Manchester-inspired vision of 'local' iconography in his 1916 *Plea for a Wider use of Artists and Craftsmen*, and the experiment with the employment of LCC students in the *Hall of Heroes* at the Arts and Crafts Exhibition Society's Royal Academy Exhibition of the same year. This exhibition had been mounted as a specific 'appeal to Public Authorities, to Municipalities, to Boards and Vestries, for more encouragement to local production',[85] and it is significant that it was at the 1923 exhibition of Decorative Art at the Royal Academy, which again included an Arts and Crafts section, that the County Hall murals were exhibited.

This, however, was after their rejection. Students had, of course, been turned down both at the Royal Exchange and in 1895, when the continuation of the Manchester decoration had been proposed, although they had been successfully employed, under E. R. Taylor's strict supervision,

[79] Ibid., p. 20.

[80] See Chapter 9.

[81] See Chapter 9 for University Hall, and for further detail of the Crosby Hall exhibition.

[82] *Report* (1911), §35, p. 23; for the murals in LCC schools, see Chapter 9.

[83] See Chapter 9.

[84] See R. Östberg, *The Stockholm City Hall: a Guide* (Stockholm, 1946).

[85] Introd. H. Wilson, *Arts and Crafts Exhibition* (1916), p. 22.

at Birmingham Town Hall in the 1890s. The architect of County Hall, Ralph Knott, and his colleague W. E. Riley, had both preferred Brangwyn's 1915 offer to paint eight panels in the ayes and noes lobbies as being from 'one of the greatest living decorative painters'[86] and must have felt aggrieved when the County Hall Establishment Committee tested *in situ* the eight student *Parks* panels, along with a further six provided by the art colleges of *Railways*, and ruled against even these on the grounds that any murals for County Hall should be 'of undoubted artistic merit'.[87] Tonks was infuriated, railing that the 'LCC and every other public body which barges into art should go and be damned';[88] with Rothenstein, Walter Bayes (Headmaster of the Westminster School of Art), and Charles Sims (Keeper of the Royal Academy), he protested in vain to the offending committee that 'rejection [of the murals] would be a lamentable sign of indifference to the claims of artists to devote themselves to public service.'[89]

The murals in fact look very dated to modern eyes. Whilst Brangwyn could have complemented admirably the Piranesian perspectives and Baroque exuberance of Knott's building, the stilted figures and elongated tree-trunks in the Royal College of Art panels, which bore over-zealous homage to Rothenstein's favoured models of Piero della Francesca and Puvis de Chavannes, must have looked as weak as the more Impressionistic mannerisms of the Slade contributions. The Westminster School of Art panels of *The Fair Ground* and *Vale of Health* at Hampstead Heath, by Norman Howard and H. Weaver Hawkins, reflect the sharp contrasts of sun and shadow of contemporary poster art, and it is not surprising they were eventually bought by London Underground to serve as decorations above the entrance to Westminster Tube Station. Although these two panels represent the most significant foray at a town hall since Lavery's *Shipbuilding* at Glasgow into the contemporary life iconography long favoured by the French, their style is ultimately a sanitized and unsatisfactory compromise between the sardonic wit of Mark Gertler's faceless machine-age mannequins in his recent *Merry Go Round*, and Laura Knight's breezy *Penzance Fair* of 1916, which was a clear compositional model.

It was while the County Hall débâcle was still being played out that the issue of contemporaneity in subjects and style, as advocated by Rothenstein, came to an even more pointed head at Leeds Town Hall. Already in his 1916 *Plea*, Rothenstein had actually included Gertler along with Henry Lamb, Stanley and Gilbert Spencer, Eric Gill, Paul and John Nash, C. R. W. Nevinson, and Dora Carrington as a new generation of artists from schools such as the Slade and the Royal College of Art, whom he felt to be the fittest to carry out his ideals of memorial and civic art with 'local' appeal. At Leeds, where he was Professor of Civic Art from 1917 to 1920, Rothenstein was instrumental in persuading the councillors and Sir Michael Sadler, the Vice-Chancellor of Leeds University, who held the purse-strings, to commission a very similar team: Stanley Spencer, the Nashes, Percy Jowett, Albert Rutherston, Edward Wadsworth, and Jacob Kramer. Sadler, of course, had sat on Geddes's 1912 Exhibition Committee with Rothenstein and had also been deeply inspired by the Hall of Heroes at the 1916 Arts and Crafts Exhibition Society show.

[86] *New County Hall Decorative Works Establishment Committee Joint Report by Architects* (25 March 1915), AR/CB/2/144, LMA. See H. Hobhouse (ed.), *County Hall* (1991) for further information about the decoration of County Hall.

[87] Letter from Clerk of Council to C. Sims (25 Oct. 1923), AR/CB/2/146, LMA. See W. Rothenstein, 'The London Parks Decorations by Art Students for the London County Hall', *Architectural Review*, 53 (1923), pp. 37–9 for illustrations of the panels.

[88] Quoted in J. Hone, *The Life of Henry Tonks* (1939), p. 186.

[89] Letter from Tonks, Sims, Rothenstein, and Bayes to the Chairman of the Establishment Committee, County Hall (17 Nov. 1923), AR/CB/2/146, LMA.

The local landscapes illustrated in the artists' pen, ink, and gouache preparatory designs (Plates 111, 112) were, however, sharply different from both the allegorical memorials of the war at the Hall of Heroes, and the vision of the nobility of modern manual labour and of man's brotherhood with nature which characterized Brangwyn's murals for the Venice Biennale of 1905[90] and his 1916 mosaics for St Aidan's church in Leeds. Both the latter had been warmly appreciated gifts to the city from one of its most prominent manufacturers, Samuel Wilson. At the Town Hall, however, John Nash's *Millworkers' Landscape* (Plate 111), in which a starkly silhouetted derelict church is shadowed by a mill behind it and dominated by a dead tree, amid deserted rows of back-to-back housing shrouded in a smoke pall from factories, was condemned by the *Yorkshire Post* as 'ugliness of form at the expense of truth'[91] whilst Paul Nash's *The Canal* is similarly devoid of human presence. A landscape of the strictly man-made, its geometric simplification speaks the uncompromising Vorticist language of the man who had included Brangwyn in his list of the 'Blasted', Wyndham Lewis. The most desolate image would have been Wadsworth's *Slagheaps* (Plate 112), a virtual abstraction lent representational significance only by a suggestion of telegraph poles. Rutherston's *Building* showed a crowd of anonymous labourers in cloth caps, but the purpose of their efforts is once again another industrial construction which relegates a Gothic church to the background. For all its avant-garde style, its juxtaposition of the workers with a massive tripod structure of crane and scaffold and its cumulus clouds were still a Brangwynesque vocabulary, but this does not seem to have been noticed.

The designs were approved by Rothenstein and the directors of the major London art galleries, Sir Charles Holmes, D. S. MacColl, and Charles Aitken. However, even though Rothenstein substituted Harold Williamson for Stanley Spencer because he felt Spencer's highly decorative washing on lines above a Leeds street to be inharmonious with the other murals, Sadler was not prepared to accept the scheme: 'though I appreciate the very great excellence of the individual designs I regard them as too discordant in character to be suitable for juxtaposition on the walls of a Town Hall.'[92]

Once again, it is the enduring status of the civic mural as an icon of power and authority expressed through what in 1867 Walter Bagehot had called 'state and show' which rests behind the final condemnation of the Leeds scheme in 1921 by Alderman Willey: 'The Victoria Hall is a magnificent building, and I, for one, would like to see it decorated, not by a discordant group of young experimenters, but by an artist of proved powers.'[93]

This iconic function of the civic mural explains why in the 1920s and 1930s it was the style of the artists trained at the British School at Rome, and their association with the Palace of Westminster, which won favour with a number of patrons, rather than either the avant-garde trend attempted at Leeds or the rather prosaic effort to demonstrate a return for ratepayers' money which, on its crudest level, undoubtedly underpinned the LCC's preference for the students of the art schools it funded. Rothenstein's influence remained of crucial importance, for he was a prominent member of the Council of the British School at Rome and, of course, one of the contributors to the 1923–7 'Rome' scheme at St Stephen's Hall in Westminster. By the early 1920s, the School's distinctive style, based on first-hand study of early Italian Renaissance models, perhaps offered the most cogent answer to date to what Sir Charles Eastlake had hoped might be developed through

[90] See Chapter 11.

[91] Quoted in A. Robertson, 'The Leeds Town Hall Decoration Scheme', *Leeds Art Calendar*, no. 74 (1974), p. 17.

[92] Ibid..

[93] Quoted in ibid., p. 19.

municipal extension of the 1840s Westminster patronage: a national school of 'historical painting on a large scale'.[94] Of the Westminster team of 'Rome' artists, Colin Gill, who had originally been at the Slade and was now an instructor at the Royal College of Art under Rothenstein, was commissioned in 1924 by Northampton Town Council to carry out a scheme he had devised for the Great Hall of its nineteenth-century building by the Gothic Revivalist E. W. Godwin. This consisted of thirteen panels of kings and local great men and also included *The Unknown Warrior*, *The Old Pillow Lace Maker*, and *A Craftsman of the Olden Time* (a 'hand-stitch' shoemaker representing 'the methods of boot and shoe making before the revolutionary introduction of machinery').[95] The latter two panels, like Gill's 'new colour scheme in red, gold and white for the hall as a whole'[96] and coats of arms on the ceiling, indicate not only an attempt to harmonize with Godwin's architecture, but also the enduring influence of Arts and Crafts ideology, which in a sense was reborn through the British School at Rome's preoccupation with the integration of art and architecture it felt had occurred in the early Italian Renaissance. The town's associations with Cromwell and Nonconformism are celebrated in the iconography, and it is clear that Gill's figure style, with its Giottesque monumentality and 'medieval' heraldic colour, was welcomed as lending an appropriate dignity to the historical lineage from which the council traced its descent.

Similar motivation and even closer emulation of Westminster are present in the mural scheme completed by 1939 at the new Essex County Hall in Chelmsford[97] (Plates 113, 114). Here, two St Stephen's Hall artists, Colin Gill and A. K. Lawrence, as well as the Rome Scholar Robert Lyon, were included in the team of painters, and Westminster-style historical episodes were used in addition to single figure motifs as at Northampton. With the Bank of England murals, which involved a similar team[98] and A. K. Lawrence's panels at Newcastle Art Gallery, Northampton and Essex represent the most direct impact of the post-war work at Westminster. This reverses the pre-war situation where Birmingham had pioneered the style—and first employed one of the artists—taken up at Westminster in 1906. Murals unveiled at Nottingham Council House in 1929 of events in the city's history and of *Merchandise welcomes Counsel and Crafts*, by Noel Denholm Davis, who had trained at the Royal Academy under Clausen and Sargent, were, however, more a revival of the German Nazarene-inspired compositions which had been produced by Dyce and Maclise at Westminster in the 1840s. Murals at Caernarvon County Council Chambers by Terence Mercer were also historical, with local landscape settings, and Maurice Greiffenhagen painted local history scenes in Braintree Town Hall Council Chamber.[99]

In identifying with the Westminster tradition of history painting, British civic and municipal patrons firmly eschewed the kind of monumental yet realistic treatment of contemporary national and city life which was to be found at the same period in Henri Martin's work for the French Second Chamber at the Palais Royal (Plate 52) and for the Mairie of the fifth *arrondissement* in Paris, or which, for that matter, was being created by Brangwyn on themes of Empire in his rejected panels for the Royal Gallery at Westminster (Plates XIX–XX, Plates 81–3). An incomplete scheme by Joseph Southall, in progress in 1939 for Birmingham Council House, abandoned the

[94] C. L. Eastlake, 'General View of the Object of the Commission', Appendix 2, *First Report* of CFA, PP XXV (London, 1842), p. 14.

[95] C. J. Glazebrook, *Northampton's Town Halls* (1970), p. 24.

[96] Ibid., p. 20. A scheme of mural decoration had in fact formed part of Godwin's original design and traces have been uncovered.

[97] See 'Council Chamber Suite, Essex County Hall, Chelmsford', *Builder* (25 Nov. 1938), pp. 1021–3, and *The Council Chamber of the Essex County Council An Account of the Decorations the Gift of Councillor William Julien Courtauld* (Colchester, 1939) (foreword by the Chairman of the County Council).

[98] See Chapter 11.

[99] These appear to post-date the First World War.

experiment with modern city-life iconography he had made in his Birmingham City Art Gallery *Corporation Street* mural of 1914,[100] and reverted to an allegorical illustration of *The Return of Peace* and *The Five Virtues* of a type which might have been devised by Crane in the 1890s. These reveal his continuing pacifist sympathies.[101] Only in a few instances, such as Wolverhampton Civic Halls, were painted decorative motifs on a modern-life subject introduced in the 1930s, as part of an Art Deco architectural ensemble. The Wolverhampton work, illustrating 'the civic and social life of the town',[102] at either side of the proscenium of the Small Hall, was carried out around 1938 by Muriel Gilbert, one of the artists of the decorations on the RMS *Queen Mary*, and is more closely related in its style to commercial art than to the tradition of mural painting originally established by Manchester Town Hall.

It is at Woodgreen Village Hall in Hampshire that the most direct response is found to Rothenstein's plea, made as early as 1916 in the context of war memorials, for the portrayal of 'familiar things', such as 'the changing life of the farm, the immemorial habits of men turning their hands to all the needs of the soil and the seasons, the great horses and their harnesses, the noble carts, the barns and sheds'.

Although designs for murals of the seasons for the Village Hall at Bourton, near Shrivenham in Berkshire, had been included in Geddes's 1912 Exhibition at Crosby Hall in Chelsea as part of a competition, it was following the war that interest developed in the creation and decoration of village halls as a means to revive England's traditional way of rural life. Vaughan Nash, who had, interestingly, been private secretary to Campbell Bannerman and Asquith during the period of the revival of mural painting at Westminster from 1906, was one of the leaders of this movement which enabled ex-servicemen to settle in country communities as smallholders, with the village hall as their social focus. Just as Lady Denham had built Balcombe Village Hall and commissioned its murals from Lord Lytton, so Vaughan Nash gave Woodgreen its hall in 1931 and launched its decoration by Edward Payne and Robert Baker (Plate XXV; Plates 115, 225). Payne was the son of H. A. Payne, one of the Westminster 1906 artists, and like Baker, trained at the Royal College of Art; both had been recommended to Nash by William Rothenstein himself. Their work illustrates in a sequence of scenes the customs and traditions of the passing seasons in the village of Woodgreen—from the *Flower Show* and *Methodist Sunday School* to the Morris dancers (Plate 115), the cricket team, and Christmas time in the Children's Ward at Salisbury Infirmary. *Village Scenes* (Plate XXV) and *A Summer's Day* (Plate 225) provide composite evocations of the community's life on the end walls. This iconography forms the natural sequel to Rothenstein's 'Rus in Urbe' project for County Hall, Eric Ravilious's and Edward Bawden's Shakespearean and traditional English themes at Morley College, and even Rex Whistler's idyllic pastorals in the Tate Gallery restaurant,[103] but they can also be seen as a modern counterpart to Clausen's rural idyll of medieval England, *Wycliffe reading the English Bible*, in the St Stephen's Hall scheme to which Rothenstein himself had just contributed, and to the pastoral emphasis in various schemes of the period in educational buildings.[104] With their nostalgic vision of an untroubled rural existence, the Woodgreen murals clearly reflect the wider preoccupation with the countryside of England which was already manifest in the publication of *Country Life* and in the 1930s was evident in

[100] See Chapter 9.

[101] See D. Farr et al., *Joseph Southall* (1980), pp. 93–5.

[102] *Souvenir Brochure Wolverhampton Civic Hall* (1938?), p. 11, in Local Studies Collection, Central Library, Wolverhampton.

[103] For Morley College, see Chapter 9; for the Tate Gallery restaurant, see Chapter 11.

[104] See Chapter 9.

Shell's famous advertisements. In their style, they offer a fascinating synthesis of lingering Pre-Raphaelite and Arts and Crafts trends with the influence of the British School at Rome, whilst their technique, like Lytton's at Balcombe, reflects the belief held by the Society of Mural Decorators and Painters in Tempera that fresco was most suitable for unpolluted rural contexts,[105] since they were largely executed *in situ*, albeit in a wax-based fresco substitute. At Woodgreen, as at Balcombe, the physical integration of the decoration with the walls which the *in situ* technique entailed additionally made it a tangible part of the rhetoric of renewal involved in the construction of village halls.

The Woodgreen murals are perhaps one of the most successful of all civic or village schemes. They incorporate over fifty portraits of local residents, but the almost Madox Brown-like delight in sunlit detail so evident from the fat sow with the litter of piglets or the cameos of milking, fruit-picking, or washing clothes (Plate XXV), is subordinated to a larger symbolic sense of the enduring cycle of human existence. Robert Baker spoke of the seasonal theme as 'something to hang things on',[106] and the murals are not just a descriptive record of Woodgreen, akin to the Mass Observation photographic project of the period, but an implicit defiance of the urban and industrial expansion and its concomitant evils which were increasingly threatening England's rural life. In the celebration of harmony between man and his natural environment and a Ruskinian emphasis on manual labour, they offer an English counterpart to Brangwyn's vision of man delighting in nature's plenty in his British Empire panels of the same period for the Royal Gallery, but their style is fundamentally different from his Baroque dynamism. Baker took conscious inspiration from the frescoes of Simone Martini at the Palais des Papes at Avignon and those in the Loire châteaux;[107] following Rothenstein's advice to him that 'if I were you, I'd go into the library [of the Victoria and Albert Museum] and study the Italian Primitives,'[108] the apple-picker on the ladder in his *Village Scenes* derives from Benozzo Gozzoli's *Golden Age* mural in the Campo Santo in Pisa and thus provides a subtle reminder of the larger symbolic theme of the murals.

Payne's *A Summer's Day* (Plate 225), filling the triangular gable of the far end wall, continues this theme by referring to classical antiquity itself. Its composition and iconography can be recognized as an imaginative reinterpretation of the east pediment of the Parthenon, with the playing children at the left who cast long, early-morning shadows, corresponding with its Helios and Hebe, and the young woman near the entrance with her basket of flowers echoing its symbolism of Demeter and Persephone. The pair of lovers and the crescent moon at the right correspond with Aphrodite, whilst the straw-hatted young man at the centre of the composition with a bottle of cider suggests Zeus and Dionysus in the pediment. Both the strong classical emphasis and the symbolic allusions in the murals to early Renaissance art also provide reminders of Rothenstein's admiration for the French Nabis. A lady called Gertrude Hooper, for example, pours flower-show tea in a tent like that of the Madonna in Piero's *Madonna of the Birth*, just as Maurice Denis imbued his *Cup of Tea (Mystic Allegory)* with Christian overtones; a portrait of Vaughan Nash occupies the place of one of Piero's angels and thereby subtly commemorates his

[105] See Chapter 9.

[106] Comment by R. Baker in discussion with the author, Sept. 1991. For details of the sitters, see S. Howell, 'Village Hall', in *Interiors* (Mar. 1990), pp. 144–57.

[107] Ibid. A lecture on the Palais des Papes decoration had been given to the Society of Mural Decorators and Painters in Tempera by E. Sands (see M. Sargant-Florence (ed.), *Papers of the Society of Mural Decorators*, vol. 3 (1936), pp. 87 ff.).

[108] Recollected by R. Baker in discussion with the author, Sept. 1991.

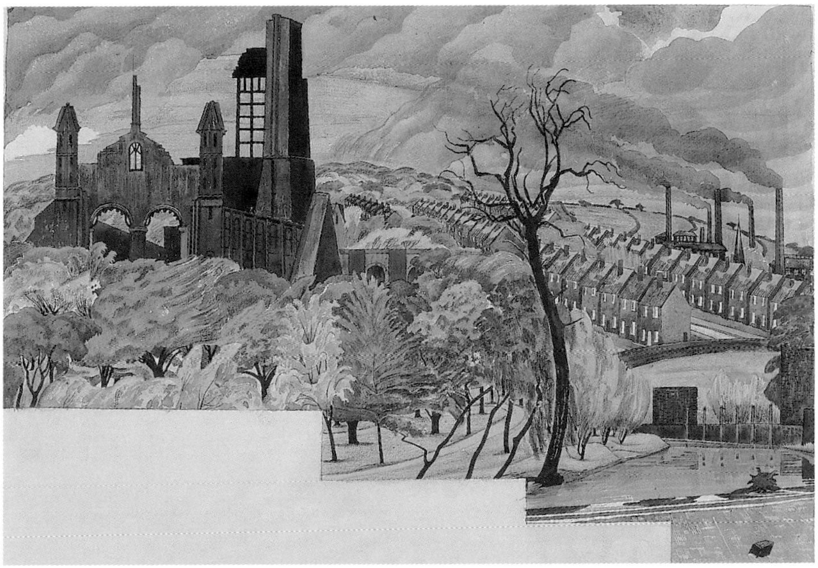

111. John Northcote Nash, *Millworkers' Landscape*, *c.*1920, design for mural for an abortive decorative scheme for Leeds Town Hall. Leeds, City Art Gallery

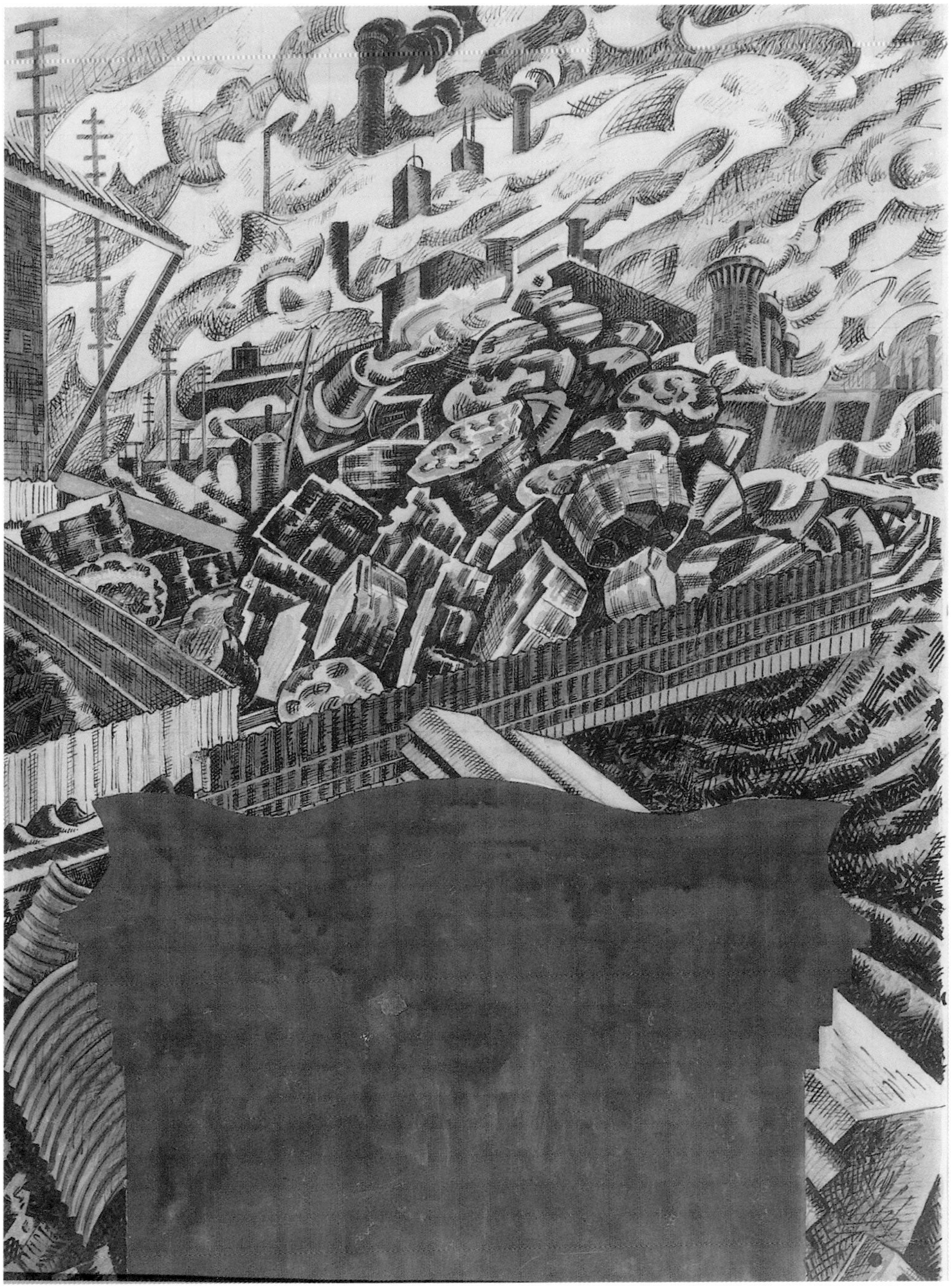

112. Edward Wadsworth, *Slagheaps*, *c.*1920, design for mural for an abortive decorative scheme for Leeds Town Hall. Leeds, City Art Gallery

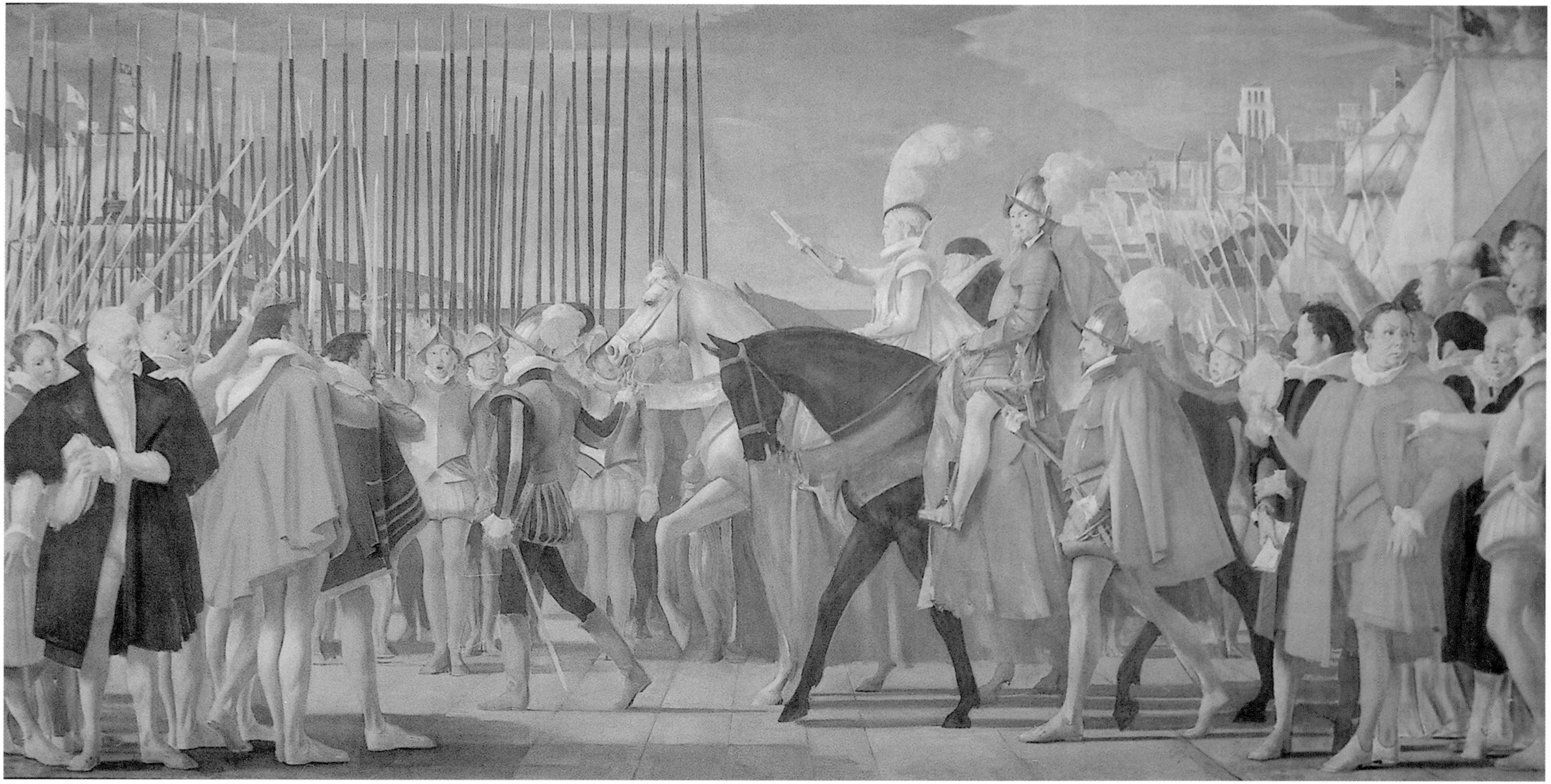

113. Alfred Kingsley Lawrence, *Queen Elizabeth reviewing her Troops at Tilbury, 9 August, 1588*, Entrance Hall, Essex County Hall, Chelmsford, 1938

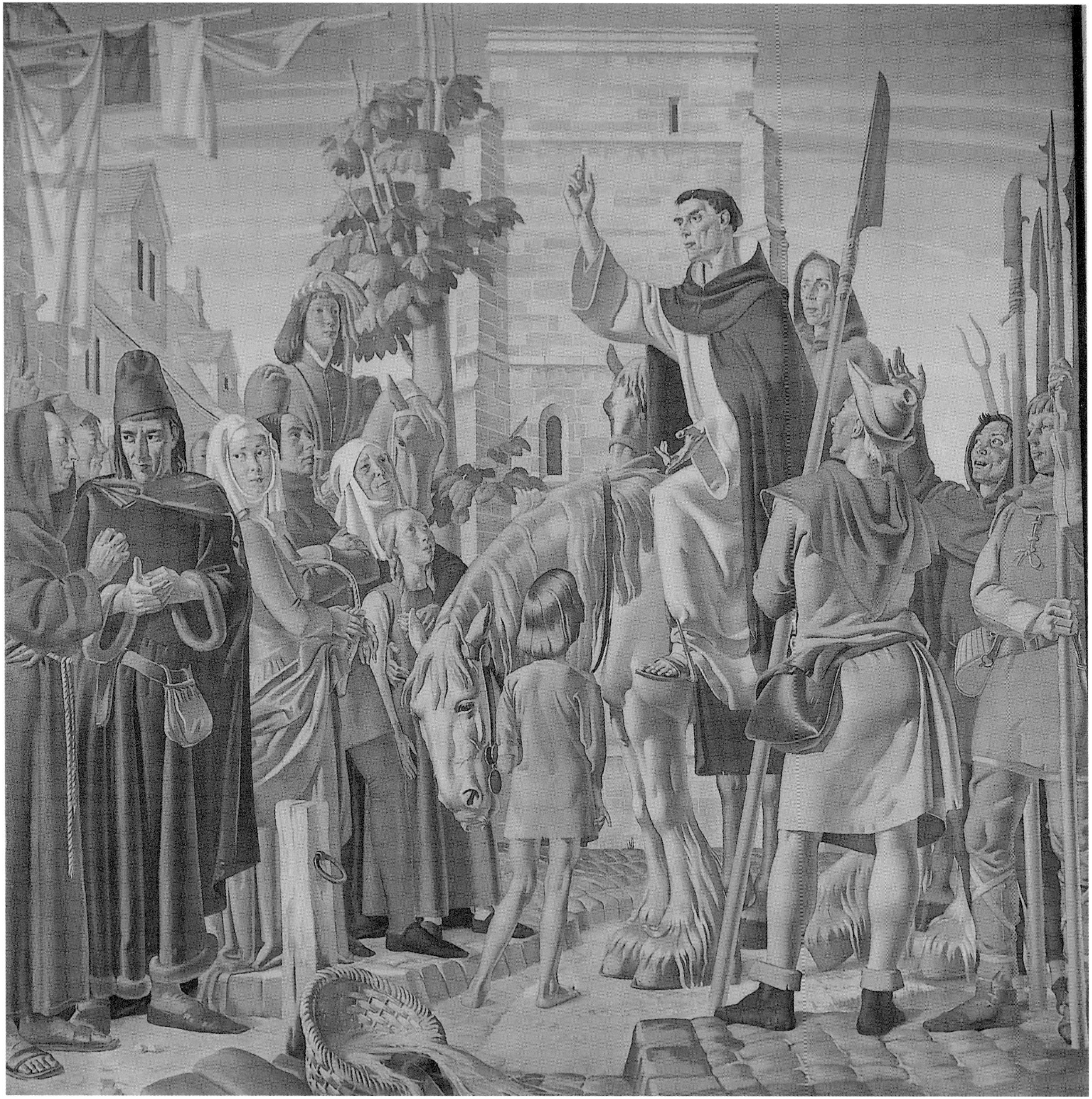

114. B. Fleetwood-Walker, *John Ball at Brentwood 1381. After the Black Death 1348–1350 came Great Unrest and a New Poll Tax caused a Peasant Rising*, Council Chamber, Essex County Hall, Chelmsford, 1938

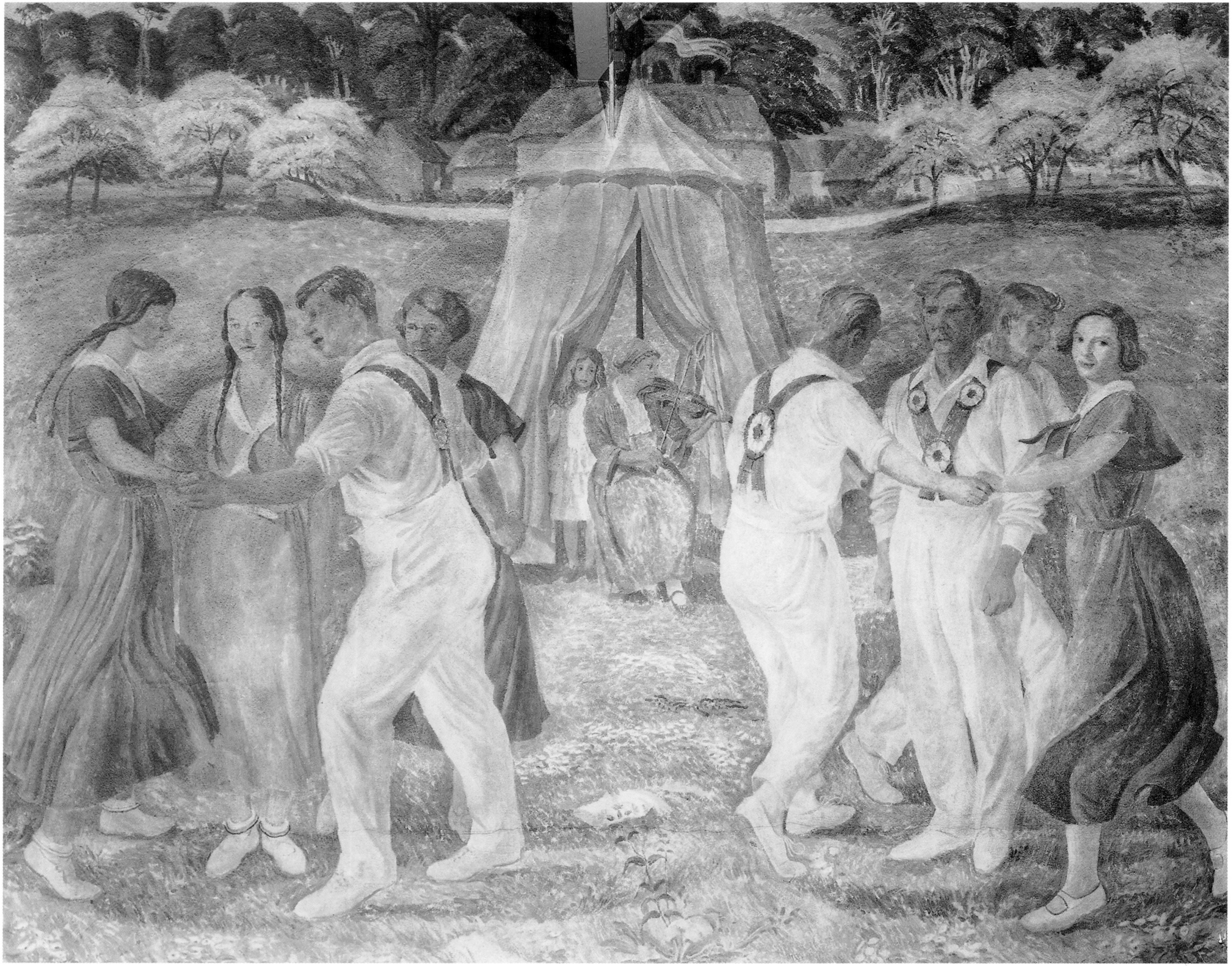

115. Robert Baker, *Morris Dancers* (*Village Team in County Competition*), Woodgreen Village Hall, Fordingbridge, Hampshire, *c.*1931–8

role, through provision of the decorated Village Hall, in the rebirth of the Woodgreen community and in consequence of England itself. Ruskin's belief that 'there should not be a single ornament put up in great civic buildings, without some intellectual intention' can hardly have been more tellingly realized, whilst sacred and secular are once again elided as in earlier civic schemes.

When Rothenstein's son, Sir John Rothenstein, mounted his photographic exhibition in 1939 at the Tate Gallery of *Mural Painting in Great Britain 1919–1939*, as 'a reflection and record of the more important mural paintings carried out in this country since the war',[109] the Woodgreen, Wolverhampton, and Essex schemes were the only examples selected from the sphere of civic or village patronage. With the St Stephen's Hall work as a centrepiece, and not a single work by Brangwyn, it was clear that he saw the legacy of his father's Royal College of Art and British School at Rome as the foundation for the future. Woodgreen and Essex were undoubtedly of key importance, but had the exhibition been selected with more awareness of the distinctive interaction between 'patron and icon' it might have been less exclusive. Swansea had, after all, been only too eager in 1933 to acquire for its new Guildhall the rejected Royal Gallery panels by Brangwyn, as an emblem of its identification with a celebrated artist who had Welsh parentage, whilst the murals at Bristol, Caernarvon, Birmingham, Liverpool, Northampton, and Balcombe were likewise an expression not merely of aesthetic principles, but more subtly, of a perceived relationship between these principles and the particular image their patrons wished to project. If their styles seemed to Rothenstein somehow less 'progressive' than those at Woodgreen, Wolverhampton, and Essex, then from an early twenty-first century viewpoint we can perhaps more clearly recognize the phenomenon of a time-lag between an ideology and its imagery which has been identified in political and economic history in relation to the emergence of a theory and its systematic expression.[110] Birmingham, for example, which under Joseph Chamberlain had pioneered municipalized water and gas supplies, free schools, and slum clearance, still settled for a sequence of historical murals in the 1890s, albeit in an Arts and Crafts update of mid-Victorian Pre-Raphaelitism, which in turn was adopted at Westminster when mural decoration was revived there in 1906. Likewise at Manchester, Madox Brown had been selected to carry out a style of work which was more a reversion to the Flemish or German history painting traditions established in the earlier nineteenth century, and thereby a symbolic statement of the council's ideals of Free Trade with the Continent, than a true reflection of the innovative Pre-Raphaelitism for which he is generally remembered today as an easel painter. This kind of 'invention of tradition' through 'civic ritual' (Birmingham's historical murals coincide with its creation as a city with a coat of arms) is as important a factor in the history of British mural painting in town, county, and village halls as at the Royal Exchange. Civic murals are also part of the revival of ceremonial which reached a climax in the years of royal and Imperial pageantry following Edward VII's accession, a period when mural painting was also revived at Westminster.

Whilst the nineteenth-century civic and county murals were a more immediate response to the recent establishment of councils as a result of the various municipal and other reform Acts and of their desire to emulate their Continental counterparts, the twentieth-century work is much more closely related to this new lead from royalty and Westminster. Its echoes are directly felt not only

[109] J. Rothenstein, *Mural Painting* (1939), p. 3.

[110] See, for example, D. K. Fieldhouse's discussion in *The Theory of Capitalist Imperialism* (London, 1967), p. xvi of the time-lag between the emergence in the late 18th century of the ideas involved in the 'theory of Capitalist Imperialism' and its expression only in the early 20th century by both the Liberal J. A. Hobson and V. I. Lenin.

in the decision to include murals in existing town halls like Chelsea, or as part of the Neo-Baroque extravagance of new ones like Belfast, but also in many iconographical references to historical links between royalty and city or county (as at Bristol). After the war, ceremonial and pageantry were translated into the use of mural painting for commemoration, but remained important until the draught of economic recession lessened demand in the late 1930s.

Yet despite their concern to express ideals and to celebrate, commemorate, or symbolize status and achievement, civic and related patrons in Britain often sought private means, on the models of the Royal Exchange and twentieth-century Westminster decoration, to finance the works they commissioned, whilst Waterhouse promoted and supervised the Manchester scheme without charge. Although there were numerous appeals for civic patronage from Geddes, the Art Workers' Guild, and Sir William Rothenstein amongst others, as late as 1939 Southall himself had to fund his murals for Birmingham. There is no ambitious civic patronage comparable to that, for example, of the Fresco Brothers in Sweden. Both their work and that of Axel Revold in Oslo Town Hall from 1938 to 1942 does, however, provide close correspondences with the use of fresco-related technique for rural themes at Woodgreen, whilst the nationalist overtones of fresco as used by the Swedish artists and the twentieth-century Swiss fresco revivalists find an echo both at Woodgreen and in Lord Lytton's work at Balcombe.

Only rarely, too, was there an organized competition to select artists, as at Chelsea Town Hall: here there was a clear emulation (probably as a result of Sargent having worked alongside Puvis de Chavannes in the Public Library murals at Boston) of French practice. The County Hall students were selected by competition, but generally there is nothing comparable to the elaborate competition procedures used in Germany for town-hall commissions. The involvement of local art clubs or art schools at Chelsea, Bristol, and in London at County Hall is only a loose parallel with the regional art contributions so important in the German tradition.

In the absence of a continuous tradition of mural painting in Britain, its revival from the 1840s thus led to a rather piecemeal emulation of selective aspects of foreign practice in town, village, and county hall commissions. If the patron's quest to project civic or local identity was paramount, some of the most interesting and successful murals were produced by those artists who, like Brangwyn, the Chelsea Town Hall team, Southall at Birmingham, and Payne and Baker at Woodgreen, found ways to make the civic icon also carry personal ideals and aspirations. At the same time, the influence of the Gothic Revival or Ruskinian philosophies of many of the early town-hall architects, like Crossland or Waterhouse, and later of the Arts and Crafts Movement ideal of art integrated with architecture, created a strong thread of continuity which runs even through many of the post-war schemes—Sir William Rothenstein acknowledged inspiration from both Manchester Town Hall and Crane—and ensures a remarkable element of consistency in a field of British mural painting which apparently offers so many contrasts of style across its individual schemes.

8
Ecclesiastical Murals

The lively and distinguished tradition of church mural patronage which had been established in Britain during medieval and pre-Reformation times was all but severed by the closure of the monasteries and the nature of Protestantism during the seventeenth and eighteenth centuries. Following the Roman Catholic Emancipation Act of 1829, however, and the rise of the Anglican Oxford Movement shortly afterwards under Newman, Keble, and Pusey, mural decoration in ecclesiastical buildings underwent a rapid revival. Despite the disappointments with fresco at Westminster, a remarkable amount of painted decoration was created in churches, monasteries and nunneries, school chapels, and even a significant number of Nonconformist chapels and churches from around 1840 to well into the early twentieth century, although not all of this was pictorial. As with any extensive movement, this ecclesiastical work is of widely varying quality; whilst it reached some considerable peaks of glory, as in Leighton's work at Lyndhurst or Brangwyn's at Christ's Hospital chapel, it also inspired a fair amount of relatively routine production. This is largely because of the dominant role of ecclesiastical decorating companies whose work formed the bulk of the commissions carried out. There is really no equivalent in Britain to the great murals of Saint-Sulpice in Paris by the *grand maître* of French Romantic art, Eugène Delacroix, or to those by his rival Ingres at Autun Cathedral. Whilst Eduard von Gebhardt's richly realistic evocation of the common crowd as a key protagonist in the parables of Christ burst open with *Breitwandpanorama* treatment the Gothic confines of the Friedenskirche in Düsseldorf in the late nineteenth century, British church muralists were by and large still remarkably conservative, continuing Gothic Revivalist styles first evolved in the 1840s and 1850s.

The involvement of 'fine' as opposed to 'trade' artists in ecclesiastical work during the nineteenth century can be summarized by a small, though undoubtedly significant, group of schemes which includes Dyce's work at All Saints, Margaret Street, London of 1853 to *c.* 1859; Leighton's at Lyndhurst Parish Church in 1863; Poynter's of 1871–3 at St Stephen's, Dulwich; Watts's at St James the Less (*c.* 1861), and the unexecuted designs of Stevens, Watts, Leighton, and others for St Paul's Cathedral, where Sir William Richmond eventually carried out mosaics in the 1890s amid furious contention. Whereas in Paris church decoration was normally municipal, commissioned by the Préfet de la Seine almost always from the winners of the Prix de Rome, patronage in Britain depended on private benefactors, priests, or congregational assent, as the Bishop of Exeter made clear as early as 1852, when he recognized 'the right of the rector to ornament his chancel' after complaints had reached him from the rural dean about proposed murals at Shevioke Church in

Cornwall.[1] By the twentieth century, we still find only isolated instances of the involvement of prominent artists in ecclesiastical decoration, which again are generally the result of enlightened individual patronage like that of H. A. Payne by Lord Beauchamp at Madresfield Court chapel in the 1900s; of Brangwyn by Christ's Hospital school in 1912–23; of Stanley Spencer by the Behrend family in the chapel at Burghclere in 1927–33; and of Vanessa Bell, Duncan Grant, and others by Bishop Bell at Berwick Church in Sussex in 1941–4. By far the greatest number of schemes were still being completed in the Gothic Revival modes of the century before. Sir Ninian Comper's 'Gothic' mural work as part of his church restoration in the early twentieth century, for example, finds its direct ancestry in his having been articled to the architect G. F. Bodley, himself a pupil of Sir George Gilbert Scott.

This may seem a curious state of affairs when religious subjects in easel painting were regenerated by the efforts of the Pre-Raphaelites and became a distinctive feature of *fin-de-siècle* symbolism. It is as though the demand for church decoration not only outstripped what 'fine art' could (or would) supply, but was, even in free churches like St Leonard's in Dunfermline in 1927, by its very nature a conservative force. To understand the character and development of ecclesiastical mural commissions, we need to appreciate the extraordinary popularity and influence in Britain of the Gothic Revival in architecture and the philosophy of ornament which accompanied it. Whilst Anglo-Catholicism provided the liturgical demand for illustration and colour upon church walls, it was the Gothic Revival as propagated by the influential Ecclesiological Society which placed a premium on painting and which made architects at least as, and perhaps even more, influential than clergy and donors in the encouragement of murals in the one form of building for which, even more resolutely than in town halls, the Gothic became the 'only true style'. Pugin's revulsion against the classical in his *Contrasts* of 1836, which eulogized the Gothic as 'Christian' and designated classical buildings as pagan temples, set the trend for virtually the succeeding century, with the Gothic mode being chosen for Liverpool Cathedral even in the twentieth century. Catholicism, Tractarianism, and Gothic Revivalism operated in interaction, but the 'architectural factor' played a distinctive and significant role.

Pugin's strictures, however, placed Roman Catholic aspiration in a quandary. Already before the Emancipation Act of 1829, Catholic confidence had been expressed with unprecedented bravura in Britain in the remarkable panoramic fresco by Agostino Mario Aglio in St Mary's in Moorfields in London, a highly theatrical classical building by John Newman in which the mural was effectively a stage backdrop with concealed illumination for the altar. Aglio had had experience as a scene painter before undertaking the mural, which illustrates the Crucifixion. The classical temple form was likewise used for St John the Baptist's Roman Catholic church in 1835 in Brighton, later to be decorated in the 1890s with murals by N. H. J. Westlake. Now, in 1836 in *Contrasts*, Pugin laid down compelling arguments for the Gothic style: in it 'alone we find the faith of Christianity embodied and its practices illustrated'; in the ground plan of Gothic churches was the cross and in 'the great height and vertical lines . . . an acknowledged symbol of the resurrection'.[2] He dedicated *Contrasts* to one of the most prominent of the Roman Catholic nobility, Lord Shrewsbury, and when Shrewsbury commissioned him to build a new church at Cheadle (com-

[1] 'The Bishop of Exeter on Mural Paintings in Churches', *Ecclesiologist*, new series, 9 (1852), p. 16.
[2] M. Day, *Modern Art in Church* (1982), p. 3.

pleted in 1846) it became a lodestone for the Gothic style, not only in Roman Catholic but also in Reformed churches. Meanwhile, in tandem with Pugin's own extensive studies of surviving Gothic buildings, artefacts, and manuscripts, antiquarian interest began to focus on the remaining evidence of Gothic church painting. L. N. Cottingham, the church furnisher, was one of the first to launch a reappraisal of medieval frescoes through his conservation in 1825 of thirteenth-century frescoes at Rochester,[3] and by the 1840s, the interest in the medieval wall paintings in the Painted Chamber and St Stephen's Chapel at Westminster[4] (Plate 12) was one of the spurs in the decision that murals should form part of the new Gothic-style Houses of Parliament, where Pugin was called in to provide the detailing and ornament for Barry's design. A last gasp of Italianate pictorialism in the tradition of Aglio and the Raphaelesque could still be found in the north, in the large mural altarpiece of the *Annunciation* and the *Agony in the Garden* in St Andrew's church, Penrith, which was completed in 1845 in oil on prepared plaster by the artist Jacob Thompson, who was trained at the Royal Academy, to replace earlier work by Matthias Reade. The landscape backdrops in its two vertical panels have strong overtones of Pugin, but apparently include the local landmark of Penrith Castle, whilst the figures were modelled from local people and are expressive and vigorous. The work forms a suitably monumental complement to the large, classical-style building and is clearly by an accomplished artist.[5] Despite such survivals of the classical, however, the 1840s, 1850s, and even 1860s became more generally the era *par excellence* of the Gothic.

ECCLESIOLOGY AND GERMANISM

During the 1840s and 1850s, the Oxford Movement under Newman (who converted to Catholicism in 1845) and then Pusey and Keble provided a focus for the doctrinal and liturgical precepts involved in the Anglo-Catholic return to ritual, but it was its Cambridge sister, the Camden Society, which emerged as the standard-bearer of medieval antiquarianism in the arts. Whilst Newman and his colleagues provided the verbal armoury in their ninety *Tracts* for the crusade against nineteenth-century materialism, preaching a return to truth 'taught . . . by many in all times before' and embodied in the catechism and liturgy,[6] the Camden Society looked to Pugin for the style to put these ideals into practice. Founded in 1839 by John Mason Neale and Benjamin Webb, it became the London-based Ecclesiological Society from 1845, having launched its polemical and extremely influential journal, the *Ecclesiologist*, in 1841. It saw its role as 'originating, exciting . . . creating, activity in various departments of art—in advising upon the furniture and decorations of churches';[7] in the pages of the *Ecclesiologist* were to be found forthright pronouncements by its High Church editor, the President of the Ecclesiological Society, A. J. Beresford-Hope; by the new Gothic Revival architects who were founder members, like G. E. Street and Sir George Gilbert Scott; and by artists like Thomas Gambier Parry, on the vital need for wall decoration as in medieval architecture. The views of the Ecclesiologists

[3] See J. Myles, 'The Church Furnishings of L.N. Cottingham, 1787–1847', *Victorian Society Annual* (1990), p. 37.

[4] See J. T. Smith, *Antiquities of Westminster* (1807).

[5] See L. Jewitt, *Life and Works of Jacob Thompson* (1882), pp. 29–31. The murals are still *in situ*.

[6] Quoted in A. R. Vidler, *The Church in an Age of Revolution: 1789 to the Present Day* (Harmondsworth, 1976), p. 53.

[7] Report of the Camden Society's Sixth Anniversary meeting in the *Ecclesiologist*, 4 (1845), p. 12.

were summed up in its mission call: 'We would have every inch glowing . . . Puritans would have every inch colourless.'[8]

The problem, however, as Beresford-Hope found simultaneously in his role as a member of Prince Albert's Select Committee on the decoration of the Palace of Westminster, was that suitable artists did not exist in Britain. Aglio, after all, who had provided the fresco at St Mary Moorfields, was Italian, and he typified the recourse to foreign talent which had come to characterize much British mural patronage in the eighteenth century. It was a long time since Sir James Thornhill's frescoes at St Paul's in 1714–19 and Wimpole Chapel in 1724; in any case, what was wanted was 'colour' and not the restrained grisaille which Thornhill had employed. Pugin's belief in 'truth to materials' led to the popularity of 'constructional polychromy' through geometric banding of coloured bricks, marble, or stone, especially after Ruskin's *Stones of Venice* drew attention to its use in Gothic Italy, but it also prompted enthusiasm for true fresco as a medium integral with the wall. As at Westminster at this period, attention therefore turned to the Nazarene fresco revival, but for Roman Catholic and High Church patrons this had an additional attraction, since the Nazarenes had used fresco as the vehicle for a distinctively Neo-Catholic nationalism, creating what Goethe satirized as 'Neu-deutsch Patriotische-religiös Kunst'.[9] As their leader Peter Cornelius put it:

> From a spiritual and physical viewpoint, these works actually belong to that spot on earth where they were created; they are in most beautiful unison with God, nature, time, and surrounding life . . . they are like a noble, excellent man whose power and high value of humanity is in general a blessing, a joy.[10]

A fresco such as that by the Nazarene follower Joseph Settegast in St Mary's church, Clapham, of *Christ and the Apostles* (Plate 116) thus turned the medium—implicitly emblematic of Christ in Cornelius's description—into the very message. It was natural that his patron, Lord Shrewsbury, a prominent Roman Catholic as well as a Westminster Commission member, should also commission fresco from Nazarenes at St Mary's Greenwich and his seminary at Oscott, both built by Pugin, although he incurred Pugin's wrath by installing an oil on canvas *Last Judgement* by the Swiss Nazarene Eduard Hauser in his church of St Giles at Cheadle. It was natural too that Beresford-Hope, who was the 'Young England' Tory MP for Cambridge, should urge Nazarene-style mural painting in the pages of the *Ecclesiologist* just as he did for patriotic reasons at the same period in evidence to the Select Committee at Westminster.

If the Cheadle *Last Judgement* threatened to betray Pugin's 'truth to materials' principle and so deny the sort of mystic symbolism described by Cornelius, its iconography had impeccable credentials. The *Last Judgement*, in the same traditional medieval position over the chancel arch as at Cheadle, had been used by Cornelius in his much acclaimed Ludwigskirche murals in Munich. These were enthusiastically described by Mrs Jameson and other critics during the 1830s and 1840s[11] as well as noted by those deliberating on the Westminster decoration, and the *Last Judgement* theme was either planned or executed as chancel-arch decoration in a group of Nazarene-inspired 'Ecclesiological' church schemes during the 1840s and 1850s (Appendix B: 1, 5).

[8] The *Ecclesiologist* (1845), quoted in P. Thompson, *William Butterfield* (London, 1971), p. 229.

[9] Quoted in W. Vaughan, *German Romanticism* (1979), p. 181.

[10] Letter from Cornelius to Joseph Görres (3 Nov. 1814) in E. G. Holt, *From the Classicists to the Impressionists* (1966), p. 100.

[11] See A. Jameson, *Visits and Sketches* (1834) and J. G. Crace, 'The Decorations of Munich', *Builder* (22 Feb. 1851), p. 119, for example.

Also popular was *Our Lord in Majesty seated on a rainbow*, which at Shevioke in Cornwall was actually part of a series of watercolour decorations in the church 'all taken from Overbeck'.[12]

The most important of these Ecclesiological responses to Nazarene models were the schemes at All Saints, Margaret Street, London, by William Dyce; and at Highnam Church, Gloucestershire, and Ely Cathedral by Thomas Gambier Parry. However, a distinctively British approach emerges which lifts the 'rainbow' motif featured in Overbeck's *Lord in Majesty* iconography onto a new symbolic plane. This can be seen both as a response to the misgivings about the lack of colour and cold linearity of Cornelius's art being voiced by many of the Westminster witnesses, and to the new rallying call of 'truth to nature' of one of the Ecclesiologists' most famous founder members, John Ruskin. Publications in the late 1840s and 1850s by Mrs Jameson and the Revd F. C. Husenbeth, and in France, Didron's *Iconographie chrétienne, histoire de Dieu* had stimulated interest in the identification of saints and religious figures by means of emblems, and hence of a 'symbolic language' of Christian art.[13] At All Saints, however (Plate XXVI; Plate 117), we find Dyce introducing a new vibrancy of colour and sense of modelled form, along with gilded backgrounds to his figures, which combine Italian Renaissance influences with the clarity of design of the Nazarenes to create a highly sensual response to Newman's call for 'the concrete representative of things invisible which would have the force and toughness to be a breakwater against the deluge'[14] of corruption in the modern world.

Dyce's mural reredos (the only portion of his commission for decoration of the entire chancel and its arch which he actually completed) can now be appreciated only though Comper's 1909 restoration. It is clear, however, that its subjects of Christ in Majesty, the Crucifixion, the Virgin and Child, and the Twelve Apostles reflected his delight in the 'excellences' of 'truth of local colour' of Pintorrichio's frescoes, and their 'profusion of gilding which on the large scale certainly contributes to reality of effect.'[15] These features he preferred to the 'method of darkening rather than shadowing' learnt 'from old art rather than nature' which he denigrated in Cornelius. Likewise, at Highnam Church the remarkable gentleman polymath and friend of Ruskin and Dyce, Thomas Gambier Parry, put his readings of 'Chevreuil, Hay, Field and Jones'[16] into effect in the iridescent mandorla of viridian, pink, and golden yellow which he painted around the figure of God in judgement above the chancel arch (Plate XXVII). Also employing expensive gilding like Dyce, he was presumably seeking to outdo even Cornelius, whose *Last Judgement* at Munich he had 'greatly admire[d]' in 1851 when he commented

> These Germans are endeavouring to establish a phase of art as the basis of a new school, which shall combine the abstracted contemplative expression of the early Pre-Raphaelite painters, with the full forms, richly massed colouring and dramatic character of more fully developed art.[17]

[12] The Bishop of Exeter in the *Ecclesiologist*, 9 (1852), p. 17. Presumably related to the Ecclesiological taste for German work was the installation at Ince Blundell Hall, Liverpool, of murals of the life of Christ painted by Gebhardt Flatz in Rome between 1859 and 1863 (see File JC21 in Walker Art Gallery, Liverpool).

[13] e.g. Mrs Jameson's *The Poetry of Scared and Legendary Art* (1848) and F. C. Husenbeth's *Emblems of the Saints: by which they are distinguished in works of art* (London, 1850); Didron's book was translated into English in 1851 (see Holt, *Classicists to Impressionists*, p. 141).

[14] B. Willey, *Nineteenth Century Studies: Coleridge to Matthew Arnold* (London, 1949), p. 88. Hope originally commissioned the French artist Henri Gerente to decorate All Saints, in 1849, but he died.

[15] Quoted in L. Errington, 'Ascetics and Sensualists, Dyce's views on early Christian Art' *Burlington Magazine*, 134 (1992), p. 493.

[16] T. G. Parry, 'Whitewash and Yellow Dab—No. II. The Use of Colour in Church Architecture', *Ecclesiologist*, 19 (new series 16) (1858), p. 373.

[17] Quoted in D. Farr (ed.), *Thomas Gambier Parry* (1993), p. 35.

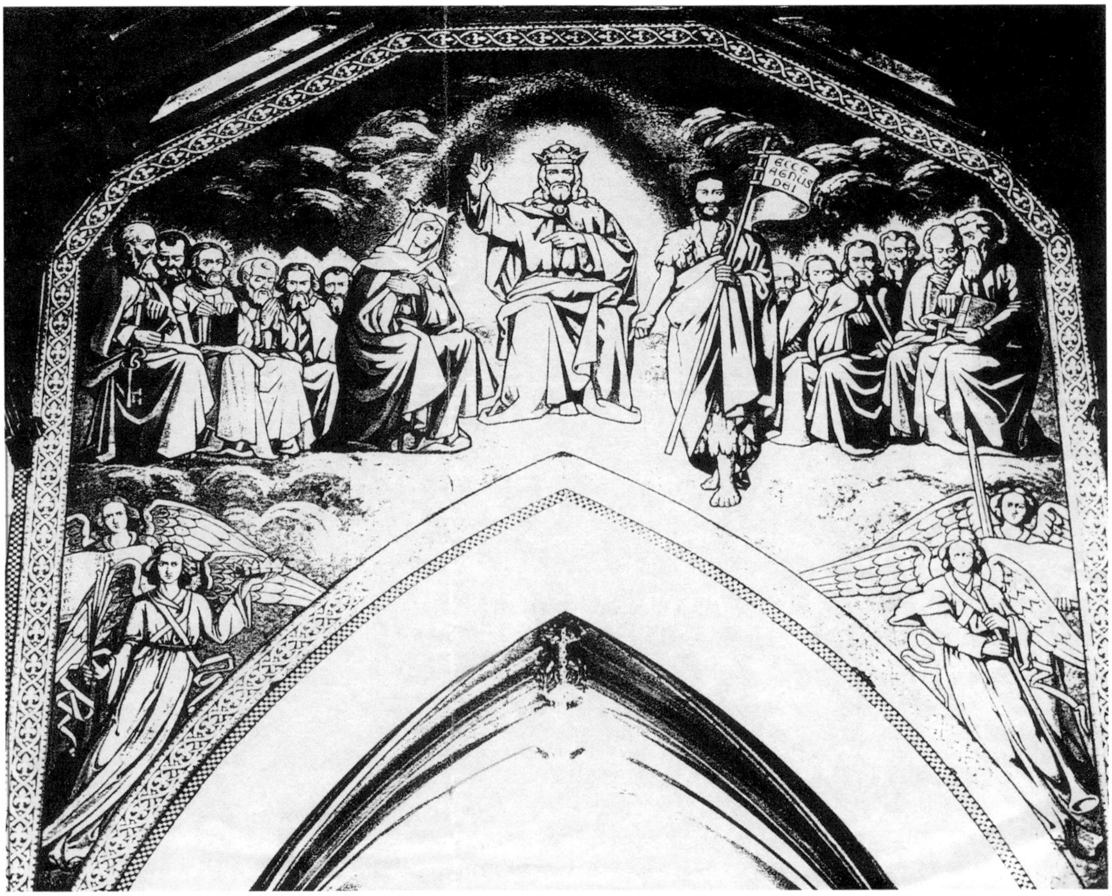

116. Joseph Settegast, *Christ and the Apostles*, St Mary's church, Clapham, London, 1854

117 (*facing*). William Dyce, design for mural at All Saints church, Margaret Street, London, *c.*1853. London, Victoria and Albert Museum

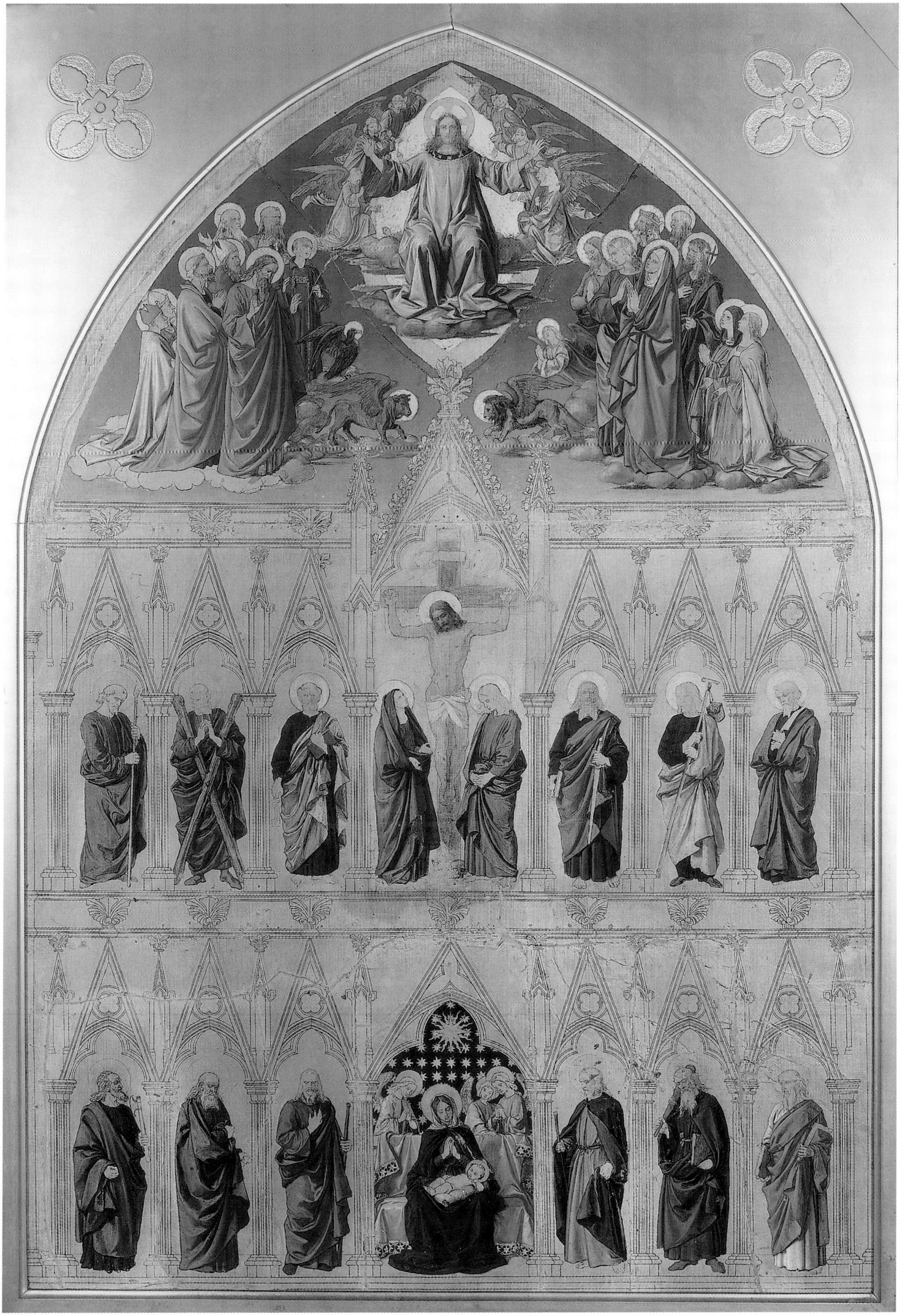

The Highnam *Doom* (1859–61), like his other murals there (completed in 1880), at Ely (1863–4), and in St Andrew's chapel, Gloucester Cathedral (1866), was carried out in part to demonstrate his new invention of 'spirit fresco', the medium to be adopted later by Madox Brown and Leighton amongst others, and which was closely related to the wax-based procedures common in the early nineteenth century in France. However, it used copal and other ingredients to obtain the vital fusion with the wall surface so important to the Nazarene, Neo-Catholic fresco philosophy. In contrast to true fresco, it permitted the use of a far wider range of colours, including cobalt, emerald, ultramarine, and Naples yellow: hence the symbolic iridescence of the Highnam 'Doom'.[18]

Beresford-Hope intended All Saints, Margaret Street, to be the 'Model Church'[19] of the Ecclesiologists. It was designed by the staunch Gothic Revivalist William Butterfield (whose pupil Henry Woodyer was meanwhile building Highnam). Butterfield had just completed the Cathedral of the Isles at Cumbrae, Bute, with its rather Ruskinian ceiling decoration illustrating the local flowers and ferns. At All Saints, however, Hope soon began to feel that Butterfield's lavish polychromy threatened to overwhelm what he termed 'the spiritualism of Gothic art'.[20] He criticized Butterfield for introducing, in addition to the murals, tiling, glass painting, and marble and brickwork which 'parricidically spoilt his own creation with the clown's dress, so spotty and spidery and flimsy it looks'.[21] In a stand against what he felt to be the dangers of the realism to which Dyce was in fact already turning in his religious easel paintings and which was evident in Dyce's Virgin (modelled on the artist's sister) at All Saints, Hope made a speech at an important meeting of the Ecclesiological Society in 1860 in which he deplored the style of the 'Preraffaelite Brethren' as being inimical to Gothic architecture:

> Surely the very essence of Gothic architecture was the imaginative scale which it created—the production of the idea of infinity within limited space . . . How then could the minute realism of Preraffaelism accord with that architecture which was essentially imaginative and spiritual?[22]

Perhaps in response to this outburst from Hope, Gambier Parry's work at Ely Cathedral, where he completed and developed a scheme of decoration for the upper arcades and ceiling of the tower and nave, begun by his Eton friend Styleman Le Strange, is more restrained and strictly archaeological; a careful homage both to the original Norman decoration which had recently been discovered in the cathedral by Parry's friend Sir George Gilbert Scott during his restoration work there, and to the 'abstract simplicity of the early painters'[23] which Parry admired as a pioneer collector of Fra Angelico, Perugino, Agnolo Gaddi, and Bartolommeo Montagna. Concluding with Christ enthroned in glory, the murals illustrate what the Dean of Ely called 'an epitome of the sacred history of man'.[24] It is possible that this ambitious elaboration of Le Strange's original Tree of Jesse theme reflected an awareness on Parry's part of the 'sacred history of mankind' being

[18] See Parry's account of his spirit fresco technique, 'Wall-painting versus the English Climate', published in the *Ecclesiologist*, 23 (new series 20) (1862), pp. 134–42, esp. p. 139.

[19] Quoted in P. Thompson, 'All Saints' Church, Margaret Street, Reconsidered', *Architectural History*, 8 (1965), p. 75.

[20] 'Twenty-first Anniversary Meeting' (discussion on 'the Praeraffaellite school'), *Ecclesiologist*, 21 (new series 18) (1860), p. 249.

[21] Quoted in Thompson, *William Butterfield*, p. 79.

[22] 'Twenty-first Anniversary Meeting' (see n. 20), p. 248.

[23] Quoted in Farr (ed.), *Thomas Gambier Parry*, p. 34. Whilst Parry's enthusiasm for early Italian art was in advance of its time, more general interest in Italian Renaissance frescoes was stimulated by the publications of the Arundel Society, founded in 1848. Advised by Ruskin, this commissioned watercolour copies particularly of deteriorating wall-paintings, and distributed engravings of these (from 1856 using colour lithography) to its numerous subscribers. These engravings were commended by G. E. Street in 'On the Future of Art in England', *Ecclesiologist*, 19 (new series 16) (1858), p. 237.

[24] Quoted in Farr (ed.) *Thomas Gambier Parry*, p. 22. A printed description of the mural decoration was issued by the Dean of Ely in 1865 (MS EDC 4/5/63, Cambridge University Library, Ely Dean and Chapter Archives).

planned at the period by Paul Chenavard for the Panthéon in Paris, or of the slightly earlier (1837) 'History of Christianity' apse painting in the Paris Madeleine church, by Ziegler, as well as of the traditional Nazarene precedents. Parry's preoccupation with symbolic iconography is clearly evident from his remark of 1859 that 'perfect art is . . . that by which an idea is completely and satisfactorily conveyed.'[25]

If Parry's belief in 'a system of pictorial art which is rather suggestive of thoughts than directly representative of things'[26] as the most suitable for Gothic architecture kept him, like Beresford-Hope, from a full commitment to Pre-Raphaelism, the architect G. E. Street was vigorously outspoken at the Ecclesiologists' same 1860 debate on what he saw as the congruity of purpose between Millais, Hunt, and Rossetti and the Gothic building style. All were concerned with 'truth', whereas the German work, he argued, was 'mere dead reproduction of an old form of art'.[27]

Paradoxically, however, the mural schemes which mark a distinctive reaction to the German and medievalizing trends of the Ecclesiologists were not in fact by Pre-Raphaelites, but rather by a group of their contemporaries and successors who were prepared to refer to the High Renaissance art of Michelangelo, Raphael, and others (which was, of course, strongly featured in the publications of the Arundel Society from 1849); as well as to modern French examples, in order to create a more full-blooded decorative style. Although Holman Hunt was commissioned in 1858 by W. J. Beaumont, the Ecclesiological sympathizer who was vicar of St Michael's church in Cambridge, to decorate its walls, this came to naught; a *Christ in Glory* surrounded by adoring angels who looked like Elizabeth Siddall, designed by the Pre-Raphaelite associate Spencer Stanhope for Christ Church, Cubitt Town in London, was meanwhile left to a secondary painter, F. A. Jackson of Ealing, actually to carry out, though Stanhope later decorated Marlborough College (Appendix B: 8). G. F. Bodley's church of St Martin at Scarborough was decorated with painting and stained glass by Burne-Jones, Rossetti, and Ford Madox Brown, with Philip Webb and William Morris providing its roof ornament, but some of its murals appear already by the later nineteenth century to have had to be repainted by another hand because their condition had deteriorated. Pre-Raphaelite religious painting seems to have been, in the event, an easel rather than a mural activity, despite (or perhaps, given its failure, because of) the Oxford Union experiment.

'IN THE PRESENCE OF THE ACTUAL SCENE': ARMITAGE, WATTS, LEIGHTON, HOLIDAY, AND POYNTER

There is no real sequel to Street's 1860 plea for church patronage for the Pre-Raphaelites to match that offered by the Oxford Union until the 'Neo-Pre-Raphaelite' style was employed by Henry Payne at Madresfield Court chapel in 1902, and in schemes of the 1900s by Henry Holiday and Harold Fayers (reported to be a pupil of Burne-Jones) (Appendix B: 7, 24). Instead, the new 'realism' in church murals from the late 1850s was created by Armitage, Watts, Leighton, Holiday

[25] T. G. Parry, 'Whitewash and Yellow Dab—No. III', *Ecclesiologist*, 20 (new series 17) (1859), p. 237.

[26] Ibid., p. 238. Parry's idiom was continued by his son Sidney's decoration of the chancel arch of All Saints, Friern Barnet, London.

[27] 'Twenty-first Anniversary Meeting' (see n. 20), p. 250. See also Street, 'The Future of Art' (n. 23).

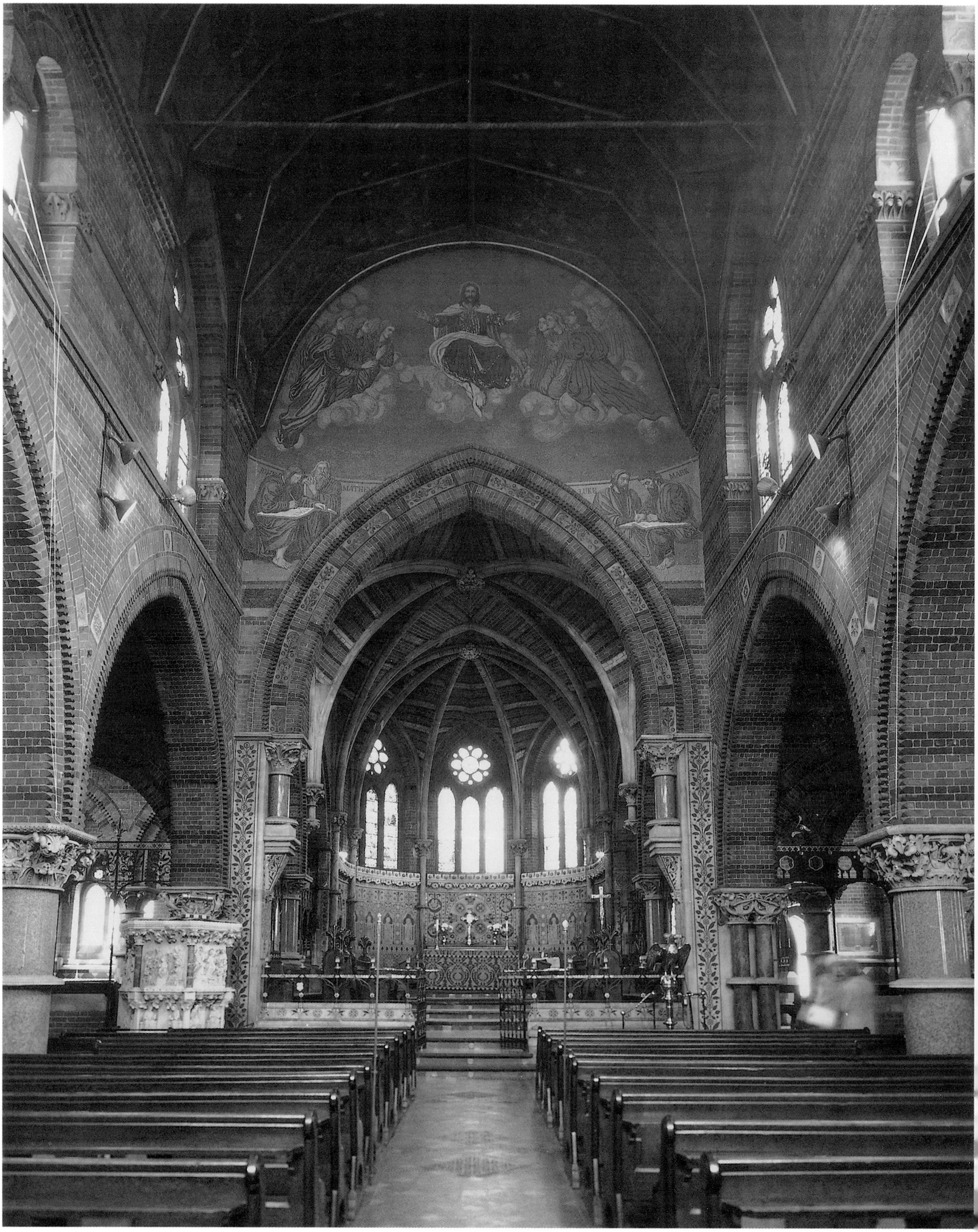

118. George Frederick Watts, *Saviour in Glory*, St James the Less church, Thorndike Street, Vauxhall, London, *c.*1860

in his early career, and Poynter, who all worked in either fresco or spirit fresco for patrons wealthy enough to afford the labour entailed by their styles and media. Meanwhile there were sporadic survivals of a Raphaelesque mode in the hands of imported Italian artists (Appendix B: 4).

Armitage's true frescoes of *St. Francis before Pope Innocent III* and *Christ and the Apostles* in St John's Roman Catholic church in Islington, painted in the 1860s(?), were the sequel to his fresco work at Westminster, but by 1870 were already 'under process of decay';[28] their style appears to have reflected his training in the *juste milieu* manner under Delaroche in Paris. The *Portfolio* admired how 'the spectator, as he looks at St. Francis and the Pope, feels himself not so much before a picture as in the presence of the actual scene.'[29] His work in this sense returned to the illusionistic tradition of Roman Catholic decoration exemplified earlier at St Mary Moorfields.

Watts, who produced designs at this period for St Paul's Cathedral, as well as a fresco of the *Saviour in Glory* at St James the Less in Vauxhall, London (a Street church) (Plate 118), seems also to have attempted a more atmospheric approach. The *Art Journal* noted that the *Saviour in Glory's* 'background is a dead yellow colour, to represent the gilded backgrounds of early Italian pictures', but also described how 'The figures rest on clouds, and the space beneath them is blue. It is intended that the whole should be light and floating, it contains therefore no heavy tones.'[30] This suggests a conscious contrast with the vibrant reds, blues, and pure gold of Dyce's style at Margaret Street, and Watts had been much enthused in 1845 by Michelangelo's Sistine Chapel frescoes, with their ethereal settings for *God Creating Adam.*

At Lyndhurst Parish Church in Hampshire, a Gothic Revival building by the Ecclesiologist William White in which a variety of Pre-Raphaelite glass was also installed, Leighton took up a theme—*The Wise and Foolish Virgins* (Plate 119)—which had been notably popular in German churches. Perhaps more forcibly even than Armitage and Watts, however, he created a new, quasi-theatrical presentation. Painted in spirit fresco in 1864 under technical instruction from Gambier Parry, his mural was a deliberate manifesto for the medium, but in place of the 'mystical' concept of the unity of image and location which inspired the Nazarene philosophy of working *in situ*, there is now a more dramatic interaction of painting and architecture. Just three metres long and nearly two and a half metres high, his mural forms a reredos so that the life-size figure of the Saviour as bridegroom, bearing a lily in the centre of the composition, acts as the immediate, radiant backdrop to the altar. He stands in a pool of light which seems almost to shine from Him, carried outwards by reflections on the angels' trumpets behind Him, and contrasting with the dark silhouette of the circular aedicule structure in which He stands. The Wise Virgins bring their lamps at His right and the Foolish ones are admonished by an angel at His left. The painted architecture gives an illusion of space opening off the east end of the church, whilst arches painted at the far right and left of the composition coincide with and extend the actual division of the wall space by the window immediately above the mural. The disposition of the Raphaelesque virgins as a frieze of elegantly draped, variously coloured figures leading the eye towards the centre from right and left nevertheless preserves a flat, decorative effect as does the shallow stage set created for the figures by the high wall against which they are arranged to right and left of the chapel structure in which Christ stands. Realistic symbolic emblems—an owl to represent sloth amidst the Foolish Virgins, a broken tree and a crack in the wall behind them which contrast with the fruiting tree and

[28] J. Beavington Atkinson, 'English Painters', *Portfolio*, 1 (1870), p. 52.

[29] Ibid., p. 51.

[30] 'Minor Topics of the Month', *Art Journal*, 7 (1861), p. 286.

sound wall on the Wise Virgins' side—guide the eye clearly to the meaning of the parable and show Leighton perhaps at his closest to the Pre-Raphaelite idiom.

Less successful is the Tree of Jesse decoration on the south wall and the angels to the right and left of the stained-glass window above Leighton's mural, which on his recommendation were entrusted to J. H. Pollen, an artist whose ceiling ornament at Merton College chapel in Oxford had reputedly inspired the murals he and other Pre-Raphaelites painted at the Oxford Union.[31] Attempting to combine somewhat crude facial realism with medieval vine-scroll ornament, Pollen's Tree of Jesse and window-frame decorations illustrate the dilemma which all too easily arose in the wake of the Ecclesiological debate over mural style. Elsewhere, when given free rein for his inclinations, Pollen designed an extraordinary neo-Byzantine Roman Catholic basilica with matching decor for J. H. Newman at Dublin University, believing the Gothic in fact to be inimical to Christian symbolism and thereby anticipating by nearly half a century the Byzantine revival at Westminster Cathedral.

Poynter's interest in fresco was probably aroused during his student years at Gleyre's atelier in Paris and he had known Leighton in Rome. At R. R. Banks's and Charles Barry's new church of St Stephen in Dulwich he was commissioned by H. A. Palmer, the incumbent's father-in-law, to paint *The Trial and Stoning of St. Stephen* and an extensive sequence of supporting murals illustrating the saint's life, which he completed between 1871 and 1873 (Plates 120, 121). Ingres's Autun Cathedral *Martyrdom of St. Symphorien* appears to have been his principal source,[32] although his scheme is now almost effaced.

Perhaps the nearest answer to Street's vision of Pre-Raphaelite church mural painting was in fact Henry Holiday's 1864 *Annunciation* for All Saints in Notting Hill, another William White church like Lyndhurst. This mural had a naturalistic garden setting with roses, lilies, and sunflower, and was reminiscent of Millais in its detail, but the figures remained firmly in the High Renaissance tradition admired by Holiday, rather than the more archaic mode used by Rossetti in his easel *Annunciation.* Holiday's later murals (Appendix B: 7), however, more properly form part of the Arts and Crafts Movement. If Street's ideas bore direct fruit in the nineteenth century, it was rather in terms of his emphasis that 'all the arts go hand in hand together,'[33] which laid the early foundations of the Arts and Crafts Movement.

Street's pupil William Morris gave focus to this ideal by setting up his firm in 1861, as a direct sequel to the Oxford Union mural experiment and in the very year that saw the demise of the Ecclesiological Society, but it produced far more stained glass than mural painting (Appendix B: 14), ousting the tired productions of the Munich glass artists hitherto favoured by the Anglo-Catholic Movement. Isolated Nazarene school murals continued to be commissioned (Appendix B: 2), but despite Parry's new spirit fresco medium and the example of Leighton, Poynter, and Watts, church mural painting by fine artists during the mid to late nineteenth century fell largely victim to the *crise de confiance* engendered by the difficulties with technique at Westminster. Although E. T. Parris had restored James Thornhill's mural paintings at St Paul's in 1853–6, mosaic (felt to be more durable than painting in a grimy urban environment) was thus favoured for the abortive scheme there by Alfred Stevens during the 1860s. Leighton and Poynter were asked to contribute to this, but Leighton's work can nevertheless be recognized as a bid, like his refusal to

[31] See Chapter 9.

[32] Noted by S.G. Wildman in *The Decorative Schemes of Sir E. J. Poynter* BA thesis (1974), Cambridge University, Dept. of History of Art. Plate 120 appears to be related to the St Stephen's scheme, even though in tempera (61 × 61 cm).

[33] G. E. Street, 'The Future of Art' (n. 23), p. 235.

countenance mosaic execution of his South Kensington lunettes soon afterwards,[34] to re-establish mural *painting*. His design *And the Sea Gave up the Dead* (intended for the dome) illustrates the Last Judgement and was inspired by Michelangelo,[35] marking a decisive departure from the Ecclesiological tradition of the medieval-style 'Doom'. Though the scheme came to nothing, Leighton developed his design as a painting (Plate 122)—which he noted was 'in the opinion of my friends the best I have ever made'—whose psychological intensity and remarkable visualization of the sea as if made of rock or stone (recalling Pater's comparison of Michelangelo's tonalities with Carrara marble)[36] make explicit its virtuosity as *painting*. Continued debate over the relative merits of mosaic and fresco eventually resulted in the mosaic decoration of 1891 by Sir William Richmond,[37] and despite Ruskin's advice in his *Seven Lamps of Architecture* that 'Pictorial subject, without . . . abstraction, becomes necessarily principal, or at all events, ceases to be the architect's concern; its plan must be left to the painter after the completion of the building, as in the works of Veronese and Giorgione on the palaces of Venice,'[38] ecclesiastical mural painting during the second half of the nineteenth century was principally the result of partnerships between Gothic Revival architects and the growing army of 'trade' rather than 'fine' decorative artists. These were often 'executants' who would either carry out designs prepared by the architect—a practice of both G. F. Bodley and J. L. Pearson, for example (Appendix B: 5, 6, 19)—or work to styles and models which by the 1890s were available in pattern books such as *The Art Decorator*. This was actually modelled on the German book *Dekorative Vorbilder*, which was much used on the Continent; also influential were the large, clear gestures of the figures in Schnorr von Carolsfeld's *Bilderbibel*, published in Britain in 1860. German influences in this sense remained remarkably prevalent, whilst the 'companies' evolved a distinctive, if often sadly debased and formulaic type of medievalism. Even though technical problems were in part overcome, a 'fine art' tradition of church mural painting as implied by Street's 'Pre-Raphaelite' ideal and seemingly heralded by the work of Armitage, Watts, Poynter, and Leighton, was probably in any case too expensive for most parishes, although the French painter Albert Besnard received a commission (Appendix B: 9), and the painter N. H. J. Westlake continued Raphaelesque effects into the 1900s (mainly in Roman Catholic churches, like St John the Baptist's in Brighton in 1916 (Plate 123), and for the architect J. F. Bentley (Appendix B: 25)). Because of their extensive involvement in nineteenth- and even twentieth-century ecclesiastical mural painting, it is thus helpful to look a little more closely at the nature of the 'trade' decorators' contributions, and their relationships with architects and 'fine' artists, even though their work was generally of only modest artistic quality.

THE CONTRIBUTIONS OF THE COMPANIES

Already in 1838, John Hardman of Birmingham had collaborated with Pugin to manufacture ecclesiastical fittings and metalwork, and by the 1850s mural painting was a regular part of the Hardman Company's operations.[39] The firm of J. G. Crace had actually carried out some work of a decorative nature at Highnam Church, but Hardman supplied its glass and became the decorator

[34] See Chapter 9.

[35] See S. Jones et al., *Frederic Leighton* (1996), p. 231.

[36] Ibid.

[37] See the debate over what D. S. MacColl termed the 'destructive decoration' of St Paul's in the April and May issues of the *Saturday Review*, 1899, and C. Harrison Townsend et al., 'Mosaic and Fresco', *Journal of the RIBA*, 3rd ser. 1, no. 8 (1893–4), pp. 245ff.

[38] Ruskin, 'The Lamp of Beauty', §XL, *The Seven Lamps of Architecture* (popular edition, London, 1906), p. 262.

[39] For the history of Hardman's, see J. Pope-Hennessy, *Victorian Church Art* (1971), p. 79.

preferred by its architect Woodyer in most of his other churches, such as St Nicholas's in Guildford (Appendix B: 17). Elsewhere, Clayton and Bell (Appendix B: 6), Watts and Company, Heaton, Butler and Bayne (Appendix B: 11) or Burlisson and Grylls were favoured, whilst other commercial church decorators included Charles James Lea[40] (Appendix B: 3, 10, 12, 13, 15). They were extraordinarily closely related: Richard Clayton, who had trained at the Royal Academy School of Sculpture and knew Rossetti, met Alfred Bell at the studio of Sir George Gilbert Scott, but by 1858–9, Bell was working with Heaton, Butler and Bayne, who had just started in practice. Holiday also undertook work for this company, whilst Joseph Aloysius Pippet, Hardman's chief artist, was a relative of J. H. Powell, who became Hardman's chief designer following Pugin's death in 1845 (Appendix B: 17). Bodley's partner Garner established Burlisson and Grylls to execute church decoration for himself and Bodley, but Burlisson was none other than Bell's son-in-law. The showcase of such firms was the great Ecclesiological Court at the 1862 International Exhibition in London, and they perpetuated styles which were essentially thirteenth- or fourteenth-century Gothic in inspiration, though simplified and sanitized to create vigorous pictorial Bibles, many in the evangelizing 'slum churches' of the Tractarian movement. Often making extensive use of stencilling, they were generally restricted in their colour range and 'very cheap', as the *Ecclesiologist* itself remarked.[41] Clayton and Bell's scheme at St Peter's, Vauxhall (Plate 124) a church built by Pearson for a poor district of London, is a good example; its pictures were attempted in fresco, but elsewhere, as at Garton-on-the-Wolds in Yorkshire, the company reverted to oil-based media (Plate 125) and at St Anne's in Derby they painted direct onto the raw bricks without any preparation of the surface. Such companies had little need for permanence; deterioration simply supplied more work in the form of restoration, as at Barton-upon-Irwell, where murals of 1865–8 by Joseph Pettit in Pugin's Roman Catholic church of All Saints, donated by the wealthy de Trafford family, were extensively repainted by Pippet of Hardman's in the 1890s in 'a type of oil'.[42] They include a highly stylized Annunciation clearly based on the strict thirteenth- and fourteenth-century models favoured by Pugin, but realism crept in even here in the form of portraits of Pugin, Newman, the parish priest, and the de Trafford family adoring the Lamb with Angels.

The products of this extraordinarily prolific commercial activity were somewhat cruelly satirized by *Punch* in 1851 in its description of a Tractarian parson with inclinations to 'Popery':

> With gold, and carving, and with paint
> His chancell he trick'd out,
> And many an olde wrynecked Saynt
> Pourtrayed the walles about.[43]

'Olde wrynecked Saynts' came in different shapes and sizes, however, and certain distinctive stylistic and iconographical trends can be identified amongst the various companies. At Garton-on-the-Wolds the Tatton Sykes family undertook extensive restoration of the medieval church of

[40] For Clayton and Bell's, see ibid.; R. Larkworthy, *Clayton and Bell Stained Glass Artists and Decorators* (Ecclesiological Society, London, 1984); and J. Allibone, *The Wallpaintings at Garton-on-the-Wolds* (Pevsner Memorial Trust, 1991). For Watts's, see. A. Symondson, 'Wallpapers from Watts and Company', *Connoisseur*, 24, no. 820 (June 1980), pp. 114–21; and for Lea (whose work was mostly non-figurative), G. K. Brandwood, 'Charles James Lea, Ecclesiastical Decorator', *Leicestershire Historian*, 3, no. 5 (1987), pp. 10–16.

[41] *Ecclesiologist*, 25 (1864), quoted in Pope-Hennessy, *Victorian Church Art*, p. 69. Many churches restricted their decoration to stencilled pattern-work and texts; typical examples are St Mary, Kilvington (*c.* 1852); and St Andrew, Caunton (*c.* 1869) (both Notts.).

[42] Information from Brian Cardy, who conserved the murals in 1991.

[43] 'Church Rats: A Ballad for the Day', *Punch*, 20 (1851), p. 184. I am grateful to Dr. G. K. Brandwood for bringing this to my attention.

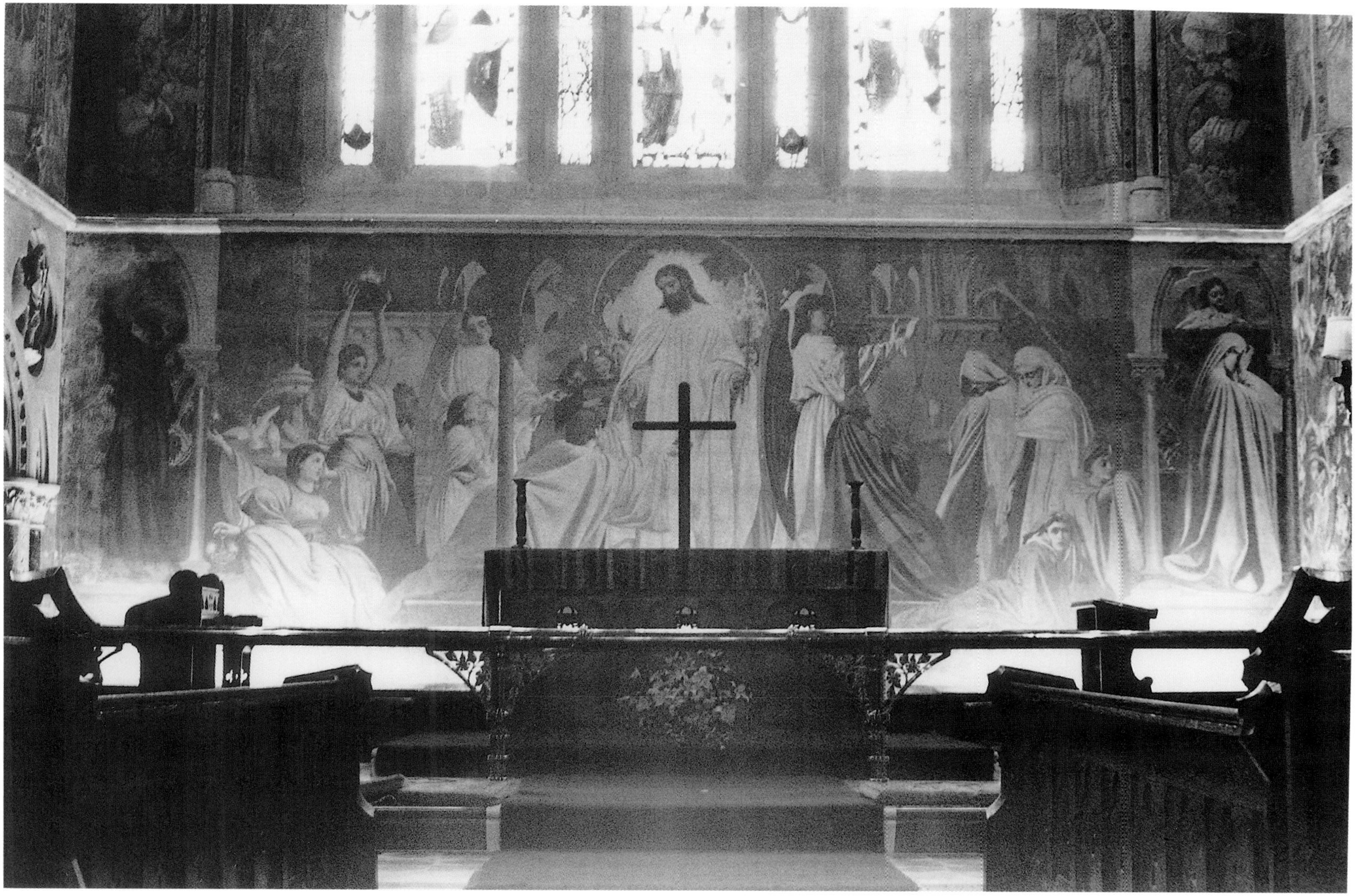

119. Frederic, Lord Leighton, *The Wise and Foolish Virgins*, St Michael and All Angels church, Lyndhurst, 1864

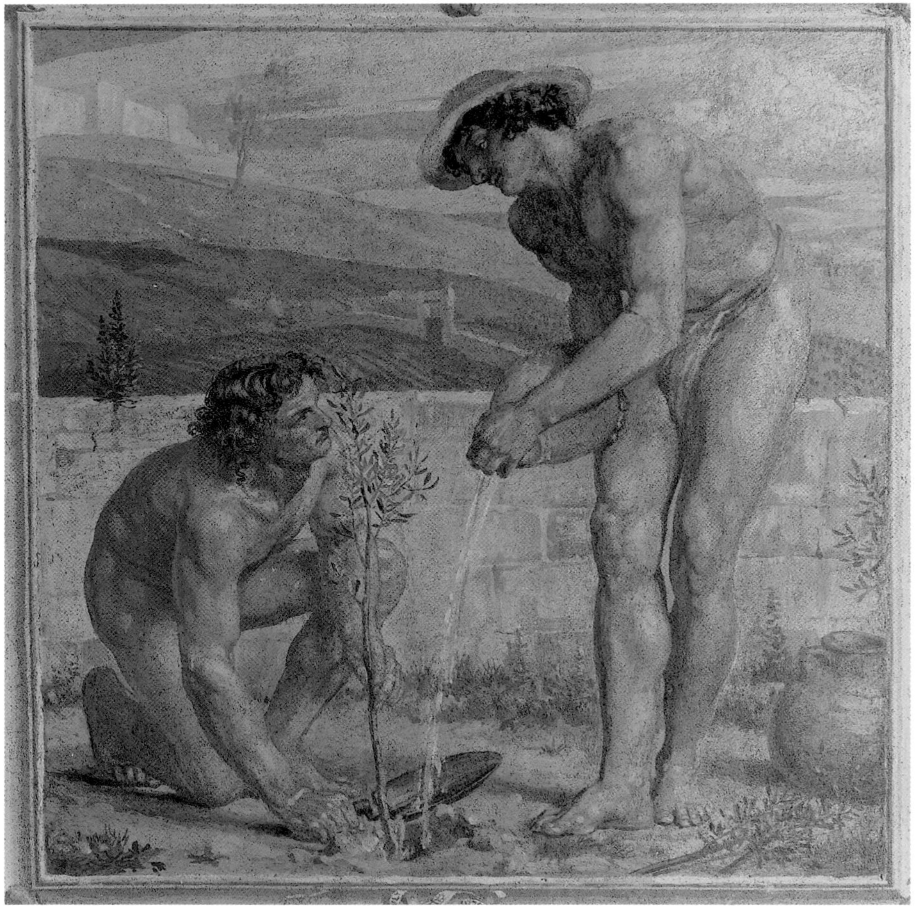

120. Sir Edward Poynter, *Paul and Apollos*, panel related to murals for St Stephen's church, Dulwich, 1872. Tempera. London, Tate Gallery

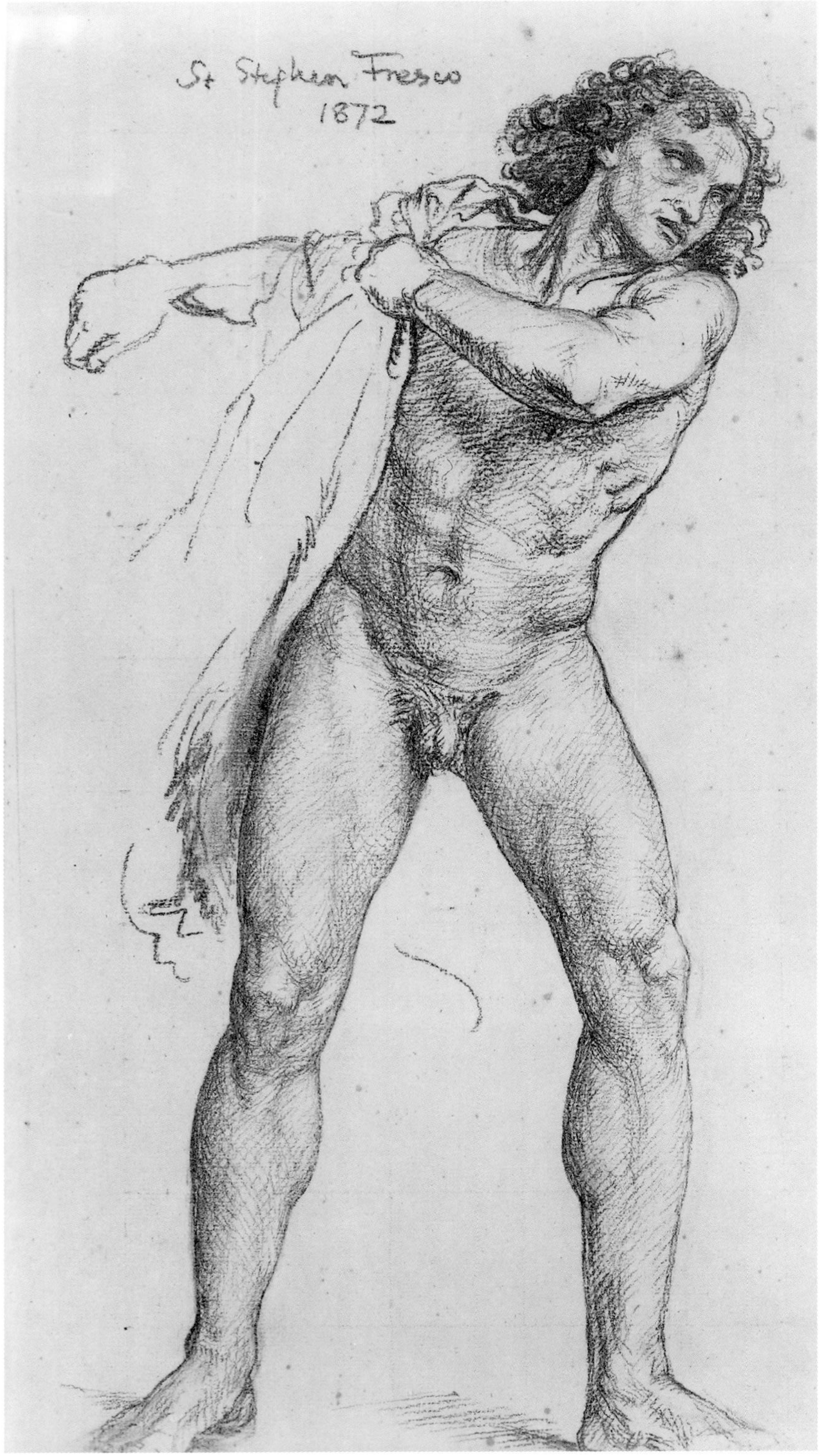

121. Sir Edward Poynter, figure drawing for fresco at St Stephen's church, Dulwich, 1872. London, Victoria and Albert Museum

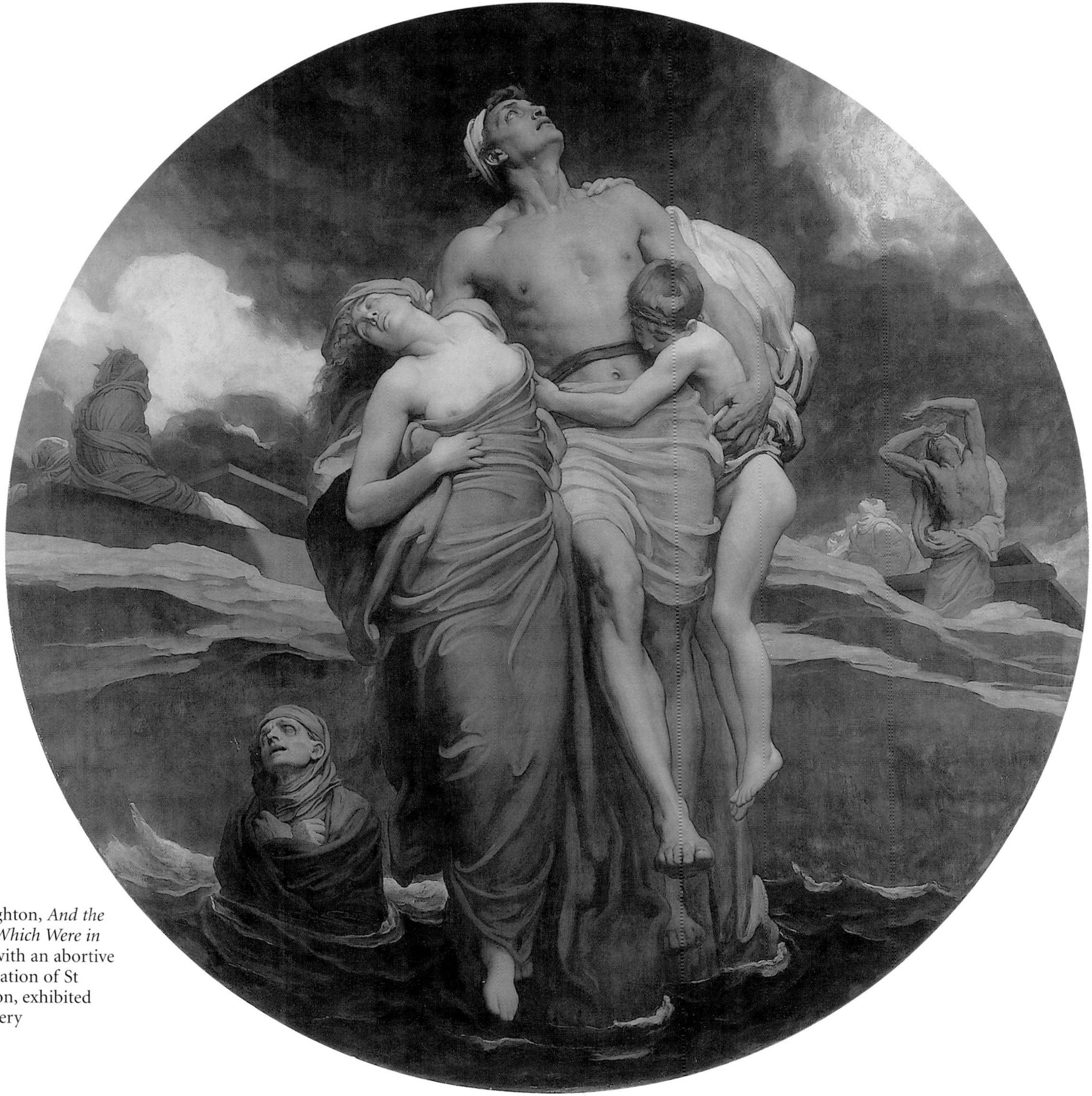

122. Frederic, Lord Leighton, *And the Sea Gave Up the Dead Which Were in It.* Painting associated with an abortive project for mural decoration of St Paul's Cathedral, London, exhibited 1892. London, Tate Gallery

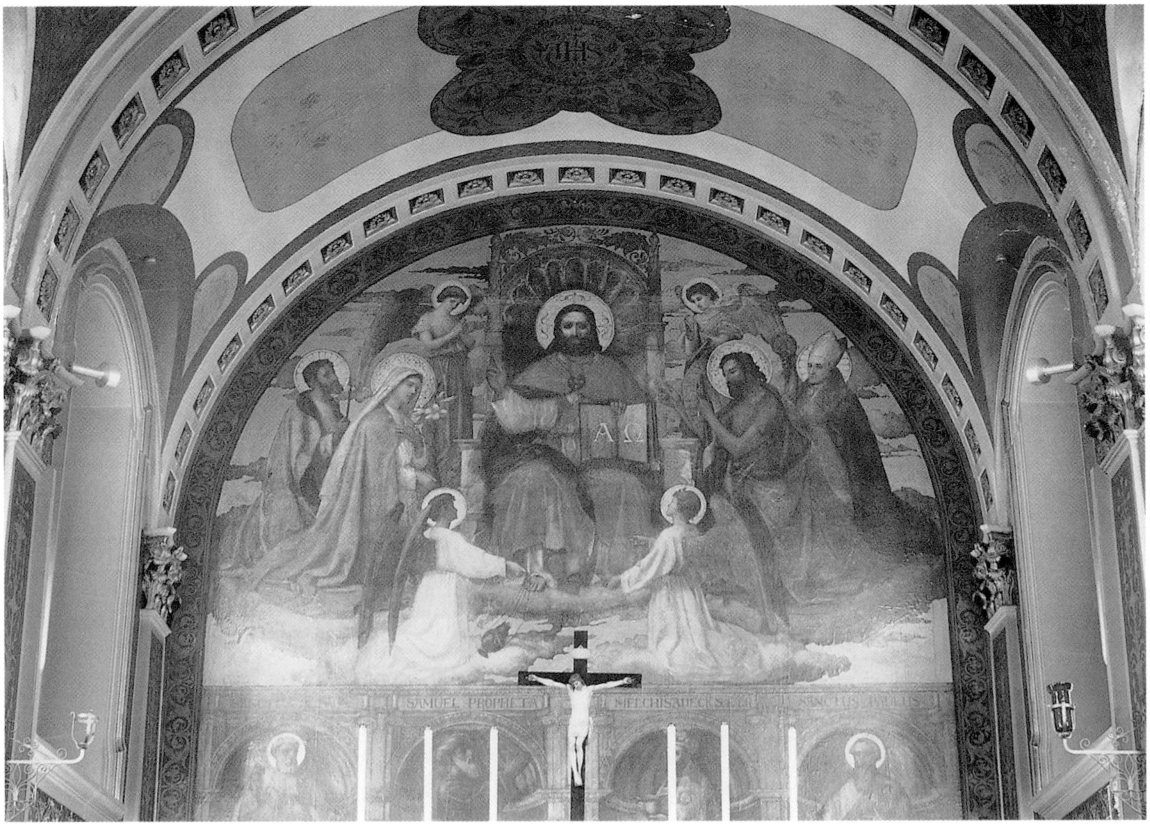

123. N. H. J. Westlake, detail of *Christ in Glory with Our Lady, St. Joseph, St. John the Baptist and St. Nicholas*, St John the Baptist church, Brighton, prior to 1916 (restored 1950s)

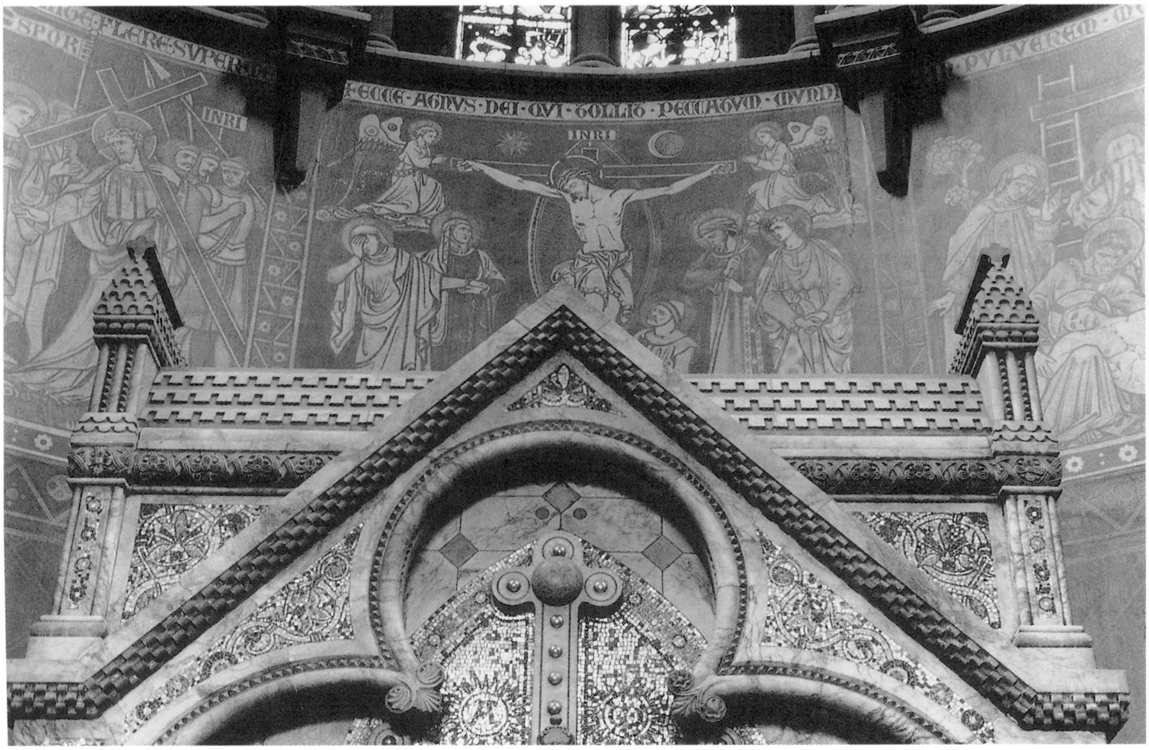

124. Clayton and Bell, detail of decoration, St Peter's church, Vauxhall, London, 1865

St Michael and All Angels, employing first J. L. Pearson and then G. E. Street as architects, and under Street, from 1865, an integrated scheme of decoration involving murals, mosaic flooring, stained glass, and furnishings was carried out by Clayton and Bell. This has now been restored in tribute to the late Sir Nikolaus Pevsner. The firm made no attempt to match the Norman architecture of the church beyond the use of trefoil round-arched aediculae; the fluttering draperies and complex figural incidents of the murals (Plate 125) belong more to the thirteenth, fourteenth, or even fifteenth centuries in their effects. Thus, the Tree of Jesse contained within a scrolling framework on the chancel arch is less a truly antiquarian facsimile than an emblem of the 'past' to which the Tractarians longed to return, and whose loss was vividly mourned by Carlyle: 'The living TREE Igdrasil, with the melodious prophetic waving of world-wide boughs . . . has died out into the clanking of a World-MACHINE. "Tree" and "Machine": contrast these two things.'[44] The lower walls show individual enthroned apostles and saints within painted architecture; the upper walls present essentially 'diagrammatic' representations, albeit it in medieval trappings, of Old and New Testament scenes to form typological oppositions between the two sides of the nave. 'Tree' and 'Machine', however, had become dangerously alike: regularity and a certain orderly predictability born of stencil technique soften the vigour and angularity of the medieval sources so that both faces and gestures are characterized by a 'modern' naturalism. Clarity of image and hence of the didactic programme had become the primary objective; inscribed scrolls carried by angels and others, and inscriptions within the dado frames reinforce the pictorial message. It is a vigorous but essentially functional style, which doggedly takes to its inexorable conclusion the distinction drawn in favour of art as 'idea' by both Beresford-Hope and Gambier Parry in the Ecclesiological discussion of realism in church decoration.

Pearson's St Peter's at Vauxhall was given a similar Clayton and Bell sequence around its apse at the same date (Plate 124), the linear drapery and open, clear gestures of the figures directly echoing the style of the sculptural angels which punctuate the frieze of episodes from the life of Christ, painted on regularly alternating blue and pink backgrounds. What the local congregation in this slum district made of the Gothic script texts in Latin is not recorded. Such a style was both shaped by and readily amenable to stencil, whose simplifications became even more didactic in the company's work at St Leonard's, Newland, Worcestershire, in the 1860s. Some spirit fresco was also employed here. By 1889, however, at churches like St Werburgh's at Hanbury near Stoke on Trent, Clayton and Bell had adopted a more complex style with heavier shading, angular draperies, and stylized sunbursts to suggest light emanting from Christ and John the Baptist, although the rather dull blue background was still preserved as at St Peter's. The company was one of the most prolific (Appendix B: 6); by the early twentieth century at St Peter's, Hersham, Surrey, its style had become intensely elaborate with sprocketed aediculae and stylized floral ornament all but squeezing the ornately draped saints and apostles from their places. For St Peter's in Bournemouth, whose architect was again Street, the cartoons of the Crucifixion for its chancel arch were prepared by the company in London and copied on to the wall in Bournemouth in 1873. Here a new technique was adopted, involving gelatine as an adhesive, which was mixed with the colours so that lime was unnecessary on the wall itself. This 'fresco' cost £150; further paintings on the theme of the Good Shepherd were added in the nave in memory of William

[44] T. Carlyle, *Heroes, Lecture V*, quoted in Willey, *Nineteenth Century Studies*, p. 126.

Wilberforce, Bishop of Winchester, who had done much to reconcile the extreme Tractarians and the Puseyites.

As this example reveals, production methods were changing, and so too was the iconography with its new memorial emphasis, although strictly Tractarian programmes still continued to be produced by all the companies as late as the 1880s and 1890s. At St Nicholas, Little Braxted, Essex, for example, the incumbent himself, the Revd Ernest Geldart, painted accomplished Tractarian murals in the companies' mediaevalizing idiom in 1884, whilst St Peter's Church at Hascombe in Surrey, built by Woodyer, the Highnam architect, was called 'a Tractarian work of art'[45] by Betjeman. Here, Heaton, Butler and Bayne realized an elaborate programme relating to St Peter in response to the High Church incumbent Vernon Musgrave's belief that 'The restoration and adornment of our Churches is not a mere aesthetic exercise, but a work mediately but surely tending to the good of souls.'[46]

The production of the designs in London by Bodley himself for St Peter's in Bournemouth is, however, of particular interest, because it marks the increasingly dominant role of the architect (Appendix B: 19). Street had already said in 1858, 'we should be better artists and greater men if we did a little less in architecture and more in painting,'[47] and it was Bodley in particular who in the later nineteenth century led a move towards a more eclectic but carefully controlled form of integrated interior, using selected artists under the umbrella firms of Watts and Company and Burlisson and Grylls, which his partner Garner had established. He had been an early friend of the Pre-Raphaelites at the Hogarth Club; not only did they work for him at St Martin's, Scarborough, but he also employed William Morris's firm at St Michael and All Angels in Brighton and All Saints in Cambridge as part of his attempt to improve the standard of church decoration. Nowadays, the Brighton church contains only a couple of enigmatic 'paper' murals, reputedly by a member of the congregation, but possibly cartoons, whilst All Saints has floral and diaper designs and texts derived from fifteenth-century sources, and a Christ in Majesty over the chancel carried out by C. E. Kempe, Arthur Hughes, and F. R. Leach, a Cambridge artist. These were designed by Bodley and reveal a far more florid style than Clayton and Bell's work, in details such as the red, almost flame-like angelic wing-feathers. Bodley also commissioned Morris and F. R. Leach to carry out the angels and foliage work on the ceiling of Jesus College chapel, Cambridge, in 1866; a letter from him to the Dean of the College reveals his close supervision of quality: 'I wd. say that Morris would find Leach a very capable & excellent executant. The design & the exact shades of the colours are all done according to the directions given to him.'[48] The most complete and ambitious decorative work by Bodley and Kempe is perhaps that at Tue Brook, Liverpool, in St John the Baptist's, where a tree of life bearing twelve 'manner of fruits', a Tree of Jesse, and much gilded low-relief plaster-work is to be found; other Kempe work includes that undertaken with W. H. Hughes in 1870–5 for a sizeable scheme (apparently devised by Lord Lanerton) of prophets and New Testament scenes at Castle Howard's chapel (Appendix B: 3).

The more naturalistic postures and plant, foliage, and flower details which characterize Bodley's approach can be clearly found in the work of his firm Burlisson and Grylls. At Holy Trinity church in Kilmarnock (Plate 126), for example, as a memorial to the son of the Houldsworth cotton-

[45] J. Betjeman, *Collins Guide to Parish Churches* (1980), p. 394, quoted in guide leaflet on *Church of St Peter, Hascombe.*

[46] Information kindly provided by Revd R. C. D. MacKenna of St Peter's Church, Hascombe.

[47] Street, 'The Future of Art' (n. 23), pp. 238–9.

[48] Quoted in D. Robinson and S. Wildman, *Morris and Company in Cambridge* (1980), p. 37.

manufacturing family, the company covered the nave walls with broad pictorial scenes rather than emblematic representations, replacing the tight rows of painted aediculae or bordered panels characteristic of Clayton and Bell with a more fluent, expressive narrative seen to best effect in the Palm Sunday procession illustration. Flowering and fruiting trees, partly stylized but still vigorously growing, contribute to the sense of light and life created by the clean bright blues, warm yellows, and pinky reds of the costumes on the white walls. More conventional scroll-work inscriptions and saints in diamonds decorate the upper walls and ceiling.

Although still working in the mediaevalizing mode, Heaton, Butler and Bayne were also venturing into more naturalistic details for garden settings in work like that at St Peter and St Paul's church, Luddesdown in Kent, by 1894. St Peter receives the keys of Heaven against a backdrop of wattle fencing and growing flowers also used behind figures by the company at Northaw Church in the 1890s. Although Bodley was dismissive of their work, it had presumably involved sufficient symbolism to meet the High Church needs of Beresford-Hope when in 1870 he employed them to paint the now whitewashed murals at Trinity College chapel, Cambridge. Stylization, albeit of a highly refined and richly decorative late medieval character, certainly persisted in the Hardman procession of Saints and Peter friezes at the Roman Catholic Cathedral of St Peter in Lancaster (Plate 127) in the early 1890s, and in work there by Eaton and Bulfield, a local firm. Shrigley and Hunt, on the other hand, also of Lancaster (Appendix B: 15), found some compromise with the sort of Heaton, Butler and Bayne plant naturalism in their 1897 decorations for St George's in Preston, which include the Adoration of the Lamb amid a decorative forest over the chancel, and reveal a more classical than strictly medieval figure type. Greater naturalism is apparent also in Cox and Sons' work (Appendix B: 13) for Norman Shaw, who was adamant on the need for 'a definite programme'[49] and deplored the piecemeal addition of decoration.

Despite such attempts on the part of the younger Gothic Revival architects to coordinate what was done to the walls of their creations, the very character of mural decoration as an attractive vehicle for memorial and commemoration, like stained glass, meant that totally coordinated schemes were rare. Individual donations of decorations, such as that in St Mary's at Long Ditton in Surrey, were much more common. Here, a Mrs Mitchell paid for a representation of the Ascension and other designs in 1909 in a church built by Street in 1878–80; the style seems even at this date to have been still the typical combination of sprocketed aediculae and linear draperies in a late Gothic manner beloved of many late nineteenth-century company painters, a combination which was, of course, completely alien to the Pre-Raphaelite 'realism' for which Street had argued so forcefully back in 1858.

As early as 1867, Bodley had complained about what he felt to be the variable quality of so much company work, commenting to the Dean of Jesus College, Cambridge, when urging the employment of Morris's firm, 'it is a great lottery what you would get from Hardman now.'[50] His own establishment of Burlisson and Grylls was, of course, an attempt to remedy this situation, but Hardman's archives offer a unique insight into the kind of commercial pressure which by the late nineteenth century meant that a wide range of artistic hands could be working for the same company, with equally variable results, whilst only the most prestigious commissions were reserved for the most talented painters. Even Joseph Aloysius Pippet, the principal artist employed

[49] Quoted in A. Saint, *Richard Norman Shaw* (New Haven and London, 1976), p. 301.
[50] Quoted in Robinson and Wildman, *Morris and Company*, p. 38.

by the firm (and, as his work at St Nicholas in Guildford shows, an accomplished exponent of 'commercial' Gothic), was put under strong pressure by Hardman by the 1890s to delegate work. Writing to Pippet in 1891, Hardman complained that

> Mr. Pugin was in a very bad way indeed when I told him that you cannot do the paintings of the S[acred] H[eart] Church, L'pool by the time they are wanted, and I could not give him any date for the completion of those for Widnes. He says he has other works in contemplation but that it is useless coming to us and he must look to other artists.
>
> From Mr. Pugin's I went to look upon? [illegible] and found Watts in despair about the Providence reredos and the Walthamstow ditto—the Dean writes to ask whether we can send out the former in June!! and the parson at Walthamstow is in a dreadful state because we can't provide the whole of his for September—
>
> All this points to the absolute necessity of a change in your method of working—I have spoken to you many times about it . . . the difficulties will always remain until you give up wanting and trying to do all the work yourself—the power of work of one man is limited and this accumulation will always be hanging over me (if we get orders) until you take to making use of others and confine your work to directing them—at times perhaps assisting them or touching up their work—but leaving off actually doing the work yourself.[51]

Pippet seems in fact already to have been 'using others', since a letter to an artist called Tipping says 'I think you know exactly the style of drawing Mr. Pippet wants viz the figures only without accessories or details,'[52] but when it came to the important work at the Guildhall in London for Sir Stuart Knill, for whom Hardman's had already carried out murals in St Mary's church at Greenwich and at Southwark Cathedral, poor Pippet was summoned to execute the decoration personally to ensure the standard expected. Within a year or two he was, in contrast, being expected to travel to locations as far away as Edinburgh and Glasgow to tout for further commissions.[53]

In 1892, for 'Decorating the church in a simple manner with emblems and Monograms of Our Lady', 'Decorating the Chancel in Oil', and 'Decorating the Nave in Destemper [*sic*]' at St Mary's in Pollokshaws, Glasgow, Pippet was paid £120,[54] and in 1893, for a variety of repairs and the repainting of two subjects at Barton-upon-Irwell, £400.[55] Such rates were substantially less than the £110 paid by Lord Lanerton in 1870–5 for one smallish mural alone to W. H. Hughes of Morris and Company at the Castle Howard chapel;[56] it is not surprising that Pippet was loth to delegate.

THE ARTS AND CRAFTS MOVEMENT

The trend begun by Bodley and Shaw towards a more imaginative unity of art and architecture reached its climax in the late nineteenth- and early twentieth-century work of the Arts and Crafts adherents (Appendix B: 5, 18, 22–4, 26–8), including that of E. R. Frampton, John Duncan, and Gerald Moira. In Edinburgh during the 1880s and 1890s, Phoebe Traquair drew on Rossetti's and William Blake's styles to evolve a personal interpretation of the Gothic Revival mode in murals for the Mortuary Chapel of the Sick Children's Hospital, St Mary's Cathedral Song School, and the

[51] Letter from J. Hardman to Pippet (22 May 1891), Letter Book Hardman 91, HA(B).

[52] Ibid., letter from Hardman to Tipping (9 Feb. 1891).

[53] Ibid., letter from Hardman to Pippet (28 Feb. 1895).

[54] Decoration Day Book (1893), Order 138, p. 11, Hardman 65, HA(B).

[55] Ibid., Order 175, p. 14.

[56] Chapel Accounts, G6/1, CHA; these also show that C. E. Kempe, who had overall responsibility for the scheme of decoration in the Chapel, was paid a total of £2,217. 8s.

Catholic Apostolic church in Mansfield Place (a building by Rowand Anderson). Her slightly naïve, overtly hand-painted (as opposed to commercially stencilled) designs, covering every inch of the wall surfaces, include portraits of her heroes Ruskin and Carlyle in conjunction with illustrations of the Psalms and St Matthew (at the Hospital) and of Carlyle and Morris in illustrations of the *Benedicite* (at the Song School) (Plate 128). Ruskin lent her thirteenth- and fourteenth-century manuscripts, and their motifs are reflected in her hybrid imagery of pictorial and emblematic motifs, which none the less remains close to commercial decorators' neo-medievalism. This approach persisted as late as 1922 in her memorial for the Manners family at their chapel (built by Detmar Blow) at Thorney Hill in Hampshire, which, along with the Song School, perhaps shows her at her best.[57] Less wilfully 'primitive' and far more compositionally assured are the rhythmic, decoratively outlined scenes from the story of King David in another Rowand Anderson building, St James's Episcopal church in Edinburgh, by Traquair's fellow member of the Decorative Section in the Edinburgh Social Union, William Hole. The Union was a philanthropic group much concerned with design reform and the promotion of the crafts. Again, Hole's work both at St James's (Plate 129) and in the early twentieth century at St Ninian's in Glasgow (Plate 130) was a form of modified naturalism within a medieval format, in harmony with his architectural setting, but by 1906–12, in his Life of Christ panels at St John's Episcopal church in Forres, he had evolved an essentially pictorial treatment with atmospheric and chiaroscural effect probably influenced by his travels in the Holy Land.[58]

Both Traquair and Hole espoused the practice of work *in situ*, though neither used true fresco, but rather oil-based or (in Traquair's case at the Song School) watercolour-related media. Edward Aveling Green was one of the few to continue the use of Gambier Parry's spirit fresco materials through his decorations of 1892–4 in St Michael's in Derby (now destroyed). These appear to have been of a more classical than Gothic tendency with strong figural forms and gestures; he also carried out work for the Duke of Bedford at Eversholt in Buckinghamshire, and murals at East Budleigh in Devon. Fresco in Britain remained a questionable entity in the wake now not only of the Westminster fiasco but also of the decay in Armitage's and Watts's church murals in London. Despite the Arts and Crafts Movement's belief in truth to materials, there was no real parallel to the Continental revival of fresco in ecclesiastical schemes at the *fin de siècle* by the Beuron monastery artists and by Maurice Denis, although in the early twentieth century Angela Latham of the Society of Mural Decorators and Painters in Tempera studied with Denis, presumably in his Ateliers d'Art Sacré.[59] Frederic Shields used fresco for two external lunettes in the Chapel of the Ascension at Bayswater, London, but his murals inside (Plate 131) were 'fixed to the wall'.[60] This project was one of the most ambitious Arts and Crafts ecclesiastical schemes, occupying Shields from 1887 to 1910 and painted for Mrs Russell-Gurney, with the encouragement of Octavia Hill, in a building purpose-made by Herbert Horne. Intended to give 'body, mind and spirit oppressed with the hurrying roar of the city's life . . . repose and a refreshing feast ever liberally spread upon

[57] For Traquair's murals, see E. Cumming, *Phoebe Anna Traquair 1852–1936* (National Galleries of Scotland, 1993); *Builder* (2 April 1892), p. 259 (Song School) and *Magazine of Art* (1895), p. 198 (Catholic Apostolic Church).

[58] For Hole's work see Mrs. Hole, *Memories of William Hole RSA by his Wife* (London and Edinburgh, 1920) (p. 83 for St James's).

[59] The Beuron work was none the less reported to the Society of Mural Decorators and Painters in Tempera (see J. Batten (ed.), *Papers*, vol. 2 (1925)); for Latham's connection with Denis, see M. Sargant-Florence (ed.), *Papers*, vol. 3 (1936), p. 68.

[60] See E. Miles, *The Life and Letters of Frederic Shields 1833–1911* (London, 1912), pp. 324, 326. The scheme was reported in the *Magazine of Art*, 21 (1898), p. 455.

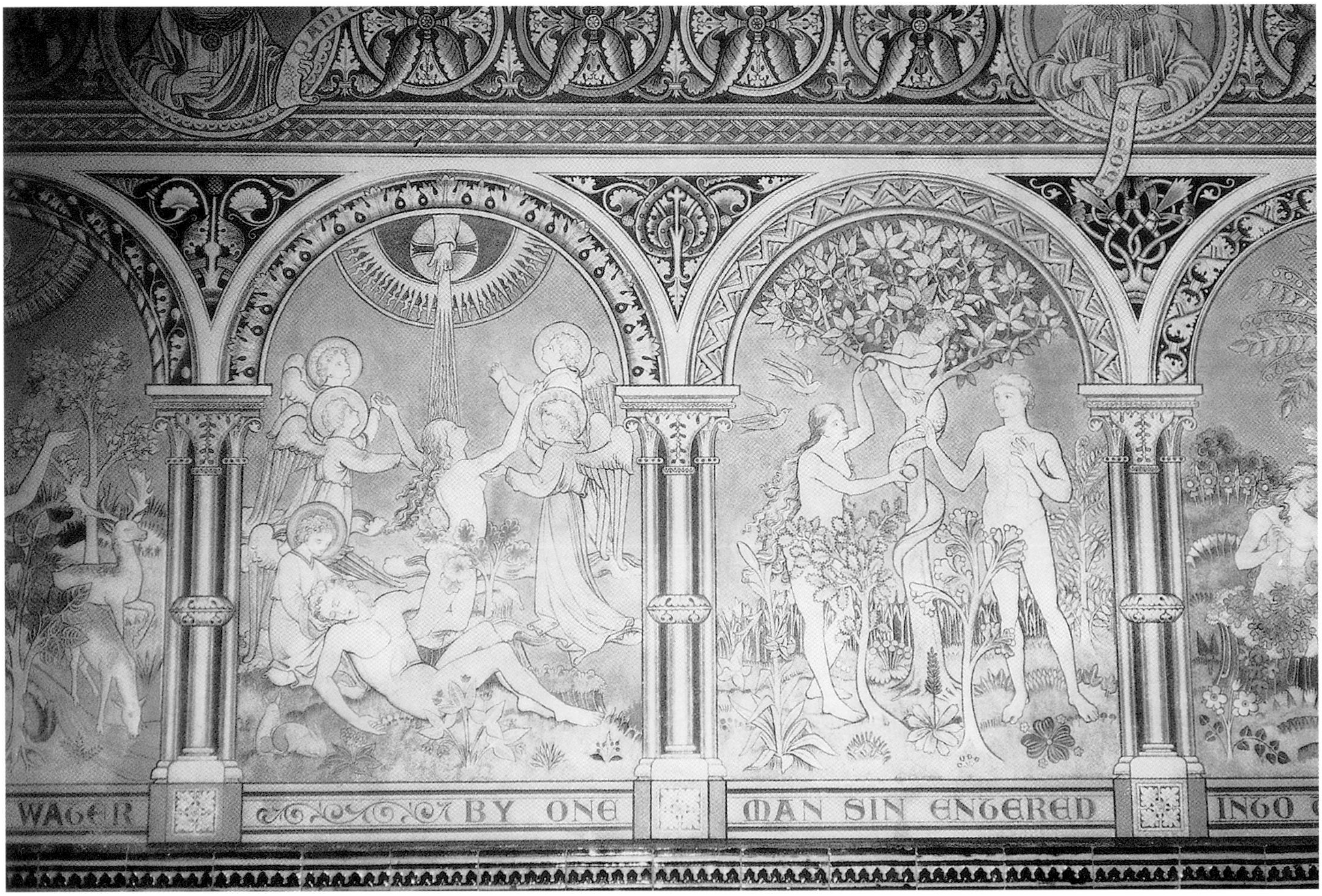

125. Clayton and Bell, detail illustrating *The Fall of Man*, St Michael and All Angels church, Garton-on-the-Wolds, 1872–9

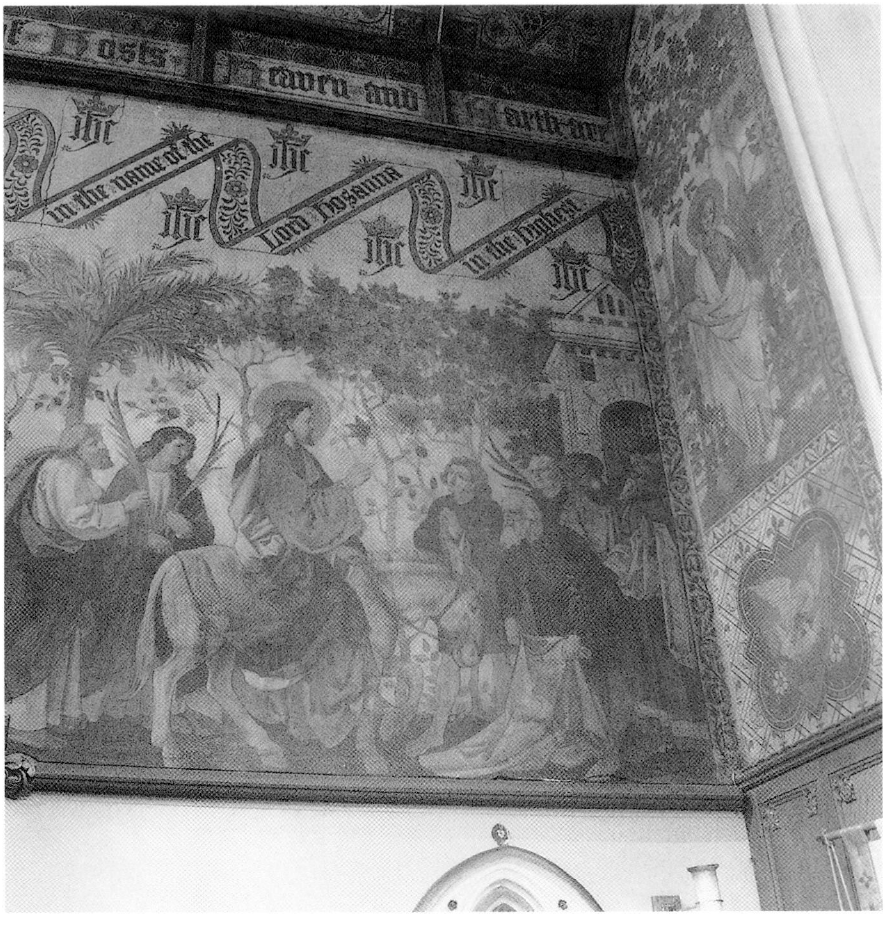

126. Burlisson and Grylls, *Palm Sunday Procession*, Holy Trinity church, Kilmarnock, Ayrshire, *c.* 1870s/1880s

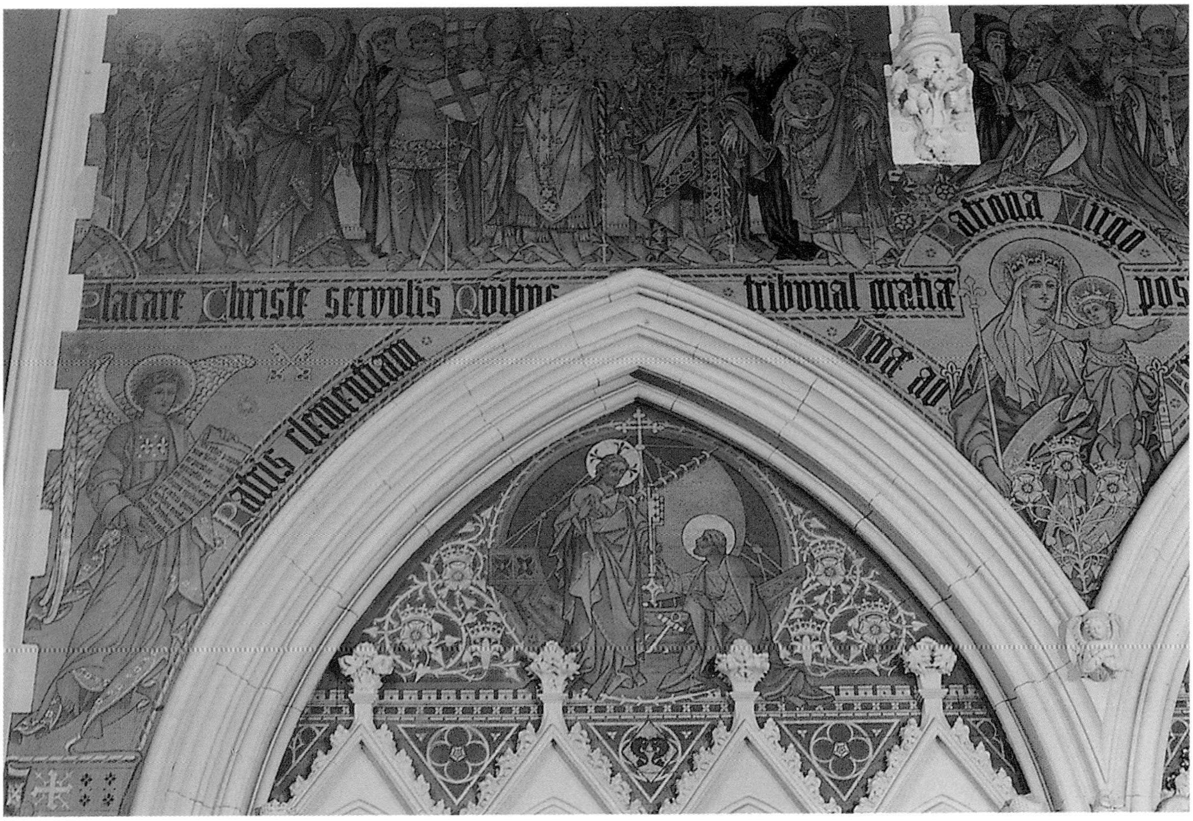

127. J. Hardman and Company, *Our Lady enthroned with St. Peter* (roundel) and procession of women saints, nave of St Peter's Roman Catholic Cathedral, Lancaster, post 1893

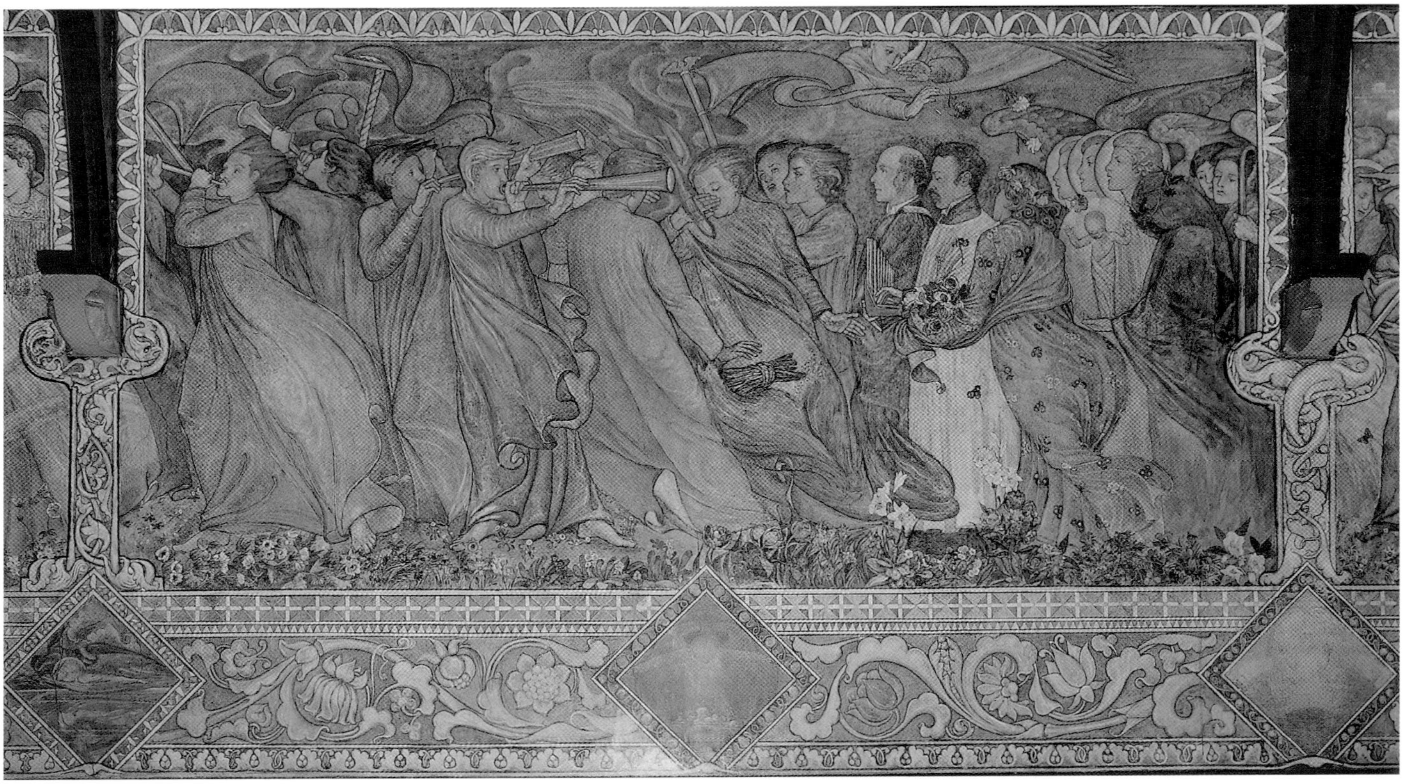

128. Phoebe Traquair, *O Ye Winds of God, O ye Fire and Heat, O Ye Summer and Winter*, detail from *Benedicite Omnia Opera*, south wall, St Mary's Cathedral Song School, Edinburgh, *c.*1889–90

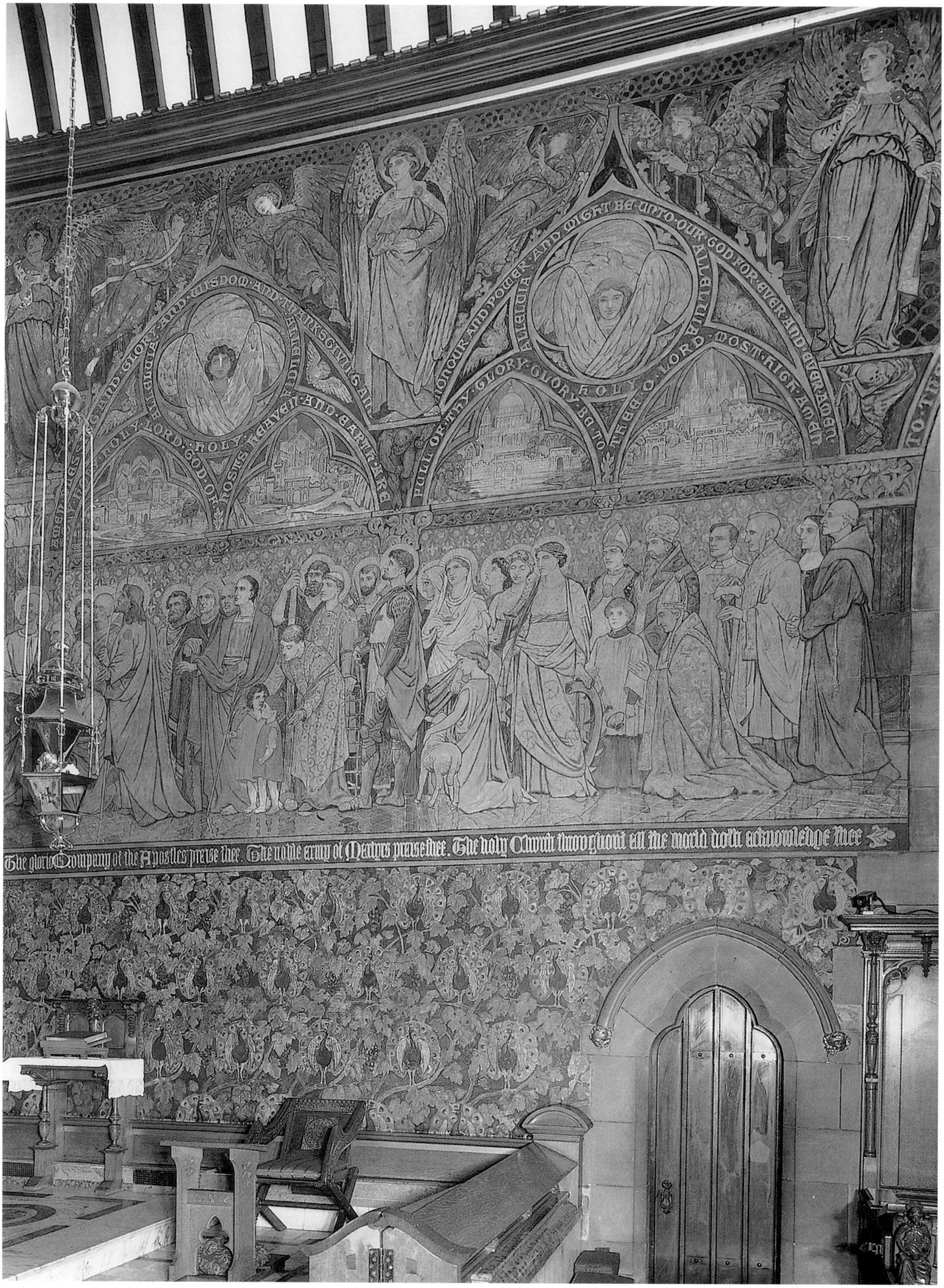
HONOUR AND POWER AND MIGHT BE UNTO OUR GOD FOR EVER AND EVER AMEN
FULL OF THY GLORY GLORY BE TO THEE O LORD MOST HIGH AMEN
The glorious Company of the Apostles praise thee. The noble army of Martyrs praise thee. The holy Church throughout all the world doth acknowledge thee

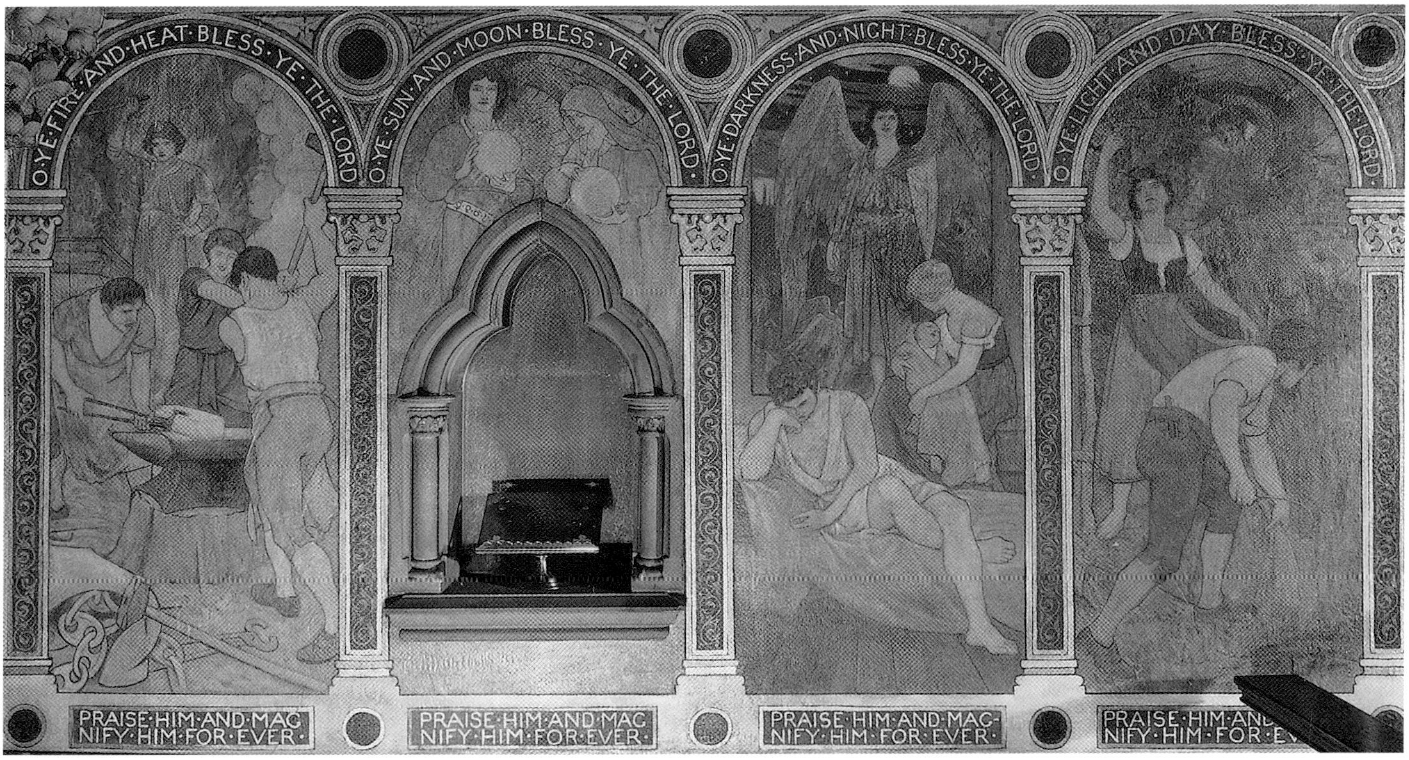

130. William Hole, detail from *Benedicite Omnia Opera*, St Ninian's Episcopal church, Pollokshields, Glasgow, *c.*1890s/1900s

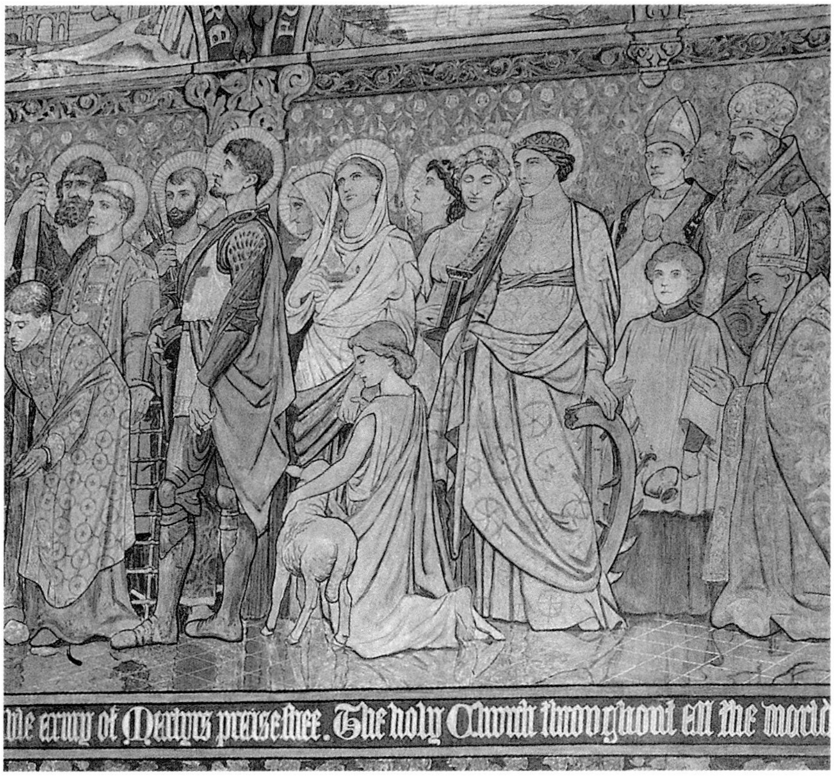

129. Facing page: (a) William Hole, *The Glorious Company of the Apostles Praise Thee* . . . part of mural decoration, St James the Less Episcopal church, Inverleith Row, Edinburgh, begun 1890s and completed 1902; Left: (b) detail

its walls'[61] the chapel and the arrangement of the murals were modelled on the Arena chapel which Shields and Horne had visited at Padua in Italy, but the dynamic, muscular figures of Shields's scheme of 'Prophets and Apostles, Christian virtues and worldly vices, Gospel and Apostolic history, types and symbols'[62] owe more to Michelangelo and Blake than early Italian art, and won Watts's admiration. The huge Ascension subject above the altar must have been the expression of Shields's personal fear of 'the thought of blind darkness . . . to a painter who truly sees . . . . But worse infinitely is the blindness of man's spirit . . . "The entrance of Thy Word giveth Light."'[63]

Other work in the Arts and Crafts idiom includes that by John Duncan and Gerald Moira (Appendix B: 26, 27), and the scheme, now destroyed, by Christopher Whall for Douglas Castle chapel.[64] One of the most extensive of any ecclesiastical schemes is W. P. Starmer's decoration, painted *in situ* and begun in 1912, in Lutyens's church of St Jude's, Hampstead Heath, London (Plate 132). Despite Lutyens's wish that his brick basilica should stand as an independent work of architecture, with bare white plaster walls, it was offered as a location for murals in one of the competitions which accompanied Geddes's Crosby Hall mural exhibition of 1912.[65] The church had connections with Canon Barnett and Starmer's work falls heir to Barnett's disciple Geddes's vision of the inspirational role of mural painting in modern society.[66] The Lady Chapel decoration, unveiled by the Princess Royal and in part a War Memorial, includes portraits of Florence Nightingale, Elizabeth Fry, Katherine Booth, and others framing one of the ceiling domes; its juxtaposition of women from all ages in illustration of female ministry clearly echoes the kind of synthetic and symbolic vision of past into present which Geddes had earlier fostered.[67] Individual portraits on the walls of Biblical women, framed by painted texts and small figural motifs, have a rhythmic, firmly outlined and subtly lit style in which the graceful poses and simplified backdrops recall Alphonse Mucha's art. Although echoes of this recur in the rest of the church decoration, it is marred by more pedestrian compositions in some of the wall panels, which are devoted to different Biblical images of the Kingdom of Heaven; the huge barrel-vaulted roof is decorated with a dramatic 'processional' sequence of painted arches and domes illustrating the Life of Our Lord. Starmer's murals were included in the 1939 Tate Gallery exhibition of photographs and designs of what was felt to be the best in British mural painting since the First World War; he completed the St Jude's work only in 1945 with a commemorative panel for the church's second vicar's son, who was lost in the *Benares* disaster.

Rather than pursue true fresco or variants carried out on plaster, like Starmer's or Aveling Green's media, the Arts and Crafts Movement tended to experiment with alternative means to integrate decoration with architecture. A number of significant church schemes of the 1890s and 1900s consequently fall outside the scope of the present survey, such as the mosaic work by the Art Workers' Guild member F. Hamilton Jackson at Henry Wilson's St Bartholemew's in Brighton; that at St Paul's Cathedral by Sir William Richmond and by Boris Anrep at Westminster Cathedral; and perhaps most notably of all, the remarkable apse decoration of 1912 by Brangwyn at St Aidan's in Leeds. Such schemes reflected the new preoccupation of architects with Byzantine

[61] Miles, *Frederic Shields*, p. 296.

[62] Ibid., p. 313.

[63] Ibid., p. 344.

[64] See the *Builder* (1 Sept. 1894 and 28 Mar. 1896) and *RIBA Journal* (1896), pp. 369–76.

[65] See Chapter 9.

[66] See Chapter 9. Muirhead Bone appears also to have been commissioned around 1918–19 to carry out a large frieze for St Jude's, but he did not take this up.

[67] See Chapter 9.

and Romanesque styles; in church mural painting the most striking example of the trend is perhaps Sir William Richmond's 1896 *Alpha and Omega* apse decoration at Christ Church in Cheltenham (Plate XXVIII). More closely related to mural painting were the coloured plaster decorations carried out during the 1890s in richly Art Nouveau vein by Mary Watts, wife of G. F. Watts, in the memorial chapel to her husband in Compton;[68] and by Gerald Moira in the library and vestry of Ullet Road Unitarian church, Liverpool. Both schemes include a Tree of Life and personifications; Moira's of the Virtues (Temperance pouring wine from an earthenware flask into a river, Fortitude with a sword on her lap, and so on) look forward to the more classically based iconography which became his forte in later painted schemes, such as those at Lloyd's Register of Shipping and the Old Bailey. Sgraffito (Appendix A) was employed by Heywood Sumner in a series of church commissions, including St. Mary's at Llanvair, Kilgeddin in Wales (where the *Benedicite* theme also used by Traquair offered, like the Tree of Life at the Compton Watts Chapel, an appropriate vehicle for the Arts and Crafts fascination with nature and creation) (Appendix B: 18). Sir William Reynolds-Stephens' murals for Harrison Townsend's church of St Mary the Virgin at Great Warley in Essex are perhaps the most famous of this group of Art Nouveau-related decorative schemes, whilst in Harrison Townsend's church of St Martin's at Wonersh in Surrey, a variant of the water-glass used earlier at Westminster was used by the American artist Anna Lea Merrit.[69]

Amongst the most vocal in support of 'art' in church architecture as opposed to the products of the decorative companies was the Arts and Crafts architect J. D. Sedding, who employed numerous craftsmen in his Holy Trinity church in Sloane Street, London in the 1890s. Fighting what he called the 'fatal notion that Art is a thing to be applied', he issued the challenge

> Are there no dead walls in our cathedrals and parish churches to be made alive by bas-reliefs and paintings? Have you no trumpery 'ecclesiastical art' reredoses to remove? Will you not prefer a good picture or sculpture to the glaring tiles and marbles, and 'holy beetles' and scribbled monograms that no one understands . . . it speaks volumes that the reredos of St. Paul's—one of the costliest pieces of sculpture of the century—should go, as a matter of course, to Messrs Farmer and Brindley, while the successors of Flaxman and Stevens are never thought of![70]

If the decoration in his own churches in fact remained fairly narrowly within a Gothic Revival mode—for example, at St Mary's in Stamford with its sub-Burne-Jones angels within panelling, emblematic vines, and Gothic initials—two Arts and Crafts-related ecclesiastical mural schemes provided a deeply individual and subtle answer to his impassioned pleading. These are Henry Payne's in the chapel of Lord Beauchamp's residence at Madresfield Court in Worcestershire, and Sir Frank Brangwyn's in the chapel of Christ's Hospital in Sussex.

The Madresfield Chapel was the inspiration for the one in *Brideshead Revisited*, by Evelyn Waugh, and the response to it there, from the character Charles Ryder, is simply 'Golly.' One of Ashbee's Guild of Handicraft likened its decoration to 'a barber's pole and an ice cream barrow'[71] and it is certainly one of the most complex and colourful ensembles of mural painting, stained

[68] Mrs Watts later created coloured gesso decoration in the Cambridge Military Hospital Memorial Chapel as a First World War Memorial.

[69] 'Keim's process' (see Appendix A) was also used by Shields in his Bayswater Chapel and by Brangwyn; it was described by J. A. Rivington in the *Journal* of the Society of Arts, 32 (1884), pp. 245–57. For Mrs Lea Merrit's scheme, see C. Harrison Townsend et al., 'Mosaic and Fresco' (n. 37), p. 248. She also painted 'frescoes' in St Martin's church, Chilworth (see the *Magazine of Art* (1895), p. 22).

[70] Quoted in A. Service, *Edwardian Architecture and its Origins* (Architectural Press, 1975), p. 271.

[71] Quoted in C. Aslet, *The Last Country Houses* (New Haven and London, 1982), p. 250.

glass, carved ornament, and metalwork created in the entire Arts and Crafts Movement. Begun in 1902 within an architectural context created some forty years before by P. C. Hardwick, the mural work (Plates 133, 134) was not completed until the early 1920s; the barber's pole quip alludes to Payne's red and white striation of the rib vaults. Payne was meanwhile chosen by Lord Beauchamp for his Palace of Westminster East Corridor mural and, like this, his Madresfield chapel reveals the distinctive Birmingham 'Neo-Pre-Raphaelite' style; it also used Southall's preferred medium of tempera, rather than fresco. In a sense, through his assimilation of traits from the Flemish and German primitives collected by Beauchamp and revered by Southall, Payne thus realized the decorative ideal which Norman Shaw recorded as being Bodley's in his battle against the companies: 'Do please let us revert to the earlier and purer character of painting . . . to the Van Eyck school, with its lovely diapers and drapery.'[72]

The chapel decoration was commissioned by Lady Beauchamp as a wedding present to her husband. Beauchamp had High Church sympathies and was a trustee of St Alban's at Conybere Street, Birmingham, where murals believed to be by Italian artists were also installed at this period. Payne's conception of the earliest portion of his Madresfield painting, on the east wall behind the reredos (itself designed by Birmingham School colleagues), thus not surprisingly falls heir to the conventional Anglo-Catholic Gothic of Hardman's, which was, of course, a Birmingham company. Christ in a mandorla, his feet on a rainbow, surmounts a tree of life, with profile angels disposed symmetrically amidst its stylized branches and a host of frontal angels framing the mandorla. Beneath, and to the right and left of the reredos, Payne began to evolve his mature style through a more naturalistic, Van Eyckian effect of pristine detail. It is this style which gives the tiny chapel its extraordinary, even claustrophobic, intensity. Lady Lettice Beauchamp and her husband kneel as in early Renaissance donor portraits (Plate 133), but against a frieze-like backdrop of intricately rambling red roses on a trellis, which continues around the other walls to convert the entire chapel into a *hortus conclusus*. In the shallow space before the trellis are placed St Michael, the Virgin and Child, and the Lygon children (Plate 134), who were born as the chapel painting proceeded, and who remain captured in eternal childhood just as the carpet of minutely observed garden flowers covering the ground preserves a timeless spring. Above the gallery on one side wall, this carpet is repeated to form a setting for a cameo of two children reading a book; angels hover and the design is clearly a visual rebus for the Beauchamp family motto 'My field is fair.' A description of the decoration, presumed to be by Payne, elucidates its specific reference to the Beauchamp wedding with a quotation from the Song of Solomon 'A Garden enclosed is my sister—my spouse' and goes on to emphasize the unity of the painting not merely with the architecture, but beyond it with the world:

> Through the open window steals the scent of blue-spiked lavender and jessamine with stars of white; the litany of gentle doves rises heavenward to the music of the hummingbees . . . every flower turns its face in praise of God . . . And the walls within have caught the glory of the world outside.[73]

This synaesthetic paean underlines the complexity of symbolic resonance to be found in the decoration and prepares us for the layers of allusion in the East Corridor mural scheme at Westminster, where Payne's subject was, of course, *Plucking the Red and White Roses in the Old Temple Gardens* (Plate XIV).

[72] Quoted in Saint, *Norman Shaw*, p. 301. [73] Quoted in Aslet, *The Last Country Houses*, p. 254.

A directly comparable, although differently expressed, extension of the boundaries of Arts and Crafts ideology can be found at Christ's Hospital. Here too, Brangwyn's murals (1912–23) take us to a realm beyond the mere relationship of art to architecture by Aston Webb and Ingress Bell, and express the artist's personal mission to promote the very unity of mankind itself: 'Art should have meaning or message, and be accessible to all—and, should be such, as to wake the feelings of the fellowship of man.'[74] Trained under William Morris, Brangwyn imposed a compelling formal unity on the sequences of seven 2.44 by 4.27 m panels plus one 2.44 by 2.13 m panel which line each side of the long, but broad, red brick Gothic-style chapel beneath the windows, using the same device of rhythmically re-echoing figural gestures and repeated floral, natural, or architectonic motifs to interlink the panels that he had recently evolved at Skinners' Hall in London. Seen from the nave, the murals draw the eye across the ranks of tiered pews beneath, into the very midst of their iconography, which consists of scenes from the lives of the early Christian saints associated with the south of England (Augustine, Wilfrid, Alban) and of Saints Aidan (Plate 135), Peter and Paul, Caxton printing Bibles, and Eliot disseminating them in the seventeenth century to the Mohicans, and a contemporary scene of hymn-singing in an East End London street. Figures are placed at the forefront of the picture plane, creating a frieze of powerful colour, and the repeated verticals—standing saints and their companions; bare tree-trunks; a cross; chair legs; a tall harmonium, lilies, and even storks' legs—combine with the horizontal accent of the high horizon in each picture, and the reiterated notes of ultramarine in sea and costumes, to elide the individual panels into a larger continuity which is both decorative and symbolic.

Appropriately for a school, the subjects emphasize children and the power of the Word to convert, from *St. Aidan training the boys at Lindisfarne* (Plate 135) to the choirboys and poor London children portrayed in the final mural of *Let all the people praise thee . . .*; whilst the panels are arranged (as again at Skinners' Hall) to create a typological relationship between opposite scenes in the chapel. *St. Ambrose training the choir in his church at Milan AD 385*, for example, partners the contemporary hymn-singing subject with its modern choirboys in surplices opposite; *The Conversion of St. Augustine at Milan AD 387* similarly relates to *John Eliot giving Bibles to the Mohicans AD 1660*, a scene which dramatically juxtaposes the exotic figures of Red Indians with the sober black Puritan garb of Eliot.

In this sense, the almost mosaic-like intricacy of the closely interlocking figure arrangements with their patterned costumes (as in Saul's conversion) or floral emblems (like the frieze of lilies in pots across the foreground of *The Conversion of Augustine*) become a cipher for the taut iconographical unity of the scheme. Whilst the subjects were determined by the headmaster of Christ's Hospital, Dr Upcott, Brangwyn clearly interpreted them to give prominence to his vision of the harmony of men as brothers and equals: Eliot shares the Word with the Mohicans; and young, aged, crippled, and clergy alike join in praise around a harmonium played by a hunchback, whose inclusion suggests a response to the First World War which intervened while Brangwyn was at work on the scheme. The murals portray no military-age men apart from the clergy, and the hunchback was modelled by a Belgian. Brangwyn was particularly affected by the war carnage and destruction in Belgium, where he had been brought up, and here he shows the power of religion and art (in the form of music) to transcend the physical suffering of his contemporaries post-1914. As at Skinners' Hall in its summative panel of *Harmony* (Plate 43), music (whether modern or that

[74] Undated comment in BD.

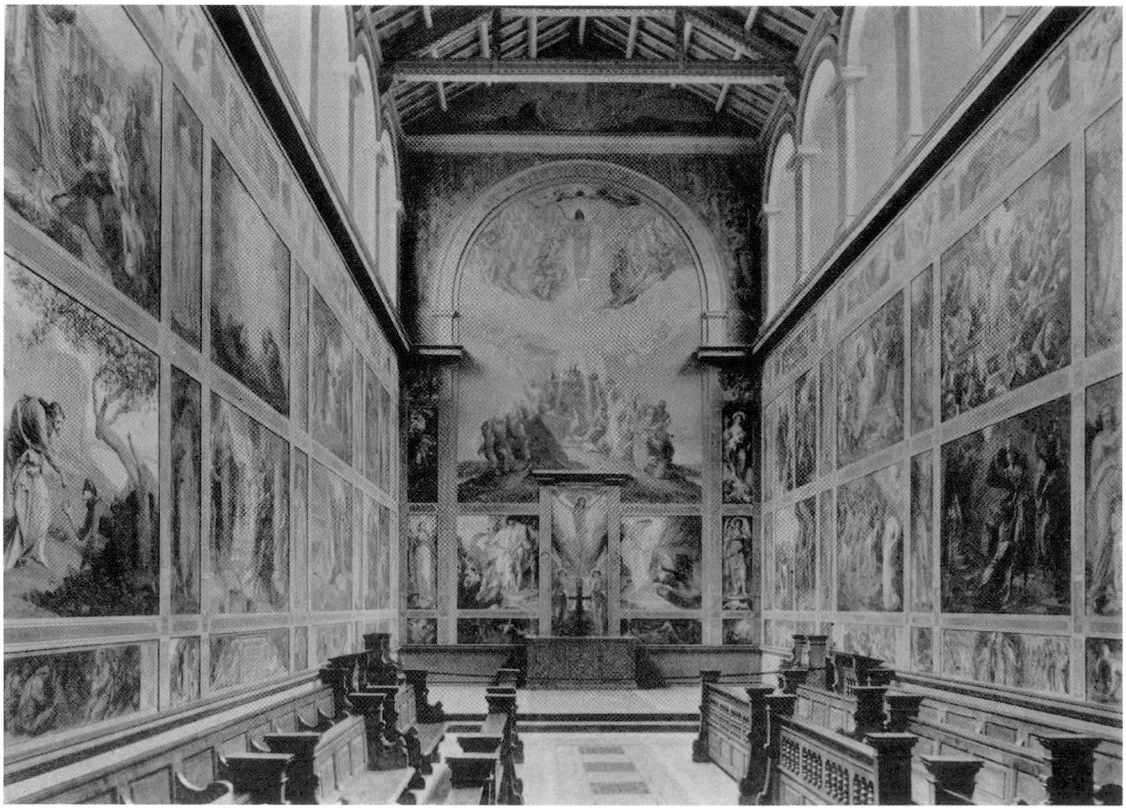

131. Frederic Shields, mural scheme formerly in Chapel of the Ascension, Bayswater, Paddington, 1887–1910 (period photograph)

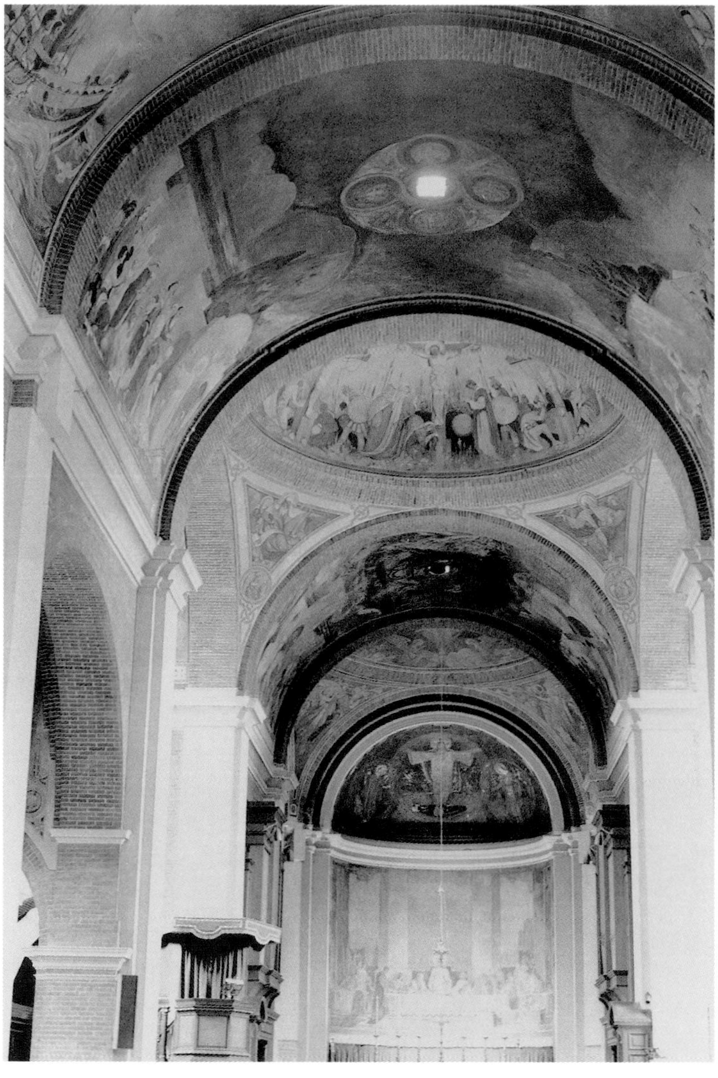

132. W. P. Starmer, murals in St Jude's church, Hampstead, London, begun 1912

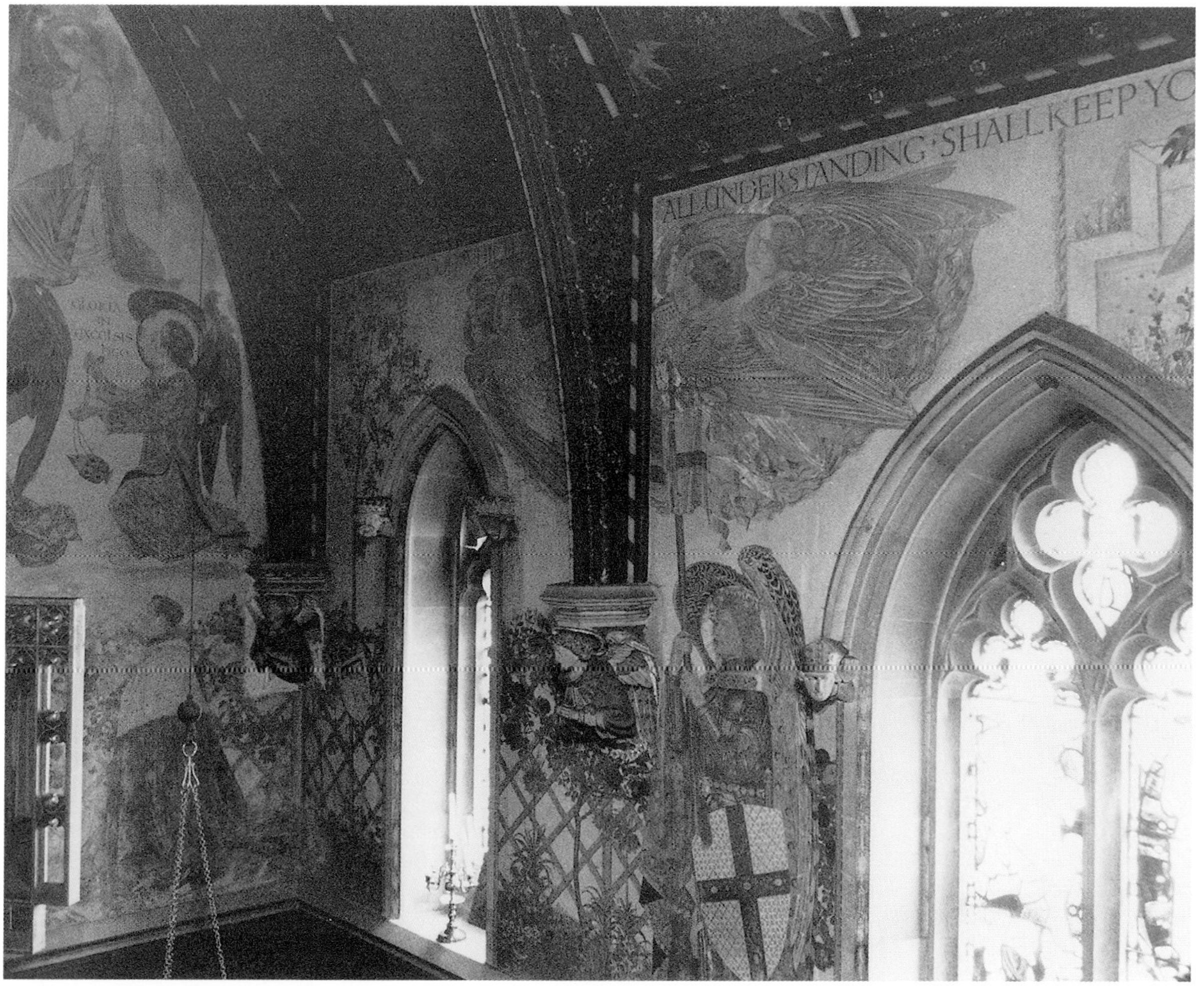

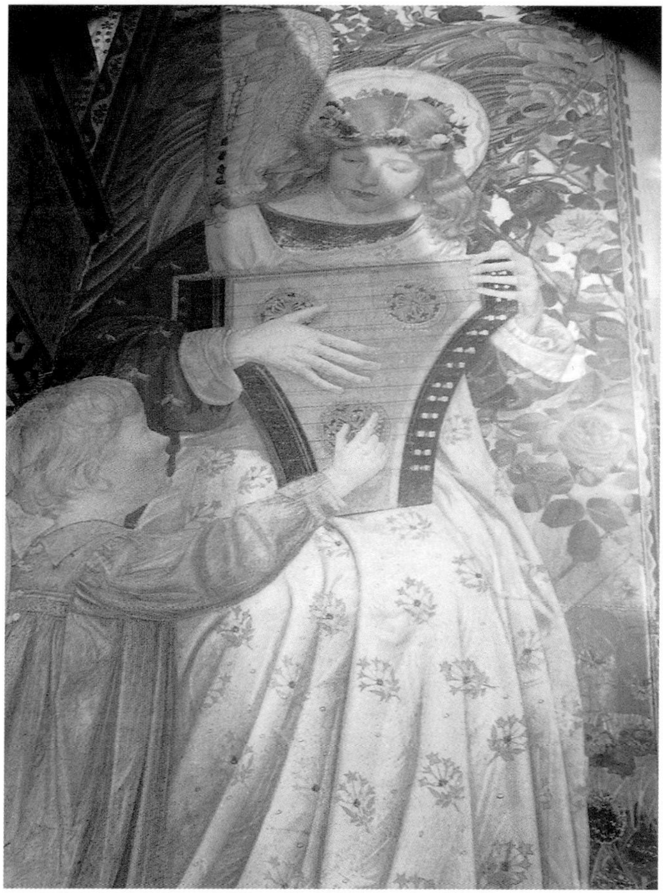

133. Henry A. Payne, detail from decoration in the Chapel, Madresfield Court, Worcestershire, 1902–1920s (Lord Beauchamp kneels to the right of the altar-wing visible at the left)

134. Henry A. Payne, detail from decoration in the Chapel, Madresfield Court, Worcestershire, 1902–1920s

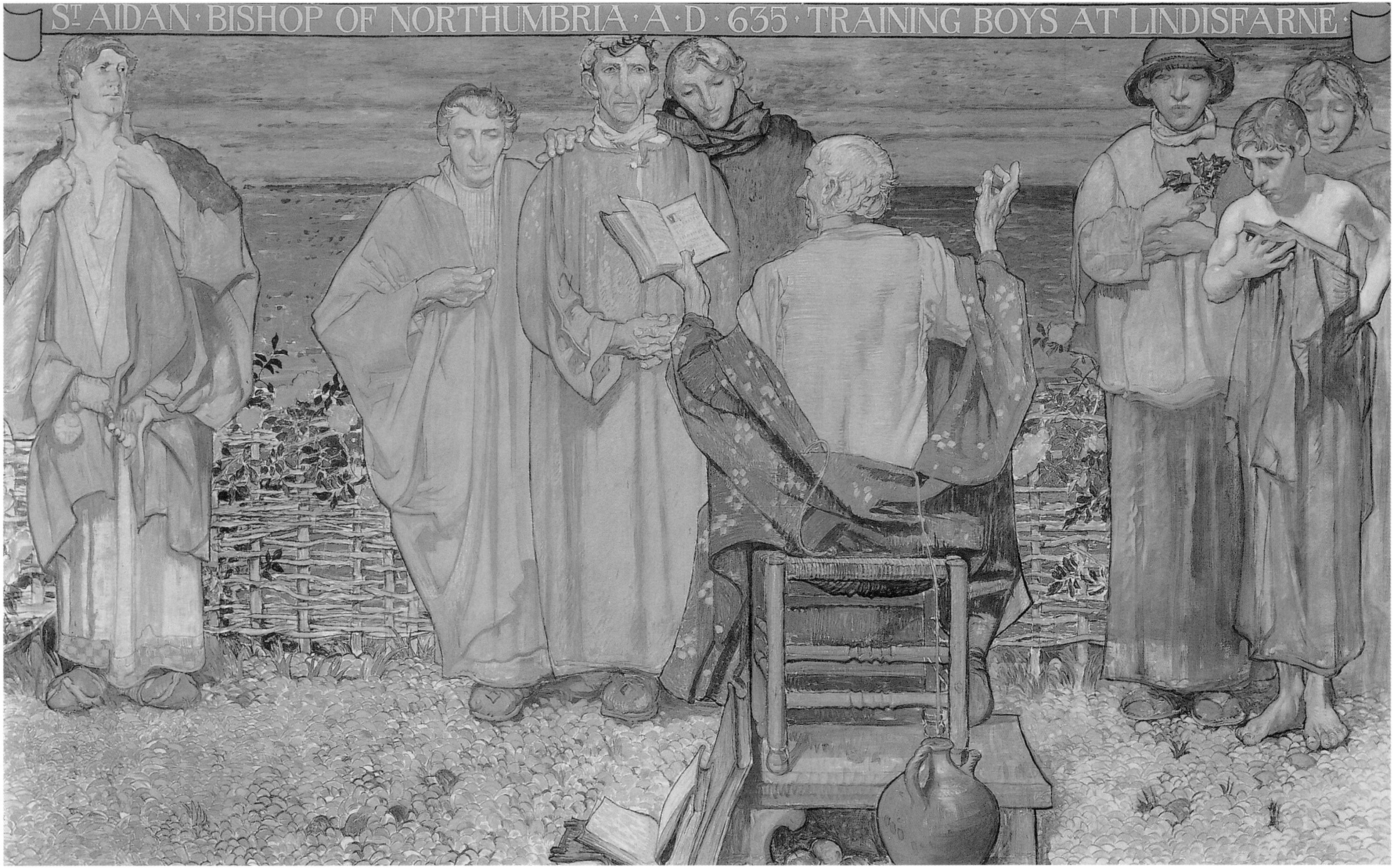

135. Sir Frank Brangwyn, *St. Aidan training the Boys at Lindisfarne*, Chapel, Christ's Hospital, Horsham, Sussex, 1912–23

of the choir of St Ambrose) is made a symbol for the brotherhood of man, both across nations and across time, and since the chapel itself was where actual choral singing took place, a subtle synaesthesia is again set up in a similar manner to that at Madresfield. Brotherhood as expressed through the Arts and Crafts 'guilds' has, as a few years later in the Royal Gallery at Westminster, become a personal philosophy of the human brotherhood of life. The primacy of the individual artist's vision now transcends the formal unity of art and architecture for which Bodley and Sedding had striven. Brangwyn's vigorous painterly technique of marouflaged oil allows the tactile traces of the artist's individual touch to become an important ingredient in the effect, just as the rich variety of humankind is conveyed in the almost caricatural exaggeration of facial forms and expressions. The stiffly painted wattle fence backdrop with flowers in the Heaton, Butler and Bayne murals at Luddesdown and Northaw churches and the almost botanical trellis at Madresfield have become the irregular, fluently touched-in fence with pink roses which separates St Aidan and his boys from the distant sea view; its shadows blue, and the pebbled ground before it a rough, prismatic mosaic of brushstrokes.

BEYOND THE FIRST WORLD WAR

The individual vision of the artist which had become dominant both at Madresfield and at Christ's Hospital, and which was being exemplified by Starmer's work in Lutyens's St Jude's, can be seen as the characteristic feature of the most significant of the twentieth-century ecclesiastical mural work. As such, it provides the first effective response to Ruskin's belief that 'pictorial subject' in buildings was exclusively the artist's 'concern', rather than subject to the architect's *diktat.* Whilst the 'Hall of Heroes' in the RA 1916 Arts and Crafts Exhibition Society's show contained murals intended for church as well as other war memorials, it was still masterminded by an architect, H. Wilson, in an echo of the Bodley tradition. Nowhere was Ruskin's ideal of the artist's primacy more vividly expressed, perhaps, than in the Sandham Memorial Chapel at Burghclere, built by Lionel Pearson to the precise instructions of Stanley Spencer, who decorated it with an ambitious programme of murals between 1927 and 1933. An admirer of Ruskin, whom he called 'a fine writer who says some fine things',[75] Spencer may have had in mind, like Shields at Bayswater earlier, the nineteenth-century critic's *Giotto and his Works at Padua*, both for the conception of the Burghclere decoration as panels in double registers as at the Arena chapel, and for the Gothic style of architecture he envisaged for his unexecuted plan for a sequel to Burghclere, Church House.

The Burghclere decoration (Plates 136, 137) evolved out of Spencer's abortive designs for murals for Steep Village Hall and Cambridge University Library.[76] Impressed by Spencer's drawings of his own wartime experiences in Macedonia, the Behrend family gave him the opportunity to turn them into murals by commissioning the chapel at Burghclere as a memorial to Mrs Behrend's brother, who had died following service in Macedonia. Although Spencer took lessons in true fresco from Mrs Sargant-Florence of the Society of Mural Decorators and Painters in Tempera, he decided to use oil on canvas, sometimes marouflaged, sometimes on stretchers, as being more practical. There are nevertheless intriguing echoes in his murals not only of Ruskin's ideal of

[75] Comment of 1916, quoted in R. Carline et al., *Stanley Spencer* (1980), p. 125. [76] See Chapter 9.

'artistic' decoration, but also of the extended brotherhood and unity themes which had evolved out of the Arts and Crafts Movement in the work of Payne and Brangwyn.

The scheme consists of Macedonian scenes and subjects from daily life at the Beaufort Hospital in Bristol, where Spencer had served as a wartime medical orderly. The hospital scenes illustrate the quotation from St Augustine's *Confessions* which Spencer had learnt from his Roman Catholic friend at Bristol, Desmond Chute: 'ever busy yet ever at rest, gathering yet never needing; bearing; filling; guarding; creating; nourishing; perfecting'.[77] They show the humdrum activities which sustain the care of man for fellow man, from *Scrubbing the floor* (a bare-roomed incident remarkably reminiscent of the Impressionist Gustave Caillebotte's straining *Floor Polishers*, although executed in Spencer's typically lean, sharp-contoured style) to *Kit Inspection* and *Filling Tea Urns* (Plates 136–7). There are obvious parallels with the sense of the sacramental within the everyday to be found in the scheme being painted at the same period at Woodgreen Village Hall by H. A. Payne's son, Edward, and Robert Baker. The meeting of public and private worlds involved in a panel such as *Kit Inspection*, where each soldier's possessions on a mat around him symbolize his fragile personal identity within the chaos of war, forms a harrowing subversion of the harmonious unity of inner and outer of the elder Payne's pre-war idyll at Madresfield. Brangwyn's *Let all the People Praise Thee* at Christ's Hospital, with its shell-shocked survivors and militarily incapables joining with the men of past and future in poignant praise, can be seen as the pivot between these old and new worlds, but Spencer too seeks for a positive, reconstructive message in his end-wall mural of the *Resurrection* as a meeting of the living and the resurrected on a Macedonian battlefield, just as he presents an almost Pre-Raphaelite, and certainly Brangwyn-esque, emphasis on common soldiers engaged in mutual help. Spencer deliberately avoided violence; his regenerative vision forms the sequel to his Hall of Remembrance painting, and a telling parallel both with Brangwyn's abandonment of war subjects at the House of Lords at the same period for 'what had been saved for the Empire' at the House of Lords, and the rejection of the landscapes of devastation intended to decorate Leeds Town Hall. If its symbolism is positive, however, Spencer's mural style remains disturbingly 'surreal' in its uncompromising clarity of focus on objects like the barbed wire and sharply silhouetted battle equipment on the bare earth of *Dug-out*; his compositions distort and exaggerate perspective and postures in a manner totally alien to Brangwyn's curvilinear, rather than geometric, forms. His art was perhaps ultimately too esoteric and uncomfortable for emulation in other schemes, but even though Burghclere stands, like Brangwyn's Christ's Hospital, as an isolated landmark in the history of ecclesiastical mural art, it poignantly encapsulates the changing mood of the times.

The nineteenth-century decorating companies staggered on until the 1920s, but with a decreasing number of new churches to employ their trade; and when the war threw into chaos their traditional iconographies of personification and symbol, ecclesiastical decoration seemed to waver. The Roman Catholic artist Archibald Jarvis updated religious iconography with such murals as the *Madonna of the Shuttle*, showing a Lancashire mill-girl;[78] whilst 'window in the wall' murals like easel paintings, such as William Aikman's St Paul and Nativity subjects at Pennington Church in Hampshire (1920s) attempted greater realism. Other twentieth-century schemes include those of James Clarke, Kitty Milroy, and Robert Tressall, and other work by

[77] Quoted in Carline et al., *Stanley Spencer*, p. 97.

[78] Believed to have been for a church in Blackburn or Little Halton.

Brangwyn (Appendix B: 20, 21, 29–36), which mark the re-emergence of independent (rather than 'trade') artists, using a wide variety of styles. The need for War Memorials, however, found remarkably little expression in church murals; the art-form had a bad reliability record and stone-carving or plaques were in any case cheaper and better suited to the primary concern of recording the names of the fallen. It was not until almost the advent of the Second World War that a renaissance of church decorative painting and an answer to a 'new style for a new age' was consciously sought through the work of Bishop George Bell of Chichester.

Already in the aftermath of the war, the vicar of St Hilary near Penzance, Bernard Walke, had encouraged the introduction of art into the life of his church through commissions to members of the Newlyn School of artists. His choir-stalls were painted with wooden panels of the lives of the Celtic saints by artists including Dod and Ernest Procter, Harold Knight, Norman and Althea Garstin, and Harold Harvey; Walke also persuaded Roger Fry to provide a St Francis altarpiece, whilst scenes from the life of Christ were painted on the Lady Chapel screen by the nine-year-old Joan Manning-Saunders. Christmas plays by Walke, some broadcast by the BBC from 1926, complemented this use of art in the church and parallel Bell's commissioning in Canterbury of T. S. Eliot's *Murder in the Cathedral* and his collaboration with artists such as Charles Ricketts and musicians such as Gustav Holst. Bell's efforts, however, launched a wider movement for art in the church in which mural painting became an important element. He later remarked that by means of his work 'the Poet and the Artist together re-entered the Church',[79] and during the 1920s his plea that 'we may seek ways and means for a reassociation of the Artist and the Church'[80] bore direct fruit in his commissions to Professor E. W. Tristram to restore medieval murals at Canterbury Cathedral and paint new ones at St Elizabeth's in Eastbourne in 1938.[81] He also arranged for Hans Feibusch to paint a Nativity subject in St Wilfrid's in Brighton in thanks for shelter from the Nazis, and in cooperation with the Central Institute of Art and Design, he organized the competition for murals at the new Bishop Hannington Memorial Church in Hove, where Augustus Lunn was selected to paint *The Great Commission* in 1941.

It was in work such as this, during and immediately following the Second World War, that Brangwyn's and Spencer's quest for new styles and iconography of relevance to the twentieth century and to the actual experiences of the common man in a sense came to full fruition in a revival of religious patronage which strictly falls outside the scope of the present book. In conjunction with the Sussex churches and 'Pictures in Churches Loan Scheme', Bell argued in the early 1940s for a new kind of decoration:

> Why should not modern artists paint our churches today, offering their gifts of colour and design in the spirit of the artists of old? . . . we have been taking too narrow a view in what we have thought of as fitting for church decoration. We have tended to have recourse to the same kind of work and the same kind of memorial or ornaments as that to which our parents were accustomed.[82]

There had certainly been new styles in the 1920s and 1930s, but with the exception of Spencer's, these were largely in the lingering shadow of the Bodley tradition of murals as adjuncts to architecture. A somewhat watered-down Art Deco had appeared in murals such as the *Risen Christ* of 1927 at St Leonard's church, Dunfermline, designed by the church's architect

[79] Quoted in R. C. Jasper, *George Bell, Bishop of Chichester* (London, 1967), p. 43.

[80] Ibid., p. 121.

[81] See G. K. Bell, 'The Church and the Artist', *Studio*, 124, no. 594 (Sept. 1942), p. 88.

[82] Quoted in Jasper, *George Bell*, p. 130.

P. McGregor Chalmers, and in the reredos mural and ceiling painting of 1935–6 by Mary Adshead for the experimental concrete church of St Christopher, Withington, Manchester, by Bernard Miller. E. S. Prior's 'Cathedral of the Arts and Crafts' at Roker, Sunderland, begun in 1905 under the philosophy that 'Architecture is an Art,' received its *Representation of the Heavens* ceiling by Macdonald Gill only in 1927; framing a sun in the form of an electric light, this too is essentially Art Deco. Eric Gill designed a mural of Christ on a wooden cross for St Peter's Roman Catholic church at Gorleston in Norfolk, which was carried out in oil on plaster by Dennis Tegetmeier in 1939 and reveals Gill's characteristic spare linearity. That Bell was in pursuit of something different—in harmony with, rather than subordinate to, its architectural context—is evident in his promotion of a scheme which marks a pivot from the pre- to post-1940 eras as much as had Brangwyn's Christ's Hospital in relation to the First World War. Taking up iconography traditional in an English parish church since medieval times, such as the Christ in Glory over the chancel arch, the murals begun in 1941 at Berwick Church in Sussex by Duncan Grant and Vanessa Bell incorporate contemporary portraits—including Bishop Bell's own—and strong colours which provoked Bell to remark 'It's wonderful. It's like stepping out of foggy England into Italy.'[83] Bell defended the project against initial parish protests, trusting on principle in the freedom of the artist to create an independent work of art, and it is revealing that Grant and Bell had visited Burghclere before embarking on their commission. Artistic, rather than architectural or doctrinal considerations, were now to the fore, and in a sense the wheel had turned full circle to a conception of religious mural painting which was as personal as that of the early nineteenth-century German Nazarenes. Clearly reacting both to the Gothic Revival and Art Deco, Frederick Etchells, who was the adviser for the scheme, said the paintings 'have not attempted to be mediaeval or anything but themselves . . . [the artists' work] like that of their ancestors, is of its own age, which does not mean that it is ostentatiously unlike that of the past,'[84] whilst Sir John Rothenstein made the extravagant claim that they were 'amongst the best paintings to be made in church or chapel in England during the present century'.[85] Given their bleak wartime context (a soldier and airman are illustrated), it is easy to see why the colourful naivety of the murals (done in oil on board rather than fresco) should have been so keenly appreciated; from an early twenty-first-century perspective, they fall into place as the natural outcome of the mood and ideals of their time. The aspects which now hold most appeal are perhaps the vibrant still-life details, like the Sussex trug with vegetables in *The Nativity* (Plate 138), and the radical iconography of *The Victory of Calvary* (Plate 139) as an androgynous Christ on a blue cross against an orange ground.

Church mural painting in the 1940s and 1950s was to return to a stylization very different from, yet also curiously comparable with the one which had held such sway in the nineteenth-century 'medieval' tradition of the companies, as Expressionist styles derived from Art Deco became a dominant force. Over the hundred years from 1840 to 1940, and amid significant and ongoing losses of church mural painting, it is the early flowering of the Ecclesiological movement in the hands of Dyce (and in certain moments, like the angel roundels at Highnam, of Gambier Parry too), along with the work of Leighton at Lyndhurst, Payne at Madresfield, Brangwyn at Christ's Hospital, and Spencer at Burghclere, which meet the eye as pinnacles of notable achievement. There was some undoubtedly accomplished work, like that of William Hole in Scotland, but also a

[83] Quoted in R. Shone, *The Berwick Church Paintings* (Towner Art Gallery, Eastbourne 1969).

[84] C. Bell, 'Paintings in Berwick Church', *Country Life* (1943), p. 1016.

[85] Quoted in Shone, *The Berwick Church Paintings.*

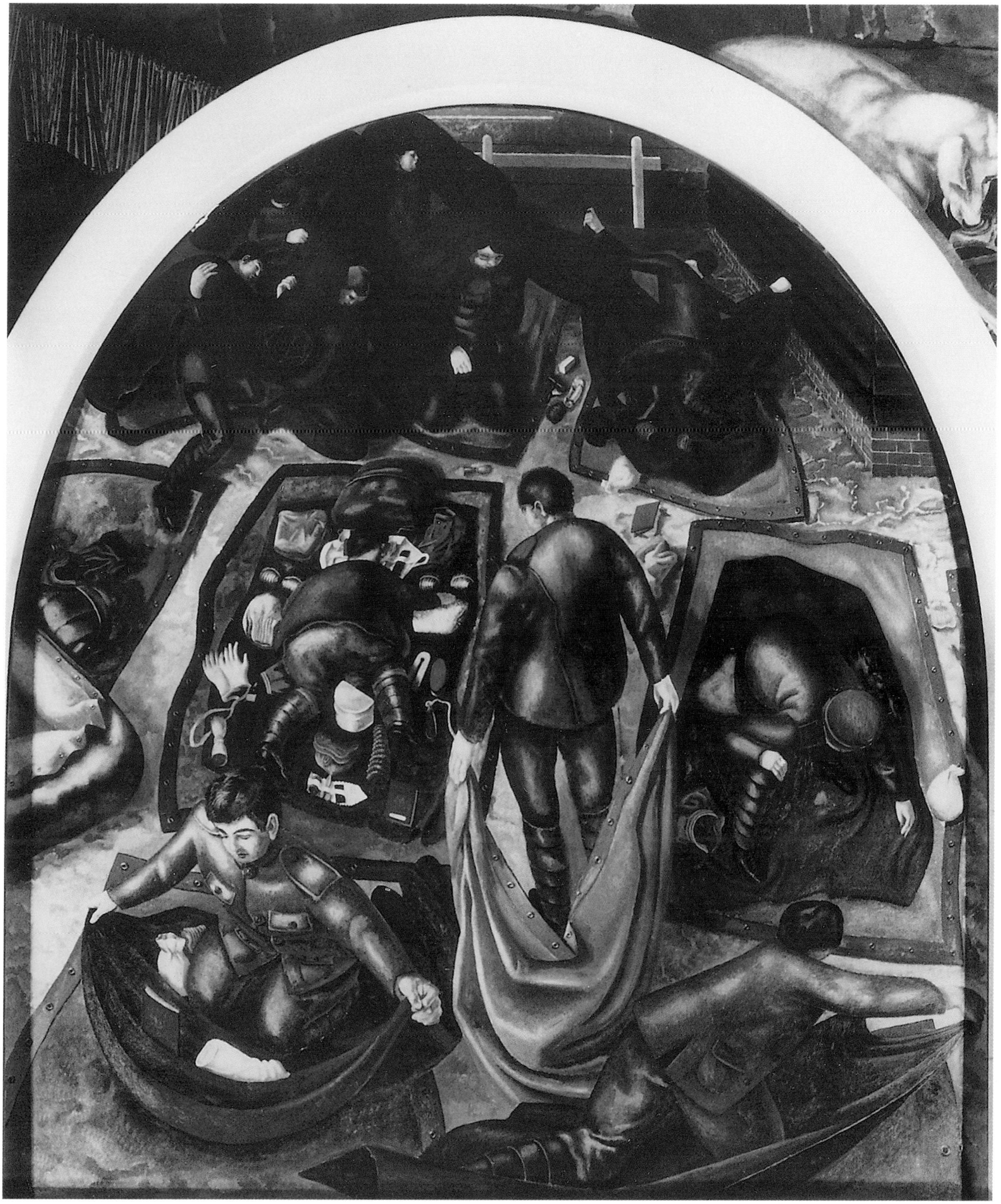

136. Sir Stanley Spencer, *Kit Inspection*, Oratory of All Souls, Burghclere (Sandham Memorial Chapel), 1927–33

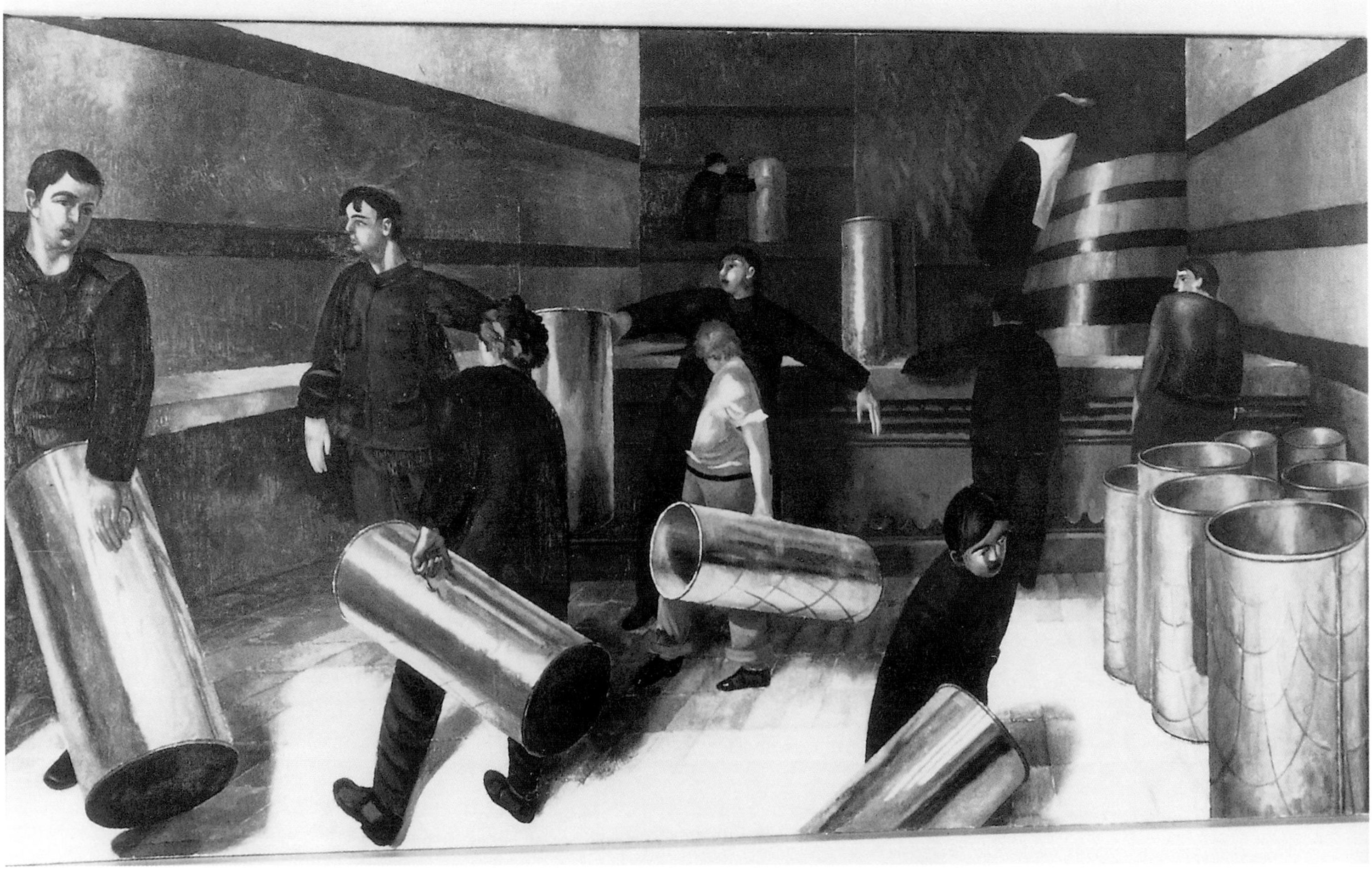

137. Sir Stanley Spencer, *Filling Tea Urns*, Oratory of All Souls, Burghclere (Sandham Memorial Chapel), 1927–33

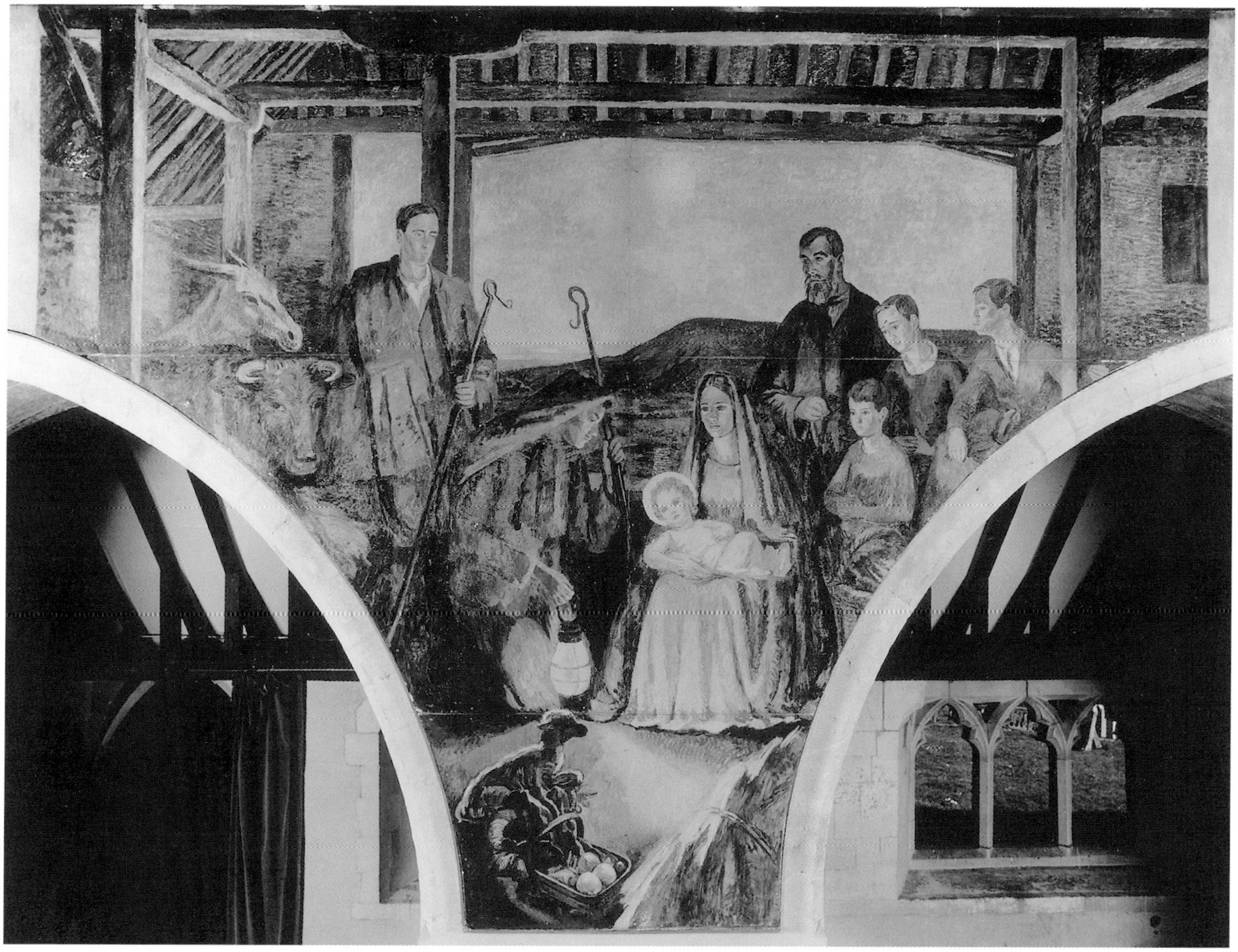

138. Vanessa Bell, *The Nativity*, Berwick Church, Sussex, from scheme begun in 1941

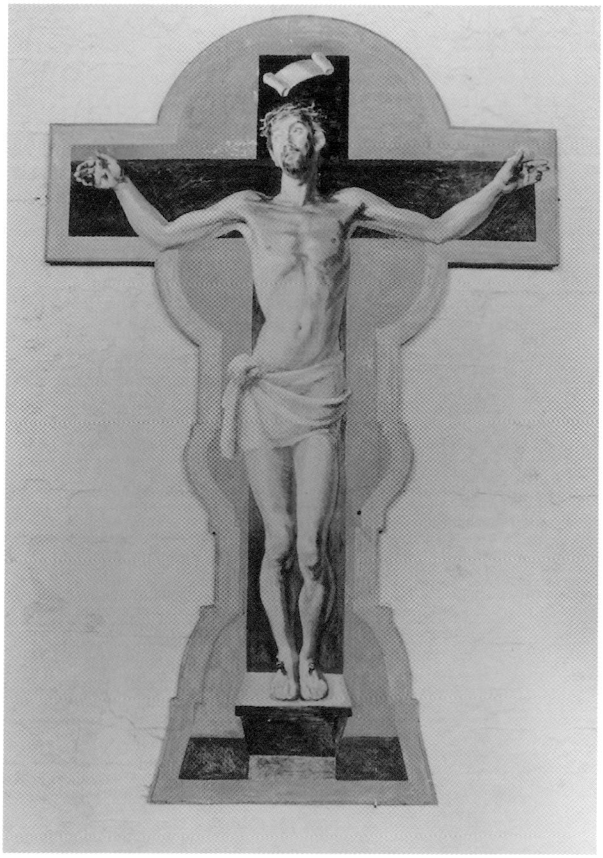

139. Duncan Grant, *The Victory of Calvary*, Berwick Church, Sussex, from scheme begun in 1941

great deal of technically proficient, yet essentially routine and uninspired pastiche medievalism by the various commercial companies. The particular demands of church patrons for specific iconography, combined with the overbearing weight of the Gothic Revival architectural movement perhaps made it difficult for all but the most original of artists working in personally congenial circumstances to create what can be called entirely successful work. By the same token, however, the great murals are particularly noteworthy, whilst the stimulus to decorative art created by the Oxford Movement needs to be seen as a highly important factor in the larger revival of mural painting in the nineteenth and twentieth centuries. In this sense Parry's work at Highnam is a significant immediate precursor to the major schemes launched by Leighton at South Kensington and the Royal Exchange, and from there in turn, at the Palace of Westminster in the twentieth century.

9

Mind and Body: Education and Welfare Murals

'Art is not an exotic supplement to life, but as inseparable from it as hygiene . . . however memories may be crammed no minds can be developed in the stupefying blankness of whitewashed schoolrooms.'[1] So urged Sir Patrick Geddes, sociologist, leader of the Celtic Revival, and Professor of Botany at Dundee University, in Edinburgh in 1889. Depressed by what he felt was the failure of State patronage at the South Kensington Museum and Schools of Design to create 'colourful reality' instead of 'wearisome colourless outline or shadow on paper', he argued that individual initiative, rather than 'governmental compulsion', was needed to win the confidence 'of some school board . . . to risk the revolutionising of their dreary whitewashed jail, in which lessons are still essentially learned parrot-wise by ear, into a paradise of childhood in which the noble lessons would be blazoned in gold and colour upon the memory through life'. He cited with approval the way in which 'the new Sorbonne is this year being frescoed by the greatest masters; while more magnificent still, the Paris Municipal Council proposes to begin the thorough mural decoration of the Paris schools.'[2] Change and decay have left only fragments of Geddes's practical remedies, but his words expose central issues in the history of mural painting in educational and welfare institutions throughout the century from 1840. The genre gathered momentum partly as a result of the didactic use of murals in the Palace of Westminster and Ruskin's belief in art for moral purposes, but it also reflected the strong Continental tradition of murals in universities, museums, and schools, such as those admired by Geddes.[3] Many of these foreign schemes, however, were State or civic commissions, fulfilling propaganda roles for ideals of good government and national identity. Patronage in Britain, in contrast, was much more various.

[1] P. Geddes, 'On National and Municipal Encouragement of Art upon the Continent' (printed paper in SUA, given to the Edinburgh Art Congress, 1889), p. 8.

[2] Ibid, pp. 7, 6.

[3] Major Continental schemes of the early 19th century included P. Cornelius's frescoes in the Munich Glyptothek and Alte Pinakothek and his and J. Götzenberger's murals in Bonn University; the Galerie des Batailles at Versailles (various artists); and P. Delaroche's *Great Artists* hemicycle at the Ecole des Beaux-Arts, Paris, which was widely publicized and emulated (see F. Haskell, *Rediscoveries in Art* (Oxford, 1980), pp. 8–15 and N. Ziff, *Paul Delaroche* (New York and London, 1977), pp. 178–82). Later schemes included W. Kaulbach's *World History* frescoes at the Neues Museum, Berlin (1847–63); Delacroix's and Ingres's ceiling decorations at the Louvre (1840s–1860s) and Puvis de Chavannes's murals at the Musée Napoléon (now Musée de Picardie), Amiens (1861–4 and 1880–2), and the Sorbonne in Paris. In Vienna, Klimt contributed to the Kunsthistorisches Museum decoration (1880s) but his controversial University panels (1890s–1904) were never installed. See G. Bazin, *The Museum Age* (Brussels, 1967); U. Finke, *German Painting from Romanticism to Expressionism* (London, 1974); W. Kitlitschka, *Die Malerei der Wiener Ringstrasse* (1981); F. Büttner, *Peter Cornelius* (1980–99); W. Vaughan, *German Romantic Painting* (1980), and C. A. P. Willsdon, 'Mural 1. Europe (i) *c.*1810–1930', in the *Grove Dictionary of Art*, 22 (1996). J. S. Sargent and Puvis de Chavannes painted murals in 1895 at Boston Public Library, USA.

Art to educate or heal, as Geddes made clear, had to appeal to the eye in vivid and potent ways. Mural paintings, in contrast to pictures in books, or the documentary films of the 1920s and 1930s, might actually shape the physical environment of lessons or therapy. As permanent images, to be seen day after day by the impressionable young or the sick or poor, they might instil values or inspire belief, like ecclesiastical decoration; many indeed used religious iconography and were located in school or hospital chapels, and some examples have already been considered in the last chapter. Britain's history and heroes were, however, a mainstay of murals in schools, colleges, and welfare foundations even up to 1940, shaping a vision of the making of the nation and its Empire which, as in the Royal Exchange or many town-hall murals, often emphasized local or institutional contributions. Realistic styles were the norm, inviting the viewer's involvement. Although by the 1920s there was a more archaeological appreciation of the past, didacticism was increasingly entwined with entertainment, nostalgia, and, from 1914, memorial purposes. Rex Whistler's Tate Gallery murals (1928) will be discussed in the chapter on 'Work and Play' because, as decoration for the building's restaurant, their character and history relate more closely to a leisure context, but other schemes, though painted for common-rooms, school halls, or refectories, like that at Morley College, find their lineage in ideas on art and education and are dealt with here. John Duncan's 1912 mural of nursery rhymes at North Morningside School in Edinburgh, or the local tales illustrated by C. R. Napier in the Junior Section of Huddersfield Public Library in 1939, reflect the emergence of child-centred principles of education. Modernism, however, as in Napier's witty distortions of reality, may not necessarily, of course, be as legible to a child as the realistic styles of earlier years. Whether located in classrooms, halls, common-rooms, or museums, 'telling a story', as in so many other types of mural in Britain, was a constant preference. Watts's *Lawgivers* (Lincoln's Inn) and Leighton's allegorical *Arts of Industry applied to War* and to *Peace* at the South Kensington Museum used an idiom more common on the Continent, and there is no real British counterpart to the psychologically charged vision of Besnard's *Life is Born from Death*, painted for the Sorbonne some seven years after Geddes's lecture, or Klimt's exploration of inner mental states in his University of Vienna murals.

Murals for museum and gallery buildings were, nevertheless, often a form of imaginative projection, conjuring distant times and places against which hallowed relics of the actual past might speak with greater meaning. Such murals are essentially agents of display; devices to frame or mediate. As Goethe had urged, they might be 'tasteful and in harmony with the [objects] displayed',[4] like Cornelius's outline 'Greek Gods and Heroes' at the Munich Glyptothek, or, as at the South Kensington Museum in the 1860s, a means of training art students through didactic illustration of historical techniques, accompanied by portraits of their greatest exponents; whilst at the Harris Museum in Preston in 1909, they were presented as part of the display themselves, much as had ocurred in the 1880s at the Natural History Museum in Vienna, where the murals illustrate the sites of the exhibits.

As Geddes's lecture reveals, there was considerable dissatisfaction with the products of the Government's art schools. A major feature of the history of educational and welfare murals in Britain is its close relationship with attempts to train artists. The fraught history of the decoration of the South Kensington Museum, begun in the early 1860s and not completed until the late 1880s,

[4] J. W. von Goethe: '. . . geschmackvoll und analog den Gegenständen' (*Über Kunst und Altertum in den Rhein und Maingegenden*, vol. 1 (Stuttgart, 1816), pp. 11ff., quoted in Kitlitschka, *Malerei der Wiener Ringstrasse*, p. 239 (author's translation).

stands out as a crisis of philosophy and practice, in which fine art values were asserted—and won—over those of the industrial or applied arts; for this reason it is discussed in this chapter even though it was a State project. Leighton's instigation at the Royal Academy in 1878 of a prize for mural decoration was an attempt to introduce a Continental-style 'Prix de Rome', and its early recipients were given wall space in the Royal Academy itself. In the twentieth century, it was in murals for colleges, hospitals, and museums in turn that the efforts of Tonks, Rothenstein, and the new British School at Rome to encourage young artists and create the still longed-for 'British School' found a major outlet.

These twentieth-century ventures, however, also had roots in the Arts and Crafts tradition carried forward by Geddes from Ruskin. A large amount of mural painting in schools, colleges, and hospitals was motivated by ideals of Christian Socialism and some of this is of interest more from a sociological than an artistic point of view, just as there is also fine individual work, like Louis Ginnett's for Brighton and Hove Grammar School, which owes its origin less to theory than to felicitous patronage and talent.

ART AND FACTS: RUSKIN, SCIENCE AND ARTISTIC EXPERIMENT

Whilst there were various schemes for schools in Britain carried out in the 1840s and 1850s by German artists, mostly as offshoots of the Ecclesiological movement (Appendix C: 1), the publication in 1859 of Ruskin's correspondence with Sir Henry Acland about the decoration of the new Oxford Museum opened up for public debate the issue of how the mind might be educated, not just through books or lectures, but also through the eye. Built with Ruskin's advice by Deane and Woodward, the Museum was created to meet Acland's need, as Reader and subsequently Regius Professor of Anatomy, for an accessible teaching collection. The most ambitious Gothic Revival structure in Britain since the Palace of Westminster, its sculptural and painted ornament were intended to demonstrate Ruskin's belief in 'combined' decoration, 'so as to produce that type of impression usually termed "sublime"—as it is felt on looking at any great series of fixed paintings'.[5] In turn, Ruskin argued that 'all architectural ornamentation should be executed by the men who design it . . . a great public edifice should be, in sculpture and painting, somewhat the same as a chorus in music'; and in a Gothic-style building in particular, it should offer 'truthful statements about natural facts, if it conveys any statement'.[6]

Whilst 'truth' and 'facts' were an admirable complement to the anatomical, natural history, and geological exhibits, 'sublimity' and 'musical' effect suggest something more emotive. The Museum, however, was being decorated exactly as Darwin's *Origin of Species* came into print. Although to many, not least the Oxford Movement churchmen, scientific enquiry and religious revelation seemed irreconcilable, Acland and Ruskin took the chance to proclaim their *harmony*. As the discoveries of science might enhance the awesomeness of the Creator, so, in turn, 'valuable

[5] Letter from Ruskin to Acland in H. W. Acland, *The Oxford Museum: Remarks addressed to a Meeting of Architectural Societies*, 2nd ed. (Oxford, 1860), p. 38. See also E. Blau, *Ruskinian Gothic: The Architecture of Deane and Woodward 1845–1861* (Princeton, 1982), pp. 5 ff.

[6] Acland, *Oxford Museum*, p. 40.

and curious examples of polished stones'[7]—the very substances identified and classified by geology—were physically incorporated in the Museum's Gothic architecture. Ornament and exhibit, like religion and science, were one; their revelation of the 'sublime' would have been even more explicit had Rossetti agreed to an invitation to paint a mural of *Newton gathering pebbles on the Shores of the Ocean of Truth.* Instead, the Reverend St John Tyrwhitt provided 'a large geological painting of the Mer de Glace, and . . . one of the lava streams of Vesuvius'[8] to complement the building's multifarious naturalistic plant and animal carvings. This must have been a somewhat startling synthesis of the Romantic sublime (Turner had painted the Mer de Glace) with 'truthful statements about natural facts'. Ruskin wrote to Acland that perhaps 'much interior imagery or colour . . . or other exciting address to the observant faculties' was not after all suited to a Museum of Science, and admitted that he was really interested in a kind of truth more moral than literal: 'The best ornamentation possible would be the painting on interior walls with frescoes by Titian, representing perfect Humanity in colour; and the sculpture of exterior walls by Phidias, representing perfect Humanity in form.'[9] No further murals were carried out at the Museum. Instead, truth conveyed by 'exciting address to the observant faculties', and inspiration from Titian, came to the fore respectively in the Oxford Union murals by Ruskin's Pre-Raphaelite followers, and the fresco by G. F. Watts at Lincoln's Inn in London.

The Oxford Union, another venture by Woodward in Gothic Revival 'art architecture', was built in 1856–7. Its Reading cum Debating Room (Plate 140) was painted with advice from Ruskin and at the suggestion of Rossetti following the *Newton* invitation, and Malory's *Morte d'Arthur*, which Rossetti had recently illustrated for Moxon's Tennyson edition, was selected as a suitable literary theme. Burne-Jones, Val Prinsep, Arthur Hughes, J. H. Pollen, R. Spencer Stanhope, Alexander Munro, and William Morris were persuaded to join the venture.[10] Rossetti later wrote, 'with the exception of Arthur Hughes and myself, those engaged . . . have made there almost their debut as painters.'[11] Though he had seen the first Westminster cartoon competition—'indeed a splendid sight'[12]—and the *Morte d'Arthur* theme suggests an echo of Dyce's at Westminster, the experiment turned quickly into riotous fun. Ruskin commented that the artists were 'all the least bit crazy and it's very difficult to manage them'. 'Truthfulness' led Morris to have a suit of armour made by a local blacksmith, only to evoke the mirth of his colleagues when its visor jammed on him. Asking a 'stalwart navvy' to model it instead for reference photographs, he found it would not bend; the navvy's 'efforts were most ludicrous'.[13] More amenable to painting was Jane Burden, later Morris's wife, who first made her début in Pre-Raphaelite art at the Union.

Since the work was carried out in tempera direct on the brick walls, it began to perish as early as June 1858, whilst the windows between the paintings made them all but invisible against the incoming light. It appears, however, that their very positioning was itself a form of symbolic truthfulness to Malory's text, developing the Nazarene philosophy of mural art as the unity of subject and place. Most of the *Morte d'Arthur* incidents selected involve light, fire, or brilliance. Pollen's *King Arthur obtaining the Sword Excalibur from the Damsel of the Lake*, in which the mystical shining sword was positioned to connect two window roundels, must have intriguingly

[7] Period quotation in T. Garnham, *Oxford Museum: Deane and Woodward* (Oxford, 1992).

[8] Acland, *Oxford Museum*, p. 28.

[9] Ibid., pp. 53, 65, letters from Ruskin to Acland.

[10] It was originally hoped that Hunt and Millais would also contribute to the scheme. See also Blau, *Ruskinian Gothic*, pp. 82 ff.

[11] Quoted in J. D. Renton, *The Oxford Union Murals* (Oxford, 1983).

[12] Quoted in L. Parris (ed.), *Pre-Raphaelite Papers* (1984), p. 173.

[13] Incidents and comments recorded in Renton, *The Oxford Union Murals*.

anticipated Tennyson's 1869 description of 'the blade so bright / That men are blinded by it'.[14] Rossetti's *Sir Launcelot prevented By His Sin From Entering The Chapel Of The San Grael* (Plate 141) likewise suggests the source for lines in Morris's *Defence of Guinivere* of 1858, 'Launcelot's red-golden hair would play, / Instead of sunlight, on the painted wall'.[15] The artists' friend Coventry Patmore—uncannily foretelling both Félix Fénéon's description of how in 'each inch' of Seurat's *Sunday Afternoon on the Island of La Grande Jatte* (1886, Art Institute of Chicago) was 'a whirling host of tiny spots, all the elements which make up the true tone',[16] and Henri Martin's application of pointillism to mural painting in the 1890s in the Paris Hôtel de Ville—spoke of the colouring of the murals as

> so brilliant as to make the walls look like the margin of a highly illuminated manuscript. The eye, even when not directed to any of the pictures, is thus pleased with a voluptuous radiance of variegated tints . . . if closely looked into, there is scarcely a square inch of all those hundred square feet of colour which has not a half-dozen different tints in it. The colours, coming thus from points instead of different masses, are positively radiant.[17]

His extravagant praise for Rossetti's contribution, 'like a steam of rich, distilled perfumes', with colour 'as sweet, bright and pure as that of the frailest waif of cloud in the sunrise'[18] suggests that just as Morris attempted by donning armour to become a Knight of the Holy Grail himself, so the students at the Union were offered Sir Launcelot's very sensation on entering the Holy Grail chapel, when 'he felte . . . a breethe that hym thought was entromedled with fyre, which smote him so sore on the vysage that him thought hit brente hys vysage. And therewith he felle to the eerthe . . . as that he had loste the power of hys body and hys hyrynge and syght.'[19] Sunk upon the ground, Rossetti's Sir Launcelot fills a corner beneath a window as if directly affected by its light. The *horror vacui* of this and the other compositions, with their near three-metre-high figures filling the foreground plane, was clearly intended not only as truth to the murals' function as surface decoration, but also as a psychological 'address to the observant faculties', and their synaesthesia is a fascinating prediction of *fin-de-siècle* developments, notably Goetze's murals at Grove House in London.[20]

If the Oxford Union scheme was an attempt to create a new kind of emotional and literary truth compared with Dyce's Arthurian allegories at Westminster, Watt's Lincoln's Inn *School of Lawgivers* fresco (Plates 142, 143) can be seen as a response to his fellow Westminster muralist J. R. Herbert's plea to 'Paint your courts of justice so as to impress witnesses with the abhorrence of falsehood.'[21] Though neither solely an educational building nor strictly a 'court', Lincoln's Inn was (and is) a training ground for barristers, and the mural, which Watts carried out at his own expense between 1852 and 1859, in this sense realized his idea for murals at Eton to enable boys to 'grow up under the influence of works of beauty of highest excellence'.[22] Spiritual illumination is indeed its underlying theme.

[14] Tennyson, *The Coming of Arthur* (1869), lines 299–300, in J. D. Renton, *Notes and Quotations related to the Oxford Union Murals* (pamphlet, 1987).

[15] Quoted in Renton, *Notes and Quotations* (1987).

[16] F. Fénéon, 'Les Impressionistes en 1886', quoted in J. Rewald, *Post-Impressionism from Van Gogh to Gauguin* (New York, 1978), p. 88.

[17] Coventry Patmore in the *Saturday Review* (26 Dec. 1857), quoted in Renton, *The Oxford Union Murals* (1983).

[18] Ibid.

[19] T. Malory, *Le Morte d'Arthur*, Book XVII, chapter 15, quoted in Renton, *Notes and Quotations* (1987).

[20] See Chapter 11.

[21] Quoted in J. Gage and C. Mullen, *G. F. Watts* (1974).

[22] Ibid.

As a convocation of thirty or so figures from Moses to Edward I, disposed on steps in the manner of Raphael's *School at Athens* philosophers, and below a dais with sculptures of Justice, Truth, and Mercy, Watts's *School of Lawgivers* closely echoes the conception of Delaroche's renowned Ecole des Beaux-Arts 'Great Artists' hemicycle of 1841 (Plate 144), and he preferred to call his mural *Justice; a Hemicycle of Lawgivers*, even though it occupies a flat, rather than a curved wall at the end of the Hall at Lincoln's Inn. He spent several months in Paris during 1855–6 whilst at work on the mural, but its personnel for the most part pre-date the thirteenth- to seventeenth-century time frame of Delaroche's, whilst their setting, in harmony with Philip Hardwick's architecture at Lincoln's Inn Hall, is Gothic. In this respect, Watts's mural is perhaps closer to the spirit, if not the Nazarene archaisms, of Overbeck's 1840 *Triumph of Religion in the Arts* (1840; Städel Institute, Frankfurt).[23] Having recently visited Italy, he clearly looked to Michelangelo's Sistine prophets for his vigorous poses, and for handling and probably also colour,[24] to Ruskin's revered Titian.

Despite these allusions to the kind of High Art forsworn by the Pre-Raphaelites—indeed, partly *because* of them—Watts's mural reveals an identification with the past just as direct as Morris's donning of armour or Rossetti's 'blinding' device which made the viewer experience Sir Launcelot's plight at the Oxford Union. For, as in his private-house schemes,[25] he portrayed contemporaries, with none other than Val Prinsep and Spencer Stanhope, who contributed at the Union, appearing as Servius and Solon, 'legislators of the ancient western world'; Armitage (who had assisted Delaroche with his hemicycle) as a Magna Carta baron (Plate 143); and Holman Hunt as the Saxon King Ina. The art of the Renaissance was thus reborn in the painters of modern times to serve the symbolic statues of Justice, Truth, and Mercy at the apex of the composition. Justinian, placed beside Moses and Theodora and directly beneath these personifications, is appropriately Sir William Harcourt, then at the start of a brilliant legal career. Just as Mahomet features in the 'eastern' legislators at the right, beside monks, scribes, and 'barbaric chieftains', so the nineteenth-century 'saviour of India', Lord Lawrence, who returned a hero in 1859 after the Punjab Mutiny, was the model for another Magna Carta baron in the register beneath (Plate 143), whilst Sir Charles Newton, who had just discovered the mausoleum at Halicarnassus (one of the 'Seven Wonders of the World') sat for Edward I.[26] Eastern, western, classical, and contemporary civilizations are thus brought together, along with the arts (Tennyson is Minos), as givers of law, whilst even Truth, at the apex of the composition, has flesh and blood character since cleaning in 1955 revealed 'her left eye [to be] closed in an unmistakeable wink'.[27]

Echoing Ruskin's vision at the Oxford Museum, Watts intended his fresco to 'pervade, so to speak, the building like a strain of Handel's music, becoming one with the architecture'.[28] Far from being an aberration, as some felt at the time, his reworking of Raphael's *School at Athens* within Gothic Revival architecture can be recognized as a symbolic projection of this integrative aim; the logical counterpart to his thematic synthesis of the 'dramatic unities of history',[29] in which the fresco medium fused subject (Justice) with time as well as place, and classical with Gothic styles. It

[23] Prince Albert had bought the cartoon for this.

[24] Although the colours have now deteriorated, in 1906 W. H. Draper noted 'the rich warmth of the whole' and 'the skilfully alternated hot and cold colouring of the individual figures' (Draper, 'The Watts Fresco', *Burlington Magazine*, 9 (1906), p. 14).

[25] See Chapter 11.

[26] Draper, 'The Watts Fresco', p. 9. H. Speed's 'Watts's "Law Givers"', *Studio*, 95 (1928), p. 406 identifies Edward I as a portrait of Watts.

[27] Anonymous newspaper cutting from the *Daily Telegraph*, believed to date from 1955, in the Watts Gallery, Compton.

[28] Quoted in Gage and Mullen, *G. F. Watts*.

[29] Draper, 'The Watts Fresco', p. 9.

is perhaps not surprising that Ruskin should have called Watts in the 1850s 'the only real painter of history or thought we have in England'.[30] If the extent to which the colour and chiaroscuro of the Lincoln's Inn fresco were originally synchronized with Ruskin's views on Titian is now impossible to gauge, it is clear that lighting effects added further levels of meaning. The traceried window opposite the mural is matched by a replica in its background, implying that the painted 'Law-givers' are 'illuminated' by the light of the same sun, shining in turn through the figures in the stained glass, which lights those who use the Hall. Real and painted worlds are joined, with the mirror held by the statue of Truth in the mural being their symbolic focus. The reciprocity of the symbolism speaks of Watts's belief, reminiscent of Turner's, that 'there can be no great art which has not for its religious basis sun-worship.'[31] It also explains the prominence given in the mural to Minos the sun-god (Holman Hunt), Zoroaster, whose followers worshipped fire, and Moses (the central figure, recalling the burning bush). Light and fire are one with Truth, very much as was also implied at the Oxford Union.

As late as 1928 Watts's Lincoln's Inn fresco was regarded as 'the most ambitious wall painting this country has produced', whilst Watts himself called it 'perhaps the best thing I have done or am likely to do'.[32] Although after it he virtually abandoned mural painting, his friend Edward Armitage embarked in 1869 on a frieze just over 17 metres long for the Dining Room of University College London.[33] This was intended as a memorial to the barrister Henry Crabb Robinson, a founder of the college, and the leader of a Germanophile circle in early nineteenth-century London which included Blake and the mural painter Jakob Götzenberger. A rare British counterpart to the genre of university mural painting so popular on the Continent, it appears to have been close in its style and informal figure groupings to the hemicycle by Delaroche (Plate 144) whose art was felt by Jacob Burckhardt to show 'human beings . . . with a reality so true to life its appears almost illusory'.[34] Armitage had helped Delaroche with his hemicycle. As if summoned up in memory by Robinson (shown seated in his study), thirty-four of his German and British friends were portrayed in the University College frieze 'somewhat over life-size'[35] and in conversation; they included Goethe, Schiller, Madame de Staël, Bunsen, Herder, Tieck, Wordsworth, Southey, and Coleridge.

'Biblical' truth was meanwhile found in 'a great experiment'[36] begun in 1862 in 'distempered watercolour' by another of Watts's friends, Lady Waterford, at the 'Tudor-Gothic' school in Ford, Northumberland (Plate 145). Ruskin contributed a 'useful critique' and 'the village carpenter, schoolmaster, gardener', as well as the schoolchildren themselves (receiving 'sixpence and a jelly piece')[37] were models for Old and New Testament scenes. These offer a worthy but rather literal amalgam of Raphaelesque poses and Pre-Raphaelite naturalism, which none the less won the praise of Holman Hunt and Rossetti. With its strong emphasis on children of the Bible, the scheme, completed in 1883, can be seen as part of the 'Christianity for children' trend exemplified in Mrs Alexander's hymns, and would of course have been a practical aid to education, since reading was taught from the Bible.

[30] Quoted in ibid., p. 8.

[31] Quoted in Gage and Mullen, *G. F. Watts* (Foreword).

[32] The 1928 view is H. Speed's, in 'Watts's "Law Givers"', p. 405; Watts's comment dates from 1904 and is quoted in Draper, 'The Watts Fresco', p. 9.

[33] University Hall is now Dr Williams's Library, London; the frieze (painted in encaustic in monochrome) is no longer visible but a portion is illustrated in H. Marquardt, *Henry Crabb Robinson und seine deutschen Freunde*, vol. I (Göttingen, 1964), plate II.

[34] Quoted in Finke, *German Painting*, p. 101.

[35] J. Beavington Atkinson, 'English Painters', *Portfolio*, 1 (1870), p. 51.

[36] Lady Waterford, quoted in Anon., *The Lady Waterford Hall, Ford, Northumberland* (Trustees of the Lady Waterford Hall, 1980).

[37] Ibid.

A late manifestation of Nazarene tradition meanwhile appeared at St Edmund's College, Ware, where Mark Barraud (son-in-law of the commercial decorator Frederick Sang) and his father Henry painted Old and New Testament incidents (Plate 146) from designs by Joseph Führich, Professor at the Academy of Fine Arts in Vienna and an early associate of Cornelius.[38] In contrast to Lady Waterford's self-contained scenes, these are presented in the form of a procession, intended to convey 'the history and triumph of religion' on the walls of the Ambulacrum 30 metres long, and suggestively complementing the daily progress of the boys on their way to lessons. Much as Führich included topical political reference in his murals for St Johann Nepomuk in Vienna, so Bismarck appears as the devil (a Barraud relation was then experiencing the Prussian siege of Paris).[39]

Efforts to establish a modern, native, decorative tradition were meanwhile revived at the South Kensington Museum from the early 1860s. Although the Government's 1863 Commission on the Royal Academy was told by Ruskin that 'wall painting in permanent materials on a large scale' should be taught in all art schools[40] and advised by Watts that 'students of the Academy might be trained by painting the walls of museums with designs from Raphael, Flaxman and others',[41] it was actually mosaic, bas relief, stained glass, and non-figurative ornament, executed by students of the National Schools of Design, which were for the most part preferred for the 'experiments in decoration'[42] at the Museum. These were masterminded by Sir Henry Cole, Director of the Museum and Secretary of the Government's Science and Art Department. From the venture, nevertheless, was to emerge the first important test in a public location and on a large scale of the medium which was to renew British confidence in mural painting in the later nineteenth century—spirit fresco.

ARTEFACTS AND EDUCATION

Just as Francis Fowke's recently completed buildings for the South Kensington Museum were those of an engineer, so its scheme of decoration bore witness to Cole's energetic utilitarianism and his view that 'Unless museums and galleries are made subservient to purposes of education, they dwindle into very sleepy affairs.'[43] The artefacts on show in the Museum were intended to allow the students of the Government Schools of Design to study the best examples of historical and contemporary design; in turn, its walls were adorned in the 1860s with conspectuses of the principal artists and manufacturing techniques of history, culminating in representations of the Lords President of Council and the Presidents of the Board of Trade as the modern leaders of artistic endeavour. This decoration still essentially reflected a Romantic ideal of instructional chronology. As Goethe put it, 'youth must always start again from the beginning and as an

[38] For Führich, see Kitlitschka, *Die Malerei*, pp. 6–11. The central section of the frieze is identical with Führich's *Der Triumph Christi* in the Muzeum Narodowe in Poznań, Poland (information kindly supplied by St Edmund's College, Ware). Mark Barraud was the brother of Francis Barraud, artist of the HMV Company's logo *His Master's Voice.*

[39] Information from manuscript history of the Barraud family by Fr Bernard Lagrue, kindly supplied by St Edmund's College, Ware.

[40] Quoted in Draper, 'The Watts Fresco', p. 8.

[41] Beavington Atkinson, 'English Painters', p. 69. Armitage also argued before the Commission for systematic training of art students in mural painting.

[42] Henry Scott (Francis Fowke's successor as the South Kensington Museum architect) and E. R. Festing (Deputy-General-Superintendant at South Kensington), quoted in J. Physick, *The Victoria and Albert Museum* (1982), p. 91.

[43] Quoted in S. Macdonald, *The History of Art Education* (1970), p. 177.

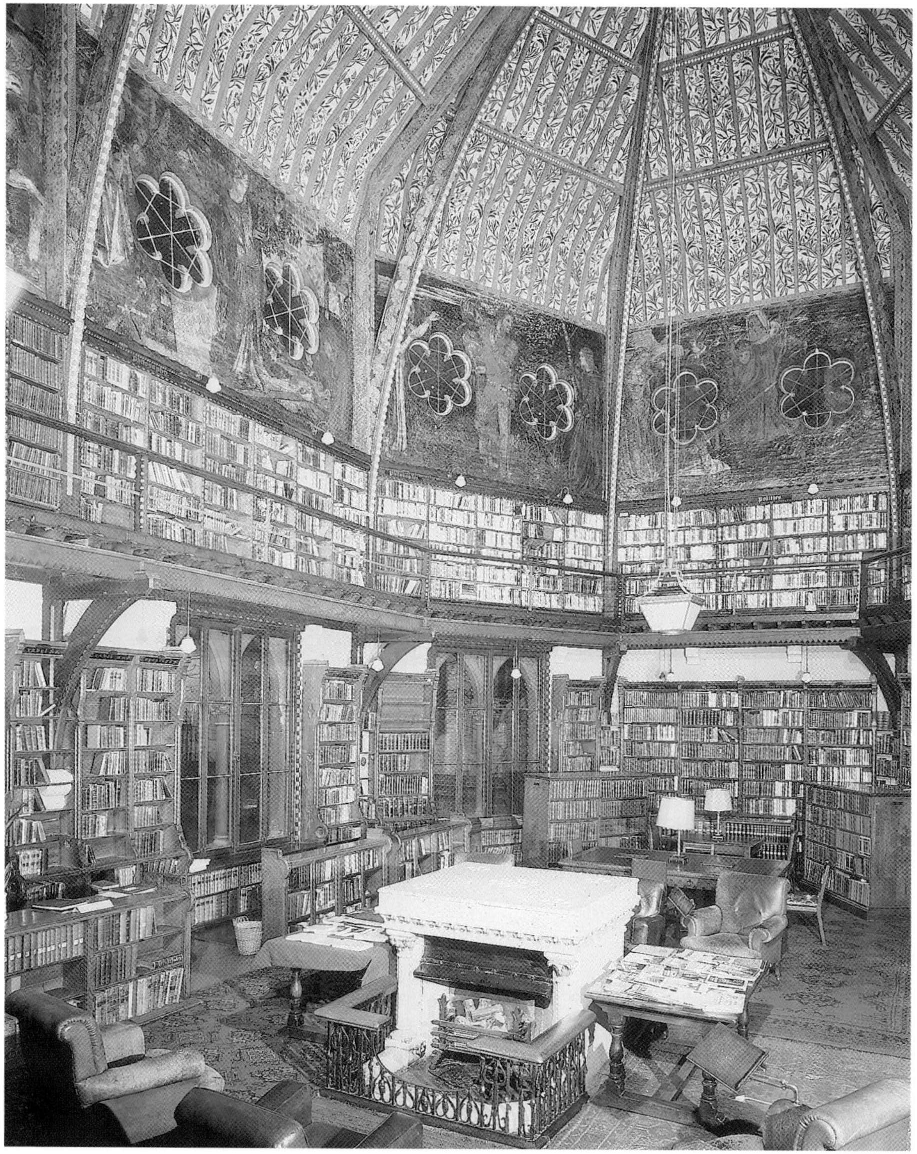

140. The Old Debating Chamber, Oxford Union Society, Oxford, showing the murals of *c.*1857 by Dante Gabriel Rossetti, Valentine Prinsep, and John Hunger Pollen on Arthurian legend subjects

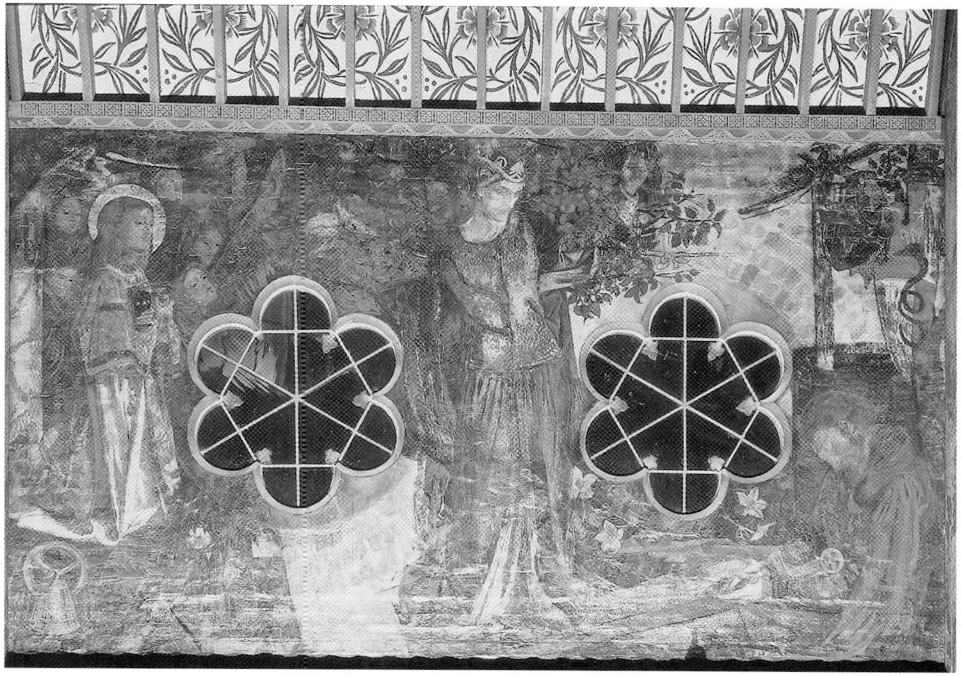

141. Dante Gabriel Rossetti, *Sir Launcelot Prevented By His Sin From Entering The Chapel Of The San Grail*, former Debating Chamber, Oxford Union Society, Oxford, *c.*1857–8

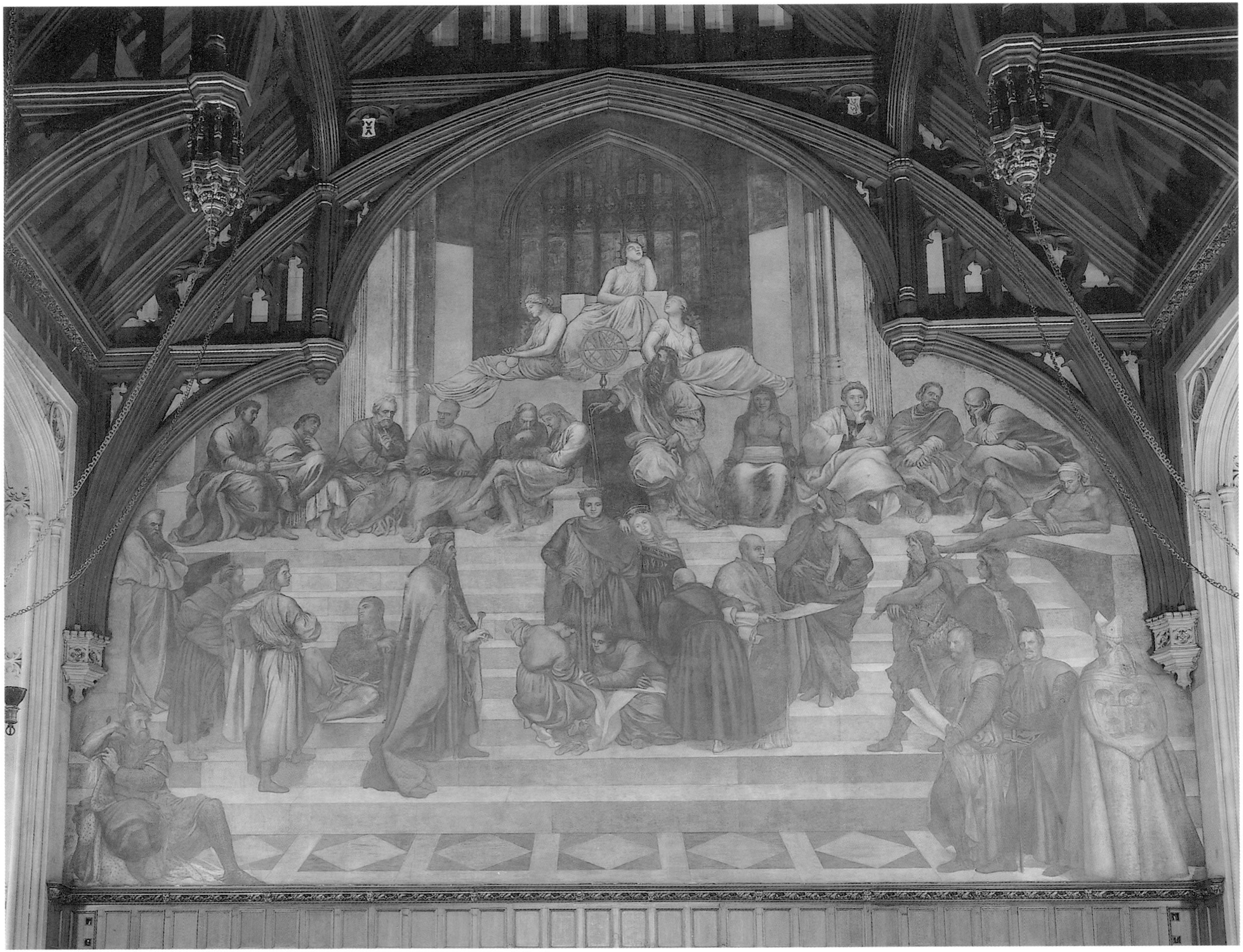

142. George Frederick Watts, *School of Lawgivers*, Lincoln's Inn, London, 1859

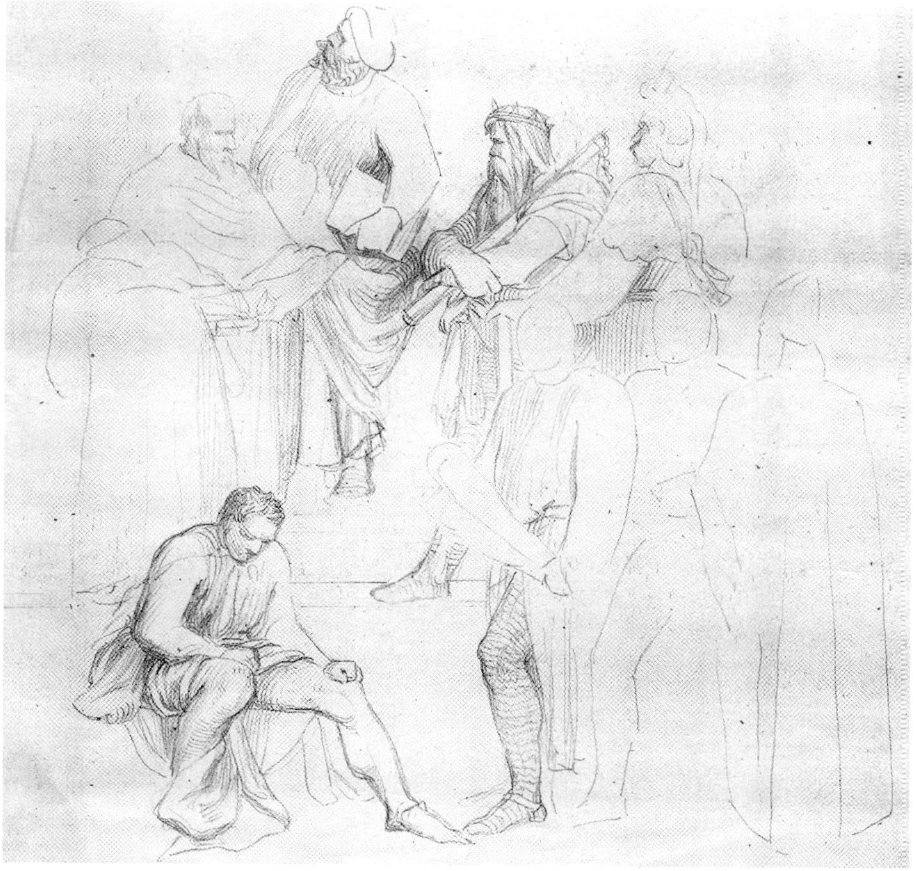

143. George Frederick Watts, sketch for *School of Lawgivers*; figures include the Earl of Pembroke with Magna Carta (third from lower right, modelled by the painter Edward Armitage), the Earl of Salisbury (second from lower right, modelled by Lord Lawrence), Archbishop Stephen Langton (far lower right), and Mahomet (centre, with book), from an album dated February 1858. Compton, Watts Gallery Archives

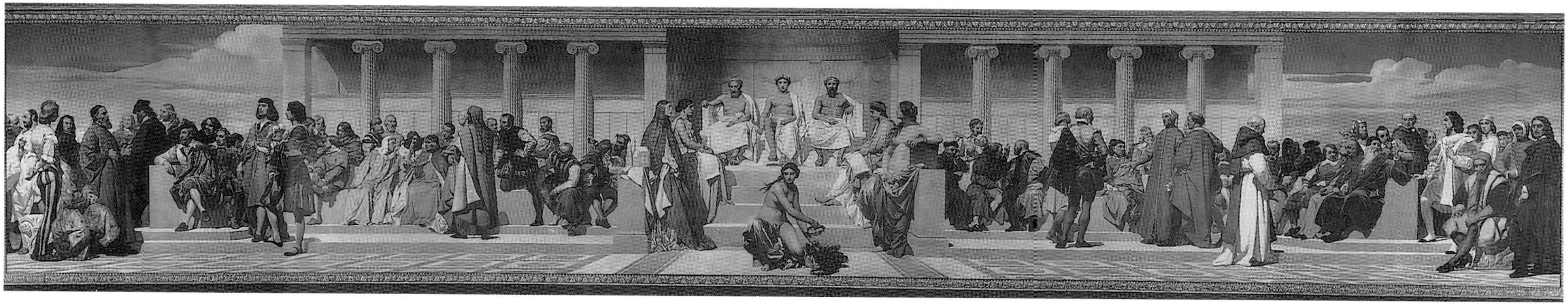

144. Paul Delaroche, hemicycle of the great artists, Ecole Nationale Supérieure des Beaux-Arts, Paris, 1841

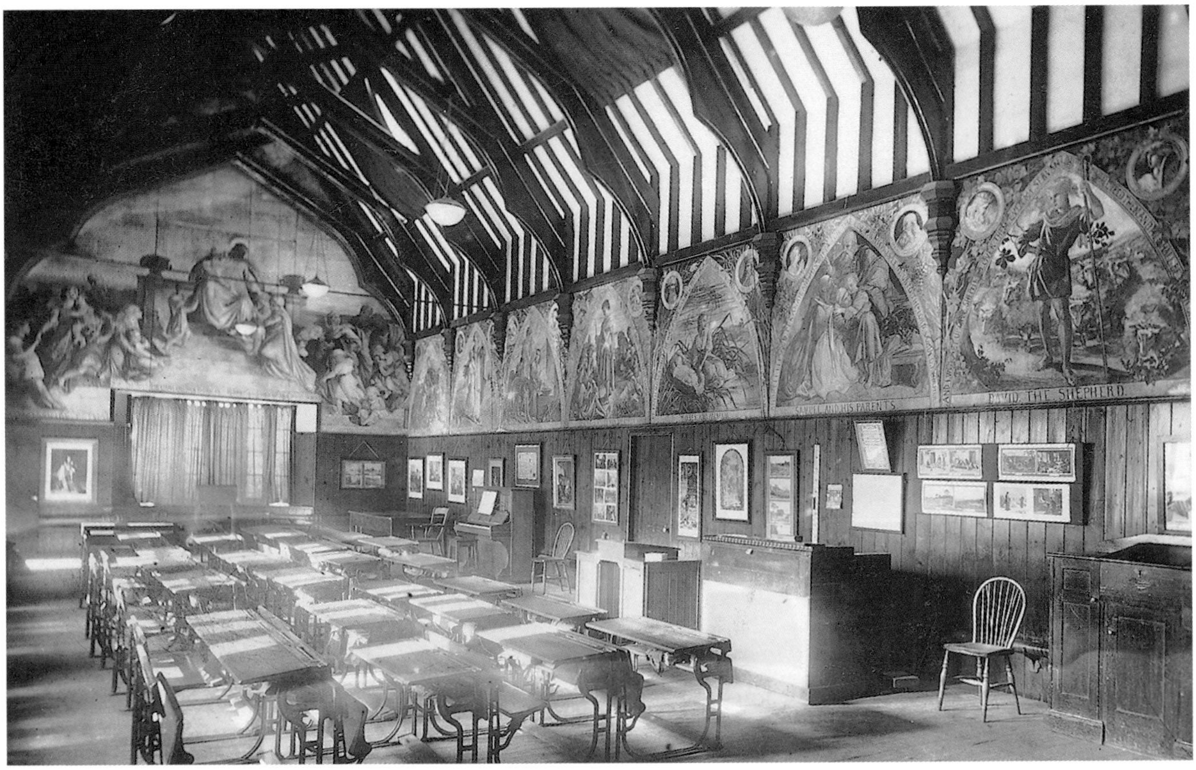

145. Louisa, Lady Waterford, murals of Biblical subjects at the Lady Waterford Hall, Ford, Northumberland (formerly the Village School), 1862–83. (Period photograph, including reproduction of Ernest Normand's *Magna Carta* mural (Plate 34) at the Royal Exchange, painted in 1900, on the wall to the right of the teacher's desk)

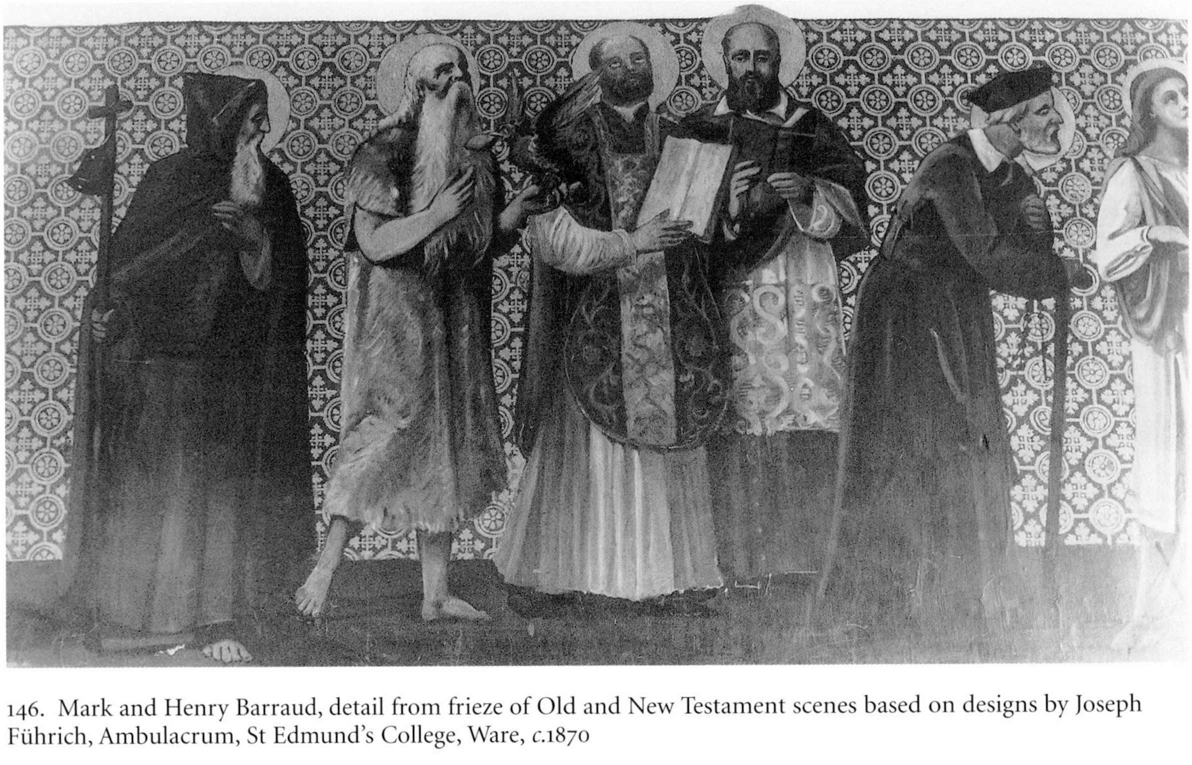

146. Mark and Henry Barraud, detail from frieze of Old and New Testament scenes based on designs by Joseph Führich, Ambulacrum, St Edmund's College, Ware, *c.*1870

individual traverse the epochs of the world's culture.'[44] If the results were prosaic compared with Watts's 'dramatic unities', the theory probably explains in part the choice of Godfrey Sykes as director of the decoration. A pupil of Alfred Stevens, he could be expected to hand the torch of 'Grand Renaissance Tradition' to his assistants Reuben Townroe, James Gamble, and Frank Moody, who after his early death in 1866 carried his designs to completion and oversaw their execution by the students.

Sykes, however, had also helped Fowke and J. G. Crace in decorating the 1862 London International Exhibition buildings, and it was the pattern-type ornament employed here, rather than the High Renaissance figurative tradition, which came to the fore at the South Kensington Museum. The festoons, diapering, and hexagonal motifs in gold, brown, blue, and white smothering its South Court, for example, were found by the *Reader* to bear 'an unfortunate resemblance to a hearthrug';[45] it was with this kind of setting that monochrome mural paintings of spinning, metalworking, and other crafts had to compete, and in due course also, two large lunettes by Leighton. Those 'fine artists' who were eventually employed in addition to Sykes, and who included (as well as Leighton) Watts, Yeames, Horsley, Poynter, Bell Scott, and a battery of lesser painters, normally had no idea whether their efforts would take shape in mosaic, painting, ceramic, or even stained glass. The symbolism of fresco, bonding subject to setting, which was so important at Westminster, the Oxford Union, Lincoln's Inn, and in churches, was now replaced with an ethos of translation, installation, and realization—executive skills in which students could be trained, but which, whatever Cole and his team may have hoped, did not necessarily lead to ability to conceive original works of art. When botanical motifs were painted on the ceiling of the Natural History Museum at South Kensington in the 1870s, for example, it was the commercial company of Best and Lea of Manchester who were called in; and they were likewise employed at Derby Museum and Library whose Gallery was built under the direction of Sir Phillip Cunliffe-Owen, Cole's interim successor from 1873 at South Kensington (Appendix C: 3). The most significant scheme by South Kensington students following the Museum was the set of historical portraits at the Royal Holloway Sanatorium in Egham, built by W. H. Crossland in 1882–4 in a similar Neo-Gothic idiom to his Rochdale Town Hall. The 'South Kensington Museum' policy indeed ran completely counter to Ruskin's insistence at the Oxford Museum that 'all architectural ornamentation should be executed by the men who design it,' whilst at first the Royal Academy actually declined 'to select artists as proposed'[46] by Cole in 1865.

Following the appointment in 1863 of the South Kensington Museum's Art Director, Richard Redgrave, who was also a prominent Royal Academician, 'to superintend experiment of National Art Students decorating the National Competition Rooms',[47] 'fine art' began to play a more prominent role in the decoration. A significant number of the Competition Room's lunettes were both designed and painted by Royal Academicians (Appendix C: 2), whilst Cole had a visit in 1867 from Yeames, who 'wished to connect himself with [our] decoration' and was prepared to reduce his price for a mural from sixty to fifty guineas.[48] Invitations were issued to other Academicians, including Stacy Marks, Poynter, Watts (who declined), and Leighton. Prinsep, as if anticipating

[44] Quoted in ibid., p. 334.

[45] The *Reader* (9 Sept. 1865), quoted in Physick, *The V & A Museum*, p. 60.

[46] Letter from Sir Charles Eastlake to Cole (19 Jan. 1865), V & A Archive, Victoria and Albert Museum, London, Ed 84/67.

[47] Science and Art Department Board Minute Précis (24 March 1863), V & A Archive, Victoria and Albert Museum, London, Ed 84/35, quoted in Physick, *The V & A Museum*, p. 83.

[48] Cole's *Diary*, quoted in ibid.

Leighton's election as President of the Academy in 1878, even portrayed him *alongside* Richard Burchett (Headmaster of the Schools of Design) and Cole, in his mural of *Distribution of Art Prizes*.

One of the deterrents to employing 'fine artists' was undoubtedly their cost. Presumably seeking to grace the Museum with the work of Maclise, then employed at Westminster, the President of the Board of Trade, Lord Granville, asked Cole in 1866 to ascertain his terms for mural painting, but the Museum could not even afford to purchase the cartoon (price £1,000) for his Westminster *Wellington and Blücher* for its collections.[49] With Sykes's death, however, artists were needed. Poynter, who had contributed, along with Morris & Co., to the decorative motifs in the Museum's Refreshment Room, was invited in 1868 to decorate the apse of its Lecture Theatre, but his ambitious design (Plate 147) was hastily abandoned when the cost of executing it in the mosaic method as 'explained at the Society of Arts'[50] was estimated at over £6,000 minimum! Its iconography, illustrating 'the general scheme of Creation', was, in fact, a vigorous manifesto for art dedicated to perfection and the ideal, instead of utility and manufacture. Genius and inspiration, not the mechanics of craft production illustrated earlier in the South Court, were now at stake: 'Beauty unveils herself to the world of Art and Poetry; youth respectfully kisses the hem of her robe . . . to the right of Beauty is a figure representing the Imaginative faculty.'[51] Though the sciences occupy the other half of the design and include Archimedes and Galileo, these too were predominantly 'abstract figures'.[52] Poynter's scheme, still loosely based on the format of Raphael's *School at Athens*, has more in common with the ideals of Anselm Feuerbach, shortly to find expression in his ceiling for the Academy of Fine Arts in Vienna—'True history painting should never descend to pictures of a particular archaeological epoch or social period'[53]—than with Cole's philosophies, and two 'murals' are indeed portrayed within it as if to suggest the very power of decoration as a stimulus to creative thought.

With the abandonment of the Lecture Theatre project, it was left to Leighton in his two vast lunettes for the South Court (cartoons in Plates 148, 149) to take up the cudgels for beauty, imagination, and the ideal. Initial plans for a mosaic copy by Moody of Raphael's *School at Athens* and a lunette by Watts, possibly illustrating 'Workmanship'[54] were abandoned for *The Arts of Industry as applied to War* (Plate 149), a theme which appears to have had its origin in Prince Albert's desire for a Crimean War Memorial but which clearly bears the stamp of Cole's belief in useful art; and (after an attempt by Poynter to seize responsibility for painting one of Leighton's designs), *The Arts of Industry as applied to Peace* (Plate 148). Leighton successfully dissuaded Cole from his plans to have *War* carried out in mosaic, and insisted that 'although my cartoon may be eventually enlarged and even roughly prepared by the students under my supervision it shall be painted by no hand but mine.'[55] A blow had been struck for the genius of the fine artist and for

49 Ibid., p. 92.

50 Letter from Poynter to Cole (20 Dec. 1870), V & A Archive, Victoria and Albert Museum, London, Ed 84/67.

51 Letter from Poynter to Cole (2 Jan. 1871), V & A Archive, Victoria and Albert Museum, London, Ed 84/67.

52 Ibid.

53 Quoted in Finke, *German Painting*, p. 133.

54 Leighton and Watts had both already contributed to the 'Kensington Valhalla' of mosaic portraits of great artists in the niches of the South Court. First plans for the lunettes date from 1863; a design was also produced by F. Pickersgill in 1871. Watts's design was described in the *Art Journal*, 5 (1866), p. 10, but he was apparently happy to cede to Leighton (see his letter to Redgrave (10 Dec. 1873), V & A Archive, Victoria and Albert Museum, London, Ed 84/67). Poynter's succession to Cole as Director of the South Kensington Museum in 1873 probably hastened the shift in emphasis in decoration towards 'high art'.

55 Quoted in R. Ormond, *Leighton's Frescoes in the Victoria and Albert Museum* (1975), p. 7. Practical reasons make it likely that he did use student help, as in his *Daphnephoria* (see S. Jones et al., *Frederic Leighton* (1996), p. 146).

mural *painting*; another was struck by his declaration to Cole in 1871 that 'the promotion of mural painting of a high class is an object for which I am ready to make personal sacrifices.'[56]

Though critical reaction to Leighton's cartoons was generally favourable, it was noted that in *Peace* he had 'seen the beauties he paints only remotely, as though in the work of some other painter, and not in the world about him'.[57] Evocation and abstraction, rather than illustration, seem, however, to have been Leighton's express goal, very much as in his decorative easel work of the 1870s,[58] and also as if to distinguish his work clearly from Sykes's monochrome *Spinners, Silk-Winders, Sculptors* and other subjects around the side walls. *War* portrays a scene suggestive of fifteenth-century Florence, filled with nobles dressing for battle with the aid of spurriers, armourers, and beautiful women; *Peace* (not finished until 1886) a Greek world in which women within a colonnaded setting adorning themselves with jewellery and men ferrying pottery by boat represent 'passive' and 'active' forms of perfect beauty. Leighton, who had been trained in Germany, wrote revealingly to Cole in 1872: 'I sincerely hope you will consent to lend my cartoons to the Vienna Exhibition [presumably the International one of 1873]—it is precisely of the order of work they care for in Germany, could appreciate and think us incapable of.'[59]

Feuerbach's sensuous yet reserved classicism or Arnold Böcklin's yearning to harmonize colour and energy with antique form offer a suggestive comparison. Whilst there are still echoes in Leighton's *War* of Raphael's *School at Athens* and, in the colonnade in *Peace* of Delaroche's hemicycle, there are also new, enigmatic elements more in keeping with nascent Symbolism. The vertiginous background of rocky landscape in *Peace* belongs to the world of Böcklin's *Island of the Dead* (1880, Kunstmuseum, Basle); a muscular boatman steers forwards to the viewer, his mouth opened in a silent cry. The women admiring themselves in hand-mirrors in the centre of *Peace* seem as if on a stage, the edge of which is demarcated by the narrow boat moored across the foreground. The allusion to Greek theatre is explicit in the masks being made at the right, but the strong directional sunlight connects the mural with reality, for it casts shadows as if entering from the window at one side of the South Court. Though it develops Watts's device at Lincoln's Inn, this ambivalence between real and imagined worlds no longer relates to hierarchical portraiture; similarly, the conjunction of the heard (the oarsman's shout) and the seen (the women admiring themselves) suggests something more synaesthetic than the rigid thematic division of 'Arts' and 'Sciences' in Poynter's Lecture Theatre design. Although, as Ormond has noted, the lunettes 'represent contrasting polarities:—war and peace, male and female; action and passivity; strength and beauty; Renaissance and Classical',[60] these are subtly interrelated. The colonnade in *Peace* is 'opened' with doorways, windows, and an enigmatic, partly drawn curtain and blind through which a woman stretches, echoing the more muscular movements of her male companions, and connecting the disciplined architectural foreground with the 'wild' landscape beyond. The women sewing flowing banners in *War* offset the vertical accent of a man trying on armour. These devices can be understood from Leighton's notebook jotting: 'Repose and serenity—grand from implied contrast—each is made beautiful by the relation to toil—potential action should therefore always be manifest where repose to have full grandeur.'[61] Art and Industry had become

[56] Letter from Leighton to Cole (16 May 1871), Nominal File 'Leighton's Cartoons and Frescoes 1868–1923', V & A Archive, Victoria and Albert Museum, London.

[57] Quoted in Ormond, *Leighton's Frescoes*, p. 10.

[58] e.g. *The Daphnephoria* (Lady Lever Art Gallery, Port Sunlight; see Jones et al., *Frederic Leighton*, no. 71, p. 177).

[59] Letter from Leighton to Cole (14 Sept. 1872), Nominal File (n. 56). E. von Steinle, Leighton's early tutor in Frankfurt, in turn often set his students to copy *War*.

[60] R. Ormond in S. Jones et al., *Frederic Leighton*, p. 38.

[61] Note in one of Leighton's notebooks in the Royal Academy, quoted in Ormond, *Leighton's Frescoes*, p. 40.

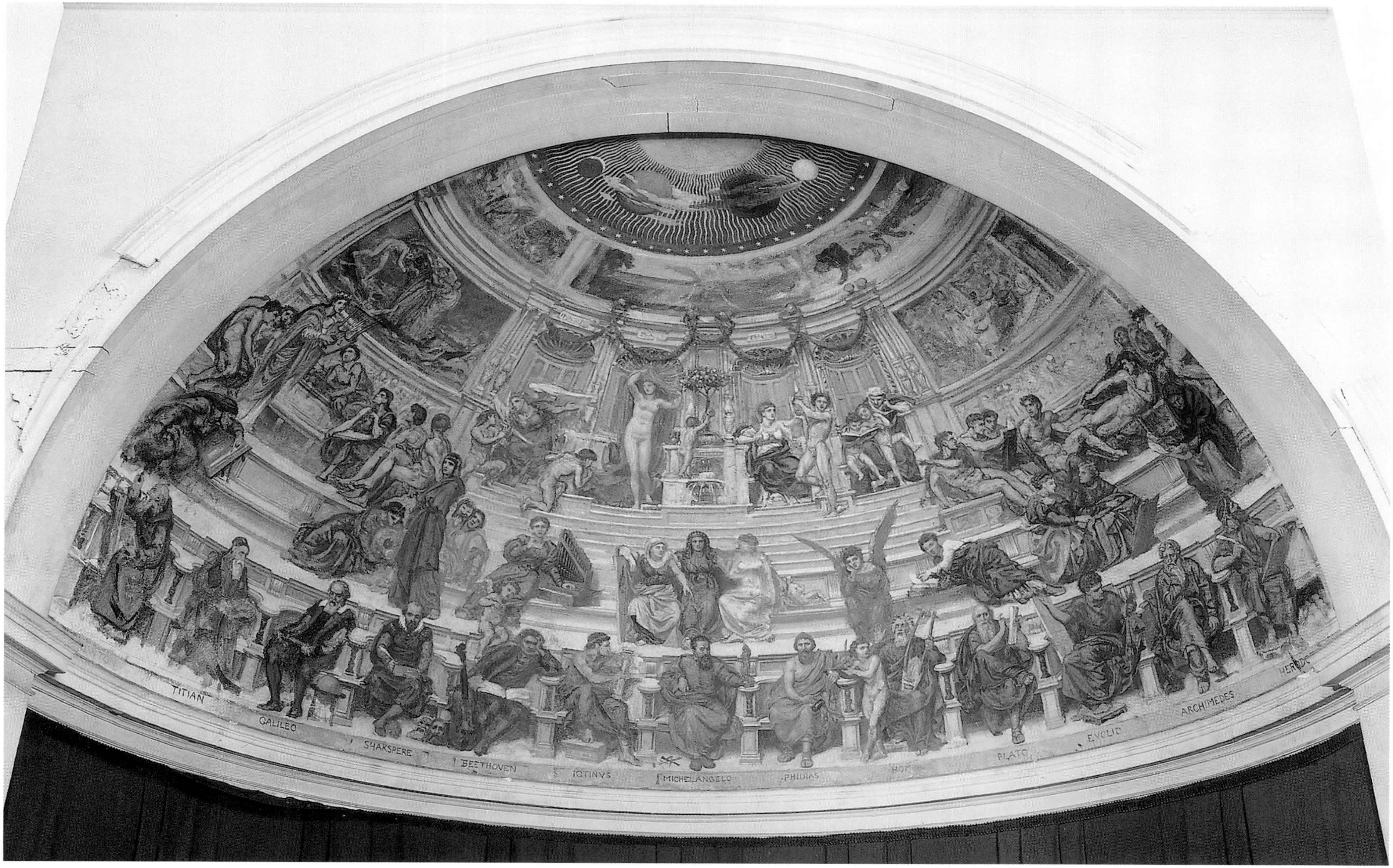

147. Sir Edward Poynter, design for decoration of the Lecture Theatre apse, South Kensington Museum, London, illustrating 'the general scheme of Creation', *c.*1866–71. London, Victoria and Albert Museum

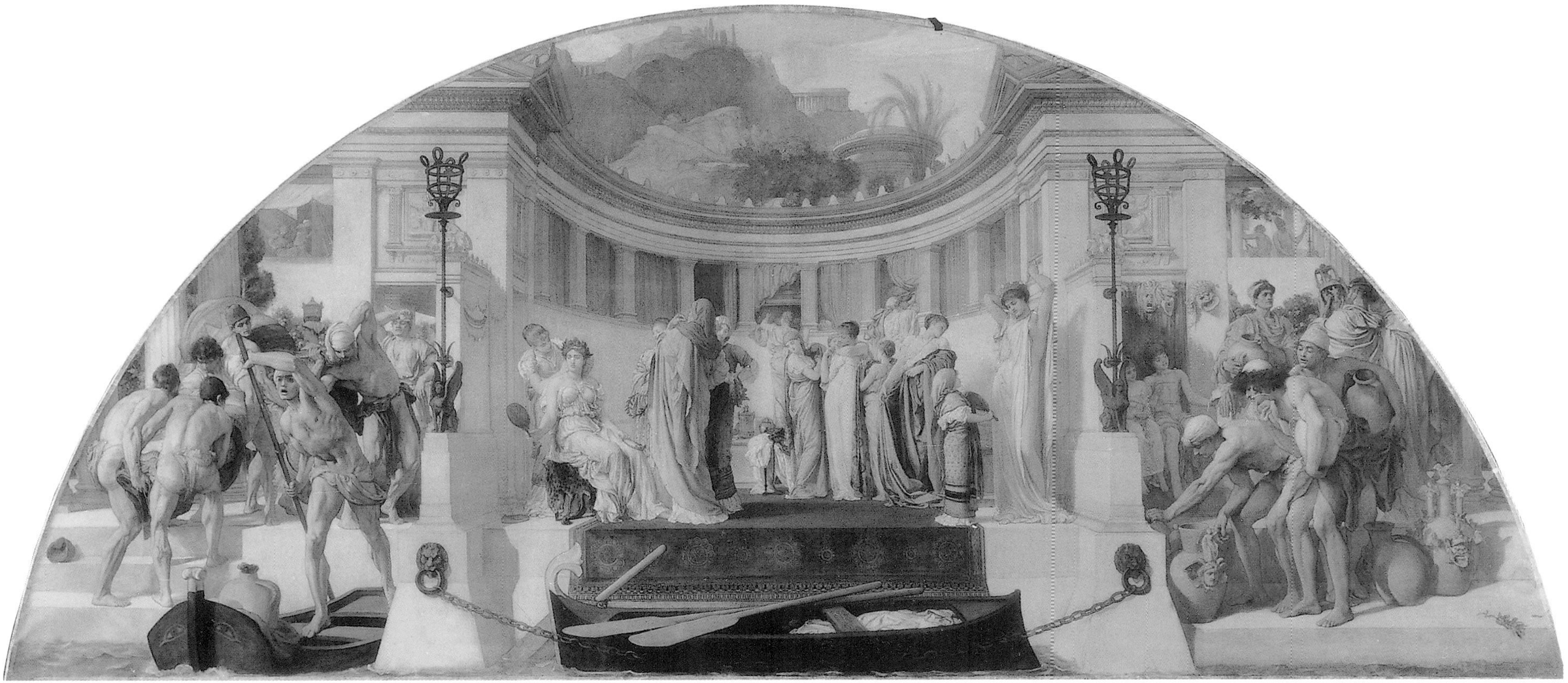

148. Frederic, Lord Leighton, *The Arts of Industry as applied to Peace.* Cartoon for mural in South Kensington Museum, London, *c.*1871–2. London, Victoria and Albert Museum

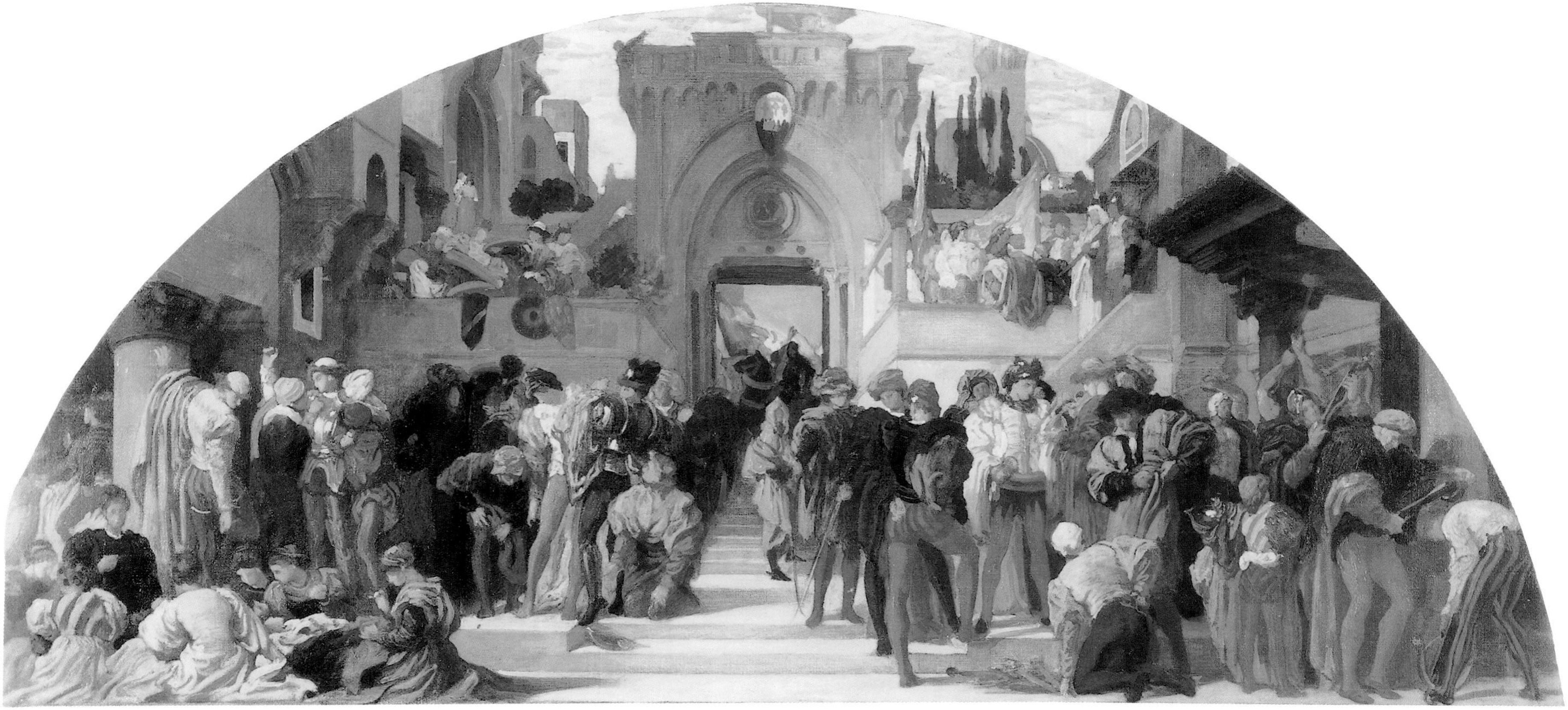

149. Frederic, Lord Leighton, *The Arts of Industry as applied to War*. Cartoon for mural in South Kensington Museum, London, *c*.1871–2. London, Victoria and Albert Museum

interdependent in a way which Cole, with his belief in 'art applied' could perhaps never have understood. In 1880, in retirement, he wrote privately of *War*, 'It looked feeble and not broad enough in treatment—pictorial rather than decorative.'[62]

An important element in Leighton's 'harmony' of opposites must originally have been the complementary colour effects now discernible only from his sketches.[63] The costumes in *War* are a pageant of warm pinks, reds, and purples against cold blue-greens, the contrast made the more vibrant by touches of white in shirts and in the bright sunlight on the upper terrace. If this combination reflects Leighton's admiration for Delacroix, his use of outline around figures may have been derived from Thomas Couture's technique[64] and would, of course, have enhanced by contrast their coloured masses. By employing Gambier Parry's new spirit fresco, meanwhile, he reinvented the earlier symbolic integration of subject and location through technique, turning an instructional demonstration (the technique was published in 1880 by Gambier Parry for the benefit of South Kensington students) into a vehicle for his larger artistic ideal of harmony.

The connection between the decoration of a museum gallery and its purpose, so important in the iconography of the earlier decoration at South Kensington, had actually been cut. Classical art was not collected by the Museum; it was the province of the British Museum. Neither the pottery and bronze artefacts in *Peace* nor the Renaissance architecture in *War* correspond with actual examples; reality, as Leighton's pupil James Ward explained, had been 'passed through the alembic of his mind'.[65] Classical deities personifying the conditions necessary to art were in turn painted, on Leighton's recommendation, by W. E. F. Britten in the soffits of the South Court,[66] but a scheme of 1880 for a mural by J. G. Crace at the National Gallery[67] was never carried out. When Sir Aston Webb proposed murals by Brangwyn for his 1909 extension to the South Kensington Museum, the pendulum had swung completely: its Director, Cecil Harcourt-Smith, took the view that 'the chief decorations of a Museum are the objects placed there for exhibition.'[68]

Art training by mural painting meanwhile effectively passed from the South Kensington Museums to the Royal Academy as a result of Leighton's 'Prize for the Decoration of a Portion of a Public Building' scheme at the Royal Academy. Several prize designs were painted in the Academy's Refreshment Room (Appendix C: 15) (Plate 150) and Girton College, Cambridge made its walls available for another (Appendix C: 6). H. J. Draper's *Spring* (1888 prize), showing youths and maidens gathering blossom and releasing doves, was carried out in spirit fresco in the hall of the Nurses' Dining Room at Guy's Hospital in 1896, and Florence Chaplin (wife of E. H. Shepard)

[62] Cole, *Diary* (22 Mar. 1880), quoted in Ormond, *Leighton's Frescoes*, p. 18. Keen interest in the lunettes was taken, however, not only in Britain (e.g. by the Gresham Committee at the Royal Exchange), but even in Australasia, where the Art Gallery of New South Wales displayed watercolour copies of them by Leighton and photographs, and an account of their technique by Leighton was published (J. Green, 'Interior Decoration', *Australasian Builder* (1892)).

[63] These are in the Victoria and Albert Museum.

[64] See Jones et al., *Frederic Leighton*, p. 61, where Leighton's inspiration from figures in Couture's *Consolatrix Afflictorum* for the women sewing at the left of *War* is also noted (these were also a stimulus for the virgins in Leighton's mural at Lyndhurst).

[65] J. Ward, 'Lord Leighton PRA. Some reminiscences, and an explanation of the methods in which the South Kensington frescoes were painted', *Magazine of Art*, 19 (1896), p. 377.

[66] See W. E. F. Britten, 'Some Thoughts on Decorative Art: the Cartoons at South Kensington', *Architectural Review*, 1 (1897), pp. 115–22.

[67] See G. Waterfield (ed.), *Palaces of Art* (1991), pp. 105–6 and watercolour design by Crace for National Gallery Hall (1887) in National Gallery.

[68] Quoted in Physick, *The V & A Museum*, p. 253. In 1910–11, Hugh Stannus's decorations on the ceilings in the Refreshment Rooms were painted over.

painted her *Hours* in 1904 in the hospital[69] (Plate XXIX). These schemes continue the allegorical idiom of Leighton's *Peace* and *War*, combined in Chaplin's work with finely observed naturalistic flowers and plants.

That Guy's was well-disposed to art perhaps reflected its connection through a former chaplain, F. D. Maurice, with the rise of Christian Socialism. Following his post at the hospital, Maurice had served at Lincoln's Inn during the years when Watts was painting his *Lawgivers*. If the prominence of Moses in the *Lawgivers* alludes to Maurice's *Patriarchs and Lawgivers of the Old Testament* of 1855, Watts in turn became a keen supporter of the Kyrle Society, founded in 1877 by Miranda and Octavia Hill with Ruskin's support. This aimed to bring 'beauty home to the people'[70] in the working clubs founded by Maurice and in schools, mission halls, and hospitals.

'LESSONING THE DEAD UGLINESS OF . . . LIVES'

The Kyrle Society made extensive use of murals (the Birmingham branch decorated no less than thirty-nine local institutions between 1880 and 1889 alone). Many were amateur works or copies but in Glasgow Fra Newbery, the new Director of the city's School of Art, led student schemes including panels by the 'Glasgow Boys' in local welfare centres (Appendix C: 4). A similar project was launched by Dublin's Kyrle Society. Meanwhile in London Canon Samuel A. Barnett, who had married one of the Misses Hill's co-workers, initiated a movement for University Extension, and from 1881 a series of art exhibitions in Whitechapel.[71] It was in Edinburgh, however, in the context of Sir Patrick Geddes's 'University Hall', that Barnett's and the Hills' initiatives bore the richest fruit.

Geddes was seeking to regenerate modern Scotland, starting with the deprived Old Town of Edinburgh, by looking to the values of the nation's ancient Celtic past. 'University Hall' in Ramsay Lodge, Ramsay Garden, the former home of Allan Ramsay the poet, next to Edinburgh Castle, became the focus of his 'little scholastic community in the heart of Edinburgh [that] symbolises a movement which while national to the core, is really cosmopolitan in its intellectual reach'.[72] Although in the 1880s, under the auspices of the Edinburgh Social Union, he had already secured mural commissions for the Irish-born artist Phoebe Traquair in the Mortuary Chapel of the Sick Children's Hospital (Plate 151) and the Song School of St Mary's Cathedral in Edinburgh (Plate 128), her work was essentially derivative and often reminiscent of that of commercial ecclesiastical decorators.[73] Scenes contrasting polluting modern industry with rural tranquillity were painted around the same time by A. G. Sinclair at the Fountainbridge Chalmers Institute, but in 1895, for the symbolic focus of University Hall, its Common Room at Ramsay Lodge, something more original, subtle, and ambitious was required. This was where such scholars as the geographer Elisée Reclus, the educationist and social theorist Edmond Demolins, the biologist Ernst Haeckel,

[69] Draper subsequently carried out the ceiling paintings at Drapers' Hall (see Chapter 3). His Guy's mural is now known only from a line version owned by the hospital, but Chaplin's (painted in oil) is still *in situ* (see the *Studio*, 22 (1901), p. 118 for design). F. Appleyard, another RA Decorative Prize winner, painted murals at Nottingham General Hospital, but these have not survived.

[70] Quoted in Gage and Mullen, *G. F. Watts*.

[71] For the Dublin Kyrle Society work, see J. McBrinn, 'Belfast's Other Murals', *Causeway* (1997). Barnett's exhibitions often included work by Watts, Leighton, Rossetti, and Burne-Jones.

[72] Geddes, quoted in E. A. Sharp, *William Sharp (Fiona MacLeod): A Memoir* (London, 1910), p. 249.

[73] See Chapter 8; T. Bonnar of the Edinburgh firm of decorators likewise restored a 16th-century painted ceiling at Riddle's Court in the Royal Mile, Edinburgh, for Geddes in 1890.

and the psychologist William James gathered each year for Geddes's Celtic Revival think-tank, his Summer Schools. Geddes turned to John Duncan, who, with W. G. Burn-Murdoch, and Charles Mackie (who had trained with Sérusier at Pont-Aven), was masterminding the art activities at the Summer Schools. Duncan had studied at the academies of Antwerp and Düsseldorf and had recently returned from Italy and Paris, where he had been deeply impressed by early Italian art, Puvis de Chavannes, and Moreau; in later life he was to comment 'The more ideas a picture gives the better I like it.'[74]

Completed between 1895 and 1898, with further panels being added by Duncan in the 1920s (Appendix C: 22), the Common Room programme (Plate XXX; Plates 152, 153) illustrates heroes and incidents from Celtic and Scottish history and literature. These were chosen for what Geddes called 'reasons manifold: poetic, historic, academic, even personal to the student's life of which they shadow forth the possible stages'.[75] Youth is represented by the warrior Cuchullin; Arthur receiving Excalibur; and the acolyte Mungo, whilst Maturity is present in Fionn fighting Swaran; Johannes Scotus Erigena (the Irish mystic), Michael Scot, and the Admirable Crichton. Decline is illustrated by Fergus, the saint whose spirit passes at death to Mungo, and by Merlin in *The Taking of Excalibur.* The central message of the murals, however, can be identified in the paraphrase of Ecclesiastes 1: 9 which is painted symbolically as part of the frame around *The Awakening of Cuchullin* (Plate XXX) over the door:

As it hath been
So it shall be.

This inscription also relates to a Columban prophesy quoted by Geddes in outlining his vision of a 'Scots Renascence'.[76] Its theme of cyclic renewal is aptly reflected by the Celtic interlace (lines without end) which borders the inscription and originally framed all the murals. *Cuchullin* launches the scheme by showing the hero rising to fight new battles after regenerative sleep; his father Lugh holds a healing potion for him and his sister brings his helmet and sword, whilst his past and perhaps future victories are 'illustrated' as if murals behind him. The theme of rebirth is vividly embodied in Duncan's 'modern' style of simplified outlined shapes and a bold red and deep green colour scheme, which betrays the influence of the Nabi art he must have encountered in Paris and through Mackie. The motif of two figures wrestling was derived from Japanese prints by Gauguin in his recent *Vision after the Sermon* (National Galleries of Scotland), and also taken up by Maurice Denis; it is also used for *The Combat of Fionn* (Plate 152), which, like Gauguin's picture, dispenses with a horizon to emphasize the psychological and decorative impact of the scene. By overcoming Swaran, Fionn restored peace to Erin.

The theme of regeneration is perhaps most strikingly conveyed in *The Journey of St. Mungo* (Plate 153). Receiving Fergus's holy spirit, Mungo is enabled to master two wild bulls to draw the saint in a wain to his resting-place. Duncan's scholarship is clearly evident in details derived from Jocelyne's *Life of St. Mungo*, such as the background river, but the elements of the story are woven into a deeply powerful image. Fergus's rebirth in Mungo (and that of Scotland, where Mungo came to Glasgow) is visually suggested both by the saltire cross formed by Mungo's raised arms as he reins in the bulls, and by the Christian cross formed by his girdle and tunic-fold. Fergus, though

[74] Comment in Notebook of John Duncan, *c*.1931–39 (NLS).

[75] Geddes, *The Interpreter of Seven Pictures of Black and White* (Foreword) (Edinburgh, 1896).

[76] Geddes, 'The Scots Renascence', *Evergreen* (Spring 1895), p. 138.

dead, intriguingly sits upright in the wain, rising immediately behind Mungo like an *alter ego* so that the viewer sees the two saints as one. The rearing bulls, perhaps inspired by Moreau's *Les Chimères* (begun in 1884, Musée Gustave Moreau, Paris), and the simplified colour scheme of reds, blues, Mungo's white robe, and the green plants on the buff, high-horizoned landscape, contribute to an almost heraldic effect. This is reinforced by the realistic flowers, scattered regardless of scale across the landscape as in the *Dame à la Licorne* tapestries admired by Duncan in Paris, or entwined like Celtic interlace. The arresting frontal viewpoint and unity of form and meaning contrast forcibly with the more literal, atmospheric rendering of the subject created concurrently by E. A. Walton in an unexecuted design for Glasgow City Chambers (Hunterian Art Gallery, University of Glasgow), and align the mural with Continental Symbolism.

Numerous other details in the murals reveal Duncan's imaginative yet historically accurate interpretation. Johannes Scotus Erigena, for example, who realized through a vision of his burning soul 'how hapless was the plight of each creature if that He who created should not also restore',[77] is shown against a rising or setting sun, whilst his soul, reaching outward to the light entering the room through the window, is an exact reversal of Cuchullin's posture at the opposite end of the wall, and is encircled with flames stylized as Celtic knotwork. The imagery suggests that Duncan referred direct to Erigena's own *De Divisione Naturae*, where rhetoric of fire and light is prominent. Similarly, whilst the 'burning' knotwork reminds us that the soul is merely a vision, its body is intensely corporeal: in keeping with his Summer School colleague Ernst Haeckel's belief in the identity of psychical and physical activity, Geddes held that 'The body without the spirit is a corpse. The spirit without the body is a phantom.'[78] Erigena's soul also calls to mind Blake's *Marriage of Heaven and Hell*, where, beneath a figure in flames, is written 'But first the notion that man has a body distinct from his soul is to be expunged.' The complex symbolism of Duncan's image, however, makes it far more subtle than the Blakean flame-enwrapped children's souls of Phoebe Traquair's Sick Children's Hospital murals. Belief in unity of body and spirit explains not only Fergus's 'living' upright posture, but also the tangible presence in *Michael Scot* of Aristotle himself, guiding the mystic's translation of his work.

Light and fire, meanwhile, recur as a visual and thematic *Leitmotiv* throughout the whole scheme. Cuchullin, a 'Sun-god', has flowing red hair; his father Lugh was King of Light, whilst Fionn, also shown with red hair, is described by Duncan's source, Macpherson's *Ossian*, in terms of light and fire. Mungo has tongue-of-fire angelic wings and flames at his ankles (again derived from Jocelyne's *Life*). Was Duncan familiar with the Oxford Union murals? The booklet published by Geddes to describe the murals certainly quotes Tennyson's lines about Excalibur, 'The blade so bright / That men are blinded by it'. The brilliant oranges, reds, and turquoises of *The Admirable Crichton* illustrate his traditional image as 'that most exquisite jewel'.[79]

Crichton alludes to Geddes's *Vivendo Discimus* ('we learn by living') motto through its pose derived from Donatello's *David*, the Biblical 'man of thought and action'. In Geddes's booklet, the entry on *Crichton* is prefaced by a definition of the 'Virtue' he represents which uses the German word for it: 'Tugend . . . Courage and the Faculty to *do*.'[80] It is, of course, in Nietzsche's *Also Sprach*

[77] Quoted in an entry on the mural by Arthur Thomson in Geddes, *Interpreter* (1896).

[78] Quoted in A. Defries, *The Interpreter Geddes: The Man and his Gospel* (London, 1927), p. 72.

[79] Quoted from 'his [i.e. Crichton's] biographers' by A. Thomson in entry on *Crichton* in Geddes, *Interpreter* (1896).

[80] Ibid.

Zarathustra that not only 'die schenkende Tugend',[81] the 'bestowing' or 'highest' 'virtue', is discussed—the one which has the character of gold, always reflecting light and therefore endlessly continuing itself—but also the doctrine of 'eternal recurrence'. This is preached to mankind by Zarathustra (based on the god of fire Zoroaster), who descends from and returns to the brilliance of sunrise. Given Geddes's extensive travels in Germany and his friendship with the evolutionary biologist Haeckel, as well as Duncan's contact with W. B. Yeats, who admired not only Blake but also Nietzsche, and with Otto Schlapp (the first Professor of German at Edinburgh University), it is likely that the Common-Room iconography of 'As it hath been, so it shall be' was at least partly influenced by *Zarathustra*. It is significant, for example, that all the murals deal with extraordinary individuals; types, in essence, of the Superman whom Zarathustra himself personifies.

It would be misleading to suggest Nietzsche as the sole source of the murals' imagery; they present a distinctively Christian reading of renewal, and parallels can also be drawn with the ideas on the continuum of experience of the philosopher William James, who attended Geddes's Summer Schools. Duncan did, nevertheless, include the typically Nietzschean image of a bacchanalian procession in his murals in Geddes's flat at Ramsay Garden,[82] as well as Darwin listening to Pan in his later Common-Room murals. Geddes, however, had evolved a modified Darwinism which posited natural selection on an energizing love both sexual and spiritual, and this idea, rather than Nietzsche's philosophy in particular, may relate to the body and soul unity in Duncan's murals. For the Dining Room at University Hall he painted the naked figure of St Andrew on the Cross, which so shocked the custodian of the neighbouring Free Church College that he tore the canvas before it was installed.[83]

Clearly, Duncan's Common-Room scheme represents a highly original and distinctive contribution to mural painting in Britain, and is one of the closest British counterparts to French Nabi decoration. Like his *St. Andrew*, however, almost all the remainder of the extensive decoration in 'University Hall' and its related rooms at Ramsay Garden has been detached or lost. Duncan's striking *Jehanne d'Arc et sa Garde Ecossaise* (cf. Plate 154), painted for the Franco-Scottish Society at Ramsay Garden,[84] was illustrated in Geddes's journal the *Evergreen*, and other drawings in this by Duncan, Mackie, and others may also record murals.[85] Further decoration for Geddes was illustrated in the *Studio* of 1898[86] and Geddes had clearly established in Edinburgh the kind of school of decorative painters so eagerly sought at South Kensington and earlier at Westminster (Appendix C: 7–9). When in turn the Board of Manufactures commissioned murals for Rowand Anderson's new Scots Baronial-style Scottish National Portrait Gallery and Museum of Antiquities building in Edinburgh in 1897, it is not surprising that W. G. Burn-Murdoch and Robert Burns, two of Geddes's artists, were asked to supply examples of their work. J. R. Findlay, the proprietor of the *Scotsman*, who had funded the building, wished to have an integrated

[81] F. Nietzsche, 'Von der schenkenden Tugend', Part I of *Also Sprach Zarathustra*, trans. R. J. Hollingdale, *Thus Spoke Zarathustra* (Harmondsworth, 1969), p. 99.

[82] See Chapter 10.

[83] C. Cammell, *Heart of Scotland* (London, 1956), p. 233.

[84] Duncan's painting of this title (The City Art Centre Edinburgh) is painted in oil on canvas and is 1.07 × 1.38 m; its size suggests it could be a detached mural. He mentioned the theme in conjunction with his Ramsay Garden murals (letters to Geddes of 18 Nov. 1895 and 3 July 1927, MS 10508 (A) and 10549 in NLS).

[85] See Chapter 10 and Willsdon, 'Paul Sérusier the Celt', *Burlington Magazine*, 126 (1984); the religious subjects by A. K. Womrath, for example, could, with Duncan's *St. Andrew*, have formed part of the Biblical/church history mural programme proposed for the 'Assembly Hall' by the artist W. Brown-Macdougall in a letter to Geddes (22 Oct. 1894) (SUA), and Duncan's 1890 Notebook (NLS) includes a list of further such subjects alongside his Common-Room titles.

[86] The *Studio*, 13 (1898), pp. 48–9 (seasonal panels by M. Hill Burton for the Dining Room of St Giles's House, apparently part of the University Hall complex).

programme of painted and sculptural decoration.[87] In the event, William Hole, who had earlier supervised student contributions to Edinburgh Social Union murals, was asked to paint the frieze of 'Great Scots' (Plate XXXI) which runs on a gold ground around the upper central hall, and the ten large scenes from Scottish history on the first-floor ambulatory and north wall. Spirit fresco was employed (his wife made tea with a burner for him on his scaffolding!) (Plate 155) and an echo of Leighton's South Kensington iconography can perhaps be found in the 'Peace' and 'War' theme which underpins the historical episodes and is also present in the façade sculpture. As at Ramsay Garden, there is, however, a specifically Christian element: the *Peace* episodes show *St. Columba Preaching to the Picts* (Plate 156) and *The Landing of St. Margaret at Queensferry.* The gathering of still figures in a landscape with a lake or river and hilly backdrop in *St. Columba* suggests that Hole was perhaps looking also to the vision of an ideal past of Puvis de Chavannes's *Le Repos* at the Musée de Picardie in Amiens, or his *St. Geneviève* Panthéon cycle in Paris (he visited France in 1897). For all their meticulous reference to historical artefacts owned by the Museum of Antiquities, the battle scenes none the less have an energy and breadth of conception, whilst *Bannockburn's* wounded receiving succour make a cross-reference to the 'Christian Peace' theme in a way which develops something of Leighton's or Watts's synthetic approaches. The 'Great Scots' frieze presents a rhythmic continuum which, in contrast to the individually framed figures of the 'South Kensington Valhalla', invites the viewer to follow Carlyle (at the start) back via Watt with a model steam engine, Sir Walter Scott, and the kings and queens to brawny Stone Age warriors, and to engage with history in a manner comparable with both the pageants mounted by Geddes, and the 'living, many-coloured, romantic history' shortly to be espoused by G. M. Trevelyan.

Though lacking money to continue his patronage after 1900, Geddes had laid a strong foundation for numerous 'educational' and 'welfare' murals in the twentieth century in Scotland (Appendix C: 11, 16, 20, 30, 32–5). One of his earliest projects had been decoration of the new Milton House Board School in the Royal Mile,[88] whose infant mistress in turn founded a progressive kindergarten on the lines of Froebel in the early 1900s, and a number of later Scottish schemes continued this connection with the child-centred education movement which had taken early root in Scotland. Duncan's 1912 composite illustration of nursery rhymes in his mural for St Peter's Roman Catholic School in Falcon Drive, Edinburgh, next door to Father Gray's church, where he met the Russian mystic André Raffalovitch, attempts to enter the child's imagination in a way which probably reflects his experience as a teacher in the early 1900s under the progressive educationist John Dewey in Chicago. Jessie M. King painted murals in schools, including Arthurian subjects for Mossend Primary School, Bellshill, near Glasgow, in a twee fantasy style halfway between the 'Glasgow Spook School' and the idiom of the Ballets Russes she had admired in Paris, and in the 1920s she advised the Lanarkshire Education Authority—dubbed by the local press 'a special kind of boss fairy that can make wonders possible'—on 'flower and fairy' schemes for nearly a hundred schools, 'transforming the usual drab plainness of such buildings into a corner of fairyland itself'[89] (Appendix C: 21). Using a modified realism with overtones of Art Deco, the murals painted in local schools and colleges by the Andrew Grant Fellows of the

[87] H. Smailes, *A Portrait Gallery for Scotland: The Foundation, Architecture and Mural Decoration of the Scottish National Portrait Gallery, 1882–1906* (Edinburgh, 1985), pp. 49 ff.

[88] By Thomas Bonnar.

[89] Quotations from press cuttings kindly supplied by Strathclyde Department of Education (30 April 1924; source illegible) and from *Daily Mail* (9 March [May?] 1929).

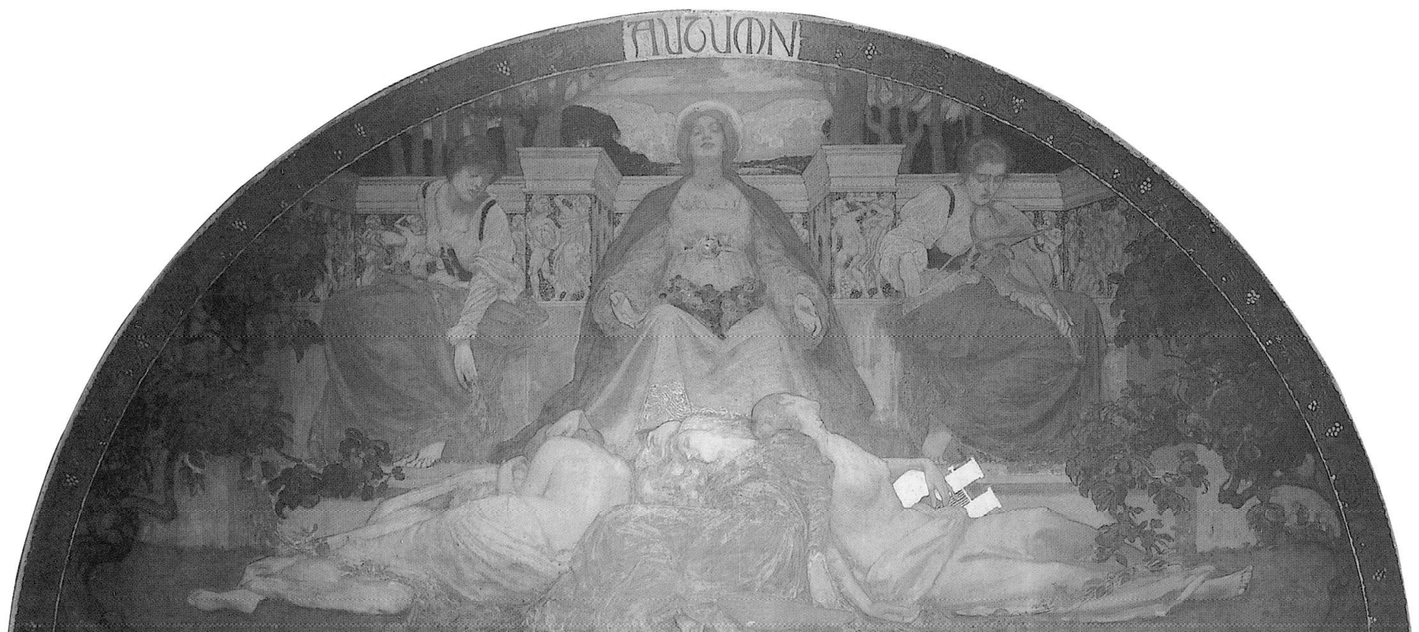

150. Harold Speed, *Autumn*, Refreshment Room, Royal Academy of Arts, London, 1898

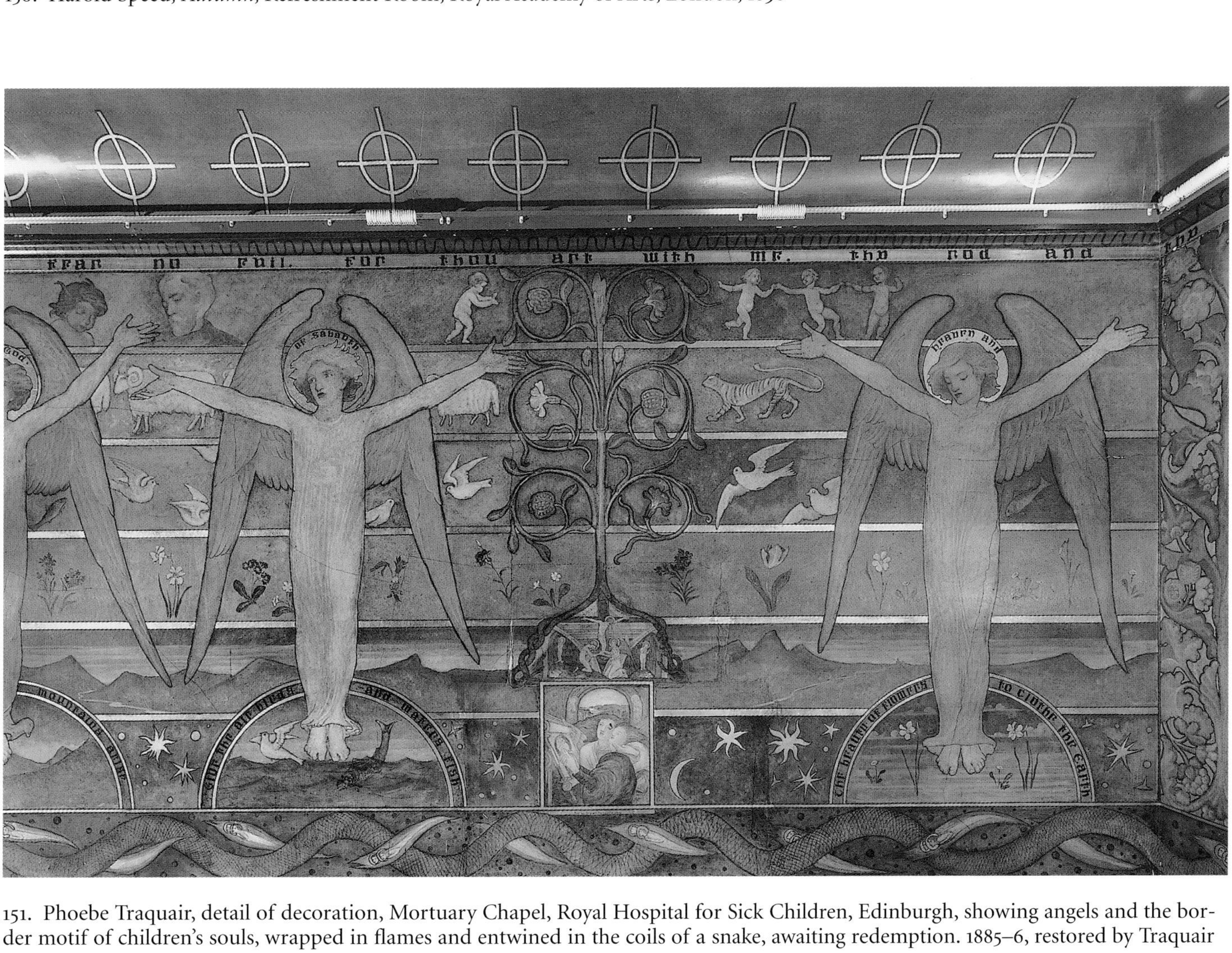

151. Phoebe Traquair, detail of decoration, Mortuary Chapel, Royal Hospital for Sick Children, Edinburgh, showing angels and the border motif of children's souls, wrapped in flames and entwined in the coils of a snake, awaiting redemption. 1885–6, restored by Traquair 1896–8

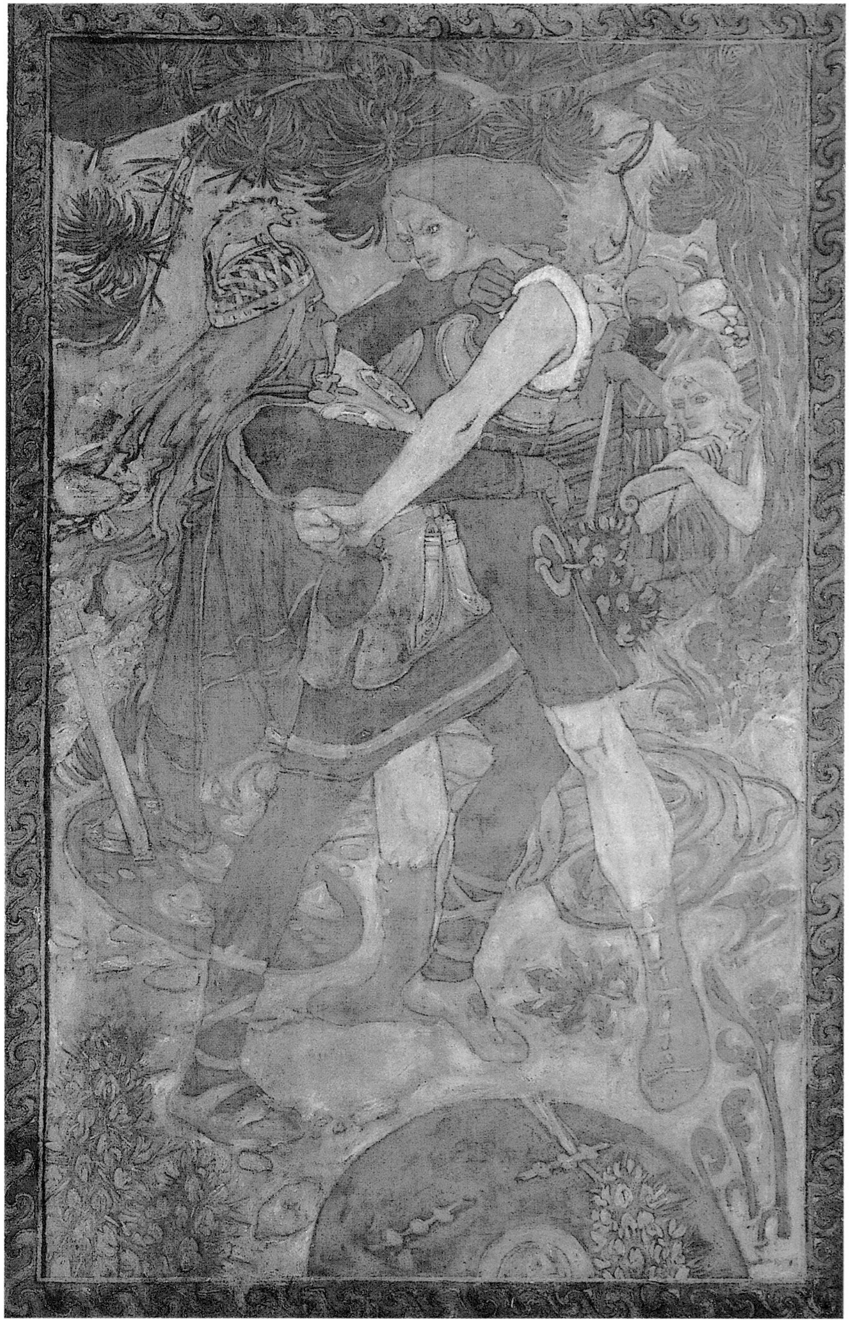

152. John Duncan, *The Combat of Fionn*, former Common Room of University Hall, Ramsay Lodge, Ramsay Garden, Edinburgh, 1895–8

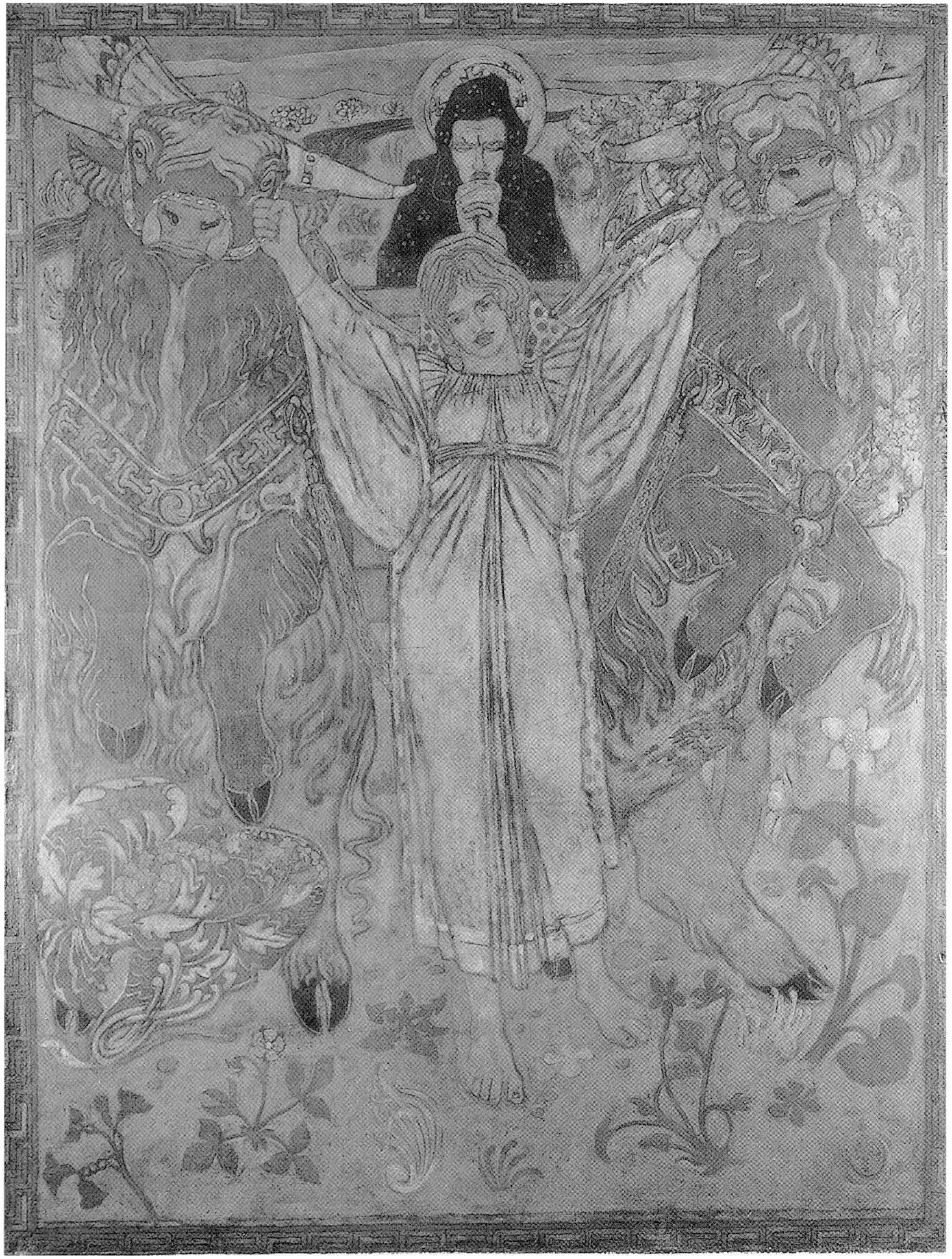

153. John Duncan, *The Journey of St. Mungo*, former Common Room of University Hall, Ramsay Lodge, Ramsay Garden, Edinburgh, 1895–8

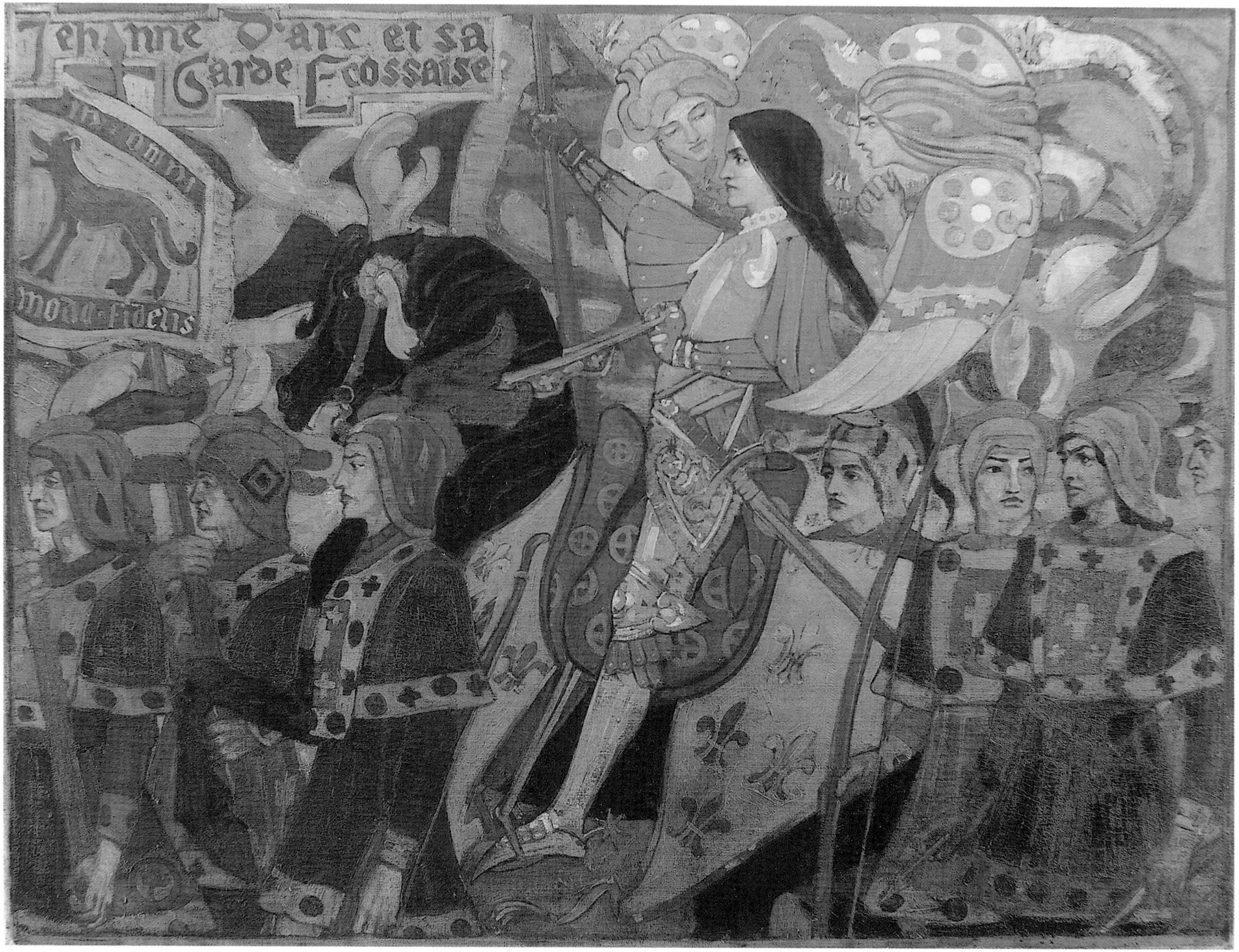

154. John Duncan, *Jehanne d'Arc et sa Garde Ecossaise*, mural or painting related to a mural formerly in the Franco-Scottish Society premises at Ramsay Garden, Edinburgh, *c.*1895. Edinburgh, The City Art Centre

Edinburgh College of Art during the 1930s were essentially a continuation of this movement. Artists included John Maxwell, whose *Neighbourhood Scenes* for the hall of Craigmillar Primary School (1935) (Plate 157), incorporating motifs suggested by the pupils,[90] also paralleled the community emphasis of the New Deal murals of the period in the USA, which were typically installed in schools. Like other commissions under the Edinburgh scheme (Appendix C: 30, 33–5) launched in 1932 by the College's Principal, Hubert Wellington, who had helped Rothenstein promote the murals by young artists at Morley College in London discussed later in this chapter, Maxwell's work illustrates a more general post-war tendency to emphasize 'entertainment' rather than 'instruction' in mural painting.

Outside Scotland in the twentieth century, a number of apparently diverse trends can be identified in 'education' and 'welfare' mural painting, which, in one way or another, none the less emerge from the 'social' view of art cultivated by Ruskin and Geddes; in several cases they were the direct outcome of an exhibition of designs for school and welfare murals at Crosby Hall in London in 1912, in which Geddes was involved. The 'mission statement' of Dorothea Beale, Headmistress of Cheltenham Ladies' College, for example—'to deliver the learner from . . . dungeon-like classrooms, and to bring into the school life . . . beauty and light . . . [children] should live . . . not in a mere material atmosphere'[91]—was essentially similar to Geddes's philosophy. So too were the ideals, bound up with his Socialist politics, of Walter Crane, Director of Art at the new Royal College of Art, which had been created from the South Kensington National Art Training Schools. He argued that 'the capacity for children for receiving ideas through the eye [should] be taken advantage of' with classroom walls 'pictured with the drama of history' and 'made eloquent with the wonders of the earth by the true and emphatic drawings of the life and character of different countries and peoples'.[92] Both Miss Beale's 'School Beautiful' movement, expressed in James Eadie Reid's 1902 *The Dream of Fair Women* above the proscenium arch in the hall of her own school (Plate 158) and other schemes (Appendix C: 12), especially in girls' schools (Appendix C: 14–15), and Crane's own decorations (Appendix C: 10) tended to favour literary, Biblical, or allegorical imagery of an essentially conservative nature.[93] Reid's Cheltenham Ladies' College mural, inspired by Tennyson's poem, portrays 'the qualities of courageous devotion and self-sacrifice'[94] through portraits of Alcestis, Penelope, Savitri (from Indian legend), and the Egyptian Queen Hatasu, each set amongst entwined foliage. Whilst this might appear to invite a feminist reading as an appropriation of masculine chivalric ideology,[95] the mural was perhaps intended, like other such schemes, as much to cultivate the 'feminine' attributes of taste and sensibility, and to associate the authority of 'High Art' with the controversial field of women's education (Reid was a pupil of Sir William Richmond). The somewhat Symbolist manner of the lunettes at Roedean of *Night* and *Morning*, by Sylvia Lawrence, a friend of Watts,[96] was unusual.

[90] See the *Scotsman* (1 May 1935) and other period press cuttings about the Grant Fellowship commissions in the archives of Edinburgh College of Art. Maxwell's *Children's Games* . . . is painted in oil mixed with wax on gesso, and is approximately 4 × 9.50 m in size.

[91] Dorothea Beale, quoting Edward Thring, in her Guild Address at the school in 1896 (A. C. Clarke, *A History of Cheltenham Ladies' College 1853–1979* (London, 1953), p. 60).

[92] W. Crane, *The Claims of Decorative Art* (1892), p. 78.

[93] Biblical themes were painted by Eadie Reid in the Chapel of Cheltenham College (the boys' school) in the 1900s. For the 'School Beautiful' epithet, see Clarke, *Cheltenham Ladies' College*, p. 50.

[94] Ibid., p. 207.

[95] Such appropriation is discussed in A. Smith, '*Masculinities in Victorian Painting* by Joseph Kestner' (review), *Art History*, 20, no. 4 (Dec. 1997), pp. 629–30.

[96] A further panel by Lawrence (Head of Art at Roedean), represents *The Good Shepherd* in a Clausen style; all the panels (in tempera) are in House sitting rooms.

Crane had actually been invited by Geddes to contribute to the decoration of 'University Hall', but had declined. Despite his ideas about 'true and emphatic' art for schools, as late as 1911 his *Painting, Sculpture*, and *Architecture* lunettes for the Royal West of England Academy in Bristol (Plate XXXII) used compositions clearly derived from Leighton's South Kensington *Peace* and *War* and present a somewhat self-conscious array of allegorical personifications, with 'modern' prismatic colour effects being elaborately 'justified' by the 'Sphere of Imagination' held by 'a winged youthful figure'.[97] In a sense, the 'true and emphatic' imagery for which he had called, and which in essence continues Ruskin's wish at the Oxford Museum to combine 'truthful statements' with 'exciting address to the observant faculties', was rather to be found in the 'documentary' panoramic scenes of the great sites of Egyptian archaeology, glowing with pink and gold atmospheric colour, at the Harris Museum and Art Gallery in Preston (Plate 159). These were painted by John Somerscales between 1909 and 1914 for the building's classical-style central hall. Begun in the very year when Harcourt-Smith declared the 'exhibits the decoration' at the Victoria and Albert Museum, Somerscales's murals (which he carried out after both Watts and Puvis de Chavannes had turned down earlier invitations to decorate the building) were sandwiched between friezes of casts from Assyrian, Egyptian, and Greek art to form an integral part of the display; the ensemble was intended to evoke the rise of Western civilization to the Renaissance. Whilst in one sense 'decoration', the murals were thus also 'exhibits', putting on show for visitors the place and time in which the 'foundations' of modern art were felt to lie.

A new and different reading both of the 'true and emphatic' and of the 'primitive' was meanwhile being offered in what the *Evening Standard* called 'the most important artistic event of 1911',[98] the completion of seven 'removable' panels painted under Roger Fry's direction for the Borough Polytechnic, on the theme of *London on Holiday*. These were *The Zoo* (by Fry himself) (Plate 160), *The Fair* (by Etchells), *Toy Sailing Boats* (by Bernard Adeney, illustrating the Round Pond at Hampstead), *Football* and *Bathing* (by Duncan Grant) (Plate 161), *Paddlers* (by Albert Rutherston), and *Punch and Judy*, by Macdonald Gill.[99] 'Truth' now lay in contemporary iconography; 'primitivism' in the 'Byzantine' style.

Suggested by Fry's Cambridge friend Basil Williams (Chairman of the Polytechnic's House Committee), the scheme followed directly on Fry's first Post-Impressionist Exhibition and was the springboard for his formation of the Omega Workshops in 1912. The sequential actions of diving, swimming, and clambering into a boat which are portrayed in Grant's *Bathing*, set in the Sepentine Pond, present *action* rather than appearance, and Adeney later explained that the 'technique of graduating the colour tone to a dark contour' borrowed from Byzantine art had been used 'to increase the rhythm of the design'.[100] Rather than fulfilling an instructional purpose, the murals were placed in the Dining Room; like Duncan Grant's *Queen of Sheba* design (Tate Gallery, London) the following year for Newnham College, Cambridge,[101] they offered recreation and even 'escape'. At the same time, however, their experiments with visualizing events in time, suggesting influence from sequential photography and cinematic images, and exactly paralleling

97 W. Crane, quoted in A. Crane, *The Walter Crane Lunettes at the Royal West of England Academy* (Bristol, 1995), p. 11.

98 Quoted in R. Shone, *Bloomsbury Portraits* (1976), p. 70.

99 The panels are now in the Tate Gallery, London.

100 Quoted in Shone, *Bloomsbury Portraits*, p. 66.

101 Tate Gallery, London. Apparently intended for the College Hall, this shows Lytton Strachey as Solomon. It arose from the Crosby Hall mural exhibition (see below) and a second design by Mrs Bernard Darwin, for 'the south wall of the lecture room passage', was commended by Henry Tonks (Minute Book of Newnham College Council, 11 May 1912, p. 262).

155. William Hole working on his frieze of *Great Scots* in the Scottish National Portrait Gallery, Edinburgh, *c.*1898

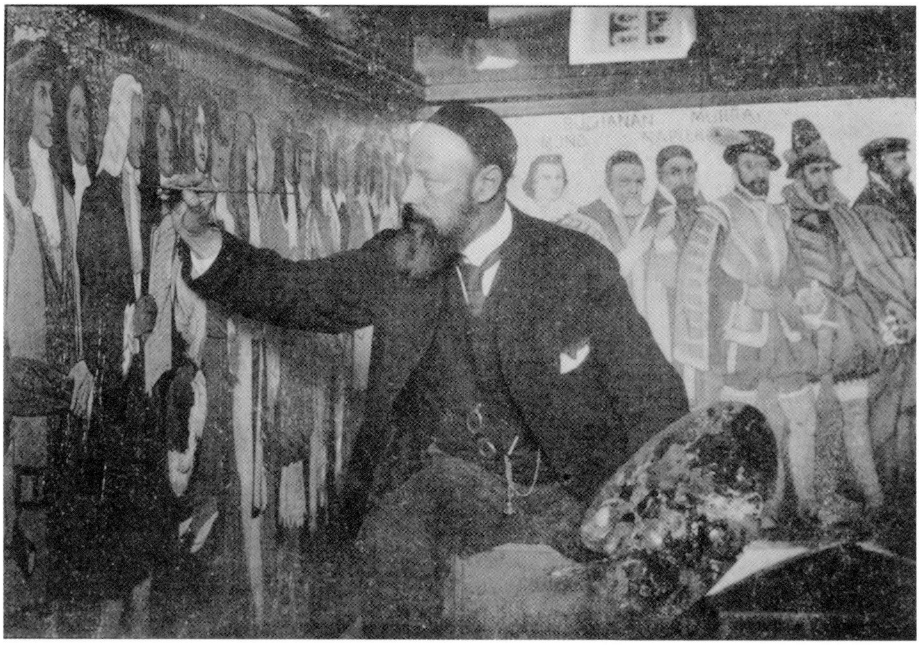

156. William Hole, *St Columba Preaching to the Picts*, Scottish National Portrait Gallery, Edinburgh, 1898

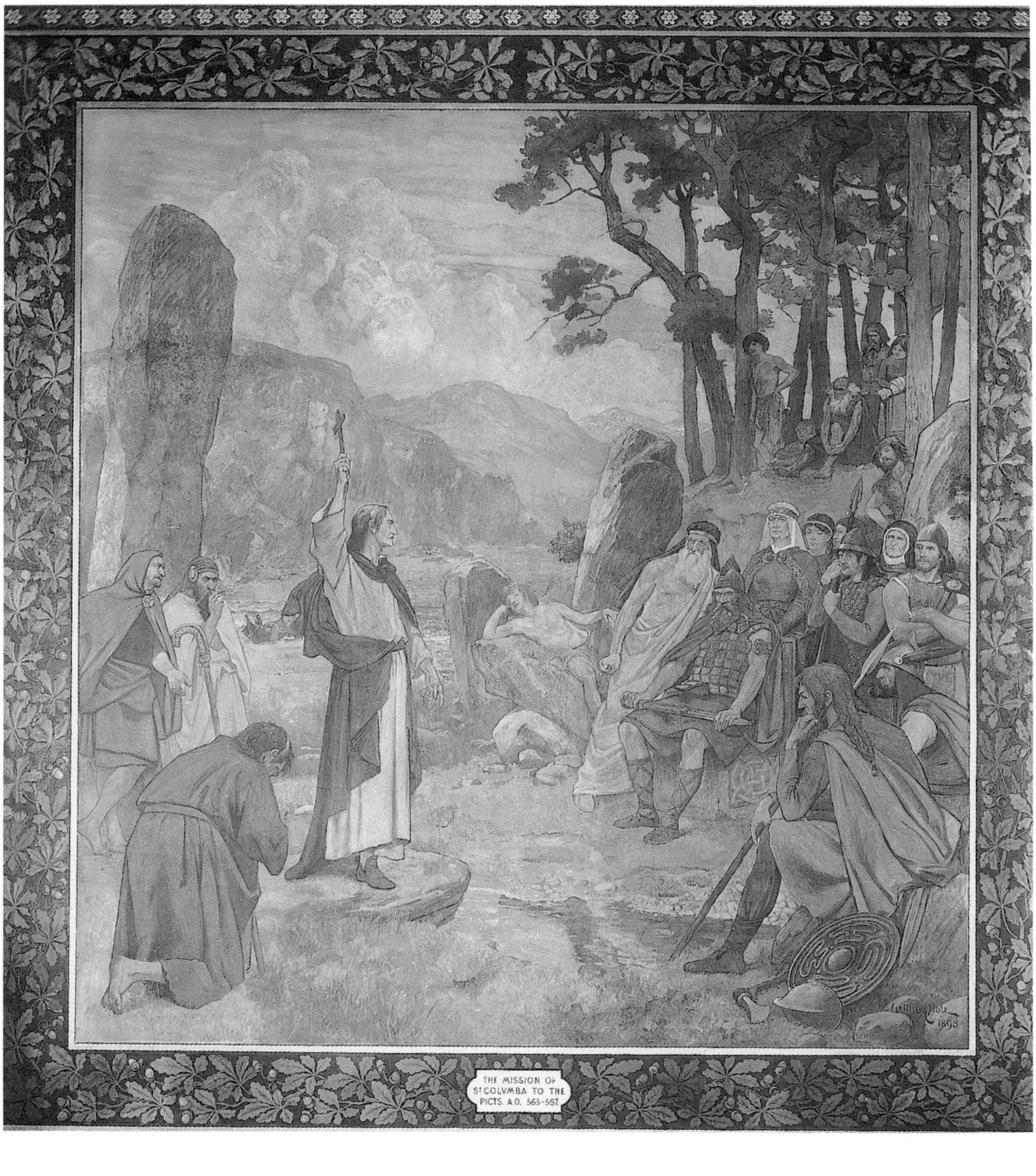

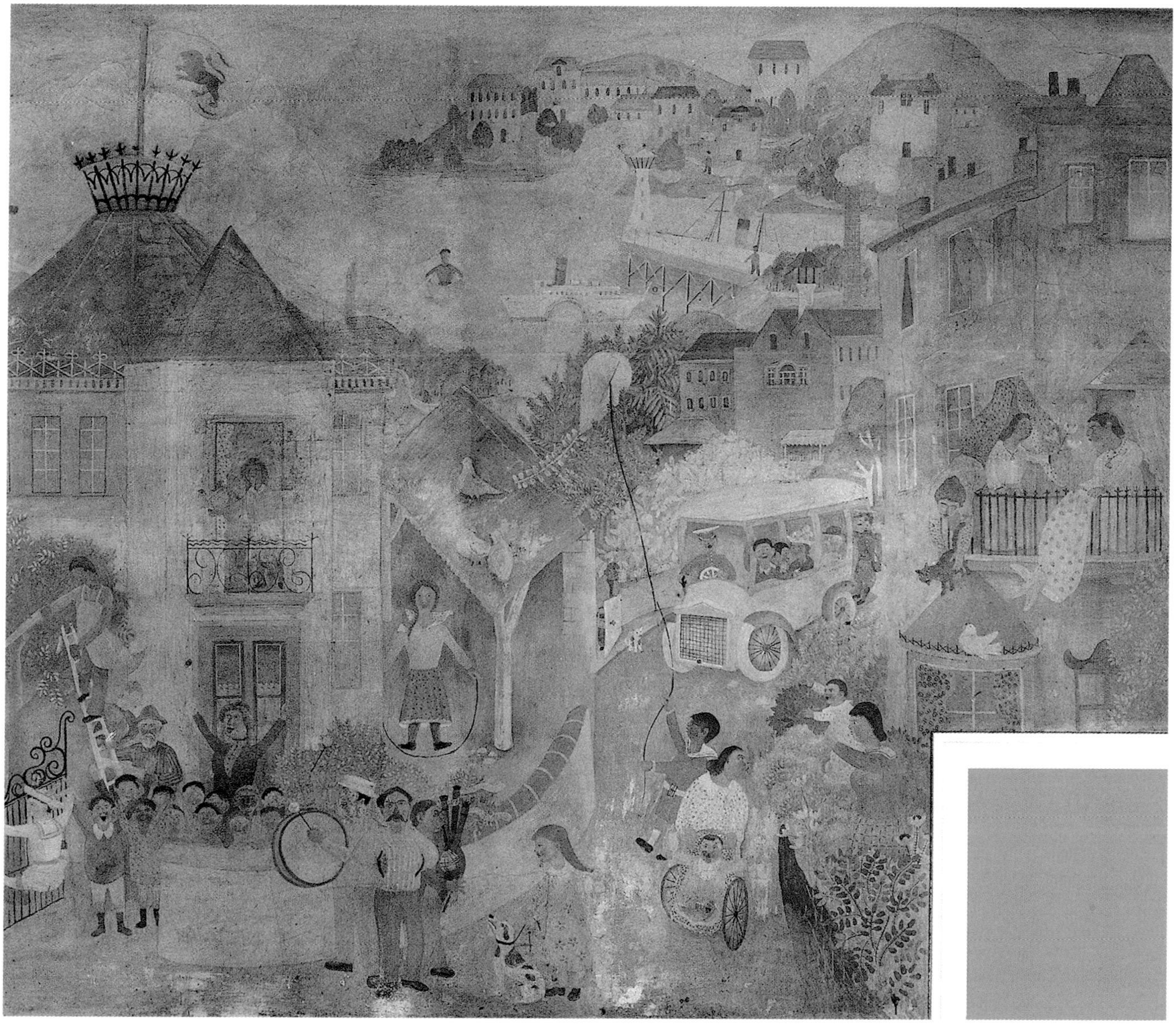

157. John Maxwell, detail from *Children's Games and Amusements*, Dining Room, Craigmillar Primary School, Edinburgh, 1934–5

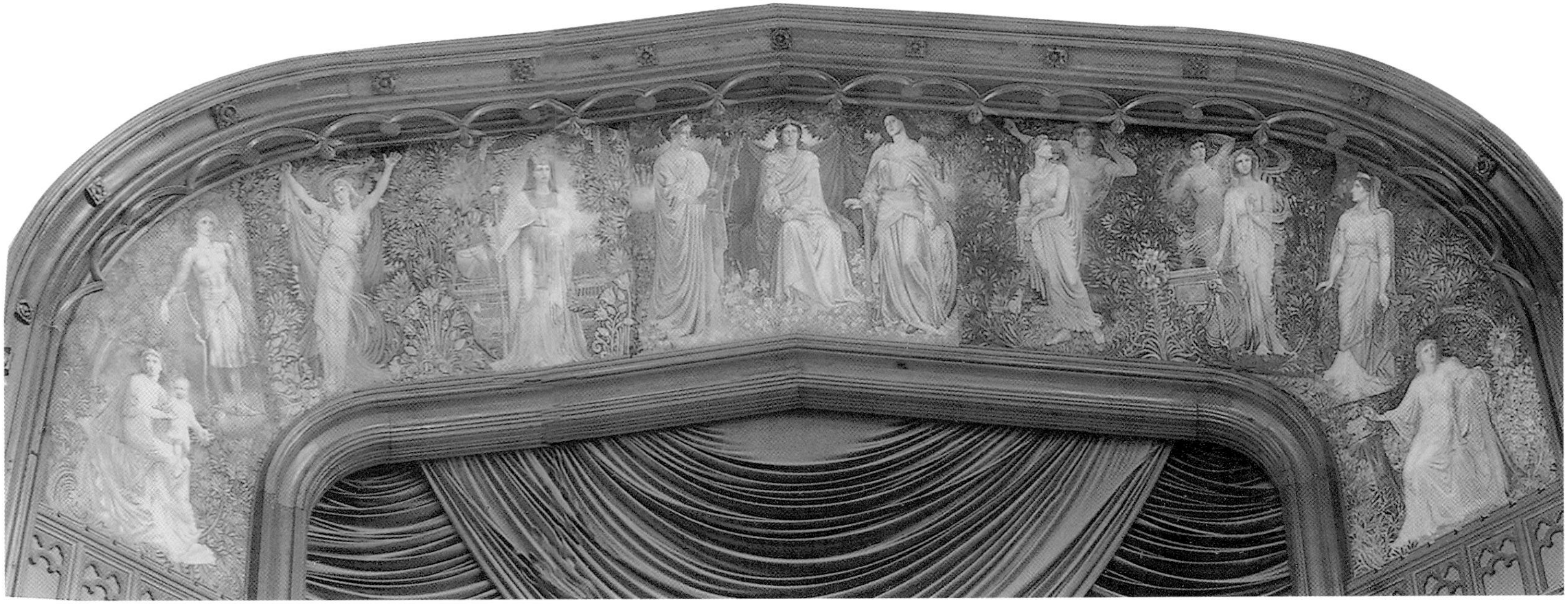

158. James Eadie Reid, *The Dream of Fair Women*, the Princess Hall, Cheltenham Ladies' College, 1902

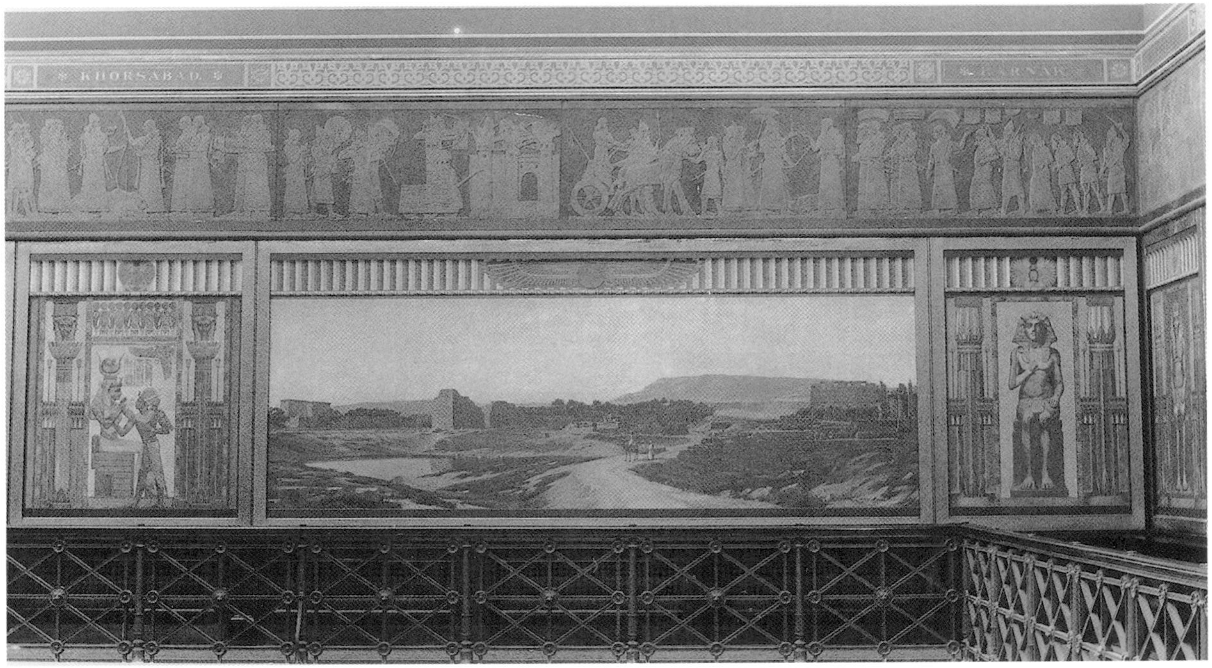

159. John Somerscales, Egyptian site, Harris Museum and Art Gallery, Preston, 1909–14 (side panels illustrating Egyptian antiquities believed to be by W. Morris-Sim)

Duchamp's 'dissociated forms' of action in his *Nude Descending a Staircase*, hint—despite the eschewal of 'meaning' in art by the Bloomsbury group—at philosophical reflection on 'time', 'place', and 'space'. Where Watts had fused these through fresco and 'dramatic unities' in his *Lawgivers* (Plate 142) (which had, perhaps significantly, been the subject of an article in Fry's *Burlington Magazine* in 1906), Grant's *Bathing*, of course, freezes fractions of an instant from contemporary London life with the aid of an artistic style, the Byzantine, which was 'intended to . . . produce a sense of the universal and eternal'.[102] In this sense, the very paradox of the Polytechnic murals as 'removable' can be read as integral to their dialogue of transience and permanence, and a kind of cipher for Fry's belief in 'significant form', the immutable element contained in all art but separate from the variables of both nature and the viewer's response. Were Fry and Grant perhaps even aware of Einstein's *Restricted Theory of Relativity*, published in 1905, and indicating the continuity of time and space?

Fry's roots were, after all, in the Arts and Crafts tradition of art for a purpose; he had learnt decorative painting in Ashbee's Ruskin Art Class at Canon Barnett's Toynbee Hall, in London. Photographs of the Polytechnic murals, 'lent by Roger Fry for the workers',[103] were given a prominent place in the exhibition of school, college, and welfare institution murals held at Crosby Hall in London in 1912, whose advisory committee included (as well as Geddes), Crane, Halsey Ricardo, Rothenstein, Tonks, and other representatives from the LCC and the major London art schools. It did not, however, have a Royal Academy representative. None of the RA Decorative Painting Prize murals were illustrated and the emphasis was on social improvement rather than the 'aesthetic ideal' which the Academy had come to represent. The exhibition was actually a sequel to one held by Geddes in Edinburgh[104] and included not only samples of the French models he admired, such as a mural design by Puvis de Chavannes, but even an 'actual piece of wall' from Phoebe Traquair's first Sick Children's Hospital Mortuary Chapel decoration, and designs for murals in Manchester Council schools by W. E. Daly which had been commended by Crane. Madox Brown's Manchester Town Hall murals, and John Singer Sargent's for Boston Public Library were also represented. Competitions for wall-painting in LCC schools and a number of other institutions were mounted in association with the exhibition. Despite its eclectic *mélange*, it looked as though a bright new era for 'mind and body' was about to dawn. In turn, challenging Fry's and Geddes's hand-craftsmanship values, the uncompromising modernity of the machine was being celebrated in the 'Rebel Art Centre' established in 1914 by Wyndham Lewis at 38 Great Ormond Street, London, as a kind of Vorticist art school. The decoration here (Plates 162, 163) included a near abstract panel above the fireplace by Edward Wadsworth, evoking a modern port scene and tellingly called *Caprice*, whilst Lewis himself contributed a mural showing a screaming head in ferocious reds.[105] This imagery, however, was to become actuality only a few months later, in war.

[102] 'Byzantine Art', *Encyclopaedia Britannica*, 11th ed. (1911), vol. 4, p. 908.

[103] *Exhibition of Designs* . . . (1912), p. 11.

[104] See advance publicity notice about the exhibition, T-GED 5/3/35, SUA. Detailed reviews of the 1912 exhibition were published in the *Builder*, 102 (14 June 1912), p. 689 and the *Building News and Engineering Journal*, 102, no. 2996 (1912), p. 798.

[105] For the Rebel Art Centre decoration (no longer extant), see R. Cork, *Art Beyond the Gallery* (1985), pp. 190 ff.

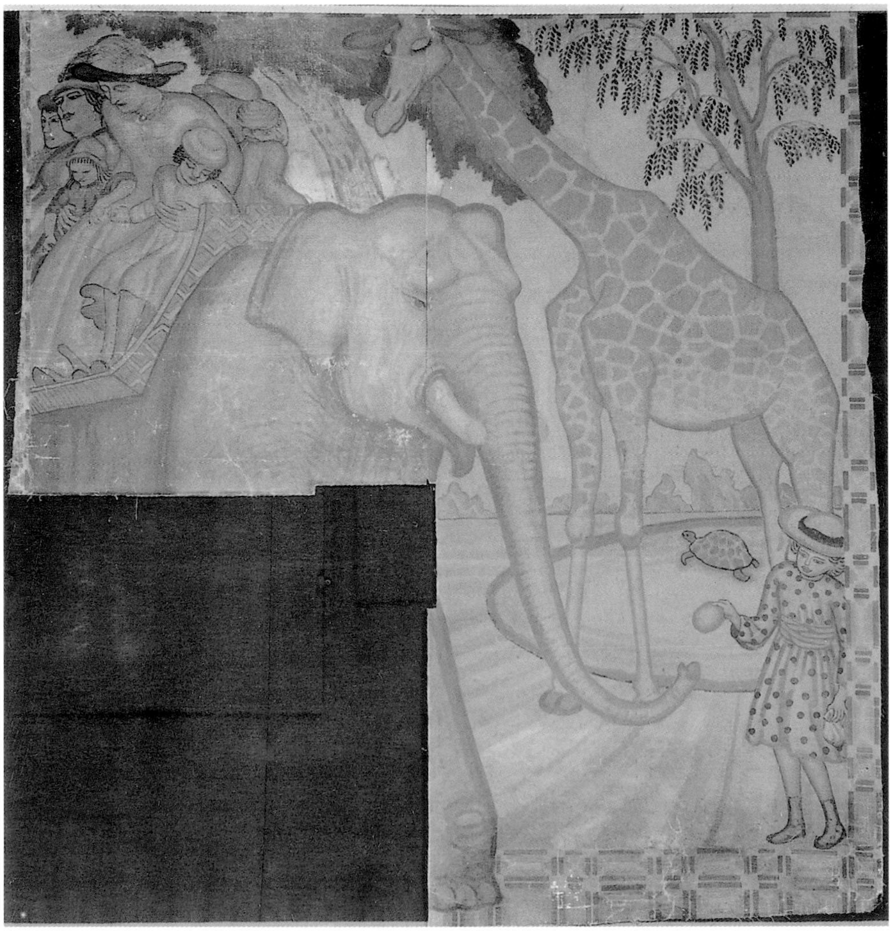

160. Roger Fry, *The Zoo*, two fragments from mural decoration formerly at the Borough Polytechnic, London, 1911. London, Tate Gallery

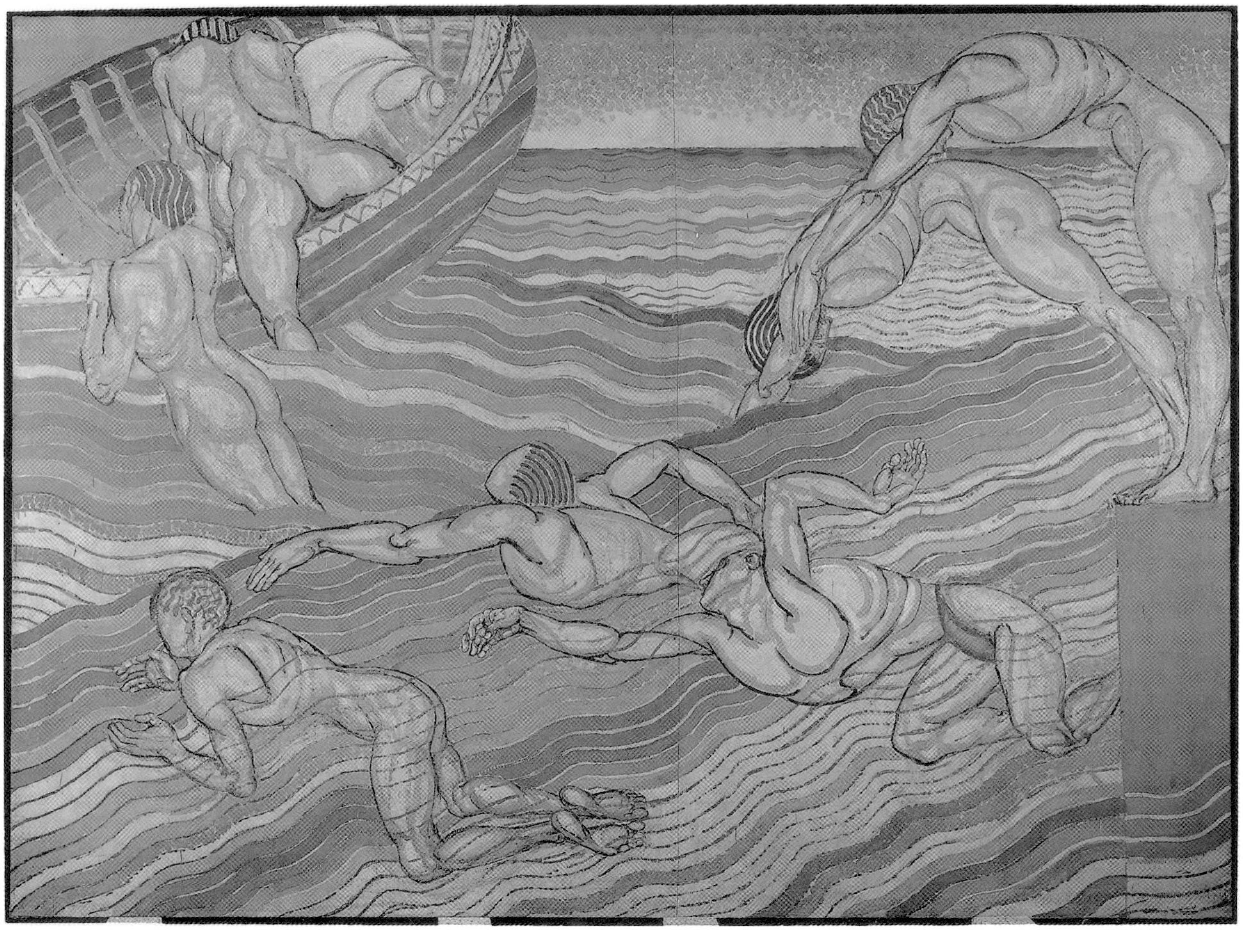

161. Duncan Grant, *Bathing*, formerly Borough Polytechnic, London, 1911. London, Tate Gallery

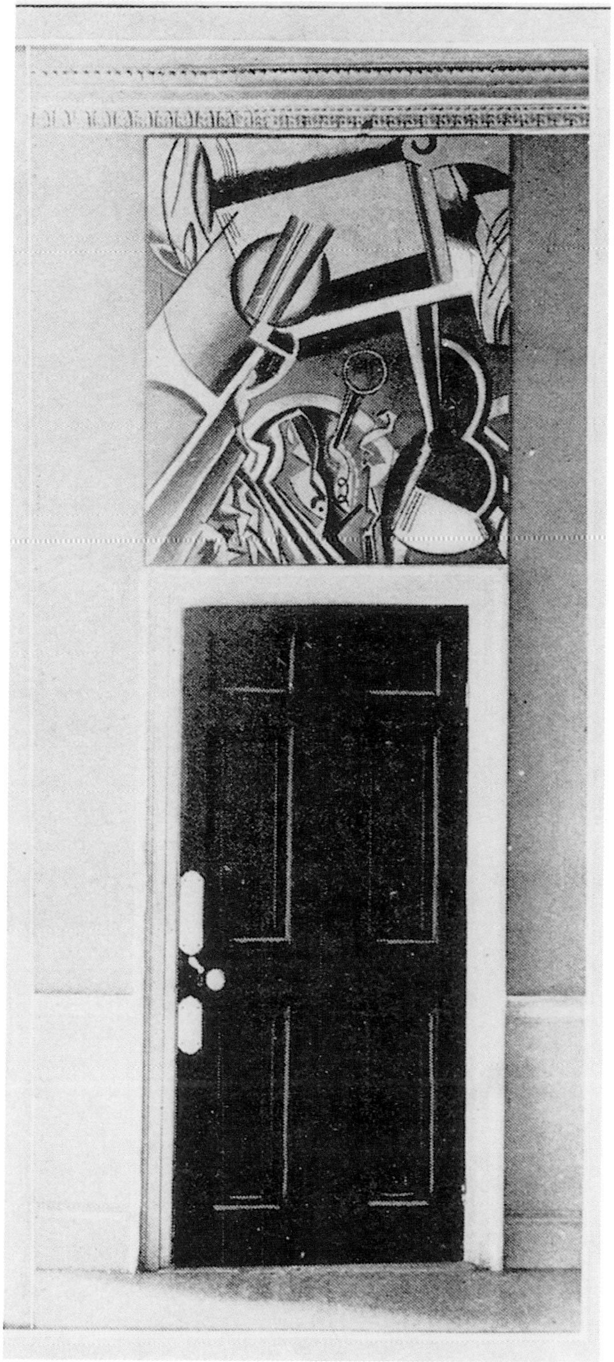

162. Edward Wadsworth, over-door mural (subject unknown) in the Rebel Art Centre, 38 Great Ormond Street, London. Period photograph published in the *Graphic* (25 April 1914)

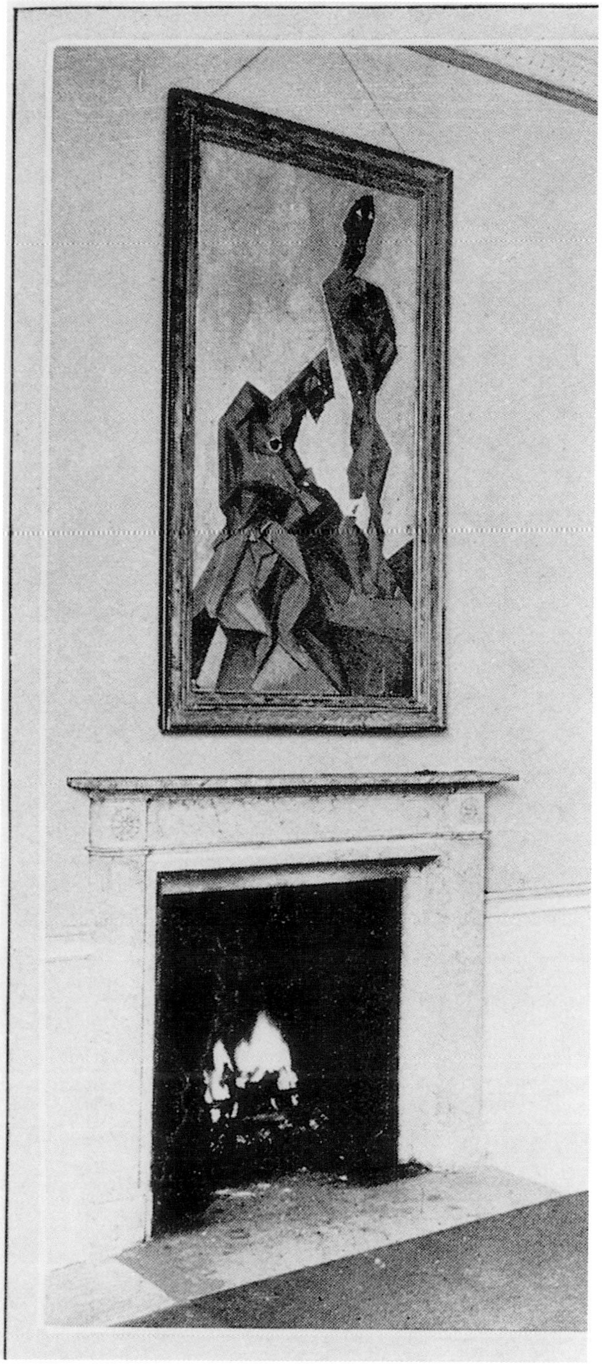

163. Percy Wyndham Lewis, painting, possibly entitled 'Group', above a mantelpiece in the Rebel Art Centre, 38 Great Ormond Street, London. Period photograph published in the *Graphic* (25 April 1914)

REMEMBRANCE, RECOLLECTION, AND RENEWAL: THE FIRST WORLD WAR AND AFTER

The First World War gave tragic significance not only to the Vorticist vision, but also to the emergent interest in contemporary subjects amongst more conservative artists. The most significant commission to arise from the Crosby Hall competitions was that given to Frederick Cayley Robinson at the Middlesex Hospital in London, funded by Sir Edmund Davis, in which the 'true and emphatic' became a potent psychological focus for the casualties of the war and those who had nursed or lost them. Where Traquair had dealt with suffering and grief through religious emblems and symbols at the Edinburgh Sick Children's Hospital (Plate 151) Robinson's scheme records its very environs—one panel, for example (Plate 164a) shows a scene of gaunt, haggard faces and listless soldiers gathering for fresh air during convalescence on the steep steps of the hospital's pillared entrance. One soldier wears carpet slippers, with his military jacket draped uselessly around his bandaged arm in a sling; another leans on a crutch at the top of the steps, looking towards a group of elderly and unemployed men. Nurses converse in the shadows at the left; a grim reminder of war's ruthlessness is provided by the harsh silhouette of a Roman equestrian statue.

A partner panel (Plate 164b) offers hope, translating Christian salvation into the secular imagery of women with a baby and young girls who wait at the entrance to the hospital with a scholar in robes, old men, and a dog whilst, at the far right, a mother kneels in prayer as her daughter thanks the senior doctor, attended by nurses, who has bandaged her arm. Above, a slender tree comes symbolically into first leaf as swallows fly past and a faint rainbow appears over tenements at the left. The sacramental overtones of the scene are emphasized by the static poses, frieze-like composition, and delicate pastel pinks and greys which offset the slate-blue uniforms and betray Robinson's admiration for Puvis de Chavannes. With the blue 'Post-Impressionist' shadows, a distinct and perhaps deliberately symbolic French accent is apparent. Another panel illustrates orphans eating in a communal dining-room; overall, the scheme was named *Acts of Mercy.* Its blend of the generic and particular compares with the monument to Edith Cavell at the same period, whilst its illustration of the sunlit outdoors—even the orphans at their meal glimpse trees and doves through the windows—points to the preference for landscape subjects in a number of hospital commissions of the 1920s and 1930s (Appendix C: 25, 28). The War Memorial by Robinson in Heanor Grammar School (Appendix C: 19) and his *Coming of St. Patrick to Ireland* mural of 1914 for the new Dublin Art Gallery, reverted to Biblical or history themes, just as heroic or 'improving' subjects such as *St. George* had been chosen for the LCC school commissions arising from the Crosby Hall competitions (Appendix C: 17). Whilst it is difficult to make meaningful generalizations about what was a very diverse range of 'mind and body' murals in the post-war period (Appendix C: 19–35), an association of healing or education and the natural world, and in turn a recognition of landscape itself as history, none the less emerge as constant points of reference. Fresh air was still the only supposed cure for many illnesses, and learning through the senses was increasingly emphasized by educationists. At the same time, remembrance gives way to forms of community recollection and even nostalgia, in place of the presentation of improving exemplars and heroes in earlier educational or welfare schemes.

A scheme begun in Brighton, Hove and Sussex Grammar School[106] in 1913 by Louis Ginnett, one of its former pupils and a teacher at Brighton School of Art, was continued as a War Memorial to the Grammar School's old boys, but eventually became a larger symbolic exploration of the continuity of civilization as manifest in the local countryside, and as representing 'that constant struggle which made modern England'.[107] The scheme was unveiled in 1939 as *The History of Man in Sussex* (Plate XXXIII; Plate 165) and whilst superficially a sequence of well-designed and realistic evocations of historical events which contributed to the making of Britain's Empire, such as *Rye. After the Armada*, it also contains a distinctive 'scientific' interpretation of the past which takes to its logical conclusion William Hole's earlier inclusion of Stone Age warriors in his 'Great Scots' frieze at the Scottish National Portrait Gallery, and reflects contemporary archaeological discoveries. The first mural, *Prehistoric Man in Sussex* (1913) showing 'primitive man returning to his Downland habitation from a raid in the Wealden forest in search of prey', literally fleshes out against a symbolic dawn the Piltdown Man whose skull, recently discovered in the region, was then believed to be genuine. The stone axes used by the figures give way in the second panel, showing the building of Bignor Roman villa against an atmospheric backdrop of the Downs, to the sophisticated tools of construction employed by Roman architects and sculptors in shaping a capital, columns, and other masonry. The half-column being measured at the left recalls the one mentioned in Samuel Lysons's account of the excavation of the villa in 1811, whilst the small boy in a green tunic at the right, holding up a drinking bowl, brings to mind Lysons's famous discovery of a mosaic of Ganymede in the villa.[108] In turn, the 'modern' basket of tools in the foreground of the mural of Parliament's deputation to the King's Gunfounder in 1642 (Plate 165) takes up the theme ('Sussex was . . . the home of the chief ironworkers of the kingdom'), and it is brought full circle[109] by the final mural illustrating the recent excavations of Hollingbury Camp (Plate XXXIII). The same rolling downland landscape traversed by the primitive hunters in the first panel recedes into soft violet and blue in *After the Battle of Hastings*, and forms the backdrop, now criss-crossed by far-off lines of modern houses, and occupied by a group of archaeologists. They are watched by passers-by in the casual dress of 1926 and a man on a motorbike (T. E. Lawrence?), having brought to light the skull of a primitive man; inspecting it is Thomas Read, the Headmaster and President of the Old Boys' Association, who had himself gifted one of the murals and followed their progress from 1913. Ginnett's comment that the figures in colourful Regency costume in an earlier panel in the scheme, *The [Brighton] Pavilion. George IV Receives a Loyal Address*, were 'descendants of the same characters we have seen under other circumstances'[110] is thus also relevant here: primitive hunters have become modern archaeologists. In turn, the young man recording the excavation on a camp-stool at the right, perhaps a portrait of Robert Gurd, then at the start of his career as an archaeological illustrator,[111] records the scene for future generations as Ginnett's mural does for future pupils. Though presented in terms of historical narrative, the sense of the evolution of history as evidenced in place is essentially comparable with the quest by Paul Nash and Graham Sutherland for the elemental and primitive within the English landscape, and it is also found in

[106] Now Brighton, Hove and Sussex Sixth Form College. Ginnett also painted New Testament scenes in the chapel at the Royal Masonic School, Rickmansworth (*c*.1935).

[107] A. E. W., 'Decorative Panels in the School Hall painted by Louis Ginnett, R.O.I. 1913–1939', *Past and Present* (July 1939) (reprinted by Brighton, Hove and Sussex Grammar School as a pamphlet).

[108] S. Lysons, 'Account of the Remains of a Roman Villa, discovered at Bignor', (Part I), *Archaeologia*, 18 (1815), pp. 216, 204.

[109] A. E. W., 'Decorative Panels'.

[110] Quoted in ibid.

[111] Gurd certainly illustrated the Bignor villa (see S. Frere, 'The Bignor Villa', *Britannia*, 18 (London, 1982), fig. 4, p. 142.

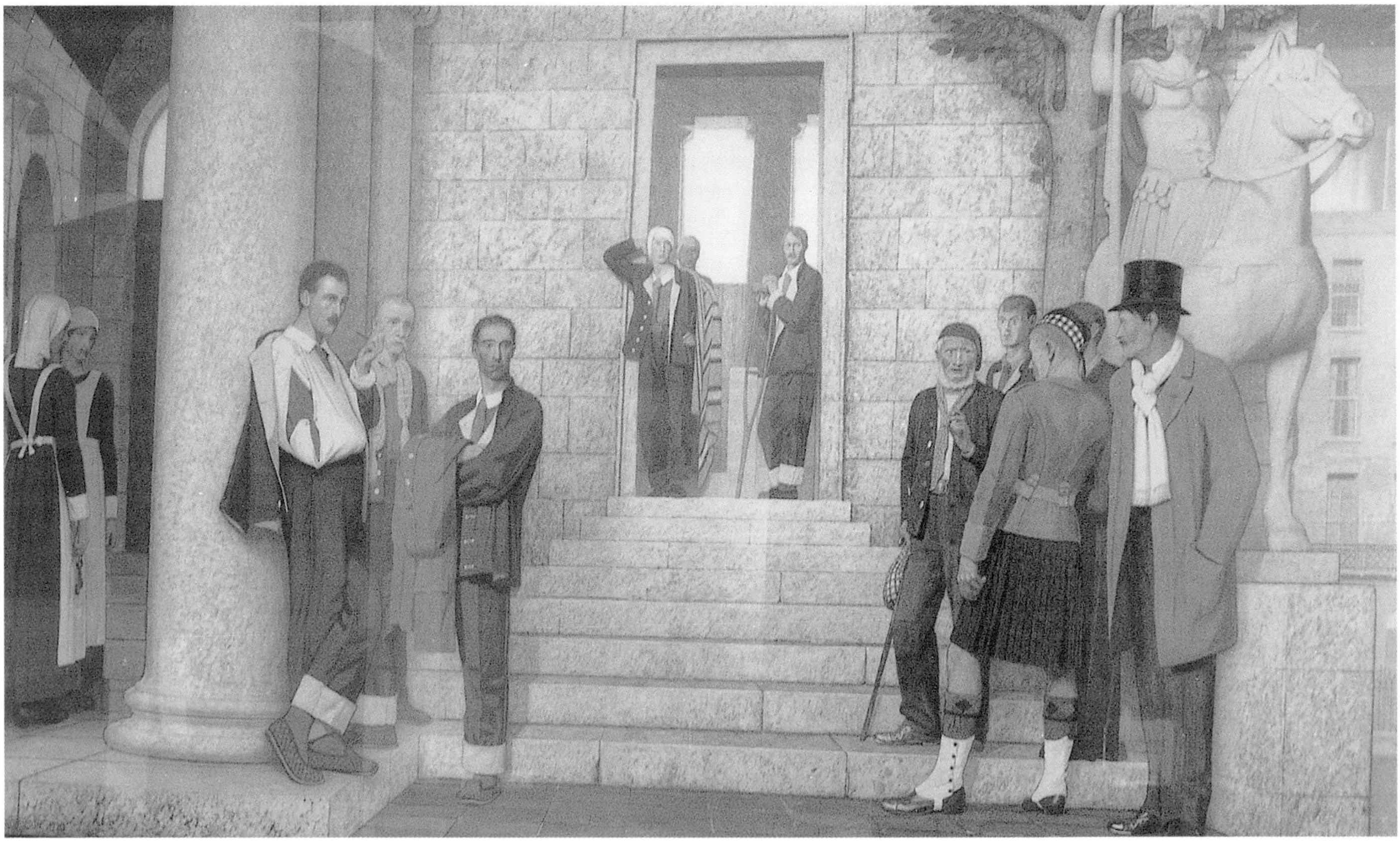

164. (a) above, and 164(b) below. Frederick Cayley Robinson, *The Doctor*, vestibule of the Middlesex Hospital, London, 1915–20

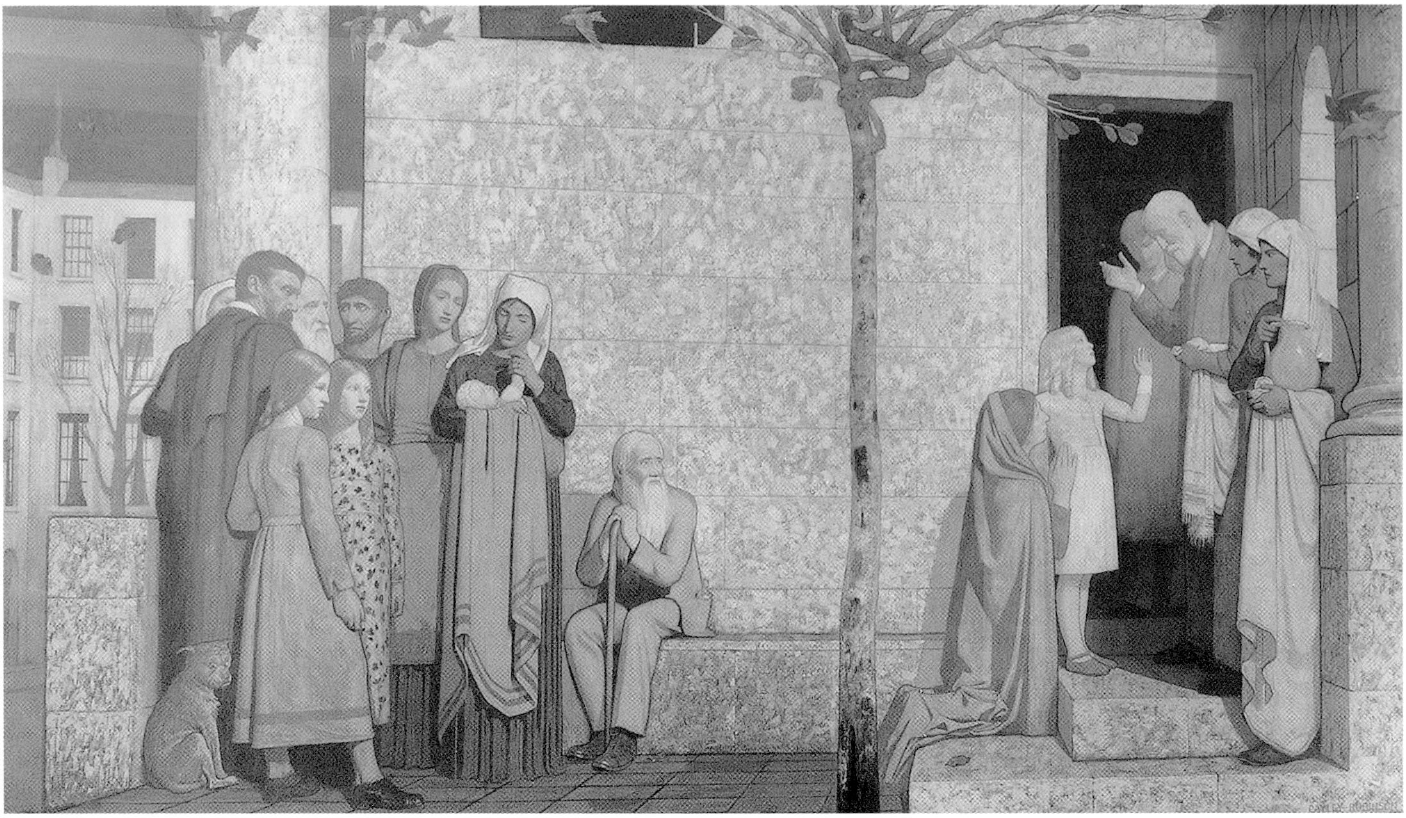

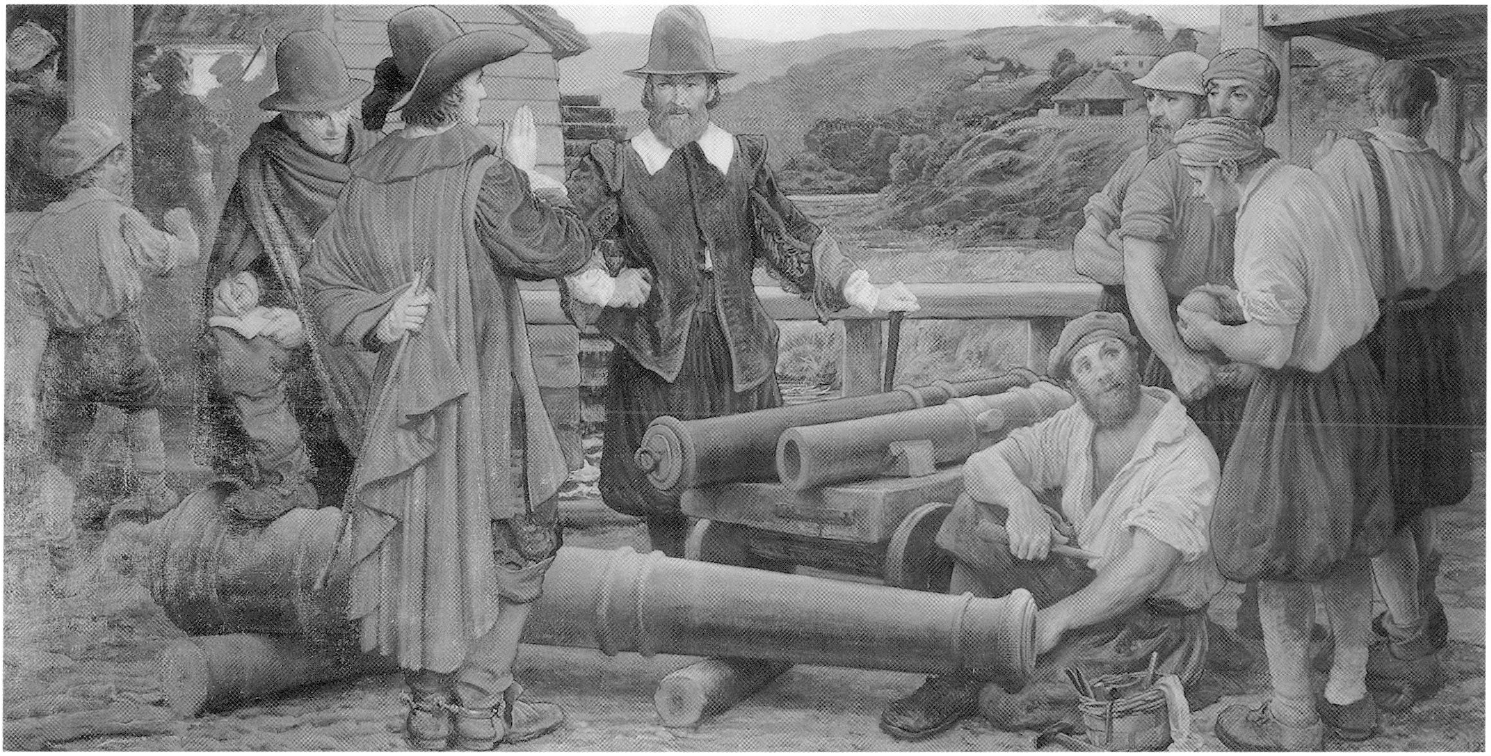

165. Louis Ginnett, *Parliament's Deputation to the King's Gunfounder, 1642*, Brighton, Hove and Sussex Grammar School (now Brighton, Hove and Sussex Sixth Form College), Hove, 1913–39

the Ulster Museum's *Ulster Past and Present* mural of 1932 by William Conor, with its dolmen axis.

In turn, 'primitive' mural techniques had begun by the period of the war to be intensively researched from Minoan and Egyptian sources by the members of the Society of Mural Decorators and Painters in Tempera. Despite his 'modern' subject-matter, Robinson's pale, fresco-like tonalities can also be seen as part of this development. Mrs Sargant-Florence's frescoes for Oakham School (Appendix C: 13), illustrated at Crosby Hall in 1912, gave impetus to theories associating the medium with health and education. Best suited to rural sites, removed from city pollution, it was felt, by extension, to be especially suited to a child's environment[112] and was used both at Bourneville School (Appendix C: 18) and by Joseph Southall in his mural of *Corporation Street, Birmingham in March 1914* in Birmingham Art Gallery (Plate XXXIV) with its motif of a toddler holding a skipping rope and reaching after flowers in a city vendor's basket. Another contemporary subject, in which the city is adversely contrasted with nature, *Corporation Street* was of course painted even as youth was being slaughtered in the fields of France. It is a powerful statement of Southall's pacifism, transmuting 'reality', through the 'pure' medium of fresco and notes of primary colour in the costumes and adjacent red van, into a powerful tribute to not only the regenerative powers of nature, but also, decorating as it does the City's Gallery, those of art. The child's mother (Mrs Arthur Gaskin), dressed in a fashionable yellow costume and fur wrap, symbolically receives a narcissus from the vendor as if some latter-day Madonna of the Assumption; the dance-like movement of the elegant figures recalls Botticelli's *Primavera.*

If Southall's mural seems strikingly to anticipate the plea made by Sir William Rothenstein in 1916 for a 'provincial culture' in which murals would convey a 'heightened sense of the beauty of familiar things'[113] as a means of reconstruction after the war, it was in turn students and artists trained by Rothenstein at the Royal College of Art, by Tonks at the Slade, and at the new British School at Rome who painted many of the 'education' and 'welfare' schemes of the 1920s and 1930s. Following his advocacy of mural painting in the *Morning Post* in 1921 as the answer to 'What is wrong with art in England?' Tonks set his students to assist him in 1922 with a broadly brushed mural for the dome of University College London, showing some of its founders, Jeremy Bentham, Henry Crabb Robinson, and Lord Brougham;[114] as a result of his 'student schemes' for children's clubs in London,[115] he secured commissions for similar projects in schools, at the Whitechapel Art Gallery, and for Nan West at the Orthopaedic Hospital in London on the theme of seasonal landscapes.[116] Though he gave the latter lavish praise in his Slade School Report of 1927–8, the murals of 1922 in the Regent Street Polytechnic by Delmar H. Banner, an Oxford history graduate, admirer of Ruskin, and student of the Polytechnic, with their lively evocation of the different crafts as practised in London history, are much more accomplished in design and colouring, as are also the local history themes by A. K. Lawrence in the Laing Art Gallery in Newcastle (1925). Painted as part of his training at the British School at Rome, Lawrence's scheme

[112] See M. Sargant-Florence, 'Frescoes of the Old School, Oakham', in *Papers of the Society of Mural Decorators*, vol. 2, ed. J. Batten (1925). Fresco was similarly advocated and used in the 1920s in hospitals (see Sargant-Florence (ed.), *Papers* . . . vol. 3 (1936), pp. 67–74.

[113] W. Rothenstein, *Plea* (1916), p. 16. Rothenstein had in fact presented his ideas in embryonic form in his evidence to the Departmental Committee on the Royal College of Art in 1911 (see *Report* (1911) §31, p. 20). Another 'Birmingham School' war memorial mural was C. M. Gere's for the College of St. Peter at Saltley (1922; destroyed); see A. Crawford (ed.), *By Hammer and Hand* (1984), p. 81.

[114] Now detached and in the collection of University College London. See J. Hone, *Life of Henry Tonks* (1929), pp. 184–201.

[115] See Appendix D, nos. 24 and 28.

[116] See Hone, *Henry Tonks*, pp. 182 ff.; C. Aitken, 'The Slade School', *Apollo* (Jan. 1926), pp. 6–7 and TGA. Apart from that at the Orthopaedic Hospital, most of these schemes are no longer *in situ*.

extended the school's new policy of requiring its students to engage 'in the actual practice of mural decoration by making designs for the decoration of wall spaces in the school building' in Rome, and it was followed by plans for scholars to paint decoration not only for the Rome premises, but also the Museum of London.[117]

It was through Rothenstein that another Royal College of Art painter, Archie Rhys Griffiths, obtained a commission to paint a mural at the Working Men's College in Camden. Completed in 1932 in a realistic but richly symbolic style, this illustrates themes of 'age and youth, the arts and labour',[118] juxtaposing a Crucifixion with a mother, child, and father working in an allotment, factories smoking on the horizon and ingenious cut-away effects which emphasize the continuity of life in a community. One shows a scene of mining beneath the ground in which an accident has just occurred; meanwhile, above ground and to the right, another cut-away reveals the interior of a house where a sick woman is being tended; the departing doctor steps into the allotment. Griffiths himself was originally a miner. Perhaps the most noteworthy training scheme, however, was that organized for Morley College in London by Rothenstein himself, with funding of £1,300 obtained by Charles Aitken (Director of the Tate Gallery) from Sir Joseph Duveen. This was a direct sequel to Duveen's patronage of Rex Whistler at the Tate Gallery (see Chapter 11). Edward Bawden and Eric Ravilious were selected to paint scenes from Elizabethan and Jacobean dramas in the Refreshment Room (Plate 166), reflecting the college's association with the Old Vic; Charles Mahoney portrayed *The Pleasures of Life in Work and Play* (scenes of London life) in the Concert Hall. All were recently qualified students of the Royal College of Art. Sir John Rothenstein called Bawden's and Ravilious's imaginatively costumed figures (which, interestingly, were again in several cases set in cut-away interiors but were far more stylized than Griffiths's) 'lively things from a fairy world'.[119] The scheme as a whole must have been both a direct sequel to the 'entertainment' emphasis at the Borough Polytechnic and a figurative counterpart to the nostalgia for a lost English landscape to be found in the artists' easel paintings of the 1920s and 1930s. The murals were inaugurated by Stanley Baldwin, the Prime Minister, in 1930 and attracted the interest of Queen Mary; they were probably an influence on Philip Ziegler's scheme of 1934 at Toynbee Hall's Lecture Theatre, illustrating the Arts and Sciences, and including *Folk-Dancing* and a sculptor modelling a bust of George Bernard Shaw. Murals showing traditional life and occupations of the region, and including portraits of local individuals, were painted in the 1930s for the Dining Hall at Coleg Harlech, Gwynedd, by Robert Baker, another Royal College of Art pupil, who also contributed to the Woodgreen Village Hall scheme.

The illustration of Britain's nature, archaeology, and traditions in such schemes of the 1930s parallels the rise of the Council for the Preservation of Rural England and the new ready access to the countryside by means of train, car, and bus, but it can also be placed in the context of the emphasis on nature study in the 'child-centred education' movement,[120] and on domestic and local heritage in the history books by Rhoda and Eileen Power, G. M. Trevelyan, and others. In a sequel to his work at Morley College, Mahoney (now a tutor at the RCA) supervised and contributed to a scheme arranged by Rothenstein at Brockley School in London during the early 1930s, in which Aesop's fables were presented as if taking place in the 'garden of England'.[121]

[117] Minute of Faculty of Painting (17 Oct. 1922), BSRA. The Museum of London scheme, if executed, is no longer *in situ*.

[118] P. Lord, *Industrial Society* (1998), pp. 190–1.

[119] J. Rothenstein, *Modern English Painters* (1984), vol. 2, p. 306.

[120] Influential developments were the *First Handbook of Suggestions for Teachers* (1928) and *The Primary Report* by Haddow (1931).

[121] See A. Powers, 'Labour of Love: Murals of the 1930s at Brockley School', *Country Life*, 181 (30 April 1987), pp. 120–1.

Further panels were painted by Evelyn Dunbar, Mildred Eldridge, and Violet Martin. The almost surreal combination of allegorical figures and botanical detail, as in Mahoney's garden scene of *Fortune and the Boy* (Plate 167), creates a visionary world reminiscent of Stanley Spencer's; Dunbar's view of the school itself amidst its setting at Hilly Fields, with its schoolboys glimpsed through a hedge of wild plants and flowers on their way to lessons, makes the association of nature, education, and well-being explicit.

Stanley Spencer had actually planned in 1922 to decorate Bedales School Refectory with a scene of an art class, and in 1933 he designed a mural for Cambridge University Library, its composition overshadowed by a Cookham blossom-tree, of *Making Columns for the Tower of Babel.* Though neither scheme came to fruition,[122] murals were painted in 1934–6 by his brother Gilbert, trained under Tonks at the Slade and like Mahoney a tutor at the Royal College of Art, in an ante-room at Holywell Manor, Oxford (an annexe of Balliol College) (Plate XXXV). These were intended to complement the aim of the Manor's architect, George Kennedy, 'to put the building on easy terms with its site and to connect its future with the fortunes of the garden and the trees planted in relation to it',[123] and Spencer received the commission after Kenneth Bell, tutor in history at Balliol, had found his *Cotswold Farm* easel painting (1930–1, Tate Gallery) 'a fizzer'.[124] The murals directly develop its pastoral imagery as the setting for their story of the foundation of the College by John Balliol. Painted at the same period as Stanley Spencer's Burghclere Chapel, they share the latter's sharp focus on domestic detail, with Bell's name, for example, being inscribed on one of the labels on the luggage being brought to Balliol by its scholars. Spencer observed the progress at Burghclere closely, and later wrote 'I too was interested in design and composition, and welcomed an agricultural setting because of the patterns that naturally appear around farms.'[125]

The white robes of the monks and bishop, and the scholars' smocks billow in forms as curvilinear as the comfortable golden haystacks in the farmyard where Balliol himself is arrested by the bishop (Plate XXXV), or the massive cartwheel in the scene of the scholars' departure for Oxford, thus becoming visually one with the rhythm of the rolling, light green and yellow hills beyond. Like Stanley, Gilbert Spencer had served in the War in the RAMC, but where his brother had portrayed directly the sombre geometry of waiting travoys, laid out before a Macedonian military hospital in his painting for the 'Hall of Remembrance' (Plate XVII), and had again included them at Burghclere, Gilbert painted rustic farm-wagons. These carry not only the scholars but also the bishop of Durham, from the Balliol story. This translation of a wartime image into the 'heightened beauty of familiar things', for which Rothenstein had called in 1916, suggests that the scheme was perhaps a form of catharsis for Spencer himself as much as an attempt to bring healthful nature into Holywell Manor; he certainly wrote of 'mix[ing] my feelings and the event of the legend'.[126]

[122] A sketch for the Cambridge University Library scheme is in the Fitzwilliam Museum, Cambridge (private collection). A mural of the *Upper Room* at Pentecost was intended to hang opposite (see TGA 733.3.1) and R. Carline et al., *Stanley Spencer* (1980), p. 125.

[123] Letter from G. L. Kennedy to the Master of Balliol College, Oxford (28 Sept. 1933), Balliol College Archives.

[124] G. Spencer, *Memoirs of a Painter* (London, 1974), p. 104. The mural scheme may also have been prompted by that painted by C. Fremantle for R. A. B. Mynors for his room at Balliol, *c.* 1929 (see J. Jones, *Balliol College: A History* (Oxford, 1997), p. 268). About this period, E. I. Halliday painted a mural for Worcester College, Oxford, showing undergraduate leisure pursuits.

[125] G. Spencer, *Memoirs*, p. 109.

[126] Ibid., p. 108.

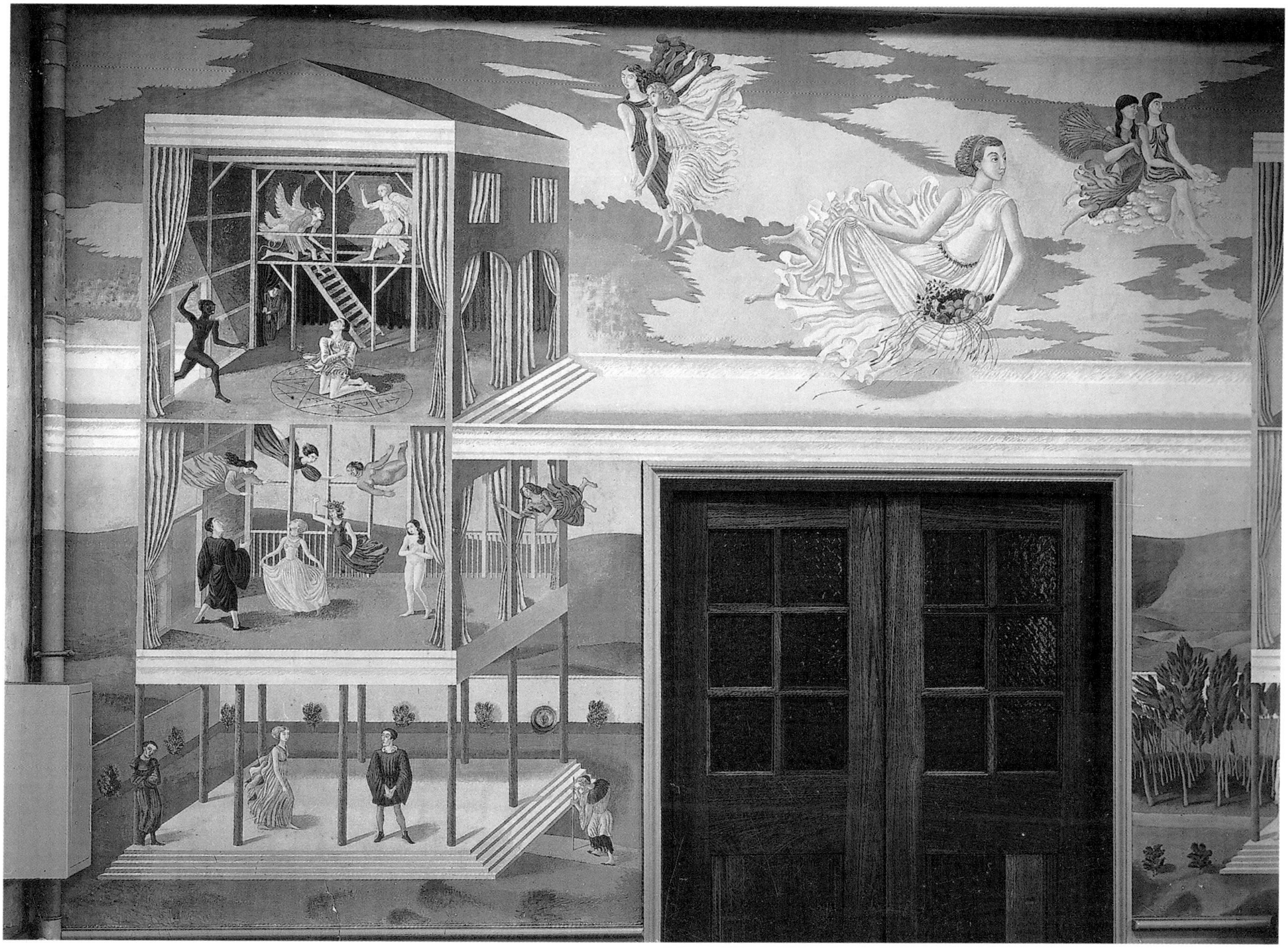

166. Eric Ravilious, *Scenes from Dr. Faustus* (Marlowe), formerly in Refreshment Room, Morley College, London, unveiled 1930. Period photograph, Archives, Morley College

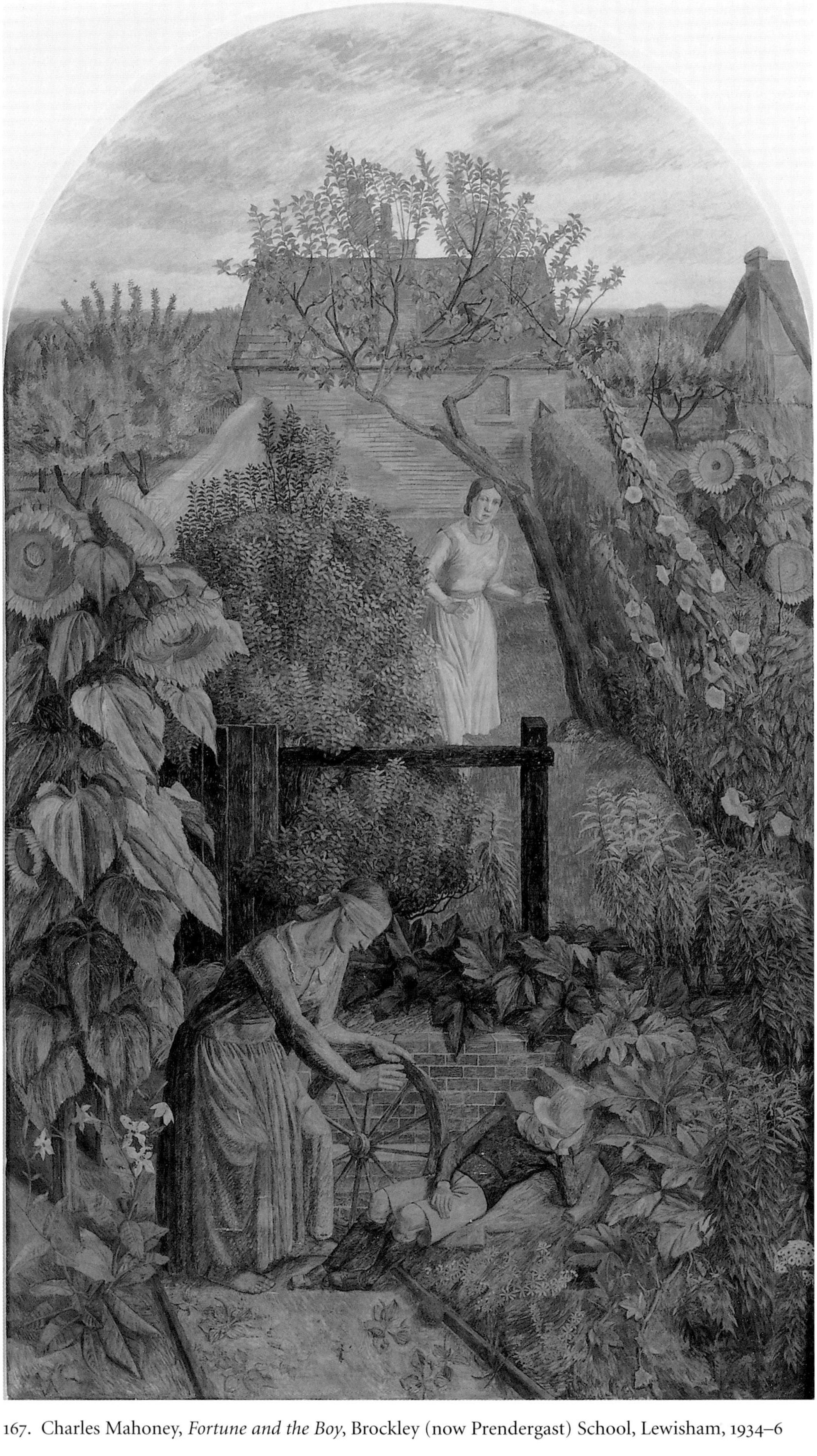

167. Charles Mahoney, *Fortune and the Boy*, Brockley (now Prendergast) School, Lewisham, 1934–6

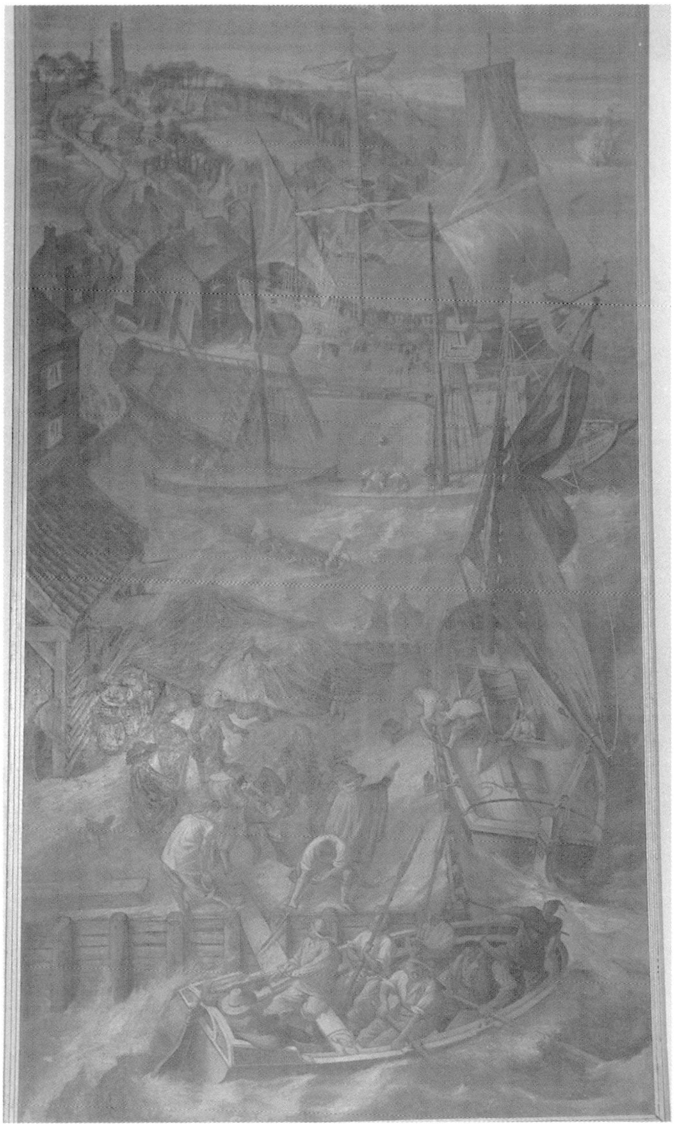

168. Alan Sorrell, *Admiral Blake refitting the British Fleet*, formerly Southend-on-Sea Public Library, 1933. Southend-on-Sea, Prittlewell Priory Museum

169. C R. Napier and pupils, *The Telling of the Stories*, formerly Children's Library, Huddersfield, 1939. Permanent Collection, Kirklees Metropolitan Council

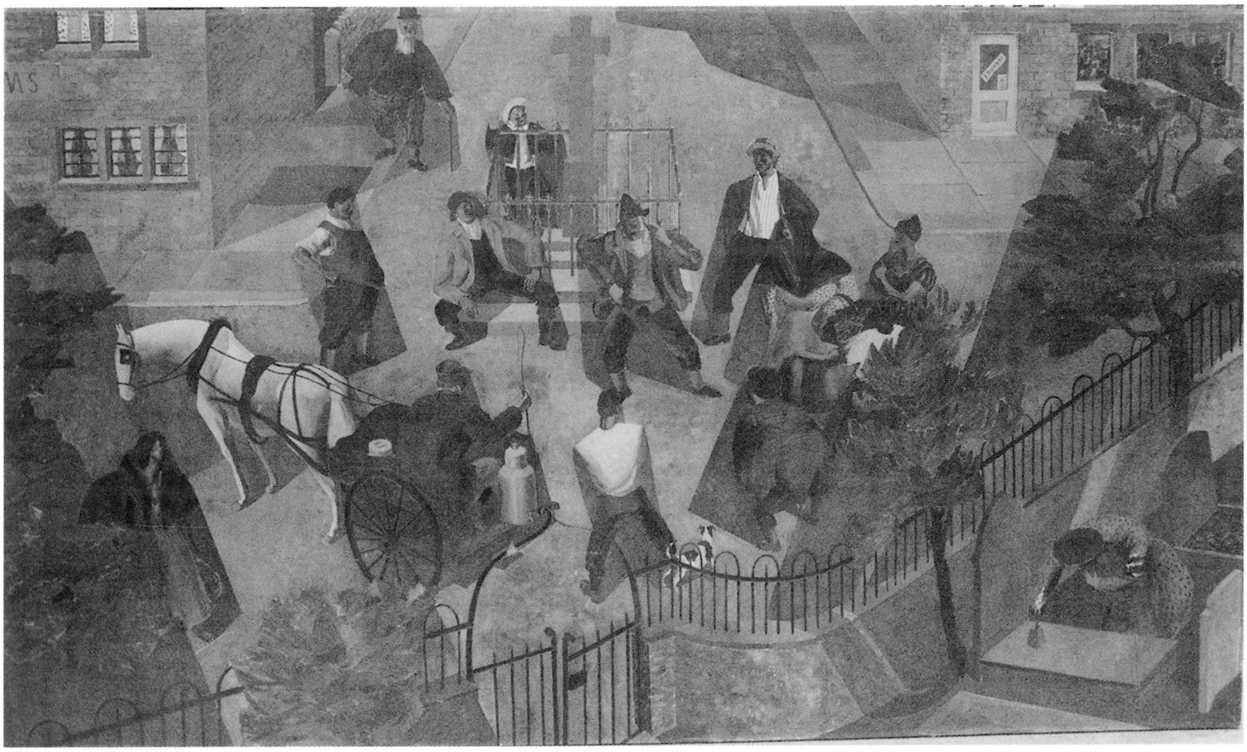

Another of Rothenstein's RCA tutors, Alan Sorrell, who had won the Prix de Rome in 1928, was meanwhile at work on 'local' subjects at Southend-on-Sea Public Library: *Admiral Blake Refitting the British Fleet, 1653* (1933) (Plate 168), *Building of the Tower of St. Mary's Church Prittlewell in the 15th Century* (1936), and *South End: The Arrival of the Coach 1800–1805* (1939). Donated mostly by local councillors, the scheme was proposed by Sorrell, who wanted contemporary themes. Instead, the murals became the foundation for his subsequent distinguished career as an artist of archaeological reconstructions. Asked to portray historical events in what was his home region, he saw his task as 'to pierce the skin of building which had spread over the hillsides, plant them again with trees, mentally demolish that ugly gasometer and the railway . . . and then rebuild.'[127] Rothenstein none the less perceptively recognized 'poetical vision'[128] when *Admiral Blake* was shown at the Royal Academy prior to installation. Its meticulous detail of naval refitting and provisioning, seen from above, appears to ascend to the high horizon with a dynamic logic. Rising masts, rigging, and curving sails guide the eye to the flag of St George silhouetted against the stormy sky atop Blake's ship. Similar narrative plotting occurs in the other panels, rendering human activity subordinate to the larger topographical scheme. The colour scheme of restrained ochres, browns, and greens creates overall harmony between the panels.

C. R. Napier's murals for the Children's Section of Huddersfield Public Library, illustrating old legends of the Huddersfield district, were begun in 1939 and painted with the aid of his students at the Huddersfield Technical College[129] (Plate 169). Like the work of Ginnett, Spencer, and Sorrell, they record a bygone age and place, which by the time of the unveiling of the murals in 1945, had acquired tragic poignancy as two of the students died in the Second World War. Decorative geometric shadows and slightly Cubist effects create a sense of whimsy, but at a deeper level, continuity across the generations is implied since the tales are told to the library's users by an old man portrayed in the central panel, and the murals are interlinked by means of the meandering path which connects one scene to the next. The figures enacting such incidents as *The Walling up of the Marsden Cuckoo* and the *Slowit Moonrakers* thus weave a world of fantasy which yet impinges on reality in its meticulous detail of local brick walls and stocking-footed, blue-uniformed bandsmen; the gawky postures suggest some influence from the Spencers. Just as Sorrell attempted to retrieve a lost topography and Spencer to honour Balliol's origins, so recollection had now become an act of faith; an inscription of folk memory on the minds of future generations. Geddes's ideal of regeneration through return to the past, like his emphasis on the natural world, had itself now been reborn.

[127] Quoted in M. Sorrell (ed.), *Reconstructing the Past by Alan Sorrell* (London, 1981), p. 10.

[128] Ibid., p. 11.

[129] The panels are now in Huddersfield Art Gallery. Napier described their original setting in a letter to Sir John Rothenstein (14 Nov. 1942), PRO No. 258 Part II, TGA.

10

Private Houses

In 1828 the pioneer collector of early Italian art, William Fox Strangways, wrote to his half-brother, Henry Fox Talbot, 'I advise the English artists to introduce fresco painting in England. May they hold out the hope of employment on the lunettes of your cloisters [i.e. at Lacock Abbey in Wiltshire]? I am more and more enraged at the supineness of the Govt. in not buying pictures.'[1] Just over a century later, in 1935, the painter Wyndham Lewis wrote: 'If you were to enquire of the artist . . . which sort of patronage he would prefer, that of the State, or of a great Corporation, or that of an individual person, nine artists out of ten would answer "Give me a rich little stockbroker every time!" . . . the individual is simple . . . the State is many things!'[2]

Although from Renaissance times there had been a flourishing tradition of private-house decoration in Britain, by the nineteenth century this had largely become the preserve of French and Italian artists.[3] If Fox Talbot in the event used his cloisters to advance another kind of experimental picture, the photograph, from 1840 a vigorous lead was none the less given to the re-establishment of a native tradition of domestic decoration through Prince Albert's commissions for frescoes at Buckingham Palace and Osborne House. Throughout the succeeding hundred years, painting for private houses, with its apparent promise of untrammelled freedom, offered a constant lure to artists and patrons alike. Lewis's astonishing 'black' interior for Lady Drogheda, created just before the First World War, was essentially a latter-day instance of the quest for the new which became closely associated with the genre following Albert's example. Although Ruskin believed that great art was public art, it was frequently only private individuals who, like 'the delightful, clever, learned' William Spottiswoode,[4] President of the Royal Society, intimate of Charles Darwin, and patron of Walter Crane at Combe Bank, had the means and inclination to gratify decorative enterprise. At the same time, of course, a private patron's personal purposes—'retreat' from society, expression of affluence, or indulgence of dreams, for example—were often the determining factor in a commission, and might lead, as in Lord Bute's castles by William Burges, to the deliberate choice of an executant rather than an imaginative artist. Whilst there are some outstandingly fine private schemes, many were essentially modest in artistic merit, often commissioned from minor local painters, or intended as no more than a form of harmonious

[1] Letter of 25 March 1828, published in M. Weaver (ed.), *Henry Fox Talbot: Selected Texts and Bibliography* (Oxford, 1992), p. 35.

[2] W. Lewis, *Art and Patronage*, BBC broadcast (1935), in W. Michel and C. J. Fox (eds), *Wyndham Lewis on Art* (1969), p. 299.

[3] See T. Bonnar, 'Ancient Mural Decorative Art in Scotland', *Transactions of the Architectural Institute of Scotland*, 3, no. 2 (1895); E. Croft-Murray, *Decorative Painting* (1965–70); and M. R. Apted, *The Painted Ceilings of Scotland 1550–1650* (Edinburgh, 1966).

[4] Description of Spottiswoode by his friend Mildred Thompson, Combe Bank Papers 33, quoted in Anon., *Combe Bank, Sundridge, Kent: A History* (Croydon, 1986), p. 17.

backdrop. For self-made men like H. I. Butterfield at Cliffe Castle (Appendix D: 14) or Joseph Grimond at Carbet Castle (Appendix D: 11), mural painting in revivalist styles was essentially a means to invent a lineage by living in 'Louis XVI' or 'Tudor' surroundings. In this situation, Whistler's infamous dispute in 1878 with the shipowner F. R. Leyland over his Peacock Room highlights tensions which, despite Lewis's comments, were at times more acute in private, as compared with public patronage. Where a talented painter and a sympathetic patron saw eye to eye, however, as at Pitreavie Castle, Fife, in the 1890s in John Duncan's *Orpheus* scheme for Sir Henry Beveridge, there were rewarding results. It is perhaps not surprising that one of the most remarkable and successful private-house schemes was Sigismund Goetze's 1913 illustration of Ovid's *Metamorphoses*, created for his own house. Its symbolic synaesthesia represents probably the closest British counterpart to the 'subjectivist dream room', bodying forth the 'chambre mentale'[5] which, in the wake of Edmond de Goncourt's *Maison d'un Artiste* of 1881, had become a distinctive feature of progressive private-house decoration in France.

Despite Whistler's assertion of 'beauty' for beauty's sake, literary themes, such as those of Duncan and Goetze, as well as history, were widely favoured by private patrons well into the first part of the twentieth century, and contrast with both the popular eighteenth-century tradition of the 'panoramic room'[6] and with emphasis on landscape iconography which emerged in domestic interiors in France at the *fin de siècle*.[7] Fuelling fantasy, such themes offered an entry into dream worlds increasingly removed from the ugliness of industrialized Britain—a Britain, of course, which many of the patrons had themselves brought into being. Perhaps for a similar reason, the revival of pre-eighteenth-century styles and techniques by the Arts and Crafts Movement had a remarkably persistent influence (Appendix D: 22–6), aided by the vigorous promotion from the late nineteenth century in journals such as the *Studio* of the concept of the 'artistic home'. In the wake of the First World War and the economic slump, the reinvention of classical and eighteenth-century motifs in *trompe-l'oeil* or pastiche form by Rex Whistler, Duncan Grant, Mary Adshead, and others (Appendix D: 29, 30, 31, 34, 35, 37–42, 46, 47), can in turn perhaps be read as a subconscious reassurance of enduring values in a changing world.

Although numerous private houses were decorated with murals over the hundred years, changes of taste and ownership have taken an often far heavier toll than happened with public, ecclesiastical, or educational schemes. Many private-house murals are known only through sketches, period accounts, or illustrations. The inevitably idiosyncratic nature of private patronage, combined with the relative absence in Britain of strong stylistic schools of decorative painting like the 'Rahlschule', whose members decorated many of the great nineteenth-century Ringstrasse 'palaces' in Vienna,[8] in any case often frustrates identification of anything other than broad characteristics or trends. In this situation, it is necessary to see its very diversity as one of the distinguishing characteristics of private-house mural painting in Britain through the century from 1840. Aspects of the philosophy of mural art and its wider social, historical, or psychological contexts, especially the concept of the *Gesamtkunstwerk*, the ideal of the integrated interior, and

[5] D. Silverman, *Art Nouveau* (1989), p. 78; the 'chambre mentale' is discussed on p. 79.

[6] See Croft-Murray, *Decorative Painting*, vol. 2 (1970) p. 60. A view of the Forth at Lylestone House in Alloa (*c*.1830s / 1840s) is a late survival of the tradition.

[7] e. g. in Nabi schemes: see G. Groom, *Edouard Vuillard* (1993) and R. Thomson, *Monet to Matisse* (1994), pp. 137–9; other examples were shown at the Paris International Exhibition of 1900 (see Y. Brunhammer and S. Tise, *French Decorative Art: The Société des Artistes Décorateurs 1900–1942* (Paris, 1990)).

[8] e.g. the Palais Sina and Palais Todesco in Vienna; see W. Kitlitschka, *Die Malerei* (1981), pp. 61–4.

the use of murals to indulge in 'escape' or make-believe, are in turn often the most valuable pointers to relationships between apparently contrasting idioms.

'AN EXPERIMENTAL MEASURE'

The Select Committee appointed in 1841 to consider the scope for decoration at the new Palace of Westminster was informed by Sir Charles Eastlake that 'the origin of the present German school in fresco . . . was owing to a private individual, a Prussian, who employed some German painters at Rome to decorate his private apartments in fresco.'[9] This individual was Jacob Saloman Bartholdy, the Prussian Consul-General, whose commission to Cornelius, Veith, and Overbeck for Biblical murals inspired both a further scheme at the Casino Massimo in Rome and King Ludwig's extensive patronage in Munich, thereby launching the Nazarene fresco revival. A similar 'experimental measure'[10] was ventured in private mural commissions by Benjamin Hawes, Lord Monson, and others who were mostly associated with the introduction of fresco at Westminster (Appendix D: 1–5), but Prince Albert's Buckingham Palace Garden Pavilion scheme appears to have been the most ambitious—and certainly the best publicized—attempt to emulate the Nazarene patrons, and it employed native British artists where Hawes and Monson had favoured Cornelius.[11] Though now destroyed, it was lavishly described and illustrated by Mrs Jameson,[12] in a volume sent by Queen Victoria to her brother the French Emperor 'comme un premier essai de cet art dans ce pays'.[13] In 1834 Mrs Jameson had already published an admiring account of the Nazarenes' work with a plea for English painters to be given similar wall-space.[14]

Just as the Casino Massimo frescoes illustrated Italian poets on Italian soil, and those at Munich included the Niebelungenlied and other national poems, so the Pavilion presented themes from Milton's *Comus* and landscapes and incidents from Scott's novels (Plates 170, 171). Again, just as Bartholdy had justified his choice of fresco as 'the medium for artists to get to know their capabilities . . . [necessitating the] working together of several young artists . . . spurred on by emulation of each other',[15] so Albert employed Etty, Dyce, Maclise, Stanfield, Uwins, Leslie, Sir William Ross, Landseer, and Eastlake each to paint a *Comus* panel, and H. J. Townsend, C. Stonehouse, J. Severn, and R. and J. Doyle the eight Scott scenes.[16]

Watching their work in progress, Queen Victoria predicted that the scheme 'will be a perfect "bijou"', but also noted ominously that 'The process of fresco painting is very curious.'[17] Etty, indeed, was defeated by it, causing Albert to substitute a panel by Dyce, and Thackeray

[9] Min. SCFA (4 June 1841), PP VI, § 596.

[10] Question from Mr Blake to William Dyce (28 May 1841), in ibid., § 418.

[11] Evidence of B. Hawes in ibid. (1841), § 752; British patronage of German artists is discussed in W. Vaughan, *German Romanticism* (1979), pp. 41, 60 et seq. A scheme promoted by C. L. Eastlake at Bowood, Wilts. from 1838 (Appendix D: 2) for the Marquis of Lansdowne is discussed in H. Smith, *Decorative Painting in the Domestic Interior* (1984) and was a counterpart to Albert's patronage of British artists.

[12] A. Jameson, *The Decoration of the Garden Pavilion* (1846).

[13] Letter from Queen Victoria to 'S. M. le Roi des Français' (29 June 1846), RA(W) Y48/57.

[14] A. Jameson, *Visits and Sketches* (1834), p. 300.

[15] Bartholdy, quoted in M. Droste, *Das Fresko* (1980), p. 20 (author's translation).

[16] Miss Rigby (later Lady Eastlake) recorded in her *Journals* in 1844 that Prince Albert himself was 'to fill up the spaces beneath' the *Comus* subjects (quoted in D. Farr, *William Etty* (1958), p. 97).

[17] Queen Victoria, *Journal* (24 Feb. 1845 and 15 June 1843), RA(W).

to complain at 'august powers and principalities ordering the works of such a great man as Etty to be hacked out of the palace wall—that was a slap in the face to every artist in England.'[18] Most of the *Comus* murals appear to have been stiff and histrionic; the liveliest was probably Landseer's characteristically vivid illustration of Comus's animal-headed troupe (Plate 171).

Mrs Jameson described *Comus* as 'like a many-sided gem . . . at once classical, romantic and pastoral',[19] and the Pavilion was correspondingly organized to present contrasting modes of mural decoration, as if they were kinds of fresco apprentice pieces. The *Comus* scenes were placed in its main Octagon, and framed with 'Cinquecento' arabesques by Ludwig Grüner (Plate 170); the Scott illustrations in a smaller 'Romantic' room to its left; whilst to the right was a 'Pompeiian' room. If the project was in part a conscious throwback to Guido Reni's decoration of a garden house, the Casino dell'Aurora, of the Rospiglioso Palace, it was clearly also a British version of a modern German Romantic *Gesamtkunstwerk*. Arabesques were so much the hallmark of Cornelius and his pupils, who used their open S shape as a cipher of the eternal, that they were nicknamed 'Germanbesques', whilst Pompeiian decoration had been revived in Munich.[20] Art, literature, and what Mrs Jameson recognized as the 'musical' and 'melodic' interaction of the contrasted styles of ornament, were made one through the fresco medium, whose symbolic power to fuse subject with setting was a central tenet of Cornelius's philosophy of mural painting.[21] Located in the grounds of Buckingham Palace, the pastoral imagery of *Comus* and the landscapes of Scott were thus made a physical part of the royal desmesne, and Milton's ideal of virtue and Scott's chivalry were made integral with the monarch's home.

Despite such symbolism, B. R. Haydon complained at the 'folly' of 'employing so many instead of placing the whole decoration in the hands of one competent man'.[22] In the Poets' Hall at Westminster, which can be recognized as the most direct sequel to the Buckingham Palace work, the artists were significantly told to 'act in concert', whilst Sir John Millais's grisaille lunettes of 1847 for a house in Leeds, illustrating *The Ages of Man, Poetry*, and *Music*, adopted a consciously angular style perhaps intended in part to create decorative unity.[23] Meanwhile, at Osborne House on the Isle of Wight, one artist only, William Dyce, was now commissioned by Albert. His *Neptune resigning to Britannia the Empire of the Sea* (Plate 172) above the central staircase is, however, a somewhat laboured attempt to combine the 'holiday' overtones of its location with inspiration from Raphael's *Galatea*, succeeding only partially in softening the hard contours of the Nazarene fresco style which both he and Eastlake deplored. Something of the *Gesamtkunstwerk* idea emerged again in the murals of *Parnassus* and the *Dancing Hours* undertaken in the 1850s in the Buckingham Palace Ballroom, but these were by the Italian artist Nicola Consoni.[24] It looked as

[18] William Thackeray, *Fraser's Magazine* (June 1845), quoted in Farr, *William Etty*, p. 98.

[19] Jameson, *The Decoration of the Garden Pavilion* (1846), p. 6.

[20] In Leo von Klenze's decoration of King Ludwig's private apartments in the Munich Residenz (see Jameson, *Visits and Sketches*, p. 278). Wilhelm Zahn's *Die schönsten Ornamente und merkwürdigsten Gemälde aus Pompeji, Herculaneum und Stabiae* (1829) was widely known in Europe. See Vaughan, *German Romanticism*, pp. 52–3 for knowledge of German murals in early 19th-century Britain.

[21] See Peter von Cornelius, Letter to Josef Goerres, 3 Nov., 1814 in E. G. Holt, *From the Classicists to the Impressionists* (1966), p. 100.

[22] B. R. Haydon: Letter to Seymour Kirkup (9 Nov. 1844), quoted in *Autobiography*, ed. Penrose (1927), pp. 587–8.

[23] For the advice to 'act in concert', see Minutes of CFA (5 Aug. 1845), (RA(W) F30/28; for Millais's scheme, see H. Smith, *Decorative Painting* (1984), p. 53 and M. Bennett, *Millais* (exh. cat., RA, London, and Walker Art Gallery, Liverpool, 1967), nos. 10–15. Landseer and Stanfield contributed to murals at Somerleyton Hall near Lowestoft, Suffolk probably inspired by the Buckingham Palace Pavilion (see M. Girouard, *The Victorian Country House* (1979), p. 418); in *c.*1842, Landseer painted 'a series of rough frescoes' (R. Ormond, *Sir Edwin Landseer* (London, 1981), p. 178) in Ardvereike Lodge, Loch Laggan, showing subjects of the chase (now destroyed).

[24] See D. Millar, 'Headquarters of Taste Early Victorian Interiors of Buckingham Palace', *Country Life* (4 Dec. 1986), pp. 1762–6. Consoni also decorated the Royal Mausoleum at Frogmore.

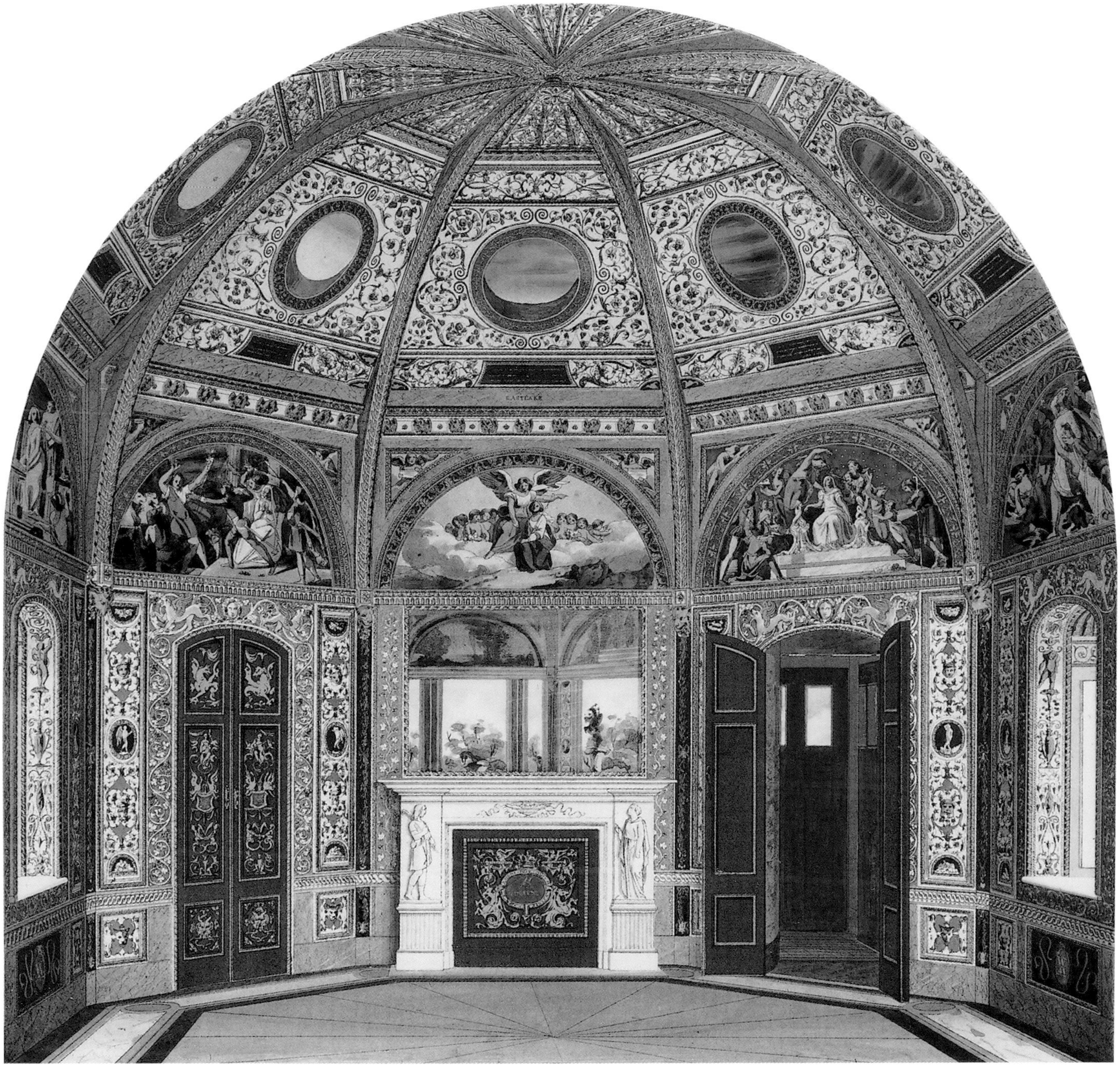

170. The Octagon Room, Buckingham Palace Garden Pavilion, showing *Comus* lunettes by Sir William Ross, Sir Charles Eastlake, and Daniel Maclise, *c.*1843–6 (destroyed), Plate 3 in A. Jameson, *The Decorations of the Garden Pavilion* (1846)

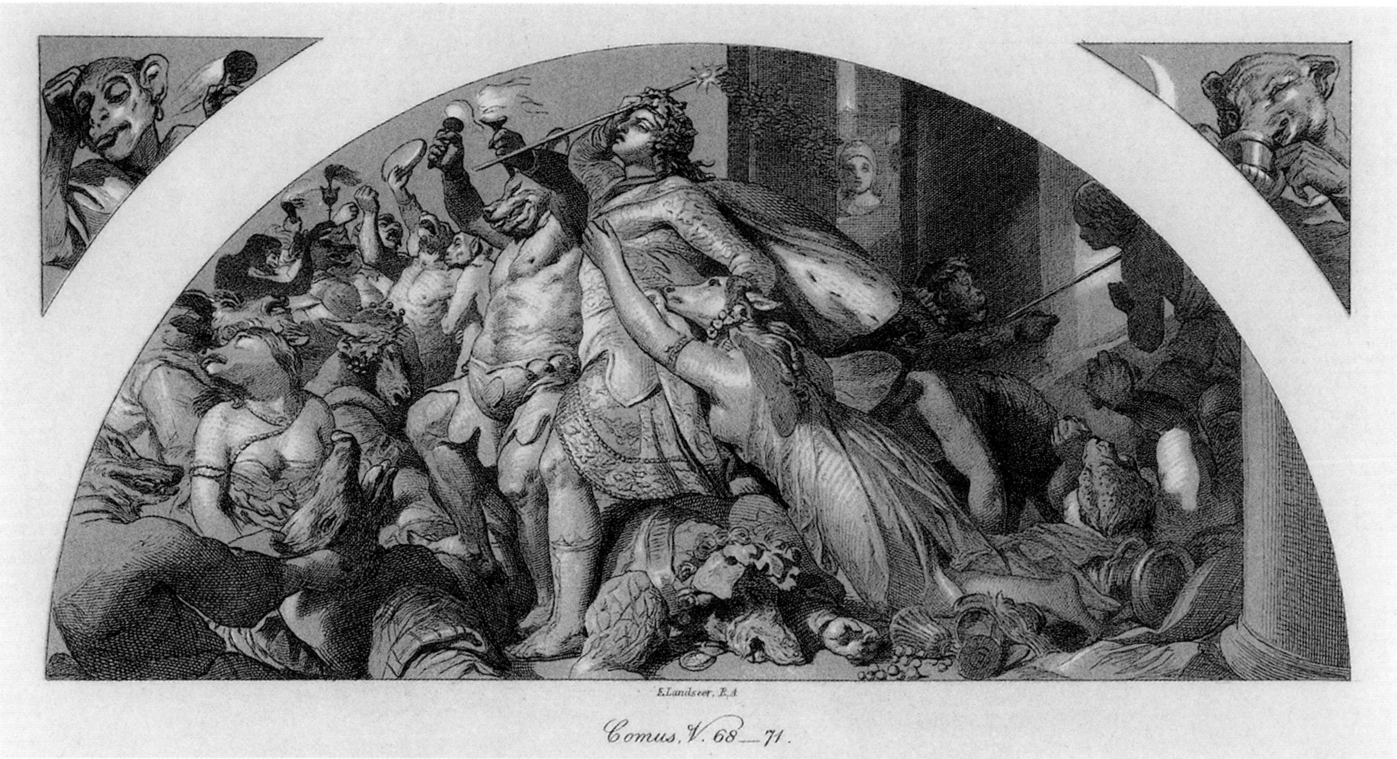

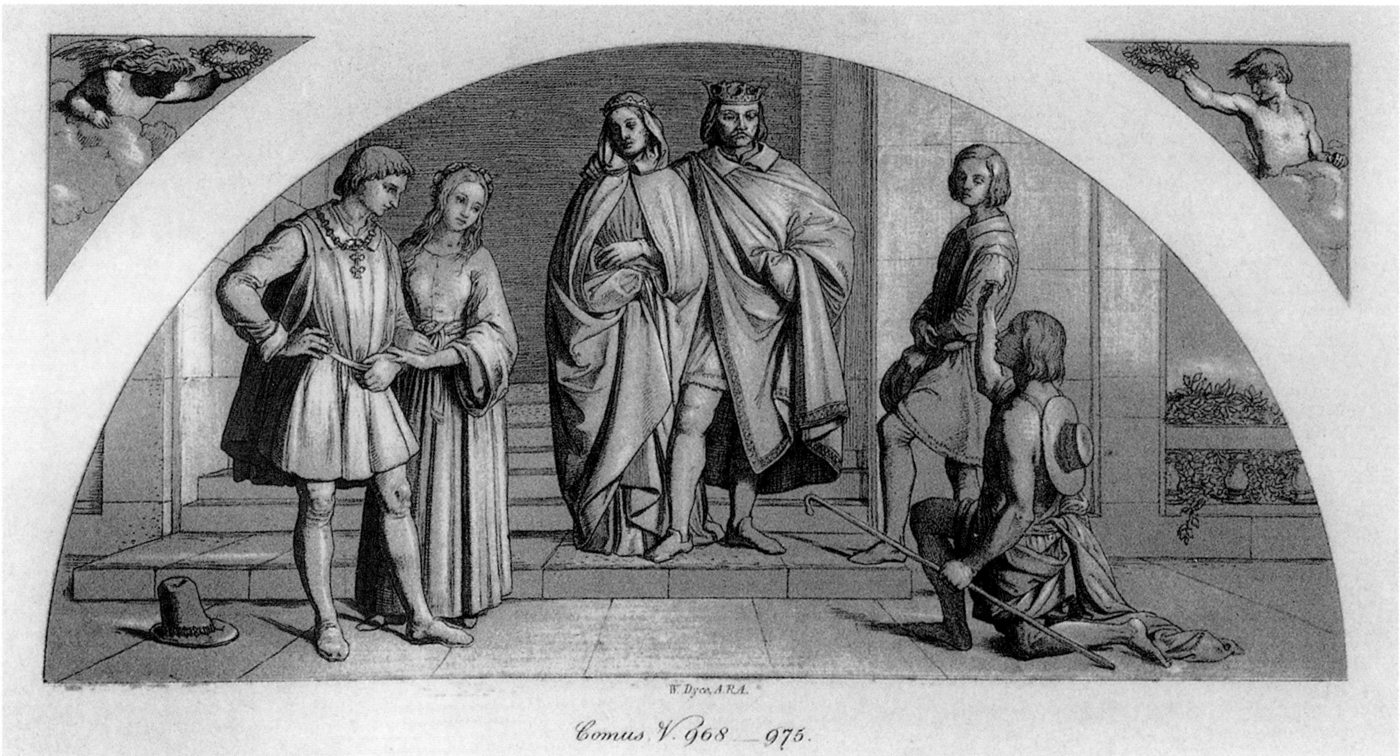

171. (top) Sir Edwin Landseer, *Comus*, verses 68–71; (bottom) William Dyce, *Comus*, verses 968–975, Buckingham Palace Garden Pavilion, *c*.1843–6 (destroyed), Plate 10 in A. Jameson, *The Decorations of the Garden Pavilion* (1846)

though Albert had lost faith in British artists; the uneven quality of his Pavilion and Osborne schemes perhaps explains why he was now advocating Germans for Westminster. It was indeed a German artist, Jakob Götzenberger, who in the year of Albert's death, 1861, completed perhaps the most symbolically complex and successfully integrated scheme of private-house decoration in Britain in the mid-nineteenth century.

Commissioned by Lord Ellesmere in about 1857 for the Great Saloon of his new Italianate *palazzo*, Bridgewater House in London, Götzenberger's scheme replaced 'great designs'[25] which its architect, Sir Charles Barry, had already formulated for decoration. Barry was displeased, but the project can be recognized both as a response to the disunity of the Garden Pavilion (its central theme was *Comus*, which had been written for Ellesmere's ancestors) and a direct reflection of Ellesmere's Germanophile sympathies as the translator of Goethe and Schiller. Götzenberger had acted as translator on Cornelius's 1843 visit to advise at Westminster, helped with Cornelius's murals for King Ludwig, and founded a fresco school as Court Painter at Mannheim. He had also known, and been admired by, William Blake. His four *Comus* lunettes mingle echoes of Blake (in the sinuous figure of Sabrina, for example) with the gentle *Gemütlichkeit* of second-generation Nazarenes like Moritz von Schwind (in the first lunette which shows Milton composing the poem; Plate XXXVI).

Placed in the recesses of the ground-floor *loggie*, the nocturnal events of the *Comus* illustrations were the initial stage in a symbolic decorative 'ascent' to the 'heavens' themselves which enacts that of Virtue in Milton's poem. Just as the association of warm and cool colours in the lunettes with 'good' and 'evil' suggests knowledge of Goethe's colour theory, so the actual light of the sun is refracted through prismatic glass at the apex of the roof; the progress of the eye towards this source would have been guided successively by the family portraits 'with allegorical attributes'[26] which appear originally to have been painted on the spandrels around the Saloon's inner central courtyard, and the twelve flamboyant, relief plaster nude sculptures of the Hours and Seasons, designed by Götzenberger and executed by Heinrich Bandel,[27] which ornament the roof supports. The 'stony fetters fix'd', in which the Lady is imprisoned by Comus's spell in the lunettes, are thus ultimately transformed into statuary emblematic of good; similarly, the fiery glow of Comus's torch and the moonlight on the waters of the Severn in the paintings below are eclipsed by the actual brilliance above of Milton's 'spheary chime', the reward in *Comus* for the virtuous soul. The symbolism of the 'music of the spheres' is reinforced by motifs of musicians in the intricate arabesque ornament which fills the *loggie* ceiling domes as well as in the musical instruments included in the plasterwork, whilst the role of the aristocracy in the attainment of Virtue is conveyed by the armorial bearings in the dome spandrels, and would have been vividly evident from the original portraits of (presumably) the very Ellesmere ancestors who had acted the first performance of *Comus*.

A revealing detail of the scheme is the tricolour ribbon worn by one of Comus's evil companions in the second lunette. In the wake of Chartism, the Tory party, to which Ellesmere belonged, still feared French-style revolution. In this sense, the Bridgewater decoration takes its place alongside a number of other private-house schemes of the period in which murals, now by British

[25] Revd A. Barry, *The Life and Works of Sir Charles Barry, RA, FRS* (London, 1867), p. 100; further discussion of the scheme is in C. A. P. Willsdon, *Bridgewater House* (1997).

[26] 'F', 'Studien zur Charakteristik bedeutender Künstler der Gegenwart LIV. Jakob Götzenberger (Nekrolog)' in *Deutsche Kunst-Zeitung. Die Dioskuren*, No. 40 (4 Nov. 1866), p. 313.

[27] See ibid. and 'Götzenberger' in *Zeitschrift für bildende Künste mit dem Beiblatt von Dr. Carl von Lützow*, 2 (Leipzig, 1867), p. 7.

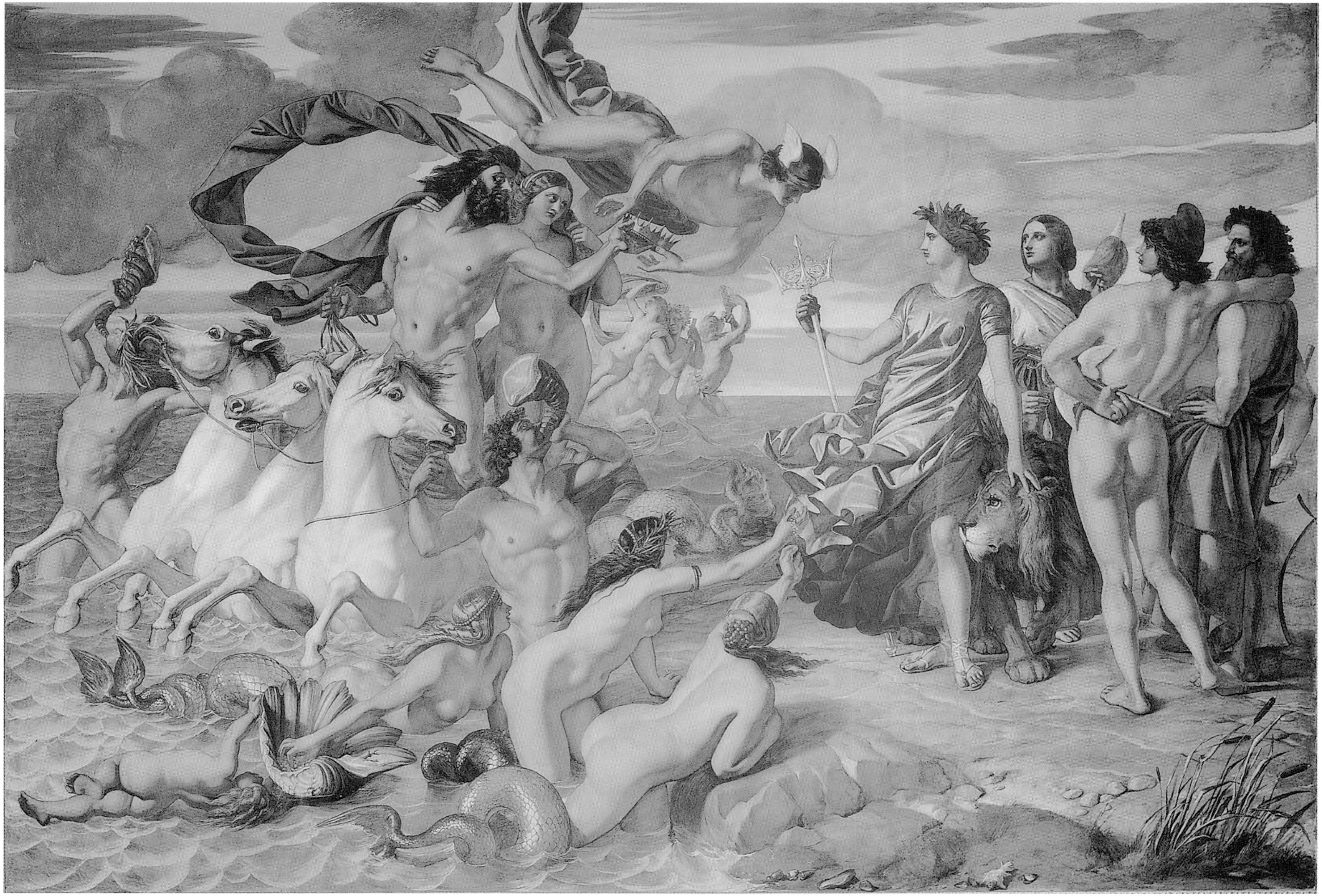

172. William Dyce, *Neptune resigning to Britannia the Empire of the Sea*, Osborne House, Isle of Wight, 1847

artists, were used to celebrate aristocratic status. These include the portraits at Scarisbrick Hall (Appendix D: 4) and the family history paintings inspired by the Westminster decoration painted by a local artist at Hartland Abbey[28] (Appendix D: 6). At Wallington Hall in Northumberland, however, the home of the Trevelyans, family allusions were set within the larger context of scenes of local history (Plates 173, 174), and a distinctively 'Whig' emphasis is evident, as well as a new 'Pre-Raphaelite' style. Here, William Bell Scott, who had studied in Germany and was an unsuccessful Westminster competitor, painted eight panels to fill the classical-style arcading which resulted from the roofing over in 1855, on Ruskin's advice, of the central courtyard, whilst Ruskin himself provided floral ornament.

The murals, painted *in situ* but now on canvas rather than in fresco, include portraits of many local personalities as historical figures, and in contrast to the Tory emphasis on the role of the aristocracy, give prominence to that of the common people in the making of history. The series culminates with *Iron and Coal on Tyneside in the Nineteenth Century*, in which Charles Edward Trevelyan himself, heir to Wallington, raises a sledgehammer as an equal alongside the brawny ironworkers of Stephenson's and Hawk's and Crawshaw's. The first painting, *Building the Roman Wall* (Plate 174) is an adaptation of the subject of Scott's 1843 Westminster competition entry, and typifies the plunge *in medias res* used throughout the scheme, which, given the murals' near life-size scale and eye-level position, makes the viewer in turn feel a part, like Charles Trevelyan, of history's process. Its Roman centurion marches forwards along Hadrian's Wall as if into the hall itself, grimly chastizing 'two Britons too lazy to work'[29] who lie across his path and whose tanned bodies are brilliantly lit by a shaft of sunlight breaking momentarily through the white clouds of the slate-coloured Northumbrian sky. These 'primitive' Britons contrast in turn with their industrious descendants in *Iron and Coal*, symbolically suggesting the Whig idea of the 'progress of history'. In *Grace Darling*, the viewer is placed alongside the survivors of the famous shipwreck as they battle in their battered boat with the raging seas; the composition as well as the realistic costume and facial detail recall the close-up boat interior of Ford Madox Brown's *The Last of England* (Birmingham Museum and Art Gallery). The Nazarene symbolic unity of subject and location through mural painting had been re-invented: past, present, and place were made one, and their identity projected through the Ruskinian 'truth to nature' of such distinctively local details as the Lindisfarne eider duck and sea-swallow in *St. Cuthbert*, or the promontory of Tynemouth Rock rising through grey mist in *The Descent of the Danes*.

RE-ENACTING THE PAST: MEDIEVALISM AND THE 'GRAND MANNER' 1850s–1870s

Scott also illustrated the ballad of *Chevy Chase* at Wallington Hall, a theme recently painted by Götzenberger for the Duke of Northumberland (Appendix D: 7): and *The King's Quair* (Plate 175),

[28] See Girouard, *The Victorian Country House*, pp. 114 and 448 for Scarisbrick; and M. Hall, 'Hartland Abbey, Devon', *Country Life* (2 Dec. 1993), pp. 96–9.

[29] W. Bell Scott, *Address* to the RIBA of 1867, reprinted in F. Graham, *Scenes from Northumbrian History* (Newcastle-upon-Tyne, 1972). 'First ideas' (sketches) by Scott for the murals are held in the National Gallery of Scotland, Edinburgh.

a poem by James I of Scotland, at Penkill Castle in Ayrshire (1865–8).[30] The patron here was the new fifteenth Laird of Penkill and friend of the Pre-Raphaelites, Alice Boyd, who is portrayed in Wallington's *Grace Darling*. The Penkill decoration marks a departure from the political or moral overtones of many of the schemes considered so far; it evokes a fantasy world of medieval chivalry in which any comment on modern society now rests in the escapist implications of its portraits of Bell Scott and his friends—Alice Boyd as Minerva, Swinburne and Rossetti as courtiers; Christina Rossetti as Lady Jane and so on. Again, however, the *in situ* technique (encaustic), and the arrangement of the mural as a frieze winding up a spiral stair-tower towards Alice Boyd's bedroom, apply the Nazarene principle of the symbolic fusion of place and subject, for *The King's Quair* describes a dream ascent to the empire of Venus. Its whimsical, rather than strictly accurate medievalism, and its delight in the natural world (other parts of the castle were liberally ornamented with birds, butterflies, and flowers by Alice Boyd as well as Scott himself) were essentially now part of the rising Arts and Crafts Movement, whose flagship interior was William Morris's Red House of 1857 with its tempera illustrations by Burne-Jones of Froissart's *Romance of Sir Degrevaunt*; they also anticipate similar motifs in the decoration at Rochdale Town Hall.

Where Bell Scott had striven for naturalism, Burne-Jones's Red House panels[31] (Plate 176) adopted a consciously archaic style based on Giotto and early Italian art. The tightly packed figures occupy a shallow picture space, taking account of the painting's function as decoration for a wall in place of Scott's illusionism at Wallington, and the scheme also complemented paintings on furniture like Rossetti's *Dantis Amor* on the settle. Rossetti described the whole house as 'more a poem than a house',[32] although Trojan War scenes planned for the stairway, and a shipful of Greek heroes planned for the hall,[33] were never carried out. The integrative approach, however, led directly to Morris's foundation of his firm in 1861, with one of its stated objects being 'Mural Decoration . . . as applied to dwelling houses'.[34] In the event the firm actually produced relatively few mural schemes, Morris's cheaper wallpapers, and other, supposedly more durable media, such as tiles, proving more attractive to patrons. Burne-Jones did, nevertheless, begin a series of murals of *St. George* in 1864 for Miles Birket Foster's house in Surrey, which was eventually completed by Charles Fairfax Murray. Now, however, his model was Carpaccio's *St. George* scheme in the Scuola di San Giorgio in Venice, rather than medieval examples.[35]

It was G. F. Watts, developing the High Renaissance sources already present in the 'cinquecento' aspect of the Buckingham Palace Garden Pavilion and Dyce's Osborne *Britannia*, and subsequently William Burges, seeking to create 'art-architecture' inspired by medieval art, who, though working in idioms diametrically opposed, made the most ambitious—and also eccentric—contributions to private-house mural painting in the mid to late nineteenth century.

[30] Vaughan, *German Romanticism* illustrates a preparatory study for Alnwick (plate 13); for Penkill, see A. Hickey, 'The Pre-Raphaelite Connection with Penkill', *Review of the Pre-Raphaelite Society*, 1, no. 2 (Summer 1993), pp. 1–11, and *Penkill Castle, Girvan, Ayrshire*, Christie's sale catalogue, 15 Dec. 1992.

[31] See E. Hollamby, *Red House* (London, 1991); seven panels were originally planned but only three completed.

[32] D. G. Rossetti, quoted in Physick and Darby, *Marble Halls* (1973), 'Red House' (cat. no. 23). Burne-Jones's style probably reflects the Arundel Society publication of Giotto's Arena Chapel frescoes (see D. Robinson and S. Wildman, *Morris and Company in Cambridge* (1980), p. 12).

[33] Roman wall-paintings illustrating Troy had been discovered in the 18th century beneath the Flavian State-rooms on the Palatine, and 'Odessey landscapes' in 1849 in a private house on the Esquiline. For the Red House interiors, see R. Watkinson, 'Red House Decorated', *Journal of the William Morris Society*, 11, no. 4 (1988), pp. 10–15.

[34] Promotional pamphlet published by Morris, Marshall, Faulkner and Company, 1861, quoted in M. Harrison and B. Waters, *Burne-Jones* (1977), p. 48.

[35] Harrison and Waters, *Burne-Jones*, p. 89.

Though Watts had hugely grand ideas—including an unrealized project for what he termed a *House of Life*, to feature frescoes illustrating mankind's development—and Burges employed a battery of executant artists to realise his multifarious schemes at Cardiff Castle, Castell Coch, and Bute Castle, it has to be said that neither achieved the artistic quality of either Bell Scott or of Burne-Jones's later *Briar Rose* panels at Buscot Park, near Faringdon, Oxfordshire.

Watts was virtually the last survivor of the fresco revival, having first employed the technique at Lord Holland's residences in Florence and Careggi in the 1840s. Whereas here, and in his murals at the Palace of Westminster, he painted literary or historical themes, in the 1850s, for Lord Somers's home at 7 Carlton House Terrace in London, he developed the grandiose type of allegory dealing with time, space, and the universals of existence which formed the basis both of his unfulfilled Euston Station project on *The Progress of the Cosmos*, and his later easel works intended less to be 'delightful to the eye' as to 'go to the intelligence and the imagination'.[36]

At Carlton House Terrace, where the murals were intended to illustrate *The Elements*[37] (Plate 177) Watts's appeal to 'the imagination' was perhaps even more modern in content than Scott's *Iron and Coal. Water* juxtaposes frolicking tritons and water nymphs accompanied by a baby floating on its back, with a primitive crustacean and some kind of flat-fish, or perhaps seaweed, which bobs in the foreground olive and azure waves and suggests the continuum of mankind with the plant and animal worlds. Darwin, who had just completed his famous monograph on the evolution of the *Cirripede Crustacea* (barnacles), to be followed by his *Origin of Species* of 1859, was the cousin of Watts's first patron, Lord Holland. This connection perhaps explains Watts's fascination in general at Carlton House with what is best described as primeval creation. Not only *Water* with its crustacean, but also the panels dealing with fire and air, include fantastical cliff coastlines (the sort of geological site where Darwin found fossil barnacles?), bordered by mysterious deep lakes or seas. The figures floating through the ether in one of the *Air* panels echo Signorelli's *Demons and Damned*, but also have the elasticity of swimming creatures. One of the two smallest panels portrays limitless ocean; the other, nudes reaching across what may be a waterfall or tornado towards a gigantic clenched fist rising between boulders.

Watts's attempt to revive the grand manner is most clearly evident in the largest fresco, nearly seven metres long, which shows a kind of bacchanalian procession with gambolling putti amidst an atmospheric landscape including Mount Olympus (Plate 177). The central figure is an unashamed quotation from Titian's *Bacchus and Ariadne*, and the idea of *Earth* is only loosely suggested by a woman bearing sheaves and two herds with a dog. Another woman, declining the attentions of a Pan-like figure at the left, is reputedly a portrait of Lady Somers, whilst a startling tricolour-winged putto, descending from a puffy white cloud as if to lend a benison to the pastoral scene of soft greens, with its distant blue sea or lake, hints at Watts's Francophile sympathies,[38] but is essentially part of the larger cosmological, rather than merely political vision of man's place in time and space which is presented in the scheme as a whole.

Such a comprehensive span, from primeval origins through antiquity to Lady Somers, suggests that whilst in France in 1855–6 in the company of Arthur Prinsep, Watts had taken note of

[36] G. F. Watts, quoted in W. Loftys Hare, *Watts* (London, n.d.), pp. 57–8. For Watts's Euston Station scheme, see Chapter 11.

[37] The murals are now detached and owned by the Crown Estates Commissioners, with some on view in their offices at 16 Carlton House Terrace, London, and others at Malvern College, Worcestershire.

[38] In 1856 Watts visited Lord Holland, Ambassador in Paris, and painted portraits of prominent Frenchmen, including Thiers and Prince Gérome Bonaparte.

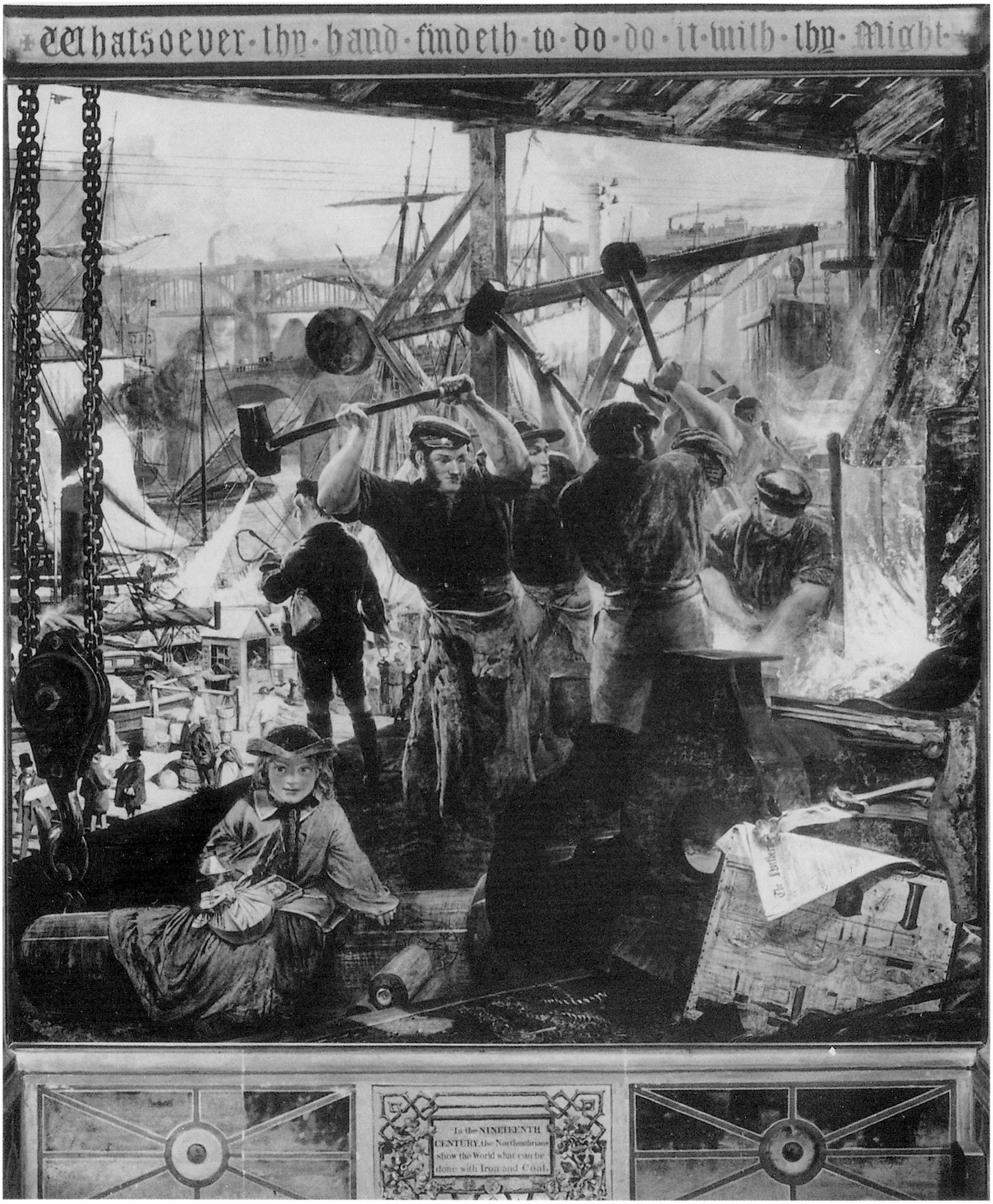

173. William Bell Scott, *Iron and Coal on Tyneside in the Nineteenth Century*, Central Hall, Wallington Hall, Northumberland, 1856

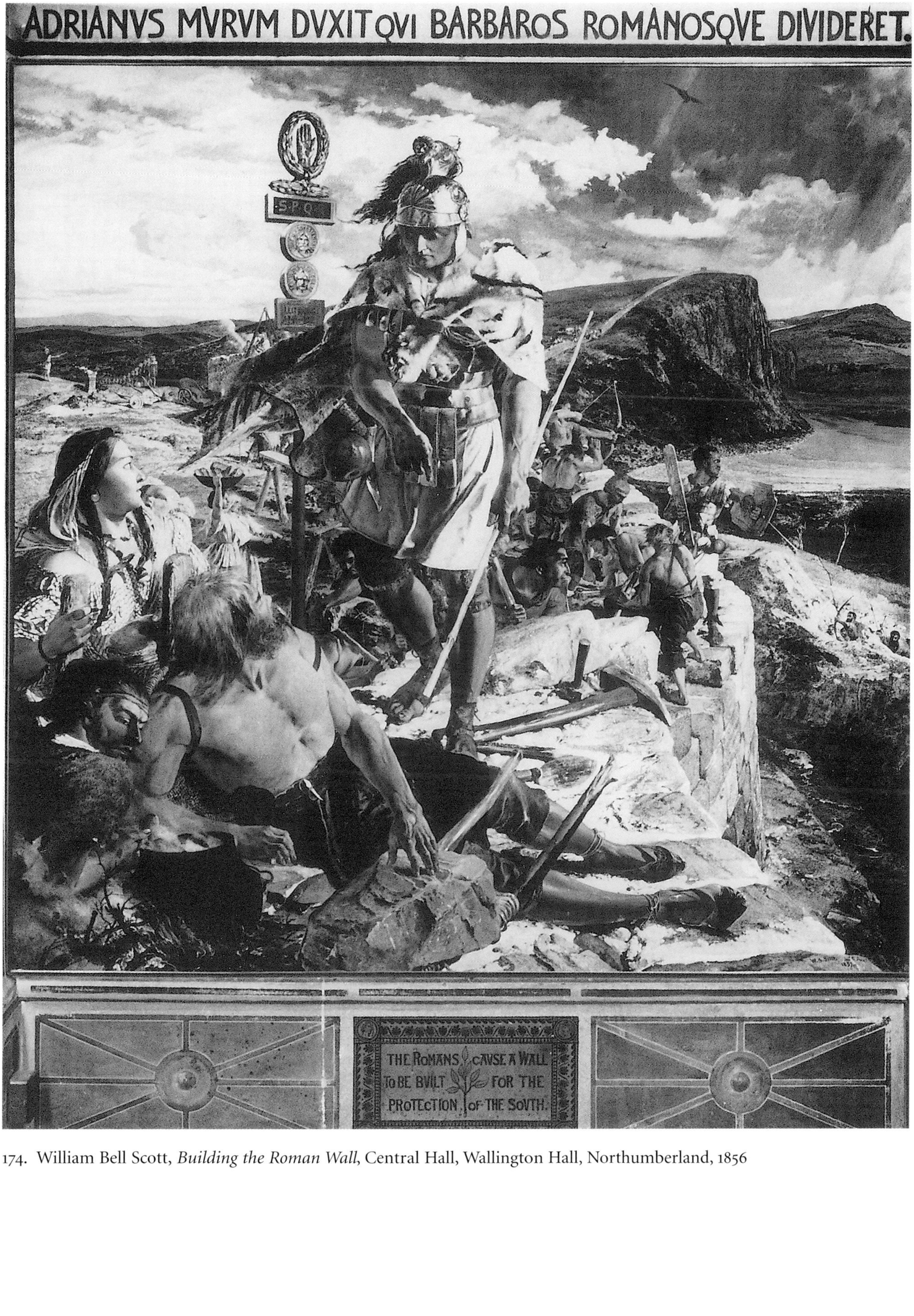

174. William Bell Scott, *Building the Roman Wall*, Central Hall, Wallington Hall, Northumberland, 1856

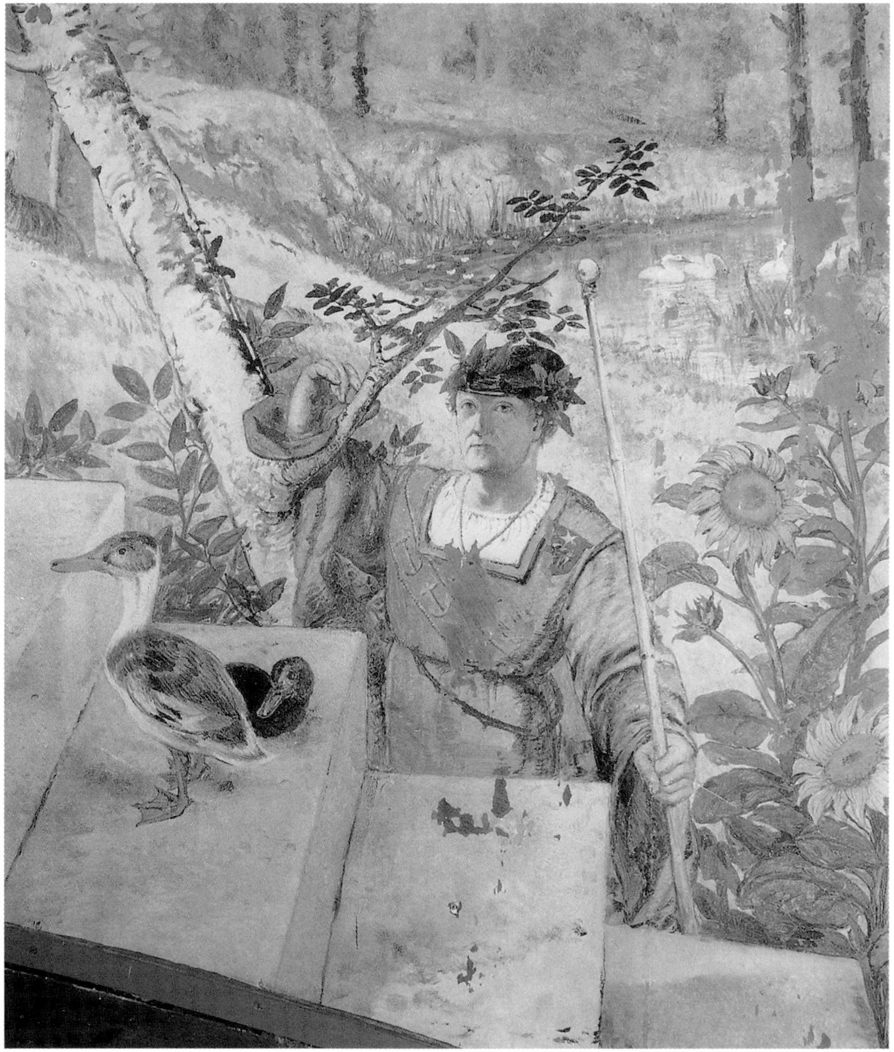

175. William Bell Scott, detail with self-portrait from *The King's Quair*, Penkill Castle, Ayrshire, 1865–8

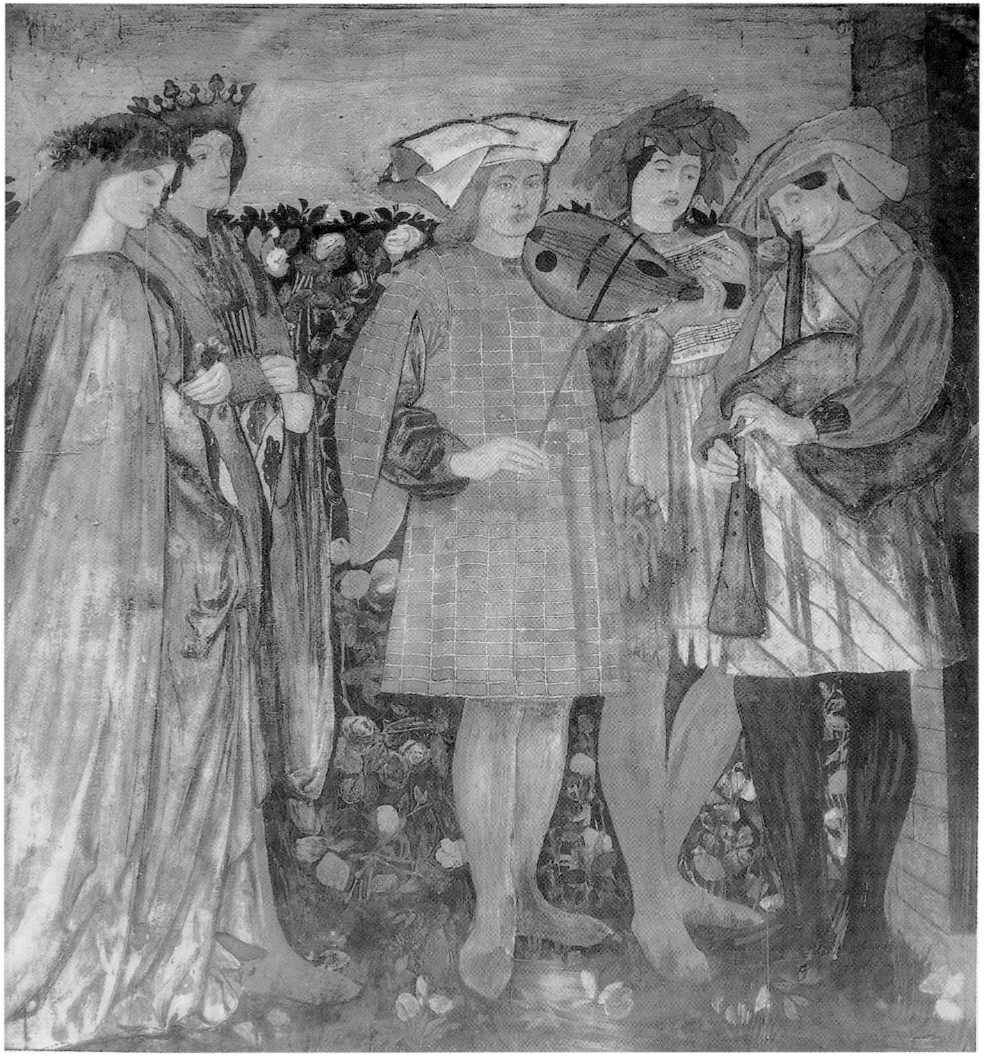

176. Sir Edward Burne-Jones, decoration at the Red House, Bexley Heath, Kent, 1850s

Chenavard's vast abortive plan for a 'History of Mankind' for the Panthéon. The *Chaos* theme of the murals Watts painted during 1855–60 for the Prinsep family at Little Holland House in London (presented by Michelangelesque nudes) certainly brings to mind Chenavard's programme, which extended from *The Flood*, with a triceratops, to Napoleon navigating the 'stream of time'. In this sense, Watts's imagery would have offered one of the most intriguing reinventions of the Nazarene philosophy of fresco, since his subject, bonded through fresco technique with place, was time itself. His murals also look towards the Symbolists' scrutiny of the creative subconscious at the *fin de siècle*. An oil painting of 1882, born of Watts's *House of Life* project, was also called *Chaos* and illustrates 'gigantic figures stretched out at full length represent[ing] a range of mountains typifying the rocky structure or skeleton'[39] of the earth; its composition was inspired by cracked and dirty wall plaster. Cosmic creation was seemingly for Watts only a cipher for the mysterious process of artistic creation itself. In this sense, he also reinvented Cornelius's belief in the 'sacred' mission of the fresco painter, whose mastery of his medium depends upon his divine genius.[40] Flawed in artistry as they are, Watts's murals were none the less a fulcrum balancing the old order of mural painting against the new artistic individualism, which would be flamboyantly proclaimed by Whistler's Peacock Room of 1878.

Watts also decorated Bowood House (Appendix D: 2) and by 1870 it was being extravagantly claimed that he had 'done more than any other man to domesticate high art in the homes of England'.[41] Even as late as 1927, the Director of the National Gallery, Sir Charles Holmes, pronounced the Carlton House Terrace scheme 'one of the most important surviving records of English work in the grand style'.[42] Watts, of course, had the benefit of sympathetic patrons willing to indulge his grand ideas. Alfred Stevens's more accomplished attempts at the High Renaissance manner (Appendix D: 8), in contrast, remained mostly incomplete or unrealized; Poynter's 1870s 'mythological games' panels for Whortley Hall were more strictly part of the Aesthetic movement and were completed by Walter Crane.[43] Stencil friezes based on John Flaxman's illustrations for Homer's *Iliad* were included by Alexander 'Greek' Thomson in the dining-room of his Holmwood House of 1857–8, at Cathcart, near Glasgow, complementing its architectural idiom. In the 1860s and 1870s, the 'domestication of high art' slipped progressively into escapism and play-acting, in which 'Italian Renaissance' became a status mode with which patrons, frequently now from the ranks of self-made industrialists, sought to give suitably lofty expression to their aspirations or ideals. The financier Charles Kuhn Prioleau, for example, engaged an unknown but highly accomplished foreign artist in the late 1860s to paint winged personifications of the Sciences in his library at 19 Abercromby Place in Liverpool. Based on Michelangelo's Sistine Chapel Prophets and Sybils, these are provided, however, with a telescope, magnifying glass, and other technical instruments! In the dining-room Prioleau's wife is portrayed as an antique matron attending the *di sotto in su* festive feast on the ceiling (Plate 178). Crace's commercial firm meanwhile continued to supply 'classical' arabesques and cherubs with occasional pictorial motifs (Appendix D: 9), as did a number of Italian decorators (Appendix D: 10), whilst from the 1870s several French artists were employed to evoke the aristocratic associations of the increasingly popular 'Louis XVI' and Rococo styles (Appendix D: 11, 14).

[39] G. F. Watts's scheme for *The House of Life*, quoted in J. Gage and C. Mullen, *G. F. Watts* (1974).

[40] Cornelius (see n. 21).

[41] Beavington Atkinson, 'English Painters' (1870), p. 67.

[42] Quoted in *Frescoes by G. F. Watts*, text at the Crown Estates Commissioners' Offices, 16 Carlton House Terrace, London.

[43] See H. Smith, *Decorative Painting*, for details of the various schemes by these artists.

In such schemes, the patron was effectively a theatrical producer, installing murals which were now usually pre-painted on canvas, rather than carried out in fresco, as part of the props for his make-believe.[44] William Burges's murals were essentially an esoteric medieval version of this escapist fantasy (Appendix D: 12). Words made pictures, however, rather than 'beauty', were his plot. Even though he had close connections with Morris's firm, he preferred the naturalistic, modified antiquarianism of Stacy Marks (a member of the St John's Wood clique), Fred Weekes, and a range of other artists such as H. W. Lonsdale, Charles Campbell, and Frederick Smallfield, mostly associated with commercial companies, who carried out his own designs.

Blurring the distinctions between painting and acting, Marks had earlier contributed to light-hearted murals showing himself and fellow artists as Shakespeare characters for Stewart Hodgeson's studio and garden house at 5 Hill Road, Abbey Road, in London.[45] At the house in Melbury Road, London, which Burges had built for himself, Marks now painted birds above the wittily carved 'Alphabet' library frieze whilst Weekes adorned the drawing-room with legendary lovers. Here, however, as in Burges's schemes in Cardiff Castle, Castell Coch, and Bute Castle (Appendix D: 16), the decoration (which also included 'Gothic' sea creatures on blood-red walls in Burges's own bedroom) must have been all but swamped by the painted furniture, riotous neo-Gothic carvings, and original medieval *objets* which jostled for attention. The props had begun to overwhelm the play.

A writer on Cardiff Castle in 1874 remarked, none the less, that 'the decorations are not only legible, but to read them is a treat to educated people'.[46] Taken as narratives rather than art, and in detail rather than ensemble, Burges's murals here, which tended to cover every available inch of wall-space, reveal a world of often mischievous and delightful wit. Literary themes abound, from Chaucer's *Parliament of Fowls* (Plate XXXVII) in the Clock Tower, to Herodotus' descriptions of the hunters and guardians of gold which inspired part of the *Mineral Wealth* decoration of Bute's own bedroom. This is thought to have been painted by Weekes, who piquantly transmuted the source of Bute's vast fortune (coal-shipping from Cardiff) into scenes, each contained within a thirteenth-century manuscript-style cartouche, which include alchemists turning lead into gold, and hatching a golden goose from a retort! The linear 'Gothic' style, however, as in the Banqueting Hall murals of *Robert the Consul* (who built the first Cardiff Castle in the twelfth century) (Plate 179) is irrepressibly Victorian. As at Castell Coch, where Burges 'hung' portraits of Bute and his family from boughs as an integral part of an escapist painted world of birds, flowers, and butterflies illustrating Aesop's fables, the retreat from modern life into a pre-industrial age is somehow too self-conscious. Only perhaps when the dogged storytelling and neo-medievalism were relieved by Aesthetic influences, as in the rhythmically interlaced branches, laden with finely observed pink and white blossom, above the gaudy birds in Cardiff's *Parliament of Fowls*, does the decoration satisfy visually. Perhaps significantly, this scheme was completed in 1889 by Charles Campbell after Burges's death; a number of private-house murals for other architects or patrons

[44] e.g. H.I. Butterfield, who issued instructions from Nice to the artist M. Leroux to paint rose garlands on the music-room ceiling at Cliffe Castle, Keighley 'as in the Cascina here' (letter from Butterfield to his son, 7 Sept. 1878, Bradford Art Galleries and Museums). For Prioleau's scheme see A. R. Allan, 'The Building of Abercromby Square (Part Two)', *University of Liverpool Recorder*, no. 97 (Jan. 1985).

[45] See R. Graham, 'Some Rediscovered Paintings by Great Artists', *Strand Magazine*, 31 (1906), pp. 537–44 and Beavington Atkinson (1870), pp. 133–4.

[46] Anon., 'Our Rambler at Cardiff Castle', *Architect* (17 March 1874), quoted in unpublished typescript kindly supplied by Matthew Williams, Keeper of Collections, Cardiff Castle. See Mordaunt Crook, *William Burges* (1981) and *The Strange Genius of William Burges*, ed. Mordaunt Crook (1981) for further details of Burges's mural decorations.

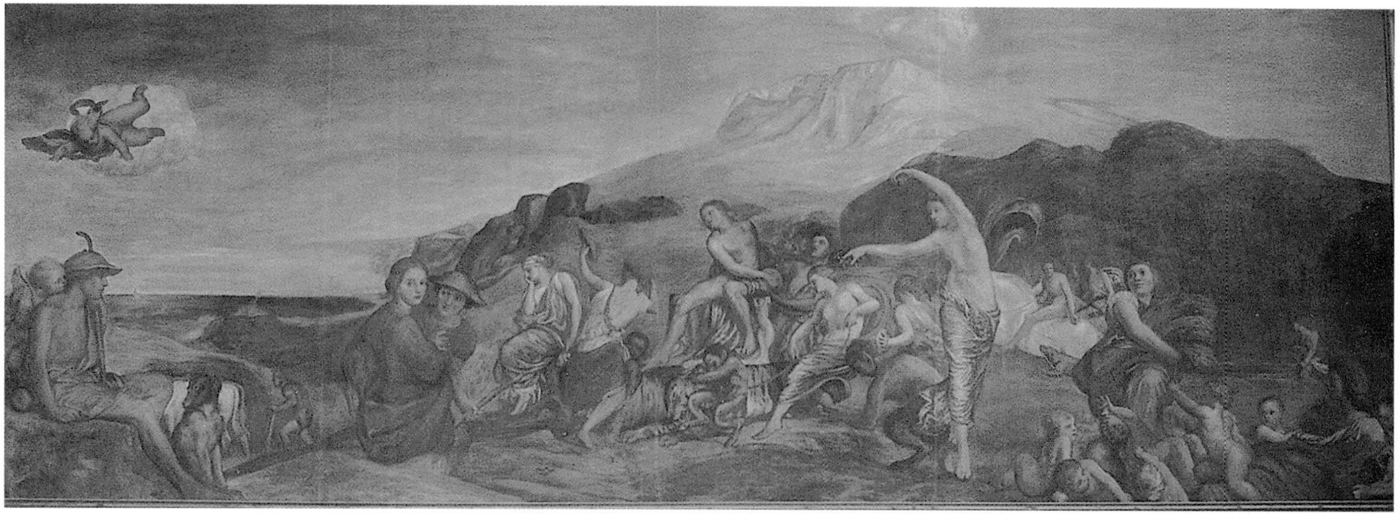

177. George Frederick Watts, *Earth*, formerly at 7 Carlton House Terrace, London, 1850s (now at Malvern College, Worcestershire)

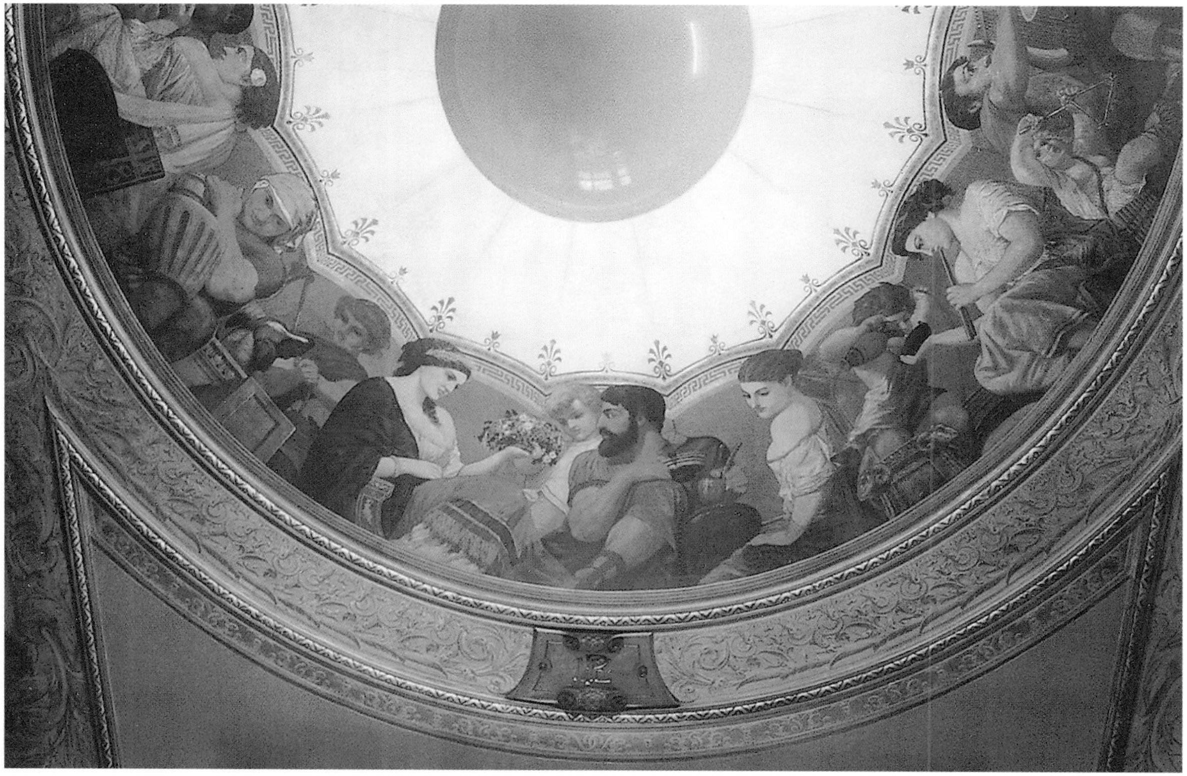

178. Unknown artist, illustration of antique feast, ceiling of 19 Abercromby Square, Liverpool, *c.* late 1860s

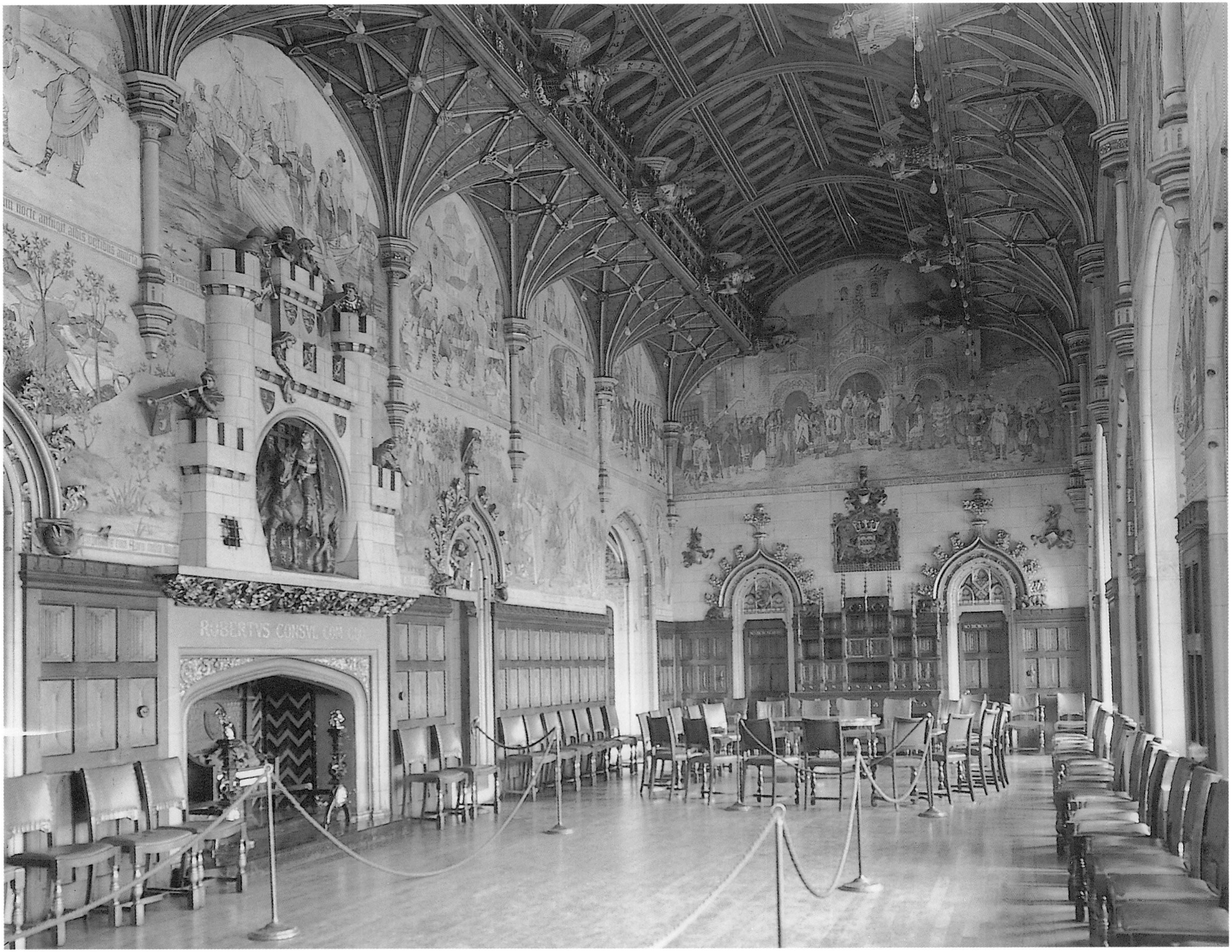

179. William Burges, Banqueting Hall, Cardiff Castle, *c.*1860s/1870s

were also carried out by Burges's artists (Appendix D: 17, 18). These include Weekes's frieze of about 1878 in the Old Dining Room of Insole Court in Cardiff (Plate XXXVIII), for the industrialist James Insole, which illustrates the seasons and derives essentially from the scheme in the Winter Smoking Room at Cardiff Castle[47] but has a liveliness reminiscent of the Austrian Moritz von Schwind's mural style.

MUSIC, MOOD, AND SYMBOL: LATE NINETEENTH CENTURY TO 1918

In advocating a return to 'mediaeval predilections' in place of inspiration from Raphael in his widely read *Hints on Household Taste* of 1868, Eastlake had already indicated that 'It is the spirit and principles of early manufacture which I desire to see revived, and not the absolute forms in which they found embodiment.'[48] Mood and atmosphere, rather than the literal re-creation of past styles, became increasingly important in private-house decoration during the later nineteenth century. By 1878 the kind of commemoration of lineage, fantasy projection, or associative games played by private patrons like Ellesmere, Prioleau, or Bute were being rudely cast aside by James McNeill Whistler's ringing declaration in his Peacock Room of artistic right over private might. Faced with the refusal of the Liverpool shipping magnate, F. R. Leyland, to pay more than a tradesman's fee for its *Harmony in Blue and Gold* (Plate 180) of peacocks and plumage patterns, Whistler retorted, 'The work of art just created alone remains the fact—and that it happened in the house of this one or that one is merely the anecdote—so that in some future dull Vassari [*sic*] you may also go down to posterity, like the man who paid Corregio [*sic*] in pennies!'[49] Art existed for its own sake—or nearly. Though Leyland's 'ambition . . . was to live the life of a Venetian merchant in modern London',[50] and he had accordingly asked Whistler to repaint Spanish leather wall panels in the dining room of his home at 49 Prince's Gate as a suitable context for the latter's *Princesse du Pays de la Porcelaine* easel painting, the artist instead created a coordinated ensemble intended to affect the sensibilities as would a piece of music. Whistler justified his 'harmony' by claiming 'I am doing the most beautiful thing that has ever been done . . . the most beautiful room,' thereby directly echoing Morris's desire to make his Red House 'the beautifullest place on earth'.[51] Whistler's Orientalism, however (the peacocks were intended to complement Leyland's shelves of blue and white porcelain), gives his scheme closer affinities with the Goncourts' cult in France of the recherché as a stimulus to the *vie intérieure*. At the same time the bird theme recalls Marks's for Burges, as well as a frieze of around 1869 by Leighton for Percy Wyndham's house at 44

[47] See M. Williams, '. . . "the example set by the late Mr Burges . . ." Gothic Revival at Insole Court. Cardiff', *Decorative Arts Society Journal*, no. 21 (1997), pp. 5–8.

[48] Quoted in C. L. Eastlake, *Hints on Household Taste* 1878 (introd. J. Gloag, 1969), p. viii.

[49] J. M. Whistler, draft letter to F. R. Leyland, 31 Oct. 1876, in R. Spencer (ed.), *Whistler: A Retrospective* (New York, 1991), p. 121.

[50] E. R. and J. Pennell, *The Life of James McNeill Whistler*, vol. I (London, 1908), p. 203.

[51] J. M. Whistler, quoted in Pennell, p. 206; W. Morris, quoted in F. MacCarthy, *William Morris: A Life for Our Time* (London, 1994), p. 158. Whistler had already experimented in 1872 with 'Oriental' effects, including two murals in the style of oriental ceramics, showing sailing ships, in the hall of his own house at 96 Cheyne Walk (formerly 2 Lindsay Row), Chelsea (see H. Smith, *Decorative Painting*, p. 91). For the cult of the 'Aesthetic' artist's house which developed in the wake of the Peacock Room, see Haweis, *Beautiful Houses* (1882). An 'Aesthetic' scheme still *in situ* is that of 1874 by T. Armstrong and R. Caldecott for W. E. Nesfield's Bank Hall, Chapel-en-le-Frith, Derbyshire (see Smith, *Decorative Painting*, p. 55).

Belgrave Square, London,[52] and there is almost Burgesian wit in the inclusion of silver shillings at the feet of one of the birds and flecks of white paint in the feathers to caricature his patron's perceived miserliness and ruffled shirt. Whistler's promotional skills none the less ensured that the scheme became a *cause célèbre* of Aesthetic decoration.

A veritable flock of bird murals by artists such as Walter Crane and Albert Moore (Appendix D: 13, 19) in fact took off as part of the taste for airy rooms with clean lines and pastel colours. Japanese and antique art, Pater's Renaissance, and synaesthesia were harnessed in the service of decoration (Appendix D: 13, 15, 19–20) which, however, was frequently very much more than mere 'art for art's sake'. Leighton's *Dance of the Cymbalists* (Plate 181), for example, consisting of 'five life-sized classical figures' set on gilded grounds and surmounted by his 'deep frieze of cormorants, storks and other wild birds'[53] at Wyndham's home was painted for the top of the stairwell and therefore suggests an allusion to the 'Music of the Spheres'. Richard Wagner was already reviving the *Gesamtkunstwerk*, whose original early nineteenth-century form would have been known to Leighton, a keen music-lover, through his training in Germany.

Walter Crane, who, inspired by Botticelli's art, asserted that 'the mural painter is not only a painter, but a poet, historian, dramatist, philosopher,'[54] looked to what he called 'the beautiful and permanent images of emblematic design' to realize his belief in the 'refining influence of art and beauty in our daily lives'. This influence made 'house decoration . . . almost synonymous with civilisation'.[55] His redecoration between 1873 and 1884 of the scientist William Spottiswoode's classical-style library at Combe Bank, Sevenoaks, includes putti bearing hourglasses who not only represent the *Hours*, but also interlink original Florentine paintings of amorini and thereby provide literal unity between past and present. The 'magnificent aluminium painted ceiling'[56] (Plate 182) in turn presents an emblematic fusion of time and space, which falls heir to Watts's Carlton House Terrace symbolism. Its central chandelier, powered by the first electric lighting system in a private house, is suspended from a 'wheel-like frame' which encloses personifications of 'the Sun, the four seasons and the signs of the Zodiac' and was intended to be 'figurative of the radiating light of the one and the revolution of the others';[57] beneath the gold and silver painted design met the luminaries of Spottiswoode's Royal Society. Just as Darwin, Huxley, and Herbert Spencer were amongst the Society's members, so the decoration carries an evolutionary theme; even the plant-stem arabesques in the window frames suggest Crane's idea, derived from meeting Darwin, that art was 'an organic thing . . . a result of that continual fierce and strenuous struggle for existence throughout nature'.[58] Allegorical schemes were subsequently painted by Crane for a number of other private patrons (Appendix D: 13); he also painted a frieze in 1883, illustrating Longfellow's *Skeleton in Armour* for a house at Newport, Long Island (now detached and in Salve Regina College).

[52] Bird murals were also painted *c.*1870s by Stacy Marks for an interior by Gertrude Jekyll at Eaton Hall, Cheshire, although his main decoration here consisted of panels of *The Canterbury Pilgrims* in the Drawing Room, and were part of the Bank Hall scheme (see n. 51).

[53] M. D. Conway, quoted in *Nineteenth Century Pictures*, Christie's sale catalogue (22 June 1990), no. 83; three of the panels were included in this sale; each is in oil on canvas and 2.21 × 1.29 m in size.

[54] W. Crane, 'Of Decorative Painting and Design' in W. Morris (ed.), *Arts and Crafts Essays* (1893), p. 45.

[55] W. Crane, *Ideals in Art* (1905), p. 110.

[56] Extract from the *Combe Bank Magazine* (1929), MS WU4/E19, Combe Bank Archive, Kent Archives Service.

[57] W. Crane, *Notes* on the decoration at Combe Bank (Dec. 1879), in *MS Notes . . . on the Walter Crane Room* (n.d.), MS WU4/E19, in same collection.

[58] Quoted in G. Smith and S. Hyde (eds), *Walter Crane* (1989), p. 20.

The scheme of fifty panels, some no more than six and a half centimetres wide, which were commissioned from fellow-artists by the painter Alma-Tadema from the late 1880s to decorate the entrance hall of his 'house beautiful at St. John's Wood' would seem, in contrast, to suggest the ultimate logic of narcissistic 'art for art's sake'; it even included two panels illustrating Alma-Tadema's former studio and showing a painting by him there.[59] Yet it was intended as an illustration of the lines from Shakespeare's *Richard III* inscribed above the mantelpiece, 'I count myself in nothing else so happy / As in a soul remembering my good friends,' which of course describe a *subjective* state of mind. Hearing the shape of panel he was asked to paint, Leighton picked up a dessert knife and asked 'My dear Tadema, what sort of subject do you expect me to paint on this?'[60] In the event this testing prescription evoked the first version of his *Bath of Psyche*. Since it is thought in fact to show Venus, goddess of love, rather than Psyche,[61] it would thus have clearly projected the ambivalence of the scheme as homage to human relationship as well as art. Despite its eclectic range, the scheme must have succeeded as a decorative ensemble where Albert's earlier Garden Pavilion (Plates 170, 171) or the Royal Exchange (Plates 1; 33–6; 38–40; Plates V–VIII) did not, precisely *because* the all but impossible dimensions of its panels forced the choice of subjects with inherently decorative potential. John Singer Sargent painted a *Javanese Dancer*, G. H. Boughton a 'tall young horsewoman',[62] Afred Parsons *Apple Blossom*, and Frank Dicksee *Andromeda*, for example, whilst there were even various landscapes and a sleepwalker, the last by Gustave Pope.

Sleep, dreams and subjective responses came to the fore in a group of late nineteenth-century schemes by artists whose background lay in the Arts and Crafts and Aesthetic traditions, but who recognized, perhaps, an inherent incompatibility between 'art for art's sake' and decoration for the home of an individual with personal ideas and aspirations. On the Continent, Marées and Böcklin had already established the primacy in mural art of 'self-realization and self-discovery';[63] and the French Symbolists were convinced that 'painting could only have been invented in order to decorate the banal walls of man's buildings with thoughts, dreams and ideas.'[64] Crane's philosophy of mural painting can be seen as a parallel to this, but the murals for private houses of Burne-Jones, John Duncan, and Charles Mackie at the end of the century perhaps came closest to the psychological dimension of Continental Symbolism, laying a foundation which was extended in the twentieth century in the work of Sigismund Goetze.

Burne-Jones said he wished 'to forget the world and be inside a picture'.[65] In his *Cupid and Psyche* frieze for an interior by Morris and Company for George Howard's house at 1 Palace Green, Kensington Palace Gardens, London[66] (Plate 183), the subjects were based on Morris's *Earthly Paradise* and included *Cupid finding Psyche asleep*. Begun in 1872, the scheme was actually completed by Crane in 1887, and though contained within a Gothic arched setting, its compositions were inspired by the Elgin Marbles, Aldus Manutius's fine late fifteenth-century printed edition, illustrated with woodcuts of the *Hypnerotomachia Poliphili*, and the work of Mantegna.

[59] The panels were each 80 cm high and varied in width from 6.3 to 20.3 cm. See R. de Cordova, 'The Panels in Sir Lawrence Alma-Tadema's Hall', *Strand Magazine*, 24 (Dec. 1902), pp. 615–30.

[60] F. Leighton, quoted in de Cordova, p. 617.

[61] See S. Jones et al., *Frederic Leighton* (1996), p. 214.

[62] de Cordova, 'The Panels in Alma-Tadema's Hall', p. 616.

[63] 'Selbstverwirklichung and Selbsterfahrung', Droste, *Das Fresko* (1980), p. 64 (author's translation).

[64] A. Aurier, 'Le Symbolisme en peinture—Paul Gauguin' (9 Feb. 1891) in *Oeuvres posthumes* (Paris, 1981), pp. 215–16, quoted in introd. by P. Jullien, *French Symbolist Painters* (Hayward Gallery, London, and Walker Art Gallery, Liverpool, 1972), p. 165.

[65] Quoted in L. D. Lutchmansingh, 'Fantasy and arrested desire in Edward Burne-Jones's Briar-Rose Series', in *Pre-Raphaelites Reviewed*, ed. M. Pointon (Manchester, 1989), p. 124.

[66] The house was built by Philip Webb; the murals are now in Birmingham Museum and Art Gallery. See B. Waters, 'Painter and Patron The Palace Green Murals', *Apollo*, 102 (1978), pp. 338–41.

Psyche's disconcerting, trance-like advance *out* of the frieze format and towards the viewer in one of the panels would have implied that the room itself was an Earthly Paradise. 'Being inside a picture', of course, suggests a critique of the 'world left behind'.[67] It is revealing that in dealing with the *Sleeping Beauty* legend in his *Briar Rose* paintings of 1889–90 (Plate 184), which were not designed as murals, but were bought by Arthur Henderson and installed to form mural decorations at Buscot Park shortly afterwards, Burne-Jones omitted the moment of awakening which brings the princess back to the present time. He explained, 'I want to leave all the afterwards to the invention and imagination of people, and tell them no more.'[68] The 'murals' however, are no longer passive stage props for the patron's fantasies as at Cardiff Castle, but instead the very dynamo of visionary experience. Their visual rhythm of sinuously interlacing boughs and foliage in muted browns and greens enfolds the princess and courtiers, but also acts upon the viewer with hypnotic power; the sleeping faces fascinate; and the prince's armour glints with cold, even surreal, intensity. The ensemble has an almost hallucinatory quality; it proved so compelling when exhibited that tours of Britain and the USA were planned. Literature (Tennyson) remained the inspiration, but the relationship between art and architecture, so dear to Morris and Burges, had been replaced by interaction with the viewer's psyche.

Though Burne-Jones attempted other murals, including *The Sleep of King Arthur in Avalon*, he failed to complete them (Appendix D: 15). Wanting 'big things to do and vast spaces, and for common people to see them and say Oh!—only Oh!'[69] he faced the same dilemma as Morris: it was private rather than public patrons who had the means and inclination to put his paintings on their walls. It took an admirer of Ruskin's ideal of public art who was also up to date with modern French developments to break this moral impasse. This was Sir Patrick Geddes, whose mural commissions at his own flat at Ramsay Garden in Edinburgh formed part of his programme at the adjacent University Hall, and in local hospitals and schools, to regenerate modern Scotland through a Celtic Revival. Fresh from the Paris 1889 International Exhibition, he argued that 'the present artistic leadership of France . . . is really due to . . . first *private*, then voluntarily associated, thereafter civic, and only *finally* national and government effort.'[70] Another admirer of Darwin, he thus sought himself to give a lead in this evolutionary sequence. During the 1890s he commissioned *The Evolution of Pipe Music* from John Duncan for the hall of his flat and *The Seasons* from Charles Mackie for its drawing-room. Further panels showing children, flowers, and plants were also carried out by Mackie, Mary Hill Burton, Duncan, and possibly also Robert Brough, E. A. Hornel, Robert Burns, and others.[71] Although all the decoration in the flat was apparently painted

[67] Lutchmansingh, 'Burne-Jones's Briar-Rose Series', p. 124.

[68] Ibid., p. 126.

[69] Quoted in Harrison and Waters, *Burne-Jones*, p. 118.

[70] P. Geddes, 'On National and Municipal Encouragement of Art upon the Continent' (printed paper in SUA, given to the Edinburgh Art Congress, 1889), p. 4.

[71] See M. Armour, 'Mural Decoration in Scotland, Part I', *Studio*, 10 (1897), p. 105; and C. Mackie's letters to Geddes (15 and 17 Oct., 1893), SUA. Norah Geddes's manuscript *Reminiscences* (NLS, p. 26) describe murals in Geddes's Drawing Room showing seasonal subjects which correspond with the 'Four panels, "The Seasons"' by Mackie in the catalogue of an Exhibition of Work of the Old Edinburgh School of Art (1895; SUA). A portion of Duncan's *Pipes* frieze illustrated by Armour was reproduced as the line engraving *Bacchus and Silenus* in the *Evergreen* (Autumn 1895) and Mackie's *Evergreen* illustrations *When the Girls Come Out to Play, Hide and Seek, Chucks,* and *By the Bonnie Banks O' Fordie* (1895–7 volumes) may therefore likewise record panels by him at Ramsay Lodge or elsewhere in Ramsay Garden. A number of the *Evergreen* line drawings are by 'Hare' and appear to be transcriptions of paintings which form the subjects of murals known to have existed (see also C. A. P. Willsdon, 'Paul Sérusier the Celt', 1984). This practice was continued in the Vienna Secession's journal *Ver Sacrum*; presumably on the grounds of expense, Geddes had commissioned line drawings as a way of recording his murals. Other seasonal or nature illustrations in the *Evergreen* which thus probably record murals in Geddes's flat include Mackie's *Lyart Leaves* and *Felling Trees*, Brough's *Roses*; Hornel's 'Japanese' *Madame Chrysanthème* (Norah Geddes's *Reminiscences* mention oriental furnishings); Burns's *Vintage, Passer-by,* and *Bathers,* and A. G. Sinclair's *Winter Harvest* (1895–7 volumes). Norah Geddes also refers to seasonal plants painted by Mary Hill Burton in Geddes's Drawing Room.

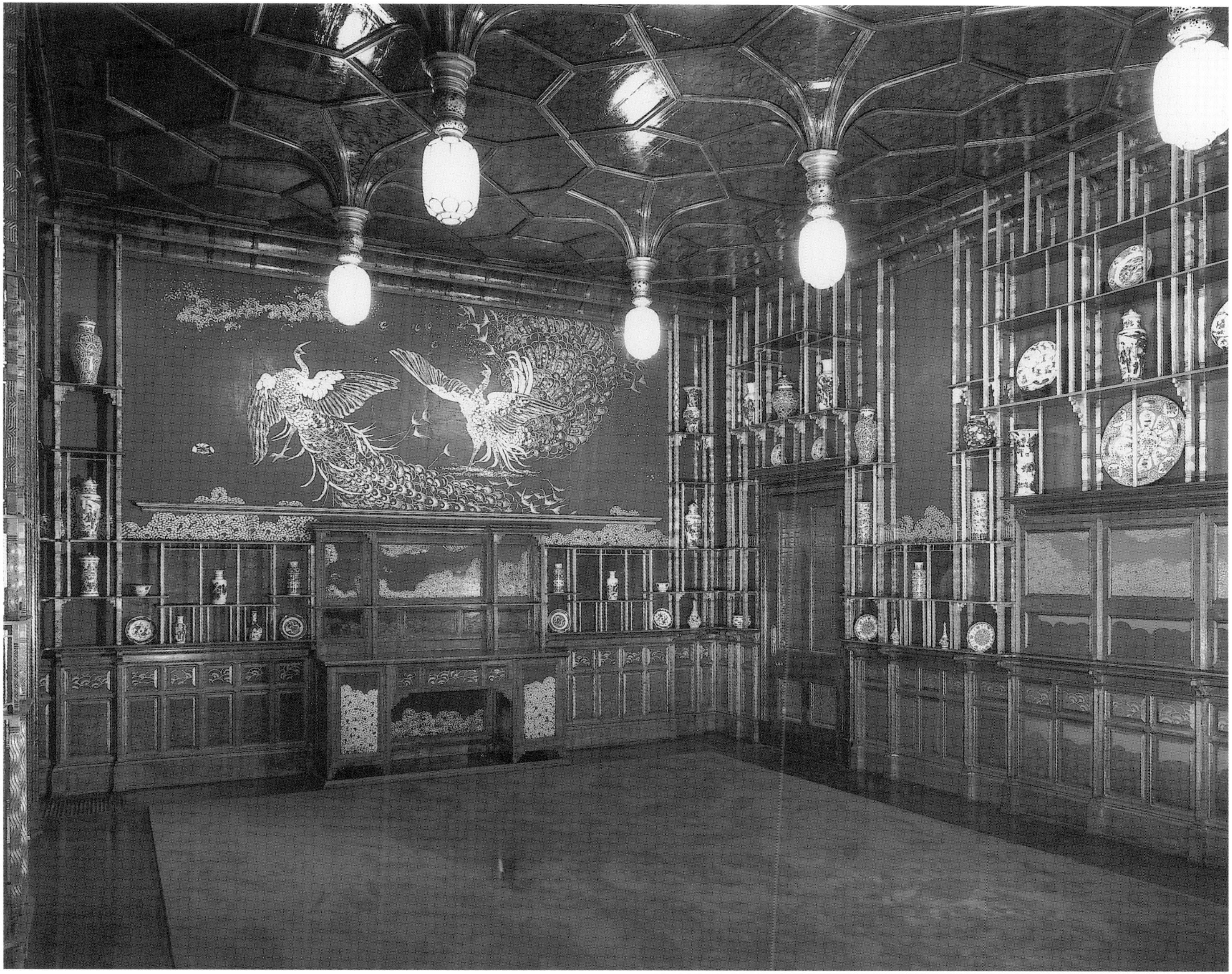

180. James McNeill Whistler, *The Peacock Room*, formerly 49 Princes Gate, London, 1876–7. Washington, DC, Freer Gallery of Art, Smithsonian Institution

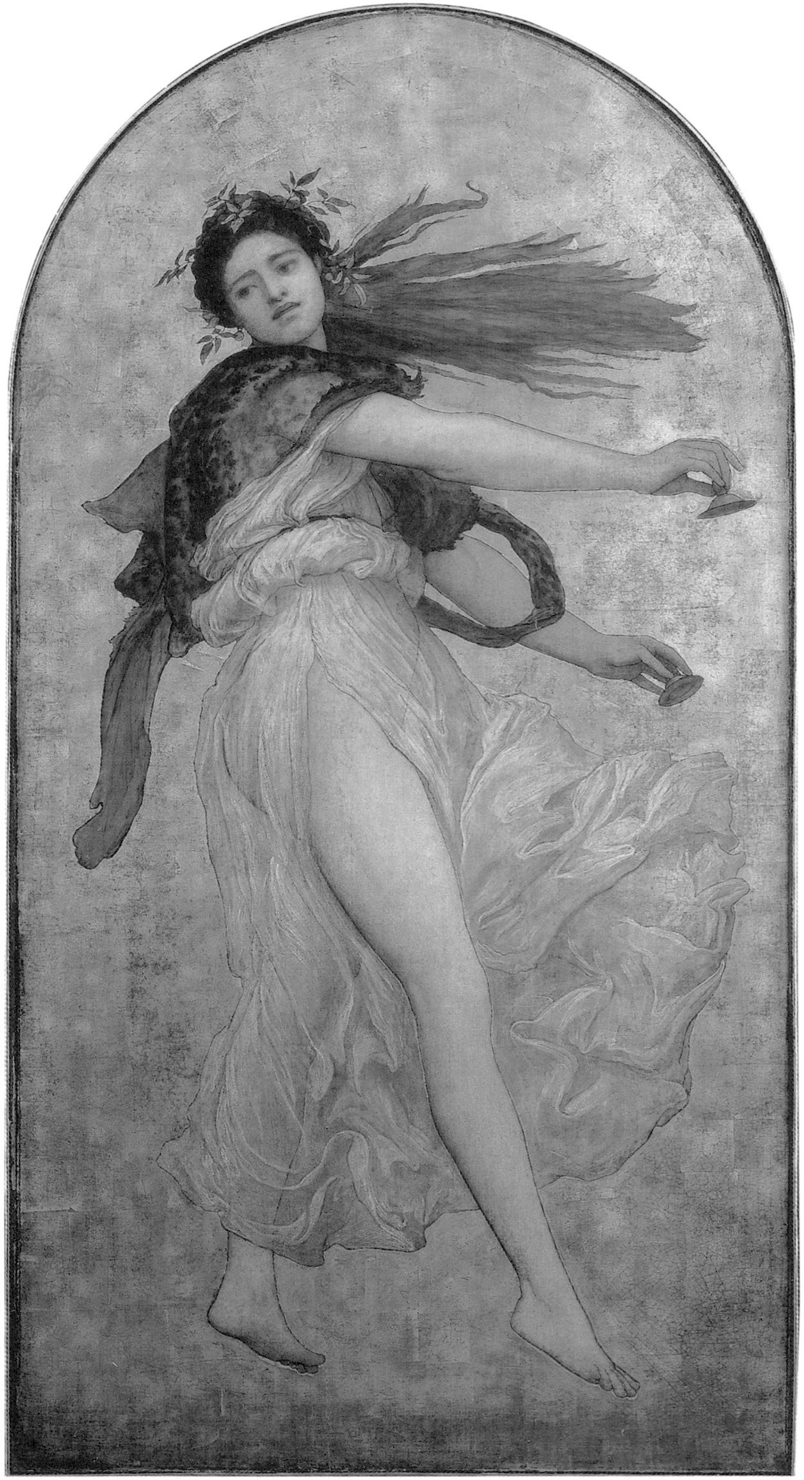

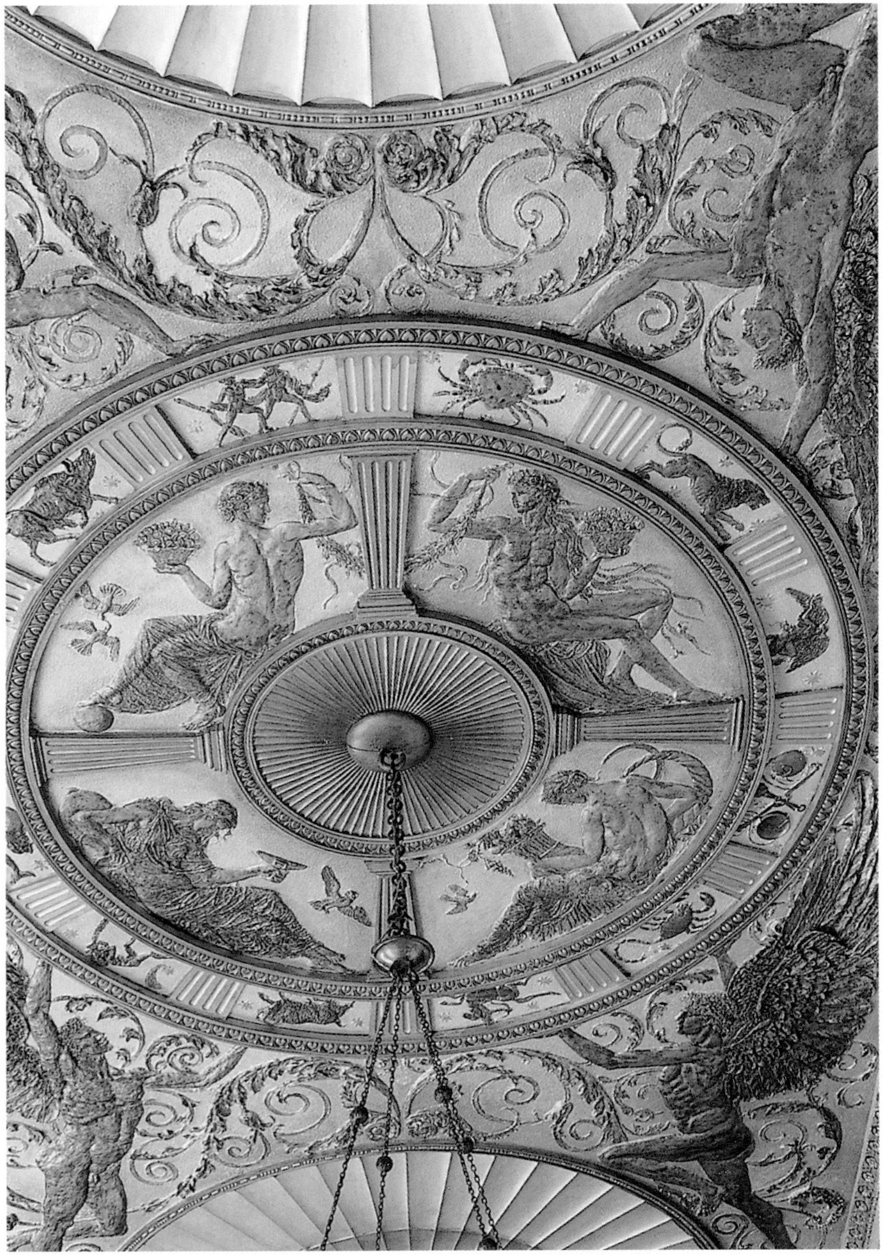

182. Walter Crane, painted bas-relief decoration illustrating Time and Space on ceiling of the library, Combe Bank, Sevenoaks, Kent, 1873–84

181. Frederic, Lord Leighton, panel from *The Dance of the Cymbalists*, formerly 44 Belgrave Square, London, *c.*1869

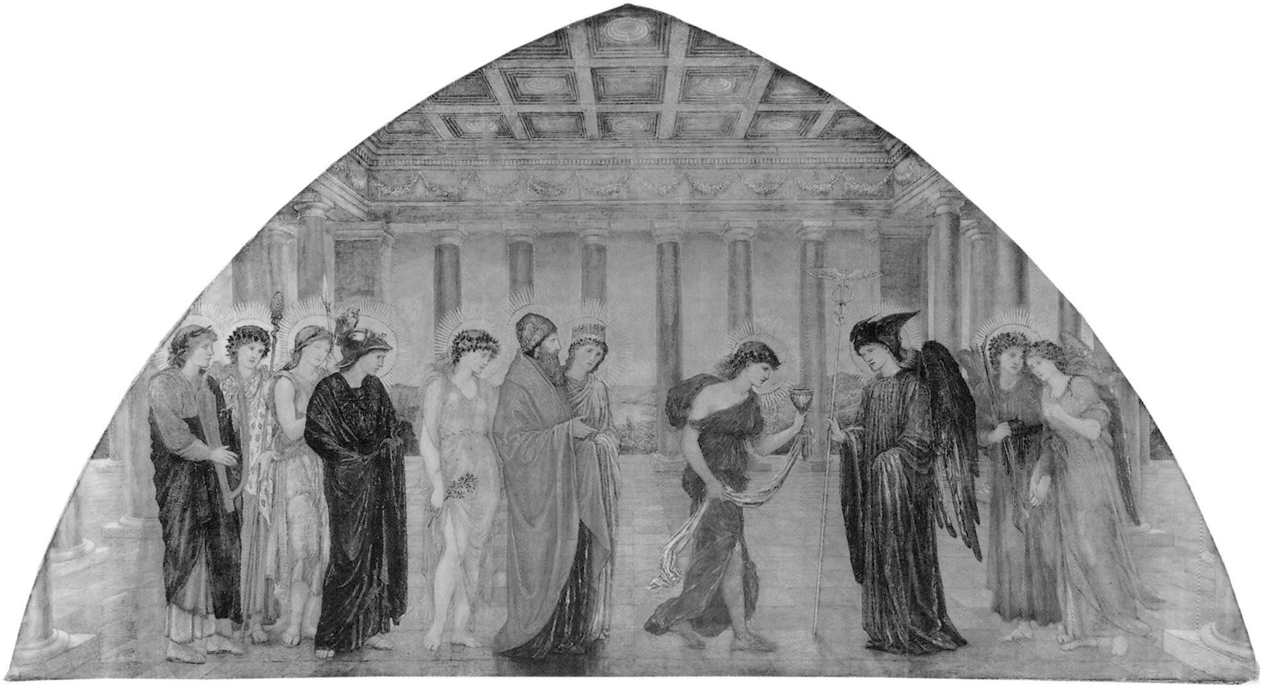

183. Sir Edward Burne-Jones (completed by Walter Crane), *Psyche entering the Portals of Olympus*, formerly at 1 Palace Green, London, 1872–87. Birmingham, Museum and Art Gallery

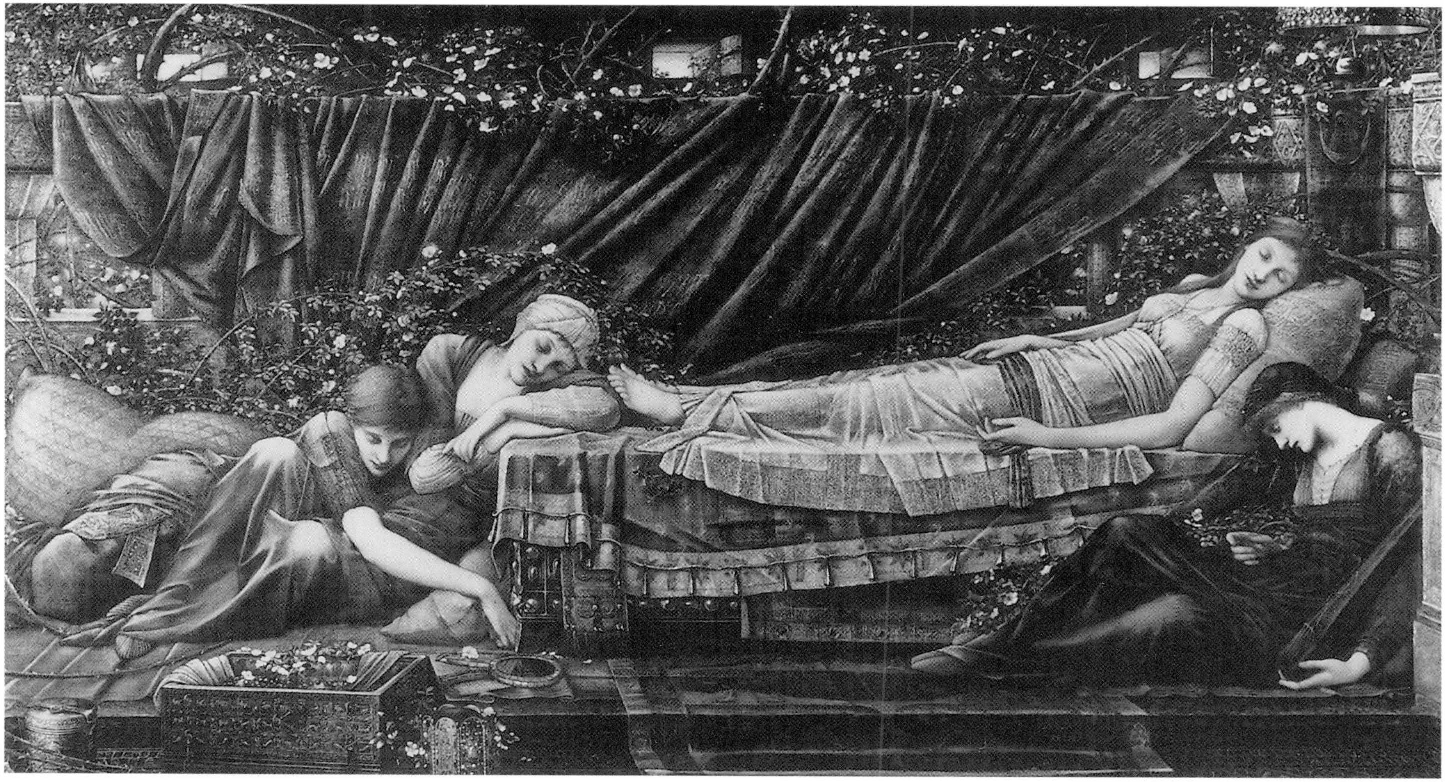

184. Sir Edward Burne-Jones, *The Rose Bower*, Buscot Park, Oxfordshire, 1889–90

over in the 1930s, a number of the murals by Hill Burton and Mackie have been uncovered in ongoing restoration of what appears to have been a very extensive scheme. Correspondence between Geddes and Paul Sérusier, with whom Mackie had studied at Pont Aven, suggests that Sérusier's *Pastorale bretonne*, an illustration in Geddes's *Evergreen* journal (Plate 185) may record another mural at Ramsay Garden.[72] Its Breton child holding a daisy in a flowered meadow, and accompanied by a woman, would certainly have complemented Mackie's *Summer* panel, which showed girls making daisy chains, raising the possibility that further *Evergreen* illustrations by Mackie, such as his *Girls Playing*, record murals no longer visible.[73]

A period reproduction of Duncan's *Pipes*, and the engraving of part of it in the *Evergreen*, show a dynamic Art Nouveau design.[74] Beginning with Syrinx, it concluded, via a spirited bacchanalian procession, with *The Coronach of Claverhouse*. True to Geddes's Celtic Revival, music's development thus culminated in its presence on the 'Highland Hills',[75] providing a symbolic transition to the landscape iconography in the drawing-room leading off the hall. Although landscape had been deemed an unsuitable mural subject by Madox Brown in his recent *Arts and Crafts Essays*,[76] on account of its distance (which he regarded as betraying the flatness of the wall), it was a popular theme in Nabi domestic murals, and one of Mackie's recently uncovered panels reveals the simplified *cloisonniste* treatment of sunlit cows and green trees through which he overcame Brown's objections (Plate 186).

The interrelationship of classical and Scottish legend in Duncan's *Pipes* was further developed in the commission which Geddes secured for him and Mackie in the late 1890s at Pitreavie Castle, home of the philanthropist Henry Beveridge. Duncan illustrated *Orpheus*; Mackie the ballads of *Hardyknute* and *Sir Patrick Spens*. Again the murals are now overpainted.[77] Duncan's appears to have been the more imaginative design, involving an ingenious narrative simultaneity. In one panel, for example (Plate 187) the viewer was asked literally to see *through* the strings of Orpheus' lyre the stages in Eurydice's rescue from the jaws of a monster personifying the Underworld and holding Pluto and Proserpine, cast into a trance by his music, in its jaws. The sinuous outlines of the monster dissolve into the spiralling vortex of Orpheus' struggle to retrieve Eurydice; the fluidity of the imagery aptly complements the synaesthesia, which intriguingly anticipates the Viennese Secessionist Alfred Roller's *Ich betrachte die Welt durch die Saiten meiner Leier* in the 1900 issue of *Ver Sacrum*. Though more pedestrian in style than Duncan's work, Mackie's *Sir Patrick Spens* frieze also included a landscape viewed partly through a harp played before it.

Although other Scots painted private-house schemes at the period (e.g. Appendix D: 21, and recently uncovered murals in Aberdeen by Douglas Strachan), Duncan and Mackie were the most in tune with Continental Symbolism's ideology of mural painting as an affective medium affording

[72] See Willsdon, 'Paul Sérusier the Celt' (1984).

[73] Mackie's *Summer* is illustrated in Armour, 'Mural Decoration in Scotland'. *Girls Playing* exists as a small oil painting (Hunterian Art Gallery, University of Glasgow) which, if not actually a detached mural, may be a preparatory sketch for one; it shares the association of childhood games and nature of both *Summer* and Sérusier's *Pastorale bretonne*. Mackie's *Evergreen* picture *By the Bonnie Banks O' Fordie* exists as a similar oil (Hunterian Art Gallery, University of Glasgow). It is clear that Geddes's flat contained a significant number of mural paintings, and possibly as many as forty or fifty panels, including those discussed in Chapter 9, may originally have decorated the Ramsay Garden buildings. Celtic Revival symbolism was evident slightly later in Dublin in the murals of 1911 by George Russell ('AE') for Horace Plunkett's house (see J. McBrinn, 'Belfast's Other Murals' (1997), p. 42).

[74] Armour, 'Mural Decoration in Scotland'.

[75] Ibid, p. 103.

[76] F. M. Brown, 'Of Mural Painting', in W. Morris (ed.), *Arts and Crafts Essays* (1893), p. 151.

[77] Several are illustrated in Armour, 'Mural Decoration in Scotland'.

entry into dreams or emotional states. Duncan was certainly reading Sar Péladan's as well as Burne-Jones's theories in the 1890s.[78] In comparison, the 'Century Guild' murals by H. Horne, S. Image, and others at Pownall Hall (1887), and those by J. E. Southall and other members of the Birmingham wing of the Arts and Crafts Movement (Appendix D: 22, 23) were far more conservative, often clinging to 'truth to materials' and medieval or early Renaissance revivalism. Fred Davis none the less adopted a more atmospheric style (Appendix D: 25), and in the early twentieth century Mary Sargant-Florence, reviving *buon fresco*, chose Maeterlinck's *Les Aveugles* as a theme[79] (Appendix D: 28). Frescoes of country subjects were painted in 1912 by Dora Carrington and Constance Lee for Lord Brownlow's library at Ashridge, Hertfordshire. Meanwhile, a tidal wave of private-house decoration arose at the turn of the century from the fashion for 'artistic' interiors, which was fostered by the Arts and Crafts Exhibition Society and the *Studio* magazine. Literary themes remained particularly popular, despite the landscapes and allegorical personifications included in the domestic interiors shown by the Société des Artistes Décorateurs at the Paris 1900 Exhibition, and the *Studio*'s illustration of Jugendstil and other Continental trends. Whilst the grand houses of the aristocracy continued to provide ready wall-space—for Christopher Whall, for example (Appendix D: 26), or Louis B. Davis, who did murals during the 1900s at Eastnor Castle in Herefordshire and Wynyards Park in County Durham, as well as in the oratory at Chenies of Adeline, Duchess of Bedford, and in the private chapel of the Marquess of Londonderry—many smaller, suburban houses were now also being decorated, often by relatively minor artists. Brangwyn, however, was employed by Sir Edmund Davis, later patron of the Middlesex Hospital murals (Appendix D: 27). In the twentieth century, commercial furnishers such as Waring and Gillow in turn included a number of painted decorations in their complete interiors in period styles.

The most remarkable and accomplished scheme of the years leading up to the First World War was undoubtedly Sigismund Goetze's decoration of Grove House, his fine Neoclassical home by Decimus Burton, in Regent's Park, London. Its seventeen panels illustrating Ovid's *Metamorphoses* (Plate XXXIX; Plate 188) in the Music Room are heirs of the famous illustrations of the text by the Carracci in the Farnese Gallery, as well as the tradition of monumental nude painting espoused by Watts and Stevens, whom Goetze admired. As a Gold Medallist at the Paris Salon, he would also have known the work of Bouguereau and Besnard. It was the Symbolist overtones of Besnard's murals, and particularly his translation into heightened colours and impressionistic brushwork of the French scientific theory of transformism[80] (itself an intriguing sequel to Watts's, Crane's, and Geddes's evolutionist ideas), which found new interpretation in Goetze's designs. Whilst in his Foreign Office decoration, begun as that at Grove House was completed, the classical nude was made the vehicle for political ideals of harmony, at home it was transmuted by Goetze into a more adventurous, highly atmospheric style of prismatic colour and loose brushwork, which presents what can perhaps best be termed a psychologically charged *Gesamtkunstwerk*.

As decoration for Grove House's Music Room, the murals were clearly intended to create an affective ambience for the concerts given by Goetze's pianist wife Constance, which often included

[78] See his Notebooks, NLS.

[79] Davis was associated with the Bromsgrove Guild, contributing with H. A. Payne and others to its decorated bedroom in the Paris 1900 Exhibition; see A. Crawford (ed.), *By Hammer and Hand* (1984), p. 70. For Mrs. Sargant-Florence's *Aveugles*, see K. Spence, 'Country Refuge from Bloomsbury Lord's Wood, Marlow', *Country Life*, 154 (15 Nov. 1973), pp. 1579–81.

[80] e.g. in his *Life is Born from Death* (for the Sorbonne, 1896): see Silverman, *Art Nouveau* (1989), p. 226.

contributions from the guitarist Andrés Segovia. Almost one entire side of the room also, via an enlarged bow window, gave onto Goetze's four and a half acre garden terraced with roses, azaleas, and rhododendrons and containing the largest beech tree in London.[81] Living flowers and plants were thus directly juxtaposed with the mythological metamorphoses into flora and fauna of the gods in Ovid's stories.

Narcissus, for example, who is shown in the panel to one side of the window, opposite Echo at the other side whom he spurned, stands amidst the flowers into which his blood was transformed after he killed himself in frustration at the vanity of seeking his own reflection. Daphne, whom Apollo turned into a bush, and other gods named after flowers, such as Hebe, as well as Venus amid her roses, are each illustrated in other panels. The 'continuum of being and the unity of all matter'[82] of French transformist doctrine, and the related concern of *fin-de-siècle* artists and thinkers with the eye as the gateway to the subconscious[83] provide a ready context for this. The mediating agent of Goetze's transcendent fusion of art portraying literature with living outdoor nature, however, was Constance's grand piano itself, which stood in the bow window, as if in demonstration of Nietzsche's belief in the Dionysian power of music to 'make the spirit free, give wings to thought'.[84] Including as it does Bacchus with his thyrsis, reaching out to Ariadne before a luminous blue sea, Pan piping to the Nymphs amidst purple flag irises in the large centre panel opposite the window; and the tambourine-playing Bacchante and cymbal-playing Faunus who flank the door opposite Orpheus with his lyre and a dryad with pipes, the mural scheme as a whole in fact shows a distinct emphasis on the 'Dionysian', which suggests that Goetze knew his Nietzsche as well as did Derain or Wyndham Lewis. Lewis, of course, had just completed his equally synaesthetic, though stylistically very different, decoration for the Cave of the Golden Calf in London.

The elegant contrapposto poses of a number of the nude gods and goddesses relate closely to items in the antique sculpture collection of Goetze's relative by marriage, Alfred Mond, first Baron Melchett, who as First Commissioner of Works supervised his Foreign Office commission. The most eye-catching feature of the scheme, however, is its extremely subtle rendering of 'transitional' light effects, such as the hot pink sun of late evening or early morning which colours the skin of the Bacchante, Apollo and Daphne, and Orpheus, and the rainbow halo of Diana which illuminates the night sky as she descends to the sleeping Endymion. Goetze's prismatic technique, which suggests he may have known Henri Martin's application of divided colour to mural painting in France[85] lends astonishing intensity to these effects, underlining their role as a symbol of the larger theme of metamorphosis. This theme is further reinforced by the more conventional personifications of the Seasons, Hours, and Winds, dressed in flowing draperies and accompanied by a profusion of symbolic flowers and fruits, and the signs of the zodiac, with which Goetze decorated the entrance hall of Grove House. Was Constance Goetze perhaps the model for these and the Music Room goddesses? Goetze certainly used his own and the Mond family as models at the Foreign Office; at Grove House this would have added an appropriately personal element to the metamorphosis symbolism.

[81] See P. Hunting, *A Short History of Nuffield Lodge* (London, 1974), p. 29; the murals were featured in a *Country Life* supplement (22 March, 1913).

[82] Silverman, *Art Nouveau*, p. 226.

[83] Emile Gallé's and Henri Bergson's ideas on this are discussed in relation to '*psychologie nouvelle*' in Silverman, *Art Nouveau*, pp. 300–1.

[84] '[Hat man bemerkt, dass die Musik] den Geist *frei* macht? Dem Gedanken Flügel giebt?', quoted in T. Meyer, *Nietzsche und die Kunst* (Tübingen and Basel, 1993), p. 102 (author's translation).

[85] e.g. in the Hôtel de Ville in Paris (1892), and at the Capitole, Toulouse (1906).

If the twin traditions of 'harmony' and 'story' in British private-house decoration had been fused at Grove House to a point of perfection perhaps never to be be recovered following the chaos of the war, George Clausen's *Morning, Golden Age*, and *Harvest* murals of 1918 for High Royd at Honley, near Huddersfield (Plates 189, 190) none the less bore testimony to the enduring strength even after the war of the Arts and Crafts ideal of synthesis. Clausen worked closely with Sellars and Wood, who had been commissioned by the owner, a Mr Norton, to reconstruct the entrance hall where the panels were installed. The 'effect of full sunlight'[86] in *The Golden Age* (Plate 189) which shows a half-nude woman contemplating an apple held aloft by a kneeling nude, with the remains of a fluted column punctuating the gently rolling landscape setting, was placed opposite the window in the simple classical-style interior, with actual daylight being in turn the agent for the transformation of the corn sown in *Morning* on the left wall into the sheaf borne by a woman in *Harvest* on the right wall. An elegiac note, however, was introduced into this affirmation of faith in a new dawn by the inclusion of scarlet poppies in the golden corn being scythed in *Harvest* (Plate 190). The monumental figures and Biblical overtones reveal Clausen's admiration for Piero della Francesca, and the scheme can be recognized as a pointer to his British School at Rome manner in St Stephen's Hall at Westminster a few years later.

In a pre-war lecture as Professor of Painting at the Royal Academy, Clausen had proposed that 'the mind naturally refers to the beauty of the great elementary things—the sky, the sunshine, and the hills, rivers, fields and trees, and in people to those things which suggest beauty, activity and health.'[87] If at High Royd these became the vehicle of poignant catharsis, then the elemental, in the sense of the 'primitive', had already begun to be explored in a very different style by Wyndham Lewis. Inspired in part by Kandinsky's *Concerning the Spiritual in Art* as well as by Nietzsche, Lewis's decoration in 1913 of Lady Drogheda's dining-room in London (Plate 191) with angular 'totemic figures',[88] placed to either side of the mantel mirror as if to guard it, replaced both the classical vocabulary of Duncan, Goetze, or Frank Salisbury at Sarum Chase (his own home) (Appendix D: 30), and Clausen's English pastoral, with the 'more savage symbols' he had discovered in 'Pacific Island masks' in the British Museum.[89] The decoration, part of an overall colour scheme of black, took psychological effect to its logical conclusion, its ritual overtones complementing the patron's interest in the occult.

OTHER TIMES AND OTHER PLACES: EXOTICISM, ESCAPISM, AND EXPERIMENTATION IN THE 1920s AND 1930s

Although Lewis's were perhaps the most avant-garde of the murals undertaken in private houses in Britain in the period 1900 to 1920, the influence of Fry's Post-Impressionist exhibitions of 1910 and 1912 and the 'primitive' exoticism of the Ballets Russes gave a modern face to the decoration produced by what Lewis scathingly called 'Mr. Roger Fry's little belated Morris

[86] L. G. P., 'Mr. Clausen's Decorations at High Royd', *Architectural Review*, 49, no. 295 (June 1921), p. 130. The murals are now in Huddersfield Art Gallery (sketches in the Whitworth Art Gallery, University of Manchester).

[87] G. Clausen, *Royal Academy Lectures on Painting* (London, 1912), pp. 237–8, quoted in K. McConkey, *Sir George Clausen* (1980), p. 12.

[88] R. Cork, *Art Beyond the Gallery* (1985), p. 183.

[89] W. Lewis, quoted in Cork, *Art Beyond the Gallery*, p. 183.

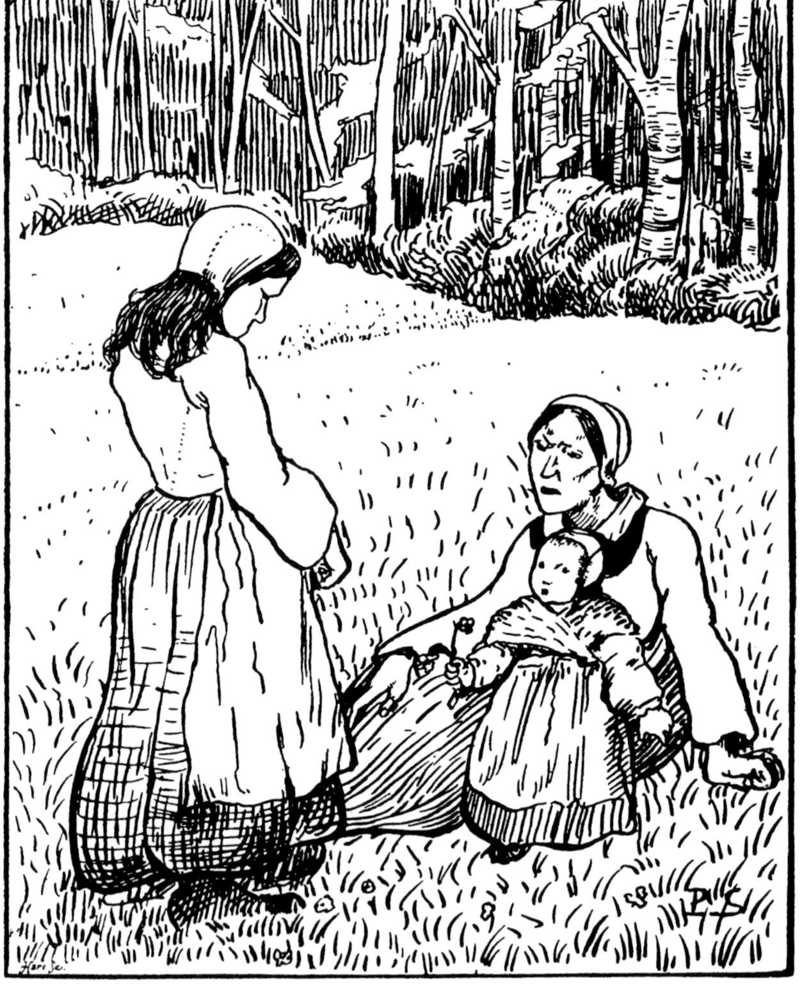

185. Paul Sérusier, *Pastorale bretonne*, 1895. Line engraving. (From the *Evergreen*, Spring, 1895)

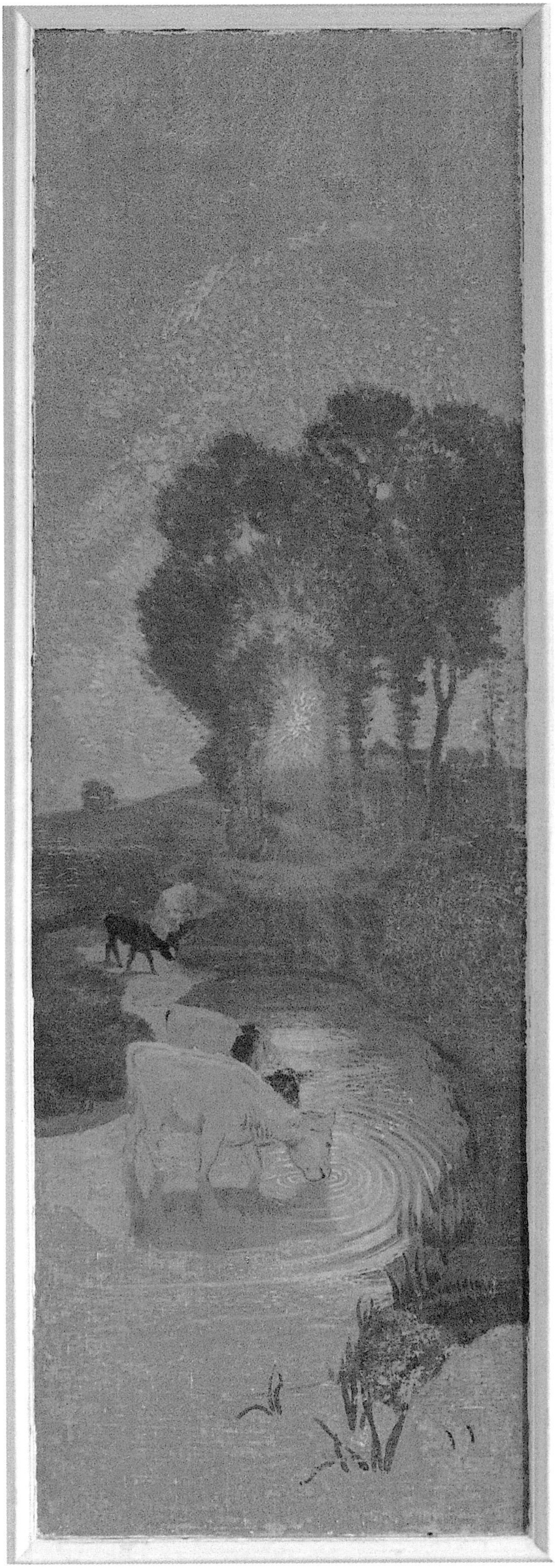

186. Mural at 14 Ramsay Garden, Edinburgh, believed to be part of a scheme illustrating *The Seasons* by Charles H. Mackie, *c.*1890s

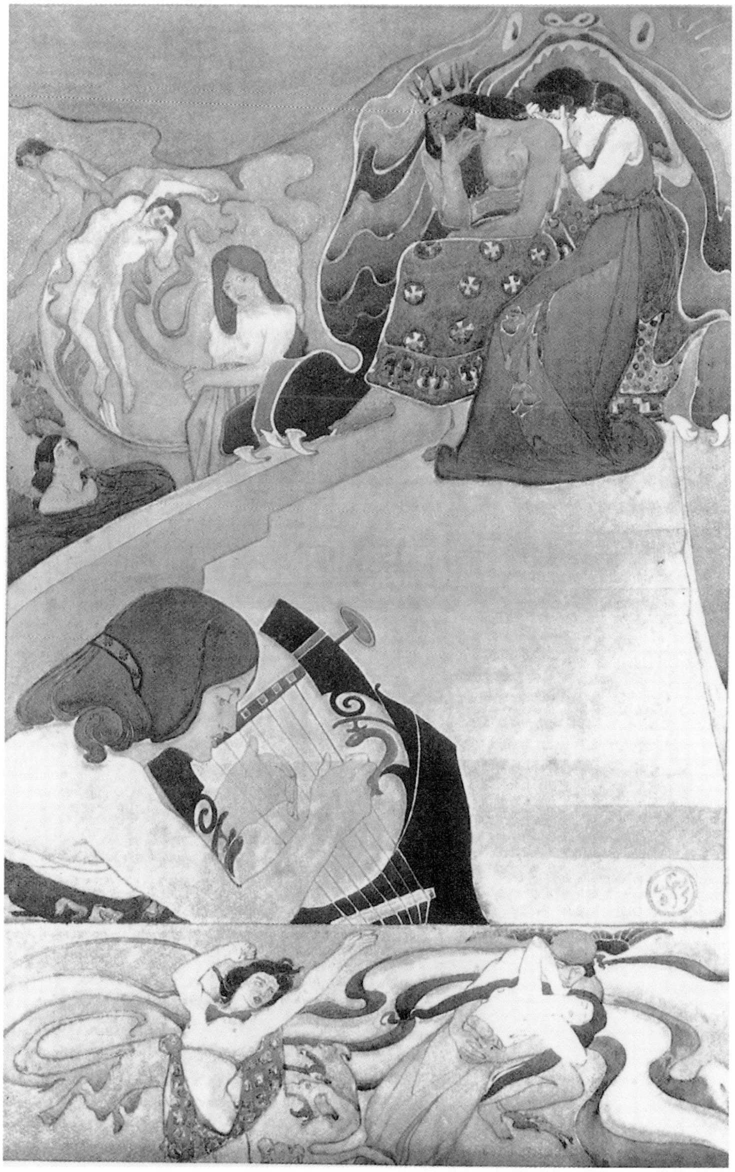

187. John Duncan, panel from *Orpheus* scheme (no longer visible), Pitreavie Castle, Dunfermline, *c.*1898

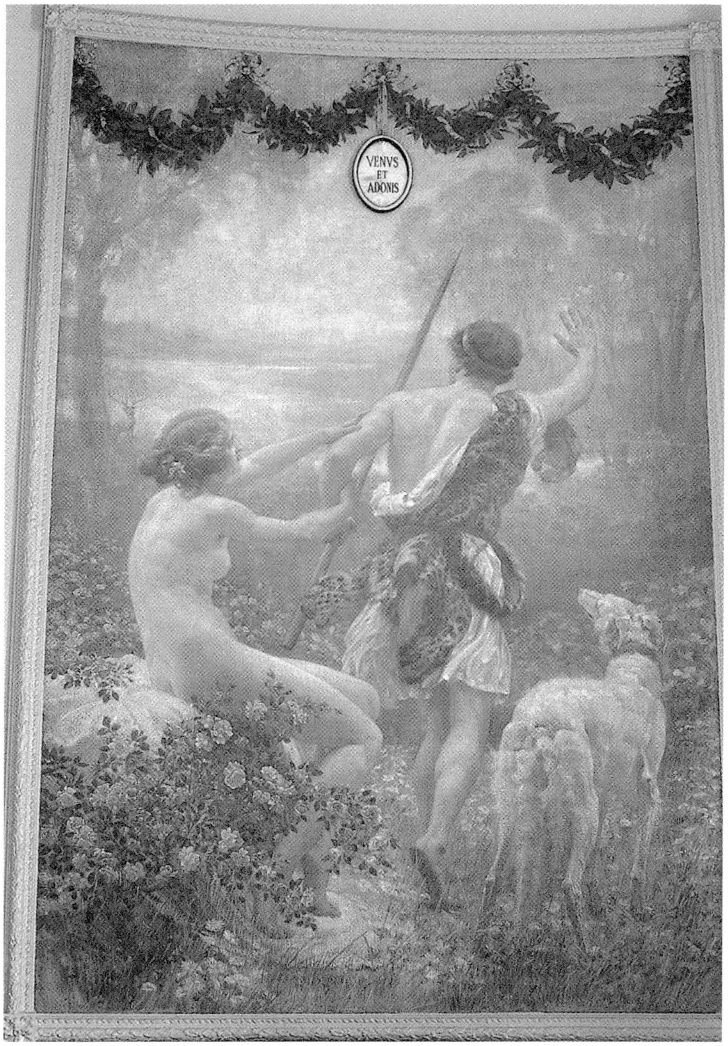

188. Sigismund Goetze, *Vénus et Adonis*, Grove House, Regent's Park, London, 1909–13

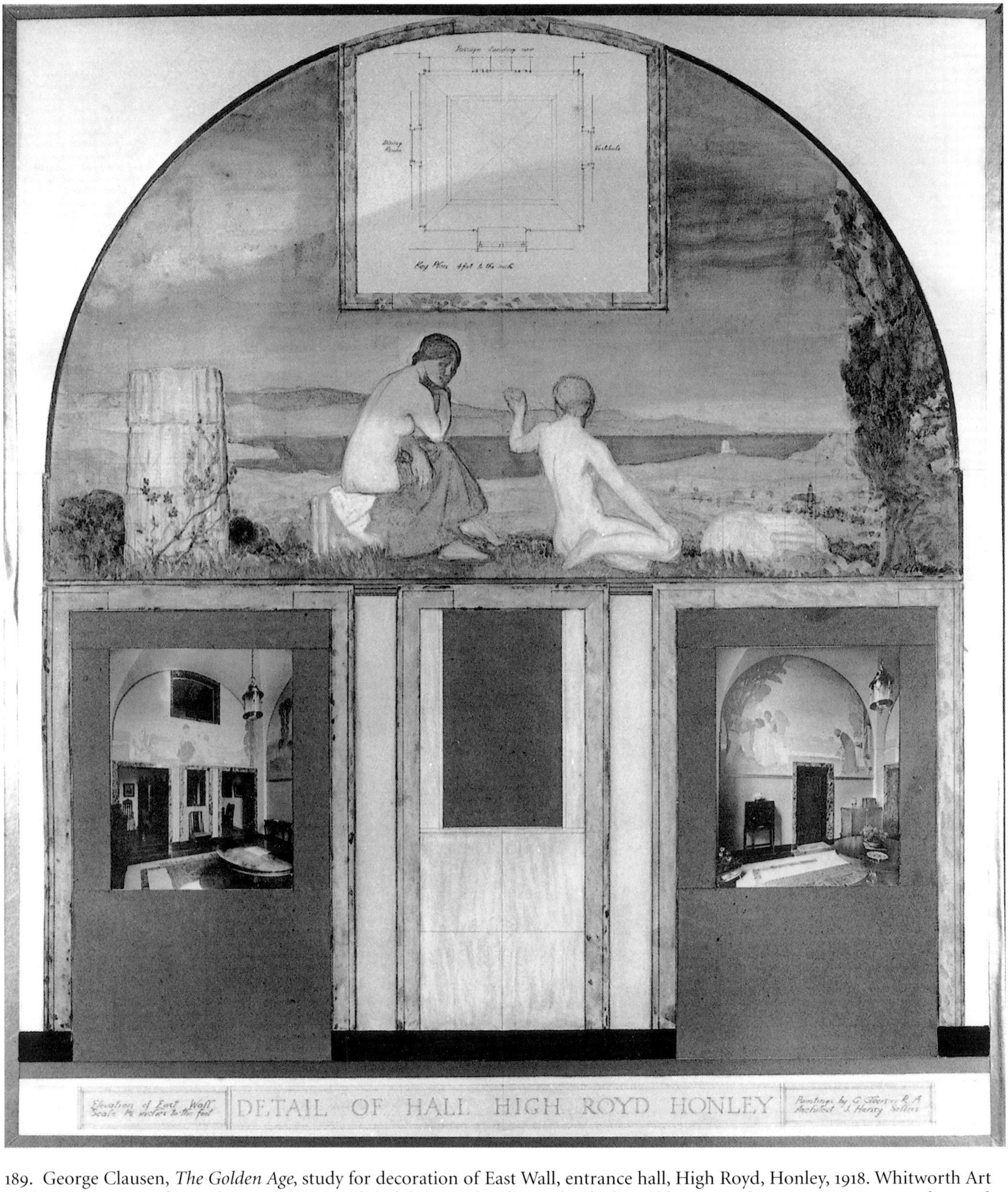

189. George Clausen, *The Golden Age*, study for decoration of East Wall, entrance hall, High Royd, Honley, 1918. Whitworth Art Gallery, University of Manchester. (Photographs of the completed murals of *The Golden Age* and *Morning in situ* pasted onto the lower half of the study.)

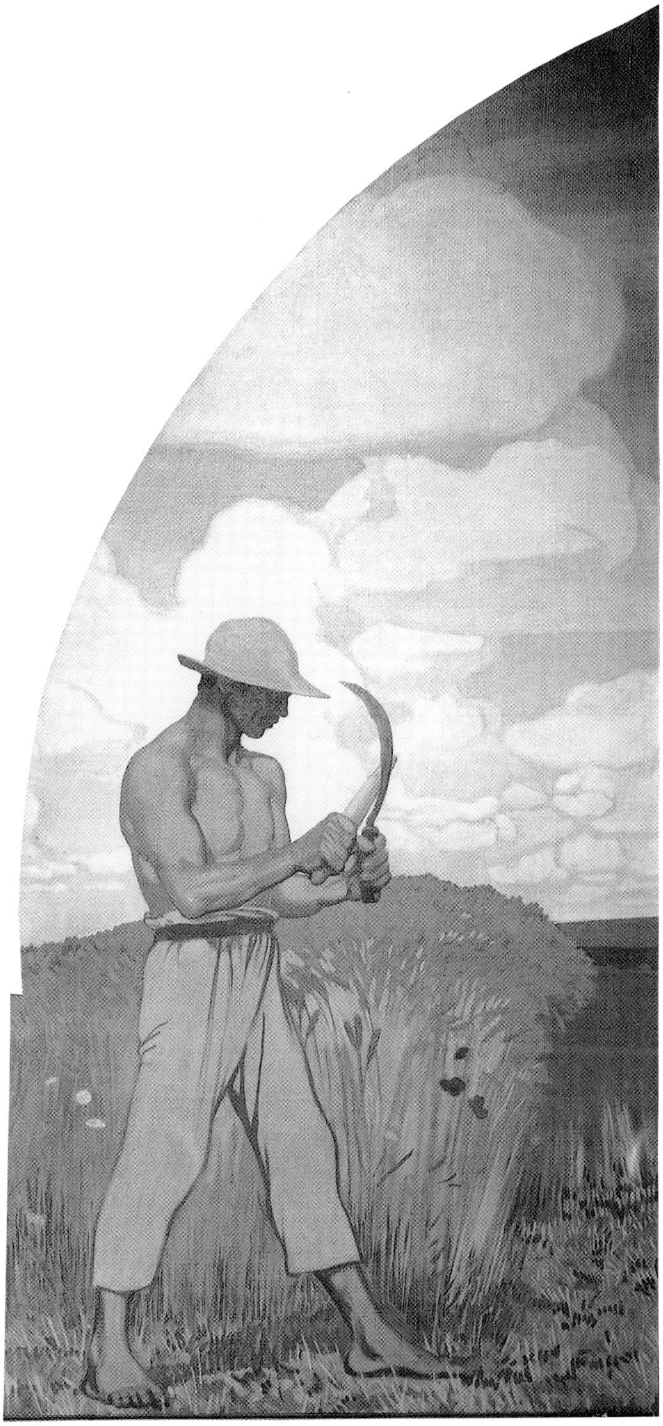

190. Sir George Clausen, section from *Harvest*, formerly at High Royd, Honley, near Huddersfield, 1918. Huddersfield, Art Gallery

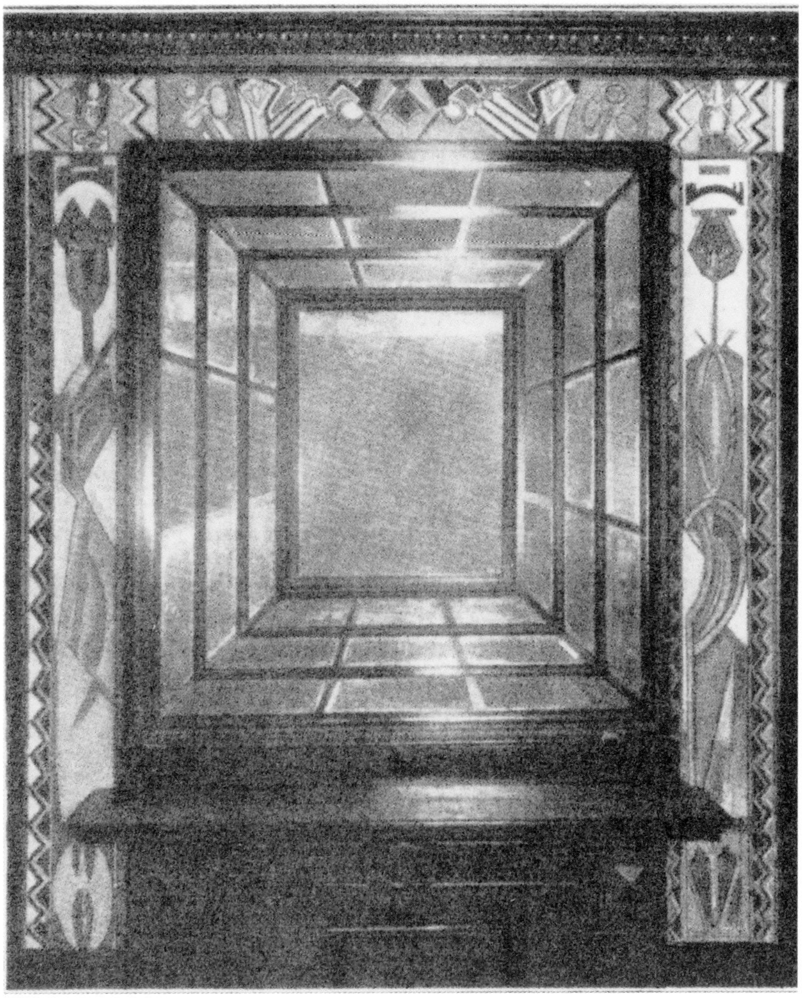

191. Photograph of overmantel by Percy Wyndham Lewis, in Lady Drogheda's dining-room, London, Plate vii in *Blast* (1913)

movement',[90] the Omega Workshops. Born in 1913 of Fry's training with Ashbee (Appendix D: 24), the workshops sought not to interact with the psyche through symbol, narrative, or 'totemic figures', but rather to exalt the artistic self-sufficiency of colour and shape, paralleling Matisse's view that 'a work of art must carry in itself its complete significance and impose it upon the beholder's eye before he can identify the subject matter.'[91] This ideal, to be further developed in Clive Bell's concept of 'significant form', was implicit in Duncan Grant's 1911 four-part mural of dancers and grape-pickers for Maynard Keynes's rooms at King's College, Cambridge (Plate 192), which was closely derived from Matisse's *La Danse* (Hermitage Museum, St Petersburg), as well as his 1912 mural of tennis-players for a room occupied by Keynes at 38 Brunswick Square, London, the home of Virginia Woolf's brother Adrian Stephen. Grant, Vanessa Bell, and Fry himself painted nudes probably inspired by Matisse's work in the entrance hall at Durbins, Guildford (Fry's house) in 1913 (Plate 193), whilst Grant and Etchells, following their Borough Polytechnic work, painted 'a fallen cab-horse with the driver of the hansom still perched precariously aloft though the cab was tilted forward with the shafts touching the pavement'[92] in the Brunswick Square room. The primary colours and spare, kinaesthetic style of such work reached the public through the bold motifs of the Omega Room at the 1913 Ideal Home Exhibition (Plate 194) which contained murals by Vanessa Bell, as well as through her 'Omega Nursery' of 1913–14 with its cut-paper elephant and jungle landscape extending even onto the ceiling, to delight children as they lay in bed. These murals marked a new mood of hedonistic pleasure in the decorative process as much as product; though the workshops closed formally in 1919, their vein by then of what Vanessa Bell called 'vast panels of moonrises and prima donna's bouquets'[93] continued well into the 1920s in the hands of Bell herself, her husband Clive, and Duncan Grant, and can be recognized as essentially a reinvention, without the narrative content, of the fantasy escapism of Burges's designs for Bute (Appendix D: 16). Although Fry went as far as to attempt to remove the traditional distinction between fine and applied art in an essay of 1917 on *The Artist as Decorator*, arguing that the artist's 'subtle sense of proportion and colour harmony' should fully equip 'him to make a definite work of creative art out of an interior' composed purely of coloured walls,[94] playful classical pastiche, verging on Art Deco, became the stock-in-trade of Duncan Grant and Clive Bell (Appendix D: 29, 31). Lewis had fallen out with Fry over the Ideal Home event of 1913; increasingly, it was a form of fantasy make-believe, enacted lightheartedly in times or places distant, rather than the deeper psychological relationships with the viewer explored by both Lewis and Goetze, as well as the *fin-de-siècle* Symbolists before them, which became the distinguishing feature of post-war private-house decoration. Whilst this can be read as escapism, idealism, or (especially in the case of the pastiche and *trompe-l'oeil* renderings of Italianate and rococo styles by Rex Whistler and others) a quest for the stable and enduring in response to destruction, carnage, and latterly, economic depression, it also represents the ultimate logic of the ideal of decorative art already formulated in France by Matisse before the war:

[90] W. Lewis, *Blast*, in W. Michel and C. J. Fox (eds), *Wyndham Lewis on Art*, p. 76.

[91] Matisse, *Notes d'un Peintre* (1908), quoted in F. Spalding, *Vanessa Bell* (1983), p. 126.

[92] David Garnett, quoted in Cork, *Art Beyond the Gallery*, p. 121 (the murals do not survive); for the Borough Polytechnic, see Chapter 9. Swags and ornamental motifs were painted by Dora Carrington in 1928 in Dadi Rylands's rooms at King's College, and several figural designs were also painted there prior to 1940 by Douglas Davidson. (Information kindly supplied by King's College Archives, Cambridge).

[93] Quoted in Spalding, *Vanessa Bell*, pp. 201–2.

[94] R. Fry, 'The Artist as Decorator', *Colour* (April 1917), p. 92.

an art of balance, of purity and serenity, devoid of troubling or depressing subject matter, an art which could be for every mental worker, be he business man or man of letters, for example, a soothing, calming influence on the mind, something like a good armchair in which to rest from physical fatigue.[95]

However, although by 1925 the artist George Sheringham was advocating 'a flowing type of decoration . . . that does not violently arrest the attention'[96] in place of pictorial subjects, narrative and representation remained firm mainstays in private houses.

Escapism through exotic *richesse* is already evident in the *Sleeping Beauty* panels commissioned by James de Rothschild in 1913 from one of the Ballets Russes artists himself, Léon Bakst. Intended to give Rothschild's house in Park Street 'the most terrific drawing room in London',[97] they were not actually completed until 1922 and were eventually installed at Waddesdon Manor (Plate 195). They reflect Bakst's contribution not only to the Ballets Russes' *Festin* production of 1909 in Paris, in which he had designed the costumes for Tchaikovsky's *Sleeping Beauty*, as danced by Karsavina and Nijinsky, but also to Diaghilev's notoriously over-elaborate 1921 *Sleeping Beauty*.[98]

The story, indeed, is presented as if taking place on steeply raked stage sets. However, despite Bakst's endeavours to 'unify' his work with its intended setting,[99] the fantastical exaggerations of scale and gesture and the sheer eclecticism and colouristic impact of the scheme as a whole tend to overwhelm the eye. Costumes are based on sixteenth-century German styles; an Egyptian hieroglyph is used to signify the Good Fairy's protection, whilst Romanesque and Byzantine architecture provide backdrops. The autobiographical significance for James de Rothschild of the Prince Charming story is presented through no less than forty-two family portraits, whilst Bakst himself, in Burgundian costume, confronts the Wicked Fairy, perhaps in reference to his belief that his own marriage had been cursed[100] (Plate 195).

It was Sir Philip Sassoon who recommended Bakst to Rothschild, and in 1920 he himself commissioned another Diaghilev intimate, Glyn Philpot, to decorate his home at Port Lympne, Kent; J. M. Sert was also employed here. Painted direct onto the plaster, Philpot's scheme perhaps reflected Fokine's *Cléopatre*, performed in London in 1911 and 1918; it consisted of a 'queer Egyptian frieze . . . of gesticulating and attitudinising figures'.[101] The walls beneath were covered with lapis lazuli. Something of the spirit of the fancy-dress costumes which Philpot designed for himself and Sassoon to wear to Diaghilev's balls must have been apparent, and it is revealing that when choosing examples for his 1939 Tate Gallery exhibition of mural painting since the war, Sir John Rothenstein preferred the more austere geometric style of Philpot's classical subjects, painted on metal foil, for Lord Melchett (Appendix D: 40).

Though Mary Adshead, recently trained under Tonks at the Slade, chose a jungle setting for her witty 'Slade School picnic'[102] of 1925 on the walls of Professor Reilly's flat in Liverpool (Appendix D: 34) (Plate 196), it was the free interpretation of the past, and particularly classical rather than

95 Matisse, *Notes d'un Peintre*, quoted in R. Thomson, *Monet to Matisse*, p. 137.

96 G. Sheringham, 'Mural Decoration', in *Reports . . . 1925* (Dept. of Overseas Trade), p. 55; Sheringham's own murals use such effects (see A. Powers, 'Rhythm in Design', *Country Life*, 185, no. 16 (18 April 1991), pp. 116–17.

97 Unattributed quotation in D. Souhami, *Bakst: The Rothschild Panels of the Sleeping Beauty* (London, 1992), p. 45.

98 See ibid., pp. 22–5.

99 Ibid., p. 37.

100 Ibid., p. 93.

101 Unattributed quotation in the *Twentieth Century Society Newsletter* (Summer 1993), p. 5. See also A. C. Sewter, *Glyn Philpot* (1951), pp. 6–7.

102 C. H. Reilly, *Scaffolding in the Sky* (London, 1938), p. 317; the murals are now in the University of Liverpool (see A. W. Moore, 'University Art Collections: a Recent Acquisition', *University of Liverpool Recorder*, no. 74 (April 1977), pp. 7–11), and correspondence from Mary Adshead in 1981 in the Archives of the University.

exotic sources which became popular in private-house decoration of the 1920s and 1930s, often continuing to provide an *entrée* to fictitious worlds. The trend can be seen as an informal counterpart to the British School at Rome idiom of the murals at St Stephen's Hall, as well as to the imaginative revival of classicism in Lutyens's architecture, perhaps revealing a hunger for a token of continuity in the 'brave new world'. Examples include Pryde's work at Dunecht (Appendix D: 32) and schemes by Basil Ionides, Geoffrey Birkbeck, John Churchill, and Margaret Angus (Appendix D: 35, 37, 41, 47) as well as the extraordinary pastiche and *trompe-l'oeil* world of Clough and Susan Williams-Ellis's Portmerion work, begun in 1920, and to which Hans Feibusch later contributed (Appendix D: 39). In Lutyens's *palazzo*-style Queen's Doll's House at Windsor, a conspectus of the grand manner was created[103] (Appendix D: 36) including Sir William Nicholson's gloomy drama of *The Expulsion of Adam and Eve from Paradise* whose labyrinthine trees and congregated beasts spread extravagantly across the Lower Hall; Gerald Moira's Neo-Baroque cherubs on the Dining Room ceiling; nymphs and allegorical figures by Charles Sims in the Saloon, and sunset gilded clouds and a morning sky by Philpot in the Queen's Bedroom. It is perhaps symptomatic of the new decorative *jeu d'esprit*, however, that this throw-back to the kind of royal patronage to be found in Tudor or Stuart times was located in a toy world rather than reality. None of Lutyens's real-life mansions were decorated with murals; he preferred the austerity of the plain wall. Likewise, although Philip Connard and Kennedy North were asked to decorate the room containing the Doll's House (Appendix D: 36), there appears to have been no other mural painting at this period in royal residences.

Perhaps the most unusual and accomplished reinterpretations of classical and past art traditions were those by E. I. Halliday, a Rome Scholar, and Rex Whistler, a contemporary of Mary Adshead at the Slade, who was awarded an Honorary Rome Scholarship in 1928. Halliday's *Hypnos* of 1925–8 for Sir Benjamin Johnson's house at Abbott's Lea in Liverpool (Plate 197) is a surreal, hallucinatory reworking of Piero della Francesca's *Resurrection*; details such as its sleeping, shirt-sleeved businessmen bizarrely juxtaposed with Italian peasant bagpipers and geometrically fissured mountains share something of Stanley Spencer's delight in the quixotic mundane, but are held in thrall by a giant apparition of the god of sleep. His *Homeric Hymn to Hermes*, painted for the Liverpool home of one Dr Livesey, placed Greek legend within an almost Art Deco rhythm of striated sun and shadow.[104] Early Italian sources were also reflected in his other private-house schemes (Appendix D: 33).

By 1930, following his Tate Gallery murals, Rex Whistler was being hailed as the head of 'the new English School of Decorators . . . who have delivered themselves from the Greeks and the Romans, from the frivolous French and the doleful Britons, who refuse to take art solemnly—from the point of view of subject matter'.[105] In 1930–2 in the Dining Room at Port Lympne for Sir Philip Sassoon, who was one of the Tate Trustees, Whistler created perhaps his most whimsical reinvention (as opposed to revival) of tradition, a make-believe blue and white striped tent 'erected' above the table, with real poles framing Palladian architectural *cappriccios* and Le Nôtre-style garden views, which include a portrait of Rudolf Stulik at the door of his Restaurant de la Tour Eiffel in London, as well as a lady and child waiting for a paddle steamer, and a bishop and clergy in

[103] See *The Book of the Queen's Doll's House*, vol. I (London, 1924), pp. 101–6.

[104] Originally in Dr. Livesey's Music Room at 10 Rodney Street, Liverpool; p. w. u.; photograph in Walker Art Gallery, Liverpool. For Halliday's private house decorations, see A. Compton, *Edward Halliday* (1997).

[105] H. Furst, 'Miss Mary Adshead's Work at the Goupil Gallery', *Apollo*, 11, no. 63 (March 1930), p. 225.

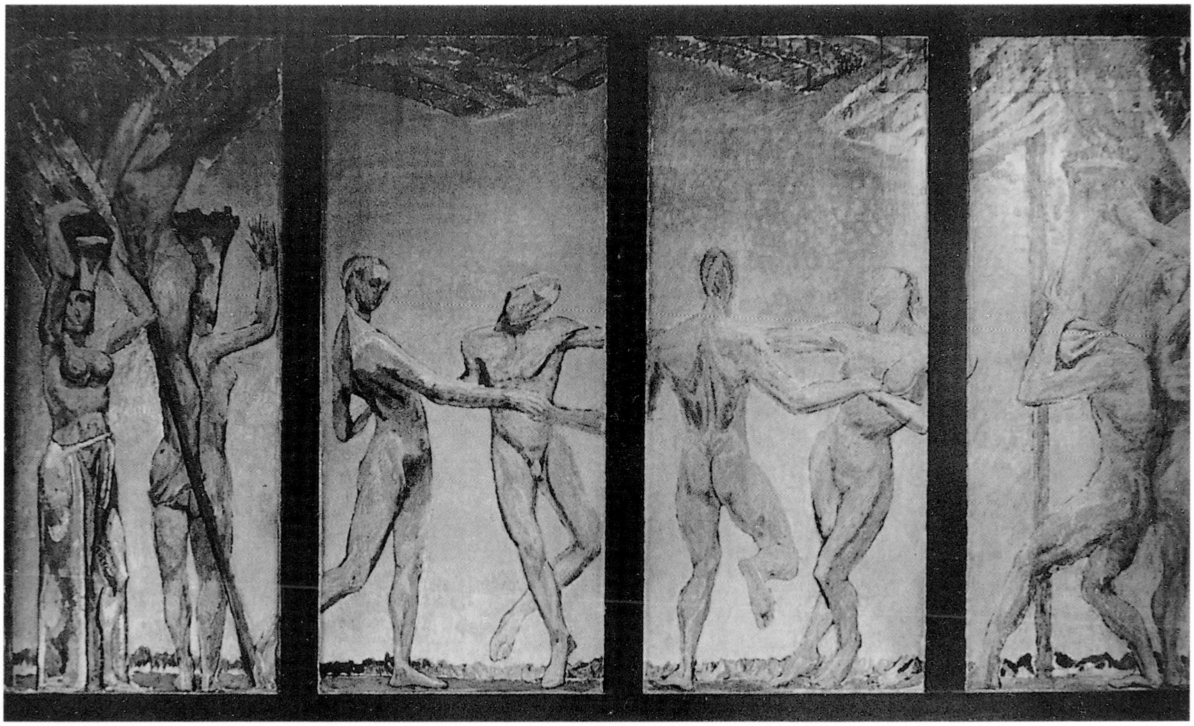

192. Duncan Grant, *Grape-Pickers*, Geoffrey Keynes's rooms, Staircase P3, King's College, Cambridge, 1910–11

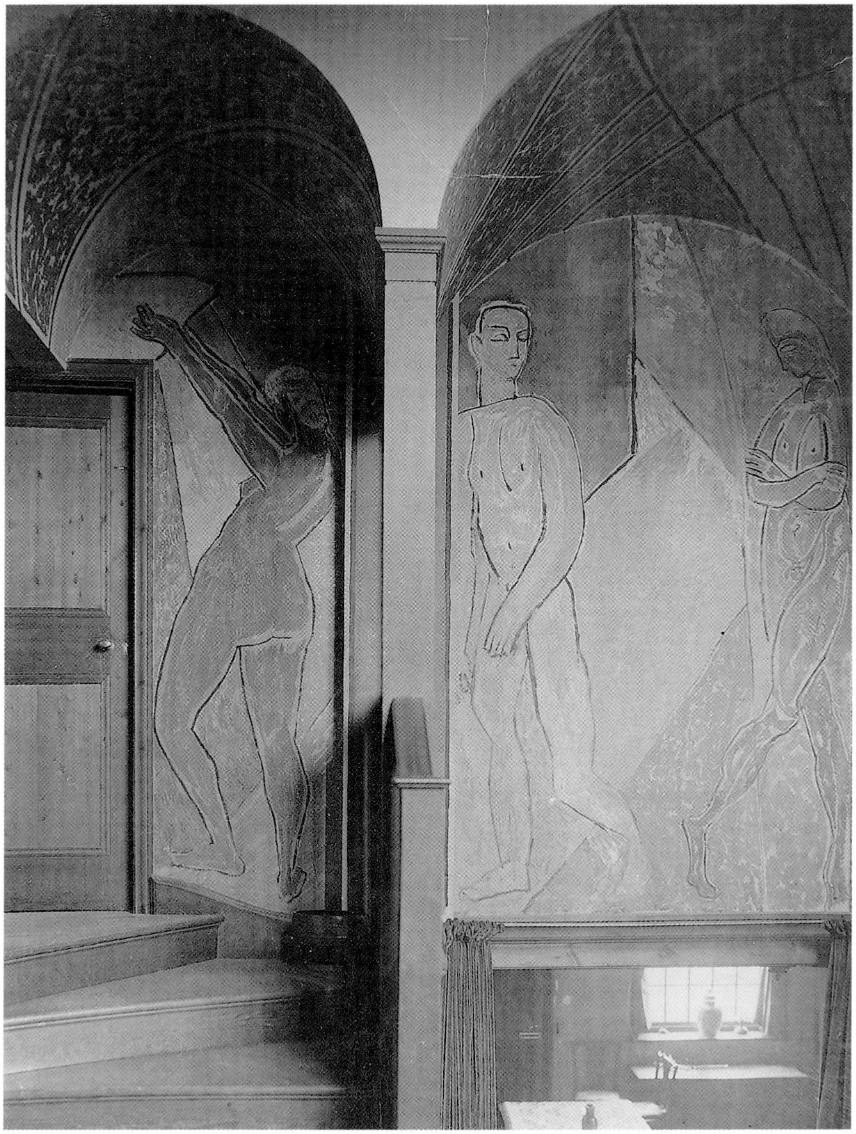

193. Period view of the entrance hall at Durbins, near Guildford, showing (left to right), murals by Roger Fry, Vanessa Bell, and Duncan Grant, 1913

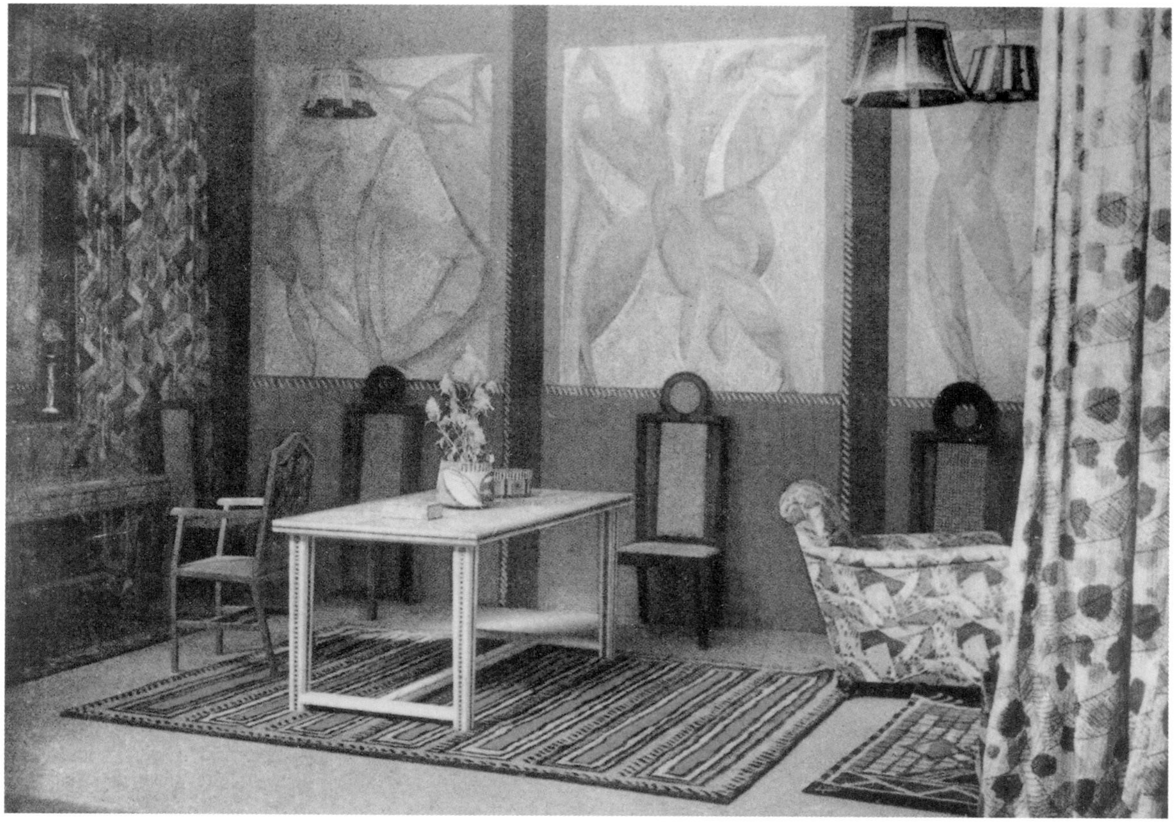

194. The Omega Workshops' 'Post-Impressionist Room' at the Ideal Home Exhibition organized by the *Daily Mail*, London, 1913. (Photograph from the *Illustrated London News*, 1913)

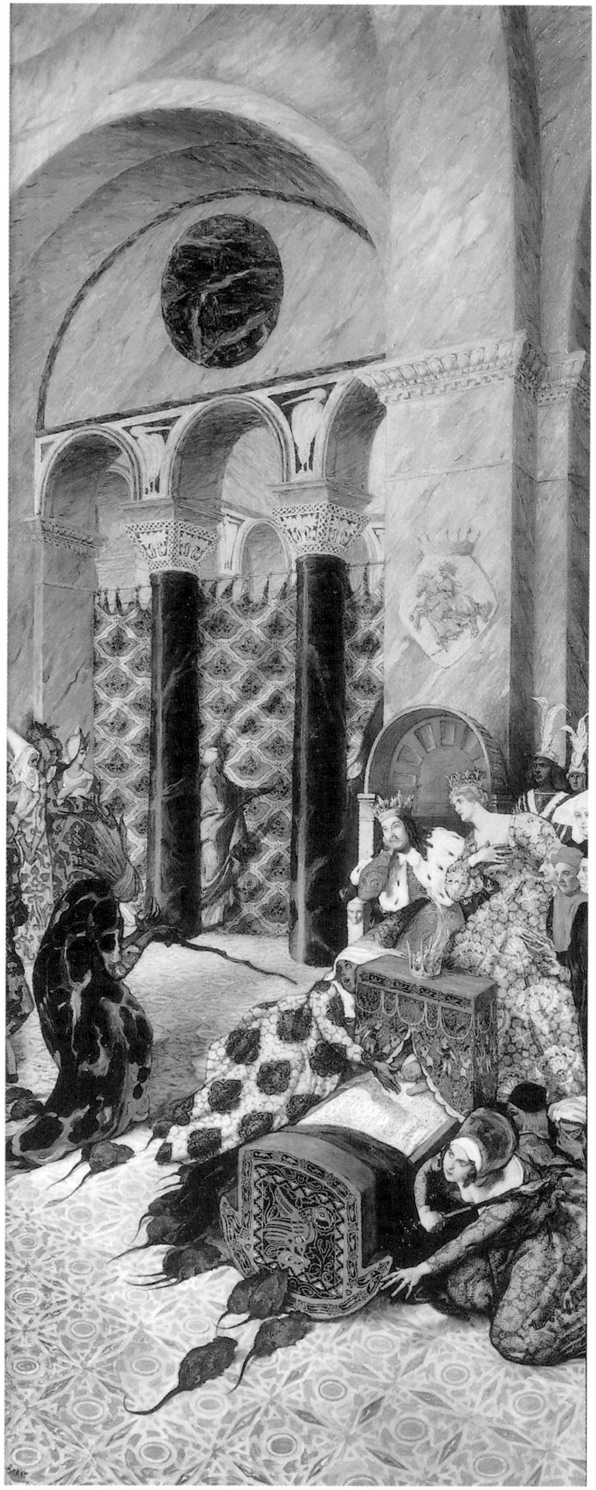

195. Léon Bakst, *The Bad Fairy Visits the Christening*, from *The Sleeping Beauty* panels, commissioned 1913, Waddesdon Manor, Buckinghamshire (including a self-portrait of Bakst, wearing a hat, the second right of the three men to the right of the queen)

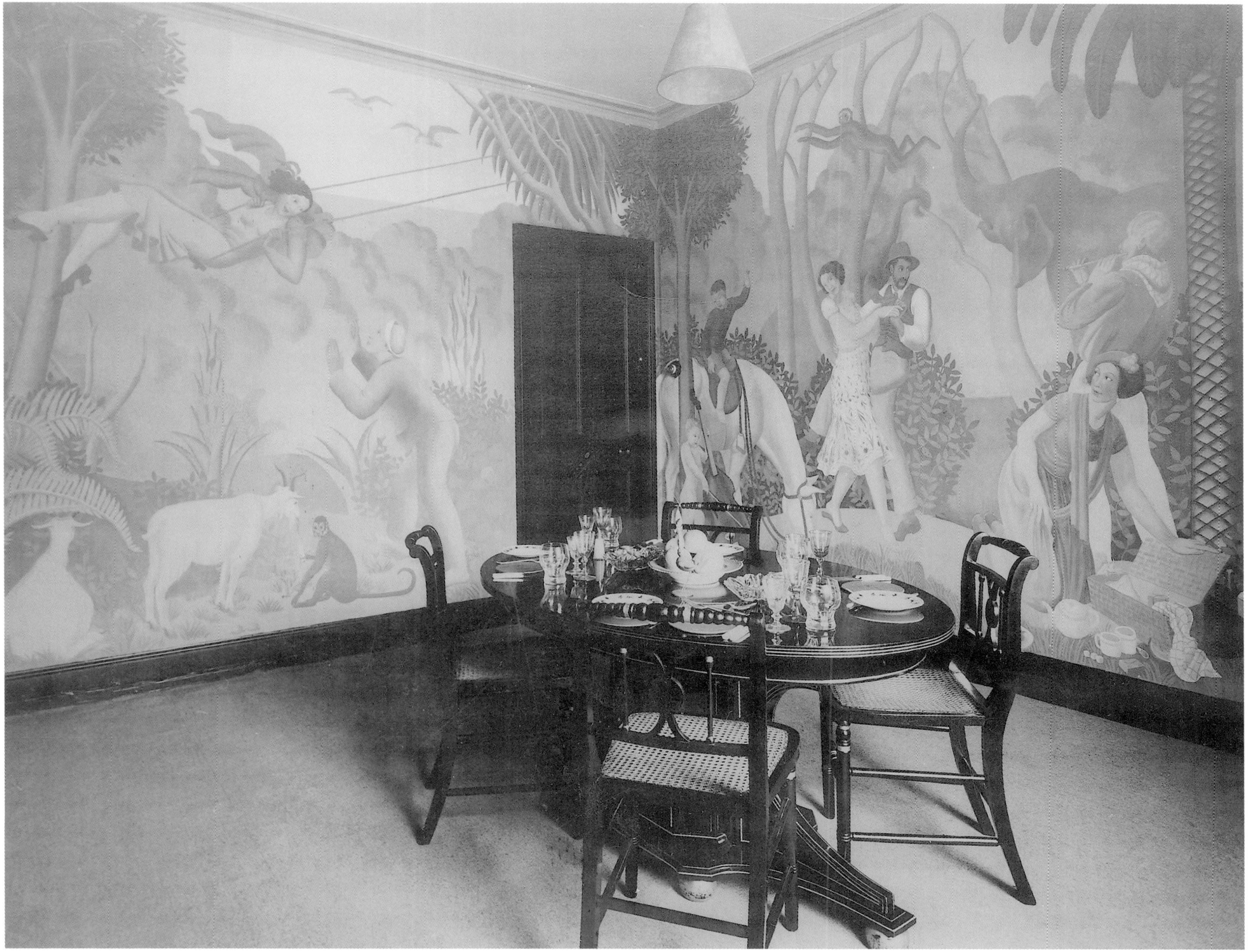

196. Period photograph showing Mary Adshead's jungle murals of 1925 in the dining-room of Professor C. H. Reilly's flat in Liverpool. University of Liverpool

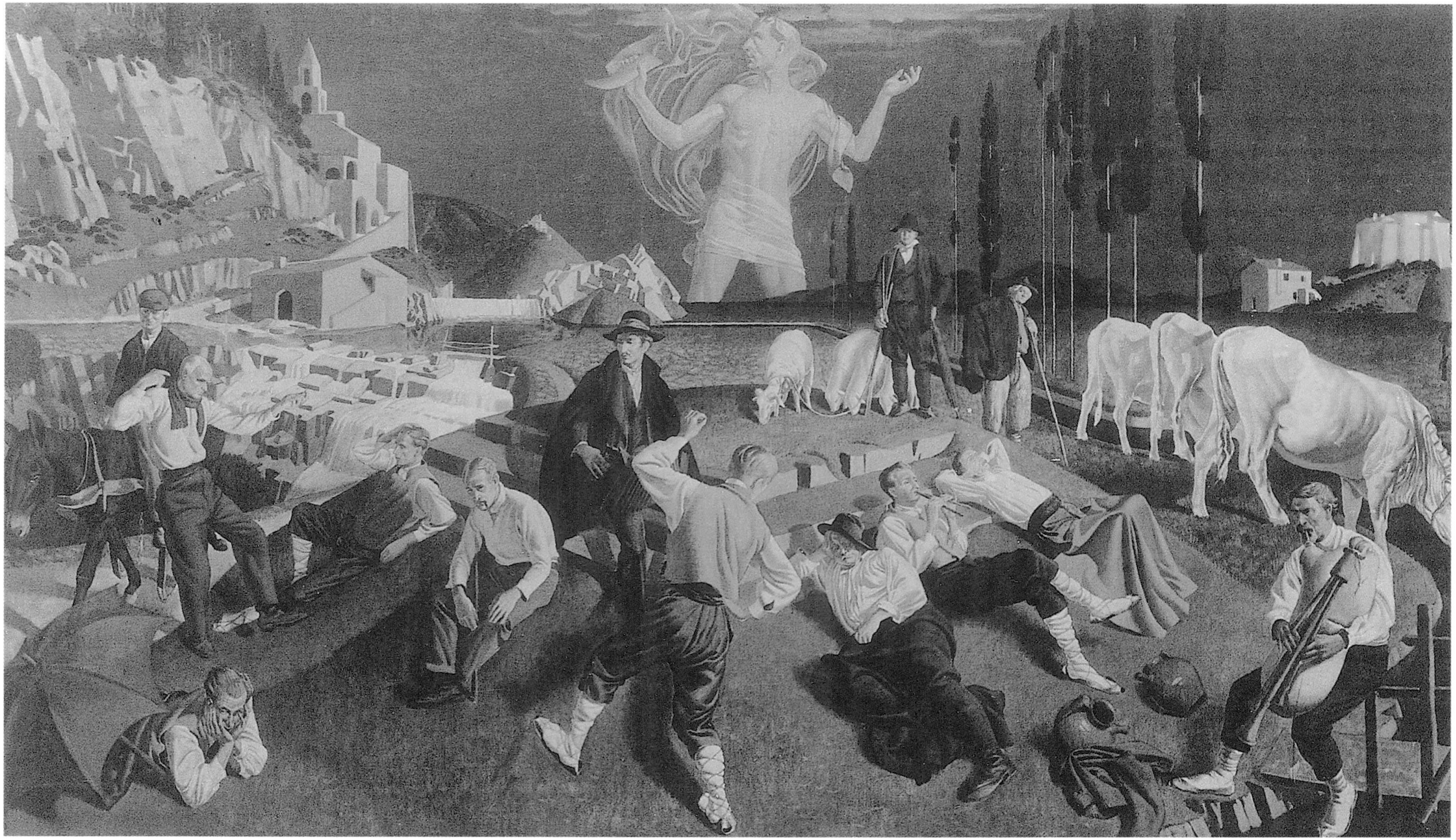

197. Edward I. Halliday, *Hypnos*, formerly at Abbott's Lea, Woolton, Liverpool, 1928. Private Collection

procession! This of course was a skit on the Regency 'Tent' decoration in the Brighton Pavilion. At Plas Newydd for Lord Anglesey in 1937 he converted the Dining Room into a Baroque *loggia* with *trompe-l'oeil* coffered ceiling, false perspectives, and a Claudean port scene apparently opening off the actual room (Plates 198, 199). Rather than bringing exotic lands or climates actually into the interior, as had Bakst, Philpot, and Adshead, a more subtle *invitation au voyage* was offered. The illusion of escape was completed with *trompe-l'oeil* motifs including an anchor, wet footprints, and mock 'bas relief' globe and compasses. At Mottisfont Abbey, where the decoration was left incomplete at his death in the Second World War, Whistler turned his virtuoso skills to mock Strawbery Hill Gothic, painting grisaille *trompe-l'oeil* 'trophies' and a cornice with a paint-pot, brush, and matches poignantly 'left behind'. He created numerous private-house schemes, mostly of a more modest nature (Appendix D: 38), and set a fashion for the *trompe l'oeil* idiom[106] (Appendix D: 42, 47).

Whistler's work was included in Sir John Rothenstein's 1939 Tate exhibition, and light-hearted identification with past golden ages appears also to have been prominent amongst the other private-house schemes he selected (including Appendix D: 41, 43, 44, 47). His choice was of course personal—Delmar H. Banner's naturalistic landscape panoramas were excluded, for example (Appendix D: 45), though, interestingly, the Earl of Huntingdon's murals at Buscot Park, influenced by his study with Diego Rivera, were included. The popularity of pastiche and period manner is evident, however, from their stock-in-trade use by the interior designers such as Oliver Messel, who from the 1920s had begun to divert taste away from traditional forms of mural painting. Such decorators (and probably also the representatives of the lingering Omega tradition) provoked a radical attack in 1932 from Paul Nash, who argued that the artist should not 'be encouraged to paint "frescoes" or panels or be allowed, for one moment, to contemplate applying his colours to any of the furniture or knick-knacks'.[107] His stance also ruled out many of the murals represented in Rothenstein's 1939 show, for he proposed that the artist

> should work entirely in terms of the substances which go to the construction or embellishment of the habitable room. His materials will range from stone to paper, glass, steel, wood, cardboard, rubber . . . He may compose with light. Infinite variety in the treatment of space, volume . . . infinite variations in textural qualities . . . temperature and vibration spread opportunity before him.[108]

These sentiments, suggesting knowledge of Mondrian and El Lissitzky's 'abstract' rooms and the *Wall Pictures* of the Bauhaus, as well as Le Corbusier's collaboration with Amédée Ozenfant, also followed to its logical conclusion Fry's earlier proposal for coloured walls, and it is perhaps not surprising that in turn in 1936 it was from survivors of the Arts and Crafts Movement, in the shape of the Society of Mural Decorators and Painters in Tempera, that a case was similarly made—in words quoted from Diego Rivera—for the association of true fresco, with its integral relationship with the wall, and 'the light soaring constructions of steel, concrete and glass which we erect today'.[109] If this effective return to the Nazarenes' respect for the primacy and symbolism of fresco met with little, if any, response, John Piper nevertheless created an 'abstract decoration' in 1939 for Berthold Lubetkin and Tecton's pioneering reinforced concrete Highpoint flats in Highgate,

[106] See L. Whistler and R. Fuller, *The Work of Rex Whistler* (1950).

[107] P. Nash, 'The Artist in the House', *Listener* (16 March 1932), p. 381.

[108] Ibid.

[109] 'The words of a contemporary artist' quoted in the preface to M. Sargant-Florence (ed.), *Papers of the Society of Mural Decorators*, vol. 3 (1936). For Rivera's statement, see his *Portrait of America* (London, 1935), p. 11.

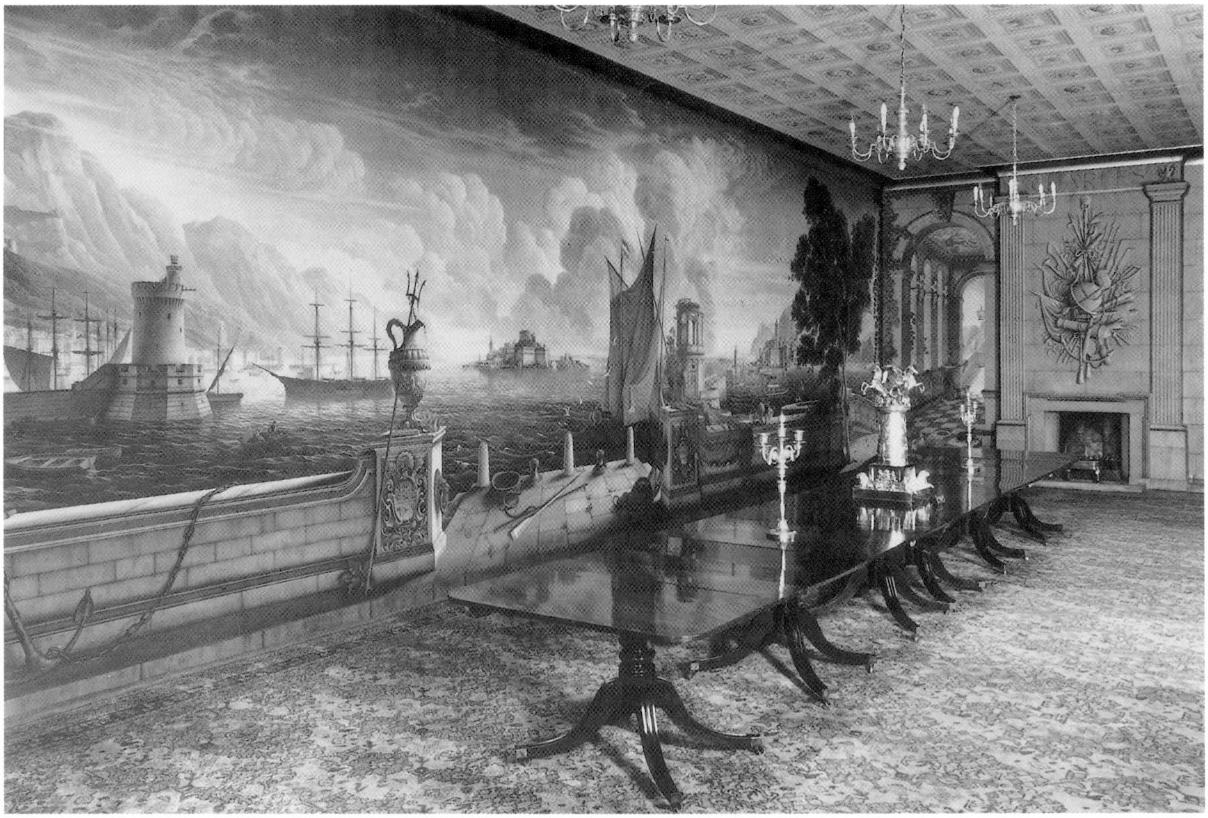

198. Rex Whistler, decoration in Dining Room, Plas Newydd, Anglesey, 1937

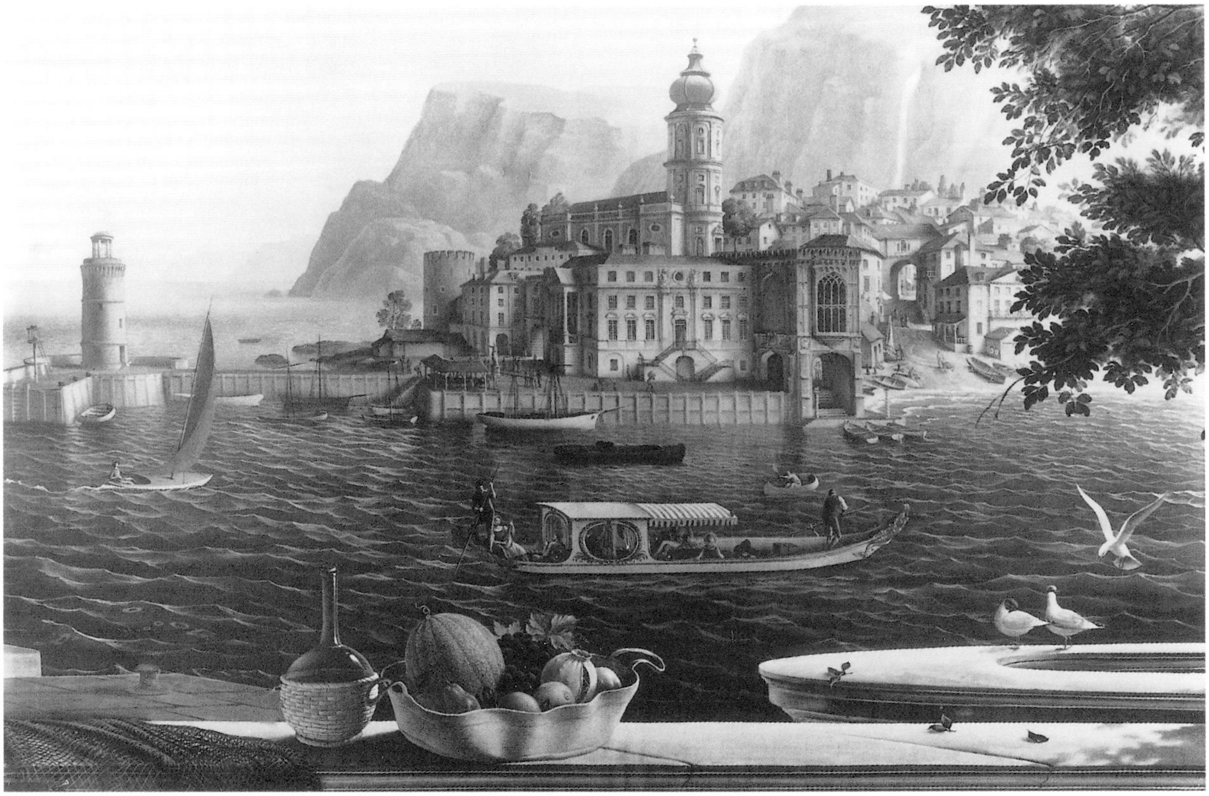

199. Rex Whistler, detail from decoration in Dining Room, Plas Newydd, Anglesey, 1937

London, thus laying a foundation for the abstract mural painting to be developed by Monnington after the Second World War at Bristol Council House. As in Prince Albert's day, private-house decoration was again the site of experiment, though abstract work had already, of course, been adopted in Britain in easel painting. Set within the context of the concepts of escape, dream, and make-believe which were so important in the domestic mural tradition since 1840, Piper's 'abstracts' should perhaps, indeed, be read less as a symptom of the so-called 'modern movement' than as the natural outcome of the essential distance from, or transmutation of, the outside world so frequently sought by private patrons for their walls throughout the preceding hundred years—metamorphosis, as it were, now reinvented.

11
Work and Play

In the early 1900s, what Walter Crane had mocked as the 'selfish, demoralising and unscrupulous demon of commercialism'[1] showed it actually shared his devotion to art. In the wake of the Royal Exchange experiment, 'A Modern Palace of Art'[2] was created at Lloyd's Register of Shipping, whilst other businesses followed more modest suit. The political struggle for London, which found expression in the Exchange scheme, likewise spilled over into both the murals for commercial premises in the capital (where the bulk of business patronage took place), and those at the Central Criminal Court (Old Bailey), a building controlled by the Corporation of London. Meanwhile, the concept of the integrated 'artistic' interior which had become so firmly established in private-house decoration not only passed into 'the business house', but was also a leading element in the 'Edwardian Baroque' of E. W. Mountford's Old Bailey. This showy architectural style, also much favoured by business and commerce in the early twentieth century as a means to demonstrate wealth and success, became a focus of lively claim and counterclaim for the 'unity' (and hence equality) of painting, sculpture, and architecture, following the RIBA's attempted professionalisation of architecture.[3] Though G. F. Watts's work at Lincoln's Inn has been discussed in the context of educational schemes, the Old Bailey is dealt with here and has a close relationship with the 'Art as Unity' trend in commercial premises, which still found resonance as late as the 1930s in Sir Herbert Baker's Bank of England. The Bank murals form the principal sequel to the British School at Rome work at St Stephen's Hall.

The murals at St Stephen's Hall also had direct repercussions, though of a very different kind, in the 1920s scheme to decorate the restaurant at the Tate Gallery in London. Many places offering recreation, such as restaurants, theatres, ocean liners, and the grand department stores which developed from the late nineteenth century, are in any case, of course, also commercial enterprises. In this sense, the distinction between 'work' and 'play' can at best be partial or rudimentary. Similarly, there is a cross-over between the educative aspects of museum decoration and the temporary murals installed in the great International Exhibitions which gathered momentum from that of 1851 onwards. Space does not permit exhaustive discussion of exhibition work, but as

[1] W. Crane, *The Claims of Decorative Art* (1892), p. 133.

[2] Anon., 'Lloyd's Registry: A Modern Palace of Art,' *Magazine of Art*, new series, 1 (London, 1903), p. 20.

[3] The Bill brought forward in Parliament in 1891 to make architecture a profession of registered practitioners and the RIBA's concurrent attempt to institute exclusive examinations provoked a 'secession' from the RIBA led by R. T. Blomfield, E. S. Prior, and others; Crane, Burne-Jones, Madox Brown, and Sir William Richmond were amongst the artists who supported this. T. G. Jackson's *Architecture: A Profession or an Art* (1892) presented their arguments for the equality of architecture, painting, and sculpture and declared solidarity with the Art Workers' Guild and the Arts and Crafts Exhibition Society, whose motto was 'Art as Unity'.

ephemeral decoration intended frequently to create a mood or an atmosphere for the vast crowds of visitors who attended these events, usually as much for entertainment as for instruction, examples have been included in this chapter in the context of 'play'. The decoration of entertainment venues often involves motives of escape, fantasy, and illusion which, though they may be linked with advertising or promotional purposes, offer an essentially different kind of art from the image-projection found in commerce, or the didactic use of art at the Old Bailey to present the even-handedness of the law and at the Bank of England to inspire trust. As aids to wish-fulfilment, sensual pleasure, or suspension of disbelief, murals in leisure and entertainment venues thus share many of the purposes of private-house decoration, whilst ship interiors were often purposely intended to evoke the illusion of being in a house (albeit a grand one) on terra firma. Yet, whilst Spencer Gore's, Charles Ginner's, and Wyndham Lewis's Vorticist decorations for the Cave of the Golden Calf Cabaret Theatre Club in London were created to provide 'surroundings, which, after the reality of daily life, reveal the reality of the unreal',[4] they were meant for *communal*, not private, enjoyment. Roger Fry called them 'evocative of a Dionysiac mood',[5] and they were clearly conceived as the means to provoke the kind of shared visionary transport on the part of club habitués which Lewis's hero Nietzsche believed the chorus collectively to have experienced in ancient Greek theatre. Even the overblown Tudor, *Chinois*, or Rococo styles so frequent in the great nineteenth-century theatres whose idiom the Cave sought to cast aside, were, like the palatial grandeur espoused by hotels and ships, essentially props for the spectacle of being seen by others in fine surroundings, rather than necessarily relevant to the function of the building.

MURALS AT WORK

Citing Hogarth ('a City man'), Alderman Boydell's 'Shakespeare Gallery', and the collections formed by the banker poet Samuel Rogers and the businessman John Sheepshanks, the *City Press* argued in 1891 that 'Art owes much to London's merchant princes.'[6] Whereas sculptural ornament had often been part of the Venetian Gothic and Renaissance architecture much favoured in the earlier nineteenth century by such men[7] as a means to reflect glory on their businesses, they had only rarely ventured on decorative *painting*.[8] Congratulating themselves in 1901 on their splendid new building in Fenchurch Street, by Thomas Collcutt in English cum Italian Renaissance style, Lloyd's Register of Shipping drew special attention to its 'higher aim':

> As a rule . . . architects and builders are not allowed time to carry out genuine artistic treatment in connection with [commercial] . . . properties, the prevailing desire being to get all such people out of the way as soon as possible, so that the prosaic work for which they are intended may be entered upon with the

[4] Cave of the Golden Calf Manifesto, quoted in R. Cork, 'The Cave of the Golden Calf' in S. Compton (ed.), *British Art* (1987), p. 132.

[5] Quoted in Cork, *Art Beyond the Gallery* (1985), p. 91.

[6] Anon., 'City Men and Art', *City Press* (5 Aug. 1891), PB 129–1993, RA(F).

[7] See B. Read, *Victorian Sculpture* (New Haven and London, 1982) and N. Taylor, *Monuments of Commerce*, RIBA Drawings Series (London, 1968); Ruskin had recommended Venetian architecture as a model for commercial buildings because the Venetians had been merchants (see 'Introduction', J. Physick and M. Darby, *Marble Halls* (1973)).

[8] The few examples of such decorative painting included Frederick Sang's 'Raffaelesque' motifs illustrating *The History of Coal* on the rotunda of J. B. Bunning's Coal Exchange (1849) (see Physick and Darby, *Marble Halls*, p. 95).

least delay. But the Committee of Lloyd's Register . . . have resolved that the new habitation should in every sense be worthy of the vast interest which they have done so much to create.[9]

This change of attitude can be directly attributed not only to the example of the Royal Exchange, where the prominent Lloyd's Register underwriter, Sir Thomas Lane Devitt, was Brangwyn's patron, but also to the Arts and Crafts predilections of Collcutt, who employed Gerald Moira to decorate both his Imperial Institute and his P & O Pavilion at the Paris 1900 International Exhibition.[10] Collcutt, however, seems to have had little difficulty in leading his patrons into more ambitious artistic waters than they had anticipated.[11] If Lloyd's origins lay in the 'ships' lists' compiled by underwriters at Lloyd's Coffee House in earlier times, the aggrandizement of its image from domestic into regal—a 'palace of art'—can be placed in the wider political context of the efforts of the City and its institutions in the 1900s to assert their historic powers amid changes in London government.

Carvings, statuary, and metalwork on the exterior of the Lloyd's Register building contrast ancient and modern shipping, implying the continuity of Britain's authority, vested in Lloyd's, upon the waves. Inside, marble panelling, stencils, stained glass by Moira, and Lynn-Jenkins's 'narrowly and brilliantly bizarre frieze . . . with its various-coloured metals, its gold and silver, its ivory and its mother-of-pearl inlays'[12] representing *Commerce*, provide the prelude to the allegorical paintings of the *Elements, Seasons, Winds*, and *Zodiac* by Moira adorning the intricately vaulted Board Room ceiling (Plate XLII). Whilst his scheme recalls the kind of iconography favoured by Crane, it is presented in a vigorous and eye-catching Art Nouveau idiom. The free brushwork and swirling draperies of the half-nude personifications aptly evoke the rhythmic surge of the surf and spume in which Lloyd's business lay; the muscular figure of *Fire*, whose torch-flames are joined with his mane of orange-red hair by the breath of a female spirit in a Loie Fuller-style scarf, would in turn have seemed to plunge from vivid turquoise 'sky' between the golden chandeliers to 'illuminate' Devitt and his colleagues as they met beneath.

The political implications of old juxtaposed with new in the sculpture and metalwork, and myth with reality in the Board Room were perhaps most explicitly presented in the two murals by Brangwyn, which were presented by donors associated with Lloyd's Register as additions to Collcutt's original scheme. *Queen Elizabeth going aboard the Golden Hind* in the Committee of Classification Room[13] was given in 1903 by the General Shipowners' Society and *The Arrival of the British Fleet after the Capture of the Plate Vessels in 1657* by the industrialist Sir John Milburn in 1907. Both subjects illustrate what were seen at the period as founding episodes in the making of Britain's modern imperial and maritime power. Men of Lloyd's such as Devitt, President of the

[9] Anon., *Lloyd's Register of British and Foreign Shipping Description of the Society's New Premises at 71 Fenchurch Street, London, E.C., reprinted from The Shipping Gazette and Lloyd's List, December 16, 1901*, p. 4.

[10] The Imperial Institute is demolished (see 'T. E. Collcutt' in M. Richardson et al., *Catalogue of the Drawings Collection of the Royal Institute of British Architects*, Vol. C–F (London, 1972), pp. 39–40); Roger Marx praised Moira's P & O Pavilion decoration in 'Les arts à l'exposition universelle de 1900 La Décoration et les Industries d'Art', *Gazette des Beaux Arts*, 2 (1900), pp. 410–11.

[11] Devitt was a member of the Lloyd's Building Sub-Committee which selected Moira on Collcutt's and Sir William Richmond's recommendation. Despite initially refusing to pay more than £1,000 for Moira's Board Room decoration (he asked for £1,680), when it was complete the Committee sanctioned an additional payment of £500 (see Minutes and Accounts of Building Sub-Committee 1900–1903 in Lloyd's Register of Shipping Archives, and C. M. Glover, 'How LR Came to Fenchurch Street', *Society* (Lloyd's Register Staff Magazine) (May 1978), p. 24)). Moira's Board Room work is discussed in F. Lynn-Jenkins, 'A Great Decorator', *Magazine of Art*, ns. 1 (1903), pp. 132–6.

[12] 'Lloyd's Registry' (see n. 2), p. 61.

[13] Now the Chairman's Office. Collcutt had left space for a mural here, but does not appear to have had a role in selecting the artist and subject.

Shipping Federation and Director of the Orient Steam Navigation Company, would have been only too aware of the 1902 Royal Commission recommendation for the municipalization of London's docks, eventually to result in the creation of the Port of London Authority in 1909. Was it mere coincidence that an allegorical marble overmantel by Harry Pegram representing Lloyd's 'influence . . . over Shipbuilding',[14] which formed part of Collcutt's original scheme, was now ousted to accommodate Brangwyn's dramatic visualization, complete with rolling cumulus clouds, shining armour, and golden sunlight, of *The Arrival of the British Fleet*? Both the prominence given in Brangwyn's two panels to the common dock labourers and Thames boats, and several of their figure groupings, offer close comparison with the *Departure of Sir James Lancaster* and *River Procession* murals in his concurrent political scheme for Devitt at Skinners' Hall; in turn, like the Skinners' panels, those at Lloyd's also translate into vivid and significant historical iconography the theme of his *Modern Commerce* for Devitt at the Royal Exchange. Here were illustrations, in Brangwyn's characteristically immediate style, of the makers of the modern Empire whose shipping Devitt and his colleagues wished to continue to control through private enterprise. One of the dignitaries welcoming Blake ashore in the *Arrival of the British Fleet* is dressed in the distinctive fur-trimmed red cloak of a Skinner: City and livery company interests now appear to have overlaid Collcutt's principles of integration between art and architecture.

It is perhaps not surprising that by 1908, the eve of the creation of the hated Port of London Authority, Lloyd's were busy redesigning Collcutt's ensemble still more dramatically, to incorporate in a new Luncheon Room twelve murals and a 6.61 by 2.4 m lunette (Plate 200), all by Brangwyn and now showing contemporary dock labour itself. Though selected by Brangwyn, this iconography can be seen as the realization of Devitt's wish (in the event overruled) to have modern subjects at Skinners' Hall; its porters shouldering the goods of Empire parallel those in Brangwyn's *Modern Commerce* for Devitt at the Exchange and his Certificate for Devitt's London Shipping Federation. Whereas Collcutt's original Luncheon Room had featured a painted frieze by E. J. Lambert on the history of shipping, the oak-panelled walls of the new room were now surmounted with muscular, flat-capped, scowling labourers whose might, still under private control when the murals were begun, was shown unloading the very tea, sugar, beer, pottery, and other goods which were transported to London under Lloyd's supervision.[15] The low viewpoint and the frontal, close-up placement of the figures would have emphasized their dignified presence as individuals amidst the wharfside filled with vessels and clouds of pink and orange steam, but each was none the less carefully related to his colleagues; exchanging a comment; sharing the weight of a meat carcass; guiding a massive packing case being desposited by a crane. Brangwyn's theme of fellowship and brotherhood at both Skinners' Hall (Plates X–XIII; Plates 42–3; 45–7) and in his recent Venice Biennale decorations[16] was now presented in iconic terms, transcending the acrimony surrounding the municipalization of London's docks to create something universal out of the modern-life imagery he had been taught to value by Julius Meier-Graefe. Lloyd's were initially disconcerted; the Board of Trade, however, perhaps recognizing both the Continental affinities of the murals and their iconic power, if not as emblems of universal brotherhood, then certainly of Empire trade, invited Brangwyn to show them at the 1913 Ghent

[14] 'Lloyd's Registry' (see n.2), p. 65.

[15] The murals are no longer *in situ* but their appearance is recorded in preparatory cartoons owned by Lloyd's Register of Shipping, London.

[16] Brangwyn's Venice Biennale work is discussed later in this chapter.

International Exhibition.[17] In 1914 they were finally installed at Lloyd's, and in 1917 further elaborated *in situ* by Brangwyn.

At the Old Bailey, the ideal of 'Art as Unity' to which its architect E. W. Mountford subscribed was associated with an even more politically charged, as well as public, venue. When opening the Courts, the Lord Mayor, as Chief Justice of the City of London, traditionally processes up the great staircase to the double-domed hall giving access to the courtrooms. Six vast lunettes were painted for this hall between 1904 and about 1908 by Gerald Moira (*Justice* (Plate 201), *Mosaic Law*, and *English Law*) and Sir William Richmond (*The Golden Age*, *Roman Law*, and *Greek Law*).[18] Richmond, the artist of the mosaics in the dome of St Paul's Cathedral, was recommended, along with Moira, by G. F. Watts, whose earlier *Lawgivers* at Lincoln's Inn[19] provided the compositional model for the gatherings of historical or representative figures in the lunettes.

Faithful to Watts's principles, Richmond was prepared to paint only *in situ*, and wearisome delays ensued.[20] Meanwhile in 1906, he argued at the VIIth International Congress of Architects in London that 'the architect can learn much from the painter and sculptor and *vice-versa* . . . the three should work together,' a proposal which was unanimously defeated by the Viennese Otto Wagner's resolution that 'The architect . . . is to be given absolute power over the co-operating craftsmen, but in a special manner over the co-operating artists.'[21] If Wagner's own Post Office Savings Bank in Vienna, with its structural elements presented as 'ornament', represents the ultimate logic of 'absolute power' for the architect, it was through the Old Bailey's paintings that Richmond seems to have promoted both his principle of the cooperative rather than dependent role of the painter, and the Corporation's cause. He had earlier in 1906 resigned an aldermanic seat on the LCC in disgust at what he saw as 'the tide of "egotistical philistinism" about the possible future of architectural beauties in London'.[22] He established the entire iconographical programme in consultation with his brother-in-law, Lord Justice Kennedy, and his own *Roman Law* surmounts what can be recognized as a critique of LCC aspiration: 'London shall have all its ancient rights.' Roman remains had been found near the Old Bailey and the Corporation identified its own achievements with those of Rome.[23] Since *Roman Law* showed 'the king as chief magistrate'[24] a direct link was in turn implied with Moira's *English Law* at the southern end of the hall, in which Alfred the Great is the central figure and the inscription reads 'Right lives by Law and Law subsists by Power.' As had been pointed out in the 1890s by Lord Mayor Knill, one of the prime movers in the Royal Exchange programme, 'It is in Alfred's time that we first hear of a municipal government.' Similar 'City' symbolism is perhaps suggested by Moira's *Justice* (Plate

[17] For the room he designed for the murals at Ghent, Brangwyn painted a second, taller lunette (now destroyed), showing a boiler under construction being lifted by crane onto a ship. See R. Brangwyn, *Brangwyn* (1978), pp. 135–6 and G. C. Siordet, 'Mr. Brangwyn's Tempera Paintings at the Ghent Exhibition', *Studio*, 59 (1913).

[18] All Richmond's murals were destroyed in the Second World War and replaced with the substitutes by Moira (which portray different topics) *in situ* today.

[19] Richmond's brother-in-law, Lord Justice Kennedy, was a member of a Lincoln's Inn Committee which in 1905 commissioned a copy of Watts's fresco by Niels Lund: see W. H. Draper, 'The Watts Fresco' (1906), pp. 8–15.

[20] Richmond's medium was tempera (see SCPW, 28 Nov. 1906 §95–6). Mountford complained about Richmond's dilatoriness in a letter to the Town Clerk (19 June 1906) (CLRO).

[21] Papers by Sir William Richmond and Otto Wagner, and Congress Resolution on 'Subject VIII': 'To what extent and in what sense should the architect have control over other artists or craftsmen in the completion of a national or public building' ('Summary of Proceedings of the VIIth International Congress of Architects', *Journal of the RIBA* (1906), pp. lviii, lx, lxii). The supremacy of the architect was a 'principle' attributed by Sir Arthur Blomfield to Viollet-le-Duc, in a discussion on 'Decorative Painting' at the RIBA in 1891 (*Transactions* (1891), p. 290: Viollet-le-Duc's article on 'Painting applied to Architecture' from his *Dictionnaire* was attached (pp. 291 ff)).

[22] Note in the *Art Journal* (1906), p. 30.

[23] See Chapter 3.

[24] Description by Richmond of his cartoons, enclosed with letter from Mountford to the Town Clerk (11 June 1907), CLRO.

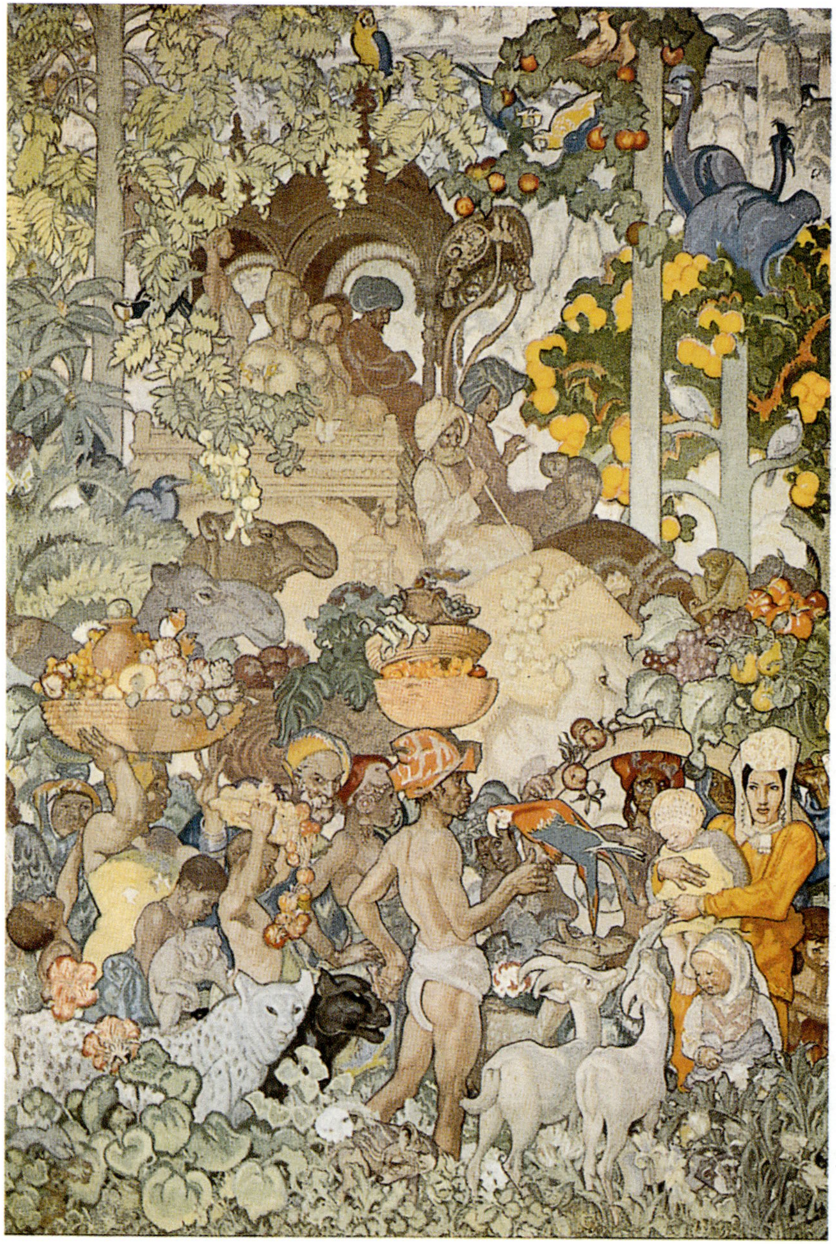

XIX. Sir Frank Brangwyn, *British Empire* mural, for centre panel, upper north wall, Royal Gallery, Palace of Westminster, London, 1924–33, now in Guildhall, Swansea (photograph taken *c.*1930–3, prior to acquisition by the City of Swansea)

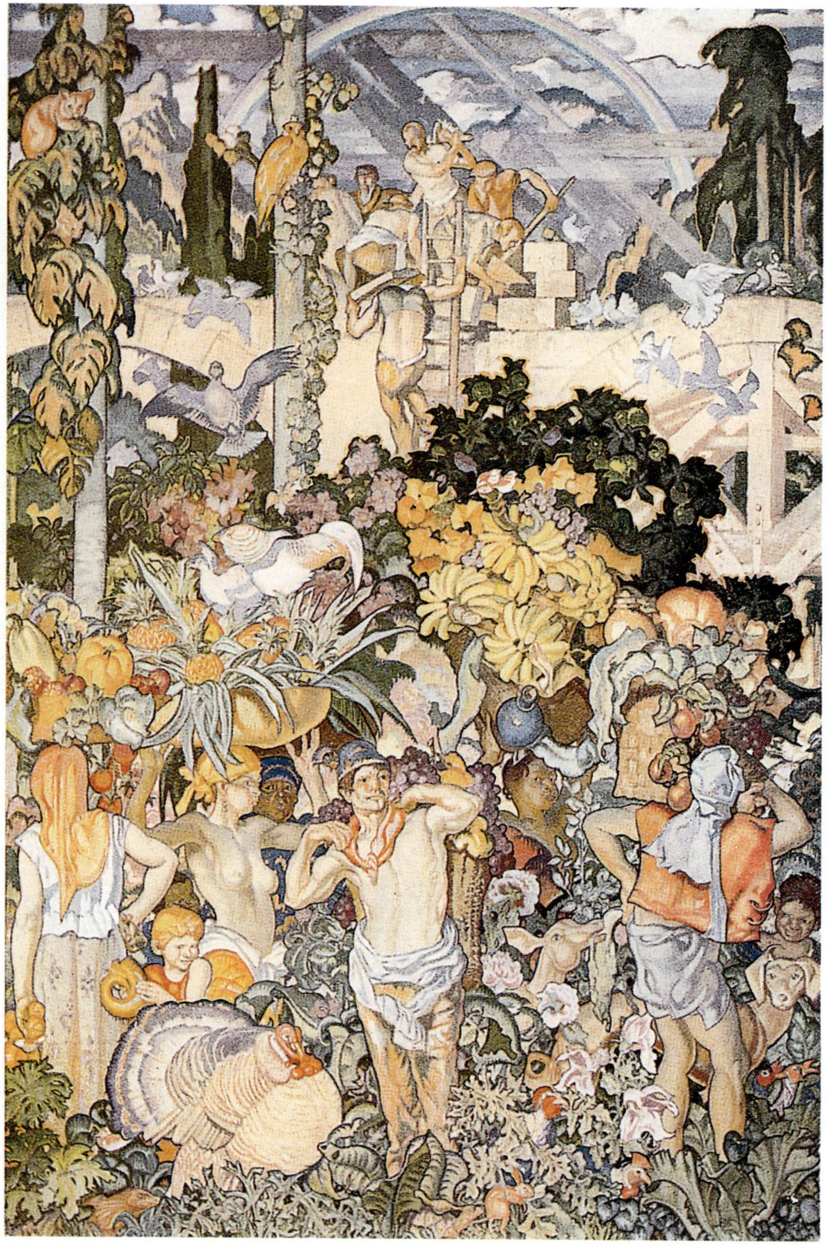

XX. Sir Frank Brangwyn, *British Empire* mural, for centre panel, upper south wall, Royal Gallery, Palace of Westminster, London, 1924–33, now in Guildhall, Swansea (photograph taken *c.*1930–3, prior to acquisition by the City of Swansea)

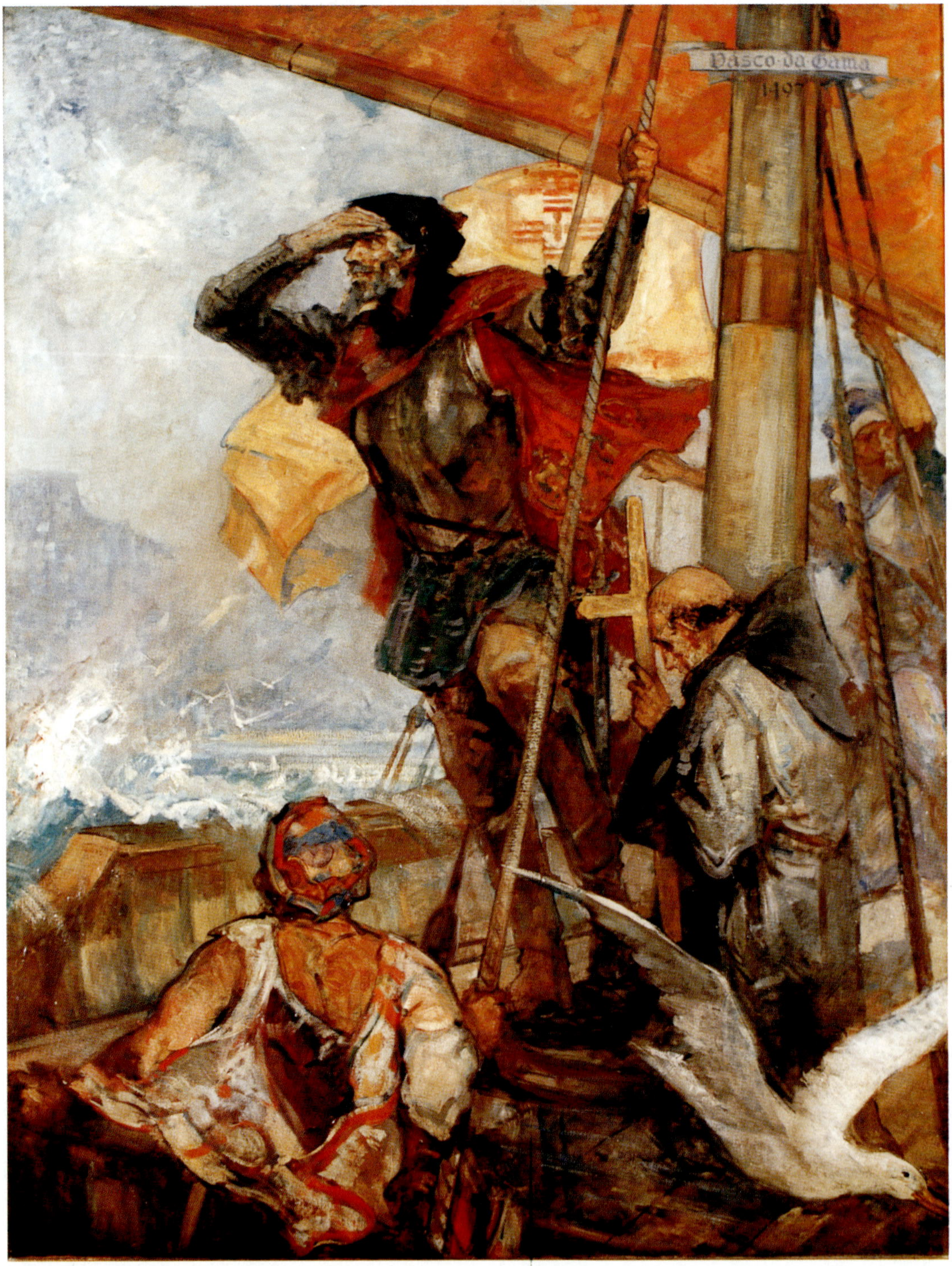

XXI. John Henry Amschewitz, *Vasco da Gama*, from *The Portuguese Navigators*, South Africa House, London, *c.*1933–4

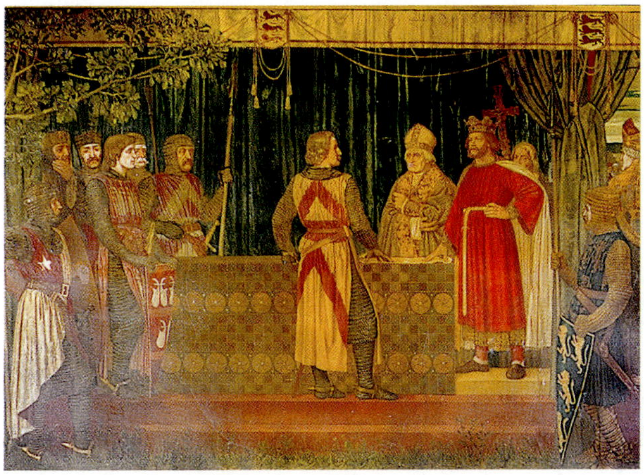

XXII. Henry Holiday, detail from *The Signing of the Magna Carta*, Great Hall, Rochdale Town Hall, 1871

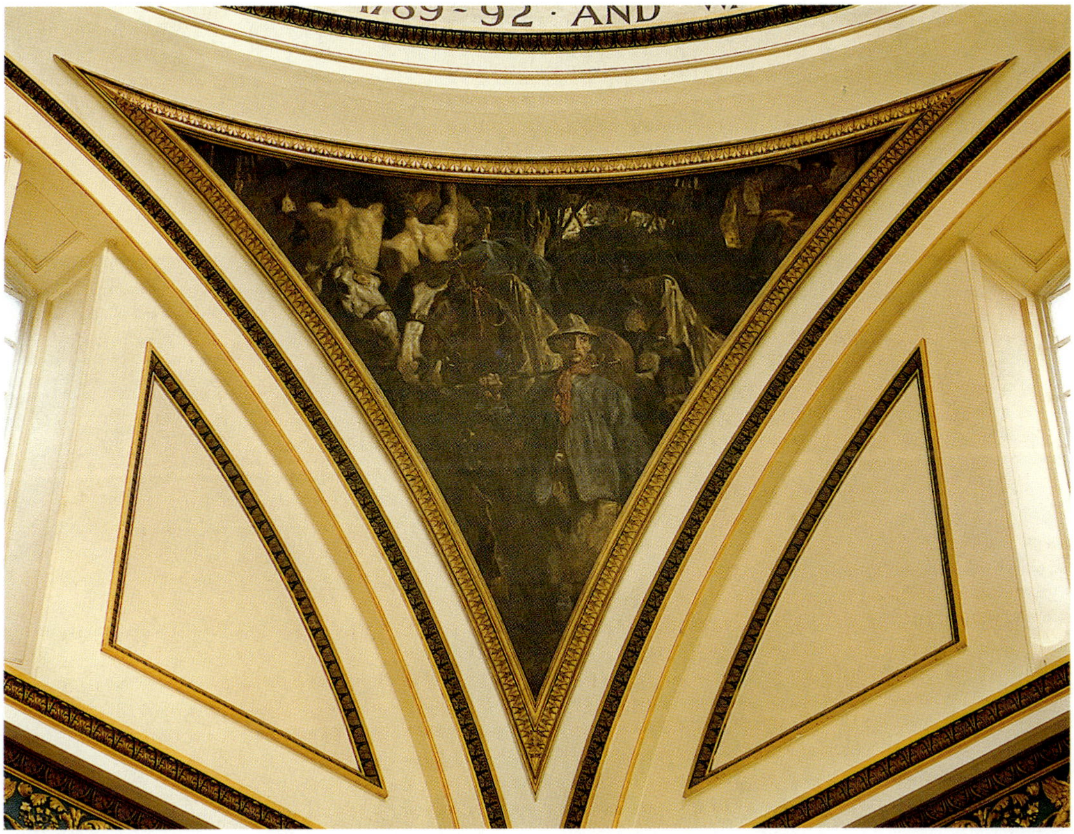

XXIII. Charles Furse, *Cotton Trollies*, dome of Liverpool Town Hall, 1901

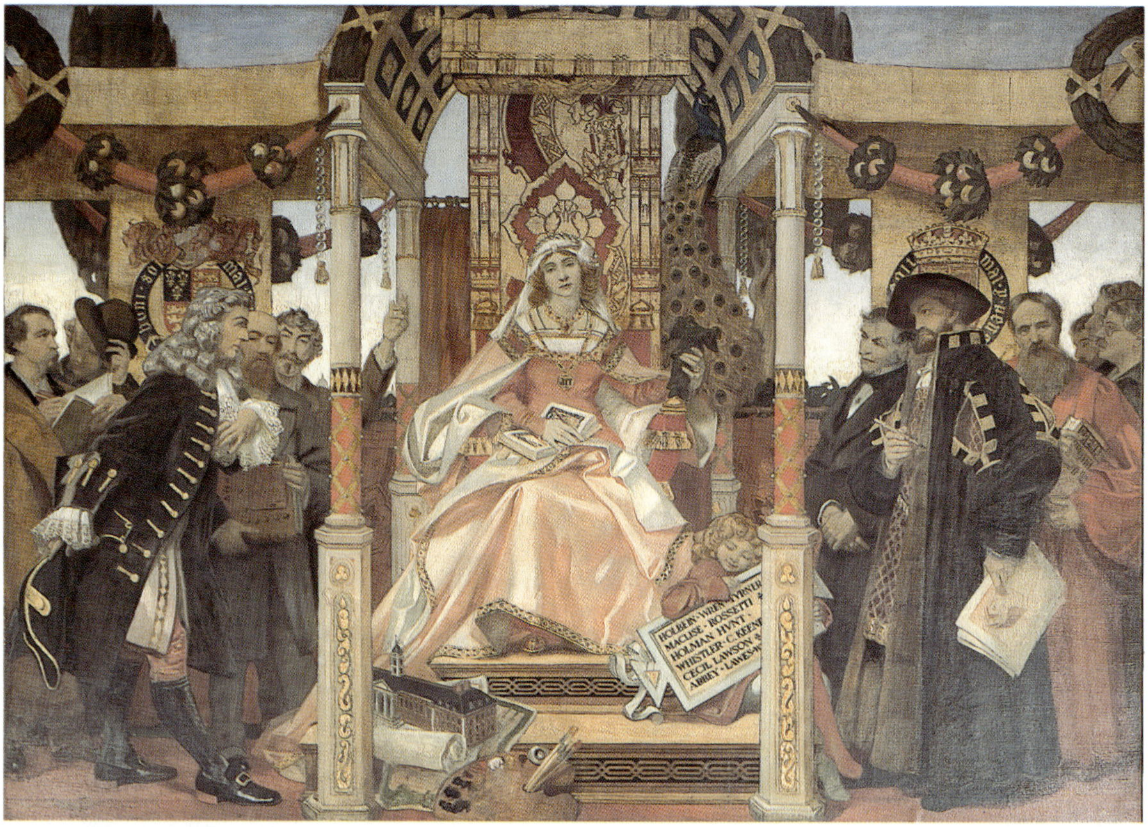

XXIV. Frank O. Salisbury, *Art*, Chelsea Town Hall, *c.*1911–13

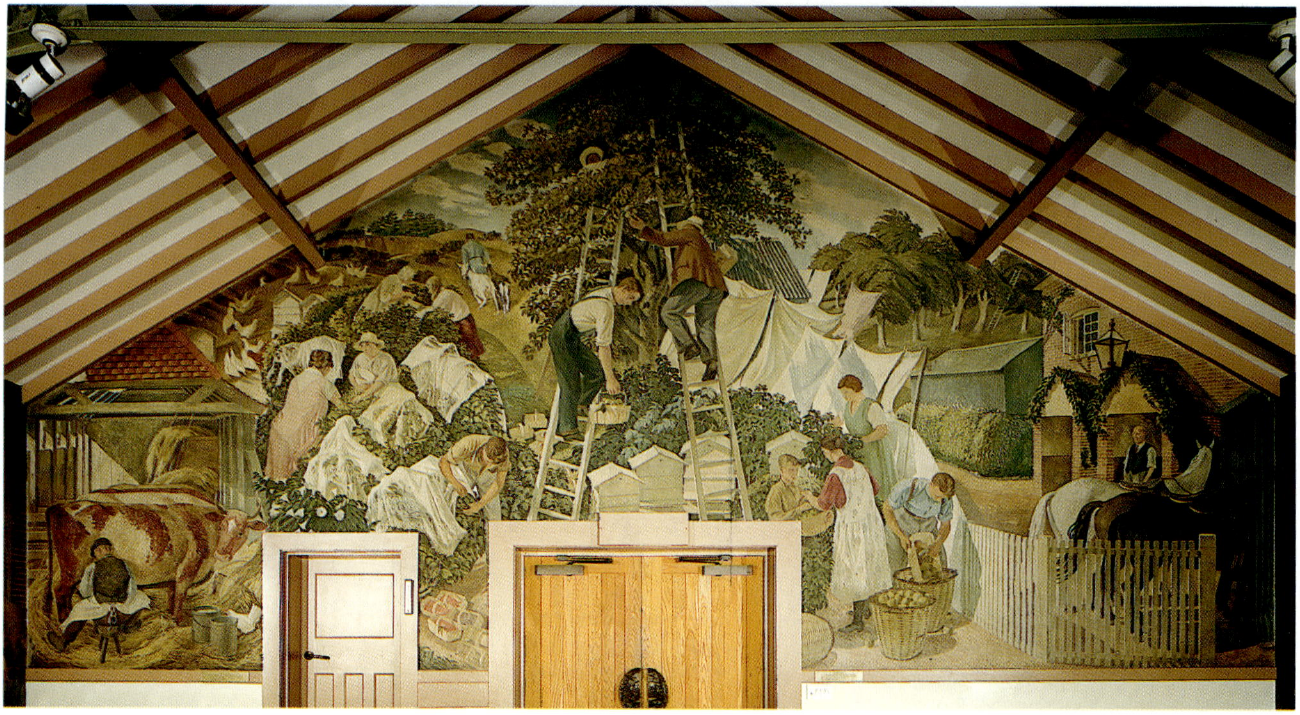

XXV. Robert Baker, *Village Scenes*, Woodgreen Village Hall, Fordingbridge, Hampshire, *c.*1931–8

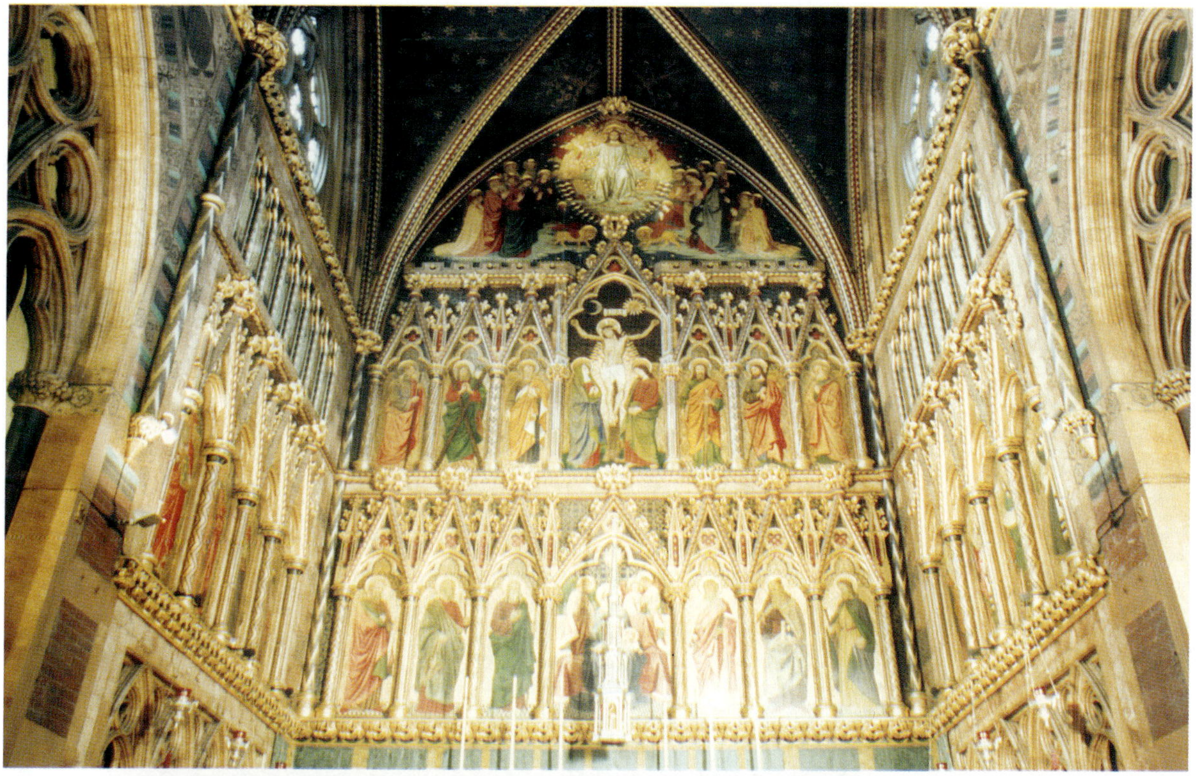

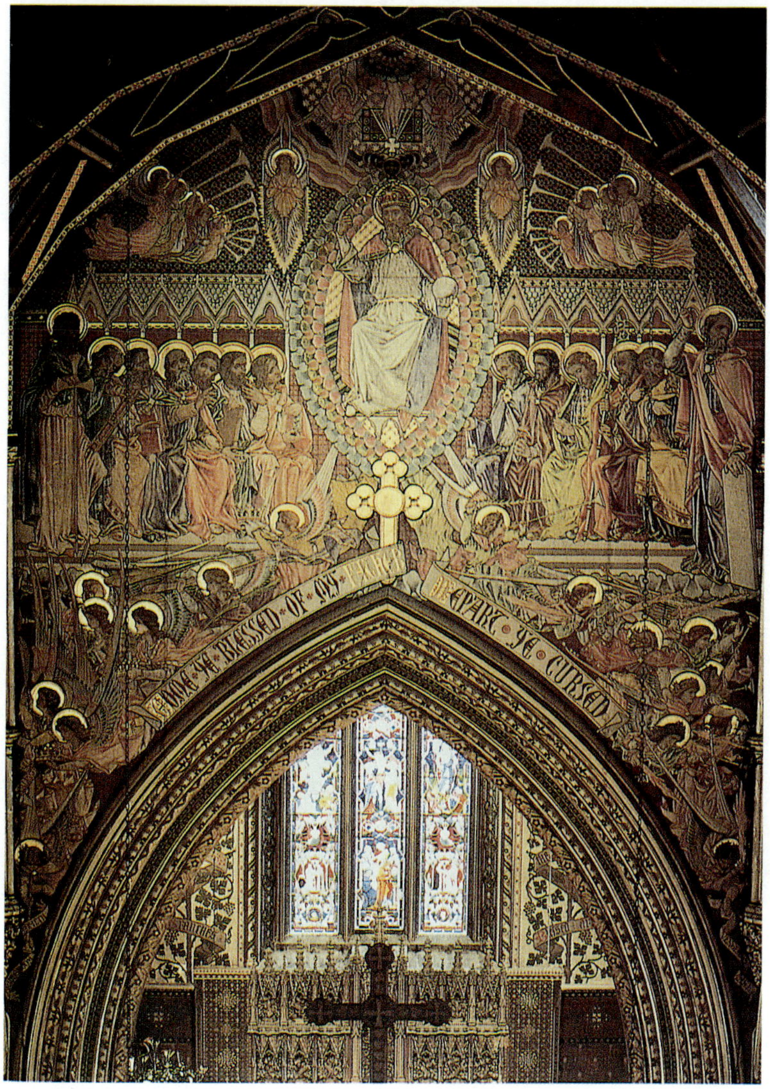

XXVI. William Dyce, *Christ in Glory and on Earth*, All Saints church, Margaret Street, London, 1853–9 (restored by Sir Ninian Comper, 1909)

XXVII. Thomas Gambier Parry, *The Doom*, chancel arch, Church of the Holy Innocents, Highnam, 1859–61

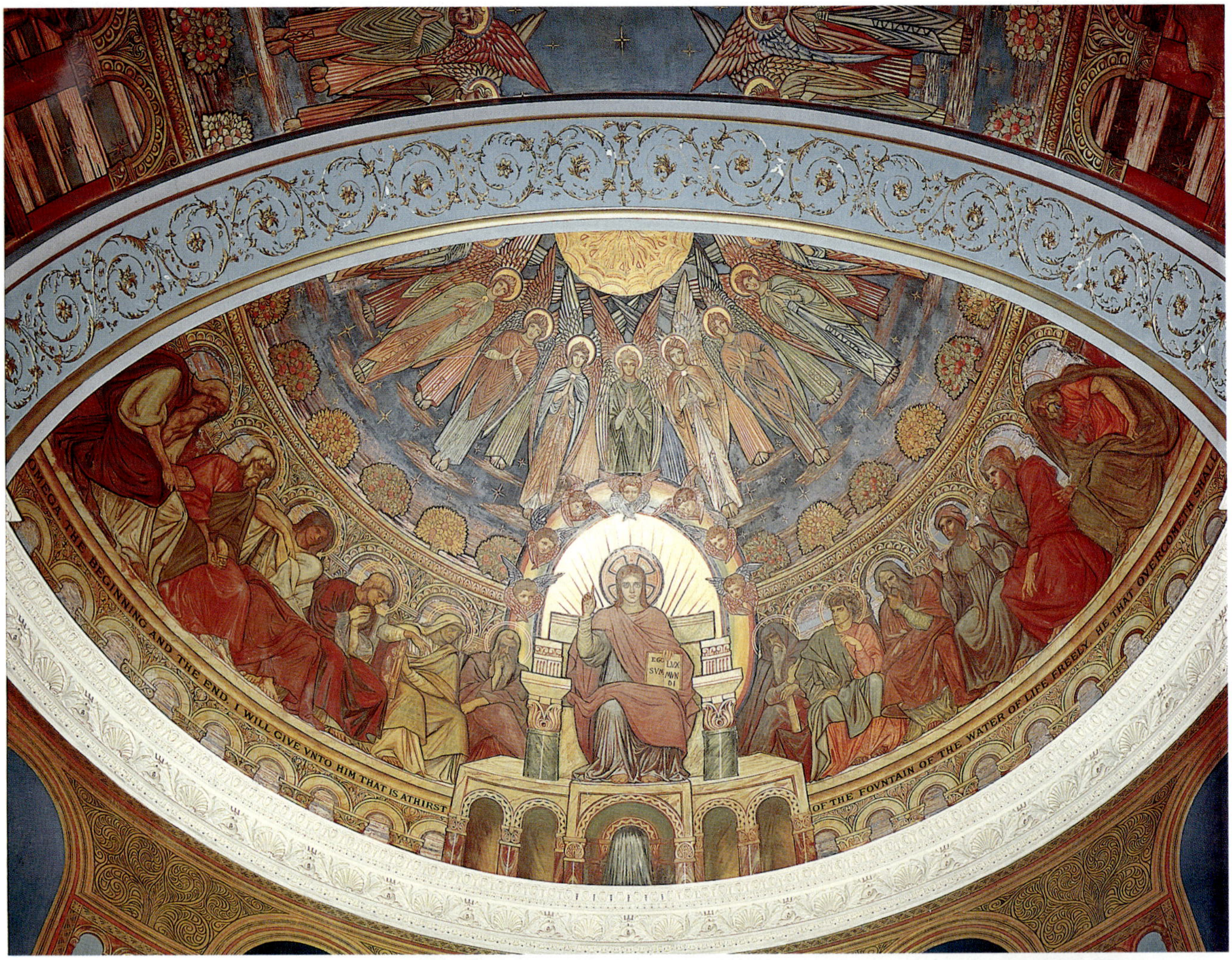

XXVIII. Sir William Blake Richmond, *I am Alpha and Omega*, apse decoration, Christ Church, Cheltenham, 1896

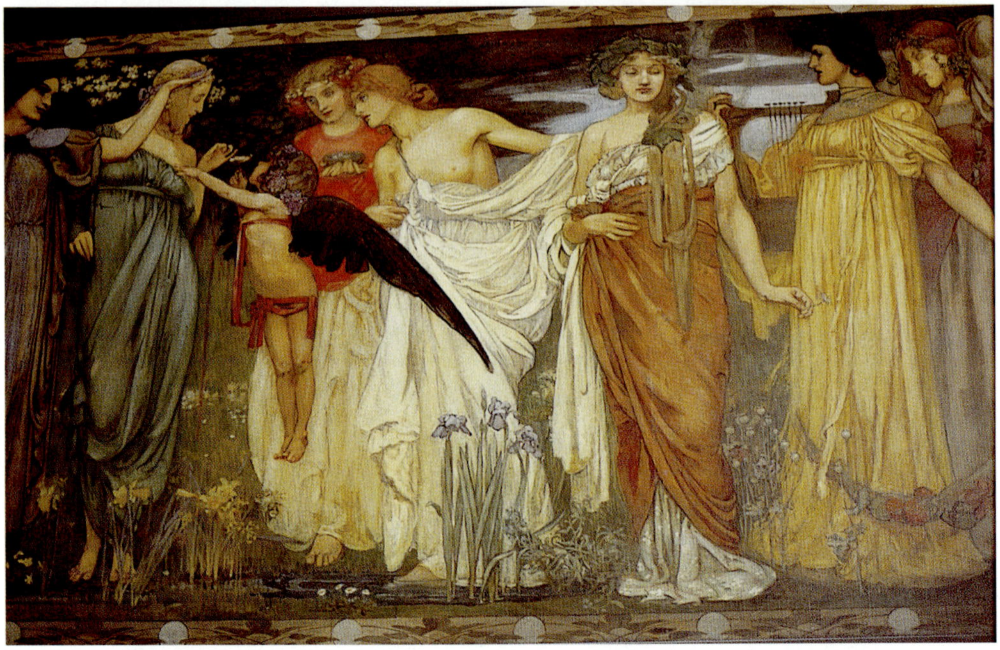

XXIX. Florence E. Chaplin, detail from *The Procession of the Hours*, Guy's Hospital, London, 1903–4

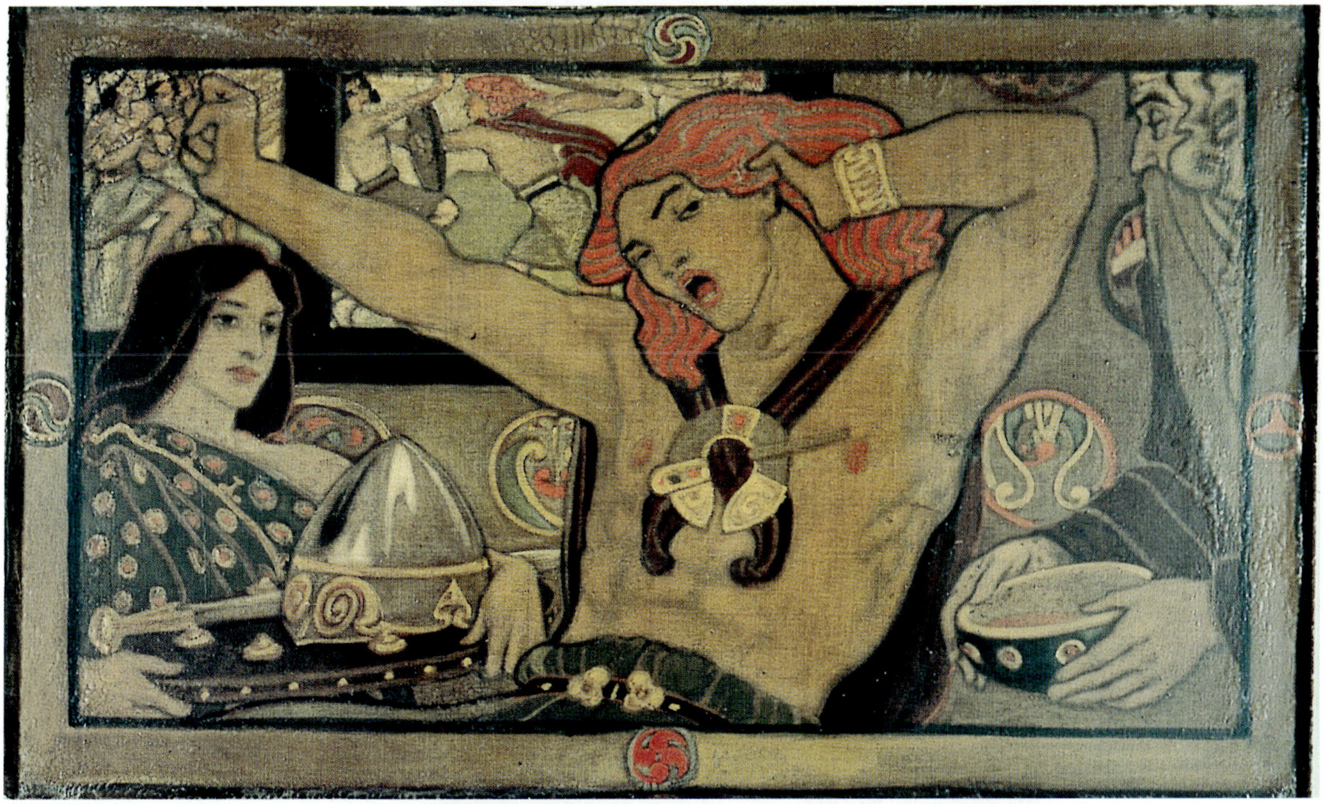

XXX. John Duncan, *The Awakening of Cuchullin*, former Common Room, University Hall, Ramsay Lodge, Ramsay Garden, Edinburgh, 1895–8

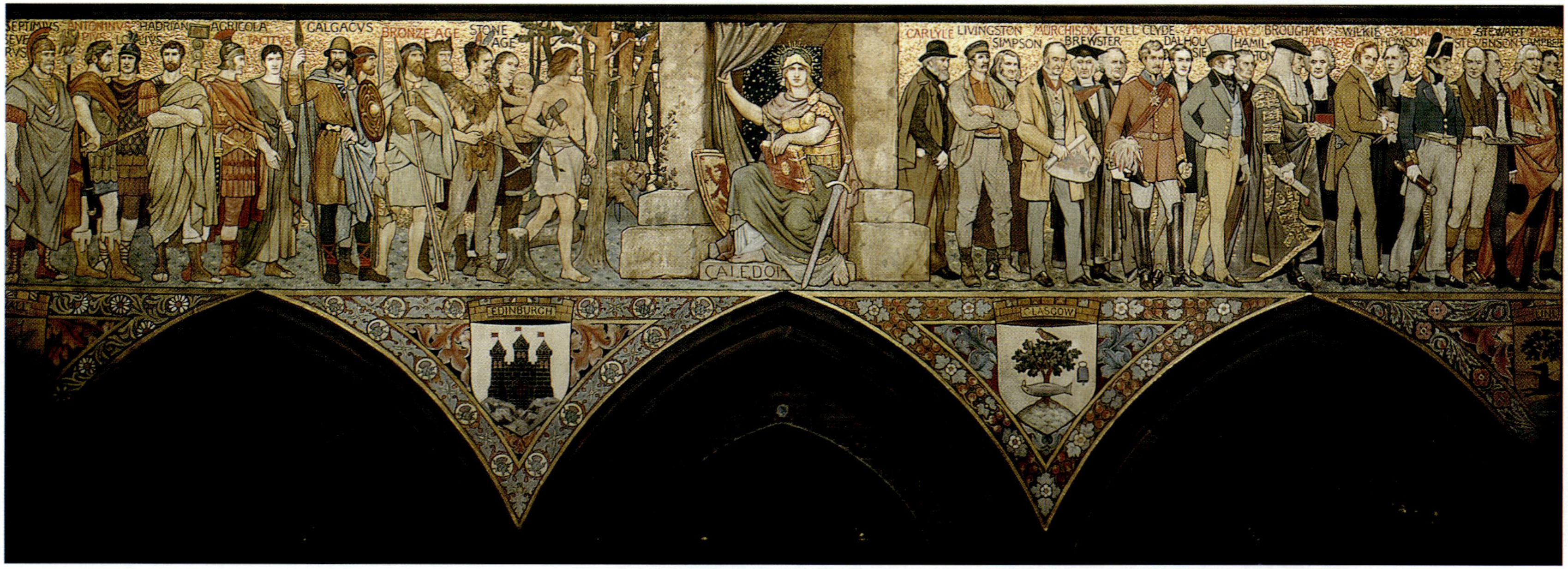

XXXI. William Hole, detail of frieze of Great Scots, Scottish National Portrait Gallery and Museum of Antiquities, Edinburgh, *c.*1898. Edinburgh, Scottish National Portrait Gallery

XXXII (*below, top*). Walter Crane, *Painting*, dome of the Royal West of England Academy, Bristol, *c.*1911–13

XXXIII (*below, bottom*). Louis Ginnett, *Excavation of Hollingbury Camp*, Brighton, Hove and Sussex Grammar School (now Brighton, Hove and Sussex Sixth Form College), Hove, 1939

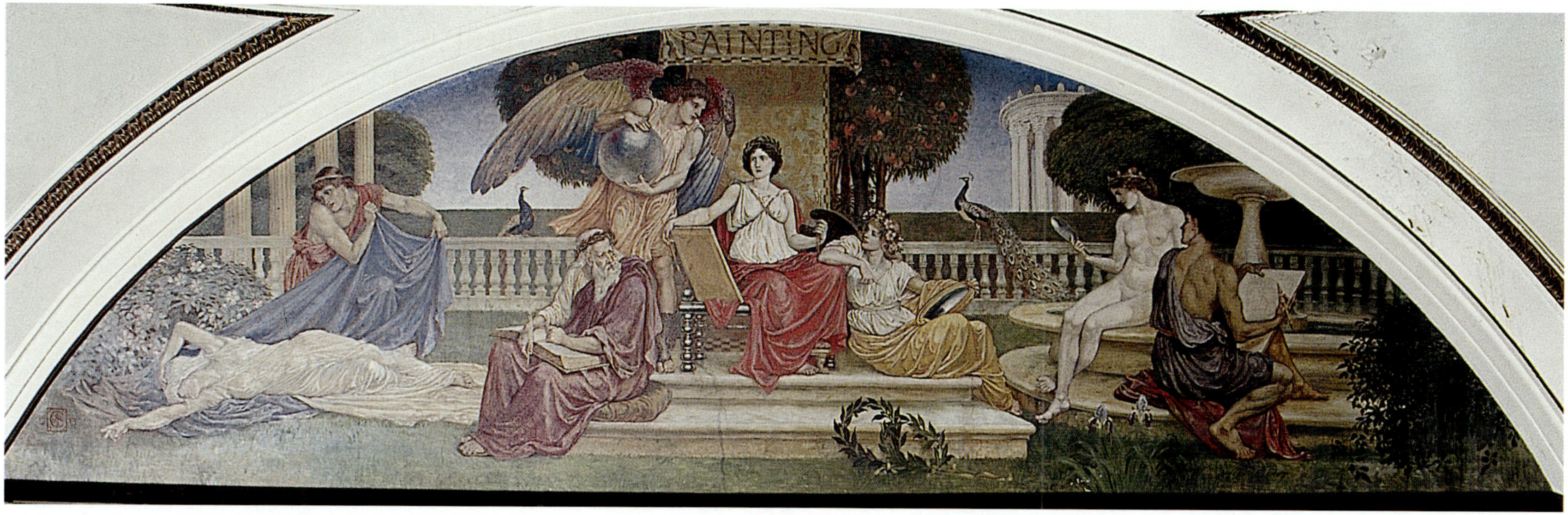
PAINTING

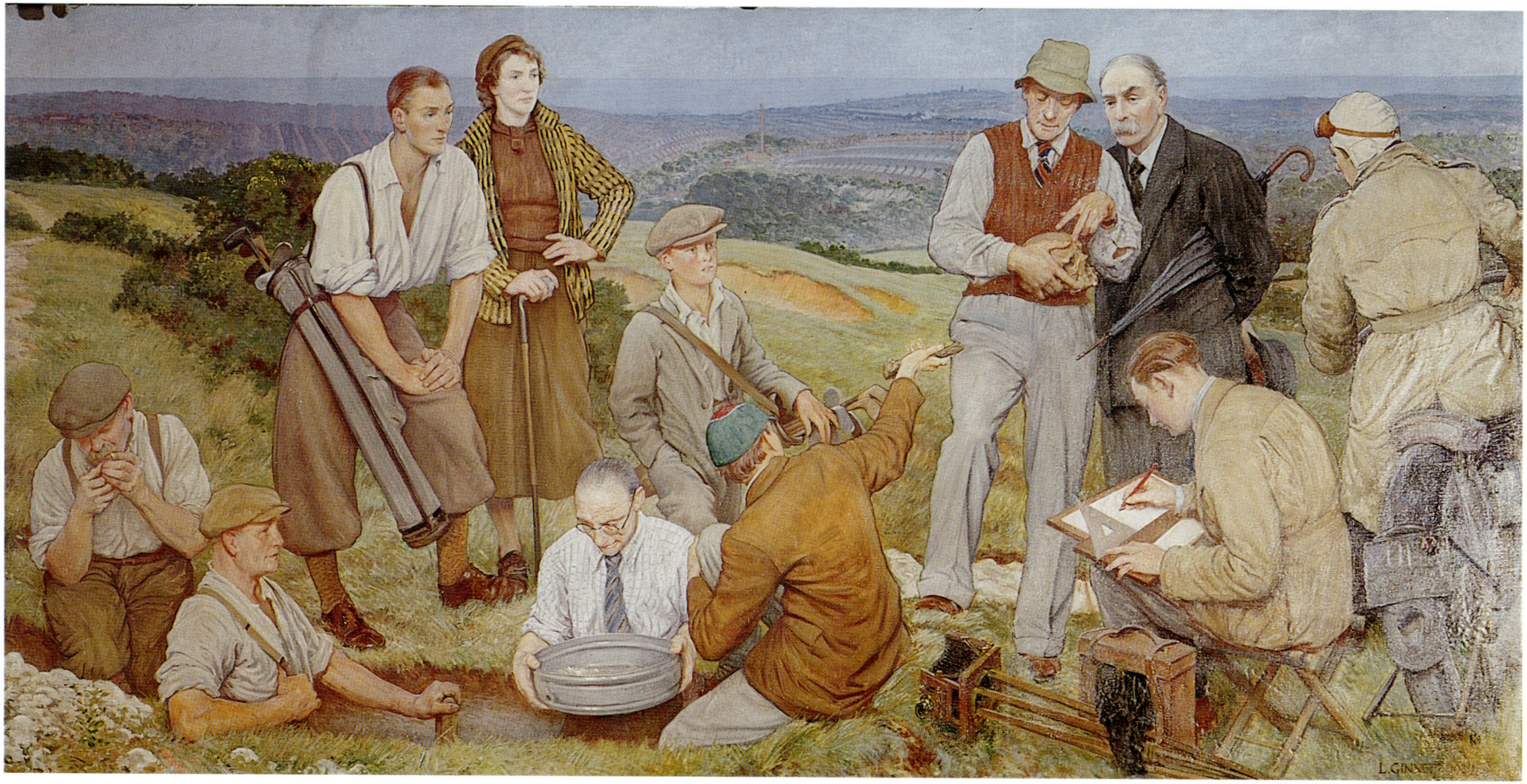

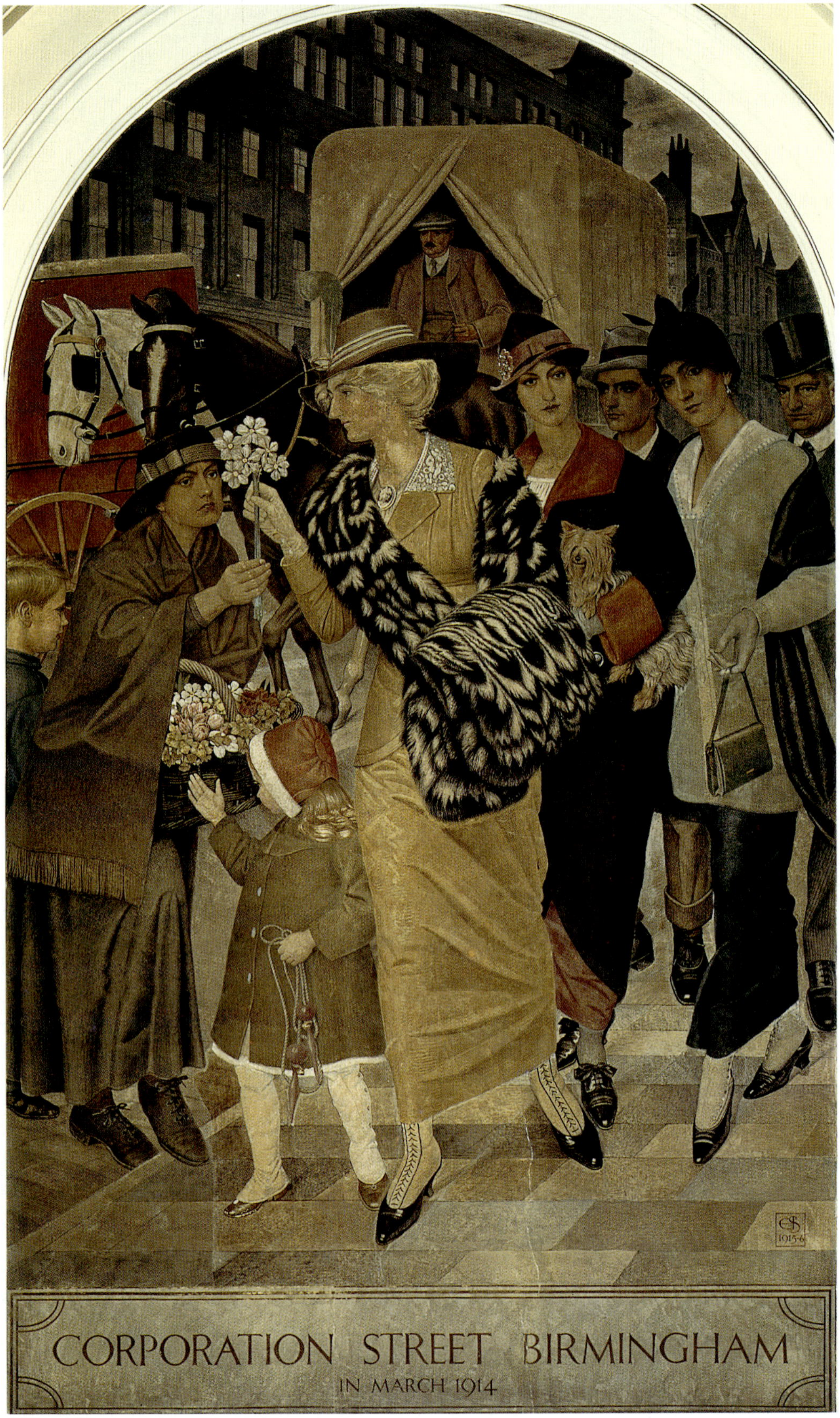

XXXIV. Joseph Southall, *Corporation Street, Birmingham in March 1914*, Museum and Art Gallery, Birmingham, 1914

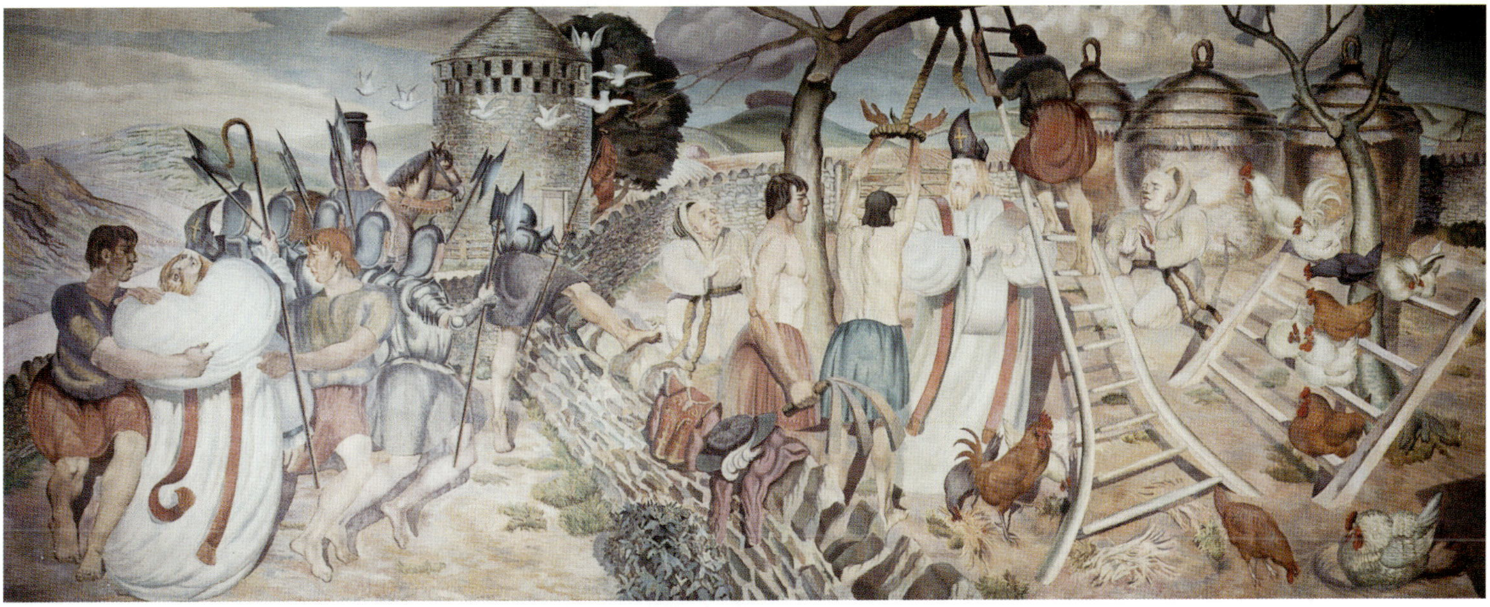

XXXV. Gilbert Spencer, detail from *The Legend of John Balliol*, Holywell Manor, Balliol College, Oxford, 1934–6

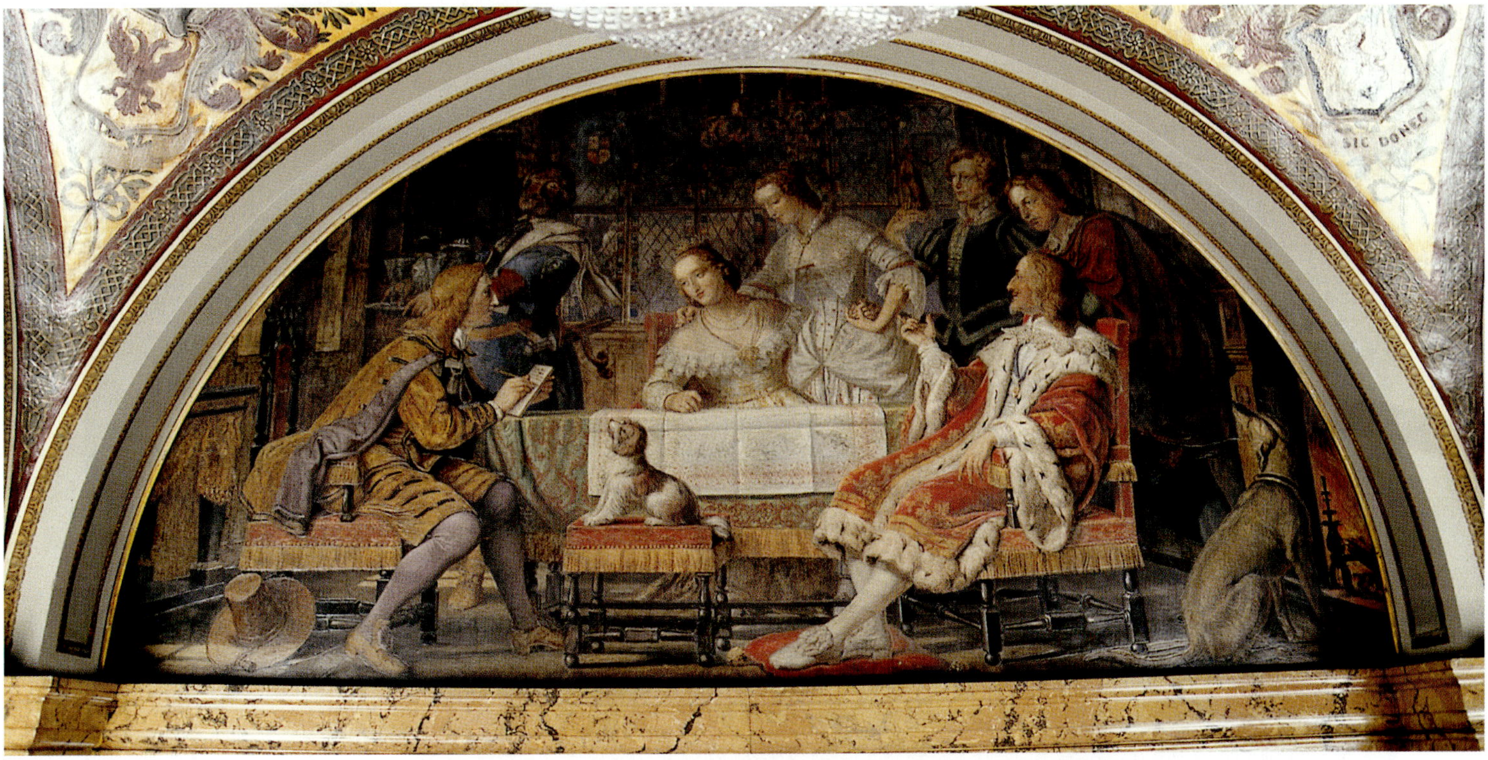

XXXVI. Jakob Götzenberger, *Milton composing Comus in the company of the Duke of Bridgewater and his family*, Bridgewater House, London, *c.*1857–early 1860s

XXXVII. William Burges, completed by Charles Campbell, detail from *The Parliament of Fowls* (Chaucer), Clock Tower, Cardiff Castle, 1889

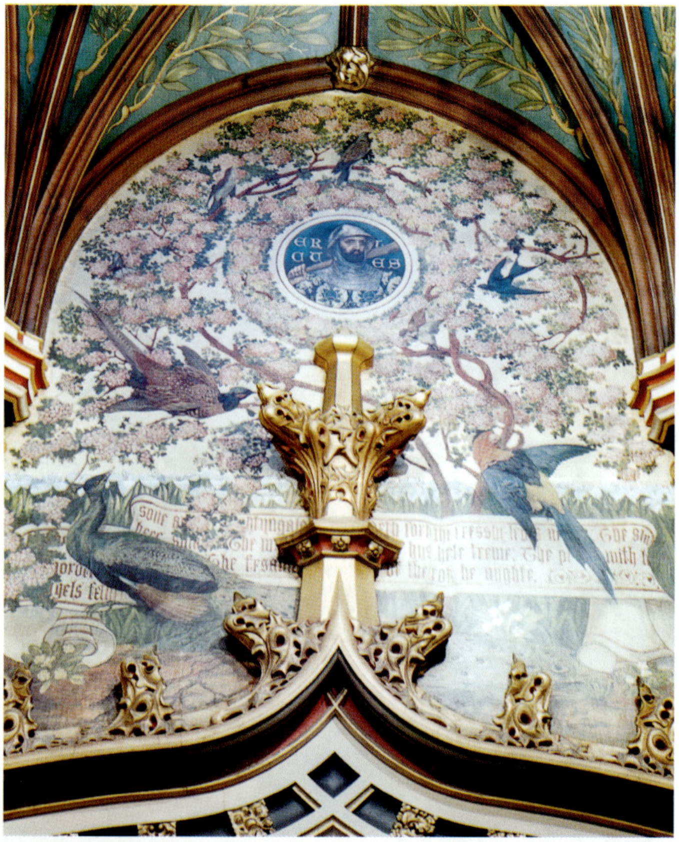

XXXVIII. Frederick Weekes, detail showing *Summer* from frieze in the Old Dining Room, Insole Court, Cardiff, *c.*1878

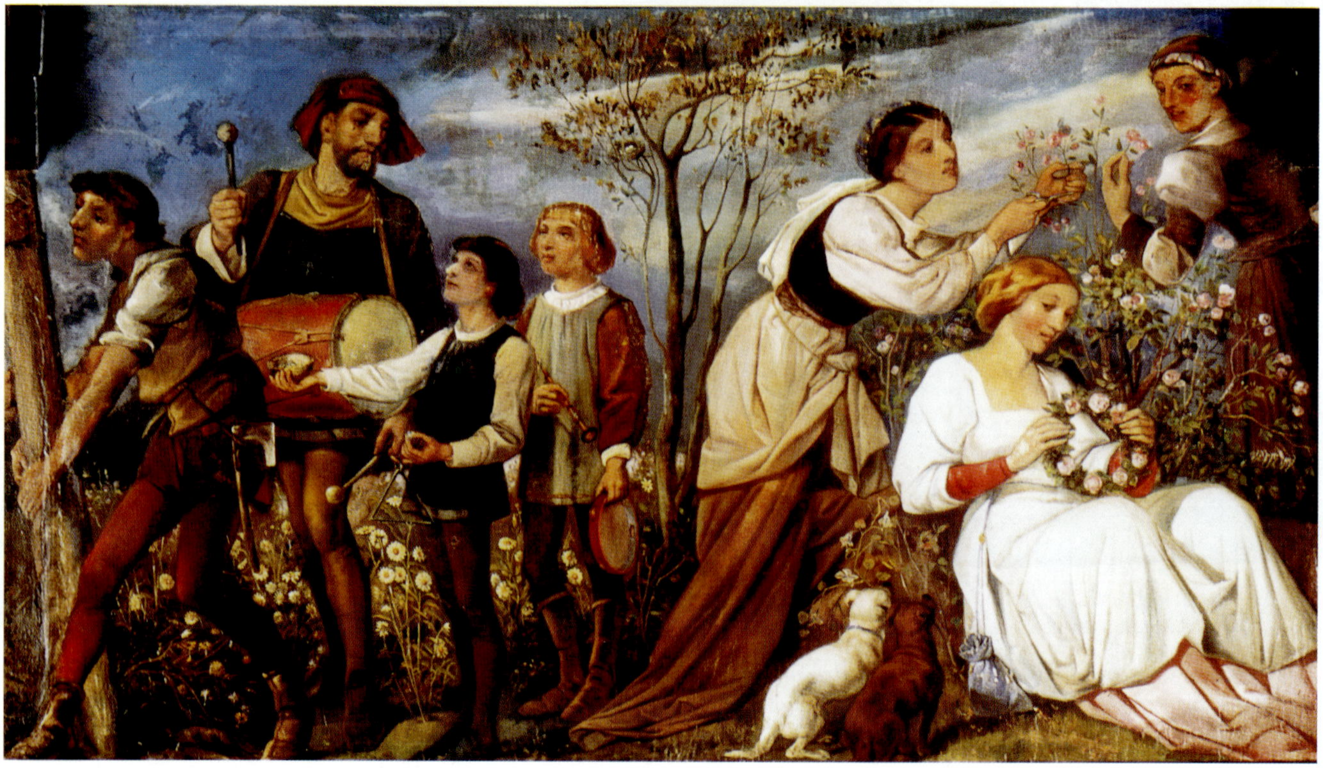

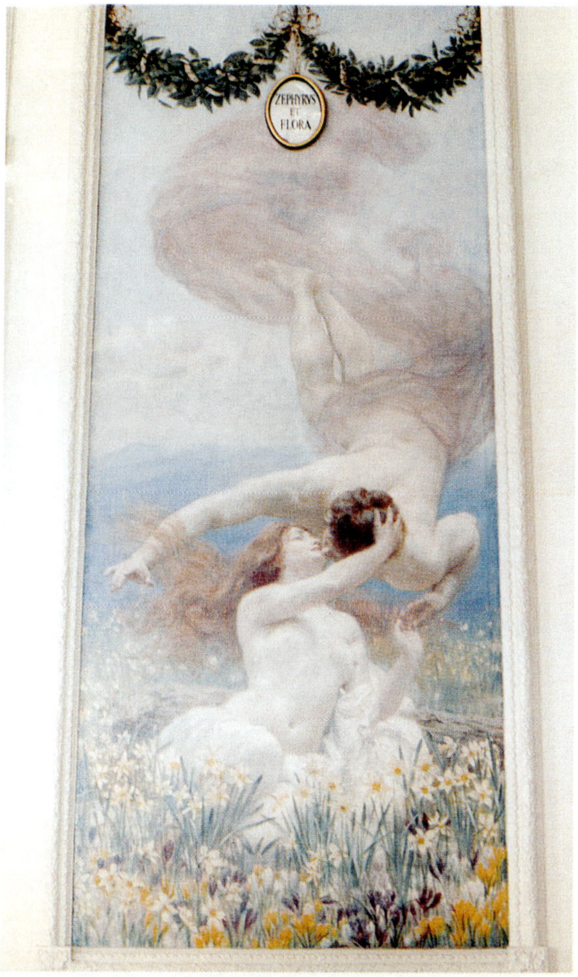

XXXIX. Sigismund Goetze, *Zephyrus et Flora*, Grove House, Regent's Park, London, 1909–13

XL. Sir Frank Brangwyn, *Blacksmiths*, originally part of the decoration of the British Room at the Venice Biennale of 1905; subsequently installed as part of an ensemble at Leeds City Art Gallery

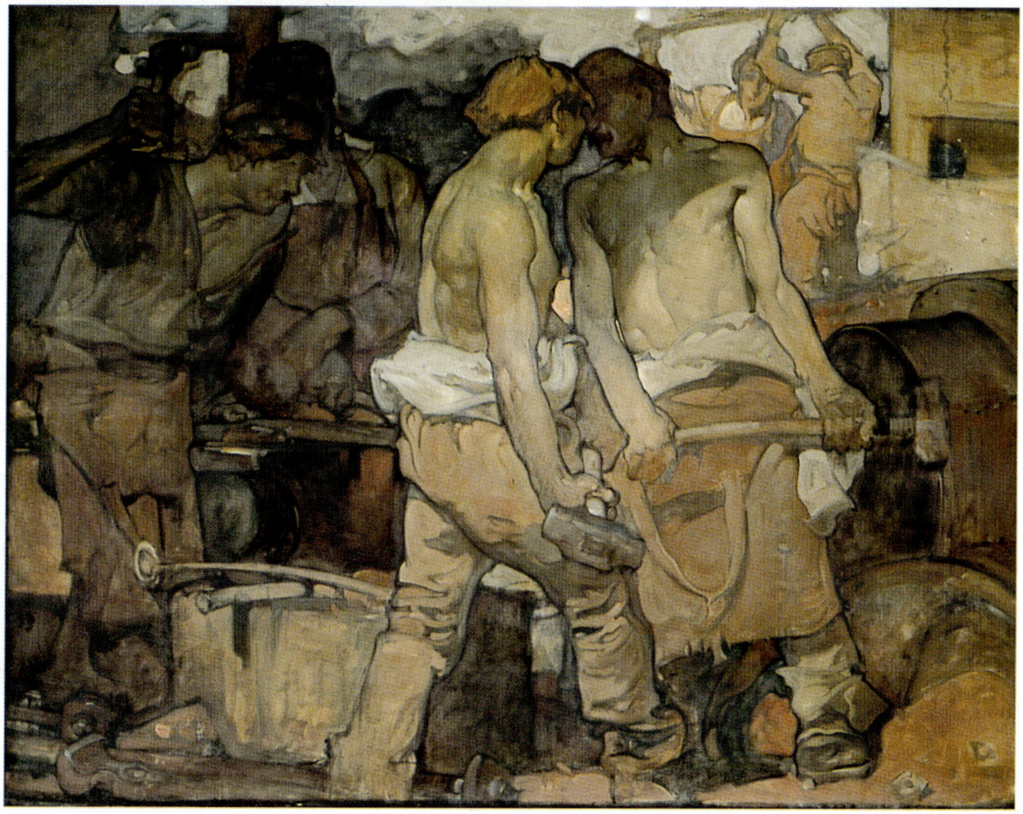

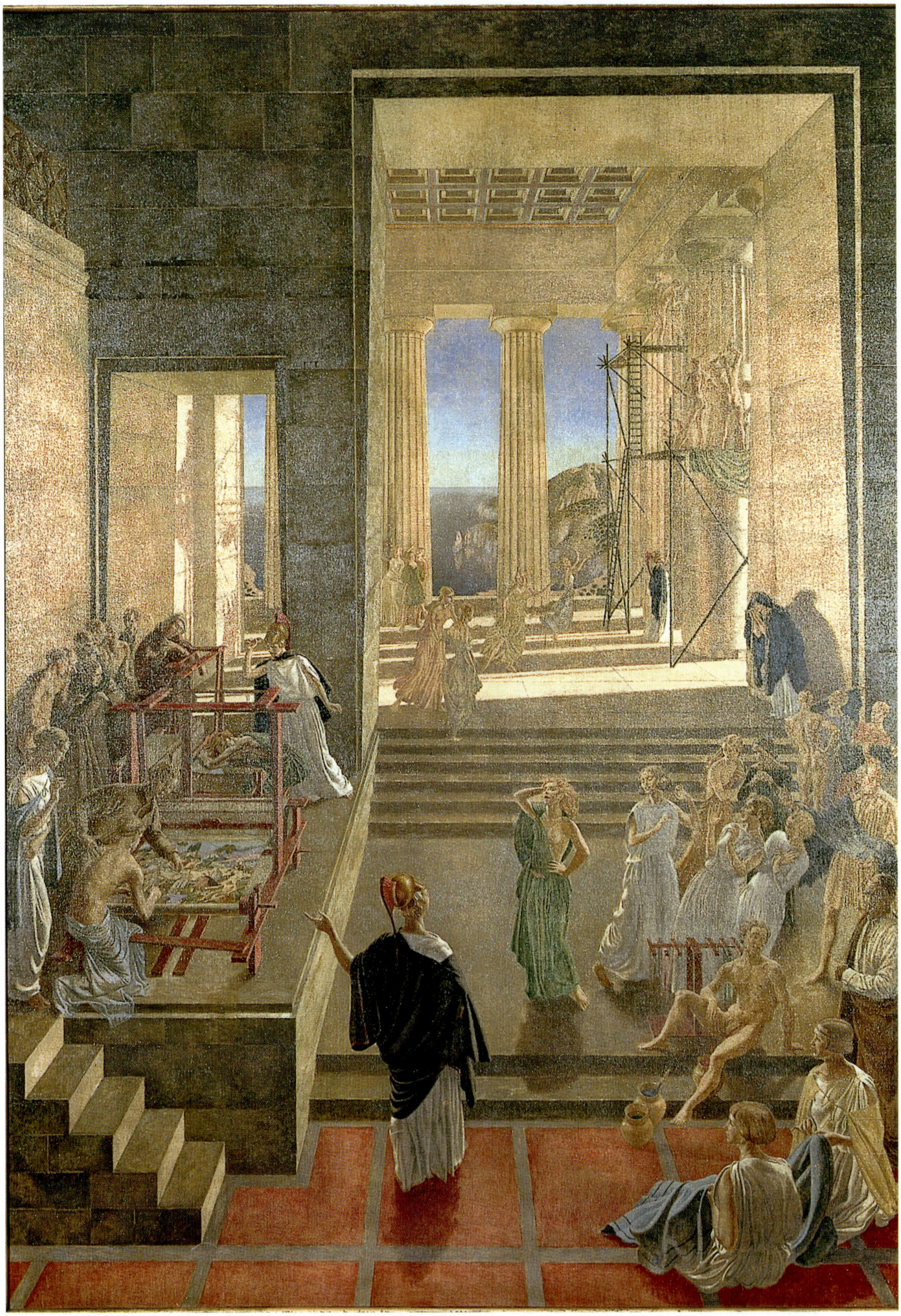

XLI. Edward I. Halliday, *Athena and Arachne*, 1929, Athenaeum, Liverpool

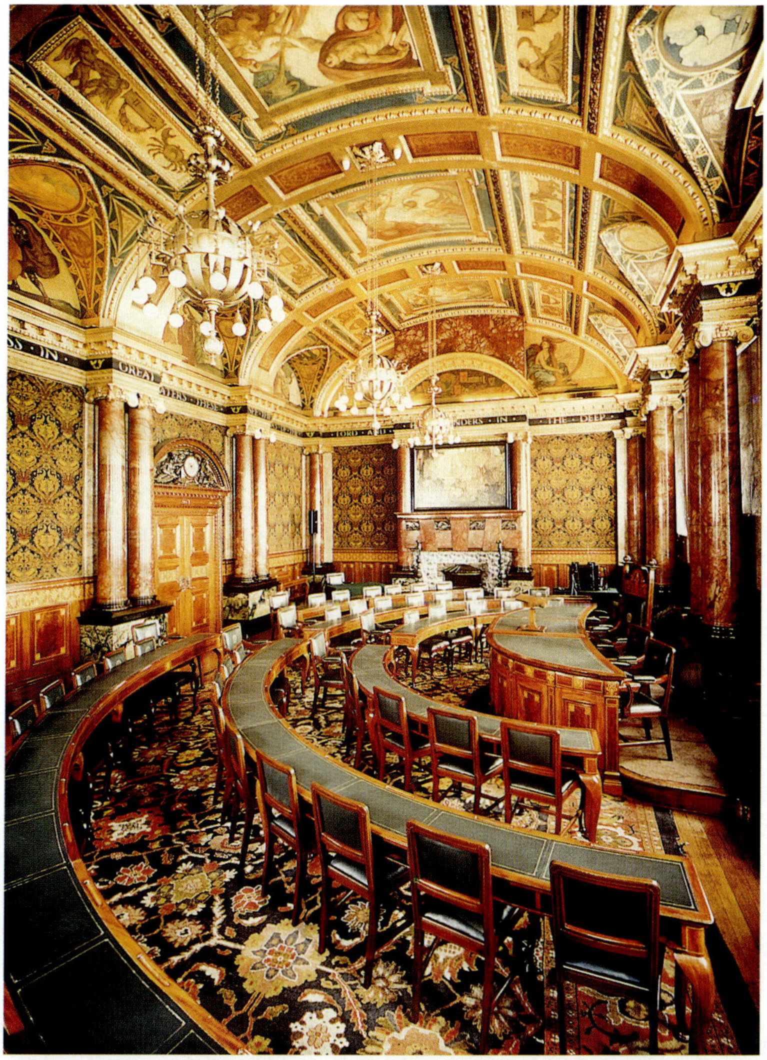

XLII. Gerald Moira, ceiling decoration illustrating *The Elements, Seasons, Winds*, and *Zodiac*, Board Room, Lloyd's Register of Shipping, London, 1902

XLIII. Frederick Spencer Gore, study for mural showing tiger-hunting in the Cave of the Golden Calf, 3–9 Heddon Street, London, 1912. London, Tate Gallery

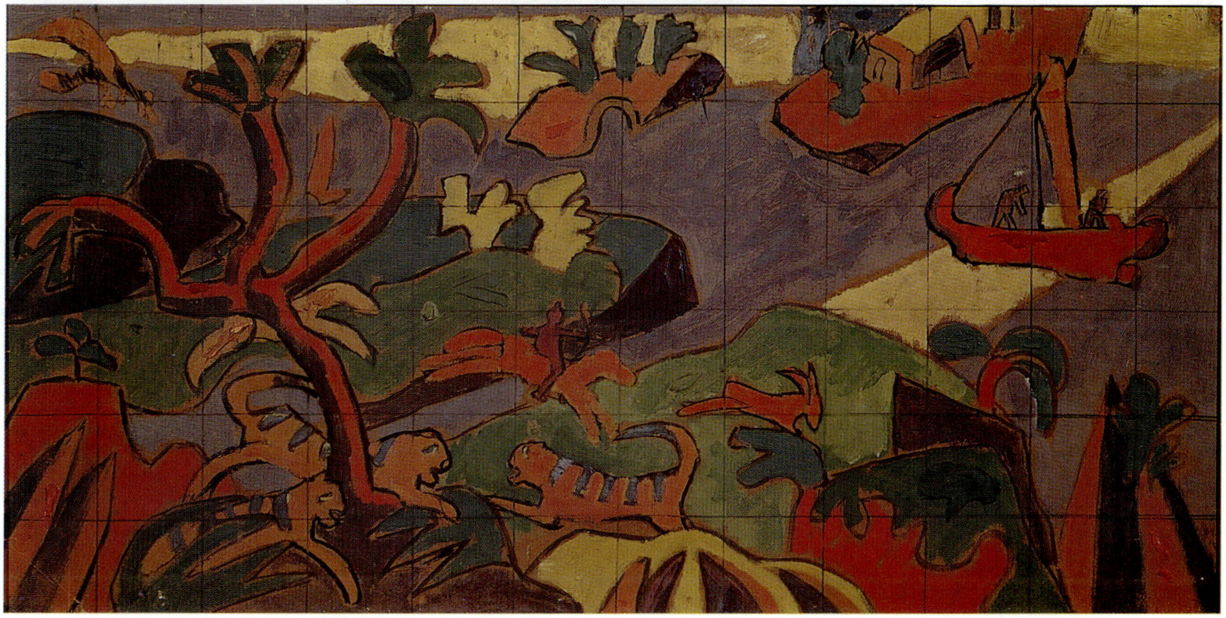

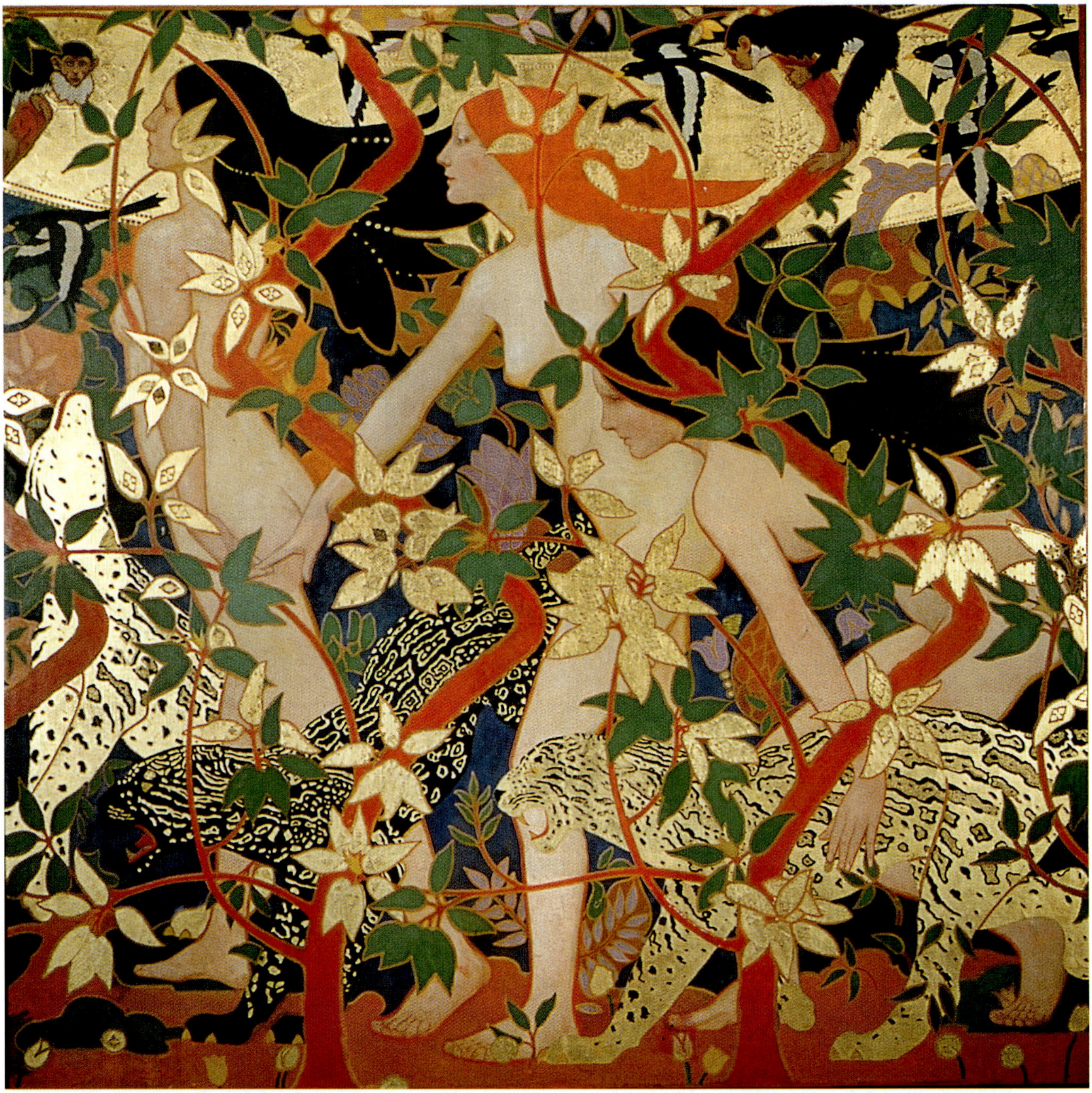

XLIV. Robert Burns, *Diana and her Nymphs*, formerly Crawford's Tearoom, Princes Street, Edinburgh, *c.* 1926. Edinburgh, National Gallery of Scotland

201), set before St Paul's Cathedral (St Paul being the City's patron saint) and above the inscription 'Poise the Cause in Justice Equal Scales.'

Moira's frieze arrangement of the figures in *Justice* contrasts sharply with Watts's tiers, however, and points to wider preoccupations than the merely political. Those who pay tribute to the blindfolded personification of Justice stand in partnership as 'equals', including the Lord Mayor, the Archbishop of Canterbury, Lord Roberts, Cardinal Newman, and the Chief Rabbi, as well as an Indian prince, a private soldier, a 'stalwart blacksmith',[25] and a mother and children. The last four are the modern-day equivalents of the 'Plebs' included in *Roman Law.* Alfred in *English Law* sits amongst his subjects before Stonehenge, Moses is amongst the Israelites before Mount Sinai in *Mosaic Law.* Richmond's *Golden Age*, a pastoral idyll showing nudes dancing to pan pipes in a cornfield before laws were needed, suggests the kind of imagery beloved of his father, George Richmond, and early friends, Samuel Palmer and John Linnell, and would have continued the theme.[26] Such 'equality', cutting across time, place, and peoples, complements the concerns at the Royal Exchange and in Lloyd's Register to show the historical continuity of the City and its institutions, and its role at the 'heart of Empire', but also, of course, echoes Brangwyn's ideal of universal brotherhood. Moira's inspiration from Brangwyn's colouristic, curvilinear style is clearly evident. At a personal level, however, the theme of 'equality' projects Richmond's ideal of partnership between art and architecture. All Moira's murals are believed to have included his self-portrait, whilst architecture is present in 'natural', 'ancient', and 'City' forms (Mount Sinai, Stonehenge, and St Paul's). It is easy to see why the Arts and Crafts adherent Anning Bell gave special mention to the Old Bailey murals in the catalogue for the 1914 Paris Decorative Arts Exhibition, at which the preparatory sketches were shown.[27]

Although Moira's work is bland compared with Brangwyn's, its monumental style and bold orange, warm red, and turquoise colour scheme is effective in the context of Mountford's grandiose Beaux-Arts architecture. No other major Edwardian Baroque building perhaps achieved comparable symbolic unity or artistic integration: schemes by Clausen for Cardiff City Hall and Sir Aston Webb's Victoria and Albert Museum extension were abortive; those at Belfast City Hall were abandoned and revived only in 1951. George Murray's 1913–14 allegorical murals at the Institute of Chartered Accountants (Appendix E: 1) were not part of its original neo-Baroque design by John Belcher, who believed that 'painting . . . must be content to subserve the purposes of the architect,'[28] and their somewhat emasculated grand manner offers rather too studied a harmony with the pale stone building. Murray's allegorical scheme at the Commercial Union in Norwich is more successful. It was again Brangwyn, working with Webb at his new Canadian Grand Trunk Railway in Cockspur Street in London between 1908 and 1910, who created what must have been one of the most splendid cooperative schemes in any building during the century from 1840. Now detached,[29] the concentrated effect of his narrow tempera frieze (Plate 202) of

[25] J. H. Watkins, *The Art of Gerald Moira* (1922), p. 23.

[26] See illustration of the *Golden Age* cartoon in E. W. Mountford, 'The New Sessions House, London', *Architectural Review* (1907), p. 139.

[27] R. A. Bell, 'La Peinture Murale' in catalogue for the International Exhibition of Decorative Arts, Paris 1914, p. xxxviii; four studies by Moira for the Old Bailey murals were exhibited (items 1091–4). The same mention appears in R. A. Bell, 'Mural Decoration' (1913), p. xxxiv.

[28] J. Belcher, *Essentials in Architecture. An Analysis of the Principles and Qualities to be looked for in Buildings* (London, 1907), p. 103. Murray, along with W. J. Neatby, also painted allegorical decorations representing the 'thread of life' and the Muses in 1908 in Skipper's 'Edwardian Baroque' Norwich Union Life Assurance Offices in Norwich (see *Celebrating Skipper 100*, p. 9, a booklet kindly supplied by Norwich Union).

[29] The frieze is now in the collection of the Department of Public Works, Canada, and is installed in the Conference Centre, Ottawa.

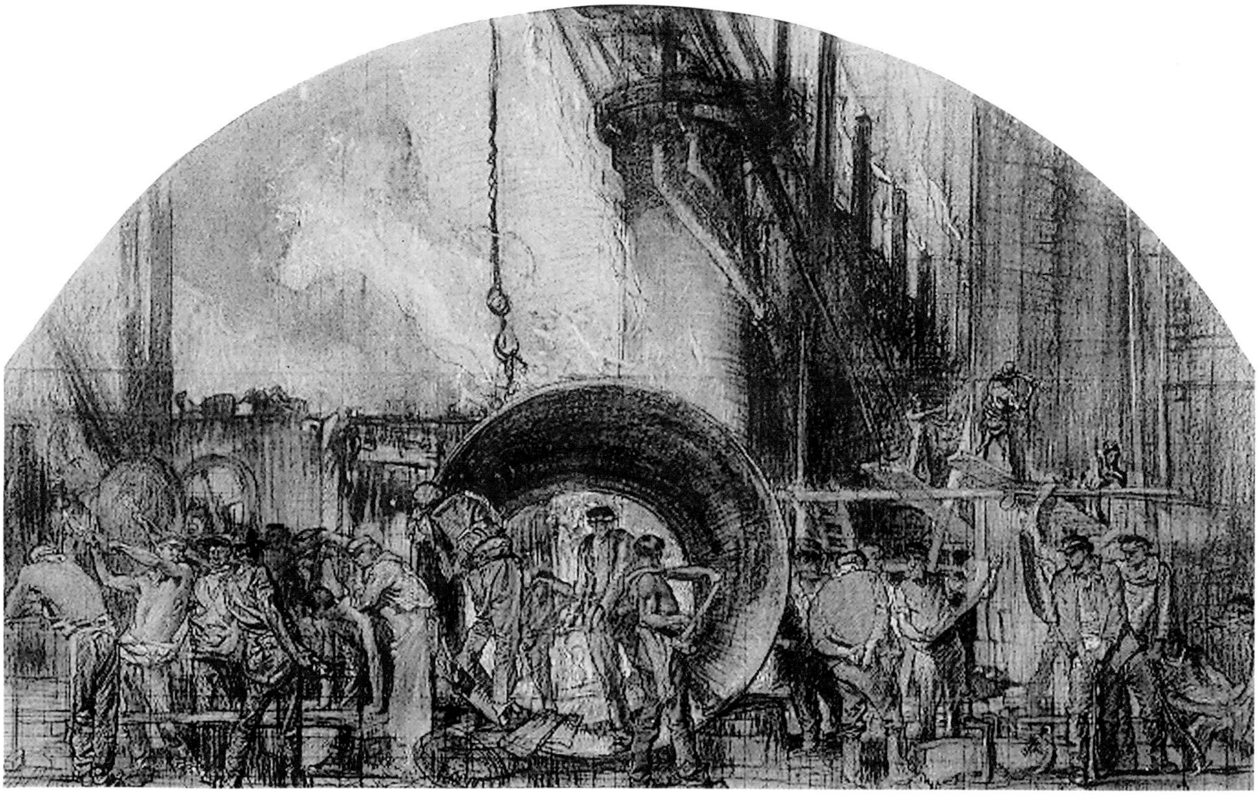

200. Sir Frank Brangwyn, cartoon showing *Dockside Labour* for lunette formerly in the Luncheon Room, Lloyd's Register of Shipping, London, *c.*1908. London, Lloyd's Register of Shipping

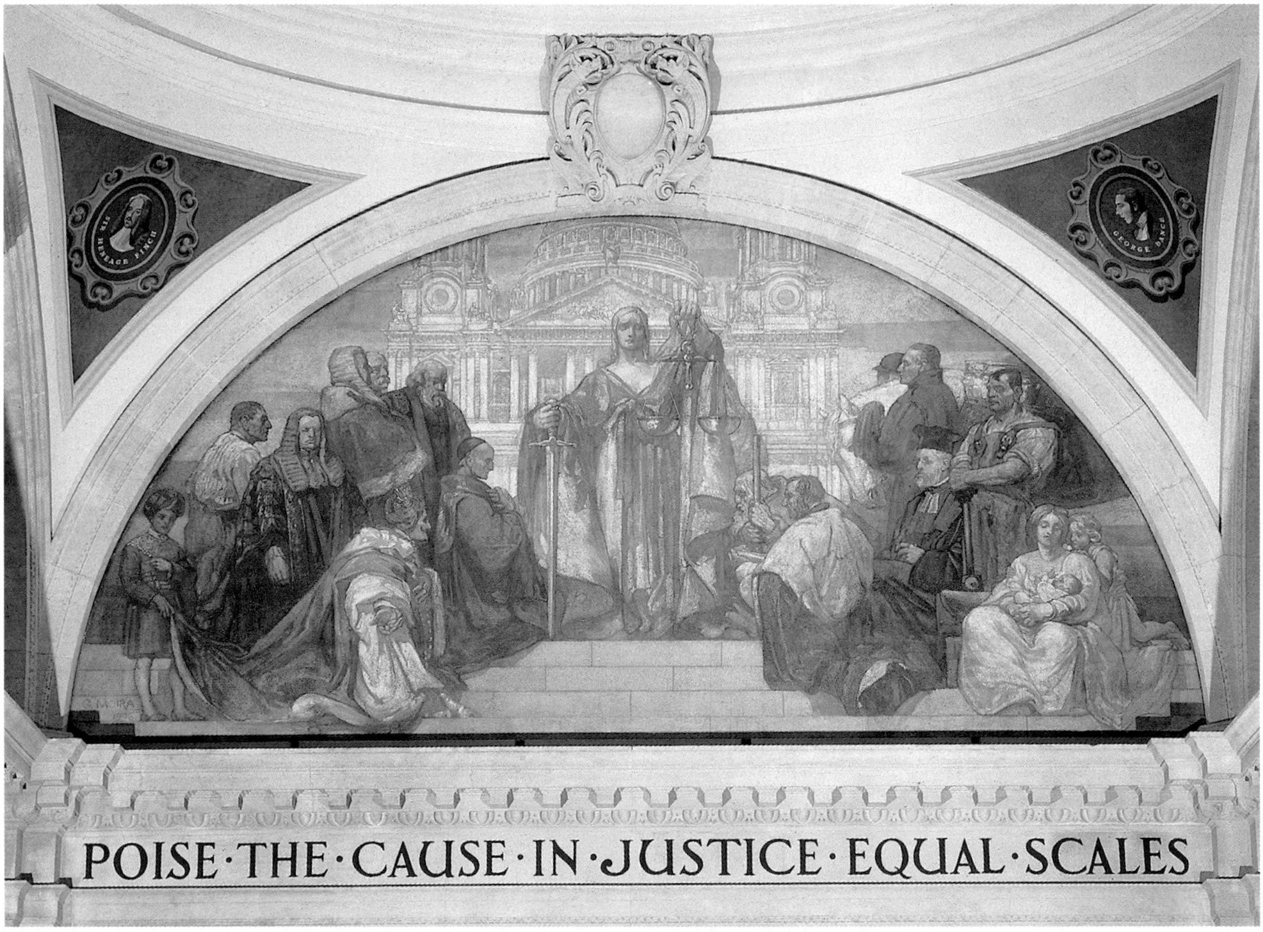

201. Gerald Moira, *Poise the Cause in Justice Equal Scales*, Old Bailey, London, *c.*1904–8

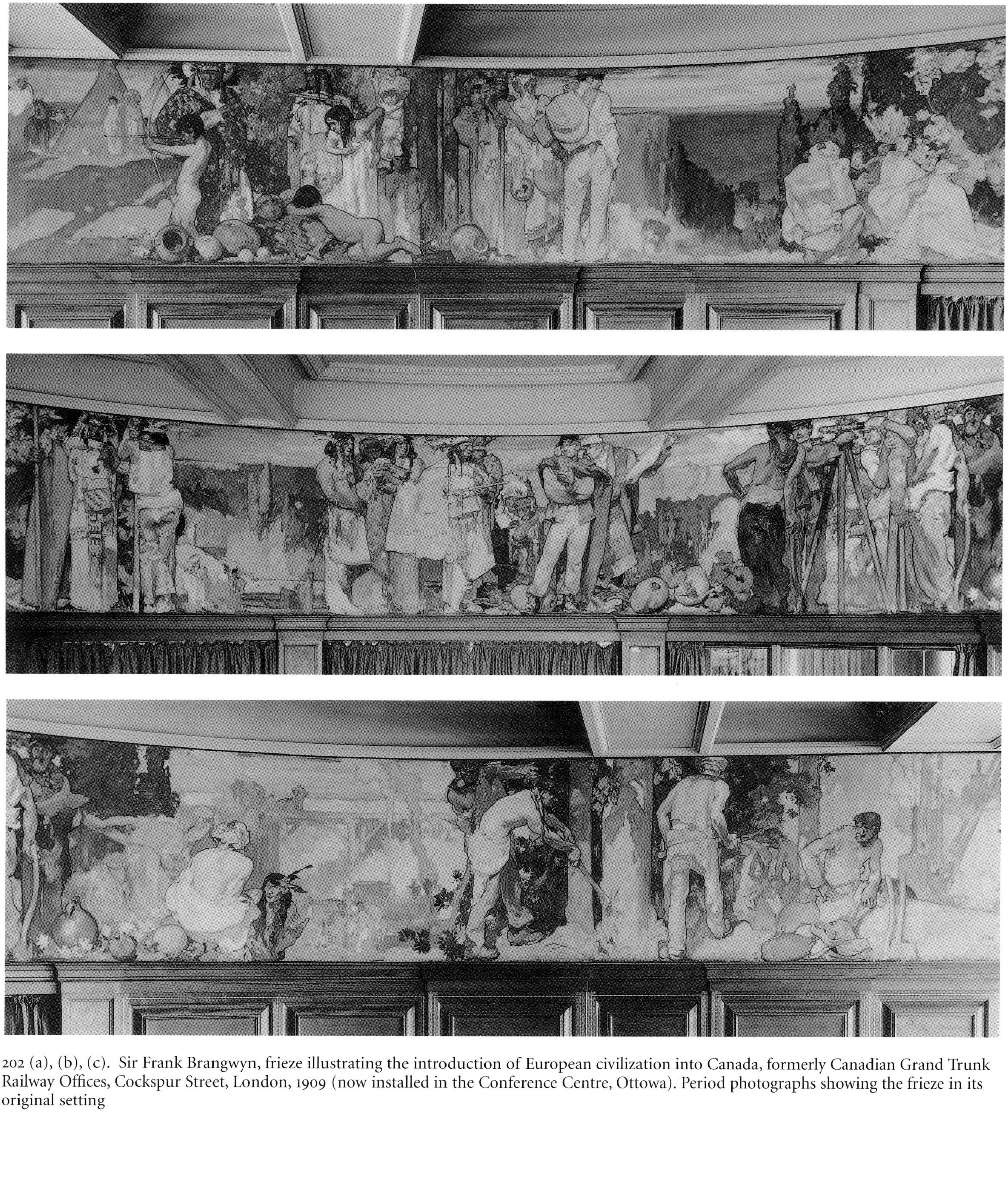

202 (a), (b), (c). Sir Frank Brangwyn, frieze illustrating the introduction of European civilization into Canada, formerly Canadian Grand Trunk Railway Offices, Cockspur Street, London, 1909 (now installed in the Conference Centre, Ottowa). Period photographs showing the frieze in its original setting

'brilliant' and 'telling colour' above the sober 'warm brown'[30] wood panelling can only be imagined. Its vigorous style, reflecting Brangwyn's admiration for Jordaens and Rubens, and so profoundly different from his fellow tempera revivalist Southall's, would have found its nearest affinities with Continental exponents of the integration of art and architecture, such as Mucha or Van de Velde. Although the *Studio* described the theme as the 'triumph of science and modern civilisation over the rude forces of nature and barbarism',[31] Brangwyn's illustration of the landscapes and peoples of the nation served by his patrons can be recognized as actually far more subtle, constituting a trial run for imagery (such as the theodolite and viaduct motifs) and the theme of native enjoyment of the fruits of Empire, which would be developed in his Royal Gallery scheme. Red Indians in feathered costumes coexist peacefully with white settlers felling trees and land-surveying; the panoramic backdrop landscape, suggesting the span from Pacific to Atlantic traversed by the Grand Trunk route, affords only distant glimpses of a train and industrial chimneys. The point of encounter at the centre of the frieze between white settlers and natives deals with a treaty (a paper scroll) and has the natives in the majority.

Conflict or tension would, of course, have been an unpalatable element in a decoration intended in part to entice the public to use the Grand Trunk Railway, and a number of details show that Brangwyn was already master of the kind of subliminal message associated with today's advertising. The native child at the far left shoots an arrow beyond the mural's frame, continuing the onward horizontal drive set up by the viaduct, theodolite, and a pointing settler, and thereby suggesting the very journey of the Grand Trunk railway traveller—swift as an arrow, yet into the unknown. Another child sleeps upon a heap of fruit, evoking comfort and sensual pleasure. To read the scheme as mere promotional propaganda, however, would be to overlook Brangwyn's recurrent personal philosophy of brotherhood; one of the Indians in negotiation with the settlers is derived from a figure in the mural of *Harmony* at Skinners' Hall. Just as the settlers felling a tree provide a symbolic link with Webb's wood panelling, so the ultimate logic of this brotherhood would have lain, as at Skinners' Hall, in its function as decoration, linking painting with architecture to invest a place of work with inner meaning.

Although the *Studio* predicted that the Grand Trunk Railway scheme 'should cause the setting-in of a fashion that may have wide-ranging results . . . [and] bring dignity and beauty into that heretofore home of hideousness, the city office,'[32] the First World War cruelly frustrated such expectation. The Palatine Bank in Manchester had been adorned around 1910 with large lunettes[33] and Crosse and Blackwell offered their jam factory for decoration in association with the Crosby Hall mural exhibition of 1912, but F. S. Beaumont's murals for Hamburg-Amerika Line's (latterly P & O's) offices (Appendix E: 2) appear to have been one of only a handful of commissions until the late 1920s (Appendix E: 6, 7). When, under the presidency of Sir Aston Webb himself, the Royal Academy mounted its Exhibition of Decorative Art in 1923, the majority of the schemes for business premises which were represented were clearly either speculative or in abeyance (Appendix E: 3–5).

The murals at the Bank of England, begun in the late 1920s and completed in 1937 (Plates 203–6), were the most significant business scheme of this period, and mark a distinctive move away

[30] Anon., 'Mr. Brangwyn's Tempera Frieze at the New London Offices of the Grand Trunk Railway', *Studio*, 48 (1910), pp. 42, 34.

[31] Ibid., p. 33.

[32] Ibid., pp. 32–3.

[33] Artist unknown; they showed 'shipping, trading and the arts' and are visible in a photograph of the Bank's Hall in the *Architects' and Builders' Journal* (5 Oct. 1910), p. 347.

from the historical iconography of their immediate precedent, the St Stephen's Hall work at the Palace of Westminster. With the exception of Francis Dodd, Sir James Guthrie, and Sir Walter Russell, all the Bank's artists—Colin Gill, A. K. Lawrence, Sir William Rothenstein, Sir George Clausen, Glyn Philpot, and Vivian Forbes—were recruited from the British School at Rome team at St Stephen's Hall, and as they had been there, they were supervised by Sir David ('D. Y.') Cameron.[34] This emulation of a State scheme can be read as a bid on the part of the Bank to project its increasingly significant national and international role, but the decoration also asserted the Bank's traditionally private identity.

The origins of the Bank lay in 'a meeting of City merchants at a private house'.[35] Its premises, newly remodelled and enlarged by Sir Herbert Baker, were accordingly, in the mind of its Director, Montagu Norman, a place where the intimate image of familiar faces should appear; what he called 'the Bank in Being'.[36] Although Baker suggested 'financial activities in English history'[37] for the larger murals, Norman thus insisted that the decoration should show

> personnel of the Bank, their work and surroundings during the after period of the War to the time of rebuilding, including the late Governor and the present Governor, and ranging from Directors and Chief Officials down to Workmen, Porters and Guards, in groups representing their habitual occupations and services in the Bank.[38]

Baker's brief as architect had been 'to preserve continuity in change—a sense of permanence in progress',[39] and in turn a related theme, not dissimilar to that of 'growth'[40] in the 'Building of Britain' at St Stephen's Hall, can be recognized in 'the Bank in Being'. Norman believed fervently that 'in a world left impoverished after the war the Bank might do something towards the healing of nations through the beneficial use of finance.'[41] Those portrayed in the murals were, of course, the agents of such 'healing'. Lord Cunliffe, for example, the 'late Governor' portrayed by Francis Dodd in one of the sequence of individual portraits in the smaller panels of the scheme, had chaired the important committee appointed in 1918 by the Government to advise on the resolution of the currency and foreign exchange crisis at the close of the war. The murals were in turn placed in the very 'rooms where the Governor works and his Directors assemble in council' in Baker's new 'Governor's House'.[42]

Dodd was told, however, to 'lessen the significance of Lord Cunliffe's heavy feet' on completion of his mural,[43] and just as Baker's massive classical architecture was a decidedly grand interpretation of the Bank's 'traditional character of a private and not a Government institution',[44] so attempts were made by Baker and Cameron to temper and adjust the 'realism' in the murals to ensure decorative harmony. The scheme was, in fact, the first major opportunity for the British School at Rome's collaborative principles to be put into action, and as such, the direct heir to the

[34] Guthrie died before his two panels (individual portraits) could be completed and neither Philpot nor Forbes in the event contributed, although it was originally planned that they should undertake five individual portraits between them. See correspondence in BEA.

[35] H. Baker, *Architecture and Personalities* (London, 1944), p. 123.

[36] Period typescript description of the plans for the murals in BEA; see also Baker, *Architecture and Personalities* p. 128.

[37] Ibid.

[38] Period typescript, BEA.

[39] Baker, *Architecture and Personalities*, p. 123.

[40] H. Newbolt, *The Building of Britain* (n.d.), p. 4.

[41] Baker, *Architecture and Personalities*, p. 124.

[42] Ibid., pp. 123, 128. Individual portraits were placed in the ground floor ante-room and Governor's Suite, and subjects involving group portraiture in the first-floor ante-room to the Court Room. 'Marble medium', a wax-based medium, was chosen, although the murals were not executed *in situ* (Memo of meeting of the artists at Baker's office, *c.*1928 (n.d.), BEA.

[43] Letter from Baker to 'Alexander' (?A.V. Alexander, Deputy Secretary of the Bank) (22 April 1932), BEA.

[44] Baker, *Architecture and Personalities*, p. 123.

attempt at partnership between artists and architect at the Old Bailey. The School's founder members in 1914 had included Sir William Richmond and in 1922 it had adopted 'associative work' and 'the collaboration of students of the various Faculties'—ideals proposed by Colin Gill and W. T. Monnington, who were to be major contributors at the Bank—as essential parts of its Scholarship syllabus.[45] Built by a leading member of the British School at Rome Faculty of Architecture (Baker), the Bank of England included not only the murals but also Charles Wheeler's allegorical exterior sculpture and Boris Anrep's floor mosaics.

Reconciling unity with contemporaneity, however, presented problems. Dodd informed Baker that 'as my panel was completed first the "Essential Harmony" you speak of is the affair of the painter of the second picture.'[46] Monnington, his wife reported, was 'worried about the trousers in his pictures he does not know whether to have them all the same shade of grey, or different in tone'.[47] Following an unsuccessful preview at the Royal Academy in 1932 of the murals completed so far, when Frank Rutter condemned them as being 'dull as ditchwater',[48] Cameron complained to Baker in 1933 of 'this extraordinarily difficult work',[49] even though a former chapel was kitted out with the Bank's internal 'architectural features properly in scale and painted in with the walls'[50] to enable Gill, Lawrence, and Monnington (the principal artists) to work side by side. Even as the scheme approached completion in 1936, however, Cameron told Baker ' "St. Stephen's Hall" was a very simple matter compared with this and the subjects creat[?ed] some scope for colour—not being dry and often ugly facts, but imaginings.'[51]

In a sense, it was perhaps the very quest for unity as much as the modern iconography which stifled 'imaginings', though the murals are by no means as uniformly uninspired as Cameron and Rutter implied. The plainness of the subdued classical décor in Monnington's *Director announcing the Bank Rate to the Chief Officials*, so obviously intended to cohere in its terracotta and pale green colour scheme and red carpeted floor with Lawrence's *Committee of Treasury* and Baker's domestic 'Governor's House', simply exaggerates the banality of its sitters' city suits and the self-consciousness of their static, architectonic poses. Clausen's portrait of W. H. Clegg (Plate 203), a tall, sober businessman bearing a sheaf of papers in the doorway of one of the Bank's corridors, is a more subtle and successful attempt to project Norman's notion of the 'Bank in Being'. Silhouetted against a partially receding vista of classical columns, the slim individual with piercing eyes seems almost interchangeable with their severe vertical accents, personifying the rigour and reliability of the Bank as if himself a pillar of its work. The shadowed threshold contrasted with pale fluted columns, with a shaft of daylight suggestively brightening the distantly viewed Bank interior, would have acted, like the subdued orange and turquoise carpet on which Clegg stands, as a continuation of the real space of the Governor's House. Placed at the forefront of the mural, the painted Clegg would thus have seemed actually to participate in the work of the Bank, whilst offering, as a portrait intended to endure for generations, an iconic link with the future.

Amongst the liveliest of the murals are the lunettes by Gill and Lawrence setting daily Bank routines against backdrops of its historic, rather than remodelled, portions. Gill's three scenes of staff moving or weighing gold (Plate 204)—the substance whose absolute value or 'gold standard'

45 Letter from the Rome Scholars appended to Minutes of Faculty of Painting, British School at Rome (17 Oct. 1922), BSRA.

46 Letter from Dodd to Baker (31 May 1933), BEA.

47 Comment of 1930 quoted in J. Egerton, *Sir Thomas Monnington* (1977), p. 10.

48 F. Rutter, 'Bank Rate in Art', *Sunday Times* (1 May 1932).

49 Letter from Cameron to Baker (2 June 1933), BEA.

50 Letter from Baker to Alexander (15 Dec. 1932), BEA.

51 Letter from Cameron to Baker (4 Jan. 1936), BEA.

had been seen by Cunliffe as vital to successful post-war renewal—involve a decorative interplay between the elemental geometry of the Old Bank's squat, round arches and the dark disc shapes of the gold-trolley wheels, giving power to Gill's characteristically angular figure poses derived from his study of early Italian art. Although by the time the mural scheme was complete Britain had actually had to abandon the gold standard, this was believed to be but a temporary measure; Gill's subjects would have presented an ideal which it was hoped might yet be rebuilt. The continuum of past, present, and future is equally suggested by Lawrence's *Old Lothbury Court with Demolition and Rebuilding Commencing on One Side*, in which the Gate Porter, F. W. Clements, clad in his traditional bicorne and red gown, is contrasted with the architect, foreman, and workmen alongside the scaffolding of the new Bank. For his *Old Threadneedle Street Courtyard with the Guard arriving at the Bank* (Plate 205), Lawrence made use not only of photographs, but also the services of a Grenadier Guard, who later recalled how 'During the summer of 1931 . . . in full uniform and Bearskin I travelled by Underground to the studio of Mr. Lawrence . . . and performed a posing session of a guardsman marching (quite a hot afternoon).'[52] Also present in this mural is the artist himself at the right, grasping a bundle of brushes as, alongside Sir D. Y. Cameron and a very youthful Monnington, he contemplates the scene to be painted.

Whilst this documentary emphasis creates the same slightly surreal ambiguity between real, ideal, and represented worlds as Clausen's portrait of *Clegg*, it would also have carried, like the portraits of Baker and his craftsmen and labourers in Lawrence's *Demolition and Rebuilding* lunette and large *Builders* panel (Plate 206), the implication that those who worked in the arts and architecture were partners with the Bank's own staff in the work of 'healing' the post-war world. At a further symbolic level, these murals also suggest the collaborative partnership of art and architecture which Lawrence had joined Baker in advocating at the Royal Academy;[53] *The Builders* had been a title set for the British School at Rome's painting competition of 1926.

So too, if the crisp linear structure of the diagonal machine-shaft, angled white paper in the press, and pointed overhead eaves combine in Monnington's *A Group in the Bank Printing Works at St. Luke's* with the sharp-focused detail of veined working hands and work-creased clothes to suggest a British counterpart to *Neue Sachlichkeit*, or a painted version of the Mass Observation photographs of the late 1930s, then even the very style of decoratively enhanced realism in the Bank murals was perhaps ultimately symbolic, rather than reactionary or anthropological. Monnington's mural, a reminder of the Bank's status from 1928 as the sole note-issuing authority in England and Wales, is as rich in subliminal power and suggestion as Brangwyn's Canadian Grand Trunk Railway scheme or Clausen's inclusion of poignant poppies in his *Harvest* panel of 1918 for High Royd near Huddersfield (Plate 190). For the sharply lit clarity of form and detail in this mural, as in the others at the Bank, is the visual counterpart to the quotation from Demosthenes inscribed by Baker around the dome of the inner vestibule of the Governor's House, where the decorations were placed: 'Truth is the best of all starting points—or foundations—for business.' Rutter may have bemoaned 'facts, facts, facts . . . untouched by a gleam of imagination or a spark of noble feeling' in 'a project of national importance',[54] but such an effect was precisely what the Bank must have sought in the aftermath of war and the rise of the Depression: art to embody 'Trust, Confidence, which breeds Credit'.[55]

[52] Letter from H. Bolton, formerly of 2nd Battalion Grenadier Guards, to Governor of Bank of England (30 July 1985), BEA.

[53] Baker, *Architecture and Personalities*, p. 175.

[54] Rutter, 'Bank Rate in Art'.

[55] Baker, *Architecture and Personalities*, p. 124.

203. Sir George Clausen, *W. H. Clegg*, Bank of England, London, *c.*1928–37

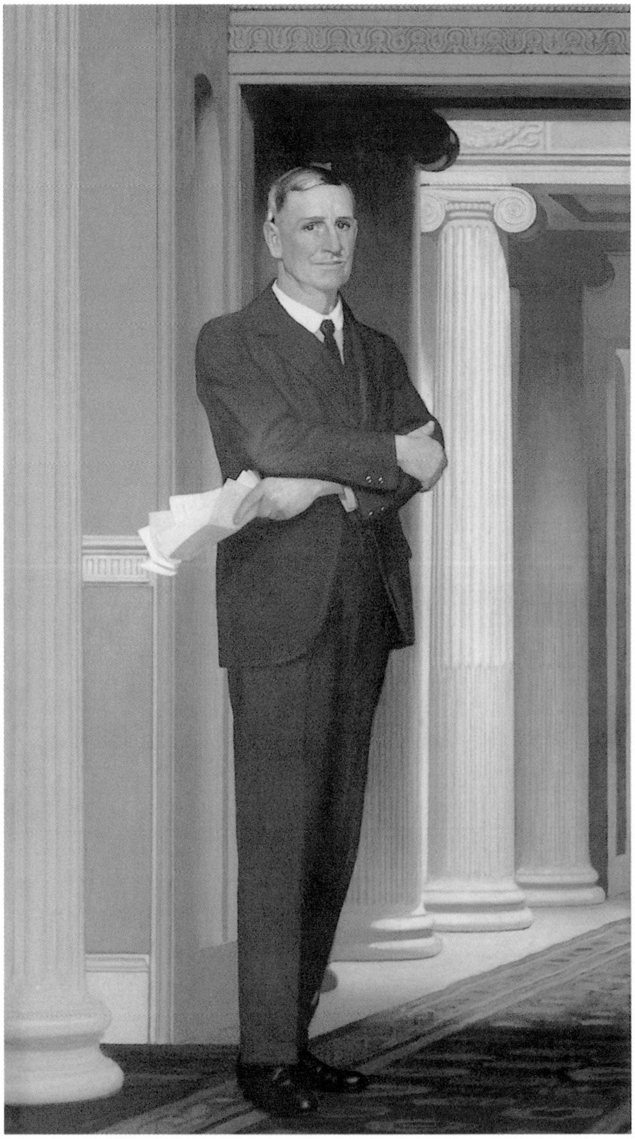

204. Colin Gill, *Moving Gold in the Old Gold Vault*, Bank of England, London, *c.*1928–37

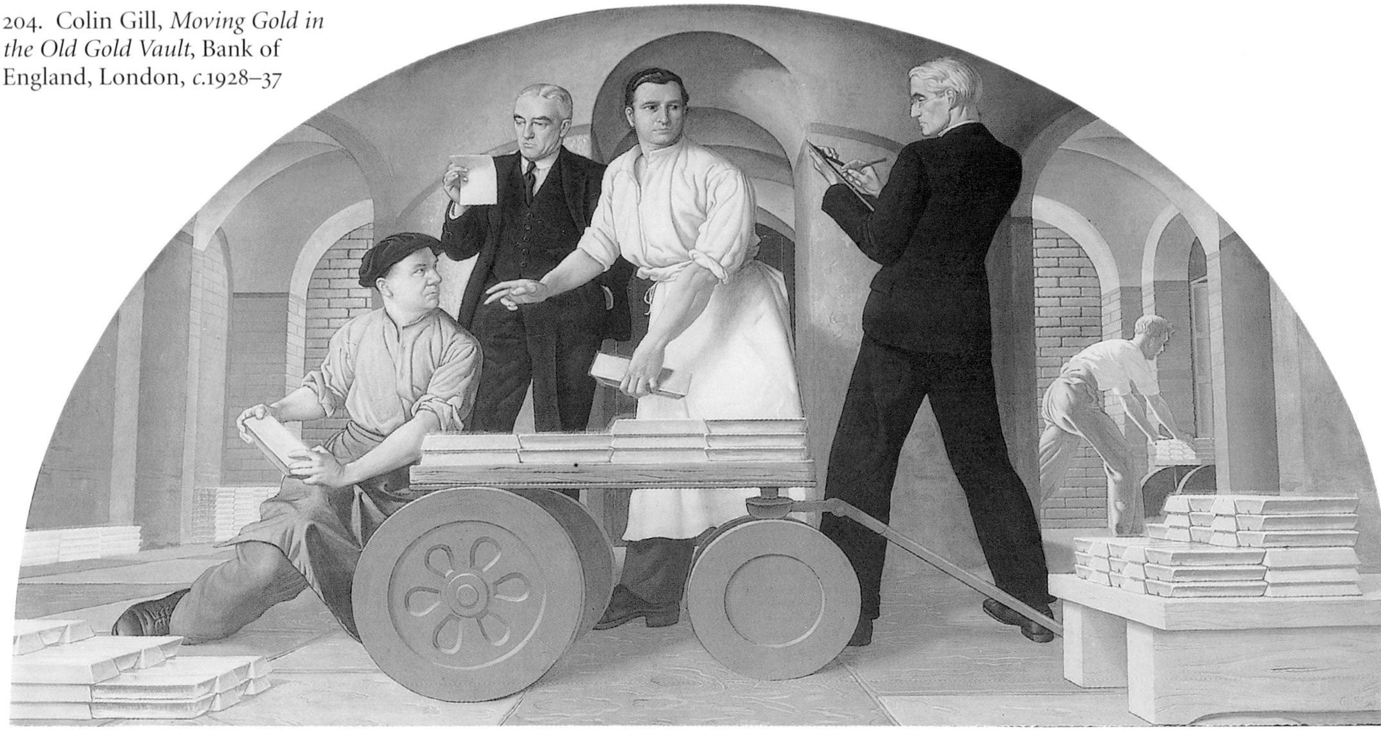

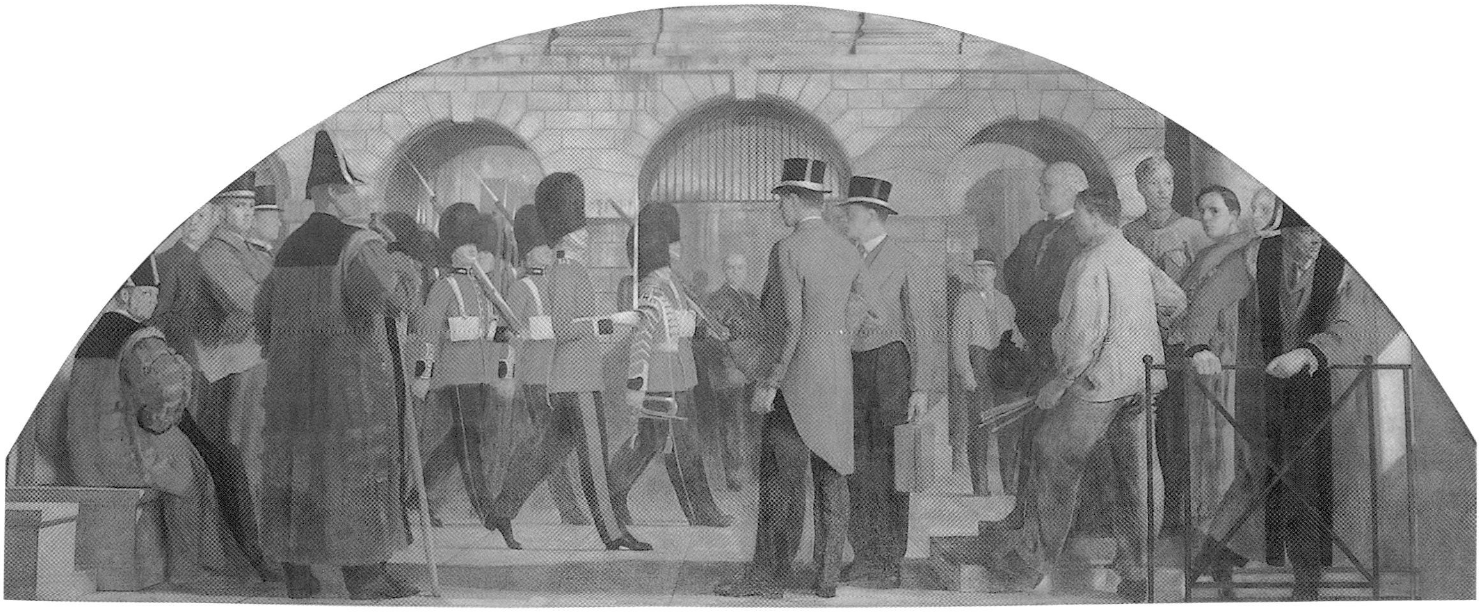

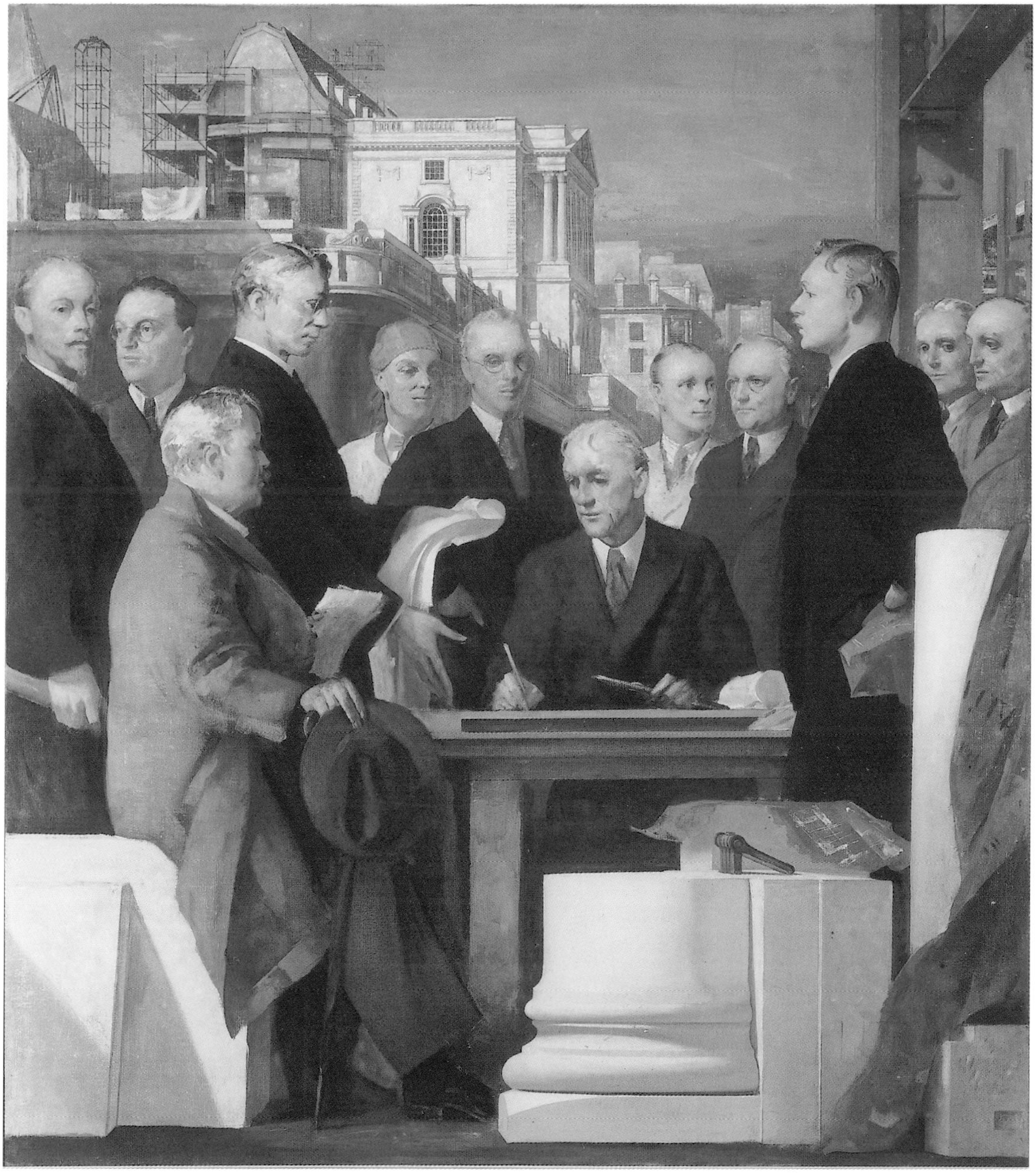

205. Alfred Kingsley Lawrence, *The Old Threadneedle Street Courtyard with the Guard arriving at the Bank*, Bank of England, London, *c.*1928–37

206. Alfred Kingsley Lawrence, *The Builders*, Bank of England, London, *c.*1928–37

The Depression, not surprisingly, saw few other murals for commerce. Colin Gill painted portraits of Founders and Governors at Glyn's Bank (another Baker building), whilst four atmospheric lunettes by Henry Lintott, probably painted in the late 1930s, illustrate sources of Scotland's wealth (*Engineering, Distilling, Printing*, and *Rural Economy*) in the former Royal Bank of Scotland in Shandwick Place, Edinburgh. These, however, are essentially enlarged easel works, having no special relationship with the Art Deco interior. At Lloyd's of London, *Neptune* and *Mercury* were painted in a flashy Expressionist style by William Walcot in 1929, and *Industry* and *Peace* in a Tiepolesque manner by Fred Taylor in 1930. Historical themes were used by other patrons (Appendix E: 8, 9).

When Sir John Rothenstein organized his Tate Gallery exhibition of 1939 on *Mural Painting in Great Britain 1919–1939*, hardly any murals at work were represented; the Bank of England scheme was absent, and panels for the Tyne Improvement Commission were rejected[56] (Appendix E: 6). Instead, it was 'public buildings', and notably 'modern hotels, clubs and liners' which Rothenstein identified as offering 'opportunities for mural painters'.[57] Significantly, he recommended that Britain should 'learn from the United States and Mexico'.[58] The recent American New Deal murals, of course, promoted recreation as an essential agent in a new cohesive social order. Philip Guston's mural of 1940 in the Queensbridge Community Centre in New York was actually called *Work and Play* and illustrates basketball players, musicians, dancers, and construction workers sharing a joint role in the creation of a harmonious society.[59] If he did not follow the Americans' promotion of murals *by* the man in the street, Rothenstein's selection at the Tate in 1939 was none the less perhaps more ideological than strictly historical, representing in essence a variation of the Arts and Crafts-influenced social philosophy of mural painting which his father, Sir William Rothenstein, had advocated. Almost a third of his exhibits were, in fact, already from the leisure locations such as theatres, restaurants, and shops which he proposed for decoration, whilst they included one of the new murals for Services' messes (Appendix E: 10). In a sense, as we shall see, the boundaries between work and play had now become blurred.

MURALS AT PLAY

Whilst business and commerce began to paint their walls at only a relatively late stage, leisure and entertainment venues have a much longer and more vigorous tradition, though many examples, by their very nature as decoration intended to amuse and divert, have fallen victim to changing fashions and tastes. In his novel *Sybil*, set in northern industrial Britain in 1837–44, Benjamin Disraeli describes a 'Temple of the Muses' which appears to have been typical of the kind of entertainment room favoured by the 'working classes' prior to a Parliamentary Act of 1843 which confined refreshment and spectacle to separate venues:

[56] A booklet about Jowsey's murals (J. Oxberry, *Mural Decoration of the Frieze in the Board Room of the Tyne Improvement Commission*, n.d.) was submitted to Rothenstein (see '*Mural Painting in Great Britain*, Organisation 1929–39', PRO No. 258, TGA) when he was choosing exhibits. The murals are now detached and in the possession of the Port of Tyne Authority, Newcastle-upon-Tyne.

[57] J. Rothenstein, *Mural Painting in Great Britain* (1939), p. 4.

[58] Ibid., p. 5.

[59] Illustrated in J. Harris, 'State Power and Cultural Discourse: Federal Art Project Murals', *Block*, no. 13 (Winter 1987–8), p. 33.

the ceiling was richly decorated; the walls were painted, and by a brush of no inconsiderable power. Each panel represented some well-known scene from Shakespeare, Byron or Scott; King Richard, Mazeppa, the Lady of the Lake, were easily recognised: in one panel, Hubert menaced Arthur; here Haidee rescued Juan; and there Jeanie Deans curtsied before the Queen.[60]

Harriet, one of the factory hands who came to the Temple to enjoy a meal and a stage performance, calls it 'just what I thought the Queen lived in', whilst Dandy Mick remarks of the *Lady of the Lake*, 'I've seen her at the Circus, with real water.'[61] If such mural decoration catered principally to the escapism, mingled with social aspiration, which drew audiences to venues like the Temple,[62] Sang and Naundorff's monochrome murals of poets and painters in the club used by Disraeli's own party in London (Appendix E: 12), like other London club schemes (Appendix E: 13), offered something more restrained. It was G. F. Watts, however, who in 1852 attempted a more ambitious combination of ideas and entertainment through his plan to harness art to that Victorian symbol of both escape and progress, the iron horse.

Frederick Crace in the 1840s had ornamented the Refreshment Room at Swindon Station with Italianate pattern motifs; in turn, perhaps aware of the official encouragement given in France during the 1848–50 Republic to murals for railway stations, the architect P. C. Hardwick had included a sequence of vast wall paintings in his 1849 design for the Great Booking Hall at Euston Station in London[63] (Plate 207). Never carried out, these panels were clearly intended to complement the line of association between modern progress and the origins of civilization implied by Hardwick's gigantic Propylaeum entrance to the station, since they illustrated the Parthenon and other antique monuments beneath blue skies. The Propylaeum at Athens flanked a *Pinakotheka* (picture gallery). Watts's scheme, however, which he offered only for the cost of the materials, is said to have envisaged *The Progress of the Cosmos* on the walls of Euston, and suggests both the idiom of his frescoes at this period for 7 Carlton House Terrace, and something approaching Courbet's vision of the 'vast railroad stations [as] new churches for painting' with murals on 'subjects picturesque, moral, industrial, metallurgic; in short, the saints and miracles of modern society'.[64] The Directors of the London and North-Western Railway, however, refused this opportunity to see the power of the railway identified not merely with mere human endeavour as in Hardwick's scheme, but—if Watts's Carlton House Terrace scheme is anything to go by—also the elemental processes of Creation itself. Likewise, Alfred Stevens met with what Brunel told him was 'a very decided objection' from the Great Western Railway's Directors to his design including life-size Michelangelesque figures for the Royal Waiting Room at Paddington Station; they wished the 'platforms or offices . . . to be as plain and inexpensive as possible'.[65] It was left to Owen Jones in his 1851 Great Exhibition decoration, and again J. G. Crace in that for the 1862 event, to associate technological progress, as represented by the modern inventions on display, with the primal, by using primary colours for what was still pattern, rather than pictorial ornament. Jones believed

[60] B. Disraeli, *Sybil*, ed. S. Smith (Oxford, 1991), p. 91.

[61] Ibid., pp. 95–6.

[62] Ibid., see note 90, p. 437.

[63] The design (a watercolour) is in the British Architectural Library Drawings Collection, RIBA. See J. Physick and M. Darby, *Marble Halls*, no. 102, p. 152.

[64] A letter of 'Sept. 27' (? 1920s) from Mrs Watts to *The Times* in the Watts Gallery Archives, Compton, states that Watts had planned the *Cosmos* iconography for the ceiling of 'a vast never-to-be-built temple' rather than for Euston station. Courbet's ideas are given in a letter from Sainte-Beuve to C. Duveyrier (22 April 1862), quoted in G. Tinterow and H. Loyrette, *Origins of Impressionism* (New York, 1994), p. 269. Ruskin was vehemently against the decoration of railway stations, as being purely utilitarian places (J. Ruskin, *The Seven Lamps of Architecture* (London, 1906), pp. 219–22).

[65] Letter from the Secretary of the GWR Company to Brunel, quoted in Physick and Darby, *Marble Halls*, p. 156.

that only these colours had been employed in the great periods of art. The strong tradition of railway station mural painting which developed on the Continent did not find a parallel in Britain,[66] and Mary Adshead's *Housing of the People* mural, shown at the Wembley Exhibition in 1924, and installed with further murals by Stephen Bone in the Bank Underground station in London in 1925 (now detached: present whereabouts unknown) remained a rare experiment. Instead, posters were preferred in the twentieth century, and murals found a place in some of the grander station hotels which were built from the late nineteenth century. Sir George Gilbert Scott's St Pancras Hotel was extensively decorated with wall and ceiling paintings, as befitted its Gothic architectural style, and as if to create a kind of traveller's Palace of Westminster; the ground-floor reception room of the Great Central Hotel of 1899,[67] a building by R. W. Edis in a neo-Renaissance manner beside Marylebone Station in London, was adorned with lunettes and roundels of feasting damsels and youths in sixteenth-century costume. Such murals were no longer for educating the mind, but for fostering illusions of life in a stately palace (Edis also designed the mural-decorated Ballroom of the Prince of Wales at Sandringham).[68]

The absence in Britain of State or civic patronage for opera and theatre perhaps precluded the kind of cultural national icon created in the Vienna Opera during the 1860s by Moritz von Schwind's Germanic opera murals and in Charles Garnier's Paris Opéra in the 1870s by Jean-Paul Baudry's integrated scheme, as well as later by the Klimt/Matsch partnership's 'History of Theatre' decorations at the Vienna Burgtheater (1880s) or those of Vuillard, Denis, and others at the Théâtre National de Chaillot (Paris Exposition Universelle, 1937)[69] (Plates 208 and 209). It was, none the less, in theatres, halls, and also restaurants that 'leisure' murals took most vigorous root in nineteenth-century Britain. Whilst Continental artists or their emulators were mostly employed to paint Italianate motifs and allegorical personifications in the 1840s and 1850s at Covent Garden and other theatres (Appendix E: 11, 14, 15), 'pictorial decoration' was supplied by 'the masters and pupils' of the Manchester School of Art at the Manchester Free Trade Hall in 1851,[70] and 'figures representing the shamrock, the harp &c., as emblems of Erin and its bardic poetry' were painted at the Ulster Hall in Belfast in the 1860s.[71] Pre-Raphaelite and Aesthetic trends emerged in Henry Holiday's, Stacy Marks's, and Albert Moore's Shakespearean or antique Greek themes (Appendix E: 17–19),[72] but by the end of the century French or Belgian artists and Rococo styles were much in favour. Huge wall and ceiling panels of gods and goddesses amidst clouds and Watteauesque parklands by Henri Brémond and Maurice Tastemain garnished the foyer of F. H. Fowler's 1882 Royal Avenue Theatre in London, for example; *Times of Day* and *Cupid and Psyche* by Arthur J. Black were to be found at Beerbohm Tree's Her Majesty's Theatre, Haymarket, and personifications of *Music, Drama*, and *Painting*, complete with thunderous clouds in turquoise skies and winged putti, by Charles Harker at the Haymarket

[66] See, for example, E. Walter, 'Le Décor' in 'L'Espace du voyage: les gares', *Monuments Historiques*, no. 6 (Paris, 1978), pp. 36–44 for French examples.

[67] Murals were included in Scott's designs for St Pancras Hotel (1868–76) (see Taylor, *Monuments of Commerce* (1968), p. 62) and have recently been restored at the hotel. The Great Central Hotel is now the Landmark, London (222 Marylebone Road).

[68] The artist of the murals is unknown.

[69] See J. Foucart *Les Peintures de l'Opéra de Paris de Baudry à Chagall* (Paris, 1980); Kitlitschka, *Malerei der Wiener Ringstrasse* (1981); E. O. Sachs's monumental *Modern Opera Houses and Theatres* (London, 1896), which gives pride of place to the Vienna Burgtheater; and B. Thomson, *Vuillard* (Oxford, 1988).

[70] Quoted in C. Stewart, *Art in Adversity: A Short History of the Regional College of Art, Manchester* (Council of the Royal Manchester Institution, 1954), p. 25. The 'Manchester Academy' would later protest at plans for foreign artists to paint the Town Hall murals (see Chapter 7 above).

[71] Quoted in J. McBrinn, 'Belfast's Other Murals' (1997), p. 40.

[72] See Beavington Atkinson, 'English Painters' (1870), p. 132 for Marks's schemes and for Holiday's work, P. Cormack, *Henry Holiday* (1989), p. 9 and illustrations in Holiday, *Reminiscences* (1914).

Theatre in 1904.[73] Such designs had nothing to do with either the subjects of the plays performed or the novel realism of Tree's productions; rather, the very disjunction of the fantasy surroundings with the plays suggests an attempt to enhance vicariously the illusions on the stage and, as at Garnier's influential Paris Opéra, to create a 'backdrop' in turn for the fashionably dressed theatre-goers.

As an accoutrement of luxury, French eighteenth-century idiom persisted into the twentieth century in the context of the Beaux-Arts Baroque of Mewès and Davies at the Ritz Hotel and the Royal Automobile Club,[74] as well as at Claridge's (Appendix E: 21). Already in 1900, however, reporting on recent murals illustrating Arthurian legend at Lyons's Trocadero Restaurant in London by Gerald Moira and F. Lynn-Jenkins, the *Art Journal* praised their refusal to engage in 'British imitation of the *chic*, dextrous painting of French and Italian decorators [which] is something like a common ice-cream or cheap vol-au-vent, not to be thought of'.[75] Amidst the flood of revivalist and pastiche leisure murals at the *fin de siècle*, there were, in fact, a number of notable exceptions. Paying tribute in 1901 to 'decorative tendencies' as 'perhaps the most strongly emergent merit' of modern English art, Hermann Muthesius identified Moira as, with Byam Shaw, 'the most outstanding representative of the decorative school' and enthusiastically described the new fibrous plaster bas-relief technique he had developed with Lynn-Jenkins (see Appendix A) in their Trocadero Restaurant frieze nearly 27.5 metres long.[76] Its combination of sculpted relief with painted colour and gold, silver, and platinum leaf must have been recognized by Muthesius as a counterpart to the mixed media employed by von Stuck and other Jugendstil artists, whilst its Tennyson imagery translated Pre-Raphaelite chivalry into Moira's characteristic Art Nouveau style.

At the Throgmorton Restaurant in London, Moira and Lynn-Jenkins applied their invention to stories from Wagner's operas,[77] and in turn a Wagnerian *Gesamtkunstwerk* effect can still be appreciated in one of their few surviving schemes, the decoration of the apse of the Wigmore Hall in London (1901), whose former glory can now be appreciated again as a result of conservation. Here, within the intimate neo-Romanesque hall built in 1890 for Bechstein's by Collcutt, Moira's collaborator at Lloyd's, *The Soul of Music looking at the Genius of Harmony* and adjacent friezes of singers with swirling banners (Plate 210) take the synaesthetic implications of painted relief—appealing to touch as well as sight—to their logical conclusion. The frontal, hieratic *Genius of Harmony* stands before gilded sun-rays, lifting a golden orb which reflects both these and the offerings of Love (roses, evoking scent); a Musician sounding his trumpet; a Composer writing music, and Psyche, who appeals to sight with her lamp. This synaesthetic bouquet, glowing with ruby red and deep green as well as gold, is, by implication, mediated to the audience though the performers on the platform immediately beneath, who in the 1900s included Busoni, Joachim,

[73] See *The Royal Avenue Theatre*, Programme for opening on 11 March 1882; A. Fish, 'Decorations at Her Majesty's Theatre', *Magazine of Art* (1898), pp. 110–11; and Theatre Files in the Research Collection, Theatre Museum, London; other examples are illustrated in V. Glasstone, *Victorian and Edwardian Theatres* (London, 1975). Harker's work at the Haymarket Theatre is one of the few schemes to survive.

[74] Original panels of arcadian scenes in the style of Hubert Robert from a French château were even installed at the RAC at 89 Pall Mall in 1911.

[75] F. Miller, 'The Decoration of London Restaurants', *Art Journal*, new series (London 1900), p. 332.

[76] H. Muthesius, 'Kunst and Leben in England' (1902), p. 69: 'Die dekorativen Neigungen sind . . . vielleicht die am stärksten hervortretenden Werte der englischen Schule' (author's translation). For the Trocadero scheme, see 'The Art Movement. Novelty in Decoration at the Trocadero', *Magazine of Art*, 20 (1896), pp. 92–7 (anon.).

[77] See J. H. Watkins, *The Art of Gerald Moira* (1922), p. 14. The technique was taken up by others including Fehr at Wakefield County Hall (see above, Chapter 7) and A. R. Martin in his 1905 decoration at the State Restaurant, 14 Dale Street, Liverpool.

and Saint-Saëns. Although the inspiration for coloured bas relief may well have been the discovery that the Parthenon frieze had originally been painted,[78] the intricately curvilinear briar-rose backdrop to the decoration has a more Celtic than classical character, and forms a suggestive echo of Charles Rennie Mackintosh's 1895 reinterpretation of the Burne-Jones motif in his stencil frieze for Miss Cranston's Buchanan Street Temperance Tearooms in Glasgow. Both artists probably also knew Guimard's and Horta's linear motifs.

Related to a pale pink and viridian watercolour of 1896 entitled *Part Seen, Imagined Part*, and showing a woman emerging from (or perhaps being transformed into) a tangled, linear rosebush, Mackintosh's decoration (Plate 211) would have contrasted strikingly with the kind of 'half-nude woman of heroic mould seated harping upon a seashore, against a gilded sky',[79] representing *Music*, which his older admirer Sir James Guthrie had painted as decoration for the 1888 Glasgow International Exhibition. Far more resolutely a-historical also than either Moira's work or the Arts and Crafts idiom of George Walton's Cranston Tearoom interiors,[80] it verged on abstraction, yet remained representational. As well as synaesthesia (the scent and sight of (tea?) roses accompanying meals and conversation), Mackintosh's 'imagined' design would have encouraged a healthful retreat, planting a garden amidst the grimy 'Second City of the Empire'. Seed-cases surmount the woman's head like a crown, implying an association between imbibing tea and nature's regenerative cycle, but the imagery also suggests, like Goetze's later Grove House murals, an awareness of French transformist theories. Besnard's *Life Is Born from Death* mural in the Sorbonne, also of 1896, had given form to these by showing a woman 'growing' from a plant.[81]

The Scottish Tearoom phenomenon also gave rise to Robert Burns's procession of *Diana and her Nymphs* (Plate XLIV) dancing amidst red and gold creepers on the walls of Crawford's restaurant in Edinburgh (*c*.1926)[82] and Art Deco effects (Appendix E: 22, 23). Stewart Carmichael meanwhile painted *The Leaders of Scottish Liberty*, including Wallace and Carlyle, for Dundee Liberal Club.[83] The most ambitious Scottish schemes for leisure or assembly venues, however, were Douglas Strachan's. His sixteen panels of 1898 (now destroyed) in the Trades Hall in Aberdeen, illustrating *Ancient and Modern Labour, Music, War, Oratory, Justice*, and *Truth*, along with the sciences, arts, and *Chief Industries* (with the latter including *Decoration*!) appear to have offered a marriage, reminiscent of that in recent decoration at the Paris Hôtel de Ville, of contemporary industrial and allegorical imagery, with Roman galley slaves and warriors appearing in *Ancient Labour*.[84]

In the long, Neoclassical-style Music Hall in Aberdeen, Strachan developed a distinctive personal interpretation of synaesthesia. The earliest portion of the scheme (1898), surmounting the organ in the apse, presents a purposeful, muscular Apollo who seemingly bounds forth with his golden lyre into the very air filled by the organ's sound. Behind him, the branches of clustered, dark green trees entwine the Muses; mortals of different ages and nations listen as they stroll on the flowery grass beneath. A Greek text inscribed under the branches translates 'But sing of

[78] Cf. the coloured version of the Parthenon frieze illustrated in Alma-Tadema's *Phideas and the Parthenon* (1868), Birmingham Museums and Art Gallery.

[79] J. L. Caw, *Sir James Guthrie* (London, 1932), p. 45. Mackintosh's watercolour is in the Hunterian Art Gallery, University of Glasgow.

[80] See H. Muthesius, 'Architecture anglaise d'intérieurs M. George Walton', *L'Art Décoratif* (1900), p. 148; K. Moon, *George Walton* (Oxford, 1993); and P. Kinchin, *Tea and Taste: The Glasgow Tea Rooms 1875–1975* (Wendlebury, 1991).

[81] Reproduced in Silverman, *Art Nouveau* (1989), p. 226.

[82] The parels are now detached and in the National Gallery of Scotland, Edinburgh.

[83] P.w.u.; see Anon., 'Notable Scottish Artist Stewart Carmichael Dundee', *Scottish Patriot* (May 1904), p. 59.

[84] See C. A. P. Willsdon, 'Scotland's Mural Renascence' (1983), pp. 15–18.

Pythian Phoebus [Apollo], of golden hair, shooting far, skilled with lyre, whom blessed Leto bore beside the famous lake.'[85] If the sun god born beside the water of the Aegean represents life itself in his passionate music-making, the panel at the opposite end of the hall, showing *Orpheus crossing the Styx* (Plate 212), portrays the water of death. Painted a few years later, it has a more atmospheric, sombre colouring, with an echo of Brangwyn's 1904 *Departure of Sir James Lancaster* at Skinners' Hall (Plate X) in the sinewy sailor seen from the back. Again, however, the design has dynamic urgency, thrusting the viewer aboard Orpheus' long sailing boat, where at the far right, the poet plays his lyre. Gazing into the distance, he turns away from an apparition of Eurydice, a visualization of the tragic image in his mind's eye. The close-up focus shows only the lower edge of the sails, compressing the subject into a narrow double ellipse which is barely contained by the frieze format, just as Orpheus, aided by music, holds his grief in check. The actual loss of Eurydice, possibly influenced by G. F. Watts's version of the subject bequeathed to Aberdeen in 1901, is amongst the other scenes from legend in the side-wall panels, which were not completed until 1910.[86]

In a lecture of 1910, Strachan praised Puvis de Chavannes's murals for their 'pattern', and drew an analogy between this quality, 'deep-rooted in every mind', and the 'arrangement' demonstrated in Wagner's *Flying Dutchman* overture; an 'arrangement' whose 'purpose . . . is to create in your mind intense realisation of storm; and to carry you forward into it until you have lost consciousness of everything save the raging night sea and the uneasy figure that looms against it, until these become the only realities'.[87] His image might be a literal description of *Orpheus crossing the Styx*, revealing the intense psychological affinity which he perceived between the arts of mural painting and music. Its rhythmic composition, punctuated by rigging and masts, offers in itself the very mechanism—the 'pattern' or 'arrangement'—by which he believed art affected viewer and listener alike.

Perhaps not surprisingly for decoration in places where people might gather for special events, or to escape from the daily routine, neither Moira's nor these Scottish examples departed from literary, historical, or mythological themes; even Mackintosh's rose-woman evokes Venus, since a tiny heart marks her transition into human form. At late as 1914, Henry Holiday's abortive *Reign of Humanity* scheme for a building which, if not exactly recreational, was none the less a place for popular gatherings, the Labour Party Hall in London, was a grand amalgam of Biblical, historical, and allegorical imagery.[88] It was Brangwyn in his murals of modern industry for the Venice International Exhibitions of 1905 and 1907, and Wyndham Lewis and his associates at the Cave of the Golden Calf (1912) and Restaurant de la Tour Eiffel (1915) in London who made a distinctive break with both the indirect mode of allegory or personification, and the revivalist pastiche so popular in hotels and theatres.

Although for a foreign exhibition, Brangwyn's four 1905 murals, showing *Excavators, Steelworkers, Potters*, and *Blacksmiths* (Plate XL) were subsequently installed with a further panel, *Spinners*, as a decorative ensemble in Leeds City Art Gallery, whilst his 1907 scheme was reused at

[85] Translation credited to Thomas Pearce in an information page about the murals kindly provided by Aberdeen City Council.

[86] Of the original ten side panels, four are now overpainted; a fifth is by Hugh Adam Crawford, RSA (1949).

[87] D. Strachan, *A Lecture on Design and Craft* (2 March 1910, Edinburgh College of Art) (published by the College), pp. 18, 10.

[88] Holiday, *Reminiscences*, pp. 459–62 (including illustration). Bernard Sleigh also painted eight panels illustrating Morris's *King's Lesson* at the Clarion Café in Manchester, where the Temperance wing of the Labour Party met (see the *Studio*, 52 (1911), pp. 58–9 and A. Crawford (ed.) *By Hammer and Hand* (1984), p. 71.

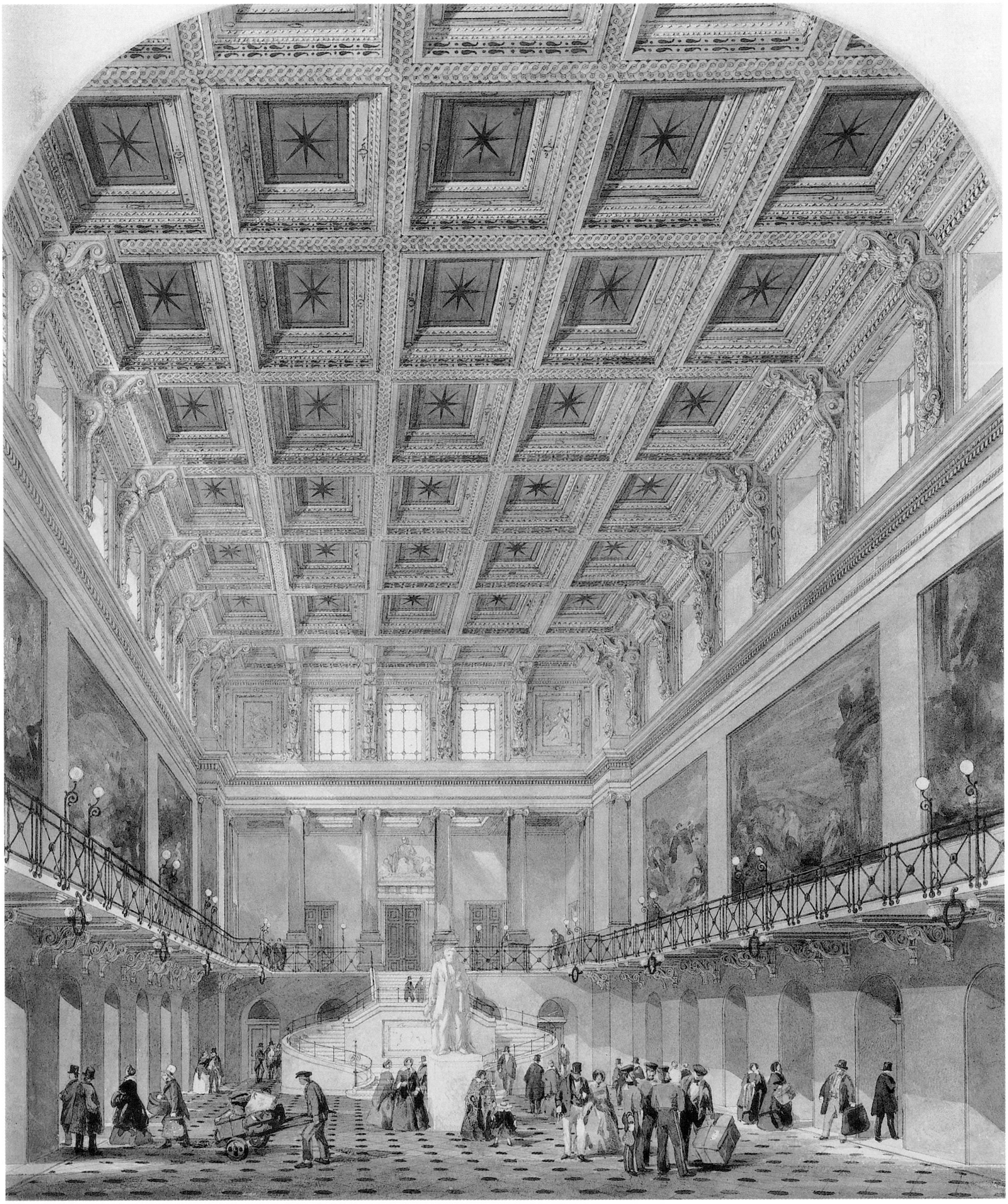

207. Philip Charles Hardwick, design for the Great Booking Hall, Euston Station, London, *c.*1849. London, British Architectural Library, Royal Institute of British Architects

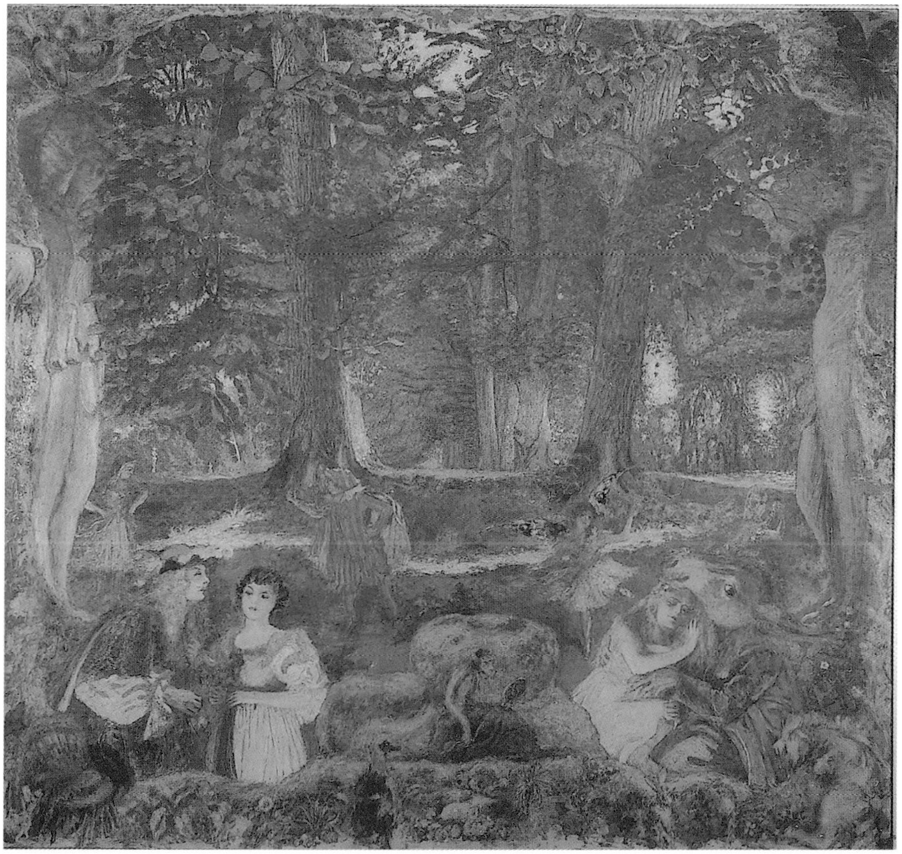

208. Edouard Vuillard, *Comedy*, Théâtre National de Chaillot, Paris, 1937

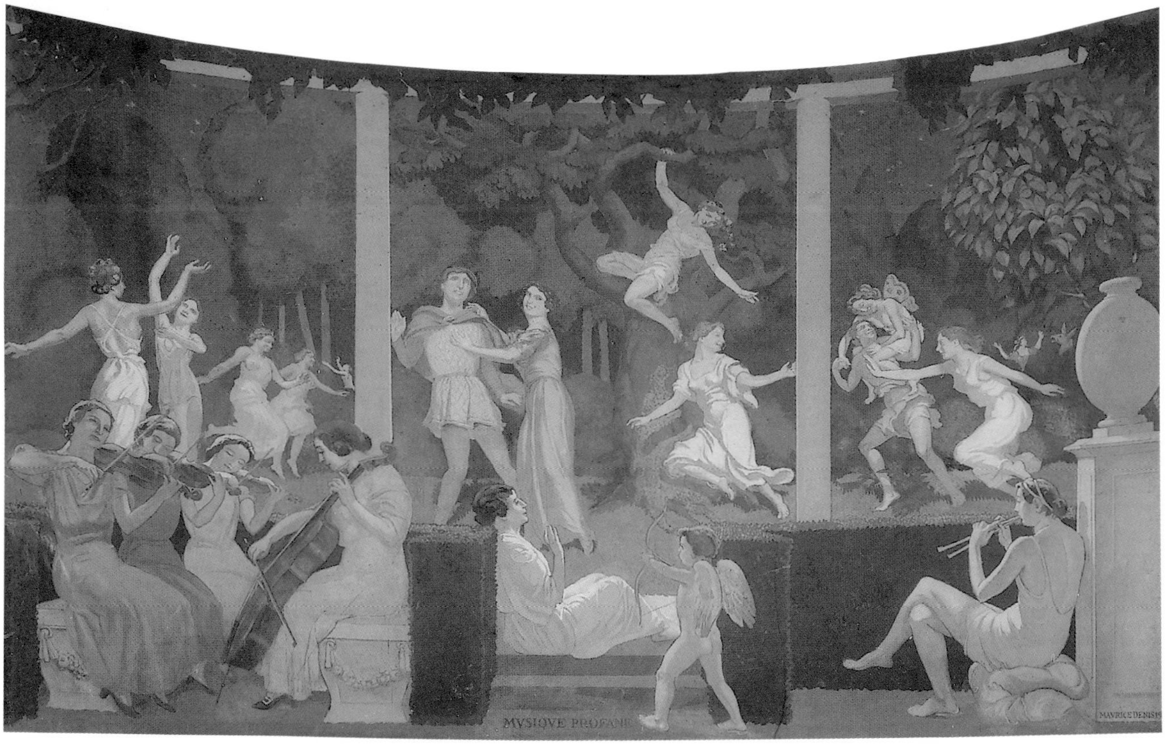

209. Maurice Denis, *Profane Music*, Théâtre National de Chaillot, Paris, 1937

210. Gerald Moira and F. Lynn-Jenkins, *The Soul of Music looking at the Genius of Harmony*, Wigmore Hall, London, 1901

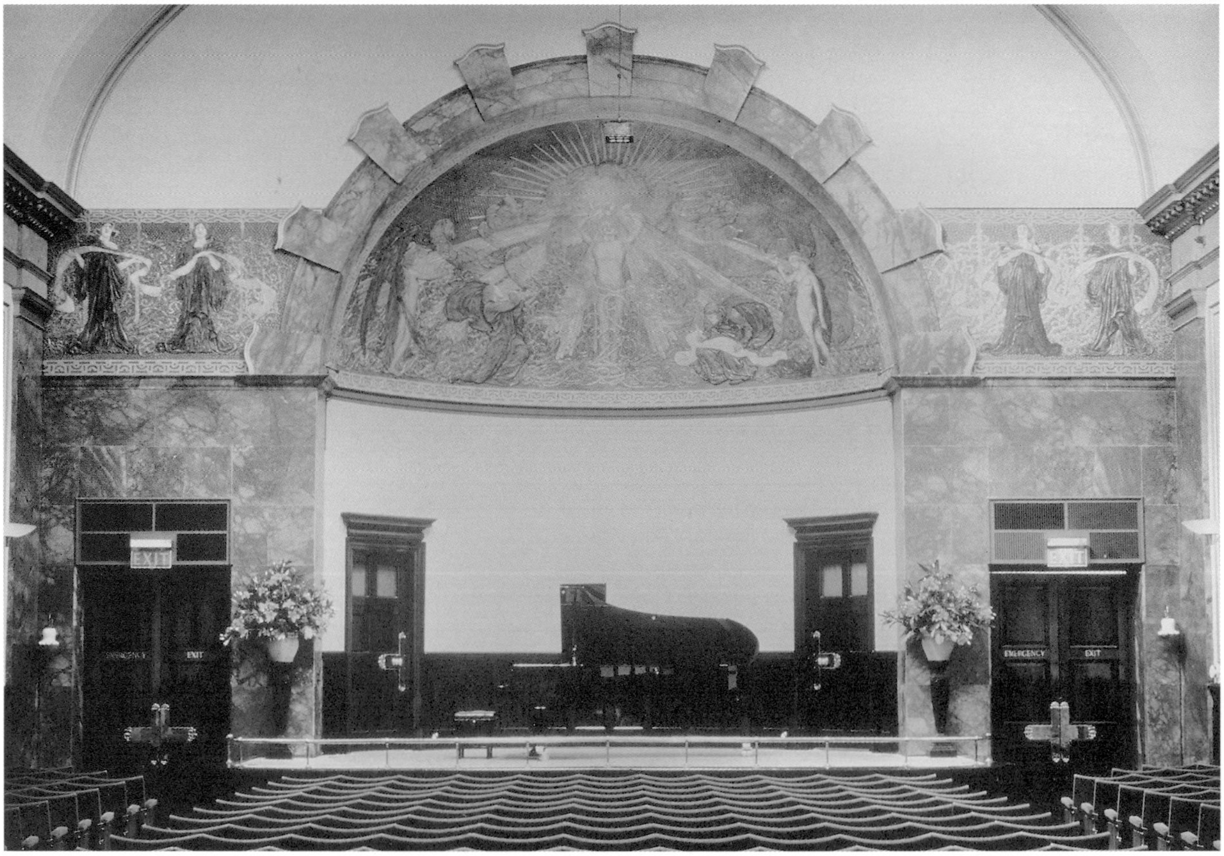

211. Charles Rennie Mackintosh, preliminary water colour design for mural (now destroyed) at the Buchanan Street Tearoom, Glasgow, *c.*1895. Hunterian Art Gallery, University of Glasgow

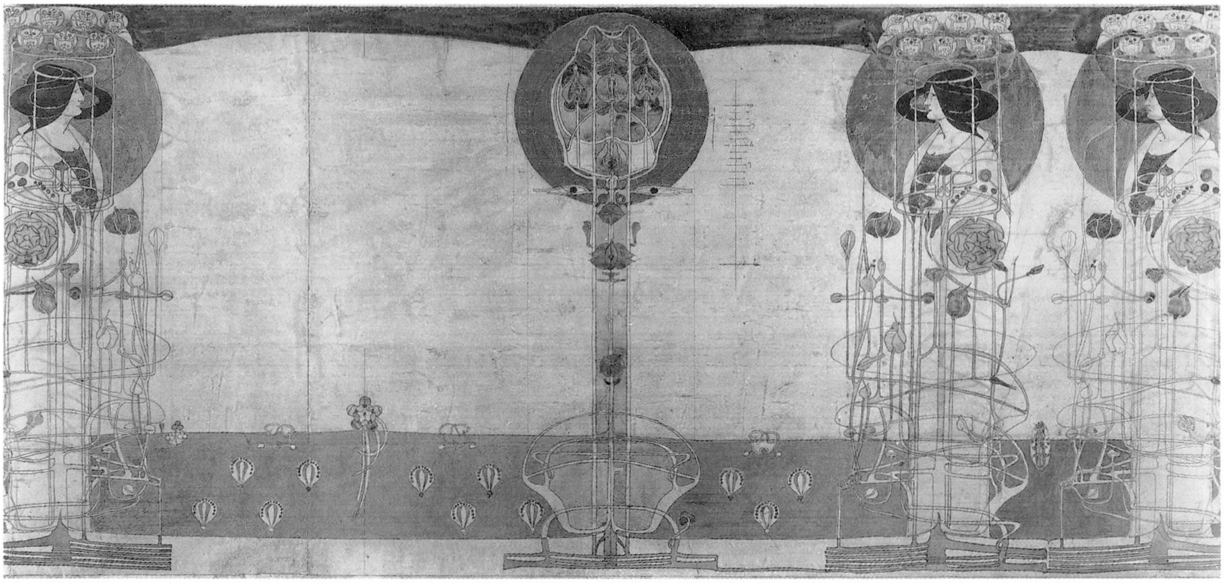

212. Douglas Strachan, *Orpheus crossing the Styx*, Music Hall, Aberdeen, *c.*1904–10

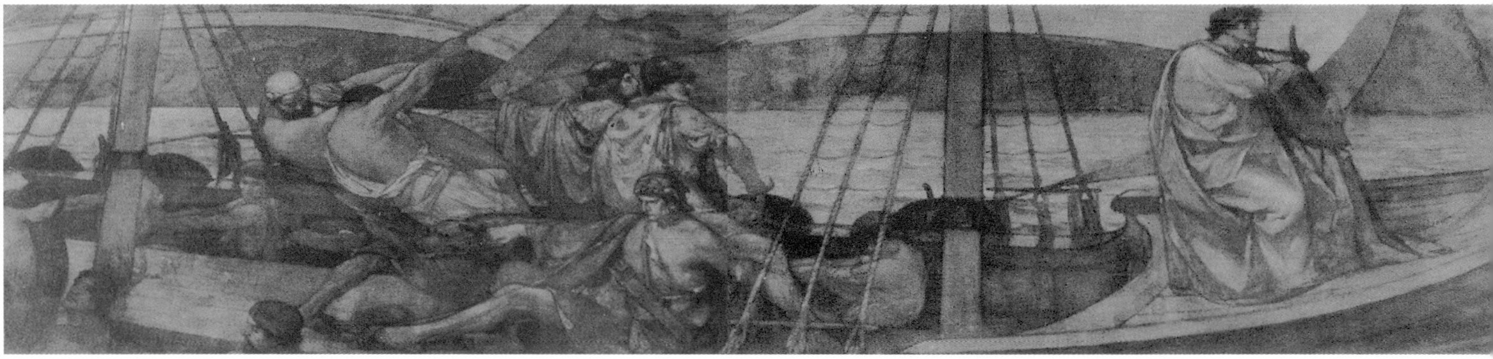

Horton House in Northamptonshire. If their original function descended from the kind of emblematic panels representing different trades or industries typical of nineteenth-century International Exhibition pavilions (Appendix E: 16, 20), their artistic vocabulary was of a kind to be developed shortly in Brangwyn's Lloyd's Register of Shipping scheme. The labourers fill the foreground plane, punctuating with synchronized or reciprocating movements the angular geometry of pink pipes and planks in *Excavators*, or of wheels, funnels, and massive machinery amidst the lurid glow of manufacture in *Blacksmiths*. The murals rediscover in an industrial context the graceful bodily movement of Brangwyn's earlier *Dancing* panel for Bing's Maison de l'Art Nouveau (Plate 13) and their theme of brotherhood in manual exertion would have amounted to a declaration of solidarity with those whose labour of art gave pleasure to the exhibition visitors. Both at Venice and in Leeds, the murals were arranged to form a decorative setting for the display of easel paintings by Brangwyn's fellow British artists. Though Wyndham Lewis promised to 'Blast' Brangwyn in his 1914 journal of that name, until, of him, Sir William Nicholson, and Sir Edward Poynter 'there would be nothing left . . . but a few Brangwynesque bubbles on the surface of the abstract,'[89] Brangwyn's vision of the artist as 'worker' and Lewis's of 'the timeless, fundamental Artist that exists in everybody'[90] are essentially not unrelated.

The Cave of the Golden Calf, where Lewis's *Kermesse* was the first mural to greet *habitués* of Madame Strindberg's nightclub as they descended to its underground rooms, can perhaps best be understood as a place intended to awaken in turn the creative impulse of those who danced the night away there. Also at the entrance stood Eric Gill's gilded bas relief of the Golden Calf, and inside, huge jungle murals by Spencer Gore (Plate XLIII) and Charles Ginner, and 'plaster images, half-human, half-animal . . . painted in clamourous colours'[91] by Jacob Epstein. Synaesthesia was again to the fore. Now, however, decoration was an agent not of passive listening, but of kinaesthetic and instinctual dance. Often led by the avant-garde dancer Margaret Morris, who, like Marinetti, was welcomed by Madame Strindberg (the former wife of the playwright), the hedonism of such dance, like the 'barbarous'[92] dramatic performances also staged at the Cave, was conceived as a latter-day enactment of the Biblical story after which the Club was named. Lewis's *Kermesse*, now known only from two related wash drawings, and a sketch by Horace Brodzky (Plate 213) likewise evidently evoked the *experience* as much as sight of rhythmic movement, consisting of 'a cubistic rendering of three festive figures, the central in rich yellow, the others in varying shades of red and purple'.[93] Like the colours, the forms were stripped to their primal essence: an angled leg; flailing arms; lines expressive of rapid and violent dancing. Lewis's description of it as 'even for a wall-painting . . . too uncouth . . . unfinished' [94] suggests a conscious projection into its very creation of the Nietzschean energy he admired, as well as an association of mural painting with what a contemporary critic called 'the primitive simplicity of the days when art was in its infancy. It was, after all, on bones and on the walls of caves that the artistic instinct found its first expression'.[95] The brotherhood portrayed by Brangwyn had become kinship; a discovery of the deepest bonds of human inheritance. Gore's and Ginner's murals,

[89] W. Lewis, *Blast* No. 2, in W. Michel and C. J. Fox (eds), *Wyndham Lewis on Art* (1969), p. 77.

[90] W. Lewis, *Blast* No. 1, in ibid., p. 25.

[91] S. Compton (ed.), *British Art*, p. 132. The Cave was at 3–9 Heddon Street, off Regent Street, London. (Plate XLIII is on paper mounted on card, 30.5 × 60.5 cm).

[92] Quoted in ibid.

[93] Quoted in R. Cork, *Art Beyond the Gallery* (1985), p. 90.

[94] Quoted in ibid.

[95] Quoted in S. Compton (ed.), *British Art*, p. 132.

portraying tiger- and deer-hunting, evoked the very iconography of the prehistoric art then being researched, but in boldly outlined Gauguinesque shapes betraying the influence of Fry's Post-Impressionist exhibitions. The 'primitive' and 'dance' elements of the ensemble were undoubtedly influenced also by the Ballets Russes and perhaps J. D. Fergusson's painting *Les Eus* (Hunterian Art Gallery, University of Glasgow),[96] but their emotional content surely found its nearest affinities in German Expressionism: Nolde had earlier painted a *Dance around the Golden Calf*, whilst *Kermesse* suggests Kandinsky's near abstraction.

The 'savage' mood was taken further in Lewis's Rebel Art Centre of 1914 and his 'Vorticist Room' for Rudolf Stulik's Restaurant de la Tour Eiffel in Percy Street, London, which included a panel of 'semi-abstract Buildings' and work by William Roberts.[97] If the Cave of the Golden Calf had sought 'after the reality of daily life, to reveal the reality of the unreal' by implicating the viewer in this very act of revelation—a process essentially still that of an earlier Nietzschean mural, the Beethoven Frieze of 1902 painted by Klimt in Madame Strindberg's and Stulik's home city, Vienna[98]—then by 1915, when Roberts painted *The Dancers* (Plate 214) in Stulik's restaurant, 'reality' could not be avoided. Neither brotherhood nor kinship now lay in the horrifying actuality of war, whose victims, as if phantoms of Roberts's recent experiences at the Front, performed in his mural a dance of death, barely recognizable as human forms. Roberts's *Diners* panel, its figures equally distorted, was added in 1919.[99]

AFTER THE WAR

In the immediate aftermath of war, few 'leisure' murals were painted. The centrepiece of the Arts and Crafts Exhibition Society's 1916 show at the Royal Academy was already a *Hall of Heroes*, effectively an installation of temporary murals of the type found in the earlier Paris or Venice exhibitions, but now given over to the grim purpose of memorial, and reverting for the most part to allegory and personification (Appendix E: 25). At the 1924 British Empire Exhibition at Wembley, something of the spirit of education through entertainment was rediscovered, but even here, remembrance was still prominent, with the Basilica being decorated by Colin Gill and A. K. Lawrence with panels including *Service, Sacrifice*, and *The Altruists*. These marked the rise of the British School at Rome as a new force in British mural painting. Brangwyn's Empire landscapes for the Pageant of Empire in the Stadium, like other murals in this and related exhibitions (Appendix E: 26, 27), meanwhile fulfilled a propaganda role shortly to be taken over by the Empire Marketing Board's films, though his Indian howdah scene, translating into exotic vocabulary his

[96] *Les Eus* (1911–12), Fergusson's largest painting, shows dancing nudes; he defined its title as meaning 'The Healthy Ones'. He married Margaret Morris.

[97] For Lewis's word 'savage', see Cork, *Art Beyond the Gallery*, p. 183. For the 'Rebel Art Centre', see above, p. 287 and Cork, pp. 190ff.; the description of Lewis's 'Buildings' panel is by his contemporary Harry Jonas (quoted in Cork, p. 222).

[98] See C. A. P. Willsdon, 'Gustav Klimt's Beethoven Frieze' (1996); as Compton, *British Art* notes (p. 132), Madame Strindberg would have been familiar with the Wiener Werkstätte's Kabarett Fledermaus in Vienna. The Cave's 'psychological' element differentiates it from the Omega Workshops' decoration of the Cadena Café in Westbourne Grove, London.

[99] For *The Dancers* (Plate 214), oil on canvas, 1.52 × 11.65 m, Glasgow Museum and Art Gallery, Kelvingrove, see cat. 45 and p. 141 in S. Compton, *British Art*, and Cork, *Art Beyond the Gallery*, pp. 214 ff. Cork suggests (p. 216) that Stulik may have been emulating the Petit Savoyard Restaurant in nearby Greek Street, where murals had been painted by C. Nevinson, E. Wadsworth, A. Allinson, and M. Gertler. Roberts's *Diners* is now in the Tate Gallery, London. All the murals were replaced with others by Frederick Gore when the Tour Eiffel restaurant was remodelled in the 1930s.

processions at Skinners' Hall, can nevertheless be recognized as a dry run for one of his Royal Gallery panels. Empire themes were in turn taken up in murals for shops in the 1920s (Appendix E: 29, 30).

For all their political topicality in the context of Britain's post-war concern to strengthen Empire trade, few, if any, of these schemes seem to have involved innovative experiment. At the Paris Decorative Art Exhibition of 1925, the British negotiated permission to interpret in a 'liberal spirit' its requirement for 'a modern inspiration and real originality',[100] perhaps in part to ensure that one of their principal mural submissions, Lawrence's Wembley *Altruists*, with its heavy dependence on Piero della Francesca, should not be ruled out of court! The Department of Overseas Trade's Report on the Exhibition none the less noted with concern the 'comparative dullness and aloofness, and the absence of the spirit of adventure'[101] in the British section.

It was perhaps no coincidence that following this disappointment, Charles Aitken, Director of the Tate Gallery, and Henry Tonks, Director of the Slade School, should have found an opportunity to promote murals in the Tate Gallery restaurant by a young British painter, Rex Whistler, whose training and style stood in contrast to the British School at Rome tradition. Although Rome Scholars had been required to produce 'a scale design for the decoration of a Hall, Concert Room or Restaurant etc.' as part of their 1924 syllabus,[102] it had been pointed out in a report on Lawrence's *Altruists* by the School's faculty that 'Piero della Francesca is not the model for every style of building, and might be too formal for a restaurant or theatre.'[103] One of the 'lessons' drawn by the Board of Trade from the 1925 Paris exhibition, meanwhile, was that 'if we are going to have any mural decoration at all it has got to be simple, and it has got to cost very little money.'[104] The decoration of the Tate Restaurant, a 'rather dark basement room'[105] was technically a State project and can be seen as a direct response to this requirement, financed as it was on a shoestring budget of £500 donated by Sir Joseph Duveen. Aitken intended it 'to induce big caterers such as Lyons etc, to give similar commissions to young artists';[106] Tonks took the opportunity to continue the encouragement of his own Slade School artists, which he had begun through his schemes for University College London, children's clubs (Appendix E: 24, 28), and at County Hall, since he told Whistler straight away that he had the job and Aitken found it necessary to pacify several Trustees, including Sir Philip Sassoon, who favoured the Rome Scholar Glyn Jones and had proposed a competition amongst Rome Scholars.[107]

Whistler's mural, called *The Pursuit of Rare Meats* (Plates 215, 216), portrays a fanciful journey, filled with witty architectural pastiche amidst rolling green countryside, whose object perhaps alludes to young British artists' eager quest for mural commissions. The journey is undertaken by the Duke and Duchess of Epicurania, and a crowd of motley followers including 'Król Duziarz' (Whistler's name in Polish). Did the mural in fact embody tongue-in-cheek allusions to the State scheme concurrently in progress by Rome artists at St Stephen's Hall? The fairy-tale style account of it written subsequently by Edith Olivier in consultation with Whistler involves anagrammatic or symbolic names including not only Ugpin (Pugin, who with Barry built the Palace of

[100] Sir H. Llewelyn Smith, 'Introduction' to *Reports* . . . (Dept. of Overseas Trade), p. 9.

[101] Ibid., p. 37.

[102] Minutes of Faculty of Painting, British School at Rome (9 May 1924), p. 58, BSRA.

[103] Letter from Dermod O'Brien to Evelyn Shaw (Hon. General Secretary of the British School at Rome) (n.d.; *c.*June 1924), BSRA.

[104] G. Sheringham, 'Mural Decoration' in *Reports* . . . , p. 53.

[105] Letter from Aitken to Sir Lionel Earle (First Commissioner of Works) (24 Oct. 1925), TGA.

[106] Letter from Aitken to Earle (31 Mar. 1926), TGA.

[107] See Minutes of Board of Tate Gallery (24 Feb. 1926) and letter from Aitken to Tonks (16 Mar. 1926), TGA.

Westminister), but also Crown Prince Etienne, 'a youth of rare beauty and promise, an aristocrat from the top of his high brow,'[108] whose name of course translates as Stephen, and who brings to mind the donation by several lords of the St Stephen's Hall murals. Król, significantly, delights in 'drawing caricatures of the people about the court',[109] but is also the member of the search party with the most up-to-date transport, a bicycle (Plate 216): was his Slade-trained art more progressive than that at St Stephen's Hall? The journey, presented as a continuous frieze around the restaurant, leads through the land of Cathay and past affectionate parodies of the Corinthian arch and Boycott Pavilions at Stowe, and a derelict 'Palace of Joisigonne' (whose name is an anagram of Inigo Jones). It also involves a ship in a tempest (an allusion to Colin Gill's storm-beaten Danish invaders at St Stephen's Hall?) as well as an attempt to 'parley' from an official 'Diplomatic' phrase book with a dark-skinned sailor carrying a cutlass (imagery from Sir William Rothenstein's St Stephen's *Sir Thomas Roe . . . envoy . . . to the Moghul Emperor*?) (Plate 69). On their return to Epicurania the members of the expedition are given honours, as were Clausen and Cameron following the Westminister scheme. The correlation with the St Stephen's Hall scheme is compelling.

Any such jests were, however, taken with good grace. Whistler's achievement was recognized by the award of an Honorary Rome Studentship in 1928, whilst the St Stephen's Hall artists were invited to the unveilling ceremony. This was performed by George Bernard Shaw, and prominent heads of business including Sir Kenneth Anderson of the Orient Shipping Line, Viscount Inchcape of P & O, and a host of managers of railway companies, hotels, and theatres were also invited. Duveen called it 'excellent propaganda'[110] and offered further finance, resulting in the murals at Morley College and a scheme at the Peel Institute, Clerkenwell. From the Tate's point of view,

> The board of this Gallery is anxious to open up new fields for the encouragement of the younger British artists. There is indubitably much talent available . . Large sums are spent in the decoration of restaurants, concert halls and other public rooms and I believe that if those concerned realized that our younger artists could decorate such rooms with individual and attractive paintings at no greater cost than that of the marble gilding and panelling usually employed . . . a School of British Mural Painters might develope[*sic*], equal to that of our mediaeval artists.[111]

If the Tate in the 1920s, aided by Duveen and Samuel Courtauld, was on one hand promoting French art through its acquisition policy,[112] on the other it was clearly seeking through mural painting to encourage young *British* artists, as if in cultural affirmation of the Treaty of Versailles. The choice for its murals of an artist from the Slade's Francophile tradition, who adopted a Claudean setting for their story, harmonized exactly with the ideal of Franco-British unity espoused by the Chairman of the Tate Trustees, Lord D'Abernon, who had negotiated the German reparations.

Though Whistler's scheme has many felicitous details, such as the *trompe-l'oeil* statues with hair made of grass in the manner of Arcimboldo's vegetable heads, the contrast of scale between its tiny, scarlet-costumed figures and the open green and ochre landscape creates a certain vacuousness. It was in a scheme of 1929 by a Rome Scholar, E. I. Halliday, for the library of Liverpool's

[108] E. Olivier, *In Pursuit of Rare Meats* (Tate Gallery, London, n.d. but post-1928), p. 10.

[109] Ibid., p. 11.

[110] Letter from Duveen to Aitken (20 Dec. 1927), TGA.

[111] 'Suggested draft for the letter to business managers inviting them personally to the opening of the Refreshment Room on Nov. 30th' (1927), TGA; this was slightly modified when actually sent.

[112] This policy was discussed by Brandon Taylor at the 'Rethinking Englishness: English Art 1880–1940' conference, University of York, 1997, in a paper entitled 'Francomania at the Tate: the 1920s'.

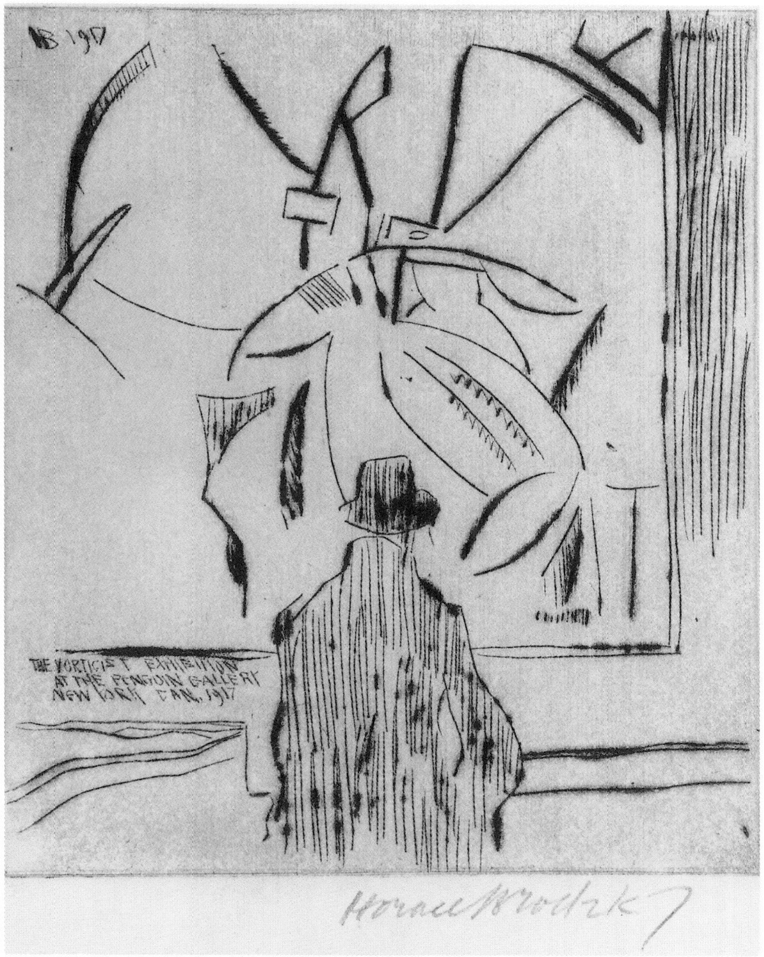

213. Horace Brodzky, *Viewing Kermesse*, 1917. Etching. Hunterian Art Gallery, University of Glasgow

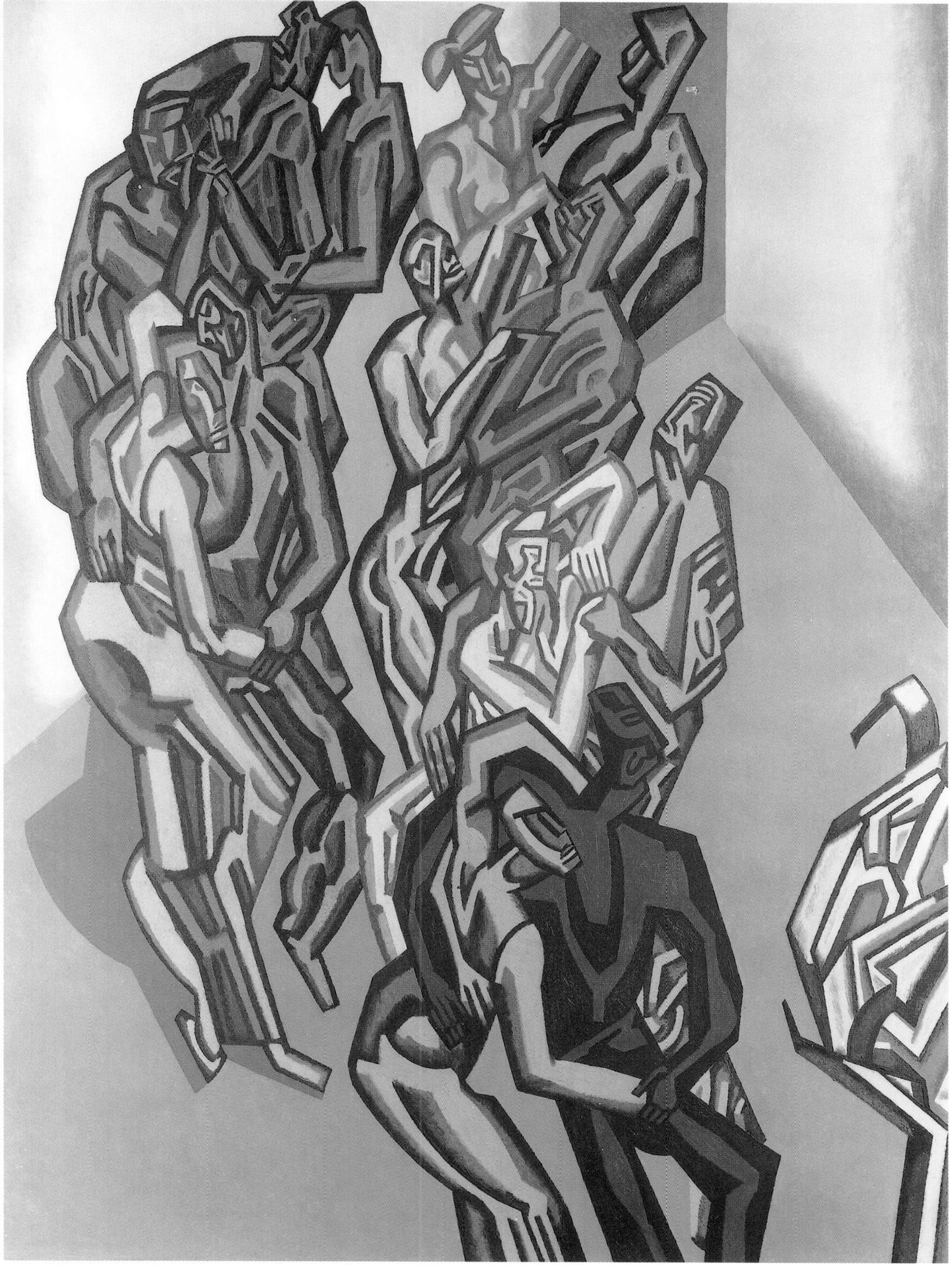

214. William Roberts, *The Dancers*, 1919. Glasgow, Art Gallery and Museum, Kelvingrove

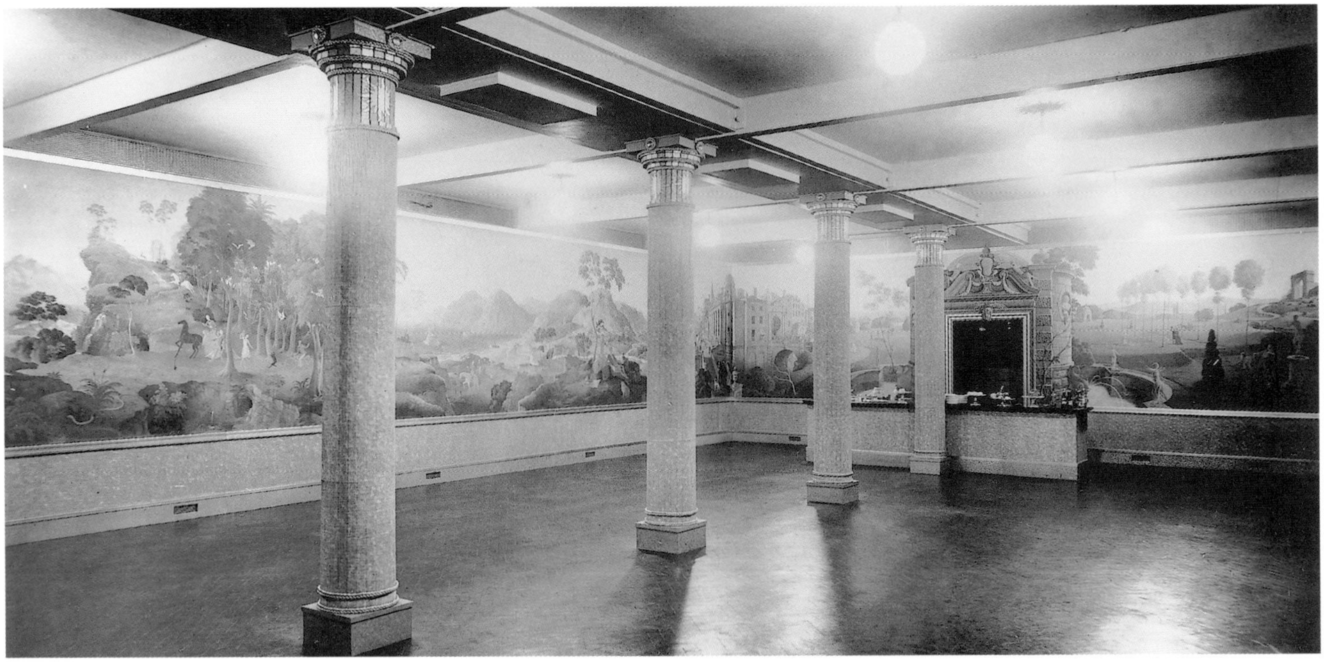

215. View of Rex Whistler's *The Pursuit of Rare Meats* decoration in the Restaurant, Tate Gallery, London, 1927, shortly after installation

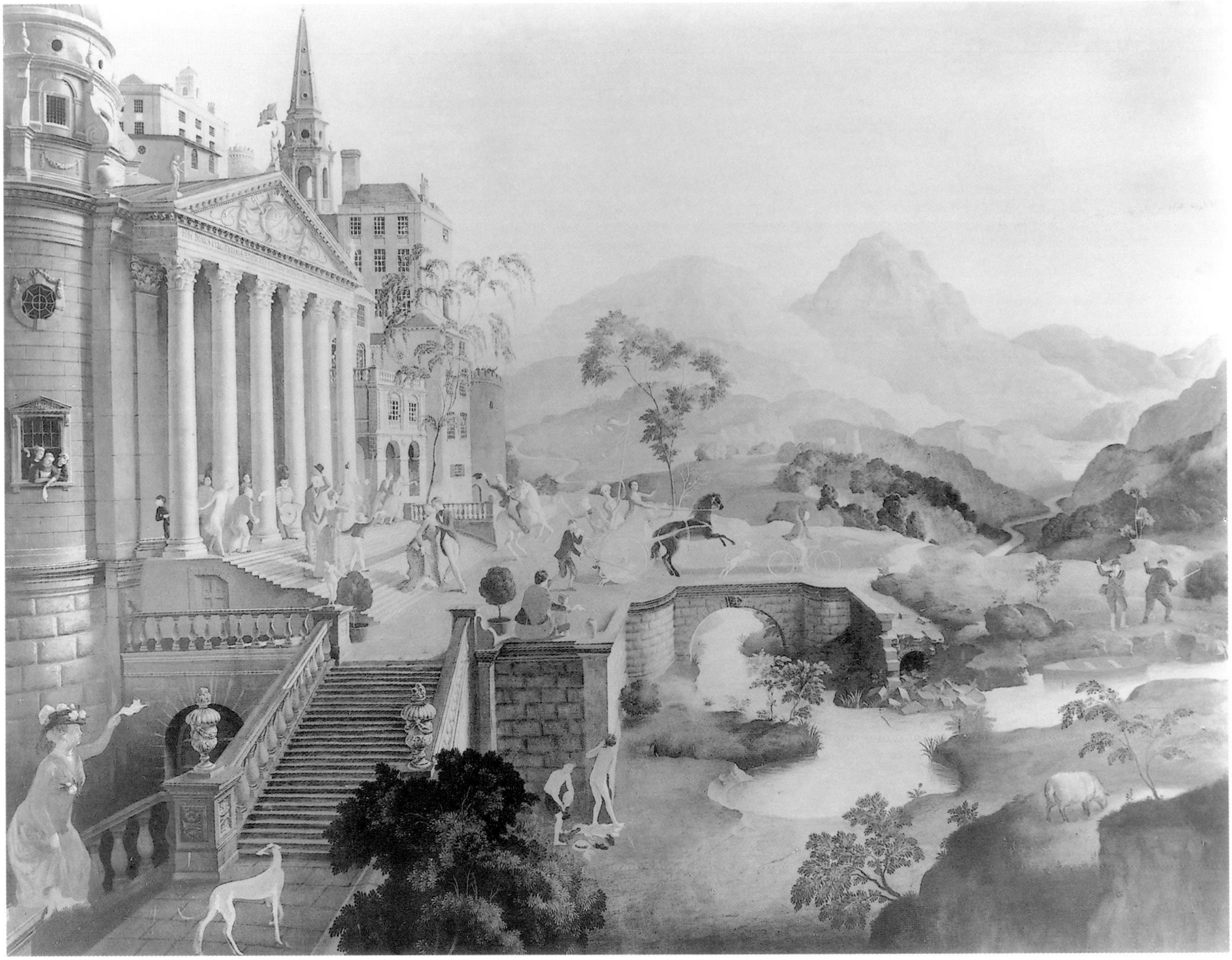

216. Rex Whistler, detail showing the departure (the artist leading the way on a bicycle), from *The Pursuit of Rare Meats*, Restaurant, Tate Gallery, London, 1927

Athenaeum Club, that a more successful integration of symbolism and decoration was perhaps achieved, whilst in turn it was in the hundreds of murals for liners and other leisure venues which followed Aitken's initiative during the 1930s that the Modernist trends displayed in the Continental exhibits at the Paris 1925 Exhibition found their sequel.

Halliday's three Athenaeum murals (Plate XLI; Plate 217) illustrate episodes from the legend of Athena, goddess of wisdom, and were donated for the Club's new premises by Sir Benjamin Johnson, who also commissioned murals from the artist for his home and his Bootle dyeworks. Though Halliday was given permission to return from Italy whilst still a Rome Scholar to undertake the commission, he created spiralling, vortex-like arrangements of figures amidst jagged rocks in *The Contest between Athena and Poseidon for the Patronship of Athens* (Plate 217) and *The Story of Marsyas* which, like the receding planes of the complex interior view in *Athena and Arachne* (Plate XLI), suggest the influence of Mannerism and Art Deco rather than the Pintorricchio and Raphael works he had been studying.[113] The simultaneous illustration in each panel of the successive episodes of its narrative, and the return to the story of *The Contest* as the subject of the tapestry woven by Athena in the final panel, *Athena and Arachne* (in which Arachne is turned into a spider for daring to compete with the goddess's skills) lend a hermetic self-referentiality to the scheme which suggests the Nietzschean doctrine of 'eternal recurrence', linking Halliday with George Bernard Shaw and D. H. Lawrence, who were inspired, like Wyndham Lewis, by the German writer. The recurrence is reinforced by Halliday's derivation of Athena's pose in the final panel, as she strikes Arachne with her shuttle, from that of Athena striking the ground to bring forth an olive tree in the *Contest of Athena and Poseidon* in the West Pediment of the Parthenon. The viewer is thus allusively returned to the subject of the first mural, just as the fate of Arachne is surrealistically foretold in *Athena and Arachne* by the shadow shaped like a spider which is cast by scaffolding around the giant classical columns in which she hangs herself after defeat by Athena. The three-dimensional web implied by the orthogonals in turn 'entraps' the *dramatis personae*, including Athena herself. The delicate olive-green colour scheme of the murals suggests Athena's olive tree, her 'gift . . . destined to bring great commercial prosperity' to Athens,[114] just as the Athenaeum Club provided social contact for Liverpool's prominent businessmen. Halliday portrayed his wife as Athena and himself as a cloth-dyer.

Halliday reverted to more tranquil compositions derived from early Renaissance sources in his murals for Booth's Shipping line (Appendix E: 31).[115] Something static, of course, was what was needed on board ship. As the architect Arthur E. Davis, of Mewès and Davis, had put it in 1911 when supervising decoration for Cunard's *Aquitania*.

> when we got well out on to the Atlantic there was one thing I craved for as never before, and that was a warm fire and a pink shade . . . If we could get ships to look like ships, and get people to enjoy the sea, it would be a very good thing, but all we can do, as things are, is to give them floating hotels.[116]

'Tudor', 'Jacobean', and 'Rococo' interiors with murals to match had been *de rigueur* in pre-war liner design, whilst the *Aquitania* of 1914, with its copies of Lagrenée and Van Loo and original

[113] See Halliday's Report on his first year as a Rome Scholar (24 June 1926) and photographs of his copies from Italian art whilst a Scholar, BSRA; for his Athenaeum murals, see E. I. Halliday, *The Athena Panels in the Library of the Athenaeum Liverpool* (Liverpool, n.d.); and A. Compton, *Edward Halliday* (1997).

[114] Halliday, *The Athena Panels*, description of *The Contest*.

[115] Photograph preserved by Walker Art Gallery, Liverpool.

[116] Quoted in V. Sekules, 'The Ship-owner as an Art Patron: Sir Colin Anderson and the Orient Line 1930–1960', *Journal of the Decorative Arts Society*, no. 10 (1986), p. 22.

painting by Van Cuygem in the 'Palladian Lounge', had been advertised as the 'Ship Beautiful'.[117] Moira's style had also been much favoured.[118] When Davis became ill in the early 1930s and Cunard turned for advice to Frank Pick of the recently formed Council for Art and Industry (who had earlier advised Aitken on his invitations to the Tate murals unveiling ceremony), a number of 'modern' names, including Christopher Nevinson, Stanley Spencer, Duncan Grant, Edward Wadsworth, Paul Nash, and Ben Nicholson were included in the list of muralists for the *Queen Mary*.[119] Meanwhile, 'fitness for purpose' was introduced as the guiding concept in Orient Line interiors following the arrival of the Bauhaus admirer Colin Anderson as a junior director. French and German liners such as the *Normandie* (with murals by Jean Dunand and Jean Dupas) and the *Europa* and the *Bremen* were showing that both in design and decoration, 'getting ships to look like ships' was realizable, and Britain was competing with these for transatlantic trade. Aboard Canadian Pacific's rather more conservative *Empress of Britain*, launched in 1930, a policy had been adopted where the artists themselves (including Brangwyn, Lavery, Heath Robinson, and Dulac) had responsibility for the overall decoration of individual areas of the interior.

In the event, Cunard decided that commercial success lay in a judicious accommodation with the 'pink lampshade', and rejected Stanley Spencer's sketch of dockyard riveters for a mural in the cabin-class ballroom of the *Queen Mary*. Refusing to paint a subject not of his own choice, Spencer pulled out of his commission. In turn in 1935, Sir Percy Bates, Cunard's director, dismissed Duncan Grant's contribution to the ship as fit only for 'the blind school',[120] provoking a bitter condemnation from Clive Bell of its remaining murals as 'aristo-comical' works revealing the 'frivolous and frightened attitude to art of rich people who are not sure of themselves'.[121] These works included Philip Connard's 8 metre *England*; Macdonald Gill's Atlantic map containing a movable crystal model of the ship; A. R. Thomson's cocktail-bar dance themes (Plate 218), and Kenneth Shoesmith's *Hakluyt* and *Pepys*—murals which, whilst easily understood, yet offered enough of Modernism to match the age. Even Wadsworth had made his nautical motif pictorially plausible by setting it upon a beach. Doris and Anna Zinkeisen had been allowed, on the *Empress of Britain* model, to design whole rooms; Doris complemented her circus and theatre panels with red curtains and a black carpet.

Shoesmith spoke up for the defence, declaring that in his commissions he had been 'subjected to no interference whatever',[122] his style, of course, like his maxim 'When you are at sea you want a rest from your own ship,'[123] offered a suitable mix of pictorial realism and decorative simplification. It was left to the Orient Line's ships, beginning with *Orion* (1935) and *Orcades* (1937) to become watchwords for the unity of art and technology. In the process, however, mural painting in the traditional sense mutated into a broader art-form, represented, for example, by E. McKnight-Kauffer's engraved glass mirror with diagrammatic motifs for *Orion*, or the wood, steel, and glass bas relief of *Neptune watching the Course of a Ship* by Ceri Richards for the *Orcades* (Plate 219). Such work was now an equal player with coordinated colour schemes and Marion

[117] See A. M. Broadley, *The Ship Beautiful—Art and the Aquitania* (London, 1914) in Cunard Archive, University of Liverpool; and for the pre-war ships, period photographs and advertising leaflets in the collection of the National Maritime Museum, London.

[118] Moira decorated 17 P & O liners (see J. H. Watkins, *The Art of Gerald Moira*, p. 33); he and Harold Wyllie also painted the five panels of British naval victories still extant in the Wardroom of HMS *Nelson*, Portsmouth.

[119] See I. Godfrey, 'Style for a Moving Place: Decorative Work on the *Queen Mary*', *Scottish Art Review*, 17 (1991), pp. 8–11.

[120] Quoted in M. Anglesea, *Kenneth Shoesmith (1890–1939)*, Ulster Museum catalogue (Belfast, 1977).

[121] C. Bell in *The Listener* (1936), quoted in Godfrey, 'Style for a Moving Place', p. 8.

[122] Quoted in Anglesea, *Kenneth Shoesmith*.

[123] Ibid.

Dorn's fabrics and curtains in a programme of interior design, orchestrated by Anderson himself in consultation with his naval architect and the New Zealand designer Brian O'Rorke, which was as fully streamlined as the ships themselves.

In essence, murals at sea had reopened the debate about the relative authority of the painter and the architect which had been so vigorous at the start of the century when Sir William Richmond had been defeated by Otto Wagner. Whereas in the 1920s and early 1930s at the Bank of England the partnership was remarkably equal, in the field of leisure murals the architecturally determined emphasis of the *Orion* and the *Orcades* decoration was matched on one hand in schemes coordinated by interior designers like Oliver Messel, whose much admired British Pavilion at the Paris International Exhibition of 1937 included murals by Mary Adshead and Hans Aufseeser; and on the other, in schemes for Bauhaus-influenced modern architecture. Surviving examples of Modernism include Eric Ravilious's decoration for Oliver Hill's Midland Hotel in Morecambe (1933) and Wadsworth's for Mendelssohn and Chermayeff's De La Warr Pavilion at Bexhill-on-Sea (1935) (Plate 220). Ravilious's *Neptune and Triton* ceiling roundel of 'primitive', Byzantinesque figures entwined in a mandorla formation complements the wide spiral staircase beneath, just as his wrap-around *Morning and Evening at the Seaside*, with its schematic evocation of fireworks on the seafront, links the theme of the diurnal round with its setting, the Circular Café. In the Tea-Lounge of the De La Warr Pavilion, Wadsworth's almost heraldic confection of spiralling nautical forms—shells, a half-unfurled map, a top, and the line of a pen-nib in action which, de Chirico-like, is transmuted into a rope at the start of an inscription recording the donation of the mural—repeats the curvilinear progress of the stair in the vestibule, whilst its grey and black ribbon motif echoes its aluminium handrail. In contrast to his *Queen Mary* work, the image is not within a pictorial setting, merely set against a sand-coloured surface.

It would be misleading to suggest that such work was typical of 1930s leisure murals. Numerous decorations were produced, both by commercial companies (Appendix E: 32) and by a body of artists who, rather than constituting any coherent School of British Mural Painters such as Aitken had hoped to found, followed widely disparate styles, not only in leisure but also work contexts. These ranged from John Armstrong's bold geometry, consistent with his *Orcades* contribution, in his *History of Transport* mural of a tractor and goods train for Shell-Mex House, or Margaret Jagger's cut-out milk-maid, leaping cow, and coat-tailed gentleman for the Meadow Milk Bar in London's Regent Street,[124] to Brangwyn's *The Printed Word Makes the Peoples of the World One* in the entrance hall of Odham's Press, London (1935–6), historical portraiture, pastiche, and comforting images of a bygone England. The historical scenes included Halliday's *Seaside of Yester-year* (1937) in the milk bar of the Dolphin Square residential complex in London, where he also painted *Seaside of Today* (Plate 221) in the cocktail bar (Appendix E: 33–7). At the 1938 International Exhibition in Glasgow, Modernist pavilions were adorned with a blend of theatricality and hard commercial interest (Appendix E: 38). Whilst this diversity provided a happy hunting ground for Sir John Rothenstein's 1939 Tate exhibition—whose goal of stimulating patronage made it a direct sequel to Aitken's Tate Restaurant scheme—it is difficult to characterize in any meaningful way, especially since much work has been lost. Clearly, however, in place of the synaesthesia and symbolism of earlier years, there was now a sharpened sense of mural painting

[124] Anon., 'New West End Milk Bar', *P. L. R. Bulletin* (13 Jan. 1936). For other examples, see Rothenstein (1939) and the file about the related exhibition, PRO No. 258, TGA; numerous schemes were also illustrated in the *Studio* during the 1920s and 1930s.

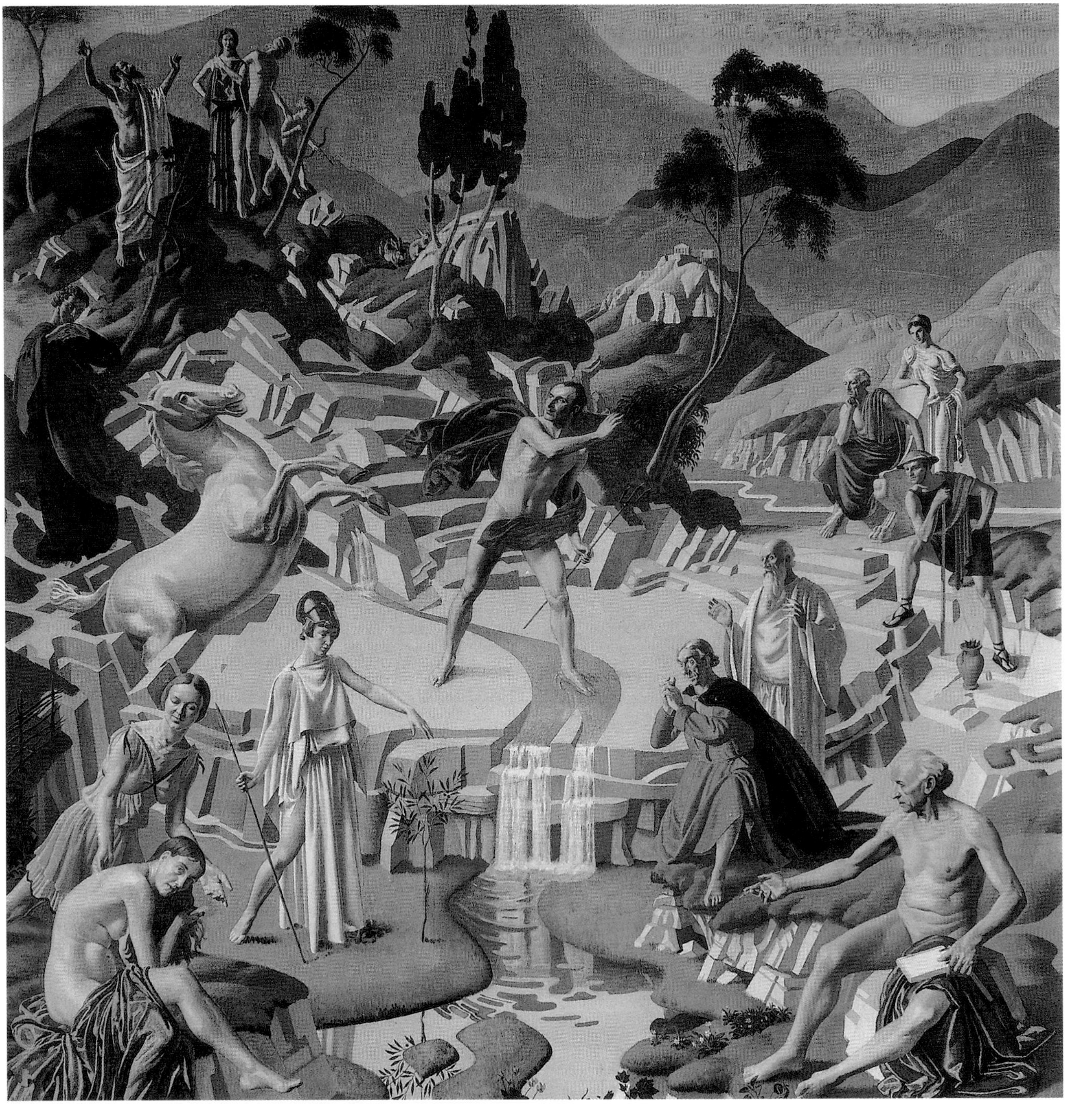

217. Edward I. Halliday, *The Contest between Athena and Poseidon for the Patronship of Athens*, 1929, Athenaeum, Liverpool

218 (*facing, above*). Alfred Reginald Thomson, *Dance* mural in Observation and Cocktail Bar, the *Queen Mary*, 1936

219 (*facing, below*). Ceri Richards, *Neptune watching the Course of a Ship*, wood, steel and glass bas relief, First Class Dining Saloon, *Orcades* II, 1937. Period photograph by Stewart Bale. London, National Maritime Museum

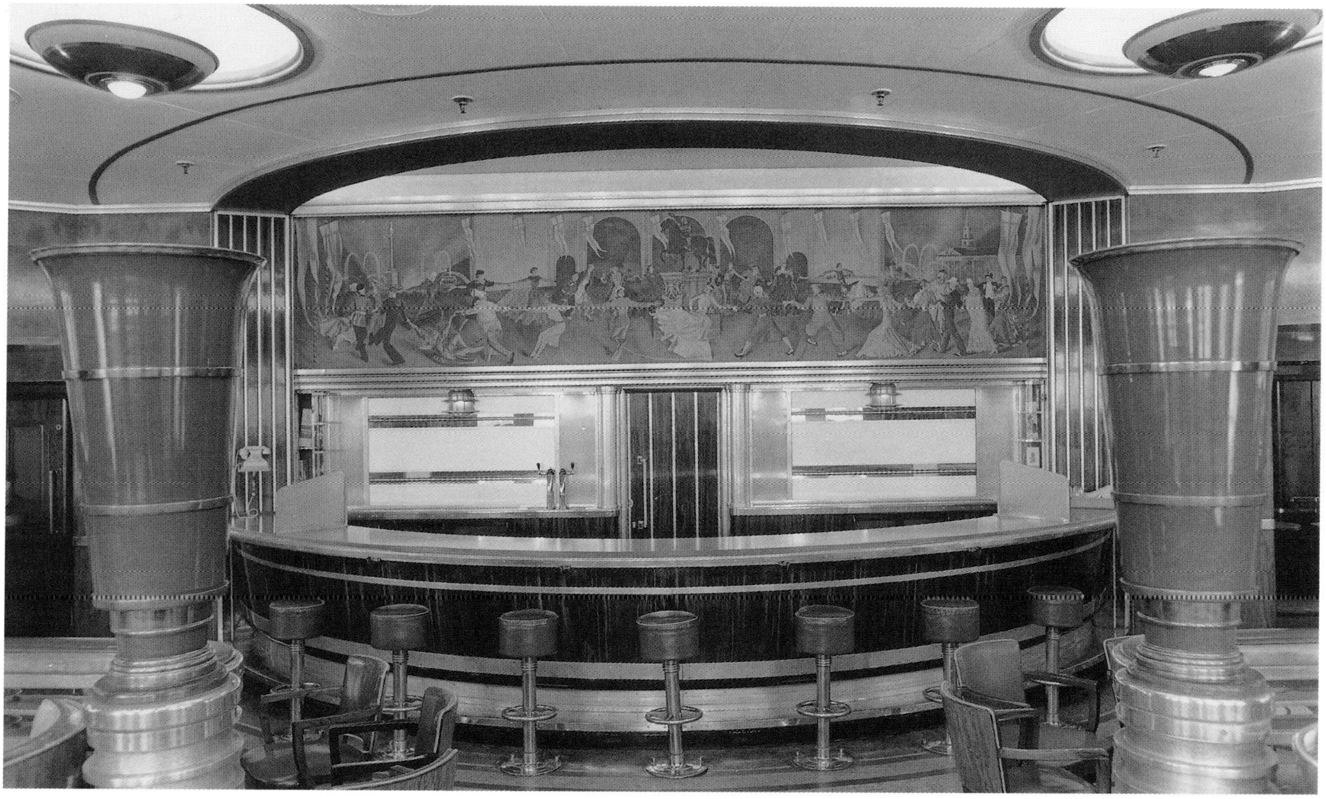

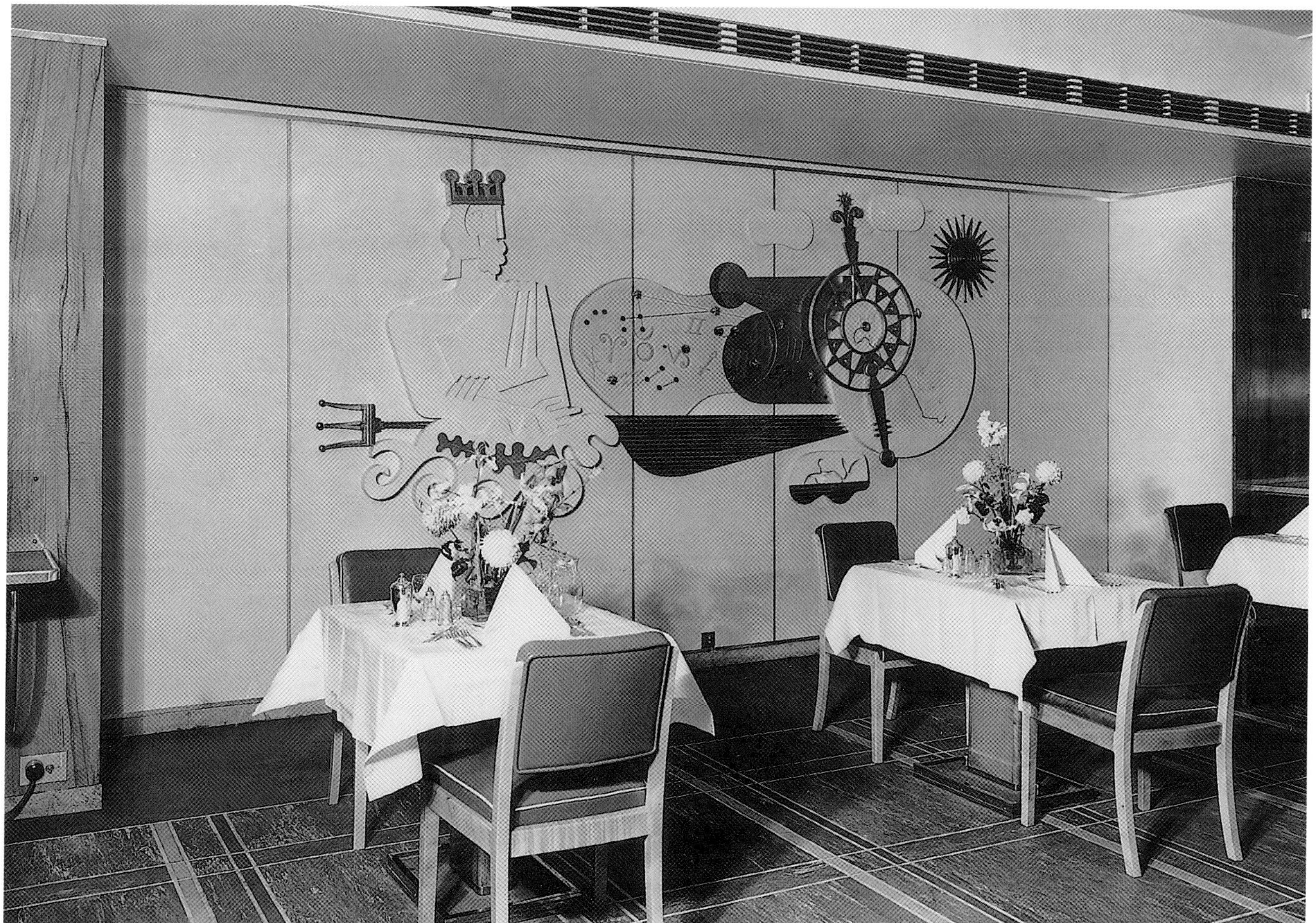

220. Period photograph taken in 1936 of the Tea-Lounge at the De La Warr Pavilion, Bexhill-on-Sea, Sussex, showing the mural there by Edward Wadsworth

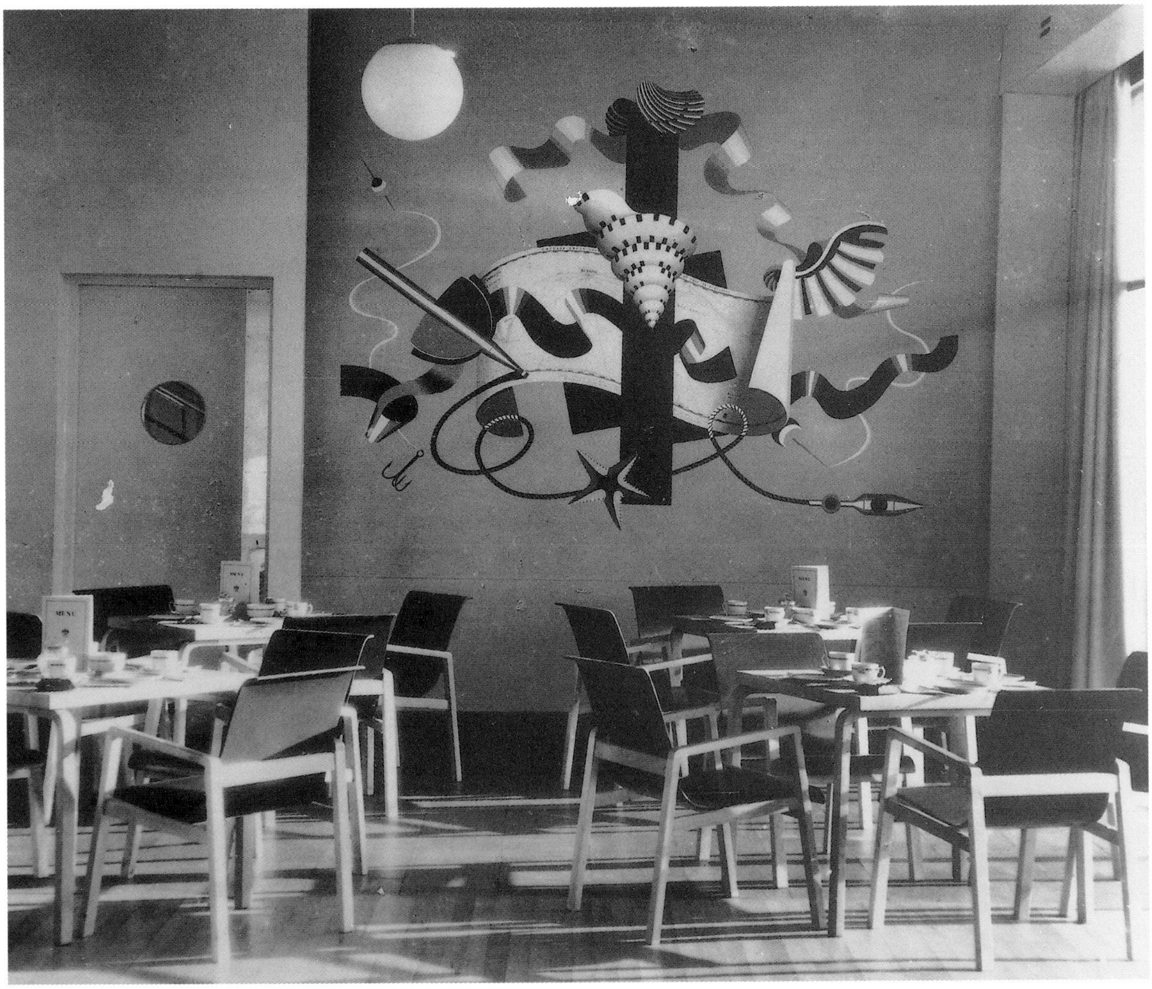

221. Period photograph showing Edward I. Halliday's *Seaside of Today* (1937) in the Milkbar, Dolphin Square, London. London, Tate Gallery Archive

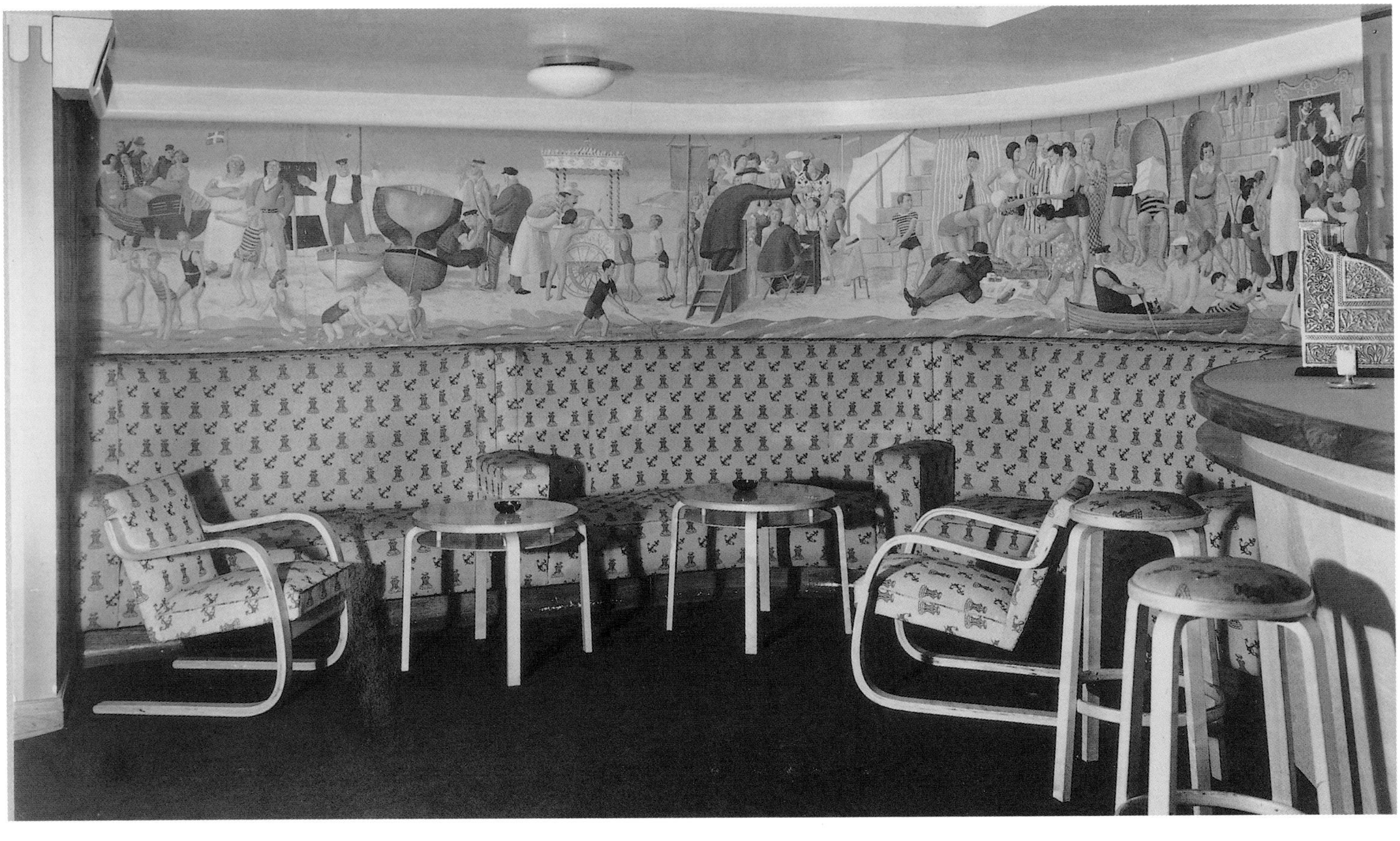

asan aid to ambience or mood, able equally to promote conversation in restaurants, escapism in the cinema, or the life of luxury on the ocean wave. At the same time there was a certain paradoxical combination of the renewed ideal of integration with architecture (and thus of mural art as something enduring) with delight in jokes, wit and economy of style, or means in which the throw-away or casual was prized. There is a sense in which mural painting as an art-form had by the 1930s become all but synonymous with leisure and recreation. Murals in schools, colleges, and hospitals, as we have seen, were increasingly for entertainment as much as instruction; the light-hearted panels for naval canteens promoted by A. R. Sturrock in the late 1930s (Appendix E: 39) in turn led directly to the war-time murals for 'munitions works . . . industrial canteens and welfare centres'[125] of an 'Art for the People' scheme intended to boost civilian morale. Play had become a vital ingredient in work.

125 W. O. Hutchison, 'Canteen Murals', *Studio*, 124, no. 594 (Sept. 1942), p. 101. Artists of these murals included Anne Redpath, Mary Armour, and William Crosbie. See also O. Hill, 'Mural Paintings in War Canteens and British Restaurants', *Studio*, 136, no. 608 (Nov. 1943).

12
Conclusion

It is monstrously absurd . . . to speak of inoculating England with the love of fresco as if that were all she wanted, and men could be sublime on a wall who were idiots on canvas. Fresco does indeed afford glorious *room* for a man who wants it; it is a splendid sea for the strong swimmer, but you might as well throw a covey of chickens into the Atlantic as our R.A.'s into fresco.[1]

Such was Ruskin's assessment in 1845 of the attempt by the Royal Fine Arts Commission to revive mural painting in modern Britain through the schemes at the Palace of Westminster. Writing as he was from his beloved Venice, surrounded by works of the great Renaissance masters, he saw little hope in the venture because 'we are a different race altogether from the men of old time; we live in drawing rooms instead of deserts; and work by the light of chandeliers instead of volcanoes.'[2] And yet by 1863, encouraged by Maclise's murals at Westminster (Plates 19, 21, 24, 25, Plate III), which he admired because 'every touch and hue of colour . . . has been put on lovingly by the painter's own hand,'[3] as well as by Watts's (Plate 27), and probably also prompted by his experience of advising on the murals by the Pre-Raphaelites at the Oxford Union (Plates 140, 141) and William Bell Scott at Wallington Hall (Plates 173, 174), Ruskin was recommending that mural painting 'should form a branch of the teaching in the [Royal] Academy, possibly the principal branch'.[4] He was, of course, witnessing in Maclise's Royal Gallery work the use of water-glass technique, that substitute for fresco which enabled the greater precision of detail that he favoured in the easel art of Millais or Rossetti, and alternative media had likewise been adopted by Morris's team and Scott. Ruskin had now reached the conclusion, as he told the Government Commission of 1863 on 'the Present Position of the Royal Academy in Relation to the Fine Arts', that

the term 'fresco painting' was a wide one . . . none of us seemed to know quite the limitation or extent of it; and after giving a good deal more time to the question I am still less able to answer [it] directly . . . but using the term 'decorative painting, applicable to walls in permanent materials', I think it is essential that every great school should include as one of its main objects the teaching of wall painting in permanent materials, and on a large scale.[5]

If Ruskin's change of heart by 1863 and the variety of techniques by then in use none the less suggest that decorative painting in the nineteenth century was as choppy a sea for critics as for

[1] Letter from J. Ruskin to his father (30 Sept. 1845), in *The Complete Works*, ed. E. T. Cooke and F. Wedderburn (London, 1903–12), vol. 4, p. 393.

[2] Letter from J. Ruskin to J. Severn (21 Sept. 1845), ibid., p. 394.

[3] J. Ruskin: Evidence to the Royal Academy Commission (8 June 1863), § 61, ibid., p. 488.

[4] Ibid., § 23, p. 482.

[5] Ibid., § 22, p. 481.

artists, what are we, nearly 150 years later, to make of its ebb and flow; of its continued swell in the twentieth century; and, at times, of the mere faint memories which are all that survive today of some of its mural schemes? Can we chart its currents and the routes its swimmers took, to write a history of murals through the hundred years from 1840? Or is a sea an entity so vast and variable as to be inherently indefinable except by contrast with the land and sky which frame it? Does the sheer diversity of patronage in the nineteenth and twentieth centuries, embracing new forms of commercial, industrial, educational, leisure, and private commission, as well as the traditional employers of Church and State, in turn demand a different kind of critical method from that suited, for example, to medieval, Renaissance, or Baroque mural art?

Whilst making a first attempt in this book to navigate Ruskin's 'splendid sea', I have also tried to find some answers to these questions by bringing other methodologies to bear; moving beyond the mere chronology of weather, wind, and the trading-routes of technique and style to probe the framing elements of place and wider context. My concerns have been to find out why, during the century from 1840, murals were painted at a given time and place; whether their presence was intended, for example, to extend horizons, embody dreams, assert identity, or invent tradition; and what spurred—and sometimes stymied—that perhaps most enigmatic element of all, the creative relationship of patron, artist, viewer, and in some cases also architect. Answers to the questions have, of necessity, been sometimes only partial, yet they offer the building blocks for a first appraisal of the characteristics, strengths, and weaknesses of mural painting in Britain from 1840 to 1940.

The nineteenth-century murals at the Palace of Westminster, for example, can now be recognized as in part unashamed propaganda for Prince Albert's vision of greater power for the monarchy within the Constitution of 1840s Britain, and those of 1906–10 as publicity banners for the new Liberal government's reforms. It is very clear that State mural painting at Westminster was consistently, from the 1840s through to Brangwyn's work for the Royal Gallery, a means to present ideas (whether those of Prince Albert or the personal ones of Brangwyn, which proved unacceptable to his patrons). But it was also a much more subtle kind of art: a symbol of national identity, in which style, technique, and iconography compose a seamless whole. The very term adopted to describe the work of the 1840s and 1850s at Westminster, 'the style of fresco', elides method and appearance. The 'large and simple forms' and 'very direct action' which it was supposed to involve (however variable the quality of the actual work produced), made it as much an emblem as an aesthetic or technique, and it was essentially synonymous with the promotion of royal prerogative in government. 'Grandeur of form' might proclaim the status Albert wished for the monarch within the Constitution. Of the artists who grappled with 'the fresco style' (Plate 222), however, perhaps only Dyce and Cope in the Royal Robing Room (Plate II, Plate 23) and the Chamber of the House of Lords (Plates 18, 20, 22) really made it work; though Cope's original 'trial sketch' in fresco for *Edward III and the Black Prince* (Plate 223) was criticized by the press because the Prince was as 'passive as though he were undergoing measurement for a pair of boots',[6] such problems were mainly overcome in the finished works. Whilst Cope's *Edward* (Plate 20) shows some anatomical peculiarities, and both his and Dyce's work has at times a rather stilted or theatrical air, it is far more successful in colour and design than the generally rather mawkish efforts in 'Poets' Hall'. Again, working in other media, Ward and Cope in the Commons'

[6] The *Spectator* (5 July 1845), p. 644, quoted in R. J. B. Walker, *Catalogue of Paintings . . . in the Palace of Westminster* (1959–77), vol. 3 p. 33.

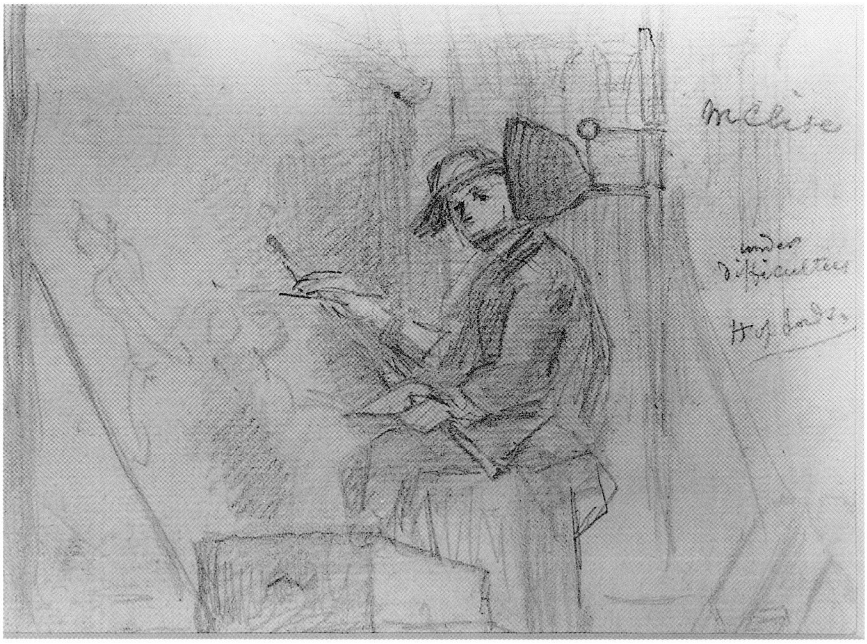

222. Charles West Cope, pencil drawing of 'Maclise fresco painting under difficulty in the House of Lords', *c.*1860s. London, Palace of Westminster

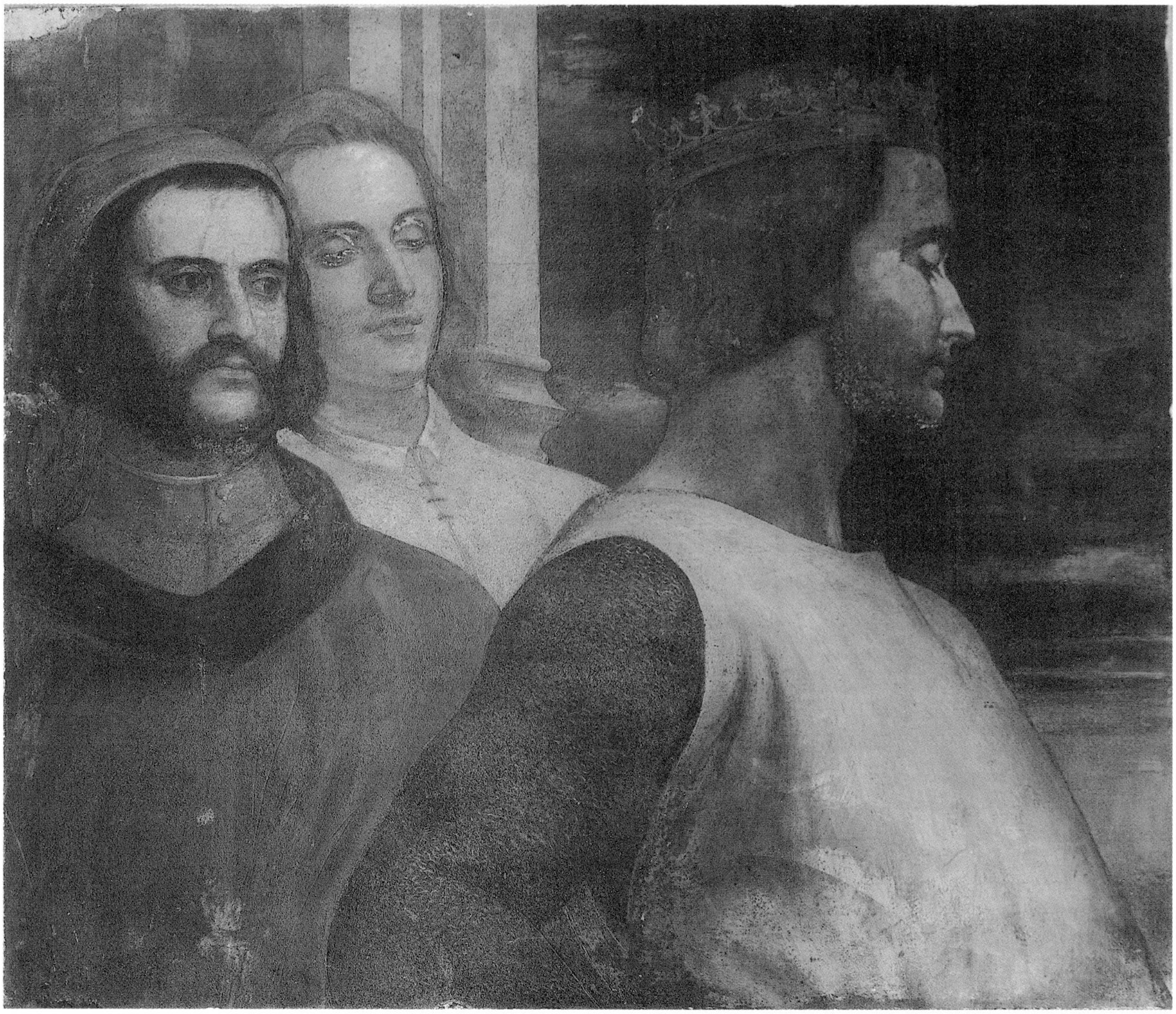

223. Charles West Cope, *Edward III and the Black Prince*, specimen of fresco, 1844, exhibited at Westminster Hall in 1845. London, Palace of Westminster

Corridor (Plate IV; Plate 28) offered a *juste milieu* form of history painting which, accomplished as it is, does not essentially differ from easel art. Maclise's Royal Gallery work stands out as a *tour de force*, but can hardly be said, as Prince Albert realized, to offer 'large and simple forms', and it has its effect less by dramatic gesture than by an appeal to the viewer's human sympathy, inviting us to identify with the common sailors and soldiers who made possible Nelson's and Wellington's victories. The painter's personal insight here arguably makes something far greater than mere illustration of the patron's ideals, much as, working for the same Royal Gallery, but in the twentieth century, Brangwyn's British Empire scheme (Plates XIX–XX; Plates 81–3) built on Maclise's sense of human brotherhood to offer a personal and imaginative if problematic response to his war-memorial commission. Here, the rhythmic harmony of composition, colour, and style itself affirms Brangwyn's vision of fellowship and renewal. The murals of the late 1930s by Jack Hastings and Clifford Wright, pupils of Diego Rivera who contributed to the anti-Fascist Artists' International Association (AIA) in Britain,[7] were more overtly political.

So too, although the nineteenth-century Tractarians and Ecclesiologists saw painting on walls as a literal means, through the fusion of an image with its physical location, to bring the spiritual values of Biblical imagery to bear upon the temporal contingencies of earthly life, it has to be said that the results rarely offer the conviction and insight which characterize the best secular murals of the period, such as Götzenberger's eerie *Comus* scenes for the *Gesamtkunstwerk* he created at Bridgewater House, Bell Scott's psychological immediacy at Wallington Hall (Plates 173, 174), or Goetze's Grove House Music Room (Plate XXXIX; Plate 188). Leighton's *Wise and Foolish Virgins* at Lyndhurst Parish church (Plate 119), Henry Payne's Madresfield Court chapel (Plates 133, 134), or Stanley Spencer's Burghclere Memorial (Plates 136, 137) represent high points of achievement in a genre which was dominated by the formulaic idiom of commercial decorating companies even into the twentieth century. In turn, the integration of painting, literature, and music which underpins Götzenberger's work (Plate XXXVI) emerges by the late nineteenth and early twentieth centuries, in private house or leisure schemes by not only Goetze but also Leighton, Duncan, Moira, and Strachan (Plates 181; 210; 212) as one of the most interesting and successful aspects of the British mural revival. Such integration shows that Britain took its place in the development of European Symbolism, not just through the conventionally cited *Yellow Book* and Aubrey Beardsley graphics, but also through the art-form which Continental Symbolists so highly prized, mural painting. The synaesthetic qualities of Wyndham Lewis's Cave of the Golden Calf decoration (Plate 213), in this sense make it not some kind of Modernist bolt from the blue, but the natural successor to these British versions of the *Gesamtkunstwerk*.

One of the most striking instances of the revelation to be had from a 'contextual' approach is the 'political' dimension of the reception given to Goetze's Foreign Office murals (Plates XVl; 54–9) and Brangwyn's Royal Gallery scheme (Plate 8). The complaints by the Lords in the early 1930s about Brangwyn's 'inappropriate' style have hitherto been taken at face value, but when set in relation to contemporary events and attitudes, they can be seen as a cover for more profound ideological concerns about changes in the Empire. Precisely *because* they are painted for a certain audience and place, murals cannot be viewed solely as mere aesthetic objects, and conversely, there may be a good case for considering whether particular pieces of easel art or sculpture might also

[7] See L. Morris and R. Radford, *The Story of the Artists International Association 1933–1953* (Museum of Modern Art, Oxford, 1983) and R. Radford, *Art for a Purpose: The Artists International Association, 1933–35* (Winchester, 1987); the AIA's work was shown in exhibitions including *Art for the People* (Whitechapel Art Gallery, London, 1939).

sometimes yield new insights if treated with a similar breadth of reference. How far, for example, does the retreat from art as propaganda, which was evident by the early 1930s in the official reaction to the British Empire scheme, as well as in the growing association between murals and leisure evident in the decoration of liners and restaurants, also provide a suggestive context for the abstract styles espoused by artists such as Henry Moore or the 7 & 5 Society? Was their avant-garde art in this sense actually more conformist than Brangwyn's own, avoiding the subjects frowned on by the censor, yet also standing as a conscious opposite to the insistent realism of the left-wing AIA?

It is obvious that such a richly symbolic or narrative art-form as mural painting, with its intimate relationship to architects', patrons', and users' purposes, offers ample justification for the conclusion reached by a number of recent writers on British art that it is time to reconsider Roger Fry's 'Modernist aesthetic theory' with its 'rejection . . . of the illustration of ideas . . . of story, sequence and temporality'.[8] Study of mural painting surely has a cardinal role to play in realizing the attempt being made by David Solkin and other historians of British art to 'reopen . . . the boundaries between modernist and other forms of painterly practice, and situate . . . all of these practices more securely within the institutional and commercial mechanisms of the modern art world'.[9] 'Institutions' and 'commerce', of course, were often the very givers of mural patronage, and their 'mechanisms'—in terms of 'invention of tradition' or self-promotion—were expressed in the decoration they commissioned for their walls. This book shows that there is a place at the art-historical table for the realist styles, story-telling, history painting, and symbolism which were dominant characteristics of the British mural revival. At the same time, however, mural painting, of its very nature, has to do with those values of design, form, and 'timelessness'[10] which Fry, Clive Bell, and the Modernist ethos sought to privilege. We can read Fry's own involvement in making murals, especially in such a context as the Omega Room at the *Daily Mail* exhibition of 1913 (Plate 194), as actually propaganda for his formalist aesthetic. Yet Ruskin's comment about the distinction between mural and easel painters also reminds us that muralists have, after all, to scale their designs to an architectural setting, fitting colouring and composition to a particular room, and must do so with skill if the viewer is to sense what Ruskin, with his nineteenth-century vocabulary, termed the 'sublime'. Whether intentionally or not, a mural carries ideas or ideals, but is far more than either a 'tract'[11] or a piece of wallpaper. It is not just an easel painting writ large, as *Punch* recognized already in 1847 when it ridiculed the struggles of Westminster competitors to meet the demands of wall-painting by adopting such 'modes' as the 'Mediaeval-Angelico-Pugin-Gothic or Flat Style' or 'the Fuseli-Michael-Angelesque way'.[12] Ruskin's metaphor of a sea, with its apparently conflicting connotations of eternity, flux, and a power part physical and part emotive (as in Matthew Arnold's *Dover Beach*, for example) may not be a bad starting-point in attempting to understand such a diverse but highly regarded art-form as mural painting was in Britain between 1840 and 1940. It was public art, decorating the walls of national and local government, the Ambassadors' staircase at the Foreign Office, churches, entertainment halls, schools, and hospitals; but it was also an intensely private medium, providing wish-fulfilment or fantasy projection in an

[8] S. Tillyard, 'The End of Victorian Art: W. R. Sickert and the Defence of Illustrative Painting', in B. Allen (ed.), *Towards a Modern Art World: Studies in British Art I* (New Haven and London, 1995), p. 191.

[9] D. Solkin, 'The British and the Modern', ibid., p. 6.

[10] S. Tillyard, 'The End of Victorian Art' p. 191.

[11] '[Mural] pictures are different from tracts', letter referring to the scheme for the East Corridor at Westminster, from Lord Carlisle to Lewis Harcourt, First Commissioner of Works (25 June 1909), HA.

[12] *Punch*, 14 (1848), p. 197, as given in Walker, *Catalogue*, vol. 3, p. 35.

individual home—and such characteristics might be richly mingled in the house of the wealthy patron who looked to mural decoration to assume a public status, or in the bank or business house which sought to gain its clients' intimate trust.

The sometimes shimmering, sometimes stormy, and in places frankly muddy waters of Ruskin's metaphorical 'sea' need to be seen as an integral part of the map of British art history if, on one hand, a rounded view is to be gained of this, and on the other, informed decisions are to be made about the conservation of mural schemes. Mural painting is a fact which has to be taken into account in any rational appraisal of British art as a whole. As this book shows, there was a significant amount of it; it was the subject of serious critical attention in its day; and a very wide range of different artists, including painters of stature, turned their hand to it, with the support of a similar diversity of patrons and architects. Historians of French art are already setting the famous names of Impressionism and Post-Impressionism alongside not only academic art, but also French mural painting, and reaching revealing conclusions.[13] The murals at the Royal Exchange in London (Plates V–VIII; Plates 1, 14, 33–6, 38–40) may not be avant-garde in style, but they constitute as tangible a part and in a literal sense, more tangible—of early twentieth-century art in Britain as the lost decoration of the Cave of the Golden Calf by Wyndham Lewis, Gore (Plate XLIII) and Epstein which has become so firmly written into Modernist and subsequent views of British art history. Yet both types of mural, in their differing ways, involve forms of ritual, wish-fulfilment, and the manufacture of identity. Clearly some of the works at the Exchange, such as Stanhope Forbes's *Great Fire* (Plate VI) or Frank Salisbury's *Alfred* (Plate V), with their taut fusion of design, psychological effect, and symbolism, are much more successful than others. Can we properly understand Fry's revulsion against 'art as message', however, unless we recognize the propaganda, commemorative purposes, and strong emotive force for their viewers of the Exchange panels? Do we adequately understand art patronage in nineteenth-century Britain if we only look at sales of easel paintings and purchases from Royal Academy and other exhibitions; the kind of art which Ruskin scorned as 'ignoble' because it was 'portable'? Are murals, in turn, not a form of documentary evidence every bit as much of a contribution to social, political, or other kinds of history as the more familiar textual sources on which this conventionally rests—letters, documents, and government memos? If in the event not precisely executed as he had planned, Prince Albert's mural programme for the Royal Gallery at Westminster, for example, which culminated in 'Queen Victoria surrounded by the sovereigns of Europe who came to prove to her their respect for her person and their readiness to cooperate with her in the maintenance of universal peace,'[14] none the less clearly adumbrates the internationalist ideals he later sought to propagate through another kind of cultural politics, the Great Exhibition of 1851.[15] In this sense it is entirely logical that mural painting, despite its 'permanent' tag, should have become increasingly popular in the pavilions of the great international exhibitions in Britain and abroad which succeeded that of 1851, and that after the Second World War, it was the 1951 Festival of Britain that provided a major focus for the continued development of mural painting in Britain.[16]

[13] e.g. R. Thomson, *Monet to Matisse* (1994) (see the chapter on 'Landscape as Decoration', pp. 131ff).

[14] See Chapter 2, note 34.

[15] For a discussion of the philosophy behind the Great Exhibition, see J. Steegman, *Victorian Taste* (1970).

[16] Cf. the establishment, 'as a result of' Sir John Rothenstein's *Mural Painting in Great Britain 1919–1939* exhibition at the Tate Gallery in 1939, of a new Society of Mural Painters with Augustus John as its President (H. Feibusch, 'Introduction' to catalogue of *Society of Mural Painters First Exhibition*, Arts Council of Great Britain, 1950), and the hope expressed in the catalogue by Philip James that the Festival would prompt commissions for the Society's artists.

Similarly, murals at Chelsea Town Hall (Plate XXIV; Plates 103, 104) can be recognized as contributions to the suffragette cause; statements in a sense yet more subversive—precisely *because* they were couched in the format and medium used by the great (and male) Renaissance masters—than the more 'familiar' agitprop embroidered banners which the Suffragettes borrowed from Trade Unionism.[17]

A full integration of the art I have discussed with the better-known gamut of easel painting, sculpture, architecture, and the graphic and applied arts of the century from 1840 lies beyond the scope of this book. Fitting its history into that of European decorative painting will clearly enrich our understanding of both British and Continental art, whilst relationships with American mural art (not least in terms of Sargent's and Brangwyn's commissions for American patrons), and with the corpus of work by such leaders in the mural genre as Puvis de Chavannes (Plates 4, 60), Hans von Marées, Alphonse Mucha, Gustav Klimt (Plates 11, 224), Henri Martin (Plate 52), Edvard Munch, Diego Rivera, Mario Sironi, and José María Sert promise further interesting conclusions. The material in the present book itself raises a variety of perspectives: reasons for the choice of medium; the visual perception of murals; the matter of how far individual mural artists shared the political or other persuasions of their patrons, and whether the beliefs evident in an artist's murals offer keys to the meaning of his or her easel *oeuvre*; the relationship between murals and the decorative easel paintings prized at the *fin de siècle*; and so on. Is there, for example, symbolism as well as an association with the choice of a Crystal Palace for the 1851 Great Exhibition, in the German water-glass medium introduced by Maclise at Westminster on Prince Albert's advice? F. W. Schelling's definition of the 'crystalline' as 'the spiritual within the material'[18] was widely known in Germany, where Maclise was sent to learn the technique; and at the Royal Gallery he of course presents Nelson's death as a secular *Pietà*. In this sense, his murals would seem to weld the temporal with the spiritual every bit as clearly as the fresco style. Such fusion, like the transformist and Nietzschean elisions of time, place, and matter in Goetze's Grove House murals, is barely amenable to the kind of starkly dialectic approach which, by pitting the belief of 'Modernist aesthetic theory' that 'pictures . . . told no stories and . . . art was timeless' versus interest in 'illustrative representation', has recently cast fresh light on an easel painter such as Sickert.[19] A flexible and wide-ranging frame of reference is necessary in mural research, without forgetting—however fascinating may be the sociological, historical, or other contextual significance of a work—the importance of genuine artistic merit.

One of the prime features of mural painting in Britain from 1840 to 1940 as compared with achievements on the Continent is, in fact, its sheer variability of aesthetic merit. Instead of regretting this, we should, I suggest, regard it as a virtue, recognizing that in the absence of a continuous tradition of mural painting and of the mural training opportunities found in France, Germany, or Austria, the experimental approach of many of the British mural artists brought heights of achievement as well as more modest work. It is, of course, easy to be starry-eyed. However interesting the work of many of the commercial decorators such as Clayton and Bell (Plates 124, 125), Hardman and Powell (Plate 127), or C. E. Kempe may seem as a phenomenon of its period and part of the Victorian Gothic Revival in architecture, its contribution to the evolution and aesthetic development of mural painting in Britain through the century

[17] For a discussion of suffragette banners, see L. Tickner, *The Spectacle of Women: Imagery of the Suffrage Campaign 1907–14* (London, 1987).

[18] Quoted in K. Hartley (ed.), *The Romantic Spirit in German Art* (1994), p. 155.

[19] Tillyard, 'The End of Victorian Art', p. 191.

from 1840 was at best minimal. Set alongside the more imaginative revivalism of certain European muralists of the period such as Joseph von Führich, it likewise shows its limitations. Even the work produced to Burges's designs (Plate XXXVII, Plate 179), or that of Phoebe Traquair (Plates 128, 151) or Stacy Marks is essentially competent and simplistically derivative, rather than inspired, often suggesting book illustration writ large, whilst some of Moira's decoration for restaurants, ships and other locations, though enthusiastically reported in the journals of the day, verges—when compared with that of Brangwyn, Mackintosh (Plate 211), or European decorators like Van de Velde or Mucha, for example—on a rather too obvious repertoire of swirling Art Nouveau forms. The murals by Fry's Omega Group (e.g. Plate 194) whilst undoubtedly a significant response to 'Post-Impressionist' and Ballets Russes influences in Britain, can seem only pale reflections when set alongside European examples like the Fauvist panels created by Matisse for Sergei Shchukin a few years earlier.[20] Many of the murals aboard the 1930s liners or in private houses, shops, and restaurants were relatively lightweight in artistic terms, offering a watered-down version of Art Deco rather than reaching the more thoughtful and imaginative approaches to wall decoration to be found in certain other British schemes of the period, like E. R. Payne's and Robert Baker's in Woodgreen Village Hall (Plate XXV; Plate 225) Gilbert Spencer's at Balliol College (Plate XXXV) or C. R. Napier's for Huddersfield Public Library (Plate 169).

There is a real sense in which the hand of the Gothic Revival lay so heavily on Britain, followed by that of Morris and the Aesthetic movement, that inertia, timidity, or working to a formula were the inevitable result. By the turn of the century, after all, as well as Van de Velde in Belgium and Mucha in Paris and Central Europe, there were muralists to be found elsewhere on the Continent such as Klimt and Koloman Moser in Vienna; Besnard, Vuillard, and Maurice Denis in Paris; Carl Larsson in Stockholm; and Ferdinand Hodler in Switzerland. It is by recognizing Brangwyn's essential affinities with these Continental artists, and in turn with Flemish Baroque art, that the symbolic element to be identified in his murals can be understood as simply natural. He, along with Sigismund Goetze, Clausen, Cayley Robinson, Louis Ginnett, Gilbert Spencer, E. I. Halliday, and a number of others working in the late nineteenth or early twentieth centuries need to be remembered, as well as the better-known names of Duncan Grant or Stanley Spencer.

In an art-form which is subject so often to the personal preferences and dictates of patrons, is there a place for the idiosyncrasies of the individual artist? Does mural painting in the industrial, production-based society of the Victorian era to the Second World War not demand, of necessity, that we focus exclusively on the dynamics of display or image creation, the patron's motives in 'inventing tradition' or presenting propaganda, or the ebb and flow of ideological positions on the relationship of art and architecture? Despite the rich illumination which, as I hope this book shows, may be afforded by such readings, there is, none the less, a perhaps distinctively British freedom from prescription in the history of mural painting in this country between 1840 and 1940, which, time after time, forces into the foreground the personalities of particular mural painters and their sponsors. In contrast to the history of murals at the same period in France, Belgium, Germany, or Austria, it is striking that work in Britain stemmed primarily from private initiative and individual principles, even though, of course, it often took an important inspiration from developments in Continental mural art. Where the decoration of town halls in post-1870 Germany

[20] 1908–11, now in the Hermitage Museum, St Petersburg.

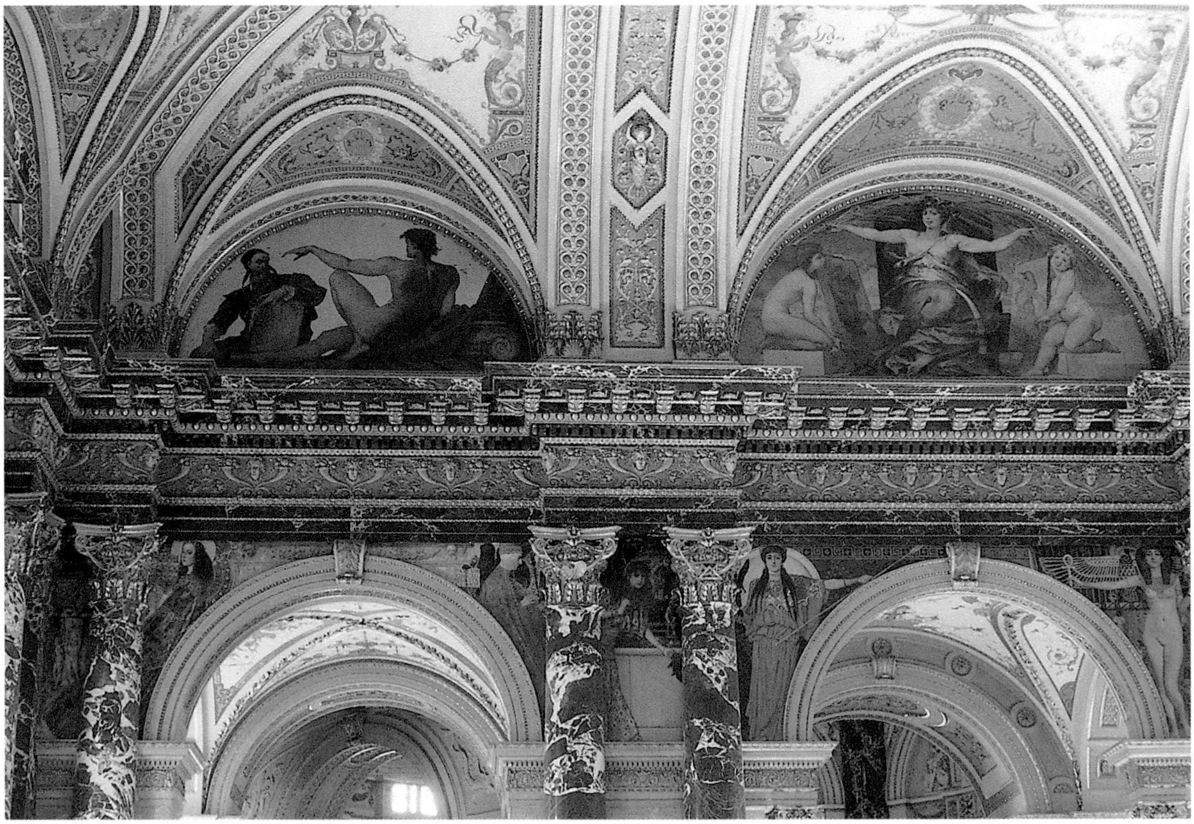

224. Gustav Klimt, *The Roman and Venetian Quattrocento* (spandrels to left); *The Grecian Antique* (spandrels to right); with *History of Art* (left lunette) and *Craftsmanship* (right lunette), both to designs by Hans Makart, Staircase, Kunsthistorisches Museum, Vienna, 1890–1

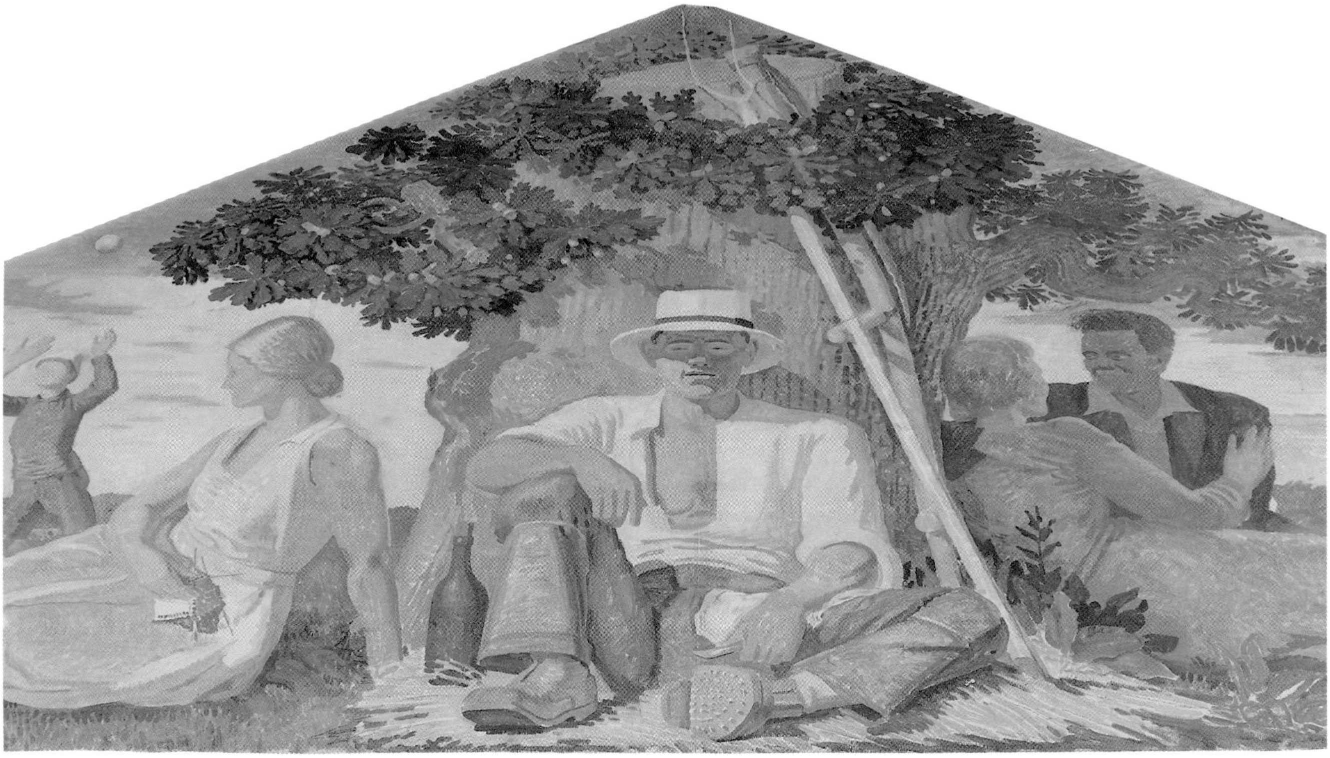

225. Detail from Edward R. Payne, *A Summer's Day*, Woodgreen Village Hall, Fordingbridge, Hampshire, *c.*1931–8

offers a coordinated effort to represent national unity and shared Germanic identity,[21] and the patronage of murals in the university, museums (Plate 224), Burgtheater (Plate 51), or Parlament (Plate 3) of *Gründerzeit* Vienna was the responsibility of the State, in Britain it was private individuals who were the prime movers and shakers of the mural revival, and who in turn, in the most successful commissions, found artists of an individual stamp to give life to their visions. The murals at the Palace of Westminster in the 1840s to 1860s, those at the South Kensington Museum (Plates 147–9), and Goetze's Foreign Office scheme are virtually the only truly State-supported projects, and even Goetze's was born of his personal choice of venue following a proposal by the Archbishop of Canterbury at a Royal Academy banquet. At Westminster in the twentieth century, it was the sponsorship of private donors from the peerage, on the model of the patronage system pioneered at the Royal Exchange, which brought into being the schemes for the East Corridor (Plates XIV, XV; Plates 48–50), St Stephen's Hall (Plate XVIII; Plates 67–71), and Royal Gallery (Plates XIX-XX; Plates 81–3), whilst the decoration of the Tate Gallery restaurant (Plates 215, 216) was funded by Lord Joseph Duveen. In a sense, an eighteenth-century tradition of dilettante connoisseurship and patronage was directly perpetuated in such ventures, and even the 1840s–1860s work at Westminster can be seen as part of this because of the dominant influence of Prince Albert and his pursuit of 'royal' ideas. For all Haydon's, Prince Albert's, G. F. Watts's, and later Lord Leighton's and Sir William Rothenstein's lofty ideals of a British School of monumental art, it was the varied approaches of independent artists, working out their own philosophies and styles of mural art with greater or lesser attention to the ad hoc guidance of charismatic patrons or promoters (such as Albert, Ruskin, Leighton, or Geddes) which tended to prevail. The public bodies or institutions which feature in this book, such as the advisory Royal Fine Art(s) Commission, the Royal Academy, or the British School at Rome, were neither State-run nor centralized. In this situation, it is perhaps not surprising that strong muralists such as Maclise, Brangwyn, or the artists of the Westminster East Corridor, seize the attention, whereas, despite their accompanying literary pamphlets by Newbolt and Rex Whistler and their symbolic iconography, the work at St Stephen's Hall in Westminster and the Tate Gallery restaurant, of which so much was hoped by Rothenstein, Tonks, and the British School at Rome, ultimately seems somewhat tame. The very attempt by the British School at Rome to foster a cohesive national style of mural painting by reference to early Renaissance models was, of course, perhaps the ultimate example of the 'invention of tradition', in which mural art now borrowed tactics so often used by its patrons. It is easy to see why the 'Rome style' appealed to the Bank of England (Plates 203–6), seeking an image of security in the 1930s. Yet the Bank wanted modern subjects, not history or classical myth; in the context of the rapid changes in art and society post-1918, the objectives of the Rome School were perhaps inherently unrealizable. Its most accomplished progeny, such as Halliday or Monnington, developed their own distinctive personal approaches, which in Monnington's case led, after the Second World War, to abstraction.

The very independence of artistic character and purpose which asserts itself through the history of nineteenth- and early twentieth-century mural painting in Britain, and which, of course, forms part of the wider diversity in art of the period, might be said, in a sense, to have actually prompted the crisis of identity which shook this art-form to the core following the First World War, and effectively brought about the demise of State mural patronage at Westminster after Brangwyn's

[21] See H. T. Wappenschmidt, *Studien zur Ausstattung des deutschen Rathaussaales* (1981), pp. 76ff. and 174ff.

Royal Gallery scheme. As the brutal reality of war and the delicacy of its diplomatic aftermath rendered irrelevant not merely the content but also the allegorical language of Goetze's Foreign Office murals, so too did the very immediacy and individualism of the images of battle produced for the Hall of Remembrance (Plate XVII; Plates 62–5) break asunder its intended coherence as a decorative ensemble. If the Royal Exchange scheme had been criticized for disunity, the Hall of Remembrance threw into question the very viability of decorative art, with its requirement for harmony both of constituent parts and of painting with its setting, as a vehicle through which to come to terms with so disruptive and destructive an experience as war; a problem later to be confronted by Brangwyn at the Royal Gallery. At the same time, the fragmentation of artistic style already so evident in easel art before the war had brought to the fore avant-garde approaches which, by 1918, were no more acceptable to the public as a focus for their sombre mood than the remote allegorical ideals used by Goetze. Even Wyndham Lewis now saw reality with a new candour, as his self-searching contribution to the Hall of Remembrance so clearly reveals (Plate 65). Films, photographs, and newspaper reports, not to mention the loss of loved ones and care for the maimed, were all so much more real than either Vorticism's distortions or the formality of High Art in public buildings. And yet the public's preference for a form of art which might truthfully represent lived experience whilst looking beyond it to the spiritual and universal were clearly revealed by the enormous popularity at the Royal Academy in 1919 of Sargent's *Gassed* (Plate 62). Recognizing the change in attitude, Speaker Whitley by the 1920s sought 'direct' appeal at St Stephen's Hall, but the results were still a compromise; history painting kept at one remove through a safe, non-controversial, Rome School style, combined with subjects which, symbolizing the quest for reconstruction and renewal, were still essentially allegories, requiring Newbolt's text for interpretation. Equally, it is arguable that neither Salisbury's ultra-conservative personifications of chivalric virtues at Liverpool Town Hall (Plate 108) nor Neville Lytton's anguished battlescapes at Balcombe Victory Hall (Plates 109, 110) provided satisfactory answers to the matter of mural war memorials. It is hardly surprising that in the years of reappraisal of the 1920s, and with the censor now tightening his grip, Brangwyn's attempt in his Royal Gallery scheme to resolve the problem of reconciling war subjects with decoration, which had shipwrecked the Hall of Remembrance project, should have gone through several radically differing stages. It is tragic and ironic that his original and imaginative solution should ultimately have foundered with yet another turn of the political tide, but it is also possible to see why the impact of the Second World War should shortly after have marked another watershed in British mural art which, in an age of yet greater artistic diversity, was arguably far more decisive even than that of 1914–18. The sequel to the State mural patronage of 1841–1933 was not permanent decoration for Parliament or government offices, or another Hall of Remembrance, but temporary mural painting for popular appreciation in the Festival of Britain of 1951; a rebuilding of Britain now undertaken not in the metaphorical images of St Stephen's Hall, but in the physical layout of the exhibition and its buildings, where art might be a focus in community renewal.

Given their individuality, and the sea changes they witnessed between 1840 and 1940, were Britain's metaphorical 'swimmers' borne on waves of any reach? Did they, in turn, make waves of lasting power? Brangwyn was essentially a one-man band, aloof from the efforts of the Rome School, Tonks, or Rothenstein to cultivate a native school of monumental art. Yet his expression of an ideal of universal brotherhood can be viewed as the logical sequel to the 'discourse of civic humanism' or 'republic of equal, active, and independent citizens' which John Barrell has shown to be the motive ideal behind the art of James Barry in the eighteenth century.[22] Not only Brangwyn's delight in the idiosyncrasies of humankind (whether in the hunchback at Christ's Hospital or the peoples of his British Empire scheme), but also that of Stanley Spencer at Burghclere Chapel, and, of course, the prominence given to the common folk of history in the murals at the Royal Exchange, all provide a continuum with Barry's open embrace of humankind's diversity in his (Royal) Society of Arts murals. Brangwyn was awarded the Society's Albert Medal in 1932. As Barrell has pointed out, the RSA murals enlarged the doctrine of 'civic virtue . . . to address all the members of a society'.[23] Is it such a long step to the emphasis on mural painting as a community art which, born of William Morris's and the American New Deal principles, was already emergent in Sir William Rothenstein's vision of local mural schemes, and Sir John Rothenstein's emphasis in the 1939 Tate Gallery exhibition? This in turn looks forward not just to 1951, but to the social philosophy behind such modern projects as the decoration of inner-city gable ends in Glasgow and other towns. Perhaps the most direct link of all between the century from 1840 to 1940 and mural art today, however, stems once again from individual initiative. The artist of panels in the Royal Exchange and Westminster East Corridor, E. A. Abbey, left money at his death in 1911 for the establishment of the Abbey Memorial Trust Fund for Mural Painting in Great Britain, but this first became operational only after the Second World War. Administered by the Royal Academy, the fund has supported numerous projects ranging from Thomas Monnington's abstract designs of 1955 on the ceiling of Bristol Council House, representing 'the nuclear age', and John Armstrong's *Bristol at all Times in its History* in the same building (1955), to murals in Ealing Hospital, London (Peter Rees-Roberts, 1979) and Wolfson College, Cambridge (Gordon Davies, 1981). A partner scheme in memory of the architect Vincent Harris, who, perhaps significantly, had worked for the LCC shortly after the construction of County Hall, was established in 1970,[24] and more recent developments include the RSA's Art for Architecture scheme.

And yet, given the richness of our nineteenth- and twentieth-century mural heritage in Britain, it is surely a matter for regret that the kind of training in mural art envisaged by Ruskin is still only seldom part of the curricula of our schools of art and architecture; and that following Brangwyn's Royal Gallery débâcle, there has been no sequel to the State mural schemes at Westminster. With novel and challenging modern architecture, developments in art techniques, and new social perspectives, it is perhaps time not just to reintroduce mural training, but also to rethink its very nature, and in turn to encourage architects to recognize it as something which can be integral with the visual and spatial environment. Already in the nineteenth century Ruskin had complained that 'to teach a young man to manage his chalk and his brush' was not enough; artists should instead receive 'an exceedingly broad and liberal education',[25] for the mural painter, such an education today surely needs to foster a wide range of interpretative as well as technical skills. Just as in Vienna at the *fin de siècle*, the Secession writer Hermann Bahr had envisaged his ideal house as one which would allow him to 'see my soul everywhere, as in a mirror', and Klimt had painted *Nuda Veritas* (Österreichisches Theatermuseum, Vienna), holding her mirror up to modern man, as a mural for the wall above Bahr's desk,[26] so the architects and mural painters

[22] J. Barrell, *The Political Theory of Painting from Reynolds to Hazlitt* (New Haven and London, 1986), p. 3; Barrell's definition is from J. G. A. Pocock.

[23] Ibid., p. 198.

[24] Both schemes are administered by the Royal Academy of Arts.

[25] Ruskin, *Works*, vol. 4, § 15 and § 17, p. 480.

[26] Quoted in K. A. Schröder and H. Szeemann (eds), *Egon Schiele and his Contemporaries: Austrian Painting and Drawing from 1900 to 1930 from the Leopold Collection, Vienna* (Royal Academy of Arts, London, 1989), footnote 47, p. 32.

of our own day might, for example, look once more to the profound psychological power of decoration—whether in a domestic context or within a State or public building—which the examples in this book have so often brought to light. The architect needs to be aware of the potential role of murals in a building, whilst the painter, through the nature of his or her training and insights, should be able in turn to reflect the ideals, aspirations, philosophies, and purposes of those for whom the building is intended. Given the foundation laid by work up to 1940 and the diverse examples produced since, the advent of a new century and a new millennium offer an excellent opportunity to create a modern sequel to the great schemes undertaken at the Palace of Westminster or the Royal Exchange. A retrospective review of the twentieth century in murals for major public buildings might celebrate developments and discoveries in science and the arts; British inventions like jet propulsion or television; benefits from medicine and in health care; and significant social or political events such as VE Day, the declaration of India's independence, or partnership with the Commonwealth and Europe. Such projects could focus national identity and—as the continuation of our earlier mural tradition—create a symbolic link between past and future generations. Training of mural artists, provision of mural space by architects in their buildings, and the patronage of State, the community, and individuals might together renew in Britain an art-form which is as old as mankind itself.

APPENDIX A

Guide to Principal Techniques and Media Used, 1840–1940

Detailed accounts of techniques and materials can be found in the various manuals and handbooks for mural painters published during the period (see the Bibliography), such as Taylor (1839), Latilla (1842), Merrifield (1844 and 1846), Thomas (1869), Gambier Parry (1880), Herringham (1899), Jackson (1904), Vallance (1908), Ward (1913), Batten (1925), Bayes (1927), and Sargant-Florence (1936), as well as in the *Reports* of the CFA at Westminster (1841–63), and (for spirit fresco and a related further bibliography) Farr (1993). For water-glass and related media and techniques, see Pursche (1998) and for sgraffito, see Demanet et al. (1996). *Wandmalerei, Mosaik (Reclams Handbuch der künstlerischen Techniken)* by A. Knoepfli et al. (Stuttgart, 1990) includes many of the media and techniques in use between 1840 and 1940.

Encaustic

A technique invented in ancient Greece of painting with hot wax colours (pigments mixed with molten beeswax and resin), which are burnt in to the wall surface after application by radiant heat (e.g. a lamp or brazier). The technique was revived in the late eighteenth and early nineteenth centuries following research into antique paintings by the Comte de Caylus and Sir Humphry Davy, amongst others, but was relatively little used after the mid-nineteenth century. It was employed by Frederick Sang in the 1840s scheme at the Royal Exchange, London, and by William Bell Scott at Penkill Castle, Ayrshire (1865–8).

Fresco

Buon fresco ('true fresco'): as used in Renaissance Italy, this was revived in the nineteenth century by the Nazarenes in Germany and emulated in Britain. Pigments resistant to lime and mixed with water are applied on *intonaco* (the top, damp layer of specially prepared fresh lime plaster); this is usually laid in patches of a size which can be painted in a day (*giornate*). As the painted surface dries, a chemical fusion occurs between the pigments and the plaster; the resultant appearance of the mural is slightly matt and chalky. *Fresco secco* involves painting on dry lime plaster with colours in a binder such as casein solution or tempera.

A mixture of *buon fresco* and *fresco secco* techniques was used by William Dyce and others at the Palace of Westminster, London (1840s/1850s), whilst *buon fresco* was further researched and revived in the early twentieth century by members of the Society of Mural Decorators and Painters in Tempera (e.g. Mary Sargant-Florence's frescoes in the Old School, Oakham, in the 1900s).

Marouflage

A procedure for attaching a painted canvas permanently to a wall (or to a slate or other form of panel fixed to a wall) by means of white lead in oil spread both over the plaster or panel and the back of the canvas. This technique (with either spirit fresco or, from around 1900, more normally oil, being used to paint the canvas), became dominant in Britain after Lord Leighton's demonstration of the modern French version of it at the Royal Exchange in 1895.

Oil techniques

Oil on canvas on stretchers, as in easel painting, was frequently used to create pictures which were let in to panelled walls or otherwise secured to the wall; from the late nineteenth century, oil on canvas fixed to the wall by means of *marouflage* was widely used, as in Brangwyn's and many of the later Royal Exchange murals (see *marouflage*). Although oil was sometimes used direct on plaster, this procedure was susceptible to problems of condensation, arising from the difficulty of ensuring a totally dry wall surface on which to paint. Various methods were adopted to avoid the reflectivity typical of oil painting, including treating the painted surface with turpentine, benzine, or 'Parris's Marble Medium'; or the incorporation of fine sand into the oil paint, as in George Walton's marouflaged *Glasgow Fair in the Olden Days* at Glasgow City Chambers (*c.*1900).

Painted bas relief

A technique for casting low relief modelled panels in fibrous plaster subsequently treated with a 'special medium' to make it 'non-absorbative', hard and durable, which was developed in the 1890s by Gerald Moira and F. Lynn-Jenkins (see 'The Art Movement. Novelty in Decoration at the Trocadero', *Magazine of Art*, 20 (1896), pp. 92–7). Surviving examples include Moira's decoration in the Wigmore Hall, London (1901), and H. C. Fehr's historical frieze in Wakefield County Hall (*c.* 1900).

Sgraffito

As developed in Renaissance Italy, this was originally a linear incision technique whereby an underlayer of coloured plaster was revealed to provide texture and contrast with the surface layer; it was revived in the late nineteenth century in a modified form by a number of Arts and Crafts artists including Heywood Sumner (e.g. at St. Agatha's church, Portsmouth, and All Saints, Ennismore Gardens, London).

Spirit fresco

A technique invented by Thomas Gambier Parry in 1859 and published by him in the *Ecclesiologist* in 1863 and in a pamphlet for the Lords of the Committee of the Council on Education in 1880 (2nd ed., 1883). Developed from encaustic procedures, it used dry plaster; the pigment was bound in a medium of gum elemi resin, white wax, oil of spike lavender, copal varnish, and turpentine, and because the same medium was also used to prime the plaster, a bonding was achieved between paint and wall surface which was felt to mimic that occurring in 'true fresco'. Professor Church later suggested modifications to improve the results. Parry demonstrated the technique at Highnam church, Gloucestershire (1859 onwards) and it was taken up by Lord Leighton at Lyndhurst parish church (1862) and the South Kensington Museum (1880s), as well as by Madox Brown in a number of his Manchester Town hall murals (1880s). Leighton used it on canvas, applied by means of *marouflage*, at the Royal Exchange (1895), but by the 1900s the technique (whether applied direct to the wall or used on marouflaged canvas) was falling out of favour.

Tempera

A method of painting developed by the Egyptians and Romans in which pigments are mixed with egg yolk and water to form an emulsion; this is applied to an absorbent gesso-covered surface, traditionally with red sable brushes, drying immediately to create a water-resistant and highly durable 'skin'. By the later nineteenth century, the emulsion was frequently created with gum or glue rather than egg yolk. Traditional tempera methods were extensively researched and adopted for wall-painting in the early twentieth century by the members of the Society of Mural Decorators and Painters in Tempera; an example is Joseph Southall's mural in Birmingham City Art Gallery (1914); Brangwyn also used tempera at Lloyd's Register of Shipping (1908–14) and the Canadian Grand Trunk Railway Offices (1908–10) in London.

Water-glass, Keim's process, and variants

Also known as stereochromy, water-glass technique was invented in *c.*1825 and further developed in Germany by Dr Johann N. von Fuchs, whose account of it was translated by order of Prince Albert for use at the Palace of Westminster (principally by Maclise in the Royal Gallery, 1850s/1860s). It involves painting on dry plaster with the same pigments as in fresco, mixed with distilled water; a hot solution of water-glass (i.e. a form of soluble glass) is applied in a fine spray afterwards to seal in the pigments. The method was further elaborated by Professor Adolf Keim of Munich in the 1880s to create Keim's process. This was used by Anna Lea Merritt at Wonersh Church, near Guildford, in 1895. Variations included use of the process on canvas, as in Brangwyn's frieze for Siegfried Bing's Maison de l'Art Nouveau in Paris (1895).

APPENDIX B

Ecclesiastical Murals: Supplementary Examples

1. Lambeth Palace chapel: W. Dyce (1840s)
2. St Thomas's church, Leeds: F. Overbeck: altarpiece mural (*c.*1840s).
3. St Barnabas's church, Pimlico Rd, London (post-1850); St Nicholas, Brighton; and St. Mark's, Staplefield, Sussex: angels, trees, ornament (*c.*1901–12): all C. E. Kempe.
4. St Malachy's church, Belfast: Felice Piccioni: murals including *The Carrying of the Cross* (*c.*1860s).
5. St Alban's church, Holborn, London: Styleman Le Strange and F. Preedy: New Testament scenes (1859); St Mary the Virgin, Madresfield, Worcs.: *Agnus Dei* and *Last Judgement*: designed by F. Preedy (about or after 1867); also a mural by C. Whall (*c.*1890s).
6. Ashley church, Northants (1865); Frinstead church, Kent; St Augustine's, Kilburn, London (designs by J. L. Pearson 1891–3); Middleham church, North Yorks.; Hersham church, Surrey (1890); and St Andrew, Kingsbury, London: all Clayton and Bell; All Souls, Haley Hill (Clayton and Bell assisted by Stacy Marks, 1859); St Mary Magdalen, Munster Square, London (begun 1867) and All Saints, Old Wolverton, Milton Keynes (1877): both Bell and Almond; St John the Evangelist, Sutton Verey, Warminster (1868); St Anne's, Derby: New Testament subjects; *Education of St. Anne*: D. Bell (1879–80).
7. Worcester College chapel, Oxford (1864, with frieze of *Te Deum* 1870); St Benedict's church, Bordesley Green, Birmingham: apse decoration (1912–13); All Saints, Paddington, London: all H. Holiday; Holy Trinity Church, Casterton, Yorks.: angels and Old and New Testament subjects: H. Holiday and J. Clark (*c.*1904) [for Clark see also no. 33].
8. Marlborough College chapel: Spencer Stanhope: 12 tempera murals (1875).
9. Unknown church in Staffs.: A. Besnard: *Christ and the Good Samaritan* (*c.*1880–3) (sketch in Musée des Beaux-Arts, Lyon).
10. St George's church, Belfast: Alexander Gibbs & Co.: New Testament scenes (1883–8).
11. St Thomas of Canterbury's church, Northaw, Herts: *St. Thomas of Canterbury, King Edward the Confessor, David*, scenes from the life of Christ, prophets, angels, etc. (1883–99); St Peter and St Paul's church, Luddesdown, Kent: *Christ drawing the Children to Himself*, angels, etc. (1894): both Heaton, Butler, and Bayne.
12. St Nicholas's church, Steventon, Hants.: C. G. Gray of Cambridge (1887 and 1889).
13. St Michael and All Angels' church, Bournemouth: Cox and Sons, Buckley and Co: frieze of saints, *trompe-l'oeil* curtains, scrolling, etc. (1889).
14. St Mary's church, Plaistow, Bromley: 'Mr. Hughes' (presumably of Morris & Co.): Old and New Testament subjects including Tree of Jesse and Majesty (1890).
15. St Mary the Virgin's church, Twyford, Hants.: Shrigley and Hunt: *The Annunciation* (late 19th century).
16. Church of the Immaculate Conception, Purewell, Hants.: Frederick Rolfe (Baron Corvo): *Coronation of Mary as Queen of Heaven* and *Mary Queen of the Universe* (*c.*1891–2).

17. St Barnabas's church, Erdington, Birmingham: *Christ in Majesty* (1894); Holy Trinity church, Winchester (1890s); and St Nicholas's church, Guildford, Surrey: Sacraments of Baptism and Holy Communion, Old and New Testament subjects, Christ in Glory surrounded by female saints (1900): J. A. Pippet of Hardman's; St James the Less church, New Mills, Cheshire: Powell of Hardman's (*c.*1880).
18. Christ Church, Church Crookham, Hants.: Archangels and *Adoration of the Shepherds* (1892–3); St Agatha's church, Portsmouth, Hants.: *Christ in Majesty* and Evangelists (1895); and All Saints' church, Ennismore Gardens, London: *Good Shepherd* lunette (1900s): all Heywood Sumner (sgraffito decoration).
19. All Saints' church, Rangemore, Staffs. (1895); St Andrew's church, Ham, Surrey: saints and prophets (*c.*1900–6); St. Bartholomew's Church, Elvaston, Derbyshire: *Christ in Majesty* (1904–5); St John the Divine's church, Kennington: all designed by G. F. Bodley.
20. St Mary's church, Cromford, Derbyshire: prophets; St Giles' church, Matlock, Derbyshire: *Agnus Dei* and angels: both A. O. Hemming (1897).
21. St Leonard's church, Ipstones (1902–3) and All Saints' church, Leek (both Staffs.): Gerald Horsely.
22. St Michael the Archangel's church, Rushall, Walsall: E. R. Frampton (1905).
23. St Mary Magdalene's church, Wandsworth, London: H. Fayers: screen and ceiling paintings of saints (1906).
24. St Mary and St Ambrose's church, Pershore Road, Birmingham: Kate Bunce (1906).
25. St Thomas of Canterbury's Catholic church, St Leonards-on-Sea: N. H. J. Westlake: *The Company of English Martyrs* (about or after 1907).
26. St Cuthbert's church, Edinburgh: John Duncan: angel spandrels; and Gerald Moira: *St Francis and the Birds* (both *c.*1910).
27. Rossall Priory, Fleetwood, Lancs: John Duncan (*c.*1900s/1920s).
28. Old Road Unitarian chapel, Middleton: F. W. Jackson: *Seed Time* and *Harvest* (1900s).
29. Bishop's chapel, Lichfield, Staffs.: J. Eadie Reid (1900s).
30. St Andrew's church and St John's church, Hastings, Sussex: Robert Tressall (pseudonym for Robert Noonan) (*c.*1902–11).
31. Holy Trinity church, Trinity Rd, London: Richard Castle: three scenes from the life of Christ; *St. Oswald, King and Martyr; St. Agnes* (1907–16).
32. St Mark's church, Hale, Surrey: K. W. Milroy: *Magnificat* and *Benedicite* subjects (1911–20).
33. St Barnabas's church, Pitshanger Lane, London: *Hierarchy of Heaven Worshipping and Adoring the Holy Trinity*: James Clark (*c.*1917).
34. St Lawrence's church, Bardney, Lincs.: A. Willett: saints, apostles, Christ and angels, and New Testament subjects (1934).
35. Campion Hall, Oxford: Daphne Pollen: *The New Jerusalem* (1935) and Sir Frank Brangwyn: *Stations of the Cross* (originally designed for a church in Amiens) (1935–6).
36. St John's church, Buckhurst Hill, Essex: B. Playne: *Visitation of Elizabeth* and *Joyous Motherhood* (1937).

A number of Nonconformist chapels were also decorated during the nineteenth century, e.g. Steep Lane chapel, Sowerby Bridge, Halifax, and Milton chapel, Huddersfield (*Adam and Eve*) (artists unknown).

APPENDIX C

Mind and Body: Education and Welfare Murals: Supplementary Examples

1. Stonyhurst College chapel, Lancs.: 'Herr Worms': *St. Francis Xavier*; 'Herr Fischer': *St. Ignatius*, and *Doctors of the Church* and angels by both artists (1852).
2. South Kensington Museum, London (National Competition Room): lunettes illustrating different types of drawing and painting, including W. Wynfield: *Drawing From Life*; G. D. Leslie: *Landscape Painting*; H. Stacy Marks: *Skeleton Painting*; W. F. Yeames: *Drawing from Life* (1860s).
3. Museum and Library, Derby: Best and Lea company of Manchester: 'edible', 'medical', and 'commercial' plants; *Caxton printing his First Impressions* (Lending Library); English oak and heraldic motifs (Commitee Room); natural history motifs (Gallery) (1880s).
4. Prisoners' Aid Society, Glasgow: murals by E. A. Walton, G. Henry, A. Roche, T. Corson Morton, and J. Nairn (1889–90).
5. Royal Academy of Arts, London (Refreshment Room): W. Reynolds-Stephens: *Summer* (1890); H. Speed: *Autumn* (1898); F. Appleyard: *Spring driving out Winter* (1902).
6. Girton College, Cambridge (dining hall): G. Hammond: *A Harvest Festival* (wall-space allocated 1890 but design not executed).
7. Edinburgh Infirmary: W. G. Burn-Murdoch: murals (*c.*1890s).
8. Outlook Tower, Royal Mile, Edinburgh: J. Cadenhead, H. Hay, and Brown-Macdougall: frieze (*c.*1890s).
9. 'Cordelius' Ladies House', Edinburgh (believed to be in the Royal Mile): W. G. Burn-Murdoch: spring landscape and flowers, and figures; and 'Ladies Hall', Edinburgh (probably the same location): J. Duncan: *Witches Frieze* (all *c.*1890s).
10. Red Cross Hall, Southwark: W. Crane: allegorical murals (1890s).
11. Gilmour Institute for Working Girls, Alexandria, Dumbartonshire (now Masonic Lodge): Harrington Mann: *Women's Work*, and frieze illustrating Scottish songs (*c.*1890s/1900).
12. Cheltenham (Boys') College (chapel): J. Eadie Reid: Biblical murals (1900s–*c.*1918).
13. Oakham Old School, Rutland: Mary Sargant-Florence: murals illustrating Tennyson's *Idylls of the King* (begun 1902).
14. Howell's School for Girls, Llandaff, Cardiff: J. M. Staniforth: Shakespearean scenes (*c.*1904).
15. Attrib, Morris & Co.: Queen Elizabeth's Grammar School for Girls, Mansfield: murals of Classical legends symbolizing the quest for knowledge (*c.*1908–23).
16. Possilpark Library, Glasgow: Glasgow School of Art students including Robertson Weir, under the direction of M. Greiffenhagen: *Astronomy, Poetry, Commerce, Science, Art* (1912–13).
17. Cable Street School, Stepney: S. North: *St. George and the Dragon* (1912–15); Commercial Street School, Stepney: L. Jacobs: murals (1912); Buckingham Gate School? Westminster: F. G. Garret: *Scenes from the*

Life of Socrates (1913); Haverstock Hill Central Girls' School, St Pancras: M. Esplin: mural (1915) (all LCC schools, London).

18. Bourneville School, Birmingham: Mary Sargant-Florence and Mary Creighton McDowell: sixteen scenes from the New Testament (*c.*1912–18).
19. Heanor Grammar School, Derbyshire.: F. Cayley Robinson: *Aeneas* (*c.*1919).
20. Langside Library, Glasgow: M. Greiffenhagen: *Mary Queen of Scots at the Battle of Langside* (1919–20).
21. Drumpark Special School, Lanarkshire: *Little Brown Seed* murals; Machanhill School, Lanarkshire: Arthurian subject murals: both J. M. King (*c.*1920s).
22. University Hall, Ramsay Lodge, Ramsay Garden, Edinburgh: John Duncan: *Napier, James Watt, Sir Walter Scott, Charles Darwin, Lord Lister* (1920s).
23. Winchester College, Hants.: C. Hawkes: 'Thule Cartoon' (mural showing school characters of the time) (1924).
24. St Elphin's School, Matlock, Derbyshire (chapel): K. W. Milroy: Biblical subjects (mid-1920s).
25. Moreton-in-Marsh Hospital, Glos.: I. Colquhoun: murals in the women's ward; and Waiting Room (waterlilies) (*c.*1920s/30s).
26. Liverpool Orphanage (Refectory): D. H. Banner: *Hermon and the Lake of Galilee* frieze (*c.*1920s/30s).
27. Goldsmiths' College, University of London: B. Swanwick: *An Opening Ceremony by the Mayor* (*c.*1920s/30s).
28. Great Ormond Street Children's Hospital (Nurses' Common Room): M. Ovey: *Tower of London* (1934); M. Ovey and/or 'Miss Stanley': *Royal Naval Hospital, Greenwich*; and *Horseguards' Parade from the Park* (1935–8).
29. North London Collegiate School: P. Angus: mural showing the removal of the school from Camden Town to Canons Park, Stanmore (1935).
30. Wardie School, Edinburgh (Hall): R. H. Westwater: *Alice in Wonderland* (1935).
31. Dame Alice Harpur School, Bedford: artist unknown: mural with aerial view of school and women's occupations from the time of the school's erection (1938).
32. Aberdeen University Union (bar): R. Sivell: murals (1938–52).
33. Craigmillar School, Edinburgh: A. Inglis: *Scenes from Children's Tales* (1939).
34. Musselburgh Grammar School, East Lothian: T. Pow: *King Arthur and his Knights* (1939).
35. Heriot Watt College, Edinburgh (New Common Room): D. Peploe: *Paracelsus* (1939).

APPENDIX D

Private Houses: Supplementary Examples

1. Trentham Hall, Staffs.: Clarkson Stanfield (1830s).
2. Bowood House, Wilts.: A. W. Calcott, C. L. Eastlake, E. T. Parris, J. Severn, C. Stanfield, T. Uwins: murals including allegories of *Music, Painting, Sculpture*, and Italianate landscapes (1838–*c*.1845); also decoration by an unknown German artist (1842); G. F. Watts: *The Parting of Alexander and Briseis* and *Coriolanus* (1858–60) (panel and fragments in Watts Memorial Gallery, Compton).
3. Gatton Park, Surrey: Peter Cornelius (design) (completed by J. Severn): frescoes (*c*.1840).
4. Scarisbrick Hall, Lancs.: E. T. Parris: medieval figures, 'men of learning and letters', royal portraits (1840).
5. Basildon Park, Berks.: artist unknown: *Divine Comedy* (Dante) (1840s).
6. Hartland Abbey, Devon: Alfred Beer: scenes from Greville and Stucley family history (1853–9).
7. Alnwick Castle, Northumberland: J. Götzenberger: *Chevy Chase* (late 1850s).
8. Harewood House, Yorks.; 9 Eton Villas, London; Dorchester House, London: Alfred Stevens: unfinished schemes (1850s and 1860s).
9. Prestwold Hall, Leics.: J. G. Crace: British poets, and views of Prestwold (mid-nineteenth century).
10. Locko Park, Derbyshire: Romoli: Cherubs and arabesques (early 1860s).
11. Carbet Castle, Broughty Ferry, Angus (1870–1); Salisbury Green House, Edinburgh: murals (1870s): both Charles Fréchou.
12. Knightshayes, Devon: W. Burges (designs): heroes and heroines of fairy-tales (early 1870s) (unexecuted).
13. 11 Palace Gardens, London: 'Aesthetic' frieze (1873); 52 Prince's Gate, London: cockatoo frieze (1878); Eaton Hall, Cheshire: allegorical design (unexecuted) (1880s/1890s); Holland Park, London: allegorical panels (1880s/1890s); Clare Lawn: allegorical panels (1888–90); Paddockhurst: *History of Transport* (1896–7): all Walter Crane.
14. Cliffe Castle, Keighley, Yorks.: F. K. Steinhardt and Leroux: family and French Imperial portraits; Shakespeare subjects; Rococo revival ornament (1878).
15. Naworth Castle, Cumberland: E. Burne-Jones: *The Sleep of King Arthur in Avalon* (1870s).
16. Castell Coch, S. Glam.: H. W. Lonsdale and others: *Aesop's Fables, Life of St. Margaret*; Bute family portraits (1870s/1880s).
17. Carlton Towers, Yorks.: N. H. J. Westlake: *Merchant of Venice* characters (late nineteenth century).
18. Milner Field, Saltaire, Yorks.: F. Weekes: murals (late nineteenth century).
19. 13 Berkeley Square, London: Albert Moore: peacock frieze (1880s).
20. 1 South Audley Street, London: Frederic, Lord Leighton: Classical subjects (late nineteenth century).
21. Knockderry Castle, Dumbartonshire: Sir James Guthrie: Biblical subjects (1880s).

22. Beaucastle, nr. Bewdley, Worcs.: *Christian at the Palace Beautiful* (1885–6); 46 Etnam Street, Leominster, Herefordshire: mermaid frieze (1885); Charlotte Road, Edgbaston, Birmingham: *Humility; Jacob and Rachel* (*c.* 1907): all J. E. Southall.
23. 50 Ullet Road, Sefton Park, Liverpool: H. A. Payne: *Undine* (*c.* 1890s).
24. 37 Cheyne Walk, London: R. Fry: Parkland scene (1890s).
25. Wootten Wawen House, Stratford-upon-Avon, Warks.: *Much Ado about Nothing* (*c.*1900); The Anchorage, 137 Handsworth Road, Birmingham: title unknown (*c.*1900): all F. Davis.
26. Douglas Castle, Lanarks. (chapel): C. Whall: murals (*c.*1900).
27. 11 Lansdowne Road, London: Sir Frank Brangwyn: *Seasons*; *Months* (1900).
28. Lord's Wood, Marlow: M. Sargant-Florence: *Les Aveugles* (*c.*1910–20).
29. 40 Gordon Square; 3 Heathcote Street; 50 Tavistock Square; 6 Gordon Place; 3 Albert Gate, London; and Moon Hall, Gomshall, Surrey: 'Omega' artists including V. Bell, D. Grant, and C. Bell: decorative panels (1913–*c.*1930).
30. Sarum Chase, Hampstead, London: F. O. Salisbury: *Life's Saga* (including *The Mystery of Creation, The Divine Overture, The Human Awakening, The Historic Struggle, The Supreme Challenge, The Final Victory* and figures and motifs symbolizing *Education, Industry, Science*, the *Arts*, etc. (*c.*late 1900s–1920s)).
31. King's College, Cambridge: D. Grant and C. Bell: *Economy, Music, Classics, Mathematics, Philosophy, History* (1920).
32. Dunecht Castle, Aberdeenshire: J. Pryde: *The Madonna of the Ruins* (1922).
33. 15 Long Lane, Liverpool: *Life of Christ* (1924); Abbot's Lea, Liverpool: *Conversion of Lydia* (1925–30): both E. I. Halliday.
34. 71 Bedford Street South, Liverpool: M. Adshead: jungle picnic subject (1925).
35. Pyrford Court, Surrey: Basil Ionides and Ranke: Classical scenes (1926).
36. Windsor Castle, Berks. (Queen's Doll's House): decorative paintings by artists including C. Conder, G. Moira, E. Dulac, Sir William Nicholson, C. Sims, etc; (State Room): Kennedy North: *Royal Coronation Procession of 1911* (*c.*1926–9) and P. Connard: *Garden Scene at Hampton Court* (*c.*1926–9) (information about the State Room decoration kindly provided by Sheila de Bellaigue from material in RA(W).
37. Bracondale Woods, Norwich: Geoffrey Birkbeck: Roman garden views (1928).
38. Dorneywood, Bucks. (hall): Landscape mural with Flora, Cupid, croquet game played by Edwardian figures, etc. (1928–9); 19 Hill Street, London (hall): Landscape mural with Cupid, view of a town, horsemen, etc. (1930–1); Trent Park, Middlesex: eight fantasy landscape panels (1936); Brook House, Park Lane, London (sitting-room): wall and ceiling paintings of architectural, landscape, and classical motifs in grisaille (1937): all Rex Whistler.
39. The Pantheon and cottages, Portmeirion, Gwynedd.: Hans Feibusch and Susan Williams-Ellis: Classical pastiche subjects (begun late 1920s).
40. Mulberry House, Smith Square, London: Glyn Philpot: *Oedipus addressing the Sphinx; Leda and the Swan* (1920s/1930s).
41. Churt, Farnham, Surrey (David Lloyd George's house): John Churchill: *Rapallo* (1920s/1930s).
42. Parnham House, Dorset: Talbot Hughes: *trompe-l'oeil* garden scenes (1920s/1930s).
43. The Beeches, Penn, Bucks.: *Poseidon and Dolphins*; *Harlequinade in Provence, Charles II at Dover*; and Horsebridge House, Billingshurst, Sussex, and Frognal Rise, London: murals: all Angela Latham (1920s/1930s).

44. The Rectory, Stedham: Cecil Todd: Shakespearean subjects (1920s/1930s).
45. Private houses, Lake Windermere, Westmoreland: Delmar H. Banner: *Cumbrian Fells from Glaramara*; *Bernese Oberland at Dawn from the Niesen* (1920s/1930s).
46. 'The Spinney', Horam, Sussex: panel: H. Aufseeser (a.k.a. H. Tisdall) (1920s/1930s).
47. Hinton Manor, Oxon. (Music Room): Margaret Angus: *trompe-l'oeil* classical statues (1935–6).

APPENDIX E

Work and Play: Supplementary Examples

'Work' Murals

1. Institute of Chartered Accountants, London: G. Murray: *Science bringing Order with Scales and Rule to Commerce, Justice,* and *Judgement and Anarchy* (1913–14).
2. Hamburg-Amerika shipping line offices, Cockspur Street, London (subsequently owned by P & O): F. S. Beaumont: ceiling and wall panels of Chinese, Indian, and other peoples, and modern shipping (1921; extension of an earlier Art Nouveau scheme of Neptune, mermaids, ships, etc.).
3. Intended location unknown: H. Davis-Richter: mural designs for 'A Merchant's Office' (*Mediaeval and Modern Power*) and for 'the Board Room of a Colliery Company' (including *Coaling*) (shown in 1923 RA Exhibition of Decorative Art).
4. Intended location unknown: N. Howard: mural design 'for offices of a marine or insurance company': *The Reclaimers* (shown in 1923 RA Exhibition of Decorative Art).
5. 'Shipping Offices, Cockspur Street', London: A. T. Bolton and G. Allfree: designs for murals (shown in 1923 RA Exhibition of Decorative Art).
6. Tyne Improvement Commission (Board Room), Newcastle-upon-Tyne: J. Wilson Jowsey: nine murals of Tyne history from *Building of Emperor Hadrian's Bridge at Pons Aeli* to *HMS 'Lion' in River Tyne, for Repairs, during the Great European War 1916* (1927).
7. Johnson's Dyeworks, Bootle: E. I. Halliday: *Conversion of Lydia of Thayatira* (1927).
8. Chartered Institute of Insurers (Museum Room), Aldermanbury, London: C. Walter Hodges: frieze illustrating the development of insurance through the ages (1934).
9. Cadbury Bros. Chocolate Factory, Bourneville: W. H. Smith: *The Meeting of Cortes and Montezuma* (1933) and *White's Chocolate House in the Time of Pepys* (1939).
10. Royal Engineers' Mess, Bulford: A. C. Overton: *Activities of the Sappers* (1938).

'Play' Murals

11. Drury Lane Theatre, London: J. G. Crace: mural scheme based on Raphael's Vatican Loggie decoration, including children symbolizing the theatrical arts, Shakespeare scenes and frieze of dancing figures with musical trophies (1836–7).
12. Conservative Club, 74 St. James's Street, London: murals of poets and painters: F. Sang and Naundorff (*c.*1840s).
13. Reform Club, London: E. T. Parris: *Music, Poetry, Painting, Sculpture* (*c.*1841–5).
14. Royal Italian Opera House, Covent Garden, London: Ferri, Verardi, and Zarra: ceiling decoration showing clouded skies and personifications of *Music, Lyric Tragedy, Comedy, The Visual Arts, The Sciences, The Seasons* (1846–7).
15. Adelphi Theatre, London: F. Sang: French Rococo motifs (1848).
16. International Exhibition Pavilion, London, 1862: R. Burchett: medallion panels symbolizing *Manufactures, Commerce,* and *The Arts and Sciences.*

17. Prince's Theatre, Manchester, and Gaiety Theatre, London: friezes showing characters from plays (1864).
18. Nottingham Theatre: frieze showing Shakespeare flanked by characters from his plays (1865); and Clifton Theatre, Bristol: frieze of *Apollo and the Muses* (1868): both H. Holiday.
19. Queen's Theatre, Long Acre, London: A. Moore: frieze showing ancient Greek audience watching Sophocles' *Oedipus at Colonnus* (1865).
20. Manchester Jubilee Exhibition Hall 1887 (central dome): F. Madox Brown: figures representing different industries and occupations (sketches held by the Whitworth Art Gallery, University of Manchester).
21. Claridge's Hotel, London: 'Mons. Felz': *fête galante* scene as part of Louis XV scheme for Ballroom (1909–10) and mural in Billiard Room.
22. Crawford's Tearoom, Edinburgh: R. Burns: *Some Ships of the Spanish Armada* (mural now held by National Galleries of Scotland) (*c.*1920s).
23. Pettigrew and Stephen's department store, Glasgow (Men's Smoking Room): M. Greiffenhagen: scenes from classical legend (panels now held by Hunterian Art Gallery, University of Glasgow) (*c.*1920s).
24. Bishop Creighton House, Fulham, London (a girls' club): scheme of murals including D. Carrington: scene of blacksmiths and anvil; W. Roberts: *Carpenters at Work*; and work by C. Gill, E. McNaught, and H. Garrett (*c.*1911).
25. 'Hall of Heroes', Arts and Crafts Exhibition Society exhibition, RA 1916: panels including C. Gere: *Cotswolds in War Time*; H. A. Payne: *His Name that sat on Him was Death and Hell followed After*; J. Southall: *The Return of Peace*; H. Speed: *Love dispelling Chaos; Henry Wilson (executed by J. Fulleylove and others): Humanity, St. George, Joan of Arc.*
26. 'Fruit Exhibition', Australia House, London: F. Leist: murals of Australian produce (exhibited at RA, 1923).
27. British Empire Exhibition, Wembley, London 1924: murals including: De Courcy Lewthwaite Dewar and other Glasgow women artists, supervised by R. Burns: twenty-three panels (Forestry Hall); C. Gardiner: industrial subjects (Rubber Hall).
28. The Highways [boys'] Club, Shadwell, London: R. Whistler and M. Adshead: panels of figures engaged in music-making, dancing, and other leisure activities in the country (1924); R. Whistler: *Comedy, Tragedy, Summer, Winter* (proscenium arch) (1925) (panels subsequently removed and presented to University College London).
29. Austin Reed's shop, Regent Street, London (Red Lacquer Room): F. Taylor: Empire landscape panels, including a scene of the Prince of Wales's 1925 South African Tour (*c.*1925).
30. Bentall's department store, Kingston-upon-Thames: H. Cawthra: panels of Tudor history (1928).
31. SS *Hilary* (Booth Shipping Line): E. I. Halliday: *The Priests and People of Poictiers ask Hilary to become Bishop* (*c.*1930s).
32. Viking Cinema, Largs: J. Houston, for Guthrie & Wells of Glasgow: mural of a Viking ship; Rialto Picture House, Kirkcaldy: Guthrie & Wells: Venetian scenes (both *c.*1930s).
33. Duncannon Tavern, London: scenes from *Pickwick Papers*; Saville Theatre, London (bar): murals including contemporary personalities: both A. R. Thomson (1930s).
34. Hatchett's Restaurant, Piccadilly (cocktail bar): *The Departure of the Bath Coach* (1930s); Good Intent Restaurant, King's Road, Chelsea, London: historic Chelsea figures: both E. I. Halliday (1930s).
35. Lord's Cricket Ground Pavilion, London: R. Pym: scene of cricket including portraits of cricketers such as W. G. Grace (1930).

36. Ibis Sports Club, Chiswick, London: M. Eldridge: *The Exploitation of the Country* (1930s).
37. International Building Club, London: E. Bawden and H. Aufseeser (also known as H. Tisdall): pastiche of landscape gardens and classical architecture; Majorca Restaurant and Ciro Club (both London): H. Aufseeser: murals (all 1930s).
38. International Exhibition, Glasgow 1938: E. Fraser: *Healing* (UK Pavilion); F. Dobson: figures symbolizing athletics, agriculture, music, and poetry (Canada Pavilion); M. Harding, to designs by J. Luke: frieze illustrating Northern Ireland's industries and tourist attractions; L. Scarfe: mural in Shell Pavilion; G. Tomlin: mural in Distillers' Building; other murals by artists including A. Inglis and M. Gray.
39. Royal Naval Canteen, Rosyth, Fife: A. Redpath: *Naval Costumes from King Alfred to 1700*; M. Trotter: *Life on the Ocean Wave* (both 1940).

BIBLIOGRAPHY

Aitken, C., 'The Slade School of Fine Arts', *Apollo*, 3 (Jan. 1926), pp. 1–11.
Aldrich, M., *The Craces: Royal Decorators 1768–1899* (London, 1990).
Andrews, K., *The Nazarenes: A Brotherhood of German Painters in Rome* (Oxford, 1964).
Anon., *Catalogue of the Cartoons sent in pursuant to the Notices issued by her Majesty's Commissioners on the Fine Arts . . .* (London, 1843).
—— *Catalogue of Works of Art for Exhibition in Westminster Hall* (London, 1847).
—— *A Description of the New Palace of Westminster* (London, 1848).
—— 'Publications of the Arundel Society: Fresco Painting', *Quarterly Review*, 104 (1858), pp. 277–325.
—— *Of the Historical Paintings in the Great Hall of the Worshipful Company of Skinners aforetime of the Craft and Mystery of the Guild of the Body of Christ by Frank Brangwyn ARA RE* (n.d. but probably *c.*1907–8).
—— *Exhibition of Designs for Mural Painting and for the Decoration of Schools and other Buildings* (exh. cat., Crosby Hall, London, 1912).
Archer, J. H. G. (ed.), *Art and Architecture in Victorian Manchester* (Manchester, 1985).
Arts Décoratifs de Grande Bretagne et d'Irlande Exposition organisée par le Gouvernement Britannique (par le Département des Expositions du Board of Trade) (Paris, avril–oct. 1914) (London, 1914).
Aslet, C., 'Madresfield Court, Worcestershire—III', *Country Life*, 168 (30 Oct. 1980), pp. 1551–5.
Atkinson, J. Beavington, 'English Painters of the Present Day', *Portfolio*, 1 (1870), pp. 49–54 (VI-Edward Armitage, ARA); pp. 65–70 (VII-G. F. Watts, RA); pp. 129–34 (XIV-H. S. Marks); pp. 163–6 (XVI-Frederic Leighton, RA).
Baldry, A. L., *Modern Mural Decoration* (London, 1902).
Barber, B. A., *The Art of Frank Salisbury* (Leigh-on-Sea, 1936).
Barlow, P., 'Local Disturbances: Ford Madox Brown and the Problem of the Manchester Murals', in E. Harding (ed.), *Reframing the Pre-Raphaelites* (Aldershot, 1996), pp. 81–97.
Barringer, T. J., 'Leighton in Albertopolis: Monumental Art and Objects of Desire', in T. J. Barringer and E. Prettejohn (eds), *Frederic Leighton: Antiquity, Renaissance, Modernity* (London, 1999), pp. 135–68.
Barrington, Mrs Russell, *The Life, Letters and Work of Frederic Leighton* (London, 1902).
Batten, J. (ed.), *Papers of the Society of Mural Decorators and Painters in Tempera*, Vol. 2 (1907–1924) (Brighton, 1925).
Bayes, W., *The Art of Decorative Painting* (London, 1927).
Beattie, S., *Alfred Stevens 1817–75* (Victoria & Albert Museum, London, 1975).
Bell, D., *The British Empire Panels of Sir Frank Brangwyn, R. A. and Preparatory Drawings and Studies in the Guildhall, Swansea* (Swansea, 1958).
Bell, R. Anning, 'Mural Decoration' in *Ghent International Exhibition: Catalogue of the British Arts and Crafts Section* (Ghent, 1913).
Belleroche, W. de, *Brangwyn Talks* (London, 1946).
—— *Brangwyn's Pilgrimage* (London, 1948).
Bendiner, K., *The Art of Ford Madox Brown* (Philadelphia, 1997).
Bland, C. H., *The Brangwyn Panels* (London, 1935).

Blunt, W., *England's Michelangelo: A Biography of George Frederic Watts, OM, RA* (London, 1975).

Boase, T. S. R., 'The Decoration of the New Palace of Westminster 1841–1863', *Journal of the Warburg and Courtauld Institutes*, 17 (1954), pp. 319–58.

—— *English Art 1800–1870* (Oxford, 1959).

Bond, M. (ed.), *Works of Art in the House of Lords* (London, 1980).

Börsch-Supan, H., *Die Deutsche Malerei von Anton Graff bis Hans von Marées 1760–1870* (Munich, 1988).

Catalogue of the Works of Sir Frank Brangwyn, RA (William Morris Gallery, Walthamstow, 1974).

Works by Frank Brangwyn, RA (exh. cat., RA, London, 1952).

Brangwyn, R., *Brangwyn* (London, 1978).

British School at Rome. Works Submitted for the Rome Scholarships, etc. (exh. cat., Grafton Galleries, London, 1920).

Brown, F. Madox, 'Mural Painting and Coloured Decoration: the Gambier Parry Process', *RIBA Transactions*, 31 (1880–1), pp. 273–6.

—— *Diaries*, ed. V. Surtees (New Haven, 1981).

Brydon, J. McKean, et al., 'Decorative Painting', *Transactions of the RIBA, ns* 7 (Section LXXXIV) (London, 1891).

Burollet, T., *Symboles et Réalités: La Peinture Allemande 1848–1905* (exh. cat., Musée du Petit Palais, Paris, 1984).

—— T., et al., *Le Triomphe des Mairies: Grand Décors Républicains à Paris 1870–1914* (exh. cat., Musée du Petit Palais, Paris, 1987).

Büttner, F., *Peter Cornelius: Fresken und Freskenprojekte*, 2 vols. (Stuttgart, 1980–99).

'J. C.', 'The Society of Mural Decorators and Painters in Tempera. The Society of Mural Decorators', *Studio*, 62, no. 256 (Aug. 1914), pp. 173–82.

Cameron, E., 'Brangwyn and the Venice Murals in the Sam Wilson Collection', *Leeds Art Calendar*, no. 59 (1966).

Cannadine, D., 'The Transformation of Civic Ritual in Modern Britain: the Colchester Oyster Feast', *Past and Present*, no. 94 (Feb. 1982), pp. 107–30.

Carline, R., Causey, A., and Bell, K., *Stanley Spencer RA* (exh. cat., RA, London, 1980).

Charles, R., *Frank Brangwyn Centenary* (exh. cat., Welsh Arts Council, Cardiff, 1967).

Christian, J., *The Oxford Union Murals* (Chicago, 1981).

—— (ed.), *The Last Romantics: The Romantic Tradition in British Art* (exh. cat., Barbican Art Gallery, London, 1989).

Clarke, H. G., *A Critical Examination of the Cartoons, Frescoes and Sculpture, exhibited in Westminster Hall. To which is added the history and practice of fresco painting* (London, 1844).

Codell, J., 'Ford Madox Brown, Carlyle, Macaulay, Bakhtin: The Pratfalls and Penultimates of History', *Art History*, 21, no. 3 (September 1998), pp. 324–66.

Compton, A., *Edward Halliday: Art for Life 1925–1939* (exh. cat., University of Liverpool Art Gallery, 1997).

Compton, S. (ed.), *British Art in the Twentieth Century: The Modern Movement* (exh. cat., RA, London, 1987).

Conway, W. M., *The Historical Paintings in the Houses of Parliament: descriptive text and key to the characters represented in the six Tudor panels in the House of Commons* (London, 1911).

Cope, C. H., *Reminiscences of Charles West Cope, RA* (London, 1891).

Cork, R., *Art Beyond the Gallery in Early Twentieth Century England* (New Haven and London, 1985).

—— *A Bitter Truth Avant Garde Art and the Great War* (New Haven and London, 1994).

Cormack, P., *Henry Holiday* (exh. cat., William Morris Gallery, Walthamstow, 1989).

Crane, W., *The Claims of Decorative Art* (London, 1892).

—— *The Origins of Decorative Art* (London, 1892).

—— *Of the Decoration of Public Buildings* (Doncaster, 1975), (Second lecture in the series given at the Arts and Crafts Exhibition Society's 5th Exhibition in the Autumn of 1896, originally published in *Art and Life, and the Building and Decoration of Cities*, London, 1897).

—— *The Bases of Design* (London, 1902).

—— *Ideals in Art: Papers Theoretical and Critical* (London, 1905).

CRAWFORD, A. (ed.), *By Hammer and Hand: The Arts and Crafts Movement in Birmingham* (Birmingham, 1984).

CROFT-MURRAY, E., *Decorative Painting in England 1537–1837*. 2 vols (London, 1965–1970).

CROOK, J. MORDAUNT, *William Burges and the High Victorian Dream* (London, 1981).

—— (ed.), *The Strange Genius of William Burges, Art-Architect, 1827–1881* (exh. cat., National Museum of Wales, Cardiff, 1981).

CUNNINGHAM, C., *Victorian and Edwardian Town Halls* (London, Boston, and Henley, 1981).

DAKERS, C., 'Sigismund Goetze and the decoration of the Foreign Office Staircase: "melodrama, pathos and high camp"', *Decorative Arts Society Journal*, no. 21 (1997), pp. 54–65.

DAY, M., *Modern Art in Church: A Gazetteer of Twentieth Century Works of Art in English and Welsh Churches*, RCA Papers, no. 12 (1982).

DEMANET, M., *Les Sgraffites à Bruxelles* (Brussels, 1996).

DORMENT, R., 'Sleeping Beauty Awakes', *Daily Telegraph* (24 Nov. 1999), p. 23.

DRAPER, W. H., 'The Watts Fresco in Lincoln's Inn', *Burlington Magazine*, 9 (1906), pp. 8–15.

—— *The Historical Paintings in the Great Hall of the Worshipful Company of Skinners* (London, 1909).

DROSTE, M., *Das Fresko als Idee Zur Geschichte öffentlicher Kunst im 19. Jahrhundert*. Vol. 2 of *Kunstgeschichte: Form und Interesse* (Münster, 1980).

EASTLAKE, C. L., *Hints on Household Taste*. Introduction by J. Gloag (New York, 1969).

EGERTON, J., *Drawings and Paintings by Sir Thomas Monnington PRA 1902–1976* (exh. cat., RA, London, 1977).

FARR, D., *William Etty* (London, 1958).

—— *English Art 1870–1940* (Oxford, 1978).

FARR, D. (ed.), *Thomas Gambier Parry 1816–1888 as Artist and Collector* (exh. cat., Courtauld Institute Galleries, London, 1993).

FARR, D. et al., *Joseph Southall 1861–1944: Artist-Craftsman* (exh. cat. Birmingham Museums and Gallery, 1980).

FEIBUSCH, H. (introduction), *Society of Mural Painters First Exhibition 1950–51* (exh. cat., Arts Council, London, 1951).

FORD (HUEFFER), F. M., *Ford Madox Brown: A Record of His Life and Work* (London, 1896).

FREEMAN, J., ASLIN, A., and ATTERBURY, P., *The Art of Frank Brangwyn* (exh. cat., Brighton, London, and Sheffield, 1980).

FROGGAT, F. G., 'British Wall and Ceiling Decoration', *Studio Yearbook of the Decorative Arts* (1908), pp. xxiii–xxiv.

FURST, H., *The Decorative Art of Frank Brangwyn* (London, 1924).

GAGE, J., and MULLEN, C., *G. F. Watts: A Nineteenth Century Phenomenon* (exh. cat., Whitechapel Art Gallery, London, 1974).

GALLOWAY, V., *The Oils and Murals of Sir Frank Brangwyn RA* (Leigh-on-Sea, 1962).

GAMBIER PARRY, T., *Spirit Fresco: An Account of the Process* (South Kensington Museum, London, 1880).

GARLICK, K., *Glyn Philpot, RA 1884–1937: A Commemorative Exhibition* (exh. cat., Ashmolean Museum, Oxford, 1976).

GIROUARD, M., *The Victorian Country House* (London and New Haven, 1979).

GOETZE, S., *Mural Decorations at the Foreign Office: Descriptive Account by the Artist* (London, n. d., *c.*1921).

GOODWIN, T., *The Art of Mural Decoration* (London, 1866).
GREEN, J., 'The Principles and Practice of Interior Decoration', *Australasian Builder and Contractor's News*, 10 no. 259 (16 and 23 April 1892) (PB98-1993 and PB118-1993 in RA(F)).
GROOM, G., *Edouard Vuillard, Painter-Decorator. Patrons and Projects, 1892–1912* (London and New Haven, 1993).
GULLICK, T. J., *A Descriptive Handbook for the National Pictures in Westminster Palace* (London, 1865).
HARRIES, M., and HARRIES, S., *The War Artists. British Official War Art of the Twentieth Century* (London, 1983).
HARRISON, C., *English Art and Modernism 1900–1939* (New Haven and London, 1994).
HARRISON, M. and WATERS, B., *Burne-Jones* (London, 1977).
HARTLEY, K. (ed.), *The Romantic Spirit in German Art 1790–1990* (exh. cat., National Galleries of Scotland, Edinburgh, and South Bank Centre, London, 1994).
HAWEIS, Mrs, *Beautiful Houses Being a Description of Certain Well-Known Artistic Houses.* 2nd ed. (London, 1882).
HAY, M. A. C., 'The Westminster Frescoes The Restoration of the Victorian Murals', *Apollo*, 135 (May 1992), pp. 307–11.
HAYDON, B. R., *Thoughts on the Relative Value of Fresco and Oil Painting as applied to the Architectural Decorations of the Houses of Parliament . . .* (London, 1842).
—— *Life . . . from his Autobiography and Journals*, ed. T. Taylor (London, 1853).
—— *Autobiography and Memoirs*, ed. A. P. D. Penrose (London, 1927).
—— *Diary*, ed. W. B. Pope (Cambridge, Mass., 1963)
HERRINGHAM, C. J., *The Book of the Art of Cennino Cennini* (London, 1899).
HOBHOUSE, H. (ed.), *County Hall*, Monograph no. 17, *Survey of London* (London, 1991).
HOBSBAWM, E. and RANGER, T. (eds), *The Invention of Tradition* (Cambridge, 1983).
HOLIDAY, H., *Reminiscences* (London, 1914).
HOLT, E. G., *From the Classicists to the Impressionists: Art and Architecture in the Nineteenth Century. A Documentary History of Art*, vol. III (New York, 1966).
HONE, J., *The Life of Henry Tonks* (London, 1929).
HUNT, F. K., *The Book of Art. Cartoons, Frescoes, Sculpture, and Decorative Art as applied to the New House of Parliament . . .* (London, 1846).
IRONSIDE, R., 'The Pre-Raphaelite Paintings at Wallington', *Architectural Review*, 92 (1942), pp. 130, 147–9.
JACKSON, F. HAMILTON, *Mural Painting* (London, 1904).
JAMESON, A., *Visits and Sketches at Home and Abroad with Tales and Miscellanies now first collected and a new edition of the Diary of an Ennuyé*, vol. 1 (London, 1834).
—— *The Decoration of the Garden Pavilion in the Grounds of Buckingham Palace* (London, 1846).
JONES, S. et al., *Frederic Leighton* (exh. cat., RA, London, 1996).
KEYSER, C. F., *A List of Buildings in Great Britain and Ireland having Mural and other Painted Decoration . . .* 3rd. ed. (London, 1883).
KITLITSCHKA, W., *Die Malerei der Wiener Ringstrasse* (Wiesbaden, 1981).
LATILLA, E., *Treatise on Fresco, Encaustic and Tempera Painting* (London, 1842).
LINNELL, J. J., and LINNELL, W., *The Prize Cartoons* (London, 1844).
LORD, P., *The Visual Culture of Wales: Industrial Society* (Cardiff, 1998).
—— *The Visual Culture of Wales: Imaging the Nation* (Cardiff, 1999).
LYNN-JENKINS, F., 'A Great Decorator: Professor Gerald Moira', *Magazine of Art*, *ns* 1 (1903), Part 1, pp. 525–33, and 2 (1904), Part 2, pp. 129–36.
MCBRINN, J., 'Belfast's Other Murals', *Causeway: Cultural Traditions Journal* (Summer 1997), pp. 39–43.
MACCARTHY, F., *Stanley Spencer: An English Vision* (New Haven and London, 1997).

McConkey, K., *Sir George Clausen RA 1852–1944* (exh. cat., Bradford Art Galleries and Museums and Tyne and Wear County Council Museums, 1980).
Macdonald, S., *The History and Philosophy of Art Education* (London, 1970).
Macer-Wright, P., *Brangwyn: A Study of Genius at Close-Quarters* (London, 1940).
Macklin, W. and Rigby, H. A., *The Decorative Paintings in Christ's Hospital Chapel* (London, 1925).
Marechal, D., 'De British Empire Panels en de Aanverwante Kunstwerken uit het Interbellum Enkele Typische Voorbeelden in het Brugse Brangwynfonds', *Jaarboek 1983–84, Stad Brugge Stedelijke Musea* (Bruges, 1985), pp. 315–20.
—— *Collectie Frank Brangwyn Catalogus* (Brugge Stedelijke Musea, Bruges, 1987).
Massé, H. J. L. J., *The Art Workers' Guild, 1884–1934* (Oxford, 1935).
Merrifield, M. P., *A Treatise on Painting (Cennini)* (London, 1844).
—— *The Art of Fresco Painting as practised by the Old Italian and Spanish Masters . . .* (London, 1846) (also reprinted, ed. A. C. Sewter, London, 1952).
Merrill, L., *The Peacock Room: A Cultural Biography* (New Haven and London, 1998).
Michel, W. and Fox, C. J. (eds), *Wyndham Lewis on Art: Collected Writings 1913–1956* (London, 1969).
Mills, E., *The Life and Letters of Frederic Shields 1833–1911* (London, 1912).
Morris, W. (ed.), *Arts and Crafts Essays: by Members of the Arts and Crafts Exhibition Society* (London, 1893).
Muthesius, H., 'Kunst und Leben in England', *Zeitschrift für bildende Kunst*, neue Folge, 13 no. 3 (1902), pp. 14–21, 49–69.
Newbolt, H., *The Building of Britain: A Series of Historical Paintings in St. Stephen's Hall, Westminster* (published for the Speaker of the House of Commons, London, n.d. [*c*.1927]).
O'driscoll, W. J., *A Memoir of Daniel Maclise, RA* (London, 1871).
Ormond, L., and Ormond, R., *Lord Leighton* (London, 1975).
Ormond, R., *Leighton's Frescoes in the Victoria and Albert Museum* (London, 1975).
—— 'Leighton and Mural Painting', *Apollo*, 143 (Feb. 1996), pp. 50–5.
Ormond, R. (introduction), *Daniel Maclise 1806–1870* (exh. cat., Arts Council of Great Britain, National Portrait Gallery, London, and National Gallery of Ireland, Dubin, 1972).
Parris, L. (ed.), *Pre-Raphaelite Papers* (Tate Gallery, London, 1984).
Phillips, C., 'Monumental Decorative Art in the Summer Exhibitions at Home and Abroad', *Art Journal*, NS (1890), pp. 162–6, (1891), pp. 184–7, and (1892), pp. 187–92.
Physick, J., *The Victoria and Albert Museum* (London, 1982).
Physick, J. and Darby, M., *Marble Halls: Drawings and Models for Victorian Secular Buildings* (exh. cat., V&A Museum, London, 1973).
Pointon, M., *William Dyce* (Oxford, 1979).
Pope-Hennessy, J., *Victorian Church Art* (Victoria and Albert Museum, London, 1971).
Port, M. H. (ed.), *The Houses of Parliament* (New Haven and London, 1976).
Poulson, C., 'The Queen's Robing Room Frescoes', in *The Quest for the Holy Grail: Arthurian Legend in British Art 1840–1920* (Manchester, 1999).
Powers, A., 'Honesty of Purpose: Painters at the British School at Rome', *Country Life* (27 Feb. 1986), pp. 512–14.
—— 'The Fresco Revival in the Early Twentieth Century', *Journal of the Decorative Arts Society*, XII (1988), pp. 38–46.
—— 'Murals of the Arts and Crafts Movement at the 1916 Exhibition', *Craft History*, 1 (1988), pp. 23–30.
—— 'History in Paint: The Twentieth-Century Murals', *Apollo*, 135 (1992), pp. 317–21.
Pursche, J., 'Betrachtungen zur Malerei mit Alkalisilikaten: Geschichte, Maltechnik und Restaurierung', in *Mineralfarben: Beiträge zur Geschichte und Restaurierung von Fassadenmalereien und Anstrichen, Veröffentlichungen des Instituts für Denkmalpflege an der ETH Zürich*, 19 (Zurich, 1998).

REDGRAVE, S., and REDGRAVE, R., *A Century of British Painters* (London, 1947).

Report of the Departmental Committee on the Royal College of Art Presented to Both Houses of Parliament by Command of Her Majesty (London, 1911).

Report on the Present Position and Tendencies of the Industrial Arts as indicated at the International Exhibition of Modern Decorative and Industrial Arts (Department of Overseas Trade) (Paris, 1925).

RICHEPIN, J., and STEINLEN, T., *Frank Brangwyn: His Work* (Paris and London, 1923).

RICHMOND, W. B., EAST, A., and SOLOMON, S. J., 'Decorative Painting', *Journal of the RIBA*, 3rd ser. 12 (25 March 1905), pp. 313–21.

ROBINSON, D., *Stanley Spencer* (Oxford, 1990).

—— and WILDMAN, S., *Morris and Company in Cambridge* (exh. cat., Fitzwilliam Museum, Cambridge, 1980).

ROLAND HOLST, R. N., 'De Muurschilderingen van Frank Brangwyn', in *Wendingen* (Mei 1918), reprinted in R. N. Roland Holst, *Over Kunst en Kunstenaars: Beschouwingen en Herdenkingen* (Amsterdam, 1923), pp. 39–47.

ROTHENSTEIN, J., *Mural Painting in Great Britain 1919–1939* (exh. cat., Tate Gallery, London, 1939).

—— *Modern English Painters: Nash to Bawden*, vol. 2 (London, 1984).

ROTHENSTEIN, W., *A Plea for a Wider Use of Artist-Craftsmen* ('A Lecture delivered at the invitation of the Chairman and Managers of the Technical School of Art at Sheffield, on the 8th November 1916') (London, 1916).

—— *Men and Memories* (London, 1931).

—— 'The Decoration of Buildings', *Journal of the RIBA*, 3rd ser., 38 (7 Feb. 1931), pp. 199–209.

—— *Form and Content in English Painting* (Romanes Lecture, Sheldonian Theatre, Oxford, 24 May 1934) (Oxford, 1934).

ROYAL ACADEMY *Exhibition of Decorative Art* (exh. cat., London, 1923).

RUSKIN, J., *The Complete Works*, ed. E. T. Cooke and A. Wedderburn (London, 1903–12).

RUTTER, F., 'The Westminster Panels', *Artwork* (Sept.–Nov. 1927), pp. 194–200.

—— *The British Empire Panels, designed for the House of Lords by Frank Brangwyn, R. A.* (Leigh-on-Sea, 1933).

SALISBURY, F. O., *Sarum Chase* (London, 1953).

—— *Portrait and Pageant* (London, 1944).

SANDILANDS, G. S., 'The Eight Wall Panels at St. Stephen's Hall', *Studio*, 94 no. 414 (Sept. 1927), pp. 155–60.

SARGANT-FLORENCE, M. (ed.), *Papers of the Society of Mural Decorators and Painters in Tempera*, vol. 3, 1925–1935 (Brighton, 1936).

SARSFIELD TAYLOR, W. B., *The Art of Painting in Oil and Fresco . . . translated from the original French treatise of M. J. F. L. Mérimée . . .* (London, 1839).

SAUNDERS, A. (ed.), *The Royal Exchange* (Publication no. 152, London Topographical Society, 1997).

SCHUBERT-SOLDERN, F. VON, 'Frank Brangwyn', *Kunst für Alle*, 25 (15 May 1910).

SCOTT, D., *British, French and German Painting: being a reference to the grounds which render the proposed painting of the New Houses of Parliament important as a public measure* (Edinburgh, 1841).

SCOTT, W. B., *Memoir of David Scott* (Edinburgh, 1850).

—— 'Mural Decorations at the Mansion of Sir Walter Trevelyan', *RIBA Transactions* (1867–8), pp. 31–46.

SEWTER, A. C., *Glyn Philpot 1884–1937* (London, 1951).

SHAW SPARROW, W., *Frank Brangwyn and his Work* (London, 1910).

SHAW SPARROW, W., and BÉNÉDITE, L., *The Spirit of the Age. The Work of Frank Brangwyn, A.R.A.* (London, 1905).

SHEPPARD, F. H. W., *The Museums Area of South Kensington and Westminster.* Vol. 38, *The Survey of London* (London, 1975).

SHONE, R., *Bloomsbury Portraits: Vanessa Bell, Duncan Grant and their Circle* (Oxford, 1976).

SILVERMAN, D., *Art Nouveau in Fin-de-Siècle France: Politics, Psychology and Style* (Berkeley, Los Angeles, and London, 1989).

SMAILES, H., *John Zephaniah Bell 1794–1883* (National Galleries of Scotland, Edinburgh, 1990).

SMITH, G., and HYDE, S., *Walter Crane 1845–1915: Artist, Designer and Socialist* (exh. cat., Whitworth Art Gallery, University of Manchester, London and Manchester, 1989).

SMITH, H., *Decorative Painting in the Domestic Interior in England and Wales c.1850–1890* (New York and London, 1984).

SMITH, J. T., *Antiquities of Westminster* (London, 1807).

SPALDING, F., *Vanessa Bell* (London, 1983).

—— *The Tate: A History* (London, 1998).

SPEAIGHT, R., *William Rothenstein* (London, 1962).

SPENCER, I., *Walter Crane* (London, 1975).

STEEGMAN, J., *Victorian Taste: A Study of the Arts and Architecture from 1830 to 1870* (London, 1970) (first published as *Consort of Taste*, 1950).

STRONG, R., *And When Did You Last See Your Father? The Victorian Painter and British History* (London, 1978).

TAYLOR, T., 'Philip Hermogenes Calderon and the St. John's Wood School', *Portfolio*, 1 (1870), pp. 31–46.

THOMAS, W. CAVE, *Mural or Monumental Decoration: Its Aims and Methods* (London, 1869).

THOMPSON, J. (foreword), *Sir William Rothenstein 1872–1945* (exh. cat., Bradford City Art Gallery and Museums, 1972).

THOMPSON, P., *Socialists, Liberals and Labour: The Struggle for London 1885–1914* (London, 1967).

THOMSON, R., *Monet to Matisse: Landscape Painting in France 1874–1914* (exh. cat., National Galleries of Scotland, Edinburgh, 1994).

TOWNSEND, C. H., POWELL, J. C., SALVIATI, G., and WESTLAKE, N. H. J., 'Mosaic and Fresco', *Journal of the RIBA*, 3rd ser. 1 (1893–4), pp. 245–64.

VALLANCE, A., *Mural Painting Revived* (London, 1908).

VAUGHAN, W., *German Romanticism and British Art* (New Haven and London, 1979).

—— *German Romantic Painting* (New Haven and London, 1980).

—— 'A "better prospect"? The First Mural Scheme for the New Palace', *Apollo*, 135 (1992), pp. 312–16.

WALKER, R. J. B.: *Catalogue of Paintings, Drawings, Sculpture and Engravings in the Palace of Westminster.* 7 vols (1959–77) with 10 vols Supplement (1965–76), held in HLRO.

WAPPENSCHMIDT, H. T., *Studien zur Ausstattung des deutschen Rathaussaales in der 2. Hälfte des 19. Jahrhunderts bis 1918* (Bonn, 1981).

WARD, J., *Colour Decoration of Architecture* (London, 1913).

WATERFIELD, G. (ed.), *Palaces of Art: Art Galleries in Britain 1790–1990* (exh. cat., Dulwich Picture Gallery, London, and National Galleries of Scotland, Edinburgh, 1991).

WATKINS, J. H., *The Art of Gerald Moira with Some Notes and Thoughts on Decorative Art, by G. Moira* (London, 1922).

WEISBERG, G., 'Siegfried Bing and Frank Brangwyn. The Gallery l'Art Nouveau in Paris in 1895', in *Jaarboek* (1985–6), Stad Brugge. Stedelijke Musea, Brugge (1987), pp. 277–86.

WELCH, C., *Illustrated Account of the Royal Exchange and the Pictures Therein* (London, 1913).

WESTLAKE, N. H. J., *Outlines of the History of Design in Mural Painting* (London, 1901).

WHISTLER, L., and FULLER, R., *The Work of Rex Whistler* (London, 1960).

WILLSDON, C. A. P., 'Scotland's Mural Renascence', *Scottish Review—Arts and Environment*, 29 (Feb. 1983), pp. 15–22

Willsdon, C. A. P., 'Paul Sérusier the Celt: did he paint Murals in Edinburgh?', *Burlington Magazine*, 126 no. 971 (Mar. 1984), pp. 88–90.
—— *Aspects of Mural Painting in London 1890–1930*, PhD thesis, University of Cambridge (1988).
—— 'Gustav Klimt's Beethoven Frieze: Goethe, *Tempelkunst* and the Fulfilment of Wishes', in M. Pointon and P. Binski (eds), *Image: Music: Text* (*Art History*, 19 no. 1, March 1996), pp. 44–73.
—— 'Mural 1. Europe (i) c.1810–1930', in *Grove Dictionary of Art*, vol. 22 (Macmillan, London, 1996).
—— 'Sir Frank Brangwyn', in *Grove Dictionary of Art*, vol. 2 (Macmillan, London, 1996).
—— *Bridgewater House: Its Murals, Sculptures and Works of Art* (published privately by TRA Ltd., London, 1997).
Wilson, H. (introduction), *Arts and Crafts Exhibition Society Catalogue of the Eleventh Exhibition* (RA, London, 1916).
Young, K., and Garside, P., *Metropolitan London* (London, 1982).

INDEX

Note: Buildings and institutions are listed by their period names, and by geographical location, except where the building has a distinctive name which is likely to be better known than its location, e.g. 'Red House', which appears in its own right rather than under 'Upton'. Cross-reference is provided in such cases. Italic numbers denote pages with illustrations.